D. P. Bailey Jr

ACKNOWLEDGMENT

TO

THE BOARD OF TRADE OF CHICAGO.

GENTLEMEN:

At length it is my satisfaction to put into your hands this volume of information relating to the growth of our City. Without bombast or vain-glorying, it is designed to exhibit fairly our relations to the Great Interior and to the Continent, which is all-important to the interests of trade committed to your special care. If it but aid a little your praise-worthy efforts to maintain a standard of commercial integrity equal to the magnitude of the interests the Board regulates, this enterprize will not be regretted by any of us. Though prepared less to advance morals than business, and for foreign rather than home use; yet no man can examine this mass of fact and testimony without impressions of weighty obligations for what has been done for our City by God and country, which will strengthen determination in honorable citizens to render our City worthy of her benefits.

Reference is made, p. vii, to a statement here of the process whereby the Board has been induced to the novel plan of taking copies for its members, and for Canadian officials. It was supposed that the statement prepared by the Secretary, Mr. Randolph, the presentation of which caused the adoption of the resolutions by over two-thirds of the members present, would here appear; and my desire was to follow it with the names of the members who had previously given their written vote in favor of the resolutions. But some of the most steadfast friends, in view of the final action having been taken by the Board as such, consider that individual endeavors for or against should be forgotten.

The following are the resolutions sanctioned by the written vote of a majority of members, to which Mr. Fairbank referred in moving the adoption of the measure at the annual meeting:

Resolved, That the Board of Directors are requested to procure one copy of the work, "Chicago: Past, Present, Future," for each member of the Board of Trade; and that with the Commercial Committee we join in the request to business men generally, capitalists and property holders, to give the work a wide distribution.

Resolved, That such a number of copies as the Directors deem advisable, be sent to Mr. F. C. Capreol, of Toronto, to distribute to the members of the Ontario Parliament and other Canadian offiicials, along with a letter printed in each copy, expressive of our interest in the construction of that important international work, the Lake Huron and Ontario Ship canal.

In no spirit of vain conceit or obstinacy has this measure been pressed to a successful issue, but with a sense of duty and of privilege which every citizen must exercise, who desires to do what he reasonably may to promote both public and private objects. Indissolubly blended by nature's God, the more we work them in harmony, the more will we prosper as individuals and as a city. But judgment of my own bantling may be biased and untrustworthy. It should not be set up against that of the citizens generally. They have come around to my way of thinking on a good many points, and they may also upon this. At all events, by the liberality, and above all the good faith, of the Board of Trade, the volume being now in condition for fellow-citizens to judge the merits, that judgment will be acquiesced in, and an additional volume be prepared after the coming census, or not, as they shall determine.

Whatever the result, my obligations to the Board of Trade, and especially to the advocates of the measure, will not be forgotten. Nor is any unkind feeling cherished for an opponent. About the proposition, men would honestly differ; and what little active opposition has been manifested, has been usually in so courteous a manner as to merely evoke moderate regret. But the aid has been given by the Board of Trade as such; and with a simple return of earnest thanks, it shall be my endeavor faithfully to further the objects of your organization, and my hope is to be a member of it while I live.

Your obliged Fellow-Citizen,

J. S. WRIGHT.

CHICAGO, *June* 10*th*, 1870.

"We the People of the United States, in order to form a *more perfect Union*, establish justice, insure domestic tranquillity, provide for the common defence, promote the general welfare, and secure the blessings of liberty to ourselves and our posterity, do ordain and establish this Constitution FOR THE UNITED STATES OF AMERICA."—*United States Constitntion.*

CHICAGO:

PAST, PRESENT, FUTURE.

"These united Colonies are, and of right ought to be, FREE AND INDEPENDENT STATES; . . . and that, as FREE AND INDEPENDENT STATES, they have full power to levy war, conclude peace, contract alliances, establish commerce, and to do all other acts and things which INDEPENDENT STATES may of right do."—*Declaration of Independence.*

QUERY.

If our National Wheel of Commerce have its Hub immovably pivoted by Nature and by Art, should not every Business Man know it?

CAUSES—RESULTS.

NATURE laid from the Atlantic Ocean into the heart of the Continent, this chain of rivers and lakes, nearly two thousand miles of the grandest inland navigation on the globe; and from the Gulf of Mexico, opened up a river navigation of many thousand miles, commingling here the sources of rivers and of lakes.

ART perfected this union by canal, which now bears to the lakes more river-valley produce than all the rivers bear to St. Louis. ART, too, made this union-point the chief railway centre of the world. By fifteen trunk lines, each 242 to over 1,000 miles long, with many branches, over 7,500 of the 11,000 miles of western railway, rapidly expanding; the Old Northwest, 600,000 square miles of the richest arable land, in the heart of the temperate zone, is already bound indissolubly to this unequaled converging point of water and railway lines. Seven of these railroads are across the Mississippi, each having, or to have, its bridge. Continuing west in nearly parallel lines, most or all will soon reach the Rocky Mountains, and beyond; and with branches concentrate at Chicago the trade of over 900,000 square miles of the richest mining region of the world. And the convergence here of three railways, which will soon reach the Pacific, render this the distributing point for the trade of the former Orient, but our Occident, at least for the Lake and River Vallies. If of the Old Northwest emporium, she must be of the present West, more correctly and definitely styled, the Great Interior; if of the Great Interior, she must be of the Continent.

CHICAGO:

PAST, PRESENT, FUTURE.

RELATIONS TO

THE GREAT INTERIOR, AND TO THE CONTINENT.

BY JOHN S. WRIGHT.

PROVINCE, GOVERNMENT, AND RESPONSIBILITY OF THE CITY.

Man's Institution—Significant Name of the first City.—"Then Cain went out from the presence of the LORD, and dwelt in the land of Nod toward the east side of Eden. Cain also knew his wife which conceived and bore ENOCH [TAUGHT, or DEDICATED, DISCIPLINED]: and he built a city, and called the name of the city by the name of his son, ENOCH."—*Gen. iv, 16–17.*

The best Government for a City.—"Therefore, saith the Lord God of Hosts, the mighty one of Israel, Ah, I will ease me of mine adversaries, and avenge me of mine enemies. Then will I turn mine hand upon thee and burn out thy dross until it be pure, and take away all thy tin, and I WILL RESTORE THY JUDGES AS AT THE FIRST, AND THY COUNSELLORS AS AT THE BEGINNING; afterward shalt thou be called a city of righteousness, a faithful city. Zion shall be redeemed in judgment, and they that return in her, in justice."—*Is. i. 24–27.*

Responsibility of a City according to Strength, Prominence, and Illumination.—"Ye are the salt of the earth: but if the salt have lost his savor, wherewith shall it be salted? It is thenceforth good for nothing, but to be cast out, and to be trodden under foot of men. Ye are the light of the world. A CITY THAT IS SET ON A HILL CANNOT BE HID. Neither do men light a candle and put it under a bushel, but on a candlestick, and it giveth light unto all that are in the house. Let your light so shine before men, that they may see your good works, and glorify your Father which is in heaven."—*Matt. v. 13–16.*

Second Edition, for the Chicago Board of Trade.

CHICAGO:
FOR SALE BY ALL CHICAGO BOOKSELLERS.
1870

HORTON & LEONARD,
Printers,
Chicago, Illinois.

CONTENTS.

Page.

Second Edition, for the Board of Trade.......... vii–x

BASIS. Fact, not Hypothesis.......... xi

Our Political Institutions.......... xii

Coöperation of Nature and Art from Abroad.......... xii

Our Railway System is immovable.......... xiv

The whole Capital of New York, and New England supports Chicago..... xv

AIMS. Not to promote Speculation, but Confidence in the Real Estate...... xvi

To show that the Great Interior must build up many great Cities.......... xvii

To show that the Great Interior, a complete Unit in Interest, must have its own Centre, which is found and established.......... xix

To show that the Chief City of the Great Interior must, probably, be Emporium of the Continent.......... xix

To show that Chicago has a Population equal to her Advantages.......... xxi

To invite Consideration of the Obligations of City and Citizens, in view of the unparalleled Benefits showered by God and Country.......... xxiii

To show Fellow Citizens their Right to prefer Expediency to Command, Privilege to Duty.......... xxiv

OBJECTIONS. "Too much Puffing of Chicago Already".......... xxvii

"Invidious Comparisons render us odious".......... xxix

"Everybody already knows about Chicago".......... xxx

"It tends to create a spirit of speculation".......... xxxii

"Too long a Story".......... xxxiii

DUTIES. To ourselves and Families.......... xxxiv

To the Church.......... xxxv

To our City.......... xxxvi

To our State.......... xxxix

To the Great Interior.......... xl

To our Nation.......... xli

To our God.......... xlii

EFFECTS. Upon the Bodies Politic.......... xliv

Upon the individual Citizen.......... xlv

Study the Past, to apprehend the Future, and improve the Present.......... 1

Former Opinions and Predictions were based upon a reasonable Hypothesis.. 2

Real Estate, especially in a growing City, is the best Investment.......... 14

General Pecuniary Revulsions may intervene, but can not change the Result 16

Public Improvements anticipated 20 and 10 years ago, as a Basis.......... 21

The Basis of our Prosperity is no longer hypothetical.......... 25

Art following Nature's Lead, Chicago has no Taxes for Railways, though she has several times more than any Rival, and nearly Two-Thirds of all West of the Toledo and Cincinnati Road, and North of the Ohio River.......... 28

The Focal Point of the Great West is fixed immovably by over 7,500 of its 11,000 miles of Railway, centering at Chicago 36
The Pacific Railways in Progress—their Effects 42
The Illinois and Michigan Canal to the Illinois River. Its possible continuation to Rock Island, on the Mississippi 52
Five Rival Railways Eastward 53
The Lake Route to the East and Europe 58
The Difference between Chicago and other Western Centres 66
The Rivals of the West—Cincinnati, St. Louis, and Chicago 73
The Northwest is the Prize contested—its Extent and Resources 111
600,000 square miles of arable Land, and water Courses, unequaled in Advantages, natural and acquired, rapidly settling with the best of Men, must give unexampled Growth to their Emporium 131
The Commerce of Chicago compared with St. Louis 140
Abundant Manufacturing Advantages of Chicago.—Rapid Progress 191
Conjunction of Coal, Iron, and other Minerals 222
Local advantages and City Expansion 249
Power of the Internal Trade to build up great Cities 300
Power of the Railway to develop and centralize 313
No other Point of Equal Convergence of either Rail or Water Communication, or of both, on the Globe 339
The Northwest and West are hereafter the Great Interior 385
Other cities no measure for Chicago 387
There is Room for them and us 402
INDEX. Use of the Facts. The Generalization 405-435
APPENDIX. Obligations of Promise, Contract and Covenant, according to the Code of Honor. Privilege and Duty of the President and Directors of the Board of Trade of Chicago, to maintain their plighted Faith in regard to the Book, "Chicago: Past, Present, Future" 1-72

Second Edition, for the Board of Trade.

BASIS—AIMS.

Although these essentials to the appreciation of this volume of fact and testimony were put on its fore front, yet their elaboration might have obtained a different reception for the first edition. The reader could put no faith in the superstructure, until he knew the solidity of the foundation; nor could he intelligently pursue the argument, until he saw distinctly at what the author was driving. By the liberality, and above all the good faith, of the Board of Trade of our City, another edition being at length called for, the opportunity is embraced to invite attention to the Basis and Aims of the discussion. With a better understanding of the object of the author, and the strength of his premises, probably fellow-citizens would not be so slow in coming to his conclusions, nor so inappreciative of their importance. In correcting what appears to be misapprehension, he is now not only concerned to maintain his own credit, but also that of the Board of Trade which has come to the rescue against general indifference, and especially the good judgment of the members who, from the outset, have been steadfast advocates of a subscription by the Board, together with the majority of members in the long catalogue preceding the title page, who gave a written vote in favor of taking one copy for each member (1,342); and also, to send copies to members of the Canadian Parliament, to encourage the increase of water facilities to the ocean. Mortifying indeed would it be to have inveigled the Board of Trade into patronage of an unworthy object. Unless an utter failure, for which no calculation is made, the endorsement by the Board of this examination into the causes of growth of our City, shall be acknowledged one of the most judicious measures ever adopted to promote our trade interests.

At length, too, the volume has its index, without which no one can judge the worth of such a mass of fact and testimony. Though a logical argument, it was never imagined that the busy men for whom it is written, would begin with the preface and read to finis, and always remember the important truths here garnered. The design was to gather facts and statistics in regard to the whole region tributary, easy to find when wanted; and, as "straws show which way the wind blows," these would indicate the Chicago-ward currents. Non-residents, for instance, interested in railroads, would value this inquiry into their growth in the Great Interior; and the index would enable him to find the information, and in obtaining it, if not very stupid, he would get hold of its relations to Chicago. So an intelligent merchant anywhere, wants all this information about the commerce of the Great Interior, and a cursory examination would show him that Chicago was its centre. So the manufacturer will find here a mass of information, just what he wants, that he will look for elsewhere in vain, and the index renders every item useful at the instant. It is prepared as a permanent work, being a very condensed, yet thorough inquiry into the growth of city and of region hitherto, which will not need to be repeated. To editors and others whose pursuits demand such information, it will be a *vade mecum*; and as succeeding generations learn to appreciate the province of this richest heritage of man, and the close relations of its emporium with the northern half of the entire globe, the facts in its early stages will have increasing interest and value.

On account of incompleteness, the first edition being sent only to our own editors, except those of Cincinnati and St. Louis, no general judgment of merits has yet been given. But the unanimous and voluntary verdict of the Chicago press, gathered in the Appendix (pages 19–22) to influence the Board of Trade, will not probably be largely dissented from. The wide distribution urged by our editors being indispensable to the obtaining of benefits; to whom rather than editors throughout the country should the book be sent? Chicago's indebtedness to them for her wide-sung praises, should have at least the slight tribute of acknowledgment by this compend of the results flowing from means and measures which they have generally advised and promoted. Dependent as we are so largely upon public opinion, should we not esteem it rather a privilege than duty to bring together these evidences of their sound judgment as to the past, to encourage them to continuance as to the future? What influence more likely to strengthen their convictions and lead to stronger advocacy of means and measures to advance the Great Interior to its destiny, than to supply each paper with this practical information, precisely what they need for reference? What editor is not concerned in what affects the destiny of the Great Interior?

A wide distribution of this, will give a demand for the additional volume, which it is my purpose to publish next year, containing the results of the census, and the progress of the three years more, which strongly confirms the claims herein; and after each National census of ten years, and perhaps each State census of five years, which States are generally adopting, a small volume, giving a summary of the progress of the Great Interior, will be acceptable to business men the world over. Nor will the end of my life end these appendices. Their practical benefits in drawing hither men and capital, will have been too strongly attested to permit the publication to be given over.

The information was never gathered for home consumption, but for foreign distribution. Chicagoans are too well understood to suppose that they can be taught anything about their City. But, in common with other active, enterprising citizens, business plans were formed, to carry which capital was wanted. To obtain the capital, it was necessary to prove the safety and profit of the operation, which depended wholly upon the growth of Chicago. No systematic examination of this important subject having been made, this was the first step to be taken. It seemed, too, that such a volume would be precisely what hundreds and thousands of other citizens would wish to use in the same way, by sending copies to non-resident capitalists, whose investments they wished to influence, or perhaps induce the owner to remove hither.

It also seemed that the subject itself would have interest at home and abroad. In this age of unexampled progress, city growth is of much importance; that instrumentality being at once the means and index of highest civilization. And with the modern powers of railway and telegraph, which strong bodies politic must wield, cities are immensely strengthened in their power and influence, while, at the same time, no such powers as these to build up cities have been known to man. To trace the operation of these forces and others upon the most marvelous city growth of the world, would, therefore, be interesting to philanthropists and business men generally; and all the more so, because incidentally it accumulated a mass of information about the Great Interior and its relations to the rest of the world, which would be in general demand.

But friends could not be made to see the desirableness of such a work, and only by persistent dint of importunity were funds obtained to stereotype and print. Thinking that an examination of the pages would remove indifference and prejudice, an edition of 1,300 copies was issued for citizens to examine, while the index was being prepared for another edition to distribute. Without the preface it might have made its way; but with "Objections, Duties, Effects," to introduce such a work to Chicagoans, it had a cool reception. If, instead of homiletics, the citizens had been told that here was the most efficacious means to make money, they would have examined the volume enough to learn its merits. But the study incident to the compilation had impressed responsibility to God and country for the untold benefits showered upon us, which these citizens should be made to realize; and for their unreasonable resistance of the benevolent enterprize, they were assaulted with answers to their "Objections," and inculcation of their "Duties." This antagonism was more natural than wise. Impatient to carry my project, annoyed beyond endurance, that in this wealthy City in which I am regarded one of the fathers, and one best qualified for this very work, that I could not by coaxing or driving obtain funds to print a volume of more importance to its growth than any other publication, it was not unnatural to think and say hard things.

Men, however, are not to be driven to duty, but led to it by their own interests. Could the Board of Trade have been driven to this liberal measure, giving this volume a proper introduction to the citizens? As our Father leads us to duty, to honor, to glory, by considerations promotive of our life and our own best good, so these sons should lead each other. In every true respect self-interest conducts to duty, duty to honor, honor to glory, and glory to self-interest, in eternal circles. Is it more to the glory and honor of Father and of sons to heed the truths on the title-page, inculcating the province and responsibility of city and citizens, than it is to our own interest?

That any injustice has been done is not admitted; only the impolicy of attempting to drive men to promote their own interests from a sense of duty. Duty, it is true, is essential in human government, because individuals are corrupt and depraved, failing utterly to discharge even duty to themselves; but how much more ennobling the motive to act from a sense of respect and honor for ourselves and our Father, than from a sense of duty. It is only by abuse of privilege that any thing becomes a duty, either toward man or God; for we are taught by highest authority, "It is more blessed to give than to receive." It is our right by inheritance to promote our own good, and happiness, and life, not so much because we owe it, even to our Creator; but as our Father seeks his honor and glory in his bounties, so to honor and glorify themselves is the birth-right of these sons. And as according to the measure of his heart a man will do as a privilege what he would scorn as a duty, it seems expedient to present for the consideration of fellow-citizens, somewhat of their privileges in regard to this volume.

Evidently, its wide distribution is even more desirable than when first published, owing to the prevalence of the belief at home and abroad, as exhibited in the Appendix, pp. 65-69, that our growth has been, and is, dependent upon ourselves. Both honor and self-interest demand of us the most emphatic correction of this fundamental error, exhibiting the truth that our prosperity has been, and is, dependent upon the most unexampled bestowments of God and country with which any city was ever favored. In that it demonstrates this truth, the value of the work chiefly consists; and for the correction of an error, shameful to sanction by silence, pernicious and weakening in its effects, should not the antidote be extensively applied?

The Table of Contents presents the line of argument, and the Index the generalization, both of which should have examination, before reading much of the body. The reader needs to see the disinterested and wide-spread sources of information, and the immense weight of fact and testimony by which the truth is demonstrated, that Chicago in the first generation has been made forever the emporium of the Great Interior; and that as such, and the same causes being certain to continue with multiplying power, another generation, *probably*, makes her emporium of the continent.

BASIS.

Fact, not Hypothesis. That which. is already accomplished, not what is possible, nor even probable—not hypothesis, but fact—is the basis of this argument. Although the Future is what is calculated, the foundation-work is what has been actually done; for, that in Chicago's progress results have been obtained according to law and nature, may be assumed until the contrary can be shown. Nor is the assumption less reasonable that they will continue to operate as hitherto, and with corresponding results; for the rule of nature and of Scripture, "To him that hath shall be given," applies emphatically to the growth of cities. That some lose ground, relatively retrograding, instead of contradicting, confirms this averment; for if truly possessed of what they claimed, possession here is surely nine points of the law. The learned Professor argues, (page 176,) that "the energy of an unlineal competitor may usurp the legitimate honors of the Imperial heir." Is that the philosophy taught in his University? Can it be true, either in law, in fact, in logic, in result? Wherever the honors can be taken away, and because they may, the presumption is more reasonable, more in accord with fact and the Bible, that instead of having, the city only "seemed to have."

In this cast of the horoscope of Chicago's future, it will be observed that improvements to be made are of small account, however reasonable and indispensable. No doubt, both railroad and telegraph are still in their infancy, and may even be superseded by more potent means of progress. Also, developments of mineral wealth in the Great Interior, as yet merely a little scratching of the surface, we know must be very insignificant compared with what a few years of scientific research will make, with the application of machinery to follow railway and telegraph. The Orient trade, too, which for thousands of years has enriched city after city and nation after nation which could obtain it, must be ours with fuller possession than our race ever enjoyed; and who can foresee the effect of that trade upon our country, especially upon that city which appears destined, by the construction of several roads from the Pacific, to be made the chief factor?

Yet, we rely not the least upon these visions of the future, magnificent, moderate though they be, apparently certain of realization from the natural current of events, as with God-given right of dominion our race "in the image of GOD created" marches on to its destiny, rooting out inferior races and possessing the whole earth. We take the natural, ordinary currents of trade as established by the Past and Present—the development of natural resources already made—the railway and telegraph as they are to-day—and from what has been done, argue on to what will and must be done. If occasional allusion be made to what seems reasonable and probable, should it be deemed irrelevant or weakening in such discussion? But let the little of that be stricken out, and the result will not be impaired. The basis is not hypothesis but fact.

Our Political Institutions. No one can understand the subject of city growth, without requisite knowledge of the laws governing. Nor can one appreciate the untold advantages of Federal Republican Democracy in building up great centres of commerce and manufactures, without much study of the science of politics. When our compound system of State and federal governments shall be apprehended, then only can we calculate the future glory of our chief cities; and then and not before can the force of Isaiah's prediction on the title-page be apprehended. So that though in such a volume this subject could only have incidental allusion, yet the fundamental truths were of course put on the lead.

Although, in ignorance of principles, we imagine State Sovereignty to be utterly subversive of National Union, faith should be placed in Illinois' motto as proclaiming the true foundation of her chief City's rights and prosperity. Solely by virtue of State Sovereignty, has our National Union existence; and as we learn the significance of *E Pluribus Unum*, and the sacredness and binding nature of covenant obligations between sovereign, free and independent States, we shall apprehend the security afforded to every civil right generated by State Sovereignty; security and support enough to bear the city that shall prove worthy, to the preëminence of being emporium of a continental republic. Only under the blaze of light and liberty shed from our fundamental documents and insignia, with a realization of the unequaled stimulus they afford to individual and corporate efforts, can we duly consider, "Chicago: Past, Present, Future."

Coöperation of Nature and of Art from abroad. Next after our political institutions, the source of our every civil right, the basis of argument to prove the future growth of a city should be, the most perfect coöperation of nature and of art. To incite to this consideration, the query prefixes the title-page, which is answered in the Causes and Results. The Results are the facts adduced to establish the truth, that the continental centre is found, and that every business man should know it; and the main Causes, of course, are either of art or nature. So that the coöperation of nature and of art, like a lens converges upon the title-page the rays of fact and testimony, casting strong light upon the otherwise mysterious subject of our future. As these rays are gathered, the important truth appears, that sources of supplies are not within ourselves, but that far beyond any city that ever grew, they are the gift of God and country; inspiring unbounded faith, that until sources fail, or we become ungrateful and unfaithful, the vivifying streams will continue to flow with multiplying benefits, according to Scripture rule.

Nature never makes a city. As Cain built the first city, we infer that this privilege is decreed to the sons; the Bible abounding with instruction similar to that on the title-page, concerning its province and ultimate perfection. No human institution is more artificial, success depending upon a conjunction of causes, which, however liberally bestowed by nature, lie dormant until operated by human effort and ingenuity. Art, however, would have a difficult task in localities neglected of nature, and easy upon sites she favored. That no city has had equal growth, would therefore be strong *prima facie* evidence that nature favored Chicago; for it would be incredible that art against nature could have raised a city from 4,479 souls in 1840, to over 350,000 in 1870. The index, under the topics, Centre, Climate, Great Interior, Lakes, Minerals, Nature, Northwest, Rivers, States by name, Water, West, etc., exhibits the unexampled concentration of nature's forces, even to the preördination of the work of art.

Yet the God of nature having ordained cities as an human institution, topics under the head of art are no less essential. Their examination shows that with adequate faithfulness and energy, art chiefly operating from abroad, concurs to ratify nature's decrees as to Chicago, however signal the failure on other sites which have unwarrantably vaunted nature's bestowments and ordination. Under Art, Agriculture, Canals, Capital, Cities, Commerce, Conjunction of Coal, Iron and other Minerals, Convergence of Rail and Water, Manufacturing, Trade, etc., an array of facts and figures are presented which would satisfy any ordinary "race of humans," who were not waiting in expectancy for some extraordinary efforts of art to supply deficiencies of nature in fulfilling her decrees. Yet Market exhibits the more effective truth, that Chicago, which less than thirty years since imported grain and provisions of all sorts from the East; is now in grain, lumber, live stock, and provisions, chief market of the world. Then, under Railroads, it appears that no equal centre for this new-found power—nearer omnipotent for centralizing than for developing,—exists upon the globe. Could effects like these have been wrought in a wilderness, and in a single generation without perfect coöperation between art and nature?

These unexampled bestowments by God and man, render the passage on the title-page from the Sermon on the Mount, especially applicable to this City. The superficial observer, it is true, considers the notorious flatness of site only emblematic of the flatness awaiting Chicago, when the exuberance of adolescence shall have spent its power; and in this application of the passage, he sees only another example of ridiculous conceit. Not so is it to the candid examiner of nature's laws. In considering (page 104), the confluence here of lake and river vallies, it was observed,—"the fact that a rain-drop here falling from the skies, could half of it run its ocean-course to Gulf St. Lawrence, the other half to Gulf Mexico, indicated the propriety of enlarging the connection, and here uniting the Great Valley of the Rivers with the Great Valley of the Lakes, in indissoluble bonds." What other considerable city occupies a hill more continental? But with this prominence, weighty obligations are engendered, largely augmented by the many and great benefits conferred by God and country. Is not due acknowledgment at least our first duty and privilege?

Our Railway System is Immovable. Though Chicago has nature's firm support, whose decrees are unmistakable and fast fulfilling, yet art being the main cause or means of progress, and the railway chief of art's appliances; could the railway system of the West be essentially changed, the argument would be unsafe if not fallacious. Therefore, immobility has careful consideration; and the volume of evidence attests, that with nature's adjuncts of lake and river, the iron network is completely interwoven far westward to the Missouri and beyond, so that no change is now possible until some new power supplants the railway. For better for worse, existing trunks must be extended, to be fed and strengthened by branches innumerable. If hitherto rival lines, designed to give trade a different direction from that taken, have been difficult to construct, will they be found less so as the system year by year increases in homogeneity, and the strong centripetal force of trade deepens and widens its natural currents, obtaining increased facilities to operate, such as less favored points and routes cannot afford to create? If the railway system east of the Mississippi, both latitudinal and longitudinal, work adversely to other cities, as the chief admit, how can trade beyond be diverted by south, or south-easterly lines? With currents there far more decidedly latitudinal, and sufficiently Chicagoward for even the Hannibal and St. Joe road, built by St. Louis right in her own State, to have deserted her; will not her few cross-lines, which will ultimately be built, become more and more feeders of Chicago roads? Why is not the Chicago, Alton and St. Louis road a fair specimen for trans-Mississippi north and south lines? The trade of that route for three-fourths the distance she had monopolized for years, and the statistics show it in large measure turned from her to Chicago by the new and stronger currents; and how can they be turned back to favor her?

Had this City built railways, or, indeed, aided in any important degree in plan or construction, adverse forces might arise to change materially the existing system. But she had neither capital nor influence at all equal either to Cincinnati or St. Louis. Besides, they had become important centres of commerce and manufactures, between them monopolizing the business of the Northwest, before Chicago began to grow. Then it was an object to reach them as it is not now, and never again can be; for various other centres are arising, some of which will successfully dispute the claims of older cities to preëminence. If, under these circumstances, Chicago has had built for her more railways than all the cities combined which have aspired to rivalry, and from forty-two miles in 1850 has already been made chief railroad centre of the world, what possible influences can work a change? That which has been done, actually compels to more and more doing of the same sort. A cursory examination will convince any competent judge that for the next ten years, railway construction of the entire country must be mainly extensions and branches of these Chicago lines, and others intermediate as the country developes and requires greater facilities. Radiating from this chief railway centre, at a distance of fifty or one hundred miles, a branch is required which often becomes a long and important trunk road.

The poverty of Chicago, which would-be rivals offer to our disparagement, is truly a strong reason in our favor. Had we enjoyed their wealth, and built our system, we could not be equally certain that foreign capital would not find other routes, with other centres more desirable. Instead of that, however, not only are former influences increasing in power, but this entire capital compels for its own profit, to further heavy investment, in order to perfect the present system. Besides, Chicago is fast attaining capital, and becoming the financial centre of the Great Interior, and will give aid where it is most wanted, and will do her most good, in constructing little branches, direct feeders of her long trunks. Relative increase of mileage compared with other cities, will be greater in merely those branches, than will be the increase of trunks and branches at any other city. What Chicago can do for herself, however, is of small account. The strength of the argument lies in the indisputable truth that:—

The whole Capital of New York and New England supports Chicago. The sagacious capitalists of the East, seeking simply their own aggrandizement, have built such roads as the East wanted, and where wanted. Of Chicago they have merely asked permission to come into the City, a boon often obtained with difficulty. Yet the East has already made her the focal point of over three-fourths of the western system.

The index, under Atlantic, Capital, East, exhibits this conjoint interest, which was urged twenty years and more ago in Boston and New York papers, to induce capitalists to do precisely what they have done. Though weak herself, Chicago has found abundant strength in her unity of interest with the wealthiest region of our country; that enterprising population to which all other sections look for capital to accomplish great undertakings. Pennsylvania has still too much to do in developing her mines and manufactures to spare capital, and she draws heavily on the States north. South of her they go to New York and New England for money, getting it abundantly, provided security and profits justify. So the West, as hitherto styled, has presented its claims, and would have succeeded had no stronger motives operated in her favor. But those far-sighted calculators, who consider permanent rather than temporary results, saw much more potent reasons why they should build roads to Chicago from the East, and from Chicago throughout the West. The Great Interior has already become, and must increasingly, the section with which they need most intimate relations. Here they look for food and raw materials, except cotton, and know they must more and more; and here they market their manufactures, the enlarging demand for which from rapid increase of settlement, as yet keeps tonnage nearly equal. Southern trade, too, they know is more secure if drawn up to the lakes. Besides these influences, strengthening year by year, they forget not the augmenting profits on their long railways, which the longer they are, the more desirable the extension of both trunks and branches.

That Chicago has had no capital; that she depends entirely upon New York and New England; that this conjoint interest has moved to the construction of the railway system here centering, our opponents constantly show to disparage Chicago. We thank them for the benefit resulting. The East in its liberality aiding public improvements, especially such as immedidiately concern themselves, have perhaps not well observed the antagonism of these anti-Chicago grooves. Should it not have influence? Still, notwithstanding their excess of liberality, three-fourths the mileage gives Chicago such prominence as the chief railway centre of the Great Interior, that already every Atlantic and Gulf city from the St. Lawrence to Mexico, is more concerned in facilitating intercourse with this than any other city. With the wisdom of the past thus demonstrated in backing up Chicago, will the sagacious business men of the East stultify themselves by changing policy? Although the natural result appear inevitable, that in only one more generation, the Queen of the Lakes must surpass any ocean city; yet to do best for themselves, the whole capital of New York and New England must support Chicago.

Other important facts enter into the basis of the argument, and at pp. 102–107 a summary is presented of nine points Chicago possesses, each essential to a city's greatness in the Great Interior, but of which no other city has any three. Is it a work of supererogation for a city to gather the evidences of these important truths, and thereby acknowledge its obligations to God and country for benefits conferred in unexampled number and measure? With this solid basis of prosperity, is not wisdom manifested in its widest exhibition? What do we so need to fulfill nature's ordinations and perfect the work of art, as to let the world know how the past growth has been attained? A half century hence the most unaccountable feature of this book will be, the indifference of the citizens to so important a presentation.

AIMS.

Not to promote Speculation, but Confidence in the Real Estate. Every thing speculative is carefully eschewed in this volume. The running title, "Past, Present and Future of Chicago Investments," is closely adhered to on every page. The query facing the title-page presents as practical, as important a question, as business men can consider, whether as affecting individual or public interests. Its demonstration is one of the most influential upon our destiny as a nation, that can be presented. From the time that "Nimrod began to be mighty in the earth," by building Babylon and other cities, there is no historic record of any nation which has not been made by its chief city or cities; and as these multiply and grow, so grows the nation. If there be a city ordained by nature, established by art as certain to be chief of the continent, what fact is more important to this practical day and generation? But our object is not merely to demonstrate this; it is the still more practical one of inviting attention to the advantages such a city offers for investments in its realty. While fact and testimony prove the unequaled opportunities which Chicago affords in commerce, manufactures, railroads, and every branch of business, it also shows that in the certain growth of the City, and consequent advance in value of real estate, is even a greater pecuniary advantage.

At p. 288 is a table of annual assessments of property since Chicago became a city, showing the real to be two to five-fold the personal. For a citizen, then, to obtain his due proportion of the values created by his own direct efforts, the active business man should have his proportion of the realty, as land is judiciously distinguished. Needing only men and money to advance Chicago to its destiny, do we not wisely to invite attention to the solid basis for both security and profit which the land of that city must afford, which, beyond peradventure, must be chief of the Great Interior, and as such, probably, emporium of the continent? Will the chief city of America cease growth when that dignity shall have been achieved? With Europe and Asia running a race to people and to develop this combination of benefits of Egypt and of Palestine; with climate and every natural advantage all which we could desire; with the commingled blood of more Caucasian families than has been hitherto obtained to rule and work the inferior races with unexampled profit, why should not a century to a century and a half make Chicago chief city of the world?

To show that the Great Interior must Build up many Great Cities. Chicago desires to have it understood, that while these expectations are reasonable, as certain of achievement as any thing human can be, she is no monopolist; and instead of desiring to see other cities, either on lake or on river, dwindling like stars to leave her a glittering sun, she rejoices in the truth that we constitute no ordinary nation, but a constellation of sovereign, free and independent States, which fact of art itself tends to create many centres, while nature, in these immense vallies of thousands of miles, has ordained sites for many great cities. Because Chicago is sure of being chiefest, it is her interest and ambition that her own section should have several chief cities; and now, as the most terrible of civil wars, the most trying ordeal of a nation, has only demonstrated our indivisible unity and strength, the superiority of many interior cities over any on the oceans, is only a question of time; a short one at that.

The penultimate section of the volume is entitled "Other Cities no Measure for Chicago," which appears to be a legitimate deduction from the preceding discussion; but the conclusion is, "Room for them and us." This important topic, it is true, did not have the consideration its importance claims, for material had been so abundant that although much copy prepared was excluded under every head, still the volume had already swelled unduly; and as this was designed to be only the first of a series, it was seen that the growth of other cities could be better examined after the census of 1870. But no one can examine this mass of fact and testimony about the Great Interior; without seeing that this is the region, this the age, to develop great cities.

Notwithstanding the waste land of the Atlantic States, observe the rapid growth of cities, especially the chief ones, though only eighty to ninety miles apart. Here the chief centres of railways, and usually on navigable water, are one hundred and fifty to three hundred miles apart, with almost no waste land. Most are fully equal if not superior to eastern cities in gathering raw materials and food for manufacturing; and as the growth of eastern cities has been chiefly made in the last thirty years, and as an effect of railways, who can doubt that for two or three generations the growth of interior cities will be more than twice that of the Atlantic? How long, then, before they are eclipsed, however rapid their increase? And grow, they will, indefinitely.

Therefore, though this first volume is not what it should be upon this point, it will be found a solid and permanent basis for every city in the Interior to measure its own growth and future greatness. Every one of them but St. Louis already gives over the contest, and they know that this is the proper city to issue a volume each new census in behalf of the Great Interior, exhibiting the relative progress of country and of cities. What city of this region is not vitally interested in this examination? What one will not welcome the volume and use it efficiently to promote their own special interests? They all know that without any mock generosity, the interest of Chicago is to do her best to build up every other city, even her closest sister, Milwaukee, which is yet as far off as New York is from Philadelphia.

That this volume is at least fair and reasonable is proved by the negative conduct of the editors of Cincinnati and St. Louis. The inquiries naturally compelled to consider relative changes of the three cities, and finding that a second edition was to be indefinitely deferred, it seemed expedient to send their editors copies, lest we should seem timid concerning comparisons instituted by us. A copy was sent each of the five chief papers of both cities, with a courteous note requesting a copy of their remarks upon it to be sent to the author. Nothing has been received, and the only allusion observed was a characteristic squib of the *Missouri Democrat*, similar to that quoted (page 395), when the walls of a brick building in process of erection were blown over, the editor remarking that no doubt Mr. Wright was correct in his elaborate work upon Chicago, in saying that they are deficient in capital. Cincinnati, as the volume attests, submits to her fate with good grace; but St. Louis kicks the goad which should spur her to proper ambition, and could she find fault with the volume, either in matter or spirit, surely would it be done. No invidious remark disgraces its pages. Even the opinion that if Kansas City can obtain the lead decidedly of Leavenworth and Lawrence, it will outgrow St. Louis, is not to injure the latter, but only the stronger to express the conviction of the certainty of many great cities in the Great Interior. Kansas City and St. Louis are nearly three hundred miles asunder, and every two or three hundred miles will make an important railway centre, throughout these hundreds of thousands of square miles of fertile and rich mineral lands.

To show that the Great Interior, a complete Unit in Interest, must have its own Centre, which is found and established. To present the points in favor of this proposition, would be to write the book over again. The trade of the river vallies above St. Louis, which she perfectly monopolized, we see has been transferred to Chicago with wonderful rapidity, as avenues to the lakes have been opened. We also see that St. Louis could not retain the region immediately contiguous to herself; for the Hannibal and St. Joseph railroad, built right in Missouri, by and for herself, works so adversely as actually to dismember her own State. Nor has war occasioned the change; a feeble tune they whistle to keep up sinking courage. Their admissions previous to the war (pp. 111-114), are conclusive that the changes began in 1857; and though, as predicted in 1861 (p. 19), the war expedited change of trade from the border cities, yet the relative figures of the two cities for the years since confirm the claim, that the transfer from the queen of the rivers to the queen of the lakes was natural and inevitable. A conclusive example of the contest and its results is given in the freight receipts of the Chicago, Alton and St. Louis railroad, and the Jacksonville branch, whereon the contest has been direct, she having the advantage of possession for years.

It remains for the relative retrograder to prove that the causes of art and nature which have wrought these changes, must again change and work in her favor. Trade being preëminently centripetal in its nature; the larger part of the trade of the whole river vallies having forsaken St. Louis as new channels have been opened by art to the centre ordained by nature; what possible forces of art and nature can be brought to bear to change the present centre of the Great Interior? Could new forces supplant the old, will they of their own inherent power supplant Chicago? If any new forces superior to railway and telegraph be brought into existence, they will be more efficient centralizers as well as developers; increasing yet more the disparity between the many cities and that one which must be at least chief of the Great Interior. Human instrumentality must make operative the new as old; and what shall induce a "race of humans," who have neglected the old, to employ the new? Would not those experienced in the old be expected to best employ the new with energy and wisdom?

Whence shall come the power to change what is evidently the natural current of events of the Great Interior? Not as hitherto shall we beg and plead for wise and just acts of Congress to advance our interests. The basin between the Allegheny and Rocky Mountains, a complete unit in its every interest, soon rules the Republic.

To show that the Chief City of the Great Interior must, probably, be Emporium of the Continent. However presumptuous and arrogant this aim may seem, one lower would fall below the natural result of the disscussion. That this million and a half square miles, the richest agricultural and mineral region of the world, has one natural and artificial centre, assures its superiority over other centres of less advantageous and smaller sections, unless the trade of the Great Interior itself can be chiefly borne to some outside centre. The struggle between Atlantic cities is for the commerce of, and manufactures for this identical region; and the admission is universal, that the party successful will be chief of the continent. Therefore, our endeavor should be and is, to show how much greater must be the traffic of such an area within itself, than with the whole world beside; that instead of our products going to New York for distribution, each town and city will obtain supplies directly from the centre of production, where the greatest variety and choice will always be found; and that manufacturers who look hitherward for consumers, will dispense with an intermediary on the sea-coast, employing factors at the central mart of consumption. The calculating East will not be long in ascertaining the disadvantages of a secondary market like New York, compared with a primary like Chicago.

Such a trade-centre would be equally desirable for manufacturers, provided other considerations concurred. Another aim has therefore been, to exhibit the superior advantages Chicago possesses to gather raw materials of every kind, and the section "Conjunction of Coal, Iron, and other Minerals," shows that nowhere can these chief ones, and lead, copper and zinc, be as cheaply brought together. The section "Local Advantages, and City Expansion," exhibit superiority upon almost every element, especially climate, pure water, good sewerage, and ease of increasing water frontage; and the section "No other Point of equal Convergence of either Rail or Water, or of both, on the Globe," shows that first essential for a large manufacturing city, the greatest possible gathering and distributing facilities. The commercial advantages are quite well understood, but these could not be a safe reliance for continental supremacy. Manufactures are even more influential; and because Chicago has in both departments advantages superior to any other city, must she be emporium of the continent.

Also, the chief commercial and manufacturing centre of the Great Interior, would be a mart of trade equally sought by other sections, as their centres could possibly be by it. More and more will foreign trade diminish relatively with domestic; and further, direct importations must rapidly increase at the interior centre, soon to come from Europe by the St. Lawrence without transhipment, or burthened at most with only the trifling cost of transfer at an Atlantic port. Especially, when in only twenty years from the first advent of the locomotive, the centre of the Great Interior has been made by foreign capital the chief railway centre of the world with more and stronger trunk lines than any other city; must not facilities be multiplied with the development of this unequaled region? If in very infancy such powers of centralization are manifested, what must be the youth and manhood?

With this broad basis, the proposition must be regarded moderate. The limit is made to probability, not because of any doubt as to the result, but for the reason that to prove the certainty, the claims of New York,

Philadelphia and San Francisco must be examined as have been those of Cincinnati and St. Louis. For that the materials are not gathered.

If Chicago be the sure emporium of the Great Interior, that is a long step continental-ward, and must suffice for the present.

To show that Chicago has a Population equal to her Advantages. With these unexampled combinations of nature and of art; with the destiny of our City as certain as anything human can be, it is nevertheless true that our destiny, and the results of these combinations, are largely dependent upon the citizens themselves. Therefore, the character of a city is an important element in the calculation of its future. If important to the individual, who is here to-day, gone to-morrow, far more so is it to the enduring city. City character, too, once formed, is as much more difficult of change, as the body politic is more permanent than the individual. Nothing more than lofty character in a city draws to it high-toned citizens, or gives faith to obligations public or private. Good government, judicious financial management, faithfulness in covenant obligations, are indispensable characteristics; and without unanimity, energy, and enterprize, no city can expect others to spend money extensively for its close fellowship, nor dependently nor independently make much progress; so that an important element of the work would be, the development of our true character.

While this would be unbecoming to do directly, the proverb "actions speak louder than words," relieves the embarrassment, and while we let them speak, the discussion naturally brings together disinterested opinions from abroad. So that although modesty in presenting Chicago's merits would not generally be charged as a prominent failing, still it is rather relieving that the index under Capital, Commerce, Manufactures, Trade, etc., affords our eastern friends sufficient assurance of faithful employment of means entrusted, to keep up their supplies of aid. As almost every city has been indebted chiefly to its own efforts for its attainments, it seems to have been imagined that this magic growth was the consequence of extraordinary qualities in our population. Undue credit has therefore been accorded us, a sweet morsel we roll under our tongue with intense satisfaction; though we are too practical, too sagacious in money-making, to desire to hold what it is to our profit to part with. We like to be regarded a smart city; yet if a better basis of prosperity can be proclaimed than our smartness, we are too smart not to make the truth known. And probably no declaration in the volume will be more generally assented to than that made in the section, "Difference between Chicago and other Western Centres," (page 70);—"The position rather than the character of the citizens has made us what we are. If with a different population, 'Chicago would be a different city'; so, too, ten times the population elsewhere located could never make a second Chicago."

While this truth should moderate self-conceit, it is also true that however great the natural and artificial advantages, they will only be effective according to skill and energy of employment. Not as Prof. Waterhouse argues (page 173), concerning the Queen of the Rivers, do we imagine that because Chicago " is ordained by the decrees of physical nature to become the great inland metropolis of the continent," that therefore " it cannot escape the magnificence of its destiny. Greatness is the necessity of its position." Our conduct from first to last proves that we believe and act upon the idea that notwithstanding nature has done far more for this site than any other known to man, still greatness, destiny depend, under Providence, solely upon the city itself. Not even the addition to nature of our railway system—art's *chef-d'œuvre*—and a cynosure to any other city, would be of much avail unless by our own endeavors they were made effective.

Paul's injunction "*work out your own salvation* with fear and trembling; FOR it is God that worketh in you both to will and to do of His good pleasure;" relates equally to affairs of time as of eternity. These sons not being mere machines, but co-workers with their Father, we shall never witness the fulfillment of nature's decrees, sitting beside a mighty river or lake awaiting the destiny to flow upon us which we deem inevitable. Man must work as though all depended upon himself, while with fear and trembling he wholly trusts, because all depends upon God. The grand doctrine is, if possible, more applicable to affairs of time than of eternity; for man as an individual is to be dealt with through those never ending ages, and knowing not what is best for him here, plans and efforts are often overruled in mercy and wisdom. But associated humanity—the family, church, city, state, nation,—ends with this life, and here the body politic is rewarded exactly as it obeys the laws of nature and of nature's God. The first law is to work, and without work where is any progress? That Chicago is an earnest worker is well known; and, though lamentably deficient in what should be done for the culture of head and heart, yet that we are not working wholly to make money, is attested by the record in these pages of what is doing in Religion and Education, Science and Art.

Yet works is not the essential nor vital principle. Next to life is faith the motive which actuates in earthly as in spiritual affairs. Faith nerves to works, and so surely produces them that literally, as James argued, "faith, if it have no works, is dead in itself." If no fruit is produced, the motive power is dead; so that as a man must have faith to "work out his own salvation" whether for time or eternity, so the city, to attain its hopes and fulfill its destiny, must have in large measure that "ground of things hoped for, the evidence of things which are not seen." These citizens manifest their faith remarkably, in utter indifference to this inquiry into the causes of our growth, confidence being unbounded that the whole world is abundantly informed. To sister cities, slow to believe that Chicago could neglect any opportunity to sound her praises, the indifference to this means of glorification would be unaccountable. Any other city which could exhibit a modicum of these achievements, however they were brought about, would scatter the information broadcast. With our well established character for sagacity and enterprise, the indifference to a volume of this sort, a wide distribution of which is demanded not more to render honorable acknowledgments for unequalled bestowments by God and country, than as a judicious financial operation to obtain more aid of the same kind, the indifference would be incredible but for the evidence afforded by the controversy with the Board of Trade, considered in the appendix. Nor is it stronger in them than in the citizens generally. With full assurance, the information is regarded not only useless, but indicative of conceit and vainglory, a meretricious vaunting of attainments which should be left to other cities who would be satisfied with *prestige*. So that conceit and vainglory, instead of inspiring to this endeavor, are its chief opponents. Any one worth teaching about Chicago, has already full information. Is this the right sort of faith? Let us have faith, proper faith in ourselves; yet does not this volume show that we have a surer basis of support than our own puny efforts, in the conjunction of forces of nature and of art? Therefore, we desire further—

To invite Consideration of the Obligations of City and Citizens, in view of the Unparalleled Benefits showered by God and Country. To make money, not to improve our morals, every man of us came to Chicago. Did we come, though, without firm belief that obligations, human and Divine, would here be regarded? Every man expected to become "a citizen of no mean city;" and will one which has been built by benefits conferred which cannot be reciprocated, be respected and honored at home or abroad, which refuses to make due acknowledgments? We came not to make fortunes as isolated individuals, but as citizens of a great city; to grow with its growth and strengthen with its strength, and our children after us. This examination into causes of prosperity shows our growth is due to extraordinary bounties of God and country. Our Father, doubtless, orders the forces of nature less for our benefit than to promote His own honor and glory; and so our country has taken its every step to promote its own interests, perfectly indifferent to its effects upon Chicago, if not actually regretting that the action of older cities, which must be pursued to advance their own interests, must result in building larger cities in the Great Interior. Is it no advantage to us to make these relations of art and nature apprehended? Thus honor and self-interest conjoining in result as they ever do with wise exercise, Chicago would belie herself not to improve this signal opportunity to render due honor for benefits conferred, and at the same time promote her own individual interests.

This idea, however, being an after-thought, not even developed in making the compilation, but an effect of the index, this impressive means of generalization would probably have a similar effect upon others, entirely obviating indifference. Citizens are generally indifferent, and some, hostile, for three reasons: 1st. Disgust with excessive laudation of Chicago. 2d. The volume seems useless, the whole world already knowing all about the subject. 3d. Inadequate realization of the little part citizens have had in our advancement, and our unparalleled obligations to God and country for our prosperity. The first two points have been considered in "Obligations" and "Duties" following, and the third is proved in the Appendix (§ xvi), by extracts from the preface of our last city directory, and from a recent newspaper.* The article there from the *U. S. Economist*, also shows how imperfectly the causes of growth are understood abroad, so that actual duty compels to this presentation of fact and testimony, giving honor where due, and at the same time showing that in the nature of things the same causes of art and nature must continue to operate, and with rapidly increasing force. But duty being too low a standard for reasoning men, we propose—

To show Fellow-Citizens their Right to prefer Expediency to Command, Privilege to Duty. "All things are lawful for me, but all things are not expedient: all things are lawful for me, but all things edify not. Let no man seek his own, but every man another's wealth." The body politic being essential to the individual, he that is wise seeks his own wealth, not individually and selfishly, but in the general good. In pursuing this worthy object, we need the best rules of conduct, and expediency commends itself as a higher standard than command; for the greater includes the less, and whatever is expedient must be lawful, though many things are lawful which are not expedient. Regarding merely our own dignity and honor, we should rise above subjection to command by seeking to do what is expedient, changing the rules of conduct given by God or man from duty into privilege. This is the one object of Paul's masterly arguments concerning law, which he applies primarily to time and to our fellow, but which we restrict to our God and to

---

* A correspondent of one of our papers from St. Louis, in a letter of April 5th, 1870, which is quite misplaced in that usually high-toned paper, says :—

"*How we Lost the Trade of Kansas.*—During all the spring comparatively few shipments of goods have been made from this city to Leavenworth, Lawrence, Topeka, and the trading centres of Kansas. A visit to the leading houses on Main and Second streets, and a few moments' conversation on the subject will draw out facts that are somewhat singular and not very creditable to the mercantile sagacity of St. Louis. The first frank admission is that Chicago undersells us, and the second is that she controls all the railroads of Kansas. Both are true. Goods can be shipped from Chicago through St. Louis to Leavenworth as cheap as they can be shipped from here to Leavenworth. Freights from Chicago to all points in Kansas are delivered with greater promptness and at lower rates to the same points, although there is an average of over one hundred and fifty miles in our favor. *Chicago has the enterprise to step in and compel the railroads to serve her interests, and if she can not do better, she buys them up. If there is any trade worth reaching that she does not already control, she at once builds a railroad to that point.*. St. Louis, on the contrary, invites New York to build and equip her railroads for her, and she sits supinely to-day aud sees Louisville and Cincinnati make new inroads in her Arkansas and Red River trades, rather than subscribe a few shares to a packet line that would secure and enlarge that trade. "Big profits or no sales," has been an axiom in our mercantile experience, and it has been damaging to our business relations with the Southwest. Another fault is a mercantile jealousy that prevents co-operation. The old houses of Southern proclivities have a distrust of the new firms that have settled in here from the East, and do not receive them cordially. They prefer to jog on in the old ruts, and too often look upon the influx of Eastern capitalists as an innovation."

Credit is due our merchants for enterprise and energy in availing themselves of the facilities for transportation to extend their trade. But except the railroad from Lawrence on to Galveston, where is a road that Chicago has bought up, or one she can be said to have built? Of the 17,000 miles of the interior, costing over $700,000,000, Chicago has never put in $10,000,000 of her own money, and has never raised, by her own influence, $50,000,000.

eternity. He says to Timothy, "exercise thyself unto Godliness. For bodily exercise profiteth little; but Godliness is profitable unto all things, which hath the promise of the life present, and of that that is to come. This is a true saying, and by all means worthy to be received."*

This point has some consideration in the Appendix, § ii., that paper being prepared not merely for that controversy, but as an example of the use of the code of honor, to incorporate in a general argument upon obligations of city and citizens, which was deemed appropriate law to accompany such a volume of fact and testimony, and it has had a year's constant study. But the effect of study being first to teach one how little he knows and how much is to be learned, as the investigation progressed, it taught prudence in presenting crude thoughts upon this profound and wide-reaching subject. So that as the present edition must soon be issued, that addition is now inexpedient though lawful, and another year will be taken for the examination. Discarding love, reason, utility and happiness as proper motives—if made even an object, they are never realized, whereas with proper motives and objects, all these glorious results flow in as subordinate means;—life, faith, honor and glory, will be found the true motives, and be made the premises to establish the rights and privileges of the sons as of their Father.

The subject will be found to have the closest possible relations to, and be the most efficient to promote, the one great object for which most of us live and labor—to make money. As we desire to do this in a legal way, we would be advantaged by more perfect acquaintance with legal obligations; as we desire to get wealth by the best and wisest means, we should be profited by knowledge of what is expedient. The religious aspect of the subject will not be presented, only the business; and we shall find that the strongest motives of self-interest equally with those of honor and glory, impel us to regard the province and responsibility of city and citizens as proclaimed upon the title-page, while at the same time we seek and use with utmost endeavor the most efficacious means to make money. This is both duty and privilege, in promoting which self-interest and honor will be found entirely concordant. No man can be too diligent in money-making, so that he seek and hold it as a means, not a paramount object or motive. Our one difficulty is that we lose sight of true honor and glory, making an end of what should be to us a humble instrument. Hence money, which next to knowledge is the strongest power of earth, we learn to love as the god of our idolatry, making it verily "the root of all evil."

With proper conceptions of our honor and our glory, these sons would not need positive command, the subjection of servants. A privilege instead of duty would it be to promote the same object for which our Father deemed no sacrifice too great, the best good of man. Man being his own worst

*1 Tim. vii., 9. Godliness is nothing more nor less than regard for our Father's laws; and whether we do this as a son to honor a Father, or merely to promote our own interests, yet even in that lowest human object, getting money for its own sake, the son is a fool who will not closely follow the commands and counsels of our Father.

enemy, he must form associations to preserve his life, the chief object. He can do nothing individually for his advancement; and could he isolated attain Gabriel's powers and wisdom, *cui bono?* He is created for association; and hence the force of Paul's deduction of the maximum of expediency as well as law, "let no man seek his own, but every man another's wealth." As a means to this ennobling end, the city is one of the most efficient; and no city having ever arisen with such a certain and glorious future, should it not be our first endeavor to know well our rights and privileges?

Let every city, too, "seek not her own, but every city another's wealth." What city ever grew which had so much to hope for from the growth of other cities, as Chicago? Most cities have their jealousies and rivalries, each considering itself injured relatively, its strength weakened, by the growth of cities in its region. Not so is Chicago. As she gets wisdom, she will learn more and more to live up to Paul's maxim, and seek her own wealth in the general prosperity. Therefore, a grander, more important theme cannot be imagined for the continental emporium, than this of converting duty into privilege, command into expediency. Now in the infancy of many cities which in a generation or two will be counted among the mightiest of earth, what can the chief one do more effective for citizens and cities, than to lead in the study of their obligations, merely regarding pecuniary profit? Let our tythes be consecrated to the holiest, most glorious object of our Father, the establishing of permanent institutions for man's improvement and elevation, and what a glory will the cities of the Great Interior become to themselves as well as to our nation and our GOD.

N. B. The endorsement of this work by the liberal subscription of the Board of Trade, is general, not special. No member has probably read it critically enough to have judged every point; and probably no other body of men would have more varied and more decided opinions concerning details.

CHICAGO, *May, 1870.*

OBJECTIONS—DUTIES—EFFECTS.

OBJECTIONS.

Not only the habitual fault-finder, the supercilious detractor, but also the candid judge, the best friend of work and author, might entertain reasonable objections to such a book. In advising with Fellow-Citizens, and seeking their aid, some objections have been too often produced to doubt that they are reasonable, and should be met to secure any considerable distribution, without which the book had better never have been written.

"*Too much Puffing of Chicago already.*"—Too true; and for that very reason, were there none still more obligatory, should an essay such as this is designed to be, be no longer deferred. Bald assertion, mere declamation, have from necessity been too much used; and to such an extent, that even many of our own Citizens imagine that we have no solid basis for our claims to greatness. Do not many conceive it impossible that Chicago should be the largest city on the continent, or even of cities inland? vain arrogance to intimate the possibility?

Other cities issue elaborate arguments, magnifying their advantages of nature and art, giving reasons for future growth, which, being never questioned, are supposed true. The annual reports of our Board of Trade, grand as they would be could their figures be contrasted with other cities to realize the immense difference, are but a dry mass of statistics, with no pretense to explain the why and wherefore of their magnitude. The nearest approach to the sort of paper required, are the annual statements of our enterprising newspapers, and their occasional articles upon special branches of business. Although these have been interesting and valuable, they fail, of course, to offer anything like a philosophic inquiry into the general causes of past progress, and of their future continuance. These statements greatly exceed older and larger cities; and as the easiest and only way to meet them, the entire western press for many years has charged us with "puffing" and "blowing." With every city but one, however, the controversy has been with all good nature; but St. Louis, seeing her laurels one after another passing upon the head of her "beautiful rival," has put more spleen and spite than fun into her hits, as these pages attest. Our editors, too confident in their truth to treat these charges seriously—too conscious of our superiority to lose temper—let their colleagues have their fun, and help them after the fashion of the *Chicago Times*:—

Chicago.—Chicago is the general headquarters of all the excellence extant among people and things. No sooner does an individual gain a more than local notoriety than he starts for Chicago. The moment a singing club or an opera troupe achieves some sort of a status, it makes its way to Chicago. Chicago is the head-centre, the Mecca, of all creation.

Strakosch has just been here. The Boston Quintette Club did the unheard-of-thing—in Bostonians—of leaving the sound of the great Boston organ to visit the Garden City. Joseph Jefferson is here. General Sherman was here the other day. Weston is coming as fast as his legs will bring him. Joe Coburn is in town. *

All these people coming here do not tax excessively either the accomodations, hospitality or cash of the Garden City. All the professionals, from a prima donna to a billiard expert, come here, get rich, and go away, and yet Chicago grows no poorer. Its capacity for giving, like its lake, is inexhaustible. No other city could stand such a drain on its resources without going into bankruptcy. All this is evidence that Chicago is one of the greatest cities on the continent.

What other city is the headquarters of the notabilities of all creation? What other employs a vast lake for a reservoir, or uses water condensed from steaming laboratories a thousand miles deep in the centre of the earth. Where is there anything like the Chicago Board of Trade, the Chicago faro banks, or the confidence men and operators of Chicago?

We are liable to be charged with extravagance when moderate, to be considered joking when in down-right earnest; for our growth is a marvel even to ourselves, until operating causes are examined. For such examination newspapers are not adapted. Their columns, filled with long disquisitions, would never be read; so that more than any other class, editors want the philosophy of a subject elsewhere studied out, which their readers can be supposed to be familiar with, the truths of which they apply practically. Reasonable hypothesis, positive but prospective results, even actual facts, are doubted or denied, simply for want of information which every intelligent business man in the country should have. Is it to be styled "puffing" to bring together the facts, and reasons of the facts? Is it not quite time that Chicago should be relieved of the charge of vain-glorious boasting, by a candid, thorough examination of the causes of her growth, and a methodical arrangement of statistics, not merely to exhibit results, but also to compare them with St. Louis?

Surely the Past, Present and Future of our young City, is a matter of transcendent importance; and if upon any one subject the public on all sides should desire to have a proper, thorough, philosophic examination of causes, it is in the title of this work. So far from claiming to reach this exalted standard, the imperfections of this endeavor are more and more realised as the great subject is more and more studied. At the same time, that has been my aim, and rising higher and higher; and such is the nature of the investigation, that only considerable industry in collecting materials, and some practical common sense in their arrangement, was wanted to work out a satisfactory result. And the chief satisfaction lies in the belief that St. Louis herself will regard the paper moderate. Upon such a theme, with such materials, the writer who would employ exaggeration would commit that contemptible wrong, a blunder. The truth itself, pressing on all sides like the atmosphere, is so full, so impressive, so satisfactory, that to resort to "puffing" and "blowing," would be to abandon native air for exhilirating gas.

"*Invidious Comparisons render us Odious.*"—A fair and just examination of the claims of Chicago to be the chief city of the West, is not invidious. To make that examination some comparison is indispensable; and should it be with second-class cities, or with the Queen of the Rivers, who has so constantly affirmed her natural right to be the first city of the Great West, that in the absence of any candid examination of her pretensions, the whole public has come to admit her claims? That either St. Louis or Chicago is to be the chief city of the West, is now universally conceded. Is it of no importance or interest to Chicago to exhibit the causes hitherto operating, which, with lightning speed, have sent her clear past former rivals, notwithstanding their *prestige*, their firmly established business, their immense wealth? Will it not hasten her advancement to show with what certainty these influences must not only continue to operate in her favor, but with constantly augmenting power, until the whole West shall be bound to her with the same close bands with which she holds Illinois, Iowa, and Wisconsin?

To establish the adverse claims of Chicago, disparagement of Cincinnati or St. Louis is not required. So far from it, that they and others must grow and rapidly to be immense cities, is one of the strongest points in the argument. But the nonsense that centrality on the rivers insures large superiority to St. Louis, is a bubble which has long wanted pricking. Nor is any injustice done in fairly contrasting lake and river advantages, and the past and future of railways.

No other city than St. Louis can complain of the manner of treatment; nor can she with any reason. If she can manfully resist the argument, and prove errors of statement, fallacies of reasoning, let her bestir herself, and show some positive strength on her side. The facts and actual results are incontrovertible; and if she complain of the ridicule of her pretentious claims to natural location, the only hook to hang a complaint upon, she condemns herself for the persistence with which she adheres to the offensive assumption. Is not that the beginning, and the end, and the substance—light as it is—of Professor Waterhouse's paper, herein quoted, and considered so able as to be incorporated in the Report of the Merchant's Exchange of St. Louis? and again that potential argument appears, evidently regarded perfect and unanswerable, being stereotyped with various others by the same author in a pamphlet, "edition 20,000 copies" on the title page, and doubtless several more editions.

"*Everybody already Knows about Chicago.*"—If that be true, how is it that St. Louis can and does maintain its claims to certain supremacy, in the judgment of candid men throughout the East? Nor need we go from this city to find many such believers.

That the West is abundantly able to build up great cities, is quite generally acknowledged. Still, even this idea is by no means apprehended as its importance demands. No section of the Union, not even New England, has stronger homogeny than the great plain between the Alleghany and Rocky Mountains. This being well understood, together with the immense benefits hitherto conferred by the wide-spread river navigation, making a unit of about a million square miles, it has been naturally and universally imagined, that because St. Louis is mistress of more than 16,500 miles of river navigation, as Professor Waterhouse effectively argues, p. 171, she "is ordained by the decrees of physical nature to become the great inland metropolis of this continent. It cannot escape the magnificence of its destiny. Greatness is the necessity of its position." Now, is it demeaning to Chicago to examine these claims which are very generally received as truth, and show their absurdity, easily as it may be done, and really without detraction? Is it judicious to trust alone to time and circumstances to correct these false assumptions; or should we present fairly the superiority of lake to river navigation, and the certainty that even the latter must pour more trade into the lakes, than into the Gulf of Mexico? Then, is it no object to exhibit the complete revolution effected by east and west railways, rendering rivers merely their adjuncts? why and how it is that Chicago has so rapidly become the greatest railway centre of the world?

Most good friends look approvingly upon Chicago as a very smart city, whose business men have wonderful energy to be able to rival the Queen of the Rivers, notwithstanding her vast superiority in natural position, in river navigation, in established trade, in immense wealth. With no investigation into the conjunction of causes operating by nature and by art to produce these unexampled results, the reason thereof is not at all apprehended by us, still less by non-residents, and none wonder at it more than we do ourselves. Yet we have a natural pride in it to which we give expression; and the *Chicago Courier* well observes:—

Chicago people may be excused for referring, on almost every occasion, to the greatness of our city, for its growth has become a marvel to all creation. Nothing proves the importance, absolute and relative, of the city of Chicago more than does the constant reference made to it by the rest of the world. Not a magazine paper, which has for its object the demonstration of enterprise, that does not point to Chicago; there is scarcely a modern book, be it descriptive, historical or romantic, that does not find one or more comparisons for Chicago; the newspapers on both sides of the Atlantic have something to say in every issue about Chicago; people in the East, who feign ignorance of everything Western, always admit that they have heard remarkable things about Chicago; foreigners, who are in fact ignorant of the geography of the country and the customs of our people, know something about Chicago. * * * * Our peculiar institutions, our unparalleled growth, our well-rewarded energy—all command respect where they do not challenge rivalry and excite envy.

The *New York Tribune*, with a singular candor, that the journals of lesser cities would do well to imitate, has recently paid a just tribute to the prosperity and enterprise of our city. It says:—

"Chicago, which in 1831, contained only twelve families, has increased during the years 1860 to 1868 from a population of 109,263 to 220,000. The assessed value of its real and personal property has increased during the same period from $37,053,512 to $192,249,644, while the municipal taxation has risen from $373,315 to $2,489,245. * * * For a period of peace, such a growth would be marvelous, and, during an era of war, no city of past or present times surpasses it. The growth of Brooklyn and of New York has been enormous during the same period. Throughout the North, and especially the West and Northwest, there has been a steady, sound, and healthy growth, of which, however, the growth of Chicago must be conceded to be the magnificent and truly unprecedented culmination."

Now, is it not quite time that Chicago ceased to be a baby-wonder of precocity, and rested upon her natural endowments and her acquired improvements as not being at all extraordinary, but entirely legitimate? a result to have been naturally expected with reasonable forecast? Until we are able to take and maintain that position, we shall continue as hitherto to be looked upon as of mushroom growth, while St. Louis from her age and strength and natural progress is compared to the solid oak. Here and there an eastern man, as the *Tribune* editor, apprehends the truth, and appreciates the natural as well as artificial superiority of Chicago. But almost universally it is supposed to be due to our greater energy and activity, which will soon give out, and then St. Louis' inherent strength, and immense natural resources, will put her speedily far in advance.

If even our Citizens doubt whether Chicago is to be the chief city of the West, as many do, is it not certain that the error must prevail extensively elsewhere? Suppose its correction be not very important to our prosperity, is it not desirable?

Then, very few have thorough knowledge of Chicago, because information like this has never been compiled. Never was there a young city to which it would have been of equal advantage to disseminate full knowledge concerning it, as to Chicago. Has the day for this entirely passed, that we may fold our hands, and consider growth attained? When will means and effort be more effective than now?

"*It tends to create a Spirit of Speculation.*" Is truth or falsehood speculative? Can a thorough knowledge of the truth do a man injury, upon either important or unimportant affairs? Some conceited conservatives deem themselves the only persons to be entrusted with full knowledge, and would make themselves custodians of the world. Said Job to such—

No doubt but ye are the people,
And wisdom shall die with you.

Men of that stripe have their use, for it takes all sorts to make up a world; and Chicago is sufficiently cosmopolitan to have bright specimens of even such.

Should these views lead some of our business men to speculate somewhat upon the point, whether it might not be expedient to become proprietors of their own homes and business locations, is it not likely to do more good to themselves and families than harm? Will speculation of that sort be a public injury? These landlords may demur to the proposition, and object to their tenants becoming landholders; but will not the stability and solidity of the City be enhanced, if in their legitimate pursuits these active Citizens become large owners of the realty of Chicago? Who should have their part of it if not these merchants, manufacturers, mechanics and head-workers who are doing most of what is done to promote public interests? With a few commendable exceptions, what have these large real-estate owners done for the City — what are they now doing — compared with the active business men? Let enough speculative feeling be generated to see the wisdom of paying more interest-money and less rent-money, saving to themselves and children the rise certain otherwise to accrue to others from their own legitimate pursuits. Moderation is indispensable in this as any other good thing; but is such a spirit of speculation to be deprecated?

"*Too long a Story!*" Will the objector please run over the table of contents, and determine what topics he would have excluded, which would not break the catenation? If the query preceding the title page be of no consequence; if the statements below it be unworthy of consideration, that is one thing. But if the statements be worthy of proof, the query to be answered affirmatively, a good deal of space is indispensable; and with further sub-division, and still more expansion, the argument would be more conclusive. Contraction could best have been used in the extracts from St. Louis papers; yet who will deny that their evidence is the most effective part of the essay? No reasonable reader, who admits the propriety of the work, will complain of length after due examination. It is literally *multum in parvo*; for many able writers and speakers are made to discuss every point with much wisdom, and superfluity is exscinded. Then the information is usable, being easily found under its appropriate head, and by the marginal notes, as well as by the index.

These, however, are only negative points. Any subject worth considering has also a positive side. Let us, then, also look at—

DUTIES.

The Bible, with no circumlocution, recognizes the existence of man in various *stati* or conditions, which we style the Family, the Church, the City or Village, the State, the Nation. They are not only indispensable to human progress, but a man out of them is like a fish out of water. After instructing us in our duties to our God, the Bible is chiefly occupied in giving laws and counsel relating to these various *stati.* Had we only wisdom to obey its laws, to heed its perfect counsel, what a Heaven should we have here upon this earth! Whatever enables us to prize more highly in any degree these relations of life; especially, whatever stimulates us to more earnest efforts to fulfil their respective duties, or to obtain more perfect knowledge thereof, is worthy our regard.

To one of these relations in particular, that of the City, your attention is herein invited; and one which seems to take close hold on every other.

Duty to Ourselves and Families.—An intelligent man does not operate hap-hazard, but according to definite plans. His success in business not only depends upon proper method, but upon sufficient and accurate knowledge of the city where he lives, of the country tributary, and of all relating circumstances. Therefore, duty to himself and family requires every good husband and father, who has had the wisdom to choose Chicago for his home, to study thoroughly into its Past, that he may correctly apprehend the Future, and improve the Present. Especially does he need to investigate all influences operating upon the extension of the commerce and manufactures of the City, and the growth of its population.

Without that knowledge, how can he plan about his business? How can he judge whether it be best to stay here as a tenant, or become proprietor in the soil? That man is a fool who chooses a place of business in which to spend years of energy and hard work, the best years of his life, and have no interest in the results except the mere profits of his business. Are *you* one of the unwise many? Even in 1860 the census made real-estate of Cook County $84,665,387; and personal only $32,076,447,—less than one-half! The value of the land has been made here, though we have not all the profits by a great deal; but of personal property, how much is foreign capital brought in? Some profits of trade, too, have been put into land; but go back only fifteen years and ascertain the amount withdrawn from business, and see what have been the relative profits since on the real-estate.

The man, however, who regards duty to himself and family, considers some other profit than merely that of dollars and cents. The first object of every man who is fortunate enough to have a wife, should be to have a home. How much of family interest, of home sentiment, can be cultivated in the *caravanserai* of a boarding house or hotel? His endeavor, too, should be, at the earliest day possible to own his home. No other influence equals this to elevate character, generate self-respect, give substance to society.

The man with large capital should begin in Chicago with buying his place of business and his residence. Of course the beginner with small capital must at first be a tenant; but at the earliest day practicable, if a manufacturer and unable to buy, he should rent a lot with the privilege of purchase, and put up his own buildings, calculating for enlargement. A merchant in three to five years can become sufficiently established, to join with others and buy lots a little back, with credit on part of the purchase, which when paid for will be ample security, with an assignment of insurance policies, for a loan to erect the store. A half dozen enterprising men can take business where they choose. So, too, with residences. Rents are enormous, because so many refuse to build for themselves. A year or two as tenant may be best, to enable a man to judge wisely as to his location. Then he should buy his lot according to his means, and become his own landlord, in a house suited to his circumstances. If a tenant of an elegant stone front thinks his family might object to coming down a peg, lest they be snubbed by some of the codfish aristocracy; let him advise with his wife, and if she approve not the change, he certainly made a mis-choice and has no better-half. The children, wife and husband who will not have enough more satisfaction in living in a moderate house of their own, to compensate for what they may lose of the society of snobs, have most certainly taken their proper places among the codfish aristocracy. Fortunately for Chicago they very little affect society, most of these Citizens having independence sufficient to do that which they deem right and best. It is only necessary to invite their attention to these considerations of their duty, and they will decide wisely.

Duty to the Church.—Although considering merely business affairs, not religious, yet the Founder of every rightful human institution having made the Church a no less essential status of the social fabric than the others, we should make it one of our chief business concerns. Notwithstanding, very many of these Citizens, to the disgrace of civilization, wholly neglect this important duty. They give money for an edifice and to support the Church organization, perhaps attend public worship regularly, yet persistently decline membership. Worse even than heathen, they refuse public acknowledgment of their God as their Lord and Master.

Even all Jews are not Church-members, much less all nominal Christians. Is not our God unreasonable in requiring acknowledgment of his claims, or we in withholding His due? Ought it to be so very difficult for one who enjoys, not only the unequaled natural bounties showered upon us, but the greater gifts of civil and religious liberty, to acknowledge his obligations? Let us think of these things, Fellow-Citizens, and we shall soon come to consider the claims of our God for infinitely greater blessings, and rejoice to be connected with some branch of His Church; and which is of small importance compared with the duty itself that we avouch Jehovah to be our Lord.

Duty to Our City.—It is this aggregation of families, creating another body politic, which we style City, which affords these unexampled opportunities to benefit ourselves and families. To the City of Chicago, then, these Citizens owe weighty obligations. The Citizens constitute the City, and mould its character and destiny; and each of us owes duty thereto according to our natural and acquired capacities and means. Our duty, too, is in proportion to the magnitude of interests involved, not merely immediate, but prospective; for as foundations shall be laid, sure and strong, so rises the superstructure, firm, secure, to its topmost stone of glory. Nor is the ground-work yet finished, although the pile itself begins to rise upon foundations well laid by the noble spirits who have been called to their reward. A few of us are yet spared, who from the very first have lent feeble aid in the holy work; and whatever regrets for other labors, have we any for time, effort or money bestowed in laying deep and broad the basis of our social fabric, with the solid stones of education and religion, superadding the various adornments of civilization? The most faithful most laments that ten times more had not been done for these chief interests, and thereby much useless, misspent work and means have been saved.

What inroads death has made upon the fraternal circle of old settlers, which, until the last few years, seemed to have almost a charmed existence! Realising more than others, as we ought to do, the immense future of Chicago, as "friend after friend departs," how should we be stimulated to the discharge of duty! "for there is no work, nor device, nor knowledge, nor wisdom, in the grave whither thou goest."

Did these Citizens all realise their duties to their City, would they run away, and stay away, to avoid, as some imagine, calls upon them for various public interests? If they have not these niggardly motives, which should cause them to be shunned when they return, they have a very simple and proper means to correct prevalent impressions, and insure a cordial welcome. Not all absent ones, however, will be put in this category, by any means.

Are many of these large bond-holders, or real estate owners, who stay at home—some of them are too miserly to spend money in traveling—are they any better than their contemptible *confrères* abroad? Were it not for the active, enterprising business men, who have very little—too little—of the real estate, what would be done? Why St. Louis makes so little headway, as their papers intimate more than charge, as they ought to do—and would do if they had proper independence—is because of the close grasp of the real estate owners to their money. Fortunately, property here is more diffused; yet our large real estate holder, who is not a down-right curse to the City, is an exception to the rule. We can only pray that in GOD's good time their wealth may be speedily distributed to more faithful stewards. Still there are notable exceptions.

To perform our duty to our City, we must know well what Chicago is to be. The importance of present efforts accords with the ratio of increase. If there is to be little change in this generation, we may leave much for the next with comparatively little injury. If, however, we can by a little investigation satisfy ourselves that the march of the City is to be far more rapid than was ever witnessed, until it becomes one of the mightiest, how imperative the duty that we make that examination, and increase our endeavors acccordingly! Our mistakes will cost our children immense sums to remedy; and this very book will witness against us that we knew our duty and did it not. This is no place to particularize; but we all know, or ought to know, that although this young City has already risen to be at least sixth, perhaps fifth, in the Union, we are still extending foundations, while we rear the superstructure. Broad, and deep, and strong, must be the base for a city of millions here to live within a generation or two. So, while some may lament that they could not have had equal opportunity with old settlers, and been more faithful; let them bless God and take courage for the abundant occasions still remaining to do their duty to their City.

The work to be done is herculean, and we need all help possible to do it. For religion and education, in churches, schools, colleges, universities and libraries; for benevolent institutions of all sorts; for academies of the natural sciences and fine arts; for again raising the grade, as it must be; for providing parks, and adorning the suburbs as they should be in the Garden City, we want all help that can be brought to do it. What means more effective, than to acquaint friends and acquaintances abroad with the superior advantages of this City for every kind of manufacture or branch of commerce? With the certain and large advance of the real estate, ensuring to every man in ten to twenty years, for merely his place of business and residence, a good estate for his family, besides the profits of a well-established business; what other city could compete with this were the facts only made known?

Nor should we fail to make it understood that Chicago rests not upon her laurels, when, with a million or two inhabitants, she shall be acknowledged Queen of the Great Interior. This vast agricultural plain between the Alleghanies and Rocky Mountains, is entirely homogeneous, and will be a unit in its interests. The whole mining region, dependent upon and closely connected with the Old Northwest, goes with it in its every purpose. As herein shown, Chicago must be the centre of a *million and a half square miles.* Is it no object to demonstrate that such a region can and will make its centre chief of all cities of America? The arguments herein advanced were written by Mr. Scott, 25 years ago, before railways were introduced, and before the mountain region was developed, proving the superiority of internal over foreign commerce to create great cities. Are not the results perfectly confirmatory, proving to every fair and candid mind, that Chicago must be the chief city of the continent?

If it be desirable to bring together this information, is it not an object to give it wide distribution? Though not without benefit confined wholly to this City, yet is not its influence dependent mainly upon extent of distribution abroad? In the East it should go to inform them of our superior advantages for business of all kinds, to bring hither both settlers and capital. In the West, and especially the South, where we have competition, the information as to the best market is wanted.

Duty to Our State.—The motto of Illinois—State Sovereignty, National Union—the most admirable epitome of the immutable principles upon which our system is based, which can possibly be framed in our noble mother-tongue; would induce me here to exhibit the perfect, absolute subordination of these Citizens and of this City, to the sovereign, free and independent State of Illinois. Yet, such is the prejudice against the doctrine of State Rights, because of its gross perversion by the school of South Carolina, it would probably create a prejudice against the book itself to show in any manner whatever that our motto is sound. Therefore, very much against my inclination, biding the good time coming, when this cardinal truth of our system will be as much honored as it is now abhorred, we must for the present purpose consider our State responsibility on a less substantial basis.

This magnificent State of Illinois, stretching from almost the southern line of Kentucky and Virginia, and almost to the northern line of Massachusetts, has been the making of Chicago. That excellent, sagacious man, who so long adorned the Federal Judiciary, Nathaniel Pope, was fortunately Territorial Delegate in Congress when initiatory steps were taken for the inchoate body politic to create itself into a perfect State, for the purpose of admission into the Union. At Mr. Pope's instance the northern boundary was extended far enough above the southern bend of Lake Michigan, to render sure that Fort Dearborn, at the mouth of the Chicago River, should be within the State of Illinois. The plan then was, in 1818, that era of good fellowship, to construct a canal from that Fort to the Illinois River, making this State a strong ligament of *National Union;* for she grasped by the imprescriptible prerogatives of *State Sovereignty,* the best navigation of the Father of Waters with her southern arm, and that of this chain of Great Lakes with her northern arm. Even if the fathers were fools, and the sons so much better informed as to the nature of our Union, was it not very natural for them to adopt our significant motto?

As early as 1830, when all north of Jacksonville was almost an entire wilderness, the canal route was surveyed; and from that day to this it has been the pride of the State to do whatever could be done for the advancement of Chicago, either by canal or railways, acts of incorporation, or other special legislation. A large part of the legislation relates to this City.

Chicago, however, is no profitless recipient of favors, for of the State income from taxes, amounting in 1865 to $2,423,141, Cook county paid $305,753; and of school tax she paid $85,578, and received $50,514. Let us make the State feel more and more the benefits of her chief City. At this point of convergence, more accessible to every county than any other, let us give them the best library of the West or of the country; the best educational institutions and cabinets of art and science; and let us be equally liberal in aid of their public enterprises, especially in the construction of their branch railways, as they are in their business support.

This State of ours, possessing unequaled advantages of soil, climate, minerals, navigable waters, and railway, with its central position, is certainly destined to be the Empire State of the Great Interior. As its chief City, exercising a powerful if not controlling influence, Chicago has corresponding responsibilities; so that every previous consideration which should stimulate to duty as the City is regarded, is increased in force by so much as our State exceeds our City. Nor let us by short-sighted selfish endeavors, impair the influence which with moderation and disinterestedness will with reciprocal confidence and regard be accorded to us. Some good Citizens conceive it of benefit to take advantage of the railway centrality and the friendly feeling, and make Chicago the capital. What advantage would it be to the emporium of the West to be the capital of the State? The whole State, instead of then being friendly, would often be jealous and antagonistic. Would not credit for magnanimity in forbearing to make the attempt, be better than the capitol? If this be our view, as it probably is with a large majority, we should make it known; for we must desire to be merely the commercial and manufacturing centre, if we continue to exercise our proper influence in the State and in the West.

Duty to the Great Interior.—Of whatever region Chicago is to be emporium, are not our duties and responsibilities coëxtensive with our domain? The farthest section has claims upon us for means to aid in laying foundations, equally with that contiguous. Nor is the most distant Territory or State much more concerned in that work than is Chicago. If we neglect their religious and educational interests, we shall suffer with them; and the little aid requisite now, will there be almost as effective as at Chicago thirty to thirty-five years ago; and probably with equal, perhaps greater rapidity. No man can tell what railroads and telegraphs will not do in that richest mining region of the world; but we know that their effect must be unexampled.

Is it not indispensable to the proper discharge of our duties to this City, that we obtain full knowledge of the region tributary to Chicago, and of the means of access? Is it not incumbent upon us to do all in our power to promote acquaintance with this immense country, especially among capitalists who have built our railways, and encourage every way the building of more, both trunk lines and branches? What more effective than to show the importance of the continuation of the seven Chicago lines, already built beyond the Mississippi, on to the Rocky Mountains and yet further? The 600,000 square miles about us, to the chief towns of which we daily and oftener send our cars,—the 400,000 miles next west, and at least 500,000 miles yet further—a *million and a half square miles*—is the domain of Chicago, destined of nature, and already assured by art, as herein demonstrated.

Duty to our Nation.—This grandest theme, involving considerations of the whole subject as to how it is that Chicago may aspire to continental commerce and manufacturing, cannot be at all discussed for lack of space. *

Notwithstanding the abundant precautions taken by Moses under Divine direction to preserve State autonomy in the Tribes of the ancient Hebrews, especially in the reversion of the land in the year of jubilee to the heirs of the original owners; yet

* As this investigation has progressed, the power of the West in our National councils, and of our corresponding responsibilities, have been very impressive. It seemed imperative duty to consider the subject, and thoughts have been prepared for an Appendix, alluded to in several places, under the title, The West the Pacificator. Seeing clearly that all our difficulties have arisen from the pernicious revolutionizing heresies of the antagonistic schools of South Carolina and Massachusetts, both extremes being too thoroughly committed to their dogmas to hope that the leading parties could be brought to see their errors; the hope of the country lies in the West. But this book has already extended beyond reasonable limits, and such a subject cannot be discussed in a few pages. Let these Citizens consider he subject, and they will soon see what a grand opportunity is ours. Let us enter into the investigaion with our whole hearts, and to all our abundant blessings shall be added that of the peace-maker.

God always addresses them as a Nation. "Hear, O Israel; the Lord thy God is one Lord." So He addresses us, though as yet without a name for this our Nation. Whatever duty we owe to our State as her faithful liege subjects, we owe it equally to the Nation; for our State by solemn compact has covenanted with every other State, that their common Agency, the Federal Government, shall have equal right upon our persons and property with the State Agency. What is our State without our Nation? And what a grand Nation have we; created not by the compact of erring, dying individuals, but by the august compact of the honored Old Thirteen, and would now consist of thirty-seven sovereign States, but for violation of their sacred compact by secession and war, whereby eleven have lost their sovereignty. Fellow-Citizens! let us study into this grandest of all subjects except religion, and learn the extent of our obligations in this Nation of States.

Duty to our God.—We cannot examine into the why and wherefore of our growth, without becoming reverently impressed with the truth that this is not man's work alone. This wonderful conjoining of diverse human efforts, accomplishing these grandest results of all time as if every man of us were working for that very object instead of accomplishing our own individual and mainly selfish purposes, can be no accident. As in every natural object which astonishes us for its beauty, its ingenuity, its perfect adaptation to its purpose, it is more unreasonable to suppose it the creation of accident, than of an intelligent Creator; so in this union of many free and independent wills, effecting these great purposes as with one mind, one soul, an over-ruling Power must govern.

This our race "in the image of God created," these "sons of God," as repeatedly entitled in the Old Testament; these "children of God," "heirs of God, joint heirs with Jesus Christ," as the Gospel teaches, probably have their chief superiority in their free and independent will. But it was used in rebellion, and man became depraved, and vicious. The great work of our God is man's restoration to the pristine perfection and glory in which he came from the Creator's hand. As doubtless the most efficacious means, He instituted the several *stati* or conditions, Family, Church, City, State and Nation; and in these several relations, we are permitted to be co-laborers with God to elevate and restore our race. For this we are to work as though all depended upon us, and trust as though all depended upon GOD, as Paul enjoins. All that is required of us is love for the work, and a willingness to do what we can for its furtherance; and our feeble endeavors are rendered effective by Omnipotent Power. Do we show that willingness by contributing of our means and efforts as opportunity offers, for the physical, intellectual, moral and religious culture of these citizens? Were these duties properly realized by this leading City, to which the entire Great West looks for an example, would so little be done for science and art, for education and religion? The trouble with us is, almost without exception, that we are too entirely absorbed in getting means, to take time to consider the equally important duty of using them. Instead of realizing more and more the weight of responsibility; as our stewardship is increased, desire to give lessens, anxiety to get strengthens. Instead of the tenth which we are unmistakably instructed should be appropriated sacredly to these various objects, we dole out the merest pittance; and when we can grasp it no longer, we soberly, considerately, determinedly, make our wills preparatory to our appearance at the judgment seat, daring to withhold GOD's dues.

Let us all, Fellow-Citizens, who are GOD-fearing men, rise to the measure of our responsibility in this regard. Whether Unitarian or Trinitarian, Catholic or Protestant, Jew or Christian,— who of us does not believe that an earnest, heartfelt thank-offering is due from this City in view of the prosperity hitherto bestowed? How immensely are our obligations increased with all other cities of the land, and above them according to our more rapid increase, for the preservation of the Union, the ark of our safety; the destruction of slavery, the chief bone of contention; and the restoration of peace. As no other considerable city ha had equal gains, should not Chicago be first to lead off in the faithful payment of tythes? Says GOD, in the closing up of that Dispensation which Christ "came not to destroy but to fulfil," to make more perfect—

Return unto me—and I will return unto you,
Saith the LORD of hosts.
But ye said, Wherein shall we return.
Will a man rob GOD? Yet ye have robbed me.
But ye say, Wherein have we robbed thee?
In tithes and offerings.
Ye are cursed with a curse:
For ye have robbed me, even this whole Nation

Bring ye all the tithes into the store-house,
That there may be meat in mine house,
And prove me now herewith, saith the LORD of hosts,
If I will not open you the windows of heaven,
And pour you out a blessing,
That there shall not be room enough to receive it.
And I will rebuke the devourer for your sakes,
And he shall not destroy the fruits of your ground;
Neither shall your vine cast her fruit before the time in the field,
Saith the LORD of hosts.
And all nations shall call you blessed:
For ye shall be a delightsome land saith the LORD of hosts.

EFFECTS.

Although man's duties relate very largely to these several *stati*, they yet depend entirely upon individual performance. So effects are produced primarily upon the individual, secondarily upon man collectively.

Upon the Bodies Politic.—It cannot but have a beneficial influence upon our own City and State, to have the relations in which Chicago stands to the Great Interior and to the Nation, well apprehended. Nor can it be without interest or benefit to every City and State of the Union to have clear conceptions of the fact that there is a City indicated by nature, established by art, as the chief commercial and manufacturing centre of the Nation. Every State and City would like to be able to present equal claims to this distinguished position. But they cannot all be greatest; and if there be one possessed of advantages affording reasonable certainty that it is to be the emporium of the continent, do they not all wish to know the reasons and judge for themselves of the probability? It is hardly to be expected that this should be received as a demonstration, notwithstanding the writer and his City may have full faith in its facts and conclusions. But it is for the general interest that so important a subject should be investigated; and it is hoped that this will not prove a one-sided, selfish, boastful presentation; but a candid examination into the Past, a just presentation of the Present, a reasonable expectation of the Future.

Nor should this effort be without benefit to subordinate corporations, upon which the prosperity of City, State and Nation largely depend. Is it of no importance that the symmetry of plan of the Chicago system of railway should be exhibited, that those concerned may see the wisdom of extending lines and filling in with branches, to perfect a system which with no concert, and traversing numerous sovereign States, by the demands of the country, and from following the natural currents of trade secured by National Union, has created in two decades, and mostly with foreign capital, the greatest railway centre of the world?

Not having been prepared in the interest of railways, but in that of real estate, it ought to be of more service to those gigantic corporations. Manufactories, too, and every other enterprise, are only considered incidentally; and if the presentation of fact and judgment be considered just and moderate, it can be made more influential to advance any one interest, than if directed to that specifically. The real-estate is our solid basis of prosperity; and if that be firm, we have the best possible ground-work for any enterprise.

Upon the Individual Citizen.—It may be that over six months' close study of a subject so consonant with my tastes and feelings, preclude sound judgment, and cause the interest in and importance of the investigation to be over estimated. Due allowance will be made for frailty, and even considerable conceit in treating of the Past, Present and Future of a City in which I helped to raise the third framed building; in which not a dozen antedate me in residence; and which no man has labored harder to advance, however imperfect and unimportant my efforts. From about one hundred souls in 1832, when on the 29th October, I was brought here by my father, a lad of 17, to have been a helper to rear a City which the 1st of April, 1868, has over 240,000 inhabitants, is something in which pride would be expected. And the one object of the book being to exhibit the superiority of this City to all others in real-estate investments; and the titles of more City property having probably passed through my name than any other, something of my own experience would be expected; and of course care would be taken to show that my pecuniary reverses were not attributable to real-estate. Study of this subject may also pervert judgment; but it would seem, that the unequaled opportunities enjoyed in the certain advancement of the real-estate, should be well employed to bring hither capitalists to engage in all branches of business.

This work was begun for a small pamphlet upon the Past, with a little material upon the Present and Future to induce parties to join me in a real-estate operation. But the printer delaying immoderately, additional material was incorporated, and it became apparent that it was best to make the paper complete, instead of adding to it by and by. The title was changed accordingly, but has been preserved as the running title to keep the point before the reader.

Such as the essay is, it is submitted to the judgment of my Fellow-Citizens. They will act upon it as individuals, and if of benefit or injury they will be affected as individuals. However received now, my faith is strong that only a very few years will attest the correctness of judgment, the moderation of estimate; and in view of doubts of past prognostications which have been more than realized, may not Fellow-Citizens be asked not hastily to condemn although they may not be prepared to adopt? At all events, let each of us realize that we are nothing as individuals, and labor more and more faithfully to improve and elevate the Family, the Church, the City, the State, the Nation; and what a glorious work will it be for our children and grandchildren to write and to read of CHICAGO: PAST, PRESENT, FUTURE.

July 1st, 1868.

THE PAST, PRESENT AND FUTURE

OF

CHICAGO INVESTMENTS.

Study the Past to understand the Future and improve the Present.

Said Solomon in that wonderful Book, which ought to be made our guide in all human concerns,— Solomon's opinion.

> The thing that hath been, it is that which shall be; and that which is done is that which shall be done; and there is no new thing under the sun. Is there any thing whereof it may be said, See! this is new? it hath been already of old time, which was before us. There is no remembrance of former things; neither shall there be any remembrance of things that are to come with those that shall come after. *Eccl.* 1: 9–11

The many important truths of this pregnant passage are not here to be considered; and even the most obvious, the vain conceit that we have so much more sagacity and invention than all before us, must be passed over. Two of the points, however, are most pertinent to the present inquiry; 1st, that there are no new principles for man to discover; and 2d, that man disregards past experience. 2 points. 1st, no new principle. 2d, experience disregarded.

Solomon does not mean that man makes no discoveries, for he afterwards says: "Lo! this only have I found, that God hath made man upright; but they have sought out many inventions." The principles, the elementary truths, are what remain forever the same; and we improve and make progress, according as we learn better and better to apply those principles to practice. To do this successfully, we need constantly to avail ourselves of the experience of the past, that time and effort be not wasted in what has already been proved vain and fruitless. Yet now, as nearly 3,000 years ago, experience is almost wholly disregarded. This accounts abundantly for the slow progress made by man in bringing things of nature under his God-given dominion. Nor are these practical truths less applicable in business affairs, than in those of the natural sciences. And, in what respect, in preference to this, is the past more worthy of consideration? Can one judge soundly as to the future, except as he regards the past? Learn principles to use in practice— —in business affairs.

This paper for those who regard experience.

This writing, be it observed, is not for the common herd, who follow one another like a flock of sheep, having "no remembrance of former things;" but for the exceptions—any rule has its exceptions —who have wisdom to consider and be admonished by the past. Nor am I pandering to the vitiated desires of those who would "make haste to be rich;" although larger profits than Chicago has afforded, and still will, can scarcely be found; and no doubt those who have wisdom to apply the past to the present, will in the future experience the truth, that "there is nothing new" as to judicious investments in Chicago. And being moderate in my expectations, doubtless enough sensible capitalists will see that it is for their interest as well as mine to adopt my plan. It might be best, therefore, to just tell in short what it is, and be done with a long story; for Solomon says also, "A fool uttereth all his mind: but a wise man keepeth it in till afterwards." You may think that all my mind upon this subject must be here uttered; yet it is not, by any means. However, as affording some evidence that I am not wholly a fool, the plan is reserved until some testimony shall be presented of my acquaintance with the subject, and you, I trust, shall have been satisfied that at all events the project is worthy of consideration. The first natural step would be to show that—

MY FORMER OPINIONS AND PREDICTIONS WERE BASED UPON A REASONABLE HYPOTHESIS.

A sound hypothesis important—

A reasonable man does not always need a long process of ratiocination to gain his partial confidence concerning a declaration; but the bare hypothesis enables him to judge whether it be worth his while to give time and attention to the argument in its support. A mere opinion, however, from most men, depends upon the strength of its hypothesis for its weight and influence. In the exceptional cases, too, the opinion only has weight according to the confidence we have in the author's ability to present a sound hypothesis, and to sustain it by true reasoning. No correct hypothesis, unless by accident—and who likes to rest upon accident in important affairs? —certainly no arguments can be adduced, without more or less knowledge of the incidents precedent; and correctness will depend almost wholly upon the proficiency of that knowledge, which if practical as well as theoretic, the more convincing. It therefore appears well to show that in previous opinions and predictions, my hypotheses were trustworthy and duly sustained; and all the better because that what are now my actual premises, and which you will readily admit are certain truths, affording a very satisfactory hypothesis for the present argument, being without precedent, were in former discussions wholly hypothetical and had to be proved; for since the days of Aristotle it has been conceded, that argument is

—should not be accidental.

The past a basis.

out of the question until parties get back to principles which they receive as truth, the argument being merely the means to ascertain the result to which the truths naturally conduct. In proportion to his wisdom, and the importance of the interests in hand, will a man use those means, tracing effects from their causes; and learning about the future from the past, know how to improve the present. What else is our Bible, the very Book of Life, but a record of the past, with the exception of a few *a priori* declarations of principles, which the Author condescends not to explain? And even the principles themselves, in the main, are left for man to discover from prophetic declarations which came to pass, or the narration of parables or historic truth. Also, the arguments heretofore used in establishing what are now premises, are here equally available. What, then, could be more judicious and reasonable, than to reapply those arguments, and observe how they conducted incontrovertibly to their natural conclusions, which experience has proved to be facts and truths, and which we shall jointly receive as indubitable premises for this discussion? Thus agreeing about our principles, and obtaining clear, well-defined conceptions of the operating influences, unless you discover fallacies and wanderings from truth's straight path, surely we shall come to one and the same conclusion.

How does the Bible teach?

Old arguments reapplied.

Besides, as a discreet man who duly estimates the worth of the past, you will appreciate one's judgment upon an important subject, according to the evidence afforded of his acquaintance with it. The best criteria of judgment, are recorded opinions and acts. Many a man claims sharp foresight after events have transpired, and thinks he foretold wonderfully. But memory being often treacherous upon such subjects, even with honest minds, it is well to have the written record. Besides, it is one thing to predict or operate hap-hazard, and quite another to have definite, positive convictions, leading naturally to the anticipated result. So that the actuating motives—the facts and views of things, the arguments and hypotheses—are no less important than the prediction or the operation. Many a numskull becomes fortunate by circumstances, and because the circumstances operate directly contrary to and in spite of his judgment. But however successful, is his opinion valuable upon that subject?*

Motives and experience important considerations—

—some move hap-hazard.

*Although famous for the sagacity of its citizens, Chicago is not without those who have made fortunes in spite of themselves; because they have not been addicted to wasteful benevolence, and have happened to own real estate which has been closely held from natural habit, and not from any appreciation of the future. One of these millionaires, when efforts were making to start the Galena Railroad, argued against it, because railroads would stop the advent of the "prairie schooners," 500 to 1,500 teams then daily arriving, and with their stoppage "grass would grow in the streets," was his sagacious declaration. Another one thought my distribution of petitions for the grant of lands for the Illinois Central Railroad was impolitic. Said he, "Why, don't you see that the railroad will enable farmers to run off their produce to Cairo while the river and canal are frozen, which if kept till spring would have to come to Chicago?" I replied, "Don't *you* see that that gives the farmers of Central Illinois the advantage over others in the choice of markets? Whatever the course of the carrying trade, you may risk the prosperity of Chicago upon the prosperity of the farmers." This, however, is the very place

Some wisdom of Chicago millionaires.

Evidence of my past sound judgment.

To write about one's self without egotism, requires too much circumlocution for this condensed paper; so that those whose stomachs are very sensitive can pass this over. Yet it certainly is important to the proper estimation of present views of the future, to consider some of the evidences of past correctness of judgment, which former transactions and recorded opinions afford. Though only a small part has been preserved, only a little of that can be here offered with any hope of its perusal; and though the object which this head presents will constantly be kept in view, yet the reader will notice the immense advance upon former prices; and although his first impression would be that the day is past to make such profits on Chicago property, I shall hope to prove to his satisfaction that it is now a better time relatively to invest here, than thirty years ago.

Same chance now as 30 years ago.

First purchases of $3,500 each in 1834.

An account of some of my transactions, prepared for the circular of 1860, are quoted p.289; to which it may be added as appropriate to this caption, that my first purchases were two of $3,500 each, in March, 1834, which I expected to share in profits with my uncle, Amasa Wright, of Brooklyn, who had written to me months before to try to get the refusal of property for him to judge of. But too little property had been sold by the State or United States, and it was too much in demand to get refusals. A copy of the letter describing those purchases, dated March 11th, 1834, was obtained at an arbitration with my uncle in 1852, from which this is extracted:—

Letter Mar. 11th, 1834.

Lot 4 B, 17, O. T., bo't for $3,500.

Last Wednesday evening I spent in endeavoring to make a bargain with Lieut. Jamison of the U. S. Army for lot four in block seventeen, of the survey by Canal Commissioners, which is (as you will see by reference to your map) [which I had made and sent him] a corner and water lot. I did not then succeed, but last Friday I bought it of him for $3500, enormous sum, half of it to be paid on the first of June, 1834, and the other half on the first of December 1834. There is a lawyer now drawing a writing in reference to the bargain, in which he (Mr. Jamison) binds himself to give a deed of the lot upon the payment of the first half, ($1750.) It is to be ready to be signed to-morrow. This may seem to you to be an enormous sum for a lot (80 ft by 150 ft) in Chicago, and I think father would not give half that sum for it. But his ideas do not keep up with property in Chicago.* I

---

for such men to make fortunes. If they will only invest their money, berate the tax gatherer, and never give anything—which is not dangerous—they will surely become rich if they live a few years however unwise their purchases.

Father's judgment of Chicago.

*While that was true, it is but justice to one of the best of fathers to add, that far nearer than most men he anticipated the future of Chicago. With great natural powers, especially in sound judgment, he had ample knowledge of the country and appreciated the West, having in 1815 and '16 traveled for his health on horseback from Massachusetts into Illinois and down to New Orleans. But he was over-cautious; and though intending to buy all the lots and land he could, he was too fearful of advancing prices by seeking purchases. He came from his New England home in the spring of 1833, intending to buy largely at the sale of school lots; but to his disappointment, and much more to mine, he only bought about $1,000 worth, six lots and two blocks.

My minority no interference.

In his absence I was my own master, my minority never interfering either here or in the East; for such was the confidence in that just man, that everybody knew that if by death he became my heir, my engagements would be sacredly fulfilled. No purchase or sale was disapproved by him, except that he thought it unwise in 1836 to sell twenty acres, in section 22, for $50,000, as I did not need so much money, and could not better invest it. Yet, had not that sale fallen through accidentally, it would have saved my property, which was worth more than my father's. But with his caution, he was out of debt, and I not. My property was swept by the revulsions of '37, and a large part of my patrimony, and the estate he left in 1840, is to-day worth over four millions.

I was subject to him, however,—as what son would not be to such a father?—and though operating

am sure that lot will in less than three months fetch $5,000.00. What makes me think so is this: There are a great many merchants coming into Chicago this summer. There are but two or three water lots that can be bought at any price. All the business is at present done on this (Water) street. Now merchants coming in are not going on to the back streets to do business, as long as they can get a building spot on Water street, *for twice what its* REAL *value is.* Lots have not yet got to near their full value. That one which I bought will within five years be worth three, and I think I may say five times what I paid for it. Chicago will within that time be as large as Detroit is now, and real estate will be worth as much. A small lot there 50x60 ft (I think it was) was sold a few weeks since for $10,000.00, and why should not business lots be worth as much here as there? These are the reasons that made me purchase that lot, and that make me think it was a good bargain. I do not suppose I could get what I paid for it back now, but I can in less than three months.

Reasons for its purchase

Chicago to be as large as Detroit within 5 years.

Wednesday, March 12th.—Last evening I made another bargain for 90½ acres of land, for which I am to pay $3,500, the same sum that the town lot cost. 73 acres lies on the North Branch of the Chicago River, and is the west half of the southwest quarter of section four in this township. [A description of that tract, and of the 17½ acres on the South Branch was here given.]

90½ acres bought for $3,500.

I do not wish to have you feel yourself under any obligations to take these lands or the town lot. But if you do not take them I shall be obliged to rely on you for the money. The money for the 90½ acres is to be paid as follows: Draft on you payable at sight for $700; $1,000 payable the first of August; $1,800 on the first of December. Mr. Noble takes drafts for these sums when they become due. He gives me a quit claim and warranty deed, [there were two tracts,] immediately. They are made out by this time, and will be signed to-morrow. I gave him a draft on you (which I hope you will accept) at the same time, and give notes in my own name for the remainder, payable as aforesaid. He does not require any endorsers, nor anything for security of payment, except the notes. This I think pretty lenient in him, and shows he has some confidence in me. I have no writings from father which could bind him (father) to any bargains I make. I ought to have had some, but I did not then think I should so soon be purchasing real estate.

His option to take purchases but must advance the money.

My notes taken in payment.

Father not bound

If you do not take these purchases, they will fall upon *me*, not upon *father*, for I want to make a little money myself. It will, to be sure, be putting some risk upon you in asking so much money of you, minor as I am. But if you do not feel secure, I can give you endorsers, for a number of good substantial men in this place have offered of their own accord to sign for me if I wish it. So you see I am not without friends, if I am here alone. Now I do not wish you to take these purchases unless you feel perfectly sure that you will make money by so doing. For my part I should prefer keeping them both if I could pay for them in any way. I have got considerable credit on them (without interest) so as not to have it crowd you in making payments.

If he wants security can have it.

No claim is laid to foresight then of what Chicago is to-day; nor was it possible with the most penetrating prescience, for no one could have anticipated the power and multiplication of railroads. But the views were sound, though youthfully expressed, and reasonably anticipated the future, as they constantly have, and as these will be found to do. The results are given p. 290. The lot is worth to-day $150,000, and the land some $500,000.

Railroads not then anticipated.

---

thus independently for myself, took chief charge of his store, until in December, 1835, he consented to sell me the remaining seven months of my minority for $2,000. I had before bought a lot of Mr. Dole for $2,000, which father desired, and it was given up to him, as was the case with nearly all his purchases, except the school lots, and a Lake street lot. So that in the division of father's estate, my brothers and sister consented to let me have that lot above my portion, in consideration of my misfortunes and of my aid in building up the estate. For not only had I been largely instrumental in purchasing, but some ten days after our arrival in Chicago, and while father was taking a cruise throughout the country, at Mr. Carpenter's instance, we went on the prairie with a surveyor and run out a quarter section each, which resulted in father's getting pre-emption for one hundred and sixty acres, seventy of which his children inherited, and are now Wright's Addition and Union Park, and worth about two millions and a half.

Aid in father's purchases.

Lot 5, B. 19, O. T., bo't for $1,200, and sold for $1,900.

The next purchase was another corner lot, 5 in block 19, for $1200, made wholly on my own account, March 17th. Of this no record exists, except as to how I raised the first payment of $300, by borrowing $17, from father's store, and $283 from C. & I. Harmon, Wm. McCorristen (a soldier) and Peter Cohen. My recollection is that before the second payment came due, 1st July, I sold to Peter Bolles for $1900. It was the first money I had made, and on the 1st of October, 1834, I opened a set of account books, with an inventory, in which stock is credited for $720—cash $560, personal property $60, and L. T. Jamison $100. Stock is debtor for $179.63. This money had been made on that lot, having made no other operation, and of course receiving no salary.

First account books.

N. 43 acres sec. 22, T. 39 N., R. 14 E., bo't at $80—

Oct. 15th I bought 43 87-100 acres of section 22, from the lake to State street, and from 12th street south, at $80 per acre. In July 1836, I sold an undivided 20 acres of it for $50,000, which was broken up by an accidental misunderstanding. It was mortgaged in 1839 for $9090 to the State Bank, and was bid in for about $4000, I think, which I expected to redeem, as most were allowed to do; but without my knowledge it was given to Mr. Ketchum in exchange for a mill property in Michigan, which never yielded much to the bank. That land is well covered with elegant residences and without the improvements is worth about $1,750,000.

—worth $1,-750,000.

Butler, Wright & Webster's Add.

Jan. 2d, 1835, I bought for $4000, payable in 4 and 6 months, 40 acres, which is now Butler, Wright & Webster's addition, to whom it was sold in New York on the 10th of April following for $10,000.

80 acres S ½ SE ¼ sec. 34, T. 39, R. 14.

Jan. 27th I bought 80 acres, south half, southeast quarter, section 34, close to the lake and now in the city, for $800. This also went to the State Bank, on the same debt. It is worth $400,000.

2 water lots in Kinzie's addition.

May 11th, I bought water lot 23, in Kinzie's Addition, for $2000; and the 13th, water lot 24 adjoining, for $3200. In December, 1837, when worth $25,000, I mortgaged them to Charles Butler, Esq., of New York to secure $8,500 for a note extended for a year. The mortgage was foreclosed and the lots bid in for Mr. Butler, for some $2000 to $3000. They are worth $50,000, and the balance of the debt by judgment took property worth over $200,000.

Bushnell's addition.

May 11th, I also bought 80 acres, which is now Bushnell's Addition, for $6,000; and the 13th, 40 acres in the same section, now called Crane & Wesson's Park, for $1300. The former is worth $1,500,000, the latter at least $200,000.

Profits 15th July, 1835, $15,000.

These will suffice to give an idea of my operations, and of advances in value. Other purchases were made and some sales, so that on balancing my books on my birthday, as was my custom, 16th of July, 1835, reckoning property at its cost, stock is credited for $25,167.76, ($1,225 cash on hand), and debited $9511.29 for indebtedness on property. The real estate inventoried at about $22,000, was worth at least four times that sum. But not having any written or printed statements of my views, the remarks, p. 290, will suffice. In 1846, having recovered from the mortification and disgust of being permitted to go to ruin, when a wealthy uncle, who had made largely directly by and through me, could with perfect ease have saved my property without risk, for he always affirmed full faith in Chicago, —having obtained renewed energies and stronger confidence in the future of the West, and of Chicago, by years of cruising and delightful intercourse among the noble hearts of the prairie farmers, I resolved again to make another fortune in Chicago property.

Began again in 1846 to make money

Having purchased block 1, in 1846, as remarked on p. 291, for $37,500, the following hand-bill was issued 3d of July, 1847 :—

B 1 O. T., bo't for $37,500.

Safe and Profitable Investment.—The undersigned offers for sale a portion of Block One, of the Original Town of Chicago, (one third or one quarter) at the rate of $75,000 for the block, lying on North Water, Dearborn, Kinzie, Wolcott and Exchange streets. It is in no spirit of speculation that the property is offered, but simply for the purpose of providing funds to use in improving the balance.

Offers to sell, 1847.

It has been owned till last year by a gentleman at the East who would do nothing to improve it, nor grant a lease except from year to year, so that this year it pays only about four per cent. on the price asked. But the undersigned will guaranty that next year it shall pay 5 per cent., the next 6 per cent., and that within five years it shall pay 6 per cent. on $100,000. He is confident the property will do much better than this; but this much he is willing to guaranty.

Profits assured.

If it can be made to pay this interest, then the property is *safe;* but therein does not consist its greatest *profit.* It must rapidly appreciate in value. Unless the friends of this young city greatly miscalculate as to its destiny, and the rapidity of its increase in business and population, property here must be greatly enhanced, and that speedily.

What was property worth twenty-seven years ago in Cincinnati, with its 10,000 inhabitants? what is it now worth, with its 100,000? That which has taken twenty-seven years to accomplish in Cincinnati, will be accomplished in a much less time here. Consider the immense power of public improvements, made in a great measure *since* Cincinnati began to increase so rapidly, to give impulse to the growth of great commercial cities, and which even now are but begun—that if the rich valley of the Miami has contributed so essentially to the growth of Cincinnati, Chicago has an equally fertile and vastly more extensive agricultural territory tributary to it—that Cincinnati has no great advantages over Chicago for mechanical and manufacturing industry—that northern Illinois is now in a much more favorable situation to push forward its chief commercial emporium, than was southwestern Ohio twenty-seven years since; and what is of vastly more importance in the consideration of this point, Cincinnati has no peculiar advantage as a commercial city, but Chicago is the *western terminus of lake navigation,* and this year will be connected by the Illinois and Michigan Canal with the great rivers of the West, so that the Mississippi and even the Missouri River, will pay tribute to us. By this route goods will be transported from New York to St. Louis at from 100 to 125 cents per 100 lbs., and often less than that. Then the very heavy lumber and coal trade which must be done here will aid essentially in our growth, and railroads will soon connect us with the lead region and other interior sections.

Comparison with Cincinnati.

It is not unreasonable to estimate that fifteen years shall do more for Chicago than twenty-seven have done for Cincinnati. Property, therefore, must rapidly appreciate in value, for there can be no drawback. No town can be named as a rival to us in the trade of the West—not even for the trade of the mineral region—nor for the South as far as St. Louis. * * *

15 years for Chicago equal to 27 for Cincinnati.

Then where can a safer or more profitable investment be found?

Reasonable as were these predictions, which were far more than realized, nobody could be made to see the truth, and that year I paid *five per cent. a month* for several thousand dollars, required to meet

Nobody convinced.

my payments. Hoping to obtain relief by profits on other operations without further increase of indebtedness, a circular was distributed in connection with Judge Thomas' report to the Harbor and River Convention.* Dated 4th of January, 1848, it thus begins :—

Circular, 1848

Investments in Chicago Property.—I am happy that a reliable document has been prepared concerning the business of Chicago, which I can send friends, and trust an examination of it will lead to the reflection whether here is not a desirable place to invest capital.

Speculation not proposed

"Western speculations," I know, have, to a great extent, lost favor with capitalists. But because so much money has been foolishly lost in visionary operations, and so much more locked up in unsaleable and unproductive property, the taxes and expenses of which are fast consuming it, it does not follow that good investments cannot be made in the West. And anything like "speculation,"—i. e. a purchase with probabilities of large profits, and more or less, or even *any*, chance of loss,—I am no advocate for; only a sober, prudent investment of capital, in property safe beyond contingency, which may be made to yield a *certain* annual income, with large profits ultimately, perhaps soon.

Such investments you may make here.

A sure income.

Property to Give a Certain Annual Income.—There is no speculative demand for Chicago property, and has not been for ten years; and though prices have been and are steadily advancing, it is a healthy growth. Sales are continually making, but they are almost wholly for investment. Lots can be bought in the central business part of Chicago, yielding a ground rent of 6 to 9 per cent. I know of a lot, for instance, held at $2500, for which the owner is offered for a five years' lease, $200 per annum and the taxes. The lessee wishes to erect a good brick building, conditioned that at the end of the lease, the lessor at his option, shall renew the lease at 7 per cent. on the value of the lot, or purchase the building at an appraisal, the value of both lot and building to be fixed by three disinterested men. The building would cost about $2,000, and would rent for $450, perhaps more. Three lots belonging to my father's estate, 20 feet front by 150 deep, which are among the best in the city, have been under lease for ten years past at $250 each, and the leases are renewed for the present year at $300. The lots are worth $4,500 each, and for a five years' lease we could get $350 per annum, nearly 8 per cent. Another lot I could have bought a short time since, and perhaps can yet, for $3,000, which is under a lease for seven years at $270, or 9 per cent., with no conditions to renew or buy the buildings. Usually lessees of ground agree to pay all taxes and assessments, the rent is paid quarterly and *punctually*, and for security, the lessor holds the improvements, which can only be removed at the expiration of the lease, and after the entire fulfillment of it on the part of the lessee. The form of lease used here is of the most stringent character.

Annual rent of lots.

Lots like these cannot always be got at a day's notice, but a person having money by him to use when good bargains are offered, would not have it on hand a long time.

Rent of stores.

Good brick stores, four stories high and well finished, costing about $3,000, will rent for $800, to $850, in the best locations. When we have 50,000 inhabitants, if rents are worth as much here as in cities of corresponding size and business, such stores will be worth *at least* $1200 per annum ; and as $500 will be an ample allowance for the building alone, $700 will be left for the lot, from which deduct $100 for taxes, and it will then pay 6 per cent. on $10,000. *This you may reasonably reckon upon within ten years.*

Suburb lots.

Property now in the suburbs can be bought at low prices, which will yield a less income, but probably greater profit in the course of ten years.

National gatherings at Chicago.

No change of capital.

*That Convention in 1847 was the first of the national gatherings, which since have been drawn to Chicago because of her focal railway position. Year by year will she increase in favor in this respect, as the rapid increase of the West, and railway extension make her still more central. Recently a St. Louis paper predicted the removal there of the National Capital. It will never be moved, I trust, from the city consecrated by the sacred memories and the name of the Father of his country. Could the West agree itself about the location, it might perhaps effect a change. But Ohio, Indiana, Illinois, and all the States contiguous to Missouri, would oppose St. Louis, because they would not like to give a close rival that advantage. So Missouri and the others would oppose any city in Illinois, and this jealousy will forever prevent the injustice of taking the Capital from the glorious Old Thirteen. If moved at all, it would be to Chicago, for the same reasons that the National Conventions come here so much oftener than to any other city.

Investments of this character must be perfectly *safe*, at least those which are rented for a term of years; and there is an almost equal certainty of a large and rapid increase. Money safe.

Increase in Value by the Growth of Chicago.—By the report, you will see the imports, exports and business of Chicago generally, have grown very rapidly, and the same causes must not only continue to operate, and with increased power, but new channels are to be opened, widely extending the range of country tributary to this market. Increase in value certain.

With no increase from abroad, business in all departments must enlarge and extend, and very rapidly in a country of the easy tillage and great natural advantages of this; but the population of Illinois, particularly of the northern portion of the State which trades here, never was increasing so fast by immigration as at present, and the settlers are of a most excellent character, and often have much wealth. The census of 1850 will show a population of about 1,000,000, being double that of 1840. * * * Growth of Illinois.

Should these views lead any of my friends to think of investing money here, I would first and earnestly advise a *personal examination.* Nothing can take the place of this, and the sooner made the better, as property is continually advancing, and in the course of a few months is likely to be much higher than at present. Examine yourselves.

Any who would be glad to give a share of the profits, (or of the losses,) to a resident, by whom investments would be made and the property managed, I should be glad to hear from; and I think a residence of over fifteen years in Chicago, with considerable acquaintance with property, ought to enable me to render considerable service. Share of profits.

I would further state, that my own means are, at present, all invested, and I have resolved absolutely not to buy any property on my own account, till I can pay for it in cash, which will not be for the present; so that those who choose to authorize me to buy, may be sure of my best efforts to get for them good bargains. Titles would be taken in their own names, or in the name of some responsible person here *in trust* for them, as would be preferred. Will not increase debt.

Any who would wish further information, I shall be happy to correspond with, and will do all in my power to make those who choose to try an investment in Chicago. so satisfied with it that they will purchase further. It appears to me a gentleman of means can do nothing so well with a few thousand dollars as to buy property in this place where he would be, to a great extent, relieved of trouble in its management, and which, to his children and grand children, would become a large inheritance. Invest for children.

Please consider this carefully and let me hear from you.

Though silent about the contiguous river property, for fear of drawing attention to it, my sole object was to induce parties to join in its purchase, if Mr. Bronson could not be pursuaded to give me an interest to take its management. But because my uncle would do nothing, nobody would look into the proposition. During the negotiation, I made the estimate of rents spoken of p. 292 and although firmly resolved, that I would not incur further indebtedness; yet the long credit obtained, and the advantages of the agreement in regard to sales, promised so strongly that capitalists could soon be led to join, that the purchase was made. Still, nobody would see the fortune waiting their reception ; and to fully present the subject, and either sell or make a permanent loan, or else sell other property, either or all of which I was willing to do, the circular of 28th of February, 1849, was prepared, thus concluding :— Nobody would invest

The preceding estimates [one of them is given, page] have been based upon the supposition that in three years $42,200 shall be expended in improvements. On every account this is desirable to have done Circular. 1849.

The three blocks can unquestionably be made to pay for themselves, and much more, with one-third that amount invested. But improvements will yield a large interest on their cost, and every good building erected will enhance the rent of contiguous lots several per cent. And the effect of expending a considerable amount, as fast as it could be judiciously done, would be very great, particularly at this time. It would give a strong impetus to the whole north side, and make this entire operation easy and safe, ensuring, not only the rents as estimated, but a considerable increase beyond.

Offer to sell cheap.

Property to be Sold Cheap.—Of this amount I can raise $25,000 out of other property during the three years; and it is my purpose to sell all other real estate, except a dwelling-house lot, and concentrate both capital and efforts on these blocks. I shall lose the future rise on the property sold, which I know will be large; but the results of the preceding calculations will not only be thereby secured, but made easy, which gives an income that should satisfy any reasonable man, and which is many fold greater than I had ever expected to have.

Rents sure.

Of the lots I wish to sell, some are now under rent; and if purchasers will lease for ten years, I will agree to sell at such a price as that they shall yield seven per cent. per annum ground rent, clear of taxes. It will be moderate to suppose the lots will double in value in ten years, which would give *seventeen per cent. per annum.* Some of the lots will doubtless double in value in a less period.

A loan sought.

A Loan of Ten Thousand Dollars Wanted.—But to sell property and get pay, will require two or three years, for it cannot be sold to advantage for cash; though I will sell at low prices for quick pay. Therefore, as I wish very much to erect a couple of warehouses this summer, I have determined to borrow, say ten thousand dollars, payable, say half in five and half in six years, and I will pay *ten per cent. interest*, semi-annually in New York city.

The security shall be satisfactory. I will give *good personal and real estate security*, and will assign to the lender the contracts for the block on which the money is expended, and will agree to to use all the money borrowed, and *fifty per cent. in addition*, upon the property given in security. Upon failure to meet the payments of interest as they become due, the whole amount of principal and interest to become due and payable in thirty days, and authority shall be given to sell the property or the contracts at public auction.

With this $10,000, and the receipts from rents and from my other property, I shall have in three years more than the $42,200 for improvements; and securing this *ground work* of my plans, the results will at least equal the calculations.

To show my perfect ability to meet both interest and principal of a loan, I will put together the surplus rents as estimated in the three previous tables :

Surplus rents.

Annual Surplus Rents above all Payments as per Foregoing Tables.

	Block 1.	Block 3.	Block 5.	Total.		Block 1.	Block 3.	Block 5.	Total.
1849....	$ 580	......	......	$ 580	1858....	$12,045	$4,478.75	$7,171.25	$23,695
1850....	1 440	......	......	1.440	1859....	13,249	5,148.05	8,241.95	26,639
1851....	3,400	......	......	3,400	1860....	14,573	5,817.35	9,312.65	29,703
1852....	560	2,518.35	4,036.65	7,115	1861....	16,030	5,716.65	9,153.35	31,900
1852....	1,528	1,163.95	1,866.05	4,558	1862....	17,633	6,432.15	10,297.85	34,363
1854....	2,561	2,687.05	4,302.95	9,551	1863....	19,396	7,147.65	11,442.35	37,986
1855....	3,674	3,025.15	4,844.85	11,544	1864....	21,335	4,590.65	7,359.35	33,285
1856....	4,867	3,571.35	5,718.65	14,157					
1857....	10,950	4,217.55	6,752.45	21,920		$143,821	$56,514.65	$90,500.35	$290,836

Estimates certain.

The result is so enormous as almost to stagger my own belief in the correctness of the preceding views and estimates. But I *know* that for at least five or six years, the surplus in the above table will be exceeded year by year, for I have only to *get rates at which I am now actually leasing*, to accomplish it; and no one can doubt that there is to be a considerable advance. But let it be observed, *if the above calculations are not half realized*, still I can more than meet payments of both interest and principal as they become due.

One of these propositions, either to buy property that will pay seventeen per cent., or make a loan at ten per cent., I am sure capitalists will avail themselves of; and it will be a favor to receive propositions soon. It is important to make arrangements for brick and for building, early in the Spring; and *a small amount will not divide a bargain, if I can get the money right away.* I prefer loaning the whole amount from one person, but may not be able so to get it, and will therefore make loans of less amount.

No success.

No railways foreseen.

Were these expectations and desires immoderate ? Could parties have seen as I did the certainty of railroad building, soon noticed, and the immense progress consequent, which must give Chicago a rapidity of progress far beyond any previous example, would these persevering efforts have been futile ? But besides the total inability to see railroads that only existed in my wild vision, that year again brought the cholera. Not obtaining relief myself, and thereby relieving others who were aiding me in borrowing money at high interest, caused the sale of block 1, in 1850, for $60,000, as noticed, p.293, and also of the half of block 3 to my brother. **Block 1 sold for $60,000.**

Though almost wholly relieved thereby of indebtedness, it was an immense reduction of my North-Side interest; and the remaining block 5 being all rented, and being still satisfied with this and the remnants of my patrimony, which had been saved by borrowing money of my uncle at twenty-five per cent. interest, to pay the bank; I thought not of any more real estate operations, and foolishly engaged in the reaper business, as noticed p. 294. To make this a success, my ambition was immoderately moved by circumstances; and to obtain capital, property was advertised—none in block 5—and sold at auction 14th October '52, in the hand-bill of which are these remarks:— **Reaper business begun.** **Property sold at auction.**

In the foregoing list is a variety of choice property, from which large or small capitalists can make investments to their minds. And the present is the time to do it. *Croakers* have been saying, even for years past, that real estate is too high. Yet up, up it goes, and never has there been a time in the history of Chicago when a future and rapid advance in real estate generally was so certain as at this time. Chicago property will approximate in value, with corresponding population and business, prices in other cities; and it is generally conceded that within seven years we shall number 100,000. If so, most of the real estate must double or treble in value within that period, and still be clear below what it is now worth in St. Louis, Cincinnati, &c. **Adv't 1852.**

Railroads that have been mostly prospective with us, are now being built to all parts of the West, and hardly a man in the city appreciates at all their influence upon this commercial centre of the Great West. If with *no* avenues of consequence except the Canal, and a short piece of the Galena Railroad, it has been impossible for our mechanics in any department to get a stock ahead, notwithstanding their constant increase, what is to be the effect upon manufactures here, with 1500 to 2000 miles or more of railroad radiating in all directions, and centering business here from regions wholly isolated from us hitherto? Yet three years effects all this; and any one who will reason from cause to effect, must acknowledge that without some great national calamity, the probabilities are that real estate here must double in value within three to five years. **Railroads sure.**

Many sagacious ones, too, prognosticate another revulsion like that of 1837 to 1840. They consider the present inflation of prices like that of 1836. No such thing. *Paper money* was the basis then, and when, to pay foreign balances, specie had to be drawn from the banks, suspension followed, and the bubble burst. Not so now. The present increase of money is the result of the discoveries in California and Australia, and there can be no doubt but these mines will for years add one to two hundred millions annually to the currency of the world. There is nothing fictitious—no danger of collapse—in this. The result is inevitable, that with so large an increase of money, its value must be lessened, or, what is the same thing, real estate and other property advance. While there may be temporary panics, got up by interested parties for particular ends, when money can be advantageously employed and invested, it must be evident to any one that to make the best use of capital, it should be put into property, as stocks, real estate, &c., which must surely increase with the increase of money. The man is not wise who hoards his funds or puts them out on permanent loan in times like these. **No revulsion** **Increase of money.**

"Having these views, then, why do you sell lots?" will be asked. I reply, because I want money for business. As evidence of sincerity in what has been said, I will make this proposition:—☞*I will take off* 15 *per cent. from the price which any lot may bring at the sale, if the purchaser will give me the privilege of buying it five years hence, at such a price as that with the income derived from the property, he shall receive* 100 *per cent. on his investment, which is* 20 *per cent. per annum.* **Why I sell.** **20 per cent. guarantee.**

No by-bidding.

To citizens it is unnecessary to state that a piece of my property when once put up at auction, is *sure to go for what is bid*, without any underhanded management or flinching. The fact of selling, at a recent auction, one lot for $950, for which we had been offered $1500 in the auction room just before the sale, is sufficient evidence that there is no chicanery or backing out from sales, no matter at what loss. But to strangers who may wish to buy, I would offer the assurance of my honor, that *every bid made is bona fide, and a lot once put up will be sold, if it does not bring a quarter of its value.* I only retain the privilege of stopping the sale, if property goes at too great a sacrifice.

The reaper ruined me.

Though success in the reaper business fully justified expectations, no doubt too much was undertaken for any one man; and owing to the circumstances stated p.294, and the general revulsions from the senseless panic of '57, and the consequent depreciation of real estate which was covered with mortgages—and they proved true to their name,—my real estate, worth in 1856 at least $600,000, and not $100,000 of the indebtedness chargeable to it, was completely swept.

Real estate tried again.

In April, 1858, a circular was printed,* though not distributed, of which these were among the opening paragraphs:—

Circular, 1858.

The money panic has brought a most favorable time to buy Chicago property. Some from necessity, and others because they are foolishly frightened, are selling at lower rates than have prevailed for several years. * * *

Results of former advice.

Ten years ago, I urged friends to buy property here. The few who heeded the advice have not regretted it. Five to ten fold has been the increase, and some receive in ground rents each year more than half the entire cost of their lots. I hold out expectations of no such advance now, as I did not then, but do most earnestly repeat the assurance, that you may now buy with great advantage, and that you will regret it if you do not. * * *

Joint-stock companies.

In March, 1860, a plan was formed of two joint-stock companies, which says:—

Circular, 1860.

A causeless panic.

About two years since I prepared a circular concerning investments at Chicago. For reasons not necessary to explain, its distribution to friends, as contemplated, has been delayed. The time, however, for its use, has now unquestionably arrived. All property but central, has depreciated on the average at least one half since 1857, and must now take an upward turn. All here consider that the crisis has been past, though but few seem to apprehend how rapidly prices must recover from so great—so unnecessary—so groundless a decline; for though property was higher than was desirable for the best good of the City, yet any one looking ahead, should have seen that the growth of the country, and of the town, would still have insured, in a few years, good profits on the investments.

Want to buy property—

I wish to avail myself of this important period, and think, at the same time, I can benefit friends. I therefore submit the circular referred to, the views of which are still applicable, and which appear to prove fairly and conclusively, the certainty of the rapid growth of the City, and the consquent enhancement in the value of property. Further consideration having shown me the difficulties in the way therein proposed for investing, from impossibility of always buying a piece of property for exactly the desired amount—the hindrance to a sale, if the capitalist wished to change his investment, &c., &c., I have been led to prepare plans for two organizations, also herewith submitted.

—to avoid debt.

Had I the requisite capital, or had I securities to give for loans, I would make more to borrow, at even extravagant interest, than to use your funds and share profits. But that is out of the question, and I shall not again go through the process of

---

Hopes still on the reaper.

*That circular has little appropriate to this place not incorporated in those subsequent. It was not prepared for actual use, for my hopes still clung to my reaper patents, or to those which had been mine. Nor, indeed, when the circular of 1860 was prepared, had I abandoned the hope of proving still that I had not misjudged about the reaper business, but that misfortunes had caused my difficulties. These circulars were, therefore, inadequately studied, and were quite imperfect, and are chiefly valuable as presenting off-hand views seven to ten years ago.

temporary loans—regular "shinning"—as in '46 to '50, and paying two to five per cent. per month interest. Doubtless money can again be rapidly made by so doing, but I have worried myself and friends enough with that system, and shall avoid it hereafter. Besides, though giving you half my profits, it is not so much lost to me, for if supplied with more cash, and not having to use credit so much, property can be bought considerably cheaper. [I had paid Mr. Bronson double the value of his property because of long credit.]

On the other hand, I flatter myself that I can take your funds and make double on it what you, or at least most non-residents would For the capitalist and agent to divide profits equally, is a very common thing here, even when both are residents, and it is still more desirable to a non-resident. Experience and knowledge are eminently requisite to success in real estate; and a residence of over twenty-seven years in Chicago, and large experience, and unsurpassed success in purchasing and managing property, justify me in claiming skill to do it equal to any fellow-citizen. **Invest on shares.** **My experience.**

And you will observe in the accompanying propositions, that you have an important countervailing benefit for dividing profits on your capital, in its safety. I have sufficient confidence in my skill and judgment, and in the future rise of property bought by me, to let you have back your capital, and a good profit—more than most can make for a term of years, with their best and constant efforts—before I receive anything for all my labor and attentions. You may think this proposition too good to be really safe, but rest assured that I shall make handsomely; and if so, you certainly will. **Capital and profit sure.**

Some of you want an income—sure—reliable, and would look more to that than to greater profits ultimately. To such the Income Company would be preferable. Property yielding rent, both improved and unimproved, can often be bought low. A short time since a lot in the centre of the city, covered with a good brick building that rents for $6,000, was sold for $24,000. Such purchases are not often to be made, but occasionally a person upon the spot, provided with funds, can find them. Your safe stocks yield you perhaps five to ten per cent., and no possibility of much increase in value. I can assure you of as much or greater annual income, and just as reliable—yes, more so—and a handsome increase of your capital besides. **Income plan—**

Others have funds that you desire to invest surely, to be relieved of care and trouble, and that will give to yourself or heirs, by and by, a large return. The other Company assures you 15 per cent. per annum for the long period of ten years. How can you better dispose of a part of your money, the care of investing which gives you much thought and anxiety? **—or no income.**

Besides the safety of a real estate investment—so far beyond that of an ordinary corporation in which the most tried and trusted officials are every little while proving defaulters—there is the ease of convertibility of any stock. **Convenience of transfer.**

Not only for the reason given in the note preceding, but also on account of the division of my efforts to two companies, and still more because of the personal liability, the joint-stock plan was soon discovered to be impracticable, and not half a dozen copies were distributed. To obviate this, an excellent charter was obtained from the Illinois Legislature:— **Joint-stock plan fails.**

AN ACT to incorporate the Land Improvement Company.

SECTION 1. *Be it enacted by the People of the State of Illinois, represented in the General Assembly,* That JOHN S. WRIGHT and such persons as may become associated with him, and his and their successors, are hereby created a body politic and corporate, by the name and style of "THE LAND IMPROVEMENT COMPANY," and shall have continued succession and exist for twenty-five years, and no longer. **A charter from State of Illinois.**

SEC. 2. The capital stock of said company shall be two hundred thousand dollars, with the privilege of increasing it to two millions, to be divided into shares of one hundred dollars each, which shall be regarded as personal property. **Stock, $2,000,000.**

SEC. 3. Said company shall be permitted to organize and go into operation when $20,000 of its capital shall have been paid in, and shall have power to contract and be contracted with, receive and convey, release and be released, sue and be sued, plead and be impleaded, answer and be answered unto, in all manner of actions whatsoever, and in all courts having competent jurisdiction, and may have and use a common seal, and alter the same at pleasure, and shall be vested **Authority.**

with all the powers and privileges requisite to accomplish the objects of its organization.

Objects.

SEC. 4. The objects of said company shall be the purchase, improvement, leasing, exchange and sale of lands and lots on the shore of Lake Michigan, or within six miles thereof; and the members may make all needful rules and regulations, and by-laws and articles of agreement, and execute all instruments in writing requisite for the profitable, efficient and safe management of the stock, property and concerns of said company, but nothing in this act shall be construed to invest said company with any banking powers, or to authorize them to make, emit or utter any bill of credit or bank notes, or other thing to be used as a circulating medium, as and in lieu of money.

SEC. 5. This act shall be deemed a public act, and take effect from and after its passage.

Approved February 22, 1861.

Plan of company.

Having then given over the reaper entirely, and setting myself earnestly to devise the plan under the charter, abundant advantages were soon discovered. But to devise a feasible method to obtain an income or not at the option of the shareholders, and also to prevent my being ousted as Actuary, required much study, and with the circular took over four months hard work.* The following was the opening:—

Circular, 1861.

Panic prices.

The revulsion of 1857, and our national difficulties, have brought a most favorable time to buy real estate in Chicago. Prices of central lots are reduced nearly one-half, and of out-property about three-fourths, and in a few years must attain former figures, and more. Of this remarkable opportunity I desire to avail myself, and think my plan of investment will commend itself to non-resident capitalists to our mutual advantage.

A chartered real estate company is rather a novelty, but has many points of excellence, especially for non-residents, who desire to invest in this most prosperous city, and would avoid the cares of personal attention, and the watching and risks of agents; and the legislature has granted a very liberal charter.

Property still low.

Although much property has regained former prices and more, as above prognosticated, much has not. Beyond any question, no other city offers equal promise of profits in its real estate; and let us here consider that—

REAL ESTATE, ESPECIALLY IN A GROWING CITY, IS THE BEST INVESTMENT.

Lots advance in value.

Land ought to be the favorite means of investing funds not wanted for active business, and is rapidly becoming so. For safety and profit, comfort and ease of management, nothing equals it. Government stocks, and many kinds of bonds are safe, it is true,—provided they are of the right kind—but not more so than real estate; and while the latter can be made to yield an income, if desired, and with at least equal if not greater certainty, advance on the land may be several fold in a few years, and little or nothing on stocks.

Stocks depreciative.

So far from ordinary stocks and securities appreciating, they probably must decline. The constant and immense increase of the precious metals, to which no limit can be put, and is yearly augmented by new discoveries, must affect all values —that is, cheapen money. Bank stocks, state and corporation bonds, and other investments at a fixed rate of interest, annuities and the like, must depreciate with

This paper hurried.

*It is regretted that this paper cannot be as strongly digested and condensed. But supposing it would be easy to remodel that to the present times, plans have been laid, and advertisements issued, that leave me time wholly inadequate. Having been carefully adapted to that important epoch, much is wholly out of date, and to obtain the same information for this period requires more time than I have. So that with the advantages of seven years more increase, this paper cannot be made equal to that. Unfortunately, only a few proof sheets were struck. the type being left standing until I could return from a visit to a friend in New York, whose advice I wanted as to changes. After two or three months' waiting, the type was distributed.

P. S. This note was added, expecting then to print only a small pamphlet.

the increase of the circulating medium of values, while other property, and especially real estate and stocks like this company, must correspondingly advance.

—even railways.

Even railroad and manufacturing and similar stocks, are to be injuriously affected, because cheapening money will stimulate competition in all operations that are very profitable, and the advantage existing companies will have over new ones, will rest chiefly in the real estate and other property obtained when a dollar bought more than it then can. In the rapid changes which are progressing, many establishments will find themselves so placed as to have lost even this benefit, being unable to compete with others in more advantageous locations.

City property gives great estates

Fortunes are often made by business and speculations of various kinds, but it is well known that most of the great estates in our country and elsewhere, have been made by holding lands. The largest and most speedy advances, too, have been in cities. Find a city which is sure to grow, and you may there, with care and skill, invest upon a positive certainty of success.

How invest surplus.

It is a pertinent inquiry, what is to be done with the money so fast being made in the various pursuits of life? For fifteen or twenty years we have put fifty to a hundred millions annually into railroads, besides what has been obtained in Europe. Investments in them are to be comparatively small in future, and how are their incomes to be used,—say one hundred millions annually—and the increasing profits in all branches of industry, stimulated and multiplied as they have been by the locomotive and telegraph? Amid the marvellous changes of modern years, it is impossible to say with certainty what may or may not be done; but it is hardly probable any new absorbent will be found equal to the railway, and it would seem that our accumulating capital must be employed in real estate and in manufactures; and the latter will very greatly affect the former at the more central localities.

In real estate and manufactures.

Views stronger now.

Events that are to stand forth upon the historic page as chief of centuries, have since 1861 given increased force to those considerations. Some talk of repudiation. Pshaw! The national indebtedness, in whatever form it may be put—and what is not needed for ordinary circulation in "greenbacks" ought to be converted into one form of stock, payable a century hence with three or four per cent. interest—will soon be highly valued the world over, and "greenbacks" and bonds will be equal to gold, and to their amount increase the circulating medium. If good for anything, they should and soon will be worth their face in gold; and the longer the time, the more premium will they bear. When their value shall be learned, what will be the difference, whether we dig $1000 in gold, and send to Europe, or send a U. S. bond for the amount, except as to the interest? Will not one buy what we want as well as the other? and this result comes inevitably, when we ourselves shall have learned the true nature and principles of our governmental system, and developed the strength of National Union based upon State Sovereignty. When the North shall be brought to see its errors concerning State Sovereignty and correct the teachings of the Massachusetts school; when the South shall learn the strength of National Union between sovereign States, and acknowledge the errors of the South Carolina school,—and how can we ever have *re*-construction without both knowledge and changes?—then shall we and other nations understand how the unexampled power displayed in war has its origin; and learning the strength and sacredness of covenant obligations, no fear can exist that indebtedness incurred in a war so high and holy as that of ours, and by States possessed of such abundant resources,

National indebtedness to be currency.

Good in Europe.

Confidence in our institutions.

Debt to be paid by posterity.

will not be paid to the last dollar. And it is the height of folly to think of putting upon this generation, or even the next, the burthen of payment of any part of it. For a long period it will be to us like so much money; and now having accidentally learned from the exigencies of war the true national currency, and when the "greenbacks" shall have supplanted the issues of the wild-cat brood of banks, we shall have the best currency of the world, and with the bonds will have world-wide circulation.

Increase of money—

Discussion of these questions would not be expected here; but he who has confidence in the perpetuity of our Heaven-ordained system, cannot doubt as to these results. And what must be the effect of this immense augmentation of the currency, conjoined with the rapid increase of gold and silver, which must be still more rapid as railways penetrate the mining districts, which, according to all indications, have but just begun to be developed? That real estate, which is the last thing to be affected, has not already been more enhanced, has been chiefly occasioned by lack of confidence in United States securities. As experience teaches us, and a permanent, sound policy is instituted, be assured the realty of the country will have a swift and permanent advancement. What can you name to compare in safety with property judiciously purchased in a city that is sure to grow?

—enhances real estate.

This the bright side.

This, however, is taking the bright view of things. Living in a world of uncertainty, adversity largely mixed with prosperity, and it not being man's province to know positively what the future will bring forth, let us also consider that—

General pecuniary Revulsions may intervene, but cannot change the Result.

Certainty of Chicago's destiny.

This topic is considerately taken, excluding, as is apparent, what would be termed Providential occurrences, as the termination of lake navigation by the removal of Niagara's rocks. Nothing less than such an event can change the destiny of Chicago. The circular of 1860 had the following:—

Neglect of past counsel.

Most of you, perhaps, are becoming wearied with this reiterated advice to invest in Chicago. Yet who of you have done as well as to have heeded my requests eight to twelve years ago? It is true, that owing to the revulsions and panic of 1857, some have property bought in 1855 and 1856, for which they could not get cost. But the present is no such period—it is like that eight to twelve years ago; and those who have, in later years, paid high prices, have only to exercise a moderate degree of confidence, and some patience, and the poorest of their purchases will prove better than money loaned at ten per cent.

Revulsion of 1857—

Let not those friends who are among these sufferers remind me that I have continually, even in 1855 and 1856, been advising to these investments. I acknowledge that I did; but they will also remember that since 1851 and 1852, I have ever coupled my advice with the statement that it was possible a revulsion might come —many prognosticated it for years as close at hand—but for my own part, I could see no reason to fear—that if prosperity continued, their Chicago investments would pay as well or better than any other; and if a revulsion came, they had only to wait a few years, and they would still make money.

The panic of 1857 came at last—and panic it was more than aught else—and though so long predicted, yet nearly everybody was taken by surprise. I confess it has brought a result which I did not anticipate. Never could I have believed that by any influences prices would again be depressed here as they now are. With such an absolute certainty as the future destiny of Chicago, which all acknowledge, I cannot understand why calculating business men do not see the intrinsic and ultimate value of property here. It is a proposition as simple and certain as that two and two make four.

—mere panic.

But we must take things as they are. The depression exists, and those who are wise, will avail themselves of it. With even more pertinacity than from 1846 to 1850—more confidence than ever in the wisdom of the advice—would I urge you not to let this golden opportunity slip. And there is this important difference in the periods—that my opinions then were predicated upon railroads, &c., in prospect, but which I was confident must be built. More—much more—than I anticipated, has been realized, and my advice now is based upon an absolute certainty. No earthly power—not even the dissolution of the Union—can divert from Chicago the business and traffic of the great Northwest.

Advantage to be taken.

In 1861, the same ideas were a little differently expressed:—

The Revulsions of 1857.—It is true I did not foresee the absurd panic and crash of 1857, or I would have protected myself. For five or six years the croakers had said one was coming, and upon its final arrival, were generally as much taken aback as others. But fortunately, while advising friends to invest, I had told them for several years that a revulsion might come—I saw no likelihood of it, though others said they did—but that if property declined, they had simply to wait with patience for the favorable change that would surely follow. So say I still, and am confident that but few purchases, even in '56 and '7, will not within ten years return the capital with good interest.

Prosperity to follow a revulsion.

Property was too high for the best advantage of the city, and for its then attainments, but a causeless and immense decline like the present, never should exist in a place possessed of the certain future that awaits Chicago, and would not if real estate operators studied causes and effects sufficiently to establish independent judgments, and were not unduly influenced by temporary embarrassments. But the depression exists, and those who are wise will avail themselves of the folly of others.

Property not too high.

Have not results thus far amply justified these opinions, notwithstanding they were written before the beginning of the conflict, when we yet had reason to hope that peaceful counsels might still prevail? But even in March the clouds were too lowering to omit consideration of current events, which, if not wholly perfect, will at least bear comparison with the judgment of the sage counselors who predicted, for I know not how long, the "end of the *rebellion* in only 60 to 90 days."

Experience confirms advice.

National difficulties anticipated.

The Effects of Secession and of Civil War.—The lamentable condition of our national affairs, is not to be ignored in considering this subject of investments. It is to affect seriously all our interests, pecuniary as well as others. But it seemed more simple to look at the prospects of the West in view of ordinary national events and progress, and then examine how they are to be affected by the present extraordinary current of governmental affairs.

Views, 1861.

That with peace and the continuance of national concerns in their usual courses, the West would have received its full share of prosperity, will not be questioned; and if upon examination it be found that these governmental troubles, and even civil war, cannot retard our progress, but may even advance it relatively, there can then be no possibility of error in choosing the West as a field for investment.

West prosper with peace—

I have endeavored in studying this subject, as also in the preceding pages, to divest my mind of its strong western partiality, and hunt up all adverse influences, and I can see no single point which is made unduly favorable to western interests, or in which injuries to that section are overlooked or under-estimated; and I confess my surprise at finding that even these deplorable, powerful national calamities must result in benefits to the West as compared with effects on other sections.

—or even war.

Views in March before the war.

Soon after obtaining my charter, I commenced the preparation of these papers, and in March wrote the one following upon our National Difficulties. Then it seemed probable that Secession would be effected, and possibly without war, and accordingly it was so discussed. Affairs since have materially changed; the war has originated in a manner wholly different from what had seemed probable; and now there is less danger that any States will be allowed to secede. Still, it is one of the possibilities that a prudent capitalist would wish to take into account, and therefore do I present my views concerning it, and the paper of March is better than anything I could now write.

West to suffer least— —large armies. West not devastated—

The Consequences of Civil War.—The preceding views are based upon the hope that our national differences are to be peacefully adjusted. Most lamentable is it to think that this may be impossible; but if the dread evils of civil war are to be ours, I do not see that thereby the results of secession, as hereinbefore presented, are to be materially affected, or that the West will be more injured than the East. With armies of a quarter or half a million on both sides, which may be expected of such people when once in earnest, it is impossible to judge with certainty what may or may not be done or attempted; but the West, with the exception of its southern border, and perhaps St. Louis and its vicinity, is not probably to be the theatre of strife and devastation. The efforts of the South will most likely be chiefly defensive.

War on large scale— —demand for agricultural products.

Whether the war be of short or of long continuance, it must be on a large scale, with an immense expenditure of money that will stimulate business and enterprizes of all kinds, creating an extraordinary demand for our agricultural produce and animals, at high rates and with great wastage; and though our government will endeavor to cut off western supplies from the South, yet dealers will find ways to get them there at an extra price. And as shown in my previous paper, the West will derive its full proportion of benefit from the free use of capital, whether caused by war or otherwise.

West soonest recuperate. West pay its part easiest.

When the means and energies of both North and South are well nigh exhausted —if indeed passion instead of reason is to rule, and bring severe and protracted war—when calm shall succeed the terrible storm, and the immense cost is to be counted and paid, what section will bear its proportionate loss more ably than the West? Which has most elasticity, and will soonest recover from the dire calamities?

War decides nothing. Differences still to be adjusted. South not to be conquered.

When the machinations of selfish, fiery zealots of the South Carolina school, and of the equally wicked, foolish, Northern abolitionists, shall have accomplished their legitimate and common purposes, and even their bitterest hate he gorged to satiety—when damages shall have ensued to our once happy country, and to humanity the world over, that ten thousand times the number of those accursed conspirators and fanatics could never repair—when rivers of fraternal blood shall have been shed, and no good effected except to demonstrate to observing nations that we have a government, and which is one redeeming and important feature of the deplorable calamity; still the differences are no nearer adjustment than before the war began. As to subjugating either section, it cannot be done unless the South is annihilated, which none but crazy men dream of.* Reason sooner or later will prevail over exasperated passions, and re-union or division will be agreed upon, either of which brings the same results before presented, with the disastrous effects of war superadded.

* * * * * * * *

War begun. North a unit. Result sure unless foreign governments interfere.

Since the foregoing was written, the aspect is altogether changed. War has begun, and in a manner quite different from what had seemed probable, and no one can predict the consequences. The refusing of supplies to, and the attack upon Fort Sumter, has made the North a unit, which it would not have been had the war differently originated. With a division of sentiment in the North, the Government would ere long have acknowledged the independence of the Confederate States. But with the present entire unanimity here existing, and much Union sentiment in the South, which would increase as the purposes and desires of our Government came to be understood and appreciated by the masses there, the result would be evident and sure, could we know that foreign governments would not interfere, though some years might be required for its accomplishment.

Misjudgment as to conquest.

*Here was my chief misjudgment. No such event being presented in all history as that of two-thirds of a nation subduing the other third; we must recognize the hand of a covenant-keeping God in substituting over covenant-breaking States, the rights of conquest for those of compact, by which they were held to National Union. But it seemed wholly improbable that the South could commit the folly of commencing the attack. Had the Federal Government begun actual hostilities, the North would not have been the unit that it became when Fort Sumter was assailed and captured.

It is a mistaken idea that this war is to be short. The blood is up on both sides, and much is to be let off to reduce either party to a temperate condition and to calm reflection. Besides, the South wholly underrate the combative power and determination of the North. They believe one Southron equal to five to twenty Yankees, and it will take a year or two of fighting to teach them proper respect for northern courage. And on the part of the North, is very general misapprehension as to the power of endurance of the South, and their relative independence. The conflict on the part of the South will be mainly defensive, which gives them greatly the advantage, and in other respects than climate.

War long and fierce.

Errors south—

—and north.

Many suppose the blockade of the coast, which will be nearly if not entirely effectual till foreign governments interfere, together with cutting off western supplies by way of the interior, is to bring the South speedily to terms. Not so. They are forewarned, and understand the necessity of providing a supply of food, and have had, and have still, ample time to raise crops; and instead of cotton, corn and wheat are being cultivated. For the little woolen cloth needed in that climate, their own flocks are sufficient, and slaves will be set to spinning and weaving on every plantation. Of course, comforts and luxuries from abroad, and even many necessaries, are to be dispensed with, but in that they will glory. No doubt for a year or two, or longer, the South can live very well within themselves. * * *

South can sustain war.

It is now certain, too, that the Border States are to be the greatest sufferers, and of the thousands of their citizens coming to the North, the West will receive much the largest part. Immense injury is to result to the cities along the Ohio and to St. Louis, and rapidly is their business from northern directions to be centered here. What changes it would have required five years to effect, in the ordinary course of events, will now be made in one or two.

Border States injured.

It is anything but agreeable to receive benefits from such a melancholy, deplorable calamity. The prosperity of the West, and of Chicago, was ample, had all other sections received of the smiles of Heaven as hitherto, and now we will do anything and everything that is right and reasonable, to bring again the blessings of peace. But it seems necessary to consider the results of our national struggle, even in its pecuniary aspect; and if, as we have seen, the prosperity of the West and of Chicago was heretofore sure, it is more so now, *relatively with other sections*, in the midst of the disasters and ruin that have come over our wretched country.

Chicago to prosper even in war.

But the war-cloud has passed; and how much of good has a gracious Providence mingled in that most terrible chastisement, a civil war unexampled on history's page! The demonstration that we are a genuine Nation, albeit we little understand its nature; the ease with which free citizens can be converted into a Nation of soldiers; the riddance of slavery, almost the sole cause of sectional conflict; the substitution of a true national currency in place of the bills of credit of the banks, with which the West has been fleeced year after year and which the Constitution prohibits, though we have never known it, and which must also be substituted for the circulation of the rotten national banks as soon as the West and South get the power;—all these great national blessings bear directly upon this question. And more important still—immeasurably more important, because it reaches the foundation principles of our Government—is the fact, which in due time will be understood, that in order to reconstruct our National Union, we must learn the principles upon which it is founded. When that great work shall have been accomplished, of which we are beginning to feel the necessity, not only we but the whole world will learn the strength and superiority of our compound system of State and Federal Governments, built upon the one solid foundation—not a split one—of the People's Sovereignty—

Blessings resulting from civil war—

—affect this question.

Principles of our government to be understood—

—dignity of citizenship.

the People by States. Then will the dignity and benefits of citizenship of free and independent States in a National Union like ours, be understood; and we shall begin to discover the essential difference in the forms of government, and the power it has in free States to create and develope the highest, noblest specimens of manhood.

War worth the cost.

Even in a generation or two shall we find benefits abundantly countervailing for the immense cost of treasure, and even of the precious life-blood; and more and more highly estimated will be the benefits, on and on for ages, as the ocean-bound Republic marches to its destiny, chief among the nations of the earth.

Adversity to come.

Affects all property.

We may, we undoubtedly shall, have our reverses, for continuous prosperity appears not to be best for man either individually or collectively. But is not other property affected as well as real estate? What is more stable than good property in a growing city? Truly, the man who looks for hard times year after year, patiently hoarding his gold instead of seeking reasonable profit in its use, will in time find an opportunity to buy even real estate at a sacrifice. But is that man likely to judge well when the right time shall have come to buy? Certainly real estate is one of the last things to rise, and is it not at last reached? Some city property has advanced; yet it was too high before the cheapening of money—as much of it doubtless was in the older cities of our country—or it must considerably enhance. The advance has already begun, and he is unwise who fails to invest surplus funds at present prices. Nor is real estate first to fall, as is generally imagined. The more fanciful the property, the quicker is it depressed. Lots and lands come last, and the better they are, the less they feel the revulsion.

Real estate to rise—

—is most permanent.

Look on bright side—

—hope and trust.

Nor is he wise who looks only or chiefly on the dark side. While duly regarding the latter, let him consider how much more of national prosperity is given to us than of adversity. The Christian—and who that is not a God-fearing Jew ought not to be a Christian in this Heaven-blessed land?—he who has proper hope and trust in his God and country, ought to regard the sure days of prosperity that have been and must be ours, rather than the days of adversity sent because we do not properly trust and obey our God in the discharge of duty to Him and to each other. The faithful steward hides not his talent for fear of loss, but manfully uses it according to his own judgment, trusting the Master for prosperity.*

Politics proper here.

*Think not that politics are improperly, and religion irreverently, introduced in this paper. The stability of our institutions are a prime consideration, in which confidence will strengthen with examination. The benefits of our compound system, too, will expand as our knowledge of its nature is increased, so that progress in the past will be as nothing to the future.

—also, religion.

Nor is the religious aspect more out of place. If individual prosperity depend upon the State and civil government, all depends upon God and Divine government. Here, however, we are considering public, national affairs, as affecting those of the individual; and States and nations have their awards in this life, where their existence ceases. We are punished for our disobedience of the Laws of Nature and of Nature's God; and the study into principles which are necessary for the proper practice of our

And our judgment must be exercised, carefully and with all possible knowledge. It is my hope to demonstrate that there is at least one city in which investments may be made with absolute certainty; for if calamities come, prosperity must follow from the nature of the case.

Proof supplied to your judgment—

To judge of the future, we must know the means of present attainment. Let us, then, next consider the—

—by the past.

Public Improvements anticipated twenty and ten Years ago as a Basis.

In 1847 I wrote a series of letters for the *Boston Courier*, to acquaint New England capitalists with their interests touching western railroads. Mr. Buckingham, in introducing them, speaks of former articles from the writer, of which I have no copy. The last letter said:—

Letters 1847 for *Boston Courier*.

These letters were commenced to urge upon Bostonians the importance and advantage to themselves, of subscribing liberally to the stock of the Galena and Chicago Railroad, and my readers will most likely think I have wandered far from my subject, in presenting, in this connection, the line of railroads from Alton to Chicago. But I have only anticipated a little. I should before have explained that the charter of this company authorizes the construction of lateral routes, and the capital is sufficient, being $3,000,000, with the privilege of borrowing $3,000,000 more. The first road to be built will be to the Indiana State Line, to be continued around the head of Lake Michigan to New Buffalo, there connecting with the Central Railroad to Detroit. From Sandwich, C. W., opposite Detroit, a railroad is being constructed to the Niagara river, which, by the wire bridge, can be connected with the New York railroads; so that probably within three years, Boston and Chicago will be connected by railroads, with the exception of crossing the Detroit river by steamboat. And passengers will also have the privilege of relieving themselves from the tedium of so long-continued a ride in the cars, by taking steamboat on Lakes Erie or Ontario, or both.

Alton and Chicago railroad.

Mich. Central route—

—3 years to Boston.

Several lateral roads will doubtless be built, connecting with the main line between Galena and Chicago, but the branch from at or near St. Charles, down the Fox River Valley to Ottawa and to Peru, the terminating point of the Illinois and Michigan Canal, will be the first, and should be speedily constructed. Then if the Alton and Springfield Railroad is immediately pushed forward, as its friends confidently expect, only 105 miles (air line) would remain to be built between Springfield and Peru, to connect Boston by railroad with the Mississippi, at the head of large steamboat navigation. A person might then start from St. Louis, and be able to reach Boston in about 63 hours, with an average speed of only 20 miles an hour. Who can say this shall not be accomplished within ten years? It might be done within five years, and surely would be if Bostonians were alive to their true interests.

Galena road and branch—

—to Alton and St. Louis

And, before going on to speak more directly of the Galena road, I cannot forbear adding yet another word, as to the peculiar interest that Bostonians have in securing the speedy—immediate—construction of this entire line from Chicago to Alton. The roads from Chicago to Detroit will be completed within two or three years, and, also, as I learn from the *Railroad Journal*, the road from Sandwich to the Niagara river. By that time, too, the Ogdensburg road will be built through to Boston, and with a line of first-class steamers running over the beautiful waters of Lake Ontario, and through the "Thousand Isles," to Ogdensburg, what route eastward would be likely to be more popular?

Important to Boston.

---

governments, will bring us at the same time to see where we have broken God's laws; for the subjects are inseparably blended in the Bible. Repenting of and correcting our wrongs towards God and each other, we shall receive of Heaven's blessings in larger measure than ever. He has not proper appreciation of his dignity and responsibility in business affairs, who takes no cognizance of such operating causes; and he is lamentably deficient in faith in both God and country, who doubts that we are to have prosperity and advancement far eclipsing that of the past. Temporary reverses we may need and suffer under, but only temporary will they be.

Lake Shore route.

The line of roads directly eastward from Chicago, along the southern shore of Lake Erie, will not probably be built till some years after the more northern route shall be finished; but it is surely to be built, sooner or later. Now, if Boston capitalists would only commence at once, and urge onward with their utmost power, the construction of the line from Alton to Chicago, they could get business so far established on their northern route before the more southern one will be built, as to secure permanently a large part of the travel and business which is quite likely to go eastward through American territory, over Lake Erie, or along its southern shore. If Boston is interested in turning the current of business northward, to avoid competition with Baltimore and Philadelphia, she is not less so in giving it the direction above named, to turn it as far as possible from New York. This her capitalists may do to a very considerable extent if they move early; and as they will surely furnish capital for the railroads from Alton to Chicago, sooner or later, because they will find it for their advantage, how much better will it be for them, to do it at once, when they will thereby be enabled to make sure of at least their full proportion of the business of the West and Southwest? * * * *

Boston to draw business north to the lakes—

—best do it soon,

Eastern cities interested—

Yes, indeed, "Eastern cities are *sure* to derive great and permanent benefits" from these and all other roads in the West, which tend to throw business upon the chain of great lakes; and of them all, no city is likely to reap so large a share comparatively, as Boston. I have before, in writing concerning the Ogdensburg road, nearly two years since, spoken of the advantages that route possessed in competing with other routes to the Eastern markets, and Boston has everything to gain and nothing to lose in getting business on to the lakes. After completing the Ogdensburg road, there are no others of so much importance to the New England metropolis, as the Galena and Chicago road, and the line from Chicago to Alton.

—Boston especially.

Rock Island road.

Another road will in time be built from Peru westward to the Mississippi, at or near the mouth of Rock river, which will, ere long, be continued on the same course to Council Bluffs on the Missouri, which would draw largely on the trade of St. Louis with the Upper Missouri, sending it eastward by way of the lakes. When will all these railroads be built? It is less to say that within twenty years every mile of them shall be completed, than to have foretold twenty years since that we should now have the works that within that time have been built. Within twenty years, I believe within a much shorter period, the iron-horse will be able to travel from Council Bluffs to Boston.

20 years build these roads to Council Bluffs!

Virginia appreciated—

I am here in the "Old Dominion," writing about the interests of Chicago and Boston. I like Virginia and its people, and can in truth say that I have never enjoyed myself so much as while partaking of their friendly hospitalities, which have, in fact, delayed this letter for several days; and I should be glad if we could become more connected in interest and feeling with this distinguished and honorable old member of the confederacy. But I *do* rejoice that the home of my adoption is so intimately united by interest and intercourse with my native State. There is no one reflection concerning Chicago and its connections which gives me more exquisite satisfaction than the close tie of a common interest by which it is united with the Old Bay State, and with Boston.

—but Massachusetts and the West united.

Boston and Chicago identified in interest.

They must go on to increase together, and Chicago and the West will be—must be—greatly aided by the far-reaching and wise efforts of Bostonians, to secure to themselves a fair proportion of the business of the country. They can hardly make an expenditure in opening avenues of trade, which will not directly benefit us at Chicago, and the citizen most ambitious for its growth, could not desire a stronger, more enduring basis of prosperity.

Railway from Boston to Rocky Mountains.

Although overwrought, yet "within 20 years the iron horse *has and does* travel from Council Bluffs to Boston," and on his return can run *five hundred and twenty-five miles, almost half the distance, further.*

Petitions for Ills. land grants.

In 1848 I distributed at my own expense, 6,000 copies of petitions to Congress, for a grant of land in aid of a railroad from the Upper and Lower Mississippi to Chicago. Three different ones were prepared for the South, Illinois and the East. Judge Douglas said they came to Washington by the hundred numerously signed and had much influence, being the earliest movement for this object outside of Congress, except by the Cairo Company. The southern said in part:—

In this measure the South-west has a large interest, as supplying the best route to the East. Even now the Lake route is much traveled, and two or three years connects Chicago with all the Atlantic cities by railroad, when it will be preferred, except in winter, to any route that will be opened for a long time. Then will this Illinois road be wanted, which will make it the best route in winter also, enabling persons to reach New York city from Cairo in three and a half days; and which, the Mississippi being always navigable to the mouth of the Ohio, would give uninterrupted steam communication between the extremes of the Union, at all seasons of the year. **Southwest interested in a road to the lakes.**

Other routes you will have in time, but with the grant of lands this would be the first entirely completed, and being very direct will give strong competition to any others, and ensure low rates of travel. * * * **This the first.**

An effort is making also for a grant of lands in aid of a railroad from Mobile to the mouth of the Ohio, to which this would be an important extension, and those interested in the Illinois roads will do all they can to aid that. We must help each other in these matters.* The South and West have a common interest in such improvements, and it is but right and just that a part of the public lands within our borders should be given in aid of works so important to us and to the public at large. **Help Mobile road.**

But no gratuitous gift is asked from Government. Thousands of acres of land, through which the road passes, will never be sold till some avenue to market is created; and only alternate sections are given. * * * **No gratuity asked.**

We therefore call upon the public spirited men of the south, as we have of the east, which is also interested in the road, to aid us. Get our bill passed, and then others can be got which are right in themselves. And it is just and politic to make this a precedent. No road in contemplation is more national in its character than that which connects the great chain of Northern lakes with the Mississippi at the mouth of the Ohio. * * * **South will aid this national work.**

The circular of January, 1848, contained the following:— **Circular, 1848.**

The Illinois and Michigan Canal.—All business with the interior has been done hitherto by teams, but the Canal to the Illinois River at Peru, will be opened in the spring, which will, perhaps, double our exports the first year. It opens to us the whole river navigation of the Great Valley, and furnishes the cheapest and most expeditious inland route between the eastern cities and the Mississippi river and its tributaries. And for supplying the whole Lake region with West India goods, cotton, sugar, etc., this is also the best channel, and that trade must be very great. Who can estimate or put a limit to the amount of business to be done on such a route? **Ills. & Mich Canal to be finished. Its value.**

Railroads with us are yet prospective, but there are four routes of so great importance, and so certain to be built, that it is proper to speak of them in connection with the future growth of Chicago. Arrangements are making to continue the Michigan Central Railroad from New Buffalo to Chicago, a distance of sixty miles, which, with the road building across Canada, connects us with the eastern roads. The Galena and Chicago railroad, 182 miles long, has been surveyed, and 35 miles of it to Fox River will be built next season. It will be finished in two or three years, and the grades being uncommonly light, and mostly descending to the lake, will permit transportation of produce and lead at very cheap rates. Branches will be made up Rock River, and into the lead regions of Wisconsin, and in other directions, and the stock must be profitable. Another is the Buffalo and Mississippi road, via Chicago to the mouth of Rock River, with the expectation that in time it will be continued across the Mississippi to Council Bluffs, on the Missouri. This has many able and influential advocates and friends; among others, Hon. Elisha Whittlesey of Ohio, and Hon. S. A. Douglas of the U. S. Senate, who are sanguine that they will be able to obtain for it a donation of lands from Congress. **Railroads prospective, but 4 certain. Mich. Cent. Galena. Buff. and Mississippi.**

*Quite possibly the influx of petitions to Congress from the South, caused the annexation of the Mobile road, extending the grant from Lake Michigan and the Upper Mississippi to the Gulf of Mexico. But the prevalent idea is wrong, that Illinois received any gratuity. Very different was this initiatory step in aid of railroads, from the munificent donations now made, and with great propriety. Alternate sections were granted, and the price of those remaining was doubled to $2.50 per acre. But the present policy will doubtless continue; and what other city will be so much aided by it as Chicago? To what other will a quarter part of the miles be added as to this city? **Grant extended to Mobile— —yet no gratuity**

Ills. Central. The fourth, and by far the most important one to us, is the road from Cairo at the mouth of the Ohio, which connects Lake Michigan with the Mississippi at the head of the largest steamboat navigation, open to the Gulf at all seasons of the year. A donation of lands by Congress in aid of this road will probably be made, as I learn from good authority, the present session, which will ensure its rapid prosecution.

National character. If not perfectly familiar with these routes, please take a map and trace them. Consider their importance in a national point of view,—see the direct interest which the extremes of the country, and the intermediate States have in their construction,—that the stock-holders of Eastern roads who have so much capital at command, have every inducement to aid in building these roads, which would so greatly augment the income of their own,—that inasmuch as Boston and New York have a vital interest in directing business on to the lakes, to prevent it from taking a more Southerly direction to their rival cities Baltimore and Philadelphia, they cannot do otherwise than aid Chicago to the full extent of their ability, in stretching its iron arms in every direction, particularly to the South—and then remember what the past fifteen years have done in building railroads, and is it an over estimate to say that fifteen years to come will see every mile of these four completed? What must be their effect upon Chicago? What other inland town can you name as the probable centre of so many and so important routes?

Boston and New York interested.

15 years to build them.

5 named. Five were named of those which are among our chief roads, the Rock Island west, and Michigan Southern east, being parts of the Buffalo and Mississippi. When only ten years had elapsed, hope had largely given place to reality, and I could exultingly say:—

Change in 10 years.

By 1858 focal point fixed. *Railroads Now Built—The Focal Point Fixed.*—Wild as were these views considered, instead of the four [five] railroads anticipated, we have *twelve* important trunk lines, about three thousand miles in length, and numerous branches of over eight hundred miles more. No longer is it "probable," but a fact, that Chicago is the greatest railroad centre in the world. And instead of fifteen years, ten see this all done. In this short time have the railroad earnings of this city grown from nothing to *over eighteen million dollars annually*.

Other roads to be feeders. Railroads will hereafter be built with more difficulty, but the present lines are so located that nearly or quite every addition in the West will be a feeder to some of them. Those most important to their several locations as well as to us are fortunately begun and will be the first finished, and six have large grants of land from Congress, ensuring their speedy construction, viz: "St. Paul & Fond du Lac," running to Minnesota with a branch to Lake Superior; the "Dubuque & Pacific," to the Missouri; the "Iowa Central Air Line," from Lyons to the Missouri; the "Mississippi & Missouri," from Davenport; the "Burlington & Missouri;" and the Hannibal & St. Joseph," across Northern Missouri, which connects with the Quincy Railroad. These last five, running westerly, will do the chief carrying for Iowa and North Missouri and send much of the business direct to this city, and are already built from thirty to eighty-five miles each.

6 west of Mississippi.

Pacific road. "The Pacific" railroad, too, in time must be built, and will connect with one or more of these roads, and though I do not as highly estimate its importance to any one city as many do, yet Chicago is as likely to be benefited by it as any other.

These predictions realized— The chief point to be made from these extracts is, not that I should have anticipated the building of these roads with such correctness, for any man of sense, who would have considered the subject with my knowledge of the Great West, would have had the same expectations; but the point is, that anticipations twenty years ago to so great an extent of what has actually been realized, prove the system to have been natural, and what the country demands, and what the keen-sighted capitalists abroad who have supplied the means, saw to be best for their own interests. Yet, however serviceable sound hypothesis may be, it is a great transition from *what is to be done* to *what has been done;* and now, be it observed, that—

—prove the system to be natural.

The Basis of Our Prosperity is No Longer Hypothetical.

The work accomplished by 1858, rendered quite sure the focal position of Chicago. Yet three years added over 700 miles, and the following list was given in 1861:— Basis quite sure in 1858.

Four Thousand Five Hundred Miles of Railroad now tributary to Chicago.—Some may like to see to what cities all these lines of railway run that are claimed for Chicago. From Lloyd's latest railroad map, I compile the following: 4,500 miles of railroad tributary in 1861.

Chicago Mil. and La Crosse	285	......	*Miles brought forward*	1344	475
Kenosha and Rockford	......	73			
Racine and Freeport	......	104	Peoria and Bureau Valley	......	46
Chicago and Northwestern	213	......	Chicago and Burlington	210	......
Milton to Prairie du Chien	130	......	Burlington and Missouri	75	......
Mill Creek to Berlin	......	33	Galesburg to Quincy	100	......
Watertown to Columbus	......	20	Hannibal and St. Joseph	206	......
Watertown to Sun Prairie	......	15	St. Louis, Alton and Chicago	285	....
Janesville to Monroe	......	33	Illinois Central	451	......
Galena and Chicago, (to Freeport)	121	......	Chicago Branch	253	......
Elgin, State Line and Wisconsin	......	41	Gilman to Galesburg	......	134
Beloit and Madison	......	37	Tolono to Camp Point	......	165
Mineral Point	......	83	Mattoon to Illinoistown	......	130
Dubuque and Pacific	111	......	Odin to Illinoistown	......	65
Farley to Anamosa	......	29	Cincinnati and Chicago Air Line	280	......
Fulton Air Line (Galena)	136	......	Pittsburgh and Ft. Wayne	467	......
Chicago, Iowa and Nebraska	82	......	Michigan Southern	243	......
Chicago and Rock Island	182	......	Elkhart to Toledo	......	142
Rock Island to Coal Valley	......	11	Laporte to Plymouth	......	30
Mississippi and Missouri	85	......	Michigan Central	284	......
Muscatine and Washington	......	46	New Albany and Salem	......	288
Miles carried forward	1,344	475	*Total miles*	4199	1475

Of the above list, the eastern ends of the Wisconsin roads, and the farther extremities of the seven last named, may not be now regarded as Chicago roads. In my estimate of trunk lines I therefore deduct nearly 700 miles, and of the branches nearly 500. But in a few years, almost every mile will belong more to Chicago than any other city; and many others, particularly in Northern Indiana, might with great propriety be even now added to the list. Branches, &c., tributary.

The remarks of 1858, anticipating roads in Iowa and Missouri, were altered in part to what *had been* done; and the change from hypothesis to fact as the basis of argument, was thus noticed:— Change in 3 years.

Capital for new lines will hereafter be obtained with less freedom, but having got about all we need, this difficulty is decidedly in our favor, destroying all danger of injurious competition, even if that possibility existed, which does not; and the present ones are so located that nearly every addition anywhere in the West, will be a feeder to some of them. Those most important to their several regions, are also most desirable for us, and fortunately are well started and will be first finished, and are all continuations of Chicago roads. Five of them have large grants of lands from Congress, insuring their speedy construction, viz: the Northwestern, running to Minnesota, with a branch to Lake Superior; the Dubuque and Pacific, to the Missouri river and onward; the Clinton, Cedar Rapids and Nebraska; the Mississippi and Missouri, from Davenport; and the Burlington and Missouri. The Northwestern is in use 213 miles. The four in Iowa are built 75 to 111 miles west of the Mississippi, and will soon be finished, and with the Hannibal and St. Joseph, which is completed and extending into Kansas, will do the chief carrying for Iowa and North Missouri, concentrating here the business of that 75,000 square miles of rich territory, which hitherto has gone chiefly to St. Louis. A manufacturer or merchant, who looked solely to that region for his market, if he sold not a dollar's worth east of the Mississippi, would seek this as the location whence he could most easily and cheaply reach his customers, even in the farthermost counties. No place within or without the borders of Iowa and Missouri, is so easy of access from all their parts as Chicago will be by these roads. * * * Chief roads secured. Others more difficult. Land grants to 5. Of Iowa and North Missouri Chicago is the centre.

Please take a map and study the location of these roads. Is not this the centre whence they radiate, not in short, but long lines of hundreds of miles? and is not the system so established that no material change can be made? Too many westerly parallel lines are built and extending, to make it practicable to converge at any point beyond us, several roads of considerable length. Nearly every one *No railway centre west of us.*

west of the Mississippi and north of the mouth of the Missouri, is a direct extension of a Chicago Road. *West of us there can be no important railway centre.*

States tributary.

It is clear as sunlight, that for Illinois, Wisconsin, Minnesota, Iowa, North Missouri, and part of Indiana and Michigan, this city must be the emporium. Kansas and Nebraska are not included, being so remote, [the Cameron and Omaha roads have just united us] but they will soon be powerful States, and some or all of the five roads above named extending to their borders, will in time be built across them; making Chicago the most easily accessible of all the large cities, to those States also, and to the territory beyond. * * *

Doubt about growth of other cities.

Of all the cities in the West, this is most certain to grow. No one doubts that these Northwestern States, so wide in extent and rich in resources, are to develop speedily, and soon to be among the most wealthy and powerful in the Union. Large cities are to arise within them, but after Chicago it is difficult to foresee which will ultimately take the lead. Cincinnati, Detroit, Milwaukee, St. Louis, Hannibal, Keokuk, Burlington, Davenport, Dubuque, St. Paul, Minneapolis, and other places, may each be good for investment, and many will so prove; but opinions differ as to their advantages and prospects, and the uncertainty time and enterprise alone can determine. No one can be singled out as sure to grow beyond the others. Even St. Louis will probably see several of them, or other western cities, outstrip her within half a century. But the citizens and friends of each—except of St. Louis and Cincinnati—concede, that however prosperous they become, all, and the whole region tributary to them, must contribute directly to the advancement of Chicago.

St. Louis may be beaten by them.

Former predictions reasonable—

My predictions hitherto, though by many deemed extravagant. were based upon fair, reasonable, business-like considerations, as are these. They were no hap-hazard guesses, but thoroughly calculated. Time has demonstrated their moderation and correctness, as it will these also. But there is an important element of confidence in progress to come, far better than any one's judgment, however well tested. Former estimates were based upon railroads *to be built*, which, though they seemed to me certain, rested upon contingency. *All the railways I then anticipated are now finished, and many more*, and their forty-five hundred miles are admirably located to accommodate the business of the West, and especially to concentrate it at this point. What might have been doubted ten years ago, is now a fixed fact, establishing here beyond a question and without rivalry, the great metropolis of the West.

—realized and more.

Basis not now problematical—

The reader will assent to the importance of the point made, as to the basis of prosperity being no longer problematical, but an assured fact. Whether strengthening confidence in present views or not, the facts speak for themselves; and any thinking man will deduce from them one and the same result, that extraordinaries excepted, the tendency of western business Chicago-ward is as sure as the revolution of the earth towards the rising sun.

—future of Chicago sure

Admission of *Mo. Dem.*

Nor will traffic come only from a due west course, but from far away to the South, as our chief rival admits. The *Missouri Democrat* of the 29th November, puts this editorial on the lead:—

Flank movement.

A Flank Movement.—A few months ago the Chicago papers contained urgent appeals to business men to subscribe to the Kansas City and Cameron road, by which, they were told, St. Louis would be flanked, a direct connection without change of cars with Kansas and the Union Pacific Eastern Division would be secured, and the business of Chicago materially increased. After a week or two we learned from Chicago papers that these appeals had been unsuccessful; that the business men of that city had declined to invest any of their borrowed capital; that, in short, not a dollar had been subscribed in Chicago to a road promising so much to Chicago trade. But, after a few weeks more, the needed capital was obtained. The capitalists whose money has created the prosperity of that city, know enough to protect their investments. Applications to Eastern men of wealth were not unsuccessful. Work upon the road was commenced. And now, within less than a year the last rail is in position, and Kansas can send goods to or receive them from Chicago with less difficulty and at hardly more expense than from St. Louis; the Union Pacific, a great enterprise in which men of this city have invested largely, is connected more directly by rail with Chicago than with St. Louis;

Cameron road not aided by Chicago—

– but by the East.

Road built—connects Pacific road with Chicago

and another link is added to that network of railroads which threatens to surround us. Until the guage of the Missouri Pacific can be changed, or the North Missouri can be pushed to Kansas City, freight and travel will have to change cars to reach this city, but will have no such obstacle to impede its course toward Chicago. Trade, like water, moves in the direction of the least resistance. Nobody has ever succeeded in making it run up hill. For the present, at least, St. Louis will have to face a considerable disadvantage in competing for all the trade of Kansas and the regions that lie to the westward. * * * Trade not run up hill.

It is not our business to grumble, but, if St. Louis does not mean to resign its trade altogether, it must work. If Chicago taps the St. Louis branch of the Pacific at Kansas City, St. Louis must tap the Chicago branch at Omaha. We must penetrate Iowa, get unbroken connection with Kansas, and open a route to the South. In all these enterprises, every business man of St. Louis has a peculiar interest. Chicago merchants can afford to neglect enterprises essential to their prosperity, because Eastern capital is already so largely enlisted in them that more can be obtained to protect what is already risked. The business men of this city have not the same resource. To be sure that enterprises of importance to them are not delayed, they must invest something themselves. They have done so already, and where would be the trade of this city to-day if it were not for these efforts? Fortunately, the time seems to be near at hand when Eastern capitalists may find it to their advantage to invest something in works which will benefit this city. There is needed only evidence that our own people have confidence in these projects, and appreciate their importance, to attract to them ample capital. We trust that evidence may not be wanting. "The times are hard," men say, and so they are. But will they ever be easier for St. Louis business, unless this city enables itself to compete with rivals on equal terms? Work for St. Louis. Chicago protected by Eastern capital. A change coming.

The views are prized particularly for acknowledging the important point, that eastern capital is devoted to the interests of Chicago, as predicted 20 years ago. Surely results are not very problematical, which depend upon the sagacious capitalists of the East, who are thus on all sides instructed as to their interests. Main point claimed 20 years ago.

The character and effects of this Kansas road had already been presented by the *Missouri Republican* of the 26th November: *Mo. Rep.* upon Kansas and Cameron road.

Kansas City and Cameron Railroad.—The completion of this road gives Kansas City an additional route of connection with the larger cities of the West and East, and will have the effect to increase the growth and trade of that youthful and growing city, and by creating competition, perhaps, may result in the cheapening of the cost of transportation to and from that place, a matter about which some complaint has, from time to time, been made. It is also expected to cheapen the price of pine lumber, by opening a market for this trade at Hannibal, as well as at St. Louis, and giving a more direct access to Chicago than formerly, in connection with that trade, the value of which can only be determined by time and experience. Another connection with the East. Cheapen Chicago lumber.

Kansas City is already considerable of a railroad centre, in this respect enjoying greater railroad facilities at the present time than any city west of St. Louis. The Missouri Pacific ends and the Union Pacific begins at or near that city. A branch of the latter projects to Leavenworth, some thirty-five miles distant. The road just completed connects with the Hannibal and St. Joseph and thence east and north. The west branch of the North Missouri will soon be completed to that point. A road in the direction of Galveston, Texas, is already being constructed, a considerable section being already under contract and even graded from Kansas City toward the southwest. All these roads, when completed, will make Kansas City a point of very considerable commercial importance. Indeed, her people expect these facilities to enable her to outstrip all her Missouri river rivals, and they seem to think possibly to become a rival to St. Louis herself. However this may be, the enterprising business men of Kansas City deserve great credit for the energy they have displayed and the success already attained. We trust they may secure at least a liberal share of the greatness which they anticipate the future has in store for them. Roads at Kansas. Pacific. Hannibal & St. Jo. North Mo. Galveston, Texas. Rival St. Louis.

Thus in the very beginning of the Pacific roads, to be put in advantageous connection with that which has been looked upon as St. Louis' own domain trenched upon.

peculiarly St. Louis' own, is certainly favorable for Chicago. Though as yet she only *hopes* to tap ours, it will be done; and it remains to be seen which can draw out the biggest streams by tapping each other's currents of business. There is, however, one point further of prime consequence in establishing the certainty that the basis of our prosperity is not to be moved; that is—

ART FOLLOWING NATURE'S LEAD, CHICAGO HAS NO TAXES FOR RAILWAYS THOUGH SHE HAS SEVERAL TIMES MORE THAN ANY RIVAL, AND NEARLY TWO-THIRDS OF ALL WEST OF THE TOLEDO AND CINCINNATI ROAD, AND NORTH OF THE OHIO RIVER.

No tax an item— The exemption from indebtedness on account of railways, is something to be considered in seeking an investment. But the cause of —the reason more so. this exemption has wonderful significance upon the very important point, whether the roads have naturally sought Chicago as their Determines whether Chicago is a natural center. focal point; or whether by dint of management, honest or dishonest, they have been hither led, and when the false influences shall be removed, they are to vacate for the benefit of some rival. If Chicago be the natural centre, and if capital has not only discovered this, but its interest conspires to maintain that centre, and to make it more and more so, we want to know it, to judge soundly as to the future.

Chicago lacks capital The chief drawback with Chicago has always been, lack of capital. Probably in no other city has so much been attempted and accomplished with the same means. The consequence has uniformly been, that the slightest disarrangement of finances generally, causes seri- Could not build her railroads. ous embarrassment, and to many ruin. Therefore, had we to depend upon ourselves for railway building, Chicago could not be the focal St. Louis rich point it now is. St. Louis, on the other hand, has immense wealth, large estates having been there accumulated in the lucrative fur trade, and from her well-established river business, before Chicago Hon. H. T. Blow upon St. Louis— was known. So that in an inaugural address to the St. Louis Board of Trade, 17th October, 1867, Hon. H. T. Blow could in truth say:

—need not go east for capital— We have too long labored under the false idea that we must necessarily go to New York, Philadelphia, or some other financial centre. Capitalists are sensitive but wise, and will seek the best portions of the world to invest their money, and we have only to commence right, and keep steadily on, to draw loans as direct —get in Europe. from central Europe as New York, or negotiate in St. Louis for millions as readily as our borowers do in London or Frankfort. Any man who will calmly reflect on all our resources, and then deny the correctness of this proposition or its feasibility, but poorly comprehends the condition of Europe at this very moment. * *

Capital seeks safety. Capital, naturally distrustful, draws back from all investments, when international conflicts threaten its security. Hundreds of millions lie idle in the vaults of bankers, and capitalists can be drawn, as readily as their coin, to a point affording good securities and fair rates of interest. Is this great valley, with its wealth and unbounded resources, such a centre? We can prove it in a single moment. Look at this Union of republican States, after passing through the severest ordeal that any nation on earth has ever known, and compare it with Europe.

Security of this nation. Thirty-six millions of people, having a perfect faith in the great principle of self-government, almost without an army! Every working man, rich or poor, hopeful and confident, all relying implicitly on the perpetuation of this noblest and best of all governments. But some well-disposed and really energetic friend will ask: How do you propose to accomplish so much now, when we have failed entirely of late to impress upon capitalists directly, the value of many of our Western bonds? * * *

False assumption injures St. L.

There is not a gentleman in this hall who does not feel the necessity and value of a close and direct communication with every portion of our State by rail, and who does not most heartily desire it, and is as heartily disgusted with the disgraceful failures of those who had assumed that they had capital and credit to complete the original system. It is this very assumption that has injured us so much, and kept us at a snail's pace on our way to Iowa, Southwest and Southeast Missouri.

Yet Chicago roads never stopped.

Remarkable is it indeed, that even in the very progress of our awful "international conflict," the building of Chicago railroads never ceased, though much retarded, for which amends are now making in more rapid prosecution than ever.

Capital finds safety. **Profits on Galena road.** **Its influence** **Other cities same advantages— —why not sought by capitalists?** **This a natural centre.**

Capital surely discovers profit and loss ultimately, and is not often wheedled into a continuance of unprofitable investments. There have been unfortunate operations in Chicago, because of unwise contracts in building and first management. But the Galena, the pioneer, was only a sample of what all might have been made, upon which the semi-annual dividends were so large, that to avoid exciting attention, the stock was "watered" over and over again. No doubt this had its influence in gathering capital for roads hitherward, besides the natural adaptation of the surrounding country to them. Still, St. Louis, Cincinnati, Milwaukee, Detroit, and other western cities, are supposed to have precisely the same advantages; and why has it been so difficult for them to get their few railways,—the fewness of which ought to have added to their profits, rendering them more desirable—when, except with the old Galena and the Northwestern, we have literally done nothing, and instead of our contriving and laboring how to get roads, they have one after another contrived how to get into the city? Surely it must be a natural centre that all the railroad men of the country, and wealthy capitalists excelled in sagacity by none, thus agree upon what is best.

Examination confirms this. **Natural connection of Eastern and Chicago interests.** **These views in 1845 to '50** **Letters in *Boston Courier*, 1847.**

At first glance it would seem that present results would only have been obtained by congruity of interest; and examination will not change first impressions. The surplus capital of our country, to which all sections look for aid, is in New York and New England. It required no keen penetration, either, to discern that the interests of that wealthy region were coincident with Chicago in drawing business from the South and West. Writing constantly for Eastern papers from 1845 to '50, to acquaint them with the advantages of the West, this congruity of interest was of course employed; and probably first in letters written in 1845 in behalf of the Boston and Ogdensburgh road, alluded to p. 21, of which I have no copy. In 1847 a series were prepared for the Boston *Courier*, in the second of which, dated on the lakes, in the steamer Louisiana, it was said:—

Conjoined interest of Boston and New York—

I have said, I believe, that the interests of Boston and New York are identical, in arranging the courses of trade from the West, as far eastward as to the New

—rivalry with southern cities.

York and Erie Railroad, and both of them must encounter strong competition with Philadelphia and Baltimore, in insuring to themselves the Western trade. Naturally, either of these two latter cities, have greatly the advantage of the former, both by being in close proximity to the West, and by the advantage of navigation on the Ohio River; and therefore if Boston and New York are to gain the ascendancy over their Southern rivals, or even equal them in facilities for obtaining Western trade, it must be by strong and persevering efforts. A few years will connect them with the Ohio river by railroads at Pittsburg and Wheeling; and it needs but a glance at the map to see how the North would be affected were a straight line of railroad to be continued on through Columbus, Indianapolis and Terre Haute, to St. Louis. The bulk of travel from that portion of the West, and all the Southwest, would be directed Eastward by that route, and much the largest portion of the trade also, making Boston and New York tributary, or at least secondary, to their Southern rivals.

They must get business to the lakes.

The only safety to these cities, is *to give the trade and travel a heavy lift to the North as near to the Mississippi as possible.* If eastward routes south of the Lakes can be cut off all the better. They might rejoice and triumph, could they be assured that the Legislature of Illinois would always do them as much good service as was rendered the past winter, in refusing to charter a company to construct a railroad from St. Louis to Terre Haute. And it is so much for the interest of our State generally to build up towns within its own borders, and to send the trade and travel through its length rather than across it, that they may be assured of our cordial co-operation to advance their ends, so far as it can be properly done, and *perhaps* a little farther.

Dog in the manger policy will not do.

But Illinois cannot long act the dog in the manger. Though every interest of our State requires that the Southern trade should be made to reach the East by way of the lakes, there can be but one method of quieting and controlling public sentiment on this subject;—there must be speedily supplied a good and expeditious route from the head of large steamboat navigation on the Mississippi, to the East, by way of the Lakes.

Road to Alton first wanted.

Best route for N. Y. and Boston.

Let a railroad be built from Galena to Chicago, and another line from Alton to Chicago, and with the present facilities for getting eastward from Chicago, together with those which will soon be added, the public will be pretty well served. The route could be shortened considerably by running east from Springfield to Lafayette, and thence up the Wabash Valley to Toledo, or from Lafayette to Michigan City, but, as I will presently show, not enough to make it an object of importance to New York and Boston; and the effort to shorten the distance by running to Lafayette, will bring them into the strongest competition with Philadelphia and Baltimore, as a road only about sixty miles long, running to the south east from Lafayette, will connect with the great central line from Indianapolis eastward.

[Then a comparison was instituted between seven routes, from the Southwest to Sandusky, every one of which is now occupied exactly as laid down, though none were then built, and it was added:—]

Chicago's interest is that of those cities.

Some *very cute* fellow may perhaps notice whence these letters come, and therefrom deduce the very logical inference that, after all, the writer probably feels *about* as much interest in Chicago as in New York and Boston. For the benefit of all such examiners into the meal tub, I acknowledge that my home—my all—(except what is away) is there located, and that I expect to prosper just according as Chicago prospers; and it is *wholly* because of the benefit that our town must derive from the construction of these great works, that I take the trouble to write these letters.

Does that injure N. Y. or Boston?

Their interest in Chicago.

But what then? Are the positions unsound, or the inferences unfairly drawn? Because Chicago cannot but grow and fatten on these railroads, is their importance in the least diminished to Boston and New York? I trow not. And if it can be made to appear—which is my object, and it is really the truth—that the interests of the great cities of the East—yes, of all New York and New England—are identified with ours, and that they must insure to us prosperity if they would prosper themselves to the largest extent, surely no friend to Chicago need desire more. Our prosperity is upon a firm foundation, for we may calculate with certainty upon the speedy construction of the Galena and Chicago railroad, and of the whole line to Alton.

Letters 1848 for *Mining Journal* and *Cour. and Enquirer.*

Though nearly the whole series could be appropriately quoted, space must not be taken. In 1848 another series was published simultaneously in the Boston *Mining Journal and Railroad Gazette*, and in the New York *Courier and Enquirer*. This was the introduction :—

Railroads are being made the effective means to unite the extremes of our wide spread country. They are literally being made the iron bands by which States separated by thousands of miles, are to be bound together in indissoluble union. As each link is added to the great chain, the patriot and philanthropist must rejoice, and do with his might what he can for its extension, till it shall ere long be fastened in all directions over this vast Republic. Railroads a bond of union.

And further, the great commercial cities find railroads yield a power which has become indispensable to their highest prosperity. As iron arms, they use them to encircle and draw to themselves distant trade, and commendable rivalry is growing up among Atlantic cities, as to which shall reach soonest and farthest into the richer regions. Iron arms encircling trade.

With all of them the almost boundless and inexhaustible West, together with the Southwest, is the chief prize for which they struggle. And to the successful competitor it will prove a prize for which scarcely no efforts could have been too great. It ensures the ascendancy of that over all other cities in the Union; and another half century makes it one of the most important,—the first, perhaps the second or third, city in the world. The west the prize.

As it is *our* business that is sought, it might be expected Western men would have their own views as to the manner in which it might be secured, and it is my hope to give in two or three short articles, the opinions prevalent in this region. They may be controverted, but I will guarantee it shall only be by those whose interests are opposed to New York and Boston. Views of western men

First, however, let me allude to the entire unity with which New York and Boston may co-operate in getting to themselves the business of the West and the Southwest. There should be—there can be—no competition between them, till the Western terminus of the New York and Erie Railroad is reached. *If true to their separate interests they cannot do otherwise than pull together to draw business on to the Lakes.* N. Y. and Boston to co-operate— —to draw business to lakes.

The roads considered were, first: The Illinois Central, which is made better than was anticipated, in that it does not deflect to Springfield, and also in taking off the Chicago branch way south at Centralia: second, the Alton and Springfield, which, instead of stopping at Springfield, by intersecting the Central, was continued on to Chicago: third, the Buffalo and Mississippi, (Lake Shore and Rock Island) with its extension to Council Bluffs, and on to the Pacific: and fourth, the Galena, with these remarks :— Roads considered. —Illinois Central— —Alton to Chicago— —Lake Shore and R. Island to Omaha— —Galena.

Railroads will probably reach no further westward than the Missouri, for a considerable time, but it is within the bounds of possibility that one will be built in time clear to the Pacific. It is, I say, among the *possibles;* and as the construction of one to Council Bluffs, would almost ensure the continuation of it whenever the attempt shall be made, either by government or individuhls, to build one to Oregon, it is surely worth a strong effort on the part of the Atlantic cities to build the line to the Missouri; which, with no business or object beyond, offers sufficient inducement within itself, as it gives directly to New York and Boston the business of a country *thirteen hundred miles* in extent. If those cities will but second the efforts of the West, and obtain a little aid for those roads from Congress, which can be given with positive pecuniary advantage to government, they will surely see them all finished very soon; and who can put bounds to the growth of cities sustained and built up by the unlimited—illimitable—trade of the great Valley of the West. Pacific road possible. Get one then to Omaha.

I have now presented four lines of railroads in the West, for the consideration of the Eastern public, and particularly for their members of Congress. Some may be disposed to jeer at the whole matter, and think that they can "see far enough into a millstone" to discover that the writer seeks probably quite as much the advantage of Chicago as of the East, in urging for help to build these long roads. Self-interest rules.

I am not disposed to deny that they are each and all to benefit Chicago, and freely acknowledge it is for that very reason I am at the trouble of preparing these East to be benefited as well as west.

papers. But does that affect the soundness of the views, as the East is regarded, or the conclusions to which they lead? Because Chicago is profited, is a tittle of the advantage to others diminished? Has not that whole region, as well as Chicago, a deep, a vital interest in the building of each and all these roads?

N. Y. and N. Eng. to get trade thro' Chicago.

Yes; it is because Chicago is backed up by the influence and power of that great and strong portion of the Union, that we are so confident of its future growth. New York and New England, if true to themselves, will secure a good part of the trade of the Mississippi Valley, *and they must get it through Chicago.* They may study and figure about it as they please, and will come to no other conclusion; and therefore I say unhesitatingly, that their public men, their members of Congress, if they neglect or refuse to render these roads all reasonable countenance and support, do not discharge their whole duty to their constituents. A very important part is left undone.

Views not visionary.

Some may consider the project visionary—that all these roads in the wilds of the West cannot be built in a quarter or even half a century. In reply I would merely remark, that in October of 1832, I left my New England home and came here to live. The Mohawk and Hudson Railroad, which I believe was the first built in the country, had then just been finished, and we went over it by horse power, sixteen miles, in about *two hours and a half.* See how much has been accomplished since that time in railroad and steamboat enterprises. A journey which then took me nearly *three weeks* I can now perform during the season of navigation in *four days and a half*, and within fifteen months it can be done in less than *three days.* If fifteen years past have accomplished so much, what will fifteen years to come do?

Results of 15 years— —what for 15 to come?

With aid of Congress will reach Council Bluffs in 15 years.

Considering the experience acquired in railroads within the past few years, the increased ability of the country both to build and to sustain them, and the greater demand for them for quick travel and transportation; and it is difficult to say where railroads will be terminated fifteen years hence. I am, at all events, willing to stake my credit for foresight on the prediction, that with reasonable aid, which Congress may and ought to render to these roads, they shall all be built within that time, and the one to Council Bluffs, also.

Predictions of 20 years verified.

More space must not be taken, though it is quite satisfactory to look over views nearly twenty years old, and observe their full accomplishment and more, and on the routes anticipated. Had Congress aided, would not more than five years have been saved? May it not be possible, that the continued reiteration of the joint interests of eastern capitalists with those of Chicago—for it was truly the string to harp on, and was pretty continuously played till 1850—had some influence to bring about the result argued for, and in which Chicago abundantly rejoices? The results had been so well attained in 1861, that in the circular it was said in continuation of the remarks, p. 26:

Right string struck.

Results attained by 1861.

Chicago roads built by foreign capitalists.

No Tax for Railroad Indebtedness.—These roads have been mostly built for us by strangers. Parties not interested in Chicago have furnished nearly the whole of the hundred and fifty millions of dollars spent in their construction, either because the roads themselves were desirable, or as feeders to Eastern roads. Nothing could more perfectly demonstrate this to be the natural centre of the West. With trifling effort and no liability on our part, have their forty-five hundred miles been stretched in all directions. Except the Galena, the pioneer road, little has been asked of us in their entire construction, but permission to reach the city; while St. Louis, Milwaukee, Detroit, and other Western cities, are weighed down with indebtedness to get the few they have, and their States have also been compelled to issue many millions of bonds to aid them. There is much satisfaction in the complete fulfilment of my prediction to this effect, made thirteen years ago, above quoted.

Other cities loaded with debt for their few.

Chicago has more roads than all her rivals—

Though Chicago has many more miles of road than all the cities united, that have been thought her rivals, she owes not a dollar on account of them; and the seven per cent. of gross earnings, perpetually accruing to Illinois from the Central Railroad, will about defray the expenses of the State government, making taxation very light. This exemption from state and city tax on account of railways, is a more important consideration in favor of Chicago investments than other cities will now admit, but which will in a few years be domonstrated.

So notorious is the fact that we have done nothing, that the financial editor of the Chicago *Times* treats the matter facetiously:— *Chi. Times* quotes a writer from Omaha.

Some person writing from Omaha to the Cincinnati *Commercial*, indulges in the following:

"The recent completion of a railroad from Chicago to Omaha—a link 600 miles long—gives an instructive instance of how enterprise can reverse the current of trade. St. Louis formerly monopolized the trade of this city and section, *via* the Missouri river. Now Chicago is autocrat of the situation. Omaha eats Chicago groceries, wears Chicago dry goods, builds with Chicago lumber, and reads Chicago newspapers. Trade turned from St. Louis to Chicago

"The ancient store boxes in the cellar have 'St. Louis' stenciled on them; those on the pavement, 'Chicago.' St. Louis might have retained the trade by building a railroad not as long as that from Omaha to Chicago; but it failed to act promptly, and has now but the feeblest hold on the trade of Nebraska and western Iowa. It is very impressive to hear St. Louis talk about its magnificent geographical blessings, its many thousand miles of tributary navigable rivers, but it should know by this time that steamboats cannot compete with locomotives. It has lost a trade here of several millions per annum; a trade that tardy energy cannot recover." St. Louis' advantages— —hard to recover

This correspondent, while he probably places a proper estimate upon the value of this railroad in a commercial point of view, and the advantages which it gives Chicago, betrays a shocking ignorance of the influences and causes which led to the completion of the railroads to which he alluded, and the general quality of the article known among outsiders as "Chicago enterprise." Chicago did not build this railroad; we very much doubt whether a half-dozen business men can be found in the city who contributed one single penny towards its construction, or thought it worth while to give encouragement to the enterprise when it was merely a railroad in prospect. Chicago has built none of her railroads. * * * Chi. builds, no railroads—

And this is not a new thing, confined to remote railroad connections. The same thing has existed here always. At no time has Chicago contributed anything towards the construction of railroads, not even a penny to the railroads which immediately centre here. Other men have constructed the railroads, and our business men have been content to grow rich upon the general prosperity which these railroads have created. The railroads have created the city, not the city the railroads, and Chicago to-day has no creative powers to expend in this direction. There have been a few men in Chicago who have made railroads their business, and have given their time and their capital to their construction, but as to business men generally lending them any encouragement or assistance, everybody knows better. —never has. Other men build them.

* * * * *

The other day one of the Wisconsin railroads, operated in the Milwaukee interest, attempted to shut off Chicago from the trade of Minnesota, by refusing to transport freight destined for Chicago, upon the same terms as freight destined for Milwaukee, and our business men were called upon to buy the bonds of a new road north from Madison, which would re-open to Chicago the trade of Minnesota. The amount realized was *contemptible*. No aid for a road to Minnesota—

Not long since delegates from Kansas City endeavored to induce the business men of Chicago to lend money, on the best possible security, to construct a short line from Kansas City to Cameron, a trifling link, which would open to Chicago the trade of western Kansas, Missouri and New Mexico. But the Kansas City gentlemen, despite their eloquence and zeal, left Chicago with less money in their pockets than when they entered it. —nor for Kansas and Cameron road.

Chicago build railroads! Nonsense! We have *permitted* others to build them sometimes, provided they would make Chicago a terminal point, and give us all the benefits resulting from their construction, without expense or trouble. It is doubtful whether we will give our *permission* much longer. * * She permits roads to come in.

Our rivals themselves have for years perceived the truth, though vainly seeking for satisfactory reasons, because of their unwillingness to admit that the city of the lakes had advantages over the city of the rivers. A slip, of which the source and date are unknown, the latter part being lost, but which was probably cut in 1861, because it was mainly from the St. Louis *Democrat*, says: Rivals see the truth, but refuse acknowledgment. *Mo. Dem.,* 1861.

Queen of the rivers losing trade of her own State.

The City that Worships a River.—In Saturday's issue we published an article from the Brunswick (Mo.) *Central City*, showing that the tide of commerce of the Grand River Valley of Missouri is now tending towards Chicago, and that St. Louis is fast losing the trade of its own State. Below will be found an article from the Missouri *Democrat* verifying the statements therein made, and revealing a decline in the trade and commerce of St. Louis which few people dreamed of:

Mo. Dem. admits the truth—

—figures given.

"Yesterday, we published a table in our commercial columns, which must have furnished our merchants, or rather the entire body of our citizens, with food for grave reflection—we had almost said, cause for alarm. We refer to the tabular statement of the receipts of produce by river and rail in this city for the current and preceding year. In the article of flour there is, it appears, a falling off this year, compared with last year up to the same date, (4th of October), of more than 200,000 barrels. The decrease in wheat exceeds 400.000 bushels; and in oats nearly the same enormous depreciation is experienced. Still, comparing both years for the same period, we find a falling off in hemp to the extent of 6,510 bales, and in whisky of 17,090 barrels.

Cause for alarm.

"This showing is calculated to inspire grave concern in all—while it calls for the serious deliberation of our capitalists and business men. Whatever may be its causes, (and we believe that they are neither occult nor remote,) no one can refuse to recognize in the figures we have quoted the register of the startling and rapid decline of a most important branch of our commerce. It may be said they only show an eddy in the current, an ebb in the sea of our prosperity, but to assume the correctness of any such hypothesis, would, it seems to us, be fatuitous in the extreme. St. Louis has been the victim of illusion long enough, and the sooner she awakes to a sense of her real position, the sooner will she redeem the past, improve the present, and forecast the future.

Victim of illusion.

Chi. trade increasing.

"In contrast to the state of things here, we find a marvelous augmentation in the receipts of produce in Chicago this year—or, more correctly speaking, of the article which is the great staple in that city—compared with last year. The quantity of wheat and flour received there last month was little less than double the quantity received in the same month of the preceding year, and exceeded by 500,000 bushels, (expressing the flour in wheat measure) the quantity received in September, 1857—a year which was distinguished by abundant harvests, and in which unprecedented quantities of grain sought the Chicago mart. * * *

N. Y. and Boston in competition with St. Louis, through Chicago.

"Without enlarging further on the foregoing topics, we will say that they are fraught with solemn warnings to the people of St. Louis, and especially to the mercantile and manufacturing classes who govern its affairs. The fact can no longer be concealed that New York and Boston have steadily come into competition with St. Louis, and with no mean success, for the commerce of the Missouri river country. Much of the produce which found its way to market solely by that river, is now transported overland to the East; and we learn from undoubted authority that a system of railroad extension is projected by the capitalists of Wall street, which will narrow the commercial territory of St. Louis to a very limited compass indeed, unless these enterprises are encountered on our part with energy and wisdom.

Wall street plans adverse.

Treason right at home—

—Mo. dismembered.

"Some weeks ago, we adverted to the sinister feeling manifested in St. Joseph, (which city is at present the frontier fortress of New York and Boston cupidity), in connection with the proposition for extending the Pacific Railroad to Kansas City, and we remarked that Missouri was virtually dismembered, in a commercial sense, by the Hannibal and St. Joseph Railroad. The statement is but too true. The figures prove it. One of our local contemporaries made the remark a text for a display of generosity at our expense and in favor of the interests which control that Railroad, and which are undoubtedly antagonistic to the interests of St. Louis." * * *

True about Han. and St. Jo. roads.

We shall see that the defection of the Hannibal and St. Joseph road is fully established, and that it is not more in the interest of "New York and Boston" than of a city a little nearer. But, lest that article be thought antiquated and valueless, an extract is taken from the *Missouri Republican*, of the twenty-fifth of November last, showing Chicago is quite a favorite city with somebody:—

Mo. Rep., 25th November, '67.

How does Chi. outstrip St. L?

Chicago—St. Louis—The Bridge.—Again and again the question recurs: How is it that Chicago outstrips St. Louis in acquiring the means whereby her business and prosperity are increased? That she does so cannot be denied. That by means of her railroads and other means of transportation, and her other acquired facilities of doing business, she has drawn to herself a great proportion of the trade of the Northwest in the large items of grain, cattle and hogs, besides many minor articles, is apparent to all. Has trade of northwest.

How did she get these facilities? Have her people greater enterprise than ours? They do not appear to have greater industry or greater economy than we have. They have not greater natural advantages or acquired capital, yet wherever anything is to be done for the good of Chicago, somebody is found to do it; whether to build a railroad or an elevator, or a cattle-pen, or a bridge, or to prevent others building them for the advantage of some other place, there Chicago is, to do or to hinder the doing, as may be for her interest; and with her sharp, shrewd, active men, always fully alive and wide-awake, usually accomplishing her desires. Keen, sharp-sighted, and long-sighted, quick and bold to the verge of audacity, persistent, and the censorious say unscrupulous, they rush on, rejecting doubts and conquering difficulties, to triumphant success and prosperity. Even just now, here in our midst, she is thought to have her emissaries, and they of her most wily, seeking her advancement by hindering our progress. * * * Who helps Chicago? No advantages, no capital—all things supplied.

Now, does not this Chicago arrangement indicate to some extent the difference between the management of St. Louis and Chicago? In Chicago it is recognized that whatever benefits one branch of trade or business benefits all, and all are disposed to assist each and every enterprise, at least to the extent of well-wishing; whilst in St. Louis it frequently happens that, when useful improvements are proposed, they are discouraged by open opposition or callous indifference, or sneering contempt of the ability of the proposers and of the soundness of their plans, or a selfish jealousy lest somebody should derive some peculiar advantage from the improvement. * * * * * Different management in St. L. and Chicago.

Too much credit by far is accorded us for our own wit and energy, which they usually deem preferable to acknowledging the truth. As we have seen, it is the wisdom of New York and New England capitalists, who have so well discerned the natural advantages which Chicago offers to promote their own interests, which has wrought the results. When the same congruity is equally apparent in St. Louis, she will not be so neglected. Not only St. Louis, however, discovers the magic power, though denying its cause, but even in that great State to the west of her, the same ideas prevail, except that the Kansas editor supposes all is really done by Chicago. Says a recent *Lawrence Tribune*:— Too much credit to Chicago—not enough to N. Y. and N. Eng. Kansas sees the truth—*Lawrence Tribune.*

St. Louis and Chicago.—The St. Louis *Democrat*, in a very sensible article recently, animadverts in strong terms against the apathy of the business men and capitalists of that city, in regard to their railroad interests. In reviewing its railroad system, the *Democrat* says: Confirms *St. Louis Dem.*

"From this review of roads now in existence, it appears that St. Louis has uninterrupted railroad communication with eighteen counties in this State, and none at all in any other State. With the bridges at St. Louis and St. Charles, it will have direct connection with Central Illinois, and with eight other counties in this State. By the transfer at Macon, we reach ten other counties—thirty-six in all. By the transfer at Kansas City, we reach part of Kansas. And this, at present, is the railroad system of St. Louis. Is it strange that our merchants find business dull? St. Louis railroads reach 36 counties—

"Chicago already has unbroken connection with sixty-nine counties in that State, with the railroads of Wisconsin, Indiana, Michigan, Minnesota, Iowa, Nebraska, and, as soon as the bridge at Quincy is completed, will have unbroken connection with the most populous half of Missouri." Chicago all the west.

This truthful statement not only clearly shows the present position of St. Louis, but tells unmistakably of the future. It shows that unless more energy, and life, and spirit, are exhibited than heretofore, instead of being the metropolis of the West, it will degenerate into a third or fourth-rate city, clipped of its power and strength by its own folly. Chicago is extending her lines of railroads to us, furnishing money to build our own lines, advertising her bnsiness throughout the State, and offering other inducements that may prove irresistible in the course of This tells of the future. Chicago lines extending.

Results sure.

time. Is St. Louis doing anything? * * * * Chicago builds her hundreds of miles of railroad, not only building up the places with which she comes in communication, but getting back cent per cent on the investment, and if St. Louis pauses at the comparatively insignificant costs of such undertakings as this, speculation as to which will gain the trade of the West is entirely unnecessary—the question being as easily answered now as a hundred years hence.

Art follows nature.

Policy to continue.

Solomon followed.

Is it not quite evident that *Art has only followed Nature's lead?* If not, it will become more and more so, until St. Louis herself shall confess—she even does already, as we shall see still more—that the Queen of the Lakes has the mastery of the Queen of the Rivers, because Art, operating with Capital, has truly followed Nature's lead. And with vigor strengthening year after year, the necessity continues for pursuing the same wise policy. Here again most truly shall it be said, "The thing that hath been, it is that which shall be; and that which is done, is that which shall be done; and there is no new thing under the sun." Beyond a question,—

THE FOCAL POINT OF THE GREAT WEST IS FIXED IMMOVABLY BY OVER SEVEN THOUSAND FIVE HUNDRED OF ITS ELEVEN THOUSAND MILES OF RAILWAY, CENTERING AT CHICAGO.

What might have been doubted in some minds in 1861, with 4,500 miles of railroads, is fully established in 1867 by 7,500 miles,—*

15 *Trunk Lines, and* 45 *Railroads, Centering in Chicago, with* 20 *Branches, more or less Tributary.*

Railways centering in Chicago 7,254 trunks, 2,211 branches.

	Trunks	*Br'ch's*
1. *Chicago, Milwaukee and LaCrosse	285	......
*Southern Minnesota	50	......
Winona to Owatonia	90	......
Milwaukee to Portage City	......	96
Watertown to Sun Prairie	......	27
2. *Milwaukee and Prairie du Chien	194	......
*McGregor to St. Paul	215	......
*St. Paul and Pacific	85	......
St. Paul to Belle Plain	47	......
3. *Chicago and Northwestern	242	......
Harvard to Madison	75	......
Janesville to Monroe	33	......
Kenosha to Rockford	......	73
Racine to Port Byron	......	181
Escanaba to Marquette	75	......
4. *Chi. and Nor. West. (to Freeport)	121	......
*Ills. Cent. (Freeport to Dunleith)	68	......
*Dubuque and Sioux City	143	......
Farley to Cedar Rapids	56	......
Warren and Mineral Point	32	......
Fox River Valley	48	......
5. *Chi. and N. W. (Junc. to Clinton)	108	......
*Clinton to Omaha	356	......
*Pacific to Rocky Mountains	525	......
6. *Chicago and Rock Island	182	......
*Pacific to DesMoines	160	......
Wilton to Washington	50	......
Coal Valley	......	11
Bureau to Peoria	47	......
Peoria to Pekin and Virginia	71	......
7. *Chi. and Quincy (to Burlington)	210	......
Burlington and Missouri	130	......
8. Chi. B. and Q. (from Galesburg)	100	......
Miles carried forward	3,718	388

	Trunks	*Br'ch's*
Miles brought forward	3,718	388
*Hannibal and St. Joseph	206	......
*St. Jo. and Leavenworth	45	......
*Atchison and Pike's Peak	80	......
*Cameron to Kansas	45	......
*Pacific, E. D	325	......
Leavenworth to Lawrence	33	......
St. Joseph to Savannah	......	15
Keokuk to DesMoines	......	162
Galesburg to Peoria	......	53
Yates City to Lewiston	......	30
9. *Chicago, Alton and St Louis	280	......
Jacksonville and Bloomington	179	......
10. *Ills. Cent. (Chicago to Cairo)	365	......
Centralia to Freeport	275	......
St. L. and Vincennes to Seymour	......	253
St. L. & T. H. to Indianapolis	......	262
Keokuk to Lafayette, G't West.	......	287
Peoria to Logansport	......	172
11. *Louisville, New Albany and Chi.	290	......
Evansville and Crawford	......	132
Jeffersonville to Lafayette	......	172
Madison to Columbus	......	45
Lawrence to Indianapolis	......	90
12. *Chi. and Gt. Eastern to Cincinnati	294	......
Indianapolis to Peru	......	75
13. *Pittsburg and Fort Wayne	468	......
14. *Michigan Southern	244	......
Elkhorn to Toledo	143	......
Laporte to Plymouth	......	30
Monroe to Adrian	......	45
15. *Michigan Central	284	......
Total tributary miles	7,254	2,211

What are trunk lines—

—direct extensions.

* Some roads styled branches in the previous list, are here reckoned as trunk lines. The Fox River Valley, for instance, and the Madison, are as valuable as the same number of miles on the Northwestern main line. So at the end of the Hannibal and St. Joseph, are several extending west that will be long lines. Also, the cross lines south styled branches, are extended as far east as Indianapolis, and they might with propriety be extended farther. The direct extensions from Chicago are marked with an

The whole business not claimed.

To claim these as Chicago roads, it is not necessary that they conduct to us their whole business. The Milwaukee and La Crosse, for example, gives much business to Milwaukee, yet more to Chicago, not only by the Milwaukee road, but also by the Northwestern. So the Alton and St. Louis gives much business to those places, yet more to Chicago than to both of them. The only point of dispute about the list is whether the Great Western, and the other three south of it, east and west, should be included. For reasons hereafter given, it is doubtful whether even the Vincennes and Terre Haute roads are of as much benefit to St. Louis as to Chicago; and certain it is that of the wholesale business on them, Chicago already does a large share, and steadily increases her proportion. If four opposition lines cross ours, Chicago, too, has four crossing them, each of which takes some of the business which has come upon them to reach Chicago. A little from each fed into each of the four to Chicago, gives in the aggregate more than any other one city derives from them. They may, therefore, well be included as branches; and if Chicago is to be the manufacturing and commercial centre which the main trunks seem to insure, those styled branches will become more and more Chicago roads. We should also take into account the—

Should cross roads be reckoned?

Chicago gets more benefit than any one city.

Other Railways West of the Toledo and Cincinnati Road, and North of the Ohio River.

Other railways in northwest.

Sheboygan and Fond du Lac	20	Miles brought forward	810
Milton to Brookfield	48	Indianapolis to Piqua	115
North Missouri (to Macon)	170	Indianapolis to Sidney	119
Pacific (St. Louis to Leavenworth)	309	Lafayette to Toledo	203
Southwest Pacific	89	Detroit to Grand Haven	189
St. Louis and Iron Mountain	87	Adrian to Saginaw	110
Seymour to Cincinnati	87		
Miles carried forward	810	Total	1,546

Of even these 1,500 miles, Chicago gets considerable business, and will have more and more from them, besides the gradual increase farther and farther into Ohio, and to the south and southwest, which is inevitable, unless the railway system of the West can be changed. We have, then, this—

Give Chicago some business—

—will more.

Total of Railroads in the Northwest.

Total roads in northwest

	Miles.
Trunk Lines tributary to Chicago	7,254
Branch Lines tributary to Chicago	2,211
Chicago Trunk Lines and Branches	9,465
Other Lines paying some tribute	1,546
Total Railroads West of Toledo and Cincinnati Road, and North of the Ohio	11,011

But, to make the calculation satisfactory to the investigator most jealous of Chicago, we suppose nothing comes from the other 1,546 miles, and abate *nineteen hundred sixty-five miles* from the Chicago roads proper, claiming *only seven thousand five hundred* of the eleven

1,965 miles deducted from Chicago list—

asterisk; and except the Atchison and Pike's Peak, and St. Joseph to Leavenworth, (No. 8.) they are all direct continuations. The road from Escanaba to Marquette, it is true, lacks the intermediate connection with the main line at Fort Howard. Yet for its length it is the most valuable of our trunk lines, for it brings the iron ore that is to make Chicago one of the chief cities in iron manufactures.

—leaves 7,500, nearly two-thirds of all.

thousand, which still leaves this city *nearly two-thirds of all the roads in the Northwest.* Is not Chicago *now* the focal point? And what possibility is there of a change, in view of the extent to which her trunk lines have already been carried to all points of the compass, except those from east to north, where we have what is still better than as many more railways, in Michigan's deep crystal bed, as we shall see. Let us ascertain the—

Change impossible.

Length of Fifteen Continuous Trunk Lines from Chicago.

Continuous lines from Chicago.

		Miles.
1.	Chicago, Milwaukee and La Crosse, to Chatfield in Minnesota	335
2.	Milwankee and Prairie du Chien, to Lake Minnetonka in Minnesota	494
3.	Chicago and Northwestern, to Fort Howard	242
4.	Chicago and Northwestern and Illinois Central, to Dubuque and Iowa Falls	332
5.	Chicago and Northwestern, to Clinton, Omaha, and the Rocky Mountains	974
6.	Chicago, Rock Island and Pacific, to Des Moines	342
7.	Chicago, Burlington and Missouri, to Chariton	340
8.	Chicago, Quincy, Hannibal and St. Joseph, Cameron and Kansas, and Pacific	676
9.	Chicago, Alton and St. Louis	280
10.	Illinois Central, Chicago to Cairo	362
11.	Louisville, New Albany and Chicago	290
12.	Chicago and Great Eastern, to Cincinnati	294
13.	Pittsburgh and Fort Wayne	468
14.	Michigan Southern	244
15.	Michigan Central	284
	Total	5,960

Where the power to work a change?

Now, if already one single city of the West, feeble in capital, nothing to commend her to favor except her position; if of the eleven thousand miles ramifying the West in all directions, Chicago actually has *over one half of the whole* radiating from her in fifteen long lines from 242 to 974 miles, on each of which she sends several times daily, running to their destination with no change of car; where is the power to come from to break up this system? Not to say that it cannot be done, who is to do it? Will not the same interests operate to continue things as they are, which have made them what they are? St. Louis thinks she can bring capital to her aid, from Europe, as we saw, p. 28., independently of New York and Boston. It is well if she can, for upon the latter she cannot rely. And as she is now the sole rival, we shall see further and important reasons for the railway system of the West to be continued and to be expanded upon the plan which already is quite well established.

Capital interested to maintain present plans.

That St. Louis has some conception of the task before her, is quite apparent. Having only to retain control of the territory of which she had undisputed sway, it is grievous to witness its sudden transfer to a rival, and she would not be hnman not to make strong efforts to resist her fate. Says a correspondent of the *Missouri Republican:*

St. Louis perceives her difficulties.

Mo. Rep.

St. Louis and her flatterers.

St. Louis and Her Flatterers.—Cities and individuals are subject to the same laws and influences which control progress or failure. There is a city in this great Mississippi Valley, which for the last forty years, has universally been considered as occupying the finest locality for permanent growth and prosperity in this extensive and rich domain of the northwest. Situated centrally near the confluence of the navigable rivers of this vast region, it became the commercial centre of that region at an early day—long ago—before the wildest imagination dreamt of any rivalry on Northern lakes or Western tributaries. During that long period, it had the opportunity and power of so fortifying and improving its condition and position, as to render all attempts to sap its trade and reduce it to a subordinate

She could have held her position.

commercial point, simply impossible. It held a midway location between the prolific cereal sections of the North and the cotton and sugar lands of the gulf States, and had the cheapest transportation facilities that nature or art can afford. In the exchange of commodities between these diverse agricultural sections, St. Louis, for she is the favored centre alluded to, grew rich and powerful. She doubled her population almost every year, and increased her wealth and business resources in the same ratio. Then was heard from one end of the country to the other the grandest prophesies in relation to the destiny of this rising metropolis. *

She grew rich and powerful.

The demands of population required other commercial centres, and these soon began their development. Not so favorably located, the new points were compelled to put forth extra efforts to overcome surrounding and obstinate difficulties. If it was necessary to *elevate a site ten feet* or more to give proper drainage, that feat was accomplished; if water transportation was not accessible, the surrounding country, *far and near, was penetrated with railroads to gather* in the richest products, and costly structures were erected to give to trade the economy and dispatch so requisite for successful competition. With no natural advantages or endowments beyond those of an ordinary character, rivals sprang up whose business, in some cases, already overtops that of this favored and lauded emporium. The truth is, St. Louis is too highly endowed. * * * Shipping points and sections on the Upper Mississippi, formerly tributary to this market, ask every now and then for aid to bring about a re-union, but the request is hardly heeded. Our railroads are not as yet completed to any paying termini, and from present appearances years must elapse before several of them, and those holding, too, the control of the country through which they are too pass, will reach their destination. We are so admirably located—so advantageously situated—that no effort seems necessary to avoid a disaster or to seek a good result.

New sites in competition.

Means they adopt.

St. L. too good to do anything.

The plains' trade naturally belongs to this market, it is very true, too naturally perhaps; but what are the facts? A city three hundred miles north of us is contending successfully for that undeveloped region, and is rapidly making connections that will nullify our advantageous position. A paper published in Lawrence, the *Journal*, on the 14th inst., gives the mail agent for Kansas and New Mexico to understand, "that by sending the mails for Kansas by Quincy instead of St. Louis, they will arrive some twelve hours earlier than they do now." We are obliged to go via Chicago to reach certain prominent points on the Missouri river. And so it goes; our citizens are tickled with the hair of flattery, while others are realizing the marrow of profit, and are satisfied with the dream of progress and power, suggested by eligible local position, while contending parties, strengthened by the necessity of exertion, are grasping the sceptre. During the winter months this market is dependent upon the Illinois Central for the outlet to the South; and yet the chance has been presented for years to obtain a communication of our own with that portion of the country. Why has not the Iron Mountain road been extended? Connections with Iowa are indispensably requisite; but with the best paying bonds offered anywhere for the purpose, and the brightest prospects for abundant freights, the extensions have not been made.

Plains trade gone to Chicago—

—even Kansas.

Scepter departing.

Inconveniences of St. Louis.

A Chariton correspondent of the *Republican*, November 28, writing in commendation of the St. Louis, Chillicothe and Omaha road, pertinently inquires:—

Chariton opinion.

Pray tell us why it is that Chicago can always find money to build railroads, St. Louis not at all? Here we are endeavoring to open up a rich country to St. Louis, and give her the trade of the Northwest, and we are left to struggle alone. If it were to reach Chicago, it would be a different story. The merchants of St. Louis can save millions by assisting us now.

Why does Chi. get money, St. Louis not?

Mr. Henry Cobb, too, writes for the *Republican* over his own name, November 25, 1867, who seems to understand the community of interest between Chicago and the East, but represents Chicago a Delilah, instead of the Queen she is, and candidly acknowledging that the sagacity of Eastern capitalists has effected the results so damaging to St. Louis:—

Mr. Cobb of St. L. perceives the truth but won't tell it.

But alas! St. Louis, that used to be a Samson in strength, and a ruling master of the commercial domain from the Allegheny to the Rocky Mountains—St. Louis, corrupted by the impolitic politicians—can one say statesmen? of Missouri—St.

Chi. a Delilah victimizing the Samson, St. L.

Louis, sinking under the consuming draughts and heavy burdens of capitalists, has fallen a sleepy victim into the lap of the artful Delilah that is cunningly watching in the garden city on Lake Michigan.

The east supplies the means. Chicago, the tool of the Philistines in the East who were jealous of the strength of St. Louis; Chicago, the Delilah, has been furnished with money by the lords of Eastern capital for shaving St. Louis of his strength, in cutting off by means of iron railways, the trade on his rivers in which his strength lay, and delivering him a seduced captive into the hands of the enemy.

What St. L. has lost. Even Pittsburgh trade comes via Chicago. Not only is the trade of the upper Mississippi river, from St Paul to Hannibal, in Missouri, cut off from St. Louis by Chicago, but also the trade of the Missouri river, from St. Joseph to Omaha, and even the Rocky Mountains; not only is the trade of the Lower Mississippi, in winter, cut off by the same hand, using the Illinois Central Railway; but even the trade of the Ohio river at Pittsburgh is this day being clipped by the Fort Wayne and Chicago Railway; as the previously mentioned thousand tons of iron, bought in the Allegheny Mountains of Pennsylvania, to be laid down on the extension of the road in the iron mountain region of Missouri, could not be brought by the Ohio River, nor by the Panhandle, by the Cincinnati or Terre Haute routes, which have heretofore been considered the channels of trade between St. Louis and the East; but the whole train of more than 100 cars, bringing these loads of iron from Pittsburgh to St. Louis, could find no other way of reaching their destination, except in being permitted to come by way of Chicago; and by the gracious favor of the Fort Wayne and Chicago road, St. Louis, in a few days, will be allowed to receive this iron—an additional evidence of humiliation.

Bridges over Miss. and Missouri rivers. Threatened loss of even southern trade. The Chicago capitalists are bridging the Mississippi river at Quincy, and even the Missouri river at Kansas City, and propose to draw off the trade of not only our Missouri Pacific Road, but also of the Southwest, even daringly striking at the centre of our State through Booneville and Sedalia, to and beyond Springfield; and, were it not for the sagacity and liberality of Mr. Thomas Allen, in giving $350,000, besides a proportion of the $375,000 bonus, for the Cairo and Fulton road of Missouri, which is of no use to him, which he did not want, and which, in its original aim, was more hostile to St. Louis than the Hannibal and St. Joe foreign movement,—were it not for this prudent sacrifice, the Chicago interests might be now extending this road from Cairo, through Little Rock, to Fulton on Red river, to draw the trade of central Arkansas and Texas, through Cairo, over the Illinois Central road; thus finally cutting off the trade of St. Louis from every side.

St. L. in fetters. Then might it be said to St. Louis, "The Philistines be upon thee, Samson!" and St. Louis might wake up and shake himself, but find that his strength was gone, that he was bound by the enemy in "fetters" stronger than "brass."

Further testimony. Further testimony of this sort comes hereafter. It is sufficient here to invite the reader's attention to a railway map, to consider

Present system admirably supplies the country. some self-evident points. Had a master mind, in the outset of railway building in the West, planned the system solely for the accommodation of the country traversed, he could scarcely have improved upon what has actually been done. Very few farmers in Indiana, Illinois, or Wisconsin, are over ten miles from a railroad or naviga-

Same doing west of Mississippi. ble water, and more than one-half are within five miles. To continue the system as devised, will do the same for the States west of the Mississippi. Who can improve that?

Had concentration been sought, same plan pursued. Or, had that master mind, with wise forethought and proper regard for permanency of the railroad interest, planned the entire system with direct reference to concentration of the business of the entire West at one centre, very little would any of the lines have been changed from their present location, and most of them not at all.

Each road has sought its own interests— Yet instead of one mind pursuing one object, either to accommodate the country or to build up a city; every one of these railways have labored to accomplish their own individual, selfish objects.

These rival, soulless corporations, each intent upon promoting its own particular advantage, or that of its connecting lines, one and the same interest, have actually been led, in spite of their strong competition, to do precisely what the wisest master mind of the world would have planned to promote the highest public good. Is not this a strong indication—nay, is it not proof positive and absolute—that there is a natural focal point, and that it surely has been found? If not, the success of the plan which the revenues of the roads, so immense in the beginning, that the Galena, the pioneer road, watered its stock repeatedly, yet constantly increasing, speak a word—and that a word which needs no watering with superfluous language—in the following table:—

—yet has promoted the best public good.

A focal point surely found.

Railroad earnings strong evidence.

The Gross Earnings of the Chief Trunk Lines of Chicago for Ten Years—**1867, $60,000,000.**

15 trunk lines, earnings 1858—'52—

	1858.	1859.	1860.	1861.	1862.
C. & Alton Railway..	$ 871,715.00	$ 732,917.00	$ 938.641.20	$ 1,098,464.89	$ 1,225,000,83
C. B. & Quincy..........	1,850,339.33	1,288,894,60	1,383,957.65	1,732,084.69	2,246,084.17
C. Rock I. & Pacific..	1,407,845.72	889,300.05	1,093,933.77	1,164,018.21	1,054,704.40
Mich. Southern........	2,309,487.30	2,714,848.00	2,019,424.96	2,075,459.08	2,250,517.91
Mich. Central..........	2,428,757.52	1,838,129.67	1,832,944.86	2,058,052.61	2,361,241.42
Great Eastern..........	....	....	....	320,825.93	331,024.48
Illinois Central........	1,976,578.52	2,114,448.98	2,721,590.94	2.899,612.64	3,445,826.88
C. & N. Western.......	....	....	....	....	....
Total...............	$10,844,723.39	$9,578,538.30	$9,990,493.38	$11,348,518.05	$12,914,400.09

—1863–'67.

	1863.	1864.	1865.	1866.	1867.
C. & A. Railway.....	$ 1,673,706.60	$2,770,483.96	$3,840,091.82	$8 695,152.86	$3,850,000.00
C. B. & Q.................	3,037,372.54	4,039,922,81	5,581,859.22	6,175,553.35	6,083,138.05
C. R. I. & Pacific......	1,529,141.02	2,143,874.78	3,359,390.80	3,154,235.68	3,574.033.71
Mich. Southern.......	2,813,831.40	3,384,294.23	4,289,465.73	4,686,445.02	4,673,192.86
Mich. Central.........	2,946,560.55	3,434,548.63	4,145,419.57	4,446,490.51	4,325,490.51
Great Eastern..........	528,364.15	850,495.49	1,112,867.12	1,317,102.11	1,287,500.00
Illinois Central......	4,571,028.38	6,329,447.20	7,181,208.37	6,546,741.47	7,100,000.00
C. & N. W...............	... .	6,820,749.75	8,243,840.28	10.161,735.45	11,680,938.76
* Total...............	$17,100.004.64	$29,673,816.85	$37,754,135.91	$40,183,456.45	$42,574,293.89

This table by no means gives the total earnings, large as they have already become. The Hannibal and St. Joseph, the Burlington and Missouri, are as much Chicago trunks, as the Chicago, Burlington and Quincy Railroad connecting them with Chicago. So are the La Crosse, Prairie du Chien, Dubuque and Pacific, etc. The earnings of these and others on Chicago trade are doubtless more than sufficient to increase the aggregate to $60,000,000. The early years of some of the roads not being given, the sum above named, $18,000,000, may be taken as the earnings in 1860. Doubtless the per cent. of increase for seven years to come will not equal the past; but without shadow of doubt the aggregate will exceed that of the last seven years at least two-fold, perhaps three-fold. How much of a city must we have by 1875 to do the manufacturing and distribute such a trade?

Not all included.

Total at least $60,000,000.

Future increase.

——* For Pittsburg & Ft. Wayno road, see page 362.

Focal point immovable because capital rules.

Further; not only because Chicago is the natural focal point of the West, of which we shall have further evidence; and not only because the system is exactly what the country traversed and to be traversed wants; but also, because the capital invested, and the capitalists who are to do the further investing requisite, will have the present system maintained and expanded, is the focal point immovable. If, under these circumstances 9,500 of the 11,000 miles of western railway have been given in perpetual lease-hold to Chicago, whence shall come the influence and wealth to work any essential change? With a clean field before them, they would be strong men to do an equal work; but with the whole field occupied, and what is not occupied, certain to extend present lines; with the whole wealth and influence of the country from New York north virtually interested in preventing innovations, and even that south, best served by keeping things as they are; is it not a truth certain as anything can be in the future, that *the focal point in the great West is fixed immovably by over seven thousand five hundred of its eleven thousand miles of railway centering at Chicago?* Of the westward lines, however, those to the Pacific merit further consideration.

Where the power to change?

Change impossible.

Chicago the fixed centre.

The Pacific Railways in Progress—their Effects.

N. Y. Times.

Said the New York *Times* Dec. 4th :—

Pacific road finished in 1870.

From the Pacific in Fifteen Days.—We are assured by the Directors of the Union Pacific Railroad that the railway from the Missouri to the Pacific will be completed in 1870, so that in three years from this date the time from New-York to San Francisco, will be less than a week. It is hard to realize that so great a distance may be accomplished in so short a time; but the results thus far attained by the Union Pacific Railroad Company are such as to inspire strong confidence in the fulfillment of its promises. Thus we find that the road is now in complete order and active operation for 525 miles west from Omaha; and the practical benefit to be derived from this fact will be well illustrated to-day or to-morrow by the receipt of foreign mails which left San Francisco only fourteen days ago. When the time usually occupied in the transit of mails and passengers from that city to this is considered, the immense advantages offered by this railway route are apparent to every business man.

This topic not heretofore considered—

—should be now.

The moderation exhibited in past opinions, which the reader now admits, however extravagant they seemed in the year of utterance, would have precluded calculation ten years ago of business by the Pacific road. But now one or more will certainly and speedily be finished; and although still holding to the opinion expressed in 1858, p. 24, that the benefits are national rather than special, this paper would be quite incomplete were it not shown that "no single city will be more benefited by connections with the Pacific coast than will this."

What is the Pacific trade?

And what is that trade? We need not adopt the chimerical ideas publicly and privately expressed both East and West, that the traffic of the Atlantic States and even of Europe must chiefly employ this route, to make it an object abundantly sufficient to excite strong contest. For the seaboard, and still less for Europe, the saving in time, in which interest is the principal item, can never justify the extra cost of carriage except upon the most valuable articles. But travel over it, even from Europe, will be immense, benefiting especially the chief cities on the route. The country, too, west of Lake Erie, may as advantageously receive its supplies direct from the Pacific as from the Atlantic. By this trade alone the city that should obtain the chief distribution, would attain high commercial importance. The trade of the Orient, from time immemorial, has enriched the cities which could command it. We need not speculate as to whether it can be secured for Europe, or even for the seaboard. The trade of the Mississippi Valley alone, is that for which we should calculate, and who can name its limits? Mere carriage is not the object; breaking bulk and distribution yields the revenues. A sober view of it was taken by the *London Daily Telegraph*, and copied into the *San Francisco Bulletin*:

For seaboard and Europe not fully available. **Is for the west.** **Trade of Orient rich.** ***Lond. Tel.***

It is nearly a year since we called attention to a gigantic public work now in progress in America, the effects of which on our own commerce, and on that of the world it is difficult to over-estimate. On the future of the United States the consequences of its completion are far beyond human foresight. This great work is the railway connecting the Atlantic and the Pacific oceans, across the entire continent of America on its widest line, spanning such rivers as the Ohio, the Mississippi, and the Missouri, and climbing over such ranges as the Rocky Mountains in the interior of the continent, and the Sierra Nevada or snow-capped peaks that border the Pacific ocean at an average distance of about 100 miles from the seaboard. Of this vast work, the portion that joins the Atlantic States to the western territories as far as the Missouri river had been completed by the private enterprise of the people in the year 1863. But from that river to San Francisco, the distance of 1890 miles to be traversed, passed through a country still uninhabited save by the trappers, the hunters and the Indian tribes. * *

Importance of the project. **Done to the Mo. river in 1863.**

The broad results are fascinating. The magnificent perspective of a line of new great States stretching across the continent—of a commercial stream diverting the trade of the world from its accustomed channels—withdrawing the silks, teas and spices of the East from the usual track—sending them straight across the Pacific to San Francisco, thence by this railway to New York, from which they will be distributed to Europe in half the time now required for their transit—and the fabulous accumulation of wealth to be gathered from the new and vast commerce—all this inflames the excitable American, flatters his national vanity, and he already enjoys in anticipation the spectacle of his country enthroned as mistress of the commerce of the world. We do not share in the belief of extravagant gains so confidently expected; but the visions of wealth and grandeur to flow from this and kindred enterprises in the United States are far from being baseless. It can hardly be doubted that a few years will show marvelous changes in the great West, where already the population is increasing five-fold in every twenty years! The centre of power in the States will be displaced, their commercial policy will no longer be controlled by Eastern manufacturers, a considerable effect will be produced on European commerce with the Indies, and various other important consequences might be suggested. We may be sure, too, that causes so great will produce effects in a variety of unexpected ways that no human being can conjecture in advance. * * * *

Extravagant expectations. **Results to be immense.**

The *New York Commercial and Financial Chronicle* also says:— ***N. Y. Com. Chron.***

The New Route to the Pacific.—The rapid progress in the construction of the Pacific Railroad, and the prospect of its completion before the close of 1870, raises the important question as to its probable effect upon the future commerce of the country. First of all, it is patent that this new highway to the Pacific must open up a vast extent of territory valuable in the precious metals and in agricultural resources. As in the case of all our pioneer roads, it is to be anticipated that population will rapidly locate along its route, and especially in those parts which offer

Pacific railway develops the west.

Increase mining.

the temptation of rich mineral deposits. Colorado, Nevada and Idaho are already contributing an aggregate supply of treasure nearly equal to the product of California; but the development of their resources is being to a large extent held in abeyance until the new road affords them the facilities of cheaper labor and safer transportation to the Atlantic. Following the mining population there must be an accession of agriculturists and traders, whose wants will have to be supplied from the interior. One of the first results to be anticipated from the road, therefore, must be the opening of a vast traffic with the rich country between Omaha City and Salt Lake City; which will, at the same time, give a new stimulus to the trade of the country, and redound to the advantage of the road.

Pacific trade.

Next comes the opening of direct railroad connection with the great port of the Pacific. Already we have a trade by steamers and sailing vessels with San Francisco, covering both ways 400,000 tons of freight annually, while the number of passengers by ocean and overland is estimated at 150,000 per annum. When the time of the journey is reduced to six days, the travel between the Pacific coast and the Eastern States will naturally be largely increased. Eastern merchandise will then be in a position to compete on more favorable terms in the California markets with the importations from other countries, and much of the staple manufactures now supplied by England may then be furnished by the factories of New England.

To develop the west is first object.

However important the Pacific trade, it is by no means chief; but as above intimated, the occupation of the great interior plain, and the resulting business, and close connection with the Pacific States, are more worthy of consideration. These are the motives, or ought to have been, which led Congress to make its liberal grants for the Omaha route, and branches from Sioux City, Atchison and Kansas. Not only have grants been made of United States bonds, but they are made a second lien, the respective companies being authorized to borrow an equal amount upon the road and its lands; and liberal land grants are also made. And one road and branches being of small account for the objects in view, as the experiment shall prove successful, we may expect other roads to be built in the same way.

One road insufficient.

Chicago wants more.—

The contest for this new and important business is mainly between St. Louis and Chicago; though Omaha, as the termination of the first through line, comes into consideration with many. Omaha being due west from Chicago, it would seem for the interest of both to have the single road, which would give so large advantages over St. Louis. Yet that is not the case. A forced monopoly by one route accords not with the genius of Chicago, and she would invite the largest competition; not only because the country needs and will have various roads for its development, bnt because she is so abundantly assured of her own impregnable position as the natural centre of the entire plain between the Alleghanies and the Rocky Mountains. With two or more routes, Omaha loses its apparent advantage; and it is only apparent as against Chicago. If this city possess the natural advantages which it is the endeavor of this paper to establish, being in truth the focal and distributing point of the Great West, could the Pacific trade be stopped at Omaha for distribution? So much of it must at all events come here that it would draw largely on the balance; and the three competing routes we shall have from Omaha direct, *via* Burlington, Rock Island, and Clinton, before the

—no monopoly.

Trade must come here.

line is open to the Pacific, insures the delivery of the business to us at the lowest posible cost.

Of the northern route, from St. Paul, the *New York Tribune* of December 21st, remarks:— *N. Y. Tribune.*

The Northern Pacific Railway.—While the Central Pacific and Union Pacific Railroad Companies are pushing on their roads, both from the eastern and western points of departure, with amazing energy and success, the Northern Company has as yet done little more than enlighten the country on the comparative advantages of its route over any other. The reason is plain. The former has a large Government subsidy, a loan of United States credit, while the latter has only a simple land-grant. These roads lie at all points nearly six hundred miles apart, and for local trade, could never be rivals. If there be any jealousy between them, it is because the Northern road, on account of its shorter distances and easier grades, must eventually be the great highway of international commerce between Europe and Asia, and between Asia and our Atlantic seaboard. But we do not propose to discuss the relative prospects of the roads from any point of view. The vast importance of either to the solid and permanent growth of the Union, to its commercial prosperity and its defensive strength, is beyond any possible estimate. In the midst of the general satisfaction which hails the rapid construction of the one, we simply desire to call attention to the grand resources which the other is likely to command—to the stupendous empire in extent and in natural wealth which it is destined to develop. In the success of the latter enterprise New York and New England have a deep interest, worthy of their most practical consideration. The commercial supremacy of the City of New York can never, of course, be disturbed, but it may be enhanced; and it seems perfectly evident that, should the trade of Asia and the great Northwest be poured into the lakes which wash the northern boundary of the State, whatever is broken in bulk, or distributed to the Atlantic States, will be drawn off to the advantage of this metropolis. * * **Northern route from St. Paul—has the advantage. Its importance. N. Y. and N. Eng. interested.**

From a newspaper slip the following statement concerning other roads aided by Congress, is condensed:—

The *Sioux City and Pacific*, has a grant of $16,000 per mile, to its intersection with the Union Pacific at Fremont. This being a continuation of the Dubuque and Sioux City Road, open 143 miles to Iowa Falls, (about half the distance to Sioux City,) supplies a route competing with Omaha, giving Chicago a fourth line from the main Pacific road. **Sioux City and Pacific.**

The *Union Pacific*, finished from Omaha to the Rocky Mountains, has received therefor $16,000 per mile. For 150 miles across the mountains she receives $48,000; and for 78 miles, to the junction with the Central, $32,000 per mile. **Union Pacific.**

The *Central Pacific*, receives for the first 7 miles from Sacramento, $16,000 per mile, and for 150 miles, across the Sierra Nevada, $48,000; thence to its junction with the Omaha line, 544 miles, $32,000 per mile. It is probably now finished 150 miles, to Virginia City, across the Sierra Nevada, the heaviest part of the work, from whence it can now be rapidly pushed forward. **Central Pacific.**

The *Central Branch, Union Pacific*, (Atchison and Pike's Peak,) has $16,000 per mile, and is already built 80 miles from Atchison. This was also to connect with the Omaha road, making another tap, though being southerly it favors St. Louis. But with the change made in the route, next to be noticed, this may run to Denver. A **Atchison and Pike's Peak.**

Atchison writer.

correspondent of the St. Louis *Republican*, writing from Atchison November 21st, says:—

Plan for Atchison road.

What you call the Atchison and Pike's Peak Railroad, is now the "Central Branch of the Union Pacific Railroad," and is not only completed eighty miles west from Atchison, with two daily trains running over it, but is nearly completed one hundred miles, with work progressing rapidly beyond that point. This road traverses the best country west of the Missouri river, and at this early day is doing a very heavy business and daily increasing, not a dollar of which goes to St. Louis for want of a connection with the Missouri Pacific Railroad; but all crosses the Missouri river at Atchison, and on to Chicago over the Hannibal and St. Joseph Railroad. The Central Branch does not turn north eighty miles west of Atchison, as you suppose, but runs out nearly due west for one hundred miles, and then bears northwest, and will connect with the Union Pacific from Omaha, at Fort Kearney, or fifty miles west on the 100th degree of longitude. And from Atchison to the point of intersection the distance will not exceed two hundred and sixty miles; and the universal opinion of those best acquainted with the country is, that as soon as completed, the Central Branch will be the main line of travel across the continent.

Un. Pacific E. D.

The *Union Pacific, Eastern Division*, has a grant of $16,000 per mile for 385 miles, where at the 100th meridian it was to connect with the Omaha line. It is built 325 miles, and being rapidly pushed; but the route has been changed by the Company. Of nnmerous extracts upon the subject, it is best set forth by a correspondent of the *San Francisco Bulletin*, writing from Santa Fe, October 4th, 1867:—

Santa Fe writer.

Change of route.

Your readers throughout California will undoubtedly be interested to know of the progress being made by the engineering parties of the Union Pacific Railway Company, Eastern Division. The railway of this Company will be completed in a few weeks to Pond Creek, a distance from the Missouri river of 385 miles, and where the Government subsidy ends. Instead of extending this road in a northwesterly course to connect with the road from Omaha *via* Salt Lake, as was originally intended, the Company have decided to make of it an *independent trunk line* to San Francisco. In order to do this it is the intention of the Company to run from Pond Creek in a southwesterly direction, into and through that portion of New Mexico lying east of the Rio Grande, to that stream; thence by either the Gila route or the 35th parallel, through to California and your city.

Another line to San Francisco.

Difficulties small.

The difficulties on that portion of the proposed route east of the Rio Grande were considered by many, before the engineering parties went over it, as almost unsurmonntable. These difficulties are proven by the survey to have been greatly exaggerated; instead of high and unbroken mountains, with passes presenting barriers impassable, the scientific parties engaged in the survey have found that the mountains are detached in their character; that the altitude of the passes is small; that there are long extents of fertile valleys and level mesas; that there is abundance of coal and sufficient wood and water; and that no serious obstacles exist, so far, on the line of the survey. There are also several most excellent crossings on the Rio Grande on the contemplated route—the banks being of rock and the channel confined to a narrow space.

Coal and water.

Two routes surveyed.

From the Rio Grande westward, as I have before remarked, two routes are to be surveyed: one by the valley of the Gila, the other *via* the 35th parallel; and whichever route may be finally selected, of this fact there can be no question, viz: that the Colorado of the West will be crossed at a point far enough south to permit iron and other materials being brought up that stream, thus materially conducing to the early completion of the road. In New Mexico it will probably be the policy of the Company to erect iron works, so that iron rails may be turned out for this part of the line. What is needed now is that Congress may be induced to grant the same aid to this route that it has already granted to the Northern. This grant will probably be effected during the coming session of Congress, and to secure it let California join with New Mexico, Arizona, and Colorado, in urging it.

Make rails in New Mexico.

Congress to aid.

No snow.

For this southern route one advantage can certainly be claimed over any other—that of freedom from snows and severe cold. I would not disparage the northern route, nor the wonderful energy displayed by its builders, but whatever may be said in regard to it, there can be no question but that two through routes are needed. Before either road can be completed both will be insufficient to carry the trade of the country. The line from Omaha by Salt Lake cannot develop the vast territory of the United States lying upon this one. This line would give an outlet to say 500,000 people residing in Southern Kansas and Colorado, New Mexico, Arizona, Southern and Middle California, Northern and Western Texas, and the rich States of Durango, Chihuahua, and Sonora, and would at once develop the vast pastoral, mineral and agricultural resources of the territory named.

Both roads wanted. *Country traversed.*

Let California shake hands with New Mexico in this matter, and assist in making patent to Congress and the people the necessity of carrying through this great enterprise.

The *San Francisco Bulletin*, of November 4th, also says:—

San Fran. Bulletin.

The engineers of the Kansas Pacific Railroad are vigorously pushing their surveys for the extension from Fort Riley, across New Mexico, to California. The road is nearly built to a point 385 miles westward from Leavenworth and Kansas City, and it is intended to lay the results of the new surveys before Congress at its next session, with a request for the same aid in bonds and lands which has been accorded the portion already constructed, and which is allowed the Union and Central Pacific roads. The surveys will extend to both San Diego and San Francisco. Gen. Palmer, the Treasurer of the Company, in a recent address to the people of New Mexico, declared that he had no contest with the road from Omaha, to San Francisco, "except to reach the western ocean before them." He believes that there is a local want for a road on the southern route, and that "before either road can be finished, both will be insufficient to carry the trade of the country, and second tracks will be required to be begun on each." Gen. Wright, the chief engineer of the Kansas Pacific Company, speaks favorably of the route through New Mexico, and says that "no material obstacles will intervene between the survey and the building of the road." Gen. Palmer speaks confidently of its completion through the Territory inside of three years.

Kansas road. *No contest with Omaha road.* *Route feasible.*

We must allow considerable for the exaggeration natural at the inception of such enterprises, but it is probable the Kansas Pacific Railroad Company means business. Whether Congress will consent to subsidize it is doubtful. If the enterprise is based on local needs and resources, as contended, it ought to rely on those. Congress has done enough in giving bonds to one great central railway across the continent. It cannot give bonds to the Southern Pacific without according them to the Northern Pacific which is just as eager an applicant; and if it grants both, there is at least $100,000,000 more added to the national debt at one fell swoop. Rival Pacific Railroads should depend upon the legitimate demand for their construction by private capital. There must be a stop somewhere to national subsidies in money, and it might better be at the point already reached. Perhaps it may be politic to make further land grants in favor of railroads, under conditions requiring their sale, at low rates, as soon as possible, to actual settlers; but the nation cannot afford to draw upon its credit any more for such enterprises. The argument of Gen. Palmer, that a road by the New Mexican route will be a great convenience, if not an actual necessity, is probably true; and we concur with the opinion that it would not compete injuriously with the Central road; but the Government ought not to be asked to build any more roads to enrich individuals. It did right to start one trunk line over the continent ten years sooner than it would have been started by private capital; in doing that it did enough in the same line to meet all public requirements.

Moderation. *Country to build its own roads.* *Land grants.*

That two or more routes will speedily be constructed through to the Pacific, cannot be questioned. With no more than two, no one place upon either can monopolize the Pacific trade, which must take its chances with the general trade of the West, and with the rest seek its natural centre, if there be one. In view of what has been done, even without Congressional aid, who can doubt that in ten or fifteen years numerous railroads will reach at least to the Rocky Mountains, and several cross them? Rival railroads from the east to Chicago, by consolidation of continuous lines, are fast settling into gigantic corporations, each interested in its line to and beyond

Competition of two roads— —have several.

the Mississippi, insuring of itself the rapid extension of lines into the rich country yet unoccupied, and which railroads will fill speedily with the best of settlers. Says Hon. J. F. Joy, President of the Burlington and Quincy Railroad, in his last annual report:—

Hon. J. F. Joy.

Interest of Bur. and Q. road in Bur. and Mo. road.

Earnings west of Mississippi.

As this Company has become largely interested in the Burlington and Missouri River Railroad, under the contract with the Company owning it, by which for a period of ten years from its date two years ago, we are to become purchasers of its securities convertible into preferred stock to the extent of $120,000 a year, it is not deemed inappropriate to bring its condition and business and prospects before our stockholders. * * * The road the past year, with only 88 miles on an average in operation, and part of it just opened, has earned $473,999.46. At this time, with only 34 miles added, it is earning at the rate of $600,000 per annum, and more, therefore, than enough to pay the interest on its mortgage debt, when fifty miles more shall be completed, and enough to pay the whole interest not only upon that debt, but upon all the securities out, and of which this Company is becoming the purchaser at the rate of $120,000 per annum. There can hardly, therefore, it seems, remain a possibility of doubt of the value of all these securities when there shall be a further section of 50 miles added to the road. Nor to those who consider the rapid development of the West, and the ease with which its prairies are subdued and brought under cultivation, and the fact that at least nineteen-twentieths of the country along the line of that road yet remains unimproved, and yet to be settled and to be made to contribute to the revenues of the road, would there seem to remain any question, either of the entire safety of the investment, now making by this Company, in its bonds to be converted into preferred stock, or of its great future value in the addition of business it will bring to the Chicago, Burlington and Quincy Railroad.

Settlement of country.

Mr. Perkins.

In the appendix Mr. Joy presents the report of Mr. C. E. Perkins the Superintendent of the Burlington and Missouri Road, in which he remarks:—

Importance of Bur. and Mo. road.

An examination of the table of distances will show that when a completed link in the line, we are sure of doing a large share of whatever business in passengers and freight may pass over the Pacific Road.

Our lands cannot be sold until the road is built through them, but with the road they will probably sell rapidly and at good prices, and unless sold within a very few years their value seems likely to be absorbed by local and State taxation.

Eastern Nebraska, and Page, Fremont, and Mills counties in Iowa, are all well settled and wealthy in agricultural communities; we shall find there a large local traffic as soon as the road is completed.

There can be no reasonable doubt that after the completion of our road to the Missouri river, the improvement of both the road and the country through which it passes, will resemble the improvement of the Chicago, Burlington and Quincy road, and the country tributary to it during the last ten or twelve years.

Way to extend Chi. roads.

On p. 94 a statement of the traffic is given, showing the increase from the Hannibal and St. Joseph and the Burlington and Missouri Roads. This is a sample of the objects, and ways and means of extending the Chicago lines. It is not necessary to decry any road; sufficient is it that these pay abundantly, insuring rapid increase.

Congress will aid Pacific road.

Yet this is not the only reliance. The aid of Congress will surely be given to many lines, the San Francisco editor to the contrary notwithstanding. Because they are certain of the one from Omaha, also that from Kansas, they would oppose further grants, because our northern lines would be recipients. But the measure in itself is every way right and desirable, notwithstanding a few sharp men make incredible fortunes out of them; and the policy is sufficiently inaugurated for these sharp men to get the grants and build the

Policy sound

roads. And shall St. Louis or Chicago reap the benefits? Both must be great gainers, but with the parallel lines started so numerously from the Mississippi, and extending indefinitely westward, at least to the Rocky Mountains, it is certain that no great centre in the far West can be formed, and which city will be able to control the business in the main? The *Missouri Republican*, of November 19th, thus presents her side:— **Will Chi. or St. L. be gainer?** **Mo. Rep.**

St. Louis and her Western Connections.—St. Louis is quite certain, ultimately, to have four connections by railroad with the centre of the continent and the Pacific coast. The Kansas branch of the Union Pacific, already built to a point 600 miles west of St. Louis, we all know about. That will connect us with Denver, and with the Omaha branch of the Union Pacific at a point 60 miles west of the longitude of Denver. At Pond creek or Fort Wallace the Kansas branch of the Union Pacific is to be extended southwest to Santa Fe and Albuquerque, and thence by the most admirable route on the continent to San Francisco. Next, there is our own Southwest Branch of the Missouri Pacific, known as the Atlantic and Pacific, which will assuredly be finished to the southwest corner of the State, and onward to Albuquerque. Congressional grants of land have already been made to the Atlantic and Pacific. **St. Louis have 4 Pac. roads.**

Then St. Louis will at an early day be in direct railroad connection with Omaha and the Union Pacific at that point. The connection will very soon be made by means of the road which is in process of building from St. Joseph to Omaha. Another connection will be made by the more direct route from Brunswick through Chillicothe to Omaha. **Connections with Omaha—**

But there is one Pacific Railroad connection in which St. Louis is essentially interested, of which very few persons are aware. We refer to that which will be effected by means of the Atchison and Pike's Peak Railroad, leading westward from Atchison. That road is built, stocked and running for a distance of eighty miles. At that point it diverges northwest over a line surveyed and located to Fort Kearney, on the Omaha branch of the Union Pacific, a distance of two hundred miles. Congress has granted to this road the usual subsidies of land and money granted to the Union Pacific. Any one who will take a map of Kansas and Nebraska will see what a direct connection this will give St. Louis with the Union Pacific Railway at Fort Kearney. From Atchison to that point is 280 miles, 80 miles built, and the rest to be built next year. From Atchison to Leavenworth, a distance of twenty miles, there is a gap. But the route for a road over that gap is surveyed and that road will be built. And then, by means of our own Missouri Pacific, to Leavenworth, St. Louis will be in connection with the Union Pacific at Fort Kearney, nearly 300 miles west of Omaha, which places St. Louis at once on an even footing with Chicago, so far as the Union Pacific is concerned, giving to St. Louis an advantage in distance, if we mistake not, for Fort Kearney is nearer to St. Louis than to Chicago. Tapping the Union Pacific at Fort Kearney, St. Louis will then be in connection with the road leading directly to Salt Lake and the Pacific. We learn that the gentlemen interested in the Atchison and Pike's Peak Road and the Fort Kearney connection will early next year press it rapidly to completion. The President of the road is R. M. Pomeroy, of Boston; Effingham H. Nichols of New York, is Treasurer. We learn that these gentlemen, and those associated with them, among whom is Lieutenant Governor Claflin, of Massachusetts, are aiming at completing this road with a view to perfecting a connection with St. Louis. Any one, upon an examination of the map, will see that the route is natural and direct, and that it is a most important matter to St. Louis to have this road built. It will in fact constitute for us the Union Pacific Railway *via* Nebraska, opening to us the same regions penetrated by the Union Pacific, and placing in our hands the necessary means for competition with Chicago on that line. **Atchison & Pike's Peak road.** **Connect with Omaha road at Ft. Kearney.** **Boston men aiding St. Louis—** **—to compete with Chicago.**

We have then:—

1. The Kansas branch of the Union Pacific, the central route, running to Denver, connecting with the Union Pacific sixty miles west and north of Denver, running southwest to Santa Fe and Albuquerque and on to the Pacific ocean. **1. Kansas route.**
2. The two connections with the Union Pacific at Omaha, one *via* St. Joseph and one *via* Brunswick and Chillicothe. **2. Two to Omaha.**
3. The connection with the Union Pacific at Fort Kearney by means of the **3. Atchison.**

—4

Atchison and Pike's Peak railway, which will make of the Omaha Branch of the Union Pacific a road tributary to St. Louis.

4. S. W. Pacific.

4. The Atlantic and Pacific, running through Southwest Missouri, and thence to the 35th parallel at Albuquerque. This road will ultimately pass down through Arizona and Sonora to Guaymas on the Gulf of California.

St. Louis' near future.

This presents the near railroad future of St. Louis, so far as its connections with the Northwestern, Central, and Southwestern Territories and States, and the Pacific ocean are concerned. The middle position of our city, on the grand central line from the Atlantic to the Pacific, insures the connections we have indicated. What has been called the Chicago Union Pacific, through Omaha, becomes ours by the inevitable necessities of our position, and through it St. Louis reaches Nebraska, Utah, Idaho, Montana, and all regions West and Northwest. Our second Pacific is insured by the road now built nearly to Pond Creek. What is needed here at home is prompt and liberal aid to be extended to those who are seeking to fill up certain gaps with roads in our own State, or immediately on our borders. Parties engaged in building the roads outside of us, to the West, do not seem to require aid. They have the means. But in our own State there are enterprises on foot, designed to perfect the railroad system of the State, which require aid. Let such aid be granted in liberal measure. Not a city or town can be named which is so greatly interested in some of these as St. Louis.

Chicago Pacific their road.

Some gaps at home to fill.

Trade of the west runs to Chicago.

It seemed expedient to take space for that argument entire. Yet, on my side to argue about business from Omaha would be useless. If Chicago cannot control trade directly in her rear, the experience of the past, which is our main premise, is useless, false; and the Queen of the Lakes will be seen crawling into her lake tunnel for shame.

Atchison road connected with Han. and St. Joe.

The Atchison road is only a few miles south of, and is connected with the Hannibal and St. Joseph road, which St. Louisians seem to have lost faith in. When the editor seriously and confidently argues that Mr. Pomeroy of BOSTON, Mr. Nichols of NEW YORK, and Gov. Claflin of MASSACHUSETTS, is building this road in the interest of St. Louis, it appears to me the editor would display more sagacity to consider the past and ascertain whether the Hannibal and St. Joseph game is not being repeated, and by the same party. A pretty keen fellow might be trapped once at the game, "heads I win, tails you lose;" but the winner would be very much of a *Sucker*, and the loser too much of a *Puke*, who was caught by it a second time. Instead of waiting to fill up that gap to Leavenworth to connect with St. Louis' "own Missouri Pacific," these Boston capitalists will "want to know" why the Macon route via St. Joseph, will not answer for St. Louis even better than the other, because shorter? If that creates "the necessary means for competition with Chicago on that line," St. Louis and Chicago can be good friends.

Funny if Mass. is in St. Louis interest.

Han and St. Joe will do the work.

Kansas route to New Mexico suits Chicago.

The Kansas route, deflecting south into New Mexico and Arizona seems promising to St. Louis. Yet if she could not hold her own business in close proximity, and which she had fastened to her by many years of intercourse, how can she draw to her from the far West, where Chicago begins competition at least even-handed? We in Chicago may overrate our abilities, but most surely if we could have had the direction of the Kansas Branch, it would have been run directly to Fort Wallace, and thence southwest through New

Mexico and Arizona, precisely as the judicious directors have determined. And it will be proved that the interest and capital of New York and Boston which incorporated the Hannibal and St. Joseph road into the Quincy and Chicago road, as effectually as it could have been done by charter, will do the same thing for this new line through New Mexico and onward.

N. Y. & Boston look out for Chicago.

In this connection it may be remarked, that St. Louis will do well if she can control even the Southwest Pacific road. A recent article in one of the St. Louis papers, which I have hunted for again in vain, felicitated that city upon the important fact that Hon. James F. Joy and others had bought 800,000 acres on that line. *Possibly* these chief shareholders in the lines from Kansas City to Chicago, are operating in the St. Louis interest. Yet sagacious as these gentlemen are known to be, if they *could* make the land operation pay as well or a little better by giving the southern business a slight bend to Kansas, would they not do it? Would it not be for the interest of that region to have a fair competition between Chicago and St. Louis which this slight change would make? The road to Galveston from Lawrence, already begun, effects the object. Let St. Louis look out for another "flank movement," for Chicago men are in it.

S. W. Pacific to be looked after.

Is Mr. Joy in St. Louis' interest?

Another flank movement.

To show that St. Louis must be pretty well occupied in "seeking to fill up certain gaps with roads in her own State, or immediately on her borders," while Chicago makes "flank movements;" a letter is taken from the *Pittsburgh Gazette*, headed "The Chicago Yankee on his Westward Way." It is dated Salina, Kansas, June 13; and July 12th the editor alluded to him as a well-informed man:—

St. Louis' occupation—

—and Chicago's.

A Kansas writer in *Pitts. Gaz.*

It is a notable fact that all the active business men here hail from Chicago, or somewhere on that social and commercial line. Many of the stores are branches of commercial houses in that city. The forwarding and commission merchants, who handle the Denver and Santa Fe trades, are Chicago men; and the wagons, reapers, mowers, threshers, shovels, spades, hoes, cooking-stoves, and everything pertaining to a farmer's outfit—and there are more of these things here than I ever saw in any town of its size—bear the same impress, and are furnished by Chicago, or by New York or New England through Chicago. This I like to see; it proves that already Chicago, which has not yet a perfect connection by rail with this road, is entrenching itself strongly and firmly in this matchless garden of the continent. It is through this avenue, and this only, that that city, and the great commercial cities of which it is the outpost, can reach the centre of Colorado, and the still more remote Territories of New Mexico and Arizona; and I am persuaded that it is destined to be their best route to California.

All business men from Chicago—

—and goods.

Chicago entrenching—

—to reach southern territories.

At present that trade is carried over the Chicago, Burlington and Quincy Railroad (the best road in Illinois) to Quincy; thence across the Mississippi to the Hannibal and St. Joseph road, which begins on the opposite bank of the river, and runs to St. Joseph, on the Missouri. Thence it goes by rail to Weston, six miles below Leavenworth. From Weston to Leavenworth it is carried by steamers. At Leavenworth it meets one branch of the Union Pacific Road. In a short time a branch road will be completed from Cameron (about fifty miles east of St. Joseph) to the east bank of the Missouri, opposite Leavenworth; and a bridge across the river to that city is the last remaining link required to complete the long and direct chain between Chicago and the Union Pacific Railway of Kansas. A branch road from Cameron to Kansas City is also in progress of construction, and another bridge is to be built across the Missouri at that point, which is the main terminus of the Union Pacific. Thus two distinct lines will unite the cities

Present Chi. route.

Cameron roads to Chicago.

Bridge Mo. river.

of the lakes, and through them all the railroad lines in and north of Pennsylvania, with this great continental thoroughfare. They are now building a bridge over the Mississippi at Quincy. So, when all that is now in rapid progress shall be completed, cars may be run from any of the cities of the Atlantic coast to the Pacific without breaking bulk. Before five years more shall have rolled round, that which lately seemed but an enthusiast's dream will be sober verity, an accomplished fact.

No breaking bulk.

Northern route *vs.* southern.

I have said that I was pleased to see the energy of Chicago in grasping this prize. It is eminently commendable, and if the cities along the other great line of the country's commerce, beginning at Philadelphia and ending at St. Louis—allow themselves to be outstripped, it is their own fault.

Trade large.

The magnitude of the trade on this road astonishes even those who are building it. Its revenue during the month of May was over $165,000, or at the rate of $1,750,000 a year. A double track will be needed through the valley of the Kansas long before the far-distant goal will be reached. J. C.

P. S.—In justice to our State, I must State the fact that all the rails and all the locomotives on this road are of Pennsylvania manufacture.

Conflict with St. L. further considered.

—The conflict with St. Louis for western business will be also considered when we compare the rivalry of the three chief cities of the West. To prepare further for this, it must be remembered that Chicago not only has her railways, but her canal and lakes. Let us look at—

Canal to Ills. and Miss. rivers.

The Illinois and Michigan Canal to the Illinois River—its Possible Continuation to Rock Island on the Mississippi.

Views 1861.

Remarks of 1848 were quoted p. 23. The circular of 1861 had the following:—

Canal important.

Such has been the increase of railroads, that the canal, which was a great national work when completed in 1848, is now almost overlooked. Its value, however, for all heavy transportation, is shown in the statement that of 15,212,394 bushels of corn received here last year, [1860] 4,326,944 bushels came by canal; and of 225,000,000 feet of lumber distributed—lath, shingles and timber not included—nearly 46,000,000 were by canal; and of sugar, molasses, etc, large quantities came by canal, and little by rail. The transportation of coal is hereafter noticed.

Corn and lumber.

Shallow-cut.

The original plan of the canal was to feed it from Lake Michigan, and much of the heaviest work was done accordingly. But in the embarrassments of the State it was deemed best to put it in operation with the least possible cost, and consequently the summit-level was raised eight feet above the lake.

Deep-cut.

The deep-cut would not affect boating on the canal itself, it being now six feet deep, and allowing the use of boats of even more draft than can ordinarily run on the Illinois river. But canal boats are loaded at various points on the river, and also on the Mississippi, and towed by steamboats to La Salle, the foot of the canal, which saves transhipment at St. Louis and other places, and it is desirable to secure a constant stage of water in the Illinois equal to the canal. By lowering the summit-level, and feeding from the lake, it is supposed this can be done at a cost of about $1,500,000, and without creating too strong a current, which would be moderate except in a drouth. The canal is a substantial work, and steam tugs as well as horses are used for towing.

Improve Ills. river.

Ills. river good for navigation.

The Illinois is even now a more reliable stream for navigation than the Ohio, or Upper Mississippi, or Missouri, but would be much improved by this sure supply in mid-summer, and the pure water of the lake would much augment its healthiness. When Chicago becomes very populous, it will also be desirable to have this constant flow of lake water for miles through the heart of the city, which the deep-cut will give, and as the canal and its lands yield good revenues, the city or State, or both, will probably in a few years make the change. The Legislature, at its recent session, passed resolutions directing surveys and estimates of the work, not only of the canal, but for improving the navigation of the Illinois river.

Deep-cut desirable for health of Chicago.

This is the shortest and best route to form a steamboat communication between the waters of the Lakes and of the Gulf of Mexico, and it is within the bounds of possibility, if not probability, that Congress may itself finish the work on even a larger scale than is now planned. It is very important to the whole country. This shortest route from lakes to rivers.

The city of Chicago has taken in hand the canal enlargement, and already let the contracts, which are in progress. It will cost the city nothing ultimately, the tolls having already reduced the canal debt to about $600,000. City enlarging canal.

The corn received by canal in 1861 was 11,735,043 bu.; 1862, 11,585,749; 1863, 10,067,081; in 1864, 4,310,864; in 1865, 8,639,108; in 1866, 9,575,569; and in 1867, 6,553,257. Lumber was shipped, exclusive of shingles, siding, dressed flooring, etc., in 1861, 41,521,-790 ft.; in 1862, 55,658,586 ft.; in 1863, 55,655,475; in 1864, 52,842,-972; in 1865, 77,794,095; in 1866, 67,951,954; in 1867, 73,029,473 feet. The total receipts are given p. 60. Corn received by canal— —lumber shipped.

It is also proposed to continue the canal almost due west from LaSalle to Rock Island, which will no doubt be done in time, to the great benefit of the whole Upper Mississippi region as well as Chicago. For while river navigation has relatively seen its best days, as will be hereafter considered, yet for bulky articles, as lumber, corn, etc., water will always be largely used where it can be; and even if produce can be marketed cheaper by shipping it down the Mississippi, it will be directly for the interest of Chicago that it goes that way. The commercial and manufacturing city of the West, would have all articles taken from and gotten to the farmers at the least possible cost to them. Her prosperity will be *pari passu* with the farmers, whoever may make the trifling pittance in a transhipment of produce. Extended to Rock Island. River still important. Interest of Chicago— —that of the farmers.

Having these unexampled facilities to gather the productions of the West, what is she to do with them? Her powers of consumption, and her distributing facilities to the eastward, then, are quite as essential as those considered; and in this respect also, Chicago will not be found wanting. Let us first examine— With these gathering powers, what to distribute? (*See also p.* 63.)

Five Rival Railways Eastward.

5 roads east.

Even in railroads to the East, no other city is our equal. The Michigan Central and its connections; the Michigan Southern and its connections; the Pittsburg and Fort Wayne and its connections; the Great Eastern and its connections; and also the Lafayette, Indianapolis and Central route through Ohio to Baltimore,—are all five, particularly the first four, strong competitors for the business here centering, insuring expedition, and care, and the lowest possible rates, in the transit of both freights and passengers to and from the various seaboard cities. Mich. Cent. Mich. Sou. Pitts. and F. W. Gt. East. Central.

The one to Baltimore is yet to be shortened, by a straight line (now building) from Piqua to Columbus, and thence to Parkersburg, Balt. has advantage—

affording the shortest route possible from Chicago to the ocean, and one which in a few years will be a strong competitor with all the others. The Philadelphia route has advantage next; and so many intermediate and nearly parallel roads are already constructed, and yet more to be constructed, that two or three rival lines will be opened to Philadelphia and Baltimore as well as New York and Boston; which the work of consolidation of short lines just commencing, will greatly expedite.

—Philadelphia next.

More roads.

Norfolk, Va., to improve.

Norfolk, also, is about equi-distant with New York; and, with the change that will be made in Virginia by the removal of slavery, that city may yet be made to equal the expectations of Washington and Jefferson. One of the first movements in that direction will be a railroad connection with the chief city of the lakes and of the interior, if there be such an one.

Seaboard rivalry.

The same reasons which have influenced the capital of New York and north in favor of Chicago, have hitherto operated upon Philadelphia and south to favor Cincinnati and St. Louis. With no outspoken declaration of antagonism, a deep, irresistible under-current of interest has led each section on the seaboard to extend its lines to draw western business. This for years has been perfectly understood, and a St. Louisian writing from New York to the ***Missouri Republican***, about the Omaha and St. Louis Road, says:

Writer in *Mo. Rep.*

St. Louis wants straight road to Omaha.

If a shorter and better road can be had from Omaha to St. Louis, than can be found between Omaha and Chicago, then St. Louis will, with equal means, and equal capacity, command the trade. With a crooked, badly graded, and poorly built road, St. Louis will stand but a poor chance to win in the lively competition which Chicago will wage for the trade which will concentrate at Omaha. The best road or none. A poor road will be but an aggravation; it will excite hopes only to disappoint them.

Who to build.

A few words as to who should take the laboring oar. And here I fear to offend. No matter what interest is suggested, other interests will feel slighted.

But when fighting, not for profit but for life, a community must put *in the lead* those who have it in their power to command success.

Mo. Pacific Co.

Phila. and Baltimore interest.

The Missouri Pacific Railroad Company possesses that power. St. Louis is the natural terminus, on the Mississippi river, of the Philadelphia, Pittsburg, Columbus, and Terre Haute line of railroads; also of the Baltimore and Cincinnati line of roads. A road from Omaha to St. Louis brings business to a point from which it cannot easily be taken away from Philadelphia and Baltimore. But if the business of Omaha is taken to Chicago, then Baltimore and Philadelphia will be brought into a direct competition, of the severest kind, with the New York and Boston roads to obtain that business.

That Co. able—

—perhaps loth.

I know of no other interest than the Pacific Company, and its potential Eastern connections, which has the financial capacity and the pecuniary inducement to build that road in a short period of time. That Company and its Eastern connections have large engagements, and may be loth to undertake a new enterprise. But their directories have men of large comprehension, and they thoroughly comprehend the greatness of the stakes involved. I think if the people of St. Louis strongly urge the enterprise upon them, they will respond as men like them have always responded—*generously. If they undertake it they will build it.*

Good local trade.

The road would have a superb local business; it would be of the very first order in amount and value, the lands being fertile and well watered.

St. L. nearest.

To St. Louis it is of extreme importance, for by its means St. Louis would be made the *nearest* and most accessible large city to the eastern terminus of the main road to California, and the intermediate States and Territories.

Who will move first in this matter? Not to build it is to surrender the California and Mountain business to Chicago without a struggle. Danger from Chi.

The Baltimore, Philadelphia, Pittsburg, Cincinnati, and their connecting roads, as I said in my former article, will be benefited if the trade of Omaha is brought to St. Louis, and injured if it is carried to Chicago; for the New York and Boston roads cannot successfully compete in St. Louis with those of Philadelphia and Baltimore, but *can* in a place so far north as Chicago. A barrel of flour from Chicago to New York would not be likely to be carried by the way of Baltimore; from St. Louis the Baltimore road can carry the barrel to New York for less money than can the Erie road. Therefore, Baltimore, Philadelphia, Pittsburgh, and most especially Cincinnati, and every railroad in Southern Ohio, Indiana, and Illinois, are deeply interested in the construction of a railroad between St. Louis and Omaha, that will have better grades and curvature, and be 100 MILES SHORTER than the best and shortest road between Omaha and Chicago. And if properly appealed to, they will certainly aid in building such a railroad. The shortest line is as important to them as it is to St. Louis. Central cities with St. L. against Chicago— —that road to Omaha.

Nor will these railroad companies care any more than I do *who* builds it. What they want, is to have the trade brought to St. Louis, where they can successfully compete for it. Unless the Omaha trade comes to St. Louis, Cincinnati roads cannot obtain one ounce of that freight, other than "chance" lots sent to fill some special order. No matter who builds.

Let St. Louis concentrate her strength on the St. Louis and Omaha railroad; and see to it that it is not made to run to the right nor to the left, to accommodate some influential officer or some flourishing village, but make it as short and level, and as curveless as possible—guard this point, for in competition it is vital. St. L.'s vital point.

But, in order to whip out Chicago thoroughly, at least in Missouri, let the Missouri Pacific company make an arrangement with the railroad company now building a railroad from St. Joseph to Omaha, by which, forever, close connections of trains, and exchanges of freights and passengers will be secured to both parties on mutually advantageous terms. This done, let the Pacific Railroad proceed to organize a company to build from St. Joseph, through Plattsburg, Richmond, Lexington, and Boonville, a branch to its railroad at a point not distant from Jefferson City. To whip out Chicago— —a new road from St. Joe—

Such a branch road will not interfere with the Brunswick and Omaha road, but would thoroughly dispose of the Chicago road, now running from St. Joseph by the way of Quincy to Chicago. —kills Han. and St. Joe Chi. road.

The greatness of the trade of the roads running east from St. Louis will also be assured if the aforenamed Missouri roads are finished before trade has been shifted, and been moulded and *fitted* to ply in large, strong, and smooth anti-St. Louis grooves; once diverted to deep adverse channels, St. Louis will find it nearly or quite impossible to recover her trade. Those Eastern roads, those cities of Philadelphia, Baltimore, Cincinnati, have as deep an interest, and their destinies will be proportionably as much influenced, in the making or not making of a successful connection with Omaha, as St. Louis itself. Clearly, St. Louis interests are their interests. But do they clearly understand this? Have they, in the turmoil of business, *studied* this connection of their interests with ours? Have our writers and speakers and railroad directors and business men and lot owners improved opportunities to explain these interests to Eastern friends? Look out for anti-St. L. grooves. East equally concerned. Is this understood?

Observe how this writer incidentally admits the significant fact of the severe competition from Chicago which St. Louis has to meet right in her own State, and the defection of the Hannibal and St. Joseph road. But the time is rapidly passing away when such considerations are to affect even Baltimore, much less Philadelphia. The last annual report of the Pittsburgh and Fort Wayne Railroad says:— St. Louis' home difficulties recognized. Such narrow views to end. Pitts. and Ft. W. Rep.

The extension of the line of road across Iowa to the Missouri river at Council Bluffs, opposite Omaha, has just been accomplished, and will this spring be worked in connection with the Northwestern Railway Company, of Illinois, as a single line from Chicago to the eastern terminus of the Union Pacific Railway, a length of four hundred and ninety-six miles. The opening of this line cannot be regarded in any other light than that of a marked epoch in the history of the city of Chicago, and must have great influence in assisting to make that city one of the Trade thro' Chi. from Pacific.

Build up Chicago.

largest inland on the continent. As your road is one of the great arteries of that city, its quickened life-blood must give new strength and growth to your interests.

Acquiesce in things settled.

It was one thing to labor to mould a system in their own interest; but it is quite another to work against a system thoroughly established. Without a doubt, they would like to draw the trade of the west through cities in their interest; but as we shall see, p. 76, the one nearest retires from the contest, and it is quite evident the other will also. Philadelphia and Baltimore will not work against the current. As the St. Louis editor says, p. 27, "Trade, like water, runs in the direction of the least resistance. Nobody ever succeeded in making it run up hill." The business of Cincinnati and of St. Louis, however, is not the object, but that of the Great West; and as that shall centre more and more at Chicago, they will extend more and more facilities, and the advantage they have in distance will be more and more felt. So that without doubt competition between the Atlantic ports, will insure increase of facilities eastward, keeping pace with increase westward. Strength of capital having lain with New York and New England, and the strong natural current of business lake-ward having favored them, they have made the focal point as advantageous to themselves as possible; and now they have still the strong competition of shorter lines to encounter against Philadelphia and Baltimore and Norfolk. Nor is the competition to be slight, did it rest on merely the present roads. The lines to New York may for a time be consolidated, though the State Legislators will doubtless discover the public interest, and with the aid of courts prevent an operation so prejudicial to the public good. But Pennsylvania and Maryland will look out for their interests, as the doctrine of State rights comes to be rightly understood and practiced; and they will never become permanently subservient to New York control. National Union upon the basis of State Sovereignty, is our solid foundation; and rival gigantic corporations, with the interests and rights of State Sovereignty to back them, will prevent the Great West from being subjected to the power of New York money.

Take trade in its natural channels. Great West the object. Atl. ports compete to reach Chi. N. Y. and N. Eng. made Chi. focal point. Competition strong. State rights our defender

New York World.

Since this paper was completed, or nearly so, the following article in the *New York World* has come to hand, dated Jan. 1st, 1868:—

Cunard line taken from Boston— —reasons—

East and West—The Port of New York.—Mr. Cunard, in his recent letter to a Boston merchant said :

"During this last autumn, when we have been sending an average of 2500 tons of freight every week, or 10,000 tons per month in our ships from this port, we have been unable to get 500 or 600 tons once a fortnight in Boston at one half of the freight we were getting here, and that was not considered sufficient inducement, as shippers in Boston complain at paying 20s per ton, when we were asking 40s or 50s."

N. Y. chief exporter. Business aggregates.

This is the whole case in a nut-shell, New York has become the great exporting as well as importing port of the Atlantic coast of North America. Our pre-eminence as an exporter is maintained not only by the shipment of merchandise that naturally seeks a market here, but by shipments to us from all directions—from Canada, from the Southern States, from the West Indies, and from Mexico—for the sole purpose of shipments hence to markets with which they have no direct communication. Being so thoroughly established, we apprehend that Boston, as well as other ports which have suffered an eclipse, will find a stern chase a very long and unpromising one.

The foundation of the commercial greatness of New York was laid when the Erie Canal was built. Her progress has been promoted by the neglect of Boston to complete her railroad communications with the West. Having allowed her opportunity to depart from her, Boston must be content to pass into comparative insignificance, to become to New York what Hull or Bristol is to Liverpool. **Erie canal made N. Y.**

The fact that New York maintains almost entirely the foremost position in the tobacco trade, which the late war gave her, is significant of the difficulty of turning trade from its accustomed channels so long as suitable facilities are afforded for its transaction. New Orleans, once pre-eminent as a tobacco market, now ranks as such below Richmond, and the influence of New York in the cotton market is greater than that of New Orleans. **N. Y. tobacco market.** **—N. Orleans**

But New York stands in great need of improving her railroad communications with the Great West. We can no longer depend upon the Erie Canal to bring our supplies of breadstuffs. Heretofore the railroads having a terminus at the seaboard have not attempted to bring much beside flour in barrels. Last spring the Erie road brought us some corn, and is now doing something in that line But the aggregate is far below the requirements of the market or the capacity of the road. It has been demonstrated at Chicago and Milwaukee, what railroads can do in the transportation of grain in bulk. What the Rock Island Railroad, and the Northwestern Railroad can do at Chicago, the Erie Railroad and the Hudson River Railroad can do at New York; and what they can do, they should do at once. The usual amount of shipping could not now find remunerative employment here, because of the deficient supply of western products, with which the West is overflowing. New York has a formidable rival in Baltimore. She drew a good deal of business from us last winter by her supply of corn received by rail. And should the James River be brought in direct connection with the Ohio, Norfolk may assume great importance as a shipping port. **N. Y. needs railroads west.** **Wants corn.** **No freight for ships.** **Balt. a strong rival to N. Y.**

What railroads can do in the transportation of merchandise is demonstrated also by the arrangement to ship cotton to New York from Cairo by rail, [and *via* Chicago] instead of by the usual route of the Mississippi River and the sea. With a close money market, and rapid fluctuations in prices, a few day's gain in time may be of paramount importance to an operator in cotton. We are receiving a few hundred bushels of corn daily from Tennessee over the Hudson River Road. Why not thousands instead of hundreds? **Cotton by rail.**

To return to Boston. The letter to Mr. Cunard details at some length the completion of numerous railroad connections with the West, and the establishment of rates for through freight over them, which promise to be very advantageous to her, although a little too late for the preservation of her steamer communication with Europe, they have already brought many advantages. They have made Boston a great flour market, partly at the expense of New York. In this branch of business we have remained nearly stationary, while Boston has doubled in a few years. The rate of freight from Chicago is but a trifle more than to New York—in fact scarcely more than from New York to Boston; while in storage, insurance, and cost of handling. she has us at a disadvantage. The same is true, to some extent, of the provision trade. The West and New England have been benefited by the system of through freights at the expense of New York, and the fact demands attention. **Boston increasing western lines—** **—advantages over N. Y.**

The admission of the severe competition New York must meet from ports south of her, is judicious. It is folly to shut one's eyes and rest content with narrow superficial views, in this broad land, where estimates of the future, and plans to control the business, should be made upon the same scale of grandeur which laid out the rivers, lakes, prairies, and mountains, with their natural products, mineral and agricultural. By rail, Baltimore always has, and always must have the advantage, for distance gives it. The *Chicago Times*, presents the current rates:— **Competition must be met** **Advantage of Balt.**

Railroad rates.

	2d class	4th class	Flour per bbl.		2d class	4th class	Flour per bbl.
New York.......	$1.50	85	$1.70	Providence.......	$1.60	90	$4.80
Boston..........	1.60	90	1.80	Worcester........	1.60	90	1.80
Philadelphia......	1.40	80	1.60	Cleveland........	61	30	60
Albany..........	1.40	80	1.60	Baltimore........	1.40	80	1.60
Montreal.........	1.54	84	1.68	Cincinnati........	60	30	60
Buffalo..........	80	45	90	Pittsburgh.......	85	45	90

Improvement in railway transportation.

Improvements, too, in railway transportation, will steadily increase the advantage even to Norfolk; and this must be an influential consideration in calculating the future. Had New York only railways, her chances would be slender, for "the foundation of the commercial greatness of New York was laid when the Erie canal was built;" and if her statesmen are wise, they will deepen that solid foundation by deepening and widening her canals, corresponding to the increase of the business of the West. It is indispensable to her; and even with it she will not long control the foreign trade from the West. For we are yet to have another and main outlet for western produce. Far better than more railroad competition, we have an independent route, the powerful regulator of even all these railways, and by which more business is transacted, and will always be transacted, than by all six of the roads, that is—

N. Y. canal— —should be enlarged.

Another route—

—the lakes.

The Lake Route to the East and Europe.

Lake Mich. drew the railways.

Michigan's billowy bosom drew to her all these iron-handed wooers. Because Chicago was the western extremity of this chain of inland seas, which afford ample room for the commerce of the world, and which have such a powerful stretch into the very heart of the continent, and reaching far enough south to supply a port in about the middle of the temperate zone, and in its very richest region,—because it is at the point of natural connection of the Valley of the Great Lakes with the Valley of the Great Rivers,—did Chicago receive her first impetus. As long as the rivers run and the billows roll, must these moving and yet immovable causes be potential in her advancement. The lakes drew hither the railroads, and the railroads abundantly reciprocate, pouring upon their consorts a stream of commerce which has already reached fabulous figures, although the land tributary is yet in the infancy of settlement. Says Mr. Parton in the *Atlantic Monthly:**—

Natural connection of lakes and rivers.

Lakes and railways reciprocate.

Mr. Parton.

Importance of Mr. Parton's articles.

*Mr. Parton's article in the *Atlantic Monthly* for March, 1867, is eminently worthy of consideration, especially in connection with his other articles upon inland cities. That upon Chicago is fair, judicious and moderate, and exhibits such careful investigation of the subject, and accuracy of statement, that no doubt those of the other cities are equally so. They have not been read for lack of time, and have not even been seen, but judging from this, I am fully confident they will confirm this argument. At all events, they bring together a vast amount of information, practical and important, throwing much light upon this subject. It is very necessary for this whole nation to understand whether there be the central city which Chicago is affirmed to be; and our capitalists and wise men should examine carefully such articles as Mr. Parton's. Having no acquaintance with him, the opinion is not given for his benefit, but

In some parts of the country railroads have temporarily diminished the importance of water communication. This is not the case with the Great Lakes, nor with Chicago's lion's share of their commerce. It is but yesterday that Astor's single schooner of forty tons, was the only vessel known to the Chicago River except Indian canoes. Chicago is now more than the Marseilles of our Mediterranean, though Marseilles was a place of note twenty-four hundred years ago. Railroads no injury to lakes or Chicago.

Water and railway carriers, and their engineers, have ardently contended that each was superior to the other. Their mistake lies in not admitting that each has its advantages for some uses, and disadvantages for others. Both are required as neither ever could have been before; for what was ancient commerce compared with modern, and how great and rapid are the changes even in these our years? Only 35 years ago, upon first visiting New York, my father showed me the enormous ship Henry Clay, of some 800 or 900 tons burthen! We are yet only in the infancy of improvements in commercial intercourse; and he who supposes they will be confined to railways, expects a supplanting of Nature's highways, and of their union by canals, in which he will probably be disappointed. The *Buffalo Commercial Advertiser*, a trustworthy authority upon such subjects, remarks:— Railway and water both indispensable. Immense growth of commerce. Water not to be supplanted. *Buff. Com. Adv.*

Railroads are a great boon to the country. An exclusive freight railway, with double tracks, can doubtless do much more than one of mixed passenger and freight traffic; but we think no sane man would for a moment claim that it would have more practical capacity for through traffic than all the five great through railway lines now in operation, and the Erie Canal. There is no method of transportation yet known so cheap as that by water. The average price of lake freights on wheat from Chicago to Buffalo, (distance 1,000 miles,) for the ten years from 1857 to 1867, inclusive, has been only 8 99-100th cents per bushel, which is a fraction less than \$3 per ton. This includes the profit of the carrier, and is three mills per ton per mile. The average cost of freight on wheat from Buffalo to New York, by the Erie Canal and the Hudson River, including State tolls and profit of carrier, has been only 15 55-100th cents per bushel, equal to \$4.62½ per ton, making the average freight per ton, from Chicago to New York, for a period of ten years, \$7.66½. The verified reports of the New York Central Railroad from 1853 to 1859, a period of six years—before we had a depreciated currency—show the actual average cost to that company to be one cent four mills and 49-100ths of a mill per ton per mile. Since that period the cost has been much greater. The distance from New York to Chicago by rail *via* the Hudson River Railroad, New York Central and South Shore Railroads, is 988 miles. At the above average cost of rail transportation per ton per mile on the Central, the cost per ton from Chicago to New York would be \$14.31 6-10ths, or \$6.65 1-10th more per ton than the average cost by the lakes, canal and the Hudson River, including profits of carrier and State tolls. This difference on the present annual eastward through movement of about 5,000,000 tons would make a saving of \$36,580,500, taking the rail freights at actual cost, and with the profits of the railway companies added, more than \$60,000,000 annually. Railways important— —water more so. Cost compared— —with railway. From Chi. to N. Y. Saving by water.

In December last the ship David Crockett arrived at Philadelphia in ninety-four days from San Francisco, with a cargo of wheat on which the freight was fifty-eight cents per bushel. At the same time the tariff rate on wheat from Chicago to Philadelphia by rail, was fifty-one cents per bushel. The ship sailed 17,000 miles, and the rail distance is less than 1,000 miles. This result shows the superior advantage in cheapness of water transportation over that of rail. San Fran. to Phila.

---

for that of the reader. The articles would be largely quoted, were they not so thoroughly digested that they need to be read entire; and the mass of information gathered from various sources, in only these few days, precludes these long articles. The reader misjudges my views and arguments if because Chicago is to be the greatest city, St. Louis, Cincinnati, Pittsburg, Buffalo, Cleveland, Detroit, Milwaukee, St. Paul, Omaha, and Kansas City, etc., are not to be great cities. This Valley of the Mississippi and the Valley of the Lakes, must make many large cities, all of which will be more or less tributary to Chicago, for she is their centre. We therefore would not decry other cities, while giving Chicago its due prominence Need to know if Chicago be central. Other cities also to grow.

Vessels large.

The vessels now being built for the grain trade on the lakes are nearly all of large class, carrying from 40,000 to 88,000 bushels of grain. It was only last week that one of our large-class lake steamers arrived at this port from Chicago with a cargo of 8,000 bushels of grain and 300 barrels of flour. These large-class vessels will soon take the place of the smaller ones now in use, when the lake freight will be diminished. The enlargement of the locks on the Erie Canal to a capacity to pass boats of six hundred tons, in connection with the large-class vessels on the lakes, would diminish the cost of transportation from Chicago to New York to an average of about $5 per ton! This would save to the producer and consumer $100,000.000 annually, in the item of transportation alone, being the difference between cost of water and all-rail transportation.

Canal enlargement.

Water carriage never to be superseded.

These facts should convince every reflecting mind that a large bulk of the commodities moving from the interior to the seaboard market will for all time to come go by the great chain of lakes and inland river in connection with artificial channels; and it should also satisfy every one that the canals will have a longer day in the future than in the past, and that water transportation can never be superseded by that of rail for heavy commodities.

Lake trade.

To give some idea of the business already done by the lakes, the following statements are compiled from the Board of Trade reports of—

Shipments of Chief Articles from Chicago by Lake for 6 years.

Shipments, 1862–'67.

Articles.	1862.	1863.	1864.	1665.	1866.	1867.
Wheat, bushels...	13,466,325	10,646,052	9,983,567	6,502,575	5,827,846	8,490,187
Corn, " ...	30,345,425	24,749,400	11,993,475	24,321,600	31,257,855	19,940,172
Barley, " ...	341,450	617,595	173,425	114,300	988,240	2,171,176
Oats, " ...	2,470,745	5,696,875	12,098,000	8,719,900	7,395,113	9,745,205
Rye, " ...	849,650	572,850	774,950	780,500	1,029,629	863,318
Flour, barrels.....	1,146,118	1,207,343	1,034,793	646,356	481,491	630,367
Beef, "	22,345	80,613	91,131	24,874	12,923	30,892
Pork, "	111,892	202,630	106,835	60,852	26,661	35,337
Green Hides, No.	60,649	75,992	186,066	129,338	63,839	86,452
Dry Hides, "	....	....	....	50,017	31,918	7,798

Receipts of Chief Articles at Chicago by Lake for 6 years.

Receipts, 1862–'67.

Articles.	1861.	1862.	1863.	1864.	1865.	1866.	1867.
Lumber, m ft.....	235,668	295,270	392,800	479,235	614,020	676,236	807,635
Shingles, m.......	79,296	131,255	152,435	131,320	193,230	197,169	234,818
Lath, m..........	32,567	23,880	41,665	63,795	62,555	118,405	145,615
Coal, tons.........	168,879	195,099	244,624	251,038	288,771	378,731	390,438
Hardware, pkgs..	....	....	....	102,162	188,904	196,693	157,653
Nails, kegs.......	....	....	100,241	49,426	21,766	30,642	53,441
Fish, bbls........	....	....	56,729	85,611	94,809	101,206	86,741
Salt, bbls.........	390,475	604,916	775,057	675,649	609,884	493,409	460,943
Salt, bags.........	....	278,789	179,182	30,404	133,923	2,381	15,006
Salt, tons.........	....	13,047	7,017	782	5,558	2,915	2,236

Figures not realized.

Of such figures we get very inadequate conceptions in a table. What number of railroads would be requisite to bring in *eight hundred and seven millions, six hundred and thirty-five thousand feet of lumber;* and shingles, lath, timber, etc., to match? Of grain, too, the dependence for transit east, corn especially, is mainly on the lakes. Of wheat, against above figures, the railways carried in 1866, 4,218,599 bu.; and of corn, 1,570,120 bu. Their accounts being made up for the Board of Trade to March 31, statements for 1867,

Railway amounts.

—'68, are not yet to be had. To do this business, the Chicago *Tribune* presents the following statements of—

Arrivals and Tonnage of Vessels and Steamboats at Chicago for 6 *years.*

Tonnage arrived 1862–'67.

Years...	Am. vessels from Am. ports. Vessels.	Tonnage	Am. vessels fr. foreign ports. Vessels.	Tonnage	Foreign vessels fr. foreign ports. Vessels.	Tonnage	Aggregate of arrivals. Vessels.	Tonnage
1862....	6,805	1,697,688	393	169,358	319	61,646	7,417	1,931,692
1863....	8,215	1,988,680	255	116,346	228	67,585	8,678	2,172,611
1864....	8,611	2,021,418	187	104,626	140	46,822	8,938	2,172,866
1865....	9,743	1,934,674	185	103,172	184	69,013	10,112	2,106,859
1866....	10,767	2,116,511	102	77,049	215	64,967	11,084	2,258,527
1867....	12,074	2,544,416	46	14,887	110	29,269	12,283	2,588,572

That table gives the totals of arrivals and tonnage arrived. The following presents the—

Number of Lake Vessels and Tonnage engaged in Chicago trade for 10 *years.*

No. vessels arrived 1858–'67.

Years.	No. vessels.	Tonnage.	Years.	No. vessels.	Tonnage.
1858............	1,548	400,301	1863..........	1,869	470,034
1859............	1,511	392,783	1864..........	648	202,304
1860............	1,576	391,220	1865..........	964	228,215
1861............	1,585	389,611	1866..........	997	51,077
1862............	1,730	454,893	1867..........	1,096	69,981

Hon. W. B. Scates, Collector of the Port gives this statement of—

Number, Classes and Owners of Vessels entered in the Port of Chicago during 1867.

Class of vessels arrived 1867.

Class of vessels.	Owned in Chicago. No.	Ton'age	Owned in other distri'ts of the U. S. No.	Ton'age	Foreign vessels. No.	Ton'age	Aggregate. No.	Tonnage.
Steamers..	8	3,181	2	2,190	....	....	10	5,371
Propellers............	13	6,020	74	51,052	8	2,859	95	59,931
Tugs	33	977	14	910	....	....	47	1,887
Barks................	41	13,899	90	28,155	26	8,308	157	50,362
Barges...............	4	1,934	1	314	....	....	5	2,248
Brigs	15	3,500	21	5,504	2	574	38	9,578
Schooners	257	43,908	395	85,648	22	5,350	674	134,906
Scows................	37	2,934	31	2,748	...	....	68	5,682
Sloops	2	16	....	....	....	....	2	16
Canal boats..........	227	19,784	....	....	....	....	227	19,784
Total............	637	96,153	628	176,521	58	17,091	1323	289,765

Space could be profitably occupied with extracts from reports of the Topographical Bureau to Congress, relative to harbor improvements, which are prepared with great care, and should be well studied to obtain adequate conception of the commerce of these inland seas. But this document is swelling to undue proportions, and very much material important to the subject must be omitted.

Reports of Top. Bureau valuable.

Lake commerce exceeds foreign

Even before our war, the lake commerce largely exceeded in value the total of foreign. Nor is that foreign commerce to be restricted to the seaboard. Direct trade with Europe, already begun from the lakes in a small way, will assume giant proportions when vessels can pass of 1,000 to 1,500 tons. With propellers of that size, exporting and importing between all foreign countries and the lakes will be profitable. Nor will the requisite improvements of the St. Lawrence be long delayed; for Great Britain has too direct and important an interest in promoting intercourse with the West, which consumes so largely of her productions, and will pay her with the cheapest food she can buy. Severance from the chief provision and grain market of the world, the port she most wants to reach advantageously, will not long be continued. Nor will the United States much longer delay the construction of the canal around Niagara Falls.

Ocean trade to be immense.

St. Lawrence to be improved.

U. S. Canal at Niagara.

Distance shortened in Canada.

Distance too, is to be shortened by a steamboat canal from Georgian Bay to Lake Simcoe and Lake Ontario, saving some 500 miles around through Lake Erie. The Ottawa River also is to be improved, shortening still more. A Canadian, who has the latter in charge, informed me last winter, at Boston, that the capital was provided and that the improvement would at once be prosecuted. Whatever lack of capital there may be, New England, especially Boston, will supply. Had she these improved connections with the West, the Cunard line would not have been lost for want of flour and grain.

Boston interested.

Propellers superseding sails.

Propellers also are rapidly superseding sail vessels; and when the simple invention shall be made, as it will be, to save caloric for steam, instead of wasting the larger half of it by the draft from furnace to atmosphere, the saving, not only in cost of fuel, but in storage room for freight, will be very great. But with present machinery, when propellers of 1,000 to 1,500 tons can load at Chicago, and carry to Europe for a trifle more than from New York, saving at least three-fourths of the cost to the latter—a project which the interests of Europe and America combine to accomplish—how long will New York hold the position she now does as the exporter of produce and the importer for the Mississippi and Lake Valleys?

Shipments from Chi. to Europe direct.

Conjunction of rivers and lakes.

The main currents of business, especially of the cereal producing States, are West to East. For this the lakes and rivers are chiefly valuable, and for this they are to be used conjointly. Their natural and artificial point of conjunction is Chicago. What this city wants is precisely what the country about her wants,—that lakes and rivers should be able to counteract the monopolizing tendency of railways. These soulless corporations, left to themselves, would combine to the oppression of the public. It would, therefore, be desirable for both city and country, that the rivers should be equal to the lakes; for the Great West demands every possible facility for its transactions.

City's and country's interest identical.

Yet with no disparagement to the immense highways with which Nature's GOD has blessed the West, and which are to be one of the strongest means of its development and progress, their use in the main is evidently to be in conjunction with railways bringing to them grain from the interior, to be borne by river and canal to the lakes. Rivers to be used with railways.

And who can estimate the extent of that commerce which the Father of Waters and its tributaries will hither bear? His feet planted in the Gulf of Mexico, his head reaching far into the North, —though not quite above these lakes,—his right arm taking hold of the Alleghanies, his left of the Rocky Mountains; what will be the limits of the agricultural products which he is annually to bear onward to their markets? When these millions upon millions of acres in the Mississippi Valley, which the plow has never touched, shall yield their abundant crops, what three points will receive as much as that one with which he most easily connects upon the lakes?* River commerce immense. Chiefly to the lake port.

*Since the above was in type, the report of Maj. Gen. J. H. Wilson, and Mr. William Gooding, Civil Engineer, of a survey pursuant to a law of Congress "to prepare plans and estimates for a system of navigation, by way of the Illinois River, between the Mississippi and Lake Michigan, adapted to military, naval, and commercial purposes," has come to hand. By a thorough examination by three surveying parties of the Kankakee, Illinois and Des Plaines, and Fox River routes,— Govt. report upon enlarging canal.

"The question of a connection through this channel with Lake Michigan, for an improvement of large capacity, has been definitely settled. * * * Question settled.

"No fact can be better established than that the system of navigation between the Mississippi and Lake Michigan, by the way of the Illinois River, should be adapted to the steamboats and barges employed in the navigation of the Mississippi and its principal tributaries, and not to ocean and lake vessels, except such as are required for the defence of our lake commerce and cities. In other words, the produce of the West, on its way to Eastern markets, must be transferred to a different class of vessels as soon as it reaches the lakes; and hence, in determining the dimensions of the canal, it will be amply sufficient for all practicable purposes to arrange it for the navigation of the largest class of river steamboats. * * * Canal to suit river boats. Transfer at Chicago.

"For a canal and river improvement of a capacity sufficient to pass such gunboats as required, and river steamers of 800 to 1,000 tons burden, from the Mississippi to Lake Michigan, no other route, in our judgment, can be compared with that by the Illinois River, and the Illinois and Michigan Canal. It follows the course of what was unquestionably once the great outlet of the lakes toward the Gulf of Mexico, and through which it is only now practicable to again turn their waters in that direction. On all other routes proposed there is a considerable ascent from the lakes to the summit, involving the necessity of an additional amount of lockage, and of providing an additional amount of water from sources much less reliable than that inexhaustible reservoir, Lake Michigan. This route best— —the old natural connection—

"The Desplaines River rises in the State of Wisconsin, and runs nearly due south parallel with the lake shore, and generally not more than eight or ten miles from it, until it reaches a point about thirteen miles, in a southwest direction, from the mouth of Chicago River. Here is a slight depression, a mile or more in width, extending across from the Desplaines to the South Branch of Chicago River, through which a part of the waters of the former river, in time of floods, flows into the lake. In this depression is what was once known as Portage Lake (as designated on the old maps of the country), but now better known as Mud Lake, a succession of shallow ponds on the same level, connected with each other and with the Desplaines River, and extending about six miles towards Chicago River. This was the portage, or carrying place, between the waters of the lakes and the Mississippi made memorable by the early French voyageurs, and so well known to fur traders. But Portage, or Mud Lake, has ceased to exist, the shallow ponds having been drained, and the impassable swamps rendered valuable land. —water channel thro' from lake to river— —used by French voyageurs.

"There can be no doubt that through this depression there was once an outlet from the lakes to the Mississippi, which was closed by the recession of the waters of the lakes. Even now, at the present stage of Lake Michigan, its surface is only between eight and nine feet below this summit. The Desplaines River, from the depression described, changes its course and runs in nearly a southwest direction until it forms a junction with the Kankakee. The river itself, except in floods, is very shallow, Ancient outlet of the lakes.

Rivers not detracted.

Therefore we have no occasion to detract from the importance of the rivers. Yet while they, with their canals, must bring to this port untold amounts of all the chief staples, the railways will doubtless bring as much more. So that it becomes an important truth in considering whether the Queen City of the West is to be upon lake or river, that while lake navigation has this positive certainty of increase, that of the rivers relatively deteriorates. Not that commerce is to forsake them, especially down the streams. It is to be im-

Relatively deteriorate—

---

being often reduced in dry seasons to a mere brook, discharging less than 1,000 cubic feet of water per minute. But the valley averages a mile wide, and is terminated on both sides by well marked terraces which become higher and higher as they approach the Illinois.

"Evidence at every step presents itself that the water, when this was the great outlet of the lakes, extended from bluff to bluff. * * *

7 feet depth required.

"It has been asserted that it is unnecessary to provide for a navigable depth of seven feet in the Illinois River, when the Mississippi River itself below the mouth of the Illinois, has at times a less depth than this. We have fully considered this objection, urged mainly against the improvement by locks and dams, and for the following reasons think it should be disregarded:

1. Miss. has it.

"1. There is usually but a short period during the season of navigation when there is not a depth of water of six or seven feet in the Mississippi below the mouth of the Illinois, and frequently the Mississippi, being high from melting snows about its source, or that of the Missouri, affords good navigation for the largest boats when the Illinois is scarcely navigable at all.

2. Miss. to be improved.

"2. We entertain no doubt that the depth of water in the Mississippi, from the mouth of the Illinois to that of the Ohio, can be materially increased during the dry season by a judicious system of improvement. The interests of commerce and navigation now require and must necessarily compel the commencement of such an improvement before the lapse of many years.

Military necessities—

"3. It is manifestly necessary to secure a depth of at least seven feet, which shall be *always available*, if this artificial navigation should ever be required for "military and naval purposes," and we deem it sound policy to secure this depth of water for commercial purposes, if it can be done without a disproportionate increase of cost. It is a well-known fact that vessels of every class are propelled at much greater speed and economy in deep, than is possible in shallow water.

—commercial.

4. 7 ft. cost but little more than 4 ft.

"4. The depth of seven feet through three hundred and twenty-two miles of navigation, traversing one of the most productive countries in the world, can be secured beyond any contingency by the plan proposed, at a cost slightly, if any, in excess of what it must cost to make an open channel navigation only four feet deep. When it is considered that it is by no means certain that the latter is practicable at any cost, and that the former would be at least three times as valuable for all purposes, there remains but little room to doubt which plan should be adopted. * * *

Adaptation of Ills. river to the work—

"There is probably no river in the United States of a length equal to the Illinois from La Salle to its mouth—222 miles—which would have its width and current so little affected by a succession of dams which would deepen the water for the whole distance on this river. The aggregate fall is only 28 62-100 feet, or an average of about one and a half inches to the mile. The river is, in fact, a natural canal, but the depth of the water is not quite sufficient for a good navigation without checking the current by placing barriers across it. These barriers or dams will not make dead-water anywhere in the channel of the river, but merely diminish the velocity of the current, and that to such a moderate extent as to be hardly perceptible to the casual observer. * * *

—a natural canal.

Canal to Rock Island.

"*Canal Connecting Rock and Illinois Rivers.*—The importance of the improvement which we have surveyed and estimated is greatly enhanced by the fact that surveys have demonstrated the entire practicability of a canal from the Illinois River at or near the mouth of the Bureau, to the Mississippi at or near Rock Island. The length of the canal would be about sixty-four miles, and it would be supplied with water by a navigable feeder, thirty-eight miles in length, from Rock River at Dixon. For a canal sixty feet wide and six feet deep, the cost together with that of the feeder, has been estimated at $4,600,000, and it would probably exceed that sum, whilst it would secure a cheap and direct navigation to the lakes, and a choice of markets to all the country drained by the Upper Mississippi and its tributaries."

Cost $4,600,000.

Choice of market.

Former views confirmed.

The above exhibits with due authority the point urged, that this is the natural route to connect lake and river navigation. The cost to pass vessels of seven feet draft and of 1,000 tons is estimated at $18,217,242. When we consider the importance of such a communication between the lakes and gulf in the event of a foreign war, and the advantages to commerce in time of peace, who can doubt that ere long the work will be done, together with the canal to Rock Island? And as the Engineers observe, the river and canal boats will not navigate the lakes. There must be transhipment at Chicago. And when a like improvement shall be made to the ocean, who can estimate the commerce at this junction of mighty rivers and great lakes, and long railways!

Results.

mensely greater than anything now known; and only relatively will they diminish, because that of the railways must be so multiplied by part of the agricultural products and by most of the other trade. Easily and cheaply can steamers tow down barges laden with the bulky, heavy articles of agriculture. Some barges go to the extreme South, for ere long the old system of cotton and sugar raising will be restored, without slavery, and the Upper Mississippi States will supply them with food. Some also goes there for export, and the more thus marketed the better for Chicago; for it will be to the gain of the farmers upon whose prosperity her own is securely based. The freights thus lost will hardly be missed by her in the vastly greater amount of produce borne to her by the barges. From the Upper Mississippi they will come down to the canal that *will be constructed* at Rock Island, and thence to the lakes. Till then they will go, with others from the Missouri, to the Illinois River, and thence to Chicago. As we shall see, this has been and must continue to be the course of trade. So that we have no occasion for jealousy of river commerce. Chicago depends not upon mere carrying or transhipment, whether more or less. She must always have far more of this than any several other cities. Yet, valuable as it is, her main dependence is upon the general business of the Great West. Therefore, as she has always done, she will seek to make the greatest possible saving to the farmer in the cost of transit; and when any other better outlet can be found for a part, she will profit with the farmers in its employment. Queen of these fresh water seas, as well as of these western railways, and her traffic sought by thousands of miles of river navigation, the whole country, east and west, must for its own convenience pay her tribute. Nor needs she more than a little pittance; for while fulfilling her commissions at a charge which a city less employed could not afford, she will have princely revenues.

—business still immense.
Course of trade.
Some goes south—
—to benefit Chicago.
Upper Miss. to Rock Island.
Mo. via Ills. river.
Chicago depends not on mere carriage—
—interest with farmers.
Small commission makes her rich.

It cannot be denied, that there is no one spot upon which a far-sighted man, who could have anticipated railway progress, would have so centred his calculations as upon Chicago. He must have anticipated that at the end of a thousand miles of lake navigation, especially bending off so far to the south, and into the heart of such a country, the railroads must there converge. What he should have foreseen, at all events is what is actually realized. There is no such position on the globe, uniting railway and water communication; nor can there be another. Many places can now be named which are certain to become large cities; but who expects any one of them to equal Chicago? And here we come to consider—

Her advantages foreseen.
—expectations realized—
—no city equal.

The Difference between Chicago and other Western Centres.

That there is a difference is very apparent. Chicago's growth is observed throughout the world. Ten years since, April 27, 1857, the English *Mark Lane Express*, in a long editorial, remarked:—

Mark Lane Exp., 1857.

First called Eng. attention to Chi.

We must take the credit of being the first paper in this country that brought the vast capabilities of the port of Chicago as a grain depot, before the notice of our merchants. We have had for the last five years an intelligent and influential shipper as our correspondent there, who has periodically—indeed, with almost every mail—sent us a market note from that city. In the month of January, 1855, he forwarded a communication in which he gave proofs that went far towards establishing his opinion, that "Chicago was the greatest grain port in the world." On the 29th last September we announced the arrival at Liverpool, of the "Dean Richmond," a vessel of 387 tons burden, direct from Chicago and Milwaukee, through the Welland Canal, which, were it but enlarged to the requirements of the trade between that city and this country, would go far towards enriching the merchants and shippers of that locality. The Welland Canal is the passage from Lake Erie to Lake Ontario, and thence into the St. Lawrence the navigation to the Pacific Ocean is free.

First vessel from Chi. to Eng., 1856.

Welland canal to be enlarged.

Trade requires it.

That such improvement must be ultimately effected in that canal from the result of the trade springing up in the prairie city of Chicago is as clear a deduction as facts and figures can give us. Ten [?] years ago there were not ten thousand people in the whole territory of Illinois. Twenty years since Chicago was a small village at the southern end of Lake Michigan, where at night the howl of the prairie wolf might be heard from all parts of its dwellings. In 1857 it is a city of more than one hundred thousand inhabitants. Then, the little village that bore the germ of a large city in its bosom, imported her beef, her butter and her flour, although growing corn more than enough for her wants. Now, the city though only budding into life, gives forth for exportation twenty million bushels of grain; while her beef, in the markets of the world can compare in weight, and bears in price as high a value as that of any other nation. At the former period railways were unheard of, and even five years since there was but one (about forty miles in length) connected with the town. In 1857, ten trunks and a great number of branch lines, counting more than three thousand miles of railway are centred in that vast grain emporium. Who then can pronounce the extent to which such a city may spread? The agricultural resources of the country in connection with it are exhaustless and wonderful; the climate is well suited to our hardy Saxon race; its mineral deposits of lead, iron, copper, and coal are reputed to be unsurpassed in richness and extent, and all are well qualified to call forth the energies of an enterprising and greatly increasing population. If, then, we look at the advance made by the city of Chicago in twenty years, it shows clearly the immense progression which is going on in the Western World.

Rapid growth of Chicago.

Large exports.

Railways increased.

Resources exhaustless.

Commerce marvellous in 1856.

Our correspondent has now forwarded us a review of the commerce of Chicago for the year 1856, but its great length precludes the possibility of its insertion. Yet so marvellous is its history, that we cannot pass it over in silence. * *

Mr. Parton.

Mr. Parton thus opens his paper upon Chicago in the *Atlantic Monthly*:—

Mr. Cobden's opinion of Niagara and Chicago.

When Professor Goldwin Smith was preparing for his voyage to America, Mr. Richard Cobden said to him, "See two things in the United States, if nothing else,—Niagara and Chicago." Professor Smith acted upon this advice, and, while visiting Chicago, acknowledged that the two objects named by his friend were indeed the wonders of North America.

Volumes could be filled with similar views already published.*

Mr. C. F. Adams in *North Am. Review.*

Boston satisfied in Chi.

*The most philosophical view of the past—equal to that of Mr. Scott, of the future, in *Hunt's Merchant's Magazine*,—has appeared since these pages were mostly in type, in the January number of the *North American*, signed Charles Francis Adams, Jr., headed "Boston," and comparing it with Chicago. But Boston may and should have much satisfaction in the results which its capital and efforts have wrought at Chicago. They should now profit themselves more directly by facilitating intercourse with the great centre of the West, which they have so largely aided to establish, and invest some of their surplus capital here in real estate and in manufactures.

Nor can any one say when they will cease, for wonder will increase instead of diminishing, that less than 5,000 population in 1840 should in 1880 require seven figures for its enumeration. Nor shall we doubt this as we study the causes operating in the past, and ascertain the certainty of their multiplying power in the future.

Change of figures in 30 years to 1880.

No doubt.

Nor is the difference perceptible only to disinterested foreign observers; for the most powerful rivals are conscious of the irresistible influences working against them. The direct admissions of the solid men of St. Louis against themselves, of which we have had some specimens, cannot be countervailed. At a meeting of the Board of Trade, held on the 1st of November last, at which the *Democrat* says "there was a good attendance of the solid business men of the city," Mr. Fagin spoke, and with more honesty than wisdom, presented points of difference so fairly that the whole is quoted, together with responsible endorsement:—

Parties near and remote see causes.

St. Louis' solid men.

Mr. Fagin's speech.

Mr. Fagin said there were gentlemen present much more competent to discuss this matter than himself, but he was prepared to say that it was a matter of vital importance to St. Louis that such a measure should be adopted. He felt it was one of the most important subjects that had come before the City Council in the history of St. Louis. I look (continued Mr. Fagin) on the commerce of St. Louis as being in a languishing condition—perishing for the want of a more vigorous prosecution of the railroad system which will connect us with the great Northwestern country. Really, in regard to this matter, I have seen nothing of very late occurrence that has struck my mind so forcibly as being of so much importance to St. Louis as the condemnation of the North wharf—connected as it is with the extension of the North Missouri railroad and the erection of elevators. I am not in the habit, as this community know, of making public speeches in reference to these matters. I can only say that I am interested, in common with every man in St. Louis, in seeing the commerce of St. Louis increased. I know very well that from the want of more intimate relations and the completion of a railroad system west of the Mississippi, our trade has decreased for years.

North wharf improvement important.

Commerce languishes—

—connect with N. W.

Condemn wharf.

Trade decreasing for want of rail ways.

Fifteen years ago most of the cereals of the Mississippi Valley were shipped to this point, and the receipts were vastly larger than they are now, and unless we immediately connect with the northwestern country by means of the North Missouri railroad, this trade will be permanently diverted from us. I look upon that road as being more vitally important to the immediate prosperity of St. Louis than any other railroad. By the extension of that road we are put in connection with a highly cultivated country. By the extension of this road into Iowa we connect, as you are aware, with every road running from Chicago to the west, and it is vitally important that we connect with those roads, with a view of drawing the trade in this direction, and at the same time inaugurate a system of railroads on this side of the river, which will make us independent of the railroad system on the east side of the Mississippi. It is of vital importance to St. Louis that this connection be made at the earliest day. The money expended on the eastern side of the river was not expended to promote the interests of St. Louis, but rather to detract trade from St. Louis, as may be seen by an examination into the tariff rates from the East to the West.

Grain trade lost.

North Mo. road of chief importance.

Connect with Chi. roads.

Roads west of Miss. benefit St. Louis—

—east side injure her.

Chicago has decidedly the advantage in this matter of discrimination because of her railroad influence. Groceries, and such articles, demanded by the Western country, can be brought to Chicago, and sold and delivered over local roads, at a less rate than you can bring them here.

Chi. advantages in railway influence.

Unless we awake to a realizing sense of our position, we shall very soon be entirely circumvented by these railroads running in the interest of Chicago, and we shall have but a very small portion of country tributary to St. Louis. We are now inaugurating a state of things, which, if properly carried out, will result to our benefit—such as the bridge across the river, the improvement of the rapids, etc. But these enterprises must be vigorously prosecuted. Some of you gentlemen will perhaps remember the condition of Louisville many years ago, when she came to a dead stand-still; and you must remember that a pause in the progress of a city like

Chi. circumvents her.

St. L.'s plans to recuperate.

Pause fatal to St. L.

St. Louis is almost fatal. In twenty-five years of time untold millions may be diverted, which it will be impossible to recover. We must either move onwards or decline. If you are prepared to see St. Louis decline, and the trade of St. Louis languish, the sooner you make it known the better, so that some of us can take care of ourselves. Twenty-five years ago Louisville was in a condition similar to St. Louis to-day. She had magnificent ideas about her resources, but by the aid of the river alone she has failed to prosper. As soon, however, as she went to work and instituted an artificial system of communication by means of railroads, she became a prosperous city. We have sat here year after year waiting for the Mississippi to float the wealth of this valley to our doors. It is useless to wait longer.

Men to take care of themselves.

Wait no longer for Miss. river.

You must remember that Eastern capital, combined with Chicago enterprise, is stretching railroads across the country, bridging the river at various points, and drawing the trade from us.

East. capital helps Chi.

With the immediate extension of the North Missouri railroad, and the pushing of the Iron Mountain railroad, we have faith to believe that the interests of this city may be materially advanced.

2 railways to help St. L.

I am interested in the prosperity of St. Louis. I take great pride in being a citizen of St. Louis, and I desire her future welfare, but I cannot conceal the fact that we are on the decline.

Pride in St. Louis.

Our receipts of grain to-day do not exceed three million bushels. Fifteen years ago they were eight millions. You cannot expect to sell goods, gentlemen, unless you furnish the means of bringing produce to this city. I insist that this measure now before the Common Council is of more importance to St. Louis than anything that has been before them for twenty years. If they fail to confirm the award of the jury in the condemnation of the North wharf, the completion of the North Missouri railroad will be of no practical benefit. It will hardly come within five miles of the required point, and you cannot afford to dray produce that distance. We have expended a large amount of money in the erection of an elevator, so that we can compete with Chicago in handling grain by sacks. The old system of handling grain is fatal to the trade—at least fifteen to twenty cents against this town. Every day that we go on 'Change we tip our hats to Chicago. "What is the price of grain in Chicago to-day?" If we do not get ten cents more here we do not get the full value.

Receipts of grain 3,000,000—

—15 years ago 8 000,000

Wharf most important thing of 20 years.

One elevator! to compete with Chicago.

Tip hats to Chicago.

I feel that I am not competent to discuss this subject properly, and I would prefer to leave it with gentlemen who are more conversant with it. I say there is a necessity for St. Louis to do something. If you do not, rely upon it that trade will be taken away from you which will not be regained in twenty-five years.

St. L. to do something—

—not regain in 25 years.

Hon. Erastus Wells, of the City Council, was next called upon. He said:

Mr. President: Being the only member of the Council present, it is proper that I should rise to say a few words.

I indorse pretty much all the gentleman has said. I can appreciate somewhat the zeal which he manifests on a subject of this character, a matter in which the people of St. Louis should feel a deep interest. * * * *

Hon. Erastus Wells endorses speech.

The difference between the cities is truly considerable, both as to what each had and has. St. Louis had wealth, as all these writers acknowledge; Chicago was poor, dependent wholly upon capital from abroad. St. Louis had the entire business west of the Mississippi, and most of it east. Thousands of miles of river navigation paid her tribute; Chicago had only the lakes and her canal. But the business that was hers, is now Chicago's; and our railroads and lakes are proved far more powerful than her rivers. Though yet small in capital compared with that wealthy city, profits are fast accumulating upon the trade taken from her; and confidence in the position, makes our credit fully equal to St. Louis' cash. Under these circumstances it might be expected of keen St. Louisians to examine causes, and another writer in the *Democrat* of Nov. 29th, (the article referred to is quoted p. 82,) prosecutes the investigation:—

Former advantages of St. Louis—

—present of Chicago.

Inquiry as to causes in *Mo. Dem.*

The Needs of St. Louis.—An article in your issue of the 23d instant, headed "What St. Louis Has, What She has Lost, and What She Needs," has attracted my attention, as it must the attention of all who have the interest of the city at heart; and while I agree with the writer in many things he has stated, I believe he has not touched the main causes which have led to the general depression now so universally felt, so little understood and so seldom discussed by the people; and with your permission I will proceed to state what I believe to be some of the principal causes that underlie our present troubles.

Needs of St. Louis—

—to know cause of depression.

The natural and geographical advantages of St, Louis are not disputed. That her commercial prosperity largely depends upon the completion of the great trunk and branch roads is admitted; that energy and a more liberal enterprise are demanded of our merchants and business men will not be denied; that greater inducements should be offered to capital is apparent to the most casual observer.

Natural advantages.

What she wants.

How stand those great auxiliaries of prosperity to-day? Is it not true that the greatest enterprises connected with the commercial and manufacturing interests of our city go begging to the world—offering bonds, the best secured in the country, at a ruinous depreciation, and find it difficult even then to negotiate? There is a cause for this? What is it?

Why causes not effective.

It will not suffice to say that Chicago or Cincinnati has outrun us in the race of progress. True, those cities have shown more energy and enterprise—the former in her great system of railroads and commercial facilities, offering every inducement to enterprise and capital, and the latter in fostering and developing her great manufacturing interests. It will not suffice to say that the State has not been liberal, even to extravagance, in her aid to public improvements; nor to say that many of our citizens have not been earnestly alive and devoted to those great measures. They have been, but with what result? On their part, disappointed hopes and broken fortunes. Look around among those liberal-minded men who for years have devoted their talent, energy and capital to public improvements, and is it not a fact that most of them have been made beggars? Is it not true that many of the most enterprising men, during the last ten years, have left St. Louis to find homes elsewhere, and is it not painfully true that while nature has surrounded us with every facility of becoming the great manufacturing city of the country, capital and genius in that line shun our city and seek investment elsewhere? The facts stated here cannot be denied. Why do they exist? What is the remedy? I know that in the points I now touch, there are many opinions worthy of consideration. * * *

Chicago and Cin. more energy.

State liberal

Still bad results.

Men, beggars and leaving.

What the cause and remedy.

The causes are "a short-sighted city government;" neglect to "improve our river navigation;" "the wharf to be opened, straightened and improved immediately;" "steamboats to be relieved from State and County tax;" "high rents and high taxation"—why, that is exactly our difficulty;—"a lot of old fogies and speculators;" and others similar. Very possibly these are influential reasons why St. Louis does not progress, for they would hardly be iterated and reiterated as they are, did they not exist. Still, would the removal of the whole of them, or even attaching the entire category to Chicago, restore the broken equilibrium, and St. Louis' supremacy? The desperate condition of the case is evident from the free use of such palliatives to soothe the patient in his rapid decline.

Summary of causes.

Would their removal save St. L.

Time was when we, too, were very sensitive, although not in a decline, and so little understood the power of our position upon Lake Michigan, that we were jealous of connection with eastern roads near to us. I recollect berating Mr. Schuyler, President of the Illinois Central, for his project of deflecting that road, to connect with the Michigan Central, fearing it would take through business to the east south of us; and St. Louis counted upon another connection of the same sort, as a means of weakening us to her benefit. For I

Chi. formerly sensitive—

—feared cut-off.

St. Louis Int., 1853. happen to have a *St. Louis Intelligencer*, Oct. 18th, 1853, which says:—

Alton railroad finished— *Still Faster—The Northern Route.*—We were surprised last evening to receive the Chicago papers of the day before. The Alton *Telegraph* explains the phenomenon by saying: "The cars are now, we understand, running to within five miles of Bloomington. In the course of the present week this remaining gap will be closed, and the cars from this city connect immediately with those of the Central Road to La Salle."

—also, "Joliet cut-off." The *Telegraph* goes on to add some comforting words to Chicago, as follows: "The link between Joliet and Wilmington will likewise be in running order in a few days. This will leave only the line from Wilmington to Bloomington to be laid, to give us an air line road to the Joliet "cut off." When the Joliet and Laporte Road is finished, which will speedily be, passengers will be put through to the East, without being compelled to go round by Chicago."

No matter now. The centripetal power of commerce was too little appreciated. Who now hears of the "Joliet cut-off?" I know not whether its trains still run, and it is not of the slightest consequence if they do.

In all our vicissitudes and encounters, however, Chicago has always been true to her interests, and the *Pittsburgh Commercial* kindly observes:— *Pitts. Com.*

Chi. prospers on account of unanimity— The prosperity of Chicago is mainly due to the fact that her citizens, recognizing the advantages she possesses, steadily act on the determination that she shall enjoy the full benefit of them. Such public spirit would make almost any place grow and prosper. Place another community there, and Chicago would be a different city. They believe in themselves, strike out boldly—and win. We wish we might have some of their spirit in Pittsburgh, which has as many advantages —but of another kind—as Chicago. We have more wealth, and, consolidated, a population nearly as large. Chicago permits nobody to run around her, but, stretching out a long and strong arm, clutches the trade and commerce of vast regions. Hence we hear St. Louis expressing dissatisfaction and alarm at the loss of trade it has heretofore shared. Though not a bright example in every respect, Chicago certainly is in this. —stretches out long arms. St. Louis complains.

Chicago united— The unanimity of Chicago has ever been a gratifying, weighty influence in its progress. Though divided by a river and branches at nearly right angles into three sections, which usually generates contention, the several divisions have had no jealousy. That public spirit and energy are distinguishing characteristics, is generally admitted. Yet, as before observed, we have had neither means nor influence to create the works which have wrought their effects. The position rather than character of citizens has made us what we are. If with a different population "Chicago would be a different city;" so, too, ten times the same population elsewhere, could never make a second Chicago. Nor is her progress attributable to any one cause, but to an unexampled combination. Nature and art have conjoined to produce results unparalleled, and that always will be unparalleled, in the growth of cities. Without Lake Michigan, Chicago would not be here; nor would its harbor be used as it is, but that it best accommodates the immense plain between the Alleghanies and the Rocky Mountains, whose vastness is only equaled by its unsurpassed fertility of soil, and its richness in mineral wealth. Then, too, the ease of connecting at this point the rivers and lakes, is another of —but poor. Position favorable. Nature and art conjoin. Lake Mich. essential. Connection of lakes and rivers.

nature's gifts; and the conjunction of these three no other city has or can have.

Of these art would naturally and wisely avail itself. But it happens further in conjunction, that the surplus wealth of the country and the chief commercial city, were interested in drawing the trade and travel of the South and Southwest to Chicago; and this conjoining of interest was so manifest and natural and reasonable, that twenty years ago it was made the main basis of argument, as we have seen, to induce capitalists to do precisely what in their better judgment they have actually done. Art avails of them— —naturally.

Besides, nature having made an end to Lake Michigan, and a little river for a harbor quite near that end, Chicago is there located, having been sought out by the Jesuits two centuries ago. The lake stretching north and south some 350 miles, and Lake Superior nearly as much more, compels the whole country to the west to pay more or less tribute to this port. This is the occasion for the concentration of the numerous railways from the north around to due west. Bridging Lake Michigan has not yet been attempted. So that not like every other city on ocean, river, or chain of lakes, Chicago has no rival, and can have none, for Lake Superior is too far north, and there is no other chain of lakes to have an end. Other lake cities rival each other, and still stronger is the rivalry between river cities. Had steamboats continued in control of the business, St. Louis would doubtless have held her relative position. But with their large supersedure by the car and locomotive, her supremacy vanished, and she has now no advantage over many other river towns above and below her, except wealth and already established influence. These it has been proved are of no account against Chicago, because of her superior focal position for railways; and as they shall be introduced west of the Mississippi, these present advantages will not hold trade against energetic enterprise, and more direct routes to the east, and especially to the lakes. Kansas, at the Big Bend of the Missouri, is a more natural point for converging railroads than St. Louis, and may yet outgrow her. Except that city and Omaha, there are now no prominent places in the West; yet without doubt several will arise as the railway system shall be developed. East of the Mississippi the system will be perfected by numerous short roads; but the chief part of railway building for twenty years will be westward to the Rocky Mountains and over them. And as before shown, it is beyond the power of man to create west of Chicago another railway centre of half—not a quarter—the roads we have and shall have. Should there be such an one, its business will be as in Indianapolis, to trundle cars from one road to another. Lake Mich. makes Chi. Concentrates railways. Chi. has no rival. Other cities rivals. St. L.'s advantages lost. Chi. focal point of railways. Kansas a good site. Railroads west of Mississippi— —but no centre.

The competition and jealousy between a dozen cities to the west will be intense, with nothing of the feeling towards Chicago, for her Rivalry of western cities—

—to reach the lakes.

supremacy will be admitted; and one of the chief objects of ambition among them will be, to create the greatest facilities for reaching the Queen of the Lakes. This is one of the chief advantages of Omaha; and this will in a few years build several other long lines to the northwest and southwest, present lines being insufficient.

Views not overwrought

These views may be thought too strong a draught upon the future to affect the immediate present. Perhaps; yet they are a thousand-fold more certain of realization than were views and arguments offered upon this same subject twenty years ago. Then I had to speak of twenty and fifteen years ahead, because of uncertainty as

Basis, what is realised.

to what Eastern capitalists might do. Now the argument rests upon what they have actually done, and their wisdom in continued action. Are not their profits sufficient to make them follow the same line of investments, where extensions shall yield equal revenues, besides

10 years to prove them.

doubling them on old roads? And now only ten years will be ample to render equally sure present predictions, as twenty have the past. Is that too long a period to consider such important causes affecting real estate investments? Are these considerations chimerical, either, or eminently practical, deeply affecting the subject presented? Are they not fairly deducible from previous considerations? The entire argument may be fallacious, but this additional point, that

Chicago has no rival—

Chicago is without a real rival, will surely prove sound unless the whole is a fraud or misconception. But the question of rivalry is to have immediate consideration. These in general are the *Differences*

—when can have one.

between Chicago and other Western Centres. When this wonderful conjunction of nature and of art can be dissevered, or the equal be found in any other city, a rival to Chicago will arise; not before. Other special advantages will be hereafter considered. In conclud-

Views, 1861.

ing this topic, the summary of 1861 is now still more relevant:—

Other cities central.

It may be said, too much is claimed for Chicago—that railroads all connect together, carrying business through to other points,—that Indianapolis, Columbus, Dayton, Toledo, Cleveland and other cities, are also great railway centres; and that the larger and more powerful cities, Cincinnati and St. Louis, are not only accessible by railroad from all sections equally with Chicago, but are more central in the Union.

The past conclusive.

To this it might be sufficient answer to point to past progress, and claim its sure continuance, which it would be difficult to give sound reasons for doubting. When Chicago was only known as an Indian trading post, each of the above places was a considerable town, but she has passed them all save two, and follows close upon

Present reasons.

them. But good reasons can be given for attainments hitherto, some of which apply more cogently to the future:

A centre of 200 miles.

1st. No one of the above towns has so extensive and rich a country dependent upon it. A circuit of fifty to a hundred miles is the largest area that any other could fairly claim, though most of them do more or less business farther off. But before the day of railroads, farmers for 100 to 200 miles around, came here to sell their produce and obtain supplies, and the business of that whole region, and beyond, is still more effectually centred here by railroads.* No one of the above cities, or any other, has half as large an area so completely identified with it.

Farmers at Chi. in 1843.

*In 1843 or '44, three *Prairie Farmer* friends met in its office, one from Vigo county, Ind., one from Clarke county, Ills., and a third from Scott county, Iowa, describing nearly a third of a circle of some 200 miles radius. After introduction to each other, I told them the gathering correctly indicated the area then naturally tributary to Chicago, and which railroads would in time secure to us.

2d. Being able to control the business of this large region, it is an object for the best men in all departments of industry to locate here; and Chicago has ever had a good name for energy and enterprise. The competition that this creates extends our area, enabling us to draw from other central points that have less dependent territory, and less business facilities; and as we outstrip town after town in the race of progress, we shall compete more and more successfully with our oldest, most powerful rivals, right in their own regions. **Energy of citizens.**

3d. No one of the towns named has half the railroad facilities with the interior possessed by this; and though business does not necessarily stop at the end of one railroad, but can be transferred from car to car and from road to road, yet it is an important advantage to a city, and to all trading with it, to be able to receive and forward in all directions, and hundreds of miles without a change. **Superior railway facilities.**

4th. The canal to the Illinois river unites the lake navigation with that of the whole Mississippi Valley, and by the shortest and best route. **Canal.**

5th. No other city at all equals this in railroad facilities eastward, four [now five] independent and through routes starting from here, creating strong competition. **Roads east.**

6th. Chicago is the western extremity of these inland seas, the navigation of which is far more valuable than the whole railway system eastward—than the thousands of miles of river navigation of the Great Valley. **Head of lakes.**

7th. The conjunction here of all these means of intercommunication — of railroads from the interior — of river and canal navigation — of railroads eastward — of the lakes and St. Lawrence—is much more powerful to concentrate business and build up a city, than can be brought to bear at any other two or three points in the West, and have centered here the produce trade to such a degree, that Chicago is already "the first primary grain exporting city in the world," and most other branches of business naturally follow the channels of produce. **Conjunction of causes— —results.**

8th. In manufacturing, which must be the main reliance for the growth of any city to a large size, no western town excels Chicago in any important respect, and few equal it, and in the chief essentials it far surpasses them all, of which further hereafter. **Manufactures.**

9th. Health—climate—topography—pure water—are all favorable. **Climate, etc.**

Having no considerable point of inferiority that I can discover, as compared with any other western city, these evident and influential causes sufficiently account for the past, and give ample promise of future progress, and some of them will be more elaborated as we proceed. **No inferiority.**

It is not superiority in one respect, however important, or even in several of much consequence, but the largest combination of the most powerful influences, that ensures supremacy in a city. No means of advancement can be named, I think, exceeding in importance any of the above; and because Chicago has not her superior in the West in a single one of them—because she combines them all in an eminent degree, and fully equal to any other two or three western cities united—has she made the unexampled progress of the past, and must make that of the future. **Combination gives superiority.**

It is worthy of remark, that the growth of cities accords with the Bible maxim: "Whosoever hath, to him shall be given, and he shall have more abundance, but from him that hath not shall be taken away even that he hath," or—"seemeth to have." **Bible rule, *Matt.* 13:12. *Luke*, 18:8.**

The latter rendering, from Luke, the more learned and precise writer, is here most applicable: for our rivals have "*seemed* to have" a good deal of business that somehow has been "taken away" and actually "given" to another that has considerable "more abundance." We propose to exhibit a literal fulfillment of that Scripture rule, by comparing the three cities that have been generally considered:— **Rivals seemed to have— —have not.**

The Rivals of the West, Cincinnati, St. Louis and Chicago.

Western rivals.

That Chicago would lead every city of the West, has not been considered probable by me, scarcely possible, until within 15 years. The above rivals standing at three corners of a triangle, the sides about 280 miles, had each an abundant area to build up the three **Superiority to St. L. not claimed—**

—nor to Cincinnati.

Opinions 1847–'8.

largest inland cities. Philadelphia is but eighty-two miles from New York, and Baltimore but 98 from Philadelphia. At first, superiority was not claimed over Cincinnati, even: not because it was doubtful, but that friends should not think me more insane than was necessary concerning the future of Chicago. Hence, in the advertisement of 1847, p. 8, and in the following from the circular of 1848, Cincinnati was only referred to as an example of what Chicago was to become:—

Chi. compared with Cincinnati.

Chicago Compared with Cincinnati.—We may also discern the growth of Chicago, from the past history of other Western cities. Cincinnati, for instance, is regarded as *the* prodigy of rapid growth; and so, indeed, it may be, having risen in population from 10,000 to 100,000, in only 23 years. This, too, has been accomplished without any particular advantage of position, the Miami canal having been finished only three years; and after getting out of range of that, there is no reason why a preference should be given to Cincinnati over other river towns, except that she has the start.

Centre of 200 miles.

Business beyond.

But take Chicago as a centre, and you may describe a quarter circle of 180 to 200 miles radius, which *must* be tributary to this market. Goods not actually bought here, and produce not sold here, must chiefly pass through this place to or from market. If Chicago were to receive not one dollar's worth of business from out of Illinois, it would still have more to depend upon than Cincinnati. But our business from beyond that quarter circle, and from the eastward, will nearly or quite equal that within it.

Manufactures.

Raw materials gathered.

Provisions.

One transportation to answer.

In manufacturing, Cincinnati has no advantage over Chicago. Steam is now considered equal to water power, and bituminous coal, of excellent quality, and in inexhaustible quantity, will be delivered at Chicago, from along the canal, at about $2.50 per ton. Cotton will be brought via the Illinois river and canal at a trifling cost; and this will be one of the most important wool markets in the country. Pig iron is brought by vessels as ballast, for little or nothing, from the manufacturers in Pennsylvania and Ohio; lead will be brought by railroad, at cheap rates, directly from the mines; and copper from Lake Superior, without trans-shipment. We have excellent ship timber in this vicinity, and pine lumber costs by the cargo $7 to $8 per M. Provisions of all kinds will always be got here at cheap rates, and labor will be as cheap as will be for the advantage of the country. We are not always to transport the raw material to the eastern manufactories, and provisions to feed the hands, and then bring back the manufactured goods for consumption. A cheaper and better plan will be to make one transportation answer, by bringing machinery and hands here; and I can see no good reason why manufacturing of all kinds may not be depended upon as an important element in our prosperity.

Population of Ohio, 900,000—

—made Cin. 6th city.

One more comparison, and I have done with Cincinnati. The total population of Ohio, even as late as 1830, was but 937,903, of which a small portion only was tributary to Cincinnati. That city then contained 24,831, having no railroads or canals connecting it with the interior, few steam boats, no connection with the East, no exports to speak of, and emigration westward was comparatively small and difficult. Yet, under all these disadvantages, the Ohio metropolis has grown to its present gigantic size, having, in 1840, a population of 46,338, which is now supposed to be doubled, and it has become the sixth city in the Union.

Illinois, 800,000—

—improvements—

—natural advantages—

Illinois has now a population of over 800,000, of which *more than half* must pay more or less tribute to Chicago. Railroads, and steamboats, and canals, which are now just beginning to be felt in their power upon important commercial points, have placed us practically nearer to New York City, the great market of our country, than even Utica was twenty-three years since. We have a prairie country of the easiest tillage and greatest fertility, with a well established business and large exports. Immigration never was so great, and never brought as much capital. The canal and railroads terminating at Chicago, which will speedily be constructed, will command, within five years, more business than is even now done at Cincinnati.

—growth of whole country—

Now if in connection with these important advantages, we consider still farther, the general advancement of the whole country in growth and power, which has been made *since* Cincinnati became so prosperous, with the increased facilities of the present day for doing business of all kinds, and the greater ability that

Illinois possesses from this time to push forward its chief commercial emporium—considering all these points, with the start we already have, and is it not reasonable to expect that fifteen years to come will accomplish as much for Chicago, as the past twenty have done for Cincinnati?

—15 years to Chi. equal to 20 for Cin.

But in 1861 the relative change had become so marked, that contest with Cincinnati was passed, and even St. Louis was soon to be outstripped, and the following table and remarks were presented:—

Changes by 1861.

Chief cities of the U. S.—

Rank in 1860.	Cities.	Population in 1860.	Population in 1850.	Increase.	Increase per cent.	Rank in 1850.
1	New York....	814,277	515,647	298,730	58	1
2	Philadelphia..	568,034	408,862	159,272	84	2
3	Brooklyn.....	273,425	96,838	176,587	182	7
4	Baltimore.....	214,037	169,054	44,983	27	3
5	Boston	177,902	136,881	41,021	30	4
6	New Orleans.	170,766	115,375	54,391	47	6
7	St. Louis.....	162,179	77,860	84,319	108	8
8	Cincinnati....	160,060	115,435	44,625	39	5
9	Chicago......	109,420	29,963	79,457	265	18

—changes in 10 years, 1850 to '60.

The eight largest cities in 1850, are still the same, though relative rank is changed; but Chicago has jumped from being eighteenth to be the ninth. In 1870 she will not be lower than fifth, probably fourth, having passed Baltimore, and possibly third, having passed Brooklyn. Philadelphia has in so full operation the means relied upon for our prosperity—manufacturing—that it *may* take till the third or fourth decade to outstrip her, should no great national changes affect the manufacturing interests of the East; but before 1900 it will be accomplished. Our rate of increase has been *more than double that of any of the thirty-five largest cities in the Union*, Jersey City and Brooklyn alone excepted, and the latter owes much of its apparent increase to the annexation of Williamsburg.

Chi. the 18th now 9th— —in '70 4th or 3d. Increase double any other city.

In 1848 I compared the advantages of Chicago with Cincinnati, and from the then wonderful progress of the latter, argued that of the former. The comparison, then considered extravagant, is tame now. Though in 1850 she was nearly four times the size of Chicago, yet her numerical increase is only a little over one-half as much. She is next to be passed, and it will soon be done.

Views of '48 tame. Cin. passed next.

I then said nothing about St. Louis, it being considered visionary by even most of our own people to suppose we could rival her, and it being perhaps doubtful which would take the lead; and being 300 miles apart, afforded ample room for two great cities. Between the rival centres of the East, New York and Philadelphia, is only ninety miles, Baltimore only ninety miles more.

Too visionary to pass St. L.—

Not till within the last six or eight years have I claimed certain superiority for Chicago. The powerful advantages of St. Louis in greater population, immense wealth, established business, and river navigation of thousands of miles of which she is the centre, precluded, in the minds of most, the possibility of our excelling. But impossibility, and even improbability, has been removed. The railroad has meanwhile been opened all over this region, and river navigation on the uncertain, changing waters of the Missouri and Upper Mississippi, has seen its best days. The locomotive, not the steamboat, is to be the carrier of produce, passengers and merchandise, as well west as east of the Mississippi; and in this Chicago has and must have large and increasing pre-eminence. And besides drawing on her territory west of the Father of waters, we are also fast increasing trade with central Illinois, upon which she has fattened.

—till 1853–'5 Her superiority. Changes made. Our advantages

Her river navigation is henceforth far excelled in value by that of the lakes; and for her greater wealth, which is relatively fast diminishing, we have a full equivalent in health and climate, hereafter noticed. In obtaining materials to manufacture, she has no superiority over Chicago, except a trifle on cotton and lead. We can get the best of iron ore from Lake Superior, as cheaply as she can from her Iron Mountain, and in lumber and copper we have the advantage.

Lakes better than rivers, etc.

With the influential aids of immense wealth, greater age and established business, particularly by steamboats, all of which have operated relatively far stronger in her favor than they can ever again, she has increased since 1850, on a population of 77,680, only 84,319; while we have increased 79,457, on only 29,963. Notwithstanding her important superiority and *prestige*—the general belief that she

Our rapid overtaking.

Her *prestige.* was to be the great city of the West, she has increased in ten years one hundred and eight per cent., and Chicago two hundred and sixty-five per cent. If within the first decade of railroads, and while they are being constructed, such direct effects as these are visible, what is to be expected of the future?

St. L. to be a great city— I have no desire to disparage St. Louis, and do not. But if one city in the West is certain to outstrip the rest, it is important to know it, and my reasoning seems fair and conclusive. She will surely grow, perhaps to a great size, and though property is higher there than here, I doubt not in both it will prove a good investment. But however large she becomes, the chances are that Chicago, in only —Chi. a greater. twenty to thirty years, will be twice her size.

Reader to compare advantages. St. Louisians of course deny the possibility of her being excelled. They vainly endeavor to account for the inequality of growth, and the papers spur their wealthy citizens to effort to preserve their business. But the reader, with map in hand exhibiting the railroad system, may judge for himself whether the ultimate and speedy supremacy of Chicago can be questioned.

St. L. Dem. confirms. This view was strengthened with extracts from the St. Louis *Democrat*, inserted p. 111; and is confirmed by recent abundant admissions. Let us first consider Cincinnati. The *New York Evening* *N. Y. Eve'g Post.* *Post*, a month or two since remarked:—

Cin. losing ground. In the triangular fight for commercial supremacy between Chicago, St. Louis, and Cincinnati, the latter seems to be losing ground. The *Cincinnati Gazette* gives one good reason for this. It is believed, in imitation of the little burgh of Erie, of peanut notoriety, the city has pursued the foolish policy of refusing to allow the Follows Erie pea nut policy. union of the railroad lines passing through its limits. With this self-imposed barrier to the free passage of through freight and travel, it is not strange that both seek the more direct east and west lines further north, or that Cincinnati begins to find herself in an eddy of the vast traffic which follows the less obstructed channels.

Railroads consolidating. The tendency is towards a practical, if not a nominal, consolidation of the great east and west railroad lines north of the Potomac and the Ohio, into two immense combinations; one line, including the New York Central and the Erie, the Harlem, and the Hudson River railroads, extending on each side of Lake Erie, across Michigan to Chicago, and thence to the great routes west, northwest and south. The other line, led by the Pennsylvania Central railroad, extends from Central Ohio, through Indiana and Illinois, and competes for the same Western trade. By Avoid Cin. both these lines Cincinnati is practically avoided. Instead of continuing the foolish obstructive policy, she ought, by all means, to encourage the through traffic, and lend her aid to the development of railroad facilities to the States south of her.

This an imaginary excuse. The *Post* presents the excuse Cincinnatians give for their relative decline. The city grows, and rapidly; but they see other cities growing faster, and imagine their own short-sighted policy is the cause of their decline. Tho' Chicago certainly has done quite differ- Other reasons. ently, yet were this the only difference, relative acquirements and *Cin. Gazette.* prospects would not be so altered. A correspondent of the *Cincinnati Gazette*, December 4th, presents facts and reasons most truthfully:—

Northwest business unimportant. *Business between Cincinnati, Chicago, and the Northwest.*—There seems to be much misapprehension in the minds of our community in reference to the importance of the business between our city, Chicago, and the Northwest, and at the same time too little appreciation of that of the immediate West, South, and Southwest. From the tenor of articles which have recently appeared in our daily newspapers, the community might be led to suppose that our business connections with the Northwest were of vital importance to the growth of Cincinnati. The writer is quite familiar with the amount of traffic which reaches Cincinnati from all points, and which is sent from Cincinnati in every direction. He therefore speaks knowingly when he says the business between Cincinnati, Chicago, and the Northwest is very much over-estimated by our community. The sum total of the whole is not half equal to the amount received from and shipped to Louisville alone.

No difference of products. The products of the regions of Chicago and the Northwest are, in the main, the same as those of our latitude, and their great market is found at the East, and their channels to reach their markets are found through the chain of great lakes, and over their numerous east and west lines of railroads. The country in that direction has been mainly settled by Eastern people, and all their affinities are with them; and their trade and travel naturally flow east and west on lines of communication far north of Cincinnati. Ninety-hundredths of their merchandise and manufactures are purchased in our Eastern markets, and the remainder is divided between Cleveland, Pittsburgh, Louisville, Cincinnati, etc., both Cleveland and Pittsburgh having the decided advantage of Cincinnati and Louisville, on account of a long distance of cheap water rates. **Line of trade north of Cincinnati.**

During the late rebellion there was quite a large business done, from Chicago to Cincinnati, in the way of provisions for our army of the Southwest. The smallness of crops in our regions very much increased the demand at that period. Since the war closed this traffic has dwindled down to a mere moiety of what it was, and we may hereafter only expect it to be of small consequence when our crops in this region fail us. **Trade during war.**

Formerly Cincinnati was the market for buying and selling by the merchants of most of the towns as far north as Logansport, Fort Wayne, etc.; but since the opening of the Indiana Central, the Bellefontaine, the Wabash Valley, the Pittsburgh, Fort Wayne and Chicago, and other east and west lines, their business is mostly done with Eastern cities. We can now only hope to command a full share from the region lying from seventy to one hundred miles north of Cincinnati. By way of illustration, we may safely say that three-fourths, if not more, of the business of the Chicago and Great Eastern Road now goes east by way of the Bellefontaine and Columbus & Piqua Roads, and *via* the Atlantic & Great Western, Pennsylvania Central, and Baltimore & Ohio Railroads. **North trade lost.** **Try to keep 70 miles.**

In view of the facts already stated, it behooves the business men of our city to cultivate and improve our connections to the South, West, and Southwest. No time should be lost in pushing forward to completion the direct road through Kentucky to Louisville, the road to Knoxville and Chattanooga, and of extending the Ohio and Mississippi broad guage both to Louisville and Evansville. * * **Seek S. and S. W. business.**

The "Queen City of the West" is quite modest in her claims of tribute; though no doubt she can "only hope to command a full share"—and only a share—"from the region lying from 70 to 100 miles north of Cincinnati." A subsequent statement of the jobbing trade of the two cities confirms this opinion. **Cin. quite modest.** **Opinion confirmed.**

The above also sustains previous claims for Chicago to railway business, and would justify claims still farther east than Indianapolis. **Chi. trade to the east.**

Time was when the business of the Northwest was the golden apple in the eye of Cincinnati.* They do well, however, henceforth to devote attention to the South and Southwest. Nor are prospects there as encouraging as they might be, were it less up-stream work to draw off what legitimately belongs to Chicago. The *Missouri Republican*, of December 19th, thus laughs at Cincinnati, and slaps its own citizens:— **When Cin. prized N. W. trade.** **S. W. not promising.** ***Mo. Rep.***

The Southern Illinois Railroad.—We announced, two days ago, a call of the merchants and capitalists of Cincinnati, to meet on Monday, to insure the completion of the railroad from Vincennes to Cairo, and thus transfer to Cincinnati the trade of a large section of Southern Illinois. The call was numerously signed. We see by the *Commercial* and the *Gazette* of Tuesday that the meeting was a failure." "Just eight persons were in attendance." A writer in the *Gazette* **Cin. meeting about Cairo road.** **8 attended.**

*Visiting Hon. John C. Wright many years ago, I assured him that Chicago was not opposed to his road to St. Louis; that a road across Illinois must of course be built, and that it was for our interest to have it direct to Cincinnati, rather than on the diagonal to Toledo. After considerable conversation, he said, that as president, he of course had great interest in that road, yet, he "cared very little for it compared with one direct to Chicago. The trade of the great Northwest is what we want." I inquired, "Why, Judge, do you expect to draw it right straight through Chicago?" "We will try for it," said he. I replied, "and we will take a strong pull Cincinnati-ward, and see which can pull hardest." Above is the result candidly, and so soon, acknowledged in the paper he so ably conducted. **Judge Wright's opinion.** **Who pulls hardest.**

says: "such a show, after the publicity of the call, was to say the least, a *joke* on our boasted Queen City. A prize-fight or a foot race would have been better attended."

Advantages. The same writer, after showing that the new route proposed shortens the distance from Cairo to Cincinnati one hundred miles, remarks:

Cut off St. L. and Chi. "Besides, it enables us to reach the Mississippi river at a point where it is always navigable, and to "tap" the Mobile and Ohio Road at its very starting point, cutting off, to a great extent, our present competition with St. Louis and Chicago, for the trade of the Lower Mississippi river, and such as does now, or may hereafter, reach Cairo, by means of railroads from the South, and centering at that point.

New route south. "Let the solid men of this city see to it, that the necessary amount of money is forthcoming, and thus secure to us another mighty feeder—a new route to the South."

Same arguments apply to St. L. Every argument which the journals of Cincinnati can use to stir up the merchants of that city to aid such an enterprise is appropriate to ourselves. We need a road leading from here, in a southeast direction, to the Illinois Central Railroad to Cairo and to Paducah. We have been invited by citizens of Illinois and Kentucky to aid in building such railroad connections with districts of country which have manifested the strongest predilection to trade with St. Louis. St. L. apathy. We are sorry to say, however, that the following remarks of the Cincinnati *Commercial*, in speaking of the apathy of Cicinnati merchants and capitalists, are not without application here:

No efforts to get roads. "That the road will be an exceedingly important one to Cincinnati, there can be no doubt, but our capitalists and business men virtually say by their cold, uncivil treatment of every project of the sort, that they want no more roads, and will make no effort to secure the construction of any more that may be controlled in the interests of this place. Business men may go elsewhere. Practically this apathy also says to those merchants who have all their small means invested in business, that they must go to some other place if they desire to extend the area of their trade, and at this word it is reasonable to expect that many will take up their treasures and go elsewhere."

Chi. takes care of S. E. Illinois. These cities need not trouble themselves about Southeastern Illinois. The road from Shawneetown to the Illinois Central, giving us that trade and much from Kentucky, will be built while other cities study about their projects to reach that important region.

Triangular duel abandoned. Cincinnati, evidently impressed with that notable example of Midshipman Easy, abandons a triangular contest; and although St. Louis refuses to acknowledge that she, too, is distanced; yet evidence of the fact is quite conclusive from admissions against herself already quoted. St. L.'s task difficult. Her vantage-ground having been lost, the conflict for supremacy, and to recover control of the immense area north and west of her, which she perfectly monopolised, is a very difficult task. *Gen. Hammond's* speech. A speech delivered in St. Louis, 21st October, by Gen. J. H. Hammond, President of the St. Louis, Chillicothe and Omaha Railroad, before the Mayor, Board of Trade and Union Merchants' Exchange, so completely presents the case that space must be taken for it entire. Omaha wants roads. *Of course*, the counties traversed, and Omaha and the whole territory west, would favor a diagonal line like this to St. Louis. Who doubts it? Will she use them? But when built, how much of the traffic from Omaha and west, except that bound specifically for St. Louis and its immediate vicinity, can be drawn that far south in preference to main lines east and west? Benefit Chi. more than St. L. And if at all correct in this general view, will not such a diagonal road give more business to Chicago roads crossing it, than that taken to St. Louis? But let us hear Gen. Hammond:—

GENTLEMEN: I shall endeavor to show you that the road which I represent is, if not the most important claiming the attention of the citizens of St. Louis, at least equal to any other. In doing this, it is not necessary to decry any other enterprise, and I confine my comparisons to distances and availability.

Omaha road most important to St. Louis.

The great effort of the present day, commercially speaking, is western connections and routes to the Pacific ocean. The Mississippi has been crossed, the western boundaries of Iowa and Missouri reached; here two routes present themselves.

Pac. connections the object.

The one toward New Mexico and Southern California presents a favorable climate and few physical disadvantages. A vigorous company has this route in hand and St. Louis has connection with it over the Missouri Pacific to Kansas City. The other route starts from Omaha, Nebraska, and pursuing the valley of the Platte to-day is in use and carries freight and passengers to the foot of the Rocky Mountains, a distance of 462 miles west of the Missouri river. This road opens a country which is fast filling up with active people and it carries all the trade of Nebraska, Colorado, Montana and Dacotah. Its trade is already immense —being mining and other supplies for the Territories and government freights— and the road pays even now. It receives a bounty from the government of $16,000 per mile with a grant of land—for the road already constructed—and has now reached the point where this bounty becomes $32,000 per mile.

Kansas route. Omaha route. Country traversed. Road pays.

From the other side of the continent the Central Pacific road has pierced the Sierra Nevadas, and is already within the Great Desert basin, and is about 700 miles from Salt Lake City. I know of my own knowledge, that from Washoe Valley to Salt Lake City the difficulties are fewer than on the route of the Pennsylvania Central and Baltimore and Ohio roads, already overcome.

Pacific end in progress.

The remainder of the route has been declared feasible by competent authority, and I refer you to the engineer's reports. It is declared that this road will be finished to San Francisco in 1870—only three years hence. The success of the managers of this road so far is an earnest that they will make good their words in the future, and you may rely on it. Those sharp business men would not be in it if it was not on the books to win.

Finished 1870. Good men.

Here then, at Omaha, is the eastern terminus of this great route, and here the strife of St. Louis and her great rival commences. I pray you, citizens of St. Louis, do not shut your eyes to the facts. Do not say peace, when there is sharp, active war. Chicago's lake facilities is the commercial equal of your river navigation. Her railroad facilities are immensely superior, and without sugar coating let me state what you are all aware of, Chicago has now the best of it, and unless St. Louis takes hold vigorously she will retain and increase it.

Strife with Chi. at Omaha. Lake and railway facilities.

Two roads bridging the Mississippi river at Clinton and Davenport cross the State of Iowa and take all the trade of that State, of Nebraska and the territories; a road to LaCrosse, and thence to St. Paul, is now completed and diverts from St. Louis the trade of Minnesota. The Hannibal and St. Joseph road, stretching across North Missouri, takes everything north of the Missouri river and west of Macon, and from North Kansas and South Nebraska. A branch road from Cameron to Kansas City, almost completed, [it is finished—see p. 27.] connects Chicago with the Fort Scott and Galveston road and absolutely places our enemy in our rear. [So thought the editor of the *St. Louis Democrat*. See p. 26.] Merchants of St. Louis will you not take the alarm and prepare to compete for this territory which is now utterly lost to you, and will so remain until you place yourselves in reliable communication with it?

Trade now sure to Chicago— —from North Mo.— —on to Texas. Regain it to St. Louis.

St. Louis is by way of the St. Louis, Chillicothe and Omaha railroad 377 miles from Omaha, 157 miles less than by any other road.

Dist. to St. Louis—

Chicago is 494 miles from Omaha by way of the Chicago, Iowa and Nebraska railroad, which is her nearest route; via Davenport, the distance is 510 miles.

—to Chi.

Thus you see St. Louis is by way of the West Branch of the North Missouri to Brunswick, and thence up the Grand River Valley, one hundred and seventeen miles nearer to Omaha, and consequently to the Pacific, than Chicago is by her nearest route. Some gentlemen may ask, How about the relative distance from Omaha to New York, via Chicago and via St. Louis? I will reach that also, and you will find that while by any other route Chicago has the advantage of one hundred miles or over, by this road, and the Terre Haute and Alton and Indianapolis connections, St. Louis is in a position at least equal to her rival, while for the trade from the territories and the Pacific seeking Cincinnati, Baltimore and the South, St. Louis by this route has it all her own way.

St. L. 117 miles nearer. How to N.Y? St. L.'s advantage to Cin., etc.

The facts already stated and the advantages in distance, are sufficient reason why St. Louis should give her energies and money to this enterprise. But in

Local trade good.

addition to this the local trade of the country through which it runs is well worth the attention of St. Louis business men.

Country rich, etc.

No portion of Missouri is more highly favored than the Grand river valley. The land is all good, it is well timbered, coal is abundant; the climate is wholesome, the latitude being that of Columbus, in Ohio, Indianapolis, Indiana, and Springfield, Illinois; and a very superior class of emigrants are coming in.

Good for railroad.

Indeed, I do not know of any portion of the State capable of supporting so dense a population. The country from the Iowa line to Council Bluffs is equally attractive, and the whole presents an easy—very easy route for a railroad. Indeed the first fifty miles is practically level and presents no obstacles at all. The people are willing and ready to do their best. Livingston county may be relied on for about $200,000, Daviess $100,000, Gentry $150,000, Chariton perhaps $100,000 in city, county and private subscriptions. Unless the St. Joseph people are sharp enough to prevent, Nodaway county will give $150,000. In Iowa, Page county has pledged already $100,000.

Subscriptions on line.

Iowa earnest.

The other counties have not named their sums, but in Iowa they are far more earnest than in Missouri, and will do quite as much. When the North Missouri West Branch reaches Brunswick, there will remain, as the road is now located to suit counties, one hundred and ninety miles to build. I have been in the habit of estimating the cost of grading and tieing at $10,000 per mile. I am now persuaded that this is the maximum cost, and that it can be done for much less; but say $10,000. The cost of grading is $1,900,000. The people think they can do this. I do not believe anything of the kind. I do, however, believe that such is their indignation towards the monopoly which now oppresses them, that they can raise in the city, county and private subscriptions, about one half of this amount. This will leave nearly a million of dollars to complete the grading, bridging and tieing of the road. The means to obtain this are, first, the city of St. Louis, which can better afford to give, donate clear and clean two million dollars than to do without the road. When St. Louis has done this she can with good countenance ask the government to extend its aid. The Chicago, Iowa and Nebraska road and the Hannibal and St. Joseph railroad, both out and out Chicago routes to the Pacific, were built by means of government aid in land grants. I know this, because I contributed money and was among the first in the Chicago, Iowa and Nebraska road. The Pacific road from Omaha is being built by the same means.

Cost of bed.

People pay half—

—St. Louis half.

Roads now "out-and-out Chi. routes."

St. L. first to be served.

Cong. to aid.

The St. Louis, Chillicothe and Omaha road is the Pacific railroad itself, and I wish to know now, why, Chicago having been served, St. Louis is not entitled to aid also. The congressional influence of Iowa, and Nebraska, and the Territories, of Missouri, of Southern Illinois, Indiana, Ohio, Kentucky, Maryland and Pennsylvania must all go for such a movement, and the managers of the Omaha Pacific road want the southern connection as much as we want them to have it.

N. Mo. director in Pac. road.

Already one of the directors of the North Missouri railroad is a director of the Omaha Pacific—James Rollins, I mean.

Kans. Pac. not to oppose.

Now then, gentlemen of the Kansas Pacific, tell me why we cannot work together in this thing? What possible antagonism is there, that we cannot combine to defeat our common enemy and give commercial supremacy to our metropolis, St. Louis.

Settle Indian difficulties.

You, of a right, ought to have government assistance in your noble enterprise. The extension of your road one mile, at a cost to government of $16,000, does more to determine the Indian question than $100,000 spent on troops.

Join forces.

Our interest lies together, and combined we can and will secure government aid to assure our success. Once graded and tied, a road running through such a country as I have described will easily bear a first mortgage to supply iron stock, and as it is a link in the Pacific road, and has its connections already established, will be a paying road from the start.

Distance to N. Y

The distance from Chicago via Pittsburg is.............................. 914
To Philadelphia.. 824
Via Columbus and Pittsburg, from St. Louis to New York..............1,074
From St. Louis to Philadelphia.. 998

Chi. less 162 miles.

This gives Chicago an advantage to New York of 162 miles; to Philadelphia of 174.

St. L. gains 117 miles.

Via Grand River Valley you gain at once on the distance between New York or Philadelphia and the Pacific 117 miles, leaving only 46 miles on the whole distance from ocean to ocean against St. Louis, and to Baltimore and Washington leaving the advantage with St. Louis.

More reduction.

When the contemplated changes are made on the line of the Terre Haute and Indianapolis route, the distance against St. Louis is reduced to about fifteen miles.

And if you will take hold of this yourselves the distance from Brunswick to Omaha can be reduced all of that—because you keep your air line and do not swerve to county seats for country aid; thus increasing the difficulties and distance. Here then, gentlemen, I offer to you a route by which you are on equal terms as regards the distance between San Francisco and New York, and which places you 117 miles, sure, and 136 miles if you will make it so, nearer to the Pacific than Chicago is. But you must be up and doing.

Equal distance.

The Illinois Central company, in the interest of Chicago, has this very week leased, for thirty years, the Cedar Falls and Minnesota State Line road thus aiming to cut you off on the North Missouri road to St. Paul, and divert by Dubuque the East Minnesota trade to Chicago. You see there is no peace—no compromise. It is open, fair, active hostility.

Ills Cent. aids Chi. No peace—war.

I will obtain every dollar I can on the line of the road in county and city, and private subscriptions, in ties, in work, in land. Then, gentlemen, St. Louis must come and help. You have no alternative; under present arrangements Northwest Missouri and Southwest Iowa can not get here. No more can Nebraska or anything west of it.

St. L. must help. Mo. and Iowa cut-off.

Every effort is being made in the country to get this great route under Chicago control. We are in concert and perfect accord with the directory of the North Missouri. When you help that road, you help us; and under the management of the able men who have recently taken hold of it, it will speedily be completed.

All help Chi. Help N. Mo. road.

With the North Missouri to eastern Iowa and Minnesota, the Branch from Chillicothe to Des Moines to central Iowa; the West Branch up Grand River Valley, via Chillicothe to Omaha, reaching out still again to Kansas City, and tapping the road up to the Kaw, south to Galveston; another road at Leavenworth; another at Atchison, with the Union Pacific reaching through New Mexico to the Gulf of California, what a future there is for St Louis.

What a future for St. L.!

It is for you to say if this glorious future shall be realized.

Natural advantages have their value, but to realize that value work is required.

To realize—work.

Do not rely on the Omaha Pacific being unavailable because of snow or any other natural obstacle.

The Ohio and Mississippi road is far away south of the Michigan Southern and Lake Shore roads, and has far less snow to contend with; but pray tell how do the stocks stand to-day in the markets of the world?

Cent. route east don't pay as northern.

I tell you, gentlemen, that to energy and industry there is no such word as fail; and you must, should St. Louis fulfill her mission and take her place among the great cities of the earth, be the movers yourselves.

Energy and industry.

Make your city, then, the emporium of both the Pacific railroads, and those who do it will not only have a niche high in the temple of fame, but strong among the solid men of the land.

St. L. emporium—fame high.

I thank you for your kind attention.

Gen. Hammond is too thoroughly master of his subject, and has too fairly presented the many and important considerations, to render comments either necessary or decorous. Instead of taking time for them, let the reader please peruse the speech again, and observe particularly how well he recognizes, the importance of lake navigation; and also makes it one of his main premises, that the Hannibal and St. Joseph road, which was built by and for St. Louis, is an "out-and-out Chicago road, and takes everything north of the Missouri river and west of Macon, from North Kansas and South Nebraska." Of course, then, it takes that east of Macon; and what in the name of reason makes Missourians the simpletons to run off all the way north to Chicago, and Nebraskians so sharp as to run off all the way south to St. Louis! A little craniology is wanted in solution. Very "vigorous" must St. Louis be, under such circumstances, to recover what was her's and is lost.

Gen. H.'s correctness. Read it again. Han. and St. Joe road to Chicago. Mo. folly. Nebraska wisdom.

Hon. H. T. Blow, in his inaugnral before quoted, p. 26, exhibits the efforts St. Louis has made, and makes, and the results:—

Hon. H. T. Blow.

—6

New Exch. required by St. Louis— The immense trade of our city, fast outgrowing the capacity of our dealers, has compelled our most active business men to devote their whole time to the daily operations of the Merchants' and Millers' Exchange. In that dense throng, where the unceasing ring of business speaks of vast and increasing operations, there is now no longer a place or time for the deliberate consideration of those great —study hard— interests absolutely requiring to be advanced and adopted—interests which must drag along slowly, unless vitalized with the spirit of sterling enterprise and pushed by co-operation which can only be attained where our wisest and most experienced —wise plans business men can, after examination, submit plans at once attractive to all classes of the community, and satisfactory to those who hold the wealth of this and other lands.

Strong court It was, therefore, necessary to organize a more deliberate court, if you please, to some extent composed of members of the Exchange, but embracing all the strong influences in our midst, having more especially in charge the great interests to Board of Trade. which I have briefly alluded. Hence the St. Louis Board of Trade was established. I cannot pass to the discussion of any industry or enterprise, however, which may ere long be advanced by your wise action, without stating for your encouragement Though so much is done— the fact, that while the Merchant's Exchange has dignified trade, advanced the commercial position of the city, and laid the foundation of many a princely fortune, educating our young men up to the highest business standard, and while our commission merchants, millers and manufacturers have evinced an individual enterprise and liberality that would enrich any community; there has never been that co-opera- —no co-operation as in Chi. and N. Y. tion with our wealthiest citizens in our great enterprises which would lead to a general advancement of the city and State, such co-operation as there is in Chicago and in New York, where by the united aid of all their individual wealth, enterprise and sagacity, the trade of whole sections of country has been drawn to them by the most rapid and economical system of transportation and travel.

* * * * *

Economy in Chicago— It is the economical principle now reigning supreme in our beautiful and energetic competitor, Chicago, which enables her to handle wheat for a cent per bushel; —cheap trade. lumber at the lowest possible rate; receive, pack and distribute her pork and cattle in every direction, and sell merchandise upon a margin which cannot be afforded, except where the extreme of this economic principle prevails. This is the true 5 times her area— secret of her success, and this makes her a splendid illustration of rapid develop- —must use her principles. ment; and while we have naturally five times the area that she has to supply, we can never progress in the same ratio except on the same principles.

Room for both cities— Both cities are a necessity to the West, and both will grow to wealth and magnificence within a few years that will surprise the most sagacious men of the day; and their wealth, power, position and advancement in everything which contributes to the elevation and happiness of a people, will come from an honorable compe- —both to grow. tition. See to it that we live up to our high privileges, and the result will be that we will continue to increase in wealth, and expand our limits long after our beautiful rival will be considered as finished, perhaps, like Venice, reposing grandly and lazily on the bosom of her Adriatic.

Chi. is not reposing, St. L. may be— The statistics of trade, rather indicate that the Queen of the Lakes is not yet "reposing grandly and lazily," but that the Queen of the Rivers may be, her business largely retrograding. Yet for —action lively— one in repose there is considerable threshing and kicking, of which the "beautiful rival" comes in for her full share. St. Louis, recumbent upon her dignity while well employing her muscle, appears quite well to apprehend that she lies on no bed of roses. Being —is being stretched. found a little short for the tall work undertaken of grasping the Northwest, instead of dallying with a Delilah, he—changing sex to follow St. Louis fancy,—finds himself in the grasp of a Procrustes upon a stretcher of iron rails, which instead of bringing him to the required height, remorselessly pulls off one after another of his limbs *Mo. Dem.* of trade. In proof of this, the *Missouri Democrat* of 23d November, presents the following:—

What St. Louis Has, What she has Lost, and What she Needs.—That business in St. Louis is not what every well-wisher could desire, is evident from the daily complaints heard on the street and in every business circle, and the reasons for the decline in business are as varied as the persons uttering them. Some say it is because we have an old fogy set of business men and capitalists, and that in consequence we have not the railroad connections we should have, and others charge it entirely upon the merchants, and claim they do not put forth the necessary efforts to sell their wares, and that our commission merchants charge too high commissions, etc., while the merchants in turn throw the blame upon the landlords for charging too high rents, and so the blame is shifted from one shoulder to another, and nothing is done to bring about a better state of things; and it is for this reason I have chosen the above heading, viz: *What St. Louis has, what she has lost, and what she needs.*

St. L. wants something—
—various opinions—
This trial to ascertain truth.

St. Louis has the natural location to become the largest city in the West, if not in the United States; and by natural location I mean her natural facilities for the reception and disbursion of values raised or manufactured in and around her, and her facilities for manufacturing in metals are superior to any other, (not excepting Pittsburgh,) from the fact that the material (viz: the coal and ore,) are almost lying side by side, and that in inexhaustible quantities.

Natural location—
—for trade and manufactures.

St. Louis has more real capital than any city in the West, and that capital is in the hands of careful, far-seeing, yet energetic business men.

St. L. rich—
—men good.

Now we come to *what St. Louis has lost.* She has lost to an alarming extent her grain trade, for instead of its having increased from eight millions of bushels per year to thirty millions, which would be no more than her proportion of the natural increase of the country, in the last ten years it has fallen off from eight millions to three millions; and who does not know that where the farmer sells his grain he buys his goods; hence if the dry goods, grocery, and other kinds of business have not fallen off in proportion to the grain trade, it is only to be wondered at.

What is lost—
—grain trade—
—merchandise.

St. Louis has lost, and must continue to lose until a different national policy is pursued toward the South, an extensive lucrative Southern trade, and outlet for her produce and manufactures, and the fact that she has lost this Southern outlet has depressed her market for grain; which taken together with the fact that Chicago has tapped at every possible point north and west of us our grain supplies, and offers cheaper facilities by handling the same *in bulk and by elevator, and by less commissions* than we offer, is telling heavily upon the commerce and prosperity of St. Louis.

South to be aided.
Chi. taps all around—
—sells cheaper.

Now we come to *what she needs;* and here is a wide field, for the question could most readily be answered by saying, what does she not need? And yet what she needs is all around her, and only requires developing. With the extensive coal-fields and mountains of iron ore at our door, it is evident the future destiny and greatness of St. Louis *lies in her becoming a manufacturing city,* and everything should be done by our capitalists and others to foster that class of industry, and if locations or other facilities are wanted to cause them to spring into existence no barrier should be placed in the way.

What St. L. needs?
Everything
—manufactures.

Again, our railroads should be pushed to completion, and when we look at the map it would be difficult to select which of our railroads should be pushed with the greatest vigor; but there is no contesting the fact that the North Missouri and Iron Mountain railroads are pre-eminently important—the first, because it passes through a thickly settled and productive country, and because it traverses across every road leading into Chicago, and it cannot fail to draw much of the trade and commerce of that section of country to St. Louis; while the Iron Mountain railroad, on the other hand, should be finished not only to Columbus, so as to secure an outlet in the winter months, but should have a branch to Memphis, for as the case now stands, we have lost a large portion of the Arkansas and White river trade, for the reason that passengers can go from Memphis to Louisville in *seventeen hours,* while it takes *twenty-seven* to come to St. Louis.

Push railroads.
N. Mo. cuts off Chi.
Iron Mount. wanted.

Again, everything should be done to *cheapen* transportation by railroad, as well as river; and by railroad we mean to see to it that combinations are not formed to the injury of St. Louis and in favor of other and rival cities, and which we have reason to believe has been done; and, so as to cheapen rates by river, every influence should be brought to bear by the city fathers, the Chamber of Commerce, the Board of Trade, and every other organization, upon the general government, to push to an early completion the work at the two Rapids, the Balize, and to remove such other obstructions as impede or endanger navigation. To join without distinction of party in recommending to Congress to reduce or repeal the cotton tax,

Prevent railway combinations—
—improve river.
—remove cotton tax—

and to repair the levees on the lower Mississippi, for until these are done the plantations of the South must remain a desert waste; and until the South recuperates, St. Louis must stagger, if she does not fall. Concert of action is needed. Crimination and recrimination will do no good. We are laboring under a combination of circumstances which it requires only that we should see, and which, by united action, we can remedy; and then St. Louis will attain that high position, commercially, which destiny points out for her.

Combination of circumstances adverse.

These views important.

"What St. Louis has, what she has lost, and what she needs," are surely topics it behooves her to consider, in aid of which these humble efforts may somewhat assist. What are her chances of recovery of what she has lost? This able advocate, while vaunting her "natural location," nearly forgets the rivers, and judiciously calls attention to railroad lines which St. Louis *wants*, and to those which Chicago already *has*. Now this writer mistakes his cue. If St. Louis possess any superiority of "natural location," it is due to the great rivers, a glorious work of nature, upon which she is very centrally located. This has ever been the string harped upon, which was passed over in considering the ***Differences between Chicago and other Western Centres***, having its more appropriate place in comparing relative advantages of Chicago with the only city that has the least show of rivalry.

Rivers neglected.

They St. L.'s basis—

—here considered.

St. L. has no natural location.

I deny point blank that St. Louis has a "natural location" entitling her to any precedence. The "natural facilities for the disbursion of values," to which this sensible writer at once brings the high-sounding phrase of "natural location" we have already considered, in comparing water and railway facilities; and that other important point of "facilities for manufacturing in metals," will have examination hereafter. If she have this "natural location," and it be also true—that "St. Louis has more real capital than any city in the West, and that capital is in the hands of careful, far-seeing, yet energetic business men;" how happens it, then, that in the very next line the writer says with italics—"Now we come to *what St. Louis has lost?*" The truth is, St. Louis has no "natural location" superior to a dozen others; and I am willing to stake my credit for sound judgment upon the prediction, that within thirty years there will be at least three cities in the west fully her equals, or certain soon to pass her. Were it not for the rivalry of Kansas, Leavenworth and Lawrence, one of these at the Big Bend of the Missouri would take the lead, and will as it is, if it can largely outgrow its close neighbors.

If she had, why is not capital and energy effective?

Other cities to beat her—

—Kansas, perhaps.

Cairo was better site—

—also Alton.

What was there in the site of St. Louis that a half century ago would have indicated her present power? The confluence of the Ohio, from whence the Mississippi has its best navigation,—highest in summer, least ice in winter—would seem to have been a far more promising position. Next to that, Alton near the Missouri and Illinois rivers, possessed important advantages. Besides, Martin's history of Louisiana says St. Genevieve had 949 inhabitants in 1799,

St. Louis 925, and Cape Girardeau 521. Who could have given any reason then for St. Louis' superiority? She had actually retrograded, for in 1788 she had 1197. Never had she the least promise of greatness,—until gradually, and with no apparent cause, the fur trade there concentrated, giving her wealth. Making money in these practical days monopolises the idea of wealth, and is rather more one of those inventions man has sought out, than a gift of nature. So, too, the animals which wore the furs, probably did it according to nature, unless they belonged to that non-descript "race of humans" we are soon to read about; but would that classify the trade among natural sciences? Then with the rapid growth of steamboats, she marched on to her prodigious increase. Nature, is it? Had she relied altogether upon the nature of her snorters, and never used any of that art in their improvement which made them famous,—the equal of which will never again be seen on the Mississippi,—would she then have achieved her greatness, or had it thrust upon her by the rude hand of nature?

St. L. had retrograded. **Fur trade started her.** **This not nature.** **Also steamboats.** **Are these nature?**

A St. Louisian writing to the Springfield (Mass.) *Republican*, while he adopts the phrase of "natural hub of the continent," goes on to show conclusively that nature has nothing to do with it, and that railroads "are obviously the cause of this new and grand impulse:"

St. L.'s ideas in *Spr.* (Mass.) *Rep.*

> There must be some veritable centralization of forces at this natural hub of the continent, to cause this upheaval in value. Speculation has not done it. That race of humans that build paper cities, air houses and castles, and figure up an immense business to astonish the commercial world, on fictitious warehouse receipts, do not live in St. Louis. It is even true of our people that they proceed entirely upon the old-fashioned cause and effect. There is here a confluence of interests already vast, and now wonderfully accumulating. Whence the tide sets in towards this great center of trade, one can hardly know without following out all the avenues that lead to and from the city. The rivers are the same old fogies they ever were—perhaps a little older and dryer—now high, and then, and just now, in fact, incontinently lower—a periodical botheration to trade. Old Mississippi is a highly respectable stream of water, but after giving St. Louis a good start, came near ruining her with false hopes. As those young F. F. V.'s used to rely upon their ancestry to carry them through life, our people relied upon the "Father of Waters" till their neighbors had laid rails all over the West, tapping the natural sources of their trade. But railroads have dragged their slow length along in Missouri, and they are obviously the cause of this new and grand impulse. * * * But railroad investments they regard at best as "roundabout." The benefits come back not so often in dividends on the identical investment as in the enhancement of commerce and general values, and that might not prove equal to them to the amount they risk. Hence, little help is obtained at home, and I am told that reliance is entirely upon Eastern capital. This ought not to be, but is nevertheless. Our sister city, Chicago, is more venturesome. If their money comes back to them around Robin Hood's barn, it is all the same to them, and hence Chicago has stretched out her iron arms in every direction, contributing largely of home capital, diverting much trade that would naturally tend to St. Louis. But St. Louis lives and grows magnificently, natbless Chicago.

Natural hub of the continent. **—a race of humans—** **Rivers old fogies—** **—Miss. nearly ruins St. Louis.** **Railroads come—** **—they cause progress.** **Slow to build them.** **Chi. around Robin Hood's barn.** **St. L. grows**

If the chivalrous Mr. Hood—his renown we have heard clear here, and now that we learn of his patronage of St. Louis, so near to us, we shall be duly respectful—if the famous Mr. Hood have his barn in St. Louis, as this writer reasonably implies, what else could be expected of a youthful sprig like Chicago, rendering due deference

Chi. respects Mr. Hood.

to antiquated fame, than to go around it? Would the dare-devil have us go right through it! As a St. Louisian, he knows the delight it would give Chicago to get around St. Louis, and this sagacious method is adopted to inform us that our movements are understood. Precisely as he says, and for the very object, we have done our best to accomplish our purpose, without even hearing about that novel "race of humans," or that the barn was there. Exertions may now be increased that we know their distinguished patron to be him of the road—is it not roads we are after? and according to present appearances, we shall soon have a strong cordon of iron bands completely surrounding her for the protection of that barn, and terribly fierce iron horses rushing hither and thither to keep out intruders, who might, by mistake put Mr. Hood himself in limbo.

St. L. shrewd

Chi. trys to get around that barn—

—success probable.

Nor is this writer less sensible upon another important point. Most assuredly "that race of humans that build paper cities and don't live in St. Louis," could never have mustered courage to aid in putting Mr. Hood's barn there, or any other such work of art; and it would not be called a work of nature, could it? And then "the rivers being the same old fogies they always were," and "after giving St. Louis a good start, [having come] near ruining her with false hopes," certainly they are not to be counted upon. Then losing the rivers, which are admitted to be nature's means, as the cause of her wonderful attainments, it becomes a profound subject of inquiry what sort of "a race of humans" that must be, which actually produces works of nature. For there is no mistake that she is "the natural hub of the continent"; and removing rivers, what else of ordinary "natural location" remains to St. Louis?

Is the barn a work of nature?

Rivers not trusty.

Who provided St. L.'s nature?

One would imagine that by this time St. Louis would have learned that it was best not to "proceed *entirely* upon old-fashioned cause and effect," but try somewhat more of those causes which seem new to her and have run off her business. But as to dependence upon "eastern capital" for means, Mr. Blow's advice, p. 28, to go to Europe, seems based upon more accurate knowledge of circumstances. Relying still, as they evidently do, upon the idea of a "veritable centralization of forces at this hub of the continent"; they will in time, if they have not already, find it quite as fanciful as anything they can discover in that other "race of humans that build paper cities, air houses and castles." If a more airy castle has been built than that of St. Louis' "central location," sight of it would be difficult. St. Louis can well say with Prospero:—

St. L. trusts old-fashioned cause and effect.

Reliance rather fanciful.

Prospero speaks for St. L.

You do look my son, in a moved sort,
As if you were dismayed: be cheerful, sir:
Our revels now are ended: these our actors,
As I foretold you, were all spirits, and
Are melted into thin air:

And, like the baseless fabric of this vision,
The cloud-capped towers, the gorgeous palaces,
The solemn temples, the great globe itself,
Yea, all which it inherit, shall dissolve;
And, like this insubstantial pageant faded,
Leave not a rack behind. We are such stuff
As dreams are made of, and our little life
Is rounded with a sleep.

Nor is this writer's correctness questioned in attributing her continued and rapid increase to railways instead of rivers. Few railroads as she has compared with Chicago, they are a powerful adjunct to her wealth, and afford the only sound reason for her present rapid progress. Are not they a work of some "race of humans" instead of nature?" True that railways make St. L. Are they of nature?

If rivers have lost their power, what then remains of St. Louis' boasted claims to "natural location"? That she has a central locality in regard to the immense business of the gigantic rivers of the West, is certain. But is every *central* position necessarily one of great *natural* advantages? and for what natural advantages was she chosen chief port of the rivers? Is she more central than Cairo or Cape Girardeau, or St. Genevieve, or Alton would be? For one hundred and fifty miles, on either side of the Mississippi, points at least equal in "natural location" and centrality, could have been fixed upon, some superior. What is St. L.'s natural location? Centrality nothing.

St. Louis has vaunted her central position, and the unwitting public have lost sight of the self-evident truth, that she is only central geographically; and that, too, of the entire Union, not of the Northwest, which, as we shall see, is her main dependence, and rightly so. Trade does not regard geographical lines or rules, except as compelled by impolitic exercise of power. When the genius of our compound system of governments shall be apprehended, and trade be left to follow the unerring laws of nature, be assured it as certainly rolls on to the great central fountain, as that the rivers flow into the sea; and that centre will not be one of mere geography. False claims deceive the public. Geographical centre nothing. Trade to seek its centre.

The truth is, the Queen of the Rivers has obtained her ascendancy under false colors.* She has no "natural location," or the magic St. L. under false colors.

* Just in time, the *Missouri Democrat*, of January 15th, remarks:— *Mo. Dem. N. Y. Mail.*

"The New York *Evening Mail* in speaking of the three rival cities of the West, St. Louis, Cincinnati and Chicago, says:—

"It is fair to say that Chicago is generally ahead in the grand total, though she has little enough to spare, for her rivals are close upon her heels. Chicago claims that in several respects she has diverted trade which would naturally go to St. Louis. General prediction, however, favors St. Louis as the great inland metropolis when the Pacific Railroad peoples the far West." General prediction.—

Yes; "general prediction" is about the only general St. Louis is able to muster into its service. One of their sensible citizens touches them (p. 39,) upon their folly in being "tickled with the hair of flattery, while others are realizing the marrow of profit." But what will satisfy such a dullard as this editor of the *Mail?* Is it not enough "that Chicago is generally ahead in the grand total," when the immense superiority of both the late rivals is taken into the account, together with the short period in which they have been outstripped?" "General prediction is the right leader for such editors, but a sensible man of business wants something of more substance in his calculations. These wind-bags need pricking, and popular notions correcting, about a question so important to the country as this, whether there be a genuine natural and artificial centre of trade, and where it is. —only general for St. L. Chicago's rapid gain over her.

wand of art in its first waving could not have dissipated her supplies, or rather sent them in torrents to her rival. She can be no "natural hub of the continent," or her *felloes* could not have so fallen from her spokes, and become fastened by other spokes into another hub where they are bound to stick, because it is natural.

Felloes do not stick.

Fur Trade started St. L.

To leave the flights of fancy upon which she has sailed in her glory, and come down to homely but patent business truths, it is undeniable that the unimportant circumstance of the fur trade gathering thither, not nature in the least, caused her remarkable advancement. The aggregation of capital, and the immense business of steamboats, have alone made her Queen of the Rivers. Sagaciously she has availed herself of these adjuncts; and while nature did nothing for her, except what has been done for scores of other places above and below her, art, and especially money, has wrought wonders in her favor. Were not nature so entirely adverse, her energy and wealth would make rivalry a hard task.

—and capital and steamboats.

Nature adverse.

Rivers her support—

As Queen of the Rivers she attained her power; and were rivers to maintain their relative importance in commerce, her prospects would brighten. But as before observed, the rivers have relatively seen their best days; and for a moment casting out of sight the marvelous changes wrought by railways, let us look at the sure decadence of what has been St. Louis' main dependence.

—their sure decay.

Tillage ruins them.

The rivers have drawn their supplies from an unbroken wilderness. Rain and snow falling upon mountain and plain, percolated the soil, and in springs and rivulets and rivers, have afforded a pretty constant supply to the main streams; though even in years past, a hot summer brought low water. But as a country is settled, the surface is quickly dried by evaporation; and surplus water, instead of gradually soaking into the earth, is borne off at once by drainage. The effect of this is seen in the Ohio river,* and Cincinnati's unfortunate predicament, the *Chicago Times* thus presents:—

Chi. Times.

Cincinnati distracted—

The inhabitants of Cincinnati seem to be in a state of mind bordering on distraction, in consequence of a phenomenon of nature which is not uncommon in that vicinity.

—about heat and water.

The phenomenon is one that results from the application of heat to water. In common language, it is known as evaporation. The rapidity of the process depends on the degree of heat. By the application of a high degree of heat, a large quantity of water may be evaporated in a short time. A moderate degree of heat, continued for a long time will produce the same result.

River down, —coal up.

The result which afflicts Cincinnati was produced by the application of a slow heat to the Ohio river. The river is dried up. Navigation thereon has ceased. Cincinnati is short of coals. Cold weather is coming. The price of coals is going up, up. The river persistently declines to go up. Cincinnati is alarmed.

Trouble semi-annual.

The situation of Cincinnati is one of semi-annual occurrence. In winter the Ohio river freezes up; in summer, it dries up. The result in either case is the same; navigation stops.

Prediction at Pittsburgh in 1837.

* Over thirty years ago in Pittsburgh, the natives were amazed to hear that Chicago was bound to outgrow her. These same reasons among others, I then gave; and they are more certain of realization upon the Mississippi for reasons given in the text.

The boasted advantages of western river navigation consist rather more in the boast than in the reality. Before railways were built, they furnished a tolerable substitute for artificial canals. But their glory, like their aqueous contents, is somewhat too readily evaporated to be enduring. Rivers fail.

Much sober truth is mingled with the irony, applying equally to St. Louis, and far more rapidly than heretofore to Cincinnati. Both the Upper Mississippi and the Missouri, are fed mostly by streams from rich plains, soon to be under the plough. The Allegheny and Monongahela from their mountain sources, are better streams for steady supply than any on the upper Mississippi; and although those from the Rocky Mountains can be depended upon for a considerable time, yet the Missouri itself is so tortuous and dangerous from its perpetually shifting bed, that it will be little used when the seven Chicago lines of railway strike her banks, except for down freights. Undoubtedly the best western river for navigation, except the lower Mississippi, is the Illinois River, having little current, and being more like a canal. Of this the navigation will be improved by feeding the canal from Lake Michigan, the deepening of which is being done by the city for sanitary purposes, and sooner or later will be completed by the Federal Government, on a grander scale. Same applies to St. Louis. Rivers to diminish. Mo. dangerous. Ills. best for navigation.

We shall have (p. 111). St. Louis' own admissions years ago as to her chance in competition with Chicago for that trade; and the same influences not only continue to operate in our favor, but with augmenting power. St. Louis was strong because the steamboat did the whole business; and with its decadence on one river after another, her supremacy disappears. What then becomes of her "natural location"? How is she the "natural hub of the continent"? Chi has it sure. St. L. fails as rivers fail. Where "natural location?"

The *Missouri Republican*, December 18th, furnishes thoughts right to the point:— *Mo. Rep.*

Railroads vs. Rivers.—Nothing is more encouraging to the business men of this city than to observe that an interest is being manifested in regard to the building of railroads, in order to place this city in more direct communication with those portions of the rich "Valley of the Mississippi," of which St. Louis is the natural commercial centre. Railroads vs. rivers.

In former times, when St. Louis was the principal, if not the only point of business in the far West, it owed its advantages to the great rivers, they being the only highways of trade and means of communication; but the times have changed, and the sooner we realize it the better. What ten years ago was a great advantage, might now be considered a drawback, not that we wish to detract from the value of our natural highways, which will continue to add to our prosperity; but we contend that our city has, in consequence of relying on the rivers as channels of trade, neglected to build railroads, and places less favored by nature, have resorted to the building of railroads, and hence have kept pace with the requirements of the age. This tardiness in constructing railroads and building bridges has given to St. Louis a name of old fogyism. St. L. chief of West, because of rivers. That now a drawback. Railroads neglected. St. L. old fogy.

It is of the utmost importance that we should build these roads which are being spoken of, and extend others which have been commenced, but we also need railroads running parallel with and in close proximity to the Mississippi river north, to tap the flourishing towns on its banks, in order to be accessible during the entire year. We experience great disadvantages to secure trade in that direction, as parties dislike to change their patronage with the change of the season. The trade of the South being now almost entirely lost in consequence of the impoverished state of that country, the West is but sparsely settled, besides being partly cut off by the railroads passing around us. It will be seen that our territory is Must build roads—along Miss. river. Trade South lost. Territory limited.

Get new quite limited, and if we want to retain our position as a great commercial emporium, we must seek new outlets and regain our old grounds. * * *

Get capital east— If our capitalists do not want to furnish the necessary means and move in the matter, let our Merchants' Exchange and Board of Trade corporations solicit the Eastern capitalists. All that is necessary is to take hold in good earnest, set forth the advantages, show them that our business men are made of the right material; that the accessions made to them of late years possess as much enterprise as any other community, and the little obstacle will easily be overcome. If this is not —or merchants leave. done our merchants will seek other points, and the cities which excel us in enterprise will carry off the prize.

Bridges essential. Do not neglect to build the bridge across the Mississippi at this point; nothing is more important at this moment. At the much less important points, Quincy, Keokuk, Burlington, Davenport, Clinton, etc., bridges have been or are being built, with all possible speed, and here we are fighting for it still. * *

Of what is St. L. centre? Oh, tell us where those treasures lie! "those portions of the rich Valley of the Mississippi, of which St. Louis is the commercial centre"! Those of the Missouri, Upper Mississippi, and Illinois Upper Miss. Val. has quit St. L. rivers, constitute quite a "portion of the rich valley"; and that trade, like "that race of humans," disregarding its every law, is eccentric instead of concentric, flying off in a tangent from its river centre, away off to a lake port. Every one of these St. Louis writers are anathematising this unnatural course of trade, and would compel it by strong bars of iron and iron horses, to come to its "natural com- Unnatural trade. mercial centre." What an anomalous, crazy, unnatural thing this upper part of the Mississippi valley must be, to entirely forget its What portions better. own centre, and run off 150 to 500 miles to find another! What other "portions of the rich valley" is she equally entitled to? Chicago would like to be informed, having no sinister purposes, but merely to make its acquaintance to see if all trade is so utterly disregardful of its obligations. In prosecuting their investigations into the afflicting Cause of evil. causes of this evil,as they have entered into pretty much everything without satisfactory results, would it not be well to inquire about Mr. Hood's antecedents, and see if he be as honest and true as such a patron should be? But understand, no insinuation is made against the august proprietor of that barn, and king of the *road.*

Art not nature makes a commercial centre. Please note the second paragraph of the above extract again—indeed, the whole is worthy—and observe how nature yields to art as the power to establish a commercial centre. Why, then, do not St. Louisians show how much more art has done to make her a centre, than was done by nature "in former times," when the great rivers [were] the only highways of trade"? Is there not more truth than St. L. old fogy— poetry in having "given to St. Louis the name of old fogyism"? If not, why still chiming so persistently upon the obsolete notion that it "is the natural commercial centre" of any district?

The St. Louis side of the argument, I trust, has been fairly presented. According to their own showing, is it not literally true, that —must revolutionize art or nature. she must revolutionize the influences of art and nature, by introducing unknown forces, or she must fail in her pretensions even more signally in the future than in the past? As the editor of the *Missouri*

Democrat remarked, (p. 27), "Trade, like water, moves in the direction of the least resistance. Nobody has ever succeeded in making it run up hill;" and he goes on to confess the disadvantages pertaining even to the Kansas trade, finding consolation in tapping Chicago trade on the Omaha line. So every one of their advocates presents difficulties which must be overcome; yet each trusts more to indefinite expectations than to any well devised plan to remedy their evils. Hope on, hope ever, is a noble maxim, but had they Hercules to give them a lift—and they have not—they must help themselves. The *Chicago Times*, with genuine disinterestedness, advises them to the only possible means of tapping Chicago trade effectually, and "taking it in the direction of the least resistance":—

Trade and water don't run up hill.

Ineffectual remedies proposed.

An effective one of *Chi. Times*.

St. Louis, in the state of Missouri, is painfully agitated by another discovery concerning Chicago. It is that "the bridge at Kansas City, and the Cameron rail-"road, are now being rapidly pushed." And the unsatisfactory conclusion to which the pushing process leads the St. Louis mind is that:

St. L. fears to lose Kansas trade.

"Within one year Chicago will have direct connection, without the break of bulk, with that branch of the Pacific railroad which is mostly owned in St. Louis, *while St. Louis will not!* Freight from Denver *via* that route, to come to this city, must change cars at Kansas City, but may go to Chicago without change of cars."

Chi. connected—

—St. L. not.

This is the latest phase which the Chicago horror has assumed in St. Louis. Of course the dilapidated newspaper concerns in that ancient borough have a remedy to suggest; in the present instance they have three remedies. One is to change the guage of the railroad between St. Louis and Kansas City, so that it will correspond with the Union Pacific gauge. This, it is said with some hesitation, "ought to be done." Another is, to complete the west branch of the North Missouri road to Kansas City, "so that cars may run over that route, without change, to St. Louis." This remedy, it is thought, is more feasible and would be better than the other. But the third remedy is the one in which the originating ability of St. Louis genius excels itself. It is thus confidently stated:

Remedies various.

One effectual—

"But there is also one other way to meet this latest manœuvre of our rival. Chicago taps the St. Louis branch of the Pacific railroad at Kansas City. Very well, then let St. Louis tap the Chicago branch at Omaha!"

—tap Chi. trade at Omaha.

With due deference to the superior genius of St. Louis, one is constrained to ask, Why not tap the "Chicago branch" at Chicago? The distance between Chicago and St. Louis is considerably less than between Omaha and St. Louis. Moreover, Chicago is a far more important commercial point than Omaha, and enjoys the superior advantage of having railway connections with every portion of the west. By tapping the Pacific railway at Chicago, would not St. Louis also tap all other Chicago railways at the same time, and draw all the commerce of the west, which now centres in Chicago, to the antique town of St. Louis? If the tapping process at Chicago would not have this effect in the fullest degree, it would have it in a degree relatively as great as it would at Omaha.

Better to tap at Chi.—

—tap the whole trade.

Did no other causes operate upon this pretentious "natural location," than this one of nature herself in impairing river navigation,—the only natural advantage she has possessed, and that only in company with many other sites,—even then must the Queen of the Rivers have succumbed to the Queen of the Lakes. God has not put man on this theatre of toil and struggle, that he, either individually or collectively, should live in idle enjoyment; but we are to be "*diligent in business*, fervent in spirit, serving the Lord;" and no man will be "fervent in spirit," who is not "diligent in business" according to his ability. Time was, undoubtedly, as these citizens honestly acknowledge, that St. Louis, with her wealth, and strong connections, could have pushed a system of improvements, which, with the many

Nature impairs natural advantages.

Man to work.

S. L's chance gone forever.

and strong natural advantages of Chicago, it would have been difficult to overcome. But that day has gone by forever, and she will have to take a quite subordinate position, willingly or unwillingly.

An affirmative as well as negative to this question.

This important question, however, of where the chief city of the West is to be—and if of the West, of the continent also—has not merely a negative but an affirmative side. St. Louis' disadvantages and relative decline are no cause of Chicago's progress, but its direct effect. Nor could these remarkably diverse results be witnessed, without positive and powerful causes. The same honest consideration of them, which I trust the negative has had, will probably afford reasonable evidence that there is a "natural location," which, with the aid of art, and the ordinary blessings of Providence, must as surely be the "natural hub of the continent," as that the continent stands.

There is a natural hub.

Chi. central.

Look at the map, and observe how near the centre Lake Michigan lies, between the Atlantic and the Rocky Mountains, and from the British boundary to the southern line of Missouri. Geography is of little account, it is true, and therefore is it first named, though with St. Louis it is the alpha and omega. No doubt a city might be made more central to the whole Union, could she take the lakes another hundred miles south. That, however, being difficult, what place south of Chicago is able to take advantage of this one point of deficiency, even as relating to the entire Union? If none, Mahomet must go to the mountain, watery though it be and rather flat.

Lake not to be moved.

Chi. centre of Ill. tho' in N. E. corner—

As before remarked, however, mere geographical centrality is of trifling consideration. Chicago, though in the northeast corner of a State stretching 365 miles south, 160 miles west, and only 45 miles north, is yet the most central city in the State, it being easier for its every county to reach her than any other. So, too, every county in Iowa has more easy access to this lake port, 138 miles from its eastern edge, than to any other place. Such centrality has significance and power in regard to commerce and manufactures, operating so effectually that, as we have seen, cut-offs are of no account; and we not only draw trade from close around St. Louis herself, but take nearly the whole of it from Southern Illinois, which she monopolized; and the prize secured is made doubly sure, because not only art but nature herself conjoins to create this centrality.

—centre for Iowa.

Nature, too, gives centrality.

Lake chain—

Nature, not art, stretched out this unequaled chain of crystal waters, over a thousand miles long, from the ocean; and here she wedded lakes with rivers. Right here close to Chicago, and on land which our children will see within the corporate limits of the city, the waters started on their opposite courses; part for the St. Lawrence and the Atlantic Ocean, part for the Father of Waters and the

Gulf of Mexico.* The union of the Valley of the Lakes with the Valley of the Rivers, truly Nature's glorious handiwork, man with genuine art has strengthened by the Illinois and Michigan canal, soon to be perfected by enlargement, permitting any boats to reach the lakes that navigate the rivers. It is therefore no illegitimate assumption of supremacy, that the Queen of the Lakes should also become Queen of the Rivers. "What, therefore, GOD hath joined together, let not man put asunder."

—union with rivers.

Queen of Lakes also Queen of Rivers.

Observe, too, how nearly every writer quoted—many more are omitted—and all in the interest of St. Louis, not merely concedes the diminished importance of the rivers in which her strength lay, but actually argues from it as a main premise, the indispensable necessity of creating more railways, the strongest means art has yet devised for the advancement of cities. Have the construction and results of railways been herein-before unfairly considered? And if she be already so injured by one of the chief lines in her own State, what magic influences will change this her poison into nutritious food? If the first few years have despoiled her of grain-trade and jobbing business, as we shall see, and from the regions where she had the whole of them, how are railway influences to work against their nature to favor her? Year by year, will she suffer more and more from "flank movements," till her flanks shall have shrunk to what she can grasp in her digits.

St. L admits superiority of art.

Railways injure her.

How to recover.

The *Chicago Times*, in reply to a St. Louis paper, generously admitting that Chicago could become a Philadelphia while St. Louis was to be the New York of the West, pithily observes:—

Chi. Times.

> St. Louis is a hundred years old. Chicago is thirty. St. Louis attained her greatest prosperity upon the "river trade," when there were no railways to divert that trade from its unnatural outlet in the Gulf of Mexico to its natural outlet on the Atlantic. Chicago is the growth of railways and railway commerce, united to the inter-ocean commerce of the great lakes. Chicago is the half-way house on the great commercial thoroughfare across the continent. St. Louis is a way-station on a side-track.
>
> All the railways St. Louis has helped to build, that have not bankrupted their builders, have contributed more to the growth of Chicago than they have to the growth of St. Louis. The reason is, that commerce moves around the globe on lines of latitude, and not on lines of longitude. St. Louis is not on the commercial parallel.
>
> If Chicago has attained in thirty years the greatness that it took St. Louis a century to attain, how long, at the same rate of relative progress, will it take St. Louis to become the New York to the Chicago Philadelphia?

St. L. an old river city—

—Chi. a railway city.

St. L not on commercial parallel.

When St. L. to become N. Y. and Chi. Phila.

While St. Louis laments the construction of even the Hannibal and St. Joe Railroad, within her own boundaries, we rejoice in it, for the last report of the Chicago, Burlington and Quincy Railroad gives the following amounts of through freight: From Quincy to Chicago, in 1866, 10,566 tons; in 1867, 9,332, a decrease of 1,234 tons. From

Loss of trade to St. L—

—increase to Chi.

* My friend, Mr. Gurdon S. Hubbard, thank GOD still living here, passed with loaded boats frequently from 1818 to 1826, from the south branch of the Chicago River through the Saginaska Swamp in high water into the Des Plaines and Illinois River. The confirmatory extracts (p. 63,) from General Wilson's report, were incorporated after this was in the printer's hands.

Natural passage from lake to river.

C. B. and Q. road. *points beyond Quincy*, in 1866, 8,754 tons; in 1867, 19,195, an increase of 10,441 tons. From Chicago to Quincy, 1866, 28,896 tons; in 1867, 35,165, an increase of 6,169 tons. To *points beyond Quincy*, in 1866, 32,230 tons; in 1867, 47,761, an increase of 15,531 tons.

Increase from Iowa. The same report shows also the direction of trade from Iowa, which was equally St. Louis' domain with Missouri: From Burlington to Chicago, in 1866, 12,271 tons; in 1867, 10,954, a decrease of 1,317 tons. From *points beyond Burlington*, in 1866, 29,921 tons; in 1867, 34,428, an increase of 4,507 tons.

Local trade greater. These figures, it is true, are small compared with local freights along the line, which to Chicago in 1866 were 432,572 tons; in 1867, 519,359, an increase of 87,787 tons. And from Chicago, in 1866, 239,365 tons; and in 1867, 264,110 tons, an increase of 24,735 tons. To be equal west of Mis. Such will be the figures in a few years west of the Mississippi, as well as east, when the country shall have become equally settled, and bridges now building afford uninterrupted communication.

St. L.'s trouble about bridge. At present St. Louis is much exercised, not only about the North Missouri Railroad, but concerning the bridge over the Mississippi. The latter, too, interests Chicago, and one of our enterprising bridge-builders, Mr. Boomer, obtained of the Illinois Legislature a charter for a bridge at St. Louis. The bridges building at Quincy, Burlington and other crossing places—the St. Louisian names them, (p. 13)—answer very well for North Missouri and on west. Still, there is a rich Chi wants it. and extensive region off southwest of St. Louis, that is best accommodated with a Chicago connection directly through our sister city, if it can be done without hitting that barn. But for some reason or St. L. opposes. other, they seem to think that if Chicago builds it, it becomes a Chicago bridge, and they are fighting it with might and main.

Will be built A bridge will be built there, however, and though jocosely treated, St. Louis will find it no joke. Were it the only bridge, that would give her consequence; but it will be one of half a dozen or more, and the direct effect of each one is to facilitate business with the East. Will aid St. Louis— To the country adjacent in Illinois, which naturally trades with her, and which we acknowledge she has, it will be an advantage, and therefore aid her; and it will help to keep the country due West and Southwest, which, without a bridge, would surely forsake her. But —yet poor as a main reliance. when counted upon as a chief means of St. Louis' growth, she may be disappointed. Most probably that one bridge of hers, will bear Chi. wants half-a-dozen. more business to Chicago, than to St. Louis, and of the half-dozen or more, each one northward becomes more and more a Chicago bridge.

Contest for territory close to St.L. Yet about this very region in Illinois, which has been conceded to her,—for we are quite as desirous that she should grow as any other of a dozen cities that are to help Chicago to her superiority over the whole of them,—of the Morgan, Jersey and Madison region, which has probably given St. Louis as much trade as any three counties, the last report of the Chicago and Alton Railroad Company speak of a new and important branch just opened, one entered as a branch in the list, (p. 36): *C. and Alton R. R. report.*

The St. Louis, Jacksonville and Chicago Railroad, which was completed to a connection with your line at a point about thirty miles from St. Louis, on the 1st day of January, 1866, is developing a large traffic; but the principal advantage to be derived by this Company from traffic originating on that line will be through its northern connection which will be much further from the terminus of your line, at Chicago, than the present connection is from St. Louis. **Jacksonville road opened.**

The traffic of that line is now almost exclusively with St. Louis and passes but a short distance over your Road; but with the northern connection made, the traffic will be mainly with Chicago, and will be a source of much greater profit to your Company, by reason of the greater distance it will pass over your route. **Takes trade from St. L. to Chi.**

Both the Quincy region and that of this Jacksonville road, equally with that west of the Mississippi, belonged to St. Louis. These are only specimens of what branches are doing and will do; and when, where and how, is St. Louis to work a change in her favor with either nature or art? One or other, or both, must operate rather differently from what they have done in years past, or the Queen of the Lakes waxes stronger and stronger, and she of the rivers relatively, and only relatively, weaker and weaker. She counts upon her ability by cross lines, as we have seen, to draw the business of the Northwest, which, as we shall see, is her chief reliance, as it is of Chicago. One of these and the first to be built, is to finish the north and south road in the valley of the Missouri, from St. Joseph to Omaha. This is so surely to aid St. Louis, that her staunch supporters of the Hannibal and St. Joe road have taken it in hand, and assure me it will be finished to Omaha by July next. Somebody is to be disappointed in regard to this north and south line, for the last report of the Northwestern Company remarks:— **This a fair example of other roads—work for Chi. against St. L.** **Cross lines wanted.** **Mo. Valley Road.** *Report of N W. R. R.*

The parties controlling the Sioux City Branch of the Union Pacific Railroad to be constructed from Sioux City, situate on the east bank of the Missouri river, in Iowa, and about one hundred miles northerly of Omaha, to some point on the Union Pacific Railroad, west of Omaha, have recently decided to construct that line of road from Sioux City, down the east shore of the Missouri river some seventy-five miles, to a point about six miles west of St. John's Station, on our Iowa line of road, and a connecting line of road from such point to St. John's Station is also being built. The intention now is to complete this new line from our road at St. John's to Sioux City this year, and have it ready for business next spring. It will prove an important feeder, bringing us the business of the rich country it traverses, the growing traffic of Dacotah and the Upper Missouri river, and will give some importance to Sioux City as a steamboat point of departure for the Fort Benton and Montana Region. **Sioux City to Omaha.** **Upper Mo. trade.**

Another line of railroad is also being now actively constructed from our present depot at Council Bluffs along down the valley of the Missouri river, on the Iowa side, to St. Joseph, Missouri, the western terminus of the Hannibal and St. Joseph Railroad. About forty-five miles of this road, from Council Bluffs to a point opposite Nebraska City, the largest town in Nebraska, Omaha perhaps excepted, is already nearly or quite completed and will be in full running connection with us this fall. This line and the line from St. John's to Sioux City, in connection with our own line along the valley of the Missouri, from St. John's to Council Bluffs, gives us the business at once of near one hundred and fifty miles along the rich valley of the Missouri to add to the earnings of our main lines from Chicago to that great valley. **Omaha to St. Joe.** **150 miles Chi. lines.**

4 Chi. roads– The Rock Island, also, comes in between the other two, and no doubt expects to share in the business; and then the Burlington and Missouri, between the Rock Island, and the Hannibal and St. Joe. With four Chicago roads, and only one or two of these cross lines –St. L. 1 or 2. to St. Louis, must she not revolutionize the nature of trade, to turn those same currents in her favor, which with only one road, and that close to her, and built directly in her interest, has set with such tremendous force against her, as that its construction is justly deemed the severest blow she has yet received? I say yet, for we shall find Another road. another line in contemplation, still more injurious. Northern Missouri and Kansas and Nebraska, will fortunately be supplied with five roads, perhaps six, competing to take their trade to the lake ports, the very best they can have, at the lowest rates. What possible chance has St. Louis to succeed against such a combination?

Mo. Dem. The *Missouri Democrat*, of Nov. 8th, urging its citizens to the importance of General Hammond's road to Omaha, remarks:—

Omaha Reg. Without strength from St. Louis, the road cannot be built. Meanwhile, the Omaha *Register* of Saturday says:

Chi. trade. "Let one go down to the warehouse of the Chicago and Northwestern railroad, on the levee, and he will give an idea of the extent of the trade which is growing up with Chicago. There is a large warehouse packed full of merchandise from that place, which an army of teams is engaged in transferring to the stores of Omaha traders. The Chicago trade is rapidly assuming enormous proportions."

Omaha telegram. Dec. 28th the *Chicago Republican* had the following dispatch from Omaha:—

Bridge built. The locomotive has come to town, and this time not on a flat-boat or as steamer freight, but on its own wheels and by its own steam across the new railroad bridge that now links Omaha to Council Bluffs. The structure is a substantial pile bridge without a draw, which latter will not be necessary through the ice-bound winter months. The bridge-builders have worked with immense energy, and have their ample reward, for the connection is now complete and without break from Chi- Continuous line 1040 mi. cago for *one thousand and forty miles* toward the heart of the continent. This gives an opportunity for the winter freight and travel to pour an uninterrupted stream across the Missouri and up the Platte Valley to the terminus of the great Pacific road. Although Gen. Casement announces that actual track-laying is suspended during the close months of winter, the interim thus helped by the new bridge will enable the railroad company to bring forward an immense amount of material and equipment for spring operations. The Union Pacific Company will build Pushing Pacific road. three hundred miles of track next season, and will inevitably add to their freight and passenger business immensely. Of course Omaha is jubilant over the new bridge, and could scarcely be persuaded to go to bed at all on Friday night. The draw will be put in in the spring, early enough to open the way for river craft.

No competition with St. L. north of St. Jo. road As for serious contest with St. Louis for the trade north of the Hannibal and St. Joseph and the Atchison railroads, it is idle to think of. When her capitalists shall see their duty—and they must mainly defray the cost and do the work—they will, in time, build two or three roads across Chicago's seven lines west of the Mississippi. Each Her lines will help Ch. one of her lines, nevetheless, will send more business into Chicago than into St. Louis.* Ultimately there will be intermediate east and

Perversion of St. L roads * The danger of this perversion of St. Louis railroads, seems to be understood by the knowing ones, for after Mr. Fagin's speech (see p. 67,) Judge Bates, the President of the North Missouri road, was called to speak, and among other things said:

N. Mo. Road and branch's "There is another matter I think it not improper to mention. There are two roads planned, and upon which some work has been done, to be connected with the North Missouri road, the Iowa Central, and west roads; but being now wide apart, we would favor a few north and south to bring traffic upon our lines.

Probably St. Louis with Cincinnati, (p. 76) will find the Northwest grapes rather acid, and conclude that "the business between Chicago and the Northwest is very much over-estimated by our community." They may, too, be quite happy, as is Cincinnati, in the "hope to command a full share from the region lying from seventy to one hundred miles north of" St. Louis. For her "full share" even of that, will not only be drawn upon by the Hannibal and St. Joe road; but she will be fortunate beyond expectations, if there be not another east and west line between her and that faithful ally. For just in time for the printer, the *Missouri Democrat*, honestly doing its duty to arouse St. Louis to its dangers, publishes the following from the *Liberty* (Clay co. Mo.,) *Tribune*, of 10th January:—

Sour grapes in northwest

70 to 100 m's very good.

Hard to keep that.

Mo. Dem. and *Liberty Trib.*

The West Branch of the North Missouri Railroad.—It is well known that the location of this road is up the bank of the Missouri river, and therefore is not of general benefit to the great majority of the people of our county. We lay no claim to much railroad knowledge, but we cannot, for the life of us, see what the road expects to gain, beyond its grade, by its present location. The history of railroads prove conclusively, that people never cross one road to ship on another, situated as close together as the Cameron and North Missouri will be. Clay county is one of the richest in Missouri, and her trade is worth something to any road; and nearly all this the road proposes to cut off and send to Chicago by her present location. The North Missouri is a St. Louis road, and is managed by St. Louis men, but we must confess that Chicago needs no better *drummer* than the present location of this road.

Trouble ab't N. Mo. road west branch.

Trade does not cross roads.

If St. Louis expects to reap any advantage from the West Branch of the North Missouri in Clay county, she must build the road so as to make Liberty a point. By the present location the Missouri will present the anomaly of a railroad traversing each bank—for the road from Pike county, Mo., through Ralls, Audrain, Boone, Howard, Saline, Lafayette and Jackson to Kansas City, will be built and that too, before the people of St. Louis get their eyes fairly open—and the interior of the rich counties on each side without any outlet except cross roads, most of them leading to Chicago. This is what St. Louis is pleased to style her splendid railroad system, but which should more properly be styled a system to build up the Eastern cities to the detriment of St. Louis.

Liberty to be a point.

Pike Co. road east and west.

Astonishing as it may appear, on a visit to St. Louis the other day, we found leading business men who were not aware that the Kansas City and Cameron railroad was running, and carrying east millions of trade that formerly went to St. Louis. How are we to account for such indifference on the part of St. Louis men?

St. L. ignorance of Cameron road.

To come to the point at once, if St. Louis expects to retain the trade of Clay county, she must build the road in question so as to compete with other roads. The people are not going to cross energetic and ably managed roads and travel 20 miles to ship on the North Missouri. They will patronize the nearest road. If St. Louis affords equal advantages Missourians will sustain and give her the preference; if not they will go where their interest points. So far as Clay county is concerned, the bulk of her trade can be retained to St. Louis by locating the North Missouri *through* Liberty. Do so, and our word for it, the road will do more trade from this county in a week than it would in three months up the river bank.

How retain Clay Co.

Trade with St. L. with equal facilities.

---

the St. Louis and Cedar Rapids, that in turn connecting with the Cedar Valley road, both running north, and it is hoped to extend them through Minnesota to St. Paul. It is important for the interests of St. Louis that these roads should be controlled by St. Louis, either through the North Missouri Railroad Company, or otherwise, or they may be so controlled as to become feeders to the roads running east and west in the interests of Chicago.

I hope the board will excuse me from further remarks."

St. L. to control or they become Chi. roads.

Quite probably they excused him. But if they did, will the roads altogether refuse freight and passengers destined for Chicago? With the direct interest that great State will have in facilitating intercourse eastward and to its chief market, will not an Iowa legislature find proper means to prevent adverse discrimination?

Iowa will take care of itself.

Remember Pike Co. road

We most respectfully ask the business men of St. Louis to give the subject their serious consideration. Let them remember the proposed Pike county road, the most dangerous to her interests yet agitated, and the certainty of its being built, and that, too, on the bank of the river opposite the present location of the North Missouri road; and also remember that the trade of a county as rich in every resource as this is, will be sought after, and will flow into the hands of the city that throws out the greatest inducements in the way of roads, etc.

Situation of Clay Co.

To understand the force of this it should be remembered, that Clay county is almost due west of St. Louis, on the north bank of the Missouri river, a little east of its great bend from its course south to east. The Cameron and Kansas road runs through Clay county on the west side, which is a Chicago road, as we have seen. This north and south Missouri Valley Railroad is expected to accomplish great things for St. Louis. But she is in a dilemma. If she run her road to the Missouri along its banks, as she might be expected to do, the business of Clay county will not seek it across a Chicago road. And if she cross the Cameron road, what becomes of business west of it?

Cameron and Chi. road.

A dilemma.

Pike County route a new one—

The Pike county route has not before been heard of. It starts from the Mississippi some 50 or 60 miles north of St. Louis, running due west, crossing the Missouri about 50 miles west of Jefferson City, making almost an air line to Kansas. Quite a proper line is it for the route traversed, and for Chicago; and though prospective, will be built before many of the roads St. Louis has upon her list of hopes.

—proper for country and Chicago.

Contest for area S. W. of Missouri.

For business south and southwest of Missouri to the Gulf, there will be some contest. If the wealth of St. Louis be largely nsed to buy up roads and let them lie idle rather than work in their natural channel, that for a time may prevent business seeking the lakes; but will it therefore go to St. Louis? Mr. Cobb felicitates himself and St. Louis, upon the "sagacity and liberality of Mr. Thomas Allen, in giving $350,000, besides a proportion of the $375,000 bonus for the Cairo and Fulton road of Missouri, which is of no use to him, which he did not want, and which, in its original aim, was more hostile to St. Louis than the Hannibal and St. Joe foreign movement,"—read the entire quotation again, (p. 40). If friend Allen can find no better use for his wealth than that, he had better come to Chicago. What a villainous scheme he nipped in the bud, if it really were a more rascally trick than that "Hamilton and St. Joe" affair! But the Illinois Central has power and inclination, and will find ways and means to afford southeastern Missouri and Arkansas and Texas an avenue to the lakes as well as to St. Louis, creating fair competition for that important trade. Did not St. Louis fear to meet it, would their solid men write such letters as that over their own names?

Mr. Allen's purchase of Cairo and Fulton road.

A villainous scheme nipped.

Difficult to control every line to lakes—

To control every avenue, however, between the region southwest of St. Louis and the lakes, will be somewhat difficult. The Illinois Central Railway will attend faithfully to Chicago interests thitherwards, though another competing route for St. Louis, and nearly as advantageous for Chicago, is opened from Little Rock, in Arkansas, *via* the Louisville and Chicago road. Even with the advantage of possessing Mr. Hood's barn, considerable knowledge of the tricks of the trade, will be requisite for St. Louis to hold that directly south of her. —or trade south of her.

But "flank movements" west are most feared and with ample cause. The *Missouri Democrat*, (p. 26), alluded to the Cameron and Kansas road, for which aid could not be gotten in Chicago, and probably for the very good reason that the Hannibal and St. Joe interest could and would take care of Chicago's interest there.* While poverty has hitherto prevented much aid to railways, capital has been and is rapidly accumulating, and unless her past record shall be falsified, and her nature essentially changed, she will do considerable henceforth to advance her own interests. This should be done, of course, where it will do most in her favor; and she evidently agrees with St. Louis in estimating "flank movements." The *Missouri Republican*, (p. 27), speaks of a road from Kansas toward Galveston being under contract and partly graded; and the papers announce the completion of 30 miles of road from Lawrence to Ottawa, part of the Galveston road, which is already connected with Chicago by the road to Leavenworth and St. Joe.

Flank movements. Cameron and Kansas road. Chi. can now help herself. Lawrence and Galveston road built 30 miles.

Now it happens that we have an instance right in hand, of the way Chicago capital is to be used. This Lawrence and Galveston road has been taken in hand exclusively by two wealthy Chicago citizens. Mr. William Sturgis is President of the Company, and its chief and efficient promoter, who is backed up by one of our millionaires, who refuses positively to allow his name to be used in this connection.† The two have spent about a quarter of a million each in building and thoroughly equipping the first 30 miles south, which has been in active use to Ottawa since 1st January. My friend assures

This a Chi. work. Mr. Sturgis president— —a capitalist with him. 30 miles built

* That was a mistake. Our citizens took $100,000 of bonds, and would have taken more had it been necessary. I relied upon what the editor said without due inquiry, and do not care to alter the text. A mistake.

† The circumstances of the case, however, justify me in taking the liberty with a friend of over thirty-five years, to say that it is Mr. P. F. W. Peck. I was not aware that Chicago men were interested in this road, until after the above was written, about completing thirty miles; when hearing that Mr. Peck had invested heavily, and Mr. Sturgis being at that time in Kansas, I went to Mr. P. for information, which he cheerfully supplied, but peremptorily refused that his name should be used. But it is too notable an example of what other millionaires can and should do, to be passed over in silence. Mr. P. F. W. Peck the capitalist.

Mr. Peck is one of about a dozen citizens whose advent antedates my own. He was a young merchant on his own account, while I was clerk for my father. In February or March, 1833, I aided to raise the frame of his store. The first frame building was Mr. Robert A. Kinzie's store, on the West Side: Mr. George W. Dole's store, south-east corner of Dearborn and South Water streets, was second; and Mr. Peck's third. Previous buildings were of logs. The first brick building was erected in 1833, on or near the corner of North Water and State streets, the brick so poorly burned that they crumbled away. The next was Mr. Heman Bond's dwelling, erected I think in 1834, where the post office now is. The third was Mr. Gurdon S. Hubbard's store, on the southwest corner of La Salle and South Water streets, erected in 1835, which for several years loomed up, the most conspicuous object from the praries for many miles. Third building in Chi. First brick.

Rev. Jeremiah Porter had organized the first Presbyterian Church of all the Northwest, (except that of the excellent Father Kent at Galena,) on the 26th of June, 1833, with 25 members, 16 of them belonging to the fort, where services were held until Mr. Peck's loft was habitable; when, without plastering, the front part was used as our church, and the rear, separated by a curtain, was the sleeping apartment of First Presb'n church in Mr. P's loft.

Sure to go on me that under the competent direction of Mr. Sturgis, and also of Major Henning, Vice President, and Col. Vliet, Engineer, it shall be built through to the State line, the end of their charter, within this year, if he and Mr. Sturgis have to furnish the entire capital, $2,000,000. Nothing can prevent this, if life be spared, but factious opposition on the part of counties traversed, which the strong friendship and liberal aid by county bonds which they have offered to induce to the enterprise, and the large interest they have in its most speedy 180 miles from Galveston in use. construction, forbid should be apprehended. I am told 180 miles from Galveston are already in use, and the intervening space will be filled by the time St. Louis shall have filled the gaps in her lines in her own State.

Small trade to Chi. Only a little traffic is expected from that distance; yet if there be any where in the Great Valley of the lakes and rivers one chief commercial and manufacturing city of easy access, all sections from the Gulf around to the Rocky Mountains, will pay it more or less tribute. Texas to be connected. Even Texas recognizes the importance of railway connection with Chicago, though there also the opinion prevails that St. Louis is "the *Houston Tel.* metropolis of the Mississippi Valley." Says the *Houston* (Texas) *Telegraph*:—

Growth of St. L. *St. Louis and Texas.*—The growth of St. Louis is one of the marvels of America. Thirty years ago it was a town of 6000 inhabitants; to-day it has a population of 229,000. It has increased nearly 100,000 in the last ten years. And it is now marching forward with giant strides to metropolitan wealth and power. It is not only the metropolis of Missouri, one of the richest States in the Union, but it is Metropolis of Miss. Val. the metropolis of the Mississippi Valley. And as the Mississippi Valley is rapidly becoming the heart of the Union, St. Louis bids fair at no distant day to be the central city of the United States. The Mississippi river above St. Louis is navigable for 800 miles, and below it for 1,345 miles; while the Missouri river is navigable Rivers 11,000 miles. above it for 3,000 miles. Altogether St. Louis has navigation for 11,000 miles. This puts her in communication by water with every town within a rich valley of 1,200,000 square miles, capable of sustaining a population of 200,000,000. When the Great Pacific Railroad is completed, which will not be very long, and St. Louis is in communication with New York on the east, and San Francisco on the west—the first 1,060 miles distant, and the second 2,300—there is no calculating the St. L. and C. rivals. rapidity of her growth. St. Louis and Chicago are rivaling each other in the race to overtake New York and Philadelphia, and these grand cities of the West will sooner approximate these great cities of the East than is generally imagined.

Railroad communication with St. Louis and Chicago will make the fortune of

---

Messrs. Peck and Porter, and the latter's study, until he erected his study on Lake street, about No. 150. There, too, we gathered the little urchins, mostly French and half-breeds, in the Sunday School.

Oldest building in Chi. New comers ought to look with reverence on that oldest building of the city, still standing on the south-east corner of South Water and La Salle streets, a humble monument to the early endeavors to plant religious institutions, where they now so abound, in this city of a quarter-million. How I would Church unity. like to pursue the subject, and speak of the excellent Methodist, Baptist, and Episcopal co-laborers in this holy work. There was no denominational division. We met in each other's churches, as most convenient; and the christian unity and love with which God started this embryo city has been one of its most influential means of advancement. But I must stop this.

Mr. Peck wealthy. Mr. Peck, with but a small amount of real estate compared with mine in 1836, has had the good sense to leave other business alone, keep his lots, and judiciously invest his income. I am poor, and he has put a quarter-million into this road, to be quadrupled if necessary. Nor is he the only millionaire that Other millionaires to follow his example. has and that will engage in these enterprises. Let them be doing in these few remaining years, that which will tell on the future of this city, more than ten-fold what the same expenditure of effort and money can do only ten years hence. We want Pecks enough of this sort to make up bushels, and what amounts will the grand-sons have to measure.

Houston and Galveston, and every energy of the State of Texas should be put forth to complete this communication as soon as possible. Not only will it make our cities great and wealthy, but it will enrich the entire State. When the people of the East, North, and Northwest, as also the Middle and Western States, can pour down into Texas by railroad, instead of going round by New Orleans, and crossing the Gulf, the revolution that will take place in trade and the increase of population are beyond our present calculation. The completion of this railroad communication, and the railroad communication with New Orleans, are the two great objects to be accomplished before Texas will fill up with population like the Northwestern States have done.

These connections important to Texas—

—to fill up like N. W.

"The Mississippi Valley *is* rapidly becoming the heart of the Union." Has it not, though, been proved a *non sequitur*, that therefore "St. Louis bids fair at no distant day to be the central city of the United States"? Geographically she is quite central of both Union and Valley; yet is it not quite significant that trade of the Valley itself, which she ought first to hold, is fast running away from her? is actually rushing, not to a point in that valley at all, but to the head of the lake valley? Where is the Mississippi Valley? Is not its chief part that Northwest, which their every writer concedes has been already lost to St. Louis, and by herculean efforts in railway building can alone be regained? What she is to the Mississippi Valley, she is to the rest of the Union, and nothing more. The Mississippi itself is only an indefinite viaduct, without head or tail, of which the lower part has incomparably the greatest value, and within ten years will actually do more business with Chicago than with St. Louis. Had it a head, somewhat could be predicated upon that important advantage. But with an indefinite number of heads, and they mere springs of supply like the sources of trade, which a city of any pretensions must have innumerably; and the very best advantage it has or can afford being a site somewhere near the centre of the Mississippi Valley, or within 150 miles of it, and upon either bank; that would hardly be accepted as sufficiently definite to be made a main premise in an argument as to either natural or artificial advantages.

Miss. Val. being heart of Union does not make St. L. so.

N. W., its chief part lost to her.

Mississippi no head.

Its benefits indefinite.

On the other hand, Chicago is not like every important inland city, located upon a long river or chain of lakes, with rivals above and below; but she occupies the sole seat of supremacy, at the farthest extremity of lake navigation; a site so prominent to far-sighted men long gone, that De Witt Clinton pointed it out as among the chief of the country.

Chi. at head of lakes.

Clinton predicted its importance.

As the investigation progresses, it will become yet more apparent, that if there is to be one central city to accommodate the entire Republic, and be so recognized, it cannot be upon any river, but must be here at the head of lake navigation. At all events, if St. Louis is to have that honor, she has quite a little job on hand, which will test the powers of her "race of humans": nothing less than to revolutionize art and nature. "Old-fashioned cause and effect," which probably includes nature, having signally failed to sustain St. Louis'

Centre of Republic at that head.

St. L. to revolutionize nature—

pretensions, notwithstanding firm faith in them; nothing remains but merely that her extraordinary "race of humans" should supersede the miserable rivers, with something of nature that will become more subservient to their Queen. Also, those false-hearted things of art, both new and old-fashioned, having forsworn allegiance to her majesty of the Rivers, and railways and canals all through the west, contemning her gracious sway and patronage; that same extraordinary "race of humans" will of course invent some new art to over-ride ordinary humans who dare to intrude upon the River Monarch in her march to greatness. For such a "race of humans" are too wise to waste their powers, however infinite; and invention or creation of new means is easier than correction of those incorrigible old offenders, who seem determined both naturally and artfully to work in favor of Chicago.

—also art.

Easier to invent new than to correct old forces.

That, however, is rather the weak side of the case, as it proves nothing positively. Who can tell what may not be done by an extraordinary "race of humans who [don't] build paper cities and air castles," but who have him of the *road* for a patron, and do live in and about Mr. Hood's barn! So that while treating the negative side of the case with that awfully tremendous solemn solemnity which befits it, the affirmative also had its appropriate consideration. Not that we are supposed to have answered the many salient points—nimble leapers are they verily over both facts and reason;—for this paper is designed for men who have observation and judgment of their own. Nor did it appear expedient to belabor with too serious consideration some of the more preposterous claims. However it may be as to the negative, it will probably be conceded that *nine* affirmative points are reasonably established, which let us glance at in reverse order:—

That the negative side—

—solemnly treated.

Affirmative has 9 points.

1st. (14.) *Cincinnati, St. Louis and Chicago, the chief Rivals.*—Whereas both the first and second cities largely led the third only 20 years since; the weakest in wealth, population, business and *prestige*, has made herself mistress of the entire Northwest, with no possibility of her dethronement except by creating new forces in nature, or by inventing an entirely new application of the old forces which have wrought the results. Yet this had been shown to be reasonably probable in considering the previous topic:—

1. Weakest beats the strongest.

2d. (13.) *The Difference between Chicago and other Western Centres.*—We found it was not one or two causes which produced the results but a remarkable combination, never before witnessed, and never to be again witnessed; because the habitable globe has no other such site, either occupied or unoccupied. Also, the more effective differences were so obvious, that we found them frankly acknowledged by those who suppose themselves rivals. Chief of these differences was Chicago's unequaled position at the head of

2. Combination of causes.

lake navigation, which had been previously considered under the topic—

3d (12). *The Lake Route to the East and Europe.*—Not only does this chain of lakes afford the grandest inland navigation of the world, but the lakes are so peculiarly located as to compel 500 to 600 miles north and south, and extending indefinitely to the Rocky Mountains and to the Pacific Ocean, to pay tribute to Chicago at the western extremity, giving this head-port so large an advantage over way-side ports, as to render it absolutely certain that she must be the emporium of the Lake Valley. So superior had the lakes proved to the many thousand miles of river navigation, that while commerce on the latter has relatively deteriorated, and at St. Louis, their chief port, has actually and largely diminished; that of the lakes has steadily and rapidly augmented, until Chicago has been for several years, and probably will continue to be for all time, the chief grain and provision market, not merely of our country, but of the world. As such, Europe must soon obtain ample and direct communication with it by the St. Lawrence. Requiring such a vastly greater tonnage to carry away the bulky articles of produce than to bring back ordinary merchandise; what other result can be expected, than that the cheap freights to Chicago, will not only render it the chief importing and exporting city between the Great West and Europe, but also for very much eastward? An influential consideration bearing upon this topic in regard to distribution from the lake port toward the Atlantic, as well as for facilitating business from the West, had been considered, and we had already ascertained the superiority of Chicago in having—

3. Lake route.

Chi. emporium.

Lakes superior to rivers.

Chi. chief grain and provision market.

Trade with Europe.

Chief for imports and exports of the West.

4th (11). *Five Rival Railways Eastward.*—These which we already have, supply far more facilities, and stronger competition, even without the lakes, their powerful regulator, than any other city possesses. Yet a sixth to Norfolk must soon be added, together with new lines to each of the others, several of which can be formed by uniting roads already in use with a few short links; which, if a little more circuitous, would carry at the same rates with other lines, to secure a share of the immense through trade.

4. 5 railways east—

—and others.

Also, Chicago has already become so completely and firmly the entrepot of the Northwest, the trade of which is the prize most coveted by every Atlantic port; that from Norfolk north, no city has an equal interest in creating the shortest, cheapest, and most numerous connections with any one city anywhere upon this whole continent, as with Chicago.

No city sought by seaboard as is Chi.

For this unexampled result, which speaks loudly, not only for this city, but for the importance of the region possessing such a centre, we had been prepared by considering facilities now in full operation

This caused by facilities west.

though constantly improving, to gather the productions of the Great Northwest, of which was first,—

5. Ills. and Mich Canal— —unites lakes and rivers. To be enlarged— —continued to R. Island.

5th (10). *The Illinois and Michigan Canal. Its possible continuation to Rock Island.*—The fact that a rain drop here falling from the skies, could half of it run its ocean-course to the Gulf of the St. Lawrence, the other half to the Gulf of Mexico, indicated the propriety of enlarging the connection, and here uniting the Great Valley of the Rivers, and the Great Valley of the Lakes, in indissoluble bonds. The value of these thousands of miles of river navigation, especially for the immense work of bearing onward to market the countless amounts of bulky agricultural products which the Mississippi Valley will soon produce, will compel the opening of water communication through to the lakes, from Rock Island direct, as well as by the Illinois River, on a scale commensurate with the trade.

Railway facilities greater.

But although the advantage of conjoining water communication of vallies which stretch a thousand miles each side of her, far exceeds any advantage of any other city of the West; yet this dwindles in comparison with railway facilities. As an opening of new routes, the effect of which upon the commerce of the whole world no man can anticipate, but which Chicago, from its advantages of direct commerce with Europe, as well as with Atlantic ports, must derive more benefit from than any two or three other cities, we had of necessity examined,—

6. Pacific railways. Several to be built. Chi. sure of most of the trade. Still not the basis of calculation— —nor montanic trade.

6th (9). *The Pacific Railways in Progress—Their Effects.*—The success of the two lines from Kansas and Omaha, which were designed to unite, but will now go through on routes several hundred miles apart, demonstrates their profits to builders and advantages to the country to such an extent, as to render certain the immediate aiding and construction of other routes. Connected with the most southern at Kansas and at Lawrence, as Chicago already is, and being sure of the chief business of every other line farther north by railways already built west of the Mississippi and Missouri, and rapidly extending; however important that trade, either from the Pacific coast or the montanic region, no city can obtain as much of it as Chicago, probably not one-third. Surely the trade of the Orient, which from ancient times has given wealth to the cities that could obtain it, is worthy of consideration in such an investigation as this. Notwithstanding, the Pacific trade being hypothetical, it was made a less basis in this estimate than business from the montanic region, which these same roads will control until intermediate lines are constructed, still more effectually to bear the traffic to Chicago. Yet even that might be regarded hypothetical, and was only incidentally introduced; the real basis being what had already been accomplished in that,—

7. Focal point of 11,000 miles of railway.

7th (8). *The Focal Point of the Great West is fixed immovably by over 7,500 of its 11,000 Miles of Railway centering at Chicago.*—

Not yet 18 years have transpired, since the first 42 miles of railway out of Chicago were finished to Fox River.* Now, 15 trunk lines run to all points of the compass—except from east to north where the lake is better than as many more railways,—each 242 to 974 miles, with numerous branches ramifying the West in all directions. 15 lines 242 to 974 miles

The system, too, has been so thoroughly established, by this long and wide out-spreading like the spokes of a wheel, that change is absolutely impossible. St. Louis, as we have seen, has been styled by her flatterers, the "natural hub of the continent." Whatever Chicago is called, she is in truth the artificial hub of the Northwest, and as such, of the Republic. Her railway spokes fasten her *felloes* to her so securely, that no rivers can wash them away; the wheel revolving with resistless power, so that no interposing wheel can come into existence. Chi. artificial hub of N. W —felloes secure.

Also, while each company has built its spoke solely to support its own interests, endeavoring to make the wheel bring grists to its own mill; yet an equal area cannot be carved out on the globe, upon which an equal number of miles of railway have been built in the same period, which so perfectly accommodate the country traversed. One half of all the railways of the West, are in these straight spokes; and over two-thirds of the remainder are supporting branches, almost as efficient stays of the wheel, as are the spokes themselves. The centre of a wheel like that, is not Chicago truly the artificial hub, at least of the Northwest? Adapted to stockholder's interest— —and to public. Chi. a sure hub.

Nor is this wheel of commerce, at the beck of any extraordinary "race of humans" hibernating toward the circumference, to be led to follow their example and disregard the laws of its very existence. While most wheels are centrifugal in their effects, that of commerce is centripetal, and most of that which comes within its whirl, will very likely find its centre. The wheel planned and constructed under such wonderful combination, would work true upon its focal pivot immutably fixed, not only by art, but by nature also; for, as we have immediately before considered— Wheel not to be changed, for—

8th (7). *Art following Nature's Lead, Chicago has no Taxes for Railways, though she has several times more than any Rival, and nearly two-thirds of all west of the Toledo and Cincinnati Road, and north of the Ohio River.*—The position of Chicago at the head of lake navigation, wrought a confluence of interest between her and the shrewd capitalists of New York and New England, which has abundantly relieved her feebleness in money. With barely asking —8. Art follows Nature. Joint interest of Eastern capital with Chi.

* The President of that Galena Railroad Company, Hon. W. B. Ogden, is now acknowledged Railway King of the West; and although he used to consider my calculations extravagant, no other man living, so far as I know, has so anticipated the importance of railways to this city, present and prospective; and to no one man is the city as much indebted for what she has in this regard, and is yet to have. Had Mr. E. K. Hubbard lived, whose early death was so deeply lamented, and who projected the Galena road, Mr. Ogden would have had a competitor who did appreciate the future of Chicago and the worth of its railways. Hon. W. B. Ogden railway king. Mr. E. K. Hubbard.

Spokes put in independently. her consent, and sometimes obtained with too much difficulty, they have built and inserted in the hub one spoke after another, giving each direction according to fancy and interest of the several builders. Wheel artistic. Yet, is not divergence wonderfully equal, and the whole wheel a specimen of artistic skill to any master wheel-wright who could have devised it? This grand triumph of art, the equal of which is not No Ch. work. found upon the globe, and probably never will be, was never planned by Chicago citizens, nor by those interested in its lands; but the most sagacious minds of the country adjusted its every part for their own individual gain, and for the good of the public. Seeking this eminent position of nature to erect their hub, a "natural location" prominent not only as the head of lake navigation, but also the point to connect the River Valley with that of the Lakes, Art surely followed Common sense ruled. Nature's lead. Not only so, but in this "world of many men of many minds," whether of an ordinary or extraordinary "race of humans," such a conjunction of human skill was never brought about without considerable common sense. That is an ingredient of character that will be admitted to partake more of nature than of art; and who can doubt that it was this lead to which art has judiciously submitted itself? Therefore, "art following nature's lead," both in matter and mind, this *chef d'œuvre* of all "races of humans," has No power to change what all interests desire. here obtained. And where is the power upon this continent that can break up that wheel or interfere with its revolutions? Nor does capital, nor city, nor country traversed, nor to be traversed, want any change; nothing but enlargement and the addition at the extremities of a few more bracing branches.

Can St. L. work a change? Suppose, then, an extraordinary "race of humans" hibernating at the extremity of a wheel-spoke which they imagine to be a "natural hub of the continent," would like to make a change, or prevent the wheel from working business into its own centre, will they be able to do more than to show their want of common sense in making such a Wheel sure to revolve. futile effort? I trow not. The wheel with its hub are sure to revolve, with sure results according to its laws, whatever any ordinary or extraordinary "race of humans" may attempt. May it not, then, enter into our calculations as a fixed fact, establishing it as a main premise in the argument, as we had presumed to do in the topic preceding?—

9. Basis not hypothetical. St. L miscalculates. 9th (6). *That Basis no longer Hypothetical.*—For any city to have fair promise upon preceding points, or even a majority of them, would be quite a feather in its cap. St. Louis has plumed itself upon actually possessing several, expecting upon that basis, especially that of the "natural hub of the continent," to secure the rest. But Prospero, p. 88, better apprehended her case than she does herself.

Promises to be tested. No city will grow indefinitely upon "that which it seemeth to have." For years it may be "tickled with the hair of flattery," and the gullible public be deceived with glittering phrases and false appearances; but time surely tests, sooner or later, the strength of a city's promises. Chicago herself has had to depend upon mere promise for ten to twenty years. But the time has at last fully come for their redemption; and she changes her base of argument from hypothesis, reasonable as it was, to acknowledged fact, solid truth.

Chi. changes from promise to fact.

Are any of these nine points hypothetic? Expansion and improvement spoken of—and necessarily in order to duly consider the future—may be more or less problematic. But what has been accomplished is a sure basis, until existing forces of nature and art shall be displaced by new inventions or new creations. And until St. Louis or some other city can claim at least a goodly share of these points, it is idle bombast to assume even to be a rival in the race with her who is already crowned Queen, not only of the Lake Valley, but of the entire Northwest.

She has these points. **A city must have several of them to be a rival.**

The five topics preceding these nine, are not so pertinent to this that they need consideration here; though another—*Public Improvements anticipated* 20 *and* 10 *years ago as a Basis*—would not be impertinent as to the natural position of Chicago. To say that improvements confidently predicted years in advance of their prosecution, and that the very lines foreseen which are now chief, were not natural, would accord more credit for prescience than I claim.

Other points omitted. **Improvem'ts natural or could not have been predicted.**

The idea has been to present somewhat in their order, the operating causes essential to the growth of the chief city of the Northwest, according to the natural configuration of the country, and present stage of inventions in art and science, leaving extraordinary influences and effects for their believers to claim and develop. Was not the result fairly, naturally, logically deduced, that by and from these causes, Chicago must be the great city of the Northwest? And now having taken that result and hastily traced back its operating causes, have we found any point disregarded, or over-estimated, or unfairly presented, which would destroy the result, or weaken or break the catenation?

Ordinary influences considered. **Causes traced to effects.** **Results traced to causes.**

Nor will it be denied, that if there be forces either in nature or art capable of supplanting all or any one of these considered, they must be wholly a new invention if not creation. Nor should that possibility militate a whit against this argument; for the Northeast would still have the same interest in centering trade here, and would use those new means for our advancement precisely as they have the old. Nor would any body who knows Chicago, suppose for an instant that we will lag behind any other city in applying improvements in art or science for our own benefit.

St. L. to invent new forces. **Chi. will use them.**

Neither will it be denied, that according to present knowledge, any city of the West to be entitled to prominence, not to say preeminence, should be able to claim of her own right at least a majority

A prominent city should have a majority of the points.

No city has three. West will build up great cities. Must help themselves. Fulfilling prophecy.

of these nine points; if not in perfection, at least in good measure. It is the literal truth, however, that except Chicago, not a city can do this. So far from it, not a single city of the west can claim any three of them. Because none can, is their relative growth so problematical. That these immense vallies of lakes and rivers, the chief and most valuable part of the whole continent, must afford many sites, both occupied and unoccupied where important commercial and manufacturing centres are to be erected, is as certain as the continuance of any "race of humans." Nature will do more or less for most of them; yet results depend mainly upon energy and industry. Even in Eden sloth was not natural to man, but he was put there "to dress it and to keep it." Now, he exercises the GOD-given right of dominion, and fulfills the prophecy—

Isa. xl., 3-5.

> Make straight in the desert a highway for our GOD!
> Every valley shall be exalted,
> And every mountain and hill shall be made low;
> And the crooked shall be made straight,
> And the rough places plain:
> And the glory of the LORD shall be revealed,
> And all flesh shall see it together;
> For the mouth of the LORD hath spoken it.

Nature of Union not apprehended. Benefits from our practice. State pride to operate.

Our country is too new, the nature of our institutions too little apprehended, to have any proper conception of the benefits of our division into sovereign, free and independent States, and yet by Federal compact created into another Nation, securing equal rights to all citizens in every State of this ocean-bound Republic, as it will soon become. Who can estimate the perfection in the science and art of Government to be developed in the experience of all these States in a century or two to come, when we shall properly apprehend our basis of State Sovereignty? When the area shall be occupied as it will be in only half a century, and this constant migration cease, and we begin to have that pride in our native State which inheritance of the paternal acres will speedily develope, what a stimulus is to be generated to give each of these States the best government with the least possible taxation.

Build great cities. Cities jealous of each other— —more of outsiders. *Jacksonville Journal.*

This State division, also, will have strong influence to build important cities, each State having becoming pride in its own offspring. Competition will create ample facilities for citizens or their own and neighboring States, to reach its chief commercial or manufacturing city or cities. While from man's nature he is jealous of his neighbor, and Blanche, Tray and Sweetheart will bark and snarl at the city that attains superiority; yet as against other States and the world outside, they will be a unit to do whatever their own chief emporium requires for its advancement. The *Jacksonville* (Ills.) *Journal*, sensibly observes:—

Chi. at home and abroad.

Chicago at Home and Abroad.—Every citizen of Illinois, when he is outside the limits of the State, finds it difficult to invent adjectives sufficient to express his admiration of Chicago, and cannot be earnest enough in his endeavors to make every one else think and speak concerning it just as he does.

He talks of it as the greatest place on the Western continent—the centre around which all creation revolves—the great hub, in comparison with which all such hubs as Boston are too insignificant to be mentioned—the favored spot upon this mundane sphere on which the sun shines more brightly, and with a more life-giving influence, than upon the common-place localities which surround this great *ne plus ultra.* Indeed, from their impassioned descriptions, it might well be considered, by the uninitiated, that Chicago was a second Garden of Eden on earth, but the moment that person returns within the limits of the State, in common with his fellow-citizens, he hurls at Chicago anathemas both loud and deep, realizing, if we may tamper with the quotation, that a city may not be without honor save in its own immediate vicinity. **Illinoisan praises it abroad.**

What are the causes of all the ill-feeling which exists against Chicago, we do not propose to discuss; probably the many scamps and rascals who hail from there, and go through the country cheating people, have given to Chicago, in the minds of some persons, an unenviable reputation; but aside from these things there are many points in the history of Chicago which it would be well for other smaller cities to make note of, and to benefit by. Among the more prominent of these points is the fact that very little of the ready money which is possessed by men in Chicago is ever salted down in some tattered stocking-leg, and hid away beneath the bricks of the fire-place, or in the innermost recesses of some closet. What Chicago does not eat and put on her back, and over her head in the shape of a roof, she expends in extending her business, in building stores and warehouses—and in making permanent and elegant public improvements. No sooner is money made than it is invested—no sooner does the interest come pouring in than it is sent out in such a shape that it will insure success in still greater business transactions. Thus Chicago grows, and thus her citizens have made her famous. Chicago fairly springs up in a night, like the fairy palace of Alladin—and rushes on most breathlessly in the race for supremacy—while her rivals, contenting themselves with the thought that what is slow will probably be sure, are content to plod along and be outstripped by the youngest contestant of them all. **Why jealous at home.** **Chi. example worthy.** **Her activity** **Thus Chi. grows.** **Others plod.**

Nothing venture, nothing have, is a maxim which Chicago has remembered—and a great many other places entirely forgotten. A great many of the capitalists of Jacksonville seem never to have learned this lesson, or at any rate are slow in putting it in practice with the means which are at their disposal. Jacksonville is a rich city, so strangers say, as they ride around her streets, and we do not doubt the truth of the assertion; but when we look around, we see but very little of it, comparatively, being used in the extension of the business of the city. Chicago is right in matters of enterprise, and numbers among its citizens some of the salt of the earth. Jacksonville boasts considerable of the latter commodity—but with the former she is not inconvenienced. St. Louis would never have been overtaken by Chicago if her citizens had been "off the same block" as those of Chicago. Money makes the mare go, but not money hid away in a strong box. **Do something.** **Use capital.** **Chi. enterprise—** **—beats St.L.**

This influence of the State alone, with none other, would insure many large cities in these immense areas of 60,000 to 150,000 square miles; for the chief motive power is to be railway corporations, to which legislatures give direction. This, it is true, might work adversely to any one central city of the West, and no doubt would, did not the general interests of every State require that all needful facilities should be afforded, and trade be allowed to find its natural channels with individuals and with States. Our prosperity rests more than we are aware upon free inter-State trade, secured by our unequaled Constitutional compact; the sacredness of which we shall learn to appreciate. It secures equal commercial privileges in all the States to all citizens, whereby such an outrage as "the Camden and Amboy" will ere long be righted; and in virtue of State sovereignty, too, because sister Commonwealths have the sacred word of New Jersey pledged to equality of rights. **States to create large cities—** **—yet must leave trade to natural channels.** **Cam. & Am. righted by State Sovereignty.**

Were Union broken Chi. would grow— Should our Heaven-ordained system of Governments be overthrown, which no one will fear when he understands State Sovereignty, even then the laws of trade would secure great pre-eminence to the commercial emporium of the Northwest. With *State Sovereignty*, however, to insure the erection of many important cities throughout the West; and with *National Union* to prevent improper restrictions, and leave trade a free course in its natural and artificial channels, we possess all opportunities that any reasonable man could desire. —with Union no favors desired.

The West a unit— While neighboring States will be jealous of Illinois, as the Tribes of Israel were of Judah when their King was chosen from the lion-tribe; yet no section of our country will be more of a unit than that between the Allegheny and the Rocky Mountains; and proud of their Queen, as against every rival, no reasonable service will be withheld to promote her prosperity. And we want no special favors only as merited. So that under our system of free Governments, if Chicago be the natural centre of trade, no earthly power can prevent the currents hither flowing; and, therefore, will she be the last city, and Illinois the last State, to permit any change in our system to impair her motto, "State Sovereignty, National Union." —proud of its Queen. Chi. and Ills. true to their State motto.

This an example of general considerations. So we might pursue every general consideration as we have the special, and if any one be less favorable for Chicago than for any other city, I am unfortunate in its non-discovery. Surely none have been perceived, and I think none can be, which are directly adverse. It would seem, therefore, that as upon the nine special and essential considerations, neither St. Louis nor any other site occupied or unoccupied can possiby claim any three of them, and that Chicago possesses the whole in full measure; she has and can have no rival, as she marches onward to her destiny, the emporium of the Northwest, and as such the artificial hub of the continent. No city having 3 of the 9 specified, Chi. has no rival.

This renders Chi. heart of continent. Thus far consideration has been mainly restricted to the Northwest. To be the emporium of that region would be ample; yet, as just remarked, that being secured, Chicago as certainly becomes the hub of the continent. Nor will even that proposition seem doubtful upon fair consideration of the premises. In this age of telegraph and railway, we must calculate and operate with their power and speed, or we fall far astern in the race of progress. Five hundred miles of distance is less, both in time and cost, than a hundred was forty years ago, except between a very few points. Changes of 40 years.

A centre draws trade from a distance. The trade of such a city cannot be restricted to its region naturally tributary, but by railways and telegrams it will draw from all quarters of the land, and gradually expand throughout the earth. Especially now, in the unsettled condition of the South, the old centres of business broken up and new forming, with the strong and natural predilections which the South and West have for each other, owing to their being agricultural, and taking a broad, expansive view of means and measures; why should not Chicago come in for her due proportion of the commerce and manufacturing of the extensive South? If so, then she will be continental. We need, therefore, to consider some points bearing upon the measure of her growth rather than its certainty, the first of which may be:— Chi. continental.

The Northwest is the Prize Contested—Its Extent and Resources.

St. Louis has thus far been our chief witness; and if better testimony could be given in our behalf, it would certainly be agreeable to read it. To judge from points already made, did she not give many and earnest assurances that she still covets the trade of the Northwest, it would be quite doubtful whether a city of the intrinsic character, and wealth, and power, the possession of which is acknowledged with pleasure, could have been in down-right contest with her "beautiful rival" for trade of one and the same region. Even in 1861, it was necessary to consider this point, and extracts were made from the *Missouri Democrat* and commented upon as follows:— St. L. good witness. Does she seek trade of northwest? Considerations in 1861.

Rivalry of St. Louis and Chicago.—Since writing these pages, it has occurred to me that some extracts from St. Louis papers themselves would throw light on this subject, and be entitled to more weight than anything I could say, and I have found a few weeks' file of the *Missouri Democrat*, one of its most influential and reliable commercial papers. I was forcibly impressed with the fact, apparent in every number, that the business of the Northwest is the prize sought there as here, and almost the same territory that is hereinbefore named as belonging to Chicago, is the main reliance of our rival. I present a few extracts: Rivalry of St L. and Chi. Northwest the prize.

"*Commerce of St. Louis—Trade North and South.*—It is by no means an uninteresting theme for St. Louisians to well on the resources ot trade, and the natural law governing commerce; but the inexorable logic of facts to practical minds, is worth more than volumes of specious theories, based upon local sympathy or sectional prejudice. St. Louis has, or has not a commerce. If she has a commerce, that commerce, like the mighty river that is our principal medium of trade, has a source and an outlet. We might as well deny that the Mississippi river rises in the north, as to deny that in its course from head lakes to St. Louis, it washes the shores of *that great empire that constitutes the right arm of our commerce.* And however much our sympathies would lead us to go to the mouth of this great artery of trade, and force commerce *up* to this point, the dictates of ease, and the dread of encountering powerful natural resisting forces, would make us seek its source, that we might glide smoothly down the natural current of this great highway, gathering the wealth of the country in our course, and deposit it leisurely at our door. * *Mo. Dem.* '61. River trade her reliance. Flows down stream.

"Then look at the Northwest. Free, industrious, self-reliant, intelligent, enterprising, cool, loyal, tolerant, contented and happy. Opening up an empire of matchless resources; subduing the wilderness; building towns, cities, railroads, school-houses, churches, colleges, and laying the enduring foundation of true civilization. Rich in the production of life-sustaining cereals which invite our commerce, and powerful in the possession of free institutions, which challenge our admiration. With soil and climate no way superior to the South, the Northwest has outstripped everything in the annals of improvement, by that policy which alone will attract an industrious population, and insure permanent happiness. While the South is prating about extra rights, the Northwest is marching on to greatness by a proper use of the rights she had under the same constitution that shelters and guards the interests of all. All sections have rights alike, and the difference in condition is dependent more upon the use of the rights we have, than on the acquisition of rights supposed to be withheld. Advantages of N. W. Outstrips the South— —by using its powers.

"This picture is not drawn from prejudice towards one, nor favor towards the other section of our common country. It is only to be deplored that the facts exist which make the contrast so glaring. Opinion honest.

St. L., no hope— —but in securing that trade.

"In view of the truth which every intelligent man must acknowledge, what hope is there for the future greatness of St. Louis, in commerce, in manufactures, in good government, in permanent wealth and substantial happiness, but in the cultivation of the most intimate and friendly relations with all sections, and particularly that portion of the country that can throw into our lap *the very trade she must secure in order to maintain her position?*"

What is N W? Rivalry for it in 1857.

"*Commerce of St. Louis.*—In pursuing this subject we must remark preliminarily that the Northwest, embracing Illinois, Wisconsin, Iowa, Minnesota, North Missouri, Kansas and Nebraska, the largest grain growing region in the nation, was paralyzed by successive failures of crops, dating back as far as 1856 and coming up to 1859. * * Then [1857] commenced the struggle between the two great rivals—St. Louis and Chicago—for the trade of the Northwest. Chicago was crippled, but St. Louis had thrown away her advantage, and now we first hear that old customers of St. Louis are making their purchases in Chicago, on terms denied them here, and of course the products of the country followed the merchants.

St. L., needs to know the truth. Iowa trade gone to Chi. Reason for diversion.

"* * Now this comparison between the action of St. Louis and Chicago may be distasteful to our merchants, but it is only drawn to show the utter nonsense of expecting to achieve commercial supremacy over an enterprising rival by a do-nothing policy, even with all the natural advantages in our favor. 'Men learn wisdom by the woes they suffer,' and it certainly occurs to us that St. Louis should rejoice to have her blunders exhibited in contrast with the success of those who have profited by her mistakes. St. Louis ought to have the immense trade of the Upper Mississippi Valley, but *inaction* won't secure it. The immense and growing trade of Iowa, for instance, which used to flow naturally to this point, has been driven away by repulsion, and forced across the country by hundreds of miles of expensive land travel to Chicago, where, in reaching the point of transhipment it has to cross the great natural highway that would bear it cheaply to St. Louis. Now there is a reason for this diversion, and it seems to us that if St. Louis does not hunt out that reason, and energetically apply herself to the restoration of that trade, that she is sadly wanting in those directing powers which will secure commercial success.

Other trade lost. Whence comes trade?

"The same with the trade of Western Illinois, Wisconsin, all of Minnesota, and North Missouri. The vast and accumulating wealth of these regions could be deposited in St. Louis much easier than it can be taken to Chicago; and why is it not done? That's the question. We may talk about our Southern trade, and quarrel over the everlasting nigger; but where does the pork, beef, beans, wheat, corn, oats, hay, horses, mules, butter, eggs and poultry, that we consume here or *send South*, come from? Do they not come from those sections of the country we have named? And without these would not our Southern trade be barren of profits? What steamer could prosecute a successful trade, freighted but one way? And who does not know that freights South depend upon Northern supply?"

St. L's. reliance. More unsafe in future than past. St. L's "toting"

It will be observed that to get the trade of the North-West, which "she must secure in order to maintain her position," the river routes are mainly to be relied upon, and the crossing of the chief—the Mississippi—in the railway transit Chicago-ward, is a strange anomaly in trade. Could this reliance upon her natural highways ever be true and valuable to St. Louis, it must have been hitherto, for the boating interest is fast diminishing, and the railroad fast increasing, and facilities for crossing the Mississippi will multiply year by year. The large ferry boats will be almost equal to the Rock Island bridge, that St. Louis has been in vain trying all sorts of means to destroy, and other bridges will no doubt be erected. But without bridges, mere transfer of cars across the Mississippi, is of small account, not at all equal to the cost of sacking grain and "toting" it on the levees if it is to go to St. Louis.

N. W. roads wanted— —none built. Han. & St. Joe road seeks its own interest.

Some effort has been made to save a portion of the trade west of the Mississip by building roads north and north-west from St. Louis. But with the exception of one intersecting the Hannibal and St. Joseph, none have been built, and nothing is said of them in those papers that I have examined, except considerable berating of the Hannibal and St. Joseph road as being adverse to the interest of St. Louis. No doubt it is managed to promote its own advantage, and if the business upon *this most southern of all the Chicago roads* west of the Mississippi has such a tendency in this direction, how is it to be upon the others?

North roads difficult.

The construction of roads northward from St. Louis to intersect the other Chicago roads, will for a considerable period be very difficult, if at all practicable, and meanwhile the five roads built or fast completing from the Mississippi to the Missouri, will have been so long established as to have attached the business of North Missouri and Iowa to these Chicago roads, and make it difficult for St. Louis to obtain even a small part. Her one or two roads—when gotten—will be unequal competitors with our five or more; and even with equal facilities of transit, except for the inconsiderable proportion going to the extreme South, what are to be the inducements to draw that business away to the South to reach St. Louis, rather than take the direct routes eastward? Not equal to East lines.

I make only one further extract: *Mo. Dem.*

"*Commerce of St. Louis—Comparative Receipts and Shipments North and South.*—When we hear talk of the great balance of trade in our favor from one section over another, we are irresistibly led to compare statistical records of such facts, so as to enlighten the public mind and prevent the inconsiderate statements of prejudiced persons from being taken as law, to the damage of commerce. Trade north and south.

"The following are the receipts of all articles of Southern production at this market for the year 1860, which do not vary much from those of the previous year: Receipts south.

		Weight—tons.			Weight—tons.
Sugar, hhds	47,637	23,818	Coffee, not grown in the South, but brought principally by way of New Orleans—sacks	109,427	3,551
" bbls	7,857	982			
" boxes	13,755	200			
Molasses, bbls	54,055	12,850			
" kegs	10,471	523			
Rice, tierces	7,078	2,300	Total receipts by river and rail		44,224

"The receipts of wheat, corn, rye, barley and oats for 1860, were as follows: Receipts north.

	Bushels.	Weight—tons		Bushels.	Weight—tons.
Wheat	3,555,875	106,676	Barley	291,130	10,065
Corn	3,516,808	100,470			
Oats	2,364,212	41,373	Total	9,886,979	263,035
Rye	158,994	4,451			

"Here we have *two hundred and sixty-three thousand and thirty-five tons of freight,* nineteen-twentieths of which came from the North by way of the river, against *forty-four thousand two hundred and twenty-four tons* coming from the South. We do not claim that these figures are correct to a fraction, but they will be found sufficiently so on examination to show the immense disparity between the shipping tonnage from the two sections of country that contribute to our commerce. But this slight exhibit is only a tithe of what we shall be able to show as we pursue the subject. The immense trade in hay, pork, flour, butter, cheese, lard, wood, lumber, etc., which nearly all come from the great North-West, will demonstrate the folly of cutting off the fountain of trade, by quarreling with the bone and muscle from which it flows. We shall show in our next, that the manufacturing interest of St. Louis is mainly indebted to the free North, for the very aliment that sustains it, and to fight away that region of country because they don't see fit to adopt our notions in their domestic relations, is simply to quarrel with our own bread and butter. 263,035 tons north. 44,224 tons south. Other items to add. Dependence of St. L. manufactures.

"But above all the trade of the mighty North-West should be sought after. The golden harvest should be garnered in St. Louis. Its railroads should be centred here. The enterprise of her people should be encouraged by throwing around it the powerful ligaments of commerce, and the whole country attracted to us by fair treatment, and the immunities of good neighborhood." Mighty N. W. trade to be sought.

As indicative of the present tendency of business, please compare the following receipts at Chicago of the articles above given as received at St. Louis: Chi. receipts of same articles.

	1860.	1859.		1860.	1859.
Wheat	14,277,083	8,060,766	Barley	617,619	652,696
Corn	15,212,394	5,401,870			
Oats	1,698,889	1,757,696	Total	32,124,961	16,104,542
Rye	318,976	231,514			

The difference in amount at the two cities, may speak for itself, but please notice that the *Democrat* says receipts at St. Louis "for the year 1860 do not vary much from those of the previous year," whereas at Chicago *the aggregate increase is about one hundred per cent.* The canal, which connects the two cities by water, and should take business to St. Louis equally as to Chicago, if she had power to draw it—the canal alone, brought to Chicago *nearly a quarter more corn than St. Louis received from all sources.* Both cities had the same regions to draw from the two years, and "nineteen-twentieths came from the North" to St. Louis; and if such is No increase at St. L.—Chicago doubles. Canal and its corn.

8—

to be the manner in which our rival is to recover her lost vantage ground—and I think it is—she is not long to be ahead of Chicago.

General opinion that St. L. is to lead.

Perhaps I am needlessly prolix, upon the advantages and prospects of these two competitors. But it has been generally conceded that one or the other was to be the great interior city of the continent, and nine-tenths have supposed it was to be St. Louis, and do still. If any reader has doubted the soundness of my claims for Chicago, these candid admissions by St. Louis against herself, must go far to sustain me.

Study railroad map.

Again I say—study a recent railroad map, and discover if you can a single point unfairly presented, either in favor of Chicago or against St. Louis.

St. L. fears realized.

These apprehensions have been more than realized. Still, St. Louis is energetic and powerful in her wealth, and although slow to realize the necessities of the case, she is becoming earnest, and a few railroads will be built. She knows the worth of the prize coveted. By years of monopoly, and when of comparatively little value, it had made her rich, and no wonder that she said, "above all, the trade of the mighty Northwest should be sought after." But how did she seek? Still hoodwinked with the delusion of river power, railroads northward, her only salvation, have been overlooked, or at least never found. They may do her no good; but her expectations fail utterly without them, and they will be built in time or times.

Prize known

How sought?

Railways neglected.

Results of contest for 11 years.

As this leading paper admitted, the struggle fully commenced in 1857; and above are results of four years, and herein of seven more. How long before she resumes mastery at this rate? Yet what possible influences can work a change in her favor? The figures of business, both in merchandise and in grain, hereafter given, cannot be gainsaid, and prove positively the truth of the above declaration, that the Northwest supplies "*the very trade she must secure in order to maintain her position.*" Has she—can she secure it? Will a road or two, or half a dozen, draw trade across our one to seven lines—probably more by the time she gets two only—when she is unable to keep trade close to her in her own State? Notwithstanding seven years more experience, the trade of the Northwest, as almost their every newspaper indicates, is still the apple of her eye. She will build one or two roads to get it; and probably when she finds them more treacherous than the Hannibal and St. Joe, she will then make up her mind that Northwest grapes are "mighty" sour.

How change them?

Cross lines not strong.

N. W. still sought—

—grapes sour.

What the prize?

And what is that prize which we have won? In 1861 I answered:

150,000 miles unequaled—

-advantages.

"It is an area of *over one hundred and fifty thousand square miles—and fast enlarging to twice that size*—the equal to which, in natural advantages, exists not on the globe in one body. Not like the old States, is it half uninhabitable, but nearly the whole the richest arable land and lakes and water-courses. Generally, it is healthy; its facilities for navigation and railroad building unsurpassed; its coa abundant; lead and copper mines superior, and its iron ore the purest and best in the world. It has limestone and other rock in abundance, marble of various kinds, gypsum, water-lime, salt springs, pottery clays, silex beds, and numerous other productions used in the arts and manufactures.

Ease of tillage.

Never was a country settled which so quickly and liberally rewarded the husbandman—the great basis of prosperity—whether in raising various kinds of grains, grasses and stock, or hemp, flax, tobacco, fruits, vegetables, etc. Not as in the older States is a generation or two worn out in subduing forests, but the farmer comes and plows and sows, and reaps a bountiful harvest the first or second year. Indian corn is the great essential in modern agriculture—"bread, meat and man

Crop first year.

ure" — and not ten cents a bushel is the average cost of its production, all through this territory tributary to Chicago. For grasses it is famous; and portions are not excelled for fruits of all kinds of the temperate zone, and wines are to be a staple production. Beyond doubt, the equal of this region was never opened to the occupancy of man.

Best region of the globe.

To exhibit how 150,000 square miles, and 3,000,000 population could be claimed in 1861, the following table was prepared. Additions are made of Kansas and Nebraska and the montanic region, together with a reasonable estimate of area and population now tributary:—

How the claim is made.

1,500,000 *Square Miles, having* 11,000,000 *Population, rapidly to become tributary to Chicago, of which* 300,000 *Square Miles, and* 7,000,000 *Population, already make it their Centre.*

1,500,000 sq. miles. 11,000,000 population.

Area. Population. Tribu'y 1861. Tribu'y 1868.

States and Territories.	Square Miles.	Population in 1860.	Tributary, 1861.		Tributary, 1868.	
			Sqr. Mls.	Popul'n.	Sqr. Mls.	Popul'n.
Ohio	39,964	2,339,511	....	....	....	....
Michigan	56,243	749,113	15,000	200,000	25,000	400,000
Indiana	33,809	1,350,428	15,000	250,000	25,000	1,000,000
Illinois	55,405	1,711,951	35,000	1,100,000	45,000	2,200,000
Wisconsin	53,924	775,881	25,000	500,000	35,000	1,000,000
Minnesota	83,500	172,023	10,000	100,000	25,000	300,000
Iowa	55,045	674,913	30,000	500,000	55,000	900,000
Missouri	67,380	1,182,012	20,000	350,000	25,000	600,000
Kansas	83,000	107,206	....	....	25,000	250,000
Nebraska	63,300	28,841	....	....	20,000	250,000
Old Northwest	591,570	9,091,879	150,000	3,000,000	280,000	6,900,000
Dakota	152,500	4,837	....	....	5,000	15,000
Montana	143,776	....	....	....	5,000	15,000
Wyoming	88,097	....	....	....	5,000	20,000
Colorado	106,475	....	....	....	5,000	50,000
Present Northwest	1,082,418	9,096,716	....	....	300,000	7,000,000
New Mexico	124,450	93,516	....	....	....	....
Arizona	130,800	....	....	....	....	....
Utah	109,600	40,273	....	....	....	....
Idaho	90,932	....	....	....	....	....
The West	1,538,200	9,230,505	150,000	3,000,000	300,000	7,000,000

Old N. W. **New N. W.** **The West.**

That is Chicago territory which transacts more business here than at any other city. New York has been and still is the emporium of the continent, for all sections have more dealings with her than with any other city. Philadelphia, Baltimore, and Boston, heavy centres of business as they are, are her tributaries. Not for several years can Chicago stand in that relation to the chief cities of the West, because New York will still be their emporium. For that reason, and that only, the whole West cannot be now claimed as Chicago's territory. The time must come, as we shall see, when the West will have far more traffic with itself than with the seaboard; and then, unless this argument be fallacious, Chicago will be its emporium.

What is Chi. territory? **N. Y. emporium of whole country.** **Why Chi. is not yet emporium of the West.**

It is difficult to realize that *six hundred thousand square miles* can really become tributary to one city. Yet to that must be added *five hundred thousand* more of the Territories already sure to us,

Area difficult to realize.

Small per cent. yet in farms.

and another *five hundred thousand* that must follow the lead of the rest. The rapidity of settlement, and the small per cent. yet cultivated of such an area, are important items. The United States census supplies the following information :—

Farms of N. W. 1850—1860. Land not in farms. Total area.

Lands of Northwest in Farms, 1850 *and* 1860, *and not in Farms.*

States and Territories.	Farms, per Census, 1850.		Farms, per Census, 1860.		Not in Farms.	Total acres in farms and out.
	Impr'd.	Unimpr'd	Impr'd.	Unimpr'd		
Ohio	9,851,493	8,146,000	12,625,394	7,846,747	5,104,819	25,576,960
Michigan	1,929,110	2,454,780	3,476,296	3,554,538	28,964,686	35,995,520
Indiana.........	5,046,543	7,746,879	8,242,183	8,146,109	5,249,468	21,637,760
Illinois	5,039,545	6,997,867	13,096,374	7,815,615	14,547,211	35,459,200
Wisconsin	1,045,499	1,931,159	3,746,167	4,147,420	29,617,773	34,511,360
Minnesota	5,035	23,846	556,250	2,155,718	50,728,032	53,440,000
Iowa	824,682	1,911,382	3,792,792	6,277,115	25,158,893	35,228,800
Missouri........	2,938,425	6,794,245	6,246,871	13,737,939	23,138,390	43,123,200
Kansas.........	....	....	405,468	1,372,932	51,341,600	53,120,000
Nebraska.......	....	....	118,789	512,425	39,980,781	40,512,000
Old Northwest..	26,680,322	36,006,158	52,306,584	55,566,558	273,831,653	378,604,800
Dakota	....	....	2,115	24,333	97,573,552	97,600,000
Montana	....	....	....	....	....	92,016,640
Wyoming	....	....	....	....	....	36,382,080
Colorado	....	....	....	....	....	68,144,000
Present Northwest	....	....	....	....	....	692,747,520
New Mexico....	166,201	124,370	149,274	1,265,635	78,233,091	79,648,000
Arizona	....	....	....	....	....	83,712,000
Utah	16,333	30,516	77,219	12,692	70,054,089	70,144,000
Idaho	....	....	....	....	....	58,196,000
The West	26,862,866	36,160,944	52,535,192	56,859,218	519,692,385	984,447,520

Old N. W. — New N. W. — The West.

Ills. in 1860 not one-fifth under fence.

What brings land into the list of *farms*, and what renders them *improved*, is not explained that I have seen. But it certainly means something less than putting land into grain or tame grass, for Illinois in 1860 had not a fifth, probably not a sixth in that condition, and this estimates over one-third *improved.* Possibly a third may have been under fence, though not very probably; and if so, it is a much greater proportion than any State north or west of her has. Of the region now tributary, which has already made Chicago the chief provision and grain market of the world, not one acre in five, probably not one in eight has yet been ploughed.

Not 1 acre in 5 yet plowed

Est. of 1861 moderate.

The estimate in 1861 having been too moderate, a mere comparison with the present would render the latter extravagant, it not being possible to have doubled area and population in seven years. But while more might then have been claimed, trade had not settled down with that firmness in new channels to render it prudent to claim what we seemed to have acquired. Seven years more of results, year by year assuring continuance of the same with accelerating ratio, will justify above figures with every disinterested, considerate judge. The present population of the Northwest no doubt exceeds 11,000,000.

7 years confirms.

Ohio not yet claimed.

Desiring to make these estimates moderate, leaving room for future increase, nothing is yet claimed from Ohio. Indiana has doubtless 1,600,000 population, and except 50 to 100 miles adjoining each Louisville and Cincinnati, the entire State gives trade largely to Chicago; yet only five-eighths is estimated. *Ind. only 5/8.* Of Illinois, St. Louis has 50 to 100 miles, perhaps, and the rest comes to Chicago. *Ills. the whole.* Missouri is estimated by Governor Fletcher to have 1,500,000 population, and only two-fifths are claimed for Chicago. *Mo. two-fifths.* A census in 1867, gives Iowa 902,040, and the whole is ours; for as remarked in 1861, (p. 25), a person who sought trade with that State alone, would come to Chicago to do it. *Iowa the whole.* Of Wisconsin, too, the whole would be estimated, but that Milwaukee has a large trade yet with New York. *Wis. allowance to Mil.* Nebraska is entirely ours. *Neb. ours.* The estimate for Kansas is doubtless most questionable; but the rapid increase will justify it, the present year making it good. *Kansas coming.*

The Territories are not counted upon except for mining trade, as that will be chief for many years. This renders a present estimate small, not that the trade is not ours legitimately, but because mining is in its infancy, and what little there is has not found its natural channel by railway. *Estimate of Territories now small.* The Pacific road, and that to Sioux City, to be finished in a few months, will take the whole trade of Colorado, and thence north. *Their trade comes to Chi.* A newspaper remarks:—

The Omaha Pacific Railroad Company have notified the Government that they intend to construct a railroad from Denver to the main road, a distance of one hundred and two miles and have it completed in October next. *Denver br'ch road.*

Other branches will also be made, and rapidly; and until other lines from the Mississippi and Missouri shall bear trade still more directly to Chicago, the Omaha Pacific will take the whole from northern Nebraska and Wyoming, and the Sioux City will be a strong competitor for that above. *Other branches.* *Omaha and Sioux City roads now take all.* The *Chicago Journal* says:— *Chi. Jour.*

Chicago and the Upper Missouri.—The commercial relations of the new Northwest and this city are becoming more and more intimate. Chicago is the metropolis of all the Northwest, of Montana and Idaho, Minnesota and Iowa, hardly less than of Illinois. *Upper Mo. trade belongs to Chi.* As the entire country pays tribute to New York, so does the entire Northwest to this metropolis. The importance of Chicago is due largely, if not mainly, to the fact that from the first it has acted upon the idea that, as Parton expresses it, "every acre with which it could put itself into easy communication must pay tribute to it forever." *She wins it.* To our people, therefore, it is a matter of no trivial interest that the Sioux City branch of the Iowa division of the Northwestern Railway, running from St. Johns to Sioux City, will be completed before the opening of spring navigation — probably in five weeks. *Sioux City road soon built.* Our informant is the Superintendent of its construction.

This important branch of the Northwestern, terminating at Sioux City, connects Chicago with the Missouri 1,039 miles, by river navigation, above St. Louis, and gives immediate prominence to our city in the estimation of the mountain people, in two essentials — that of trade and travel. *Takes Upper Mo. trade.* The better to complete this line of communication with Montana, a line of fleet, light-draft steamers, especially constructed for navigating the Upper Missouri, has been projected, and will ply this coming season between Sioux City and Fort Benton. *Steamboat line in connection.* The exorbitant freights and high rates of insurance on goods shipped from St. Louis, resulting partly from the many dangers and difficulties attending the navigation of the Missouri as high up as Sioux City, and partly from the absence of competing lines from points above St. Louis, are items of importance, which, if no others were wanting, would serve to divert a great commercial channel from St. Louis where it has heretofore been *Lower Mo. difficult of navigation.*

Trade with Chi. natural.

compelled to go, to Chicago, where, this season, it will *properly and naturally come.* With one-third of river navigation overcome (and that the most dangerous and difficult) — with from twelve to fourteen days saved — steamers leaving Sioux City, conveying freight and passengers, delivered in three days from Chicago, will be able to make two, and possibly three, trips to the headwaters (instead of one, as heretofore,) before the close of navigation.

Montana paper.

To illustrate the more clearly, take the following facts, for which we are indebted to a Montana exchange:

Extent of their trade. Long trips from St. L.

"During the past season, forty-nine steamers, transporting upward of seven thousand tons of freight, and nearly three thousand passengers, reached Fort Benton from St. Louis. The average time of these boats in reaching their destination was sixty days. The Octavia made Benton, from St. Louis, in thirty-five days. The Zephyr was wafted through in ninety days! Steamers, such as are to be put on the line from Sioux City, ought to make the 'voyage' from that point to headquarters in from twenty-five to twenty-seven days, with one hundred to one hundred and twenty-five tons of freight and full passenger list."

Shows advantage of Chi. route.

* * * These facts are important as showing a great saving of distance, time, and cost of transporting goods to, and the shipment of treasure from, and so demonstrating a material divergence in the channels of trade, important alike to the people of Chicago and the vigorous and thrifty communities of the mountains.

37,000 miners want connection East.

With a population already of 37,000 people — with thousands of adventurous men adding to her numbers yearly—with a gold product only second to California, and with silver mines that promise to equal, if they do not excel, those of Nevada, Montana has little patience and less disposition to suffer longer that isolation which, more than any other Territory, has been her lot in the past.

Helena Gaz.

The *Helena* (Montana) *Gazette*, Nov. 28th, announces her opinion in the case of—

Chi. *vs.* St. L. Trade goes to best bidder. St. L. inert. Chi. active. Sioux City road. Steamboats to connect. Benefits to Montana. Her trade sought. *Dubuque Herald.* Mountain trade large. Come to Dubuque.

Chicago vs. St. Louis.—Rapid and cheap transportation, to a country isolated as is Montana, is the medium to the *ultima thule* of commercial advantage; and whatever the predilections of our merchants may be, or the convenience and advantage of their business relations elsewhere, it is every day becoming more apparent that Chicago is making the best bids, or, what is the same thing, offering greater inducements for Montana trade, than even St. Louis, that has grown wealthy off of western traffic, and should be willing to spend a portion of that wealth in opening up to us commercial facilities. While St. Louis, like an overgrown boy, reveling in the plenitude of animal life, is inert from the lassitude of inaction, and suffering, absolutely from the growing pains of expansion which it cannot prevent without doing violence to nature, Chicago is straining every nerve to accomplish the great result of securing the Montana trade. Besides the lease by the Illinois Central Railroad company of the Dubuque and Sioux City railroad, that immense corporation, exerting its influence in the interests of Chicago, will, by spring, without fail, connect at Sioux City by means of a road to St. Johns, on the Missouri river, 35 miles above Council Bluffs, and thence without change of cars, a distance of about 70 miles, to Sioux City. By putting on a line of boats thence to Fort Benton, that place will be made the Chicago depot of supplies to Montana, and our merchants will be able to buy either in Chicago in February or March, or at Sioux City in March or April at Chicago rates, with freight added, and transport their goods to Fort Benton in a numerous line of light-draft Chicago bottoms, at a cost of about four cents for river transportation and insurance, and two and a half for railroad. These are bright prospects for Montana, but the rays of our light will not fall on St. Louis, unless she makes a determined and present effort, which, from present appearances, we should judge she is not likely to do. As an illustration of the high estimate placed upon our trade by Chicago, Dubuque, and Sioux City, we quote from a *Dubuque Herald*, of a recent date: "As an example of what may be expected, we may point to the immense business now derived by Omaha from the upper Missouri. We learn that the bank deposits of that city are not less than $2,000,000. The handling of the gold from the mountains, brought by steamers and mackinaw boats down the Missouri, require the presence of large amounts of capital. A single mackinaw boat is frequently loaded with 200 pounds of gold dust. Open to Sioux City communication with the east, and these same steamers and boats will make that place their southern landing, and their business, passenger and freight, will be done there. This immense business in the minerals of the mountains and the agricultural products of the plains will be brought to our doors on the extension of the D. and S. C. R. to the Missouri river." With this view of the active interest being shown by Chicago capital in securing to us commercial advantages, and the apathy shown by St. Louis, we cannot help but be impressed with the conviction that St. Louis has "lost her grip," as commerce, like water, will travel in the lowest channel and seek an outlet where there exists the least impediments. This branch road from Chicago to Sioux City is now completed to Onawa, some 30 miles below, and half of the intervening distance is graded, being a gap of but fifteen miles of grading and thirty miles of track-laying to be completed between now and spring, and the bridging of the Floyd, just below Sioux City. If St. Louis is determined to "shake us," *regnant* Chicago say we.

Chi. seeks

St. L. regrets

Trade like water.

Regnant Chi.

To indicate something of the rapidity of increase, and present value of that trade, an extract is taken from a letter in the *Chicago Republican*, urging the importance of the Sioux City road :—

Increase rapid.

Chi. Rep.

The fact is, Sioux City is the first point reached by the upper Missouri river and Montana trade, where it gets rail communication with Chicago and the East. And as by taking the boats at Sioux City in place of St. Louis, over one thousand miles of difficult river navigation is saved; Chicago cuts St. Louis entirely off from this trade, and can secure it for herself if the Dubuque and Sioux City road is built on the direct line to Sioux City, for it would then be *the* "thoroughfare" for the whole of this trade. * * * *

Sioux City route best—

—cuts off St. Louis.

It will be seen that the direct line to Sioux City is the only one that will give Chicago enterprise a fair chance to compete for this important trade, whose history is the best index to its value. In 1864 the entire Montana trade was carried by two steamboats from Sioux City to Fort Benton, on an experimental trip. In 1865, the number was increased to thirteen boats, with 1,600 tons of freight. In 1866, to thirty-seven boats, and 4,600 tons of freight. In 1867, to fifty-three boats, and 7,300 tons of freight, at a cost, for freight alone, of over half a million dollars.

Best for Chi.

Increase of Montana trade.

The *Missouri Democrat*, of January 21st, said :—

Mo. Dem.

The Colorado Trade.—We have frequently had occasion to point out the necessity of the trade of Colorado and the other Territories on the line of the Eastern Division railway being secured to St. Louis—its natural outlet—but circumstances have, thus far, almost entirely prevented it. We now wish to refer particularly to the trade of Denver—that city being the entrepot of nine-tenths of the merchandize which the Territory of Colorado consumes. Since the construction of the Omaha line of the Union Pacific railroad, Chicago and New York have enjoyed undisputed possession of this trade, and it amounts to a sum of no mean importance, as we published several days since—shown by the statistical report of the Denver Board of Trade for 1867. This report shows that 17,122,000 pounds of freight were received from the East. St. Louis should have furnished the greater portion of that amount. Whereas, she furnished but an infinitesimal fraction. This is owing to the fact that there exists no means by which freight can be transported to Denver, over the St. Louis route, except by express or ox trains. The former is too expensive and the latter too slow. We published, a day or two ago, a statement showing the comparative business of St. Louis and Chicago during 1867. It was very satisfactory to our city*—Chicago being many hundred thousand dollars in arrears. To make the discrepancy still greater, we only require the Western trade, which will naturally come to St. Louis when we furnish a line of communication. The people of Colorado, we have always been assured, and are now assured, are very friendly to our city, and are anxious that something should be done by which freights can be ordered over the St. Louis line at a tariff which will stand comparison with that over the Chicago line. What is required until the Eastern Division railway extends its road to Denver, as they will do at as rapid a rate as is possible, is a fast freight line from its terminus to the commercial centre of Colorado.

St. L. must secure Colorado trade.

Chi. and N. Y. now have it.

Denver trade

St. L. has very little.

Ox trains—too slow.

St. L. beats Chicago.

West. trade make her still better.

Fast freight line wanted.

---

* Yes; and satisfaction was rather short-lived, probably. The only statement of the sort that I have seen, was that of the Commissioner of Internal Revenue; in which, as hereafter shown, the blunder was made of giving the Chicago trade for only six months. Throw off half of our business, and then St. Louis is a little ahead. We, too, can say, that "to make the discrepancy still greater, we only require the western trade." But instead of having to add, "which will naturally come to St. Louis when we furnish a line of communication"; we can and do say—that which *does* come to Chicago by roads already built. The difference is very trifling, only that between ox-trains and railway trains.

St. L. crowing over a blunder.

Trade naturally goes to Chi.

The *Democrat*, the very next day, January 22d, shows the good prospects St. Louis has in Colorado. No doubt the people are friendly with the city, with which what little trade they had was transacted; yet if in Clay county, in Missouri, it will go to Chicago if it be for their interest, as we saw (p. 97); St. Louis should bear no malice against Colorado for choosing railways over ox-trains or even horse expresses. Says the *Missouri Democrat* :—

Railways better than ox-trains.

Mo. Dem.:

Action of Denver abo't railroad to Cheyenne.

Denver News

The Denver Pacific Railroad Movement.—Judge Usher and Governor Carney addressed the Denver Board of Trade, on the 13th inst., deprecating the voting of bonds by Denver to the Denver Pacific Railroad. Maj. Johnson and Gen. Hughes responded for the Denver movement, and their views are embodied and endorsed by the *News*, of the 14th, as follows: "Our city has been long enough deluded by promises and hopes. If we expect anything we must go to work ourselves. This we have done, and this we propose to continue to do. When a half million of bonds are voted, and a road graded and tied from Denver to Cheyenne, or some point on the Union Pacific railroad, we shall then have some reliable assurance of a railway connection. If this action embarrasses the eastern division we are very sorry, but we cannot help it. The Denver Pacific must go on. We assure Governor Carney and Judge Usher, that we have the warmest sentiments of friendship for their road, for Leavenworth and St. Louis. We reciprocate their expressions and will extend a hearty welcome to their road when it comes. More than this, they shall have substantial aid when we can afford to give it. But when they attack the Denver Pacific road, our own enterprise, and present diplomatic reasons why we should not vote bonds, they must expect no response, but only a firmer adhesion to the position Denver has taken. We will enter into any agreement they wish, save one, and that is to abandon the Denver Pacific railway. If to obtain this is the object of their visit, we predict that it will be a failure, and so it should be."

Sorry to embarrass St. L. road.

Will welcome them—

—aid them.

But will have their own road.

Chi. now able to help.

Chicago has now attained a position that she can do something for her own protection, and for the extension of her commerce and manufactures. Although every influence hitherto favorable, especially that of the conjoined interest of eastern capitalists, must operate continuously and with multiplying power; it will not prove a slight stimulant to continue the same course, that their judicious aid in the past will henceforth enable Chicago to be an energetic, liberal contributor to means promoting joint interests, chief of which will be to extend the railway system exactly as it has been established. Who can doubt that this sure policy, continues nearly every one of the seven Chicago lines west of the Mississippi, and perhaps two or three intermediate ones, onward to and into the Rocky Mountains within ten years, most of them within five? Nothing beyond is calculated upon, though several will go to the Pacific, for it will suffice that they reach into the mountains to secure to us the entire area above listed, and we leave a little for future additions.

An encouragement to East.

Continue 7 lines west—

—to Rocky Mountains and beyond.

Lines compete with each other.

Can competing lines be established? They can and will compete with each other to obtain the business and deliver it at Chicago. That will be the only serious competition, for should long diagonal roads be constructed, they would only be feeders to the trunks. Whence shall funds come to build roads enough to interfere with these powerful spokes of the Chicago hub? Starting from this natural and artificial centre, the long lines diverge, and quite evenly,

Rival roads difficult.

taking in the entire region from Mexico to the British Possessions. Being itself considerably south of the centre of latitude of the Northwest, what possible influences can be generated to draw this trade away off from its natural and direct route eastward, 150 miles south to St. Louis, upon the very verge of the Northwest? She will have part of the Kansas trade, but less and less from each line north.

Difficult to draw trade 150 miles south to St. Louis.

As before remarked, competition on the southern road from Kansas, begins at least even-handed; and what forces will there operate in her favor, which failed in her own State? She will display more wisdom and ability than she has yet done, if she can draw her part of the far-west trade through Kansas, or the chief city that will there arise. Competition directly in her rear will afford ample employment without seeking it so far from home. Were the west bank of the Missouri the shore of a lake, what a site would Kansas City be! But St. Louis can take no advantage of Kansas' deficiencies, for she is still more deficient.*

Competition at Kansas.

A rival to St. L.

Site good.

---

* The Great Bend of the Missouri, affording a site more nearly approaching that which Lake Michigan affords than anything else in nature, and creating a centre which art will surely regard; it is natural that we should have a sympathy with the embryo city there, which, within 20 years, will count its hundreds of thousands; and we would like to have it determined whether it shall be Kansas City, Leavenworth, Lawrence or some other. Since pp. 99 and 100 were stereotyped, a private letter, written by Col. Vliet, Engineer of the Leavenworth, Lawrence and Galveston Railroad, to a friend to acquaint him with the advantages, present and prospective, of that road, was lent me for perusal, and I have obtained permission to make some extracts, exhibiting at once the undeveloped resources to be developed in the Southwest; and also the important fact that already they look to Chicago for their market. Three-fourths of the immense herds of cattle that Kansas and the Indian Territory are annually to export, will come to the Chicago stock yards. Says Col. Vliet:—

Great bend of Missouri river a site.

Col. Vliet's letter about Galveston road.

"In natural and undeveloped resources, the country along the proposed route of the L. L. & G. R. R. presents a most inviting field in that part lying within the State of Kansas; the extreme fertility of the soil, and its adaptation to the production of all the grains and fruits of the temperate zone, and especially of wheat and wine are acknowleged by all acquainted with the country, are fast becoming proverbial. The mildness of the climate, the gently undulating surface, and the facilities for grazing will render it eminently favorable for stock and wool growing.

Route desirable.

Products

Climate.

"Having become well acquainted with the country from Lawrence to Humboldt, I can testify from personal knowledge that it has not been over-rated. It will not suffer in comparison with the richest portions of Illinois or Iowa. As a whole, it is perhaps not as well adapted to the growing of corn as some portions of those States, though the bottoms are unsurpassed in this particular, but will equal or surpass them in the production of wheat, fruit, stock and wool. I have recently returned from a trip across the Osage lands from Humboldt, south, to the State line. The great fertility of the Neosho Valley and its large supply of timber are widely known and appreciated. and are unquestionable. But my route led me over the uplands, between the Neosho and Verdigris. Here I was agreeably surprised. With the exception of occasional small isolated ridges, the lands are less undulating than those to the north of them, and more fertile, rivalling in this respect the bottom lands themselves. My course was mostly over prairie, on the divide between the waters of these two streams. * * *

Personal knowledge.

Osage lands.

"The route, along the line proposed, is exceptionally singular. No parallel route of equal practicability exists on either side of it, except in its immediate neighborhood. To the east of it the Ozark Mountains of Missouri, and the mountainous regions of Western Arkansas, interpose an effectual barrier to any practicable route short of the meridian of Little Rock — over 150 miles to the east. To the west, the country rises rapidly. The valleys of the numerous large streams have generally, an east and west direction, and are separated by high ridges which would lie directly across any parallel route on that side.

Only practicable route.

"The country about the junction of the Canadian and the Grand (or Neosho) Rivers with the Arkansas seems to be a focal point, toward which large streams flow from nearly all directions, having a common outlet through the Arkansas to the eastward. Here, the Neosho (or Grand) and Verdigris come in from more than 100 miles to the northward, interposing a valley between the mountain ranges on the east and the ridges to the west, which is unexceptional as a railroad route and in which our line will be laid.

A focal point

The route for railroad.

Chi. to seek best trade.

Chicago, with every other city that has ability to combine the two chief interests of civilization, commerce and manufactures, if she be wise, will give special attention to those States who will be her best customers in both. Therefore will time, means and effort be given as necessary, to secure the traffic of the Rocky Mountains. Double the population elsewhere in the West, will not supply a trade equally valuable with that of the mines. Mining will be their business, except to raise their grain and potatoes. Buying almost everything and being free livers, they will soon employ a set of traders who will make it a specialty, adapting themselves to the necessities and caprices of their customers. For the reason that it is a peculiar trade, it is inclined to aggregation, seeking those who understand it, and sticking to them. Each 50 to 100 miles, the entire breadth from Mexico to the British line, will have a railway, branch or trunk, direct to Chicago. Probably no city intermediate will have more than three, and two of them short branches. Must not the trade of those cities, as well as of the mining region in their rear concentrate at Chicago? What city west would have a greater, or even a tenth, of that which the focal point of the mining region would gather?

Rocky Mts. superior. Buy everything. Trade peculiar. Numerous lines to Chi. Focal point.

464,000 miles more— —Chi. territory.

That million miles listed above as the Northwest, does not include New Mexico, 124,450 miles; Arizona, 130,000; Utah, 109,600; and Idaho, some 100,000 miles, an aggregate of 464,050 square miles to be added in a very few years as also Chicago territory, without reckoning Nevada and the Pacific States, whose trade will seek chiefly their own cities. Excluding them, about ONE MILLION SQUARE MILES of the richest mining region of the world will have numerous railroads to it and through it, all leading to one city. Were she not the acknowledged emporium of the Northwest, what city could

1,000,000 miles mining territory. Emporium will take trade.

The Poteau coming into the Arkansas from the south, and the mountain fork of Little Run running in precisely the opposite direction from the Poteau to the Red River, would furnish almost exact continuation of the valley of the Neosho or the Verdigris, and only interrupted by the neck or ridge at the sources of the Poteau and Mountain Fork, connecting the Sans Bois Mountains of the Indian Territory with the mountain ranges of Southern Arkansas. How formidable an obstacle this neck or ridge may prove to be is unknown; but a slight detour will carry us up the valley of the Canadian to the west of the Sans Bois Mountains in the direction ef Preston. On this line the Engineers, on the preliminary survey for the Pacific Railroad, near the 35th Parallel, report the summit between the Canadian and waters of the Red River as only fifty feet above the former stream. Through this natural door-way will be built, and must forever remain, the Grand Avenue which shall furnish the great Empire west of the Mississippi its best communication with the markets of the world, and unite Texas and Mexico with Kansas, Nebraska, Colorado, Arkansas, Missouri, Iowa, and through Chicago with the regions about the lakes. It will be, perhaps more than any other road in the country, a grand trunk road; for while the topography of the country is such as to promote the construction of several very important branches—no competing route is practicable, except almost right along side of it. Should this road first occupy the ground, it will be poorly managed, indeed, if it does not timely make such additions to its accommodations as to always hold undivided possession.

Sans Bois Mountains. A natural doorway— —to lakes. No competition.

"At Lawrence, the L. L. & G. R. R. will, by means of the railroads already completed or immediately to be built, have direct and unbroken access to all the markets of the country. It leads towards Chicago, and in that direction the attention of the people along this line is strongly directed. * *

Railroads built to Chi.

"The 'Great American Desert' is already an admitted fiction of the past; and the rapid settlement of the rich valleys along, and in the immediate vicinity, of the U. P. R. R., as its construction progresses, is demonstrating that the country is not without value in an agricultural point of view. Yet, the fact remains that Western Kansas and Eastern Colorado are not particularly attractive for farming purposes.

Gt. Am. Desert a fiction.

compete with her for the mining trade? But with that advantage, and with special efforts surely to be made to secure it, what city can rival her successfully? She will get and hold that far easier than from much intervening territory. What sort of figures, too, will be requisite to compute such a trade from such an area? What other city of the West would not be satisfied to take Chicago's chances for that alone? Its vastness

Mining is yet prosecuted in the crudest manner. Science and improved machinery will probably augment its profits more than any other branch of industry, speculative as it is. Railways, too, are to carry very much of the streams of settlement through and over the agricultural lands to the eastward of the mountains, except directly on their routes. It is only 20 years since the first gold was discovered in California, and see what has been already done, almost without railways. They have far more efficiency in developing a mining than an agricultural region; and who can doubt that the present decade will accomplish twice-over what two have done, a four-fold increase? Mining to improve— Only 20 y'rs since gold was discov'd.

It was my design here to present extracts exhibiting the wealth of this mining region, but their accumulation renders it impossible to do the subject justice, and the last coming to hand must suffice. A correspondent of the *Chicago Republican*, for whom the editor strongly vouches, and whose letter bespeaks close observation and moderation, writes Jan. 1st, from Wyoming, soon to be a Territory set off from Dakota, and that region through which the Omaha railroad is being built:— Mining information abundant. Cor. *Chi Rep*

The principal value of this region will consist in its grazing advantages. It will be peculiarly adapted to wool-growing; but will hardly be able to compete in the raising of cattle, horses, and mules with the milder climate further South. * * * * * Good for cattle and sheep

"On the other hand, the L. L., & G. R. R., as already shown, has its course in its whole extent through a country unsurpassed in agricultural resources, which will furnish, from the beginning, a large, permanent and constantly increasing local business. It is destined to supply a vast region, now destitute, with two essential articles of lumber and coal; a region wanting only these to become equally eligible and valuable with any other in the same latitude. It opens to the whole North and East of our country its most valuable avenue to the great beef growing region from which they must soon draw their principal supply. On its completion to the Gulf, it will furnish a through route of unequalled advantages to not less than four States of the Union. Striking the Gulf at an angle where its coast treads almost in direct extension of this route, it reaches at Galveston, and will traverse, by an entension already projected, and which will be built almost or quite as soon as the L. L. & G. R. R. can be completed, the extensive sugar country lying along the Gulf coast from Galveston to the Rio Grande and beyond, the only source within the Union from which the deficit in sugar for home consumption, over and above the productive capacity of Louisiana, can be made up. Pursuing its almost undeviating course, the route which we initiate at Lawrence will cross the Rio Grande, and, passing through the City of Mexico, will compete at Acupulco for the trade of the Indies over a route some hundreds of miles shorter, much cheaper, and every way better than any practicable route from Lawrence or Chicago to San Francisco. This route superior. Beef region. Galveston —continuance. Sugar region To Mexico and Pacific.

"This is no chimera. The Eastern cities, and St. Louis, Cincinnati, Cairo, Memphis, Vicksburg and New Orleans will equally require the route from Galveston by way of the City of Mexico to form a much needed connection with the coast of the South Pacific. Every mile of the way is teeming with the richest productions of the earth. Already the opposing currents of emigration coming from the East and the West are eddying among the mountains of Idaho, Montana, Nevada, Utah and Colorado There is no outlet except to the South. Thitherward 'manifest destiny' points the way, and the L. L. & G. R. R. may be the pioneer enterprise which shall give the initial impulse and derive the principal profit arising from the transportation connected with the movement." * * No chimera. Emigration to the South.

Gold discoveries in Wyoming.

The first discovery was made upon Willow Creek, a tributary of the Sweet Water, fourteen miles northwest of Pacific Springs, and ten miles north of the old South Pass telegraph station. One of the party, Henry S. Redell, Esq., riding along, leisurely, one day upon his horse, discovered a white boulder lying upon the side of the hill near by, which attracted his attention by its unusual appearance, and which, upon examination, he found to be literally covered with gold. After he had satisfied himself that his eyes were not deceiving him, and the excitement of the moment, naturally caused by so rich a discovery, had subsided, he began the search for the source from whence this boulder must have had its birth, and within a few moments he was richly rewarded by the discovery of the famous Cereso Lode. Out of this mine men have made as high as $130 per day with a hand mortar. Four tons of quartz hauled to Springville, Utah Ter., yielded $28,000—so report says, and I have no reason to doubt it. At present the company are paying $200 per ton to have the rock hauled five hundred miles to be crushed, with a result of from $2.000 to $4,000 per ton. In three or four cases rock has been pounded in a hand mortar which yielded $10 to the pound of ore.

Cereso lode.

Its richness.

Mines opened.

Here follows a marvelous list of mines so soon opened, although the first was only discovered in June last, and the writer continues:—

Estimate moderate.

I have given you a fair average of the mines thus far found in this rich mineral section, about which so much has been said, so many strange stories told, and where so many wild rumors have had their origin. But after all not overestimated. Some one hundred and fifty leads have been located, all within a small circle of some six by fifteen miles, while the great mineral belt in which the mines are found extends from Fremont's Peak south to the junction of the Grand and Green Rivers, a distance of some 300 miles, and in width from 30 to 60 miles. Only the small portion above referred to above has been prospected, and that even only run over. Three gulches have been discovered which prospect from three to thirty cents to the pan, with from three to nine feet of pay—no stripping and plenty of water. In the Cereso Gulch, they averaged during the fall $30 per day to the hand. Reliable reports which have just reached us, bring the tidings that a very rich gulch has just been struck some 20 miles east of the South Pass, on Wind river waters. The gulch is reported as five miles in length; pay, nine feet, and that all the way down, with plenty of water, and good for from an ounce to $30 per day to the hand. Rich diggings are also reported as just discovered at Devil's Gate, on the Sweetwater, where gold has been found for years, but never before in paying quantities. The best prospects ever obtained in all this region, until within the last few weeks, were found in the Great Basin of the Sandy's and Sweetwater. Near the base of Fremont's Peak, in the new Pacific District, prospects are good that very rich placer mines will be discovered during the spring and early in the summer. As but very little prospecting, has, as yet, been done, we know but little of what these hills and valleys contain. * * *

150 leads.

Good yield.

New discoveries.

Field unknown.

Improves with development.

All of these, and the many other mines, upon which more or less work is being done, all grow richer as they are developed. Four mining districts have been organized, viz: Shoshonee, California, Mill, and Pacific. Three cities are already laid out—South Pass, in the Shoshonee District; Hamilton, in the California District; and Pacific City, in the Pacific District. About six hundred men and six women now occupy this section, so wonderfully rich in gold, silver, copper, iron, coal, coal oil, and mineral springs, not to speak of the magnificent and fertile valleys of Wind river, the Pass Agiles, Sweetwater and Green rivers (Valley of the Lakes), which for fertility of soil, grandness of scenery, salubrity of climate, as well as in point of location, near the great thoroughfare across the continent, the Pacific railroad; then again for timber and water, and last but not least, their mineral wealth and home market—all combine to make this the spot which never was and never will be surpassed in this country or in the world. The Pacific railroad will pass within fifteen miles of the mines, and be completed as far as this point by the 1st of August, this year. The telegraph is within nine miles, and will be completed to the towns as soon as the weather will permit. * * *

3 cities.

Various minerals.

Natural advantages.

Pacific railroad.

Coal and iron.

In passing from Cheyenne to the mines, we cross the great coal and iron belts, which extend from the western base of the Big Horn mountains westerly to Green river, and thence to Salt Lake, and southerly to Mexico. This entire region abounds in veins of coal from 5 to 11 feet in thickness, and of a superior quality, resembling cannel coal, now bituminous, having the hardness of anthracite coal, resembling it in appearance, and ranking next to it. There is probably not less than 10,000 square miles of this lignite formation, and that, too, in a region of country where there is a great scarcity of wood, and also where are found positive evidences of as fine iron mines as any in the world. Immense deposits of iron are

10,000 miles of coal.

Iron immense. Silver. Region new.

found upon Boulder Creek, and huge mountains of it in the Iron Mountain range. In fact, so far as outward indications can be taken as proof, there is not less than an area of 100 miles square, covered with beds of rich iron ore. West of these we find a silver belt, rich in the precious metal so far as has been tested. The extent of this silver section is not known, only that indications show an extent of leads about ten to twelve miles in length by three in width. Specimens of silver ore from this section, worked in Nevada, have given wonderful results. But this section, like all of this grand mineral region, is as yet almost entirely unknown. West of this silver belt we find the Sweetwater gold mines, rich and extensive.

Provisions, etc., dear. Trade to Salt Lake—going to Chicago. Neglect of Chi. merchants.

Provisions of all kinds are already scarce, and will be more so before spring. Flour, $20 per 100 lbs., and none to be had. Pork, 75c; beef, 30c; bacon, $1; tea, $5; coffee, 75c; potatoes, $9; butter, $1; cheese, 50c; axes, $6; picks, $7,50; glass, $1 per pane; boots, $15@24; nails, $1 per ℔. Lumber, $100; shingles, $10. No tools, powder, fuse, or anything else with which to work the mines. There are but two little shops or sort of stores in all this region. Clothing, blankets, etc., are about four times as high as at Salt Lake City, and there double the price of almost any other western city. The trade has been thus far with Salt Lake City, but with the opening of spring it will turn eastward toward the railroad, when Cheyenne, Omaha, and Chicago, will each secure their share, providing their business men use proper exertions, and not like Chicago in the past, allow St. Louis to take three and a half millions of dollars in gold of her trade directly out of her hands for want of a little exertion. In my entire trip through Montana and Idaho, I never saw a Chicago advertisement in one of their papers. Let not this be true in the gold region of the Sweet-water.

Most valuable mining region. 50,000 people in a year. Chance for business men—not drones. Law rules.

After a most careful and thorough investigation and prospecting of these mines, I am fully convinced that in richness of ore, extent and permanency of mines, ease with which the rock will be worked, and last, but not least, the small expense with which machinery will be transported hither, and put into place when once on the ground, these mines are more valuable than any other ever discovered in the country, and second to none in the world. A year from to-day 50,000 people will be found on the very spot where, in July last, forty-five Indians held the reins of government in their own hands. But their day has passed, and with the coming spring there will be a grand rush for this new "49" of the Rocky Mountains. Let every one come prepared with provisions, clothing, and tools to last them until the middle of July. Those coming from the West and Northwest must get their outfit of horses, provisions, etc., at Salt Lake City. Montana and Idaho must outfit at home, while those of the East have the choice of Cheyenne or the terminus of the railroad, which will probably be some seventy miles west of there, and within 110 miles of the mines. Horses and mules will find no trouble in reaching the mines after the first of May; before that it may be doubtful. There are fine chances here for business men—live, energetic, straightforward, accommodating men—who can see beyond the present penny to dollars in the future. I have seen no place as yet, in all the mountain region, for drones or men who wish to make a fortune without hard labor; no place for outlaws; too many vigilanters for them. Law and order prevail, and the people are determined that such shall be the future.

Act prudently. All depends on effort.

I would not advise any man, young or old, to rush to the mines, but look the matter over carefully and candidly, and then decide. Large nuggets are not picked up on every hillside, or in every valley, but on the contrary, hard, earnest efforts here as elsewhere only will be successful. It is true that fortunes are and will be made here in a single hour by some, but this is generally if not always the result of the most persistent effort, while others are always poor and always will be, perhaps always ought to be. * * *

Other mines too far away. Progress rapid. Cheyenne 8 000. All sorts of minerals. Grand scenery.

When we look at Nevada, Idaho, Montana, and even poor Utah—not to speak of California and Oregon—and see what they are, situated so far away from "America," or in other words, their base of supplies, what must we expect from this new and rich mineral region, over which already the iron horse begins to prance, after having carried or drawn his heavy load to the only door of the mines? Cheyenne, born on the 2d day of last August, and to-day boasting of 8,000 inhabitants, is but the index of what is to be. When August next shall have come, the railroad then within sight of these cities on the summit; just think, 37 hours from Chicago, *via* the Northwestern and Union Pacific railroads, and you find yourself upon the summit of the Rocky Mountains, in the regions of gold, silver, copper, iron, coal, coal oil, and in the finest agricultural region of the entire West, as well as in the land of the elk, deer, antelope, buffalo, and the delicious mountain trout and where sunrise and sunset scenes, the old mountain storms, the magnificent landscapes, put Bierstadt's famous "Storm in the Rocky Mountains" and "Yo Semite Valley" in the shade. Will our business men and capitalists then take their

A Country as God made it. families to Saratoga, Nahant and Long Branch to spend the weary heat of summer? I think not. Let them try one trip where they can see a country as God made it, where they can see the perfection of workmanship, and the charms of the fatal social air of fashionable watering places will lose their charms. Let men be Keep Cool. careful. Excitement will run high. Fortunes will be made and lost in a day. Some will win, others lose. Many will praise while others will condemn the country. Let every man be cool and deliberate; think well before he acts, but if Be in earnest he decides to cast his lot in this "new Northwest," do it with a will, and then in the end he will be sure of success.

Confirmation. Confirmatory of this statement concerning this new mining region of the Sweetwater,—and who can say that in a million square miles many such A letter from Salt Lake City. will not be discovered, perhaps even surpassing this?—an extract is taken from the *San Francisco Bulletin*, January 18th:—

Sweetwater Mines. Va. City *Enterprise.* *The Sweetwater Mines.*—We are permitted, says the Virginia City *Enterprise*, to make the following extract from a letter received by a gentleman in this city, from a friend in Salt Lake City. The letter is dated January 2, 1868.

"I wrote you a few days ago about the Sweetwater mines, and told you what I knew and thought of them at that time. Since then I have seen several letters from there, and have talked with some men from the mines—*and they are to be believed.* New discoveries. There are discoveries being made every day, and such as will throw everything in the shade that has been found in the last seven years. It is hard to believe, but it is so. They have also enough rock in sight to run two or three such mills as the Gould & Curry, for years, and of that character that men are now making from $5 Rich placers. to $20 per day, pounding it out in common iron mortars. They have also discovered placer mines that will pay well and give employment to 20,000 men, and are still finding more. Within 25 miles of the mines is one of the finest valleys in the world. In this valley at the present time, they have green grass nearly knee deep. Towns growing. There are at this time, about 600 men in the mines and valley. South Pass City is growing fast; it contains two stores, a carpenter shop, blacksmith shop, etc., but nary whisky mill. If I were fixed, I would go there immediately, and get a small stock of goods from St. Louis and rush it in ahead of all others. With $2,000 I 15,000 by 1st July. could make $10,000 next summer. There will be at the least calculation, 15,000 men in the mines by the 1st of July next. We receive letters here (in Salt Lake City) from New York, Ohio, Wisconsin and many other States, inquiring about the Sweetwater mines, and all say that there are many persons in the East that think of coming to the mines in the Spring, but first wish to know something of their Turn out well. character. Now, my honest opinion is, that the Sweetwater mines will turn out well."

If half the above is true, the new mines are the "biggest thing out," Who Good for prospectors. says there is no place left for our prospectors? They will find a perfect paradise in the Sweetwater country for at least two years.

Extent of wealth unknown. The extent of mineral wealth we can know little of, spread over a *million square miles.* Nor is it confined to precious metals, as they are styled, but the more precious ones of coal, iron, etc., abound. Withal, rich valleys for agriculture furnish a home supply of the main articles of food at large profits. So that while extent of wealth is wholly unknown, it is Unequalled. well ascertained that its equal exists not on the eastern continent, at all events.

Facilities to reach it will be afforded. For such a country, with such resources, all needed facilities should and will be afforded. The probability of building speedily several lines through to the Pacific with Congressional aid, has been considered; and since these Cin. *Railroad Record.* pages were in type, the Cincinnati *Railroad Record*, of January 23, comes to hand, containing so just and sound an argument, that space must be taken for parts:—

Govt. lands for railroads.

Government Lands for Railroads.—We observed with regret, that in the late political canvass in Ohio, some of the Democratic orators pronounced against any more grants to railroads. We have not observed this in other parts of the country, and we may safely assume that it will *not* be a popular doctrine with that party. In our opinion, it ought not to be so. Nothing is more certain, than two facts, that great lines of commercial intercourse create far *greater wealth* than they ever cost; and what is of equal importance, *furnishes employment* to tens of thousands of people, who without this resource, would have found it difficult to get along.

They create wealth.

There is also another fact of great moment, in connection with lines through a new or wild country: This is, that it makes *new settlements and cultivation* with great rapidity.

Settle a country.

Take, for example, the line of the Union Pacific Railroad. That line is now five hundred and twenty miles in advance of what was, three years ago, the frontier settlements, and in that five hundred miles, towns, ranches, settlements have sprung up the whole way to the foot of the Black Hills. Now it would have taken twenty years, or more, to have made a line of continuous settlements that distance. These settlements form the points of departure for other settlements laterally; so that in ten years from this time, the whole line of western settlement and population will be at least three hundred miles in advance of what they would have been, if the Pacific Railroad had not been made.

Effects of Pac. road.

But, these settlements become the centers of industry and commerce; and in this way the *basis of taxation* is constantly and rapidly increased; and it is by broadening and strengthening the basis of taxation that our debt can be paid, and the financial burdens of the country sustained.

Aid taxation

It is true, that the Government is not likely to make money by the mere *sale* of lands; for it has abandoned that policy, by the Homestead and Pension acts. But it makes money for the nation in a far more extensive and beneficial way, by advancing the settlement and cultivation of the country.

Sale of land no object.

But, how can Pacific Roads be made on the Southern and Northern borders, if they are not aided in some way? If the Government gives lands, and to that we shall now confine ourselves, it absolutely gives nothing *from* itself, but something which is immensely *beneficial* to the roads.

Govt. shall give something.

If there be only one Pacific Road, the settlement of the lands will only extend along that line, and be not more than a twentieth of that vast region, which *ought* to be occupied. It is necessary, therefore, to have lines both north and South of the Central line.

Several roads needed.

It has been supposed that most of the great region lying between the Mississippi States and the Rocky Mountains was barren; but this delusion is wholly passed away. Nine-tenths of it will in the end prove both arable and rich. Hence, the Government has the same motive to promote their settlement, as it had to promote the settlement of Illinois, by giving lands to the Illinois Central. It will have vast bodies of cultivable land on either side of the road, open to sale or actual settlement. Even in the mountain region this will be the case to a considerable extent. * * * * *

Ill. Cent. an example.

If it were a question of mere calculation in the Government, of mere pecuniary interest, it would be, as it has been, the clear duty of the Government to grant lands for the construction of Railroads in its unsettled territories.

Give for mere money—

But there are considerations higher than that; there is the consideration, which is so often spoken of, and so often pressed, and which every year presses harder, that of opening up great commercial routes across the continent.

—and higher objects.

But it is quite evident that no one road will do. Just take up the map and look at the vast country, from the Straits of Fuca to the Gulf of California! Now, if this country were connected with all the trading points of the interior, running into San Francisco as they do into New York, it might do; but it neither is so, nor can be for a great length of time.

Immense area to be reached.

We want, and must have, *three* great Pacific Roads; one on the route from Mackinaw to Puget's Sound; another from the Mississippi (it may be the Kansas branch) to the Colorado; and the third now making, the Union Pacific.

Must have three roads to Pacific.

These views are judicious; but while three routes to the Pacific may answer, we must and will have five to seven or more to the Rocky Mountains.

Yet more to Rocky Mts.

Whatever old fogies may say about the absurdity of opening such an area to settlement, with a breadth of hundreds of miles this side vacant, it will be done. Members of Congress who will not take a broad, statesman-like view, and legislate wisely for the whole Republic, and its most rapid

M. C's must do their duty

development, will be speedily left at home, until a majority in Congress will understand the will of the sovereign people. Such a land-proprietor as

U. S. a large land owner. Uncle Sam, must employ means commensurate to dispose of his wild lands.

Land Office Report. The *Washington Chronicle* gives this interesting summary of a report I have been unable to obtain for this paper :—

Hon. J. S. Wilson. *The Future of our Country.*—Hon. Joseph S. Wilson, Commissioner of the General Land Office, has submitted his annual report to the Secretary of the Interior. The report consists of five hundred and seventy-six pages of manuscript, besides a special accompanying document of over one hundred pages. In the regular report the statement is made that about 7,000,000 acres of public lands have been disposed of during the past year. There is yet the immense amount of

1,400,000,000 acres public land. 1,400,000,000 acres of public land, including the newly acquired Russian Territory. The report is made up to the 15th day of October, which ends the fiscal year. There are thirty maps fully descriptive of the States and Territories, together with the most elegant and carefully prepared map of the world that has ever been gotten up in any country, accompanying the report.

Points considered. The special paper inclosed with the report is one of the most interesting, instructive and valuable documents that has ever been gotten up in this country. It fully elaborates upon the mineral wealth of the United States; its gold and silver

Minerals. products, the same in comparison with the rest of the world; the quantity of gold, silver and other precious metals; the quantities now in existence in this country and in the world, and by this means showing the comparative wealth of this

Pacific slope. country. The paper speaks in detail of the great Pacific slope—1,000 miles long and 680 miles wide, with an area of over 831,000 square miles, or about 5,000,000,000 of acres—sufficient to inhabit 100,000,000 of people. The great wealth and increase of this country and its future prospects are thoroughly treated upon. The

—railways. great Pacific railways are fully explained, and the tide of the Atlantic and Pacific shown.

Trade of East— The trade of the Indies, of China, of Japan, of all the Eastern World must flow into this country, and through this country to the rest of the world. To San

—to N. Y. Francisco, and thence to New York, all the precious metals of the Eastern World will find their markets for the world. Mr. Wilson shows how we are now three

Ahead of Eng. thousand miles ahead of England in our routes to China, Japan and the Indies. He shows in full the necessary division of the trade to this country, and its effects on our public lands on the Pacific slope and in the Mississippi Valley. He gives on the map of the world, every rail road line completed or in contemplation in this

Pac. railroad finished 1870 country. He speaks in detail of the various Pacific railroads, announces the important fact that by October, 1870, the main road will be finished, and the great steam horse will carry us from New York to San Francisco direct.

Railroads— He says there are now 37,000 miles of completed railroad in this country, which, since their commencement, is at the rate of 1,000 miles a year. He further says that there are in course of construction 17,860 miles of railroad. For these

—aids by Congress. roads completed, and for those in contemplation, the government has donated over 184,800,000 acres of land, and to the Pacific roads over 24,000 [?] acres of land. He speaks in detail of the immense increase of the wealth of the country by the warranted advance in public lands bordering on all these roads. Mr. Wilson's treatise

Domestic trade $5,000,000,000. on our domestic and foreign trade, in these papers, is invaluable to our commercial world. He demonstrates that our present domestic trade is over $5,000,000,000.

Asia trade with San Francisco and N. Y. He shows conclusively that we are bound to absorb the immense trade of Northern and Eastern Asia, by way of San Francisco and New York. He gives full details about the Suez Canal; shows how England has been acquiring immense wealth from Indian possessions—her present income being over £78,000,000 in tariffs for the last year just from that source; shows how we are 3,879 miles nearer

Advantages of water. to Melbourne, Australia, than England or France; tells us all about China and Japan, and our increasing trade with those countries; gives the names of all the cities for trade, and how the shipments are made to San Francisco, then to New York, and then to Europe, and through our own country; gives an interesting account of the trip of the steamer Colorado from San Francisco to Japan in twenty-seven days, and her return in three weeks, laden with rich freight. The same trip from London or Paris would take sixty days each way. Rapidity of travel, Mr. Wilson contends, will draw the travel and the trade. The teas and silks of China and Japan must come through us to the rest of the world. The trade was worth $260,000,000 last year to our European neighbors. We'll get this trade. It is rapidly coming to us. We get this trade.

Mr. Wilson's learned and instructive digest of the trade of the world since the time of Alexander the Great up to the present time is altogether the best written article on the subject we have ever had the pleasure of perusing. His description of our great country, its railroads, rivers, canals, and other internal improvements; his full description of the Pacific slope, with its 100,000,000 acres of undisposed public lands, and its great Pacific railways, is a State paper which every man in this country, desirous of being informed of our true national greatness and prosperity and prospects of the future, will eagerly seek for. Mr. Wilson reports that there is room enough on the Pacific slope for forty new States. He thinks that by the commencement of the next century we will be a united country of one hundred States, with the control of all the great treasure shipments of the world. He says this country has commenced her grand imperial course, with the control of the Eastern trade in her power, and that the immigration and natural growth of the country will place us at over one hundred millions of people by the year 1900. He speaks of the civilizing influence of our great democratic institutions, and their effect upon the rest of the world. Ancient trade described. Also our country. To have 100 States by 1900—100,000,000 people.

Mr. Wilson has been a long time preparing this elaborate paper, with the accompanying map of the world, which has also been so well prepared. He has consulted over one thousand different volumes, been in constant correspondence with the principal officers of the European Governments who could give him information on the various subjects of which he treats, received much information and data from the State Department, and our Ministers and Consuls throughout the world; has had the assistance of the surveyors and mineralogists of our Interior Department, and now lays before the people, through the Secretary of the Interior, one of the most valuable public documents this country has ever received from any of its public officers. Thorough research. Much aid. Valuable document.

In preparing this paper, the facts outside of the General Land Office matter have been detailed by Mr. Wilson, so as to show the value and influence of our public lands, and their great wealth throughout this country for years to come. We hope to see the report and accompanying manuscripts printed by order of Congress and freely distributed throughout our country. Value of lands developed.

With the power of the entire railway system east of the Mississippi to urge requisite liberality on the part of the National Government; with that liberality well inaugurated by judicious grants; with the whole public inciting to rapid railway extension; with strong competition between these gigantic corporations of the East to extend their lines into this mining region, really the *ultima thule* to most of them; and with the certainty that she is the centre of that million miles, Chicago will make her arrangements to receive that trade; and thousands who wish to engage in it, will locate at Chicago as the place to get it. With that energy and enterprise for which she has credit, will not her merchants and manufacturers, and railway interests, together with the power behind the throne, be very sure to make whatever effort and sacrifice the invaluable prize may render needful? That their eyes are fixed upon it is evident from the previous article from the *Journal*, and here is another from the *Chicago Republican*:— Means to secure trade being certain—Chi. prepares to receive it. Energy given to it. —*Chi. Rep.*

Chicago and the Territories.—There is a very prevalent belief among Chicago residents that the Garden City is so weighty, and under such tremendous headway, that it will run itself. This is true, if the distance to which the city will run itself be limited. An immense fly-wheel, driven at a high rate of speed, will, if nicely Chi. and Territories. Headway strong.

—yet fly-wheel may stop.

balanced, continue in motion for a very long time. Chicago, being immense and well balanced, will likewise run a very long time. But if the propelling power be taken from the wheel, it will, in time, stop; the same is true of Chicago.

Chi. must not be— —like St. L.

Chicago, without the building of another mile of railroad, or the lifting of the finger of anybody to extend its business or connections, would keep in motion longer than any other city, under similar circumstances, in the United States. To sit still, and allow the machine to run itself, would be to imitate St. Louis. Possessed of a good deal of water power, that city has been under the impression that it needed no effort. It had, for three-quarters of a century, no rival, and hence it never appreciated the necessity of exertion. It waited for trade, and growth, and wealth; and they came. To-day they are still waiting for trade, and growth, and wealth; and they are coming—to Chicago.

How trade comes to Chi.

Keep up present rate.

Now, what we want in Chicago, is not to fall into the belief that our wonderful prosperity will always continue so prodigious without being urged or assisted. We can sit entirely still and grow faster than the most enterprising city, outside of Chicago, in the country; but this is not sufficient. We must keep up our present high rate of progress, and, to secure this result, effort is necessary.

Chi. to extend her lines.

With the return of business, Chicago ought to be extending its connections through every territory in the West. The Union Pacific railroad, is of course, a Chicago railroad, and Chicago will reap all its benefits. We shall get all its trade, if we do nothing; we can do more than this by a little effort. We can keep in advance of the building of the road, and secure all the streams which may be induced to run into it. Whenever a construction train advances three miles, it should find a Chicago agent there, waiting to send an order to Chicago. We should be ready to run branches from the main line up and down every valley, till we have taken in Denver and the gold mining regions of Colorado, the rich deposits and heavy trade of Montana, and the silver mines and other valuables of Nevada. A very little effort is all that is needed to give Chicago exclusive control of every square inch of territory west of the Mississippi and Missouri rivers Beyond the Missouri river lies a country the richest in all the world. There is scarcely a known fruit, or wine, or mineral, or fur that it does not produce. Chicago must be made the reservoir into which the Pacific streams of this domain must pour their golden wealth.

Keep in advance.

River branches.

A little effort secures all.

How these things must be brought about, any one knows. Nature, position, have accomplished already three-fourths of the task. There remains to Chicago to build here and there a branch railroad, and to establish at every point its agents.

N. W. a prize to be coveted

This great Northwest, of such diversified and abundant resources, both agricultural and mineral, is beyond doubt the prize coveted by every section; and what sort of a people would they be who were indifferent to its possession? Would it be unnatural, however, to give it to a city within its own limits, could one be found sufficiently central and accessible? Has not commerce natural laws, vibrating toward its centre as does the needle to the pole? What obeys laws if trade does not? Is forced trade reliable or profitable? Nor does distance impair effects, so there be but one centre as there is but one positive pole. The nether is of no account in either. Although the 1,500,000 square miles, would make twenty-six such countries as England and Wales, and seven of France; and although London is emporium of the former, and Paris so completely of the latter that she rules the Empire; yet neither has as many spokes in its wheel of commerce, as has the Great West in its hub.

Its own City should have it.

Trade obeys laws.

26 Englands.

7 Frances.

No centre equal to that of N. W.

N. W. able to build up its emporium.

That the Northwest has its centre, and that not of mere geography, we shall ascertain, if we yet have not, and we shall learn the power of internal commerce to build up great cities. What other section is able to impart eminence to its commercial and manufacturing emporium, should the Great Northwest fail? Although certain as the rising and setting of the sun, that of this 1,500,000 miles, Chicago is to be the centre, made so both by nature and art, without power in any ordinary "race of humans" to work a change; yet the magnitude of prospect renders realization difficult. If in the judgment of more moderate citizens, the vision is too grand for accomplishment, too chimerical for earnest thought,—in short, too much like St. Louis' "general prediction"—let us come down to a plain matter-of-fact view, that— Prospect difficult to realize. A moderate estimate.

600,000 SQUARE MILES OF ARABLE LAND AND WATER COURSES, UNEQUALED IN ADVANTAGES NATURAL AND ACQUIRED, RAPIDLY SETTLING WITH THE BEST OF MEN, MUST GIVE UNEXAMPLED GROWTH TO THEIR EMPORIUM. Old N. West 600,000 Sq. Miles.

Adding less than 15,000 miles for the Pacific railway west of Nebraska, and the above statement only includes the area already directly bound to Chicago by these 11,000 miles of iron bands; of which over two-thirds, as we have seen, are specially Chicago roads; and every mile more or less beneficial. From Ohio to Kansas and Nebraska, with the country intermediate, has been styled the Northwest. Yet with this cutting down, the area would give ten kingdoms like England and Wales, and two and three-quarters of France. This already secured by railroads. Old N. West equal to 10 England's. 2¾ France's.

Of the abundant testimony concerning the unequaled natural advantages of this area, we choose that which is most likely to be disinterested, because outside the region. Where shall one find an inquiring, capable, honest mind within the bounds of this Republic, who is not interested, deeply interested, in the development, prosperity and relating facts of the Great Northwest? From a report of the Board of Trade of Buffalo in 1863, copied into that standard work, *Hunt's Merchants' Magazine*, the following is extracted :— Testimony concerning it. Everybody interested. Report *Buffalo Board of Trade.*

In 1800, in all the territory west of New York and Pennsylvania and Northwest of the Ohio River, there were no considerable settlements, except in Ohio, which was then territory containing a population of only 45,365. There was, by the census of 1860, in the lake basin, a population of 9,474,358, against 4,100,425 in 1840, and 6,080,609 in 1850. Population 1800—1860, '40, '50.

The cereal product of the lake basin States was, in 1840, 267,265,877 bush.; in 1850, 434,862,661 bush.; in 1860, 679,031,559 bush.; in 1862, (estimated) 900,000,000. Cereals of Lake Basin.

In 1840 the surplus cereals moved to the seaboard out of the lake basin was about 5,000,000 of bushels, against 145,000,900 bushels in 1862. Surplus 1840—'62.

The Erie Canal and the Mississippi River were, from 1825 to 1838, the only avenues of transportation for the products of the West to the seaboard. The surplus cereal products exported from those States bordering on Lake Erie, including flour estimated as wheat, were all included in the receipts at Buffalo, which receipts in 1836 were only 1,239,357 bushels. Avenues 1825. In 1836, 1,238,357, bu.

The first grain received at Buffalo from Lake Michigan was in 1836, being a small cargo of 3,000 bushels of wheat from Grand Haven, Michigan, by the brig John Kinzie, R. C. Bristol, Master. The first grain received at Buffalo, from Chicago, was a small cargo of 1,678 bushels of wheat, shipped by Newberry & Dole, of Chicago, Oct. 8, 1839, on the brig Oceola, Francis P. Billings, Master, and consigned to Kingman & Durfee, Black Rock, now North Buffalo. 1st grain from L. Mich. 1836—Chic. 1839

In the year 1862, the surplus cereals exported from Lake Michigan, were from Chicago, 57,676,741 bushels, from Milwaukee, 18,723,000 bushels. Other ports (estimated) 10,000,000 bushels, making a total of 86,399,741 bushels. Surplus 1862

Such are the changes of less than twenty-five years. With such results before us, what may we reasonably expect will be the increase of the next succeeding twenty-five years, when all the circumstances are so much more favorable than were Changes 25 years. What next 25?

The area. those of twenty-five years ago? The States bordering and tributary to the lakes, embracing Ohio, Indiana, Michigan, Wisconsin, Illinois, Minnesota, Iowa, Missouri, Kansas, Kentucky, Nebraska and Dakota, have an area of 501,027,260 acres, only

Rapidity of Settlement. 56,221,908 of which were improved lands in 1860, against 26,680,340 acres in 1850. In the single decade from 1850 to 1860 no less than 25,146,341 additional acres were taken from forest and prairie and turned into farms. During this decade the population had increased 3,393,749, being 55 8-10 per cent. or an annual increase of over 5½ per cent.

3 per cent. increase in Union. 100,000,000 in 1890. The annual increase in the population of the whole of the United States, since 1790 has been three per cent. and a fraction. By this rule which has proved correct through seven decades, applied to the remaining portion of this century, the population will be upward of one hundred millions in 1900.

Half to be in lake and river valleys. If this fertile region of the country shall continue to increase in population, at the same rate per cent, for the remaining portion of the century, that it has during the last decade, more than half of the population of the United States in the year 1900 will be in the valleys of the lakes and the Mississippi.

Increase of int. improvements. The progress in internal improvements in these northwestern States, shows stupendous results. There were twenty-eight miles of railway in 1840, 1,354 in 1850, 11,782 miles in 1860. In 1830 these States had no artificial canals. In 1860 there were completed and in operation 1,556 miles of canals, besides nearly one thousand miles of slack-water navigation, answering all the purpose of canals.

3 divisions—Pac., Rivers and Lake Valleys, and Atl. & Gulf. Within the present limits of the United States and Territories there are three millions of square miles, which may be geographically divided as follows: Pacific slope 750,000 square miles, Mississippi and lake valleys, 1,350,000 square miles, Atlantic and gulf slopes, 900,000 square miles.

Middle, 1,350,000 sq. m. This great middle division of 1,350,000 square miles, embracing nearly one-half the national domain, is drained by the Mississippi and its tributaries, and the Great Lakes; the waters of the former finding an outlet in the Gulf of Mexico, and the latter in the Gulf of St. Lawrence, through the River St. Lawrence, extending through 20 degrees of latitude and 30 degrees of longitude.

Mineral Wealth. This vast area of country abounds with extensive deposits of iron, coal, copper, lead, gold, silver, and quicksilver the coal being always near the iron deposits, and the quicksilver near those of gold and silver; the former being necessary for the manufacture of the iron, and the latter for economizing the gathering of the more precious metals.

Rich arable land. The rich alluvial soil of the Lake and Mississippi Valleys, will make the richest and most productive agricultural district in the world. By the year 1900, the fifty

Division of Labor. millions of people inhabiting these valleys, dividing their labor between agriculture, manufactures and trade, promoted and advanced by the productive wealth of the gold and silver mines of the Pacific slope, will, from necessity, give life and vigor to a domestic commerce that will be equal to that of all Europe, and from which will result a more extended foreign commerce than has ever been the lot of any nation to enjoy.

No country equal. There is no country on earth that has so many natural advantages for a large and extended internal trade, or can be so easily made available by artificial aids, as the great West and North-west. * * * *

Canals completed. These connecting links [canals from lakes to rivers] in the great internal water highway being completed; the proposed improvement of the Canadian canals will,

St. Lawrence and Miss. Lake arms. when accomplished, extend an arm of the sea from the Gulf of St. Lawrence into the heart of the great West, while from the Sunny South comes another arm from the Gulf of Mexico.

Also Va. route. Between these two great water highways is a projected canal from the Ohio river, through Virginia to the ocean; besides the Pennsylvania canals, and the canal system of New York, with its trunk line, the Erie and Oswego. New York need

St. Law. route strongest. never very much fear this Southern arm of the ocean, but the Northern arm has power now, and when the plans and purposes of the Canadian Provinces shall have been carried out, there will be such an augmented power as to sweep onward to the ocean, via the St. Lawrence, nearly all the vast prospective commerce, the infancy of which has been shared by the Empire State.

Chance for future growth. Of this succinct statement, two points will be specially observed; rapid increase, and small proportion of land yet under cultivation. The census of 1870 will no doubt exhibit quite as favorable results to the Northwest in relation to growth, notwithstanding the war, which not only withdrew hundreds of thousands from the plow, but enlisted those spirited, active men, who would mostly have come into the West. But the census of 1880 will exhibit far greater relative changes, rendering certain the prediction above, that "more than half the population of the United States, in the year 1900 will be in the valleys of the lakes and the Mississippi." Ten years to come will give this region double the increase of railways of the past ten, and mostly direct extensions of Chicago lines west of the Mississippi. As before remarked, the gigantic corporations from the eastward will have fierce rivalry in extending present lines and creating new feeders in the prolific West; and with the mining business as a rich object of attainment, will open new lines through the present wilderness to be at once converted into farms and towns.

1900 will give N. W. half the whole population.

10 Years double railways.

Rivalry of Eastern lines

Of the mass of information gathered about the progress of the West, only a little can be given. Nor does the point need amplification. Who is ignorant of the growth of the Northwest? Beginning in the South, the Governor of Missouri says in his Message:—

Progress of N. W. is known.

Gov. of Mo.

Thirty-six months have not yet passed since that epoch, from which our prosperity dates. An intelligent, energetic, liberty-loving immigration has come from older free States and from foreign nations, and has materially aided to repeople the places made waste by war. We have invited and cordially welcome free labor; the churches have been repaired and filled with worshippers. On the prairies, in the forests, and along the rivers, spires have risen, making new temples and new altars erected and dedicated to our God. The increase of educational facilities is one of the surest proofs of our progress. Four thousand eight hundred and forty schools are now filled with over two hundred thousand children. The University is being crowded with students, and has taken rank with the first colleges in the nation. The Capital State School Fund has more than doubled; cities, towns and counties have in many instances trebled their population; the exchanges resound with voices of active men, the steamboats and long trains of cars are bearing our productions to markets. The prairies, forests, hills and valleys, are being everywhere beautified with new-made homes. Capital, by millions, has come to us, and manufactories have arisen, and are vocal with busy industry. The mines are re-opened and new and valuable discoveries of ore have been made. Two hundred and forty miles of railroad have been built without thereby increasing the State indebtedness; two hundred and ninety-two miles are in process of construction, and eight hundred and twenty miles more are projected.

Progress since war.

Religion regarded—

—and education.

Great prosperity.

Access of means.

The debt of the State has been reduced about $11,000,000. Our population has increased to at least one million five hundred thousand, and taxable property has been augmented in value by importations and by additions consequent on our general prosperity to $4,554,863,895. Our credit as a State has not only been restored, but raised to a standard higher than it has ever reached since the reception of the internal improvement debt. With these fruits of a loyal and progressive rule before us, we may well be strengthened in our attachment to the principles by which these wonders of transformation have been wrought and made firm in our resolve to push forward to new victories, fraught with new and greater blessings, until we have laid sure and steadfast the foundation upon which we mav safely rest the future of our State.

Debt reduced.

Population increased.

Stand by our political principles.

Gov. of Kansas.

Says the Governor of Kansas in his Message:—

The immigration to the State since January, 1867, has comprised not less than fifty thousand persons, and with a reasonable appropriation, might have been increased to one hundred thousand. No State in the Union offers greater inducements to the immigrant than Kansas; with 80,000 square miles of fertile soil, well

50,000 settlers in 1867.

Unsurpassed advantages.

adapted to the production of all kinds of grain, fruit, etc., with a a mild, genial climate as desirable as one could wish, with an abundance of the best quality of timber, water, stone, marble, coal gypsum, salt, and almost every other natural advantage, there is no reason why Kansas, with a proper effort should not receive a large proportion of the vast immigration westward.

Mercht. Mag.

As to the extreme North, extracts are made from an article in *Hunt's Merchant's Magazine*, of Nov. 1865 :—

Minnesota. Rapid growth.

Minnesota was erected into a Territory of the Union in 1849, with a population of 4,049 souls. Here it becomes a political community and takes its statistical start. Eight years later, when preparing to take its place in the sisterhood of States, a census was taken, which showed that its population had increased to 150,037. In the meanwhile the assessed valuation of real and personal property had risen from $514,936 to $35,000,000.

In 1865 250,000.

Thus, in less than ten years, had arisen from the wilderness, a State equaling in population more than one sovereignty of Europe, the structure of a thousand years. This same State contains now (1865,) not less than 250,000 inhabitants, and possesses a taxable valuation of not less than $50,000,000.

Newer States grow fastest. Facilities greater. One day work of 30.

It took Ohio, Indiana and Michigan, each, thirty-five years from their foundation to reach the same status. Illinois gains the same point in twenty-five years, Wisconsin, Iowa and Minnesota had each 250,000 fifteen years after being erected into separate Territories. It would appear from this that the further we progress into the wilderness the greater and more rapid the influx of population. This, however, may be explained by the greater facilities now enjoyed than those vouchsafed to the immigrants of an earlier date. They had to break the untrod wilderness, unmarked by even ordinary roads, while the immigrant of to-day reaches his destination by railroad and steam navigation. So much for facilities, and as to time, the work of thirty days is now compressed into a single day. Other elements have also favored later times,—adverse policy has driven to our shores millions of foreigners, refugees from tyranny and starvation, and the vast increase of population in the older States has compelled the young and able to seek new homes in the West. It is not wonderful, then, that the extreme portion should receive this foreign and domestic overflow, which, passing the older settlements, seeks new fields on which to expend its forces. The progress of Minnesota since it became a State, in population, land occupation, and wealth, is shown in the following table :

Progress of Minn.

Progress of Minnesota in Population and Property.

	Fiscal Year.	*Population.*	*Land—Acres.*	*Real Estate.*	*Pers'l Prop'ty*	*Total.*
From 1858—	1858..........	155,000	5,182,309	$34,533,144	$7,313,634	$44,846,778
	1859..........	163,000	5,957,645	28,349,116	7,227,176	35,576,392
	1860..........	172,022	6,404,491	32,021,913	4,629,907	36,753,408
	1861..........	190,000	7,171,559	34,066,830	5,914,683	39,981,513
	1862..........	215,000	7,274,318	24,791,888	5,040.831	29,882,719
	1863..........	230,000	7,580,161	25,100,198	6,560,570	31,660,768
—1864.	1864..........	250,000	8,026,285	33,111,956	8,500,000	41,611,956

Irregularity explained.

The above valuation is for taxation. The apparent falling off from the valuation of 1858 is caused by change in the assessment laws. The depression in 1862 and 1863 is the result of Indian hostilities in those years, which temporarily disorganized the frontier counties, which, though appearing in the land column, are absent for valuation.

Mo. Dem.

The shipments of wheat exhibit the rapidity of growth, which are taken from the Missouri *Democrat*, Jan. 1st :—

Wheat of Minn. 1867.

Wheat Shipped from Points in Minnesota for 1867.—The following table gives a comparative exhibit of the exports of wheat from Winona for a series of years, commencing with 1859:—

From Winona.

Year	Bush.	Year.	Bush.	Year.	Bush
1859	130,000	1862	1,203,161	1865	2,543,146
1860	405,000	1863	1,251,830	1866	3,256,482
1861	993,133	1864	1,854,795	1867	2,348,759

Other points

From despatches sent by reliable persons, we compile the following table of shipments from other important points:—

Ports.	Bush.	Ports.	Bush.	Ports.	Bush.
Red Wing	628,535	Wabasha	333,704	La Crescent	15,200
Hastings	536,000	Minneiskee	205,000	Pickwick	36,000
Lake City	342,622	Mendota (East)	60,897		
Total					2,157,958
Add Winona					2,348,759
Grand Total*					4,506,717

Rapid strides of N. W.

The census exhibits the great strides which the States mainly tributary to Chicago are making, compared with the rest of the Union, in corn and wheat.

Increase of wheat and corn. —1840—'60.

Corn and Wheat Raised in Five States, as per U. S. Census.

States.	*Corn*—1860.	1850.	1840.	*Wheat*—1860.	1850.
Indiana	71,588,919	52,964,363	28,155,887	16,848,267	6,214,458
Illinois	115,174,777	57,646,984	22,634,211	23,837,023	9,414,575
Wisconsin	7,517,300	1,988,979	....	15,637,458	4,286,131
Iowa	42,410,686	8,656,799	1,406,241	8,449,403	1,530,581
Missouri	72,892,157	36,214,537	17,332,524	4,227,586	2,981,652
	309,583,839	157,471,662	69,526,863	69,019,737	24,427,397
Total U. S.	838,792,740	592,071,104	317,531,875	173,104,924	100,485,944

Total U. S.

Proportions of N. W.

It will be noticed that these five States produced in 1840 about one-fifth in corn, in 1850 about one-fourth, and in 1860 over one-third the entire crop of the Union. In 1850 they produced about one-fourth of the wheat, and in 1860 nearly forty per cent. In 1850 Illinois was fifth in the Union, in

—of Illinois.

*The financial editor of the *Chicago Republican*, just returned from a long visit to Minnesota, says their exports of wheat were about 6,000,000, of which 4,500,000 came to Chicago, despite Milwaukee endeavors to shorten its transit to the Lake.

Chi. Rep. says 6,000,000.

wheat; and first in 1860. In 1840, she was seventh in corn, in 1850 third, and in 1860 first, producing about one-seventh of the entire Union.

General satisfaction of settlers.

One may travel over the entire Northwest, and wherever he stops to enquire—and if he stop long enough to hear a word, he is sure of the information—that all things considered, that is the very best site that can be found. Usually quite well informed about the country, they admit that *that* location is advantageous for such a reason, and *that* for some other; but considering every advantage, this is *the* choice of all; and reasons are as plenty as blackberries. Nor are their reasons baseless; and hence the universal satisfaction which every man has all over this 600,000,—this 1,000,000,—this 1,600,000 square miles, that he is in the very garden-spot of creation.

Reasons good.

Has the N. W. a centre?

For such a land we are endeavoring to ascertain whether it has a business centre, and where it is; and under the next topic, we shall have quite good evidence that as to commerce the centre has been found, and is already well established; and the topic succeeding will exhibit like results as to manufactures. But these pursuits depend almost entirely upon the well ordering of government. Political influences should therefor have equal consideration with physical. They have not, however, for the very abundant reason that we ourselves have had no knowledge of the fundamental principles whereby our compound system of State and Federal Governments is operated. Ignorant ourselves of the very basis upon which our grand superstructure rests,—a Federal arch spanning a continent from ocean to ocean, and stretching from torrid to frigid zone,—how could we show foreigners it's strength and beauty? Indoctrinated with heresies in the very origin of our Governments; * no old and sound text-books reprinted to inform us concerning principles of political science, in the application of which the excellence of our system consists, and overwhelmed with a flood of errors; very little has the superiority and beneficence of our Governments been employed to bring immigrants from less favored nations.

Influence of Govt.—

—equal with physics.

Ignorance of principles—

—its cause.

Influence of Govt. not used.

Ignorance caused war.

Imperfectly as we ourselves have understood the relations and obligations of free and independent States in National Union,—so imperfectly that ignorance at the bottom, and passion to inflame, generated a conflagration unexampled in civil wars—it could not be expected that foreigners would take the lead in developing essential differences in forms of Government, displaying their own vast inferiority. Therefore, the chief operative influence hitherto in bringing settlers, has been the natural advantages of the country; nor has that been a weak inducement. The U. S. census gives the following figures:—

Foreigners will not display their own inferiority.

If true, important.

* Being unwilling to make such a charge as this without offering some evidence that it is not baseless, an Appendix is added to consider in short this and kindred topics; which, if true, it will be admitted must have very great influence upon this question of immigration.

Total annual Immigration from 1841 *to* 1860. Annual immigration.

1841..........80,289	1846..........154,416	1851..........379,466	1856..........200,436
1842..........104,565	1847..........234,968	1852..........371,603	1857..........251,306
1843..........52,496	1848..........226,572	1853..........368,645	1858..........123,126
1844..........78,615	1849..........297,024	1854..........427,833	1859..........121,282
1845..........114,371	1850..........369,980	1855..........200,877	1860..........153,640

—1841—'60.

Total, 20 years..........4,311,465
Total from 1820 to 1840..........750.949 From 1820—'40.

Total immigrants for 40 years..........5,062,414 Total 40 years.

As approximating the immigration since 1860, we can compare with the above those of New York as given by the New York *Journal of Commerce*:— *N. Y. Jour. Com.*

Immigrants arriving annually at New York, from 1848 *to* 1867. Immigration at N. Y. 1848—'67.

1848..........189,176	1853..........284,945	1858..........78,589	1863..........156,844
1849..........220,791	1854..........319,223	1859..........79,322	1864..........225,916
1850..........212,603	1855..........136,323	1860..........105,162	1865..........196,347
1851..........289,601	1856..........142,342	1861..........65,529	1866..........233,398
1852..........300,992	1857..........183,773	1862..........76,306	1867..........242,371

Last year Germany sent 117,591, Ireland 66,134, England 33,712, Scotland 6,815, Sweden 4843, etc., nor are we without accessions from contiguous territory. One of our papers gives the following item:— From several European States.

Emigration from the Canadian Dominion to the United States has been so large within the past few months that the Canadian authorities manifest signs of alarm. In the Legislative Assembly, at Quebec, on Thursday last, notice of a motion was given that the Committee on Emigration be instructed "to inquire into the primary cause of the emigration of citizens from the Province of Quebec to the United States, and that necessary means be taken to prevent the same." Canadian immigration——their fears.

The tide, it will be observed, largely fluctuates. But if war retarded, its results will accelerate immigration. Who can doubt that causes hitherto so effective will operate with increasing power? Almost every immigrant draws others; and now to natural advantages of rich, cheap land, are to be added the increasing facilities of intercourse; and far above them will political considerations have power. No confidence has hitherto been possessed in the stability of our institutions; so that not only superiority has been ignored, but no calculation could be based upon perpetuity. Those who have considered the subject, as few have, were satisfied in the belief that such a people as we were known to be, would have some sort of tolerable government. But our war has demonstrated the strength of our National Union, as well as the inherent power of a government of the people, proving it strongest right where De Tocqueville pronounced it weakest. Now being compelled, in order to reconstruct our shattered but not destroyed Union, to thoroughly study into the principles of State Sovereignty, it will be seen that a like danger can never arise in future; for we have been taught a lesson that will

Immigration to increase. One draws others. Confidence in our institutions. Strength of Govt. demonstrated. State Sovereignty to be apprehended

Confidence strong.

last for all time, and confidence unbounded will be inspired in the perpetuity of our institutions.

South to grow.

Benefit other sections.

N. W. to have political power.

The South we hope will receive more settlers than hitherto, for a large cotton product gives strength to the entire country, while it makes a larger demand upon the Northwest for bread-stuffs and meats, and a draft upon the East for manufactures, which compels them also to draw upon the West. Yet the West as hitherto is to have the chief part of foreigners, so that the fast increasing political power of the Northwest, is an important item in these calculations. She has never had justice done her, not even by New England, * which ought to be foremost upon every occasion in her offspring's cause when right and just. But power will soon be ours; so effectively, that one trembles at the fearful responsibility inevitably to devolve upon us, to the weal or woe of the entire Republic. The following topic was considered in 1861:—

Responsibility great. Views, 1861.

Increasing power of N. W.

Loss of other sections.

Census Returns of Illinois, Iowa and Wisconsin.—The recent United States Census gives valuable indications touching this subject of Western investments. Since 1850, Illinois has increased 860,487—more than any other State; Iowa, 482,704; and Wisconsin, 470,490. *They have gained ten Members of Congress, while all the other new States have gained only nine, and the old States have lost twenty-four*, which indicates fairly and clearly the relative changes in the Union now progressing.

Same to continue.

Chief stay of Chicago.

Relative increase compared.

Probably in 1870, these three States will again have proved the largest gainers, and in the same order, for they are still sparsely settled, and no newer region more inviting can be opened to occupation. They are the chief dependence of Chicago, though much business must here concentrate from other States, and their astonishing growth shows the increase of their metropolis is not in advance of the country. Their total population now is 3,162,745, to 1,349,075 in 1850, being an increase of 134 per cent. The gain throughout the Union has been about 35 per cent., but in New England was only 14½ per cent., in the Middle States, 37 per cent., and in the whole Northwest, from Ohio to Kansas inclusive, and north, and containing 9,091,984, was over 68 per cent.

Mr. Scott's prediction—

—its moderation.

1910, 70,000,000.

To accomplish Mr. Scott's predictions, hereinafter presented, that "the great interior plain would, in fifty years, have seventy millions," the per cent. of annual increase can be largely diminished. Suppose the present decade, instead of 68 per cent., the Northwest increases *only sixty per cent.*, gives in 1870, 14,547,174; the next, 55 per cent., gives in 1880, 22,548,119; the next, 50 per cent., gives in 1890, 33,822,178; the next, 45 cent., gives in 1900, 49,042,158; and the next, 40 per cent., gives in 1910 68,659,021. These per cents. are surely moderate, and the addition of Kentucky, Tennessee, etc., included by Mr. Scott, will make a larger aggregate than seventy millions.

Of this Chi. is centre.

Of this "great interior plain," it is claimed that nature has indicated, and art already established, Chicago as soon to be the largest city, probably excelling in only twenty or thirty years any two or three within its broad and rich domain.

Another important topic was also noticed in 1861:—

Character of settlers.

Character of the Settlers.—To develop and employ the advantages so bountifully bestowed by nature, Providence has sent a suitable people. A Western traveler is

A Mass. M. C. upon the Ill. Cent. R. R. Bill.

Why he opposed it.

* I speak not without knowledge. When the Illinois Central land grant was passed, I was in Washington for three weeks laboring for it. Massachusetts members I saw repeatedly, and as a son of the Bay State and a Whig, plead with them to make her vote a unit in favor of a bill so important to us and the whole country. One of them acknowledged it was right and expedient, but refused to vote for it because western members would vote against the tariff. I finally told him about these words,—for I have repeated them many times since,—you are a pretty Representative of Massachusetts. A man of your cloth—he was a clergyman—to violate your oath, and vote against a bill you admit is every way desirable and just because western men will not violate their oaths and favor protection which they conscientiously believe to be wrong. If Massachusetts expects to make Whig and tariff votes out of the West, she must send to Congress different men from you.

Hon. George Ashmun friendly.

She then had different men there, and an adroit movement of Hon. George Ashmun, saved our bill, which his colleague would have been glad to kill.

always impressed with the superiority of the settlers, and often is the remark made concerning them,—"No wonder the West grows so fast."

In enterprise, intelligence, activity, energy, they are unsurpassed, seldom equaled. My long connection with the *Prairie Farmer*, and extensive acquaintance, enable me to speak understandingly on this point. Immigrants also have greater wealth than formerly. Capital being liberally rewarded as well as labor, more and more wealthy settlers come in as the advantages of the West are made known. Travel gives knowledge.

The character of American immigrants cannot be improved. For twenty to thirty years, the most active, enterprising, intelligent, liberal-minded men of the East, have been pouring into the West. This is what gives the West a uniform character for energy and progress, excelling all other sections, as is universally acknowledged.* But foreign immigration can and will be changed immensely for the better. Not that we refuse a welcome to the poorest or most ignorant, so that they come with a strong hand and honest heart. We want them, and shall have tens where we have had units. But this land of ours offers inducements to men of character, in the superiority of its political institutions, quite equal to its physical advantages. We have not used this influence as it should have been, because unaware ourselves of the truth. Proud of our country, and zealous in our claims to precedence, it has been wholly zeal without knowledge, as I propose to show in the Appendix before referred to. When difference between the forms of government shall be demonstrated, and the superiority of our own established as never having been equaled; who can doubt that the knowledge will have an influence upon immigration never before known, especially in the higher circles of society, who can appreciate the importance of this? And in large measure it will seek the West.

Best men come west.

Foreign immigration.

All welcomed.

Higher classes to come.

Have not used our advantages.

Knowledge of our superior Govt's will bring settlers.

Besides, instead of the African who, in two generations, will have almost disappeared, we shall have millions of Coolies; and the South with that labor, will again produce cotton, rice and sugar, enjoying a prosperity as much superior to the past, as the Chinaman is superior to the Negro. They cannot afford to turn their labor to produce food and manufactures. These will again be supplied by the North; the latter by the Northeast, until gradually the Northwest shall have attained the ascendant, by its advantages in obtaining raw materials and food, as we shall soon see.

Coolies to come.

South to prosper—

—to benefit North.

---

*Nearly twenty years ago Dr. M'Guffey, that efficient patron of common schools, as well as accomplished Professer of a University, visited Chicago with reference to investments. After spending a few days, he desired to see the country and people, and asked me for letters of introduction along the route from Elgin down Fox River, and thence to Alton. Visiting him at the University of Virginia a year or two after, he informed me that on arriving at a village he presented his letters, and offered to deliver a lecture upon education. Notices were at once posted and information circulated, and in the evening he would have a good audience in the church, or school house, or court house. He said that he had never lectured to such audiences, displaying equal intelligence, energy, and noble character; adding with emphasis, "It is no wonder that Illinois grows so fast."

Dr. M'Guffey's opinion of Illinois settlers.

Having travelled with my horse and buggy all over Indiana, Illinois, Wisconsin and Iowa, before the advent of railways, to interest the farmers in their paper, and make them write for it, I am able to confirm Dr. M'Guffey's opinion. Never was any country blessed with an agricultural population,—the controlling power, thank God—equal to that of the Northwest.

Prairie Farmer experience.

Benefits of war. The predictions of 1861, (p. 18) as to the nature of the war, were not more correct than as to its effects. Confirming those expectations to the full, one of the best newspapers, the New York *Evening Post*, says of—

N. Y. Evn. Post.

Strong N. W. *The Strong Northwest.*—While the Southern States send up a piteous cry for relief from almost universal destitution, and the manufacturing and commercial States of the East are pervaded by a general feeling of depression, it is a comfort to know that there is one part of the country—and that a considerable one—where prosperity and financial soundness are the rule, and poverty and depression the exceptions. States included.. We refer to the Northwest, and include in this designation the States of Indiana, Michigan, Illinois, Wisconsin, Iowa and Minnesota—formerly included in the old "Northwestern Territory," and now the homes of between seven and eight millions of the most energetic people within the United States.

Prosperity general. A friend who has just returned from a visit to this region confirms our previous reports as to the general thrift and prosperity which pervade it. The main interest, of course, is agricultural, and this is in a position of peculiar independence. During Out of debt. the war the high prices paid for products of the farm enabled the agriculturalists of the West to get free from debt. Tens of thousands of mortgages for purchase Farmers independent. money and improvements were lifted from their farms during the first three years of the war, and since then good crops sold at high rates, have enabled the farmers to improve their farms, buy stock, and otherwise intrench themselves against the contingencies of the future. Thus, as a class, they occupy an unusually strong and safe position. If a general financial storm should arise they are fully prepared to weather it in safety and even comfort.

Feel N. W. pulse at Chi. The pulse of the Northwest can be felt better at Chicago than anywhere else, and there our informant found among business men a feeling of staunchness and confidence that was decidedly comforting. The business of that city, since the gather- Injury to East helps Chi. ing of the last crops, has been enormous. The very causes which have damaged the manufacturers and wholesale merchants of the East have helped the merchants of Chicago. With a falling market the small dealers in the interior have preferred to make small and frequent purchases near home, rather than to lay in large stocks at the East. The numerous large and handsome stores that are building in Chicago attest the great increase in its trade from this and from more permanent causes. Increase of commerce. Among other indications of the growing commercial importance of that city is the fact—pretty well authenticated—that the largest of the new stores now in course of erection there is to be used as a branch by Mr. A. T. Stewart, of this city.

Manufactures growing. With the prosperity of the agricultural and mercantile intersts of the Northwest, of course, the manufacturing interests have not suffered. By the simple operation of the laws of demand and supply, manufactures adapted to the wants of the people have sprung up along all the water-courses of this locality, and have now obtained an importance and stability hardly to have been expected in so young a Rock River Valley. country. In some parts of the Northwest, particularly along the benutiful Rock River valley, the number of manufacturing establishments reminds one of the busiest inland districts of New England.

Such is the N. W. Such is the Old Northwest, such its resources, and its connection with that city which it has already made its emporium. Whatever merit this Reasoning from past to future. paper possesses, is due to the one means employed, of reasoning from the past and present to the future. As evidence of the power of this region to continue what we have so well begun, let us look at—

Commerce of Chi. & St. L.

THE COMMERCE OF CHICAGO COMPARED WITH ST. LOUIS.

Com. indispensable. Whatever apparent advantages a city may have, commerce is indispensable to their development and profitable use. Why it proves effective, is not easily answered, especially with modern improvements for handling merchandise and produce of all kinds. Manufactures, we can readily perceive, build up cities, because employment is afforded to a multitude. But a few persons can handle an indefinite amount of mechanism or agricultural products. Yet mere commerce has always, and always will, build up cities, according to its magnitude. Will build up cities.

The highest civilization, begetting the greatest division and subdivision of labor, renders commerce an indispensable adjunct. Some countries, some sections of a country, are best adapted to certain productions, as is the South to cotton and sugar and rice. They can better afford to buy grain and meat from the Northwest, and manufactures from the Northeast, than to turn land and labor to their production. The merchant comes in to facilitate exchanges to their mutual advantage. No one thing more bespeaks superiority of modern civilization to that of Greece and of Rome, than their degradation of commerce and our exaltation of a labor absolutely necessary to high culture. Heathen as they were, they knew not that GOD had ennobled labor, setting man at work even in Eden, "to dress it and to keep it." Nor was commerce without honor among other nations renowned in antiquity. Tyre was a great city before Athens and Sparta; and Hiram, its King, was a friend of Solomon's. Said Ezekiel concerning Tyre:— Division of labor— —requires commerce. Ancients degraded it. God ennobles it. Tyre renowned.

O thou! that art situate at the entry of the sea,
Which art a merchant of the people for many isles,
Thus saith the LORD GOD.
The inhabitants of Zidon and Arvad were thy mariners:
Thy wise men, O Tyrus, that were in thee, were thy pilots.
The ancients of Gebal and the wise men thereof were in thee, thy calkers:
All the ships of the sea with their mariners were in thee, to occupy thy merchandise.
Tarshish was thy merchant by reason of the multitude of all kinds of riches;
With silver, iron, tin, and lead, they traded in thy fairs.
Javan, Tubal, and Meshech, they were thy merchants;
They traded the persons of men and vessels of brass in thy market.
They of the house of Togarmah traded in thy fairs
With horses and horsemen and mules.

Ezekiel, xxvii 3, 8, 9, 12-14.

The whole of that grand description could be appropriately quoted, for this city is also beside this inland sea, and its commercial power is to be the means of drawing manufactures, and the cause of all its greatness. Its merchants will continue to be, as they already are, its princes; and they will mould its character more than any other class. Let them realize their responsibilities to GOD and country; remember always that "a just weight and balance are the Lord's;" and constantly "bring all the tithes into the storehouse," * and they will draw down upon themselves and this city, the Appropriate to Chi. Merchants control. Their responsibility. To give tithes.

*Since this article was written it has been my good fortune to hear Rev. Mr. Martin, of Nevada present the claims of the mining country, and I cannot forbear suggesting, especially to these liberal-minded, sagacious merchants and manufacturers, the propriety of giving largely for a few years to establish religious institutions in that region. Truly as that GOD is Author of Malachi's declarations—what a befitting close to the prophetic and ushering in of the Gospel Dispensation!—will He bless them who pay Him the tithes on the increase which He gives. Who can doubt. that if Chicago would spend $100,000 in that way—and if she spent five times that, and twice-told all that she now gives to kindred objects, still the tithes would not be given—yet, if she would spend in that important field, whose commerce is here to converge, $100,000 annually, who doubts that it would be a judicious investment? "If you like the security, down with the dust." Rev. Mr. Martin of Nevada. Chicago to give to mining regions.

blessings of a covenant-keeping GOD, averting curses that came upon Tyre for pride and self-confidence; offenses still more rank in Heaven's sight, in this nineteenth century of the Christian era. While we glory in our unequaled blessings, let it be with heartfelt acknowledgments to the Giver; and let our acknowledgments be more in dollars, and our words will have more heart and weight.

Thereby show thankfulness.

Responsible for improving our advantages.

Weighty is this responsibility to GOD and country, for the improvement of the unequaled commercial advantages here bestowed. Nature, as we have seen, has made it one of the most prominent cities of the world for trade; and art has wonderfully manifested its wisdom in following nature's ordinations. No city could possibly have such commercial facilities without a respectable commerce; and to afford some evidence that art has made no mistake in its endeavors, and that nature's benefactions are not wasted, it will be well to look at some of the statistics. A comparison, too, with St. Louis as far as possible, will serve to show whether the relative decline—not actual, for we hope always to see St. Louis prosperous—does not sustain previous views and declarations.

Commerce already large

Relative decline of St Louis.

Int. Revenue Returns. *Chi. Tribune.*

The annual returns to the Commissioner of Internal Revenue, afford a true index to the relative business of American cities. The *Chicago Tribune*, Jan. 8th, 1868, publishes the following:—

Chi wholesale trade.

Tax 1 mill.

Wholesale Trade of Chicago.—The Report of Special Revenue Commissioner David A. Wells, which appears in our columns this morning, contains a table giving the gross returns of sales by wholesale of goods, wares, and merchandise, for the last financial year, in all the chief cities of the Union. A tax of one mill on the dollar is levied on the sales, and by multiplying this tax by 1,000, the total value of the sales at wholesale are accurately arrived at. According to the figures in Mr. Wells' report, the business of Chicago stands eighth on the list of American cities—stands even below St. Louis and Cincinnati, and but little above that of San Francisco. Believing that a gross error existed in the Commissioner's figures, we sent to the Assessor's office for an abstract of the wholesale returns made to that office, and subjoined is the result of the examination. The sales, as reported by Mr. Wells, are as follows:

Mr. Wells' error in making Chi. 8th.

1st statement of 9 chief cities.

New York...	$1,976,565,000	Baltimore.......	$307,076,000	Cincinnati......	$180,753,000
Philadelphia	616,697,000	New Orleans...	367,591,000	Chicago.........	174,245,000
Boston.........	646,407,000	St. Louis......	234,891,000	San Francisco	161,225,000

Chi. only for 6 months.

The return for Chicago is evidently made for but six months, and must be a blunder of the copying clerk in Washington who furnished the figures to the Special Commissioner. Here are the amounts returned each month for the year past on which taxes have been paid by our wholesalers:

Returns from Dec. 1866—Nov. 1867.

Dec. 1866.........	$22,340,000	April, 1867......	$31,024,000	August, 1867....	$21,433,000
Jan. 1867.........	24,286,000	May, "	37,918,000	Sept. "	23,059,000
Feb. "	25,905,000	June, "	52,817,000	October, "	39,532,000
March "	25,718,000	July, "	46,764,000	Nov. "	40,791,000
Total sales					$391,587,000

Chi. 4th city

From these figures it is seen that Chicago stands fourth on the list of American cities in respect to magnitude of business. New Orleans and Baltimore stand much higher than we supposed. But both are below Chicago. The trade of 1866 was better in this city than in 1867, and if our monthly returns had begun with July, 1866, instead of December, 1866, the year's business would foot up more than four hundred millions: but we give the figures as they were furnished, it being too late to-night to get them for the last six months of 1866. Diminished trade 1867.

The *Missouri Democrat* published this, Jan. 16th:— *Mo. Dem*

The Large Cities.—For some reason or other, the newspapers of Chicago and Cincinnati have not given especial prominence to the following table of statistics given in the last report of Special Commissioner Wells. It is a statement of the aggregate business transacted in the leading cities of the country, by wholesale and retail dealers in merchandise and liquors, and by auctioneers and merchandise brokers, during the fiscal year ending June 30, 1867. The figures are obtained from official sources, from the returns of taxes on "sales" and "licenses." From this table it appears that St. Louis exceeds both Chicago, Cincinnati and San Francisco, in the amount of its business. The table is as follows: Trade of large cities. St.L. exceeds Chi.

New York....	$1,976,565,000	Chicago.........	$174,245,000	Cleveland.........	$56,117,000
Philadelphia.	616,697,000	San Francisco.	161,225,000	Mobile............	54,291,000
Boston.........	646,407,000	Providence.....	78,904,000	Buffalo............	51,783,100
Baltimore.....	307,076,000	Pittsburg.......	76,240,000	Detroit............	50,471,000
New Orleans.	367,591,000	Louisville......	72,949,000	Charleston.......	36,574,000
St. Louis......	234,891,000	Brooklyn.......	61,448,000	Newark...........	34,396,000
Cincinnati...	180,753,000	Milwaukee.....	58,165,000		

20 Cities.

From this table it appears that the business of this city exceeds that of Cincinnati over fifty-four millions, and that of Chicago over sixty millions. Baltimore and New Orleans are fourth and fifth on the list, and Boston and Philadelphia compete very closely for the second place. A single fact like this is a sufficient reply to all the blowing of our friends in Chicago, for in spite of the rapid growth and boasted enterprise of that city, and in spite of the reasonable anxiety of St. Louis people not to be out-maneuvered in the work of internal improvements, the fact still stands that St. Louis continues to lead both her rivals. To hear Chicago men talk, one would suppose that Cincinnati was a mere village, but though Cincinnati brags less, it does more business than Chicago with all its boasting. St. L. exults. Chi. "blows" Cin beats her.

With the figures of the previous year to warn St. Louis, superabundant caution was not requisite to prevent hasty use of a statement that our papers had already corrected; which correction could not have been overlooked by St. Louis editors, who give Chicago papers more attention than any others, and are perpetually on the sharp scent after any mistakes of fact or argument. The same day (16th January,) that article appeared in the *Democrat*, the *Chicago Tribune* had the following:— St. L. should be cautious. Sharp after Chi. *Chi. Trib.*

The Business of the Cities—Important Correction.—When we published the report of the Hon. D. A Wells, Special Commissioner of the Revenue, we called attention to what appeared to us an important error in the table exhibiting the aggregate amount of business transacted in the leading commercial cities of the country. The comparatively low figures placed to the credit of Chicago we were certain were incorrect, and we so stated at the time. It appears that the Commissioner accepted the compilation of the table from a clerk in the Treasury Department as correct, but, upon revising the whole report, the errors in that table were discovered, and the statement will appear in the printed volume correctly. In the meantime, we spread before our readers the table as it originally appeared, and as upon revision and correction the facts really exist. It will be seen that there is a very large change in the figures showing the business of Chicago. In the table as just published Chicago ranked the eighth in the amount of business, and below Baltimore, Correction of Mr. Wells' report. Change as to Chi.

Was 8th, is 5th.

Why New Orleans is larger.

Boston trade.

St. Louis and Cincinnati, when in point of fact Chicago ranked fifth in the amount of business, and largely exceeded the three cities named. The fact that New Orleans shows a larger return than Chicago is due to the sales there of the large cotton crop of 1866, with portions of that of 1865, at prices ranging from forty to forty-five cents per pound. The sales of New Orleans which will be returned for the fiscal year 1868, will probably fall below one-half of those of 1867, as the price of cotton has fallen to fifteen or sixteen cents per pound. On the other hand, the fine crops of 1867, which are being marketed in Chicago, at high prices, will carry the sales of this city, for the fiscal year ending July 1, 1868, far above those returned for the last fiscal year. The immense returns of Boston are due to the fact that nearly all the raw materials for the manufactures of New England are purchased there, and nearly all the goods and wares made in those six States are sold and handled there. The buying and selling of all New England are done in Boston.

Changes in other Cities.

Cincinnati gains by the correction and St. Louis loses. Louisville and Milwaukee gain largely. Buffalo stands ahead of Pittsburg, but her trade consists chiefly of the grain shipped from Chicago, on which her warehouse owners receive a commission for removing it from the lake vessels into the canal boats.

Traders included in list.

The following is the table, as originally published and as officially corrected, showing the aggregate amount of the business transacted in the leading commercial cities of the country, by wholesale and retail dealers in merchandise and liquors, and by auctioneers and merchandise brokers, during the fiscal year ending June 30, 1867, as deduced from the returns of taxes on "sales" and "licenses," the tax being one mill on the dollar:—

Trade of 20 cities.

Cities.	Correct Am't.	As originally published.	Cities.	Correct Am't.	As originally published.
New York	$3,313,608,058	$1,976,565,000	Milwaukee	$110,675,000	$58,165,000
Boston	928,173,000	646,407,000	Providence	91,876,000	78,904,000
Philadelphia	662.097,000	616,697,000	Buffalo	81,850,000	52,783,000
New Orleans	526,795,000	367,591,000	Pittsburg	80.839,000	76,240,000
Chicago	342,182,000	174,245,000	Mobile	77,383,000	54,291,000
Baltimore	324,966, 00	307,076,000	Brooklyn	69,676,000	61,448,000
Cincinnati	213,254,000	180,753.000	Detroit	62,757,000	50,471,000
St. Louis	213,033,900	264,891,000	Cleveland	55,302,000	56,117,000
San Francisco	151,367,000	161,225.000	Charleston	46,769,000	36,574,000
Louisville	116,216,000	72,949,000	Newark	36,428,000	34,396,000

Is St. Louis malicious?

One would imagine that St. Louis would avoid further ventilation of this subject, lest she become a stench in the nostrils of other cities, which admire generous emulation and despise malicious misrepresentation. Although her editors had seen that correction of Mr. Wells' first statement, as this article proves, the *Missouri Democrat* has the effrontry to publish the following editorial 4th February:—

Mo. Dem.

A Chi. story.

Denies Mr. Wells' report.

A Chicago Story—A Chicago paper complains that St. Louis people publish as correct the table given by Mr. Wells, the Commissioner of the Revenue, in his official annual report, showing the business of the cities of the country. From that table it appeared that the aggregate business of St. Louis was much larger than that of Cincinnati, and that of Cincinnati much larger than that of Chicago. The Chicago paper now says, "the fact is as all intelligent readers know that Chicago and Cincinnati lead St. Louis."

Authority demanded.

We demand authority for that statement. The table given in the official report referred to cannot be disproved by the mere assertion of any newspaper.

Chi. pretends to make correction.

Mere blowing.

No voucher.

A Chicago paper not long ago, came out with a statement that Mr. Wells' figures were erroneous, and giving what it called a corrected table, which differed from that of the official report very largely, the figures for New York alone being changed several hundred millions. But for this pretended "corrected report" no authority has been given, and it rests as far as we know upon the mere assertion of the newspapers of a city more given to "blowing" than any other in that country. If the statement is correct it can be substantiated by official records, and the signature of the proper officers of the government. In that case, it will appear that Mr. Wells is precisely what the whole country now thinks he is not—so gross and careless a bungler as to incorporate statements wildly inaccurate in his official reports. If, on the contrary, the statement cannot be officially substantiated, then the report of Mr. Wells will continue to command general confidence, and the Chicago papers will be called upon to tell an admiring public who it was that invented a table to hide the nakedness of the Garden City. Let the statement be substantiated or frankly own that it is a mere advertising dodge. Invention to hide Chicago nakedness.

Our "beautiful rival" should keep her temper in the contest, for "whom the gods would destroy, they first make mad." If we are to judge of her prospects from her spleen, she must be nearer destruction than we believe, or desire. Her malevolent charges have been treated with due contempt; that article never having been noticed by one of our papers, that I have observed. But bringing together full information touching the subject, and in form for preservation, it appears judicious to present an official endorsement notwithstanding the offensive demand. General Mann favors me with the following note:— Let St. Louis keep her temper. Proper contempt.

UNITED STATES INTERNAL REVENUE, COLLECTOR'S OFFICE,
1ST DISTRICT, ILLINOIS.
CHICAGO, Febuary 21st, 1868.

Gen. Mann's official statement for 1867.

J. S. WRIGHT, ESQ.

Sir: In reply to your note of this date, making inquiry in relation to the amount of sales returned to this office for the past year, I respectfully submit the following statement taken from the records of this office. This exhibit embraces sales of auctioneers, which were omitted in previous report made by one of my Deputies, and published in several of our papers.

You will observe that this statement is for the calendar year—hence the discrepancy between this and the report of Special Commissioner Wells, who estimates for the fiscal year.

Sales in Chicago, 1*st Dist. of Illinois, for the year ending Dec.* 31*st,* 1867, *upon which the tax of* $1, *per thousand was paid into this office.*

January	$24,635,520	May	$38,837,870	September	$23,357,920
February	25,987,640	June	44,764,090	October	40,176,380
March	25,792,760	July	48,115,090	November	41,174,510
April	31,109,870	August	21,863,620	December	40,758,770

Sales $406,574,040.

Total....................$406,574,040

Respectfully Yours,
O. L. MANN, Collector.

Will that satisfy the Queen of the Rivers? Quite self-satisfied that she has distanced both; she finds greatest comfort in that Cincinnati, too, should lead Chicago. How likes she marching down herself to the third place? However absurd the truth may be in her estimation, by what rule of ethics does she hold us responsible for merely copying the absurdity from a responsible source? St. L. below Cin. instead of Chi.

St. Louis being Queen of the Rivers, her sex makes her splenetic; for Mr. Cobb says, "Alas! St. Louis, that *used to be* a Samson in strength!" Whatever she was, she now must be a feminine to exhibit such weakness. She discredits the Great West, to make up faces, insinuate shameful conduct, and call bad names in this way. How much better to follow the example of that other city of the West, whose philosophic endurance does honor to the She wants philosophic endurance—

—like Cin. *Cin. Enq.* old Roman whose name she bears! The *Cincinnati Enquirer* generously admits the truth, and wisely endeavors to find reasons for the growing disparity:—

Cin. not equal to Chi. We know that the old saying, "Comparisons are odious," pertains very strictly whenever an attempt is made to state the relative position of Cincinnati and Chicago; but fear we can no longer compare, that we can only contrast.

Trade sales less. The list of sales of Chicago merchants, published a few days since, leaves no room to doubt that we have a formidable rival in the Illinois giant, which threatens to leave us far behind in the race. It is humiliating, indeed, to think that with all our advantages to enable us to maintain our present position as the greatest commercial city of the West, we may be compelled to yield the palm to our more enterprising Northern sister. Why so? Why is this so? Why, with a better geographical position naturally, and a more extensive field of resources at our command, with almost a half century start, are we to be superseded by a city recently founded, and with not a tithe of our advantages?

Press responsible. We believe that the press are, to a certain extent, responsible for the general apathy which exists in regard to our public enterprises, by the constant propensity Old Hunkers rule. to cater to the old hunker element. When go-ahead citizens attempt some project for benefiting the city, the Old Hunkers raise a cry about taxes, these newspapers Chi. not so. echo the cry and the enterprise is speedily killed. It is not so in Chicago—they are wide awake to their interests, and the press and people accord. Chicago Differences. tunnels for two miles under the lake to get pure water for her citizens, while we continue to sip our decoction of Deercreek sewer. While Chicago is on the alert for any rail road connection to increase her trade, and ready with the money to secure it, we are blind to the great advantages of a Southern railroad connection, and allow other places to step in and carry off the prize.

Chi. makes a harbor—. While Chicago scoops out her prairie mud, and rides the largest lake vessels in her manufactured river, Cincinnati allows Millcreek to overflow its banks once in two or three years, and render nearly valueless, hundreds of acres of desirable land almost in the very heart of the city. While Chicago builds wharves and docks —builds wharves. for her shipping, we cannot get our press to favor an appropriation for the construction of our West End wharf, a necessary outlet for the carrying trade of one-third of the city and of five rail roads, whose depots are within one square of that location.

Room for all 3 cities. All these cities have plenty of room, and each will be large, nor cease to grow for a century, if ever. Cin. graceful— But while Cincinnati gracefully yields to her fate, being content with what she cannot prevent, St. Louis vents spite and —St. L. spiteful. malice. Even a calamity like our recent fire, destroying a large block of iron fronts and other beautiful buildings, some $3,000,000 of property, is *Mo. Rep.* cor. attributed to a desire to sell to insurance companies. The *Missouri Republican* publishes the following from a Springfield correspondent:—

Sell to Insurance Co's. Much of the business of our metropolis is based on want of capital, or borrowed money. When sales are slow, and creditors sharp, there is no alternative but to sell to insurance companies. One considerable portion of the recent great fire is said to be such a sale. Buildings in Chicago are neither more frail nor combustible; stocks of goods no more inflammable, than such buildings or stocks elsewhere. Chi. safe from fire— The security of the buildings, the efficiency of the Fire Department, the vigilance of the Police, and the inexhaustible supply of water from the lake tunnel, have furnished themes on which the press of that city have immeasurably enlarged. —yet $3,000,000 burnt. Yet, on the first serious check of trade, $3,000,000 of property is destroyed by fire in less than three hours. The alarm of fire is given after some of the buildings Don't want fire put out. are destroyed, the fire steamers arrived late, the water supply was short. The public mind outside of Chicago, and, as is suggested there also, has hit upon one Insurance Co's. buy. solution; it is hinted in these paragraphs; Chicago was compelled to sell to somebody, and, as no buyers were in the market, insurance companies were constrained to purchase.

Truly must a city conceive herself hard pushed in the contest, to publish such base stuff, whether paid for or gratuitous. It was very satisfactory to cut the two preceding extracts from the *Chicago Post*, of February 5th, inserted together without a word of comment * under the caption, "Chicago abroad. The late fire. Chicago and Cincinnati contrasted." Insult harmless.

Lest our unamiable neighbor,—uneasy in her position at the extremity of one of our spokes, which she imagines a secure hub,—having faith in nothing except her "natural location," should also call for a verification of General Mann's figures, we give a partial statement of returns of leading firms to the Commissioner of Internal Revenue for two years, compiled from lists in the *Republican* and *Tribune*. The former presented that of last year as well as this; the latter classified them as to business, and here they are combined. The *Tribune* prefaced its list:— St. L. wants faith. Returns of 2 years to Com. Int. Rev. *Tribune.*

From partial returns made to the Assessor of Internal Revenue for this district, we present the following list, comprising a trifle more than one-half of the firms in Chicago whose sales for 1867 exceed half a million of dollars. Scores of the heaviest firms in the city are not included, as will be observed, their returns not having been made. As the law does not require returns to be made until just before the 1st of May, it will be impossible to give anything like a complete list until that time. The following will serve, however, to illustrate to rival villages the ordinary run of business in Chicago: Returns of 1867 incomplete— —1st May to make returns.

The *Republican* remarked:— *Republican.*

The figures show that twenty-one firms transacted a business exceeding two million dollars each, and seventy-six exceeding one million dollars, within the year; while one hundred and seventy-six make returns surpassing half a million. 21 over $2,000,000.

Fifty-nine firms did business in this city in 1866 to the extent of one million dollars and over, and fourteen exceeded two millions. The highest return was that of Field, Palmer & Leiter. Business 1836.

We also publish for the purpose of comparisons, the returns of as many of the firms in question as were published in the *Republican* of May 21, 1866, for the year 1866. Two years.

In this latter exhibit, several omissions will be seen. These are caused in several cases by changes in the firms, and in the instance of the live stock brockers doing business at the Union Stock Yards, from the fact, that owing to some mistake, their sales were not included in the regular business returns made for the year 1866. Cause of omissions.

---

*We, in Chicago, have a good deal to be proud of, and by no means least, is our newspaper press. We little realize how much we are indebted to our editors, not merely for ability, but for their correct appreciation of the dignity, courtesy and magnanimity which becomes the Queen of the Northwest. Obligation to Chi. press.

P. S. A squib of the *Times*, which throws hard shot when necessary, opportunely indicates tone and temper:— *Chi. Times*

"The Chicago papers are the conduits of the feelings and sentiments of the inhabitants of that "goodly city."—*St. Louis paper.*

A "conduit" is something in the nature of a sewer; but sewers do not perform the function of conducting "feelings and sentiments." A "conduit" is, also, a sluiceway, but a sluiceway does not conduct "feelings and sentiments." A "conduit" is, likewise, a "vessel, canal, or pipe for conducting water or other fluids;" all of which are different from feelings and sentiments. None of these various definitions of a "conduit" seems to corrorborate the St. Louis assumption, that a "conduit" is a Chicago newspaper. The application of the term "conduits" to Chicago newspapers, seems, therefore, to be a misnomer, since they are conceded to be vehicles of feelings and sentiments. But, as the newspaper concerns in St. Louis are chiefly employed in conducting "water or other fluid," it might not be improper to call them "conduits." What is a conduit.

Chicago Trade.—Sales of some of the Leading Houses for 1866 *and* 1867.

Dry Goods and Clothing

DRY GOODS AND CLOTHING.

Firms.	1866.	1867.
Field, Leiter & Co	9,220.967	9,071,597
Farwell, J. V. & Co	6,948,328	7,109,714
Tuttle, Thompson & Wetmore	583,010	558,488
Ross & Gossage	863,958	551,112
Shay, J. B. & Co	550,174	541,543
Fisk, D. B. & Co	614,728	539,517
Beardsley, C. & Co	....	516,399
Wills, Gregg & Brown	252,822	693,182
Frank & Meyer	266,716	1,024,000
Hamlin, F. N	....	901,283
King, Kellogg & Co	829,539	892,979
Bowen, Whitman & Winslow	3,458,876	2,422,505
Richards, Crumbaugh & Shaw	795,800	602 000
Carson, Pirie & Co	691.634	733,996
Fiske, Kirtland & Co	390,523	615.321
King, George W. & Co	946,468	636,250
Wadsworth, P. & Co	804,552	506,562
Hunt, Barbour & Hale	1,012,605	1,667,946
Keith Brothers	562,542	1,550,762
Clement, Ottman & Co	....	639,920
Kohn, H. A. & Bro	....	794,000
DeForrest & Co	319,650	512,600
Hill, D. & Sons	....	581,000

Grocers.

GROCERS.

Firms.	1866.	1867.
Doane, J. W. & Co	1,957,615	2,605,493
Cook, G. C. & Co	1,589,469	1.932,474
Reid, Murdock & Fisher	1,250,397	1,375,423
Hindsdale, Sibley & Endicott	1,362,399	1,368,897
Hoyt, Wm. M. & Co	689,483	1,122,488
Sprague & Warner	720,000	1,002,200
Flanders, George W. & Co	2,523,000	2,335,000
Norton & Co	888,659	938,076
Beckwith, C. H	862,200	937,214
Day, Allen & Co	2,369,272	1,953,712
Peck, Clarence I	....	1,829,826
Shores, Staley & Co	666,740	618,444
Taylor & Wright	1.569,687	1,668,425
Thompson, H. M	766,546	904,950
Stearns & Co	1,149,622	1,693,984
Gray, Phelps & Co	1,324,231	1,405,089
Durant, Bros. & Powers	848,589	780,518
Ewing, Briggs & Co	599,614	828.706
Knowles, Cloyes & Co	497,150	527,598
Barrett, Cossett & Co	347,872	663,624
Stearns, Forsyth & Co	861,617	845,815
McKindley, Gilchrist & Co	819,130	840,138
Whitaker, Harmon & Co	1,133,390	1,498,358
Corbin, C. R. & Co	507,617	727,387

Hardware.

HARDWARE.

Firms.	1866.	1867.
Hale, Ayer & Co	1,521.814	1,338,529
Hibbard, Spencer & Co	1,183,387	1,408,894
Sturgis, F. & Co	851,584	947.584
Blair, William & Co	1,111,410	1,047,852
Jones & Laughlin	805,541	770.473
Markley, Alling & Co	664,642	609,325
Hall, Kimbark & Co	980,858	981,900

Commission.

COMMISSION MERCHANTS.

Firms.	1866.	1867.
Hoard, Bro. & Co	2,105.570	1,167,200
Ash, I. N. & Co	669,910	1,165.430
Walbridge, Watkins & Co	924,039	1,155,246
Hobbs, J. B. & Co	....	832,354
Woodruff, W. M	793,600	831,660
McCormick, C. H. & Co	531,800	958,140
Pulsifer & Magee	1,056,140	1,240,466
McDonald & Trego	....	1,684.640

COMMISSION MERCHANTS.

Firms.	1866.	1867.
Armour, H. O. & Co	2,191.324	2,880.464
Munger, Wheeler & Co	1,128,251	2,614,702
Hastings, L. R	....	1,209,290
Higgins, L. & D	2,324,488	2,390,529
Erwin, D. W. & Co	....	1,209,630
Morse, Albert & Co	959,250	1,204.710
Gregg & Hughes	1,217,633	1,117,626
Culton & Sprague	....	1,387,097
Dow, Quirk & Co	1,689,680	1,625,940
Eichold, A. & Co	....	717,357
Burton, Horace	474,654	702,671
Underwood & Co	2,056,085	1,979,702
Munn, Norton & Co	3,535,468	3,829,670
Maitland & Scranton	2,000,010	3,536,310
Hutchinson, B. P. & Co	1,468,766	3,277,796
Lyon, J. B	1,758,230	3,164,310
Rumsey Bros & Co	....	3,110,859
Culver & Co	1.419,650	1,885,600
Pickering, A. H. & Son	....	912,160
Nelson, Murry & Co	709,835	910.939
Phillips & Bros	254,629	905,150
Kelly, David	....	891,910
Priestly, Howard	319 646	887,186
Peters, A. A. & Co	1,450,806	1,531,756
Goodyear, C. B	2,209,079	2,488,120
Davis, Pope & Co	2,247,220	2,444,356
Robbins, E. V	2,237,631	2,435.578
Bacon, Ennis & Co., (8 months,)	....	1,356,430
Blair, Densmore & Co	1,642,763	1,473,645
Dole, J. M. & Co	1,486,073	1,466,604
Green, Harley	....	1,441,572
Howe, G. M. & Co	632,470	874.960
Randolph, Charles & Co	1,040,919	1,651,756
Wright & Beebe	451,674	977,163
Hamilton & Mitchell	466,508	968,789
Gilbert & Field	1,636,889	1,812,020
Shiek, Wagner & Co	561,228	1,795,329
Boyington, Foster & Co	....	585,074
Baldwin, Stone & Co	434,299	583,023
Cummins & King	....	581,111
Nichols, M. S	659,089	806,119
Newhall, G. Jr	552,704	805,397
Sherman, Hall & Lyman	1,267,890	1,236,846
Lewis, H. F. & Co	416,621	934.424
Wright, A. M. & Co	337,991	845,238
Sharp, J. S. & Co	216,628	528,042
Webster & Baxter	403,000	1,070,180
Reineman, Moses	435,150	586,552
Low, Brother & Co	1,228,426	788,270
Sturgis, McAllister & Co	502,093	531,974
Ellis, O'Connor & Co	747,310	765,639
Hall, D. A	....	562,518
Rogers, A. A. C. & Co	284,000	660,732
Comstock, C. (agent,)	571,967	575,826
Chapman, J. & H. C	....	615,083
Lawrence, Nixson & Butler	1,472,621	1,757,361
Brown, Thomas Jr	....	538,880
Colvin, W. H., (7 months,)	....	647,490
Burton & Adams	257,000	475,000
Houghtelling, W. D	1,063,630	454,367
Pettit, Smith & Co	440,423	430,481
Jesup, Kennedy & Co	931,377	429,574
Loomis, J. Mason (6 months,)	565,074	421,000
Pottle, J. W. & Co	406,027	493,885
Penton, D. H	362,675	483,014
Dhillips & Bros	254,629	905,050

Paints and Oils.

PAINTS AND OILS.

Firms.	1866.	1867.
Chase, Hanford & Co	1,070,606	1,189.218
Page & Sprague	473,785	658,104
Lewis, Ham & Co	....	730,746

Chicago Trade.—Sales of some of the Leading Houses for 1866 *and* 1867.*—Continued.*

Live Stock.

LIVE STOCK.

Firms.	1866.	1867.
Conger, L.W.	....	1,046,850
Adams, Jesse.	....	1,118,304
Start, John.	....	794,340
Bentley, George.	....	545,216
Conover, H. H.	....	572,508
Wallwork, John.	....	569,755
Keenan, W. T.	....	1,495,602
Gregory, A.	....	1,193,293
Mallory, H. E.	....	844,233
Adams, John.	....	2,108,528
Eldridge, Isaac.	....	2,099,510
Adams, George.	....	2,031,026
Strader, Jacob.	....	1,631,842
Mallory, H. C.	....	1,016,693
Conger, R. P.	....	1,051,850
Conger, M.	....	1,053,850
Reeves, J. D.	....	920,993
Waixel, David.	....	613,661
Waixel, Isaac.	....	612,679
Adams, E.	....	746,965

Packers.

PACKERS.

Firms.	1866.	1867.
Hough, R. M. & O. S.	667,604	787,604
Cragin & Co.	1,244,510	2,960,762
Kreigh, D. & Co.	1,141,765	964,671
Kent, A. E. & Co.	1,079,700	1,100,530
Tobey & Booth.	449,463	576,577
Culbertson, Blair & Co.	2,721,570	4,277,160
Burt, Hutchinson & Co.	750,000	750,000
Reid & Sherwin.	1,250,397	1,334,871

Miscellaneous.

MISCELLANEOUS.

Firms.	1866.	1867.
Meeker, A. B.	924,015	1,118,629
Ford, B. M. & Co.	....	517,120
Schwab, McQuade & Smith.	396,046	516,445
Fuller, Finch & Fuller.	1,955,549	1,790,749

MISCELLANEOUS—*Con.*

Firms.	1866.	1867.
Allen & Mackey.	1,042,885	1,319.277
Wrisley & Bros.	....	726,199
Smith & Dwyer, (6 months).	....	528,229
Dake, J. M.	265,488	998,900
Mitchell, J. J.	262,985	992 051
Brown, W. F.	....	846,431
Dawson & Miller.	475,299	566,978
Hill, D. & Son.	....	519,883
Jackson, S. D.	827,731	631,376
Norton, Tuttle & Co.	888,659	739,972
Nichols, Thomas	....	637,962
Peck, C. J.	171,000	643,279
Rogers, H. W. & Bro.	....	539.390
Stiles, Goldy & McMahon.	1,614,550	1,045.660
St. John. A. H.	....	538,878
Thompson, Elisha.	....	845,952
Winans, Matthews & Co.	....	512,560
Whitaker, Harmon & Co.	1,233,390	1,49[illegible],358
Laflin, Butler & Co.	723,290	742,632
Griggs, S. C. & Co.	486,957	505,601
Lord & Smith.	....	573,202
Burnhams & Van Schaack.	706.733	513,013
Mears, Bates & Co.	926,524	884,213
Western News Company.	665,114	675.476
W.B.Keen & Co,	448,334	595 000
Brown, Thomas Jr.	....	538,880
Matson, N. & Co.	278,759	523,659
Farr, James J.	....	497,187
Beck & Wirth.	386,105	478,163
Hollister & Phelps.	685,577	476,501
Holt & Balcom.	306,689	475,208
Fairbanks, Greenleaf & Co.	328,424	466,084
McDonald, J. D. K.	....	455,300
Grant, Buck & Co.	311,874	450,514
Reed, J. H. & Co. (7 months).	....	450,188
Morse, Loomis & Co.	....	449,601
Law, Robert (Agt. for 9 months).	445,913	446,089
Webster & Gage.	....	435,100
Union Stock Yards & Transit Co.	....	428,043
Ryerson, Otto & Co.	....	426,735
Tolman, Crosby & Co.	214,104	415,776
Wesiecker & Co (4 months).	393,229	400,061
Dogget, Bassett & Hills.	990,781	840.138

The *Republican* had this editorial:— *Chi. Rep.*

Our Trade in 1867.—In another part of this issue we give a list of sales by our leading houses in the several departments of trade for the past year, presenting only those amounts in excess of four hundred thousand dollars. For the sake of comparison we give corresponding statements for the previous year. We readily accept each and both lists as inaccurate and incomplete. The necessity of the creation of such a list is one of the least popular features of our internal revenue system. Solid merchants are not fond of exhibits of their business, and are not inclined to favor their publication by the press. But as the list is created and a part of the current news, it has in Chicago a present value which even its inaccuracies cannot defeat. It must stand confessed that the errors, corrected, would very largely swell the list in individual and aggregate statements. It would add very many names not given at all. But in the list as it exists we see very much that is suggestive of the growth of our commerce, and its distinctive features during the past year of depression and financial disturbance. There has been in that period an immense accession to the trade and business of Chicago. Our field as a wholesale center has widened and our merchants in a better and more thorough manner have filled it. It is discouraging, indeed, to have handled these immense stocks of goods in the past year with so little profit or perhaps a heavy loss. The market has tended steadily downward, and houses of great prosperity and solidity in former years have seen their business largely increased without other compensation realized than that they have held and widened their field. And this is the morale of the exhibit given

Remarks upon trade list.

Imperfect.

Still valuable.

Too small.

Business increases.

Present trade hard.

Increase natural.

elsewhere in the list referred to of the extension and development of the business of our city. In this there is nothing spasmodic, but steadily cumulative. This increase of trade has sought us on natural and irresistible grounds, which will con-

Pay by and by.

tinue to help its accession, reserving its harvest of advantage for the general revival of mercantile prosperity when values are once more settled. As surely as the latter period is to arrive, so surely is the advantage to follow. Chicago has put

Chi. a centre

forward, year by year, more prominently its claims as a center of trade second only to one other in the country, and this it will become, helped by causes to which each season is lending increased force.

Map shows it.

The study of the map, with its features of climate and natural resources, its routes by water and rail, gives the best of all keys to our destined prominence as a trade center. This is to be the market of the great staples of the Northwest, and for the supply of the Northwest. More than this, we are soon to be one of the

Trade of Orient.

principal stations on the world's greatest route of intercontinental commerce. In less than five years the trade of the East Indies will seek this route to the markets of both hemispheres, and this current once established, as old, in its first conception, as the dreamings of Columbus, we shall see in our mercantile community the best and strongest representatives of the branches of trade thereon dependent.

No chimera

This is no chimera. It is being soberly discussed and accepted in older cities by veterans in commerce who, not long ago, were gravely deprecatory of undue ambi-

Old houses coming.

tion in our young city. If there is one thing more marked than another in the general aspects of the trade of the country, it is this growing conviction, and its early promised fruits in the tendency of old houses on the seaboard, and in cities once our rivals, to make their branch or principal establishments here. It is a fixed fact that notable pioneers of this class are to occupy some of our business palaces now in process of erection or projected. We are at no distant day to find our miles of

Commerce to increase.

lumber yards, our immense grain warehouses and live stock and provision enterprises, only a portion of the framework of our mercantile undertakings, which will include silks and teas and their kindred merchandise in the hands of original importers, giving us a market unsurpassed in breadth and variety, with marvelous facilities for its handling and delivery to all parts of the country. If any doubt this, let them file away this forecast of our future, which will not grow old among their memoranda, until it is fulfilled to the letter.

Unfortunately I have no statistics of St. Louis houses for this last year.

Chi. Tribune

The *Chicago Tribune* made the following preface to its list of 1866–67, annexing names of houses in Cincinnati and St. Louis whose sales exceeded a million :—

Comparison of St. L. Cin. & Chi.

We present below a highly important comparative exhibit of the trade of Chicago, Cincinnati and St. Louis. The subjoined lists give the names of all wholesale dealers in the respective cities just mentioned, whose sales for the year May 1, 1866, to May 1, 1867, amounted to one million dollars or upwards. They are copied from the Government revenue records, and, being certified on oath, the contrast which they afford—however surprising their comparisons may be to the astonished burghers of Cincinnati and St. Louis—cannot be disputed.

No rivals.

Hereafter. the preëminence of Chicago as the Metropolitan city of the Northwest will be a matter of record. Figures sometimes do lie, but the truth of these must be so indubitable that we suspect we shall hear no more from either of the rival wood-stations on the Ohio and Mississippi, about their aspirations to be reckoned as rivals of Chicago.

Milwaukee excepted.

We omit from this interesting comparison, Milwaukee, because we have not the space for a list of Chicago *retail* merchants, any one of whose sales exceed the returns of the heaviest wholesale dealer in the village up the Lake.

Amts. compared.

The following figures show that last year in Chicago there were *fifty-nine firms whose sales exceeded one million dollars*; in Cincinnati *fifteen*; and in St. Louis *sixteen.*

The heaviest sales reported by a single house, amounted in Chicago, to *nine millions two hundred and twenty thousand nine hundred and sixty-seven dollars*; in St. Louis to $3,127,223; and in Cincinnati to $2,700,000.

In Chicago *fourteen* houses report sales exceeding two million dollars; in Cincinnati, *four*; and in St. Louis, *one.*

Cincinnati Houses over $1,000,000, 1866–7.

Cin. houses over $1,000,000.

Glenn, Wm. & Sons	$2,700,000	Schwab, Peter & Co	$1,236,900
Grotenkemper, H. & Co	2,600,000	McAlpine, Polk & Hibard	1,191,835
Shillito, Jno. & Co	2,504,247	Rineskopf Bros. & Co	1,100,500
Bishop, R. M. & Co	2,405,289	Stix, Louis & Co	1,100,100
Addy, Hull & Co	1,469,000	Gibson, Early & Co	1,069,332
Gibson, Daniel & Co	1,395,000	Tweed & Sibley	1,032,800
Pearce, Tolle, Holton & Porter	1,326,855	Lowry, Perrin & Co	1,000,517
Moore, Robert A. & Co	1,282,389		

St. Louis Houses over $1,000,000, 1866–7.

St. L. houses over $1,000,000.

Lamb & Quinlan	$3,127,223	Homeyer, H. A. & Co	$1,350,000
Roe. J. J. & Co	1,841,640	Benton, W. H. & Co	1,272,557
Jameson, Cotting & Co	1,790,039	Bell, H. & Sons	1,243,748
Ames & Co	1,700,000	Dodd, Brown & Co	1,203,000
Barr, Duncan & Co	1,686,378	Davis, J. C. & Co	1,200,000
Taeger & Co	1,676,354	Merriman, J	1,180,000
Weil, J. & Bro	1,384,162	Green & Co	1,103,221
Whittaker, Francis & Sons	1,383,788	Underhill & Eaton	1,100,846

The following table from the newspapers is confirmatory, showing the amount of sales made in six Western cities in 1867. The figures give the sales of general wholesale dealers, general retail dealers, wholesale liquor dealers, retail liquor dealers, auctioneers, and commercial brokers:

Confirmation

Trade 6 W. cities.

CHICAGO.	PITTSBURGH.	ST. LOUIS.	DETROIT.	BUFFALO.	CLEVELAND.	
$250,607,830	$35,859,330	$114,999,100	$32,145,490	$52,275,800	$24,032,630	Wholesale,
38,830,968	20,307,640	34,286,706	12,371,814	10,313,010	12,415,972	Retail
17,564,960	2,113,420	29,015,750	2,995,585	5,170,865	2,708,330	Wholesale Liquor.
30,462,920	7,404,645	24,989,662	14,308,290	13,035,820	13,344,780	Retail do.
2,154,930	658,240	6,273,320	237,210	408,540	377,010	Auctioneers.
2,551,100	14,066,320	3,470,420	698,820	96,980	2,264,160	Com. Broker
$342,172,708	$80,409,595	$213,034,958	$62,757,209	$81,301,015	$55,142,882	

Relative changes.

St. Louis kept the lead for several years in jobbing, after losing largely in grain trade, as they admit. No doubt the war aided, as predicted in 1861, (p. 19,) to expedite changes, which were inevitable. Still, the immense increase is a marvel to ourselves. The report of the Board of Trade in 1860, said :—

Trade statistics 1860.

We present the following valuation of property which has arrived at and departed from our city, with a great deal of reluctance. It has been compiled at the request of many of our business men interested in such statistics. The best judges in such matters pronounce our estimates low.

Fair estimate

The table has been prepared with great care, under the supervision of J. J. Richards, Esq. In valuing the articles enumerated, the receipts and shipments for each month are valued at the average prices during the month ;—this has been a work requiring much labor, but insures its correctness.

Figures small.

The value of our Imports and Exports in 1858, as reported to the United States Government, by Col. Graham, was $174,896,011,70. We see no reason why the figures presented herewith should fall short of that year, unless Mr. Richards

Low valuation. places a lower valuation on property where the value cannot be correctly ascertained, than was fixed by Col Graham; our commerce in the products of the soil as well as in most other articles of trade in 1860 having greatly exceeded that of 1858.

Value of commerce 1860.

Valuation of Property Received and Forwarded by Lake, Canal and Railroads, in 1860.

Imports and exports.

Description of Property.	Imports.	Exports.	Description of Property.	Imports.	Exports.
Flour	$3,285,646.14	$3,385,940.20	*Brought forward*	$40,901,990.37	$36,675.618.65
Wheat	12.579,249.48	11,048,611.53	Salt	482,814.59	327,320.10
Corn	7,215,278.96	6,781,555.74	High Wines	698,807.50	733,758.75
Oats	525,547.78	295,161.92	Fish	154,366 50	22,029.75
Rye	184,291.10	94,606.28	Wool	300,736.80	293,732.15
Barley	841,022.14	153,342.37	Coal	786,480.00	122,184.00
Live Stock	9,349,926.10	5.681,207.87	Wood	373,819.00	....
Provisions	1,051,780.92	2,349,2[illegible]8.88	Pig Lead	638,915.60	503,523.96
Hides	1,235,730.98	1,634,986.54	Butter	188,943.89	208,300.67
Lard	530,759.02	1,144,171.93	Broom Corn	161,511.04	186,315.52
Tallow	12,153.30	284,488.00	Mill Stuffs, Meal, &c.	40,140.08	36,501.02
Grass Seed	424,264.44	863,333.78	Vegetables	64,450.74	25,966.53
Lumber	4,166,340.01	3,462,988.61	Other Property	52,274,640.78	33,574,716.14
Forward	$40,901,990.37	$36,679,618.65	Total	$97,067,616.89	$72,718,957.24

Total value of Imports $97,067,616.89
Total value of Exports 72,718,957.24

Aggregate value of Imports and Exports $169,781,574.13

Remarks, 1861. My paper of 1861, had these observations, now still more applicable :—

Jobbing trade. *The Jobbing Trade.*—The same report gives amounts as follows: dry goods, $15,000,000; groceries, including sugar refinery, $8,200,000; iron and hardware, $3,650,000; and boots, shoes, clothing, etc., (estimated) $5,000,000. Total, thirty-one millions, eight hundred and fifty thousand dollars. The Report says, "Our advantages as a commercial city are equal if not superior to any inland city on the continent."

Keeps pace with produce. It is a gratifying fact that our jobbing trade is almost four-fifths the amount of all our produce exports, which are about forty millions of the above list, showing that the trade of the country follows the channels of produce and centers here, instead of going chiefly to New York, as is generally supposed. It should do so, Advantages of Chi. over N. Y. for each of these thousands of merchants, scattered all over the West, can step into a car at night and be here in the morning, and replenish his stock, and be home again the next morning. These frequent supplies of fresh goods are always desirable, and economical of interest. Then, too, the saving in expensive trips to New York is an item; and the Chicago jobber saves something in rent and other expenses over the New Yorker; and shipping in large quantities, can often save a trifle in transportation and insurance. Also, manufacturers in the East are fast learning their interests. For western supplies, it is a useless expense to pay transportation to a sea-board city, and commission there, which could all be saved and more by shipping directly hither. Besides, a Chicago house, that by railways and telegraph is in constant communication with every town, can know the condition of its customers—watch "lame ducks" and guard against losses—far better than any New York concern, however sharp.

Those figures now small. Large as we deemed these figures only eight years ago, they are small now. That Chicago should so soon have become the fifth city in gross commerce, abundantly substantiates the above reasons; though I have to confess to having followed the common notion, that other trade follows the channels Views more applicable against St. Louis. of produce. Having been presented mainly as against New York, the positions are far more easily sustained as against St. Louis. Ten years ago, when competition really began, she had the whole trade along the Mississippi, and west of the Illinois river, and of Central and Southern Illinois. Against her established trade and large capital, the work of the last decade has been very severe compared with what it is to be henceforth. True it is, as before remarked, that the war came to our aid, shaking off the hold of both St. Louis and Cincinnati. But time enough has elapsed to show that neither can regain its hold.

Having already completely distanced both these old colts, we shall lead them a race upon a track of business trying both wind and pocket. St. Louis, to her own shame, boasts of superiority in the latter; and would feign believe that our strength lies mainly in the former, in "blowing" up our trade statistics. Let her hug delusion to her heart's content. It is her sole reliance. Time, however, will soon be called for the winner by a long misjudging public; and another decade will cause St. Louis herself to acknowledge her secondary position. Having considered trade in general, let us look at some of the details.

A race ahead

St. L. boasts of Capital.

Results soon known.

The Grain Trade.—The ninth Report of the Board of Trade, for the year ending 30th March, 1867, gives the—

Grain trade.

Shipments of Flour (reduced to Wheat) and Grain from Chicago, for the past Twenty-nine Years.

Chi. shipments since 1838.

Year.	Fl'r. & Wh't. Bushels.	Corn, Bushels.	Oats. Bushels.	Rye. Bushels.	Rarley. Bushels.	Total. Bushels.
1838	78	....	....	....	....	78
1839	3,678	....	....	....	....	3,678
1840	10,000	....	....	....	....	10 000
1841	40,000	....	....	....	....	40,000
1842	586,907	....	....	....	....	586,907
1843	688,907	....	....	....	....	688,907
1844	923,494	....	....	....	....	923,494
1845	1,024,620	....	....	....	....	1,024,620
1846	1.599,919	....	....	....	....	1,599,619
1847	2,136,994	67,135	38,892	....	....	2,243,201
1848	2,286,000	566'460	65,280	....	....	3,001,740
1849	2,192,809	644,848	26,849	31,453	....	2,769,111
1850	1,387,989	252,013	186,054	22,872	....	1,830,938
1851	799,380	3,221,317	605,827	19,997	....	4,646,291
1852	941,470	2,757,011	2.030,317	127,028	17,315	5,878,141
1853	1,680,998	2,780,253	1,748,493	120,275	82,162	6,412,181
1854	2,744,860	6,837,899	3,239,987	148,421	41,158	12,932,320
1855	7,110,270	7,547,678	1,888,533	92,023	20,132	16,633,700
1856	9,419,365	11,129,658	1,014,547	19,051	590	21,583,221
1857	10,783,292	6,814,615	316,778	17,993	....	18,032,678
1858	10,909,243	7,493,212	1,498,134	127,008	7,569	20,085,166
1859	10,759,359	4 217,654	1,174,177	134,404	486,218	16,771,812
1860	15,892,857	13,700,113	1,091,607	156,642	267,449	31,108,759
1861	23,855,553	24,372,725	1,633,237	398,818	226,534	50,481,862
1862	22,508,143	29,452,610	3,112,366	871,796	582,195	56,484,110
1863	18,298,536	24,906,930	9,909,175	683,946	943,252	54,741,839
1864–5	10,687,055	12,740.543	16,470,929	898,536	527,431	47,124,494
1865–6	15,718,348	25,228,526	10,598,061	1,022,200	645,089	53,212,224
1866–7	21,330,484	32,953,580	9,564,223	1,489,895	1,398,528	66,736,660

Some flour and grain comes from the east to go directly back. The main currents, however, are from the south and west, which will rapidly augment as new acres along present lines are brought under the plough, and as the power of the chief grain market of the world shall be applied to distant regions, and facilities of access be increased. Compare these with the fol-

Supplies from South and West.

St. L. trade reports.

lowing, taken from the "*Annual Statement of the Trade and Commerce of St. Louis, for the year 1867, reported to the Union Merchant's Exchange, by Geo. H. Morgan, Secretary,*" to whose politeness I am indebted for copies of that and the previous year:—

Receipts Flour and Grain 12 yrs.

Receipts of Flour and Grain at St. Louis for Twelve Years.

Year.	Flour, bbls.	Wheat, bu.	Corn, bu.	Oats, bu.	Rye, bu.	Barley, bu.	Total.*
1867..	944,075	3,571,593	5,155,480	3,445,388	250,704	705,215	17,848,755
1866..	1,208,726	4,410,305	7,233,671	3,567,000	375,417	548,796	22,178,819
1865..	1,161.038	3,452,722	3,162,313	4,173,229	217,568	846,229	17,657,251
1864..	815,144	3,315,828	2,369,500	4,105,040	140,533	326,860	14,331,481
1863..	689,242	2,621,020	1,361,310	3,845,876	205,918	182,270	11,662,404
1862..	647,419	3,550,336	1,734,219	3,135,043	253,552	290.925	12,201,170
1861..	484,000	2,654,738	4,515,040	1,735,157	117,080	201,484	11,643,499
1860..	443,196	3,555,871	4,249,782	1,832,634	159,974	339,974	12,354,215
1859..	484,715	3,568,732	1,639,579	1,267,624	123,058	242,262	9,264,830
1858..	687;451	3,835,759	892,104	1.690,010	45,900	291,660	10,162,688
1857..	573,664	3,281,410	2,485,786	1,624,058	30,442	176,062	6,466,078
1856..	323,446	3,747,224	938,546	1,029,908	....	....	7,333,908

*This is an addition of my own to compare above aggregates, the flour being multiplied by five. The Chicago table, it will be noticed, is only of shipments, and St. Louis of total receipts.

Years not corresponding.

The Chicago Board of Trade Reports, being now made up from 1st April, 1866, to March 31st, 1867, the last three years do not exactly compare as to time. The *Chicago Republican*, in its annual statement, January 1st, gave for 1867, of flour received, 1,814,286, bbls.; shipped, 1,859,985 bbls. Of wheat received, 13,090,868 bushels; shipped, 10,360,458 bushels. Of corn, 23,018,827 bushels; shipped, 20,213,790 bushels. Of oats, 10,988,617 bushels; shipped, 9,732,146 bushels.

Chi. items, 1867.

Is trade from same region?

The respective amounts speak for themselves. With such disparity, it might be imagined, notwithstanding all we have seen about St. Louis' efforts to obtain the trade of the Northwest, that Chicago had a more highly productive region tributary than St. Louis. But comparing routes and supplies to both cities, exhibits the same sources in the main.

Routes and receipts at Chi. 1866 '67.

Routes and Receipts of Flour and Grain at Chicago, 1866–7.

By	Flour, Barrels.	Wheat, Bushels.	Corn, Bushels.	Oats, Bushels.	Rye, Bushels.	Barley, Bushels.
Lake........................	47,752	236,832	2,210	4,041	412	5,546
Ill. and Mich. Canal....	45,317	83,834	9,575,569	1,417,436	67,423	24,691
C. R. I. and P. R. R.....	179,316	1,420,163	4,279,190	982,761	313,059	484,927
I. C. R. R..................	80,173	892,260	5,929,080	2,375,520	171,610	366,500
C. and N. W. R. R.......	1,386,913	8,078,061	3,042,561	3,792,178	591,210	586,824
C. B. and Q. R. R.........	173,473	1,190 004	8,324,281	1,714,687	508,524	300,810
C. and A. R. R............	51,379	131,347	2,572,520	257,275	30,190	45,870
C. and Mil. R. R.........	32,484	240,162	346	5,011	....	25
C. and Gt. E. R. R.......	2,676	1,396	170,740	99,002	578	1,125
P., Ft. W. and C. R. R..	694	568	28,448	44,606	334	600
M. C. R. R..................	15,156	10,873	4,434	20,548	585	8,519
M. S. R. R..................	6,737	735	259	916	....	9,081
	2,022,060	12,286,287	33,929,632	10,713,981	1,683,925	1,834,418
Teams, (estimated).......	....	15,000	50,000	120,000	20,000	45,000
Flour manufactured in Chicago.....................	452,528	....	....	....	....	....
In store Mar. 31, 1866.	23,616	1,075,602	499,754	984,897	112,827	269,624

Routes and Receipts of Flour and Grain at St. Louis for 1867.

St L. grain routes and receipts 1867

From	Flour, bbls.	Wheat, bu	Corn, bu.	Oats, bu.	Rye, bu.	Barley, bu.
Upper Miss. River........	119,106	1,194,563	909,620	1,584,844	122,987	322,317
Lower Miss. River........	71,849	120,149	14,290	5,820	81	11,349
Illinois River..............	83,074	439,049	1,510,118	819,799	54,750	107,529
Missouri River............	3,366	462,616	329,697	109,536	11,052	8,722
Ark. and White Rivers..	95	....	....	....	....	546
Cumb. and Tenn. Rivers.	169	....	....	....	....	....
Ohio River.................	694	1,154	162	....	....	506
Ohio & Miss. R. R.........	183,843	51,547	545,582	193,652	5,117	57,664
Chicago, A. St. L. R. R..	85,604	228,391	840,021	253,851	17,488	35,005
St. L. A. & T. H. R. R..	228,094	252,563	683,788	248,590	19,401	86,490
Pacific R. R................	19,419	322,163	166,865	89,400	5,963	57,117
North Missouri R. R.....	22,807	134,614	62,657	127,332	6,262	6,937
Iron Mountain R. R.....	1,184	9,464	30	2,564	103	1,033
Wagons	124,771	355,320	92,650	10,000	7,500	10,000
Total Receipts.............	944,075	3,571,593	5,155,480	3,445,388	250,704	705,215
Flour Manufactured......	765,298	....	....	....	....	....
In store Jan. 1, 1867.....	53,687	285,809	40,000	20,000	....	52,000
	1,763,060	3,857,402	5,195,480	3,465,388	250,704	757,215

Trade seeks a centre for distribution.

The doubling up of transportation to and from an important commercial centre, is worthy of notice. Parties who wish to purchase go thither, and take back what sellers have just sent over the same road. More and more will this be the case, though largely so already, as will be observed by comparing the following with receipts on opposite page. Amount of lake shipments, and variety of ports, will be observed.

Routes and Shipments of Flour and Grain from Chicago, 1866–7.

Routes and shipments of grain from Chi. 1866-'7.

By	Flour, Barrels.	Wheat, Bushels.	Corn, Bushels.	Oats, Bushels.	Rye, Bushels.	Barley, Bushels.
Lake—						
To Buffalo...............	274,013	3,297,571	2,464,000	6,725,545	894,804	917,840
To Oswego...............	300	1,272,800	1,406,045	145,950	....	32,200
To Ogdensburg.........	45,680	300,375	495,150	630	100	....
To other Am'n. Ports	139,029	433,600	705,110	389,618	83,250	20,000
To Ki'n. and Mon'l...	2,611	82,650	1,602,600	21,750	82,000	....
To Sarnia.................	17,335	5,000	179,985	1,200	....	....
To Colborne.............	50	400,900	1,818,715	110,170	52,875	18,200
To Collingwood.........	....	....	124,800	....	1,600	....
To Goderich.............	2,548	450	203,550	250	....	....
To other Ca'n. Ports.	25	35,000	93,600	....	15,500	....
To Bergen, Norway...	....	....	4,400	....	....	....
By Ill. & Mich. Canal..	218	235,758	125,555	99,182	8,586	60
By C., R. I. & P. R. R..	27,554	....	....	....	....	....
By I. C. R R................	70,005	192,960	350	70,000	15,900	67,200
By C. & N. W. R. R.....	2,562	228,567	110,976	56,898	10,815	19,812
By C., B. & Q. R. R......	2,162	171,099	6,606	....	2,504	21,450
By C. & A. R. R..........	27,718	62,422	....	31,385	....	11,175
By C. & M. R. R.........	301	17,279	26	86	....	1,020
By C. & Gt. E. R. R.....	338,454	1,031,218	16,490	353,959	130,790	150,094
By P, Ft. W. & C. R. R	535,303	1,390,734	180,312	692,490	127,915	48,870
By M. C. R. R............	262,072	604,702	434,828	182,727	124,947	62,872
By M. S. R. R............	419,947	578,964	820,532	682,588	43,809	36,735
	2,179,785	10,341,549	32,953,580	9,564,223	1,489,895	1,398,528
Flour in City Mills......	....	2,262,640	....	....	....	....
City Consumption and unaccounted for........	237,724	295,104	....	1,524,473	....	....
Used by Distillers and Br's., and acct'd. for..	....	....	703,068	....	215,575	601,242
In store March 31, 1867.	62,693	477,596	822,788	730,182	111,282	149,272
Total....................	2,498,204	13,876,889	34,479,386	11,818,878	1,816,752	2,149,042

The following table enables the reader to see and judge for himself of the extent of St. Louis trade; and we only regret that our statistics are not kept, so as to furnish a parallel:—

Receipts of Leading Articles at St. Louis for Twelve Years.

ARTICLES.		1867.	1866.	1865.	1864.	1863.	1862.	1861.	1860.	1659.	1858.	1857.	1856.
Bacon	Casks and bbls	12,384	13,374	10,171	17,731	16,014	21,185	22,610	17,477	10,380	21,578	14,789	22,983
"	Pieces	58,004	50,103	62,496	170,998	230,092	106,315	106,000	46,287	18,356	47,859	8,549	32,148
Barley	Bushels	705,215	548,797	846,229	326,860	182,270	290,925	201,484	339,974	242,262	291,660	176.062	....
Beans	Packages	10,751	8,198	18.118	21,492	52,227	39,871	32,602	12,065	18,973	19,714	7,168	....
Beef	Tierces and bbls.	6,798	306	3,008	3.394	2,427	....	....	3,933	5,645	13,192	6,930	1,758
Bran	Sacks	86,581	104,185	55,347	7,432	3,606	....	....	56,351	55,592	65,003	23,564	11,647
Brooms	Dozens	8,427	19,712	17,144	10,267	6,891	8,750	13,105	18,599	21,641	19,248	20,642	20,686
Butter	Packages	21,326	33,537	36.288	14,183	18,827	16,151	24,062	27,384	27,250	15,979	6,070	....
Cattle	Head	74,164	103,359	94,307	114,149	33,171	....	....	57,815	31,208	15,488	4,024	2,442
Castor Beans	Packages	32,998	14,539	14,652	6,686	1,806	....	....	4,020	1,119	5,044	2,320	....
Cheese	Boxes	76,118	32,848	49,846	18,931	22,404	34,828	23,500	37,306	39,389	11,963	....	....
Coffee	Bags	98,617	90,567	66,016	71,790	25,824	61,536	91,850	110,147	144,202	140,165	109,051	136,365
Corn	Bushels	5,155,480	7,223.671	3,162,310	2,369,500	1,361,310	1,734,219	4,515,040	4,249,782	1,639,579	892,104	2,485,786	938,546
Cotton	Bales	40,508	21,585	89.215	83,060	26,833	39,430	....	....	....	....	....	....
Dried Fruit	Packages	24,023	25,864	21,093	20,986	22,828	32,375	37,840	42.773	29,776	37,998	10,366	29,918
Flax Seed	Packages	20,347	28,411	21,851	30,908	10,081	....	....	1,725	2,579	5,590	3,368	7,264
Flour	Barrels	944,075	1,208,725	1,161,038	815,144	689,242	647,419	484,000	448,196	484,715	687,451	578,664	323,446
Grease	Packages	1,437	867	1,153	4,497	4,556	4,871	3,130	3,052	3,891	3,169	2,281	3,065
Gunnies	Bundles	3,252	7,910	9 622	2,626	1,947	....	....	9,260	8,877	6,793	6.588	8,018
"	Bales	9,044	15,895	6,226	8,284	1,996	....	....	15,184	6,970	4,438	7,471	4,194
Hay	Bales	178,992	124,165	266,511	166,005	171,138	226.017	114,745	150,810	58,064	35,656	24,336	16.857
Hemp	Bales	30,750	18,759	40 846	64,078	56,337	78,317	28,568	68,673	68,796	81,423	80,094	53,737
Hides	Pieces	146,421	160,470	202,211	203,105	147,687	132,888	159,196	170,888	237,662	208,414	144,468	115,068
"	Bundles	11,910	6,981	....	....	....	....	....	....	....	....	....	....
Lard	Bbls. and trcs.	21,666	15,313	19,948	29,341	33,489	41,382	40,108	41,200	44,471	60,488	55,074	80,675
"	Kegs.	13,567	7,238	2,084	2,471	2,717	5,993	11,815	17,728	9,025	15,114	9,831	15.995
Lead	Pigs	144,555	149,584	116,636	93,085	79,828	95,800	115,250	238,241	264,380	303,897	162,555	204,656
Malt	Sacks	39,171	31,372	45,004	31,877	12,794	....	....	13,064	9,880	22,216	23,243	....
Molasses	Barrels	9.103	6,807	12,863	14,222	6,872	4 297	11.605	56,673	60,778	42,256	60,523	66,458
Nails	Kegs	190,634	171,137	89,336	60,426	55,167	49,133	92,948	180,538	164,767	110,101	173,665	76.625
Oats	Bushels	3,445,388	3,567,253	4,173,229	4,105,040	3,845 876	3,135,043	1,735,157	1,832,684	1,267,624	1,690,010	1,624,158	1,029,908
Onions	Packages	40,315	53,368	102,970	30,229	19,875	22,605	19,135	61,918	38,044	27,610	25,644	....
Pig Iron	Tons	30,027	41,386	21,704	17,387	16,165	11,720	8,780	19,037	16,778	17,565	22,944	19,079
Pork	Barrels	92,071	56,740	66,822	71,559	34,256	51,187	116,445	117,079	96,230	126,950	102,876	92,990
"	Packages	11,486	8,285	16,144	5,681	6,299	6,515	11,358	18.302	12,895	9,125	8,907	15,196
"	Pieces	730,461	343,202	338,223	721,161	865,287	487,580	751,318	920,915	804,888	588,921	492,549	796 377
Potatoes	Packages	173,865	262,338	323.190	266,569	120,161	87,622	160.300	312,057	214,111	225,396	154,761	105.150
Rope	Coils	15,844	16,094	11,528	2,622	4,887	17,846	22,000	42.035	64,198	69,321	46.484	57,880
Rye	Bushels	250,704	375,417	217,568	140,533	205,918	253,552	117,080	159,974	123,058	45,900	30.442	....
Salt	Barrels	141,674	134,542	170,814	133,362	89,683	102,588	....	36,387	36.083	43,663	45,665	36,759
"	Sacks	79 ,025	88,013	83,221	46,698	56,818	107.508	....	399,576	328,280	451,275	303,170	460,806
Sugar	Hogsheads	19,730	14,686	17,889	16,780	9,028	23,468	83,750	47,637	53,172	53,891	31,141	54,331
"	Barrels	19,819	12,119	8,199	6,076	6,450	....	....	7,851	9,096	8,493	5,551	9,720
"	Boxes	29,924	43,607	29,410	551	....	4,170	8,0	13,7	6,695	13,966	8,828	26,274
Tallow	Packages	7,875	12 883	10,874	7,144	3,606	4,871	3,130	4.506	3,619	4,507	2.493	....
Tobacco	Hogsheads	18,584	13,669	16,483	42,490	19,325	13,050	8,510	11,956	9,006	6,721	5,646	6,829
Wheat	Bushels	3,571.593	4.410,305	3,452,722	3 315.828	2.621,020	3,560.336	2,654,738	3,555,871	3,568.743	3,835,759	3.281,410	3,747,224
Whisky	Barrels	37,455	58,157	38,014	40,407	54,862	70,374	72.790	102 356	100,092	122,265	125.547	95,821
Wool	Bundles	12,040	9,205	10,559	8,129	6,259	6,176	2,860	7,696	5,121	3,671	2,935	....

Steam Elevators.—Such amounts of grain could never be handled in reasonable time for western operators, except by steam machinery. It seems like magic to compare present facilities with Mr. Dole's horse-power elevator, which, with Messrs. Peck's, Wheeler's, Walker's and others, supplied requisite facilities, till that ingenious spirit, Capt. R. C. Bristol, erected in 1848 the first steam elevator. Mr. Wheeler says that down to Jan. 1st, 1855, the whole storage room was not over 750,000 bushels. So that the total only thirteen years ago, was but little over the average of one of seventeen elevators now, and every one before 1855 has gone out of use.

Steam Elevators. First in 1848. Rapid increase to 17.

Along the river, and south branch, and lake basin, these huge, sombre piles of 2x6 and 2x12 joisting, laid flat, rise high above surrounding structures. Their sides studded with iron plates, which are heads of large rods to hold against lateral pressure, bespeak the heavy stores they safely hold. Thinking an account of the *modus operandi* would be interesting, I went for information to the elevator last built by Messrs. Armour, Dole & Co., which was certain to have all improvements. An old settler, Mr. Baker, was in charge, who began to build in 1854 the elevator of Messrs. Gibbs & Griffin, on a lot leased by me to them. After politely showing me through and explaining the operation, I asked him for the further favor of writing out what he had spoken, and here you have it:—

Mode of stucture. Armour, Dole & Co.'s. the last. Its operation

Chicago has superior advantages in handling and storing grain, not only on account of steam elevators, but in absence of current, and the even stage of water. These are serious inconveniences on the Mississippi, and other large western rivers. Then the wide prairie affords ample yard-room for cars, which the railroads and proprietors of elevators have wisely provided.

Advantages of site.

Few persons, however, even of the old settlers in Chicago, have correct ideas of the ease and speed with which grain is handled. This is the *modus operandi* of Messrs. Armour, Dole & Co's new elevator on the South Branch, running from the C. B. & Q. Railroad.

Speed of handling.

The building is 312 feet long, 84 feet wide, and 130 feet high, machinery driven by a 400 horse-power engine. It is divided into 150 bins, 65 feet deep, with storage capacity of 1,250,000 bushels. The yard will hold 300 or 400 cars. Two switch engines, when in full operation, are required to put in and take out cars. Two tracks receive each ten cars, unloaded at once in 6 to 8 minutes, each car having its elevator, conveying the grain to its large hopper-scale in the top of the building. There weighed, it is spouted to the bin appropriated to that kind and quality. To carry grain to the several bins renders the elevation necessary. Allowing 15 minutes to unload each set of 10 cars, 400 are unloaded in 10 hours, about 140,000 bushels.

Building and machinery. 10 cars unloaded in 8 minutes; 140,000 bush in 10 hours.

Shipping facilities equal receiving, there being six elevators for that work, handling each 300 bushels per hour, or 180,000 bushels in 10 hours. The grain is run out of the bins to another set of elevators, which throw into large hoppers at the top of the building, in which it is weighed, and sent down in spouts into the hold of the vessel. The same Company have another elevator on the opposite side of the slip—for a slip at right angles to the South Branch is cut to lay vessels alongside the warehouse—and ten other large elevators and 5 smaller, afford the same facilities. Any one of 13 of them, too, will unload a canal boat of 5,000 or of 6,000 bushels, in an hour and a half to two hours; an aggregate from 65 canal boats alone of 357,000 bushels in 10 hours.

Shipping facilities. Another Elevator. 15 more such Unload canal boats.

List of Chi. elevators and capacity.

Names of Owners and Capacity of Chicago Elevators.

Warehouses.	Receive from	Capacity.
J. E. Buckingham & Co., A	Illinois Central Railroad and Canal	700,000
J. E. Buckingham & Co., B	Illinois Central Railroad and Canal	700,000
Flint, Thompson & Co., A	Chicago & Rock Island Railroad	750,000
Flint, Thompson & Co., B	Chicago & Rock Island Railroad	1,250,000
Munn & Scott, City Elevator	Railroads and Canal	1,250,000
Munn & Scott, Union Elevator	Chicago & Alton Railroad and Canal	700,000
Munn & Scott, North Western Elevator	Chicago & Alton Railroad and Canal	600.000
Munn & Scott, Munn & Scott	Chicago & Northwestern Railroad & Canal	200,000
Armour, Dole & Co., A	Chicago, Burlington & Quincy Railroad	1,250,000
Armour, Dole & Co., B	Chicago, Burlington & Quincy Railroad	850,000
Munger & Armour } Consolidafed into Munger, Wheeler C Co.	Galena & Chicago Union Railroad & Canal	600,000
Hiram Wheeler } Consolidafed into Munger, Wheeler C Co.	Galena & Chicago Union Railroad & Canal	500,000
Galena Elevator } Consolidafed into Munger, Wheeler C Co.	Galena & Chicago Union Railroad & Canal	500,000
W. H. Lunt, Iowa Elevator	Canal	300,000
O. Lunt & Bro	Canal	80,000
Finley & Ballard, Illinois River Elevator	Railroads and Canal	200,000
Vincent, Nelson & Co	Railroads and Canal	250,000
Total Bushels		10,680,000

St. L. Elevator.

Trade Report.

THE *St. Louis Elevator.*—The day of small things is too recent with ourselves to despise it in our neighbors. Therefore the following is quoted with all due respect from the Secretary's *Report* to the *St. Louis Union Merchant's Exchange*, for Dec. 31st, 1866 :—

Wheat statistics. Lack of handling facilities. Advantages of river route. N. O. Elevator built by St L. Grain to be handled in bulk. Some toting.

The receipts and exports of grain show an increase over 1865. The receipts of grain (and flour reduced to wheat) for 1865, were 17,657,252 bushels; for 1866, 22,279,072 bushels. Exports for 1865, 13,427,052 bushels; for 1866, 18,835,969 bushels. These figures may look small compared with those of some of our neighboring cities, but the fact that our city is yet deficient in conveniences for handling grain in bulk, will account for the disparagement. The St. Louis Grain Elevator has demonstrated the fact that grain can be handled in bulk advantageously, and with proper facilities for shipping to New Orleans and transferring at that point in bulk, grain can be delivered at the Eastern cities and foreign ports cheaper, via the Mississippi River, than by any other route. The cost of transporting a bushel of wheat from St. Paul to New York, via St. Louis and New Orleans, with four feet of water on the rapids above Keokuk, and the proper facilities for transferring at the two points named, would be at least twenty cents per bushel less than by any Northern route, and, it is believed, that with a canal around the rapids, the cost would be less. The Mississippi Valley Transportation Company are prepared to handle grain in bulk, and a transfer elevator for New Orleans, built by St. Louis parties is now fast approaching completion, and will be ready by opening of navigation. Efforts are being made to secure facilities for the erection of elevators and warehouses at East St. Louis that will give our neighbors an opportunity to get their products to market without the expense of sacking and handling. Experience and the success of other cities has clearly demonstrated that in no way can grain be handled so cheaply as in bulk, and if St. Louis would compete for the grain trade of the West and Northwest, her merchants must encourage and facilitate in every possible way, enterprises that look to that end. The bag system must still be retained in a measure, for the interior trade of the States south of us, where grain is not, and perhaps cannot be handled in bulk; but while we may retain this very important branch of our shipping demand, wo can, at the same time, look to making the Mississippi the great pathway of the products of the Northwest to foreign markets.

Prof. Waterhouse.

In the same Report is a paper in advocacy of St. Louis' extravagant claims to preëminence, from the pen of "Professor S. Waterhouse, of Washington University," which has this very expressive paragraph :—

Benefits of the elevator.

The effect of improvements upon the business of the city, may be illustrated by the operations of our city elevator. The elevator cost $450,000, and has a capacity of 1,250,000 bushels. It is able to handle 100,000 bushels a day. It began to receive grain in October, 1865. Before the first of January, 1866, its receipts amounted to 600,000 bushels, 200,000 *of which were brought directly from Chicago.* Grain can now be shipped, by way of St. Louis and New Orleans, to New York and Europe ten cents a bushel cheaper than it can be carried to the Atlantic by rail.

An honest Professor would of course tell the whole truth; but a sharp man of business would hardly have deemed it dishonest to have put in plain type the statement that one third of the first receipts of "*the* St. Louis Elevator" came from Chicago. That italicising is truly no malice of mine. A simpleton might wonder why St. Louis, supposed to be so much more powerful than Chicago, and competing with her in drawing grain from the same primary sources, has to go to her rival for one-third of her wheat. But a learned Professor has sagacity to call attention to the never-failing source *the* elevator has to rely upon.

Honesty rather than keenness—

—to exhibit St. L.'s. dependence on Chi.

But while the Professor would thus honor Chicago, it would seem from the Report that the Secretary is not equally friendly. He remarks under the caption,—

Secretary Board of Trade.

Wheat.—The receipts of Wheat at this port notwithstanding the light crop of 1866, which caused a falling off in receipts at other points, have increased, being 4,410,305 bushels, against 3,452,722 bushels for 1865, an increase of nearly 1,00,000 bushels.

Wheat receipts, 1865-6

The St. Louis Grain Elevator Company, having given the facilities for handling the grain in bulk has no doubt added to our receipts. The bulk of the receipts have been taken by the millers, but there has been an export demand from Cincinnati, Paducah, and other points on the Ohio River, and for nearly all the country mills in the neighborhood of St. Louis; and shipments have been made, by Illinois River and rail, to Green and Jersey counties, Illinois; and considerable amounts have been sent by rail to Ohio and Indiana. Prices have ruled as high and oftentimes higher than in other markets, and have been governed entirely by the supply and demand. St. Louis has no combinations of railroad or other interest to control her wheat market, and shippers can forward their grain to this port without any fear of its being slaughtered for the benefit of speculators.

Increase due to Elevator.

St. Louis market independent.

Exports for the year were 635,187 bushels, of which 277,976 bushels were shipped by Ohio river boats, and over 210,000 bushels by Ohio and Mississippi, and St. Louis Alton and Terre Haute Railroads, to points in Ohio and Indiana.

Exports 1866

Stock on hand at the close 285,809 bushels, about equally divided between fall and spring wheat, of which 96,515 bushels spring and 97,890 bushels fall were in elevator.

Stock on hand.

A city that has been unable to obtain any considerable railways to form even one combination, may solace itself with the avoidance of danger by their absence. But we have become so desperate in that chase around Mr. Hood's barn, and are so involved in combinations, that we have less fear, as to their effect in slaughtering poor victims, than our quiescent sister, who, eschewing railway combinations, is now looking to barge combinations as a *dernier* resort, as we shall see. Nor are we sharp enough in tricks of the trade to see how the holder of a Chicago warehouse receipt is to be slaughtered by "combinations of railroad or other interest to control her wheat market," which would not victimize the holder of "the St. Louis elevator" receipt. Her large milling facilities, which honesty requires should be considered under the topic of manufactures, no doubt enable her to pay

St.L. eschews combination.

Chi. desperate.

How Chi. to be a victim & St. L. escapes.

when she is short something above market price. But how long will her large capital suffice for that? Suppose that some month, a week's Chicago receipts were cast upon her market,—and does she not expect to grow at least to that?—would prices then rule high?

Chi. likes a stable market— St. Louis and Chicago differ essentially in what constitutes a market's superiority. Stability when other great markets stand; ponderosity, so that the wants of a few millers make no impression; rise and fall with the markets of New York, and Liverpool, we are proud to say are our characteristics, invariable except as means and cost of transportation vary. Nor can our market be moved, without moving other chief markets of our country and world. —St. Louis a vibrating one. On the contrary, St. Louis even boasts of an independent market; one so independent that it vibrates with the necessities or caprices of its millers. What other market knows or cares for the difference? The difference of opinion, however, concerning a market's essentials, is to be cared for, which, as would be expected, corresponds with the difference in figures. The difference. One is genuine commerce; the other a peddling concern. But even for a peddler she must lack in some essential qualities, for if so independent, and able to pay "oftentimes higher than in other markets," why are receipts so small? St. L. wants more than one Elevator Has she already more than she can handle? We hope so, for if a city 280 miles from Chicago, with the pretensions which St. Louis has had to the trade of the whole Northwest, and with so productive an agricultural region immediately contiguous, cannot show better figures, and a demand for increased facilities beyond what "THE St. Louis elevator" can supply; it will be lamentable evidence that we err upon the main premise, the great productive power of the Northwest. The trade report gives the—

St. L. Elevator receipts, Oct. '65— —Jan. '68.

Amount of Grain Received and Disbursed by the St. Louis Grain Elevator Co., from October 24, 1865, to January 1, 1868.

	Receipts.	Disbursements.	Balance Jan 1, 1868.
Wheat	1,877,272.35	1,776,254.37	101,017.58
Corn	382,623,35	382,623.27	....
Oats	130,870.17	130,289.12	581.05
Barley	268,238.15	266,655.24	1,582.39
Rye	37,986.31	37,986.31	....
Malt	1,364.04	1,364.04	....
Total bushels	2,698,355.	2,595,173.	103,182.

2,698,355 bu.

Another elevator— Fortunately, it appears from the Trade Report for 1867, that the subject of increase has consideration:—

—at East St. L. Its benefits. The East St. Louis Elevator Company, organized during the past year, is vigorously at work erecting an elevator and warehouse on the east bank of the river, opposite the foot of Pine street. This enterprise is destined to be of great benefit to our city in the saving of drayage and ferriage on merchandise destined for re-shipment South, as well as attracting the grain trade of northern, middle and southern Illinois to our city, by offering facilities for handling in bulk. That this can be accomplished was demonstrated during the past year, and only failed of success from the fact that there were no facilities at East St. Louis for unloading the cars, which so retarded the business of the railroad companies that shipments in bulk were prohibited.

To count in receipts at East St. Louis, in Illinois, is a good deal like our reckoning those of Milwaukee, in the State of Wisconsin, which we are not yet compelled to do to maintain a respectable lead. But we trust that now they are alive to the fact that "toting" days are over, something by the name of St. Louis, either in Illinois or Missouri, will do its part towards maintaining the reputation of the West, by drawing grain to such an extent as that at least one new elevator shall be built annually for some years. And even then, when the barge system shall be well introduced, as it speedily will be, she will have to show more commercial energy than hitherto, or five times the number of river barges will come to Chicago that will go to St. Louis.

St. L. in Mo. or Ills. to build an elevator a year.

Barges then come to Chi.

A gigantic trade of 50,000,000 or 60,000,000 bushels of grain, would of course breed speculators, and some dishonest ones. Nor would it be surprising, amidst constant examples of fraud and defalcation in large sums, and with opportunities which this immense warehouse system affords; that Chicago should in this respect also be equal with other cities. Yet the first instance of that sort in the elevator business is yet to come. Bought and sold according to sample, the seller's grain goes with others to the bin or bins appropriated to that kind and grade; and the buyer's grain is drawn from these bins according to his contract. The Chief Inspector, Mr. O. L. Parker, furnishes this account of—

Guards against fraud.

None yet.

Mr. *Parker.*

Grain Inspection.—All grain arriving by rail or canal is inspected by inspectors appointed by the Chicago Board of Trade. This system, the result of ten years' experience, is believed to be the most perfect of any yet established. Supervised by one chief inspector, the city is divided into six districts, each having an old experienced inspector at its head. All inspections into store are made in cars or on canal boats. The kind of grain and its grade is marked on a ticket attached to the car door, giving date, name of road, number of car, and inspector's name. These tickets are taken off and preserved by the elevator company and the grain stored in bins as these tickets designate, under the supervision of an inspector stationed in the elevator and employed by the Board of Trade. Books of entry are placed in the exchange room every day during 'Change hours, after which, they go to the Chief Inspector's office, and the details are copied into large books, accessible at all times. The average weight of wheat is also given, and reasons for grading when necessary.

Grain inspection.

Into store.

All grain is inspected out of store unless otherwise ordered; the main reason being to determine whether it comes out in the same condition as it went in. In out inspection a sample is saved and a certificate issued. If the party owning the grain requires, the inspection is made as it runs on board the vessel or cars. This record is also kept in the Chief Inspector's office from returns made by deputies.

Out of store.

In case of an error in judgment, or difference of opinion between inspector and owner of grain, it is referredto a committee of three members of the Board of Trade, styled the Inspection Committee, whose decision is final.

Differences arbitrated.

The full force of inspectors in the busy season of lake navigation, is about thirty-five men; through the winter about twenty-three. The Inspector's office has a cabinet of distinct varieties of wheat, and other grains, from different States, which if well examined by producers, might be of incalculable advantage to improve seed wheat, and also benefit the buyer.

No. of inspectors.

Cabinet of samples

—11

Course of honest men.

Laws, with governors, are only "a terror to evil doers and a praise of them that do well;" and the late Chief Inspector, Mr. T. T. Gurney, remarks in the last Annual Report of the Board of Trade:—

Inspection system. Cordially sustained. Some mistakes.

The system of warehouse inspection adopted December, 1865, has met with general and deserved approval. My opinion is, that it cannot be dispensed with, while your board continue to superintend the inspection of grain. It is proper in this connection to state that your inspectors have been cordially sustained by all the parties to this great interest, in no one instance have they or either of them been interfered with while in the discharge of their duties. It is unquestionably true that mistakes in the inspection of grain have occurred, but they have been of a character that could not be avoided, neither can they in the future be avoided unless damaged grain be classed as rejected.

Premature marketing.

With these unexampled facilities for handling grain, and thorough means of protecting buyer and seller against fraud in quality; yet these very means stimulate endeavors to reach market prematurely, especially in corn. The chief grain market of the country and of the world, would be deficient in discharging its duty to producer and consumer, did it not prepare requisite facilities for—

Grain drying. Mr. Marsh's dryer.

Grain Drying.—In transit hither, especially by river and canal, in which grain business will have the largest relative increase, grain is often wet. With proper facilities for drying, the water would do little injury. One of our oldest citizens, Mr. Sylvester Marsh, early gave attention to this and obtained several patents for a dryer. A warehouse was built for the purpose in 1860, and worked by Mr. E. K. Hubbard, who used it with great success until burnt in May 1867. In 1865 Messrs. Munn and Scott attached Marsh's dryer to their elevator, which has not been used in consequence of extra fire-risk. But a desideratum so great to all grain dealers would not long be disregarded, even if extra insurance required severance from elevators built mainly for storage.

Wheat curing.

Though valuable for wet grain, it also cured wheat too hastily marketed. Much is sent direct to market without sweating in the stack; and by dampness in the bin or vessel, or car, becomes unfit for bread.

Corn curing. Losses by heating. Spoilt for food. Should be better prepared.

Nor is saving value of a kiln-dryer in wheat at all equal with what it is in corn. The liability of new corn to heat is generally known. The early volumes of the *Prairie Farmer* will show the consideration given the subject, and the enhanced value of the corn crop, when corn and corn-meal should be duly prepared for long transit, especially on the ocean. One would suppose that losses in transit to New York, much more to Europe, would have brought into general use a drying process. Corn is little used as food for man compared with what it would be if supplied to house-wifes in proper condition. Ordinary meal becoming speedily stale, it is no wonder that it is little sought in Europe, little even in the land of its origin. One of the most palatable, nutritious, healthy articles of diet in proper condition, and obtained at such small cost; it is unaccountable that more has not been done to prepare it properly for market.

It was therefore very satisfactory to learn upon inquiry, that the National, one of the smallest elevators, but with large facilities to transfer grain from canal to lake craft, belonging to Messrs. Vincent Nelson, & Co., has a grain dryer attached by Messrs. Murry Nelson, & Co. With much experience in grain trade on the lakes and railways, after trying various patents, and corresponding widely with others seeking the same desideratum, they have erected a dryer at large expense under H. H. Beach's patent, which is already a complete success. They do not, however, decry Mr. Marsh's but prefer the one chosen. It drys 1,500 to 2,000 bushels per hour of new corn so that it will keep in any climate, without changing the bright, natural appearance of the grain, and leaving upon it no smell of heat, or acrid, or parched taste, or appearance of having been subjected to any mechanical process whatever. This machine is available for wheat, or any grain damp or wet, or in anyway out of condition, and is claimed to be the first to dry and cure grain on a large scale for commercial purposes, having a capacity to dry cargoes without unusual delay. A full account of its operation would be interesting, but space is precious.

Vincent, Nelson & Co.'s grain dryer.

Beach's patent.

1,500, to 2,000 bu. per hour.

Any grain cured.

A tower seventy-five feet high, built of brick and iron, fire proof, receives the grain at the bottom, where it is elevated to the top, and passes slowly down over perforated iron plates, the motion of the falling grain being constant and uniform, regulated by slides or valves at the bottom. The grain in motion forms a solid column seven feet wide and three inches deep. There are two columns of grain, and a furnace at the bottom supplies hot air, which is evenly distributed by suction-fans, so as to pass constantly and equally through the grain the entire heighth of the kiln. Temperature is regulated by thermometers set in the walls at several points, avoiding all danger of over-heating. Impurities or foreign substances are passed off in vapor or steam. Then it is thoroughly cooled before being passed to the bins in the elevator by the same process, except cold air instead of hot is used, which contributes further to dry as well as cool. Every person interested—and who is not, in all that saves or adds to the accumulated industry and labor of the farmer, as represented in these vast storehouses—should witness for themselves this saving of grain, otherwise lost to the owners and the world, and the price of bread consequently enhanced. The time is coming, if not at hand, when our western farmers must save very much of what is now wasted in their fields, enough to make other farmers rich; and certainly not the least of what their hard toil has successfully garnered, should be allowed to depreciate or become worthless in the hands of our merchants, millers, warehousemen, or carriers. If this dryer suffice not, half a dozen will be erected; and if a better process can be devised, to what other city will it be more valuable? Who can and will pay more for improvements in grain trade, especially in corn, than the chief grain mart of the world?

Mode of operation.

Those interested should see it.

Farmers must save.

Grain not to be wasted

What is requisite will be done.

Live Stock Trade.—When a city counts swine receipts by the million, it would certainly be a distinguishing feature had it not others equally important. Although Cincinnati, previous to 1861–2, when Chicago passed her, had never packed 500,000 in a season,—and most if not all then received

Live Stock Trade.

Chi. no Porkopolis.

were packed,—she had the euphonious cognomen of Porkopolis. Although about four-fold her highest number are here marketed, yet we escape the name.

Cattle Trade. *Tribune.*

Cattle, too, are counted by the hundred thousand. The *Chicago Tribune* in its last annual exhibit, thus describes the rapid growth:—

Rapid growth since 1860.

It is only a few years since the Live Stock trade of Chicago was considered of but trifling importance, and, indeed, aside from supplying the then somewhat limited demand for home consumption, the trade in this product—prior to the year 1860—had not attained sufficient eminence to be classed with our leading commercial interests. But the same causes which combined to make Chicago the largest interior

Causes.

grain market in the world, have built up the Live Stock trade to its present gigantic proportions. The rapid development of the great Northwest, and the construction of an almost perfect network of railroads, stretching out in all directions from this, the great centre—thus affording unequaled facilities for the marketing of stock—

States tributary.

are chief among the causes contributing to this result. The increase in population and wealth in the States of Illinois, Indiana, Iowa, Wisconsin, Minnesota, Kansas and Nebraska, and the remarkable development of the resources of these States, have rendered Chicago the leading market for supplying the large and increasing wants of the East. It is the chief collecting point for the immense herds of beeves which annually graze on the vast prairies of the West, and for the enormous crop of hogs which is annually raised by the farmer and stock-breeder. By reference to

'55, 10,715 head rec'd—'64, 336,627.

table given elsewhere it will be seen that in 1855 only 10,715 beeves were received in Chicago, while in 1864 the number amounted to 336,627. In 1855 the receipts of hogs amounted to only 302,068, which number in 1863 had increased to 1,990,509, and for the year just closed—notwithstanding the partial failure of the corn crop, the arrivals of hogs amounted to 1,696,748 head. Such an extraordinary development of resources, and such an increase in trade and commerce, are without parallels in history—ancient or modern.

Trade varies.

This trade, however, like all other branches of business, has had its vicissitudes, but each year has added something to its extent and importance, until to-day it takes rank as the leading Live Stock market of the world. And when we consider

Small area yet producing.

that but a small fraction of the territory, of which Chicago is the natural outlet, has yet been populated and developed, the future of the trade in this product can scarcely be conceived. The extravagant rates of freight demanded by the railroads running

High freights derange trade—

East from this point, was the principal drawback encountered during the past year. Through the summer months, owing to the "fight" going on between the different companies, the tariff was reasonably low, and business prospered correspondingly, but in the latter part of August the spirit of soulless extortion again took possession

—injure roads.

of these corporations, and the evil results at once became apparent. Much of the stock that would otherwise have come here, has, on account of the suicidal policy of the railroad managers—who, unfortunately, are not gifted with penetration enough to see that a continuance of exorbitant charges will kill the goose that lays the golden eggs—been compelled to seek an outlet through some other channel. It is to be hoped that this evil will be speedily remedied.

Hogs rec'd and shipped from 1858–68

Receipts and Shipments of Hogs at Chicago for Ten Years.

Year.	RECEIVED.			FORWARDED.		
	Live.	Dressed.	Total.	Live.	Dressed.	Total.
1858	416,225	124,261	540,486	159,181	82,832	192,913
1859	188,671	82,533	271,204	87,254	22,992	110,246
1860	285,149	107,715	392,864	191,931	85,233	227,164
1861	549,039	126,863	675,902	216,982	72,112	289,094
1862	1,110,971	237,919	1,348,890	446,506	44,629	491,135
1863	1,343,863	333,894	1,677,757	733,213	123,272	856,485
1864–5	1,267,097	143,223	1,410,320	517,656	18,781	536,437
1865–6	871,468	327,364	1,178,832	538,035	125,531	663,566
1866–7	1,071,399	270,257	1,341,656	549,499	123,270	672,769
1867 to Dec. 31.*	1,696,748	134,496	1,831,247			

*This is taken from the Annual Report of the Union Stock Yard Co., Jan. 15th, 1868.

The Trade Report of St. Louis gives no receipt of Hogs or Cattle for a series of years, and the general table of receipts of leading articles (p. 156,) does not include hogs, though it does cattle. In the last two reports, (here cattle are omitted,) are these statements of— No St L. returns for a series of years.

Routes and Receipts of Hogs at St. Louis for 1866 *and* 1867.

Receipts of Hogs at St. L. 2 years.

Routes and No.

Routes.	1866.	1867.
Upper Mississippi River	17,969	27,812
Lower Mississippi River	....	416
Illinois River	11,266	5,199
Missouri River	8,570	12,882
Ohio & Mississippi R. R.	10,474	29,461
Chicago, Alton & St. Louis R. R.	30,215	64,399
St. Louis, Alton & Terre Haute R. R.	47,926	37,560
Pacific R. R.	12,810	56,589
North Missouri R. R.	36,765	63,170
Iron Mountain R. R.	117	753
Drove in, estimated	41,510	15,000
Total receipts	217,622	313,241
Shipped during the year	13,358	28,627
Taken by Packers and Butchers	204,264	284,614

The *Missouri Democrat*, in its annual review, Jan. 1st, states the monthly receipts of stock, for 1867, this being the aggregate; cattle, 90,380; sheep, 90,201; hogs, 224,640. *Mo. Dem.* states receipts 1867.

The St. Louis Trade Report, however, supplies this valuable table, enabling the reader to ascertain the proportion of trade in hogs Chicago has obtained.

Entire Pork Crop of the Country for 18 *Years, from* 1849–50.

Entire pork crop from 1849–67.

Year.	No. Hogs.	Year.	No. Nogs.	Year.	No. Hogs.
1849–50	1,652,220	1855–56	2,489,502	1861–62	2,863,666
1850–51	1,332,867	1856–57	1,818,468	1862–63	4,069,520
1851–52	1,182,846	1857–58	2,210,778	1863–64	3,261,105
1852–53	2,201,110	1858–59	2,465,552	1864–65	2,422,799
1853–54	2,534,770	1859–60	2,350,822	1865–66	1,705,955
1854–55	2,124,404	1860–61	2,155,702	1866–67	2,425,254

Receipts and shipments of Cattle at Chi. from 1852–68.

Receipts 11 *Years and Shipments* 15 *Years, of Cattle at Chicago.*

Year.	Received.	Forw'ded.	Year.	Received.	Forw'ded.
1852..................	....	77	1860..................	177,101	97,474
1853..................	....	2,657	1861..................	204,579	124,145
1854..................	....	11,221	1862..................	209,655	112,745
1855..................	....	8,253	1863..................	300,622	187,068
1856..................	....	22,502	1864–5..............	303,726	262,446
1857..................	48,524	25,502	1865–6...	348,928	310,444
1858..................	140,534	42,638	1866–7..............	373,277	260,833
1859..................	111,694	37,584	* 1867..............	329,188	

* Stock Yard Report for the year.

Sources of supply.

To compare sources of supply, the following compilation is made from the Board of Trade Reports, and for last year from the *Republican*:—

Routes and Receipts of Hogs and Cattle at Chicago for three seasons, from 1*st of April* 1865–6, 1866–7, *and till December* 31, 1867.

Routes.	HOGS.			CATTLE.		
	1865–6.	1866–7.	1867, Dec. 31.	1865–6.	1866–7.	1867. Dec. 31.
Lake..................	....	10	....	216	181	
C. & R. I. R. R....	162,579	194,534	236,959	50,182	49,099	41,241
Ill. Cent.,............	151,682	166,250	289,213	41,264	39,351	53,882
C. & N. W. R. W...	348,258	422,046	407,957	92,218	77,025	50,189
C. B. & Quincy.....	387,690	403,949	527,839	115,887	139,291	119,931
C. & Alton...........	110,351	104,949	151,227	40,462	58 691	54,143
C. & G. East........	4,977	8,168	7,617	543	143	1,347
Mich. Cent...........	14,964	14,956	19,939	3,544	844	1,466
Mich. S. & N. Ind.	6 0	19,470	35.544	686	403	1,056
C. & Mil..............	7 9	....	....	3,110		
Pitts. Ft. W. & C..	4 2	6,854	8,750	816	87	439
Driven into Yards.		470	2,703		8,163	5,500
	1,198,832	1,341,656	1,696,748	348,928	373,277	329,194

Provide adequate facilities.

For such a trade adequate facilities should be afforded, as they have been for other articles. A plan of the stock yards will be found preceding the title-page. From a pamphlet description the following is extracted:—

Chi. largest live stock market.

Not only is Chicago the greatest pork, lumber and grain market, in the world, but it is also the greatest live stock market. This will be established by figures, in the present article. The signs of the times are sadly awry if this child of the prairies and the lakes does not likewise become the greatest manufacturing city in the world, ere its years of adolescence merge into the vigorous, muscular action of middle age.

Rival railways unite—in Union stock yards.

Probably no enterprise in the history of Chicago has combined so many corporations and capitalists together into one great company, as the Great Union Stock Yards. Railroad companies, that have heretofore been rivals for the live stock trade of the West, and often at war with each other upon this subject, are now a unit, working together as architects of this great undertaking Their tracks have been extended to a common centre, and nine of the former competing roads now

Large estimates for future.

connect directly with the Great Union Stock Yards. The broad prairie that stretches southward from the city is now traversed and re-traversed by their different branches, all tending toward the great bovine city of the world. Packers and commission dealers, whose extensive establishments have heretofore demanded their entire attention, are now found at this nucleus; prospecting upon the results of the enterprise, laying plans for the future, and prognosticating the prosperity that is to follow the opening of this great cattle mart. Their estimates for the future might be considered chimerical by the Rip Van Winkles of other and less go-ahead cities; but Western men know the extent of the broad prairies of Illinois, and neighboring States, which stretch away like the *pampas* of South America, yielding pasturage for innumerable herds of cattle, found nowhere else in the country.

Early sales of stock.

Packing business a branch.

Among the first business transactions of the hamlet, now grown into this great city, was buying and selling cattle and swine; large herds of which were easily driven to market here, slaughtered and shipped to other points. The packing business was only another branch of this trade, and beef packed in Chicago was to be found in the marts of Liverpool, long before the growing Western town from whence it came had a "local habitation and a name" among the cities of the continent.

Col. Hough's beef at World's Fair.

Increase of Chi. trade.

Dealers come here.

Railroads.

Basis solid.

At the World's Fair, held in London several years ago, the attention of Queen Victoria and Prince Albert was called to several tierces of beef, from the packing establishment of the Houghs in Chicago; and they were awarded a premium. Thus the produce of the new city began to grow in the estimation of foreign dealers, and an impetus was given to the trade. Steadily advancing, the exports from our harbor began to look like those of much older cities; and St. Louis and Cincinnati lost their laurels—the latter ceasing to be the recognized "porkopolis" of the land. Reaching out like a young giant, the new commercial port seized upon the produce of the prairies of Illinois and the West, and put an embargo upon the growth of older towns, less centrally located. Dealers in live stock soon left their old landmarks in Cincinnati, St. Louis and Louisville, and established themselves in the Garden City; the places that had known them knowing them no more, unless it was to hear of their prosperity and increasing wealth. Railroads sprang into existence, and cut the prairies in every direction, while the lakes were whitened by the unfurled sails of thousands of vessels; and the great rush of business which now blesses Chicago as a metropolis, was established permanently, upon a basis having for its foundations millions of acres of productive lands, great natural resources, and untold commercial advantages.

Yards began last June.

Sewers.

On the first of June, of the present year, ground was broken for the new yards. The first thing to be done was to drain the land—a work of no small importance. An immense box sewer was constructed along Halsted street, to serve as a main discharge for the drains and sewers. This structure is half a mjle in length, running north and south, and four feet in the clear. Constructed on the most improved plans, these drains and sewers, underlying the yards in every direction, perform their work in the most admirable manner. The soil is now in good condition, and no inconvenience will be experienced from wet land or standing water. In this particular the great bovine city will be far ahead of the populous and crowded human city which it adjoins, and of which it is destined to become an important part.

30 miles drains.

The total length of the drains and sewers is about thirty miles. They have caused a wonderful transformation in the level, wet land of the prairie, which it has heretofore been considered impossible to drain. The argument deduced from this is, that all the low land surrounding Chicago is valuable for building purposes, and that it can be thoroughly drained, so as to afford a solid foundation for structures of any size.

Foundation of yards.

Planking.

The Foundation of the Yards.—The tract of land selected as the site of the yards was now thoroughly drained, and what a short time before was a marshy prairie, covered with rank grass, appeared dry and firm, admitting of the passage of loaded wagons, and the laying of railroad tracks over it. Lines of rails were soon constructed, leading from different railroads, which were to transport the immense amount of lumber required for the construction of the yards, to the spot. Large sills of timber were placed upon the ground, across which were laid three-inch joists. Upon this foundation the planking was commenced. That portion of the yards to be used for cattle pens was planked with three-inch pine plank, placed firmly upon the joists and nailed thereto. Two-inch plank was similarly placed upon those portions where the hogs are to be kept. The planking being raised from the ground affords the water and refuse from the yards an opportunity of draining off to the ground, where it immediately finds its way into the drains and sewers which underlie the whole, thence into the main sewer on Halsted street, and into the river. The entire planking, like the draining, was done in the most substantial manner, no expense or pains being spared to make it firm and solid, so that no accidents might result in the future from its sinking or breaking through, beneath the tread of the herds destined to pass over it. A portion of the planking was done by contract, and the remainder by the company. As many as 1,000 men were employed upon it at one time.

Work thorough.

Streets and alleys.

345 acres.

The Streets and Alleys.—The entire 345 acres comprised in the yards are laid out into streets and alleys, in the same manner as a large city. Through the center from north to south runs a broad avenue which has been named E street. This great central thoroughfare is one mile in length, and seventy-five feet broad. It is divided into three sections, like a bridge, to facilitate the driving of cattle through it. Droves passing to the south will take one section; those passing to the north, another, meeting on the way without the slightest inconvenience or stoppage. The drover's whip will not be called into requisition in passing through this avenue, as all will be "fair sailing." This street runs through the entire grounds, and is paved with Nicholson pavement; the blocks used being the refuse ends of plank, etc., which economy greatly reduced the expense. There is not a finer or smoother drive in Chicago than this well paved and finely rounded street; and there will be no more sightly one, when the yards are filled with innumerable herds of cattle and swine, and teeming with the activity of buying selling and transferring stock. Running parallel to avenue E are other streets, leading to the railroads that surround the yards, on all sides, but the south.

Main street has Nicholson pavement.

Streets rectangular.

These streets are crossed at right angles by others, running east and west. The principal one of these passes by the hotel, and has been named "Broadway" by the workmen. It is indeed a broad avenue, and will probably retain that name, as it leads from the Hough House to the bank and exchange building, where the life and excitement of the yards will center. It is sixty-six feet wide, planked with heavy timber, and traversed on the south by a raised sidewalk.

500 yards and pens.

The Yards and Pens.—There are five hundred of these enclosures, all lying on the different streets, like the buildings of a city, and all properly numbered. In size these inclosures vary from 20x35 to 85x112, while others are precisely the size of a car, calculated to hold just one car-load of stock. The cattle pens are open, but those designed for hogs are covered with sheds, and so arranged as to prevent the hogs "piling," which they are inclined to do in cold weather.

Barns and cribs.

Hay Barns and Corn Cribs.—The yards are provided with six hay barns and six corn cribs, situated in different parts of the enclosure, convenient to different sections of pens.

Railway facilities.

15 miles track.

Various roads accomdated.

The Railway Facilities. Perhaps the greatest feature of these Yards is that of the different railway accommodations. Nine of the principal railroads of the West find a common center here. There have been constructed fifteen miles of track, as branches, which connect these roads with the Yards, besides many switch tracks and side runs. Upon the north are tracks of four railroads—the Great Eastern, the Michigan Central, the Michigan Southern and the Pittsburg and Fort Wayne, These roads all run in from the east, and their tracks are so arranged by the side of "shoots" that whole trains can be unloaded at once. On the north, and parallel to the "shoots" belonging to these roads, are others, running nearly parallel. They are for the accommodation of two roads, the Chicago, Burlington & Quincy and the Illinois Central, which also approach the grounds from the east. The east and west sides of the yards describe an inward curve, along which are platforms and "shoots." The Chicago and Rock Island railroad owns those upon the east, and the Chicago and Northwestern and the Chicago, Alton and St. Louis, those upon the west, where their tracks are constructed. By the act of incorporation all the roads have the privilege of running over each others tracks, but so ample are the arrangements that this will seldom, if ever, be necessary. The yards are provided with water tanks for the engines, wood yards, turn-tables, and everything that is required at a great depot, which in fact these grounds are—the greatest in the world.

Platforms and shoots.

Ample depot arrangements.

Loading and unloading—

Loading and Unloading Facilities.—The facilities for loading and unloading cargoes of cattle at these Yards are unsurpassed. Each road has 1,000 feet of platform, which is provided with "shoots," leading directly into the yards and pens of the division appropriated to the use of such road. When a train of cars loaded with live stock arrives, it draws up in front of the "shoots." Gates are so arranged that they open across the platform, extending to the cars, and thus form an enclosure through which the stock passes directly into the Yards. These gates enable a whole train to unload as quick as one car. Several of the "shoots" are made double, so that the upper and lower floors of a car load of hogs can be passed out at the same time. This arrangement is so perfect that there is little chance for an accident to happen to the stock, as they pass down the avenues formed by the gates, and are thence driven into the pens. As many as 500 cars can be loaded or unloaded in this manner at the same time, the whole operation occupying only a few moments. This fine arrangement is considered one of the greatest features of the Yards.

—entire train.

500 cars at once.

Supplying the Yards with Water is the next topic, which is wholly superseded by the following from the *Republican*, March 4th:—

Water supply-

Artesian Well at the Stock Yards.—Yesterday morning connections were made between the new artesian well and the water-supply tanks at the Union Stock Yards. The pipe which conducts the water from the well is five inches in diameter. It is estimated that no less than 440,000 gallons of water will flow into the tanks every twenty-four hours. The pipe is curved to the top of the receptacle, which is at least sixty feet high. An overflow pipe is also connected with the tank, which carries off the surplus water to the Chicago river. The Hough House is supplied with water from the well in question, and the guests express entire satisfaction in regard to its excellent quality.

Artesian Well

440,000 gals. pure water in 24 hours.

Hough House supplied.

In the afternoon the depth of the bore was finally measured, and gave a return of 1,190 feet. At that distance is a kind of seam or well—so far as can be ascertained—eight feet deep, which is always full of water, and from which the stream mounts toward the earth's surface through the bore. It was at first believed that the water would have to be supplied to the tanks by the pumping process, but the experiment of this morning shows conclusively that the fount from which the water springs must be at a height of upward of sixty feet above the level of the well's oriffice, for, as is a well known fact in the science of hydrodynamics, water will always rise to its own level if unobstructed.

Depth 1,190 feet.

Head over 60 feet.

Then follows a description of minor items, of the hotel,—the Hough House is 130 by 188 feet deep, 6 stories high, well built of brick, with a slate roof,—the exchange building and bank, cottages, stores, workshops, etc., for which space cannot be taken. Many omissions have been made where not marked.

Hough House, &c

Because stock trade is so immense, can these unequaled facilities be supplied for its transaction. Because the energy and capacity of our active business men and of railroad directors keep pace with public requirements, are requisite facilities provided. Because they can be and are here supplied as they can be at no other city, must the stock-trade grow here indefinitely with the entire West. We have little conception of the herds that will be raised in Texas and the Indian Territory, which will chiefly be marketed here. Butchers from the chief cities will come and buy a car load or two, selecting just what they want, and saving at least one seller's profit. And if any other improvements are wanted to accommodate the business, what other city will be more likely to discover and employ them?

Immense trade affords large facilities.

None equal.

Herds from a distance.

Other improvements soon.

The paper quoted from speaks of the enhanced value of real estate. Without a doubt the Company will actually make more, perhaps twice as much, in the rise upon its land as in profits of the business. That is one of the chief advantages of business here, that the merchant, manufacturer or operator, who has sagacity to buy his place for business and for his home, will, in that alone, leave a good estate to his children. How foolishly our

Enhances land.

That a Chi advanta ge.

Business men should buy.

citizens act in this matter, paying rents and giving rise to their landlords; instead of paying interest and keeping profits to themselves—profits made by their own industry, and which few landlords are entitled to, either for foresight in their investments, or any efforts to promote public interests.

Lumber trade.

Lumber, Shingles and Lath.—For many years this young city has held the position of the largest lumber market in the world. Figures have been so enormous,—and last season largest of all—that I designed to compare receipts at the other chief points with this. But space cannot be wasted with that superfluity. A circular of Messrs. Woolner & Garrick remarks:—

Other markets. *Woolner & Garrick's* circular.

Alb. receipts half those of Chi. Trade fair.

The total receipts of lumber at this port will more than double the total receipts at Albany, where, up to the 8th of November, only 357,000,000 feet were received against 760,000,000 feet here. If we look at the business in a general view, without going into a detailed case here or there, it may be safely said that the trade has been pretty fair, with a decent remuneration to all parties. The stocks on hand here in the spring were so light that the loss on them was unimportant to the holder. A number of speculators with limited means and less capacity for or knowledge of the manufacture of lumber, but enticed into it by the splendid results of former years, have paid dearly for their experience, and will necessarily retire from the trade, leaving the business to more able and sagacious hands. It is to be hoped that the products of the woods for the coming winter will fall short rather than exceed those of last season.

807,635,000 feet 1867.

Receipts the past season were given, P. 61, except of some hard-wood lumber by rail—lumber *eight hundred seven millions, six hundred and thirty-five thousand feet;* shingles 234,818,000; lath, 145,116,000. The last report of the Board of Trade says of the market of 1866–7:—

730,000,000 feet 1866. 647.000,000 feet 1865.

The receipts of Lumber during the past year were 730,057,168 feet, against 647,145,734 feet for the year previous, an increase of 82,911,434 feet. About five per cent. of the receipts were brought hither by Railroad from Indiana and Michigan—consisting mostly of hard wood lumber. Notwithstanding that the receipts showed such a material increase, the trade was prosperous and the market was very uniform throughout the season of navigation. The extension of railroads to the far West is constantly opening up new sources of demand, and the trade must steadily increase each succeeding year.

Receipts lumber, &c. 11 yrs., shipments 8 yrs.

Receipts Lumber, Shingles, Lath 11 *years, Shipments* 8 *years.*

Year.	RECEIPTS.			SHIPMENTS.		
	Lumber.	Shingles.	Lath.	Lumber.	Shingles.	Lath.
1856	441,961,900	185,876,000	79,235,120	....	....	....
1857	459,639,000	131,832,000	80,130,000	....	....	....
1858	278,943.000	127,565,000	44,559,000	....	....	....
1859	302,845,207	165,927,000	49,102.000	226,120,389	195,117,700	28,236,585
1860	262,494,626	125,894,000	36,601,000	225,872,340	168,302,525	32,170,420
1861	249,308,705	79,366,000	32,637,000	189,376.445	94,421,186	31,282,725
1862	305,674,045	181,255,000	23,880,000	189,279,079	55,761,630	16,966,600
1863	413,301,818	172,364,878	41,768,000	221,799,330	102,634,447	30,293,247
1864–5	501,592,406	190,169,750	65.953,900	269,496,579	188,497,256	36,242,010
1865–6	647,145,734	310.897,350	66,075,100	385,358,678	258.351,450	61,516,895
1866–7	730,057,168	400,125,250	123,992,400	422,313,266	422,339,715	74,265,405

St. L. Rep. deficient. *Mo. Dem.*

The St. Louis Trade Report has no lumber department, nor does the Annual Review in the St. Louis *Journal of Commerce* allude to it. The *Democrat*, January 1st, remarks:—

St. Louis is not at present as important a distributing point for lumber as some of her near neighbors, yet considerable is marketed here, and prices at this point are looked for with much eagerness by all the raftsmen in the upper country. We have numerous readers among the pineries of the Wisconsin and Black rivers of Wisconsin, and Minnesota side of the St. Croix, and away up in the more northern pineries of the headwaters of the Mississippi and Otter Tail lake regions of Minnesota, and knowing they will read with interest a statement of the business of the year, we give it as near as possible, without pretending to exactness, as there is no record kept of the receipts by river which can claim the merit of absolute perfection. Other cities larger in lumber trade Upper Miss.

Lumber.—Receipts by raft have been not far from 40,000,000 feet during the year. Receipts by rail have been too inconsiderable to notice, not amounting to more than 80,000 feet. Very few changes have taken place in the price of lumber during the year. In May the new cuttings began to be looked for, and as early as the first week sales to arrive of over half a million feet, were made at $24 to $26, afloat and on the bank. The floods everywhere prevailing at this season did considerable damage to booms and retarded receipts, but rather stiffened prices. The market held up through May, and into June, but before July 20 prices were somewhat depressed, and we note sales of 450,000 feet Chippeway, at $18 to $19 afloat. In August the market regained its tone, and $20 in the water, and $23 on the bank were paid, with light receipts and good demand. There was an increase in receipts, however, in the next six weeks, and prices declined to $17@17 50 afloat for Chippeway, at which price the market remained steady for the balance of the season. 40,000,000 feet 1867.

Shingles.—Receipts have been very light, approximating 10,000,000 by all routes. Shingles

Lath.—Receipts were fully 4,000,000 during the year, but the demand was more than up to the supply. Lath.

That is, she received about *five per cent.* of the Chicago amount of lumber, and still less of shingles and lath. Our stock on hand in 1858 was 173,474,033, in 1867, 171,068,504, the two highest amounts; and intermediate years the surplus runs down to the lowest in 1863, 73,000,000. Allowing the average to be 120,000,000, we carry over about three times her entire receipts. She would probably do better, had she proper gratitude for what she has. No account seems to be made of receipts from Chicago. Could shipments by rail and canal to St. Louis have been ascertained, they would have shown her indebtedness here quite as much for lumber as for wheat. It is an ungrateful slight to run away off to the head waters of the Mississippi to find interested parties, and forget Chicago. 5 per cent. of Chi. receipts. Ungrateful. Chi. slighted

For several years our shipments have been only about one-half the receipts, showing consumption of 100,000,000 to 300,000,000. How *could* Chicago grow as she does, had she such a miserable little lumber market? With neither capital nor time to build of brick to meet pressing demands, it will be a cheaper means to stop her growth for St. Louis to set her Allens to buying and burning Chicago lumber, instead of buying up adverse railroads. And burning property to make insurance money being peculiarly a Chicago trick, would it not be easy for their sagacious business men to arrange with our lumber dealers to their mutual advantage? Evidently we are in a condition to need preservation, however it may be with St. Louis, and we will next consider— Chi. consumption. A plan to stop our growth.

Chi. Salt receipts 12 yrs.

Receipts and Shipments of Salt at Chicago, for Twelve Years

Years.	Received, Barrels.	Forwarded, Barrels.	Years.	Received, Barrels.	Forwarded, Barrels.
1855	170,623	107,993	1861	390,499	319,140
1856	184,884	83,601	1862	612,003	520,227
1857	200,946	90,918	1863	775,864	579,694
1858	334,997	191,279	1864–5	680,346	483,443
1859	316,291	257,847	1865–6	611,025	444,827
1569	255,148	172,963	1866–7	496,827	452,587

St. L. Salt receipts 12 yrs.

Receipts of Salt at St. Louis for Twelve Years.

Years.	Barrels.	Sacks.	Years.	Barrels.	Sacks.
1867	141,674	79,025	1861	No record.	No record.
1866	134,542	88,013	1860	36,387	399,576
1865	170,814	83 221	1859	36,083	328,280
1864	133,362	46,698	1858	43,[illegible]68	451,275
1863	89,683	56,118	1857	45,665	308,170
1862	102,538	107,508	1856	36,759	460,806

Relative changes in trade.

The St. Louis *Democrat*, it will be remembered, stated in 1861, p. 112, that the contest with Chicago fairly began in 1857. Then we were ahead even in salt, supposing two sacks equivalent to a barrel, and the last five years we double and triple her. Our consumption in that time, deducting shipments from receipts, equals her gross receipts into less than 100,000 bbls; a two months stock for us, and six for her.

Chi. receipts Wool 12 yrs.

Receipts and Shipments of Wool at Chicago, for Twelve Years

Year.	Received, Pounds.	Forw'ded. Pounds,	Year.	Received, Pounds.	Forw'ded. Pounds.
1855	1,943,415	2,158,462	1871	1,184,208	1,360,617
1856	1,853,920	575,908	1862	1,523,571	2,101,514
1857	1,106,821	1,062,781	1863–4	2,831,194	3,435,967
1858	1,053,626	1,038,674	1864–5	4,304,388	7,554,379
1859	918,319	934,595	1865–6	7,639,749	9,923,069
1860	859,248	839,269	1866–7	12,200,640	12,391,933

St. L. receipts Wool 11 yrs.

Receipts of Wool at St. Louis, for Eleven Years.

1867	12,040 pkgs.	1861	2,608 pkgs.
1866	9,205 "	1860	7,696 "
1565	10,559 "	1859	5,121 "
1864	8,129 "	1858	3,671 "
1863	6,259 "	1857	2,935 "
1862	6,176 "		

St. L Trade report.

In the receipts of wool it is impossible to give an estimate as to the number of pounds, as it is received in different kinds of packages. The exports being entirely in bales, may be averaged at 200 pounds to the bale, making the exports for the three past years in pounds, 2,385,600 for 1867, 1,711,400 for 1866, 1,878,800 for 1865.

Here, too, we lead her, and more than four-fold.

Are not these items abundantly sufficient to establish the correctness of Mr. Wells' report as amended? And although the reports of both cities have been carefully compared, I can see no one item except receipts of lead, and in flour manufactured, in which she is ahead. Doubtless, however, in some articles, as sugar, her trade is largest. I regret not having figures 20 years ago to exhibit her large supremacy which in only about half that time —for railroads had little power till 1856 or '7, when the contest really began, as they say—has not only been destroyed, but our own established to an almost equal degree. This, it may be repeated, has been done in the very field which she wholly possessed, and felt herself as secure in holding, as that of her own State, or even her own county. With the current thus setting hither irresistibly, are our business men likely to oppose? Will they not, on the other hand, be on the alert to avail themselves of the *prestige* now in our favor, which hitherto has been in hers? No one can estimate the benfits to her of the hitherto unquestioned belief of the public, that she had an impregnable natural position, and the confident expectations that she must become the great inland city. She was no genuine Samson, as Mr. Cobb imagined, (p. 39); for this her hair has been proved false, in which her imagined strength lay. Shorn even of this, her fancied supremacy vanishes. Yet only supremacy has gone. Even if the city at the Big Bend of the Missouri also eclipse her, still she will grow speedily to half a million, perhaps a million. All depends upon her own energies. Cincinnati, acknowledging that she is beaten, and realizing the necessity of great effort to resist the Chicago-ward tendency of business, is in a proper state to maintain her true relative position; and the sooner St. Louis comes to the same condition, the better for her.

These items sustain Mr. Wells.

Old figures wanted.

Current set-

—shall we oppose?

Prestige gone.

Still to grow to 1,000,000.

Cin. wise—

—St. L. to follow.

So får, however, from realizing the force of what they themselves admit on all sides, as we have seen, and no one of them can deny, that whatever advantage they had in the river trade in the day of steamboats, has vanished in the day of railway ascendancy; they still vaunt and rely upon their "natural position." Prof. Waterhouse published in *Hunt's Merchants' Magazine* July, 1866, an interesting paper upon this grandiloquent theme, which if true, proves this paper false. It is reprinted with some alteration in the St. Louis Trade Report for 1866 under the caption,—

Still relies upon natural advantages.

Prof. Waterhouse.

MISSOURI:

St. Louis the Commercial Centre of North America.

St. L. com. centre of N. A.

St. Louis is ordained by the decrees of physical nature to become the great inland metropolis of this continent. It cannot escape the magnificence of its destiny. Greatness is the necessity of its position. New York may be the head, but St. Louis will be the heart of America. The stream of traffic which must flow through this mart will enrich it with alluvial deposits of gold. Its central location and facilities of communication unmistakably indicate the leading part which this city will take in the exchange and distribution of the products of the Mississippi Valley. * * *

Ordained by nature.

Geog. centre.

St. Louis very nearly bisects the *direct* distance of 1,400 miles between Superior City and the Balize. It is the geographical centre of a valley which embraces 1,200,000 square miles. In its course of 3,200 miles the Mississippi borders upon Missouri 470 miles. Of the 3,000 miles of the Missouri, 500 lie within the limits of our own State. St. Louis is mistress of more than 16,500 miles of river navigation.

Other points. Conclusion as to centrality. Prospective railways.

Where the asterisks are above, latitude, longitude, etc., are given, and a table of distances from other points on the long rivers, Ft. Benton on the Missouri, being 3,100 miles; and another table of distances by rail from chief cities interior, and on the Atlantic and Pacific coasts. What else is necessary to prove St. Louis' centrality? Hence the next paragraph. A description follows of St. Louis as she now is; a list of railroads within the State, 950 miles including that traitorous Hannibal and St. Joe road; and losing sight of this, and that other routes might prove equally disadvantageous to St. Louis, though serviceable to the State—is not that the reason that "Missouri" heads the article?—the Professor introduces a magnificent prospective of railways, which must prove St. Louis' centrality, if it had not been done previously.

N. Mo. road.

The Directors intend to complete the extension of the North Missouri to the Iowa line, where it will connect with the whole system of Iowa railroads, by the first of July, 1867. The work upon the west branch of the North Missouri, whose ultimate destination is Kansas City and Leavenworth, is rapidly advancing.

10,000 miles contemplated. Chief terminal points.

A vast enlargement of our railroad facilities is contemplated. More than 10,000 miles of new lines have been projected on the west side of the Mississippi. A quarter of a century may elapse before the completion of these extensions; yet the very conception of them shows that the public mind is alive to the importance of ampler means of communication with the States and Territories of the Far West. Most of these roads have received grants of land from the Government, and upon some of the lines the work is already far advanced. The terminal points of the most important roads are:

Lake Superior—Gulf—Pacific.

Superior City and New Orleans, *via* St. Paul, St. Louis and Memphis
St. Louis and San Francisco, *via* Kansas City and Salt Lake.
Kansas City and Ft. Benton, *via* Omaha.
Leavenworth and Galveston, *via* Lawrence.
St. Louis and San Diego, *via* Springfield.

N. W. trade may be diverted. S. W. sure.

The extension of this last line from Rolla, merely to the southwest corner of Missouri would be an incalculable benefit. The trade of the northwestern roads may be partially diverted from St. Louis by the construction of rival lines. But the Southwest Branch, by its advantages of situation, will compel all connecting lines to be subsidiary to itself; and its commerce, constantly swelled by the traffic of tributary roads, must necessarily flow to St. Louis.

S.L. learning prudence. Wonderful progress. Relative decrease— —why?

Railways, especially important lines, are not better apprehended than difficulties; and is not here seen an inkling of following the lead of Cincinnati, and depending upon trade south and southwest? That would be prudent. Then follows an interesting statement of the present business and its accomodations—which is truly wonderful, even if San Francisco and Chicago have eclipsed her in speed—when the Professor perceives that, notwithstanding this natural location, all these river facilities, many railroads built and more prospective, her large wealth, her thoroughly established trade; that relative progress is not maintained, and that much is to be done. In immediate connection, too, he considers why she has declined relatively, finding the main cause in the "rebellion,"—

The length of these lines of transportation, the slowness of our present means of communication, and the magnitude of our territorial population and trade, forcibly illustrate the necessity of a Pacific Railroad. Pac. road needed.

The foregoing summaries exhibit the commerce of the Mississippi Valley with the mountains. But while St. Louis does not monopolize the trade of the gold regions, it yet sends to the territories by far the largest portion of their supplies. Even in cases where merchandise has been procured at intermediate points, it is probable that the goods were originally purchased at St. Louis. Mining trade monopolized

During the rebellion the commercial transactions of Cincinnati and Chicago, doubtless exceeded those of St. Louis. The very events which prostrated our trade stimulated theirs into an unnatural activity. Their sales were enlarged by the traffic which was wont to seek this market. Our loss was their gain. Rebellion hurt St. L.

The Southern trade of St. Louis was utterly destroyed by the blockade of the Mississippi. The disruption by civil commotions of our commercial intercourse with the interior of Missouri was nearly complete. The trade of the Northern States, bordering upon the Mississippi, was still unobstructed. But the merchants of St. Louis could not afford to buy commodities which they were unable to sell, and country dealers would not purchase their goods where they could not dispose of their produce. Thus St. Louis, with every market wholly closed or greatly restricted, was smitten with a commercial paralysis. The prostration of business was general and disastrous. No comparison of claims can be just which ignores the circum stances that, during the rebellion, retarded the commercial growth of St. Louis, yet fostered that of rival cities. South. trade destroyed—North injured. St. L. paralyzed.

Nothing more clearly demonstrates the geopraphical superiority of St. Louis than the action of the Government during the war. Notwithstanding the strenuous competition of other cities, our facilities for distribution, and a due regard for its own interests, compelled the Government to make St. Louis the Western base of supplies and transportation. During the rebellion, the transactions of the Government at this point were very large. Govt. action proves centrality.

That St. Louis should have been made the base of supplies was quite natural, because of her contiguity to the seat of war; though without doubt it was owing quite as much to the prevalent absurdity we are endeavoring to combat, that she is the *natural* centre of the Republic. But it happens unfortunately for our "beautiful rival" of the rivers, that before the war began, as we ,saw pp. 111—114, business was altering its currents according to natural laws. It was predicted in 1861, p. 19, "that changes it would have required five years to effect in the ordinary course of events, will now be made in a year or two." Were they not? Prevalent absurdity helps St. L Currents changed before war.

But how happens it that these years of peace exhibit receipts of grain at Chicago in 1865, in round numbers, 45,000,000, at St. Louis, 17,000,000; in 1866, Chicago 53,000,000, and St. Louis 22,000,000; in 1867, Chicago 66,000,000, and St. Louis 17,000,000? The inference is natural that Chicago must have a superior territory to St. Louis, from which to draw her supplies. But this has been provided against by the tables exhibiting the same sources. Directly against fact and reason, the Professor argues or rather asserts:— Why no return with peace? Same area supplies both.

The National exigencies forced the Government to select the best point of distribution. The choice of the Federal authorities is a conclusive proof of the commercial superiority of St. Louis. St. L. central because a military depot.

The conquest of treason has restored to this mart the use of its natural facilities. Trade is rapidly regaining its old channels. On its errands of exchange, it visits the islands of the sea, traverses the ocean, and explores foreign lands. It penetrates every State and Territory in the Mississippi Valley, from Alabama and New Mexico to Minnesota and Montana. It navigates every stream that pours its tributary waters into the Mississippi. Peace restores advantages.

Is that true? If there be any truth in that, why are directly contrary results witnessed? Does not the Professor know that truth is always consistent with itself? If "trade is rapidly regaining its old channels," the leading business men and papers of St. Louis have a sad method of demonstration, as these pages attest. They will do well to seek instruction from this Professor. But notwithstanding the grandiloquence with which the lie is given to all these other writers and speakers, the Professor himself goes directly on to say:—

Prof. W. contradicts himself.

Difficulties of St. L.

But St. Louis can never realize its splendid possibilities without effort. The trade of the vast domain lying east of the Rocky Mountains and south of the Missouri river, is naturally tributary to this mart. St. Louis, by the exercise of forecast and vigor, can easily control the commerce of 1,000,000 square miles. But there is urgent need of exertion. Chicago is an energetic rival. Its lines of railroad pierce every portion of the Northwest. It draws an immense commerce by its network of railways. The meshes which so closely interlace all the adjacent country gather rich treasures from the tides of commerce.

Chi. energetic.

Her railroads.

Chicago is vigorously extending its lines of road across Iowa to the Missouri river. The completion of these roads will inevitably divert a portion of the Montana trade from this city to Chicago. The energy of an unlineal competitor may usurp the legitimate honors of the imperial heir. St. Louis cannot afford to continue the masterly inactivity of the old *regime*. A traditional and passive trust in the efficacy of natural advantages will no longer be a safe policy. St Louis must make exertions equal to its strength and worthy of its opportunities. It must not only form great plans of commercial enterprise, but must execute them with an energy defiant of failure. It must complete its projected railroads to the mountains, and span the Mississippi at St. Louis with a bridge whose solidity of masonry shall equal the massiveness of Roman architecture, and whose grandeur shall be commesurate with the future greatness of the Mississippi Valley. The structure whose arches will bear the transit of a continental commerce should vie with the great works of all time, and be a monument to distant ages of the triumph of civil engineering and the material glory of the Great Republic.

Trust in nature not safe.

What St. L. must do.

Why does nature fail at St. L?

If so *naturally* tributary to St. Louis, why this indispensable effort? Is nature so false to its votary—and where can a more devout worshipper be found than the Queen of the Rivers?—as that "the energy of an unlineal competitor may usurp the legitimate honors of the imperial heir?" Is that a sample of logic or ethics taught in Washington University?

Practical advice to be heeded.

But considerations of Chicago, give the Professor's thoughts quite a practical turn. It remains to be seen whether St. Louisians will heed the counsel and do what they may and should to retain trade west and south of them, which otherwise surely comes to Chicago. We, too, want "the structure whose arches will bear the transit of a continental commerce, should vie with the great works of all time;" for surely as that time and bridge last, it bears more to Chicago than to St. Louis. That naturally brings in the subject of the bridge at St. Charles over the Missouri. Then "persistent" efforts could induce the Government to establish a naval depot at Carondelet. Then THE elevator comes in, quoted p. 156, which introduces the final and sure means of attaining what nature against herself withholds, and art has hitherto failed to supply. Alas that nature in the domain of the Queen of the Rivers, is so derelict towards her most faithful devotee that barge-trade is the only remedy! Is that according to art or nature?

Other means to help nature.

Barges the chief reliance.

The facilities which our elevator affords for the movement of cereals, have given rise to a new system of transportation. The Mississippi Valley Transportation Company has been organized for the conveyance of grain to New Orleans in barges. Steam tugs of immense strength have been built for the use of the company. They carry no freight. They are simply the motive power. They save delay by taking fuel for the round trip. Landing only at the large cities, they stop barely long enough to attach a loaded barge. By this economy of time and steady movement, they equal the speed of steamboats. The Mohawk made its first trip from St. Louis to New Orleans in six days, with ten barges in tow. The management of the barges is precisely like that of freight cars. The barges are loaded in the absence of the tug. The tug arrives, leaves a train of barges, takes another and proceeds. The tug itself is always at work. It does not lie at the levee while the barges are loading. Its longest stoppage is made for fuel.

Miss. Val. Trans. Co.

Its business, towing.

Mode of operation.

Steamboats are obliged to remain in port two or three days for the shipment of freight. The heavy expense which this delay, and the necessity for large crews involve, is a great objection to the old system of transportation. The service of the steam tug requires but few men, and the cost of running is relatively light. The advantages which are claimed for the barge system are exhibited by the following table:—

Steamboats compared.

	Tug and Barges.	Steamboats.
Stoppage at intermediate points	2 hours.	6 hours.
" " terminal "	24 "	48 "
Crew	15	50
Tonnage	25,000 tons.	1,500 tons.
Daily expense	$200	$1,000
Original cost	$75,000	$100,000

Relative delay and cost.

In addition to the ordinary precautions against fire, the barges have this unmistakable advantage over steamboats: they can be cut adrift from each other, and the fire restricted to the narrowest limits. The greater safety of barges ought to secure for them lower rates of insurance. The barges are very strongly built, and have water-tight compartments for the movement of grain in bulk. The transportation of grain from Minnesota to New Orleans, by water costs no more than the freightage from the same point to Chicago. After the erection of a floating elevator at New Orleans, a boat load of grain from St. Paul will not be handled again till it reaches the Crescent City.

Fire risks.

Cheapness.

Freight to N. O.

At that port it will be transferred by steam to the vessel which will convey it to New York or Europe. The possible magnitude of this trade may be inferred from the fact that in 1865 Minnesota alone raised 10,000,000 bushels of wheat. Three quarters of this harvest could have been exported, if facilities of cheap transportation had offered adequate inducement. In 1866, higher prices. which produced the same practical result as cheaper freightage, led to the exportation of 8,000,000 bushels.

Thence to Europe.

Minn. surplus.

From the 1st of May to the 25th of December, 1866, the tow boats of this city transported 120,000 tons of freight. This new scheme of conveying freight by barges bids fair to revolutionize the whole carrying trade of our western waters. It will materially lessen the expense of heavy transit, and augment the commerce of the Mississippi River in proportion to the reduction it effects in the cost of transportation. The improvement which facilitates the carriage of our cereals to market, and makes it more profitable for the farmer to sell his grain than to burn it, is a national benefit. This enterprise, which may yet change the channel of cereal transportation, shows what great results a spirit of progressive energy may accomplish.

Revolutionize river trade.

National benefit.

The mercantile interests of the West imperatively demand the improvement of the Mississippi and its main tributaries. This is a work of such prime and transcendent importance to the commerce of the country, that it challenges the coöperation of the Government. A commercial marine which annually transfers tens of millions of passengers, and cargoes, whose value is hundreds of millions, ought not to encounter the obstructions which human efforts can remove. The yearly loss of property, from the interruption of communication and wreck of boats, reaches a startling aggregate.

Miss. to be improved.

For the accomplishment of an undertaking so vital to its municipal interests, St. Louis should exert its mightiest energies. The prize for which competition strives is too splendid to be lost by default. The Queen City of the West should not voluntarily abdicate its commercial sovereignty.

St. L. to work for it.

Europe to help fulfill prophecy.

If the emigrant merchants of America and Europe, who recognize in the geographical position of St. Louis the guarantee of mercantile supremacy, will become citizens of this metropolis, they will aid in bringing to a speedier fulfillment the prophesies of its greatness. The current of western trade must flow through the heart of this valley.

St. L. to keep pace with West.

The march of St. Louis will keep equal step with the West, located as it is, at the intersection of the river which traverses zones, and the railway which belts the continent, with divergent roads from this centre to the circumference of the country.

Growth immense.

St. Louis enjoys commercial advantages which must inevitably make it the greatest inland emporium of America. The movement of our vast harvests and the distribution of the domestic and foreign merchandize required by the myriad thousands who will, in the near future, throng this valley, will develope St. Louis to a size proportioned to the vastness of the commerce it will transact. This metropolis will not only be the centre of Western enchanges, but also, if ever the seat of Government is transferred from its present locality, the capitol of the nation.

Universal friendship.

St. Louis, strong with the energies of youthful freedom, and active in the larger and more genial labors of peace, will greet the merchants of other States and lands with a friendly welcome, afford them the opportunities of fortune, and honor their services in the achievement of its greatness.

Sum of the the argument.

That is the conclusion, and in large measure the substance, of an argument supposed to prove the truth of its caption; at least to be in its favor. Why *Missouri* is put prominently on the lead, doth not appear. Perhaps it will be influential to bring traitors in the Hannibal and St. Joe region, and others in the "flank movement" region, to their allegiance, and generate a patriotic spirit in filling up those gaps. For as "St. Louis is ordained by the decrees of physical nature to become the great inland metropolis of this continent; it cannot escape the magnificence of its destiny." Neither Professor Waterhouse, nor any other good citizen desires to see nature fail in any of its ordinations. Yet, if "greatness is the necessity of its position," either nature or art has made a good deal of mistake; or such changes in the relative business in favor of Chicago and against St. Louis, would not have been witnessed.

Nature not to be proved false.

Art or nature blunders.

Are barges the perfection of art?

Has it, then, come to this, that nature herself depends upon barge trade to fulfil her ordinations?* Is the barge system of transportation so superior to all other appliances of art, that it can more than counterpoise the lack of railways, and even make good nature's deficiencies? Evidently nature's highways are still relied upon; and with this wonderful perfection of art in barge-towing, nature's decrees are to be fulfilled! What else is there of the argument?

How can barges benefit St. L?

How, in the name of reason, is this barge system to benefit St. Louis? She will have less than ever to do in the grain trade. While "toting" was in vogue from the little steamers above to the mammoth steamers below, she

---

Value of Prof. Waterhouses's paper.

*The Secretary remarks in the Trade Report, introducing Professor Waterhouse's paper:—

"The following interesting letter is one of a series of papers from the pen of of Professor S. Waterhouse, of Washington University, and will be found full of interest to the people of this city and State. Professor Waterhouse is about publishing his articles in pamphlet form, and all classes of our citizens should assist him in his work, as it will be the means of diffusing useful and valuable information concerning the great State of Missouri, and St. Louis, its commercial capital."

Rather Pickwickian.

Although a view of the Professor looking at the future grandeur of St. Louis with barge-spectacles reminds one somewhat of the venerable Mr. Pickwick, the author is evidently sincere and earnest, and must be treated accordingly.

had the profit of the "toting." But with barges loaded up the river for New Orleans, not only "toting" is dispensed with, but St. Louis elevators too. If St. Louis can rejoice in a commerce consisting in tying a barge for hours or days to her levee; or in seeing a squad towed past her without stopping, she will no doubt have her abundant grounds—or rather *water* which is her natural glory. But at Chicago a transfer is made; and though at small cost, yet the immense amount yields good revenues. An extract has been taken from a Chicago paper, the *Republican*, I think, upon this point; though it is over-generous in admitting that barges will be towed over the lakes:—

Dispense with toting.

A transfer at Chi.

Chi. papers upon—

The Northwest and Transportation.—The people of Minnesota are looking forward to the time when a Northern Pacific Railroad shall open to that section of the country another commercial outlet. Senator Ramsey's proposition for the construction of such a railroad, and the purchase of British Columbia and the Hudson Bay territory, only reflected the prevailing sentiments of his constituents. But with all due deference to the opinion of the citizens of that State, we would suggest that the desideratum of Minnesota lies in quite a different direction. The Atlantic, and not the Pacific, is the ocean to which Minnesota grain should go.

—the N. W. and transportation.

Minn. to seek Atl. not Pac.

If the experiment now being tried, of transporting grain to Liverpool by way of New Orleans, instead of New York, proves successful, the great bulk of cereals exported from the Mississippi Valley will drift down stream, and from the barges be loaded into ocean vessels by means of floating elevators. We believe the experiment now being tried by Mr. Merry, of Dunleith, will prove the practicability of the plan, and that a revolution is to be wrought in the transportation of trans-Mississippi grain. Narrow selfishness might make Chicago envious of a project which threatens to break in somewhat upon its grain monopoly; but this city can afford to be generous in sentiment and free from jealousy, and, as a matter of fact, it is. If the producer can do better by sending his grain down river than across the country to New York, he ought to have the facilities for doing it. Steam is of necessity more expensive than water, cars than barges, and if the farmers of the Mississippi Valley can command better prices for their products by down river shipments, we are glad of it. Every dollar saved in the cost of transportation is so much added to the actual wealth of the country.

Barge system on trial.

Probable success.

For Chi. interest—

—with the farmers.

In a few years the canals and the lakes will enable barges loaded on the banks of the Mississippi to reach the ocean without breaking bulk. Until then river transportation will, in the event the Merry experiment succeeds, increase rapidly in importance, and Chicago will indulge no mean envy because the Mississippi does not pour its wealth of water at her feet, the charges of provincial newspapers to the contrary notwithstanding. Eventually, the belt of country rich in mineral and agricultural resources, which extends for a breadth of from six to twelve degrees across the continent west of the Upper Mississippi and Lake Superior, and embracing Minnesota, Dakota, Montana, Idaho, Oregon, Washington, and north of the international line, the great valley of the Saskatchewan and British Columbia, will have railway facilities from ocean to ocean; but all this generation will pass away before that consummation will be reached. In the meanwhile the river on the one hand, and the system of railways, lakes and canals on the other, will be the grand highways of that region.

Barges via the lakes.

Northern belt to have railways by-and-by—

—meanwhile use rivers, etc.

The trade report for 1866, p. 21, has the following:—

St. L. tonnage 1866.

Tonnage of St. Louis and other Ports as Compiled July 1, 1866.

RIVERS	Steamers.	Barges.	Total.	Registered Tonnage.	Carrying Capacity.	Estimated Value.
Lower Mississippi River........	55	30	85	43,345	74,800	$3,970,000
Arkansas and White Rivers....	16	.....	16	3,232	5,925	378,000
Cumberland and Tenn. Rivers.	18	.....	18	3,505	5,925	282,000
Upper Mississippi River........	44	67	111	16,560	30,695	1,625,000
Illinois River........................	16	25	41	5,535	10,355	488,000
Ohio River..........................	45	.....	45	11,217	19,800	1,088,000
Missouri River.....................	71	.....	71	23,232	39,525	2,545,000
Total..............................	265	122	387	106,626	186,015	10,376,000

Transient barges not reckoned.

Barges find favor.

To move heavy freights.

In the list of barges above only those belonging to the regular packets are included. A great number of transient barges and canal boats arrive by Illinois and Upper Mississippi rivers, which are not registered at our port, and not included in the tonnage. The "barge system" is fast finding favor with our merchants, and will, at no distant day, be the prevailing mode of transporting heavy freights, while the fine packets which now grace our western waters will be run *on time* for passengers and light freight. The Mississippi Valley Transportation Company has, during the past summer, demonstrated the fact, that this is the cheapest mode of moving produce and heavy freights, having since May 1st, carried from this port over 110,000 tons. And when the plan of moving grain in bulk is established, the tow boats and barges will add to the commerce of our city by giving cheap freights and saving an immense amount of expense in the shape of handling, tarpaulins and damage.

Compare St. L. and Chi. figures.

Has not the immensity of St. Louis' river commerce been made an important item in calculating St. Louis' superiority? Compare those figures with Chicago lake trade, p. 61. To compare this last year, the following is taken from the Trade Report:—

St. L. Departures 1867.

Departures from St. Louis, 1867.

DATE.	Lower Miss.	Upper Miss.	Missouri.	Illinois.	White.	Cumberland.	Arkansas.	Tennessee.	Ohio.	Yazoo.	Total Steamers.	C. B. and Barges.	Total.	Tonnage.	Wharfage.
January........	12	3	......	......	......	......	3	3	......	......	21	1	22	9,547	$ 833 20
February.....	66	30	2	21	1	2	5	5	9	......	141	16	157	41,469	3,806 00
March.........	81	68	12	53	2	3	8	4	23	1	255	82	337	113,719	7,092 55
April...........	64	83	35	54	2	......	4	3	28	4	277	102	379	123,869	7,977 45
May............	61	87	28	40	2	......	5	6	21	......	250	106	356	113,837	8,217 50
June............	53	87	44	86	1	......	3	5	18	......	247	79	326	107,830	6,681 70
July............	55	87	46	34	......	......	7	4	7	......	240	60	300	104,001	6,298 70
August........	61	102	40	37	......	......	3	3	5	......	251	54	305	109,159	7,288 35
September...	59	102	45	27	1	......	......	3	4	......	241	100	341	109,103	6,813 00
October.......	73	121	20	20	3	......	......	2	6	......	245	146	391	114,282	7,438 40
November....	59	95	28	24	2	......	......	5	9	......	222	161	383	105,782	7,762 90
December.....	47	21	11	4	3	......	......	2	......	......	88	40	128	33,772	5,426 05
Total..........	691	886	311	350	17	5	38	45	130	5	2,478	947	3,425	1,086,320	$75.685 80

That is, her total tonnage is *one million, eighty-six thousand, three hundred and twenty tons.* That of Chicago on the lakes alone, not counting canal boats and barges, is *two million five hundred and eighty-eight thousand, five hundred and seventy-two tons;* over twice and a fourth that of St. Louis. Besides, a boat merely touching at St. Louis, either up or down, the tonnage is counted. But to figure at Chicago, it is there destined. S. L. tonnage, 1,086,-320—Chi. 2,588,-572 tons.

Had we St. Louis figures 10, 20, or 30 years agone to compare with Chicago and observe the progress of one, the relative decadence of the other; it would at least prove, that if the old-fashioned barge system is to be put to the new-fashioned work of stopping both decadence at St. Louis and advance at Chicago, it must be by the process peculiarly St. Louis' own, of inventing new forces in art and nature. Supposing, however, that the barge system *can* do this, *how* shall it be done? Preceding Professor Waterhouse, the Secretary himself had said, pp. 8 and 9 of his report:— Old figures wanted. How barges to work.

It is the desire of the people of the Upper Mississippi Valley to trade with St. Louis. The high reputation and business standing of our merchants is well known, and with the same facilities for transportation, a good share of their products will come to us for sale, and in turn our merchants will supply them with the articles they do not produce. From statistics gathered it is shown, that of 15,000,000 bushels of wheat shipped from points above Rock Island, but 1,000,000 came southward; of 318,000 hogs, none come to this market. The reason is self-evident. The people wish to trade with us, and are loud in their complaints against railroad monopolies, but are powerless because they have no alternative. St. Louis is already a great commercial city, but with these obstacles removed, her resources might be doubled. U. Miss. Val. wants to trade with St. L. But can't. Reason, railways prevent.

The question is very simple, Will barges solve this difficulty to the relief of St. Louis, and "the people of the Upper Mississippi Valley?" They want to give St. Louis the trade; St. Louis wants them to do it. Here is an argument showing not only how it may be done without violence to nature, but by due employment upon its grandest highways, of a most neglected means of art. Who can question either argument or conclusion? No matter that a Chicago Professor, who should start off with such a heading, and conclude with such a demonstration, would be regarded a butt-ender blunt as his barges; the St. Louisian, with a grand flourish of nature, and with the submerging power of a long string of butt-enders, would bury in oblivious waters any futile attempt to question the supremacy of her Majesty of the Rivers. Will barges solve difficulty? An argument—of butt-enders.

If, when the barge system was not in vogue, grain trade had already forsaken the river for the lake route, as the whole evidence attests, how will this new means, rendering still greater facilities to transport grain from any river port directly through to the lakes without a change, benefit St. Louis? That being a hypothetical question is not suitable for discussion here; but the Secretary throws light upon the subject in his succeeding and last Report, pp 7 and 8:— Barges helps lake trade. *Sec. Report.*

The trade of a country follows the products of its soil, and in proportion as we attract to our market the harvests of the country, manufactories, trade and merchandising will increase and prosper. Where the grain is sold there will the goods Trade follows produce.

be bought which are needed in exchange. Trusting too much to natural advantages, and retarded by the late war St. Louis has not advanced as rapidly as her geopraphical position would seem to have warranted. Hitherto our great market was in the Southern States, which had given their whole attention to the raising of cotton and sugar, necessitating the importation of breadstuffs. The change in the entire labor system, and the destitution almost universal in the South, has so interfered with the production of the great staples that they have of necessity been small buyers in our market, and have been compelled to raise food to sustain life. It is not unlikely that this change in the agricultural condition of the South will continue, even when her old prosperity has been regained. For while, with proper encouragement and a settled plan of labor, the cultivation of cotton and the sugar cane will be adopted as the most profitable, yet it is more than probable that the planters and farmers of the South will hereafter depend more upon themselves for the food they eat. Thus St. Louis will be obliged to seek another market for the products which will come to her from the North and West, and must open up other avenues of trade.

Geographical position not well supported.

South to depend on itself.

St. L. seek another market.

Facilities requisite.

First, we must have the proper facilities for handling, storing, and shipping produce cheaply. Next, we must establish, through New Orleans, facilities for exporting direct to the South American and European States the surplus product of the Mississippi Valley. This accomplished, the trade will flow to St. Louis as naturally as the great river flows to the Gulf. And as trade seeks an outlet southward, the railroad interests west of the Mississippi, so long languishing, will receive new impetus. The great States yet to be established in the far west will of necessity be in a measure dependent upon some point near the Mississippi, and with proper energy St. Louis will secure that trade; for with a direct export trade via New Orleans, furnishing the quickest and cheapest mode of transportation, the products of other countries must naturally come back to us by the same channel, to be distributed throughout the West. Much has been done in the past year towards the accomplishment of these projects.

Trade flows naturally to St. L.—

—and foreign trade.

Railroads spoken of by Directors.

The Report goes on to discuss river improvements making and to be made, and though the Secretary says nothing about railroads, the report of the Directors, p. 13, remarks:—

Adverse circumstances beginning of year.

The year opened with high values in produce, supported, as it was soon found, by a scarcity almost equivalent to the results of a famine; and the new crops, although more abundant, have been kept away from us much by low water, with a six months' protracted drought, and diverted to railroad communications east, necessitating with us higher prices than consumers expect to pay in the heart of a great producing region, and especially damaging to our trade with the South, so illy prepared by a succession of two poor crops and the condition of their section to be free buyers.

Causes considered.

This alteration of our old abundance and activity in trade has drawn the attention of our merchants to examination into the causes, and the year has been very active in conventions and deliberations.

Facilities to learn about St. L.

Commencing with the River Improvement Convention in February, followed by the Senatorial Visits in June, and the Millers' Convention in July, there has been afforded, during the past year, much opportunity for strangers to know more particularly of us and our surroundings and resources, and gives me pleasure to say it has caused a light expense to the Chamber, and has resulted in establishing a friendly feeling and coöperation among the cities of the Mississippi Valley, favoring advantageous results in the near future.

Good feeling.

Visitors call their attention to railroads.

The Chamber has also had much attention called to railroads, by visits of parties connected with the many roads pointing here; and it is gratifying to notice the universal wish, both North and South, East and West, to make St. Louis the point for their connections, requiring of us but good will and zeal in seconding their endeavors to be our customers.

What prevents a rush to St. L?

Now, with not only the Northwest and St. Louis friendly, but the whole country waiting to rush into its natural centre, what can be the adverse influences which prevent St. Louis from attaining that destiny which has not only been ordained by nature, but which the whole country demands?

If all these conventions prove ineffective to bring art to fulfil its duty to nature, will not the barges, as they make obeisance to the Queen of the Rivers with the screaming whistle, as in long lines they sail past her, or with elegant curve turn bows up-stream to tie up for a while, fulfil these reasonable expectations and desires?

The Secretary argues, that as "the trade of a country follows the products of its soil," it must come to St. Louis. But does he not prove too much for a sound argument? Goes not the trade with its barges on to New Orleans? How is that to benefit St. Louis? Sec. proves too much—sends trade to N. O.

The war it will have been observed, is made by the Secretary and Professor, the cause of decline in grain trade. But the quotations, pp. 111–114 were made expressly to disprove that position from their own papers in 1861. Col. Foster's able Report at the Ship Canal Convention in 1864, remarks:— The war not cause of decline. *Col. Foster's Rep.*

The Committee of the Chicago Board of Trade, in a recent report, say: *Chi. Board of Trade.*

"In the early settlement of the West, the Mississippi was the only outlet for the products of the country; but the opening of the New York and Canadian canals, and of not less than five trunk railways between the East and West, has rendered the free navigation of the Mississippi a matter of secondary importance. Miss. formerly a necessary route.

"The heated waters of a tropical sea, destructive to most of our articles of export; a malarious climate, shunned by every Northerner for at least one-half of the year; and a detour in the voyage of over 3,000 miles in a direct line to the markets of the world;—these considerations have been sufficiently powerful to divert the great flow of animal and vegetable food from the South to the East. Up to 1860, the West found a local market for an inconsiderable portion of her bread-stuffs and provisions in the South; but, after supplying this local demand, the amount which was exported from New Orleans was insignificant, hardly exceeding two millions of dollars per annum." Gulf difficulties. Only local demand at South.

The annual report of the Secretary of the Treasury, for the year ending August 31, 1860, shows the amount of bread-stuffs and provisions exported to foreign countries from New Orleans and New York respectively, as follows:— *Treas. Rep.*

Exports from N. Y and N. O.

Articles.		From New Orleans.	From New York.
Wheat	Bushels	2,189	1,880,908
Wheat	Barrels	80,541	1,187,200
Indian Corn	Bushels	224,382	1,580,014
Indian Meal	Barrels	158	86,073
Pork	Barrels	4,250	109,379
Hams and Bacon	Pounds	890,230	16,161,749

The total receipts of grain of all kinds, at that port, in no single year exceeded 14,500,000 bushels, either for exportation or consumption in the interior, which are about the receipts at Milwaukee, or Toledo. In 1859-60, the receipts were as follows:— N. O. equal to Mil. or Toledo.

Grain exports.

FLOUR. bbls.	WHEAT. sacks and bbls.	CORN. sacks and bbls.	OATS. sacks and bbls.
965,860	339,348	1,722,637	659,550

These facts show conclusively that, with the navigation of the Mississippi unobstructed, the great mass of western exports would flow through other channels. Grain seeks other channels.

St. L depends on direct shipments to Europe— Several articles from St. Louis papers have been extracted showing their confident expectations from direct shipments to Europe. But space need not be taken. Could a quarter of the whole products of the Mississippi —Chi. wants it. Valley go to market by the Mississippi instead of lakes, it would be to the advantage of Chicago. No such portion will go except occasionally; but Her interest with farmers. could it, the competition would inure to the benefit of the farmers, as we shall see; and Chicago prospers precisely with that interest. She has and always must have so much shipping business, that her advantage lies in making the utmost possible of rival routes. We hope sincerely that St. Louis may realize her full hopes from barges; yet, for every one unloaded at St. Louis, may not ten be discharged at Chicago?

Generosity costs Chi. nothing. But upon this question of river and lake competition, Chicago can afford to be generous, for it can cost her nothing. If St. Louis take advantage of nature in down-river navigation, she must take with it the more than Climate against river route. counterbalancing disadvantage of nature in climate. This subject has had thorough consideration by competent parties. In the introduction to the Considered in *U. S. Census Reports.* U. S. Census of 1860, the question of production and of marketing facilities is discussed. After considering internal grain trade, exhibiting lake shipments, and direct trade between the lakes and Europe, we have the following, p. clv:—

Grain trade of Miss. Valley. *The Grain Trade of the Mississippi River.*—The grain trade of the Mississippi and Ohio rivers has, for upwards of a quarter of a century, occupied an important place in the commercial history of the United States. In the early part of the present century, before the era of canals and railroads, the tide of emigration forced itself into the valleys of these rivers and laid the foundation of what soon became large River towns before lake towns. and flourishing settlements. Before Chicago, Milwaukee, and Toledo had existence, other than as small trading posts, Cincinnati, on the Ohio, and St. Louis, on the Mississippi river, were comparatively large towns, with a trade and commerce Miss. natural outlet. which attracted capital from all parts of the world. The Mississippi river was the natural outlet for this trade to the ocean, and New Orleans became at an early day the only exporting point for the grain products of the west.

Settlements along Ohio and Miss. rivers. The valley of the Ohio river, embracing the States of Ohio, Indiana, and Kentucky, was settled first, and the grain trade of that river proper is therefore the oldest. But the fertile lands of the river tier of counties in Illinois and Missouri soon attracted the attention of agriculturalists, and the grain trade of the Mississippi river proper followed; and as we have shown in a previous chapter, before steamboat Barges used. navigation had made much progress. the grain was shipped chiefly in rude barges and carefully floated down the Mississippi to New Orleans, where it found a market, and was shipped to foreign ports. And even, at no distant date, all the western grain and flour which found a market in New York or New England was shipped to New Orleans in steamboats, and thence around the Atlantic coast in Ocean ships.

This the origin of barges. Its inefficiency. Here is the origin of the barge trade, now expedited by tugs instead of river current. To show its inefficiency, in contrast with previous lake shipments, tables are given for a series of years of flour and grain from Cincinnati, St. Louis, and New Orleans, and the Editor remarks:—

Change of trade from rivers to lakes. A comparison of the foregoing tables with those illustrating the grain trade of the lakes and of the Erie canal, demonstrates the revolution that has taken place in the grain trade of the west. The trade and commerce of the Mississippi river, so far as relates to grain and other produce, has not kept pace with the development of the territory through which it runs, and for which it is the natural highway to the ocean. The old theory that "trade will follow the rivers" has in some respects been disproved. The artificial channels of trade, canals and railroads have tapped the west and carried its products eastward across the continent. The grain trade of Illinois, Iowa, Missouri, Wisconsin, and even the greater portion of that of Indiana and Ohio, have been diverted almost entirely to the lakes, the Erie canal, the St. Lawrence river, or the six great trunk lines of railroads that lead from the heart of the west to the seaboard. The Mississippi river has been bridged at Rock Island, and another bridge is just being completed at Clinton, farther up. The lines of railroads which extend from Lake Michigan to this river are being pushed forward with great rapidity to the Missouri river, and into Kansas and Nebraska, and there is every probability that the grain of these frontier States will also find a market by way of the lakes. Even now grain is being received at Chicago from Kansas and Nebraska *via* the Missouri river, the Hannibal and St. Joseph railroad, and the Chicago, Burlington and Quincy railroad. As an outlet to the ocean for the grain trade of the west, the Mississippi river has almost ceased to be depended upon by merchants. There are several reasons for this change:—

Artificial channels East.

Miss. bridges.

Take trade West of Miss. to lakes.

Miss. almost abandoned for grain.

First.—The risk of damage to grain and flour that may be shipped during the summer months through the southern latitudes of the Gulf of Mexico, as compared with the transportation by the northern routes, viz., around the lakes and through the Erie Canal, or *via* the St. Lawrence river. This applies particularly to corn, which is more liable to become heated than any other kind of grain.

Reasons, 1, Climate.

Second.—The uncertainty of river navigation during the summer months, in droughty seasons, and the vexatious and ruinous delays that are apt to occur in consequence.

2, uncertainty.

Third.—The speedy transportation by railroads and canals on the northern route, as compared with transportation by river to New Orleans, and thence by ocean ships around the Atlantic coast.

3, railroad speed.

Fourth.—The superior advantages which New York during the past ten or fifteen years has attained as an importing point, as compared with New Orleans, thus offering greater inducements to ocean shipping to trade with New York.

4, N. Y. superior to N. O.

Fifth.—The rapid growth of the cotton, sugar and tobacco trade at New Orleans, to the exclusion of almost every other branch of trade and commerce.

5, magnitude of other products.

A glance at the table of receipts of grain at New Orleans during the six years previous to the blockade of the Mississippi river, as compared with the great movement of grain during the same period eastward by the Erie canal and the St. Lawrence river, shows clearly the diversion which has taken place in this trade. The entire receipts of grain in New Orleans in 1860 amounted to only 5,198,927 bushels, while the receipts during the same year at the single port of Chicago, amounted to about fifty million of bushels, while Milwaukee received about ten million. The exportation of grain from New Orleans to foreign countries had also fallen off year by year, till in 1860 the entire amount exported was only 2,189 bushels of wheat 224,382 bushels of corn, and rye, oats and small grain to the value of $1,943, while during the year 1860–'61 there were exported from New York 23,859,147 bushels of wheat, 9,268,729 bushels of corn, and 2,728,012 barrels of flour.

N. O. receipts and routes East.

Compared with Chi.

Diminished exports.

Amts. at N. O. and N. Y.

In the late autumn, winter and early spring, some four months, the heat is not a difficulty; but then the sources are frozen up. Still, considerable amounts can be brought by rail to St. Louis, whence the river is usually open, also to Cairo and other ports; and we sincerely wish they could always send abroad far more than they ever will.

Notwithstanding obstacles—

—hope that route can be used.

Chi. Journal.

Indicative of the present course of trade, the following is clipped from the *Chicago Journal*, March 30th:—

Export bread-stuffs to Gt. Brit.

Export of Breadstuffs.—The following shows the export of Breadstuffs from the United States to Great Britain and Ireland, from 1st September, 1867, to dates undermentioned.

5 Atl. ports.

FROM	Flour, brls.	Wheat, bu.	Corn, bu.
New York, March 18	293,737	4,736,899	3,910,296
New Orleans, March 11	253	36,947	253,148
Philadelphia, March 14	13,201	33,889	300,701
Baltimore, March 14	5,679	....	397,288
Boston, March 14	13,824	....	2,302
Other ports, latest dates	39,034	4,029,676	. 45,917
Total, 1867–8	365,228	8,837,411	4,906,652
Total, 1866–7	88,226	2,890,247	4,761,052
Increase	277,002	5,947,164	158,600
Total, 1865–6	112,798	1,055,236	5,434,499
Total, 1864–5	81,839	1,367,136	61,159

To Continent.

To the Continent.

	Flour, brls.	Wheat, bu.	Corn, bu.
New York, March 4	37,882	284,759	33,251
Other points, latest dates	13,245	81,231	....
Total.			
1867–8	51,127	365,990	38,261
1866–7	2,207	53,220	8,261
1865–6	10,962	71,722	9,985
1864–5	50,962	71,722	9,985

Only produce trade considered. Maxim wrong that trade follows produce. Other trade seeks railway. How can St. L. get it?

Following up the recent and strongest St. Louis arguments, has led us to consider almost exclusively one branch of trade, that of produce, in which it would seem Chicago has nought to fear. From their stand-point, that other trade follows produce, their line of argument is not surprising; nor would Chicago fear competition did that maxim hold true. But hereafter that will be shown to be erroneous. Years before the war, as she herself admits, she had largely lost grain-trade, yet held jobbing trade, of which the war, however, loosened her hold. By what means is she to regain it? That, of all branches, seeks the railway; and with our roads already built, ramifying the territory in every direction upon which she depended, and she in vain struggling to get a few cross lines,—more feeders to Chicago than to St. Louis,—how is she to prevent the disparity in trade statistics, not only from continuing but increasing?

We have before considered results where competition was direct, and the last report of the Chicago & Alton Road having since come to hand, an extract is taken confirmatory of the expectation expressed in the previous report quoted, p.95:— *Chi. & Alton R. R. Rep.*

The gross earnings exceed those of the preceding year by $197,708,62 or about 5½ per cent. The receipts from passenger traffic being $36,588,92 less, and from freight traffic $234,297,52 more than in 1866. Increase 1867.

The increased amount of earnings from freight traffic is mainly due to the accession of business from the St. Louis, Jacksonville and Chicago road since its connection with your line at Bloomington, on the 23d of September last. Although the two lines were connected at that date, the remaining three months of the year were occupied by the St. Louis, Jacksonville and Chicago Company in constructing sidings and station buildings, and in procuring rolling stock necessary for the transaction of its business. The amount of traffic contributed to your line was, therefore, much less than it would have been, had that Company been fully prepared for business when the connection was made. The amount of your earnings on joint business with that line, received mainly during the last three months of the year, was, exclusive of the 10 per cent. bonus paid to them per contracts dated January 25th, 1864 as follows: On passenger traffic, $40,950,08; on freight traffic, $214,514,05; making an aggregate of $255,464,13. Freight increase due to new road, St. L., Jacksonville & Chi. Not yet full trade.

While the cash receipts from passenger traffic on your line are less, the number of passengers carried exceeds that of the preceding year by 14,674; the number in 1866 being 516,543; and in 1867, 531,217; the increase being in local traffic. Increase of passengers.

The number of local or way passengers carried in 1866 being 477,578, and in 1867 494,601, showing an increase of 17,023, or about 3½ per cent. The proportion between the number of way and through passengers being 93 per cent., of the former to 7 per cent., of the latter. Local travel.

The average amount of fare paid by way passengers during the year, is found to be one dollar and seventy-one cents.

The increased tonnage of freight in 1867 over 1866, is equal to nearly 18 per cent. The proportion between through and local freight being 12 4-10 per cent., of the former, to 87 6-10 per cent., of the latter. Local freight

Every Chicago road westerly and southerly, will increase local traffic in like manner. Only a small part of the arable land contiguous to any road, is yet under culture. Morgan and Jersey counties transacted nearly their whole business with St. Louis, being only 30 to 80 miles distant, and we 200 and over. This is wholly changed by opening a branch road through that rich country, connecting with Chicago by the main line from Alton, at Bloomington. Is that region to be considered exceptional, because in Illinois, and favorable to Chicago? Then consider tendency in the far West. Nor is the *Atchison* (Kansas) *Free Press*, of March 10th, more correct in comparing results, than in contrasting operating influences between Chicago and St. Louis:— All local traffic thus to increase. Trade diverted from St. L. to Chi. *Atchison (Kan.) Free Press.*

A Comparison.—There are two great business centres in the West—Chicago and St. Louis. Each of them is extending its arms to draw to its bosom the trade which otherwise will fall to its rival. There was a time when St. Louis was the centre of all the trade of the West; that was when nearly everything depended upon the trade in furs and the French were the only white inhabitants of the Mississippi Valley, and the region of the upper lakes. When Cincinnati was but a hamlet, gathered around Fort Washington, and but few pioneers from Pennsylvania and Virginia had begun to penetrate the forests of Southern Ohio and Indiana, the French had already an occupancy of all the tributaries of the Mississippi, and St. Louis was the focus of all their traffic. Merchandise found its way up that stream from New Orleans, and was at St. Louis exchanged for furs and peltries, which the *voyageurs* brought in from every valley of the West. Long after the West was transferred from the French to the Government of the United States, and emigration had poured its myriads from the Eastern States into the Mississippi Valley, St. Louis continued to retain the character it had early formed. Its merchants were St. L. and Chi. compared. St. L. had trade. Fur trade. St. L. on its dignity.

staid, substantial men. The current of their business flowed on as smoothly as the placid waters upon which all their commerce floated. The nervous, far sighted, often reckless Yankee was not there, or if he came he could not unloose the purse strings of those whose wealth was necessary to extend speedily from that point the arms of a railroad system over the West. And so it is, in a great measure, to this day.

St. L. strong before Chi. started. Chicago had not begun to spring up until long after St. Louis had become opulent in her quiet wealth and ease. But shrewd and active merchants at length set their stakes at Chicago. At first they bought grain by the wagon load, and sent it all by schooners down the lakes. Chi. railroads. Then they commenced the construction of railroads. In all directions they caused them to push their way out over the prairies to bring in the production of the ten thousand farms, opened upon the exhaustless soil of all the States over which the ordinance of 1787 had spread its ægis of freedom. Merchants. St. Louis merchants clung to the fogyism and the faith of their correspondents away down the Mississippi. Chicago merchants comprehended the most progressive ideas Elevators. of modern commerce; and they sent out their iron rails, and erected their towering castles for the reception of all the grain of the Northwest. Cairo cut off. Chicago railroads cut St. Louis off on the east, away down to Cairo, long ago; cut across the State of Missouri to the Missouri River, long ago, and penetrated the heart of Iowa, and cut Routes West. across Wisconsin to Minnesota. Now they reach across Kansas by two lines—one by the way of Cameron, Kansas City, and the Eastern division, Pacific; the other by the Central Branch, Pacific, from Atchison. They cross Nebraska by the Pacific Trunk, to the Rocky Mountains. They reach the Territory of Dakota at Sioux City. And everywhere these iron arms are being rapidly lengthened out.

Nebraska trade. Chicago merchants bought Nebraska grain two years ago, and paid more for it than would St. Louis merchants, though the latter could bring it to their own mills without change of bulk. And it is not only grain, but the beef and the pork of the Northwest that the Chicago merchants monopolize by their superior enterprise. We published the other day the statistics of Chicago beef and pork packing. St. Louis can make no such showing.

Transferring exchange. While Chicago has gathered up the produce of the West and marketed it in every Eastern city and in Europe she has kept her exchange accounts even. The grain merchant does not from his sales bring currency from the East to buy more grain with. He gets a bill of exchange. This is transferred to the Chicago dry goods and grocery merchant.

Chi. enterprise. To every point from whence comes grain to the Chicago market, Chicago dry goods and grocery merchants send bills of goods. Every Northwestern town is visited by the Chicago merchant, and orders solicited. Every newspaper in the Northwest teems with inducements offered by Chicago merchants to retail dealers. These inducements are real and they are accepted. The Chicago merchant has his arrangements for shipping complete. His transfers, if any, are made with the utmost facility. Every stream is bridged or is being bridged. Not many months hence Chicago will reach the uttermost confines of every Northwestern State without breaking bulk.

St. L. spasmodic. Modern St. Louis men are working out a railroad system—but at a slow pace. St. Louis merchants, at the spring rise in the rivers, manifest much spasmodic life, and they sell considerable bills of goods. But the unceasing enterprise, the unfailing energy of the Chicago merchant is wanting among the merchants of St. Louis.

2 errors— These views are sound upon every point save two—1st, that any amount of effort on the part of St. Louis, could have averted her fate; 2d, that Chicago citizens have built our railways. These lie at the basis of this —fundamental. discussion, as to whether the Northwest has a natural centre, and where it is. Chicago hands have been reached out in all directions, but whence comes Is "St. L. commercial centre of N. A.?" the moving power, the soul? Whether the pretension that "St. Louis is the commercial centre of North America" be true or not, is a momentous question upon which the entire business mind of the continent needs to be settled. With becoming seriousness, I trust, it has been considered, despite ridiculous pretensions, inclining to ludicrous treatment. Some points, too, have been iterated and reiterated; yet do not prevalent impressions justify? When the

truth is known, words can be saved; and till known and acknowledged, reiteration is indispensable. It is quite problematic, however, whether the more effective method be not that of the *Chicago Times*, which thus medicates:— Repetition necessary. *Chi. Times.*

The Troubles of St. Louis.—St. Louis attributes all her failing, losses and troubles to Chicago. If there were no Chicago, St. Louis would be increased; it would be the centre of trade, commerce, piety and civilization. It would supply the world with food and with light, with religion and beer. But Chicago has grown up to the windward of St. Louis, Chicago has grown up between St. Louis and the sunlight, and the venerable old town spends its long winter evenings when it is cut off from all postal or railway and ferryboat communication with the rest of the world, in gossip and scandal about its younger, handsomer and dashing sister, Chicago. St. L's troubles. Chi. interferes.

St. Louis has a "railroad system" running West, which was intended to bring all the trade of Western Missouri, Kansas and the farther West to that city. It so happens that each of the roads in this "system" has a connection with some other road which communicates directly with Chicago. The people of St. Louis, unable to understand why Missourians and Kansasians should go to Chicago to purchase goods, got up a theory that the roads made a discrimination in freight in favor of Chicago against St. Louis. Upon this theory the newspapers and the Board of Trade have been denouncing the railway officers, and accusing them of directing trade from that city to the metropolis upon Lake Michigan. The railroad officers make answer, showing that the discriminations in freight charges are largely against Chicago and in favor of St. Louis, and yet trade has preferred to come to Chicago. The figures of freight charges are thus given:— Railroads designed for her benefit— —run to Chi. Unjust discrimination charged.

"During the past season the rates of freight have been as follows:— Rates compared.

	1st class.	2d class.	3d class.	4th class.
New York to St. Louis	$2.42	1.90	1.40	1.00
New York to Chicago	1.88	1.60	1.27	82
New York to Kansas City	3.19	2.54	1.99	1.48
Chicago to Kansas City	1.30	1.15	97	77
St. Louis to Kansas City	60	50	40	40

Now it readily appears from the above figures that the rates of freight instead of being in favor of the Chicago merchants are really largely in favor of our St. Louis people; for instance, adding the rates from St. Louis to Kansas City to the New York rates we have: First class, $3.02; second class, $2.40; third class, $1.80; fourth class, $1.40, as the entire from New York on goods purchased in St. Louis, while on the same goods purchased in Chicago the cost of transportation from New York to Kansas City would be: First class, $3.18; second class, $2.75; third class, $2.24; fourth class, $1.59." Against Chi. in favor of St. L.

The reason why trade will pass by St. Louis and come to Chicago is as great a mystery as ever in St. Louis. The Board of Trade have given up all attempts to explain it. The Academy of Sciences will investigate it as soon as the absent members can find a cake of ice upon which they can safely cross the river to their native shores. Mystery why trade comes to Chi. instead of St. L.

It is also an important consideration that these rapid and immense relative changes have been accomplished, not only against long-established currents of business, but against large wealth. Prof. Waterhouse remarked:— St. L's large wealth. *Prof. Waterhouse.*

Our commerce is aided by ample banking facilities. There are in St. Louis, in addition to more than 20 private banks, 32 incorporated banking institutions, with an actual capital of $15,000,000. The character of our banks stands deservedly high in the financial world. St. L. banks.

To boast of superior capital and larger banks, is to glory in her shame. Says the *N. Y. Evening Post*, January 18th:— *N. Y. Eve. Post.*

St. Louis versus Chicago.—St. Louis having been rather worsted in the recent dispute with Chicago as to the relative value and importance of the two cities in St. L. *vs* Chi.

some of their commercial, political, and social aspects, has now found a feature in which it thinks it can equal its rival. This is in the business of its banks, not the river banks, but the financial institutions so called. The regular annual statement of the two cities has been published, and St. Louis finds to its great satisfaction that in the amount of banking capital in circulation, and in deposits, the banks of Chicago are inferior to its own. Seventeen St. Louis banks have a capital of $9,-283,610, that of twelve Chicago banks is $5,200,000. The eight national banks of St. Louis have a circulation of $3,118,091, against $3,930,277 of the twelve national banks of Chicago. In deposits the St. Louis banks hold $13,682,545,39 to $12,567,-752,01, in those of Chicago. These differences in favor of St. Louis cause great exultation in the Journals of that city and one of them remarks, "St. Louis continues as heretofore, to lead her fussy and boastful rival by a large amount."

St. L. asserts superiority, in banks.

She exults.

This point, however, is less alluded to as touching St. Louis than to benefit ourselves. With this commercial superiority, unexampled facilities for transacting business near and remote, very desirable opportunities to invest capital must be afforded. This we need to have well apprehended abroad by large and small capitalists. One of the chief benefits from this discussion, is the evidence presented upon this essential point. Notwithstanding our progress, no city of half the size and trade has so little cash capital. Herein to the initiated is the chief wonder at our advancement; and although considerable wealth is being accumulated, yet probably no other city offers equal inducements for capital, either regarding safety or profits. Yet care and skill in choice are quite as requisite here as elsewhere; perhaps even more important, because of unexampled opportunities. With proper discretion, all sorts of investments may be made, in loans, banks, railway stocks, real estate, or in active business of any kind, with safety at least equal to other cities, and much stronger promise of profits.

Chi. needs capital.

To prove this our object.

No city offers equal inducements.

This very important topic has spun out immoderately. Yet who can forbear to consider, that, with these unexampled commercial advantages, responsibilities of Chicago merchants are correspondingly multiplied to GOD and country. Let us realize these responsibilities, and employ all these advantages now in these early years of development, so that while our sons shall bless their fathers, each succeeding generation shall thrice bless us, and the Father of our spirits who moved us to the work. Considering the lofty responsibility of a merchant-prince of Chicago, not merely to the poor Indian and Negro, who will soon have disappeared, but to the Mongolian, which is next to feel Caucasian power, as in fulfilment of Paul's prediction at Athens, and in possessing our GOD-given right of dominion, we go on to occupy the whole earth; nothing could be a more fit conclusion of this, and appropriate introduction of the succeeding topic, than this extract from an address of that most excellent Christian, Dr. Channing, before the Mercantile Library Company of Philadelphia, in 1841:—

Our responsibilities for these advantages.

Inferior races to be cared for.

Dr. Channing.

Commerce is a noble calling. It mediates between distant nations, and makes men's wants, not as formerly, stimulants to war, but bonds of peace. The universal intellectual activity of which I have spoken, is due, in no small degree, to commerce, which spreads the thoughts, inventions, and writings of great men over the earth, and gathers scientific and literary men everywhere into an intellectual republic. So it carries abroad the missionary, the Bible, the cross, and is giving universality to true religion. Gentlemen, allow me to express an earnest desire and hope, that the

Commerce noble—

—Christianizing.

merchants of this country will carry on their calling with these generous views. Let them not pursue it for themselves alone. Let them rejoice to spread improvements far and wide, and to unite men in more friendly ties. Let them adopt maxims of trade which will establish general confidence. Especially in their intercourse with less cultivated tribes, let them feel themselves bound to be harbingers of civilization. Let their voyages be missions of humanity, useful arts, science, and religion. It is a painful thought, that commerce, instead of enlightening and purifying less privileged communities, has too often made the name of Christian hateful to them; has carried to the savage not our useful arts and mild faith, but weapons of war and the intoxicating draught. I call not on God to smite with his lightnings, to overwhelm with his storms, the accursed ship which goes to the ignorant, rude native, freighted with poison and death; which goes to add new ferocity to savage life, new licentiousness to savage sensuality. I have learned not to call down fire from heaven. But in the name of humanity, of religion, of God, I implore the merchants of this country not to use the light of a higher civilization to corrupt, to destroy our uncivilized brethren. Brethren, they are in those rude huts, in their wild attire. Establish with them an intercourse of usefulness, justice, and charity. Before they can understand the name of Christ, let them see his spirit in those by whom it is borne.

Merchants to be generous.

Extend civilization.

Do not corrupt.

Teach Christ in acts.

Allow me to say a word to the merchants of our country on another subject. The time is come when they are particularly called to take yet more generous views of their vocation, and to give commerce a universality as yet unknown. I refer to the juster principles which are gaining ground on the subject of free trade, and to the growing disposition of nations to promote it. Free trade!—this is the plain duty and plain interest of the human race. To level all barriers to free exchange; to cut up the system of restriction, root and branch. To this, a free nation should especially pledge itself. Freedom of the seas; freedom of harbors; an intercourse of nations, free as the winds; this is not a dream of philanthropists. We are tending towards it, and let us hasten it. Under a wise and more Christian civilization, we shall look back on our present restrictions as we do on the swaddling-bands by which, in darker times, the human body was compressed. The growing freedom of trade is another and glorious illustration of the tendency of our age to universality.

Free trade.

The interest of man.

We tend towards it.

Manufacturing Advantages of Chicago—Rapid Progress.

Whether due regard for commerce would lead to free-trade at an early day, as Dr. Channing seems to have thought above, may be questioned. What we would like to have,—what man may yet attain unto in his perfect day,—is one thing; what we should have, and what restraints should be put upon our freedom as we are to-day, is quite another.

Present free trade doubtful.

For man's best good, various interests have been created, all of which the Creator has bound together by indissoluble bonds. We exist, however, not merely as individuals, but as families, States, Nations. In these varied relations, our rights, duties, interests, sympathies, vary; and we err greatly in misapplying those of one condition or *status* to another. The State, the source of our every civil right, as Aristotle taught, "is first founded that men may live, but continued that they may live happily." Its nature being wholly different from the individual,—the latter a weak, dependent, dying creature; the former immortal, if the laws of its being be duly regarded, and independent and omnipotent as anything human can be—so are the laws governing. The various *stati*, too, are instituted to advance the best interests of the individual, facilitating his progress for time, the better to qualify him for the future world. These *stati* end in time, but man individually is for eternity.

All branches to be cared for.

Duties vary.

Nature of States

Laws to be regarded.

In these several *stati*, man has his responsibilities, in each of which he must regard the Laws of Nature and of Nature's GOD thereto applying. While individuals should seek the best good of individuals the world over, States are to seek the best good of States the world over. Peace, next to honor and glory, is the highest good, and war the greatest evil of States. Hence, it is the first object of all GOD-fearing nations to preserve peace. No means to this is more effectual than to be prepared for war. The best preparation is that every nation, as far as it may, possess within itself the means requisite to its defence, existence and comfort. So far as it depends upon other countries for luxuries, and still more necessaries, so far is it at the mercy of its enemies, if they possess power to cut off its supplies. He as an individual who disregards the fundamental truth that he is in a world of contention and struggle, is no more unwise than the State which prepares solely for peace.

States seek peace.

Must be independent.

Commerce not to be disregarded.

At the same time, the diversity of climate and of productions is not to be overlooked, and a country can best obtain its supplies of many articles from foreigners, paying in something which it produces advantageously. By commerce a nation avails itself of the capital and labor of other nations; and the higher the civilization, the more will it be employed. But entire free-trade seems to belong to that blessed condition of man ages hence when he learns war no more. The wise statesman does not imagine that wisdom will die with this generation, and deals with man as he is, not as he ought to be. While he would promote commerce by all legitimate means, he at the same time does his best to render his country independent and self-sustaining. Commerce and manufactures are alike indispensable to a nation's prosperity and greatness, and each should have due care and encouragement from the Government, which is instituted solely as an agency to promote the State's best good. Man's Creator not having given hearts to States, we can exhibit wisdom in some better way than by endeavoring to convert States into philanthropists. Especially should that truth be realized here in this New World, which has been kept back from our race until our present stage of progress. Our duties are here, not in Asia or Europe. Yet what better good can we do even to them, than to pursue that policy which is best calculated to draw here their superabundant men and money? And to the philanthropist, what other field promises equal results.

Future free-trade.

Commerce and manufactures both needed.

States no philanthropists.

Gov't to care for all interests.

The interests of the State—of this Nation of States—should be cared for by the Government to which they have been so largely committed, according to their relative importance. One is not to be neglected for another, but each and all should have due attention. Immense as is the commercial interest, it dwindles in comparison with either agriculture or manufactures, both as to men and capital employed. But while agriculture tends to diffuse, manufactures are the most powerful means to concentrate population. This tendency to concentration, as we shall see, is the one subject of all others to be considered in ascertaining the destiny of Chicago; and therefore the past

Manufactures concentrate.

and future of manufacturing in our country, is a most important element in the computation. Nothing more comprehensive, just, appreciative, has come under observation, than the "Preliminary views" to the volume upon manufactures in the U. S. Census of 1860, from Mr. Edmunds:— *Editor of U. S. Census.*

Nature, in the wide dominion allotted to man, has given him the means, in some latitudes spontaneously, but everywhere through *labor*, of supporting life from the products of the soil, whilst he has been invested with the faculty of reason and invention, whereby to discover the secret agencies of the material world, and so direct them as to change its products into new forms—forms of utility, endless variety, and beauty—all ministering to the end of promoting the comfort, prosperity, and happiness of our race; and these are classed by political economists under the general name of manufactures. Nature gives means — —man employs them for his good

The agriculturalist opens the earth, and so disposes the seed that, aided by heat, moisture, and the silent but ever active agencies of nature, he secures the reward of his diligence and skill. Farmer's work.

The preceding volumes of the Census of 1860 indicate the population in that year of this Empire-Republic, and the agricultural products which the labor of our people, in the diversity of our soils and climate, has brought from the bosom of the earth in such abundance as not only to support thirty-one and a half millions of inhabitants in 1860, but with an immense surplus for foreign markets. His products

The statesman or historian, in glancing over the past seven or eight generations to the period when feeble settlements were first established on these then barbarous shores, and in an unopened wilderness, will trace the causes of our progress and advance in civilization. He will find in our constitution and laws security to persons and property—the incentives to individual enterprise. * Security of our Constitution and Laws.

It has been forcibly said that the "accumulation of capital which has taken place in England during the last hundred years, and which, besides enabling that nation to defray, with little difficulty, the cost of so many protracted and destructive wars, has covered the land with cities and all sorts of improvements, and the ocean with ships, would either not have taken place at all, or but in a very subordinate degree, had there been any serious doubt about its present or future security, or about the abilty of the owner to employ it, or bequeath at pleasure." English security— —basis of prosperity

These elements of steadiness and security are found in our political system, the spirit of which is against monopolies, and favors freedom of industry and trade. Our policy is in no respect exclusive in dealing with great industrial interests; it invites competition at home and from abroad, encourages immigration, conceding to foreigners, after a limited period of residence, the privileges of a native-born citizen. It opens up to all the vast fields of the public domain, the common inheritance of our people, and presents a surface of every variety of climate and soil equal to the support of the human race, according to the ratio to a square mile of the Belgian population. From these broad acres liberal donations have been conceded for the establishment of schools, colleges—agricultural and mechanical—universities, and works of internal improvement on a stupendous scale. Same elements ours. Nothing exclusive. Benefits.

---

* The importance of this truth will grow with its consideration. Too little do we ourselves, much less foreigners, appreciate the stimulus and moulding power which Government exerts upon individual character. Those who give any attention to politics being completely engaged with the most practical affairs of government, the rest wholly absorbed in practical enjoyment resulting from the employment of the unequaled natural advantages here so profusely spread—no more the direct gift of our God than are our political advantages, and of even less moment for time, far less for eternity—the science of our wonderful compound but not complex system, has had too little attention. With the rights of conquest of eleven of these States cast upon us, we shall find more wisdom, more knowledge of principles of political science, requisite in the children to preserve, than in the fathers to frame our system. Yet meagre as was their knowledge, ours is still less. These practical citizens will not plod on much longer in the difficult paths of reconstruction of our shattered but not destroyed Union, without inquiring whether more light from political science will not avail us; and when they find we have the solid basis of State Sovereignty, not the false one of consolidated National Sovereignty,—not even partly so, as Madison taught—then will the superiority and strength of our National Union begin to be apprehended, together with the immense benefits of free Governments upon individual citizens and subjects. Too little attention to politics. Rights of conquest compel to study. Find basis State Sovereignty.

Raw materials abound. We have within the bounds of the Republic the raw material for almost every branch of manufacturing industry. In veins of gold and silver are found wealth unmeasured and incalculable. These, the universal representatives of values, predominate in *intrinsic* worth over the *labor* in any form bestowed upon them in manufacture. The Union also holds in its territory the useful metals of iron, Labor gives them value. copper, lead, and tin, of untold extent, in which *labor* constitutes the chief value, as shown in the diversified forms in which skill has fashioned these metals, from the main spring of a watch, where the artist's genius imparts a hundred-fold value over that of the raw material, to articles of domestic use, and from these up to the complex and gigantic machines which do the manual labor of hundreds of thousands of men.

Converts to use and ornament. Other products, as sand and soda, of inconsiderable value in their crude state, are capable of transmutation into beautiful and useful forms, subservient to domestic use—in the adornment of temples of worship, in stained and colored glass of living hues, and in other forms of excellence and taste, embellishing palatial edifices, and giving light and comfort even to the lowly cottage; then in the form of telescopic power, whereby the eye of science watches the sidereal procession by land and sea, Rags made into paper. and realizes the value of the teachings of these celestial objects. Even rags, valueless in their crude state, the skill of the manufacturer transforms into paper, the medium of recording the doings of men in social and business life, and perpetuating, in written forms, the result of scientific philosophic thought, the rise progress, decline, and fall of nations, the means whereby the people, through the press, are continually in council in our own land, and the great truths of natural and revealed Benefits of land culture. religion are everywhere dissemminated. The man of observation sees our prosperity in the driving of the ploughshare over wide fields between the two great oceans of this half continent, and from the inland seas of the North to the Tropics; in Cities and towns. establishing over two millions and forty-four thousand farms, and in creating cities rivalling some of the proud capitals of Europe which had been founded a thousand years ago. These, with towns and villages number twenty-eight thousand, and Manufactories. contain a fraction less than five millions of houses. Our manufactories number one hundred and forty thousand four hundred, besides machine shops of great capacity and value, the former converting the raw material of wool, cotton, hemp, hair, hides, and other products, into the multitude of forms known to civilized life, the latter creating machinery of immense strength, of exact movement, huge engines of labor, moved by the irresistible force of steam, indicating the intellectual power and skill of our citizens, whilst our shops and ship-yards are continually renewing and All linked by railways. increasing the commercial and naval tonnage. The industry of our people has linked our cities, manufactories, and machine shops by lines of railway much greater in lineal extent than the circumference of the globe, and connected by the electric telegraph the most distant points of the Republic. Not content with these triumphs Petroleum. of manufactures and machinery, the genius of man has demanded of the earth her oily treasures, and, by powerful engines, is enriching the country by securing this valuable product, the element not merely of light, but of permanancy and lustre in color in the manufacture of woollen and other fabrics.

Adam Smith. Dr. Adam Smith, in his treatise on the "Division of Labor," states that "the most opulent nations, indeed, generally excel all their neighbors in agriculture as Manufactures chief. well as in manufactures; but they are eminently more distinguished by their superiority in the latter than in the former."

British example. This declaration of the great political economist is illustrated in the vast wealth brought to the British shores by manufacturing instrumentality.

Britain 1337. In 1337, five and a quarter centuries ago, the English were nothing more than shepherds and wool-sellers. An act of parliment in that year interdicted the exportation of wool, and the use of any but English cloth, forbidding the importation of foreign cloths, yet inviting foreign manufacturers to domiciliate in the country. Progress dates from mannfactories. The wonderful progress and wealth of that nation are traced from the time of the establishment of manufactories in the kingdom, and to the use of their machinery, the aggregate capacity of which is equal to the manual labor of the whole human race.

U. S. progress in 50 years. What strides in that direction have the United States taken in the last half century! In the year 1810, by order of the Secretary of the Treasury, the returns of marshals in relation to our manufacturers were then arranged by a skilful agent. The results are, that the goods then manufactured by the loom from cotton, wool, flax, hemp and silk, besides instruments and machinery manufactured—hats of wool and fur; manufactures of iron, gold, silver set-work, lead; of soap, tallow candles, wax, spermaceti, and whale oil; of hides, shoes; of wood, oils, refined sugars, paper,

marble-stone, slate, glass, earthen manufactures, tobacco, dye-stuffs, drugs, paints, cables, and cordage—amounted to..$127,694,602.
Omitted articles, or those imperfectly returned estimated at..........$45,068,074,
To which add value of "doubtful articles," having connection with agricultural pursuits, cotton pressing, flour and meal mills for grinding grain, &c. estimated at..$25,850,795.
Making in the year 1810, the aggregate manufacturing values of........$198,613,471.

Total, 1810, $198,000,000.

What were the values of this branch of American industry in 1860? The exact figures, according to the Census tables, are $1,885,861,676.

1860. $2,000,000,000.

To this amount, obtained from actual census returns, let there be added a moderate estimate for omissions, and for non-return of minor and inconsiderable establishments, and the aggregate values, in 1860, of our manufactures, reach the enormous sum of two thousand millions of dollars, having been multiplied ten times within the fifty years ending in 1860, whilst our population in the same period has increased four and a half fold.

Ten-fold in 50 years.

Reciprocal benefits of agriculture and manufactures.

These amazing results, whilst measurably affected by the wealth of our soil, its successful tillage and abundant harvests, are yet directly traceable to the science, artisan-skill, industry, and energy of the American people in the great department of manufactures; results, realizing to the nation the truth hereinbefore mentioned, that the most opulent nations are more distinguished by their superiority in manufactures than in agricultural interests; and yet, in the ratio in which the former are increased, is the landed estate enhanced in value—these great interests reciprocally acting upon and advancing each other.

General advantages of our Nation.

With unlimited raw material at hand to supply almost every variety of manufactures; with a railway system completely connecting every important point east of the Mississippi, and rapidly extending so as to carry the work to the Pacific; with a line of river and canal communication reaching the principal interior marts of the country, we have the elements and the means within ourselves of a domestic trade of surpassing value; and, with a river and ocean commerce equal to thirty thousand vessels, the United States have become a formidable competitor for the lion's share of the trade of the world.

Carnot's exception of the Am. Republic.

Carnot, the war minister of France, the man who "organized victory," in resisting, in 1802, the decree creating Napoleon consul for life, spoke generally of the instability of republics, tracing the same to the fact of "being hastily put together in the midst of civil commotions, enthusiasm always presiding over their establishment." But that distinguished statesman singled out from these the American republic. "*One* only," said he, "has been the work of philosophy." *Organized in the calm of peace*, this republic subsists, full of wisdom and vigor; the *United States of North America* present the phenomenon, and their prosperity constantly receives accessions, which excite the wonder and admiration of other nations. *

Its success.

Why failure of France as a Republic and our success.

* And why our success and the failure of France to establish a Republic? No doubt difference of character of people was an important element; yet far more effective was our regard for the wisdom of their great Montesquieu, in employing Federalisim, and their disregard in Consolidation. Under Providential guidance we adhered closely to our noble motto, *E. Pluribus Unum*, and our ship of State has made progress upon life's ocean unexampled in the world's history; and theirs, started under the vain-glorious banner, *The Republic One and Indivisible*, soon went under the bloody waves of the French Revolution.

Study requisite to appreciate our system.

That study into the nature of our Governments and Union, which hitherto we have been too practical to give, will enable us to apprehend the wonderful results obtained by our combination of State and Federal Agencies. The difficulty has been, and always will be until man attains perfection, to govern enough and not too much. The exercise of political power is one of the most self-aggrandizing influences with which we have to do. Checks must be employed in the best of States, with the best of rulers, or the best of Governments becomes oppressive. The gradual institution of checks in the British system, has brought it to its great perfection. Although no Republic, as Lord Brougham, John Stuart Mill, and other conceited Britons represent; they have judiciously engrafted upon their root of Monarchy the principle of Republicanism, or Representation, whereby it is rendered the most perfect example of Limited Monarchy ever known. We have engrafted this same principle upon our root of Democracy, the Sovereignty of the People—the People by States. It is the possession of this Sovereignty by the People, compelling to the exclusive use of Representation, that alone constitutes a Republic. Rome under the Cæsars was as much a Republic, as Great Britain is a Republic. We want to understand these things and learn at once the intrinsic benefits of our compound system, and its superiority to anything the world has ever enjoyed. This division of the exercise of State Sovereignty to two co-ordinate and independent sets of agents, State and Federal, and the sub-division to distinct, co-ordinate Departments, Legislative, Executive and Judicial, has given us undoubtedly the most admirable system of checks and balances ever devised.

Checks essential. Adopted in Gt. Britain.

State Sovereignty. We a true Republic.

Superiority of our checks and balances.

Lesson taught. Thus was it reserved for the New World to teach the Old that "*nations may tranquilly exist under the dominion of liberty* and *equality*."

The Union in 1800. Such was the Union at the opening of the present century, in the infancy of its political being. What has it accomplished since? It has advanced with gigantic strides towards its high destiny in the three elements of a nation's power—agriculture, Results 1860. manufactures and commerce. The results are recorded in the census volumes of 1860; but it has gone further; it has successfully quelled the greatest revolt known to ancient or modern times.

Politics and physics wisely blended. With profound wisdom are physical and political considerations thus blended to consider the future of manufactures. Of the power of politics we can have no conception, until far more study is given it than hitherto. Nor are the best informed any exceptions. No man has so much knowledge of the nature and superiority of our institutions, that he can learn no more; Our contrary teachings— and the pernicious, fundamental errors, generally prevalent,—the destruction of National Union by the school of South Carolina, against which the most gigantic of civil wars has been required to shield us; the subversion of State Sovereignty by the school of Massachusetts, now our chief danger—prove that if there be any certainty in the fundamentals of politics, our —prove egregious errors. teachers of one school or the other, or of both, have erred most egregiously; or else, that common-sense which is usually accorded these citizens, is withheld in their political practice. *

No place for this discussion. But this opens too wide a field to have proper consideration here. We certainly shall find, that the nature and strength of National Union based upon State Sovereignty, has never been apprehended even by ourselves; and these Providential events compel us to a thorough examination, which must Effect on manufactures. have a direct and powerful influence upon this subject of manufactures, in which, possessing already such a variety and abundance of raw materials, labor and capital are chief essentials.

Common sense rules. Errors of the fathers. Chisholm *vs.* Georgia. * The truth is, that right against our teachers, under Providential guidance, these practical citizens have conducted their affairs with wonderful success. The fathers came very near to a rejection of this frame of Government, because of erroneous teachings of some of its chief friends and framers. Then, in *Chisholm vs. Georgia*, the first important case before the Supreme Court, the sound decision was given that these States could be sued. But Attorney General Randolph had argued, and the Court wove it into their *obiter dicta*, that the United States could not be sued; and where is the authority from that day to this which has ever suggested that the Court's teachings might have been wrong, being in direct conflict with the Constitution itself? Why should not either State or Federal Government be liable to have its claims and obligations adjudicated in a court of justice? Because the Queen of Great Britain, as the source of all law within her dominions, cannot be made amenable to her own court of justice; shall that exempt either State or Federal Agency from amenability to these sovereign States, by whose enactment alone either Government has existence?

Blackstone's nonsense. We are so completely indoctrinated with Blackstone's nonsense of the sovereignty of the legislature, that we have no conception of the Sovereignty of the People, and the excellence of the system we actually have to keep our Governments and officials to their proper duties, and the fulfilment of their just obligations. Error of 11th Amendment. That absurd *obiter dictum*,—though as usual the practical part of the case, the decision was correct,—led those practical citizens at once to adopt the 11th Amendment; for they rightly determined, that if some how or other a supreme authority had gotten over them which could not be held accountable to the laws of the land—not even to the supreme law of the land by which alone every part of the Federal Courts of Claims. Government existed—these sovereign States at all events should not be sued. We are gradually feeling our way back, by instituting Courts of Claims,—though not yet at all trusted; and when our teachers shall study a little more of the principles, they will tell us that our Courts, not Congress, are the proper adjudicators of all such questions.

The examination of principles will, in the first place, correct prevalent belief, that there is no essential difference in the forms of government. That our Creator thought there was a difference, which has never yet been done away, is shown by the earnest remonstrance against a change, when Israel said, "Nay, but we will have a King over us;" and we shall learn the reciprocal operation of government upon people, and of people upon government, and more than ever realize and acknowledge the goodness of our GOD in giving us the very best system of government ever devised, either regarding the individual or the body politic.

No difference in forms of Gov't an error.

Obligations to GOD for our system.

The strength and sacredness of covenant obligations, especially on the part of States and Nations, will be appreciated as never hitherto. This more than aught else will generate unbounded confidence in the perpetuity of our institutions; and while the privileges of American Citizenship will be more highly valued than ever, the liberty-loving in Europe will see more and more that they are never to be enjoyed except by removal here. The obligations there between Monarch, Nobility and People, are no less sacred, than these between these States; and so long as a government is reasonably well administered, there is no right of revolution. . Our Declaration of Independence, will be acknowledged a perfect exponent upon this right. As a consequence, we shall have an increasing immigration, not only from the low, but from the higher classes and even the nobility, many of whom will see the benefits of giving junior members of a family equal opportunities with the first-born. Relief for dissatisfaction with government, is to be found individually in the right of expatriation; in regard to which our teachings and practice are undoubtedly right, and Rutherforth and other British authorities wrong. Israel's law is surely the Law of Nations on that point; and when any Nation, be it Great Britain, or France, or even our good friend Russia, shall authoritatively dare to call in question the rights of expatriation, and of the transfer of a subject's allegiance from her to one of these States, which thereby obligates the Federal Agency of that State to render its faithful liege subject all due protection against any foreign power; that protection to the humblest subject will surely be rendered, cost what it may, unless the stars and stripes cease to wave in heaven's breeze. European diplomatists may higgle, and assert prerogatives too long unquestioned; but no civilized Nation dare resort to *ultima ratio regum* with the United States upon that point. The full benefits of these political considerations cannot be estimated without thorough examination; yet who will refuse to acknowledge their importance in multiplying immigrants, many of whom will be manufacturers?

Strength of covenant.

Europe cannot have our system.

Our teaching of the right of revolution.

Europeans to come here.

Britain wrong about expatriation.

If denied—

—we fight—

—if necessary.

The chief part of our labor, however, for manufacturing, also mining, agriculture, building railroads, etc., is to come from the ancient Orient, but the American Occident. Thither the star of destiny points our Caucasian way to the spot where GOD created Adam, and gave him and his posterity dominion of the whole earth. As a means preparatory, we are no doubt to

Ancient Orient our Occident.

Millions of Asiatics to come.

have millions upon millions of Mongolians, Malayans, Hindoos, etc., to develop the unequaled natural advantages here enjoyed and elevate our race to its ultimate glory. Two or three Pacific railroads, creating intimate commerce with China and other Asiatics, are to have more effect to develop manufacturing by cheapening labor, than any other instrumentality that can be conceived. What other section will receive more of them than the Great Vallies of the Rivers and of the Lakes?

Develop manufactures.

Capital to be drawn from Europe.

Next to labor, capital is essential. What means so efficient to draw hither the superabundant capital of Europe, as to strengthen confidence in our institutions? Developments which we ourselves must make of the sacredness of covenant obligations, in order to maintain our governmental system, and the earnestness and sincerity with which on all hands our declarations will be made to pay every dollar of our liabilities, together with increasing knowledge of our immense resources, will satisfy the world that our indebtedness of every sort, city, county, State, Nation, will surely be paid. When any one of these States shall refuse to obey the adjudication of the Supreme Court, and refuse to pay a just debt, of which there is not scarcely a possibility; it will be found a question affecting the credit of every State, and a violation of covenant obligations, for which a remedy will surely be found, and in virtue of State Sovereignty, too, for the preservation of which these States formed the first, and then the "more perfect Union." What is State Sovereignty good for without faith and honor? When that august prerogative, the Sovereignty, the *summum bonum* of the State, shall once be realized together with its corresponding obligations, never can one of these States refuse to fulfil its engagements; and if one should, the benefits of a National Union of free and independent States, will be found sufficient to protect the State from a fate worse than *felo de se*.

Confidence in our promises to pay.

State rights our safeguard.

State Sovereignty to be appeciated.

Dispute about part of the bonds.

Had we correct apprehensions upon these points, could we so dispute about paying part of the Federal bonds? We endeavor actually to make an issue in the coming Presidential contest, concerning payment of part of the bonds, as if we expected to continue indefinitely the present shaving system of National Bank issues, and never have specie payments. We shall return to the one as we relieve ourselves of the other, and substitute the true national currency of green-backs; and then, what is the difference whether principal or interest be payable in specie or not? Now, we are selling these securities to foreigners for thirty to forty per cent. discount; the best security in the world, and which we shall pay dollar for dollar. During the war it was to be expected, but how much longer should this state of things continue with peace? It mattered little about discount so long as traffic in bonds was chiefly at home; but selling abroad at a discount is a dead national loss.

Return to specie payments.

Loss upon our securities.

Pay dearly for capital.

We are certainly paying dearly for the use of foreign capital; and as indebtedness on account of the war is yet to be immensely augmented, and Europe will seek it more and more, it is of prime consequence that we soon learn enough of the economy of politics, to ascertain the difference between two-thirds of a dollar and the whole of it, and find some speedy way to rid ourselves of national banks, save interest to the Nation by using greenbacks for currency, and return to specie payments, the only possible way to get the whole dollar. Then shall we have abundant means to obtain capital for manufacturing and for railroads, of which the West will obtain its due proportion.

Way of relief.

Means for manufactures.

As to the prospects of Chicago to obtain its own proportion of Western benefits, the following general observations from the circular of 1861, are appropriate :—

Chicago's share. *Views* 1861.

Commerce alone seldom if ever makes a large city. A few persons can sell and handle millions of dollars worth of property. But a strong commercial point draws to it all kinds of business, chief of which is manufacturing. New York is our principal city for both domestic and foreign trade, but far more of her people are concerned in manufactures than in mere selling and shipping. Though all materials must there be brought from a greater or less distance, and high rents and extra expenses incurred, yet its advantages as being an important business centre are more than an equivalent.

Manufactures, not commerce builds large cities.

Example of N. Y.

So it is to be at Chicago. As already intimated, the West abounds in raw materials, and nowhere else than here can coal, lumber of various kinds, iron, copper, lead, wool, cotton, food, etc., be more easily and cheaply brought together. Were it not so, its advantages of distribution would, as in New York, offset considerable expense in procuring materials. It must ever be an influential consideration to a manufacturer to make his location where daily or oftener he can put his articles on a car that, without change, will carry them to his customers in all directions, and hundreds of miles distant. But having unsurpassed facilities for gathering materials, combined with unequaled means of distribution, Chicago must become a great manufacturing city.

Same at Chi.

Advantages of distribution.

Gathering materials.

Not long is the present system to be pursued. From these lakes, lumber is sent all the way to New England, and food for the hands that carry it and manufacture it, and they build our furniture, carriages, etc., in large proportion, and even many farming tools, wagons and the like, and they, or somebody besides ourselves, do nearly all our other manufacturing. Perhaps in cotton and wool, and all finer branches, their capital and experience may enable them for some time to hold superiority, but of common articles, that cost a good per cent. on their value to transport, the West will soon be its own producer, and will steadily gain in all.

West to manufacture for itself.

Climate and healthiness, and other local advantages hereafter noticed, are also favorable and important influences, and the extensive home market the West affords is another. If correct in the previous suggestion, that much of the increasing capital of our country is to find employment in manufactures, is it not reasonable to believe that the advantage an establishment would have at Chicago in obtaining materials and food, and in supplying western consumers, would in many articles enable it to ship eastward and abroad in successful competition with the New England producer?

Various advantages.

Manufacture some for East.

If manufactures are to be speedily increased by the necessity of employing money advantageously, no one point will receive more of it than Chicago, which removes our chief obstacle—lack of capital. The next difficulty is in the supply and price of labor, which in these days of information and of rapid intercommunication, and with so migratory a people, cannot be very considerable.

Capital will come.

Labor also

Railroads themselves require a large amount of manufacturing, in their cars, engines, etc., and had Chicago no other manufacturing business except that resulting from her railway system, it would build up a large city.

Large railroad manufacturing.

We have already a great variety of manufactures commenced in a small way, and though the life's blood has been drawn out of them by the enormous rate of interest paid on all money borrowed, and though suffering with all other business by the depression of the times, yet a brighter day is about to dawn, capital must increase for their benefit, and soon prosperity will attend upon them as in few cities in the country.

Great variety.

Prospects good.

Slow growth hitherto gives more in future.

Our lack of capital, especially as compared with St. Louis, has been felt more in manufactures than any branch of industry. But if relative progress therein has not equaled commerce, it only proves that growth in future is to be accelerated as capital shall increase. Still, we have never been ashamed of our manufacturing statistics, and this table is taken from the *Chicago Democratic Press*, exhibiting—

Dem. Press.

Chi. manufactures 1855.

Chicago Manufactures in 1855.

Manufactures.	Capital.	Hands.	Value of Manufrs.
Iron Works, Machinery, etc.	$1,102,000	1,395	$1,926,500
Agricultural Implements	454,000	480	649,790
Railroad Cars, etc.	750,000	550	950,000
Brass, Tin, Copper Ware, etc.	142,000	188	377,200
Type, Printers' Furnishing, etc.	15,000	12	....
Carriages, Wagons, etc.	417,000	792	702,104
Lead Pipe, etc. (estimated)	20,000	75	50,000
Planing Mills, Sash Factories, Shingle Mills, etc.	374,000	396	749,684
Cabinet Furniture, etc.	300,000	530	455,500
Marble and Stone	578,000	676	588,900
Whisky, Ale, Porter, Beer, etc.	397,500	180	826,645
Oils, Soap, Candles, etc.	361,000	104	464,130
Gas, Coke, etc.	....	....	126,442
Leather	150,000	130	290,000
Brick	56,000	220	260,000
Saddlery	52,000	120	142,000
Musical Instruments,	16,000	38	45,000
Daguerreotypes, Photographs, etc.	43,500	47	70,000
Jewelry, Silver Plating, etc.	77,000	37	80,100
Quick Lime	80,000	110	96,000
Confections	24,000	60	80,000
Stoves	80,000	92	195,000
Wooden Ware, Brooms, etc.	90,000	48	120,000
Blank Books and Stationery	26,500	66	124,000
Barrels	30,000	100	105,000
Glue	10,000	15	4,072
Ship Building	60,000	250	300,000
Hats, Caps, etc.	17,000	30	40,000
Mill Stones	5,000	14	23,418
Trunks	50,000	80	180,000
Lithography, Engraving, etc.	10,000	15	20,000
Saleratus	6,000	8	18,000
Matches	5,000	21	18,000
Boots and Shoes, Clothing, Millinery, Tobacco, Crackers, Bread, Coffee and Spices, Surgical Instruments, etc.	506,500	1,866	1,954,006
	$6,295,000	8,740	$11,031,491
Recapitulation of 1854	4,220,000	5,000	7,870,000
Increase during 1855	$2,075,000	3,740	$ 3,161,491

$11,031,491.

Table carefully prepared.

The above table was compiled with great care by Mr. Ballantyne, then of the *Democratic Press,* now of the *Republican*, who visited every establishment. A similar one was prepared in 1856, giving figures upon some items here omitted, and omitting some here given. But it is not necessary to repeat unofficial statements of consecutive years, particularly as we have none of St. Louis whereby to compare relative progress. In no invidious spirit, but merely to invite attention to a point worthy of consideration it may be observed, that could figures be obtained, they would exhibit the immense advantage St. Louis has had, not only in capital, but in established manufactures, the result of her wealth. Relative figures in 1856 and

St. L. was much larger in manufactures.

previously I have been unable to find, but in 1860 she was more than double of Chicago. The panic and revulsion of 1857, so disastrous to the whole country, was more severe at Chicago than any other city, because deficiency of capital compels use of credit to a large extent, which in the general collapse was temporarily destroyed. Then in 1857 and '58 the farmers having poor crops, and being unable either to buy or pay for what they had bought, as I learned to my ruin in reapers, manufacturing was slow in regaining natural channels. Still, manufactories must have been steadily growing, both in variety and in number, or the census of 1860 could not have exhibited so large increase. The remarks of 1861 quoted, p. 199, were made before the statistics of the census had been published. Though well sustaining the opinion concerning increase, the eight years since, as we shall next see, have done vastly better. These are the —

Panic of '57

Poor crops '57–8.

Still good increase. Shown by census.

Better since

Statistics of Manufactures in Cook County Illinois, per U.S. Census 1860.

U. S. Census 1860.

Manufactures, Cook Co.

MANUFACTURES, COOK CO.	Number of Establishments.	Cost of Raw Material.	Capital Invested.	Number of Hands.	Annual Cost of Labor.	Annual Value of Products.
Agricultural implements	1	$6,000	$25,000	27	$10,680	$35,000
Mowers and reapers	1	96,210	500,000	200	54,996	414,000
Thrashers and powers	2	15,890	137,000	67	26,160	80,000
Alcohol	2	333,750	17,500	10	3,600	520,000
Bags	1	70,000	1,000	14	3,648	93,000
Blacksmithing	9	7,210	18,050	27	10,848	30,150
Bone black	1	990	8,000	10	1,800	8,500
Brass founding, &c	6	51,490	54,000	98	31,820	186,000
Book-binding and blank books	1	3,330	1,000	7	1,872	9,800
Boots and shoes	66	95,543	75,800	256	80,724	216,231
Boxes, packing	5	42,045	24,000	70	39,360	86,040
Boxes, paper	2	2,050	4,500	9	2,304	8,000
Bread	11	238,364	121,800	128	46,740	391,688
Brick	5	15,795	95,700	266	85,800	139,200
Brushes	1	145	200	2	384	600
Camphene	1	180,325	6,000	2	480	190,000
Carpentering	10	34,390	15,250	50	19,560	73,975
Carriages	25	55,595	253,000	188	74,028	213,070
Carriages, children's	1	1,480	6,000	4	1,200	11,100
Cars and car repairing	3	37,500	130,000	82	38,280	82,000
Car wheels	1	43,560	10,000	8	2,160	56,000
Cigars	6	12,285	6,650	22	8,100	65,715
Cisterns	1	1,000	1,000	3	1,140	3,100
Clothing	26	328,846	113,900	399	115,944	540,709
Coffee and spices, ground	8	158,090	62,000	27	11,640	192,700
Coffins	4	8,984	9,200	7	3,240	12,000
Confectionary	5	84,400	15,000	26	11,088	143,950
Cooperage	29	77,723	205,450	243	96,836	178,765
Coppersmithing	1	460	250	1	300	1,100
Cordage	1	1,340	100	3	900	2,500
Cotton batting and wadding	1	10,000	1,200	5	1,440	15,000
Engraving	2	2,150	3,300	12	5,700	12,550
Flour and meal	8	970,550	193,000	78	32,700	1,185,125
Furniture, cabinet	18	68,311	83,750	212	59,484	247,863
Gas	1	60,000	768,000	140	48,000	245,000
Gas fixtures	1	2,000	7,000	13	4,800	15,000
Glue	2	57,660	12,500	60	17,280	80,840
Hardware, files	1	1,062	2,000	3	1,200	4,320
Hats	4	10,930	10,400	16	6,780	24,780
Hay pressing	1	....	25,000	22	6,600	18,000
Iron castings	6	89,675	129,000	96	39,180	221,000
Iron, railroad	1	445,000	200,000	195	96,000	660,000
Carried Forward.	277	$3,717,128	$3,347,500	3,908	$1,104,296	$6,600,871

[*Continued.*]

U. S. Census 1860.

Statistics of Manufactures in Cook County Illinois, per U. S. Census 1860.

[*Continued.*]

Manufactures, Cook Co. concluded.

Establishments, 469.

Materials, $8,026,670.

Capital, $5,571,025.

Hands, 5,593.

Labor, $1,992,257.

Product, $13,555,671.

MANUFACTURES, COOK CO.	Number of Establishments.	Cost of Raw Material.	Capital Invested.	Number of Hands.	Annual Cost of Labor.	Annual Value of Products.
Brought Forward.	277	$3,717,128	$3,347,500	3,608	$1,104,296	$6,600,871
Iron work, ornamental	1	1,950	2,000	10	3,600	6,000
Jewelry	5	15,257	4,800	10	4,740	27,000
Leather	3	16,620	81,500	12	3,984	25,628
Leather, morocco	1	20,000	10,000	7	2,100	34,000
Lightning rods	1	5,100	10,000	12	3,600	20,000
Lime	1	9,980	18,000	10	3,000	37,822
Liquors, distilled	1	110,300	60,000	36	14,400	216,000
Liquors, malt	14	214,882	445,500	140	44,664	572,240
Liquors, rectified	6	119,360	92,000	37	18,012	271,480
Looking-glasses and picture frames	2	1,290	2,500	6	1,956	4,800
Lumber, planed	6	356,875	49,000	74	19,992	417,828
Machinery, Steam engines, &c	16	249,084	846,000	597	234,120	582,500
Malt	1	9,240	2,000	2	600	10,250
Marble and stone work	4	131,000	177,000	182	69,840	227,000
Matches	2	487	1,800	6	1,920	4,375
Mattresses	3	1,240	1,150	3	900	2,600
Millinery	12	72,075	26,600	75	22,740	133,400
Mineral water	2	37,000	13,000	11	3,660	53,000
Musical instruments, piano fortes	2	7,050	15,500	7	2,820	23,600
Painting	4	4,531	4,500	19	7,680	22,805
Plastering	2	2,880	1,400	10	8,240	9,000
Pottery ware	1	250	300	1	600	1,000
Printing	19	190,716	307,700	356	154,428	525,022
Provisions—Pork, beef, &c	5	1,443,825	155,000	146	27,885	1,626,142
Regalia, Masonic	1	4,500	1,000	5	1,320	7,000
Saddlery and harness	13	21,681	26,325	52	17,244	56,707
Sash, doors, and blinds	13	124,164	188,800	278	96,936	373,247
Scales	1	945	5,500	10	4,800	10,000
Sewing machines	2	446	2,800	4	1,080	3,050
Shingles	4	27,300	35,000	72	12.864	61,000
Ship and boat building	2	1,505	2,500	8	2,160	3,700
Shirts	3	7,964	1,600	27	7,104	23,581
Silver-plating	1	2,500	2,000	6	2,520	11,000
Silverware	1	25,520	20,000	9	4,320	34,000
Soap and candles	11	121,837	48,300	43	14,712	242,680
Staves	1	14,000	5,500	12	3,600	32,500
Sugar refining	1	727,000	13,000	75	27,000	860,000
Tin, copper and sheet-iron ware	10	22,002	20,150	28	10,440	37,983
Trunks	3	14,616	15,000	26	9,216	47,620
Turning, ivory	1	2,600	1,000	1	480	3,300
Turning, wood	3	1,260	2,500	4	1,800	4,800
Type founding	1	6,210	25,000	16	4,824	24,600
Vinegar	2	6,000	3,000	4	1,200	12,840
White lead	2	153,000	24,000	29	12,000	283,000
Wigs and hair work	2	4,600	8,000	7	1,860	18,700
Total.	469	$8,026,670	$5,571,025	5,593	$1,992,257	$13,555,671

87 articles in 1860.

Chi. 16th city. Increase from 1850.

Mo. and St. L., 1860.

Of 631 articles in the list of the Union, Cook county had only 87. Chicago was then 9th among the cities in population, had in manufactures a capital $5,422,225., producing a value of $11,740,684., making her 16th in the scale of manufactures. But her relative increase that decade was large. The total of Illinois manufactures in 1850 was only $16,534,272, and $57,580,886, in 1860, raising her from 15th to the 8th State. Chicago had nearly one-fifth. Missouri in 1850 was 10th, producing $24,324,418.; in 1860 she was 11th, producing $41,782,731.; of which St. Louis county had actually $27,610,070.

Subsequent increase unknown.

It would be interesting and profitable to ascertain subsequent increase both in value and variety. But supposing statistics had been regularly gathered as formerly, no means have been taken, and it is impossible to obtain them for this first edition, except upon a few articles. The U. S returns of Internal Revenue ought to and will afford a true result; but the clerical force is inadequate to foot last year's returns for several weeks. Knowledge of what has been done, however, is chiefly valuable to indicate what may and should be done. An enterprising manufacturer any where —in Old or New England—who looks largely to the West for a market, must see at a glance, the advantages of this point, whenever manufactures can be introduced in sufficient variety and amount to support each other and draw hither labor. Meanwhile, those who shall have come early and have established themselves at home and abroad, will reap ample reward for foresight and energy. On this account rather than to display growth, would information about miscellaneous manufacturing be valuable. From Edwards' city directory we compile the following—

Valuable to indicate what may be done.

Advantage of early comers.

List of Manufactures in Chicago, May 1867, *and Number of Establishments.**

Manufacturing establishments in Chi., May, 1867.

Agricultural Implements	3	Candle	5	Elevator Builders	1
Alcohol and Spirits	7	Candy	5	Embroidery Stamps	1
Ale Boxes	1	Cans	1	Engine Builders	6
Atificial Flowers	1	Card Engravers	1	Engravers, Bank Note	1
Artificial Limbs	4	Carpenters and Builders	109	Engravers, Card	4
Artists	21	Carpenters and Joiners	3	Engravers, General	21
Axles	1	Carp. and Stair Builders	1	Engravers, Lithographic	13
Axle Grease	1	Carpet-bags, Valises, &c	3	Engravers, Wood	4
Bags	5	Carriage Builders	30	Family Medicines	1
Bakeries	107	Chain Pumps	1	Fence Builder	1
Bank Vaults	2	Cattle-Brands	1	File	1
Banners and Ensigns	1	Chair Factories	3	Filter	2
Barrels	2	Chemical Works	8	Fire Shovel	1
Baskets	2	Children's Carriages	3	Fire Works	1
Bedsteads	2	Children's Clothing	2	Flavoring Extracts	3
Beef Extract	1	Chronometer	1	Flour Mills	19
Bellows	1	Cigar Box	2	Flour Mill Machinery	1
Bent Carriage Timber	1	Cistern	2	" Sacks	1
Billiard Tables	2	Cloak	1	Foundries	13
Binder (Shutes ready)	1	Cloak, Shawls, Mantillas	4	Fringes	1
Bird Cage	1	Clock	3	Furniture	25
Bitters	5	Clothing	15	Fur	2
Blacksmiths	84	Coal Hods	1	Galvanic Batteries	1
Blank Books	12	Coffee and Spice	7	Gas Stove and Lamp	1
Block and Pump	1	Coffin	2	" Light and Coke	2
Block Letter	1	Collar	4	Gents Furnishing Goods	71
Boat and Yawl	4	Coopers	44	Gilt and Rose W. Mouldings	2
Boiler	11	Contractors and Builders	20	Gilt Block Letters	1
Bone Dust	1	Copper and Sheet Iron Ware	2	Glass Factories	3
Book and Edge Gilders	1	Copper Smiths	5	Glove and Mitten	1
Book Binders	14	Cords and Tassels	1	Glue Factories	8
Boots and Shoes	207	Cork	2	Gold and Silver Platers	4
Boys Clothing	3	Cotton Presses	1	Gold Leaf	1
Brass Cock and Faucet	3	Curled Hair	1	Gold Pen	4
Brass Founders	7	Dental Instruments	2	Grain Separators	1
Brass Tubs	1	Distillers	11	Grate and Fender	1
Breweries	36	Dress makers	138	Grist Mills	3
Brick	14	Dyers and Scourers	16	Guitar and Banjo	1
Broom	5	Eaves Trough	1	Guns and Pistols	4
Brush	6	Electro Plates	3	Hair Jewelry	4

[*Continued.*]

* The lists from which this is compiled, giving name and location of each house, cannot be exaggerated But very many kinds of business have different branches, under each of which a firm that prosecutes both as *cigars* and *tobacco*, is listed. It is too tedious to compare and see what cigar makers are not included in the tobacco lists; and as most tobacconists make cigars, the latter list is wholly omitted. So horseshoers are omitted, because most are doubtless in the list of blacksmiths. Though less, both in variety and number than it might be made, this prevents exaggeration, and the amounts are still abundantly satisfactory.

The list not exaggerated.

Manufacturing establishments in Chi., May, 1867.

List of Manufactures in Chicago, May 1867, *and Number of Establishments.*

[*Concluded.*]

Hair Workers, (Wigs, &c.)	4	Paper Bag	3	Spring Bed	3
Hand Stamps	1	" Box	7	Stair Builders	6
Harness	38	" Collar	5	Starch	2
Hat and Bonnet Block	1	" Hangers	14	Stave and Shingle Joiners	1
" Frame	1	Pattern	2	Stave Cutting Machine	1
Hats	5	Perfumery	2	Staves and Headings	2
" Caps and Fur	2	Photographic Galleries	40	Steam and Gas Pipe Fitters	6
Hay Press	1	Piano Stool	4	Steam Engine and Boiler	20
Hominy and Split Peas	1	Pickle	2	Steam Engine Governors	1
Hoop Skirt and Corset	9	Picture Frames	22	Steam Guage	3
Horse Collar	4	Pipe	2	Steel Stamp Cutter	1
" Nail	2	Planing Mills	27	Steel Works	1
" Power	1	Playing Cards	1	Stencil Cutters	9
Hose Carts	1	Plow	1	Still and Cistern	1
Hosiery	2	Plumbers	51	Stocking Weaver	1
Hot-air Furnaces	3	Pocket-book	2	Stove Founders	2
Ice Cream	1	Powder	2	Stove and Furnace	4
Indellible Ink	1	Printers, Book and Job	41	" and Hollow Ware	8
Indigo and Washing Crystal	1	" Card	1	Straw Goods	3
Ink	4	" Commercial	2	Sugar Cane Mills	1
Iron	3	" Furniture	1	Surgical Instrument	2
Ivory Turners	3	" Publishers	42	Surveyors "	1
Jappanned Ware	3	Pumps	6	Syrups, Plain and Fancy	5
Japanners	1	Reapers and Mowers	6	Tailors	148
Jewelers	37	Rectifiers	2	Merchant Tailors	88
Kerosene Oil Safe	1	Regalia	2	Tanners and Curriers	19
Labels, Cut and Gum	1	Ribbons	1	Tea Caddies	1
Ladder	1	Roofs	17	Teeth, Porcelain	1
Lanterns	2	Rolling Mills	2	Telegraph Instrument	1
Lard Oil	5	Roofing Paint	1	Threshing Machine	2
Last	1	Rope	4	Tin Ware	1
Leather Belting	2	Saddle and Harness	26	Tinners Goods	1
Leather	7	Sails, Awnings and tents	4	Tinsmiths	18
Lightning Rod	1	Sash Doors and Blinds	84	Tobbacco	60
Lime	8	" Lock	1	" Pipe	1
Linings	1	Sausage	3	Travelling Bag	4
Linseed Oil	2	Saw	7	Trunk and Valise	13
Lock	1	" Mill Machinery	1	" Box	2
Locksmiths	11	" Smithing	1	" Lock	1
Locomotive Lamp	1	Scale	3	Truss and Bandage	1
Machine Belting	1	Screen	1	" Hoop	1
" Twist	2	Scroll Sawing and Turning	3	Type Foundries	3
Machinists	21	Sculptors	1	Umbrellas and Parasols	5
Maltsters	7	Seal and Stencil	1	Upholsterers	26
Mantillas	1	Seamless Bags	1	Varnish	6
Marble Workers	10	Sewer Builders	10	Ventilator	2
Match	4	Sewer and drain Pipes	2	Vermicelli	1
Mathematical Instruments	3	Sewing Machine Frame	1	Vinegar	14
Mill Pick	1	" Silks	2	Violin	1
Millers	3	Shingle	7	Wagon	59
Mineral Water	1	Shipsmiths	6	Water Proof Wagon Cover	1
Model	2	Shirt	13	Whip Lash	1
Mouldings	8	Shoe and Harness Wax	1	Whips	4
Musical Instrument	3	Shoulder Braces	1	White Lead	5
Mustard	3	Show Cases	9	Wig and Toupee	3
Muzzles	1	Sidewalk Builders	1	Willow Ware	3
Office Furniture	2	" Vault & Deck Lights	1	Wind Mill	1
Oil Electric	1	Seives	1	Window Shade	4
Oil	7	Silver Plated Ware	2	Wire Works	5
Oils, Lubricating and Illumin...	2	" Platers	6	Wood Carvers	4
Organ	3	" Ware	2	Wood Working Machinery	1
Packing Houses	38	Soap and Candle	16	Wooden Ware	4
Painters, Banner and Sign	14	Soda Water	8	Woolen Factories	2
" Carriage	9	Sofas and Chairs	2	Writing Fluid	1
" House and Sign	81	Spice Mills	4		
Total					2,848

No. 2,848.

318 kinds. There are *three hundred and eighteen* different branches of manufacture, against 87 in 1860. Then Cook county had 469 establishments. Now this list of the city alone containes 2,848; and doubtless many branches, and

Five-fold increase. still more shops, have been overlooked. That, however, is over six-fold increase in numbers, and over five-fold in variety, in eight years; being only three less in variety than the census gave New York City in 1860. What

Chi. a certain centre for manufactures. other information is requisite to establish the claims of Chicago to superiority in manufacturing? Why have these thousands of mechanics come here in the last eight years? Their establishments are of course mostly small concerns, though rolling-mills, and some foundries and machine shops would be respectable anywhere. And the least of them will in a few years have grown to large establishments, or have given way to others who had more energy, and capital. Let us look at the progress of two or three as indicative of the rest, the newspapers having recently compiled information.

Chi. Times. Leather manufacture.

Leather Manufacture.—The *Chicago Times*, 26th March, well observes :—

Everybody now concedes to Chicago unrivalled commercial advantages, from which have sprung her wonderful growth and development; but those who are acquainted with the progress made here in the mechanic arts are not so large in numbers. The railroads that radiate from the city in every direction, and the white sails that catch the busy gales of the lake, are elements in the greatness of Chicago that all must acknowledge from their very obviousness; but the sound of grinding wheels, the clank of hammers, the flash of the forge, the roar of the furnace, and all the peculiar phenomena of a manufacturing town, must be sought for in their respective localities, or they will not so readily be seen. And it is not exaggeration to say that Chicago is rapidly adding to its purely commercial character that of a varied and extensive manufacturing activity. Hardly a day passes that does not see some new branch of manufacturing industry, requiring skill and capital, introduced among us. But a few days since it was announced in *The Times* that forges were to be set up on the South branch for the reduction of Lake Superior iron ore, and it is believed that, if these are successful, as they are almost certain to be, they will be but the initial steps in a very extensive business.

Ignorance of our progress in mechanic arts.

Manufactures rapidly increasing—

But it is not alone new manufacturing interests that are beginning to attract a wide interest. The success of most of those that have been established for a sufficient length of time, and under sufficiantly favorable circumstances to test them, has induced a general belief that Chicago is shortly to be as noted for its industrial as for its commercial pursuits.

—already a success.

Antiquity.—Among those branches of the former art that have become established here, is that of the manufacture of leather. The art of tanning is one of the oldest in the world. From the mythical days, men have been habituated to the dressing of skins for personal comfort and for economical ends. Among the lost arts, that of tanning could never be numbered, and science in the present age has lent its aid to perfect what the experiments of former times have bequeathed.

Antiquity of leather.

Its Extent.—From small beginnings, the leather-dressers of Chicago have grown into a powerful guild; and the business itself involves in its management, at the present time, over a million and a quarter of dollars. Including all the separate establishments in the city for the making of leather, large and small, there are 35. These are, for the most part, situated along the North branch of the river, and within the city limits, although there are two or three tanneries along the other branch of the river. The pungent aroma of hemlock bark and neat's foot oil, and the rubric hue of the landscape in this vicinity, arising from the exposure of the skins to the air and light, sufficiently mark the broad acres that are devoted to the tanner's and currier's skill. The buildings that have been erected, and the machinery introduced, are of the most substantial and approved styles and patterns for the most part, and there seems to be no reason why the manufacture should not be very greatly extended beyond its present proportions.

Extent of Business.

35 tanneries.

Substantial arrangements.

The principal elements for the successful establishment of the business are hides, and bark containing a sufficient quantity of tannin. The first is a staple article of export in Chicago, and the bark of the hemlock, which grows in abundance across the lake in Michigan, and which can be transported to Chicago at a very small expense, supplies the other main item in the establishment of the business.

Hides and bark.

Large supplies.

All the leather tanned in Chicago is what is called hemlock leather, since no oak growing in the north has yet been found with a sufficient quantity of tannin to permit of the economical and successful manufacture of leather from it.

All hemlock.

The demand for the home-manufactured leather is at present fully equal to the supply, and the rapidly-developing boot and shoe manufacture in the city is constantly increasing the demand.

Home demand

The *Times* describes the chief establishments, which we condense : Union Hide and Leather Co. employed last year 100 men, tanned 50,000 hides.

Labor and product of large tanneries. Chicago Hide and Leather Co. can tan 35,000 hides per annum (vats not now full) employ 20 to 30 curriers. Bristol & Engle employ 40 men, tan about 18,000 hides per annum. Chicago Sole Leather Co. tans 10,000 hides per annum, with 20 men. Grey, Clark & Co. tan 40 to 50,000 hides per annum, and 60 to 70,000 sheep-skins, employing 70 men and using 4 to 5,000 cords of bark. Garden City Hide and Leather Co. tan 20,000 hides per annum. Eliel & Co. tan 18,000 hides, and 10 to 12,000 kip and calf-skins, employing 40 men. Grey, Marshal & Co. tanned last year 11,412 hides, employing 30 men. The editor adds:—

Small ones. There is a large number of smaller tanneries, employing from 1 to 8 or 10 men, and there are in these about 100 men employed, and from 40,000 to 50,000 hides transformed into leather.

Enlarging. Nearly all the manufacturers of leather at present located in the city are making arrangements for the enlargement of their business, and it is not improbable that, within a very short time, the business will be double its present magnitude.

Reasons for increase. Compared with the figures of the census of 1860, p. 202, these are quite satisfactory. Nor is this trade at all what it will be. Here should all the hides stripped, and all that come in a green state, be dressed. Having unsurpassed facilities for obtaining bark from the entire lake region, where the hemlock abounds, no reason can be given why the hides of the whole west should not come here to be converted into leather. Less and less should they be shipped, though owing to the packing business, we actually ship Receipts and shipments of hides. more than we receive. In 1866–67, we received 20,125,541 lbs., and shipped 23,234,791 lbs.; in 1865–66, received 19,285,178 lbs., shipped 20,379,955 lbs.; in 1864'5, received 20,052,235 lbs.; shipped, 27,656,926 lbs. So that this branch of trade, with the reputation Chicago leather has obtained, offers great inducements to manufacturers and capitalists. One trade, too, begets another; and as closely connected, let us look at—

Boots and shoes. *Boots and Shoes.*—This business is even more remarkable for its growth, because labor is a heavier item, in which we are deficient as compared with *Chi. Times.* New England, the chief manufacturing region. The *Chicago Times* March 27th, gives a history of foot-covering and adds—

Extent of business. Mass. amounts. *Where the Best Shoes are Made.*—In the United States the manufacture of shoes has reached the highest perfection. The shoes of Massachusetts have a world-wide reputation for their beauty of form, and they excel those of any other part of the world. A century ago the town of Lynn was famous for its manufacture of shoes, and at the present time about 10,000,000 pairs of boots and shoes are made in this town alone, and in the state of Massachusetts in 1860 there were made nearly 33,000,000 pairs of shoes, and 11,500,000 pairs of boots.

Phil. next. Outside of the New England States, Philadelphia is the city of next note as a manufacturer of boots and shoes.

In Chicago— —began 1859. *Boot and Shoe Manufacture in Chicago.*—About nine years ago the subject of the manufacture of boots and shoes for the jobbing trade was agitated in Chicago, and one or two firms undertook the business in 1859 and 1860. It was thought to be an experiment, and by some of the best dealers it was believed that it would prove successful. The war coming on soon after at first had a tendency to prevent the successful execution of these experiments; but after a year or two it was found Increase. that the increased demand for shoes for the army stimulated the business, and accordingly other manufacturers came to the city and embarked in the trade, until, at the conclusion of 1865, a half dozen large manufactories were well-established, and doing a paying business. At the present time more or less new firms for the manufacture of shoes, put up their signs each year, while almost invariably those who have gained a foothold remain.

Superiority of Chicago Leather.—Chicago-made boots and shoes had not been tested more than two years, before it was found that they were decidedly superior to eastern ones in durability, and a demand was created, which has grown each year until, by the Assessor's returns last year, there was more than $1,500,000 worth of boots and shoes made in Chicago in 1867. One cause for the superiority of Chicago-made goods is, the better quality of leather made here. It is said that Chicago-manufactured leather is decidedly superior to that made east, owing to the skill of the tanners, and their greater care in the handling of hides during the process of tanning. So decided have the preferences of the farming communities of the northwest settled in favor of Chicago boots and shoes, that every wholesale jobber in the city is compelled to manufacture or to purchase these goods. With a single exception, all the shoes and boots at present made in the city are of the staple calf and kip skins, and comprise men's, women's, boys', and youths' sizes. All the lighter serge goods sold in this city are manufactured at the east.

Work superior.

Leather superior.

Chi. work preferred.

Extent of the Business.—The proportion of Chicago-made boots and shoes to those of eastern manufacture, as at present sold in this city, is from 20 to 25 per cent. The business is rapidly growing in importance, and almost every manufacturing dealer for the coming year will increase his product from 15 to 20 per cent. over that of last year. The following is a statement of the amount of business done last year by the most prominent manufacturers of the city, as compiled at the United States Assessor's office.

Extent of business.

Increase.

Chief manufacturers.

Whitney Bros. Co. ....$	294,593	E. Chapin..........................$	92,316
W. D. Wells & Co.	197,888	T. B. Webber & Co.	54,100
McDougal, Nicholas & Abbot.	154,807	S. Walker & Co.	53,140
C. M. Henderson & Co.	131,936	S. Nelson & Co.	46,034
Davis, Sawyer & Co.	219,453	C. McFarland.	37,539
Fargo, Fales & Co.	102,059	Gillette, Aiken & Follett.	26,196
Dogget, Basset & Hills.	84,194	Haight & Bowen.	17,655
Chapin & West.	80,229	Griffin & Palmer.	12,159
J. L. Watson.	79,113		
Phelps, Dodge & Co.	72,670	Total.	$1,656,081

Machinery.—In all these wholesale establishments labor-saving machinery is used and anxiously sought after, for on its uses the proprietors chiefly rely for their profits. In no department of shoe-making has there been a greater revolution than in that of stitching. The work that was once performed slowly and with great tediousness by the awl and bristle, is now done in a twentieth part of the time by a sewing machine. The lap-stone has given place to iron rollers for hammering and spreading the leather; the knife and pattern for shaping soles have fallen into disuse, and a single blow with a steel dye does the work better and in a tenth part of the time required by the old method. Skiving machines, splitting machines, and a multitude of other appliances and inventions diversify the old trade of shoe-making, and render a—

Machinery used.

Its superiority over hand-labor

Division of Labor absolutely necessary in a wholesale manufactory. In the best establishments of this city, a boot in its manufacture, requires to pass through the following hands: The roller, the heel cutter, the outsole cutter, the insole cutter, the heel maker, the sorter of soles, the counter-fitter, the cutter of uppers, the crimper, the trimmer, the fitter, the stitcher, the bottommer, the finisher, the treer, and the packer, making 16 distinct operations and operators. In doing this work it is remarkable with what speed some of the workmen learn to operate. A single man can cut 6,000 soles per week, or 3,600 uppers; he can crimp 96 pairs of boots per day, or bottom 6 pairs in the same time.

Division of labor.

16 operations.

Female Labor.—All the light work, such as attending the sewing-machines, stitching the uppers, fitting, etc., is done by females, nearly all of whom receive good wages.

Female labor.

Many of the large jobbing manufacturing establishments are in connection with the wholesale boot and shoe establishments at the head of Lake street.

The *Times* adds a description of the 18 chief manufactories, number of hands, kind of work, amount, etc., for which space cannot be taken. They

Description manufactories omitted.

each employ from 75 to 140 hands, and many speak of large increase this year.

Increase of business since 1860.

According to the U. S. census of 1850, Illinois' total of this manufacture was $478,925.; and in 1860 was $1,133,458, Cook county having 66 establishments, capital $75,800., producing a value of $216,231. It is mere guess work to judge of present product, but deducting the 18 above, if the other 189 produce a proportionate amount with the census of 1860, over $600,000 should be added for small manufacturers, making over $2,250,000.; an increase more than ten-fold in eight years.

Present product, $2,250,000.

These items fair indices to others. Others more impressive.

These items afford satisfactory indications of progress made and making in general manufactures. Yet they are less impressive than others for which Chicago is already famous. If packing of provisions have such tendency to centralize, which requires little machinery, is of universal demand, and more than almost anything else would be supposed most advantageous nearest the place of production; how much more the thousand and one little articles of manufacture, which find purchasers only here and there, to say nothing of great ones requiring extensive facilities for manufacture? That city which attains preëminence in ordinary manufacture, surely wants only time and capital to develope equally the extraordinary, unless laboring under great disadvantages in obtaining raw materials. Of the ordinary, no safer guide of judgment can be found than that of—

Success in ordinary, success in extraordinary branches.

Chi. Times.

Pork and Beef Packing. *

Pork and Beef-packing. Its beginning.

History of Business.—The first packing house in the city commenced operations in 1835, when 3,500 hogs were cut and packed by Gurdon S. Hubbard. Since that time the business has increased with the growth and prosperity of the West, until it has assumed its present proportions as one of the three or four leading branches of business in this great commercial city. During the season of 1861–62 one-fifth of the whole number of hogs packed for market in the Western States were put up in the Chicago packing-houses. They furnished nearly one-fourth of the total product of these States during the season of 1862–63, and more than one-fourth the succeeding season; while during the season of 1864–65 almost one-third of the hogs packed in the Western States were packed in Chicago.

Increase.

Chi. chief packing city. Advantages.

These figures show Chicago to be the most prominent packing point in the world. It has secured that position by the advantages of its position and the perfection of its communications, both natural and artificial. To the east, cheap transportation of provisions is afforded by lakes and canals; while from the west, numerous lines of railroad furnish the only means of carriage which can profitably, be used for the transportation of live stock. Living animals must be transported rapidly, for they rapidly become unfit for butchering. Canals and rivers never can compete with railroads for this class of freight. The country reached by railroads which lead into Chicago is especially productive of corn, and consequently well calculated for the production

Corn abundant.

* Nothing better upon this important branch has been noticed than the article quoted in *Hunt's Merchants' Magazine* from the *Chicago Times*, from which these extracts are taken. But I have earlier recollections of the business.

My earliest recollections of pork-packing.

My first winter in Chicago, 1832 '3, I boarded with that whole-souled friend, and natural gentleman, Mark Beanbien. The "Hoosiers" drove in a lot of hogs, of the breed more famous for the time they could make, than for the lard they could yield. The bipeds staid a week or two to kill and pack the quadrupeds, and it was my privilege to have the former for fellow-boarders. They were never too busy with killing, and never wasted time with washing, to keep them behind at meal times. Mrs. Beaubien—a noble woman was she, and devoted Christian mother, who corrected many of my New England anti-Catholic notions—tried her best to get some of the "slap-jacks" to me, but the hog-killers were so on the alert, that two week's fighting for my living, impressed upon my memory pretty effectually the early days of Chicago pork-packing; rather a contrast to present operations. Nor am I very old either.

of hogs and cattle. These can be raised for this market at a profit even in the interior of Missouri, Iowa, and Minnesota, although the freights on grain from points so distant make it a profitless crop unless fed to stock. Little of the grain received in this market is raised west of the Mississippi. The rates of freight will not permit it. The territory from which we receive live stock is four or five times as extensive as that from which we receive grain. Great as is this branch of business, it is yet in its infancy. Chicago must always be the great live stock emporium, and the great provision manufacturer for the Eastern and European markets. Put into hogs and Cattle.

The advantages of this business, however, are not limited to the citizens of Chicago. Our packing-houses are of immense importance to all the producers of stock. Everything which in any way facilitates the transportation of produce from the farm to the consumer is of great value to the producer. Hogs and cattle when reduced into barrels of pork and beef, of lard and tallow, are not only materially reduced in weight, but put into a much more convenient and manageable form. A few days confinement in cars tells wonderfully on these stock. The shipper must not only pay freight on good butchers meat, but also on blood and bones, horns and hoofs and all manner of offal; he must hire men to care for them, and buy hay and grain to feed them. Barrels of provisions, on the contrary, submit to be rolled about from wagon to car and warehouse; they will rest contentedly and without injury on the longest journey, with no one to watch over and take care of them; they require no outlay for either food or drink, and are neither decreased in weight or injured in quality by hard travel or long keeping. Benefit to stock-raisers. Saves in transportation.

There is every reason why the cattle and hogs of the West should be butchered and packed;—in other words, should be manufactured into provisions,—before they are exported; and it is not to be wondered at that Chicago and Cincinnati have become the greatest packing points in the world. The causes which are now operating will continue to operate, and we can hardly fix a limit to the increase which may be expected in packing operations. The great weight of grain compared with its value will always tend to discourage shipments of bread-stuffs to distant markets, and we must expect to see trade in live stock and provisions increase more rapidly, and reach greater proportions, than the grain trade. Packing business at Chi. and Cin. natural. To increase.

There are many reasons why it is desirable that the farms of the west should be devoted to raising stock rather than grain for export. Besides the difference in the cost of transportation which has just been mentioned, a very important consideration is the difference in the effect on farming lands. Repeated crops of wheat and corn will eventually exhaust even the rich soil of western prairies. Flocks and herds enrich the field which feeds them. Continued cropping of prairie farms will sooner or later leave the land, like that of the e xhausted plantations of Virginia, barren and unproductive, while a system of culture which includes the raising of animals, and consequently the production and use of fertilizing agents, will preserve and increase the productive capacity of this magnificent agricultural country which is now deservedly known as the garden of the world. Stock-raising improves the farms.

No statement of beef-packing at St. Louis is found. The *Mo. Democrat* gives a list of pork-packers, aggregating 204,132 hogs up to 1st January, thus prefaced :— Packing at St. L. *Mo. Dem*

Provisions.—St. Louis as a packing city is surpassed in the amount of her business, by both Cincinnati and Chicago, but in the reputation of her prepared meats she stands unrivalled. Ames' "breakfast bacon," Whittaker's "star hams," Maxwell & Patterson's "Magnolias" are known far and wide, while the quality of the barreled meat and lard her packers put up is too well known to need a reference to. But when St. Louis learns to do less swearing by her rivers and determines to put more capital, energy and faith into the construction of railroads, into the agricultural regions of her own and sister States, she will find the result of her packing seasons ever so much more in her favor. St. L. exceeded by other cities. To swear less by her rivers.

They take consolation for present losses in future hopes, never to be realized. If Cincinnati could not hold what she had, what advantages over her in provision trade has St. Louis, that she can now draw successfully against Chicago, with the multiplying facilities here, which St. Louis can never have? How can St. L. realize her hopes?

The Pork Packing Association makes the following report of last season's business:

Statistics of the Pork Packing in Chicago, 1867–8.

NAMES OF PACKERS.	Live Hogs.	Dressed Hogs.	Total No Hogs.	Av'ge Gross W'g't.	Av'ge Net W'g't.	Av'ge yield Lard.	Mess Pork bbls.	Clear Pork, bbls.	M. O. Pork, bbls.	P. M. Pork, bbls	Ex. P. Pork, bbls.	R'mp Pork, bbls.	S. P. Hams. Tcs.	Lard, Tcs.	Cumberland Middles, lbs.	S. Clear Middles, lbs.	S. Rib Middles, lb
Culberston, Blair & Co.	102,020	8,021	110,041	244	194	27	13,621	169		3,972	564	35	7,320	9,495	2,155.000	491,000	2,354,000
Cragin & Co.	71,146		71,146	250	200	28	11,583			1,862	287	560	6,000	6,500	1,497,000	268,000	431,000
Burt, Hutchinson & Snow.	64,073	2,753	66,826	258	206	30½	10,615		648	1,054	1,321	100	3,172	5,231	662,000	1,088,000	1,414,000
A. E. Kent & Co.	54,000		54,000	244	194	27	4,123		160	3,162	635		1,500	4,500	650,000	825,000	1,100,000
Jones, Hough & Co.	33,580	17	33,597	236	186	27	1,221				151	180	364	2,878	685,000	240,000	654,000
Reid, Sherwin & Co.	34,094		34,094		195	29¼	5,820			460		106		3,160	840,000	252,000	630,000
D. Kreigh & Co.	26,310		26,310	249	196½	28	4,388		213	385	167	378	2,427	2,418	398,000	50,000	877,000
Tobey & Booth.	31,801	270	32,071	250	197	27	2,219			188	352		600	2,700	400,000	106,000	520,000
Kelly Bros.	33,700		38,700	237	189	32	3,500			300			300	3,200	1,200,000	100,000	500,000
G. W. Higgins & Co.	5,192	30,219	35,411		176	25	776		200	750	200		1,000	2,703	447,000	615,000	994,000
H. O. Armour & Co.	25,400		25,400	245	195	25	3,700		450	800	780	250	440	2,117	675.000		220,000
C. M. Favorite & Co.	18,397		18,397	242	191	27	2,362		837	663	180		202	1,565	189.000	69,000	840,000
V. A. Turpin & Co.	23,734		23,734	246	194	30.40	2,223			623		240	2,285	2,259	311,000		778,000
Joseph Jones.	22,000		22,000	227½	182	29.22	897			341			556	2,000	757,000	55,000	475,000
G. S. Hubbard & Co.	15,318	1,559	16,877	247	198	28	2,744	164	980	362	219	67	949	1,525	161,000	84,000	182,000
Leland & Mixer.	11,135	239	11,374	234	185	24,60	1,193		648	994	981		905	900		250,000	
Flint, Thompson & Co.	8,287		8,287	257	201	33	1,632						786	869	118,000		87;000
Freeman, Ruggles & Co.	12,000	10,248	22,248	245	181	22	1,175			725	500	300	800	1,600	400,000	135,000	750,000
H. M. Chapin & Co.	9,025		9,025		179½	22	400			2,075	325	72	652	600	160,000		108,000
McLaury, Ray & Co.	16,235		16,285		207	28	1,052			150	180		810	1,481	215,000	440,000	277,000
R. McCabe & Co.	1,100		1,100		190					200				100			
Shaw & Co.	10,500		10,500	238	190	27½	1,174				100		350	960	130,000		350,000
John Nash.	12,200		12,200	227	177	25				225				810	214,000	9,000	123,000
W. M. Tureman.	5,040	7,589	12,629	235	172	24½	500		60	265			120	770	224,000	74,000	122,000
Thorne & Co.	12,884		12.884	250	192	27½	1,472			150	725	96	1,129	1,142	228,000	10,000	407,000
Wm. Coker & Co.	5,281	1,788	7,069	245	195	21	1,030		25				100	452	142,000		247,000
Barter & Whitehouse.	3,531		3,531		292½	32½	278			95				380	38,000	28,000	145,000
L. Richberg.	3,500	2,633	6,183		190		200							515			
H. Brinkworth.	2,000	6,000	8,000		185		100							680			
T. D. Booth & Co.		3,800	3,800		195	24	300							380			
S. McKichan & Co.	9,223	8,498	17,781		195	28	2,075			870	160			1,576	132,000		338,000
H. W. Smith & Co.		2,003	2,003		198	32	267	200						170			
Geik, Hayes & Co.	470	3,228	3,698		214	28½	1,125		151					300			
Sweetser & Galloway.		3,786	3,786		179	26								800			
L. French & Co.	1,200	1,625	2,825		190									240			
— Wolfer.		5,348	5,348											480			
— Orvis.		2,150	2,150											195			
— Colling.		935	935											84			
— Boehm.		550	550											50			
— Metzger.		1,800	1,800											162			
— Tucker.		1,500	1,500											135			
— Sanderson.		1,000	1,000											90			
Dugan Bros.		980	980											88			
— Linscott.		500	500											45			
— Schoenthaler.		1,000	1,000											90			
W. C. Reed & Co.		1,800	1,800											162			
Totals for the season.	684,386	111,839	796,225		198	27,56	83,765	538	4,472	20,171	7,827	2,384	32,267	68,007	13,023,000	4,684,000	13,923,000
Totals for the season 1866–7	471,173	164,559	635,732		227⅔	38	142,623			9,792	10,665	3,432					

The page not receiving all the figures, it should be added, that there are also of long-clean middles, 1,691,000 lbs.; long-rib middles, 605,000 lbs.; rough sides, 3,980,000 lbs.; dry salted hams, 38,200 lbs.; dry salted shoulders, 11,644,000 lbs.; long-cut hams, 25,118 pieces. Additions to table.

The editor of the *Commercial Report and Market Review*, says;— *Com. Report.*

Quite as prominent a feature is the difference in the kind of product manufactured—the amount of barreled pork showing a large decrease and of cut meats a corresponding increase. This is partly the result of the decrease in net weight of the hogs cut, packers especially in the opening of the season making very little barreled pork, in anticipation of a heavier run of hogs; the principal cause, however, was the anticipation of liberal English and Southern demands—the former for English cuts, and the latter for bacon. This anticipation has been fully met, as our table of shipments elsewhere given will show—the former demand having already taken a liberal supply, and the latter stimulated largely by the advance in cotton, being lately and now a liberal purchaser, and to this as well as a revulsion in the feeling of despondency generally prevailing at the opening of the season, may the upward turn in the market be attributed. Cut meats instead of barreled— —for Eng. and South

Mr. Gillette Secretary of the Pork Packer's Association, supplies— *Sec. Pork Packers.*

Statistics of the Beef Packing in Chicago, 1867–8. Beef-packing 1867–8.

NAMES OF PACKERS.	No. of Cattle.	India Beef, tcs.	India Mess, tcs.	Prime Mess, tcs.	Mess Beef, bbls.	Ex. Mess Beef, bbls.
Culbertson, Blair & Co.	7,025	....	1,178	2,482	4,569	3,146
Cragin & Co.	8,510	....	2,090	3,582	9,000	500
A. E. Kent & Co.	7,132	....	2,977	5,687	1,432	51
Jones, Hough & Co.	3,780	....	1,302	501	3,239	1,215
D. Kreigh & Co.	2,414	....	....	....	4,123	....
Favorite & Co.	1,984	....	....	....	3,217	79
Joseph Jones	1,650	....	1,200	350	150	600
G. S. Hubbard & Co.	1,852	....	236	442	2,380	....
H. M. Chapin & Co.	999	34	742	508	....	....
Total for the season	35,346	34	9,725	13,552	28,110	5,591
Total for the season 1866–7	26,998	....	....	....	....	....

35,346 head.

In March, 1857, 11 years ago, *Hunt's Merchants' Magazine* said of— *Hunt's Mag.*

The Chicago Beef Trade.—Every day, says a cotemporary, we meet in some journal or other, convincing proof that a new branch of agriculture or industry is advancing with incredibly rapid strides, and building up cities and great populations as it advances. We remember some obscure hamlet, some quiet village, which we once visited in youth, and are startled some day by receiving from it a newspaper containing proof that it has grown up to cityhood just as rapidly as we have advanced to manhood. Chi. beef trade. Rapid changes.

One of these indications is shown in the extent of the provision trade of Chicago, Illinois, some particulars relative to which we find in a reliable German cotemporary, the *Illinois Staats Zeitung*, which is addicted to statistics. Those who follow the markets may be aware that Chicago-salted provisions bring a markedly high price in eastern cities, and that they are well known in England. During the late great war, contracts were directly made with a Chicago house to supply the allied army with a vast quantity of salted beef, and in 1855 not less than 63,000 barrels of that provision, requiring 29,000 oxen, were prepared in that city. During 1856 the amount has, of course, diminished, there being no extra cause of demand, so that, as it is said, the horned cattle keep pace with the hogs. Increase. Highly esteemed.

Facilities for Slaughtering and Packing.—The trade in animals here centering, would create extensive packing facilities; while these facilities would also draw the stock. Nor is it a slight advantage, in a trade so Packing facilities.

Advantages at Chi. variable as that of provisions, to locate a packing establishment where an unlimited supply of hogs or cattle can be had if packing be desirable. If the trade promise well, the packer can select the stock wanted; if otherwise, it goes to other markets. Year by year must Chicago have more and more of this advantage, so that her relative importance as a stock market will more and more, augment. Information concerning packing houses would be expected, which Mr. Wells supplies by describing the largest in his *Commercial Express*, January 30th.—

Com. Exp.

Description of largest establishment.

At the corner of Eighteenth and Canal streets is located their packing-house, a substantial brick structure of four stories, 200 by 210 feet, with adjacent yards, and exterior stock-ways for driving either cattle or hogs up to the level of the floor where they are to be introduced within the building. Hogs are taken in at the top of the house, where the whole floor is divided into pens, which will easily hold 4,000. Cattle are taken in on the second floor, through small pens, holding two or three each, easily supplied from the adjacent yards. Without going into details of the slaughtering operations, it is sufficient to say that when the season is at its height, 300 cattle and 2,000 hogs per day can be disposed of, neither branch of the business interfering with the other. The appliances of machinery dispense as much as possible with manual labor, everything is done or handled with the greatest ease, regularity and rapidity, and yet, when the house is in full blast, 300 persons find active employment.

Slaughter 300 cattle, 2,000 hogs daily.

Cooling.

Lard.

One whole floor of the building is devoted to the hanging of carcasses for cooling, another to bulk meats, another to barreled meats. The lard room contains nine enormous rendering tanks, one high-pressure, and the others low-pressure, the preference being given to the latter. In this room is also a lard-purifier, an immense kettle, into which all the lard from the tanks is drawn, for a second process, which renders it absolutely perfect before it passes into the tierces. This purifier is a peculiar feature of this establishment, and to its use is doubtless to be attributed the fact that their brand of lard has borne the highest price in this market all the season.

Purifier.

Skill.

The most skillful and experienced workmen are employed in all the processes, besides which the proprietors give their constant supervision to every department. In the selection of stock, the materials for the methods of cure, the putting up for market, and the storing and subsequent handling, their motto is excellence in every grade of product.

More storage

The firm have hitherto experienced some disadvantages from want of sufficient storage which they are now remedying, and propose to further remedy. A brick structure of equal size with the present, and contiguous to it, is projected and will be ready for the next season's operations. A wooden storehouse 400 feet long and 66 feet wide, of only one floor, is already completed and occupied. It has double filled walls, double windows, double ceiling and roof, so that an even or nearly even temperature may be preserved; never freezing in winter, and sufficiently cooled in summer by an adequate number of ice bins, constructed at intervals through the centre.

Future increase.

Future Increase of Provision Manufacture.—Immense as are these figures, what are they compared with the future? As we have seen, Illinois and the States adjoining are the chief producers of that grandest American staple, Indian Corn, which John Taylor of Caroline, pronounced "bread, meat and manure." This of all grain should be put in the most concentrated form for transportation, its cost of production on the farm being under ten cents a bushel. Hon. S. B. Ruggles of New York, at the Ship-Canal Convention, considering the benefits of "cheapening the transportation of western products through the proposed enlarged canals," remarked:—

Corn, great staple.

Hon. S. B. Ruggles.

Grain raising in west just begun.

For who, in all this large assemblage, regards for a moment these 520,000,000 bushels as the full measure, or even a tythe of your product, when the whole of your 260,000,000 acres shall be brought into full and careful cultivation? True, it already exceeds the whole cereal product of the British Islands, and nearly approaches that of carefully cultivated and carefully governed France; but can a man be found upon these magnificent western waters small enough, or stupid enough to assert, that these eight great States have now reached their full maturity, have now got all their growth? What human being in his senses, not wholly idiotic, or utterly blinded by political bigotry, or lust of political power, could assert that this God-given, exuberant and all but virgin West has now reached its "culminating point?" For one, I stand awe-struck and amazed at the immeasurable prospect opening before us. I can see nothing smaller, nothing more diminutive, nothing less stupendous, than a yearly product of cereals, to be measured not, as now, by hundreds, but by thousands of millions of bushels—a result so vast, so solemn, so fraught with consequences so momentous to our nation and to the world, that I can but bow with reverential gratitude before such a wonderful manifestation of the providence of our great Creator. Never before in human history did He lay out a garden so wide-spread and fertile; never before did He provide a granary so magnificent for the use of man.

Thousands of millions of bushels.

For what was ancient Sicily, the "granary of Rome," or the fertile plains of the Po, or the exuberant valley of the Nile itself, compared with this our great continental garden, pouring forth yearly volumes of food so enormous and yet so inevitably, resistlessly increasing? In view of such a power to feed our race, who will venture to depict or limit the commercial and the political destiny of this unequaled portion of the earth? Was it thus specially endowed and set aside by the Great Architect of Nations merely to feed the petty State of Illinois, great as it is, and large enough to hold a half dozen Sicilies; or the still more petty State of New York, with all its golden gates of commerce; or rocky little New England, with its thousand and one "notions" on land, and its ever "victorious industry" both on land and sea; or even the whole majestic Union of these temporary jarring American States, soon, I trust, to be happily pacified?

American superiority.

Benefits not home restricted.

No, my fellow countrymen, the manifest destiny and high office of this splendid granary, of which this Chicago of yours and of ours is the brilliant centre, stands out plain as the sun in heaven. It is unmistakably marked by the finger of God on these wide-spread lands and waters, that it is to be our special duty to feed not ourselves of this New World alone, but that venerable, moss-covered fatherland—that old father world of ours across the ocean—as the pious Grecian daughter nourished her aged sire—to carry abundant food, and with it the means of higher civilization and refinement, and that too in the truest Christian spirit, to that over-crowded but under-fed, European Christendom to which we owe our common origin. Let us then come fully up to the measure of this world-wide idea. Let us, by cheapening the transit of food to our seaboard, prepare vigorously to carry out the predestined and providential arrangement of God himself to increase the happiness of man.

New world to feed the old.

Cheap transit wanted.

And now, my esteemed friends, let us make a slight descent; let us talk a little about hogs, and the glorious West as a gigantic hog-pen. I must really beg you not to laugh, for I am profoundly serious, and do earnestly assure you that the hog is a very praise-worthy, interesting, and important animal. For how, let me beg to ask, could you possibly, without his benevolent and efficient aid and cöoperation, bring down the whole of these five hundred millions of bushels of grain to the sea? How could such a mountain mass of cereals, and especially of Indian corn, ever be sold or disposed of? But, thanks to the ingenuity of man and the necessity of the case, the process has been found. The crop is condensed and reduced in bulk by feeding it into an animal form more portable. The hog eats the corn, and Europe eats the Hog. Corn thus becomes incarnate; for what is a hog but fifteen or twenty bushels of corn on four legs?

Hog—don't laugh at him.

Great corn carrier.

Corn incarnate.

It is among the many providential features, of which this subject is full, that a striking revolution has taken place just within the last two troubled years, in the destiny of the American hog. By a new process of curing or preparation, brought in, as I am told, from England, the animal has suddenly become extensively marketable in Europe.

New mode of curing.

Heretofore, the quadruped has passed after death in brine, obedient, perhaps, to the traditions of New England, where a pork-barrel in every family is a sacred institution. But Europe did not relish, and would not eat the hog in brine—so that a great hog-reformation is now in vigorous progress through these interior States, in packing the animal, not in brine, nor in a barrel, but in dry salt, in a

European trade.

light, cheap wooden box. In that shape Europe has recently consented largely to eat him. But let us ascertain precisely and statistically just how far the tickling the palate of the Old World has already advanced. In the year 1859, the exports of pork in the box (barbarously denominated "cut meats" in the official tables) were only nine millions of pounds. In round numbers they rose to twenty millions in 1860, to seventy millions in 1861, to one hundred and thirty millions in 1862, and during the present year, 1863, will probably very nearly ascend to three hundred millions of pounds. Inverting the calculation, and bringing the "cut meats" back to "hog" again, this export is equivalent to an army of one million and a half of these interesting animals, marching across the ocean. After this, will you, can you laugh at the hog?

Cut meats exported, 1859, 9,000,000 lbs.

1863, 300,000,000 lbs.

Fiscal effects.

At any rate, you will consent to be more serious when you perceive the fiscal effects of such a swinish exodus on our national treasury. These three hundred millions of pounds are worth in Europe thirty millions of dollars, sending back imports, paying in duties nine millions of dollars in gold.

Lard.

Nor is this quite all. We have a little more of "the whole hog" in a fiscal point of view. The skill of our artificers in pork expresses out the very quintessence of the creature into lard, an humble element which has suddenly risen from its ancient culinary office of making cakes and greasing kitchen utensils, to the more exalted duty of illuminating houses, and oiling the millions of wheels of our locomotives, and other labor-saving machines. Not only has it literally smoothed our way to this very convention, in this great hog-manufacturing city, but it is exerting its world-wide influence in relieving the whales within the Arctic and Antartic circles from the indefatigable pursuit of that same rock-bound but vigorous New England.

Increased use.

Requisite facilities to be opened to the world.

Who can doubt that all requisite facilities to promote intercourse between consumers, and the great provision market of the world, will be speedily supplied? If the natural operation of causes, with limited facilities hitherto, have concentrated at Chicago the beef and pork of the West, until it has already become the chief provision market of the world; what must be the effect upon that market, to open to the whole world a free and direct transit to it of vessels of 1,000 to 1,500 tons burthen?

Provision manufacture to increase.

More and more, too, will live stock be manufactured. Wheat and corn can be sent east to manufacture with advantage, because in bulk it is handled with facility, eats and costs nothing by the way, and the offal is more valuable on the seaboard. But each of these items operate largely in favor of packing at Chicago. The offal, both expensive and offensive at lesser markets, is here converted into glue and fertilizers, and other valuable products. Messrs. Baugh and Sons, from Philadelphia, under the name of the Northwestern Fertilizing Company, supply this information:—

Baugh & Sons.

Utilizing offal.

Utilizing of Offal.—At their Depot in the city, box-cars are always ready to receive the material as it comes from the packing houses; and each day the cars are taken to their works, 13 miles from the city, where they have erected an immense building in which the material is at once converted into a merchantable condition by patented driers and mills. Heretofore the material has been dried in the sun; but it is now taken from tho car, immediately dried, disinfected and ground ready for market.

Flour.—We now come to an item in which time and capital give large superiority to St. Louis:— **Flour.** *Trade Rep.*

Flour Manufactured in Chicago for Seven Years. Manufacture 7 years.

MILLS.	Barrels.	MILLS.	Barrels.	YEARS.	TOTAL Barrels.
Oriental Mills..........	86,200	Chicago City Mills......	30,000	1865–6..........	301,776
State Mills..........	73,157	Marple's Mills..........	23,895	1864–5..........	290,137
B. Adams & Co..........	53,641	Empire Mills..........	18,000	1863–4..........	223,128
Michigan Mills..........	51,850	Star & Crescent Mills..	500	1862..........	260,980
Ionic Mills..........	47,285			1861..........	291,852
Maple's Mills..........	35,000	Total in 1866–7..........	452,528	1860..........	232,000
Lake Street Mills..........	33,000				

The *Chicago Republican*, in its statement 1st January, presents— *Chi. Rep.*

Statement of Flour Manufactured at Chicago since 1860. 3 years manufacture. List of mills.

MILLS	1865.	1866.	1867.
B. Adams & Co..........	47,428	69,112	85,000
J. D. Cole, Jr. (Ionica mills)..........	36,162	45,000	46,415
Empire mills..........	9,000	18,000	10,000
Lake Street mills..........	18,500	45,000	45,000
Michigan mills..........	35,500	46,629	45,000
Oriental mills..........	40,000	57,000	97,300
State mills..........	45,000	70,000	78,500
City mills..........	25,300	28,783	35,000
Maple's mills..........	12,600	40,000	27,000
Marple s mills..........	....	20,000	33,586
Star and Crescent mills..........	....	500	69,700
Robinson, Rice & Co..........	....	....	16,000
Garden City mills..........	....	....	10,500
National mills..........	....	....	22,000
Other mills..........	20,000	3,500	3,000
Total.	288,390	445,524	574,096

In 1864 the amount manufactured amounted to 255,058 brls; in 1863, 236,261; in 1862, 260,980; in 1861, 291,852; in 1860, 232,000. Man. 1860–64.

Flour Manufactured by St. Louis Mills for 17 *Years.* St. L. man 17 years. *Trade Rep.*

Year	Barrels	Year	Barrels	Year	Barrels	Year	Barrels
1851..........	408,099	1856..........	678,496	1860..........	839,165	1864..........	782,560
1852..........	383,184	1857..........	662,548	1861..........	694,110	1865..........	743,281
1853..........	457,076	1898..........	825,651	1862..........	906,860	1866..........	818,300
1854..........	503,157	4859..........	863 446	1863..........	758,422	1867..........	765,298
1855..........	603,353						

High Wines Manufactured in Chicago for 11 *Years.* High Wines manufactured, Chi. 11 years. *Trade Rep.*

YEAR.	Barrels.	Gallons.	YEAR.	Barrels.	Gallons.
1856..........	27,550	1,653,000	1862..........	61,703	3,702,180
1857..........	50,000	3,000,000	1863..........	77,524	4,850,022
1858..........	60,000	3,600,000	1864–5..........	58,855	3,498,345
1859..........	53,000	3,180,000	1865–9..........	7,514	476,592
1860..........	62,400	3,744,000	1866–7 (City & County)...	42,516	2,550,724
1861..........	89,915	5,394,900			

The offal in high-wines, flour, starch, and other grain products, is worth so much more at the sea-board than here, that these manufactures will never Disadvantage in grain manufacturing.

attain the proportion of provision manufacture. Besides, grain in bulk is more cheaply handled than in barrels

These branches indices of others.

Obstacles in starting manufactures.

Present increase remarkable.

These items suffice to indicate something of what Chicago must become in manufactures with capital and time brought to bear upon the abundant resources of the Northwest. Time is requisite, the demands of a newly settled country not being for luxuries, but necessaries; and what of these is not produced of the soil, comes mostly from abroad. With appliances of machinery now-a-days in all sorts of manufactures, the distant establishment can with profit send products to supply those who must depend wholly upon manual labor. To erect buildings and machinery on any considerable scale, large capital is requisite; and considering the paramount claims of agriculture, and of railways to move its products, is it not a wonder that since 1850 so much should have been done for manufactures? We might estimate for the present, but guess-work is not the basis of these calculations. Nor does the intelligent reader require long argument to convince him of the importance of this City for manufactures. The unexampled growth in eight years past, both in variety of articles and number of shops, surely indicates what is to come; even were it at all doubtful whether a point of such unexampled commercial facilities was to concentrate manufactures.

N. Y. manufactures— —yet imports everything.

No advantage over Chi. but age and capital.

New York, though she imports every thing, her food as well as raw materials, is actually our chief city in manufactures. The superficial examiner attributes her greatness to commerce. No doubt commercial facilities have drawn to her manufactures; but probably five, perhaps ten, of her denizens are dependent upon manufacturing, to one dependent upon commerce. Comparison with New York comes hereafter to obtain some idea of what our own growth is to be. But what single advantage has New York except age and capital, which Chicago possesses not in larger measure? What were her distributing facilities twenty years ago—what even are they to-day—compared with what this young Queen of the West already has?

Phil. compared.

Chi. has advantages of both cities.

Philadelphia comes next, her marvelous growth being due to superior advantages for obtaining food and raw materials, particularly coal and iron. Chicago, as we shall see, as much excels Philadelphia in gathering as New York in distributing. Therefore our measure of progress in manufactures is to be calculated by combining that of the two chief cities of the East, with due allowance for age and capital in their favor, and every other advantage in our favor that can be conceived.

Rapid increase already.

When reach N. Y. and Phil. figures.

Of course this City, yet in her teens in manufactures, could not vie in products with those which can boast of centuries of solid growth. But if from manufacturing 87 articles in 1860, she has 318 in 1867; and if in 1860 the whole of Cook county had but 469 shops, and in the City alone 2,830 in 1867; how long before she overtakes in products the 6,298 shops of Philadelphia, as enumerated by the census of 1860, with their variety of 365 articles, and the 4,375 shops of New York with their 321 varieties?

The number of shops we may not speedily equal, but the variety we shall; and like New York, with less shops the product will be relatively greater. The total of New York was in 1860, $159,107,369; and of Philadelphia, $135,979,777. When we shall have looked a little farther into operating causes, it will not be deemed extravagant to expect that the census of Chicago in 1880 will at least equal the latter figures, possibly the former.

By 1880 equal Phil. in 1860, if not N. Y.

As remarked, in 1861, p. 199, had we no other manufacturing to do but to furnish Chicago railways, that would build up a great city. Two heavy rolling mills are now employed almost entirely in re-rolling railroad iron. No doubt steel is to supplant iron rails, which will be made mainly from the charcoal iron of Lake Superior, in obtaining which no other city has equal advantages with Chicago, as we shall see under the next topic. But if mere iron is to be used, none is equal to that of Lake Superior. All branches of railway manufacture will follow; and with the advantage of so many home railways to supply, we can compete successfully with any city in furnishing any railway. The only drawback is lack of capital, which will surely find its place of safe and profitable investment. The *Railroad Journal* said eleven years ago, in 1857:

Railway manufacture important.

Advantage in Lake Superior iron.

Railroad Journal 1857

Manufactures of Machinery in the West.—Had the railroads of the West been built upon local means they would have been stocked with machinery manufactured west of the Alleghanies. The capital of the West is held mostly in lands and agricultural improvements, to the holders of which iron and steam engine-making would be a new and doubtful business. The western people do not seem fully awake to the advantages they possess for the prosecution of this branch of industry. Chicago, for instance, has 2,500 miles of railroad trunk lines, and 1,500 miles of branch lines immediately tributary thereto, and about the entire equipment of engines for those roads is built or building at the East. Chicago has one establishment for the manufacture of locomotives, but this is wholly inadequate to the wants of the market, the capacity of its capital and machinery being equal only to $100,000 worth of work per annum, while the value required to stock the above 4,000 miles of road would be full $7,000,000; or enough to employ *fourteen* such shops, each five years to complete.

Manfr. machinery in the West.

Large railroad demands.

We should say that no better investment could be made than in these branches of business in the large western towns. We have advocated such investments at Cleveland and Detroit, and for the same reason we should recommend Chicago as another extremely favorable point. Not that we suppose that *one* establishment, or *one* city will derive all the profits of this business, for as well might one flour mill or one saw mill supply the domestic wants of the West. The demand for engines is such, that each important city must be able to produce them, at least cities having such elements of success as Cleveland, Detroit, Chicago and St. Louis. The successful prosecution of engine building at one of these towns will naturally be an inducement for others to go into it.

Chi. a good point.

Many cities.

Manufacturing has now obtained sufficient foot-hold to strengthen itself, and must inevitably grow faster in proportion than population. Mr. Edmunds observed concerning the U. S. census, p. 195, that while population had increased four and a-half fold in 50 years, manufactures had increased ten fold. A corresponding relative increase, probably greater will be seen throughout the West, especially at the chief manufacturing centre, if there be one.

Manufactures to strengthen.

No city to monopolise. No one city of the West, however great its superiority, is to monopolize manufactures. They will spread more or less to every town and hamlet, with all branches of industry, and the Great West will have various important centres of manufactures as of commerce. Yet the West to have a centre— Yet, as the business of the whole country has built up manufactures at Philadelphia and New York, so will that of the Northwest operate upon its centre or centres; and with immensely greater effect, as we shall presently see, because never was there such a centralizing power as the modern railway system, and never was it brought to bear on such a country. —save profits to themselves. Profits hitherto given to the East by the West, because neither time nor capital have sufficed to create manufactures, will gradually be withdrawn to their own region; and by so much as the Northwest excels in vastness, in richness, in feasibility of occupation, in means of intercommunication, will the manufacturing city or cities of the West be advanced. *U. S. Census.* The editor of the U. S. Census Statistics, Mr. Edmunds, forcibly remarks:—

Increase of manufacturing in the West. The rapidity with which manufactures have increased in the West, as well as the East, render it highly probable that in future there will be a much greater home demand for agricultural products of all kinds than existed for a few years previous to the war. Some of the largest coal fields in the world exist in the Western States, while iron and other metals are found there in great abundance. Causes operating. Everything is favorable for building up a great manufacturing interest. Whatever may be the result of the war in other respects, it seems certain that the price of manufactured articles must also continue high. The interest on our national debt and the increased yearly expenses of the Government, will require heavy duties on foreign manufactures, and this, in addition to the heavy expenses of transportation, will give the manufacturers in the West all the protection that can be desired. Immense mineral resources. The discovery and development of the immense mineral resources of our Western Territories, and their astonishing richness in gold, silver and other metals, also favor the idea that in a few years the centre of population will be found in the West, whither it has been marching with steady progress, rather than in the Atlantic States. Home manufactures. Most of the produce which is now sent East at such a great expense, will be consumed at home, and the farmers of the interior will thus obtain a more equable market, at fair remunerative prices.

Cost of labor chief obstacle. The chief drawback in our manufacturing is scarcity and cost of labor. But with only existing facilities of intercourse, how long is this to last to our disadvantage? Hitherto the world has looked to the East for population and wisdom. None more than we have realized and practised the truth,

Westward the course of empire takes its way.

East changed to West to pursue our destiny. But the end of the West, *ultima thule*, has at length been reached; and now, still in fulfilment of the destiny of our race, we make of the Orient, our Occident. What was the East we make the West that we may go on conquering and to conquer. No doubt that ultimately, ages hence, when untold myriads of inferior races shall have been brought to the knowledge of JEHOVAH, they will have passed away; Asiatic laborers coming. but meanwhile they are to be made hewers of wood and drawers of water until we shall have attained our GOD-given dominion and occupy the whole earth.

Nor should we be impatient, and endeavor to expedite the decrees of Providence. Let us wait in full confidence that the Infinite Creator will in

His own good time, give the race "in the image of GOD created"—these "sons of GOD"—their full dominion. Not with Great Britain should war and conquest lead our way; but Providence indicates our course through the peaceful paths of commercial intercourse. From instinct the Japanese and Chinese seem to favor the United States above other Caucasian Nations, perhaps anticipating the sway under which they are ultimately to come. Mr. Burlingame's appointment is only a first step to the influence which we shall acquire by a uniform course of honor and good faith. Nearest to them, they will naturally learn to look to us for protection against Europe. Shall we not render it as may be necessary? *

Let us bide our time. Commerce opens our path. Asia to depend on us.

With myriads from Asia, here congregating as laborers who will never be Citizens; crowds from Europe, both laborers and capitalists drawn hither by the august privileges of Citizenship, which will be awarded to all of our race upon due qualification; both Europe and Asia uniting to give this intermediate region advantage over the other to supply the necessities of their native land; what limit can be put to the power of manufactures here to be developed? No other land so abounds with all varieties of raw materials; in none is food more cheaply produced; in none is climate more invigorating and health more general. With the multiplication of human wants by civilization, and corresponding means of supply; what have been the attainments of the last century, half-century, quarter-century, compared with what each of these periods will witness here in this land of freedom, and especially in the West? When we come to practice upon such questions, these practical Citizens are a good deal more agreed than they seem to be when discussing abstract questions of politics. The *Merchant's Magazine*, which has been regarded a free-trade journal, in Nov, 1866, said of—

Labor from Asia and Europe. Materials abundant. Improvements increasing. *Merch. Mag.*

American Manufactures and Emigration.—While we are not the advocates of special legislation on the part of our Government for the purpose of planting among us particular branches of industry, especially such as are not well adapted to our country, or to the genius of our people, we cannot refrain from taking deep interest in the development of manufacturing enterprise. Perhaps there is no vocation or department of labor more essential to national greatness. We may cultivate the soil, and render it sufficiently productive to nourish the inhabitants of other countries. We may dig the precious ores in quantities ample to supply every nation; we may produce the fibre for every spindle and loom; but so long as we require from other countries the principal manufactured wares necessary to our comfort, we lack a necessary element of independence. Our commerce, which

Am. manufr. and emigration. Mnfr. essential to a nation.

---

* Let us study into the principles of political science, that in our ignorance we commit against Asiatics, no such wrongs as against the Cherokees, for which the Supreme Court of The United States is more responsible than Georgia. In our peculiar circumstances we need to have thorough knowledge of the well established code of International Law, which we have had no hand in founding, but which we shall endeavor faithfully to practice, and hold any other Nation responsible for its infringement against our rights. Our rights in part will be to protect the weak against the strong; and interest may move there, too. Let us patiently bide our time, and European jealousies will work out our opportunities. No nation ever had so much to gain from sound knowledge, thorough practice, of the Laws of Nature and of Nature's GOD—none so much to lose from malpractice and ignorance—as this Nation of States united. Let us study them to appreciate the superlative excellence of our system, and that with no misstep we may march on to our destiny.]

We need to understand our rights and duties as States, and a Nation.

Commerce made a means of vassalage.

ought to be a reciprocal exchange of values created by industry, is rendered to a large extent, an agency to place us under a form of vassalage; for the taking of the products of the soil and mine abroad for manufacture, is but an element of dependence which tends to enfeeble a nation. Such a country is liable, upon the sudden recurrence of a war, to find itself in a pitiable condition indeed, deprived as it is, to a great degree, of the means of defence.

Dependencies not allowed to manufacture.

So conscious of this have the governments been that have held countries and colonies in subjection, that it was long the practice to discourage, and even to prohibit, the people of such colonies engaging in manufactures. When Parsena conquered Rome he forbade the working of iron in that State, compelling it to depend upon the forges and furnaces of Etruria. The Philistines, when they overrun the country of the Israelites, permitted no smith to work among them. The European nations of modern times, so far as lay in their power, carried out a like policy. The Dutch Government made manufacturing a penal offence in the colony of New Netherlands; and the British Parliament enacted laws against slitting mills and other branches of industry in their American provinces. But it is unnecessary to multiply instances. It is evident that a state of dependence is not one of power.

Eng. supremacy.

This subjet is invested with new interest by the events of the present period. Up to this time England has been able to retain her manufacturing supremacy, and the product of her looms now fill the markets of the world. Hitherto, her mills have produced at so low a price as to preclude successful competition. It was more profitable for the planter to raise cotton, and the farmer wool and breadstuffs for the manufacturing towns of England than to erect factories at home to convert the raw fibre into cloths, muslins and other articles of prime necessity. Statesmen often sought to change this condition by special legislation, not being sufficiently far-sighted to perceive that they were attempting to set aside the omnipotent laws of trade. They have always failed, of course, to take away from England her supremacy. It was not legislation which could remedy the matter, but a law higher than man could devise.

A change coming.

Agencies are, however, now in operation, which are almost certain to modify this condition of things, and to give our people greater importance among manufacturing nations. We place no dependence upon the remarkable declaration of Mr. Gladstone, in regard to the exhaustion of the coal beds of England. It is a contingency too remote to be taken into calculation, while science and commerce can both be pressed into service to obviate the difficulty. But there is another agency at work,

Loss by emigration.

more rapid in its influence and more sure to accomplish the result. We refer to the equalizing movement now going on in the emigration that is taking place at prodigious and constantly increasing rates.

Cheap labor made Eng.

The supremacy of England as a manufacturing country has been due to the cheap prices of labor. Her dense population has produced manufactured goods at rates low enough to enable the merchant to undersell Americans, even in our own markets. As long as this condition could be maintained we were dependent upon that country for our supplies. But there has been a change taking place for several years.

Wages increasing.

Better living.

The wages of English operatives have been steadily increasing. With this improvement in their circumstances comes naturally the acquirement of more expensive habits. Better food has been obtained, better clothing worn; not only has the importation of breadstuffs been continued as heretofore, but other articles, like beef and the products of the dairy, have been added to the requirements of the laboring population. The European supply of these products is annually falling shorter, and the demand is at the same time increasing rapidly. This necessarily tends not only to keep up the rates of wages, but to make it necessary to increase

Laborers leaving—

them, and is telling upon the manufacturing enterprise of the country. Thus, while the better classes of operatives—the more skillful laborers—are swelling the multitude of emigrants that are coming weekly to the United States to better their

—others better paid.

condition, those who remain are demanding, and must receive, a large increase in their rates of wages.

Cheap labor enables her to control.

The cheapness of labor has enabled England to control the enterprise of other countries. She could import cotton, wool, and other raw material for her factories, and breadstuffs for the operatives, and, by reason of the low price of work, could keep the price of manufactured goods lower than they could be afforded where labor was better remunerated. But this is impossssible when a considerable

No sudden change.

increase of wages shall have taken place. Of course, we predict no immediate violent change. The influence of this movement, however, which is even now being felt, will gradually work out the result indicated, enabling our manufacturers to successfully compete in foreign markets. In all particulars, except the one of labor, our advantages have ever been greatly superior. We produce the raw material for most classes of manufacture, not only cotton and wool, but the most important metals; our country is an immense coal field; almost every State in the Union abounds with water power enough for all the mills and forges of the world, and generally running waste; we produce all the food required for laborers. With the enormous influx, then, of population, we will have the last impediment removed to successful competition with every other country.

Labor our difficulty.

Materials abundant.

Immigration our relief.

This does not involve the necessity of reducing the price of labor as low as the rates in Europe. To be sure, whenever values shall become properly adjusted, there will be important modifications in that particular. But another element in computation will exist of which our laborers will have the principal benefit. While the operatives in England require that both material and food shall be shipped to them at enormous waste of capital for transportation, our workmen will have all these supplied at their hand from our own fields. The importance of this fact can readily be perceived.

Price of labor not to be low.

Our advantage in transportation.

Another important consideration is the fact that a few years will give to the United States the control of the commerce of China and the other countries of the East Indies. The Pacific Railroad, when finished, will with its collateral routes, make a speedy transit from ocean to ocean, all Asia will thus be brought into communication with the United States in a period of time many days shorter than can be effected with any commercial town of Europe. We thus not only gain this eastern trade, but have the facility for easily distributing our products and manufactures in the East, giving us a transit to an extensive market, cheaper because nearer, than any other country possesses. Hence we see that emigration—this equalizing movement—must in the end necessarily work out a change which will be hastened and rendered more certain and complete by other agencies now or soon to be at work.

Commerce with Asia.

Pac. railway.

These judicious thoughts scarcely need application to the West. Who doubts that in the process of events, never so rapid as here, that the chief manufacturing for the West is to be done by the West? No one interest is more concentrative in its nature than manufactures. And if commerce without manufactures, before their power was at all felt in the West, has already made Chicago the centre; will not this powerful adjunct render sure what has been so well begun? As we we have seen, though without direct comparison, our distributing facilities excel New York; and as we shall next see, our gathering facilities of chief metals and coal excel Philadelphia. With unequaled supplies of food and lumber, unsurpassed local advantages, as we shall also find, what can prevent Chicago from having the same preëminence in all sorts of manufactures that she already has in provisions? Could we never look beyond the western boundary of Iowa, what other city ever had such a manufacturing business as this 600,000 square miles will surely give its emporium? Were we compelled to look solely to the west of Iowa, having never a dollar's worth of business this side, what other city ever had such a trade as that 1,000,000 square miles of mining region must give somewhere? What other city is likely to get an equal amount of it with Chicago?

West to manufacture for itself.

To have its centre for this—

—as N. Y and Phila.

Country east of Iowa abundant—

—also that west.

But the clinching of the argument lies in the driving home by these gigantic corporations, each one striking for its own interest, of these long stretchers of iron rails. What other place can a manufacturer find, not merely in this land of great enterprises, but on the continent, or on the globe itself, at which he can place his wares simultaneously, several times

Railways a clincher.

15 daily routes of distribution—

daily, upon fifteen different cars, running to every desirable point of the compass, from 242 to 1,000 miles and over without a change? This advantage, which no city will probably equal, but which will be here increased by five to ten or more trunk lines within ten years, would countervail for many disadvantages, did any exist. But these have been sought for in vain. To pass over silently any which were perceived, in a discussion purporting to be full and fair, would be injudicious; stamping the entire argument as superficial, if not dishonest. No one is discovered except lack of capital and labor. In lumber of all sorts, and in food, as already shown, Chicago is peerless. Yet, her chief strength lies in—

—to be increased.

No obstacles intentionally overlooked.

Conjunction of Coal, Iron and other Minerals.

Conjunction of coal, iron, etc.

Chi. has neither.

Chicago has neither coal nor iron in close proximity, as yet discovered. Nor is it essential in even heavy iron manufacture that she should have. Philadelphia brings both fuel and iron from a distance, yet eclipses interior towns where ore and fuel are found side by side; and New York at even greater disadvantage eclipses Philadelphia. It would be very possible, therefore, for a city to import wholly its pig iron or blooms, and yet have great preeminence in iron manufacture. It would seem, however that Chicago must be able in large measure to take crude iron ore and transform it into engines, locomotives, nails and watch-springs.

Nor Phila., nor N. Y.

Chi. can have iron ore.

Strange as it may appear, the examination begins with an article in the interest of St. Louis. But it is the best exposition met with of the incalculable mineral wealth, deposited by nature upon the same grand scale which spread out prairies, dug channels for lakes and rivers, and reared mountains on the east and on the west of this unequaled valley.

Views favorable to St. L.

The superficial examiner might think that the prosperity of Chicago depended upon a monopoly of iron and other chief manufactures. On the contrary, as we saw in regard to commerce, she desires the largest freedom, and the general diffusion of manufactures. Because Chicago is the centre of the richest area of the globe—of 600,000—of 1,000,000—of 1,500,000 square miles—not only rich in agricultural productions, but in mineral wealth—must she become the great city of the continent. Should that wealth be locked up to the injury of the country, that tribute might be paid to Chicago? Nay; but because of wide-spread abundance, can each city, town and neighborhood have manufactories of their own; and of their prosperity and extending wants, all of them will require now and then an article from the central city. Then, some articles, as bar-iron, nails, heavy machinery, etc., will be chiefly produced here. The more use can be made throughout the interior country of nature's rich gifts, the richer becomes Chicago from its dependent country, albeit it may have large cities. If not dependent, the wealth or poverty of the country makes no difference to the Queen of the Lakes; if dependent, we desire its every section to make the best possible use of natural advantages, that each may do its part to raise

Chi. desires no monopoly.

Centre of 1,500,000 sq. miles.

Each locality to have manufactures.

Country to use its wealth—

—to advance Chi.

the emporium of the West to that position in the scale of the Union which the West itself may claim. Therefore, we begin with an article from the *Merchants' Magazine*, October, 1866, entitled:— *J. A. Blake.*

MINES AND MANUFACTURES IN THE MISSISSIPPI VALLEY.

Mines and manufr. in Miss. Val.

By J. A. Blake.

A trip through some of the leading mining States of the west, for the purpose chiefly of recording developments already made but secondarily of pointing out new fields of promise, has led us at the termination of our travels to combine in one article a review of mining statistics, and from their connection with and almost absolute control of another branch of industry, to point out and urge both the facilities and necessities for manufactories in the Mississippi Valley. If we succeed in showing where the chief workable minerals are, how they may be mined, and what the profits shall be, what the natural elements of successful manufacturing are, how widely they exist, and what markets they may control, we shall have accomplished our object. Mineral wealth promotes manufactures.

The chief mining States of the Mississippi Valley are Missouri, Illinois and Iowa. Missouri has a total area of 67,380 square miles. * * In the absence of any regular scientific survey we are left in doubt whether there is not even better mining territory in the enormous area yet unexplored. Thirty-one valuable minerals have been found. The enumeration is as follows beginning with the most important and extensive: iron, coal, lead, zinc, copper, platina, kaoline, hydraulic cement, nickel, cobalt, metallic paints, emery, plumbago, silver, gold, salt, sulphur, petroleum, silica, granite, marble, fire-clay, fire-rock, chalcedony, agate, jasper, alabaster, pipe-clay, salt-petre, muaganese, and tin. Mo.—variety of minerals.

The iron ore deposits of Missouri comprise the famous Iron Mountain which with a hight of 228 feet and an area at its base of 500 acres it is thought will give for every foot from summit to base an average of 3,000,000 tons of ore; Pilot Knob whose hight is 1,118 feet is known to be solid iron to 440 feet below the surface where the base has an area of over 200 miles; and Shepherd Mountain, 660 feet high, a mass of the finest magnetic and specular iron ore. * * The ore is mostly specular, yields 56 per cent. of pure iron; the product of which is strong, tough and fibrous. Iron ore. Quality.

The coal measures in Missouri have been discovered in upwards of 40 counties. Coal.

* * * * *

The area of lead-bearing rocks in Missouri is said to be over 6,000 square miles. Lead.

* * * * *

Copper has been found in 18 counties in Missouri. * * * Copper.

Illinois has an area of 55,409 square miles, nearly as large as all New England. She is the richest agricultural State in the Union, and yet one-fifth of her entire area is mineral territory. Coal, lead, gypsum, silver, gold, petroleum, iron, salt, copper, zinc, freestone, lime and silver have been found. We have in a former communication spoken at length of the location, extent and quality of these minerals. It will be sufficient for the purposes of this communication to present a few statistics. Ills.—variety of minerals.

The Illinois coal field is estimated by Prof. H. D. Rodgers to contain 1,227,500,000,000 tons. The Pennsylvania coal field contains 316,400,000,000 tons. All the coal fields of North America, 4,000,000,000,000. The coal fields of Greal Britain 190,000,000,000. The Illinois coal measures then, contain four times as much coal as those of Pennsylvania, nearly one-third as much as all those of North America, and over six times as much as all the coal fields of Great Britain. It will take 100,000 years to exhaust them. The prominent seams are the Belleville and La Salle, occupying the southern and middle parts of the State. Mining is now chiefly carried on in St. Clair, Madison, Randolph and La Salle counties. The present annual product of the entire State is about 1,500,000 tons. St. Louis, Chicago, the markets of the Upper Mississippi, and the home consumption are supplied mainly or in part by Illinois coal. Last year, Southern Illinois sent 10,000,000 bushels of coal to St. Louis markets, of which the St. Louis, Alton and Terre Haute carried 6,000,000, and the Ohio and Mississippi road 4,000,000 bushels. Coal, its extent. Chief seams. Product of South. Ills.

There are three staples in which Illinois is singularly "strong." We mean wheat, coal and lead. If she is not first in the former, she certainly is in the latter. For 20 years the entire lead product of the country has come from the famous Galena mines in Joe Daviess county, which, with judicious and regular working, would Galena lead mines.

have been not only amply sufficient to shut off any foreign demand, but even to create a foreign market. A few mines circling Galena have supplied and smelted 15,000,000 pounds a year.

Extent. The great Galena lead district occupies a portion of three States, extending East and West 87 miles, and North to South 54 miles. This belt includes 62 townships in Southwestern Wisconsin, 8 in Eastern Iowa, and 10 in Northern Illinois. The portion included in Wisconsin and Illinois is directly accessible to Galena, and is called the "Galena Mines." This district has an area of 1,000,000 acres. The ore has been struck in every direction all over this great field. The lead is found in horizontal veins, varying from half an inch to ten inches in thickness. It is sometimes found in solid masses of great weight. The average of pure lead in the ore is about 70 per cent.

Iron abundant. Iron has not been extensively worked in Illinois, though it exists in workable quantities. It abounds in the Northern part of the State. In Hardin County, on the Ohio, large deposits have been found. Several furnaces are in operation. In Monroe and Randolph there are said to be extensive deposits of iron ore. About four miles north of Jonesboro', in Union County, and two and a half miles west of the Illinois Central Railroad, there is a ridge rising abruptly to the hight of 200 feet, called Iron Mountain. The base of the hill, for 50 feet or more, consists of fossil shale intermixed with masses of hematite iron ore.

Silex, etc. The best qualities of silex for glass manufacture are found in Alexander and Pulaski counties. Salt in Hardin, Saline, Effingham and Pope counties. Petroleum in Clark, Livingston and La Salle; copper in Monroe, Fulton, Rock Island and Jo Daviess; crystalized gypsum in St. Clair; quartz crystal in Gallatin; gold in Jo Daviess and Fulton; and silver in Stevenson county.

Iowa. Iowa has a total area of 57,045 square miles, nearly the size of Illinois. Her area has not been ascertained. The State has not seen fit to order a geological survey. But from what appears on the surface of the country merely, is sufficient evidence of very great mineral wealth.

Variety of minerals. Lead, coal, copper, hydraulic limestone, and iron have been found. Her coal field is very extensive throughout the valley of the Des Moines. Lead is abundant in the Northeast; copper along the river opposite Jo Daviess county, Illinois; and hydraulic limestone in several of the central counties in the valley of the Des Moines.

We wish in the light of facts now presented, to argue the advantages that these rich mineral areas afford for manufactures.

Manufactures generally to spread— Space cannot be afforded for the interesting argument in favor of manufactures, naturally deduced from these premises. The inexhaustible amounts, and wide distribution of coal, iron and lead, promise a general spread of common manufactures, to the great benefit of all interests; and the great variety of minerals will enable a central manufacturing city to obtain all requisite materials for extraordinary products. —help a central city.

Prof. Waterhouse. We are also indebted to Professor Waterhouse for another paper in the *Merchants' Magazine*, March, 1867 :—

THE ILLINOIS CHESTER COAL FIELDS.

By Prof. Waterhouse.

Ills. Chester coal. Some researches which I have recently made on the subject of our iron interests have led me incidentally to investigate our available resources of coal fit for the manufacture of iron. The following results are derived from authorities which seemed entitled to credence. If there are errors in the statements, it is thought they are not of sufficient magnitude materially to affect the soundness of the general conclusions.

Location. The Chester coal bed is located in Randolph, Jackson and Perry counties, Illinois. Eighteen thousand acres has been tested, and three strata of coal found. The situation and richness of these beds are indicated in the following figures :

Strata.

Veins.	Depth.	Thickness.
First	36 feet.	6 feet.
Second	77 "	4½ "
Third	119 "	6 "

The quantity of coal in the area already examined is, according to the common methods of measurement, 450,000,000 tons. So vast an amount fatigues the imagination. The quantity is practically inexhaustible. The coal deposits of Illinois alone are said to exceed those of the United Kingdom of Great Britain. Quantity.

The Chester mines are accessible and convenient. There seems to be a providential design in their location. In the immediate neighborhood of our colossal mountains of iron, there are immense beds of coal fit for the purposes of smelting. The coal field lies only twelve miles from the Mississippi River, fifty miles from the iron mountains of Missouri, and seventy-two from St. Louis by river. A railroad from Chester to the mines is now contemplated. This road will connect with the St. Louis and Cairo Railway, which has been already surveyed. It will be twelve miles long, and cost $300,000. Contiguous to Iron mountain. Railway to be built.

The quality of the Chester coal is superior. Its freedom from impurities fits it for the manufacture of iron. It has less than one per cent. of sulphur, and is comparatively free from bitumen. It has been tested in the blast-furnaces of Ironton, Ohio. Tried by practical men, it has borne the severest tests, and proved its superiority to the coal from the mines of Brier Hill. Heretofore this Ohio coal has been regarded as the best in the country, but now it must yield its preëminence to the Chester mines. Iron manufacturers assert that this Illinois coal makes a better and stronger metal than the Scotch pig. Quality superior—to Brier Hill.

The value of these exhaustless coal fields to the Western country may be inferred from the fact that there are, in the whole Mississippi Valley, but three other places where coal suitable for the manufacture of iron is found. Coal to make iron in three places.

The mines of Pittsburg yield golden revenues. The shipments from that port during last November were 2,600,000 bushels, and the net profits $800,000; 650,000 tons were landed at Cairo for marine and manufacturing uses. St. Louis annually consumes 400,000 tons of coal, at an average of $3.75 a ton. In 1866 Pennsylvania shipped to the tide water upwards of $67,000,000 worth of coal. There is no substantial reason why the Chester mines should not yield a corresponding wealth. Pitts. mines. Pa. product.

The strongest economic motives urge the West to develop its own coal fields. Coal from the Chester beds can be delivered on the banks of the Mississippi at $1.50, and at St. Louis for $2.20 a ton. West to develop its coal.

This coal can be used for manufacturing purposes. But it is a strange illustration of the indifference of Western men to their own interests that blacksmiths within thirty miles of the Chester mines are using for their forges an inferior coal from Pennsylvania. The freight from Pittsburg is more than the total cost of the Chester coal. The Pittsburg coal must be converted into coke before it can be used for smelting iron ore; but the Chester coal requires no change. It can be used in its original state. Steamboatmen prefer this coal. It generates more steam, and is free from clinker. On the lower Mississippi, Pittsburg is bringing $6.00 a ton. Illinois coal can be furnished for one-third of this price. Chester coal valuable for manufg. Compared with Pitts.

Dr. Litton, Professor of Chemistry in Washington University, has recently analyzed two specimens of Chester coal, with the following results: *Dr. Litton.*

Analysis of Chester coal.

Moisture	2.78	per cent.
Volatile Combustible Matter	31.62	"
Carbon in Coke	61.23	"
Ashes (light colored	4.37	"
Coke	65.60	"
Sulphur	.37	"

Sulphur and Bitumen are the chief elements which unfit coal for the manufacture of iron. The amount of these substances in the Chester coal is surprisingly small.* Little sulphur and bitumen.

The early doubt that mineral coal could be used, without coking, to make iron, is now dissipated by conclusive facts. In Pennsylvania and the Mahoning Valley, raw mineral coal is not only employed in making iron, but it is actually driving charcoal furnaces out of competition. Raw coal affords a far intenser heat than coke. The richness of our ores and the superiority of our coal greatly increase the productive capacity of our furnaces. Coking unnecessary.

The fortunate invention of the Bessemer process of smelting iron, will still further enlarge the results and diminish the cost of production. But even if it is necessary to reduce the Illinois coal to coke, there is still a profitable difference in our favor. The cost of coking Pittsburgh coal is 70 cents per ton; that of Chester, 50 cents per ton. Bessemer process.

*Of what is the "volatile combustible matter" composed? suggests Col. Foster. A query.

15

Coal used raw. Benefits to St. L.

But practical experiments show the fitness of Chester coal, in its raw state, for the manufacture of iron. The importance of this fact can scarcely be exaggerated. It will lead to the erection, in the vicinity of St. Louis, of the largest iron works in the United States. It is difficult to magnify the possible extent of this industry. Thirty thousand tons of iron were recently shipped from Ironton to Pittsburgh to fill a single order. Doubtless a portion of the iron manufactured from this ore is brought back to St. Louis. Our dealers would, therefore, incur a triple expense.

Cost of iron at Pitts.

Freight of ore to Pittsburgh, per ton	$7 00
Freight of manufactured iron from Pittsburgh, per ton	8 00
Cost of manufacture, per ton	8 00*

Chi. rejoices in St. Ls'. prosperity.

We rejoice in the prospects of St. Louis for manufacturing. The more numerous and larger the cities of the Great West, the larger must that become which shall be emporium of all. Therefore Chicago rejoices in the special advantages of each, the general of all.

Both must import materials. St. L. cannot supply Chi.

Neither St. Louis nor Chicago having coal or iron in close proximity, they expect their commercial and distributing facilities will enable them to compete with sites more favorable for one or the other or both minerals. As between these chief points, the difference in cost of transportation would be the first item to be considered, though there are others. Were Chicago compelled to draw coal from Chester, iron from the Iron Mountain, she would have to lose the first manufacture, and take pigs and blooms. But would that profit go to St. Louis? The furnaces on the Mississippi that could supply Chicago, would have so wide demand from other cities of the West, that to save a few cents per ton each on ore and coal, would be a good profit. To Sulphur Springs on the Mississippi, just above Chester, is 40 miles from Ironton. There, or in the vicinity, will coal and iron come together, pigs and blooms costing Chicago the extra tonnage by river and canal with no handling. If we depend on Chester coal also, the same extra cost lies against us, perhaps $2. per ton on iron and coal. Against this, we have, as we shall see, an important advantage in climate; and how far could St. Louis distribute manufactures upon the 11,000 miles of western railway, listed p. 36, before her advantage will have been doubled, tripled and quadrupled in railway freights? So that had we no sources of supply but those of St. Louis, we could still compete with her successfully. But we have other dependence. First—

Near Chester the place. Cost Chi. $2. per ton extra. Offset in freight facilities.

Prof. Waterhouse hard on Pitts.

*Were the Professor's subsequent calculations given, some sharp fellow or other might set himself to analysing them, and imagine something wrong in the figures, casting discredit upon other statements which are doubtless correct. One would suppose that such a "triple expense" was enough for poor Pittsburgh to bear; but the iron-hearted St. Louisian cyphers it out, that "a daily product of pig metal would cost at Pittsburgh $588.00; St. Louis, $226.80. Difference in favor of St. Louis furnace, $361 20." All this Pittsburgh has to bear, besides the extra cost of 20 cents per ton for coking. Anybody but a St. Louisian would have let Pittsburgh off at a less cost than $23 for iron made from Pilot Knob ore, delivered at St. Louis; for that makes him pay $7 per ton for freight of ore, and then $8 back, ($1 extra because it is now manufactured and must go down stream most of the way), besides $8 per ton to the manufacturer, (to which Pittsburgh will not object). The Professor, however, not only makes the cost of "Chester coal less than one-half that of Pittsburgh," but says that "irrespective of the difference between the prices of Chester and Pittsburgh coal, a furnace at Pilot Knob, with a daily capacity of 24 tons, would save $250 every twenty-four hours." The practical part, therefore, had best be exscinded, lest it should weaken the scientific, which is, no doubt, fair and truthful.

Lake Superior Iron and Copper.—This unequaled region of the globe for the supply of these priceless minerals, is the chief dependence of Chicago. The canal around St. Marie's Falls was opened in 1855, previous to which a little ore had been hauled below the falls for shipment. That season 1,447 tons were shipped; and 1867, *five hundred thousand, two hundred and thirty-one* (500,231) gross tons of ore and iron, according to the *Lake Superior Mining Journal.* Mr. S. C. Baldwin reports the shipments of ore alone *five hundred and thirteen thousand and sixty-two* (513,062) *tons of* 2,000 *lbs.* This is nearly one-sixth of the total U. S. product in 1860, according to the census:

Lake Superior iron and copper.

1855, 1,447 tons iron ore—

—1867, 500,231 tons gross.

From the first use its superiority has been acknowledged by competent judges, and the Editor of *Hunts' Merchants' Magazine*, in his Journal of Mining for January, 1857, spoke of—

Merch. Mag. 1857.

THE IRON OF LAKE SUPERIOR.

The superiority of Lake Superior iron over that obtained from any other locality has been often proved in our pages to our readers, but our attention has again been called to it by an article from the pen of one of our cotemporaries, whose scientific knowledge has contributed not a little to the interest of our pages and the enlightenment of our readers. The article in question speaks for itself, and we will now only refer to tenacity and strength of this iron as compared with that of other localities. The following results obtained by Professor W. B. Johnson, will show the exact position of the different metals:—

Superiority of Lake Superior iron.

Strength compared with others.

				Strength in lbs. per square inch.
Iron from	Salisbury Connecticut, by means of	40	trials	58,000
"	Sweden "	4	"	58,084
"	Center County Pa. "	15	"	58,400
"	Lancaster County Pa. "	2	"	58,061
"	McIntire, New York "	4	"	58,912
"	England (cable bolt) "	5	"	59,105
"	Russia "	5	"	76,069
"	Carp River, Lake Superior, determined by Major Wade			89,582

Thus it will be seen that Lake Superior iron is about one-third better than all other kinds but one, and that one kind is far inferior.

One-third better.

There is no doubt but that when once the most perfect mode of manufacturing it is attained by experience, it will prove better than the above estimate; but even should it not, the present position which it occupies is a sufficient guaranty of its excellence.

That suffices.

In speaking of this, the Buffalo Express says some of this iron was recently tested in Shepherd's Foundry in that City, with a view to try its tenacity. A piece of rolled-iron, of the thickness of one's wrist, was subjected to various processes, and, after bending across an anvil, twisting it in opposite directions, and in fact, employing upon it all possible force and skill, the experimenters were compelled to acknowledge that they never before had known any iron capable of such stubborn resistance to breaking force. The fracture of this pig metal glistens like steel, and the fibre of the rolled-bars is tougher than that of any other iron known to the trade. Of the different qualities found there it is not necessary to speak, as it varies in the same mines, yet it can be reduced to about the same average in nearly all of them. We learn, on good authority, that the Eureka ore, which has generally been considered of inferior quality, makes the best iron manufactured at the Wyandotte Mills; and that it improves the other ores materially when mixed with them. The increased demand for the Jackson and Cleveland Mountain ores is sufficient ground for the assumption that they are the best to be obtained without the aid of the comparison given above, but with the addition of scientific tests there is no longer room for doubt. It has frequently been placed in the most trying places, and subjected to the severest tests, but we have yet to learn that it has been found

Tried in Buffalo.

Fibre tough.

Best at Wyandotte Mills.

70 per cent. iron.

wanting. A chemical analysis of the ores of this region make them yield about 70 per cent. though in many instances they will far exceed that, and of the quality we need no further evidence than that heretofore given in our pages.

Col. Foster's Report most satisfactory.

The most complete, satisfactory account of the Lake Superior iron district met with, is that of the accomplished geologist, Col. J. W. Foster, in 1865, to the Board of Directors of the Iron Cliffs Company. The whole is important to a full understanding, but space can only be given for extracts. In Part I, Geology, after describing the geographical position, he gives—

Area of iron ores—

Area of the Iron Ores.—There is no region of the earth where the ores of iron are developed on a scale of such grandeur, or concentrated in such a state of purity as on the southern shore of Lake Superior. Dannemora, Nijny Tagilisk, Elba, or Missouri may contain isolated deposits equally rich; but these combined would occupy a mere patch on the surface over which the ores of this region are known to be distributed.

—150 miles E. and W., 6 to 70 N. and S.

This area is somewhat irregular in outline; its length, east and west, is about 150 miles, with a variable width, north and south, of from 6 to 70 miles but the greatest concentration of these ores thus far observed, is in Township 47, north, Ranges 26, 27, and 28 west.

Mode of Occurrence.

Mode of Occurrence of the Iron Ores.—It may be stated, as a general rule, that the great iron deposits of the district occur in close proximity to the igneous rocks, mainly greenstone. This rock forms nearly all of the prominent peaks of the region, not in continuous ranges, but in a succession of dome-shaped knobs, while the iron ores repose upon their sides or dip beneath their bases, so that the greenstone appears rather in the form of intercalated beds than as wedge-shaped masses.

Knobs or ridges.

The whole region has been subjected to a powerful denudation, and the greenstone being the more unyielding rock, has been left in the form of knobs or of ill defined ridges. I cannot recall an instance where it forms a true axis of elevation.

Beds 400 or 500 ft thick

The beds of iron ore often attain a thickness of four or five hundred feet, and may be traced longitudinally for five thousand feet, but they are far from being persistent in character.

Quartzose materials abound.

The quartzose materials so abound that it is only in pockets, or lenticular bands, that the highly concentrated ores are found. This is seen at all of the mines which have been extensivsly worked, and the necessity of sinking below drainage has already arisen, and preparations have been made to meet it, by driving adits and by erecting pumping machinery.

Varieties of ore.

Ores of Iron.—The iron ores of this region may be arranged under the following heads: 1st, Magnetites; 2d, Red Hæmatites; 3d, Brown Hæmatites; 4th, Manganesiferous Ores; 5th, Argillaceous Ores. [These are described and the location.]

Worth, little known as yet.

Localities of Iron Ore on the Company's Lands.—With our present knowledge of these lands, it is to be presumed that we know very little of the metallic wealth which they contain. Even of the known deposits, few have been systematically explored, and I have information as to the existence of others which I have been unable personally to inspect.

The explorations in the future will undoubtedly prove as successful as in the past.

Great variety, pure, exhaustless.

Enough, however, is known, to give the assurance that these lands contain a combination of ores not before observed in the district, of great purity, exhaustless in quantity, and most favorably situated for mining and smelting. [After 15 pages of description of the various mines, Col. F. adds:—]

More examinations develop more merits.

I here close my enumeration of the observed localities of iron ores on the Iron Cliffs Company's lands. Further reconnoisances will doubtless add largely to the list. I have not had the time carefully to examine and pass upon the merits of but few of these deposits. To arrive at a true estimate of value, the explorer must lead with his axe and hammer, to be followed by the miner with his pick and

Superficial views insufficient.

shovel, and then by the chemist with his crucibles. He who professes to judge of the value of a deposit at a single glance, has powers of observation which I cannot claim. The "mountain masses," of which so much has been said, whether in Dannemora or Missouri, or on Lake Superior, are not all merchantable ores. I saw the Cleveland and Lake Superior mines at a time when I could not direct at what point 20 tons of merchantable ore could be extracted.

Enough, however, has been revealed to enable me to assure the Company that they have an abundance of first class ores, and some of them containing valuable properties heretofore undetected in the region, to answer all of the requirements for local use and for exportation, in positions accessible to railroads, and high above drainage. The latter consideration is a matter of prime interest in all mining enterprises. The disadvantages of working under drainage are not simply the cost of lifting the water by powerful pumps, nor even the increased expense of sinking, compared with throwing down. For while there may be a sump hole deep enough to collect the water, it still permeates through the seams and fissures of the rock, which renders repeated charging and firing in the same holes almost impossible, and the drilling and firing much less effective of results. In the mines now principally worked the necessity of soon working under drainage is already recognized, and preparations for that purpose are making. At the Tilden and Foster mines, breasts 100 feet in height can be attained at an inconsiderable expense, compared with the benefits to be attained.

First class ores abundant. High mining—its advantages. 100 feet breast.

Mode of Mining.—These ores are wrought in open quarry. Belts of peculiar richness, varying from 40 to 100 feet and even more in width, are found intercalated with jaspery and argillaceous materials, which close up, and again expand. In approaching these belts, it is often necessary to trench, or tunnel through an unproductive rock at right angles to the prolongation of the ore-deposits, which, when reached, are worked in open trenches, often 500 feet in a linear direction, and often with a breast of sixty feet. It is necessary to throw down the ore with blasts. The jumpers used are made of 1¼ inch steel, expanded into bits of 1¾ inches. The holes are sometimes sunk to the depth of 14 feet, using for the purpose sinking hammers of the weight of about 8 lbs. The degree of hardness in the ore is variable. The superintendent of a mine informs me that he has known three men to work 11 hours to penetrate a foot in a jaspery ore; and again, in a red hæmatite, the same foree has been penetrated 14 feet in the same time; but the average sinking in the granular or specular ore is about 8 feet a day. It not unfrequently happens that a single blast, where the miner has availed himself of the seams in the ore, throws down 1,000 tons.

Mode of mining. Blasting. Ease of drilling varys. Blasts throw down 1,000 tons.

The deep holes are generally charged with from 2 to 7 feet of powder, and covered with from 1 quart to 2 quarts of sand; and it often happens that the first blast merely shatters the rock, and repeated charges are required to throw it down. The amount of ore thrown down ought to average 5 tons to a man each day. The ore is broken up with heavy sledges, loaded into carts, which convey it to covenient platforms, from which it is dumped into cars. The cost of mining a ton of ore at this time, when miner's wages are $2,50 a day, is from $1,25 to $1,50 a ton.

5 tons a day an average. Broken with sledges. Cost $1,25 to $1,50.

Then in Part II, Metallurgy and Commercial values, Col. Foster considers—

The Lake Superior Ores. Their Peculiar uses and Application.—I propose to enter into the metallurgy of these ores so far as they possess qualities which do not appertain to the impure carbonates of the Coal Measures of Western Pennsylvania and Northern Ohio. The furnaces which have sprung up in this portion of the Appalachian coal field, are the great consumers of the Lake Superior ores. This consumption, great as it is, will, with the development of the country and with enlarged facilities of communication, assume still more collossal proportions.

Uses and application of ores. Pa. and Ohio chief consumers.

From these ores, with skillful manipulation, can be made an iron of almost any desired strength, ductility, or tenacity; capable of being drawn into the finest wire, or forged into the most ponderous anchor; of being rolled to the thinness of paper, or the thickness of an armour plate; of being converted into a needle for the finest cambric, or a cable to sustain the weight of a loaded train; of being softened so as to receive the slightest touch of the graver, or hardened to take almost the celestial temper of Michael's sword.

What the ores will make.

Foreign Ores Analogous to those of Lake Superior.—Of all the foreign ores, those of Sweden, in their mode of occurrence and in the peculiar qualities of the iron, present the strongest resemblance to those of this district.

Foreign ores analogous.

England derives her main supplies from the argillaceous ores of the Coal Measures and the Lias, while the balance is made up of the spathic carbonates and the red hæmatites of the Carboniferous and the brown hæmatites of the Oölite.

Eng. supplies.

In France and Belgium, the limonites furnish three-quarters of all the iron ore; Prussia, on the other hand, has a large variety from which to select, such as brown and clay iron ore, black band, red and spathic ore, bog ore, and to a limited extent magnetic ore.

France and Belgium.

Russia.

In Russia, the magnetites enter largely into the production of iron, which has a reputation second to that of no other country. [An account of the Swedish mines is omitted.]

Analysis. Free of sulphur. Little manganese hitherto. Now found.

Analysis of the Lake Superior Ores.—While these ores are as free as those of Sweden from all those substances which impair the value of iron, and which the most careful manipulation has failed thus far to eliminate, they surpass them in one respect, in their freedom from sulphur which in the Swedish ores is, as we have seen, got rid of by calcination—a process to which the Lake Superior ores are not subjected. On the other hand, the Swedish ores contain a notable percentage of manganese, which, in the ores heretofore shipped from Lake Superior, has been found in a hardly appreciable amount; but now, ores rich in this substance are known to exist, and under circumstances to be made available. [Analyses are given from Foster and Whitney's Report, and some by Bar, published in Paris 1857. The "Impure Carbonates of the Coal Measures," exhibits the injury of sulphur and phosphorus in most ores, which is followed by "The Effects of foreign Ingredients on the quality of Iron and Steel," thus concluding—]

Free from hurtful— —abound in good qualities.

From this somewhat extended review of the chemical composition of iron ores, it will be seen that on the one hand, while those of Lake Superior are characterized by an almost entire freedom from those substances which are hurtful to the manufactured product, on the other they possess, and particularly in the recently discovered manganeseferous ores, qualities which will neutralize, to a certain extent, the defects which appertain to the coal measure ores of Ohio and Pennsylvania.

Mixture of ores— —gives best iron.

Admixture of Ores.—The standard of iron has vastly improved since iron-masters resorted to admixture, either of the different ores to produce pig-iron, or of different qualities of pig-iron to produce the bar. In this way it is maintained a better iron is produced than from any single ore, however meritorious; and fortunately, at this day, the means of intercommunication are so direct that the iron-master may command the pig-metal of half a continent, and make his fusion with little enhanced expense.

Buffalo furnace.

At the Union Works, at Buffalo, which for completeness of structure, including all details, I believe to be unsurpassed in the country, the admixture is as follows:

Its mixture.

5-13 Lake Superior, yielding	65 per cent.
5-13 " Champlain "	60 " "
2-13 Clinton, N. Y., silicious, yielding	45 " "
1-13 Blackband Tuscarawas, Ohio	45 " "
Average	58 6-13 " "

Silica added in flux.

As these ores are not silicious enough, *per se*, to make a good cinder when brought in contact with lime, a limestone containing 15 per cent. of silica is selected as a flux in preference to a pure carbonate.

Lake Cham. ore cheapest.

The Lake Champlain ores are delivered at Buffalo cheaper than those of Lake Superior. Other things being equal, the latter would be substituted to the extent of 10-13.

To make 1 ton iron.

To make a ton of iron are required,—Anthracite, (Pittston Valley,) 3,600 lbs. Combined ores, 3,600 lbs. Limestone, 1,000 lbs.

Cost of ingredients.

The cost of these ores in Buffalo in 1863, was—Lake Superior, $7,00 per ton; Lake Champlain, $6,40 per ton; Clinton, Oneida County, $4,05 per ton; Black Band, Tuscarawas, $7,00 per ton.

Pittsburgh mnfr.

At Pittsburgh, each manufacturer uses the product of different furnaces, to produce, as his experience suggests, the precise quality of iron fitted for the use intended, whether castings, bar-iron or steel.

Chooses from a variety.

He has a wide range to select from, for to this point is sent the product of the furnaces from Eastern and Western Pennsylvania, Ohio, Tennessee, Kentucky, and Michigan, and made from a variety of ores—the brown and red hæmatites, the specular and magnetic ores, and the argillaceous ores of the Coal Measures, and with a variety of fuel—the anthracite, the hot and cold blast charcoal, the raw bituminous coal, and the coke.

Required materials.

At Pittsburgh, to make a ton of pig-iron, are required—Lake Superior iron, 1½ tons; Coke, 125 to 130 bushels; Limestone, ½ ton.

For rich Lake Superior ores— —can pay $12 per ton.

The effect of making the burden of the furnaces entirely of the rich ores of Lake Superior is to increase their yield, and this yield is estimated as high as 60 per cent. as compared when the lean ores of the coal measures are employed. The iron-master, therefore, of Northern Ohio, or Western Pennsylvania, can well afford to pay $12 per ton for the imported ores from Lake Superior, rather than $5 per ton for those which occur in the vicinage.

Hitherto, the ores sent from Lake Superior have been of a single character, if we except the limited shipments of red hæmatite from the Jackson mine; but the explorations on the Company's property show that there exist in economical quantities, at least six varieties of ores, and each free from noxious ingredients, from which the iron-master may make his combinations to produce an iron of almost any desired quality. These varieties I recapitulate: magnetic, specular, red oxide, brown hæmatite, argillaceous oxide, and manganesiforous ore. Only 1 kind exported. Varieties large.

That these ores smelted separately would produce a homogeneous iron is not to be expected; but that each possesses certain properties, differing one from another, in reference to elasticity, extensibility, tenacity, hardness, etc., is evident from the whole history of iron metallurgy; and in discussing these properties I regret that my judgment is formed on the chemical composition of the ores, rather than the result of actual working. Of this great fact I am convinced, that the highest capacities of the Lake Superior ores have not been developed. Benefits of mixing. Judgment scientific, not practical.

Special Qualities of the Iron Ores. Steel Manufacture.—It is a well established fact that the finer varieties of steel are only made from the specular and magnetic ores. The famous Indian wootz is made from a magnetic ore containing about 40 per cent. quartz and 58 per cent. magnetic oxide. Steel mnfr.

In 1862, Great Britain, notwithstanding she smelted over 4,500,000 tons of pig-metal, imported upwards of 36,200 tons of iron from Sweden, Russia, and Madras, mainly for steel purposes. The Dannemora iron prepared for steel purposes costs the Sheffield manufacturer £30 per ton, which is five or six times more than the price of ordinary coke iron. The enormous price of foreign iron has led the English manufacturer to resort to the home product as far as possible, which, with the extreme care in its fabrication, is found to be suitable for the ordinary uses of steel, but the finer varieties are still made from the product of specular and magnetic ores. Eng. supply.

It is evident that the time is rapidly approaching when the United States will no longer be dependent on England for steel. Within the past few years Pittsburgh has entered largely into its manufacture, making every variety, from the coarse steel for ploughshares to that for articles destined to receive the highest temper and polish. U. S. to make its steel. Pitts. mnfr.

In 1862, she produced of Cast Steel, 5,350 tons; other kinds, 14,850. Increase.

Compare this with the product of other countries and we shall be struck with its magnitude. England produces annually 40,000 tons; France, 14,954 tons; Prussia, 5,453 tons; Austria, 13,037 tons. Foreign mnfr.

In this province, I foresee a large demand for the specular and manganesiferous ores of Lake Superior.

The Bessemer Process. [An interesting account Col. F. thus concludes:—]The great desideratum, so far as relates to the uses and applications of iron, is *cheap steel*, and those who are interested in such matters were disposed to hail the Bessemer process as the harbinger of such an event. It is of immense importance to the railway interest alone, in the substitution of the steel for the iron rail, since experiment has shown that it is eight times as durable, while at existing prices it is not eight times as expensive; and there are thousands of other interests in which the substitution would be equally beneficial. Bessemer process. Steel for railways.

The specular ores of this region, rich in iron and in their freedom from phosphorus and sulphur, and the manganesiferous ores in close proximity, offer the most promising field in the world for the realization of this great problem. What ores best for this process.

The various uses of iron are considered, Railroad Bars, Armour Plate, Gun-Metal, Car Wheels, Wire Rope, showing Lake Superior iron suitable; then a "Table showing the tensile Strength of Wrought Iron" is introduced, of which the most important tests having been given, p. 227, it is here omitted. Col. Foster thus considers— Various uses. Strength.

Strength of Lake Superior Ores.—The French irons, which show no very remarkable tensile strength, are made from the limonites. French iron.

The Russian iron, which shows a strength unsurpassed except in a few instances, is made from the magnetic ores. Russian.

The Phillipsburg wire drawn iron, which shows such marked tenacity, was made from the magnetic ores of the Andover mine, which, unfortunately, has become exhausted. Phillipsburg.

Salisbury, Ct., and Pa. The iron of Salisbury, Ct., Centre and Lancaster Counties, Penn., is made from the brown hæmatites, and in charcoal furnaces, and is fully equal to the standard of the best English iron.

Major Wade's test of Lake Sup. iron. The specimen of Lake Superior iron, which shows a greater tensile strength than any on record, was made in a catalan forge, and drawn out from a bloom at the Jackson works. It was selected by me on the spot, and placed in the hands of Major Wade of the Ordnance Bureau, whose office it was to test the strength of guns made for the Government, and the results of his experiments are given in the above table.

Best admixture— *En resumé*, it is believed that the following admixtures of Lake Superior ores, will produce iron of the required qualities:

—for various uses. For steel, the specular ores with 10 per cent. of manganesiferous ores. For iron requiring great tensile strength, specular ores. For soft iron, easily turned, for machinery, where extraordinary strength is not required, the brown hæmetites. For railroad iron, where hardness and tenacity are required, specular ores with the addition of 10 per cent. of the manganesiferous ores. For gun metal, a union of the specular and brown hæmatites, with 10 per cent. of the manganesiferous ores. For casting car-wheels, equal mixtures of the specular and brown hæmatite ores. For smooth castings, brown hæmatite. [The Production and Shipment of Ores, are omitted, as we have later information.]

Distribution of Lake Superior Ores.—The subjoined statement, though not claimed to be strictly exact, is believed to be nearly so:

Places where Lake Sup. ores were used, 1864.

	Furnaces.	Roll. Mills.	Gross Tons.
1 Buffalo	4	1	28,000
2 Pittsburgh	7	25	50,000
3 Shenango Valley, New Castle, Sharon, Middlesex... &c	10	3	56,000
4 Brady's Bend, Pa	3	1	5,000
5 Mahoning Valley, Youngstown, Niles, Mineral... Ridge, &c. Ohio	12	2	60,000
6 Black River Loraine County, Ohio	2	....	2,500
7 Cleveland, Ohio	1	1	5,000
8 Massilon and Dover, Ohio	3	....	....
9 Toledo, Ohio	1	....	2,000
10 Detroit	3	1	16,500
11 Lake Superior	6	....	12,000
12 Miscellaneous, mainly for furnace linings at Wheeling, Zanesville, Ironton, Cincinnati, Kittaning, &c	....	....	4,500
	52	34	241,500

Buffalo. 1. *Buffalo* has become a leading mart in iron manufacture. The Union Iron Works comprise three furnaces and one rolling mill. The annual product is about 24,000 tons of pig-metal, which is consumed by the rolling mill, producing bar iron of extra sizes, such as rails, girders, propeller shafts, etc. Pratt & Co. have, within the past year, erected a furnace of 8,000 tons capacity. The fuel employed is anthracite.

Pittsburgh. 2. *Pittsburgh.*—Of the seven furnaces two are owned by Laughlin & Co., two by the Lake Superior and Pittsburg Company, and three by Graff & Bennett,—each of which has a capacity of making twenty tons of pig-iron a day. The best coal for smelting is obtained on the Connelsville Railroad, sixty miles from the city, from a 12 feet seam. It is a soft coal, too bituminous to use raw, but makes an admirable coke.

Shenango Valley. 3. *Shenango Valley.*—These furnaces are owned as follows: J. M. Crawford & Co., 1; Reis, Brown & Berger, 1, New Castle; James Wood & Co., 4; Coleman, Westerman & Co., 1; C. M. Reed & Co., 3,—Middlesex. Some of the furnaces will produce 6,500 tons of pig.iron annually, but the average will not exceed 5,600. Some are run entirely with Lake Superior ores, while others are run with a mixture of local ores. The fuel employed is raw coal obtained from a seam near the base of the coal measures.

Brady's Bend Iron Co. 4. *Brady's Bend Iron Co.*—This large company, whose works are located on the Alleghany River, have thus far used the Lake Superior ores sparingly; but with improved reilroad communications with Lake Erie, which will soon be open, they will hereafter become large consumers.

5. *Mahoning Valley.*—These furnaces are owned by the following firms: Brown, Bonnel & Co., 1, Wm. Ward & Co. 4, Niles; Jouth Ward, & Sons, 2, Mineral Ridge; Brier Hill Co., 2, Crandal, Tod & Co., 1, Eagle Furnace Co., 1, J. B. Canfield, 1, Youngstown; and McCrary, Bailey & Co., 1, Lowelville. Mahoning Valley.

The ores employed are mainly Lake Superior, with the kidney rock, and black-band ores of the neighborhood. The proportions are the iron-master's secret, but he produces an iron of great strength and tenacity. Throughout this region occurs a coal known as "Brier Hill," which is used in iron smelting. It has a slaty cleavage, is of a glossy jet-black color, does not soil the fingers, ignites rapidly, does not agglutinate, gives a white ash, and is free from clinker and sulphur. Chemically, it gives upwards of 61 per cent. of fixed carbon and less than three per cent. of ash. About 2½ tons net, of this coal are required to produce a ton of pig-iron. Each furnace consumes about 7,000 tons of ore annually, and produces about 5,600 tons of pig-metal. [Minor points are omitted; also, remarks upon the Local Consumption of Lake Superior; and upon Fluxes.] Brier Hill coal. Other places omitted.

The Prospective Demand for Iron.—It is not reasonable to suppose that there will be an over, production of this most precious of metals. Its use is so intimately connected with the history of the civilization of man, is so thoroughly incorporated with every branch of operative industry, that we can hardly conceive of any material benefit to be conferred on the race, which shall not be dependent on this substance for its accomplishment. Few persons estimate its full value in all that relates to the production, the transformation, and the distribution of the materials of wealth, extracted first from the sea, the soil, or the deep recesses of mines; then fashioned by a variety of processes, chemical or mechanical, into articles for food, raiment, shelter, locomotion; and finally distributed to the race for consumption in every quarter of the globe; and yet in every transformation, Iron has performed a most important part. Prospective demand for iron. Its intrinsic worth.

The railway interest of the United States alone requires an amount of iron for its annual maintenance equal to the national production a quarter of a century ago. Wants of railways.

There are in the loyal states over 34,000 miles of railway completed, or under construction, originally requiring over 3,000,000 tons of rails, and requiring an annual replacement of 370,000 tons; or if we embrace the whole Union, there are nearly 50,000 miles of railway, originally requiring 4,600,000 tons of rails, and an annual replacement of 575,000 tons, which is in excess of the whole product of the country in 1850. Although our railways have been constructed largely of English iron, the financial condition of the country is such and is likely to remain so, that we have largely ceased to import, and must depend on our local resources. Their extent. To use American iron.

Iron Product of Principal States, 1850 *and* 1860. (*U. S. Census.*)* *U. S Census.*

Product iron ore and pig iron, 1850, 1860.

States.	Tons of Ore Mined.		Tons of Pig Iron.	
	1850.	1860.	1850.	1860.
New Hampshire	5,000	1,000	200 }	3,224
Vermont	7,676	4,500	320 }	
Massachusetts	27,909	25,000	12.287	13,700
Connecticut	35,450	20,700	13,420	11,000
New York	46,385	176,375	23,022	63,145
Pennsylvania	877,283	1,706,476	285,702	553,560
New Jersey	51,266	57,800	24,631	29,048
Maryland	99,886	79,200	43,641	30,500
Ohio	140,610	228,794	52,658	94,647
Indiana	5,200	....	1,850	375
Michigan	2,700	17,900	660	10,400
Wisconsin	3,000	4,500	1,000	2,000
Missouri	37,000	42,000	19,250	22,000
Kentucky	72,010	73,600	24,245	23,362
Virginia	67,319	23,217	22,163	9,096
Tennessee	88,810	53,220	30,420	18,417
Total.	1,563,004	2,514,282	555,469	884,474

*These figures vary from my copy of the census. The table of ore in 1860, including that manufactured, was 3,218,275 tons. The total pig was 987,559 tons. The above table is only of the "principal States." Error as to Mich.

Increase with bituminous coal.

This table is instructive as showing that, in those States where charcoal is the fuel employed in smelting, there has been no increase, and, in many instances a falling off; but the great increase has been in those States that could resort to the coal fields of Pennsylvania and Ohio for fuel. [The table of annual product of other Nations is omitted.]

Competing ores.

Competing Ores.—The specular and magnetic ores have been introduced into the Ohio Valley from two other sources, in competition with the ores of Lake Superior, viz: Missouri and Lake Champlain. It falls within the sphere of this report to discuss the question of additional supplies.

Mo. ores.

Missouri Specular and Magnetic Ores.—In the counties of Iron and St. Francois, from 80 to 90 miles south of St. Louis and 60 miles west of the Mississippi River, occur the famous Iron Mountains. These are three dome-shaped hills, known as the Iron Mountain, Shepherd's Mountain and Pilot Knob. The former is distant from St. Louis 81 miles, the latter 86 miles.

Freight favors Lake Superior.

These mines are separately considered, and though the yield "is hardly as rich as the Lake Superior," yet the item of transportation is so much in favor of Lake Superior, that Col.. Foster observes:—

These ores used in N. Y., Pa., O.

Mo. ores South.

Demand increasing.

But apart from these considerations, my impression is, that with a restored country, and commerce flowing through its accustomed channels, the Lake Superior ores will monopolize the markets of Western New York, Western Pennsylvania, and Northern Ohio, while the Missouri ores will seek their appropriate fuel in Southern Illinois, Southern Ohio, and Kentucky. * * From the foregoing details, I think we may assume that, with the enlarged facilities for transportation ready to go into operation on the opening of navigation, and with an equalized scale of labor in mining, the Lake Superior ores will be used throughout a widely extended circuit, whose outer margin will reach central New York, the western slope of the Alleghanies in Pennsylvania, central Ohio, and northern Illinois.

Rapid increase of Lake region.

These mnfg. towns to beat Eng.

To produce our own iron.

This circuit embraces the most favored portion of the United States. Here population duplicates itself each decade of ten years, and to keep pace with this growth the iron product should duplicate itself also,—to say nothing of the multiplied uses which spring up as a people advances in wealth and refinement. It is the chosen seat of agriculture, and contains a coal field long enough and broad enough to cover Great Britain. It requires no prophetic power to foresee that, within this area and for all time, there will be an almost unlimited demand for these ores. Pittsburgh, the Mahoning. and the Shenango Valleys, to say nothing of Buffalo, and the ports on the southern shore of Lake Erie, will, as seats of iron-manufacture, outstrip Yorkshire, Staffordshire, and South Wales; and fifty years hence, when our resources shall have been thoroughly developed, our descendants will wonder, that, with an exhaustless supply of the purest ores, with the cheapest of all modes of conveyance —lake navigation,—and with ample supplies of fossil fuel suitable for smelting, in a healthful climate, and amid a productive soil, we were so long dependent on foreign sources for that most precious of all metals—IRON.

These views trustworthy.

These facts and opinions, prepared by one of the most accomplished, most practical geologists of the country, after careful exploration of the Lake Superior region, and with extensive knowledge of the whole subject of mineral supply and of its uses, are worthy of more than ordinary credence.

Results confirm judgment.

Advantages of Chi. in transportation—

—mixing ores.

The rapid increase of demand for these ores each of the three years since these mines were explored, abundantly confirms Col. Foster's judgment as to the superiority of these ores. If so valuable as to bear transportation into the interior of New York, Indiana, Ohio and Pennsylvania, supplanting the home product in even both these last States, the chief iron States in the Union, what advantage in iron manufacture must Chicago have, with her conveniences for obtaining this superior ore? The necessity of mixed ores, and the abundant variety Lake Superior affords, is a very important feature.

Touching further upon some of these advantages, Col. Foster appends to his Report the following paper, which was originally prepared for the *New York Tribune* and had been inserted in *Hunts' Merchants' Magazine*:— *Dr. Lamborn.*

ADVANTAGES OF LAKE SUPERIOR REGION FOR PRODUCING CHARCOAL PIG.

Lake Sup. charcoal iron.

BY DR. R. H. LAMBORN.

The proper development of the iron industry of the United States demands a steady and abundant supply of first class charcoal metal, suitable for working into car-wheels, cannon, tires for locomotives, boiler plate, and for the vast present and prospective requirements of the steel maker in the departments of cast steel, puddle steel, and, above all, for use in the Bessemer or Pneumatic converter. The relative quantity of charcoal to mineral coal iron produced in the United states has decreased with the increasing production of the vast anthracite furnaces of Eastern Pennsylvania, and with the discovery of pure bituminous coal in Ohio, while scores of charcoal furnaces, scattered through the Eastern States, have gone out of blast through the appreciation in value of timber lands, caused by the demand which has sprung up for fuel for other purposes through the building of ways of internal communication, and the demand for surface for agricultural use. These causes are, year by year, making the Eastern States less suitable for a large charcoal iron production. Where, therefore, are our manufacturers in the early future to look for their supply of this necessary raw material? England sends to Sweden, Norway, Russia and Nova Scotia for her best brands. Large demand for charcoal iron. Diminishing supply in East. Eng. supplied from Sweden, etc.

If we follow around the same northern isothermal zone in which these countries are located, we reach, upon our great lakes, a region designated by nature in the most extraordinary manner as our future domestic source, of a vast amount of excelent charcoal iron; and it is with no desire to disparage the importance, and value of the charcoal district of Northern New York, Connecticut, Northern New Jersey, and Central and Western Pennsylvania, that this article is written; but rather with the hope of drawing the attention of the skillful iron-masters of those districts to a most promising field for enterprise, and for the exercise of their peculiar knowledge—a field already inviting development, and which must continue to increase in importance as long as the iron and steel industry of the United States continues to enlarge. The belt of country along the southern shore of Lake Superior, extending 40 to 60 miles into the States of Michigan and Wisconsin, is one of the richest mineral regions on the globe. A district producing copper on the north already sends to market some 16,000 tons of the metal; a region producing—with argentiferous galena and sulphide of copper—silver and gold, is in process of development southward of this copper belt; while from Lake Monistique in Schoolcraft county, to a point as far west, at least, as the Penokee iron range, 100 miles west of Ontanagon, are found immense deposits of iron ores of all varieties common in igneous rocks, magnetic oxide, red hæmetite, brown hæmatite, as well as the water formed bog ores. These first mentioned ores, where developed, occur in vast beds adjoining hornblendic dykes, and in chloritic slates, and they exist in such quantities that they may be considered as practically inexhaustible. Same zone supplies us. Lake Sup. rich in minerals.

One-eighth of all the iron now made in the entire United States is dug from the mines of Marquette county, and yet, ten years ago, a piece of Lake Superior ore was a curiosity to most of our practical Metallurgists. * * * Supplied one-eighth the iron of U. S., 1865.

The development of the manufacture of pig from charcoal, in the county of Marquette, has been even more remarkable, as the difficulties to be encountered in building large structures, erecting new machinery, and collecting necessary labor in a distant and hyperborean region, are numerous and serious. Increase of charcoal iron more remarkable.

The earliest iron made was produced directly from the ore in what is known as the Catalan Forge. This manufacture was commenced in 1847 by Everett & Jackson, at the Jackson Forge. After it followed the Marquette Forge, then the Collinsville Forge, and lastly the Forestville Forge, all in the same vicinity, near Marquette. They made iron with more or less success for a few years, but are now in ruins, or so greatly dilapidated that much time would be required to repair them. Iron first made 1847. First works in ruins.

The production of pig iron from charcoal commencing at the Pioneer Works, near the Jackson mine, in 1858; 1,627 tons were sent to market that year. This manufacture has increased by the erection of new furnaces, until at present the Increase.

Pioneer, the Collinsville, the Forestville, the Morgan, the Northern, and the Greenwood Furnaces are in activity. The progress of the trade has been as follows:

Mnfr. 7 yrs. In 1858......1,627 tons were exported.
" 1859......7,258 " " "
" 1860......5,660 " " "
" 1861......7,970 " " "
In 1862......8,590 tons were exported.
" 1863......8,908 " " "
" 1864......13,832 " " "

Total ore 1865, 925,000 tons. The total quantity of ore already extracted, chiefly from the three first mines, is not less than 925,000 tons, nothing but "surface" or "patch work" has yet been done. All the mineral has been quarried from the shallow openings in the sides of the iron hills. No pumping machinery has yet been erected, and only Mines inexhaustible. recently have adits for drainage been begun. The surface rock indicates in many points that but a portion of the most easily obtainable ore has been quarried, and it is safe to estimate that several millions of tons are proven to exist in the three or four oldest mines, with every likelihood of vast quantities in the beds below water level.

Other localities. In addition to this are hundreds of localities where iron is known to exist in a belt of thirty miles in length, and at more than a dozen localities companies have been formed or mines commenced. Great skill is not necessary in working these ore Ease of mining. quarries. The operation consists in blasting from a ledge of ore large masses, which are subsequently broken into fragments by other blasts, by the sledge or, sometimes, in the most refractory cases, by means of a fire of huge logs.

4,000 tons by one blast. At the Jackson Mine, a hole 18 feet in depth and two inches in diameter, loaded with powder and exploded last March, brought down 4,000 tons of ore. The holes Facilities for handling and shipping. are all bored with good steel drills, managed by two strikers and one turner. The fragments of ore are loaded into one horse carts, hauled a few hundred feet to the railroad, thrown into six ton four-wheel-cars, and carried to the wharf at Marquette, where they are unloaded into pockets or hoppers, shoots, and thence into the vessels that transport them to the furnace on the lower lakes; or are transferred by wheel-Cost. barrow from the hoppers to the vessel or steamboats. The laborers at the mines receive $2, per day, work ten hours and pay $20, per month for their board. The average product of each laborer including all whose names are on the pay-roll, miners, drivers, trackmen, repairers, etc—is 2 to 2½ tons of ore per day per man. In some cases an average of five tons per day per man has been taken out by a small gang. Ninety-one cents per ton freight is paid on the railroad to Marquette, and the price of ore on the vessels is now $5, per ton.

Freight to Cleveland and Pitts. The freight from Marquette to Cleveland is $3 per ton, thence to Pittsburgh $2 to $2.50. So that ore may be laid down at the great iron manufacturing city of the Union at from $10 to $11 per ton. The lowest rates which have prevailed, I am informed by my friend H. B. Tuttle, of Cleveland, were those of 1861, when ore could be placed in Pittsburgh for $7 per ton, as follows: Cost at Marquette $2.50, Cost at Pitts. $7.00. freight to Cleveland $2, freight thence to Pittsburgh $2, insurance commission, etc., 50 cents; total $7. * * * * * * *

Process of charcoal mnfr. The long winters with their five consecutive months of snow, during which charring in pits is attended with many difficulties, renders this plan the most expedient. Charcoal is now being delivered at the furnace at 11 cents per bushel by contract. The flux used is a limestone found near the railroad, and which does not cost over 35 cents per ton of iron. The ore produces from 55 to 65 per cent., a soft hæmatite from the Jackson mine being the favorite mineral used of all the smelters. It requires 25 bushels of charcoal to reduce one ton of iron, and the Cost. furnaces produce from 10 to 18 tons in 24 hours. The cost of making iron is now about $30 per ton; but it is asserted that under the most favorable circumstances iron has been made at $14 per ton, and contracts have been entered upon for its manufacture by furnace owners with their managers at $16.50 per ton, delivered on board at Marquette. The foregoing facts will enable any one familiar with the iron business to judge the relative advantages of the region under discussion as a locality for the production of pig iron.

Future encouraging. The future of the manufacturer is encouraging; and in case the internal revenue taxes, joined with an inadequate tariff, do not force the business across the Atlantic, it will develope even more rapidly in the future than the past. Land, from which may be cut an average of 50 cords of wood per acre, may be bought at from $2.50 Competition in freights— to $4 per acre in hundreds of places along the shores of the lakes. We have seen that there are already two competing lines of railway leading from the mines to the lakes. The lakes are free to all navigators who may desire to carry ore, and in five years there will be from 12 to 15 mining companies competing for the market. This combination of circumstances will secure the delivery of ore at any point on the shore of the lake that may be selected, at rates most advantageous to the manufacturer, while the various increasing uses for charcoal-iron will always cause an ample demand for the product of his furnace. —and mining companies.

The Editor of the *Chicago Republican* kindly consents that extracts may be taken from an unpublished letter from a special correspondent:—* *Cor. Chi. Rep.*

The principal feature of Escanaba is the magnificent ore dock built by the Chicago & Northwestern R. R., a structure which has not its equal in the United States. This dock contains 196 pockets for loading ore, each pocket holding 40 to 60 tons, from which 4,000 to 5,000 tons of ore have been loaded in one day. The Company are now building another dock inland, which will be used for storing ore, and will have a capacity of 20,000 tons. This will be especially useful in winter, as by means of it and the dock on the shore of the bay, the Company will be able to accumulate ready for instant shipment on the opening of navigation, which takes place on Green Bay at least three weeks sooner than on Lake Superior. Escanaba—shipping facilities.

The railroad and dock have hardly been opened two years, and already the business done over each is immense. In 1866 the shipments of ore from Escanaba were as follows: From the Jackson Mine, 53,963 tons; New York, 33,462 tons; Cleveland, 18,518 tons; Iron Cliffs Mnfr. Co., 3,470 tons; Iron Mountain mine, 6,855 tons; a total of 116,268 tons. Increase of shipments—

In addition to the amount shipped there were also in store 7,482 tons, 900 lbs. of ore at the end of 1866. During the same year 689 tons of pig metal from the Pioneer and Morgan Furnaces were shipped from Escanaba. That these shipments are but the beginnings of an immense traffic there can be no doubt. The Peninsula R. R. branch of the Chicago & N. Western R. R. has already lapped round its rival, the Marquette & Bay De Noc R. R., and now its tracks extend into the Jackson, Cleveland, New York, Iron Mountain and Iron Cliff mines. To the two latter it affords the only outlet. The same enterprise which forestalled the slow moving Marquette and Bay De Noc R. R. Co., in the construction of the road from Negaunee to Escanaba, may also be depended on to tap every iron mine in the district; and although as a matter of course, Marquette will always have a large share of the ore and iron sent forward for shipment, yet Escanaba must continue to grow in favor, and may ultimately outstrip its northern sister. Not only is the Bay De Noc a safer anchorage than Marquette, but vessels of a larger class can lay at the docks, since no vessel drawing more than ten feet of water can enter Lake Superior, that being the depth of St. Mary's Canal. In point of distance, too, Escanaba is nearer to every port on the lower lake than Marquette, while sailing vessels bound there avoid all the vexatious delays and expenses of the passage through the St. Mary's River and Canal. Besides all this, Escanaba is open to navigation at least two weeks earlier in the spring and later in the fall than any port on Lake Superior. —yet further. Energy of N. W. railroad. Safe harbor—large draught. Distance less. Early navigation.

It is eminently desirable that Chicago merchants should inform themselves somewhat respecting capabilities of the Lake Superior mineral districts for production, and their value as customers. Trade valuable to Chi.

The *Marquette Mining Journal* remarks upon— *Marquette Jour.*

The Future Supply of Lake Superior Iron Ore.—The season now closing has been marked by a greater development of the leading interest of this region—the production of iron ore—than in any other year since the mines were opened. Future supply of iron ore.

Until this year it has been doubtful whether the supply of 67 per cent. ores would keep pace with the annually increasing demand, but it may now be considered certain that no limitation of the business will ever take place by reason of the inadequacy of the supply. 67 per cent. ores abundant.

---

* This correspondent was employed the winter of 1866-7, to explore the mining region of Lake Superior, and several letters have been published in the *Republican* giving full information. This last being a sort of *resume*, has been waiting for a convenient occasion ever since. Thorough investigation.

Supply increasing. The highest yearly product of any single mine previous to 1867 was about 90,000 tons; this year the Lake Superior Company and the Jackson Company will each produce about 125,000. The Cleveland Company, the Pittsburgh and Lake Angeline Company, and the New York mine, have also this year all increased their production about 50 per cent. over that of 1866. Machinery aids. The introduction of machinery, and the system of deep mining in the older mines, will enable them to maintain without exhaustion, a large production from year to year, although its cost will be somewhat increased, compared to that of the merely surface operations of their earlier history. Mines improve downwards. Generally speaking, the deposits of ore in these mines enlarge as they are worked downward, giving promise of an unfailing supply for the future.

New discoveries. On the New, or Magnetic Range, there is the same gratifying assurance of a future increased production. The discovery made last fall at the Washington mine of the continuance of the deposit eastwardly, proves to have been of great importance. A heavy belt of perfectly pure ore has been traced for nearly half a mile on this location, to which the entire operations of the company have been transferred. The product of this range has hardly been felt as yet, but it will hereafter figure largely in the sum total. The mine recently discovered near the Champion Furnace, about four miles west of the Washington mine, is probably upon the same range. The deposit here is of large extent and great purity, and the new mine just opening upon it will be able to make a good product next season. Under ground mining. The system of underground mining has been adopted already at the Edwards mine on the new range. The greater regularity of the occurrence of the deposit on this range, and their nearer correspondence to regular veins are calculated to facilitate this mode of mining, and to insure a large and uniform crop.

More hæmatite. A large deposit of soft hæmatite of good shipping quality has also been discovered during the past year on the land of the New England Company, and that of the Lake Superior Company adjoining, from which a considerable supply of this kind of ore can hereafter be derived. Demand increases with supply. The aggregate production of ore during this year from all the iron mines in this country is about 450,000 tons. The demand has held good up to the last days of navigation, and but little, we understand, remains undisposed of at Cleveland and Erie. It is a matter of encouragement to our local interests that in a year characterized by so much general depression of business the demand for our products has actually increased fifty per cent. over any former year. One or two years of general commercial and manufacturing following each other (which it would not be unreasonable to expect unless our national energy is to be crippled by political blunderers and plunderers), and we shall produce and export a million tons of ore a year.

Lake Sup. Mining Jour. *The Lake Superior Mining Journal*, February 1st, furnishes this statement of—

Products of Marquette Co., 1867. *Marquette County. Its Business, Product and Improvements for the Year* 1867.—Rapid as has been the development of the iron interest of Lake Superior, the year 1867 stands out in its history as unprecedented. A decade has scarcely passed since the first shipment of iron ore from the mines of Marquette County was made, and yet the grand result of the year just closed is a *half million* tons—equal to one-fourth of the entire product of the United States.*

Population increasing. The population of the county, as made up from reliable estimates, has been increased during the year by about 4,000. The total population now, cannot fall short of 14,000, showing an increase of 40 per cent.

Mines described. An account follows of each mine, its product, disposal, and increase. Also of the Marquette and Pacific Rolling Mill Co., and the Iron Bay Foundry. Shipping. Of shipping for 1867, the clearances were, steamboats, 521; vessels, 404; total, 925; tonnage 442,431. Clearances 1866, No. 765; tonnage, 381,345; an increase in No. 160; in tonnage, 61,086. The

---

Exaggeration injurious. * This statement, seen in other quarters, is a gross error. The U. S. Census, of 1860, states the annual product to June 1st, of ore mined, 908,300 tons; used in furnaces, 2,309,975 tons; total, 3,218,275 tons. The increase of Lake Superior ore is an abundant wonder, which exaggeration only destroys.

figures of The Marquette and Ontonagon Railroad are for 1867, tonnage east, 309,122; west, 30,959; total 340,081; for 1866, 236,976; increase, 103,105. Passengers 1867, 58,963; 1856, 35,591; increase, 23,372. The Editor adds remarks and tables following:—

Mar. and Ont. R. R.

The Marquette & Ontonagon, as also the Peninsular Railroad, has been taxed to its utmost to furnish transportation for the immense amount of freight pressed upon it. It has moved as many as 3,000 tons in a single day. Both roads are engaged in increasing their rolling stock this winter.

Full business.

The active capital employed in Mining and manufacturing has been increased not less than $1,000,000. The aggregate sum invested in the iron business is now about $5,000,000.

Increased capital.

Produce of Lake Superior Iron Ore, 1867.

Produce Lake Sup. ore, 1867.

Companies.	Gross tons.	* Net tons.
Jackson Iron Co.	126,391	133,280
Cleveland Iron Co.	75,822	81,480
Marquette Iron Co.	7,827	5,894
New York Iron Co.	47,000	48,024
Lake Superior Iron Co.	120,178	108,560
Pittsburgh & L. A. Iron Co.	46,607	51,967
New England Mine	9,075	9,943
Edwards Mine	4,980	5,577
Washington Iron Co.	25,440	24,726
Iron Mountain Iron Co.	5,000	3,918
Iron Cliff (estimated)	1,000	* 39,693
Total Iron ore	469,320	513,062

Manufacture of Lake Superior Pig Iron, 1867.

Lake Sup. pig, 1867.

Furnaces.	Tons.	Furnaces.	Tons.
Grenwood,	5,339	Bancroft,	3,051
Morgan,	5,050	Pioneer,	6,980
Michigan,	4,131	Northern,	1,730
Collins,	4,630		
Total, Pig Iron, tons,			30,911
Total, Iron Ore,			469,320
Total, Iron Ore and Pig, tons,			500,231

Product of Iron Ore and Pig Iron in Marquette County, from 1858 *to* 1867.

Product ore and pig from 1858 to '67.

Year.	Iron Ore.	Pig Iron.	Value.	Year.	Iron Ore.	Pig Iron.	Value.
1858	31,035	1,629	$ 249,202	1863	185,257	9,813	$ 1,416,935
1859	65,679	7,258	575,529	1864	235,123	13,832	1,867,215
1860	116,998	5,660	736,496	1865	195,256	12,283	1,590,430
1861	45,430	7,970	419,401	1866	296,872	18,437	2,405,960
1862	115,721	8,590	984,977	1867	469,320	30,911	3,475,720

* Mr. S. C. Baldwin, Superintendent of the Peninsular Railroad, before the publication of the Marquette paper, had supplied this statement of the ore products, which nearly accords; as in the last item, instead of "Iron Cliff," which is omitted, Mr. Baldwin gives amount "furnished to local furnaces," which in the other statement is included in the product of each mine.

Mr. Baldwin's statement.

First export 1855. Exportation began in 1855, when the Sault St. Marie Canal was opened, with 1,445 tons; in 1856, 11,594 tons were exported, and in 1857, 26,184 tons.

Mr. A. B. Meeker. Mr. A. B. Meeker, who restricts his trade to coal and iron, particularly the latter, furnished the Marquette paper quoted, and adds these remarks:—

Routes for ore. Of this quantity of ore, 469,000 tons, 300,000 were shipped to Cleveland, Ohio, the balance to Detroit, Erie, Buffalo and Toledo. Of pig iron the greater part was shipped to Chicago. First cargo at Chi. 1867. The first cargo of ore, 355 tons, was received from Lake Superior at Chicago in Dec. 1867. For shipment to Indiana and consumption here, 75,000 tons will be needed in 1868. This is a wonderful increase; but it is estimated that in the next five years, shipments of ore to Chicago will largely exceed those to Cleveland or any other port. Advantage of this route. The Lake Superior ores, *via* Escanaba, can come to Chicago at least $1 per ton less than to Cleveland. Escanaba, the terminus of the Peninsula Division N. W. R. R., is to be the great shipping port for Lake Superior ores, situated as it is on Lake Michigan, at the entrance to Green Bay, with one of the finest harbors on the whole chain of lakes. To Chicago it is 36 hours sail; to Cleveland 5 days, besides heavy cost for towing up and down Detroit River from Lake Huron to Erie.

Good Ia. coal. In Clay and Parke counties, Indiana, an excellent quality of splint or block coal has been discovered the past year, superior to the block coals of Mahoning Valley, Ohio, and Shenango Valley, Pa., for smelting ores. Three blast furnaces have been constructed in the last six months at Brazil, Indiana, to smelt Lake Superior ores with this coal. To smelt Lake Sup. ores. They are a great success, making pig iron, it is averred, with less coal than is being done by any other bituminous coal in the country.

To come through Chi. The Lake Superior ores for these furnaces, must be shipped from Chicago; and return ore cars can bring coal, as iron made in Indiana, Ohio and Pennsylvania, is largely shipped to Chicago, this being the great distributing point of the northwest. A Chi. iron Co. In this connection, some large capitalists here have formed a stock company of $250,000, to construct two blast furnaces, having capacity to make 60 tons pig iron per day, furnace to be in blast by 15th Sept. next. Other mills. Other parties are getting ready to erect mills to make bar and sheet-iron, nails, railroad spikes, etc. Ill. coal. It is confidently expected that our own coals, such as Wilmington and Vermillion, will smelt ores. The former, from the mines of the Rhodes Coal Co., has been tested for that purpose, and pronounced, by good iron men, a great success. Illinois has eight times the coal area of Ohio, and it is not reasonable to suppose that the Creator of all things would place this vast quantity of fuel so near to Chicago, and the great iron region of Lake Superior, and not have it used right here. Chi. a distributing point for West. The greater part of the supplies for the iron and copper regions of Lake Superior, are now shipped from here, six steam propellers being constantly engaged in the trade, during the shipping season, besides large shipments *via* Chicago & Northwestern R. R. to Escanaba. Has ¾ Lake Sup. trade. Three years ago Detroit and Cleveland had the great bulk of the trade, while now Chicago has at least three-fourths of it.

Chi. Jour. Mr. Meeker has organized an Iron Company here, thus noticed in the *Chicago Journal*:—

Mr. Meeker's Iron Co. *The Manufacture of Pig Iron at this Point.*—Several weeks since we made mention of the fact that experiments had been made in smelting Lake Superior Iron Ore in this city by Illinois Coal, from the Rhodes Coal shaft at Wilmington. Trial of Wilmington coal. The trials proved successful, and it was satisfactorily demonstrated that Iron of a very good quality could be made at a figure much below what it costs to lay the article down here, either from Lake Superior, Pennsylvania, Ohio or Indiana.

Capital $250,000. With facts and figures indisputable as to the pecuniary profits of such an enterprise, some of our prominent merchants have organized a company with a capital stock of $250,000, to be called the "Chicago Iron Company." Two blast furnaces, with a capacity to smelt thirty tons each of iron per day, will at once be erected, and put in operation just as soon as navigation opens and a supply of iron ore can be obtained.

Among the list of subscribers to the stock of this new enterprise, we find the names of A. B. Meeker, E. T. Watkins, P. L. Yoe, S. B. Cobb, Jerome Beecher, John B. Turner, George L. Dunlap, Perry H. Smith, Cyrus Bentley, George Armour, Hiram Wheeler, F. Haskell, Hugh T. Dickey, and other gentlemen largely identified with the interests of our city. Stockholders

To say that the manufacture of iron in this city is a matter of great importance, is speaking of it lightly when the advantages to be derived from it are fully considered. Chicago is naturally the grand distributing point for the West and Northwest, and the steady increase of fully 33⅓ per cent. per year in the sale of both pig and other manufactured iron, during the past five years, demonstrates the fact beyond all question. Important to Chi.

Chicago is not only the best distributing point, but it is the best port on the whole chain of lakes at which to deliver iron ore, it having the advantage of fully $1.00 to $1.50 per ton, in the shape of freight, over Cleveland. Chi. best shipping port for ore.

Escanaba, which is destined to be the great shipping point for the Lake Superior ores, is within 300 miles, and vessels from the lower lakes will gladly bring as ballast, Canada and Lake Champlain ores. Good Wisconsin ores can also be obtained, and 60 miles south of Chicago lies immense bodies of "bog ore," which assays 52½ per cent. It will thus be seen that Chicago can obtain at a lower figure a greater variety of ores than any other city or port in the United States. Wis. ores. Ill. ores.

The next question to be solved is the supply of fuel for smelting purposes, which is easily done by stating the fact that raw Illinois Coal can be laid down here in large quantities at $3 to $4 per ton. Indiana Coal, of a quality very little inferior to Brier Hill, at nearly the same figures. Pittsburgh Coke and Anthracite Coal can also be laid down here at a very small advance on the cost in Cleveland. With all these advantages, Chicago can unquestionably compete successfully in the manufacture of Pig Iron with any other city in the Union, and in place of having to pay tribute to Pennsylvania and Ohio, the State of Illinois will in the course of a few years manufacture all, or nearly all, the iron which this great Western country will need. Coal—Ill. Indiana. Pitts. Coke and Anthracite.

The success of the manufacture of Pig Iron here, once established, will insure the erection of mills for the manufacture of bar iron, nails and other descriptions of hardware—indeed Eastern capitalists are already here looking into the feasibility of at once putting into operation a first-class nail mill, and it may with truth be said that Chicago is yet in its infancy, and destined to be the greatest manufacturing point in the United States. Business will increase.

Mr. Baldwin, Superintendent of the railroad to Escanaba, says the cost of ore at the mines in 1867, was $4, and will probably be $3, this year, and railroad freight $1.75, freight to Chicago $1.50, making total cost $6.25 to $7.25, per ton. Mr. Meeker has contracted for his supply delivered here, at $6.50. Suppose we have to use Brazil coal, the cost per ton on cars is $2.75, freight $3, is $5.75, per ton. *Mr. Baldwin.* Cost of Lake Sup. ore. Brazil coal.

It requires, say 2 tons each of ore, $13, and coal, $11.50, making $24.50, and allowing $5.50 for cost of smelting, makes the very best of iron in pigs cost $30, per ton. These are outside figures, to be reduced upon each item. Doubtless competition will reduce the cost of ore, $1, to $2. Then freight will be some reduced by strong competition usually with the fleet of grain vessels, which will load in part with coal on Lake Erie, to throw off at Escanaba, and then load with ore or iron for Chicago. Down freights largely exceed up freights, and Chicago will usually have coal brought from Lake Erie, and iron from Escanaba, for a small profit above cost of handling. From $1.50 to $3, will be saved on coal. The Pennsylvania and Ohio coals will be brought down by competition to $4, or $4½ on Lake Erie, and freight to $1, or $1.25; and these coals of long-tried use, we can rely upon both in quality and amount at under $6, per ton. We are constantly hearing of Pig cost $30. To be reduced in—ore and freight— —coal and freight. Pa. and O. coals sure.

other coals equally as good and even better; but when we know that within 100 miles of Chicago, a coal as good as Brier Hill or Ormsby can be had, it will be a bright day to Chicago manufacturers. Next to them, as at present advised, the Brazil coal spoken of by Mr. Meeker, has been best tested and not found wanting. With a straight railroad, saving some 70 or 80 miles out of 250, which is contemplated, and will speedily be built, taking down ore and bringing back coal, freight will be reduced more than half. First cost, too will be less than $2.75, and this coal can be delivered for $4,50 per ton.

Brazil probably next.

To cost $4.50.

Besides, the tests of Wilmington coal afford strong evidence that we have inexhaustible beds of good quality within 50 to 60 miles of Chicago. In addition to the experiment alluded to by the *Journal*, p. 240, Mr Walker, President of the Chicago & Wilmington Coal Company, informs me that 30 tons were used by Capt. Ward at Detroit, successfully smelting Lake Superior ore. It is regarded by its friends one of the best coals brought here, the demand exceeding the supply. The railway freight is $1.40 per ton, and at $2.50 on the cars, the cost is $3.90. Even if not equal to the Brier Hill, it will take the place of that in many uses, leaving that for the special purposes for which it is wanted, and bringing down its price to the lowest possible figure.

Wilmington coal good.

Costs $3.90.

Our railways understand the interest they have in promoting the consumption of Illinois coal. The Wilmington comes by the Alton road, and their entire coal freight as yet is in this to Chicago, of which their last report thus speaks:—

Railways to give cheap freights.

Chi. & Alton Rep.

> The coal traffic of your line is yet in its infancy. Beginning in 1865 with 6,000 tons, it increased in 1866 to 71,090 tons, and in 1867 to 146,050 tons. A large number of new mines are being opened, from which an increased amount of coal will be taken the present year.

6000 tons '65. 146,050 in 1867.

> This branch of our traffic is one that must be specially cared for. The coal upon your line, when mined extensively and cheaply, as it soon will be, if proper encouragement is afforded, will contribute largely to your future income, and diminish operating expenses by reducing the cost of fuel burned upon your locomotives.

This traffic to be cared for.

> It will not only contribute to enhance the value of your property as already stated, but an All-Wise Providence has placed an almost continuous deposit of coal below a soil unsurpassed in fertility, for a distance of two hundred and thirty miles, traversed by your railway.

Coal field under road, 230 miles.

> The northern portion of this immense coal field is much nearer to Chicago than any other, (being only 55 miles) and your railway will, at no distant day, be the means of transporting nearly all the coal consumed in that city.

Nearest Chi.—only 55 miles.

We trust that concluding declaration is not to be realized, for it would become an oppressive monopoly. The Illinois Central, Rock Island, and Burlington and Quincy, pass over the coal field and transport more or less coal, and probably on other roads good quality will be found, though the Alton Road will have some advantage in distance. We shall have more roads, too, south and southwest. Then, along the canal and Illinois river, which affords the cheapest transportation, good coal may be found. We yet know very little about our immense coal field.

Competition indispensable.

Other railroads.

Canal and river.

The Chester coal is another reliance, we hope, for the cost of water transportation will not largely exceed that of railway from Wilmington. This hope is strengthened by the success of an experiment at Carondelet, near St. Louis, smelting Iron Mountain ore with Chester, or Big Muddy coal. A meeting of congratulation was held "on 'change at 12 o'clock" where speeches were made and these resolutions adopted:— Chester coal. Successful trial at St. L. *Board of Trade reslutions.*

Whereas, The iron furnace at Carondelet, smelting the ores of Missouri with the coal of Illinois, is now in successful operation, not only yielding iron in large and increasing quantities, but producing it in quality suited for the most valuable uses of mankind; and Mo. iron ore—Ill. coal.

Whereas, The entire success of this experiment, with the richest ores known, and with coal to be had in quantities as unlimited as our mountains of iron, opens a new era in the iron production of the continent, and will secure to Missouri preëminence, in the domestic iron trade of America; therefore, —secures to Mo. preeminence.

Resolved, That we, the Union Merchants' Exchange of the city of St. Louis, congratulate the people of Missouri and Illinois on the auspicious event, and invite capital, skill and labor from all parts of the world to share with us the riches that nature has provided. Congratulate Mo. and Ill.

The speeches, very appropriate, would be interesting. Though of course advocating St. Louis as the chief point of Manufacture, they sustain the important point of the general distribution of iron works throughout the vallies of the rivers. Their expectations, so far as that St. Louis is to be a great manufacturing city, will surely be realized; further deponent saith not, for it would prove nothing. St. L. made the centre. To be a great mnfg. city.

The *Illinois State Journal*, Dec. 31st, 1867, furnished an account of an experiment by the Sangamon Coal and Mining Company:— *Ill. State Jour.*

* * * This new development of coal, which has been so throughly tested, is from the mine of the S. C. & M. Co., located at Howlett, in Sangamon county, Illinois. This company own nearly 1,500 acres of coal territory, lying together in a body on the south fork of the Sangamon, and on the line of the Toledo, Wabash & Western railroad. This company commenced their operations in June last, and have developed a stratum of coal averaging six feet in thickness, probably the richest in quantity and quality yet discovered in the West. It was from the mine of this company the coal was taken that was subjected to the tests above mentioned. * * * * * * * Sang. Co. coal tried with success.

In every instance the quality of the iron produced was as good as that produced by any other coal. The shortness of the time required, as compared with that of anthracite coal, is ample proof of the great heating qualities of the coal, while the quality of the metal proves its freedom from those foreign impure substances heretofore so deleterious to the use of Illinois coals. Iron superior.

With these developments, which at all events are very favorable indications, it would appear incredible that in this greatest known coal-field of the world, good qualities should not be found. Explorations thus far teach us that we have much yet to learn; and for the far reaching view which we are taking, it would not be unreasonable to draw considerably upon the future to sustain the future. But this we have done no further than to calculate to some extent upon what man will do from what he has done. Calculating upon the profound arcana of nature is quite another proposition, which is not necessary. Judging from the past, nature will probably be found as favorable to Chicago as other points; but why draw upon it These points promising. Much to learn. No hypothetic basis. Reality suffices.

when not necessary? From what we have seen, Chicago can have a never failing supply of good bituminous coal from Lake Erie at $6, with plenty of competition to reduce the price $1 to $2 per ton. At the highest figure, she can make her pig iron out of Lake Superior ore at $30.

Iron at highest, $30—

If we cannot make pigs and blooms to sell to others, what other city can save enough on ore and coal to supply us cheaper than we can make it? With an unlimited supply of coal and iron at these figures—and iron probably comes down to $25, and coal on the average to $3.50—what reason can be given that with reasonable time and capital Chicago should not have the same position in iron, that she has in her provision-manufacturing?

—probably $25. Coal $3.50.

Nor need we to seek any other region to supply than that naturally tributary to Chicago.

Large region to supply.

Messrs. Hale & Ayer sold last year over $190,000 worth of nails, and Messrs. Hibbard & Spencer over $200,000. These are only part of the nails, and nails only one of the items, to produce which Chicago affords these abundant facilities.

Sale of nails.

How long before capital will discern these unequaled opportunities to use Lake Superior iron, which certainly has nothing superior to it in the known world? Well is the present stage of our race denominated the "Iron Age," for it has been the chief means of progress; and our advancement in future will be commensurate with the improvements we make in using this solid, unyielding basis of prosperity.

capital will discern its interest.

Our leaps onward in the scale of progression, will only be limited by the artistic skill employed in giving spring to the dormant energies locked up for ages in Lake Superior Iron Ore, which, if not developed specially for the benefit of Chicago, at least inure to her primarily and throngh her to the whole Nation. Nor does Chicago superiority end with iron. In other chief minerals she has great facilities to obtain supplies.

Leaps with steel springs.

Houghton Gazette.

Lake Superior Copper.—The *Houghton Gazette* gives the product of each mine last year, from which this abstract is taken:—

Lake Sup. copper; Product '67.

Copper Produce of Lake Superior, 1867.

District.	No. Mines.	Largest Mines. Tons.	lbs.	Smallest Mine. Tons.	lbs.	Total, 1867. Tons.	lbs.	Total, 1866. Tons.	lbs.	Increase. Tons.	lbs.
Portage Lake,........................	14	1,175	565	17	8	6,424	565	5,050	1,747	1,373	0,818
Keweenaw,........................	13	1,086	1,077	2	0	3,801	777	3,023	691	778	86
Ontonagon,........................	10	329	832	14	114	1,509	1,210	1,701	1,250	192	40
	37					11,735	552	9,775	1,688		

Product 1845 -1867.

Copper Product of Lake Superior, 1845-67.

Year.	Tons.	lbs.	Year.	Tons.	lbs.
1845 to 1854........................	7,642	......	1862........................	9,062	......
1855 to 1857........................	11,312	......	1863........................	8,548	......
1858........................	3,500	......	1864........................	8,047	......
1859........................	4,200	......	1865........................	10,790	1,156
1860........................	6,000	......	1866........................	10,375	1,688
1861........................	7,400	......	1867........................	11,735	552
Total,........................				90,037	1,396

The correspondent of the *Chicago Republican* adds to his remarks upon iron, p. 237, the following upon copper and upon the Lake Superior general trade:— *Cor. Chi. Rep.*

With regard to the Copper District, my preceding letters contained notices of one hundred and thirty different mining companies. Of these companies seventy-eight have suspended operations; in some cases temporary, in others probably lasting. The number now operating is fifty-two, with what result in each case has been stated so far as could be ascertained. Of these companies working and nonworking, Messrs. Dupee, Beck & Gayles, of Boston, publish a list of 107, stating severally the amount of capital paid in. This list, corrected up to September last, gives the capital paid in by the Shareholders of 107 mining companies at $13,465,500. On this investment $5,570,000 have been returned as dividends to the Shareholders of eight companies. (130 companies. 52 at work. Capital $13,465,500.)

The operations of all the companies have resulted in a gross product of 86,588 tons of mineral copper. Figuring this at 75 per cent. of ingot copper, which will probably be a little under the mark, will give 64,941 tons as the total product; the value of which estimated at an average price during the past twenty years, $500 per ton, would amount in round numbers to $39,000,000. During the past year (1866) the product of mineral Copper was very nearly 10,471 tons, which at 75 per cent. ingot would give 7,854 tons. Reckoning the average price during the past year at 30 cents per lb., or $600 per ton of 2000 lbs. we should have $4,712,400 as the value of efforts for one year from the copper districts of Lake Superior. It would be no exageration to say that at least $4,250,000 of this amount was spent in the district itself, in wages to laborers, and in paying miscellaneous expenses, machinery and mining supplies imported for the development of the mines. In aid of this, also, assessments to the amount of $1,375,000 were paid during the same time by the shareholders of the different companies. (Total to Dec. 1866, 86,588 tons. $39,000,000. 1866, $4,712.400. Mining trade.)

The iron region is pressing hard after the copper district, as a producing, exporting community. Already in bulk it largely exceeds that of the copper district; and increasing rapidly in amount, it will before long be equal in value. The total ore shipped from Marquette and Escanaba since 1856 is 1,297,039 tons, of which 285,243, tons were shipped the past year, (1866.) The price per ton on board vessel is $5,00, making in round numbers $1,425,000 as the value of exports of ore during the past year. (Iron increasing. Shipments from Marquette and Escanaba.)

Shipments of pig iron must also be taken into account. So far as can be ascertained, shipments during the season were 16,187 tons out of a product of 18,437 tons; the balance made after the close of navigation will of course come forward during the coming season. Estimating price last year at $55,00 per ton, would give $890,285, as the value of shipments of pig iron during 1866. These estimates, which are offered only as approximations, but are believed to be substantially correct, make the value of exports of ore and pig iron during 1866, $2,315,285. Adding to this the figures of copper, gives $7,026,605 as the value of copper and iron exported 1866. (Pig iron. Ore and pig, 1866, $2,315,285.)

To this sum must be added something for furs, fish, and root crops, in which a considerable trade is already done. The proportion of this sum which is spent in the district, or rather, which is employed in purchasing supplies for its population, and the operations of the mining companies, may be estimated from a consideration of the following facts: Practically the whole industry of the country is directed to the development of its mines. Where does all this business go? What proportion of it comes to Chicago? A very small part indeed. Of the iron ore shipped, about one-fourth goes to Erie, three-eighths to Cleveland and Pittsburgh, while the remaining three-eighths is distributed between Detroit, Toledo, Milwaukee, Chicago and other points. Of pig iron, about eight thousand tons have been shipped to Chicago. (Other products. All mines. Where trade and ore goes.)

Chicago having no capital for mining, the trade from Lake Superior at first went naturally to Detroit and Lake Erie, and no effort has been made here to obtain it until the past few years. The character of the trade, and its tendency toward Chicago, are points of importance as affecting iron transportation; for vessels trading there have nothing but iron and copper (Chi. had no capital for this trade. Its tendency to Chi.)

for return freights. The following statement has been prepared at my request by one well acquainted with this subject:—

Mining Lake Sup. dependence.

The mineral district of Lake Superior has scarcely any resources, except these derived from its great Mineral Wealth. But very little attention is paid to agriculture, although it has some very rich soil. As a general thing, the seasons are found too short for the maturing of crops, with the exception of potatoes and hay. The majority of the laborers have been brought up in England, Ireland and Germany, in a mining country, and consequently are accustomed to the art of mining from childhood. In consequence of these facts all the necessaries and comforts of life must be imported.

Purchase everything.

Detroit first interested.

Detroit having interested itself largely in the mining enterprise of Lake Superior, belonging to the same State, and establishing at once a regular communication by water, of course was the uniform choice as the depot of supplies for the district. In 1850 the propeller Manhattan, was moved across the Portage. The "Napoleon," a schooner moved over previously, was also constructed into a propeller. The propeller Monticello followed in 1851, and the side wheeler Baltimore in 1852. These four formed a regular line on the Upper Lake, connecting at Sault St. Marie with steamers from Detroit and Cleveland. In 1855 when the Sault St. Marie Ship Canal was opened, Detroit and Cleveland put on a line of seven boats, transporting largely freight and passengers. They run without competition, and charged high rates for freight and passengers. It is well known that Detroit grew rich out of this trade.

First steamboats.

Connected with Detroit and Cleveland.

Chi. did nothing.

Chicago, even at that time by far the best market, made no effort to obtain this important trade. The facilities for transportation were too limited and unreliable to induce business and mining agents to go into that market to purchase, as often freights had to lie for weeks in warehouse, and besides was subjected, particularly in the latter part of the season, to exorbitant rates. Some seasons one, some two boats were on the route, and they did not pretend to run regularly, but would make trips elsewhere when more profitable. Under these circumstances the Lake Superior people preferred to pay higher for supplies at Detroit and Cleveland, although they knew well, that the Chicago market was by far most advantageous. In 1864 the Cleveland, Detroit and Lake Superior Line, consisted of 12, mostly first class steamers, while Chicago had but one side wheeler, (for a part of the season) and two propellers on the route. Messrs. Leopold & Austrian, an enterprising business firm, one or both residents and active business men there for over 25 years, have since 1850 established trade at different points of the copper region. With their large experience, they comprehended the situation and determined to establish a reliable line of steamers from Chicago, with reasonable rates of freight all the season round. They purchased the propeller Ontonagon, 640 tons, and put her on the route 1865. The current of trade at once set for Chicago, so much so, that these gentlemen purchased the propeller Norman, 540 tons. The Ontonagon was mostly rebuilt the winter '64 and '65, costing about $30.000; and these have formed the past two seasons the Lake Superior People's Line Steamers, doing an extensive freighting and passenger business. They transported last season over 7,000 tons of merchandise, from Chicago alone, though rates charged for freight were quite too reasonable for profit. There were the past season, also three outside propellers, making five steamers, besides sail crafts. All of them will take their places on the route again this coming season.

No regular line of boats.

Detroit and Cleveland had 12 boats 1864.

Leopold & Austrian.

—established a Chi. line 1865, 2 boats.

7000tonsfrom Chi., 1867.

3 other propellers.

Cleveland and Detroit line declining.

The Cleveland, Detroit and Lake Superior Line, on the other hand, has melted down from 12 steamers, to half of that number and the prospect is a further decline, with an increase on the Chicago route, as by the erection of furnaces now in progress, the down freight will largely increase. Although the copper district of Lake Superior is now passing through a severe crisis, its wealth is such, that the final result can not be doubtful. The existence of inexhaustible deposits of copper and iron is proved beyond doubt; and should a tariff on copper, be laid which is before Congress, it would stimulate mining materially, and all business connected with it. At all events, great improvements may be expected, and Chicago for the future may be looked upon as the depot of supplies for the Lake Superior country, which position it gained for itself through many advantages offered in its market and the satisfactory manner in which transportation is now done.

Trade valuable.

Chi. to furnish supplies.

Boats to Escanaba.

Two steamers, the George L. Dunlap, and the Saginaw, as hitherto, run in the interest of the Northwestern Railroad from Green Bay to Escanaba, together with the Washington, creating direct competition with the Marquette route for supplies to and shipments from the iron region. The Lake Superior trade, too, is naturally ours, in that during winter the only connection is by the Northwestern railroad, which, though only finished to Green Bay, will soon be extended to Escanaba, with branches to different ports on Lake Superior. This the only winter route.

Bog Iron Ores.—Should these be found beneficial to mix with Lake Superior ores, they are profusely scattered in northern Indiana, Illinois and Wisconsin. They have been found within 40 miles of Chicago, and may be nearer. Bog iron ores.

Galena Lead Mines.—Mr. Blake's remarks, p. 223-4, suffice to present the abundance of this valuable metal. Lead manufactures are already extensively prosecuted at Chicago, and their increase *pari passu* with others is very sure. Galena lead mines.

Zinc also abounds. The following is from *Hunt's Merchants' Magazine* Oct., 1865 :— Zinc. *Hunt's Merch. Mag.*

Zinc Manufacture in Illinois.—The existence of rich zinc ores in various parts of the country has long been known, and numerous attempts have been made to turn them to account. As far back as the Revolution we find these experiments beginning to be made and continuing till some 12 years since without success. The first remunerative results were realized in New Jersey by converting the zinc ore, known as Franklinite, into the white oxide of zinc for paint. Similar works were erected in Pennsylvania at Bethlehem, using the calamine or carbonate and silicate of zinc. The market was soon stocked with the zinc white now so extensively used as a pigment instead of white lead. Practical men having thus turned their attention to the ores of zinc, several attempts were made to reduce them to a metallic state, in New Jersey, Pennsylvania and Wisconsin. These attempts were generally failures, and the belief was confirmed that metallic zinc could not be successfully manufactured here. One exception is found in the Bethlehem works of Pennsylvania, and another in the subject of this article, the zinc works of La Salle, 90 miles west of Chicago. Manufacture at LaSalle, Ill. N. J. and Pa. Difficulties—failures. Two exceptions.

The country is indebted to Messrs. Mathieson and Hegehler, two highly intelligent Germans, and graduates of the Mining Academy of Frieburg, for the first success in this direction. These gentlemen came to America in 1857, and began their experiments at the Lehigh zinc works, in Pennsylvania, where they produced, as it is believed, the first metallic zinc of American make. Learning of the superior richness of the Wisconsin ores, they went West in 1858, and examined the zinc ores of the lead region, which had been described in the geological reports of Wisconsin in 1853. Satisfied of their value and abundance, they looked for fuel and facilities of manufacture and transportation. La Salle, with its rich deposits of coal, building material, and unequaled means of land and water transportation, presented these conditions in the highest degree, and they at once decided to make it the location of their works. At first they rented a small temporary furnace, and, in a quiet and unpretending way, began experiments upon the ores, coal, and fire-clays within their reach. The fire-clay for their first retorts was brought from Germany, all American fire-clays then known failing to stand the intense heat required. Great difficulty also was experienced in adjusting the old machinery and processes of Europe to the new materials. For nearly five years these men labored with a patience worthy of all praise, overcoming one obstacle after another by a rare combination of scientific knowledge and practical skill. So numerous have been their changes in the old methods of treating the ores of zinc, that they may justly claim to be the inventors as well as builders of their present furnaces. They have at last achieved a most triumphant success. Their new works are being constructed in the most permanent manner, and when completed will be the most extensive and perfect in the world. Founders of LaSalle works. Examinations. Locate at LaSalle. Obstacles. Five years' labor—brings success.

The daily yield of the three furnaces is about four tons. The coal used is mostly slack or waste of the mines, of which about six tons are required to produce 4 tons per day.

a ton of zinc. The amount of ore consumed is about five tons, or 2,400 pounds to each ton of metal produced. The zinc made here is said to be the best in the world. Telegraph zincs are already extensively manufactured for Western consumption. The ore used is obtained from the iron region of Wisconsin, 100 miles north of La Salle. It is found in great quantities among the rubbish of the old lead mines, where it has been thrown aside by the miners under the name of "dry bone." It often attends the lead ore as the matrix, or vein stone, and is in bad repute from the tendency of such veins to give out. The miners say the dry bone eats out the galena. The ore resembles a dirty limestone, and in its natural state gives no indication of the brilliant metal which it holds. Heavy deposits of it have been opened in mining for lead, but the surface supply is adequate for present purposes. The ore is roasted at the mines, and parts with carbonic acid and water, which form 33 per cent. of its weight. It is then put on the cars and transported to La Salle, the Illinois Central Railroad, with commendable liberality, charging only a nominal price for transportation, to encourage the development of the manufacture. The price of zinc in the pig is now about $200 per ton. The product of the La Salle furnaces is mostly sold in New York, where it is rolled and manufactured. The proprietors intend erecting rolling mills next season for the manufacture of sheet zinc. One of them is now in Germany securing the means and skilled labor for a still further expansion of the enterprise.

Ore from Wis. — Heavy deposits. — Ill. Cent. railroad liberal. — Zinc sold in N. Y.

Still successful.

Upon inquiry, I find success still attends this enterprise. The rolling mill is in operation, able to convert into sheet-zinc 14,000 lbs. per day, while the works produce about 7,500 lbs. of metallic zinc each 24 hours.

Fire Clay.

Fire Clay.—Notwithstanding the La Salle fire-clay is not considered good, Dr. J. V. Z. Blaney, says it is because care is not taken in its extraction, to keep the pure stratum separate from that above and below—that he has had superior specimens from there, which he has subjected to the severest tests.

Silex.

Silex.—An inexhaustible bed of pure white sand exists within half a mile of the canal in La Salle county, some 10 or 12 miles in length, as it appears at Utica and at Marseilles. By canal boat it is brought at small cost; and with Galena lead, glass manufacture is to become extensive. Already three work-shops are started.

Chief minerals gathered at Chi. — Insures mnfg. largely. — Further developments. — Not hypothetical.

However inadequately the matter has been handled, the intrinsic force of its own elements must convince any candid investigator, that no other point can claim superior advantages to Chicago, for gathering the chief minerals, —iron, coal, copper, lead, and zinc. Superiority is not claimed upon any one of these, though it should be conceded on iron and copper; but upon the five, no one of the ten or fifteen largest cities is equal to Chicago. Advantages in this respect alone would insure the growth of a large manufacturing city. Nor is it merely to these chief minerals that her superiority is restricted. Although the surface of the Great West has not yet been even skimmed, and we can know nothing of its hidden wealth, yet look at the lists above given, already known to exist. The objector will say, "But mining of them is untested and we know not whether it will pay cost, and you profess to base your argument upon fact, not uncertain hypothesis." True; yet is it not certain from discoveries already made, that the West is the most prolific in minerals, and in greater variety, than any other known region of the world? More scientific knowledge, more practical experience, may be required for their development. But as we saw in zinc, science and art will come together, and coöperate to the development of as great a variety of minerals as any two or three Nations ever had. We depend not upon a few thousand, or a few hundred thousand miles for our resources; but fifteen hundred thousand square miles make Chicago its emporium, of which a million is the richest mining region of the world. With the chief ordinary minerals in close proximity, rendering it the centre of manufactures for the entire West, the extraordinary would naturally come thither to be fashioned for their various uses in art and science. With the river as well as railway system bearing its chief products to its centre, what other equal point of conjunction of minerals of all kinds, ordinary or extraordinary, exists on the globe?

Developments sure.

1,000,000 sq. miles of mining.

What other equal point of convergence?

Local Advantages and City Expansion.

Local advantages.

We have seen the unequaled advantages Chicago possesses in lake, canal and railway to bring together and to distribute men and their property. As a natural consequence of these advantages, irrespective of any supposed difference in energy and enterprise, we have seen the young Queen of the Lakes surpass Cincinnati, whilom Queen of the West; and then St. Louis, which had attained supremacy, and still fancies that the departure is only temporary, soon to return to prove the correctness of nature's decrees. The examinations of commerce and manufactures, while abundantly confirming previous views, afford still stronger promise for the future; and we have seen the solid basis which nature creates for these chief motive powers of human progress, in the inexhaustible stores of agricultural and mineral wealth. The gold and silver of the world must in large measure be distributed from Chicago; and the inexhaustible supplies of the still more precious minerals of coal and iron, leave little else to be desired to maintain in the future the progress of the past. With this wonderful combination of causes to advance this City, has nature failed in her ordinations as at St. Louis,—if St. Louisians blunder not egregiously about nature's designs—and created counteracting influences to retard the growth and prevent inordinate excelling? Converging here this abundance of nature's best gifts, which art with natural wisdom has aided and strengthened, are they brought to a site where their profitable employment is difficult or impossible?

Gathering and distributing advantages—

—of commerce and mnfrs—

—of agricultural and mineral wealth.

Has nature failed?

Is site deficient?

It has been generally believed that Chicago is located in a swamp. On the contrary, nature has had equal success in the site, as in all other adjuncts, to a great city. It is not beautified with hill and dale, rocks and running brooks, for then this immense system of railways would have been subjected to heavy cost to get into the city and to make sites for their depots and grounds. Very inconvenient, too, would it have been to transact business with water craft, were the river and branches in a deep valley. There never was a site more perfectly adapted by nature for a great commercial and manufacturing city, than this. The cost of grading, removing

Site desirable for a mnfg. and commercial city.

Expense of other cities saved. rocks and hills, and filling vallies, which in most cities equals the first cost of the land, or even more, is here entirely saved. Let us consider some of the points:

The ground. No swamps. *The Ground.*—So far from being a swamp, with miry beds, its solid substratum keeps the surface wet Too nearly on a level for the rain to run off, it must evaporate or soak into the soil. Almost uniformly, except near the lake, a rich black loam of one or two feet or more is gradually mixed with clay until it becomes pure, or hard-pan intervenes. Occasionally a Solid foundation. bed of quicksand occurs, rendering piling requisite for a sure foundation; but probably no other city ever arose where the ground was so perfectly adapted to solid building by nature, and where so little must be done by the Rich soil. occupant. The rich loamy soil affords a natural velvet turf of blue grass and white clover, and rapid growth to shrubs and trees; and when the land about the city shall be properly laid out for suburban residences, and beautified with parks and fountains, we shall become fairly entitled to our pretty *sobriquet*, The Garden City.

The Grade. Our own blunders. *The Grade.*—The natural level could hardly have been bettered. Blundering has been wholly in us, in failing to perceive the designs of nature, and the rapidity with which this flat prairie was to be covered with one of Dug out streets. the chief cities of the land. We actually dug out the streets to drain the surface of the blocks, as if a little building on the corner of an 80 feet lot was always to be the sole occupant. Most of us never dreamed such a crazy vision as that of raising the entire surface with brick and mortar four or Basements not valued. five stories. Cellars being out of the question, we could not well consider the value of basements; nor had they much value so long as most buildings were two stories or less, and plenty of vacant ground along side. A rise or two was made, until in 1855 the grade was put up some four feet, and we all remember the ridicule of the barricade at the corner of Lake Grade should have been higher. and Clark streets, where the sidewalk was raised to the new grade. We now see the mistake that was made in not putting it still higher. Perhaps it is inexpedient to again raise it on the south side north of Monroe street;* Can be in most parts. but south of that, and in the north and west divisions, it can, and should, and will be put up so that the bridges from those sides will be nearly on a level, and the railroads be able to come in on a low grade.

Should be on account of drayage— Either one of these objects is abundantly sufficient for doing this. In this flat city, with our Nicholson pavement, which will be universal, a team can draw all that can be put on the truck, were it not for rising over the bridges. In the mere item of drayage it is worth the cost. But for our —railways. railways the change is indispensable. They should be able to come and go on high speed, saving both time and expense. The slow rate now

---

Mr. Potter Palmer wants higher grade. *Mr. Potter Palmer says his buildings erected and erecting, would be worth $50,000 more with four feet more in the basement; and he would welcome any elevation, if not more than six inches. But if too great an undertaking for the most part of the South Division, let not all the rest of the City be deprived of the benefits of a higher grade.

required by ordinance is necessary, and even with this precaution, every few days some one is seriously injured, and within ten months nine have been killed. Nor would it be very important to relieve the roads of this inconvenience, were not the city limits to be extended in a very few years in all three directions. When trains must run five to ten miles, taking an hour to an hour and a half, it becomes quite an expense to them and an annoying inconvenience to passengers.

Injury to citizens. 9 killed.

Give speed to railways.

Subsequent items in small type are taken from my pamphlet of 1861 :—

Harbor and River Frontage.—Two branches, one from the north and one from the south, lying almost parallel with the lake shore, and navigable for several miles, unite in the centre of the city, forming the main river, which runs at a right angle nearly a mile, to the lake, and is fifteen to twenty feet deep. Piers extend into the lake, between which vessels enter the river, and south from the piers another extends parallel with the shore, forming a basin or outer harbor, which can be indefinitely enlarged as commerce requires.

Harbor and river frontage.

On this basin and on the river and branches, are located the railroad depots, grain warehouses, lumber yards, packing houses and manufacturing establishments of all kinds, for which the double banks of the two branches afford ample room for many years. Canals or slips are also being constructed from the branches, in digging which, the material, blue clay, is used in brick making. The expansion of river facilities by digging these slips, is the only means we have to obtain material here for brick.

Extent of water fronts.

To be increased constantly.

The Chicago Dock and Canal Improvement Company.—Hon. W. B. Ogden obtained a charter from the Illinois Legislature for this company to improve the lake shore property north of the piers. M. D. Ogden, Esq., is President; Mr. S. H. Fleetwood, Treasurer; Mr. Franklin Hatheway, Secretary; Mr. R. A. Connolly, Chief Engineer and Superintendent.

North side harbor improvements.

Dock Co. officers.

By constructing the piers at nearly a right-angle to the shore, the sand, which has a natural drift from the north, has been stopped, the accretion compelling the extension of the piers about 2,100 feet. For several years the sand drifting past the end of the pier, has erected banks, obstructing navigation, and costing much for removal. To improve this shore accretion is the object of this Company, which will not only be immensely profitable, but promises to obviate effectually the difficulties hitherto experienced concerning the harbor.

Harbor difficulties.

This improvement remedies them.

The Dock Company commences by constructing a powerful breakwater 700 feet east of the light house due north, inside of which will be docks and slips. This breakwater catching the drifting sand affords material for docks. The Company will at first extend these works north only about 500 feet, but that gives about 1½ mile more of dockage. Their pier from the north end of the breakwater to the shore will cause accretion to the north, which they will improve in like manner. About $80,000, were expended last year, and $150,000 will be this year, wind and weather permitting. It is an enterprise worthy of the Railroad King of the West, and will make of a large part of the neglected north-side lots, first-class business property. Notwithstanding what we have seen, few have any conception of the area which the business of this City is speedily to require. If others of these large real-estate

A breakwater.

½ mile of dockage.

Enterprise worthy of Mr. Ogden

Other real estate owners should do so.

owners were alive to the progress and future demands of the City, would they neglect the unexampled opportunities offering? In all parts of the City similar well considered enterprises can be profitably undertaken, and render great public service.

Health.

Health.—That Chicago is very healthy, is apparent to every visitor. Statistics of mortality confirm this impression, having always shown a less per cent. of deaths here than in other American or foreign cities, and still more in our favor of late years, owing, as is supposed, to our sewerage system, which works admirably, and improves year by year as the city becomes more densely populated, and the sewers more used. *

Purifying river. Pumping into canal. Canal to be fed from lake.

Purifying the River.—In the dry weather of summer, when the river might be unwholesome, the canal to the Illinois river, which enters the South Branch four miles up, is supplied by pumping water from the branch, filling it and the river with pure lake water. In a few years the canal may be lowered and fed from Lake Michigan, sending a continuous flow of crystal water for miles through the heart of our city, and we can have this now, whenever necessary for sanitary or other purposes, at the inconsiderable cost of working the pumps. †

Climate. Cool summer nights. Bracing for labor. Difference in St. L.

Climate.—Doubtless the cool nights in summer are also important promoters of this healthiness. The temperature by day is about the same as in other places in this latitude, though we are seldom without a breeze from some quarter, which in winter and spring is not so very comfortable. In summer, a cool breeze usually comes off the lake in the evening, that makes sleep refreshing and invigorating, an important consideration in favor of extensive manufacturing, in which profits depend considerably on the vigor and health of workmen. A conductor on the Chicago and St. Louis road, who last summer spent nights and days alternately in the two cities, told me that he arose at St. Louis from his bed weak and exhausted, and at Chicago fresh and vigorous.

Pure water of Lake Mich. Our improvements.

Water Supply from Lake Michigan.—Having no streams and indifferent wells, until the first artesian was bored, our reliance for water has been upon Lake Michigan. Nor need we anything better than its cool, crystal waters. At first elevated by the old Hydraulic Company, and then by the City, by steam pumps into a tower, and thence distributed by pipes throughout the City; the only change has been in the mode of obtaining the supply, and increasing the facilities of distribution. But these changes are immense. Instead of impure shore water, we now draw two miles out, in water 30 feet

---

Sewerage. Paid for by city. Wisdom of this.

* *Sewerage*—Yet more in regard to this than perhaps any other public improvement, we have fallen behind the growth of the City. Candor requires the confession, that although still the healthiest city except Philadelphia, we have deteriorated; and in the judgment of Dr. Rauch, the capable head of the Board of Health, because of non-extension of drains. There being no danger of the grade being lowered to interfere with drainage, but being certain to go up to its benefit, there is no reason why the system should not be prosecuted to the full demand of the City, now that prices are moderating. For this permanent improvement, it has been wise in the Council to defray the cost by loans instead of assessment. Though the use of drains cannot be assessed as of water, yet it is equally proper in one as in the other that the whole City should pay the cost; and it is an important consideration to the poor man in buying his out-lot that he has not this heavy assessment to pay. To be sure, the man in the heart of the city, who pays proportionally on land worth $2,000 a front foot, would prefer to pay assessments on his individual lot; yet is it any injustice to make the whole property pay its quota for such a common good? With all the expenses this generation must bear in laying foundations, is it judicious to put upon it the cost of a permanent improvement like that?

City now lowering canal.

† Since 1861 the river has been intolerable, though relief has been obtained by means of pumping water into the canal. The City has now arranged to deepen the canal to set the current from the lake for which it will doubtless be ultimately reimbursed, in making steamboat communication from the Lakes to the Gulf of Mexico, a truly national work which will be prosecuted. The State, however, guarantees the payment. Notwithstanding more drainage is needed, yet the Board of Public Works put down in 1866 over nine miles of sewers at a cost of $225,000. The report for 1867 is not yet published.

deep, so that it is never moved upon the bottom, and is free from all shore influences. At the surface the water in June was 60°, and at the bottom 51½°.

For this wonderful triumph of engineering skill, we are indebted to Mr. E. S. Chesbrough, * who conceived and planned the whole enterprise; though for the admirable execution, the keeping in their true course the miners from both ends of this subterranean channel and bringing them together, he awards chief credit to his assistant, Mr. W. H. Clarke, one of our oldest, most esteemed citizens. Considering the darkness, difficulty in using instruments, the foul air, it will be regarded by all capable judges a very distinguishing work to both planners and executors.

Mr. Chesbrough planned the tunnel.

Mr. Clarke's assistance.

The contract having been let to Messrs. Dull & Gowan, of Harrisburgh, Pa., ground was broken with due ceremonies by the city officials 17th March 1864. The shore-shaft having been sunk 69 feet, direction was given by Mr. Clarke to the tunnel proper. On July 24th, 1865, a huge crib of timber and iron with numerous water-tight compartments was launched and towed to its proper place in the lake, its gates opened, and it sank to its bed on the bottom of the lake, in about thirty feet water, the top extending a few feet above the surface. Except the centre well, it was filled with stone. In the centre were placed one above another, iron cylinders, 9 ft. diameter, 2½ in. thick. Their weight sunk them several inches into the clay, and the water was pumped out, and the clay dug away, allowing the cylinders to settle about 27 ft. The horizontal shaft has a descent to the shore shaft, of 2 ft. to the mile.

Excavation begun March 17, 1864.

Crib sunk.

Centre well.

The shore end of the tunnel had been finished 4,815 ft. when the crib end was begun on the 22d Dec. 1865. Could it be possible for these horizontal shafts, begun two miles apart, to even touch each other? The 30th November 1866, the shore shaft having been excavated 8,275 feet, the lake shaft 2,290 feet, leaving two feet between; Mr. Chesbrough, Mr. Clarke, the contractors, miners in two parties proceeded from each end to the centre, and at the appointed time, 20 minutes to 4 o'clock, the miners speedily removed the intervening clay, opening the shaft two miles and seven feet in length, five feet in diameter horizontally, and two inches more perpendicularly. The brick-work, was out of line only about seven inches.

Work at both ends.

Meet and open tunnel through 30 Nov., 1866.

Only 7inches out of line.

As the excavation progressed, two courses of brick were laid in water-lime, any space between the brick and wall of clay being carefully filled. The entire cost of the tunnel has been $457,844,95. A new engine has been obtained to elevate the water in the tower, costing $112,350. The report

Brick walls.

Entire cost.

---

* For our drainage system, and for all our public works, we are under great obligations to this accomplished engineer. A mere salary is no proper reward for these years of patient industry, and honest, faithful effort in promoting and directing the great public improvements. To the credit of the City some of our leading Citizens have realized these obligations, and last thanksgiving day was apropriately chosen to send Mr. Chesbrough $11,000, by Messrs. Ogden, Blatchford, Scammon, Laflin, McCagg, Munger and others. May all our faithful servants have like recognition of their merits.

Obligations to Mr. Chesbrough.

Gift of $11,000.

Cost of water-works $2,373,919. of the Board of Public Works to March 31st 1867, soon to be published, makes the total cost of water works $2,373,919,80. The report says of—

Report Board Public Works. *Income.*—Water rents collected, deducting $75.026 refunded, $301,048,81. Profits of tapping pipes, $968.78. Total income for the year $302,017.59. Excess of income over interest and expenses, $84, 520.05, a greater excess than has before occurred. Increase of income of year ending March 31st 1867, over that of year preceding, $48,903.10. Increase of interest and expenses for same time, $15,521.53.

Water income March 31st, 1867.

Water pipes. *Water Pipes* laid during the year 1866, of either 4, 6, or 8 in. diameter, were 60,550 ft., 11 miles, 2,470 feet.

Pipe laid 5 years.

Cost of Distributing Pipes Laid for 5 Years.

Cost.

Years.	Amount Laid. Feet.	Total Cost.	Cost per Running Foot. About.
1861	13,761	$12,008.00	87¼
1862	50,881	39,197.00	77
1863	68,691	75,241.00	1.09½
1864	62,657	104,828.00	1.67¼
1865	73,494	146,332.23	1.99

Artesian wells. *Artesian Wells.*—Quite possibly the lake tunnel would not have been bored, had the petroleum fever operated here a little earlier. Boring for oil resulted in striking the first artesian well, of which enterprise Mr. Geo. A. Shufeldt, Jr., was chief promoter, and in a pamphlet the wells are fully described. Space can only be taken for the chief points:—

Mr. Shufeldt's first.

Water struck, Nov. 25, '64 at 711 feet. The drill continued to go down until, at the depth of seven hundred and eleven feet, the arch of the rock was penetrated, and the water suddenly burst forth. This was about the 25th of November, 1864. The water flows at the rate of about six hundred thousand gallons per twenty-four hours, through an orifice four and a quarter inches in diameter at the bottom. The temperature is 58° F. and is uniform. It is clear as crystal, as pure as the diamond, free from all animal or vegetable matter, and from any injurious mineral substances, and its composition is such that it is better adapted for drinking purposes, and for health, than any other water known.

600,000 gals. in 24 hours. 58° F. Clear and pure.

Finest well known. Taking into account the low temperature of this water, the great depth from whence it comes, its head, or the force with which it comes to the surface, and the quantity discharged, it may be said to be the finest Artesian well in the world. There is no well known which discharges so large a quantity of pure healthy cold water. There is one well—that of Passy, near Paris—of large bore, which furnishes more water; but it is warm, and can only be used to supply the lakes in the Bois de Bolongne, and for irrigating purposes. The water of the well of Grenelle, also, is unfit for other than mechanical uses, and this is true of the majority of deep wells in this country.

Passy well. Grenelle well.

Tubed 35 ft. deep. Immediately after reaching this water, we proceeded to tube the well through the thirty-five feet of surface rock, which was much broken by the commotion and upheaval. To that end a four-inch pipe was inserted and driven down forty feet, until it reached the solid marble. This tube, or pipe, is now carried twenty-five feet above the surface, and out of the top of this pipe the water flows into a flume, and is conveyed to the water wheel, twenty-feet in diameter, which is used as power to drive the drills and machinery for other wells which are now in process of construction. * * *

Rises 25 ft. Works a pump.

Second well, 694 ft deep. The second well is located about nine feet distance from the first; is 694 feet 4 inches in depth, to the surface of the water; was commenced on the 8th of May, and reached the water on the 1st day of November following. There are no striking geological differences in the two wells, the rock penetrated being almost the same in character, and exhibiting the same signs of oil. The water in the new well is entirely free from the odor of sulphur perceptible in the first well; this is owing to the fact that the vein of sulphuretted hydrogen gas which enters the well before it reaches the fountain was not touched in boring the second well. Free of sulphur.

This water may now be considered as the clearest, purest and best in the world. On the surface of the ground there is none like it, and no other Artesian well approaches it in purity or temperature. Clearest, purest, best in the world.

In the absence of any accurate measurement, we conjecture that the two wells are now flowing about twelve hundred thousand gallons per day. 1,200,000 gals. daily.

F. Mahler, Ph. D. gives this analysis:— *F. Mahler, Ph. D.*

Analysis.

1000 parts of water contain:	
Carbonate of lime	0.2220
Carbonate of magnesia	0.0241
Sulphate of lime	0.1049
Sulphate of magnesia	0.2250
Sulphate of soda	0.0050
Chloride of sodium	0.1380
Silicic acid	0.0050
Alumina and potassa	traces
Sum of solid mineral substances	1.0137
Carbonic acid, free	0.1533
Total of all constituents	1.1670

The *Chicago Times* in a lengthy paper describes the boring of the two wells at the stock yards, and the peculiarities of the several strata:— *Chi. Times.*

A well 8 feet in depth was dug, in which, on the 14th of May, 1866, drilling was commenced. * * * Several minor streams of water were encountered, but it was not until the 30th of October that the final stream was reached. On this day 22 feet were drilled, making a total depth of 1,032 feet. From this well 65,000 gallons of water were yielded daily, and for a time it was supposed that, with this great increase of the company's water-power, it would be enabled to fully satisfy the requirements of the yards; but the lapse of a very few months showed the necessity of at least a second visitation to the depths below. Stock yard wells. 1st well, 1,032 feet deep. 65,000 gals. daily.

In sinking the second and last artesian well at the stock-yards, three distinct veins of water were encountered. The first vein was struck in the thick bed of limestone following the second shale, and yielded about 15 barrels an hour. After passing this stream, no water was seen until the 90 feet of limestone under the first sandstone had been reached. In this rock a very extensive spring, flowing at the surface of the well about 65,000 gallons a day, was opened. The third and large vein was struck in the bed of hard limestone, 1,190 feet from the starlight. 2d well. 3 veins of water. 3d vein 1,190 feet deep.

The following table will show the depth from the surface at which the several *strata* commence, and the beds in which streams of water were found. Water was not found at the depths indicated, but was in the rocks which commenced at those depths:

Various strata passed through.

Distance from surface.	Nature of rock.
Beneath surface earth	Hardpan.
40 feet	First limestone.
300 feet	First shale.
400 feet	Second limestone.
420 feet	Second shale.
550 feet (first water)	Third limestone.
877 feet	First Sandstone.
1,010 feet (second water)	Fourth limestone.
1,100 feet	Last Sandstone
1,130 feet	Sand and limestone.
1,160 feet	Same, but harder.
1,172 feet	Last limestone
1,190 feet	Same.

Stream 8 ft. deep. Strong current. The vein from which the greatest supply of water was obtained appears to be about 8 feet in depth, so far as can be ascertained by sounding. The current is a very strong one, and is apparently passing from the northwest to the southeast. This fact was ascertained by lowering into the bore, by means of a fine wire, a long lead plummet. The weight would descend steadily until it reached the stream of water, when it would instantaneously be snatched or jerked out from the perpendicular line from the directions indicated. In relation to the velocity of the stream, one of the attendants explained that it was "about the swiftness of a catfish." The experiment with the plummet explains this remark.

Two wells together. Raise the water 45 ft. The two wells are both beneath the same shed, and fill tanks that rest side by side. Each tank is elevated 45 feet from the ground, and has a capacity for holding 114,000 gallons. The wells are 59 feet apart north and south, in which distance the strata has a "dip" or inclination of seven feet to the northeast. In the old well the first bed of sandstone is 20 feet thicker than in the new one. The *stratum* of underlying limestone is exactly 20 feet thinner. With this exception, both borings present materially the same features.

Difference of water. 1st, sulphurous. *The Water* in the wells presents a marked and singular difference. In the old well it is strongly impregnated with sulphur. So thorough is the impregnation, that the water not only smells and tastes of the substance, but deposits it profusely upon the bottom of the trough in which it is received, and in the tank in which it is collected. After exposure to the air for a few hours, the sulphur is partly precipitated and partly carried off by the air, leaving a perfectly colorless and tasteless fluid.

2d, chalybeate. In the second well, on the other hand, there are no sulphurous evidences; but the water is strongly charged with one of the oxides of iron. It has no perceptible odor, but its chalybeate characteristics are very apparent to the taste; and to the eye, in the iron-brown deposit which covers the bottom of the receiving trough. Both waters undoubtedly possess excelent medical properties, and, if only situated in some fashionable watering-place, would undoubtedly boast a national reputation.

No analysis. As yet neither has been analyzed, so that nothing is known of them, beyond their prominent distinguishing features,—the impregnation, respectively, with the metalloid sulphur on the one hand, and the metal iron on the other.

600,000 gals. daily. Rises 45 ft. Head, 175 ft. *The Force of the Water* of the last well is sufficient to discharge 600,000 gallons a day, at the surface. In carrying itself to the height of the tanks, an altitude of 45 feet from the ground, it loses so much force that only 450,000 gallons are discharged at this point daily. It is estimated that a further height of 130 feet, being 175 from the surface, the water would assume a stationary position, and would readily obey King Canute or "any other man," if he told it to rise no farther.

Supply stock yards. The wells are both now in running order at the stock-yards. They are the only means used in the supply of the immense amount of water there constantly required, and prove highly successful in every respect. As living realizations of the laws of science; as proud exemplifications of the energy and will of our people, they should command the interest and attention of every believer in Chicago and her institutions.

Value of these wells. Promise others. Perhaps throughout the West. It is difficult to over-estimate the value of this discovery of water with such a head. These wells being about 5 miles apart, the first two 3¼ miles from the lake, and about 2¼ west of the north branch of the river near Chicago avenue; the others east of the south branch, and about 2½ miles from the lake, they seem to promise supplies in all parts of the City. Should it be deemed best to use the lake water for ordinary purposes, these wells will still be valuable for manufactures, fountains, etc. Should these subterranean rivers be discovered extensively in the West, it will be regarded one of the best of nature's rich endowments.*

Whence the lake supply? No river supply. *For thirty years it has been a matter of speculation with some, where these lakes obtain their supplies. On the west side of Lake Michigan, within 12 miles of it, the streams bear the surface water into the Mississippi. The Kankakee, another Mississippi stream, heads far up in Michigan. No considerable streams flow into either of the lakes, the whole not equaling the evaporation, perhaps not half of it; and whence can the supplies come for Niagara's cataract? My theory has been that they were fed in

Building Materials, Brick, Stone, and Lumber.—Being the chief lumber market of the world, that affords the cheapest and readiest material for building. The demand being strong and constant, we build quickly as possible, and we learned in the very beginning to economize in its use, and to dispense entirely with timber except for the sills. The first "balloon" frame, as they were christened, of which Chicago had heard, was erected by Mr. George W. Snow, in the autumn of 1832. They are now, however, too well known to require description. Besides their economy, their lightness renders moving easy, and almost daily some can be seen rolling to the outskirts to make way for better buildings. In this respect they have been of immense service, for had cheap brick buildings been erected, many would have remained to disfigure the site for long years. They are strong enough for all ordinary uses.* But the high insurance and low rent:

Building materials. Lumber chief.

Balloon frames.

Mr. Snow.

Facilitate good buildings.

---

their deep beds by subterranean channels from the Rocky Mountains, as the surface streams there are inadequate to carry off the rain and snow. The discovery of subterranean streams by Capt. Pope, now Major General, and others, seemed to countenance this theory, and these artesian wells confirm it The great head must come from some elevated source; and what region more probable than the Rocky Mountains? If so then boring may discover currents throughout the west.

Subterranean channels from Rocky Mts.

*While these buildings are strong enough when once erected, and many years have endured high winds; yet in process of erection, and especially if the wind blows into an angle allowing no outlet, it would be disastrous. A block of ten buildings was thus blown down. The *Post* described the occurrence, which the *Times* quoted, on the 13th April, and added facetious comments. It afforded a rich treat to our amiable sister of the rivers, and the *Mo. Democrat* of the 15th gave a half column for both articles; and close alongside, as the first and chief editorial, gave vent to St. Louis jealousy in this characteristic manner; which, not to be charged with mangling, is given entire:—

Balloon frame strong

Blown over in building.

Mo. Dem.

A Chicago House.—A stranger, visiting Chicago, will be gratified to observe the rapid erection of buildings in every direction, and upon close observation, will find in the quality of the buildings erected new evidence of the peculiar enterprise and goaheadativeness of her people. Perhaps, at first blush, the structures may seem to him somewhat light, airy and ephemeral. He may wonder how on earth people manage to make little sticks standing on end support a wide roof, several floors, and the machinery for crowded factories or stores. The structures look as if they were not meant to stand over night; the idea that they will last a lifetime is too ridiculous to be entertained; and the city, with its wooden houses supported by a few splinters, assumes to the observer the aspect of a big card-castle or cob-house, which some zephyr may one day blow away altogether. But this is a most ungenerous and narrow view of the matter. These flimsy structures are only evidences of the wonderful enterprise of Chicago builders and inhabitants. The builders are enterprising, because they put up buildings (so called) with an impossibly small quantity of material. The inhabitants are enterprising, for, realizing that they have here "no continuing city," and that they are to "tarry but a night" until trade moves somewhere else, they hold themselves ever in readiness to go ahead any whither at as little pecuniary sacrifice as possible. Perhaps their houses are frail, but they will last as long as the merchant expects to stay. Like the tents of the Arabs, they are all the better for not being permanent, or enduring.

A Chi. house.

Not stand over night.

Chi. enterprise.

Frail houses last long enough.

With all this good sense and wonderful enterprise, however, Chicago people are guilty of one slight fault. They do not make their buildings quite light enough. Unfortunately, structures so frail will tumble down at times, perhaps while crowded with people. Common humanity would dictate that they should be so light and airy that their fall could never by any possibility crush or bruise anybody. A very slight improvement in the construction, the least possible change in the thickness—beg pardon, the thinness—of the sticks and shavings of which these structures are built, would attain this most desirable consummation, so that a Chicago house would be not only as light, as cheap, and as easily moved as a tent, but as harmless to its inmates whenever it falls—as fall it often must. Thus, on Monday, a block of ten stores and buildings, in process of erection on Clark street, three stories high, was blown down and of the sixty persons at work in the building at the time, though none were killed, several were injured. Now, this is unpardonable. The sticks ought not to have been heavy enough to bruise anybody. The *Post* justly calls it "an indefensible and damning crime" [The *Democrat* probably imagined this remark in order to turn his period. At all events, nothing of the sort is in either article quoted.] for a builder to put into a Chicago house sticks of such unreasonable weight. Here was one man frightfully cut on the head! Had the building been light enough nothing of the sort could have happened. Another had a leg broken! Let the builder be instantly indicted, who has dared to put into such a house a stick big enough to break anybody's leg. The *Tribune's* report, elsewhere copied, states that the scantling for the second story were "simply nailed upon" the scantling which supported the first, and the third, again, was sustained by other scantling "simply nailed" upon the uprights of the second. Now, this *is* "damning and indefensible." To put *nails* into such a house! Of course the "scantling" ought to have been tied together with thread.

A Chi. fault.

House material too heavy.

Block blown down.

Injury unpardonable.

Builder to be indicted.

Strange—passing strange, is it not?—that a city whose "structures look as if they were meant not to stand over night," should so completely have over-mastered the Queen of the Rivers; that solid city of solid growth, of solid wealth, and if she is to be believed, all the solidity of nature to build her up! If a

Strange that such a flimsy city overmasters St. L.

17

comparatively of a wooden building, compels the owner of a lot which becomes worth $600 or $800 a front foot, to either lease the lot, or sell, or build. As a consequence, the central business part of our City, with its brick, Joliet stone, and iron, is not surpassed by an equally compact area of any other city in the country.

City well built.

For brick manufacture we have unlimited resources for clay, as before remarked, in digging slips; and sand the lake furnishes; and for fuel the waste coal largely suffices. The price is exorbitant, the demand being constantly above the supply. But most of our buildings are faced with Joliet limestone, of which the quantity is inexhaustible, and being along the canal, is brought at small expense. It cuts easily when first quarried, and becomes very hard upon exposure; and with some fifteen years of use it promises to be an enduring stone. A greenish light cream-colored tint at first, the iron in the composition oxydizes upon exposure, and in a year or two becomes a deep rich cream. Not sombre like brown stone, not dazzling as white marble, the eye rests upon it always with pleasure, and the oldest buildings are the richest, and have an appearance of age beyond their years. Especially in the light and shade are the buildings remarkable. No other material gives to the projections, as caps, sills, pilasters, cornices, etc., more pleasing and stronger effect; and it increases with age. The Masonic Temple, Portland Block, Mr. Ogden's corner on Clark street, the Marine Bank, etc., are among the oldest, as they are richest looking in the City. But no block has been erected so ornate, so effective in its angles to bring out light and shade, as that designed by Mr. Van Osdel for Mr. Potter Palmer on State street. On the diagonal corner, Mr. Palmer is erecting a splendid block of white marble from Canaan, Connecticut. By this favor to the City, we may see the superiority of home material.*

Brick abundant. Joliet stone. Durable. Rich cream color. Great effect. Mr. Palmer's finest block. His marble block.

Our wide streets afford unusual opportunity to enjoy architectural beauty, and probably that is one reason why we have so many fine buildings. At all events, our excellent architects have set the current, and it will run indefinitely; and by the time we shall have a million inhabitants, Chicago will be as famous for the beauty of its buildings as for its rapid growth.

Wide streets afford good view. Chi. well built.

---

mushroom city like Chicago can accomplish this, of what sort of milk and water elements must St. Louis be composed, to be thus surpassed in everything? Will spiteful snarling of this sort—and that even false—mend their case? Besides taking space for the *Times*' and *Post's* articles, it seems this Chicago accident was so important to St. Louis, that a third notice of it was inserted in the same paper from the *Tribune!* The reiteration will make the world believe that Chicago is not only blowing up, but is blown up with its cob-web castles. But why does not St. Louis make more headway against "the city with its wooden houses supported by a few splinters, which some zephyr may one day blow away altogether?" Is she waiting for "the merchant" to leave his "card-castle or cob-house," and go to the solid city? At present too many from St. Louis seem to venture the balloon frames, to render it expedient for those already here to go to her relief.

Snarling all she can do. Why does not St. L. make headway?

*Mr. Palmer's block now building is 100x150 feet; the basement stone, 1st story iron, 4 stories marble, and an atic with French roof. The marble costs $99,000, in New York. The building will cost $800,000, An addition will be made of 60x150 feet when the present lease upon it expires. It is said to be the most splendid commercial building in the world.

Mr. Palmer's marble blk. to cost $300,000.

Could information be obtained, it would be found that building materials were actively employed. The *Republican*, Dec. 30th, 1867, contained a statement obtained from architects, though imperfect as some declined to give information. The list contains 87 stone fronts, costing $1,744,000; 106 brick, $1,331,500; 112 wood, $620,700; a total of 305 buildings, costing $3,696,200. In addition, the Centennary Methodist Church cost $60,000; a Lutheran $6,000; Scotch Church, $12,000; Historical Society building, $36,000; Academy of Sciences, $35,000; Rush Medical College, $50,000; Michigan Southern and Rock Island depot, $200,000; water works, $200,000, etc. Not one in ten of our buildings are of this permanent character, or employ an architect. They are built for temporary use; and in these buildings seven-eighths of the Citizens reside. No doubt over 3,000 good comfortable dwellings and places of business were erected in 1867.

Building active. *Republican.* 305 buildings cost $3,696,200. Other buildings. Most buildings temporary. 3,000 in '67.

Financial Condition.—Besides the school fund above, the City has its various public buildings, of which the land is appraised at $234,000; the property of the fire department, $225,000; dues on wharfing privileges, $90,000; school furniture, $51,000, etc.

City finances. Property.

The following model message of our Mayor, Hon. J. B. Rice, at the instalation of the new Common Council, 4th May, is inserted entire:—

Mayor Rice.

GENTLEMEN OF THE COMMON COUNCIL OF THE CITY OF CHICAGO—The debt of this City is $6,530,382, and is made up as follows:

Message 4th May, 1868.

BONDED DEBT.

Water loan	$2,483,000
Sewerage loan	2,149,000
Municipal loan	1,852,500
Floating debt	44,182

Total debt $5,530,382.

As the income from water rents will pay the principal and interest of the water loan, that portion of the city debt may properly be deducted from the above amount, as also the debt for deepening the canal, the payment of which is guaranteed by the state. These two items: water loan, $2,483,000, and deepening the canal, $450,000, amount to $2,933,000,—leaving the debt of the city, which is to be paid by taxing the people, $3,597,682. There is now $272,000 in the sinking fund.

Water debt pays its way. Real debt $3,597,682.

Among the many questions of importance that will be submitted for your consideration and action, I will call your especial attention to the building of a house of correction, extending the Court House building to La Salle street, establishing a hay market off the lines of the business streets in a location that will be convenient for both buyers and sellers.

Improvements wanted.

The city of Chicago is prosperous beyond precedent. The population is increasing rapidly. All business in competent and faithful hands is successful. Let the City, in facility for doing business, in convenience, cleanliness, and security, keep pace with this favorable condition of its people. The taxes are said to be high. The money collected from the citizens is all expended for the purposes named in the various appropriations; and I believe that in every department of the city government every officer has faithfully discharged his duty, and that the people have received a full return for all the money they have paid.

City prosperous. Taxes faithfully applied.

The cost of sewerage, as already observed, should be defrayed for years by loan, and doubtless will be. The municipal loan includes money borrowed for school houses and other public buildings. What other city of

Sewerage debt judicious.

Taxes 1868. equal size has so small a debt and so much property to show for it? The Comptroller states special assessments last year, $1,029,322, and regular city taxes, $2,417,081.

Estimate for City Expenditures, 1868–9.

Estimate for city expenses, 1868–9.

Street cleaning and repairs	$ 292,957.01
Sidewalks	29,300.00
Street obstruction	3,200.00
Street improvements:	
Balance to complete works began	35,589.52
South division	111,488.19
North division	270,482.90
West division	201,882.51
Street lamps	3,000·00
Chicago harbor	83,300,00
Land damages to be paid from the general fund, for new bridges	15,000.00
Bridges, repairs and maintenance	30,285.00
Bridges, salaries of tenders	30,860.00
Bridges, new	117,209.74
Public buildings	11,000.00
Purchase of city docks	25,000,00
Dock lines, expenses of surveys and maps	18,000,00
Public parks	65,000.00
Salaries, not including commissioners	11,000.00
Office expenses	6,650.00
Total	$1,365,205.53

$1,365,205.

Character of our population. *Character of our Population.*—Because Chicago from early date has had world-wide reputation for energy and enterprise, it has drawn a corresponding population. Energy and enterprise. These invaluable traits duly exercised in the progress of these years, have become fixed, distinguishing characteristics, according to the ordinations of nature's God. This is said in no spirit of vain glorious boasting, but as a truth necessary to understand the past, and to apprehend the future. With any man who is desirable as a Citizen, this should be a very influential consideration. Character made by busy men. At the same time it must be confessed, that our character has been made by the active men, busy in some mechanical, mercantile or professional occupation. So long as they continue in business they do their part in public affairs; but when they withdraw and settle down upon their property, it is too often a settlement upon themselves—a withdrawal from public interests, a perfect absorption in their individual concerns. Private men selfish. To cultivate this spirit of selfish aggrandizement, growing with declining powers, is not only their burning shame, but a grievous public wrong. A shame and wrong. How could their wealth have been made but for the aid and superior advantages afforded by the City? Do obligations to their City cease now that they are able to cease from daily toil, and add their thousands upon thousands yearly from interest and rent receipts, and rapid increase in the value of lands and lots? Their obligations to the city— Nay; now that they have withdrawn from active business, whereby they aided in the public growth, are not obligations increased to do what they may to improve and beautify the City, and build up the various institutions of religion, of science, and —increase with liesure.

of art, which this aggregating of humanity enables a city to create, and which it is bound to create as an antidote to the incidental ills flowing from these ulcers upon the body politic?

But those who choose to turn into fossils instead of keeping powers of head and of heart in healthy exercise, are only exceptions. The work accomplished in religious, educational and philanthropic purposes, compares favorably with other cities, and gives promise that in these respects as in business, Chicago will not be in the rear. It should be and is our hope and aim, that this young City, made up in large measure of the most active, energetic, enterprising of the older States, should set other cities an example of what may and should be done by these centres of civilization, to improve and elevate humanity. Money made so easily and abundantly as it is here, will be liberally spent.

There are exceptions. **Work done gives promise.** **Chi. to be an example.**

As yet we have had to labor mainly in foundation-work, with little time or means to adorn and embellish. But in this we are beginning; and with the wonderful prosperity Providence bestows upon our endeavors, can there be any lack of means if Jew and Christian only faithfully render to GOD His tenth? Nor are tythes to be given specifically to religious objects, so called; that is, in benefactions to GOD, in contradistinction to those to man. Are we not religious if we labor to attain Divine objects? For what else is the Bible given, except to teach us the works of GOD for man? For the benefit of these sons of GOD, even the death of the Eternal Son was not too great a sacrifice. Is it not made our religious duty, the evidence of our regard for JEHOVAH, that we do what we may to benefit our fellow? Except the offering of the heart in gratitude and adoration, what else is there in religion but to benefit man? All through the Old Testament,—

Adornment beginning. **The tythes sufficient means.** **To be used for divine objects—** **—to benefit man.**

What doth the LORD require of thee,
But to do justly, to love mercy,
And to walk humbly with thy GOD? *Micah. vi. 8.*

The Gospel is only an advance upon the same teachings, according to the progress of our race. If we "do justly" and "love mercy," what physical or spiritual want of man will be uncared for? We have done something for these great purposes of life, yet little compared with what would have been done had a half the tythes been rendered. Those of us who from the beginning have seen the results of the little we have done for the cause of GOD and humanity, what abundant encouragement have we to give as we have opportunity of both means and effort! How should the truth come home to us,—

Gospel same teaching. **Tythes not half given.** **Old settlers to work.**

Whatsoever thy hand findeth to do, do it with thy might; for there is no work, nor device, nor knowledge, nor wisdom, in the grave whither thou goest. *Eccl. ix. 10.*

If duty devolve upon old settlers in view of their opportunities past and present, are new settlers relieved? Enjoying the fruits of past bestowment of means and effort, actually entering into others' labors, their obligations

New settlers also.

Obligations greater. Easy to lead old settlers.

are correspondingly augmented to render service for what they enjoy. Yet no extra service is requisite. The best of us are so far deficient in duty, that by faithfully rendering the tythes to the high and holy cause of GOD and humanity, new settlers may place themselves in advance of many even of the old settlers. Where we bestow our money we shall give our work.

Churches. Methodist first clergyman. Father Walker's log building. Presby'n church there organized.

Churches.—From the beginning religion has had attention as the foundation of social and civil institutions.* In the winter of 1832–3 Father Walker, a good old Methodist itinerant made his headquarters here, and bought a log building standing on the west side of the north branch, near the railroad bridge. The front part was used for worship, and the rear as his dormitory. About June 1st, 1833, the troops in Ft. Dearborn were changed, and Rev. Jeremiah Porter, whom a few of us are left to remember with affection, came with the new troops as chaplain, and organized the first Presbyterian Church (as noticed p. 99,) in Father Walker's building. Next, a most excellent man, Rev. Mr. Freeman, a Baptist, arrived. Dr. John T. Temple, the proprietor of the first line of stages into Chicago from Detroit, an energetic Baptist, with a few others, came in 1833 and put up the first church building, on the corner of Franklin and South Water streets; and Baptists and Presbyterians held services alternately, and had a joint Sunday School until a Presbyterian church was erected late in 1833. It stood facing north at the northwest corner of the alley and Clark street, north of the Sherman House. The Methodists erected a small church on North Water street, between Clark and Dearborn, in 1834.

Baptist church first. Union with Presby'n. 1st Presby'n church. 1st Meth.

Father St. Palais came, I think, in 1833, and erected a Catholic church near the corner of Lake and State streets, in 1834. A most accomplished scholar and gentleman, and devoted Christian, he now honorably fills the eminent chair of Bishop of Vincennes. Rev. Mr. Hallam was a faithful pioneer in Episcopacy. They organized a church in 1834, worshipping in Mr. Watkins' school room on North Water street, near the Methodist church, where all of us young men aided to adorn the room for Christmas. Bishop Chase several times held service in the Presbyterian church. They erected the first brick church, the old St. James, in 1835.

1st Catholic. 1st Episcopal.

As before observed, it is one of the most delightful reminiscences that churches were instituted with so little denominational feeling and jealousy. Without a doubt, the genuine Christian fellowship which has prevailed, has been one prime cause of not only our religious, but temporal progress; and may we not yet hope that the glorious work of union goes on until we

No denominational jealousy.

Chi. needs good influences. Influx of vice.

*It must be acknowleged, that we have more than ordinary need of the safeguards of religion and of all other less controlling influences, to stem the torrent of vice hither setting. The very causes of our business progress, drawing to us people from the ends of the earth, brings vicious equally with the virtuous. Indeed, the former are more likely to seek out such a cosmopolitan place than are the latter; and this City is believed to be a very sink-hole of iniquity, because one can scarcely take up a newspaper any where, without finding in it some description of a shocking crime at Chicago.

FIRST BAPTIST CHURCH.

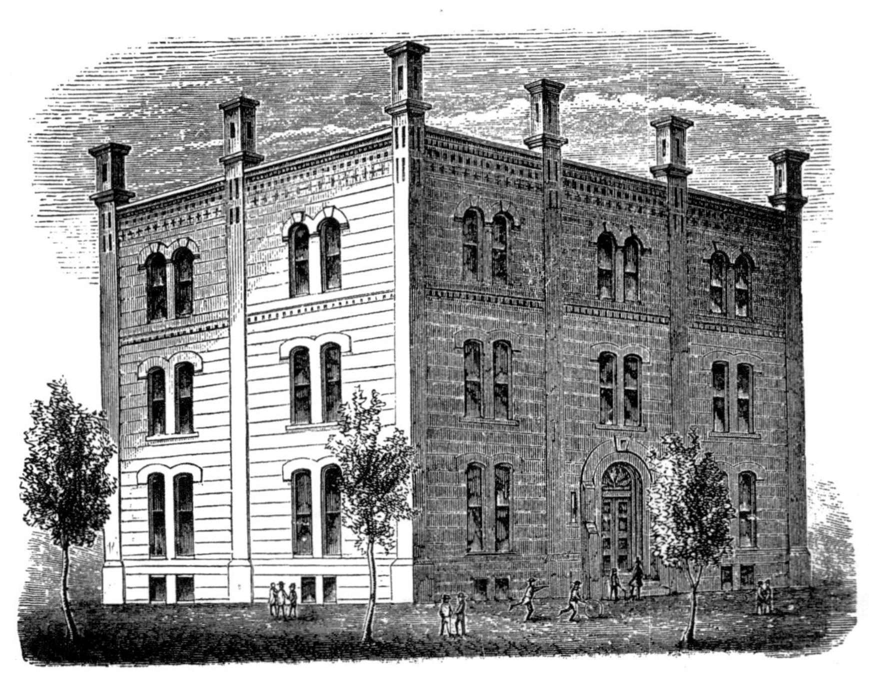

OGDEN SCHOOL.

learn to practice John's teachings (I John iv. 1-4), and Protestants and Catholic, Unitarian and Trinitarian—all who "confess that Jesus Christ is come in the flesh"—shall recognize each other as brethren? Then, each in the family to which his tastes and habits best adapt him, the diversity will give the strongest possible unity. Is not this an object for the Christians of Chicago to labor for, to pray for, to believe in? From those feeble saplings, what trees have grown, and what strong off-shoots!

All Christians to recognize each other.

Should be an object for Chi.

List of Churches in Chicago.

Baptist	15	Methodist	12
Mariners Bethel	1	German Methodist Episcopal	6
Christian Church	2	Norwegian Lutheran	4
Congregational	7	Presbyterian, New School	10
Episcopal	13	Presbyterian, Old School	8
Evangelical	3	Presbyterian United	3
Evangelical Lutheran	4	Reformed Dutch	2
United Evangelical	4	Roman Catholic	18
First Mission Building, Church of God.	1	Swedenborgian	2
		Unitarian	2
Independent	1	United Brethren in Christ	2
Jewish Congregations	3	Universalist	2
Total			125

List of Chi. churches, May, 1867.

Number, 125.

A moderate estimate of the cost of these churches would be $2,000,000; the most expensive being the First Baptist, which cost $175,000.

Cost $2,000,000.

With churches, the various philanthropic societies have grown up, and in no city are benevolent operations more thoroughly organized. That we do not give as we should, is not for lack of system, or of urgent applications, but because with most of our countrymen we have not yet learned with what directness and positiveness God requires of us the tythes. When we shall learn to consecrate the tenth part of our increase—as we surely shall, if our blessings are continued—how will the influence of our City be strengthened!

Benevolent societies.

Tythes to be given.

Education.—This subject, also, from the first has had earnest attention, especially our public school system. It seems but yesterday since in 1835 the first public school house was erected on Clark street, on the church lot.*

Education.

1st public school house.

---

*To Mr. W. H. Wells, to whom as Superintendent we are so much indebted for the present efficient system of public schools, am I indebted for the knowledge that that building was the first erected specially for school purposes. But the honor is due to my sainted mother. Having then plenty of money, it was spent very much as she desired. Interested in an infant school, she wanted the building, and it was built. Afterwards, learning myself to be interested in educational efforts, and means having been lost in the reverses of 1837, I set to work conscientiously to make some money to use in that sacred cause. My plans were accomplished, and I had property enough; but instead of sticking to my resolutions, against my mother's earnest entreaties, I became a slave in the reaper business, and was ruined by it, as I deserved to be. Had those solemn resolutions been kept, to devote myself entirely to the cause of common schools throughout the State; my means were abundant, I should probably have done some good, should have gladdened my dear mother's heart, and doubtless had an estate of a million. Nor is my unfaithfulness a solitary example. How many business men know when to stop their special efforts to make money, and set themselves to work as honest, earnest stewards, to employ their means in advancing the cause of God and humanity? How many who have ceased business labors, have engaged in these other labors?

Mr. Wells my informer.

My interest in common schools.

Resolutions not kept.

Do others do better?

My account book shows Mr. Joseph Meeker was paid for building it, $507.93. Quite a contrast to the last Annual Report of the Board of Education, which presents this statement of—

Value of Chicago School Houses, Lots, etc., 31*st August*, 1867.

Value of school houses and lots, 31st Aug. 1867.

	Date Erec.	Mate-rial.	Height.	Size.	How heated.	Value.	Size of Lot.	Value of Lot.
High	1856	Stone.	Three Stories.	53 x 90 feet.	Steam.	$ 30,000	203 x 186	$ 20,300
Dearborn	1844	Brick.	Two Stories.	60 x 80 feet.	Stoves.	8,750	130 x 162	78,000
Jones	1844	Brick.	Two Stories.	53 x 71 feet.	Stoves.	10,500	150 x 212	45,000
" Branch,	1858	Wood.	Two Stories.	26 x 45 feet.	Stoves.	2,200	50 x 106	5,000
Scammon	1846	Brick.	Two Stories.	50 x 72 feet.	Stoves.	10,500	203 x 205	30,450
" Branch,	1862	Wood	Two Stories.	60 x 36 feet.	Stoves.	4,000		
Kinzie	1845	Brick.	Two Stories.	46 x 71 feet.	Stoves.	10,500	197 x 90	16,745
" Branch,	1862	Wood.	Two Stories.	56 x 39 with wing 26 x 44 ft.	Stoves.	5,000		
Franklin	1851	Brick.	Two Stories.	45 x 70 feet.	Stoves.	10,500	181 x 264	18,100
" Branch,	1862	Wood.	Two Stories.	56 x 39 with wing 26 x 44 ft.	Stoves.	5,000		
Washington	1851	Brick.	Two Stories.	45 x 70 feet.	Stoves.	10,500	200 x 116	8,000
" Branch,	1852	Wood.	Two Stories.	56 x 39 with wing 26 x 44 ft.	Stoves.	5,000		
" "	......	Wood.	Two Stories.	....	Stoves.	500		
Moseley	1856	Brick.	Three Stories	78 x 58 feet.	Steam.	24,000	200 x 224	25,000
" Branch	......	Wood.	One Story.	22 x 44 feet.	Stoves.	800		
Brown	1857	Brick	Three Stories.	60 x 84 feet.	Steam.	26,000	262 x 122	20,960
Foster	1857	Brick.	Three Stories.	60 x 84 feet.	Furnace.	26,000	200 x 172	12,000
" Branch,	1855	Wood.	Two Stories.	26 x 42 feet.	Stoves.	2,000		
" "	1862	Wood.	Two Stories.	44 x 53 feet.	Stoves.	4,000		
" "	......	Wood.	One Story.	....	Stoves.	1,500		
Ogden	1856	Brick.	Three Stories.	60 x 80 feet.	Steam.	25,000	179 x 108	12,530
Newberry	1858	Brick.	Four Stories.	74 x 78 with wing 50 x 58 ft.	Stoves.	35,000	200 x 148	8,000
Wells	1865	Brick.	Four Stories.	68 x 86 feet.	Steam.	35,000	250 x 180	7,500
Skinner	1859	Brick.	Four Stories.	74 x 78 with wing 50 x 58 ft.	Steam.	35,000	145 x 189	11,600
Haven	1862	Brick.	Four Stories.	68 x 86 feet.	Steam.	30,000	150 x 170	19 500
Cottage Grove	1866	Wood.	Two Stories.	77 x 68½ feet.	F. & Stoves	13,500	200 x 231	6,400
Bridgeport	......	Wood.	Two Stories.	28 x 66 with wing 24 x 40 ft.	Stoves.	2,000	115 x 237	3,000
Holstein	......	Wood.	One Story.	24 x 72 feet.	Stoves.	1,800	100 x 145	1,500
Walsh Street	1866	Wood.	Two Stories.	76 x 68½ feet.	Stoves.	13,500	158 x 195	7,000
Pearson St. Pr'y	1866	Wood.	Two Stories.	76 x 68½ feet.	F. & Stoves	13,500	239 x 108	15,730
Elizabeth do	1866	Wood.	Two Stories.	76 x 68½ feet.	Stoves.	13,500	206 x 164	16,258
Rolling Mill do	1855	Wood.	Two Stories.	42 x 46 feet.	Stoves.	1,800	288 x 288	4,000
Total value of School Buildings						$416,850		$392,573

$416,850.
392,573.

More to be done.

More has been done the last than any previous year; yet *the work must go on.* With all the increased accommodations, and their crowded condition, still children cannot obtain admission. For at least two or three years to come as much should be done annually as in the past year. At the dedication of another school-house, christened after my old friend, Mr. Philo Carpenter—a few months older resident than myself—the *Chicago Post* reports:—

Carpenter school-house dedicated.

Ald. Holden.

Ald. Holden congratulated the patrons of the district on having this day dedicated to the cause of the education of their young this beautiful building. He congratulated not only the patrons of that district but every citizen of Chicago on having this beautiful and substantial edifice added to the large number heretofore erected and dedicated for purposes of educating all of the youth of our City. He said to acquire grounds and erect such buildings as this, costs money and large sums. He said he would show in part what had been done during the last municipal

Schools cost money.

HAVEN SCHOOL.

WELLS SCHOOL.

year, in the way of paying out money for these purposes, showing the following sums to have been expended:

Dore school lot		$10,500.00	Expenditures for schools 1867–8.
Dore school building		42,830.55	
Heating the same		10,976.25	
Furniture for the same		3,000.00	
Carpenter school lot		10,000.00	
Carpenter building		43,983.85	
Furniture		2,500.00	
Holden school lot		6,000.00	
Holden school building		47,619.60	
Furniture for the same		2,500.00	
Lot for Hayes school		9,950.00	
Hayes school building		33,762.00	
Lot on Reuben street, near Sampson		5,000.00	
Building on the same in process of erection—to cost	$53,000		
Wentworth avenue lot		7,000.00	
Jones school lot		27,500.00	
Walsh school		5,300.00	
Rolling mill lot		4,224.00	
Balance on Cottage Grove building		2,850.00	
Building at the corner of Elm and Rush stseets		7,000.00	
Total		$282,496.25	$282,496.

To this is to be added some $40,000 more, making the total about $320,000, and leaving on hand $180,000 for building purposes. Total, $320,000.

To meet the named expenditure, seven per cent. school bonds, having twenty years to run, have been issued and sold. The council were authorized to issue and sell school bonds to the amount of $500,000, by an act of the legislature at its last session. Sale of city bonds.

He also stated the income from the school tax levied for school purposes for the municipal year 1867 to be $387,486.99. From State Fund, estimated at $30,000. From rents, $41,260.15. Total, 458,147.14. School income from taxes.

He said there had been paid out from the School Tax Fund, $384,645.25. Of this amount $261,695.06 was for teachers' salaries. Not however for the year 1867, for $43,500 was paid out in 1866 more than the appropriation for the year, hence the sum had to be made up in 1867, thus leaving on hand quite a margin for future expenses. Expenditures $384,645

Besides this property, the City has a school fund, to which belongs, according to the last Report of the Board of Education :— School fund.

Real estate within the limits of the city, appraised at	$651,206.67	
Amount of real estate outside of the city,	43,375 00	
Money loaned—Principal,	52,040.00	
Wharfing Lot Fund,	61,129.00	
Total School Fund,	$807,750.67	$807,750

This yielded for the fiscal year, 1866–7, of rents and interest, $42,859.30. The real estate is to increase rapidly in value. Block 142, estimated at only $78,990, is under lease until 1880, at 6 per cent. upon an appraisal to be made each 5 years The next appraisal is in 1870, which will be over $1,000,000. We shall have a school fund, if present property is held, of several millions in a few years. Income $42,859. Land rapidly enhancing

Besides the above receipts from the school fund, the receipts from the State were $29,616.79; and from the three mill school tax, $234,445.92. The payments for support of schools (not including new buildings) was $296,672.89, an average cost per pupil of $18.10. Other receipts. Expenses 1867–8. $296,672.

The following is the estimate of expenditures the present year :—

Estimate 1867–8.

Current expenditures	$487,500
Heating and ventilating apparatus, furniture, out houses, fences, sidewalks, etc., for buildings now erecting	103,000
New buildings and sites for the same	307,000
Total	$897,500

$897,500.

Schools have had careful attention.

Nor has attention been bestowed merely upon buildings and funds. From the beginning our best men have given close attention to the subject of popular education, as lying at the foundation of democratic government. But the public have no more realized the importance and the future of common schools, than that of any other interest of the City. Who does not remember the ridicule even to hooting at Mr. Ira Miltimore on account of the Dearborn school house, the first of the large ones erected in 1844, and which even that far-sighted man, Mayor Garrett, in his inaugural in 1845, advised should be sold or converted to some other use? To their credit, the Board of Education, because their duties compelled to consideration, have always been in advance of public sentiment. In 1854 they obtained the aid of Mr. J. C. Dore of Massachusetts as Superintendent. He classified and systematised the schools, and stimulated to the erection of the High School, finished 1856. That year he resigned, and Mr. W. H. Wells was appointed, each having a school building appropriately named after him. Mr. Pickard, the present incumbent, was appointed in 1864. We have been very fortunate in our Superintendents, and too much praise cannot be accorded them for their zealous efforts. Yet to the Board of Education who have given so much time and labor are we primarily indebted. Mr. Wells in his report of 1858 gave a history of the schools, and remarked :—

Ridicule of first school house. Board of Education have led. Mr. Dore, Supt. Mr. Wells, Supt. Mr. Pickard, Supt. Obligations to Board. *Mr. Wells' Rep.*

In the future the early workers will be honored.

> When in the far distant future the philosophic historian shall write the history of our City; when the character and the acts of successive generations shall be weighed in the scales of impartial judgment; when material wealth shall be regarded in its true light, as a means to an end; when social enjoyment, and intellectual cultivation, and moral worth shall be rightly estimated, as essential elements of prosperity in every community—then will the wisdom of those who have laid the foundation of our public school system be held in grateful remembrance; then will the names of Scammon, and Brown, and Jones, and Miltimore, and Moseley, and Foster, and their coadjutors, be honored as among the truest and most worthy benefactors of Chicago.

Public schools best. Relative increase of pupils.

The increase of pupils is beyond that of population, as it ought to be. Too many are out of any school; and the public schools ought to be and are the best, drawing more and more from private schools. In 1855, to 80,000 population, 2,154 pupils attended on the average; in 1860, to 109,260, the average was 7,582; in 1867, to 200,418, the average was 16,042.

Common schools our bulwark.

The common school is the bulwark of our institutions. What means equal it to nationalize the foreign element? What more effective to bring them hither than these influences of education? To the person who has heart and capacity to appreciate the constituent elements of character, there is no one thing which would more commend Chicago to him for residence, than its devotion to the cause of common schools. They have ever been our pride, and are still the chief object of interest to exhibit to appreciative strangers. Said Mr. George C. Clarke, President of the Board of Education, in the last annual report:— Devotion of Chi. to them. *Mr. Clarke, Pres.*

A careful comparison of our schools with those of other cities, can but occasion considerable, and, surely, a pardonable satisfaction. Comparison satisfactory

One is surprised to see how much has been accomplished in the forty years that have passed since Chicago was a mere trading post, and how plainly in the front line of progress, in all that pertains to public instruction, the City stands to-day. Ideas that other cities are just experimenting upon, with us are established facts; improvements that older organizations hesitate to adopt are already incorporated into our school system. And this, perhaps, is due to our youth, just as, because of their age, older cities have deep-seated evils that require years to eradicate. Change in 40 years. We lead others.

Among the elements of improvement possessed by us, one of chief importance is the Graded Course of Study, adopted in 1861, upon the suggestion, and under the direction of W. H. Wells, Esq., while Superintendent, which has been in successful operation since that time. This course has been the chief model on which many similar courses in other cities have been constructed, and it is now almost daily consulted for ideas, in the establishment of similar plans in cities of far maturer age than Chicago. Graded course. Mr. Wells.

Our City Normal School has been in successful operation for ten years, and the most satisfactory evidence of its efficiency is found in the fact that the best teachers employed by the Board are graduates of this school. Out of three hundred female teachers now in our schools, nearly one-half received their training here, and our only regret is, that the number is not greater. Normal school. Supplies teachers.

The Training Department, inaugurated some two years ago, has been steadily growing in excellence and value since that time, and is now an indispensable part of our Normal School. Training department.

In close connection with this is our monthly Teachers' Institute, established in 1857, and continued regularly since then. Yet while such an Institute is generally conceded to be a necessity in any comprehensive school organization, in one or two of the largest cities the obstacles offered to the inauguration of it have not yet been fully overcome. Teacher's Institute.

In the matter of school structures, we have at last, after repeated trials, secured a plan that is rapidly being copied in other cities, as the best *general* arrangement of school accommodations in use. Best school houses.

Evening schools have become thoroughly a part of our system, and, though we do not claim to have originated them, we were among the first to adopt and introduce them. Evening schools.

In one other particular the schools of Chicago are conspicuous, and that is in the salaries paid to teachers; although not what they should be, they are higher, on an average, than in any other city of the United States, with, perhaps, two exceptions. Teacher's salaries.

Science and Art.—Nor have we altogether neglected the higher institutions of learning. They are yet in their infancy; but in nearly every department the foundations have been begun, and seem laid solidly. No amount of effort or of means can thoroughly establish scientific institutions; time is indispensable. What we have done, however, shows that material wealth is not the sole object of regard, and gives promise that no more in intellectual than in commercial pursuits, will Chicago be in the rear. The long list of private schools, academies and seminaries, shows that too many pupils are out of our public schools; and the former must be very good or they could not exhibit this successful competition. Science and art. Time indispensable. Some work done.

Rush Medical College. *Dr. Blaney.*

The Rush Medical College is probably the oldest scientific institution. At the dedication of their new edifice, 2d Oct., 1867, Dr. Blaney, the President in his address remarked:—

Opened 1843. Dedication 1845. Enlargement 1855. New dedication 1867.

"The first epoch was marked by its organization, by the appointment of a Faculty, and the opening of the first course of Lectures, in December, 1843; the second by the dedication of the first building erected for its use, on the site of the present building, in 1845; the third by the enlargement of that building to meet the growing demands of its classes, in 1855; and this, the fourth epoh, is marked by the assemblage this evening of this large and respectable audience to assist in the dedication to the service of medical education of the large and imposing edifice in which you are now convened."

Dr. Brainard. Chi. school suggested 1843. Important to have an institution at Chi.

* * "Not content with total inanition, as a tentative experiment, Dr. Brainard opened a private school of anatomy in his own rooms on South Clark St., which, with small numbers in attendance, he continued for several years. Meanwhile, he accepted and acceptably filled the chair of Anatomy in the St. Louis University for two years. It was during the session of 1842 and 1843 of that institution that the speaker first met Prof. Brainard, in St. Louis, and learned from him his views in regard to the establishment of a medical school in Chicago; and it was then concerted that should certain contingencies arise during the following summer, a school should be opened in Chicago in the autumn of 1843. Those contingencies were the opening of schools of medicine at several points in Illinois and Indiana. The fact was fully conceded that the movement would be premature, and in advance of the demands of the profession in the Northwest. But it was deemed important, in view of the probability that Chicago, then a town of between 5,000 and 6,000 inhabitants, would continue to be, as she then was, the largest of the numerous towns then struggling for supremacy on the great lakes, that it should be occupied as the site of a medical school, before other schools in other towns should obtain the prestige of priority in their establishment." * * * *

Other schools beaten. Building enlarged 1854. New building 1867.

Meanwhile schools had been opened at Jacksonville and St. Charles, Ill., and at Laporte, Ind.; but in the winter of 1847-48, this institution remained master of the field, with a class of 140, and with thirty-three graduates. With various changes in its faculty, and with but little variation in the number of its students and graduates, it continued to labor for the improvement of the profession until 1854, when the building first erected was deemed too small and not sufficiently commodious, and was enlarged at a cost of $10,000. This enlarged building was first occupied November 5th, 1855, and was continued in use until the close of the last session, when, urged by the imperative demands of the overflowing classes which had sought its portals, the faculty determined upon the erection of the noble edifice in which you are this evening assembled—a structure commensurate with the enormous expansion of this great Northwest, and worthy of the important uses it is intended to subserve.

Obstacles removed— —by wise location.

It would not be becoming in me to enlarge upon the weary years of labor expended, the hope deferred, the struggles for life and success experienced in the effort to build up an institution of this kind—prematurely organized, and in a forming and unappreciative community—but I cannot refrain from the remark that much of the position which this College now sustains is due to the foresight which located it in a city, which, by its unprecedented growth, and attainment of universal acknowledgment as the metropolis of a territory unequaled in its resources, present and future, has carried along with it, in its advance, every public enterprise, which, having a worthy object in view, has proved itself adequate to the constantly increasing demands of the communities which are its tributaries.

Mayor Rice.

Mayor Rice followed, and in his remarks said:—

20 years ago 22 students— —1866, 300. Paid its own way.

A little over twenty years ago, as the President has just told you, the faculty of Rush Medical College delivered lectures to a class of twenty-two students. Last year their lectures were delivered to a class of over three hundred students, and there would have been more to receive the valuable education which is to be gotten here, if there had been room for more. One remarkable part of the history of this college is, and perhaps it is unprecedented, that the entire establishment—all the vast expenditures for its erection—has been borne by the professors of the College. There has been no joint-stock company, and no aid from state, county, or city;

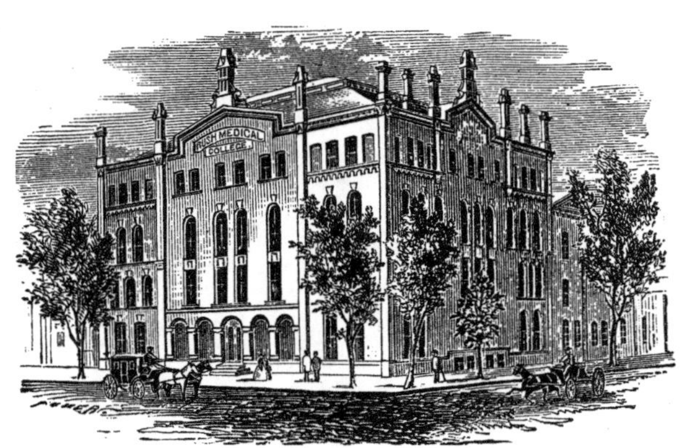

RUSH MEDICAL COLLEGE.

no endowments; but the whole sum, seventy thousand dollars, paid by a few earnest men, that the doors of this great building should be thrown open to the thousands of men seeking instruction, from every part of our globe, and coming here where they are sure to find it. Cost $70,000.

The graduates 1866-7 were 79; 1867-8, 126; total graduates about 1,150. The faculty is thus constituted:— Graduates, 1,150.

J. V. Z. Blaney, M. D., President, Professor in Chemistry and Pharmacy. Jos. W. Freer, M.D., Professor Physiology and Microscopic Anatomy. J. Adams Allen, M.D., LL.D., Prof. Principles and Prac. Med. E. Ingals, M.D., Treasurer, Prof. Materia Medica and Medical Jurisprudence. DeLaskie Miller, M.D., Secretary, Prof. of Obstetrics and Dis. of Women and Children. R. L. Rea, M.D., Prof. of Anatomy. Moses Gunn, A.M., M.D., Prof. Prin. and Prac. Surgery and Clin. Surgery. Edwin Powell, M.D., Prof. Military Surgery and Surgical Anatomy. Joseph P. Ross, M.D., Prof. Clinical Medicine and Disease of the Chest. Chas. T. Parkes, M.D., Demonstrator of Anatomy and Prosector in Surgery. Edwin L. Holmes, M.D., Lecturer on Diseases of the Eye and Ear. Corps of Lecturers and Instructors in Spring and Summer Course: Wells R. Marsh, M.D., Prin. and Prac. Med. and Dispensary Physician. John E. Owens, M.D., Surgery and Venereal Diseases. Wm. C. Lyman, M.D., Surgery and Surgical Diagnosis. Curtis T. Fenn, M.D., Obstetrics and Dis. of Women, etc. Chas. T. Parkes, M.D., Anatomy, etc. W. C. Hunt, M.D., Microscopy and Histology. Faculty. Lectures and spring instructors.

The Chicago Medical College is another thoroughly established institution, located on State Street near 22d. The lot and building cost $20,000, and are paid for. It has a fine library, museum and chemical laboratory. Beginning in 1859-60, with 83 students and 12 graduates, they increased both each year, until in 1867-8, students were 115, and graduates 50. Total 9 years, 222. Chi. Medical College. Began 1850. Graduates, 222.

The faculty consists of: N. S. Davis, M.D., President of Faculty, Professor of Principles and Practice of Medicine and of Clinical Medicine. W. H. Byford, M.D., Professor of Obstetrics and Diseases of Women and Children. Edmund Andrews, M.D., Secretary of Faculty, Professor of Principles and Practice of Surgery, and of Military Surgery. John E. Davies, A.M., Lecturer on Organic Chemistry and Toxicology. H. A. Johnson, M.D., Professor of Diseases of the Chest. J. S. Jewell, M.D., Professor of Descriptive Anatomy. J. H. Hollister, Professor of General Pathology, and Public Hygiene. Ralph N. Isham, M.D., Professor of Surgical Anatomy, and operations of Surgery. M. O. Heydock, M.D., Professor of Materia Medica and Therapeutics. ————, A.M., Lecturer on Inorganic Chemistry. R. J Patterson, M.D., Professor of Medical Jurisprudence. Daniel J. Nelson, M.D., Professor of Physiology and Histology. J. M. Woodworth, M.D., Demonstrator of Anatomy. E. O. F. Roler, M.D., Assistant to the Professor of Obstetrics. S. A. McWilliams, M.D., Assistant to the Professor of Anatomy. Faculty.

In medical graduates Chicago is next after Philadelphia and New York. In Theology the Congregationalists have a seminary well inaugurated. Their present building is on Warren street, 50x65, four stories. The main building, fronting on Union Park, they expect to commence this season. Their professorships are endowed with $30,000 each, and funds are now being raised for two more. The library has 3,000 volumes. Students last year 46; alumni 77. Theol. Sem., Congregationalist. Alumni 77.

Directors: President, E. W. Blatchford, Esq., Chicago; Vice President, Hon. I. G. Foote, Burlington, Iowa; Secretary, Rev. G. S. F. Savage, Chicago, and twenty-one other prominent Clergymen, and others, throughout the West. Treasurer, Rev. H. L. Hammond, Chicago; General Agent, Rev. W. H. Daniels, Chicago. Directors.

Faculty. *Faculty*: Rev. Joseph Haven, D.D., Illinois Professor of Systematic Theology; Rev. Samuel C. Bartlett, D.D., New England Professor of Biblical Literature; Rev. Franklin W. Fisk, D.D., Wisconsin Professor of Sacred Rhetoric. Department of Ecclesiastical History at present filled by Prof. Haven.

O. S. Pres. Theol. Sem. The Presbyterian Theological Seminary of the Northwest, is under the auspices of the Old School branch. The present building cost $16,000, and it is planned for enlargement. It is located on 20 acres within the City, corner of Fullerton Avenue and Halsted streets, donated by Hon. W. B. Ogden, and Mr. Sheffield of New Haven, Conn. Five acres contiguous were donated by Messrs. Lill and Diversey. It has been wisely provided that none of this land can be sold for 25 years. It is now worth $75,000. The endowment fund is $125,000, in which Mr. C. H. McCormick judiciously invested $100,000 of his reaper profits. He will no doubt reap more good of the same sort. There are also 6 scholarships of $2,500 each. The library has about 8,000 volumes. There were 11 graduates in 1861, 14 in 1867, and a total of 47.

Land $75,000. Endowment $125,000. Graduates, 47.

Trustees. Faculty. *Trustees.*—Roswell B. Mason, President; Henry G. Miller, Vice President; Samuel Howe, Secretary; Eliphalet Wood, Treasurer; Horace A. Hurlbut, James H. Knapp, Cyrus H. McCormick, Wesley Munger, Robert Reid. *Faculty.* Willis Lord, D. D., McCormick Professor of Didactic and Polemic Theology;——of Biblical and Ecclesiastical history; Leroy J. Halsey, D. D., Professor of Historical and Pastoral Theology and Church Government; and Charles Elliott, D. D., Professor of Biblical Literature and Exegesis.

Meth. Epis. Northwestern University— The Northwestern University in charge of the Methodist Episcopalians, has a larger endowment than any other. A lot was bought in 1852, for $5,000, which fortunately is still retained, being now worth at least $70,000. But the next year it was decided to purchase land outside, and a site was chosen 11 miles north of Chicago, upon the lake shore, where they purchased from one and another for nominal sums over 400 acres, naming the town Evanston. * The University is the land proprietor; and though considerable has been sold, and a town has grown up of about 2,000 inhabitants, yet the value of unsold lots and lands was $132,150, June, 1867. A circular of Prof. Noyes, Financial Agent, of that date exhibits in detail the assets which are here condensed: Productive funds, (nett) $190,427, unproductive property $370,322., a total of $560,749. The walls of the main building are nearly erected. The students last year numbered in the University 41, preparatory department, 105. The number of graduates I have not been able to ascertain.

—at Evanston. Lands, $132,150. Funds, $560,749.

Officers. *Officers of the Board:*—Hon. John Evans, M. D., President. James G. Hamilton, Vice-President. Thomas C. Hoag, Treasurer. Henry S. Noyes, Secretary.

Evan's * Without disparagement to other active promoters of educational interests which have been developed at Evanston, it may and should be remarked, that to Hon. John Evans, M. D., after whom the town was appropriately named, the public is largely indebted for the success which has there been witnessed. As Governor of Colorado Territory, with the capital of which, Denver, Chicago will this year be united by rail, he can now better appreciate the far-reaching wisdom of founding here educational institutions for the benefit of the wide West, the Great Interior.

NORTHWESTERN UNIVERSITY.

G. P. Randall, Architect, Chicago.

Executive Committee:—Hon. John Evans, M. D., James G. Hamilton, Orrington Lunt, George C. Cook, Jabez K. Botsford, Henry S. Noyes, Thomas C. Hoag. Executive Committee.

Faculty and Instructors:—Evans Professor of Intellectual and Moral Philosophy. Henry S. Noyes, A. M., Professor of Mathematics and Astronomy. Daniel Bonbright, A. M., Professor of the Latin Language and Literature. James V. Z. Blaney, A. M., M. D., Professor of Chemistry, Emeritus. Oliver Marcy, A. M., Professor of Natural History and Physics. Rev. Louis Kistler, A. M., Professor of the Greek Language and Literature. Rev. David H. Wheeler, A. M., Professor of the Eaglish Language and Literature. Rev. Henry Bannister, D. D., Acting Professor of Hebrew. Rev. Miner Raymond, D. D., Acting Professor of Mental Philosophy. Edgar Frisbie, A. M., Instructor in Mathematics. Rev. Louis Kistler, A. M., Librarian. Faculty and Instructors.

The Garrett Biblical Institute was founded by the will of Mrs. Eliza, widow of Hon. Augustus Garrett, who bequeathed two-thirds of her estate to trustees for this object; the Institute to be under the direction of the Methodist Episcopalians, and designed to prepare young men for the ministry. The example of this superior woman, whom all the old settlers remember with profound respect and warmest regard, ought to have been more imitated, and would be could the importance of present efforts, and the value of means for their promotion be more realized. Hon. Grant Goodrich, one of the trustees, in an address commemorative of the noble benefaction, remarked:— Garrett Biblical Institute. Mrs. Garrett's example. *Hon. G. Goodrich.*

How humanity towers up into almost God-like grandeur and power, when it thus becomes the co-architect with God, of results so mighty—blessings so beneficial and immortal! It demonstrates man's origin divine—his brotherhood to Christ—his heirship to heaven. Such honors are unattainable by the tallest archangel "that bows and burns before the throne of God." How illustrious is life, how noble are its toils and labors, when crowned with such results! How amazing that such noble, God-given powers and capacities should be wasted and prostituted in acquiring wealth to gratify the mean ambition of worldly display, or to curse our children with its possession, when ends and blessings so lasting and beneficent may be attained by it. Man a co-worker with God.

In 1855 the Institute was incorporated and opened, a building having been erected at Evanston for the purpose. Last year, as a centennary contribution, Heck Hall, a building 45x160 ft. was erected for a dormitory. The first class of 8 graduated 1858. Last year 10 graduated. The total graduates is 93. The present number of students in the Institute proper is 40; in the preparatory department, 60. None of the property bequeathed has yet been sold, and its present value is between $300,000 and $400,000, rapidly increasing. Opened 1855. 93 graduates. Property over $300,000.

Trustees.—Hon. Grant Goodrich, President. Orrington Lunt, Esq., Secretary and Treasurer. Rev. Thomas M. Eddy, D.D. Rev. Luke Hitchcock, D.D. Rev. Hooper Crews. John V. Farwell, Esq. Trustees.

Faculty.—Rev. Daniel P. Kidder, D.D., Professor of Homiletic and Pastoral Theology. Rev. Henry Bannister, D.D., Professor of Exegetical Theology. Rev. Miner Raymond, D.D., Professor of Systematic Theology. ———— Professor of Historical Theology. Rev. F. D. Hemenway, A.M., Adjunct Professor of Biblical Literature. Faculty.

The Methodists have also at Evanston a female college. It is evident from these statements, that however indifferent Methodists have been as a Energy of Methodists.

denomination to the means of highest mental culture, they are wide awake to the subject here in the West, and are actually so far on the lead at this centre, that it will trouble other denominations to overtake them.

Baptists. University of Chi. Judge Douglas the leader. The University of Chicago, under the patronage of the Baptist denomination, is next to the Methodist in endowment. To that noblest son of the West, to the far-sighted Stephen A. Douglas, are we indebted for the initiation of this important educational enterprise. In 1855 he made the contract for ten acres of land, and in 1857 the corner-stone of the central building was laid in his presence. In 1858 the south wing was occupied, and in 1866 the main central building was finished and occupied. The value of the property with endowments is $400,000. The north wing, expected to cost $50,000, Hon. W. B. Ogden has engaged to build as soon as $100,000 are raised to pay off existing liabilities. Mr. William Jones, whose late decease has removed another of the esteemed old settlers, was a contributor of $30,000. Hon. J. Young Scammon* erected the observatory, at a cost of $30,000, in which the Clark telescope is placed, the largest and best refractor in the world. The College graduated 10 last year, and the Law School 20. The College has now 77 scholars, and the Preparatory Department, 160.

(Margin: Property $400,000. Mr. Ogden, $50,000. Mr. Jones, $30,000. Mr. Scammon, $30,000. Clark telescope. Scholars.)

Officers. *Officers of the Board.*—Hon W. B. Ogden, President. Hon. Charles Walker, 1st Vice President. Hon. J. Y. Scammon, LL.D., 2d Vice President. Hon. J. H. Woodworth, Treasurer. Cyrus Bently, Esq., Secretary.

Faculty. College. *Faculty of the University.—Collegiate Department.*—Rev. John C. Burroughs, D.D., President, and Professor of Moral and Intellectual Philosophy. James H. Boise, A.M., Professor of the Greek Language and Literature. Alonzo J. Sawyer, A.M., Professor of Mathematics. J. H. McChesney, A.M., Professor of Chemistry, Geology, and Mineralogy. William Mathews, A.M., Professor of Rhetoric and English Literature. Alonzo J. Howe, A.M., Professor and Principal of the Preparatory Department. J. William Stearns, A.M., Professor of the Latin Language and Literature. Joseph O. Hudnutt, A.M., C.E., Professsor of Civil Engineering and Natural Sciences. Truman Henry Safford, A.B., Professor of Astronomy, and Director of the Dearborn Observatory. Henry Booth, A.M., Hoyne Professor of International and Constitutional Law. Charles Gardner, A.B., Tutor in Greek.

Law Department. *Law Department.*—Hon. Henry Booth, Dean of the Faculty, Real Estate, Personal Property, Contracts, Commercial Law. Hon. John A. Jameson, Criminal Law, Personal Rights, Domestic Relations. Harvey B. Hurd, Esq., Evidence, Common Law Pleadings, Practice.

Theol. Sem. Independent of the University, yet using some of its rooms and other advantages, the Theological Seminary has been commenced, and they expect to erect a building for its use this year.

Trustees. *Trustees*—President, M. L. Pierce, La Fayette, Indiana; 1st Vice President, Rev. J. M. Gregory, LL.D., Champaign, Ill.; 2d Vice President, Charles N. Holden. Chicago; Recording Secretary, Rev. E. J. Goodspeed, Chicago; Treasurer, Dea. Edward Goodman, Chicago, and 27 Trustees among the first men of the West.

Faculty. *Faculty of the Seminary.*—Rev. G. W. Northrup, D.D., Professor of Systematic Theology. Rev. G. W. Warren, A.M., Professor of Biblical Literature and Exegesis. Rev. J. B. Jackson, A.B.. Professor of Ecclesiastical History. ———— Professor of Homiletics and Pastoral Theology.

Mr. Scammon's liberality. * Mr. Scammon is one of our most active promoters of all good works, and one of the most liberal givers. Had we a thousand to give equally—not then one where we ought to have five—no public enterprise would lag for lack of means.

Surely Episcopalians will not long neglect a point so central, as to have already drawn the other large denominations to lay here the foundations of Universities, designed to be severally their chief institutes of education for the West. In other cities, two or perhaps three denominations may have their higher seminaries of learning; but where is another city in which so many have been congregated? With the railways, and for precisely the same reason, have these various educational enterprises made a rush for Chicago. At the gathering of the Baptists here in 1867, in considering the Theological Seminary in connection with the University, the accomplished Dr. Hague of Boston, remarked :—

Episcopalians will follow.

No equal aggregation of seminaries.

Dr. Hague.

Did you ever read the seventeenth chapter of Acts—the sermon there? What a sermon! No other man then on earth could have preached it. How adapted to the congregation met on Mars Hill! Paul there spoke not as a Jew, but as man to man, meeting his Greek hearers on their own ground. How does this come about? Paul was born in Tarsus, where was a university next in eminence to that at Athens. There he learned his Greek. Thence he went to Jerusalem, and at the feet of Gamaliel learned his Hebrew. Then when these and other elements of culture had been matured in fine combination, Jesus converted him and claimed him for himself. The highest style of man is always made by such combinations of efficient elements.

Paul an example.

Thoroughly educated.

Elements to be combined.

God has made Chicago to be a great centre of trade. It is destined also to be the great Baptist head-quarters, a fountain of life and influence to the West. This it must be, in spite of everything. Had he the wealth of Peabody, he would put a million of dollars here in Chicago. He would make the University so attractive that it should distance every other. He would put beside it a Seminary equal to it in all respects. Here you may raise up other Pauls.

Chicago a centre.

Baptist headquarters.

Dr. Ide, another noble representative of Massachusetts also observed :—

Dr. Ide.

We were accustomed to say, in the earlier stages of the late war, that "Generals are born," and there was a disposition to scoff at the idea of "made Generals." After a few defeats we found out that generals are much better for being made after they are born. Ministers are better for being made after they are born. They must, indeed, first be born. If you take up a man whom God has not marked "Preacher," you can never make him a preacher. But when you have such a one, give him the appropriate training and you make him a man. Here, in the Northwest, properly trained ministers, and enough of them, are a great want. How mighty are the interests that rise before us here! How immensely important that these masses of immortal minds shall be acted upon by other immortal minds, so as that souls may be saved. It is, too, important that the Northwest should educate its own ministry. You must have for your ministers men born upon your soil; men who have breathed the same atmosphere, been moulded by the same influences, who know you and whom you know. How many seminaries, then, shall you have for this work? He would say just as few as possible. The East has made a great mistake on this point.

Generals and ministers made, not born.

Wants of the West.

To educate its own men.

Should have few seminaries.

Let it be remembered that there are things essential to a theological seminary which money can not buy. There is something going to the training of a scholar, the development of a man, which endowments can not procure. It is a scholarly atmosphere; it is the surroundings and associations tending to develop the whole man. A man trained in seclusion always shows that he has been so trained. It would take all the praying men of the church ten years to pray such a man alive sometimes. You must put a minister, for his education, where men are the thickest; of course that is Chicago.

Essentials other than money.

A scholarly atmosphere.

Educate among men.

There is much wisdom in these ideas, of the most practical character. The course pursued at the East, or in any other country, is no index to what is expedient here; though if we profit by example we may avoid some of their mistakes. The old institutions were begun when 100 miles

East no index to West.

No centre there.

Here a focal point.

Chi. institutions not inferior.

Whole West will aid them.

East also.

Chi. will help.

Supply oil for common stock.

was equal to 1,000 now; and since the later ones have been initiated, no single great centre has been recognized to which all interests, all eyes were directed. The law of gravitation is here to be regarded equally as in physics. An institution at the focal point of a railway system covering already 600,000 square miles, soon to be 1,000,000, and then 1,500,000 miles, will have important advantages over any other. The occasions which parents will have or can easily make to come to the emporium of the Great Interior, where they can see their sons or daughters, would of itself be controlling were institutions not inferior. These of Chicago will not be inferior. Their grade depends much upon the benefactions; and to what institutions are the whole West so likely to contribute as to Chicago? Some will give to neighborhood seminaries; but more and more will the Great Interior cultivate a feeling of pride in having here the first institutions of the land. Then, too, we still look to the East to aid in these philanthropic enterprises, of such vast national importance, as providing ample means to educate the men in heart and head who are soon to give the laws to and rule the Nation. At what other place can they plant universities whose dollars in them will yield equal revenues? Besides, Chicago herself can and will do much for these objects of cherished affection, of noblest ambition. The gifts we have already seen will be but a drop to those to come, as the power and beneficence of previous benefactions shall be witnessed. The seat of these luminaries, it will be her special province to supply oil in common for their use, and such adjuncts as no single institution could hope to have *.

Different sects no injury

We must differ.

Agree to differ.

Nor will rivalry and jealousy operate to the injury of this intellectual brotherhood. The denominational divisions, instead of weakening, will be found an element of strength, as we apprehend the wisdom Paul reveals, of having but one body, the Church of Christ, yet many members, as these different organizations, each to perform its proper functions. Theology is a head-matter, religion a heart-matter; and we commingle them so differently according to our various tastes, temperaments, habits, education and circumstances, that the more we study theology, and the more we prize religion, the more shall we value our own chosen means of promoting both. But we

---

A library needed.

Especially upon politics

* One of these adjuncts would be an extensive library of rare books. Here, of course, should be the library to which these various institutions and the entire West would resort upon occasion. Especially in regard to politics, and the entire science of government, in regard to which investigations are to be made as they have not been since Aristotle and Cicero wrote, in order to bring us effectually out of our difficulties, and establish our governmental system on a known and sure foundation; does the Great Interior, the power of the Nation, need a complete library. Superficial politicians, if the words may be conjoined, may scout the idea; but if man needs all possible aids for the study of his nature individually; that more complicated structure of man collectively, the body politic of the State, we shall find far more difficult to apprehend. Only because of our total ignorance about it does it appear so simple.

Dr. Cogswell would make selections.

That thorough bibliographer, Dr. Cogswell, famous for gathering that noble library, the Astor of New York, told me last summer that he would be delighted to begin the gathering of a library for Chicago; and with his experience $500,000 would procure a better library than four times the money in most hands. Some of our business men should engage in this.

shall value them merely as a means to an important end; and best for us, not for all. Here and there a man may be changed from one sect to another; but the best, most desirable effect is to make him think less and less of denominational distinctions, and more and more of the one brotherhood in Christ. We shall learn to well practice the maxim, "in essentials, unity; in non-essentials, liberty; in all things charity." Besides, the imperfections of humanity pertain less to man collectively than individually; and without a doubt the chief result of rivalry among these institutions will be to stimulate efforts for improvement, and to do the most to render Chicago the literary centre of the Great Interior, if not ultimately of the Nation.

Think less of sect.

Associated humanity less imperfect.

The Lake Forest University is an enterprise initiated by the New School Presbyterians in 1856. They purchased a tract of beautiful land 25 miles from Chicago, on the lake shore, and laid out a town ornamentally, called Lake Forest. It will be the location for the various branches of education of that denomination for this region, and may and should absorb their efforts throughout the West, until thoroughly established. Owing to the pecuniary resources of the chief beneficiary, no more has yet been done than to establish a good academy for boys. One for girls it is expected will be built this season. They have, in cash funds and loans, $70,000, academy worth $30,000, bequest and subscriptions for female seminary, $30,000, and lands worth $100,000; a total of $230,000.

Lake Forest University, N. S. Pres.

Efforts delayed.

Academies instituted.

Funds, $230,000.

The Catholics have been among the pioneers in intellectual culture. In 1843 the See of Chicago was erected, and the Rt. Rev. Dr. William Quarter was appointed Bishop. Arriving in Chicago on May 5th, on 3d of June this sagacious, energetic prelate opened the college, afterwards converted into the University of St. Mary of the Lakes, and chartered, 1844. The Bishop also established an Ecclesiastical Seminary in 1846, which has been their main object, and supplies the diocese with clergymen, the majority of whom are graduates of St. Mary. It is in excellent condition, under the charge of Dr. Magoffin, a young priest, Chicago-born, and for ten years educated at Rome. The university is temporarily suspended. It has 37 graduates, the lamented General Mulligan among the number.

Catholics.

Bishop Quarter.

University of St. Mary of the Lakes.

Theol. school

Dr. Magoffin.

37 graduates

Having seen already four universities well begun, and in the first score years of the City's existence, and schools of theology, of medicine, and of law in full and vigorous operation, what is to prevent these institutions from growing with even pace with the immense country upon which it and they mutually depend? Where else would efforts in behalf of these fundamental institutions of society be more effective?

4 Universities begun. Schools of theology, medicine and law.

Where more effective?

The Chicago Historical Society was organized in 1856, through the efficient efforts of the Rev. Mr. Barry, with 19 members, and was chartered in 1857. They have just erected a fire-proof building, 40 by 90 ft., designed to be the right wing of the future main edifice. The collections number

Historical Society.

Building erected.

Collections 100,000. about 100,000, and 15,000 bound volumes. There are 60 active and life members. The officers are:

Officers. President, Walter L. Newberry; Vice Presidents, William B. Ogden and J. Young Scammon; Recording Secretary, Librarian and Treasurer, Thomas H. Armstrong; Corresponding Secretary, E. B. McCagg.

Academy of Science. The Academy of Sciences was begun by a few lovers of nature in 1857. The efforts of the enthusiastic naturalist, Major Robert Kennicott, whose early death was so deeply lamented by friends and lovers of scienee, made the Institution in the main what it is, though Dr. Stimpson is an efficient successor. Major Ken-nicott in Arctic America. Major K. spent three years in Arctic America under the auspices of the Smithsonian Institute, gathering specimens in natural history, but with the understanding that a complete series of the specimens should be at his disposal, which he hoped Chicago would provide for, having Beginning of museum. always lived here or in its close vicinity. Funds were raised by subscriptions of life memberships of $500 each, and the specimens were arranged in Another trip. rented rooms, under the direction of Major Kennicott. In March, 1865, he left under the direction of the Western Union Telegraph Company, to aid in examining the route for a telegraph to connect Russia with America. But the continuance of his scientific examinations, and gathering of specimens, was a prime object; the Trustees of the Academy supplying apparatus for this.

Major K's death. In May, 1866, the Academy met with the sad reverse of Major Kennicott's decease in Russian America, at Nelato, on the Yonkon River.* Loss by fire. Another sad calamity occurred that year in the burning of the Metropolitan block, in which the Academy occupied rooms, whereby the library was injured much by water, and 18,064 specimens were burnt, and 4,772 damaged. Dr. Stimpson Director. At the annual meeting, January, 1867, Dr. Stimpson, who had had charge of the museum in Major Kennicott's absence, was elected Director

---

Announcement of Maj. K's death. * At the meeting of the Academy of Sciences, called in consequence of the sad intelligence, Mr. George C. Walker, the President, thus concluded the announcement, to which many of us could heartily respond, especially myself who had association with Mr. Kennicott for several years as an assistant in the *Mr. Walker.* *Prairie Farmer*: "I had known him from boyhood and watched the expansion and the growth of his mind, and especially the effect of his first tour to the north, and though he had grown in years, he His devotion to science. seemed not to have lost any of the enthusiasm and singleness of devotion to the absorbing themes of science. His short but eventful and useful life, is a most valuable lesson to all our young men. It shows that a thorough devotion to any pursuit, will be sure to command success now as it ever has in the past. Robert Kennicott whom many of us have known from boyhood, has made for himself an honorable name among the scientific men of the nation—a name of which, as citizens of Chicago, and An example to be followed. members of this Academy, we may all be proud. His bright example and persevering efforts, should stimulate the young men of our City and State to a life of usefulness, stern labor and earnest devotion to some noble pursuit, that, like Robert Kennicott, they may have an honorable name when their work is done."

Mr. Walker's example. It is not improper, I trust, to observe, that Mr. Walker practices what he preaches, and to his influence and energy the public is mainly indebted for the purchase of the lot and the erection of the building. If not misinformed, too, his purse defrayed most of the cost of the first volume of Transactions; a work creditable for elegant typography as well as for scientific research. Let others follow Mr. Walker's example, and choose their special object of public interest to love and to promote.

in place of his deceased friend. The following is the list of property as stated at the annual meeting, January 1868:—

Cook County bonds, $20,000, cost	$17,400	The property
Mortgages on real estate	7,660	
Real estate, dwelling house and lot	21,623	
Subscription notes available	5,000	
Total	$51,683	
Permanent fund	50,000	
Surplus	$ 1,683	

The fire-proof building erected in the rear of the lot and now occupied with their museum, etc., has cost $45,162, most of which has been paid by subscriptions. The intention is as soon as funds are obtained, to continue the building to the front. Up to 1865, the museum contained 39,559 specimens; in 1865 were added (supposed) 10,000; in 1866, 17,558, and were burned 18,064; in 1867, 12,158 were added, a total of about 60,000 specimens. Mr. George C. Walker is President, Mr. Daniel Thompson, and Dr. J. H. Rauch, Vice Presidents; Dr. Wm. Stimpson, Secretary; Dr. G. H. Frost, Librarian. Building cost $45,162. 60,000 specimens. Officers.

Other institutions could be advantageously considered, but these chief ones can be taken as samples of what is being done in other departments. Chicago herself is not yet an institution, but is being instituted emporium of the Great Interior. From what we have seen it will be admitted, that important as are the material interests of such a centre, which, as we have seen, are abundantly cared for, the immaterial yet more real elements of progress, the means of intellectual and of religious development, are having consideration. In these endeavors to care for and promote the highest interests of humanity, we have had large encouragement by the liberal benefactions from the East; and to those who look for the best means of bestowing their tythes, where can they find any other place of deposit, where the revenues will have equal increase on and on for ages?—yea, for all time, for *ultima thule* has been reached. Nor are the elegant adornments of civilization at all neglected. While the solid bases of education and religion have the first care of these eminently practical Citizens, they are behind no other city of the same age in attention to the— These are samples. Intellectual and religious culture. The East aids. This the place. Fine arts not neglected.

Fine Arts.—Mr. G. P. A. Healy, who had resided many years abroad and had acquired eminence in his profession, after spending some years in the eastern cities, upon visiting Chicago in 1855, and travelling over the interior, decided to make this City his home; and chiefly because at that early day he foresaw the attention that would be accorded to the fine arts. No mere wielder of the brush, though it be with a master's power, he appreciates his profession, and the influence it may and should have in the advance of civilization. From the very beginning he has looked forward to the establishment here of the finest galleries of paintings and statuary that will be found in the country. Finding art appreciated and liberally Mr. Healy Chi. a centre of art. Fine galleries.

remunerated, the result was only a question of time. Nor is he now a solitary laborer in his art. The 21 scenic and portrait artists, and several sculptors that have followed and find quite steady employment and fair remuneration, are effective coöperators in making this the centre of art at least for the West. In what other section will wealth be made more easily or spent more freely for the highest works of art?

21 painters, several sculptors.

Liberal Patronage.

Painters.

Mr. Diehl, a Chicagoan from two years of age, has executed a Macbeth that is very highly esteemed. Mr. John H. Drury, Mr. Fishe P. Reed, Mr. Arthur L. Pickering, (a pupil of Mr. Healy's,) Mr. Wm. Baird, Mrs. St. John, and Mr. Henry C. Ford, have high reputation, and no doubt others might and should be named.

Sculptors.

Mr. Volk.

Nor is statuary neglected. Mr. Volk came to Chicago in 1855, and Hon. Stephen A. Douglas became his patron, and by his aid he was enabled to pursue his studies two years at Rome. His statue of Douglas and also his statuette and busts are speaking likenesses of our great statesman. He had equal success, too, with Mr. Lincoln's bust, which was made shortly prior to his nomination for the Presidency. It received high commendation at the Paris Exposition. Mr. Volk's "Youthful Washington," representing him at the cherry tree, is also a fine work of art. He has also executed a bust of Dr. Brainard, and various other works; and the Douglas monument was designed by him.

His works.

Attention to monuments.

Chi. Jour.

Mr. Volk, truly, has a worthy ambition to render his noble art something more serviceable to man than merely to gratify the sense of the beautiful. Or rather, he would employ the sense for a high and holy object, honoring the dead with beautiful monuments. Says the *Chicago Journal* in a long notice of Mr. Volk:—

Chi. attends to her dead.

Monuments by our own artists.

Mr. Volk.

> Chicago, ever progressive, foremost in business, hopeful in science, enthusiastic in music and her drama, genial in art, while she thrives as a city of the living, is alike with those that have passed before, building steadily her cities of the dead. Already the sacred resting places are adorned with impressive monuments, and these chiefly the work of our own artists. While some few have strayed from abroad, and some from older cities, our chief pride must properly rest with those designed and executed at home. As in other things, we can well afford to be courteously independent of our eastern brethren in matters partaining to monumental art. In this, perhaps, we are most largely indebted to our fellow citizen, L. W Volk, whose untiring energy, devoted love for art itself, and the consummate skill with which he has united pure sculpture with monumental architecture, has made him worthy of a far greater tribute than we may be able to pay in this article. Springing from a family whose lives have been devoted to monumental sculpture; studying from boyhood the practical details of the profession, at the same time stealing quietly into the mysteries of pure sculpture as an ardent student, and finishing with a two years' course among the famous works of Rome, he now occupies the rare position of "a prophet *with* honor in his own country."

He leaves for Rome.

Mr. Volk leaves soon for Rome to establish there a studio, remaining part of the time, and executing commissions already ordered.

Mr. Seibert.

Mr. Seibert is another sculptor of established reputation.

Theatre and opera.

The theatre and opera, too, are duly cared for. One of our young men, very successful in his enterprises, resolved to give Chicago a superior place

CROSBY'S OPERA HOUSE.

of public entertainment; and the Crosby Opera House is acknowledged to be one of the finest in the country. In it, too, is a fine picture gallery, surrounded by 16 studios for artists. The Academy of Design is here located in a fine room, with numerous pupils; and many other rooms are occupied by music teachers, many of them of high repute. Three of the large stores are occupied with music dealers and publishers; so that within itself it supplies an elegant art collection. We have also Mr. McVicker's theatre and Col. Wood's museum with theatre attached, and several subordinate affairs.* Music is much cultivated, and the Philharmonic Society, under the leadership of Mr. Balatka, takes rank among kindred organizations in older cities.

Crosby's OperaHouse. An art centre. McVicker's and Wood's. Mr. Balatka.

But all this patronage of art is not to be credited to Chicago. The refinement and culture of the West is not here embodied. This City is merely a fair representation of the Great Interior, which with strongest delight furthers the éffort of its emporium to provide means of improvement and enjoyment for its widely scattered patrons of science and of art. The entire West has a fair proportion of off-shoots from the best families of the East and South; and many also from Europe, and the number of these is to increase immensely. Any fine performance brings them to town from hundreds of miles; and they will come more and more. With our fifteen trunk lines, a few from along each railway sprinkled among our city attendants make a large audience. Upon this point, the extent of patronage in the fine arts and the dependence of the country upon the City, probably music affords the best illustration.† Says the *Chicago Courier*, April 1st:—

The country patronage. Its culture Ease of reaching city. Patronage of fine arts. *Chi. Courier.*

Ten years ago, Messrs. Root & Cady inaugurated the first business in Chicago, for supplying the trade with everything pertaining to music and musical demands. They began in a room that measured 20 x 65 feet. They found themselves without any of the facilities necessary to carrying out their designs, which was to make a complete publishing and furnishing music-house. Within that time and from the most modest beginnings, they have built up a business, which, in its line, is unsurpassed by any in this country, and may now claim to be the great central musical publishing house of the country.

Root & Cady's establishment.

---

* Even this slight allusion to the opera house and theatres will be offensive to some whose favorable judgment is highly valued. Yet in this place something of the sort would be expected. Nor do I subscribe to the entire ostracism of theatricals. The truth is, the world of the stage is like the world of books. Each book must be judged by itself; each art by itself. The wholesale denouncer of the stage must denounce Shakespear, whose wonderful delineations of human heart and passions, place him in the judgment of all competent critics, next to the Bible. The improvement in the character of the stage has been wonderful in 20 years; and although equal change is impossible in a like period in future, yet the religious world fail greatly if they neglect this means of human improvement, which will increase in power with civilization. But having said this much, it is due to the public to acknowledge, that defence is necessary, because the view is doubtless opposed by almost the entire religious community. Nearly every one who sends a copy of this book to a friend, will do it in spite of this heresy, because he sees enough other countervailing good.

Notice of theatres. Not to be ostracised. Change in theatres. My views not generally approved.

† Probably no other house equals that of Messrs. Root & Cady in publishing music; though we have three other considerable concerns. But the West sustains here 15 dealing establishments in musical instruments, and 7 manufacturing.

15 music dealers, 7 mnfrs.

Present accommoda- tions.

A few details may serve to give a good idea of what these gentlemen have been able to accomplish by energy and business management. Instead of one small room, they now occupy portions of three large buildings. Their store, one of four, under Crosby's beautiful Opera House building, measures 30x180 feet; their basement below, in which every inch of room is economized, measures 30x200 feet; their printing office, in another building, is 50x60 feet; they employ in all between forty and fifty people regularly. The printing office, which is used exclusively for their own musical publishing business, contains nine presses, which are worked by steam, regular compositors, engravers, press-men, etc. They require and use nearly $200 worth of white paper each day. They get up their own books as well as sheet music, and are just at present, among other jobs, completing a new book of church music by Geo. F. Root, Esq., which promises to be one of the most successful publications of the kind in this country. This immense business of printing and publishing music has been built up by Messrs. Root & Cady, gradually, but rapidly and efficiently, as may be inferred.

Printing office.

Mr. Root's church music.

N.Y. and Boston only excel in business.

For many years, Messrs. Root & Cady have had the reputation of being the most extensive publishers of music outside of New York and Boston. Their war songs went broadcast throughout the land, stirred many a heart to patriotism, and their fame extended to other countries across the Atlantic. But in addition to their own catalogue they have recently bought several others, together with the engraved plates, so that they are now enabled to present perhaps the very largest list of musical publications in America. Their own, and those plates which they have recently made their own, weigh over twenty-five tons and fill two immense vaults. The editions are sold even more rapidly than they can be worked off at present, and the proprietors are preparing to secure additional facilities.

Largest list of music.

Character of our press.

Newspapers.—Nor would this notice of local advantages be complete, were the press omitted; those reflectors of sentiment and of character, as well as efficient promoters of public interest, which have become one of our most thoroughly established institutions. High toned and chivalrous, properly appreciating their vantage ground, they discuss questions with no jealousy, no animosity. Outside of New York City, no press in the land furnishes more national information; none takes a broader national view of means and measures. While leading the West, and ever true to its interests, the Chicago press is eminently metropolitan. We have 9 dailies, 26 weeklies, and numerous semi-monthly and monthly papers and magazines, discussing nearly every conceivable subject; for the West is emphatically the region of greatest variety of vigorous thought, of unbounded intellectual freedom. The first number of the *Chicagoan*, devoted to literature and arts, remarks upon—

None more national.

Metropolitan.

9 dailies, 26 weeklies.

Chicagoan.

Chi. as a business centre.

Chicago as a Business Centre.—That Chicago is to be by far the greatest city of the West, and that even now it surpasses any of its western rivals, are propositions meeting the hearty assent of all its citizens. To convince the residents of other cities, whose natural prejudices incline them to dispute these propositions, we are in the habit of telling of the wonderful rapidity of the growth of Chicago in all material wealth—of the vastness of its trade in dry goods, in groceries, in grain, in cattle—of the thousands of new buildings each year erected, and of similar flattering facts.

Proud of its business.

To be literary metropolis.

There is, however, another field in which Chicago is to assert supremacy over all other cities in the West, and certainly stand unrivaled in the Northwest. Chicago is to be the Literary Metropolis of the West.

Much done.

Already much has been done in this direction. We have not yet the great libraries and monster publishing houses of older cities, but these are soon to come. The book-trade of our city is already immense, and Chicago-made books are no rarity. No one asks, "Who reads a Chicago book?" The greatest advance yet made, however, is in periodical literature.

Most residents of Chicago will be surprised to learn that we have full *seventy-five* periodicals regularly published here—from dailies to quarterlies. The influence and ability of the Chicago political press is generally conceded; its religious press surpasses in circulation, and certainly equals in ability, that of any city west of the Atlantic slope; its agricultural press nearly or quite equals in circulation that of all the West besides. That little has been done, as yet, with purely literary periodicals, is not surprising. In the nature of things these cannot precede and must be content to follow, in the order of time, those devoted to politics, religion and special professions. **75 publications. Ability. Literature slow growth.**

There is now, however, that literary taste and culture here which demand more attention to the supplying of purely literary reading, and the time is not very far distant when Chicago will have able and successful literary Magazines and Quarterlies—as, we believe, it is now come when we may have a successful literary Weekly—when we shall have publishing houses whose fame shall be national. **Taste to grow rapidly**

There is a natural and desirable tendency to concentrate leading publishing houses in a few places. The great books, the popular magazines, the influential reviews, the leading newspapers, will always come from a few centers. Every indication points to Chicago as destined to be the publishing center of the Great West. **Tendency to concentration. Chi. publishing centre of West.**

Soon, very soon, will this Great Interior rule in the world of mind in its every province. Shall it be to the weal or woe of our Heaven-blessed land? Let those who realize the future of our country, give to this central region, now in its forming period, their best efforts, their wealth—yea, themselves, and the longer they live, the more will they rejoice in having made the gift. **Shall West rule for weal or woe?**

Public Parks.—Very little has yet been done either to improve or obtain public parks. The same deplorable want of realization of the future in this regard has been displayed that has marked our course in every public movement. But in the previous estimate of expenditures, $65,000 for parks this year was included. Twenty years ago or thereabouts, it was proposed to buy land outside of the City, for a large park in each division, to be improved in after years and connected by a wide avenue, to be extended to and along the lake shore at the north and at the south, surrounding the City with avenues and parks. The land could have been bought for less than one-tenth of present prices. Had it been purchased, it would have been too far in, and could now be sold for enough to buy other park property, and supply a munificent fund that would have given us the most extensive parks of any city in the world without costing a dollar. That opportunity is lost forever; but every years' delay largely increases the cost of an improvement that must and will be made. There are, however, other important considerations touching this subject. **Public parks. $65,000 for them. Plan 20 yrs. ago. Price increased tenfold. Delay increases cost.**

Lake and River and Wide Streets for Ventilation.—Chicago is peculiarly situated. A necessity in any other city is not one of course here. No other within my knowledge has equal ventilating facilities without parks. The centre and most densely settled part will be along the lake, three miles south of the river, two miles north, and two miles west from the lake. The lake with its pure air is ever open on the east. The river extending eastward from about the centre, where its branches unite from the north and south quite equi-distant between the lake and western borders, are soon to **Means of ventilation. Lake on east side. River & branches thro' centre.**

Wide streets.

be filled with pure lake water.* These afford much ventilation; and to these must be added our wide streets. We therefore have less need of parks in the heart of the City; and though in most cities a necessity, they are a serious interruption of business from which we are exempt.

Horse railways. 80 ft. streets. Phila. plan. To be improved.

Wide Streets and Horse Railroads.—Not a small benefit is it that the central part of the City has 80 feet streets; and the main avenues north and south for miles are of that width and wider. This not only gives abundant light and ventilation, but affords ample room for that important auxiliary to city locomotion, the horse-railway. Upon this level site, with rectangular streets, we shall ultimately and speedily adopt the Philadelphia plan, of a single track running up one street and down another. Two tracks, even on our wide streets, are a serious inconvenience; but a single track interferes very little with ordinary vehicles. The use of street cars has only just begun. How long before some ingenious man obtains a patent for a steam car superseding horses? In no city in the land are street railways more available than here, or improvements of more benefit.

Chi. Post. Horse railway traffic 1867.

From the *Chicago Post* the following items are obtained, of—

Street Railway Traffic, 1867.

West Division. 6,059,724 passengers.

West Division Railway.—Average receipts per day, \$868.47; average expenses per day, \$726, number of miles run during the year, 823,821; average receipts per mile run, $38\frac{1}{2}$ cents; average expenses per mile run, $32\frac{1}{3}$ cents; number of fares collected, 6,059,724; average cost of carrying passengers, $4\frac{3}{8}$ cents; number of round trips made, 153,999; average number of passengers carried per round trip, 39, or $19\frac{1}{2}$ passengers each way; eithty-three and five-eighths per cent. of receipts used to pay running expenses.

South Division. 5,530,636 passengers.

South Division Railway.—The average receipts per day during the year 1867 were \$837,61, and per month \$25,447.27. The average receipts per car per day were \$21,14. The total number of five cent passengers carried was 4,269,080; cash, or six cent passengers, 1,311,556, and children at three cents each, 4,008. The number of passengers carried to the Union Stock Yards were 164,416. The total expenses of the company during the year was \$281,695.20.

North Division. Interruptions. 2,566,739 passengers.

North Division Railway.—Three miles of the line on Clark street, etc., were taken up and relaid during the past year, and the Clark street line was cut up in laying sewers and pavement 180 days. The Chicago avenue line has not been in operation since September last, on account of the improvements in that street.

During the year there were carried 2,566,793 passengers, and the cars were run 437,067 miles. The number of passengers carried per mile run was 5 87-100. The receipts per mile run were 38 48-190 cents, and the expenses $28\frac{3}{4}$ cents per mile run.

Cars, 144. Horses, 899. Men, 543. Miles, 48¾.

Division.	*Cars.*	*Horses.*	*Men.*	*Miles.*
West	55	356	245	26
South	53	375	198	$12\frac{1}{4}$
North	26	168	100	$11\frac{1}{2}$
Total	144	899	543	$48\frac{3}{4}$

N. Branch to be filled with lake water.

* It was quite an oversight not to have spoken, p. 252, of the facilities we can easily have, and shall have, to throw the lake water into the north as well as south branch. The bridge at Wells street can be filled solid except the width of the draw, which should have gates to be closed at certain times, when not inconvenient, as at night and Sundays, to stop the flow of water. Then by cutting a canal from the north branch to the lake, or by laying a pipe, the supply of lake water for the canal could be thence obtained, either by constructing a protection to the canal entrance, or by elevating the water by an engine from the lake.

Ordinary Railways.—This is another important consideration. No other city has equal facilities with our 15 trunk lines, for reaching its suburbs. Several near the lake shore south do not spread much for several miles; but so admirably are the others distributed, that we only need one S. S. W., another W. S. W., another W. N. W., and another N. N. W., to have all that could be desired. Ordinary railways. 15 lines. 4 wanted.

The S. S. W. is one of the surest; for the Evansville road through Vincennes and Terre Haute to Rockville, 132 miles, is already built. The Brazil coal, the value of which we have seen, would take it at Terre Haute or Rockville. Thence it is about 22 miles to Danville, where good coal has also been discovered. Thence it is about 120 miles to Chicago, traversing the country nearly midway between the Ills. Central and the New Albany and Salem, making the closest possible connection between the rich valley of the Wabash and Lake Michigan, and opening the shortest route into Kentucky, through Hendersonville. S. S. W. to Danville, Wabash and Evansville. Midway route.

For the W. S. W. there are three very proper lines. 1st. A straight road from Petersburg, crossing the Illinois river at Marseilles, and through the heart of Kendall county. 2d. From the centre of Pike county Ills., midway between the Burlington and Quincy and the Illinois river, which would encourage the building of the road across Missouri, south of the Hannibal and St. Joe. road, spoken of p. 97. 3rd. A road from Keithsburg or New Boston to Amboy and Batavia. W. S. W. 3 routes. Petersburg. Pike Co. Keithsburg.

For the W. N. W., competition of the Illinois Central with the North-western, will soon build a road from Freeport through Byron and Elgin. W. N. W. from Free-port.

As to the N. N. W., when some of the managers of roads which are rivals to the Northwestern in Wisconsin, see their folly in endeavoring to direct trade from its natural centre to Milwaukee, and desire to make their roads pay well to stockholders, they will seek the shortest routes to Chicago; and a contest will probably arise between them to accomplish the object first. This will give us one or two at least. N. N. W., several from Wis.

Each of these six or seven routes is through a very rich country, about equi-distant from existing routes, and all able to make a road pay by local traffic alone. No one who has any faith in Chicago can doubt, that most or all of them, will be so far built in less than five years, as at least to be running trains out of Chicago. And the routes of new lines into the city, will be chosen with direct reference to accommodating suburban trade; for its profit will be to all the roads an important censideration, and at the same time, the sharp competition of so many gigantic corporations, will insure unequalled accommodations at reasonable charges. All desirable. To be built in 5 years. Accommo-date the city. Sharp com-petition.

But all these hopes and expectations, moderate as they are, are still hypo-thetical. A sensible man would consider them, and a reasonable man admit they were almost certain. Yet not being quite certain, we must rest upon the 15 lines we already have. With these alone no other city has an equal They are hypothetical 15 lines we have. No city equal facilities.

number of acres within ten miles of its limits upon a railroad or equi-distant from it, with Chicago.

Railways. Expansive power.

Expansive Power of Railways.—The unexampled facilities these railways may and should afford, will cause the City to expand, covering a far larger area than almost any other city to be found. They not only afford facilities for rapid connection with the centre and suburbs, but they compel expansion by the large area each road requires for its own accomodation.

C. B. & Q. depot grounds. Own 83 acres in city. Need more.

Mr. Hjortsberg, Engineer of the Chicago, Burlington & Quincy Railroad, furnishes a statement in detail of the land they own exclusive of the right of way. In the south division they have 0.807 acres, and in the west division 82.247 acres, a total of 83.054 acres. Even already they are cramped for room, though with much foresight and considerable good luck, they have unusual advantages of connection with other roads. They probably have more land within the city, however, than any other railway. All is used for merely depot purposes, their machine shops being at Aurora; and besides, for passenger trains they use the depot of the Illinois Central and Michigan Central Companies. Every one of these railways will require 75 to 150 acres each for mere depot purposes; and this will no doubt be found the best place for repairs, and their shops will require much more.

Each road needs 75 to 150 acres.

C. B. & Q. road has 11 miles city track.

The Burlington and Quincy road has 11.06 miles of railway track of its own, within the City limits. Perhaps none other has as much, but many of them must have even more. What is the present business on any of these long railways, compared with what it will be only five years hence? Wise directors will waste no more time, but purchase ample ground for their accommodation. They need not wait for lower prices, nor fear having too much; and if they should have a surplus, it will prove the best possible investment. As before observed with regard to the stock-yards, more will be made on the land than on the business of the yard.

Roads sho'd buy ample grounds.

Facilities to reach suburbs.

But while railways crowd out the City, they afford ample means to recompense for area used, converting into a comfort what would otherwise be a serious inconvenience, by facilitating access with the suburbs. These unequaled railway facilities, however, will be of little practical benefit, if they must be restricted to the speed of a horse railway. As intimated, p. 250, a grade must be instituted for the exclusive use of railways, so that trains can start every few minutes from the centre of the City at high speed without endangering life or limb by use of the track for other purposes. It will be an expensive undertaking to both roads and City; yet the benefits to both will prove the investment judicious. The City is bound at any cost to protect its Citizens; yet, as before observed, nine have been killed, (so Dr. Rauch informs me) within ten months by the railroads, within the City limits, and doubtless 50 to 100 have been seriously injured. No matter that railways are liable for damages; does money pay for a lost husband, father, son? Is it ever compensation even for a lost limb?

Must run quick. Independent grade required. It will pay. Railway casualties.

These will be multiplied.

But we have this list of deaths and of probable casualties, within only the present limits, with only the few trains now running. With limits doubled, with trains quintupled, what will be the increase of casualties? Nor is it possible for the City to afford protection if only one grade is used, except to dispense with railways. With the utmost care, accidents will occur if ordinary streets must be used by railways. To dispense with them is to lay Chicago flat as a flounder. Who considers that a possibility? Even ten-fold sacrifice of both life and limb would first be endured, and still would we cry welcome to the railways. No possible means to obviate the difficulty can be imagined than that of giving railways their own independent grade.

Change of grade only protection.

Benefits already sure.

In Boston, or any where that a railway can be bridged over, the benefits are very striking. We see it here along the river and south branch. Probably in no other city could such a work be done with so little cost and inconvenience. Irrespective of the railway grade, the improvement will pay doubly for its cost. The increased value of the basements in this City of wide side walks, will more than pay; and the saving in drayage by putting the bridges upon a level, will pay over again in dollars and cents. Then add the benefits of sewerage, and convenience to citizens of passage everywhere unobstructed by trains and locomotives in perpetual motion, and who can doubt that the change will be one of the best paying investments that the City ever made?

Improve basements. Save drayage.

Sewerage.

Individual convenience.

Benefits to railways.

The advantage to the railways will scarcely be less. They must every year pay more for casualties; and the first session of the legislature the city limits will be widely expanded, and speed be reduced to six miles an hour for a couple miles more; and not long before a couple more.

All will favor change.

This improvement is one that every railway man would not only favor, but urge its immediate prosecution. They need to know what is to be done to plan their grounds and buildings accordingly. If they want it they must work for it. City officials, who are appointed to care for these chief public concerns, who will neglect to give all requisite efforts to the success of a scheme so indispensable to the City, are not faithful stewards. No one can question the desirableness of such an improvement, which would give Chicago advantage over every city of the world for railway trade. Nor can any reasonable man who appreciates the future of railways for this City, doubt that ultimately the railways will be given a grade to themselves. Every year's delay only increases obstacles and costs, continues the existing inconveniences to citizens and railways, and sends more victims to beds of pain, and others to their graves.

City officials should aid.

Give Chi. unequaled advantages.

Delay intolerable.

Indefinite expansion.

Room for Indefinite Expansion—its Benefits.—As before observed, the land contiguous to the City is all that could be desired for suburban purposes of a great city. Instead of mountain grandeur, we have for those who regard scenic effect, the equal grandeur of expanse, in the illimitable spread to the horizon of lake and prairie; doubtless a powerful influence in giving that breadth and comprehensiveness which is a preëminent characteristic of prairie-reared men.

Grandeur

No expense to prepare site. But no one site has everything in perfection. If to some tame for want of rocky hills, deep ravines, bottomless bogs; to others countervailing exceptions would be a full equivalent. To have the surface prepared to hand by nature, instead of expending several fold the first cost to bring it to usable condition, would be somewhat of an item to most men, even those quite given to fancy. Then what our environs lack in variety, will be amply compensated for in beauty. Beauty in place of variety.

No choice of land. For ten miles around, except upon or near the lake shore, there is little choice of land. The water view is invaluable, and its limited amount will raise it to a high price, although near the City it is the poorest soil we have. But from the Calamink to Waukegan it will be occupied mainly by those doing business in Chicago. After leaving the lake a short distance, there is little choice. For ten miles and more it is good arable land. Though varying in elevation, all needs under-draining to remove surface water; and when drained some of the wettest will be the richest, best land. Even Mud Lake may prove no exception. The Northwestern depot is 10 feet above low water mark; and the railway rises gradually out to Harlem, 9 miles, which is 45 feet above. Burlington & Quincy depot is 11 feet above low water; Lyons, 13 miles out, is 41 feet. All good land. Elevation at Harlem. At Lyons.

Benefits. 1st. Health. We have, then, abundant room, and what are the benefits of expansion? 1st. *Health.* Free ventilation is an advantage that needs no argument. This is best secured by expansion. 2nd. *Keeping prices moderate.* Should the suburbs be chosen by the wealthy, as they may and should be, the interior will be left for business, and for the homes of common laborers. To keep down prices of land for manufactures and other business, and for the homes of mechanics and other laborers in their vicinity, is of the utmost importance to the progress of the City. That so large a part of the laboring classes are land-owners, is one of the most encouraging and important suggestions to be offered. Let our City be ruled by lot-owners, and there will be less official mismanagement and corruption. For one to three miles or more outside, the land may and should be made more valuable than that within a mile of the limits, either out or in. 3rd. *Beauty.* A city may be splendid, but cannot be beautiful, built up in solid blocks. Of splendor we soon weary, but "beauty is a charm forever." Nature has given us ample means to make here a beautiful city, with small cost. It depends alone upon the plans we lay for the future city which is surely to be here, whether it be made as inviting in regard to beauty as to business. Could suburban owners be induced to join in plans to lay out the land ornamentally with winding streets; little parks set out at once with trees and shrubbery, on which ultimately an elegant church or school house or both should be built,—temporary ones being used meanwhile on some side street—so that architectural beauty could be enjoyed; the current thitherward could soon be set, and lots of various size be occupied with pretty cottages and stately mansions. The fine soil would soon supply beautiful shrubbery and trees, and the artesian wells water for fountains and other uses. 2. Low price of lots. Laborers to own lots. Out lots more valuable. 3. Beauty. It depends upon ourselves. To be laid out ornamentally. Soon desirable.

Garden City. Obstacles. 1. Many owners 2. Slow trains. Removal uncertain.

To a plan so desirable, and which would at once make us truly the GARDEN CITY, there are, however, weighty obstacles. 1st. Sub-division to numerous owners renders concerted plan and action difficult. 2nd. Impossibility at present of reaching the suburbs with reasonable speed. The second doubtless is chief, the removal of which would soon bring owners to see the desirableness of an arrangement which would in a few years enhance values several fold. Yet probably neither is sufficiently certain to render it indispensable that every land owner should immediately double his prices.

Indefinite liability. A charter remedies. Charter Land Improvement Company. Delay in use. Soon to organize. Others also. Some oppose. Tax them. It is just.

But it is one thing for a land-owner to see what is for his interest, should everything work favorably; quite another to consent to put his land into a company, rendering himself liable indefinitely. This indefinite liability can only be obviated by an act of incorporation; and having given much consideration to the improvement of suburban property, as the only means of accomplishing my plans, I asked of the Legislature the Act of Incorporation of the Land Improvement Company, (see p. 13), which is all that could be desired. The intervention of the war, and subsequent engagements in other affairs, has prevented prosecution of the plan, although several applications to purchase the charter have been made, and the funds any time would have been a great relief; yet having been obtained to be used by me, and having that distinct understanding with our members, Senators Ogden and Blodgett, and Representatives, Brown, Scammon, Wilmarth and Haines, it has been kept intact. It is now my intention soon to organize a company under that charter, and show what can be done in the way of improving suburban property. The scheme will be popular on all sides, and numerous organizations will result, effecting general improvement in outside property. But there always will be selfish, picayune men, who will oppose any such movement. Such usually abhor the tax collector, and the most effective dose to relax their grasp of land will be to bring it for three or four miles outside within the City limits. The payment of City taxes a while will set them to inquiring some way to make their land pay, or else cause them to sell. No just man can object to this, for land that would not be worth $5 per acre were there no city here, is by the City itself given a value of $50 to $2,000 per acre, though most of it is without the slightest improvement or very little at best. Why should not such property pay its proportion of City expenses?*

Ultimate city limits. Triple go'vt not wanted. Only 3 or 4 miles at present to come in.

* The time will come, it is to be hoped, when the City will be relieved of town and county organizations, extending the City say to Lake County north, to the Des Pleines west, and down the river to Willow Spring, thence southeast to the State line near Thornton; so that the City authorities can regulate all sorts of manufactories that will affect the City. The present system of triple government is not merely a useless expense, but every way injurious. Within that area every acre has its value almost entirely from contiguity to Chicago, and it should be under City rule and pay City taxes. But it may not be expedient at present to ask that this be done. Three or four miles, however, in each direction should undoubtedly be added to the City the first session of the legislature, and make these do-nothing landholders pay their part. Some of the largest landholders will no doubt urge the change, but the picayunes will fight it.

Certain advance of property.

Certain Advance of City and Suburban Property.—Notwithstanding the uncertainty as to what may be done for the improvement of Chicago; that it surely grows and rapidly, and its property immensely augments in value, is a fixed fact, and one of our chief local advantages. As we have seen, the future of this City is certain, and we have yet to consider topics whereby we can judge correctly of the rapidity and magnitude of growth; but no man can put his finger on any other site which has this certainty. Not that it is at all doubtful, whether cities in the West are to grow, some to a large size; but however confident the friends of each may be, as we saw p. 107, no other city can claim any three of the nine points made in favor of Chicago, most of which are essential, and all important to any city. It is, therefore, to Chicago a Local Advantage, and a very important one, that parties may here invest in real-estate with an absolute certainty of its advancement. This lot or that may be most valuable, but all Chicago property must largely advance in price.

No other city equally certain.

An important local advantage.

Object in coming to Chi.

A person changes his home wholly to improve his pecuniary circumstances. He locates most advantageously to pursue his favorite calling. He must have a place to do business and to live. Chicago being a favorite place of resort, buildings of all descriptions have been difficult to get, and rents correspondingly high, so that laboring classes especially have been compelled to rent or buy a lot and erect their own house. They could not afford to hire and must build for themselves. As a consequence, property is very much distributed. Many a blacksmith and shoemaker, whose earnings by his trade have been larger than they could have been almost anywhere else, finds himself now in comfortable circumstances merely from his house lot; and if energy and foresight led him to buy a shop lot, he is a rich man.

Rents high.

Obliged to buy.

Many made rich.

Real and personal advance.

The difference in the advance of real and personal property is not observed as it should be. The Comptroller's Report, 1st April, 1867, contained the following statement:—

Population 1837–'66.

Population of the City of Chicago from its Incorporation, in 1837, *to October* 1*st,* 1866, *with Valuation of Property and Income from Taxes:*

Valuations, real and personal. Taxes.

Mayors.	Years.	Population.		White persons under 21.	Valuation of real estate.	Valuation of pers'nl Property.	Total Valuation.	Income from taxes.
W. B. Ogden.........	July, '37	City Census...	4,170		$ 236,842		$ 236,842	$ 5,905 15
Alexander Lloyd..	1840......	U. S. Census..	4,479		94,437		94,437	4,721 85
Aug. Garrett........	1843......	City Census...	7,580	2,694	962,221	$ 479,093	1,441,314	8,647 89
Aug. Garrett........	June, '45	State Census..	12,088		2,273,171	791,851	3,065,022	11,077 58
J. P. Chapin.........	Sept. '46	City Census...	14,169		3,664,425	857,231	4,521,656	15,825 80
J. Curtiss............	Oct. '47	City Census...	16,859	7,603	4,995,446	853,704	5,849,170	18,159 01
J. H. Woodworth..	Sept. '48	City Census...	20,023		4,998,266	1,302,174	6,300,440	22,051 54
J. H. Woodworth..	Aug. '49	City Census...	23,047		5,181,637	1,495,047	6.676,684	30,045 09
J. Curtiss............	1850......	U. S. Census..	29,963		5,685,965	1,554,284	7,220,249	25,270 87
C. M. Gray...........	Dec. '53	City Census...	59,130	17,404	13,130,677	3.711,154	16,841,830	135,[illegible]62 08
L. D. Boone.........	June, '55	State Census..	80,000	31,255	21,637,500	5,355,593	26,992,893	206,209 03
Thomas Dyer.......	Aug. '56	City Census...	84,113		25,892.308	5,843,776	31,736.084	396,652 39
John Wentworth..	1860......	U. S. Census..	109,260	52,861	31,198,155	5,855,377	37,053,512	373,315 29
*F. C. Sherman....	Oct. '62	City Census...	138,186	58,955	31,580,545	5,552,300	37,139,845	564,038 06
F. C. Sherman......	Oct. '64	City Census...	169,353	65,947	37,148,023	11.584,759	48,732,782	974,655 64
John B. Rice........	1865......	State Census..	178,492	82,966	44,064,499	20,644,678	64,709,177	1,294,183 54
John B. Rice........	Oct. '66	City Census...	200,418	89,150	66,495,116	19,458,134	85,953,250	1,719,064 00

*The figures here given are for the territory within the present city limits. The population within the old city limits in 1862, was 133,768.

Last year the assessment was made at the fair cash value, which previously had been nominal. Thereby personal property was assessed at $53,487,824; real-estate, $141,415,940; yielding taxes of $2,517,143.50. Of the personal much has been brought in; but the value of the real has been made here, and in by far the chief part, by the energetic, rapid use of the former. Is it wise for the active man to take to himself only the profits upon his business, which is itself aiding to increase values all around him, and two to three-fold faster than his own? Is it no object to locate in a city where a person can have the positive certainty of doubling ordinary profits in the legitimate operations of his business?

1867, real, $141,415,940.
Personal, $53,487,824.
Citizens to own lots.
Advantage of location.

But where is the benefit if a man neglect to avail himself of his opportunity? The hazards of trade are proverbial. Real-estate in a growing city is almost the only sure thing in which to invest with a certainty of rise besides ordinary interest. Every business man then, should buy his home lot, at least, when he is able, and to put it beyond the risk of trade, *convey it to some friend in trust for his wife and children.* If he could do so with his business lot all the better. No man has any right to go on indefinitely in the hazards of trade, and make no provision for his family against calamity. I speak from sad experience, having lost two good estates made in Chicago property, by unwisely engaging in other business.* As an example to be shunned, and at the same time exhibiting something of what has been done in Chicago property and can be done again; and the folly of relying wholly upon business however promising,† an account of my early transactions, before referred to, is taken from a pamphlet of March, 1860:—

Trade hazardous.
Real estate sure.
Business men to have some.
Duty to family.
My experience.
Views 1860.

In 1832, at the age of 17, my father took me to Chicago with a stock of merchandize. The town then contained some 150 people, exclusive of the garrison, two framed stores, and no dwelling except those built of logs. After remaining a few weeks, examining the country south and west, and satisfying himself that he had made the right location, he left me to shift for myself. In 1834, he removed his family to Chicago and lived till 1840, having his first convictions strengthened year by year, that it was rapidly to become one of the largest cities of the country, and of the world.

arrived at Chi. 1832.
Father's opinion.

Though a mere boy, I, too, became impressed with the advantages of the point which was the western extremity of the great lake navigation, with a certainty of its connexion, by canal, with the Illinois and Mississippi rivers, and which was the natural commercial centre of a country so fertile, and so easily tilled, and so vast in extent. In the winter of 1833 and 1834, I induced a wealthy uncle to take some

My early impressions.
First purchases 1834.

---

*To what else does Paul refer, when in the midst of his directions to Timothy concerning the duties of widows, he remarks? "But if any provide not for his own, specially for those of his own house, he hath denied the faith and is worse than an infidel." It is a man's duty to pay his debts, especially to protect endorsers, but it is also duty to take care of his family; and when he has a competence and can honestly set aside property, he ought to do it and put it beyond contingency. This is not to advise that they have separate interests. They are joined in one, and their interests should be and are indissoluble.

Paul's directions.
1 Tim. v. 8.
No separate interests.

Let these energetic, successful husbands see to it that their families are made safe against poverty by a Chicago lot or two conveyed in trust for their benefit.

Give your wife a lot.

†My mistake was worse, for property which had been settled upon my wife, and for which I had received money, was used by me, with no security to her; and then when my reverses came in 1857, not expecting to be seriously embarrassed, and fearing that my property would be tied up by judgments, all was assigned to secure endorsers. It is one of the important events of my life, that under like circumstances would surely not be repeated, highly as are obligations to endorsers regarded by me.

A mistake.

Benefits to my uncle.

purchases which I had made, expecting to share in the profits. He took them, and has made out of those and other operations, through me, several hundred thousand dollars, but all the benefit to me, directly or indirectly, has been $100 He came to Chicago in the Spring of 1835, and the next day after his arrival, said if I would sell his lot—one of those which I had bought about 15 months previously for $3,500 —for $15,000, he would give me *one hundred dollars!* I sold the lot that day for cash, and the $100 was reckoned into my credit in our final settlement in 1838.

Sound reasons.

The letters that I then wrote, I had an opportunity to examine a few years ago, and they show that I operated in no speculative, hap-hazard sort of way, but at that early day, even, had sound and abundant reasons to prove the certainty, and the rapidity of the growth of that embryo city. [Extracts from one are given p. 4.]

Railroads not then foreseen.

Are now a sure basis.

No one could then have anticipated the power of railroads to build up great commercial points, and their wonderful multiplication, especially from Chicago. These have not only expedited the development of the west, but concentrated and bound to its great commercial centre with iron bands, the business and traffic which at great cost otherwise, would still have come here. They have served to fix, beyond all peradventure, what some might then have regarded as problematical —that is, which city in the west is to have the supremacy.

Purchases for myself 1834. Profits.

Sales in N. Y. $50,000.

In 1834, I began to operate in real-estate on my own account, and in February, 1835, went to New York to buy merchandise, and sold for $10,000 a 40 acre tract which had cost $4,000, the profits of which more than paid for all my other purchases. Thereafter increasing my operations, I sold in the Spring of 1836 to various parties in New York, real-estate for over $50,000, receiving about two-thirds of the pay cash in hand, and giving my individual obligations to make the conveyances when I came of age, the July following. My father would have been my heir, in the event of my death, and they knew he would fulfil my contracts.

Worth $200,000 in 1836.

No aid.

I had, then, in 1836, acquired a property of over $200,000, without any assistance even from my father, never having used his money for my operations, the store being his, and for conducting it, only my expenses had been paid. My uncle was the only relative who could have aided me, and he never would, even temporarily. So far from it, he was in my debt continuously from 1834 to our final settlement in 1838.

Crash of 1837.

Business begun.

Small indebtedness

But 1837 brought ruin to me, as it did to nearly all who owed anything; though it was not so much speculation in real-estate as engaging in mercantile business that involved me. At that age it seemed desirable every way to have regular occupation to promote good habits, and in accordance with my father's wishes, I purchased in 1836 a warehouse and dock-lots, to engage in the shipping business, which cost $23,500. My whole indebtedness was about $25,000. I had nearly $20,000 due to me, which was supposed to be well secured, it being chiefly the final payments on property of which over half the cost had been paid. To provide ample means for business, I sold in the autumn of 1836 a tract adjoining the city for $50,000, quick pay. This trade was unfortunately broken up by the merest accident, and thereafter I had no opportunity to sell at what was deemed a fair price. I came in possession of the warehouse 1st May, 1837; and though having small cash resources, I thought best to commence business, hoping there would soon be a favorable turn. But all went down—down, and I was soon inextricably involved. The money used to buy those lots for business, not speculation, would have carried me through.

Business my ruin.

Sacrifices.

By 1840, my property had all gone; one piece that had been worth $100,000, went for $6,000; another that had been worth $12,000, went for $900, and so on.

Prairie Farmer begun.

Its reputation.

Having been connected with an agricultural society, as its secretary and manager, the farming interest had a good deal engaged my attention. Seeing the importance of having a newspaper devoted to it, and of having an organ for the interchange of experience in prairie culture, and believing I could at least make out of it a living till something better offered, I commenced in the autumn of 1840, the "Prairie Farmer," and was for several years its sole editor; and though without any experience in farming, yet it is gratifying to know that from its commencement it has been regarded one of the most practical, reliable agricultural papers in the country. I retained its proprietorship till 1857.

Travels throughout the West.

From 1840 to '45 I traveled most of the time, and in all parts of the west, to acquaint myself with the influential farmers, and make them write articles for their paper. I became, of course, well informed about the country in all respects; and witnessing its rapid settlement, and the development of its unequalled, inexhaustible resources, I would anticipate what even twenty to thirty years must accomplish, when its few hundred thousand population must be increased to millions, and railroads so laid down as to bring nearly every farm within twenty miles of one, or of navigable water. *

Anticipations of the West.

I saw how immense must be the productions of so rich a country—how large its wealth, and naturally the effect that all this growth must have upon its chief commercial centre—my home—was considered.

Effect upon Chi

I resolved in some way to get a larger interest in property here, and in the autumn of 1845, went to New York to try and obtain funds. Having leisure, I wrote a series of of fifteen or twenty articles for the *Commercial Advertiser* and the *Evening Post*, about the various agricultural products of the West, their profits, etc., the minerals—manufacturing advantages—the canal—railroads that would be built, etc., etc., but not till the subject of the State debt was reached, was the rapidity of progress realized. Illinois bonds were then only worth about 25 to 30 cents on the dollar, and three years of accrued interest not reckoned, so prevalent was the impression that we could never pay the State debt; and such a fearful load was it considered, that immigration hither was considerably affected. But it was shown fairly and conclusively, that by 1858 or '59, our State would pay her full interest without any increase in the then rate of taxation; and for two years we have done this, and our bonds are above par.

Wanted some Chi. lots.

Articles about Ills.

Anticipations as to State debt.

No prediction gives more satisfaction than this. Little as the public were influenced by those views, improbable as all then regarded them; to look back upon, they now appear plain common sense, just such as any business man who would study the subject, ought to have arrived at.

Views reasonable.

Though no one would see the future of the West and of Chicago as I did, my own confidence had never been so strong. The examinations incident to the preparation of those newspaper articles brought more clearly to view than ever before, the abundant resources, and great natural advantages of the immense territory tributary to Chicago, and my determination was strengthened to buy property here.

Confidence strengthened.

Desire to have property.

By examinations I found Frederic Bronson, Esq., would sell a block on long credit for $30,000, with only $1,000 paid down. It was upon the river, near the heart of the City, and somewhat improved. I made prudent estimates of its present and prospective rental, and found it could be made to pay for itself with a small outlay. But I could make no one so see it. There was not the least confidence in Chicago, it having been for ten years a synonyme for all that was wild and visionary. Mr. Dyer of Chicago also had commenced prior negotiations with Mr. Bronson, and not wishing to interfere with him, my endeavors were postponed till their negotiations should be closed.

Block 1 for sale for $30,000.

Could be made to pay for itself.

I had no means of my own to buy with—could get no one in New York to think favorably of my projects—knew not where else to apply, and after months of vain attempts, returned home, having purchased nothing. In April, 1846, Mr. Bronson sold this block to Mr. Dyer for the $30,000. A few months after I bought it of him for $37,500, having ninety days in which to secure the $7,500 advance, and the $1,000 he had paid. By much solicitation, my brothers were prevailed upon to give this security, and the Bronson contract was assigned to me.

Failure to buy.

Bought from Mr. Dyer, $7,500 in advance.

I clung to this block, preferring to pay this large advance, rather than buy other property; because, having no capital or means of raising any, it was necessary to get such as, by its income, would pay for itself. I knew this would do it, and it was the only piece of the sort, in any considerable amount, to be found. This was large enough, 320 by 600 feet, to be an object, particularly as I was confident that by the time it was paid for in ten years it would be worth $200,000 and over. It was actually worth in 1856 over $450,000.

Reason for preference.

320 x 600 ft.

Worth in '56 $450,000.

By the spring of 1848, I had, as calculated before the purchase, with a few hundred dollars expenditure, made the rents about equal the annual payments of principal and interest.

Expectations realized.

Doubtless it would have been better to have been satisfied with this purchase. But in its improvement we had effected an arrangement with the city by which the river was to be widened up to the line of this block, and also along the six blocks next west of it. I saw the benefits that were to accrue from making dock-lots 189 feet deep, with an 80 feet street in the rear, and wanted a share in them.

Still wanted more!

* Less than fifteen years have seen this done for Illinois, and much more. But few farms are ten miles from a railroad or navigable river, and more than half are within five miles. It is also in good part accomplished for Iowa, Wisconsin, North Missouri, and all the rest of the country centering at Chicago

Change of 15 years to 1861

1 ½ block of Mr. Bronson. Mr. Bronson still had a block and a half of this river property, and in the spring of 1848, I went to New York to see what could be done with him. He asked $45,000, at least double what it was worth, and was willing to give long credit, but wanted annual interest. That I knew the rents could not meet at once, the property being chiefly occupied with the shanties of Irish squatters; and till the river bank was excavated, which would require a year or two, it would be impossible to get much revenue. I therefore insisted upon having interest for a few years added to the principal, and the result was to close contracts for the purchase, at $50,000, on 16 years time, $2,500, payable in six months, which was secured on the contract for the other block, and no other payment of principal for three and a half years, when interest commenced at six per cent, payable annually. Payments of principal then began at $1,000 a year for four years, then $2,000 a year for three years, and so on, so that no heavy payments came due till 1860.

Terms of purchase at $50,000.

Long credit.

Contract provisions for safety. To guard against the possiblity of failure, should my estimate of rents prove fallacious, I had a clause in each contract, authorizing the sale of a lot, or half a lot—the proceeds to be applied in payment of the contracts. There were also four separate contracts, so that upon an emergency I could sell a part of the purchase and not lose the whole.

Results pre-calculated. The negotiations, and making contracts, occupied some three weeks; and meanwhile I carefully estimated what the property would yield in the sixteen years, with $26,000 to expend within two and a half years. I frankly told Mr. Bronson my plans and expectations, and offered to join him in the profits if he would let me manage the property, and he advance the funds to improve it. That would have been preferable to buying, as it would have saved the labor and annoyance of "shining" to raise money for the improvements which were indispensable. That estimate I now have, and it gave, as the net value of the improvements in 1864, *after meeting all payments of principal, interest, taxes, etc.*, the sum of *one hundred and forty-seven thousand dollars*—the surplus rents being used each year upon the property; and the value of the land over $400,000. The rents have far exceeded that estimate, as I said they would. Two of the lots, equal in value to about one fourth of the purchase, for two and a half years, with no improvements except excavating the river bank and building the dock, have yielded a ground rent of $7,000—the lessee paying all taxes and assessments; and he has put on a grain elevator that cost about $100,000, that is security for the rent.

Desire to avoid debt.

Large profits

Ground rent of two lots $7000.

Plans were sound. Upon these two purchases I look back with much satisfaction. It is true I failed to induce capitalists to join me, as I had hoped. Getting credit for six months on the first payment, I thought would save me from advancing even that. But though in error on that point, nothing else was misconceived. There was nothing fortuitous or accidental in the whole operation, but it was perfectly calculated from beginning to end, and all possibility of failure effectually guarded against. *

All calculated.

Others could not see the result. Though paying double what the property was worth in cash or on short time, yet I could not get the cash, and knew that the three and a half years of credit without interest, would bring all straight. But though so clear to me, there was not a man in Chicago, to my knowledge, with whom Mr. Bronson would have made the contracts, who would have taken the purchase off my hands. On this point there is strong evidence. To induce parties abroad to join and advance capital for improvements, I had nine of our leading and best citizens, and all operating more or less in real-estate, examine the estimate of rents made at the time of purchase, with a written statement of my views and reasons thereon. They acknowledged,

9 citizens examine estimates.

Second purchase unwise. * That was so in 1860; but subsequent reflection causes doubt as to the wisdom of the second purchase Notwithstanding it promised so well, had my firm resolution not to further increase indebtedness been adhered to, the sacrifice of block 1 would not have been made, nor of other property. Could others have been made to see results as they appeared to me, and have advanced funds, the whole project would have been successful, and property been worth $1,500 a foot, which is now not worth $500. No central part of the city offers a more inviting field than that very property, with the railroad ousted east of Wells street, as it ought to be. Yet wretchedly as the property has been managed, and notwithstanding the opportunity for profits still remaining, at present value the increase in twenty years is over *500 per cent.* besides all the rents, and I predict it will be as great a per cent. in twenty years to come, if there be any proper management of the property.

A desirable purchase now.

that though the results were so astounding, they could discover nothing unfair or improbable in the views or calculations, and they signed the following certificate: Signed certificate.

"The undersigned have examined an estimate made by John S. Wright, of rents on lots, 3, 4, 5, and 6 of block 3, * Original town of Chicago, supposing $10,000 to be expended in improvements within two years and a half, together with the annual surplus of rents above the payments of $19,250 of principal, and all the interest in sixteen years; and we concur with him, in the main, in the views and estimates therein contained. Chicago, June 9th, 1848." [Signed]. B. W. Raymond, Geo. W Dole, George Steel, John H. Kinzie, E. S. Wadsworth, Thos. Dyer, John P. Chapin, W. H. Brown, and Geo. Gibbs. [Only two of whom now live. What shadows we are; what shadows we pursue instead of true riches!] Full endorsement of my estimates.

On the 28th of February, 1849, I printed a circular, and in conection with the above certificate, said: *Circular 1849.*

"Five of the first signers gave the papers a minute and critical examination, and the first two examined them thoroughly by themselves, and also together The others studied them less critically, but satisfied themselves of their general correctness, and most, if not all, expressed the opiniou, that, extraordinary calamities alone excepted, the results would be realized. One of them (W. H. Brown, Esq.) a few days since casually expressed some distrust of the operation, and I subsequently told him that I wished to use his name in connexion with the certificate, but could not rightly do so as long as he had doubts about it; and upon re-examination of the estimates, he expressed himself satisfied.' Views well considered. W.H. Brown

They could not but "concur in the views and estimates," for they were reasonable and moderate, yet their total lack of confidence in their attainment was evinced by the fact that three and a half blocks more of this same north-side river property were nearly all in the market, yet for years no one bought in it but myself, with a single exception, and that exception the more strongly confirms my statement. Mr. Wadsworth, one of the above signers, and considered one of the most sagacious of them, and who carefully studied and discussed the papers with me, sold the winter of '48 and '49, to Mr. Steel, another of the signers, two lots next adjoining one of my blocks, for one quarter cash and the balance in 1, 2 and 3 years, at a rate *considerably less than half the price I had paid.* Though very conscientious, and in all honor and integrity certifying as above, yet he could not bring himself to realize that the result must come. As do most real-estate operators, he went with the current. I have joked him several times since for his folly, for the lots he sold for $4,500 would have since brought $80,000, and are to-day worth $50,000. He has made no use of his money that would have paid at all equal to this, and I know of no other purchase as good. The buyer, it happens, was one of the signers, but he did not credit the results certified to any more than did the others, for he was, and is, a wealthy Scotchman, and could and would have bought every one of the lots if he had supposed there was a fifth part of the profits in them that he has realized. Concurence reasonable. Yet not believed. Mr. Wadsworth. Mr. Steel. Evidence of their disbelief.

In '46 the best lot on the north side, 80 feet on the river and North Water street, and 189 feet on Clark (a bridge) street, was offered for $6,000; and for years I urged friends to buy it. The owner kept advancing his price, till in January '50, I induced a couple of Virginia friends to take it at $9,000. In '56 that lot was worth over $110,000, and is now worth $70,000, and has all the time yielded a good ground rent. Another north side lot.

But these purchases, though apparently so judicious and profitable, were a heavy load to me and my brothers for years. I could not make capitalists see through my spectacles, and none would lend me the aid of their money. The widening of the river cut off rents largely for two years, and the excavation, building of docks, warehouses, etc., had run me into debt, at two to five per cent. a month, and a brother was an endorser, greatly against his will, for $15,000 to $20,000. In the spring of '50, he insisted upon relief, and having our affairs disentangled, and learning that the Galena Railroad would buy one of the blocks for a depot, he urged its sale. He had acted generously towards me—few brothers would have done as much—and his request was reasonable, notwithstanding it involved such a sacrifice of my expectations. The block first bought for $37,500, was sold to the Company for $60,000. † Purchases a heavy load. Block 1 sold 1850—for $60,000.

---

* This was the half block, about two-fifths in value of the purchase—the other block, about three-fifths costing $30,750. I did not care to trouble them to go through the calculations for the latter, for if correct for the half block, they would be found so on the whole purchase. Two-fifths of purchase, $19,250.

† Let it not be imagined that the depot was regarded an important desideratum by me. In converting the nine lots into wholesale property for groceries and iron, as was my expectation, by supplying stores Depot not desired by me.

The personal considerations required.

Though prolix and tedious in discussing these operations, it is not from foolish conceit. The egotism is as distasteful to me as to you, but seems required. Whether I have judgment or not in real-estate transactions to make your money safe and profitable, is the point considered, and how can it be so well shown as by what has been done? The reasons and motives influencing me are also important, for if the transactions were accidental instead of calculated, they would give no assurance for the future. Therefore is this statement presented, and though from necessity "blowing my own trumpet," yet it is fair and truthful. It may not be in my power to make just such operations again, but I shall be sadly disappointed if ten years hence, with my life and health, I do not show some as good relatively as were those. Increased knowledge and experience ought to be of some service; and at all events no purchase will be made without due investigation, and you shall always have a good reason if you ask me.

Experience valuable.

Reaper works.

I made some profitable exchanges, but no considerable purchase of property till '55 I bought 52 acres on and near the North Branch, for my Reaper works, for $72,000.

Ocupation wanted.

Until '51, the management of these blocks had given me constant work. They were then mostly rented, yielding several thousand dollars beyond annual payments, and I wanted more occupation. I did not wish to buy more property, being satisfied with what I had done and knowing that a few years would make it a fortune large enough for me and my family. Manufacturing suggested itself, for which Chicago possesses great advantages, all kinds of raw materials being as cheaply brought together here as at any city in the Union, while it excels all others in distributing facilities. My connection with an agricultural paper informed me of the great demand the prairies would make on Chicago for farming implements, and the large acquaintance and warm friendships made among the leading and most enterprising farmers all over the West, would give great advantages in selling what I might make. It seemed that with a good practical man as a partner, a safe and lucrative business could be easily built up of a most agreeable character, and it was much more congenial to my temperament than sitting still to wait the rise on real estate. Besides, though having no desire to be immensely wealthy, I wanted more income to use year by year.

Advantages for mnfg.

Prairie Farmer.

Mnfg. agricultural implements.

Partnership formed.

I therefore formed a partnership with an experienced mechanic at the East, but after getting the business started, he decided not to remove to Chicago, and I had to abandon my plans or go on alone. Not being fond of backing out, I continued the business in a small way at first, hoping month by month, and year by year, to find a suitable partner. Mr. Atkins, too, had given me a half interest in his Self-Raking Reaper for patenting and introducing it, which I saw had great merit, and having become warmly interested in this most ingenious invention, I did not like to relinquish it. No other harvester ever had such success. I built the first in '52, forty in '53, three hundred in '54, twelve hundred in '55, and there had been no complaint or difficulty with them of any account; nor had any taken so many premiums.

Atkin's self-raker.

Its complete success.

It was my ruin.

But this unequaled success led me on to my ruin. It is not necessary to the present purpose to follow through the success and disasters of the reaper business.*

Reasons for its purchase.

40 x 180 feet, at low rents to begin with, it seemed advantageous to have a railway track for the accommodation of the stores, and I started the project of selling block 5 for a depot. But Mr. Newberry would not consent to that, because as the owner of the contiguous property, it would appear that he was rendering the railway serviceable to himself; and Mr. Turner wanted it as far east as possible, in order to facilitate connexion with the Illinois Central by a bridge. Entirely against my own judgment and plans, circumstances compelled the sale of block 1 instead of 5, and precisely the result which I predicted to Mr. Newberry, has come. The value of the entire river property has been destroyed. I would never have consented to the arrangement, had it not been my purpose to fight the railroad in their use of the street, where they had no rights, and compel them to exchange with me block 1 for 5; and west of the latter they could have used it as they pleased. I knew the whole city would be with me, because of the immense inconvenience of constantly running of cars and engines back and forth across Clark and Wells streets. But absorption in my reaper successes, postponed attention to real estate.

River property destroyed.

Cause of disaster in reaper business.

*An explanation, however, is due to myself: In the winter of 1854-5, the unvarying success leading me to build 1,200 machines for the ensuing harvest, it seemed reasonable to expect to build 3,000 machines for 1856, and that winter I employed a competent person to purchase lumber, mostly ash, in Ohio. It was carefully piled on docks at Conneaut, Fairport, etc., for summer freight, which had previously been $2, to $3, per M. The summer of 1855, there being no down freights, and a vast amount of railroad iron to come up, vessels asked $8, to $12 for lumber. In October I contracted at $6.25, but the

Lumber bo't in Ohio.

Nothing of that kind is herein proposed, and sure am I that I shall not again be so caught. Suffice it here to say, that the reaper involved me inextricably in '57, and has swept away all my real-estate, worth to-day half a million.

Some good friends, because of past predictions, and from engaging in those north-side purchases which no one else would touch, have considered me at least a little wild and visionary. But with these explanations of motive, and of calculation, I do not see that I am amenable to the charge. The purchases of those blocks were too thoroughly scrutinized and planned to be even doubtful; and certain it is, I was not so elated with success as to engage in other operations of a like character. I was satisfied with the property made, but wanted more income, and hence engaged, not in anything speculative, but in a regular staid business, that with more experienced aid in its conduct, would have realized all my anticipations.

My plans not visionary.

Staid business.

So with regard to predictions. With my knowledge of the west, and fondness for investigating all subjects bearing upon its prosperity, I could not but anticipate the results, as would have others viewing from my stand point. I could not overlook railroads, and in some degree appreciated their immense power to develop a country, and build up great cities. In the investigations incident to the writing of several articles for New York and Boston papers, in 1848 and '9, about western railroads, laying down five or six roads that must be built, I was forcibly struck with the congruity of interest between Chicago, and the cities of New York and Boston, in bringing business to the lakes, to make it tributary to those cities and to the intermediate routes. I endeavored to demonstrate the importance of extending to Chicago the eastern lines of railroad, and thence argued that when once they reached here, competition would ensure the construction of all paying roads. Has not the result justified the predictions? True it is, the competition and railroad mania have done for us much more than was anticipated, but was it not a natural result of interest that eastern capital should build roads from here as from no other point? That it has been done is a fact, and I see nothing visionary in the predictions.

Predictions reasonable.

Causes of observation.

Railway anticipations

N. Y. Boston and Chi. united in interest.

Results realized, and more.

Nor was the Illinois Central Railroad an exception. That was regarded a wild goose chase; but looking back, it seems a natural, reasonable operation for Congress, as a great land proprietor, to have given each alternate section of land to build a road through a region otherwise inaccessible, and then double the price

Ill. Cent. no exception.

---

vessels took railroad iron again at better rates. Another contract was made as soon as possible at higher figures, and two cargoes arrived, but winter closing two or three weeks earlier than usual, two cargoes of thick lumber, and most important to have well seasoned, were frozen up in the St. Clair river. There was no seasoned lumber of the sort here, and mills were engaged in Indiana and Michigan to saw to bill. But we could obtain none till February, and then entirely green. Super-heated steam kiln-dryers were constructed; but being obliged to go east in March, my partner, an energetic, driving man, but utterly unfitted to direct a large business, would not wait for the lumber to season, and Mr. Hollingsworth, the foreman, informs me that much was put in entirely green. The result was, of course, a universal failure under the burning sun of harvest. Payments had to be put over, and a cash outlay incurred of $30 to $50 on each machine. Still, the farmers were universally pleased with the machines, and the circular of 1857, showed stronger confidence than ever, nothwithstanding their difficulties. Then in 1857, and '58 the farmers had no crops and could not pay; and with the utter prostration of real-estate, my property was entirely swept, not paying my endorsers, though subsequent advance in real-estate will save them from loss. Had the business been kept up, as it should have been, there was property in stock and reaper dues that would have paid all. Besides, I had not misjudged as to the superiority of self-rakers. The Atkins was the pioneer in this important improvement, and the patents could have been made to control upon the essential point, the delivery by one rake out of the way of the team on the next round. Nearly all reapers now built are self-rakers, and probably none equal to the Atkins. Every little while I hear of one of the machines still running and giving the highest satisfaction; and with more nerve the business would have been saved and been largely profitable, and all my debts have been paid with small loss to any one. The dues to me for reapers sold would have paid my debts had the business been kept up.

High freights.

2 cargoes frozen up.

Green lumber used.

A consequent failure.

Farmers unable to pay.

Business abandoned.

Self-rakers preferred.

Business should have been saved.

Having said this much to show that failure in the business was the result of circumstances beyond my control, it is due to my brothers, the endorsing creditors in whose behalf the assignment was made, to add; that under the pressure of the times, and with this heavy load upon them, most persons would have endeavored as they did to take care of themselves, without risking more in a business which had not only sunk my large property but also heavily involved them. It is one of the examples of the uncertainty of all business, exhibiting the wisdom and necessity of having some means of family support placed beyond such dangerous contingencies.

No blame to brothers.

Should have some stay besides business.

Years of labor for it. **of the other sections, so that it cost the Government nothing. I do not regret that for years I worked for this, and spent three weeks at Washington when the bill was passed. It is one of those visionary schemes, resulting in such practical benefits, that for one I am proud to have had a hand in its accomplishment.**

Opinions not visionary then or now. Probably no one would now consider former opinions visionary, even at their dates of expression, but reasonable and certain from my stand-point. So will these be found in the future. And in my best judgment, according to the views most men take of future operations, Chicago is to-day a safer city to invest in than ever hitherto. More money is now required, and doubtless the per cent. of increase will be less, especially upon inside property. But business which has been almost wholly confined to South Water and Lake Streets, has within only two or three years broken its old bounds, and Randolph, Washington, and Madison, and the cross streets, have advanced several hundred per cent. The same effect will be seen on other streets within a few years. The uncertainty where, however, affords ample scope for the exercise of judgment. Very much depends upon contingencies as well as foresight and energy, in a city having so many powerful influences, not only old but new, constantly arising to shift business centres.

Chi. safer than ever. Business changes. Others to come. Chances offering.

10 per cent. sure. But one thing a buyer may rest upon, that any property bought at fair value, will with the rents, if rent-paying, yield more than ten per cent. per annum, exclusive of taxes. If out-property, from which no income can be had, the greater increase will more than equal the rent of inside. The natural growth of the City insures this, and more. Besides this, a buyer takes his chances for superior judgment or favoring circumstances, and may make far more. It was my intention here to cite instances of both species of property. But they might be regarded exceptional; and the assessment roll itself, p. 288 proves the statement as to the past to be clear within bounds. "The thing that hath been, it is that which shall be."

Natural progress. Further chances. Evidence.

Revulsions may come. Very possibly, even very certainly, a revulsion from a causeless panic like that of 1857, or from some efficient cause, like that of 1837, may come. If so, it will surely send down values as then, for we still lack capital very greatly, and use credit so extensively, that its injury works financial ruin. But, as several times repeated, the man who is able to hold his real estate, will soon find old values returning, together with good profits. No property on earth is safer than Chicago lots.

All right in the end.

Opportunities great. Small buyers can do well, better than in almost any other city; but to large capitalists, or to those who would make a combination, and engage energetically in improvements, no other city offers equal inducements. Consider the field offering in that enterprise of the north-side Dock Company; such another as the South Branch Canal Company; Mr. Potter Palmer's improvement of State Street, any and all of which can and will be repeated, if equally sagacious, energetic men, control the property. Then

Examples.

we need a large cemetery;* and the field of operations in suburban property is almost coëxtensive with the prairie. Because of the constant fluctuations, contingencies always arising upon which no one can calculate, the far-sighted and industrious have unusual opportunities. Chance for smart men—

Nor is it indispensable that a capitalist should be a resident to avail himself of some of these opportunities. Assuredly, a man here who has full knowledge of the City and watches his opportunity, and has funds to avail himself of the necessities of others, or of other occurring changes, has an important advantage. But by a liberal commission, or what is better, giving the agent an interest in profits, very profitable operations can be made. The man underrates Chicago shrewdness who supposes he is smart enough to come here and pick out the best bargains, and take them away from our own operators. —for non-residents. Pay liberally Don't be too smart.

> The liberal soul shall be made fat:
> And he that watereth shall be watered also himself,— *Prov. xi. 25.*

will be found true in this regard as in higher interests. It needs no argument to prove that any non-resident can afford to give largely of profits to secure the best efforts of competent agents; and none more competent or more honest can be found anywhere. But if they can honestly make a good trade either to buy or sell, they will surely do it, or they would not be such agents as you would desire; and how can the non-resident obtain their best services except by making it for their interest? Our agents good. But will make a good bargain.

Some of these Citizens are selfish enough to wish to keep all profits to themselves. They consider it a direct loss to the City for non-residents to become our land-holders. But these very prudent, sagacious calculators may remember with advantage, that active enterprise in behalf of Chicago, depends not upon residence here. How many of our chief land-owners have done as much for their own City, as Mr. Charles Butler of New York, Mr. Nathaniel Thayer of Boston, Mr. Joseph E. Sheffield of New Haven, Mr. Erastus Corning of Albany? No doubt public interests and profits otherwise influenced them; yet, has not their interest in Chicago property itself stimulated somewhat to their efforts in behalf of our railways and other public improvements? These were among the pioneers in creating the mammoth system of inter-communication now centering here. Who of Some citizens selfish. All helpers not residents Mr. Butler. Mr. Thayer. Mr. Sheffield Mr. Corning.

---

*It is no disparagement to the enterprising persons who saw the injudicious location of the cemetery to be now converted into Lincoln Park, and gave us Rose Hill and Graceland, to say that they are totally inadequate to the necessities of our future City. Nor are they judiciously located. All the lake shore is wanted for residences, and the property contiguous to a cemetery is largely reduced in value. The best location we have is northwest of the City, where a railroad will run by the time the land could be put in condition. Sections 28 and 29, 32, and 33, of T. 40, R. 13, would be very desirable, and somewhere in that vicinity land should be bought for the purpose and a charter obtained. The *Journal* truly observes, p. 278 that the Citizens give attention to cemetery adornment. But to obtain this effectually, we must know that the cemetery is so located as to be permanent, never to be interfered with by the growth of the City. Upon all these important public concerns we can now plan with certainty for the future city sure to be here; and failing to do this are we not derelict in duty? Present cemeteries inadequate. One wanted N. W. Must have one large and permanent.

What grumbler has done so much? these selfish grumblers have done as much, or ever will do as much for this City, as either one of these gentlemen, or twenty other non-residents who could be named? Is it unreasonable that they should have a small share in the wealth their liberality and enterprise has generated, the enhancement of the real estate which their own railroads have created, and compared with which their railway profits are insignificant? Let these grumblers consider the proverb above. No city has more to gain from faithful practice of that liberality; none more to lose from its disregard, and Infinite Wisdom gave it equally to guide our conduct in pecuniary as in spiritual concerns.

Is not a share their due?

Liberality our interest.

Non-resident railway men to have a share.

Practicing this principle, then, should we not be glad to have those non-residents **have some of the lots**, who with no proprietorship in the soil have yet contributed the means to build our canal and railways? No matter that they did it because the investment promised well. The same motive actuated the curmudgeon to buy his lot, who makes a fortune by sitting lazily on his haunches; while the railway invester makes his pittance. Besides, we have more railways to build. It would seem that only about two-thirds as many more roads can ever be built direct from Chicago, as have been in the last fifteen or sixteen years. But each one of the present fifteen, and then the ten more, will for years want extension and branches. The trunk lines will nearly every one be good paying roads; and if so, what must be the business they will pour into Chicago? What must be the effect upon its real estate? Will it not stimulate stock-taking and railway-building, that wealthy capitalists who for good and abundant reasons prefer residence elsewhere, should own a good slice of Chicago property?

More roads to build.

They will pay.

Further stimulus to own Chi. lots.

Non-residents do more than citizens.

But why argue against the bootless notions of these niggardly churls? Dozens of non-residents could be named who are fairly entitled to more of the profits on the realty of Chicago, than any equal number of land holders; and it is the literal truth, that except Hon. W. B. Ogden, no Citizen has drawn capital for our railway system equally with Hon. James F. Joy, of Detroit, who I believe owns not a dollar's worth of Chicago property. The Chicago, Burlington & Quincy Railroad, a combination of different enterprises, has had steady conduct without the ups and downs which characterize most railways, exhibiting fairly what can be done with Chicago roads honestly built and managed, and duly regarding public interests and those of stockholders. All railroads are not managed for the stockholders, and many have to find satisfaction in the knowledge, that if they make less, their officers make more.

Hon. J. F. Joy's aid.

Management of C., B. & Q. road.

If stockholders fail, officers make.

Railway men to buy Chi. lots.

Doubtless some of these railway owners will take this view of the case and agree that the time has fully come for them to obtain an interest in Chicago property. Some will prefer to buy independently and own separately. Others will see that associated capital has equal advantages in land operations as any other, and is even more desirable. A great public improvement like that north-side Dock Company, can only be prosecuted

Various ways.

Companies necessary.

under a charter, because there must be a combination, and prudent men, however willing to take a known amount of risk, will not involve themselves indefinitely. Only by companies, too, can suburban property be judiciously laid off and improved in a large body. Individual owners will not agree, and their interests must be committed to a directory. Notwithstanding both public and individual advantages in the proper planning of the suburbs, we shall go on indefinitely making our additions with none but straight streets, until companies are organized for the purpose. With a capital of only a million or two, a company would have strength and make vastly greater profits than individuals, while at the same time accomplishing public benefits which are beyond the reach of single efforts.

Suburbs never improved without them.

Most profitable.

A company of this kind offers important advantages to non-residents in particular, provided they can be sure of competent and honest managers. They will be relieved of the difficulty and labor of individual purchases; will be certain to have the average growth of the City, probably more in the first enterprises; can make transfer by assignment of stock certificate; can convert it easier into cash upon necessity; and have no risk from warranty of title.

Best for non-residents.

Advantages of a Co.

Taking this view of the case, the charter was obtained in 1861, as noticed pp. 13, and 287. Although it has lain idle, it has not been from want of appreciation or confidence, but on account of other occupation from a sense of duty.* My fear has been constantly that some one would engage in a similar project, yet no one has. Property is rapidly advancing and will probably never be lower, and no time should be lost in organizing and purchasing the land. But we have no spare capital for such an enterprise, and my hope is that some readers abroad will percieve the reasonableness and certainty of the project, and make due inquiries and become shareholders. The inauguration of one such will be speedily followed by others, as soon as charters can be obtained; and the quicker the better both for shareholders and the City.

Charter of Land Imp. Co.

Time to use it

Capital from abroad.

One brings others.

This long topic, however, should be ended. The ownership of Chicago lands or lots, must be conceded to be be a chief and abundantly satisfactory Local Advantage, by whatsoever means attained. The non-resident who has information and fails to employ some means or other to obtain more or less of Chicago property, commits a blunder which he will regret in less than

To own Chi. lots a local advantage.

Neglect of non-residents injudicious—

---

* A plan was prepared immediately after obtaining the charter, which contains some novel features without complication. An annual dividend is to be declared out of the profits (there will be none for a year or two,) which the shareholder can draw in cash or scrip, the latter being convertible into stock; for the capital, as sales are made, will be constantly invested in contiguous property and put under improvement. Unless needed, the dividends will always be taken in scrip. I shall be bound to give my undivided attention to the Company, and make no purchase except for it. The plan in substance is to offset my charter and experience against capital. If any think my services are put too high, let them look into the plan. Those who prefer to take 20 per cent. per annum on their stock can have the option, and I take the balance. If a project can be offered that is absolutely safe, with a reasonable prospect of such a profit for a term of years, am I not entitled to an equal share?

Some features of my Co.

Dividend optional.

Efforts equivalent to capital.

20 per cent. per annum.

—of residents criminal.

ten years ; but the resident who can possibly do this, even in a small degree, and labors year after year to build up the City with no recompense but his regular business, grievously wrongs himself and family.

Other topics touching this

But to appreciate the immense Local Advantage of owning Chicago lands and lots, some further topics must be carefully considered. We have seen, it is true, that the matchless facilities of inter-communication, by lakes, railways, canal and rivers; the unequaled progress hitherto; the firm establishment of commerce; the marvelous growth of manufactures; the conjunction of minerals, with cheap food and lumber; and now these local advantages, all combine to assure a certain and rapid growth, and consequently entire safety in the real estate. But there are still other considerations which not only confirm both as to rapidity and certainty, but also afford satisfactory means to judge of the magnitude of growth. Upon this important point, let us first consider,—

Points already establish certainty

Others to judge of magnitude.

Internal trade—its power.

Power of the Internal Trade to Build up Great Cities.

Material supplied by others.

It will be admitted, that except to devise the plan of discussion, which naturally presented itself, my chief labor has been to arrange the abundant material. Under this topic, original views would be out of place; for Mr. J. W. Scott, the widely known Editor of the *Toledo* (Ohio) *Blade*, has too fully discussed it for me to add to the argument. Not only so, but the quarter of a century which has intervened since the papers were published in Hunt's *Merchants' Magazine* (1843,) has brought to maturity this pure truth, as the same time would the pure juice of the grape or of rye. The three papers should be given entire, did room permit.

This from an Ohioan.

Age improves quality.

Internal Trade of U.S.

INTERNAL TRADE OF THE UNITED STATES.

By J. W. Scott, of Toledo, Ohio.

Population hitherto on sea-board.

Almost up to the present time, the whole weight of population in the United States has lain along the Atlantic on shore, and near its tide waters, and a great proportion of their wealth was connected with foreign commerce, carried on hrough their seaports. These being at once the centres of domestic and foreign trade, grew rapidly, and constituted all the large towns of the country. The inference was thence drawn, that as our towns of greatest size were connected with foreign commerce, this constituted the chief, if not the only source of wealth, and that large cities could grow up nowhere but on the shores of the salt sea. Such has been the experience of our people, and the opinion founded on it has been pertinaciously adhered to, notwithstanding the situation of the country in regard to trade and commerce has essentially altered. It seems not, until lately, to have entered the minds even of well-informed statesmen, that the internal trade of this country has become far more extensive, important, and profitable, than its foreign commerce. In what ratio the former exceeds the latter, it is impossible to state with exactness. We may, however, approximate the truth near enough to illustrate our subject.

Imagined superiority of foreign commerce.

Internal trade not realized.

Annual earnings $1,500,000,000.

The annual production of Massachusetts has been ascertained to be of the value of $100,000,000. If the industry of the whole nation were equally productive, its yearly value would be about $2,300,000,000; but, as we know that capital is not so abundantly united with labor in other states, it would be an over-estimate to make that state the basis of a calculation for the whole country. $1,500,000,000 is probably near the actual amount of our yearly earnings. Of this, there may be $500,000,000 consumed and used where it is earned, without being exchanged. The balance, being $1,000,000,000, constitutes the subjects of exchange, and the articles that make up the domestic trade and foreign commerce of the United States. The value of those which enter into our foreign commerce is, on an average about $100,000,000. The average domestic exports of the years 1841 and 1842, is $99,470,900. There will then remain $900,000,000, or nine-tenths, for our internal trade. Supposing, then, some of our towns to be adapted only to foreign commerce, and others as exclusively fitted for domestic trade; the latter, in our country, would have nine times as much business as the former, and should, in consequence, be nine times as large. Although we have no great towns that do not, in some degree, participate in both foreign and domestic trade, yet we have those whose situations particularly adapt them to the one or the other; and we wish it constantly borne in mind, that an adaptation to internal trade, other things being equal, is worth nine times as much to a town as an adaptation in an equal degree to foreign commerce. It may be said, and with truth, that our great seaports have manifest advantages for domestic, as well as foreign commerce. Since the peace of Europe left every nation free to use its own navigation, the trade of our Atlantic coast has probably been five times greater than that carried on with foreign nations; as the coasting tonnage has exceeded the foreign, and the number of voyages of the former can scarcely be less than five to one of the latter.

Trade $1,000,000,000. Foreign $100,000,000. Domestic $900,000,000. Internal trade 9 fold advantage. Coast trade 5 times greater than foreign.

Now, what is the extent and quality of that coast, compared with the navigable river and lake coasts of the North American valley? From the mouth of the St. Croix to Sandyhook, the soil, though hard and comparatively barren, is so well cultivated as to furnish no inconsiderable amount of products for internal trade. In extent, including bays, inlets, and both shores of navigable rivers, and excluding the sand beach known as Cape Cod, this coast may be estimated at 900 miles. From Sandyhook to Norfolk, including both shores of Delaware and Chespeake bays, and their navigable inlets, and excluding the barren shore to Cape May, the coast may be computed at 900 miles more. And from Norfolk to the Sabine, there is a barren coast of upwards of 2,000 miles, bordered most of the way by a sandy desert extending inland on an average of 80 or 90 miles. Over this desert must be transported most of the produce and merchandise, the transit and exchange of which, constitute the trade of this part of the coast. This barrier of nature must lessen its trade at least one half. It will be a liberal allowance to say, that 4,000 miles of accessible coast are afforded to our vessels by the Atlantic Ocean and Gulf of Mexico. Of this only about 2,500 miles, from Passamaquoddy to St. Marys, can be said to have contributed much, until recently, to the building of our Atlantic cities. To the trade of this coast, then, are we to attribute five-sixths of the growth and business, previous to the opening of the Erie canal, of Portland, Salem, Boston, Providence, New York, Albany, Troy, Philadelphia, Baltimore, Washington, Richmond, Norfolk, Charleston, Savannah, and several other towns of less importance. Perhaps, it will be said, that foreign trade is more profitable in proportion to its amount, than domestic. But is this likely? Will not a New York merchant be as apt to make a profitable bargain with a Carolinian, as with an Englishman of Lancashire? Or, is it an advantage to trade, to have the wide obstacle of the Atlantic in its way? Do distance and difficulty, and risk and danger, tend to promote commercial intercourse and profitable trade? If so, the Alleganies are a singular blessing to the commercial men living on their western slope. Some think that it is the foreign commerce that brings all the wealth to the country, and sets in motion most of the domestic trade. At best, however, we can only receive by it imported values, in exchange for values exported, and those values must first be created at home. [The different effect of foreign and domestic trade are considered, showing that we export necessaries and import luxuries, which is not condemned, but the point is made, that if they were our own products the commerce would have equal value. Then the error is controverted, of "attributing the rapid increase of wealth in commercial nations to foreign commerce."]

Ocean and inland navigation compared. St. Croix to Sandyhook. —to Norfolk— —to the Sabine— —4000 miles. 2,500 miles have made the Atlantic cities. Domestic trade profitable as foreign. Other points considered.

Will it be said that, admitting the chief agency in building up great cities to belong to internal industry and trade, it remains to be proved that New York and the other great Atlantic cities will feel less of the beneficial effects of this agency than Cincinnati and her western sisters? It does not appear to us difficult to sustain by facts and reasoning, the superior claims in this respect of our western towns. It should be borne in mind, that the North American valley embraces the climate, soils, and minerals, usually found distributed among many nations. From the northern shores of the upper lakes, and the highest navigable points of the Mississippi and Missouri rivers, to the Gulf of Mexico, nearly all the agricultural

In internal trade will Cin. have advantage over N. Y.? Variety of our products.

articles which contribute to the enjoyment of civilized man, are now, or may be produced in profusion. The north will send to the south, grain, flour, provisions, including the delicate fish of the lakes, and the fruits of a temperate clime, in exchange for the sugar, rice, cotton, tobacco, and the fruits of the warm south. These are but a few of the articles, the produce of the soil, which will be the subjects of commerce in this valley. Of mineral productions, which at no distant day, will tend to swell the tide of internal commerce, it will suffice to mention coal, iron, salt, lead, lime, and marble. Will Boston, or New York, or Baltimore, or New Orleans, be the point selected for the interchange of these products? Or shall we choose some convenient central points on river and lake for the theatres of these exchanges? Some persons may be found, perhaps, who will claim this for New Orleans; but the experience of the past, more than the reason of the thing, will not bear them out. Cincinnati has now more white inhabitants than that outport, although her first street was laid out, and her first log-house raised long after New Orleans had been known as an important place of trade, and had already become a considerable city.

Agricultural exchanges North and South.

Mineral products.

Will exchange be on sea-board or inland?

N. O. and Cin.

It is imagined by some, that the destiny of this valley has fixed it down to almost exclusive pursuits of agriculture, ignorant that, as a general rule in all ages of the world and in all countries, the mouths go to the food, and not the food to the mouths. Dr. Chalmers says: "The bulkiness of food forms one of those forces in the economic machine, which ends to equalize the population of every land with the products of its own agriculture. It does not restrain disproportion and excess in all cases; but in every large state it will be found, that wherever an excess obtains, it forms but a very small fraction of the whole population. Each trade must have an agricultural basis to rest upon; for in every process of industry the first and greatest necessity is, that the workmen shall be fed." Again: "Generally speaking, the excrescent (the population, over and above that which the country can feed,) bears a very minute proportion to the natural population of a country; and almost nowhere does the commerce of a nation overleap, but by a very little way, the basis of its own agriculture." The Atlantic states, and particularly those of New England, claim that they are to become the seats of the manufactures with which the West is to be supplied; that mechanics, and artisans, and manufacturers, are not to select for their place of business, the region in which the means of living are most abundant and their manufactured articles in greatest demand, but the section which is most deficient in those means, and to which their food and fuel must, during their lives, be transported hundreds of miles and the products of their labor be sent back the same long road for a market.

Valley have something beside agriculture.

Dr. Chalmers.

Agriculture the basis.

Error of New England.

But this claim is neither sanctioned by reason, authority, nor experience. The mere statement exhibits it as unreasonable. Dr. Chalmers maintains, that the excrescent population could not, in Britain even, with a free trade in bread-stuffs, exceed one-tenth of all the inhabitants; and Britain, be it remembered, is nearer the granaries of the Baltic than is New England to the food-exporting portions of our valley, and she has, also, greatly the advantage in the diminished expense of transportation. But the eastern manufacturing states have already nearly, if not quite, attained to the maximum ratio of excrescent population, and cannot, therefore, greatly augment their manufactures without a correspondent increase in agricultural production.

Population not over 10 per cent. above food.

New England nearly reached this.

Most countries, distinguished for manufactures, have laid the foundation in a highly improved agriculture. England, the north of France, and Belgium, have a more productive husbandry than any other region of the same extent. In these same countries are also to be found the most efficient and extensive manufacturing establishments of the whole world; and it is not to be doubted that abundance of food was one of the chief causes of setting them in motion. How is it that a like cause operating here, will not produce a like effect? Have we not, in addition to our prolific agriculture, as many, and as great natural aids for manufacturing, as any other country? Are we deficient in water-power? [The abundance of this is shown, and also of coal for steam-power.]

Agriculture the basis of prosperity.

To be so here.

Will laborers be wanting? Where food is abundant and cheap, there cannot long be a deficiency of laborers. What brought our ancestors (with the exception of the few who fled from persecution) from the other side of the Atlantic, but the great abundance of the means of subsistence on this side? What other cause has so strongly operated in bringing to our valley the 10,000,000 or 11,000,000 who now inhabit it? The cause continuing will the effect cease? While land of unsurpassed

Food brings cheap labor.

Cause hitherto.

fertility remains to be purchased, at a low rate, and the increase of agriculture in the West keeps down the relative price of food; and while the population of the old countries of Europe, and the old states of our confederacy is so augmenting as to straiten more and more the means of living at home, and at the same time, the means of removing from one to the other are every year rendering it cheaper, easier and more speedy; and while, moreover, the new states, in addition to the inducement of cheaper food, now offer a country with facilities of intercourse among themselves greatly improved, and with institutions civil, political, and religious, already established and flourishing—are farmers, and mechanics, and manufacturers—the young, the active, and enterprising no longer to be seen pouring into this exuberant valley and marking it with the impress of their victorious industry, as in times past? [Growth of New York is then considered, and the immense river navigation of the West.]

Must continue.

Best settlers pour into this valley.

But our interior cities will not depend for their development altogether on internal trade. They will partake, in some degree, with their Atlantic sisters of the foreign commerce also; and if, as some seem to suppose, the profits of commerce increase with the distance at which it is carried on, and the difficulties which nature has thrown in its way, the western towns will have the same advantage over their eastern rivals in foreign commerce, which some claim for the latter over the former in our domestic trade. Cincinnati and her lake rivals, may use the outports of New Orleans and New York, as Paris and Vienna use those of Havre and Trieste; and it will surely one day come to pass, that the steamers from Europe will enter our great lakes, and be seen booming up the Mississippi.

Interior cities to have some foreign trade.

Atlantic outports.

To add strength and conclusiveness to the above facts and deductions, do our readers ask for examples? They are at hand. The first city of which we have any record is Nineveh, situated on the Tigris, not less than 700 miles from its mouth. Babylon, built not long after, was also situated far in the interior, on the Euphrates. Most of the great cities of antiquity, some of which were of immense extent, were situated in the interior, and chiefly in the valleys of large rivers, meandering through rich alluvial territories. Such were Thebes, Memphis, Ptolemais. Of the cities now known as leading centres of commerce, a large majority have been built almost exclusively by domestic trade. What country has so many great cities as China, a country until lately, nearly destitute of foreign commerce?

Large cities inland.

Nineveh.

Babylon.

Thebes, etc.

Chinese cities.

To bring the comparison home to our readers, we here put down, side by side, the outports and interior towns of the world having each a population of 50,000 and upwards. It should, however, be kept in mind, that many of the great seaports have been built, and are now sustained, mainly by the trade of the nations respectively in which they are situated. Even London, the greatest mart in the world, is believed to derive much the greatest part of the support of its vast population from its trade with the United Kingdom. [The table of 67 outports, and 142 interior cities, the chief of the world, is omitted.]

Comparison of outports and inland.

London.

Table omitted.

If it be said that the discoveries of the polarity of the magnetic needle, the Continent of America, and a water passage to India around the Cape of Good Hope, have changed the character of foreign commerce, and greatly augmented the advantages of the cities engaged in it, it may be replied, that the introduction of steam in coast and river navigation; and of canals and railroads, and McAdam roads, all tending to bring into rapid and cheap communication the distant parts of the most extended Continent, is a still more potent cause in favor of internal trade and interior towns. The introduction, as instruments of commerce, of steamboats, canals, rail, and McAdam roads, being of recent date, they have not had time to produce the great results that must inevitably flow from them. The last twenty years have been devoted mainly to the construction of these labor-saving instruments of commerce; during which time, more has been done to facilitate internal trade than had been effected for the thousands of years since the creation of man. These machines are but just being brought into use; and he is a bold man, who, casting his eye one hundred years into the future, shall undertake to tell the present generation what will be their effect on our North American valley when their energies shall be brought to bear over all its broad surface.

If invention favors foreign—

—it also does domestic trade.

Railways, etc., new invention.

A bold man to foretell this effect.

Let it not be forgotten that, while many other countries have territories bordering the ocean, greatly superior to our Atlantic slope, no one Government has an Interior at all worthy a comparison with ours.

No inland country like ours.

It will be observed that in speaking of the natural facilities for trade in the North American Valley, we have left out of view the 4000 or 5000 miles of rich and accessible coasts of our great lakes, and their connecting straits. The trade of

Lake valley not noticed.

these inland seas, and its connection with that of the Mississippi Valley, are subjects too important to be treated incidentally, in an article of so general a nature as this. They well merit a separate notice at our hands.

Int. trado No. II.

INTERNAL TRADE OF THE UNITED STATES, NO. II.

Natural advantages of Interior. The lakes. Stretch south— —east. Lake and river valleys closely connected. Varied surface. Minerals.

Providence has evidently designed the temperate regions of the interior of North America for the residence of a dense population of highly civilized men. Throughout its southern and middle regions, which are elevated but a few hundred feet above the level of the Gulf of Mexico, the deflected trade wind bears from that sea the vapors, which, falling in showers, give fertility to the soil, and swell to navigable size their numerous and almost interminable rivers. Towards the north he has spread out, and connected by navigable straits, great seas of pure water, to equalize and soften the temperature of that comparatively high latitude, and to aid in irrigating the surrounding countries. And he has so placed these seas, as to give them the utmost availability for purposes of trade; for, while they reach to the highest latitude to which profitable cultivation can be carried, they stretch away south almost to the very heart of the great valley. Towards the east they approach the Atlantic, and extend westward towards the Pacific, more than a third of the distance across the continent. To give the lake and river countries easy access to each other, he has placed them nearly on the same level; and strongly pointed out, and indeed, in some places, almost finished, the great channels of intercourse between them. To invite and facilitate migration from Europe and the old states, he has provided the St. Lawrence and Mississippi rivers, and cut a passage through the Appalachian chain, where flow the turbulent Mohawk and majestic Hudson. His munificence ends not here. He has diversified its surface with hills, vales, and plains, and clothed them alternately with fine groves of timber, and beautiful meadows of grass and flowers. Beneath the soil, the minerals of nearly every geological era, and of every kind, which has been made tributary to man's comfort and civilization, are properly distributed. [The country is described and its then settlement.]

Erie canal. Enlargement required. Two more canals. Two railroads from lake to ocean. Lake trade makes Atlantic city chief.

In anticipation of the early settlement of the fine country bordering on these waters, and its capacity to furnish the basis of a large commerce, the Erie canal was projected and opened. But its banks had hardly become solid, its business men been got into train and reduced to system, before the discovery was made that its capacity would little more than suffice for the business of the country through which it runs, and of course, that it would soon be inadequate to the passage of the trade then just springing up, with indications of vigorous growth, on the upper lakes. Wild as were thought the visions of Morris and Clinton by the strictly practical men of their day, it turns out that what were considered visions were but practical deductions, falling short of the truth instead of exceeding it. Ten years after the chimerical grand canal was completed, men, having the reputation of being eminently practical, thought they saw the necessity of making it about three times as large, and forthwith entered upon such enlargement. Practical men in other states have believed, perhaps prematurely, that such portion of the lake trade as they could divert from this New York route would pay them for the outlay of so many millions as will be necessary to construct two more canals, and the same number of railroads, from the Atlantic to the lake waters. Not only are cities and states entering upon a competition for this trade, but there are indications that a few years will witness an active emulation between the United States and Great Britain, in endeavors, on the one hand, to retain, and on the other to acquire it. On all sides it is admitted, that the city of the Atlantic coast which receives the bulk of our eastern business will be the leading city of that border; and if it is not now admitted, it soon will be, that the emporium of the Mississippi Valley which commands the best channel of intercourse with the lakes, must be and remain the Queen City of that valley.

Large area. Shores 5,000 miles. Take trade of river valley.

But what is it that makes this lake country of such commanding importance? In the first place, it is of great extent. Its navigable shores, including bays and straits, measure more than 5,000 miles. Not only do these command a large country lying back, in many places, much beyond the head waters of the streams which flow into them, but, by means of canals and other artificial aids, no inconsiderable portion of the Mississippi Valley is made tributary to their commerce. This is owing to their affording the cheapest and best route to New York and

Canada. Even with the small canal between Buffalo and Albany, levying tolls high enough to have already paid for its construction, we find a strong inclination to that route, not only for the foreign and eastern manufactures that are purchased in the great Atlantic Emporium, and brought into the lake and Mississippi Valleys, but for the farming produce of sections of country that formerly floated it down to New Orleans.

Draws from N. O.

The strong tendency of business toward the lakes instead of the rivers, was even then perceptible and well argued. Also, the increased facilities of the enlarged Erie canal, Chesapeake & Ohio, Pennsylvania canal and railroad, Welland canal, and the N. Y. Central, the Erie, and the Baltimore & Ohio Railroads, and Mr. Scott proceeds :—

Other eastern routes.

Such are the great works made and making; and for whom? surely not for the two or three millions that, within a few years past, have fixed their homes in the lake countries. No! but for the anticipated tens of millions of intelligent and industrious freemen, who will, as a moderate forecast enables men to see, in no long course of years, spread over, and clear and cultivate and beautify these pleasant and fertile shores. Whatever other error may arise from making the past a basis of calculation for the future, that of a too sanguine estimate could hardly be committed, in treating of any civilized country of the present day, much less of ours, the most rapidly progressive of the whole family of nations. To exhibit the growth of the principal upper lake towns, from 1830 to 1840, we here give their population at those periods :—

For whom made?

No danger of over-estimate.

Growth of lake cities, 1830–40.

	1830	1840		1830	1840
Buffalo	8,653	18,213	Toledo	30	2,053
Erie	1,329	3,412	Detroit	2,222	9,102
Cleveland	1,076	7,648	Monroe	500	1,703
Sandusky City	400	1,433	Chicago	100	4,470
Lower Sandusky	351	1,117	Milwaukee	20	1,712
Perrysburg	182	1,065	Huron	75	1,488
Maumee City	200	1,290			
			Total	15,138	54,706

Showing an increase which, if the numerous villages that have commenced their existence since 1830 were added, would more than quadruple their number in ten years. The increase of business on the upper lakes has been in a greater ratio than even ten to one. Indeed it has nearly all grown up since 1830. If the reader doubt this, let him examine and compare the account of the collector of canal tolls at Buffalo for that year with that for the past season, and add to the last the produce passing through the Welland canal.

Four-fold in ten years.

But it should not be forgotten, that while the relative amount of products of the soil, in proportion to the population, is rapidly augmenting, our cities and towns are beginning to receive a large accession of mechanics, manufacturers, and other business men, which will more and more tend by its increase, to keep down exports to the East.

Towns growing.

The intercourse between the agricultural and manufacturing regions of our country will doubtless increase as fast, and be productive of as much mutual benefit, as any friend of both sections now anticipates; but the home trade within the limits of our North American Valley will grow much faster, and possess a vigor as superior to the former, as do the great arteries near the heart to those of the limbs of the human system. Western commerce with the Atlantic border, is analogous to that of the Eastern and Middle States with Europe.

Trade to grow between sections—more still in North American Valley.

This trade has been a rapid development, but by no means in proportion to the augmentation of that with their own coast and Interior. The foreign commerce of Philadelphia, for instance, is no greater than it was in 1787, when the population of the city and liberties did not exceed 40,000, while its home trade has increased ten-fold, and its population become more than five times 40,000. It will probably

Domestic trade increases most. Philadelphia

Lake ports exceed the whole colonies.

surprise many of our readers to be informed that the exports and imports of our upper lake region, the past season, have probably exceeded in value those of all the colonies on an average of six years preceding 1775. According to Pitkin, the annual exports from the colonies of those six years, amounted to £1,752,142, and the imports to $2,732,036. The average annual amount of the exports and imports of this upper lake country for the last three years, would be estimated low at $20,000,000. Such are the results of the infantile labors of the young Hercules of the Lakes.

Vallies of lakes and rivers— —give valuable trade.

The basins of the St. Lawrence and Mississippi constitute nearly all the great Interior Valley. Each of these basins, when settled to a fair extent, will have a vast commerce of its own; and it will be interesting to ascertain through what channels, and through what towns the great intercourse that will naturally grow up between them, will be carried on. The time will come within the present century, when the trade between the northern and southern portions of the North American Valley will become more important than that of the whole valley with the eastern States and Europe. Until that period arrives, the channels which command most of the eastern business will be of paramount importance.

Routes west compared. Distance favors Maumee.

The Ohio canal, the Miami, from Maumee to Cincinnati, and the Illinois & Michigan, from Chicago to the Illinois river, are compared; and the greater *distance* by Chicago gave the then result in favor of Maumee.

Chi. route to increase in importance. Trade north and south.

When the day shall arrive that witnesses the predominance of the home trade of the North American Valley, over that which is carried on with the Eastern States and Europe, and the intercourse between the northern and southern portions of it takes the place of that which is now carried on with the old States; and when, also, the shores of the upper lakes shall be brought under cultivation, and become densely settled, the just claims of the Chicago route to participate largely in the trade between the lakes and the central and lower Mississippi Valley, will be greatly enlarged. Then she will be the port from which supplies of southern productions will be drawn for all the borders of the great Lakes, Michigan and Superior, and the northern shores of Lakes Huron and Iroquois; and through which will be sent southward most of the surplus productions of those extensive regions. But the Miami canal, as soon as completed, will fall into possession of a well peopled and highly cultivated region of great extent, whose productions will rush through from both extremes the moment it is rendered navigable.

Miami and Pittsburgh routes. Expense favors Maumee.

And Mr. S. argues on in favor of the Miami route, and then compares it with the Pittsburgh route, and the ocean, gulf and river routes *via* New Orleans, where *expense* favors Maumee.

N. O route cheapest. Climate injures flour. Lake route best— —safest.

Productions sent from the West, having greater weight and bulk in proportion to their value than merchandise coming the other way, can better afford to pay insurance, and, other things being equal, would incline to the New Orleans outlet, as the cheapest. The cost of taking flour to the New York market from all places on the Ohio below Cincinnati, (at which point it will be about equal,) will be less this way than by the Miami canal. But flour taken from the West through New Orleans, brings less in the great Northern markets than that which goes by the lakes, by more than the ordinary cost of carriage from the mouth of the Ohio to Cincinnati. This is well known to be owing to the great liability to damage in going through a hot climate. As a final market, New Orleans is, in general, very fluctuating and uncertain. These facts assure us that nearly all the surplus flour within reach of the canals leading from the lakes into the Mississippi Valley, will take the northern road to market. For safety from the bursting of boilers, there is no steam navigation in the States, and perhaps not in the world, equal to that of the lakes. On the ocean, the use of salt water, and on the western rivers, the use of muddy water for the boilers, has probably occasioned a large proportion of the explosions that have so greatly augmented the risk of navigation on the Mississippi waters. The pure waters of the lakes has proved eminently favorable to safe steam navigation; and the numerous harbors along the American shore of Lake Erie, have lessened the riks, and given it an advantage in that respect over the others—Ontario, perhaps, excepted.

Foreign products imported for the West.

But it may be said that, at no very distant day, a large portion of the productions of foreign countries brought into the great western marts for sale will be imported directly from the regions in which they are produced; and that the assuming of New York as the great centre of supply, will fail in regard to these, and thus affect the conclusions heretofore drawn. An examination of the various inlets to this foreign trade will not, however, much vary the results on the routes we have contrasted and compared. Is the St. Lawrence, the route for the European supplies adopted? The Miami and Illinois canals will still be the channels for its transport to a great part of the Mississippi Valley. Is the Mississippi the chosen channel for the introduction of what are usually called West India and South American products to the upper lakes? Still are these the only rivals in their transportation. Will the Mississippi challenge comparison with the St. Lawrence, in our anticipated European trade? Such comparison can only result in the triumph of her northern rival. It would not be difficult to prove that, when the canals now being made around the obstructions to navigation from Montreal to the upper lakes, shall be finished, so as to admit sea-going vessels to their ports, freight and insurance, between Liverpool and the ports of Cleveland, Maumee, and perhaps Chicago, will be lower than to the port of New Orleans. The distance from England or France by the St. Lawrence, to the ports of Lake Erie, is less, by more than 1,100 miles, than to New Orleans by the Gulf of Mexico. On the St. Lawrence route, the distance by river and canal, requiring the aid of steam or horse power, may be about 200 miles; and by the Mississippi, from its mouth to New Orleans, upwards of 100 miles. The advantage possessed by the latter of the saving of tolls, can hardly be an offset against the 1,100 miles additional length of voyage. Each route will have some peculiar advantage. The northern will build, man, and own the shipping employed on it; whereas the southern will depend on ships foreign to her port. The southern will be open all the year; whereas the northern will be barred by ice half the year. The favorable effect upon a trade, of being carried on by a maratime people, in their own vessels, from their own ports, is made manifest by contrasting the trade of Boston and Portland, with that of Charleston and New Orleans.

Canals still the channels. From N. O. also. Superiority of northern route. Distance less 1100 miles. East route its advantage. Northern own their vessels.

INTERNAL TRADE OF THE UNITED STATES, NO. III.

Int. Trade, No. III.

The increasing tendency to reside in towns and cities which is manifested by the inhabitants of all countries, as they make progress in the arts and refinements of civilization, is sufficiently obvious to most men who think on the subject. But it is not so apparent to those whose attention has not been particularly turned to the matter, that the improvements of the last century have so much strengthened that tendency as almost to make it seem like a new principle of society, growing out of the combined agency of steam power and machinery. Mr. Hume, who had as clear apprehension of the relations of the various conditions of society, and the operation of the causes modifying them, as any man of his time, expresses the opinion that no city of antiquity probably ever contained more inhabitants than London, which, at the time he wrote, near one hundred years ago, was estimated at 800,000. He thought there were internal and inherent causes to check and stop the growth of the most favorably situated cities when they reached that size. Taking the then existing condition of society as the basis of his reasoning, it seems probable that he judged correctly. Neither the spinning jenny, nor the power loom, nor the steam engine, nor the canal, nor the McAdam road, nor the railway, had then been brought into use; nor had the productive power of the soil, aided by science and art, been, at that time, tasked to its utmost to bring forth human sustenance. Mr. Hume looked with the eye of a philosopoer on the past and present, but, in predicting of the future, his mistakes were nearly as numerous as his vaticinations. To judge of the future by the past may seem safe and philosophic to those who believe not in the certain advance of mankind towards a more perfect condition and nature. So to judge was in accordance with the sceptical mind of Mr. Hume. Let us avoid, as far as we may, his mistake; though to us it seems not practicable to avoid falling into some degree of error of the same sort, when we undertake to foretell future conditions and events, in a rapidly progressive community.

Tendency of population to cities. Strengthened by new improvements. *Hume.* No city over 800,000. Modern inventions unknown. Man's constant progress.

What has been the effect of the improvements, physical and moral, of the past century, on the growth of towns? and what is likely to be their future effect, aided by other and probably greater improvements, on the growth of towns, during the

What the effect of modern improvements in towns.

hundred years to come? We define a town to mean any place numbering 2,000 or more inhabitants. It is to Great Britain we are to look for the main evidences of the effects of the labor-saving improvements of the last century.

Changes in England and Scotland.
Advance of towns east.

The changes in England and Scotland are described, and the greater relative growth of the towns is noticed; also the effect of railways, in giving more rapid advance to the towns over the States in New York, Pennsylvania and Ohio, which is placed under the next section, and our author observes:—

20 U. S. towns grew 55 per cent. —whole country 34.

The increase of the twenty largest towns of the United States, from New York to St. Louis, inclusive, from 1830 to 1840, was 55 per cent., while that of the whole country was less than 34 per cent. If the slaveholding states were left out, the result of the calculation would be still more favorable to the towns.

Tendency to towns—
—stronger in future.

The foregoing facts clearly show the strong tendency of modern improvements to build towns. Our country has just begun its career; but as its progress in population is in a geometrical ratio; and its improvements more rapidly progressive than its population, we are startled at the results to which we are brought, by the application of these principles to the century into which our inquiry now leads us.

U. S. pop. 1840, 17,068,-666—
—1940 to be 303,101 641.

In 1840 the United States had a population of 17,068,666. Allowing its future increase to be at the rate of $33\frac{1}{3}$ per cent for each succeeding period of ten years, we shall number in 1940, 303,101,641. Past experience warrants us to expect this great increase.

Century estimates omitted.

The figures for the century are omitted, being beyond the present calculations.

Estimates for 50 years.
1890, 72,000,-000.
Distribution.
⅓ in agriculture.
Rapidly improving.

But lest one hundred years seem too long to be relied on, in a calculation having so many elements, let us see how matters will stand 50 years from 1840, or forty-seven years from this time. The ratio of increase we have adopted cannot be objected to as extravagant for this period. In 1890, according to that ratio, our number will be 72,000,000. Of these 22,000,000 will be a fair allowance for the Atlantic slope. Of the remaining 50,000,000, 2,000,000 may reside west of the Rocky Mountains, leaving 48,000,000 for the great valley within the states. If to these we add 5,000,000 as the population of Canada, we have an aggregate of 53,000,000 for the North American Valley. One-third, or say 18,000,000 being set down as farming laborers and rural artisans, there will remain 35,000,000 for the towns, which might be seventy in number, having each half a million of souls. It can scarcely be doubted that, within the forty-seven years, our agriculture will be so improved, as to require less than one third to furnish food and raw materials for manufacture for the whole population. Good judges have said that we are not now more than twenty or thirty years behind England in our husbandry. It is certain that we are rapidly adopting her improvements in this branch of industry; and it is not to be doubted, that very many new improvements will be brought out both in Europe and America, which will tend to lessen the labor necessary in the production of food and raw materials.

Tendency to towns in old countries.
Less in U. S.
Reasons.
Change coming.
Cincinnati.

The tendency to bring to reside in towns all not engaged in agriculture that machinery and improved ways of intercourse have created, has already been illustrated by the example of England and some of our older States. Up to this time, our North American Valley has exhibited few striking evidences of this tendency. Its population is about 10,500,000; but with the exception of New Orleans, Cincinnati and Montreal, it has no large towns. As a whole, it has been too sparsely settled to build up many. Too intent on drawing out the resources of our exuberantly rich soil, we have neglected the introduction of those manufactures and mechanic arts that give agricultural productions their chief value, by furnishing an accessible market. This mistake is, however, rapidly bringing about its own remedy. In Ohio the oldest, (not in time but in maturity) of our western states, the arts of manufacture have commenced their appropriate business of building towns. Cincinnati, with its suburbs has upwards of 50,000 inhabitants; a larger proportion of whom are engaged in manufactures and trades, than of either of the sixteen principal towns of the Union, except Lowell. The average proportion so engaged in all of these towns is 1 to 8.79. In Cincinnati it is 1 to 4.50. Indeed our interior capital has but two towns (New York and Philadelphia) before her, in number of persons, engaged in manufactures and trades. Our smaller towns, Dayton, Zanesville, Columbus, and Steubenville, having each about 6,000 inhabitants, have nearly an equal proportion engaged in the same occupation. Smaller towns.

These examples are valuable only as indicating the direction which the industry of our people tends, in those portions of the West, where population has attained a considerable degree of density. Of the ten and a half millions now inhabiting this valley, little more than half a million live in towns; leaving about ten millions employed in making farms out of the wilds, and producing human food and materials for manufactures. When in 1890, our number reaches 53,000,000, according to our estimate, there will be but one-third of this number (to wit, 18,000,000) employed in agriculture and rural trades. Of the increase up to that time, (being 42,500,000) 8,000,000 will go into rural occupations, and 34,500,000 into towns. This would people sixty-nine towns, with each half a million. These indications. 10,000,000 now in farms. In 1890, 34,500,000 in towns.

Should we yielding to the opinion of those who may believe that more than one-third of our people will be required for agriculture and rural trades, make the estimate on the supposition that one-half the population of our valley, forty-seven years hereafter, will live on farms and in villages below the rank of towns, the account will stand thus; 26,500,000 (being the one.half of 53,000,000 in the valley) will be the amount of the rural population; so that it must receive 16,500,000 in addition to the 10,000,000, it now has. The towns, in the same time, will have an increase of 26,000,000, in addition to the 500,000 now in them. Where will these towns be, and in what proportion will they possess the 26,500,000 inhabitants? Suppose half in agriculture. Then 26,500,000 in towns. Where?

These are interesting questions, and not so impracticable of an aproximately correct solution, as, at first blush, they may seem. Solution easy

One of them will be either St. Louis or Alton. Everybody will be ready to admit that. Still more beyond the reach of doubt or cavil is Cincinnati. We might name also Pittsburg and Louisville; but we trust that our readers, who have followed us through our former articles, are ready to concur in the opinion that the greatest city of the Mississippi basin will be either Cincinnati or the town near the mouth of the Missouri, be it Alton or St. Louis. One Alton or St. Louis. Chief town of Miss. valley.

Within our period of forty-seven years, we have no doubt it will be Cincinnati. She is now in the midst of a population so great and so thriving; and, on the completion of the Miami canal, which will be within two years, she will so monopolize the exchange commerce at that end of the canal between the river and lake regions, that it is not reasonable to expect she can be overtaken by her western rival for half a century. For 47 years Cin. will lead

But such has been the influx of settlers within the last few years to the lake region, and so decided has become the tendency of the productions of the upper and middle regions of the great valley to seek a market at and through the lakes, that we can no longer withstand the conviction that, even within the short period of forty-seven years, a town will grow up on the lake border greater than Cincinnati. The following facts it is believed, will force the same conviction to our readers: A lake town to beat Cin. Reasons.

The States of Ohio, Indiana and Illinois, are bordered by both Lake and river. All have large river accommodation, but Illinois has it to an unrivaled extent; whereas it has but one lake port. River avs. Ills. superior

Now let us see what has been the relative and positive growth of the river region and lake region of these states, from 1830 to 1840. Southern Ohio, including all south of the national road, and the counties north of that road which touch the Ohio river, had, in 1830, 550,000 inhabitants, and in 1840 730,000; showing an increase of 180,000—equal to 33½ per cent. Northern Ohio, in 1830, numbered but 390,000, which in 1840 had increased to 805,000; exhibiting an increase of 413,000, or 105 per cent. In 1830, Southern Ohio had 160,000 more than Northern Ohio; whereas, in 1840 the latter excelled the former 75,000. This preponderance of the lake region has not been owing to the superiority of its soil, or the beauty of its surface; for, in these respects, it is inferior to its southern rival. Relative growth of river and lake regions. Ohio in 1830 and 1840.

Let us now see how the river and lake regions of Indiana compare in 1830 and 1840. The national road is the dividing line.

Ind. in 1830 and 1840.

Southern Indiana had, in 1830,	252,000	
Northern Indiana " "	89,000	
Southern Indiana had, in 1840,	397,000	
Northern Indiana " "	278,000	
Southern Indiana in 1830,	252,000	Gain 145,000, or 58 per cent.
" " 1840,	397,000	
Northern Indiana had in 1830,	89,000	Showing a gain of 189,000, or 212 per cent.
" " " 1840,	278,000	

Such has been the rapidity of settlement of the northern counties of Indiana, for the three years since the census was taken, that we cannot doubt that the north has nearly overtaken, in positive numbers, the south half.

Ills. more striking.

Illinois exhibits the preference given to the lake region, in a still more striking manner. A line drawn along the north boundaries of Edgar and Cole counties, and thence direct to the town of Quincy, on the Mississippi, will divide the State into two nearly equal parts. The three counties, Morgan, Sangamon and Macon, we divide equally, and give two-thirds of Adams to the North, and one-third to the South.

Changes 1830 to 1840.

Southern Illinois had in 1830,	122,732	
Northern Illinois " " "	33,852	
Southern Illinois had in 1840,	242,873	
Northern Illinois " " "	232,222	
Southern Illinois in 1830	122,732	Showing a gain 120,141, equal to 97 per cent.
" " 1840	242,873	
Northern Illinois had in 1830,	33,852	Showing a gain of 198,370, equal to 586 per cent.
" " " " 1840,	232,222	

N. half largest.

There can be no doubt, with those who know the course of immigration, that Northern Illinois, at this time, contains many thousands more than Southern Illinois.

Increase not only in per cent. but amount.

It may be said that the lake region of these States, being of more recent settlement, and having more vacant land, has chiefly on that account, increased more than the river region. This might account for a higher ratio, but it would not account for a greater amount of increase. For instance; the State of New York between 1820 and 1830, had a greater amount of increase than any western state, though most of them increased in a far higher ratio. So by the census of 1840, it appears that the amount of increase of Ohio, for the ten years previous, was about three times as great as that of Michigan, although the ratio of increase of Michigan was more than nine times as high as that of Ohio.

These compared.

Let us compare, then, the amount of increase of the lake and river regions of these states:

N. half 1830 to 1840.

Increase from 1830 to 1840 of	Northern Ohio	413,000
	" Indiana	189,000
	" Illinois	198,370
		800,370

S. half 1830 to 1840.

Increase from 1830 to 1840 of	Southern Ohio	180,000
	" Indiana	145,000
	" Illinois	120,141
		445,141

Ark. and Mich.

Arkansas and Michigan, were it not that the latter has the advantage of not holding slaves, would afford almost a perfect illustration of the preference given to the lake region over the river country. Each has extraordinary advantages of navigation, of its peculiar kind. No State in the valley has as extensive river navigation as Arkansas, and no State can claim to rival Michigan in extent of navigable lake coast.

Relative growth 1830 to 1840.

In 1830, Michigan had a population of	32,538
" " Arkansas " "	30,388
In 1840, Michigan numbered	212,276
" " Arkansas "	97,578

These facts exhibit the difference in favor of the lake country sufficient to satisfy the candid inquirer that there must be potent causes in operation to produce such results. Some of these causes are apparent, and others have been little understood or appreciated. The staple exports, wheat and flour, have for years so notoriously found their best markets at the lake towns, that every cultivator, who reasons at all, has come to know the advantage of having his farm as near as possible to lake navigation. This has, for some years past, brought immigrants to the lake country from the river region of these States, and from the States of Pennsylvania, Maryland, and Virginia, which formerly sent their immigrants mostly to the river borders. The river region, too, not being able to compete with its northern neighbor in the production of wheat, and being well adapted to the growth of stock, has of late gone more into this department of husbandry. This business, in some portions, almost brings the inhabitants to a purely pastoral state of society, in which large bodies of land are of necessity used by a small number of inhabitants.

Potent causes— —little understood. Grain seeks the lakes. This draws immigrants. South stock-raising.

These causes are obviously calculated to give a dense population to the lake country, and a comparatively sparse settlement to the river country. There are other causes not so obvious, but not less potent or enduring. Of these, the superior accessibility of the lake country from the great northern hives of emigration, New England and New York, is first deserving attention. By means of the Erie canal to Oswego and Buffalo, and the railway from Boston to Buffalo, with its radiating branches, these states are brought within a few hours' ride of our great central lake; and at an expense of time and money so small, as to offer but slight impediment to the removal of home, and household goods. The lakes, too, are about being traversed by a class of vessels, to be propelled by steam and wind, called Ericson propellers, which will carry emigrants with certainty and safety, and at greatly reduced expense.

N. dense, S. sparse. Lakes accessible. Propellers.

European emigration hither, which first was counted by its annual thousands, then by its tens of thousands, has at length swelled to its hundred thousands, in the ports of New York and Quebec. These are both but appropriate doors to the lake country. It is clear then, that the lake portion will be more populous than the river division of the great valley. This is one reason why the former should build up and sustain larger towns than the latter.

Increase from Europe in lake region. Gives large towns.

A comparison is instituted between Cleveland and New Orleans, and Alton and Chicago, exhibiting the superiority of the lake towns.

Cleveland and N. O. Alton and Chicago.

The facts we have adduced, taken altogether, seem conclusive in favor of the lake towns. As a body they come out of the investigation decidedly triumphant. But how shall we decide on their relative merits? There are several, whose citizens would claim preëminence for each—Oswego, Buffalo, Cleveland, the Maumee town, (be it Maumee City or Toledo) Detroit and Chicago.

Lake towns superior. Which to lead.

The relative advantages of those towns being fairly considered, the range was narrowed to Cleveland, Maumee and Chicago. The water power of Maumee, cheap fuel, facilities of procuring wheat, wool and cotton, lead to the following conclusion:—

Cleveland, Maumee and Chicago. M. to lead.

As a point for manufacturers and mechanics, the aids and facilities above mentioned give Maumee an incontestable superiority over Cleveland and Chicago. Let us now compare their commercial advantages: Those of Cleveland have been already set forth to some extent, in comparing her claims with those of Buffalo. In the exchange of agricultural products of a warm and of a cold climate, Cleveland by her canals and her connexion with the Ohio, can claim south, as against the Miami canal, no farther than western Virginia and eastern Kentucky. Maumee will supply the towns on the Lakes Erie, Huron, and probably Ontario, with cotton, sugar, molasses, rum, (may its quantity be small) rice, tobacco, hemp, (perhaps) oranges, lemons, figs, and, at some future day, such naval stores as come from the pitch-pine regions of Tennessee, Mississippi and Louisiana. Chicago will furnish a supply of the same articles to Lake Michigan, Lake Superior, when that lake becomes accessible to her navigation, and perhaps the northern portion of

Advantages of Maumee over Cleveland. Chi. market extensive.

But Maumee region most settled in 47 years.

Lake Huron. How important these commodities are in modern commerce need not to be enlarged on in a magazine whose readers are mostly intelligent merchants. During the forty-seven years under consideration, the countries to be supplied with these articles from Maumee will continue to be more populous than those depending on Chicago for their supply. This position seems too obvious to need proof. It is clear, then, that as a point of exchange of agricultural products of different climates, Maumee has advantages over Chicago—the only place on the lakes that can set up any pretension of rivalry in this branch of trade.

Chi. only rival.

Rival merits of these towns.

What are the relative merits of these towns for the exchange af agricultural products for the manufactures of Europe and the eastern States? The claims of Cleveland, in this respect, have already been considered; and to some extent, also, those of Maumee.

Cleveland area.

The control of Cleveland south and south-east, embraces a country of about 40,000 square miles; being a quarter larger than Ireland. For early spring supplies, and light goods, this domain may be invaded from Philadelphia and Baltimore; but for the shipments east, and the bulk of goods from New York and Europe, it belongs legitimately to Cleveland.

Maumee area.

Maumee will have in this trade the chief control of not less than 100,000 square miles—say 12,000 in Ohio, 30,000 in Kentucky, 30,000 in Indiana, 10,000 in Illinois, 13,000 in Tennessee, 5,000 in Mississippi and Alabama, and 5,000 in Michigan—to say nothing of her claim on small portions of Missouri and Arkansas. This domain is half as large as the kingdom of France, and twice as fertile.

Maumee canals.

The Miami canal, connecting Maumee with Cincinnati, will, with that part of the Wabash and Erie which forms the common trunk after their junction, be two hundred and thirty-five miles long. The Wabash and Erie canal, from Maumee to Terre Haute, will be three hundred miles long. Of this, all but thirty-six miles at its northern extremity, will be in operation the present season. By means of these canals, and the rivers with which they communicate, great part of this extensive region will enjoy the advantage of a cheap water transport for its rapidly increasing surplus.

Chi. may equal M. in area.

Not equal in 47 years.

Chi in future power unknown.

Canal to Rock Island.

Chi. only rival of M.

After 47 y. may do something.

Chicago, on the completion of the Illinois canal, may command, in its exchange of agricultural for manufactured products, an extent of territory as large as that controlled by Maumee. Admitting it to be larger, and of this our readers must judge for themselves, it does not seem to us probable that within forty-seven years it can even aproximate, in population or wealth, to the comparatively old and well-peopled territory that comes within the range of the commercial influence of Maumee. We have not sufficient data on which to calculate the extent of country that will come under the future commercial power of Chicago. That it is to be very great, seems probable, from the fine position of that port in reference to the lake, and an almost interminable country south-west, west, and north-west of it. An extension of the Illinois canal, to the mouth of Rock river, seems destined to give her the control of the eastern trade throughout the whole extent of the upper Mississippi, except what she now has by means of the Illinois river. She will also probably participate with Maumee in the lake trade with the Missouri river and St. Louis. On the whole, we deem Chicago alone, of all the lake towns, entitled to dispute future preëminence with Maumee. The time may come, after the period under consideration, when the extent and high improvement of the country making Chicago its mart for commercial operations, may enable it at least to sustain the second place among the great towns of the North American valley, if not to dispute preëminence with the first.

Superior advantages of M.

When we properly consider the future populousness of our great valley; the tendency of modern improvements to build up large towns; the great and increasing inclination of population and trade to and through the lakes, and the decided advantages which Maumee possesses over any other lake port, we need not fear being over sanguine in anticipating for the leading town on that port a growth unrivaled by any city whose history has been recorded.

Conclusions not popular.

Facts incontrovertible.

The conclusions to which we have come, in this and the preceding articles on internal trade, are not expected to be universally or generally acceptable. Many of them run counter to the hopes and preconceived opinions of too many persons for us to expect that they will be considered with candor, or judged with impartiality. The facts therein contained will be encountered with less alacrity. On these we rely. For these we ask a dispassionate and fair examination.. If other and different conclusions are deducible from them than those we have drawn, it would give us pleasure to acknowledge our error, and correct it. But if, after a thorough examination of the subject, we have gone beyond the anticipations of men, who, with more ability, have bestowed much less thought on it, let them not condemn merely because our conclusions seem to them extravagant; but let them examine for themselves, or, if they will not do that, let them hesitate before they pass a hasty judgment on what we have investigated with the utmost care, and with an earnest desire to arrive at the truth.

Let critics be moderate.

Not give hasty judgment.

The concluding paragraph presents both the noble spirit in which this profound examination was conducted, and the gist of the argument. Based upon *facts*, facts as they then existed, exhibiting fairly and conclusively the superiority of the lake to the river basin; have not the twenty-five succeeding years abundantly confirmed the deductions from preëxisting facts and changes? Yet these very opinions and statements, although a quarter century old, were scarcely more discredited in their origin than they are to-day by the mass of our countrymen, and even a large proportion of our own Citizens. Nor is any other argument needed now to demonstrate the moderation and reasonableness of these views, than this with two or three corrections, not of the facts, but of their application. Mr. Scott in comparing the Chicago route with Maumee, made distance the criterion, which largely favored the latter in consequence of the detour of the lakes northward. Then Pittsburgh and Maumee were compared as to expense.* The mistake was in not making time and expense together the elements of calculation.

Noble spirit.

Truths sustained by 25 years' experience.

Still doubted

Argument sustains these views.

Mr. Scott's slight mistake.

The chief error, however, lay in miscalculating the rapidity of changes in favor of Chicago. His careful study and far-sighted vision, discerned changes that would probably intervene in favor of Chicago after 1890. But they have come in less than half the time named, in consequence of multiplying railways as by a magician's wand. Even my own predictions, wild as they were esteemed, were far short of the reality. And as the next step to sound judgment concerning future relative power of the chief interior city compared with that of the sea-board, let us consider the—

Rapidity of changes not calculated.

My own predictions too moderate.

Power of the Railway to Develope and Centralize.

Railways develope and centralize.

Since time began, no such power as the railway to develope the hidden resources of a country, and give them world-wide distribution, has been known to man. Nor was it ever brought to bear upon such another region as the Great Interior. Somewhat of the nature and capacity of this section we have learned. It seems to have been kept back by Providence from occupation, until both railway and telegraph should have been brought into existence to connect all parts of the civilized world with this storehouse of nature's richest treasures. Midway between the ancient Orient and

No other equal power.

No such area to work upon.

Kept back for railway and telegraph.

* At the Harbor and River Convention held here in 1847, I sought out Mr. Scott and told him of my collecting materials to answer his papers in Hunt, pointing out his mistake. He inquired how, and upon explanation at once admitted that Chicago must be the great City; and ten years after he published the paper, p. 394, in our favor. But my engagements then and for several years in individual concerns precluded the preparation of the answer.

Mr. Scott admitted the mistake.

Am. in centre. Occident, the Occident now our Orient, and the Orient our Occident, it is made our glorious duty to develope and employ the wealth which ages have been appointed to gather, that it might be used in these years of wonderful progress to advance the best good of man, the highest glory of our GOD.

We must see results. However careless or ignorant we may be concerning our destiny, we cannot altogether close our eyes to the remarkable occurrences along our pathway, in which we are chief performers, and the result of which is so unmistakable. Providence directs. We can no more fail to recognize the direction of Providence in man's work than in that of nature. As remarked pp. 40, 41, these individual, soulless corporations, each seeking its own special interests, have yet operated so directly for the public good, that we could scarcely desire any important change in any existing line of railway. Roads rightly located. Not 40 years since first railroads. Not yet forty years have elapsed since the first horse-power railroads of Quincy, three miles for stone, and Mauch Chunk nine miles for coal, were built, and under the next topic we shall ascertain present progress. Yet even now no other equal area on the globe has either so many miles of railway, or the lines so admirably located to accommodate the country traversed, as this north eastern quarter of the Great Plain between the Alleghany and Rocky Mountains. Northwest best accomdated. Agricultural product: unexampled— This is that region whose agricultural products already astonish statisticians, though not one of twenty acres has yet been touched by the plough; but which the railways are peopling with such rapidity, that were the settlers to be restricted to agriculture, they would soon glut the markets of the world. —supply the world.

Means of mnfg. But to save from this calamity, nature has here showered in equal profusion, as we have seen, the chief essentials of manufacture; and in conjunction, art supplies by her railways and water communication, abundant facilities to bring together materials, and to interchange among ourselves, and also to transport to various regions of our country, and to the whole world, all such products as we can most advantageously produce. Gathering and distributing facilities. To develop these advantages and employ them in the most active, efficacious way for man's benefit, is made our first duty, and the evidence of our regard for the Creator. Duty to develope. What we do for ourselves and for our race, it is true, must be done under a sense of our obligation to the Infinite Giver, or we fail to come up to our privileges as co-workers with our GOD. Recognise the Giver. But that sense of obligation is all that the Creator requires of us in performance to Himself; and should this be difficult for recipients of such unexampled benefactions? Yet even the measure of our realization of GOD's goodness, is determined by what we do for our fellow-man. Work for our fellow-man. Let the doubter study James, on this point. The soul is only reached through the body, and every effort made to benefit the physical condition of man, is a very direct means to adopt to advance the glory of our GOD. A co-worker with GOD. We need of all things to realize these truths, in order to properly fulfill our duties and faithfully employ the means our GOD has given us to promote His own great work, the advancement of our race.

For this work no such means have been entrusted to man as the railway, and its hand-maid, the telegraph. What could answer more specifically to Daniel's vision and prophecy, that "many shall run to and fro, and knowledge shall be increased?" While we build them to make our dollars, as is our duty, will it detract from their profit to recognize our duty to GOD in their construction? Will it diminish the satisfaction of pecuniary profit to well apprehend the truth, that that is the least of railway benefits?

Railway and telegraph best means.

Dan. xii. 4.

Pecuniary profit least

The effect of railways in the West is a most difficult matter of judgment. Being yet in its first-half century of existence, and most of that period confined to old settled regions, starting from one prominent town to run to another; we can hardly judge therefrom what the effect is to be in a new country. All the criteria worth a straw are supplied alone by the West. Especially as to the development of the country is the West a measure to itself. Of what value is experience in our old States, or in Europe, to estimate progress here?

W. railway progress difficult to estimate.

Its own measure.

Nor do we lack experience of our own. The difficulty is our application of it, and our incredulity in following it out to its legitimate results. In that eminently National work, the U. S. Census, in a very able introduction of clxxii pp. to the agricultural volume considering the various questions affecting this chief interest of our country, and toward the conclusion, "Influence of Railroads upon Agriculture" is presented, which is very naturally confined to the West. After showing that railroads have in no way injured agriculture, the demand even for horses having been augmented, Mr. Edmunds observes :—

Our experience.

U. S. census 1860.

Mr. Edmunds.

We now proceed to show the positive advantages which all departments of agriculture have derived from the construction of railroads. So great are their benefits, that if the entire cost of railroads between the Atlantic and Western States had been levied on the farmers of the central west, their proprietors could have paid it and been immensely the gainers. This proposition will become evident if we look at the modes in which railroads have been beneficial; especially in the grain growing States. These modes are, first, in doing what could not have been effected without them; second, in securing to the producer very nearly the prices of the Atlantic markets, which is greatly in advance of what could have been had on his farm; and third, by thus enabling the producer to dispose of his products at the best prices at all times, and to increase rapidly both the settlement and the annual production of the Interior States. A moment's reference to the statistics of internal commerce will illustrate these effects so that we can see the vast results which railroads have produced on the wealth and production of the country.

Positive benefits of railways—

—special to grain growers.

Means of benefit.

If we examine the routes and tonnage of the trade between the Atlantic cities and the central western States, we shall find some general results which will prove the utter incapacity of all other modes of conveyance to carry on that trade without the aid of railroads.

No other means adequate.

A comparison is instituted between the tonnage of canals and railways in 1862, and Mr. Edmunds remarks :—

Canals and railways.

It is evident, therefore, that railroads not only carry two-thirds of the freights to and from the West at the present time, but that such is the rapid increase of western products, and the surplus carried to Atlantic or foreign markets, that the time is near when all that can be carried by water will be but a small proportion of the whole. The transportation by wagons is no longer possible to carry the

Railroads carry two-thirds.

surplus products of the Interior States to either foreign or domestic markets. In fine, in the absence of railways, the cultivation of grain beyond the immediate wants of the people must cease, or the surplus perish in the fields. Such was exactly the state of things in the West before the general introduction of railroads. The grain-fields of Ohio, Indiana, Illinois and beyond the Mississippi, have been mainly cultivated because railroads made their products marketable and profitable. In one word, railroads have done what could not have been done without them.

To grain indispensable.

Give the West market

Railroads secured to the producer very nearly the prices of the Atlantic markets, which was greatly in advance of any price which could possibly be obtained in western markets. It might be supposed that if the carriage of a bushel of grain from Sandusky to New York was reduced from forty cents a bushel to twenty cents, the gain of twenty cents would inure, in part at least, to the consumer; but experience shows this is not the fact. This gain of twenty cents inures to the producer. In proof of this it will be sufficient to adduce two or three well known facts. The prices of flour and meat at New York (estimating them at the gold standard) have not been reduced in the least, notwithstanding the immense quantities of the products of grain imported into that city. On the other hand the prices at Cincinnati, on the Ohio, have doubled, and in some articles, such as pork, have trebled. The great bulk of the gain caused by the cheapness of transportation has gone to the producer. This depends on a general principle, which must continue to operate for many years. The older a country is, the more civic and the less rural it becomes. That is, the greater will be the demand for food, and the less the production The competition of the consumer for food is greater than that of the producer for price. Hence it is that Europe, an old country, filled with cities, makes a continual demand on this country for food. Hence it is that New England and New York, continually filling up with manufacturers, artisans, and cities, must be supplied with increased quantities of food from the interior West. And hence, while this is the case, prices cannot fall in the great markets. Hence it is that the cheapening of transportation inures to the benefit of the agricultural producer. New England consumes more than a million barrels of western flour. The transportation is cheapened a doller per barrel; and thus, in New England alone, in the single item of flour, a million of dollars net profit is put into the pockets of the western farmer by the competition of railroads; for a large portion of this flour is carried over the Massachusetts Western railroad. It is entirely true that the manufacturer of New England shares, on his side, in the gain of cheap transportation; but we are here considering simply the influence of railroads on agriculture.

Increase farmer's profits.

N. Y. prices not reduced.

At Cin. doubled and over.

Old country to be fed.

Prices cannot fall.

New England flour increased $1,000,000 in profit.

In the western markets the gain to the farmer is palpable in the enhanced prices of every article. At Cincinnati, in 1848 and 1849, (which was the beginning of the greatest railroad enterprise) the average price of hogs was $3 per hundred. In 1860 and 1861 it was double that, and has continued to increase. This was a net gain to the farmers of Ohio alone of from three to four millions of dollars. In the entire west it was a profit of more than twenty millions on this single animal. For if there were now no railroads, this product could not be carried to market except on foot, which would take away half the value. No further illustration of this point need be made. Take the market prices of New York and Boston, on the Atlantic, and of St. Louis and Cincinnati, in the West, at an interval of twenty years, and it will be seen that the cheap prices of the West have gradually approximated to the high prices of the East, and this solely in consequence of cheapening the cost of transportation, which inures to the benefit of the farmer.

Prices high in West.

Ohio $3,000,000 gain in hogs

West. prices grown to East.

By thus giving the farmer the benefit of the best markets and highest prices, railroads have increased the agricultural productions of the interior States beyond anything heretofore known in the world. We have already shown that this increased production, or rather its surplus, could not have been carried to market without the aid of railroads, more than two-thirds of the whole being carried off by that means. Let us now reverse this operation and we find, on the other hand, that railroads have stimulated and increased production. The Northwestern States are those in which the influence of railroads on agriculture is most obvious.

Railroads stimulate agriculture

Especially in N. W.

In the five States of Ohio, Indiana, Illinois, Michigan, and Wisconsin there were comparatively few miles of railroad prior to 1850; but from 1850 to 1860 the construction of roads was most rapid. In 1850 there were only 1,275 miles of railroad in those States, but in 1860 there were 9,616 miles. Let us now examine the profits of those States in 1850 and 1860, and see how the progress of railroads has sustained and stimulated agricultural production. The following table shows the

West. built since 1850.

Effect of railways.

increase of the principal vegetable and animal production in the five States of Ohio, Indiana, Illinois, Michigan, and Wisconsin in the ten years from 1850 to 1860:

	In 1850. bushels.	In 1860. bushels.	Increase per cent.
Wheat	39,848,495	79,798,163	100
Corn	177,320,441	280,268,862	58
Oats	32,660,251	51,043,334	50
Potatoes	13,417,896	27,181,692	100
Cattle	3,438,000	5,371,000	59

Produce five N.W. States, 1850-60. Increase per cent.

This increase is decidedly beyond that of the population; showing that the products of agriculture are, in those States, profitable. The aggregate in those States of wheat, rye, corn, oats, barley and buckwheat, in 1850 was 255,240,444 bu., in 1860 was 422,369,719 bushels.

Greater than population.

Then the concentrated form into which corn is put, in pork, beef and whisky, is considered; and prices at Cincinnati in 1826, '35, '53, '60, show that flour doubled, corn increased four-fold, hogs three-fold, and lard double. The benefit of obtaining distant manufactures is presented, and Mr. Edmunds remarks:—

Corn concentrated.

Again, the influence of railroads on the value of farming lands is too great and striking not to have been noticed by all intelligent persons. We have, however, some remarkable instances of the specific effect of certain railroads; we have, for example, the immediate effect produced on the lands of Illinois by the Illinois Central railroad. That company received from the government a large body of land at a time when the government could not sell it at $1.25 per acre. Since then the company has constructed its road and sold a large part of those lands at an average of $11 per acre, and the greater part of the lands of Illinois is fully worth that. Notwithstanding the rapid growth of population, the larger part of this advance is due to railroads. The following table shows the advance (by the census tables) of the cash value of farms in the five States mentioned in the ten years from 1850 to 1860.

Farming lands enhanced.

Ill. Cent R. R.

Lands worth $11.

Due to railroads.

	1850	1860
Ohio	$358,758,602	$666,564,171
Illinois	96,133,290	432,531,072
Indiana	136,385,173	344,902,776
Michigan	51,872,446	163,279,087
Wisconsin	28,528,563	131,117,082
Aggregate	$671,678,075	$1,738,394,188
Increase in ten (10) years		$1,066,716,113

Advance of farms in value, 1850, 1860.

$1,066,716,113.

It is not too much to say that one half this increase has been caused by railroads, for, we experience already the impossibility of conveying off the surplus products of the interior with our railroads. Putting the increase of value due to railroads at a little more than one-third, we have four hundred millions of dollars added to the cash value of farms in these five States by the construction of railroads. This fact will be manifest if it is considered that the best lands of Illinois were worth but a dollar and a quarter per acre prior to the construction of railroads, and are now worth twenty dollars. We need not pursue this subject further. If the effect on the central western States has been so great, it is still greater in the new States which lie beyond the Mississippi. They are still further from market, and will be enriched in a greater ratio by the facilities of transportation. Indeed railroads are the only means by which the distant parts of this country could have been commercially united, and thus the railroad has become a mighty means of WEALTH, UNITY, and STABILITY.

Half effect of railways.

Land $1.25 now $20.

West of Miss. still more profitable.

Benefit of railways to agriculture. Mr. Edmunds' views are unquestionable; and though he does not say it, yet the result is inevitable, that agriculture, more than any other department of labor, is benefited by railways. This must indefinitely be the predominating interest of the West. This chief in West. Besides a virgin soil of unsurpassed fertility and ease of tillage, no department of industry is deriving more benefit from inventions of machinery to save labor and time, and in none is the face of the country and the nature of the soil better adapted to their use. With even present means of transportation we can feed western Europe cheaper than can any other country. Feed Europe. Mouths come to food. But, as Mr. Scott argued, p. 302, the mouths are to go to the food, and more and more who depend upon the West will come from the old States and from Europe, and for their food and clothing, do their part to develope the Great Interior. Arguing as we do, and must, from the past to the future, the report of Hon. S. B. Ruggles, Delegate from the United States to the International Statistical Congress at Berlin, in 1863, supplies valuable information. *Hon. S. B. Ruggles'* report to Berlin Congress. Progress of U. S. After examining area and progress of population of the United States, "advance in the material wealth" is considered, which, excluding slaves, was $8,048,825,840; the official valuation having been in 1850, $6,174,780,000; and in 1860, $14,222,618,068; and Mr. R. continues:—

10 years' increase of property. The advance, even if reduced to $8,048,825,840, is sufficiently large to require the most attentive examination. It is an increase of property over the valuation of 1850 of 130 per cent., while the increase of population in the same decade was but 35.99 per cent. In seeking for the cause of this discrepancy, we shall reach a fundamental and all-important fact, which will furnish the key to the past and to the future progress of the United States. Cause railways and canals. It is the power they possess, by means of canals and railways, to practically abolish the distance between the seaboard and the wide spread and fertile regions of the interior, thereby removing the clog on their agricultural industry, and virtually placing them side by side with the communities on the Atlantic. 11,212 miles in West 1850, to 1860. During the decade ending in 1860, the sum of $413,541,510 was expended within the limits of the interior central group, known as the "food exporting States," in constructing 11,212 miles of railway to connect them with the seaboard. The traffic receipts from these roads were in 1860, $31,335,031; in 1861, $35,305,509; in 1862, $44,908,405.

Saved 5 times $44,908,405 in transportation. The saving to the communities themselves in the transportation, for which they paid $44,908,405, was at least five times that amount; while the increase in the exports from that portion of the Union greatly animated not only the commerce of the Atlantic States, carrying those exports over their railways to the seaboard, but the manufacturing industry of the Eastern States, that exchange the fabrics of their workshops for the food of the interior.

Increase of each section. By carefully analyzing the $8,048,825,840 in question, we find that the six manufacturing States of New England received $735,754,244 of the amount; that the Middle Atlantic, or carrying and commercial States, from New York to Maryland inclusive, recived $1,834,911,579, and that the food-producing interior itself, embracing the eight great States of Ohio, Indiana, Illinois, Michigan, Wisconsin, Minnesota, Iowa and Missouri, received $2,810,000,000. West, $2,810,000,000. This very large accession of wealth to this single group of States is sufficiently important to be stated more in detail. States described. The group, taken as a whole, extends from the western boundaries of New York and Pennsylvania to the Missouri river, through fourteen degrees of longitude, and from the Ohio river north to the British dominions, through twelve degrees of latitude. 441,167 sq. miles. It embraces an area of 441,167 square miles, or 282,134,688 acres, nearly all of which is arable and exceedingly fertile, much of it in prairie and ready at once for the plough. There may be a small portion adjacent to Lake Superior unfit for cultivation, but it is abundantly compensated by its rich deposits of copper and of iron of the best quality.

Into this immense natural garden, in a salubrious and desirable portion of the temperate zone, the swelling stream of population from the older Atlantic States, and from Europe, has steadily flowed during the last decade, increasing its previous population from 5,403,595 to 8,957,690, an accession of 3,554,095 inhabitants gained by the peaceful conquest of nature, fully equal to the population of Silesia, which cost Frederick the Great the seven years' war, and exceeding that of Scotland, the subject of struggle for centuries. Increase of population. 10 years 3,554,095.

The rapid influx of population into this group of States increased the quantity of the "improved" land, thereby meaning farms more or less cultivated, within their limits, from 26,680,361 acres in 1850, to 51,826,395 acres in 1860, but leaving a residue yet to be improved, of 230,308,293 acres. The area of 25,146,054 acres thus taken in ten years from the prairie and the forest is equal to seven-eighths of the arable area of England, stated by its political economists to be 28,000,000 of acres. Increase of farms. 25,146,054 acres in 10 years.

The area embraced in the residue will permit a similar operation to be repeated eight times successively, plainly demonstrating the capacity of this group of States to expand their present population of 8,957,690 to at least thirty, if not forty millions of inhabitants, without inconvenience. Capacity 8-fold that.

The effects of this influx of population in increasing the pecuniary wealth as well as the agricultural products of the States in question, are signally manifest in the census. The assessed value of their real and personal property ascended from $1,116,000,000 in 1850 to $3,926,000,000 in 1860, showing a clear increase of $2,810,000,000. We can best measure this rapid and enormous accession of wealth by comparing it with an object which all nations value, the commercial marine. The commercial tonnage of the United States was in 1840 2,180,764 tons, in 1850 3,535,454 tons, in 1860 5,358,808 tons. Wealth increased—$2,810,000,000.

At $50 per ton, which is a full estimate, the whole pecuniary value of the 5,358,808 tons, embracing all our commercial fleets on the oceans and the lakes and the rivers, and numbering nearly thirty thousand vessels, would be but $267,940,000; whereas, the increase in the pecuniary value of the States under consideration, in each year of the last decade, was $281,000,000. Five years increase would purchase every commercial vessel in the Christian world. Annual increase above whole commercial marine.

But the census discloses another very important feature in respect to these Interior States, of far higher interest to the statisticians, and especially to the statesmen of Europe, than any which has yet been noticed, in their vast and rapidly increasing capacity to supply food, both vegetable and animal, cheaply and abundantly, to the increasing millions of the Old World. In the last decade their cereal products increased from 309,950,595 bushels to 558,160,323 bushels, considerably exceeding the whole cereal products of England, and nearly, if not quite, equal to that of France. In the same period, the swine, who play a very important part in consuming the large surplus of Indian corn, increased in number from 8,536,182 to 11,039,352, and the cattle from 4,373,712 to 7,204,810. Thanks to steam and the railway, the herds of cattle which feed on the meadows of the upper Mississippi, are now carried in four days, through eighteen degrees of longitude to the slaughter houses of the Atlantic. Capacity to supply food. Increase of cereals. Swine. Cattle.

It is difficult to furnish any visible or adequate measure for a mass of cereals so enormous as 558,000,000 bushels. About one-fifth of the whole descends the chain of lakes, on which 1,300 vessels are constantly employed in the season of navigation. About one-seventh of the whole finds its way to the ocean through the Erie canal, which has already been once enlarged, for the purpose of passing vessels of two hundred tons; and is now under survey by the State of New York for a second enlargement, to pass vessels of five hundred tons. The vessels called "canal boats," now navigating the canal, exceed five thousand in number, and if placed in a line would be more than eighty miles in length. Figures difficult to realize. Erie canal.

Who doubts the efficiency of railways as the chief instrument of these marvelous results? Who imagines, either, that Mr. Ruggles found a false key to unlock the causes of unexampled increase of production over that of population in the past which will fail to unlock the future? The water facilities nature has supplied in our grand chain of lakes, are not to be ignored; nor the close conjunction of lake and river vallies, which art has Railways the power. Water facilities valuable improved and is carrying on unto perfection. Yet undoubtedly as Mr. Edmunds showed us, p. 315, the railways are moving and are to move more and more our agricultural products to the East. How small is the proportion of our food products which we export; yet were that little retained, usually our prices would be sunk to at least a very moderate remuneration. So in transportation. Only the most bulky, and that in which a few days' delay is of no importance, goes by water; yet this relieves the pressure on the railways, and prevents prices of freight from reaching the exorbitant figures which might be expected, were we subjected entirely to soulless railroad corporations. Then as to gathering here the products of the farm, what other means are at all comparable with the railway?

Relieve pressure on railways.

Gathering facilities.

Nor is the railway valuable only as a means to develope a country. Nothing equals it for centralizing. Man is naturally gregarious, attaining highest culture in the largest centres of civilization. As our destiny is onward and upward to a glory of which we can form no conception, and we undoubtedly are working it out under Divine conduct, while at the same time we pursue our own individual plans; we show our highest wisdom in the large use we make of this chief centralizing power. What we need is to consider somewhat the ultimate results of our labors and plans, and not restrict ourselves to the narrow superficial views which pertain to us merely as individuals. We want to realize more what we are as CITIZENS—Citizens of this City, of this State, of the Great Interior, of the Nation.

Centralizing power of railways.

Its use wise.

We operate as Citizens.

A city, indeed, is styled an ulcer on the body politic of the State, and with entire correctness. The strongest hope of our country under GOD is the fact that the Great Interior is to be the controlling power; and because the power here lies in the rural population. But does the ulcer make itself? What is it but the natural gathering of noxious matter from the body politic itself, the effect of unhealthy action in its various parts and members? Until inherent corruption is remedied, cities may be the best vent for the body politic; as in the human system ulcers frequently save limb or life.

City an ulcer

Does not make itself.

A vent for corruption.

Nor are cities wholly evil. Far from it. From time immemorial they have been the centres of civilization. If they accumulate the evil of the State, they are equally prominent in their influence for good. Man works out his destiny by his associated powers; and the worth of a great city which is ruled by true principles, and actuated by high and holy purposes, it is impossible to over-estimate. Is it not our highest ambition to render Chicago such a city?

Centres of civilization.

Associated effort needed

Worth of a true city.

The tendency of population to towns in consequence of modern improvements, has for over a quarter of a century been widely observed. Prof. George Tucker in his philosophical examination of the Progress of Population and Wealth in the United States in Fifty Years, analysing the censuses from 1840 back to 1790, remarks upon—

Modern tendency to towns.

Prof. Tucker.

Cities and Towns.—The proportion between the rural and town population of a country is an important fact, in its interior economy and condition. It determines,

Cities and towns.

in a great degree, its capacity for manufactures, the extent of its commerce, and the amount of its wealth. The growth of cities commonly marks the progress of intelligence and the arts, measures the sum of social enjoyment, and always implies increased mental activity, which is sometimes healthy and useful, sometimes distempered and pernicious. If these congregations of men diminish some of the comforts of life, they augment others: if they are less favorable to health than the country, they also provide better defences against disease, and better means of cure. From causes both physical and moral, they are less favorable to the multiplication of the species. In the eyes of the moralist, cities afford a wider field, both for virtue and vice; and they are more prone to innovation, whether for good or evil. The love of civil liberty is, perhaps, both stronger and more constant in the country than the town; and if it is guarded in the cities by a keener vigilance and a more far-sighted jealousy, yet law, order and security are also, in them, more exposed to danger, from the greater facility with which intrigue and ambition can there operate on ignorance and want. Whatever may be the good or evil tendencies of populous cities, they are the result to which all countries, that are at once fertile, free, and intelligent, inevitably tend.

Growth of cities marks progress.

Evils have countervailing benefits.

Civilization promotes their growth

A table is given of 31 towns, all in the country which in 1840 contained 10,000 and upwards, giving respective population in 1820, '30, and '40 and the decennial increase, and Prof. T. observes :—

31 towns of 10,000 inhabitants.

It appears from the preceding table, that the population in all the towns of the United States, containing 10,000 inhabitants and upwards, is something more than one-thirteenth (10-128) of the whole number; that ten of the States, whose united population exceeds 4,000,000, have as yet no town of that rank; and that in the other sixteen States the ratio of their town population to their whole population, varied from something less than one-third to less than one-sixteenth part. It further appears that the increase of those towns has been nearly the same. from 1830 to 1840, as from 1820 to 1830; and that, in both decennial periods, it exceeds that of the whole population nearly as 50 to 32.

1-13th of entire population.

Other points observed.

Tables follow of all the towns in the United States containing less than 10,000 and over 2,000, concluding with a general table, valuable chiefly as exhibiting the small proportion of the towns in the Northwest to population. The following is a summary of the sections, with the Northwest in detail :—

Towns of 2,000 and upwards.

Few in N.W.

Proportion of Town Population in U. S., 1840.

Proportion of towns in 1840.

Sections and States.	Population of Towns.		Total.	Ratio to whole Population.
	Of 10,000 inhab'nts and upwards.	Between 10,000 and 2,000 inhabitants.		
New England	215,166	574,767	789,998	35.3
Middle States	833,205	231,889	1,065,094	20.8
Southern States	82,684	65,680	148,364	4.4
Southwestern States	114,865	27,988	142,853	6.6
Missouri	16,469	....	16,469	4.8
Kentucky	21,210	13,764	34,974	4.5
Ohio	46,338	43,906	90,244	5.9
Indiana	....	12,786	12,786	1.8
Illinois	....	11,708	11,708	2.4
Michigan	....	9,102	9,102	4.3
Northwestern States	84,017	91,266	175,283	4.2
Total	1,829,937	991,590	2,821,527	18.6

Towns of 10,000.

Towns of 2,000.

Ratio to whole population.

Towns in New England and New York.

The fact is noticed that in New England and New York the proportion in small towns is augmented by the township being called a town, and Prof. Tucker concludes:—

⅛ of population in towns.

If the proportion in the whole United States could be correctly ascertained, by the correction of the errors adverted to, it would probably be found that those who live in towns aud villages containing at least 2,000 inhabitants, are not much more nor much less than one-eighth of the entire number.

Railways stimulate their growth

The effect of railroads, and of transportation by steam generally, is to stimulate the growth of towns, and especially of large towns. It is, therefore, likely that our principal cities will, at the next census, show as large a proportional increase as they have experienced in the last decennial period.

Examination of other censuses wanted.

It is to be regretted that a like examination of the last two censuses has not been made with that of Prof. Tucker's. But speculation upon what may be is too foreign to indulge even upon such a point. The anticipated effect of railways has been realized, and nowhere more than in the West.

Growth of towns. *Mr. Scott.*

Mr. Scott, answering the query on p. 307, "What has been the effect of the improvement on the growth of towns?" thus continues that paragraph:—

First canal 1760. Date of other inventions. Facilities of intercommunication. *Mr. Slaney,* M. P. Increase of mnfrs. and mechanics in England. Growth in towns. In 1831 ⅓ in agriculture. In 1841 ¼. Changes in Scotland— —in Eng.

* * * The first canal was commenced in that country by the Duke of Bridgewater, no longer ago than 1760. The invention of the spinning jenny, by Hargreaves, followed seven years after. Not long after this, the spinning frame was contrived by the ingenuity of Arkwright. In 1775, Mr. Compton produced the machine called the mule, a combination of the two preceding. Some time after Mr. Cartwright invented the power-loom, but it was not until after 1820 that it was brought into general use. The steam engine, the moving power of all this machinery, was so improved by Watt, in 1785, as to entitle him to claim, for all important practical purposes, being its inventor. At the same that these great inventions were being brought into use, the nation was making rapid progress in the construction of canals and roads, and the duplication of her agricultural products. Indeed, great part of her works to cheapen and facilitate internal trade, including her canals, her McAdam roads, and her railways, have been constructed within the last thirty years. The effect of these, in building up towns, is exemplified by the following facts: Mr. Slaney, M, P., stated in the House of Commons, in May, 1830, that "in England those engaged in manufacturing and mechanical occupations, as compared with the agricultural class, were 6 to 5, in 1801; they were as 8 to 5, in 1821; and 2 to 1 in 1830. In Scotland the increase had been still more extraordinary. In that country they were as 5 to 6, in 1801; as 9 to 6, in 1821; and in 1830, as 2 to 1. The increase of the general population for the preceding twenty years, had been thirty per cent.; in the manufacturing population it had been forty per cent.; in Manchester, Liverpool, Coventry, and Birmingham, the increase had been fifty per cent.; in Leeds it had been fifty-four per cent., and in Glasgow it had been one hundred per cent." The increase of population in England and Wales, from 1821 to 1831, was 16 per cent. This increase was nearly all absorbed in towns and their suburbs, as the proportion of people engaged in agriculture has decreased decidedly with every census. More scientific modes of culture, and more perfect machines and implements, combined with other causes, have rendered an increased amount of human labor unnecessary in the production of a greatly augmented amount of food. In 1831, but one-third of the people of England were employed in the labors of agriculture. In 1841, very little more than one-fourth were so employed. In Scotland, seven of the best agricultural counties decreased in population from 1831 to 1841, from one to five per cent.; whereas, the counties in which were her principal towns, increased during the same period from 15 per cent. to 34.8 per cent., the latter being the increase of the county of Lanark, in which Glasgow is situated. The average increase of all Scotland for those ten years was 11.1 per cent. According to Marshall, the increase of population in England for the ten years preceding 1831, was 30 per cent in the mining districts; 15½ in the manufacturing, and 19 in the metropolitan, (Middlesex county;) while, in the inland towns and villages it was only 7¾ per cent.

Railways increase towns.

The railways which now traverse England in every quarter, and bring into near neighborhood its most distant points, have been nearly all constructed since 1830. Their effect, in aid of the other works, in augmenting the present great centers of population, will, obviously, be very considerable; how great, remains to be developed by the future. London, with its suburbs, has now about 2,000,000 of inhabitants; but she is probably far below the culminating point of her greatness. The kingdom of which she is the commercial heart, doubles its population in forty-two years. It is reasonable, then, to suppose that, within the next fifty-years, London and the other great *foci* of human beings, in that kingdom, will have more than twice their present numbers; for it is proved that nearly the whole increase in England is monopolized by the large commercial and manufacturing towns with their suburbs.

London to grow.

Growth in Eng. chiefly in towns.

So in U. S.

Will similar causes produce like effects in the United States? In the States of Massachusetts, New York, Pennsylvania, and Ohio, the improvements of the age operated to some extent on their leading towns from 1830 to 1840. Massachusetts had little benefit from canals, railways, or steam power; but her towns felt the beneficent influence of her labor-saving machinery moved by water power, and her improved agriculture and common roads. The increase of her nine principal towns, commencing with Boston and ending with Cambridge, from 1830 to 1840, was 66,373, equal to 53 per cent; being more than half the entire increase of the State, which was but 128,000, or less than 21 per cent. The increase, leaving out those towns, was but 11 per cent. Of this 11 per cent., great part, if not all, must have been in the towns not included in our list. * * * * * *

Mass.

9 towns more than half State increase.

Growth in N. Y.—

The growth of two towns in the State of *New York*, during the same period, is mainly due to her canals. That of the fourteen largest, from New York to Seneca, inclusive, was 204,507, or 64½ per cent.; whereas, the increase in the whole State was less than 27 per cent. and of the State, exclusive of these towns, but 19 per cent. Of this, it is certain, that nearly all is due to the other towns not in the list of the fourteen largest.

—in Pa.—

Pennsylvania has canals, railways, and other improvements, that should give a rapid growth to her towns. These works, however, had not time, after their completion, to produce their proper effects, before the crash of her monetary system nearly paralyzed every branch of her industry, except agriculture and the coal business. Nine of her largest towns, from Philadelphia to Erie, inclusive, exhibit a gain from 1830 to 1840 of 84,642, being at the rate of 39⅓ per cent. This list does not include Pottsville, or any other mining town. The increase of the whole State was but 21¾ per cent.

—in Ohio.

Ohio has great natural facilities for trade, in her lake and river coasts; the former having become available only since the opening of the Erie canal, in 1826, and that to little purpose before 1830. She has also canals, which have been constructing and coming gradually into use since 1830. These now amount to about 760 miles. For the last five years, she has also constructed an extent of McAdam roads exceeding any other State, and amounting to hundreds of miles. Her railways, which are of small extent, have not been in operation long enough to have produced much effect. From this review of the State, it will not be expected to exhibit as great increase in town population, from 1830 to 1840, as will distinguish it hereafter. The effects of her public improvements, however, will be clearly seen in the following exhibit: Eighteen of her largest towns, and the same number of medium size and average increase, contained, in 1830, 58,310, which had augmented, in 1840, to 138,916; showing an increase of 138 per cent. The increase of the whole State during the same period was 62 per cent. The northwest quarter of the State has no towns of any magnitude, and has but begun to be settled. This quarter had but 12,671 inhabitants in 1830 and 92,050 in 1840.

More rapid hereafter.

Increase of 18 towns.

These opinions confirmed.

Confirmatory of these anticipations as to England and our old States, we have the paper following; for although nothing is said specifically about the centralizing power of railways, and the relative growth of town and country is not even alluded to, the argument is the more effective for the present purpose. Though only discussing the general results of railways, yet the chief point—and the one of all to be regarded in old settled countries—is clearly demonstrated, that increase of imports and exports is *pari passu*

A country grows with its railways.

Commerce and mnfrs. centralize. Railway extension and results. *Mr. Baxter.*

with railways. What is this but to exhibit their power in concentration, involving the two chief elements of cities, commerce and manufactures? So that the most satisfactory paper which has come under observation, upon this very important point, is this by R. Dudley Baxter, M.A., which was read before the Statistical Society of London, November, 1866, and was reprinted in the *Merchants' Magazine*,* July, 1867, entitled, "Railway Extension and its Results." The entire paper should be carefully studied. After an introduction, and speaking of the early difficulties, and exhibiting growth to 1865, this topic is presented :—

Distribution of English railways. London the centre. Other cities. Paris. Madrid. Other European cities. United States.

Distribution of Railways in the United Kingdom. * * The manner in which this railway mileage is distributed through England deserves some attention. A railway map will show that the general direction of English lines is towards the metropolis. London is a centre to which nearly all the main lines converge. Every large town is, in its degree, a centre of railway convergence. For example, look at the lines radiating from Leeds, from Hull, from Birmingham, or from Bristol. But all those lesser stars revolve, so to speak, round the metropolis as a central sun. A great deal may be learned of the character and political state of a country from the convergence of its railway lines. Centralizing France concentrates them all on Paris. Spain, another nation of the Latin race, directs her railways on Madrid. Italy shows her past deficiency of unity, and want of capital, by her straggling and centreless railroads. Belgium is evidently a collection of co-equal cities without any preponderating focus. Germany betrays her territorial divisions by the multitude of her railway centres. Austria, on the contrary, shows her unity by the convergence of her lines on Vienna. The United States of America prove their federal independence by the number of their centres of radiation.

Manchester and Liverpool. Converging points. Mnfg. and commercial centres.

The national character of the English nation may be traced in the same way. Though our railways point towards London, they have also another point of convergence—towards Manchester and the great port of Liverpool. The London & Northwestern, the Great Northern (by the Manchester, Sheffield & Lincolnshire line), the Great Western and the Midland run to Manchester and Liverpool from the south. The Manchester, Sheffield & Lincolnshire railway, the London & Northwestern, Yorkshire & Carlisle lines, and the network of the Lancashire & Yorkshire Company converge on them from the east and north. The London & Nortwestern Welsh railways and the Mid Wales and South Wales lines communicate from the west. Thus our railway system shows that Manchester and Liverpool are the manufacturing and commercial capitals of the country, as London is its monetary and political metropolis, and that the French centralization into a single great city does not exist in England.

Checks upon power— —in Great Britain— —in U. S.

Admirers of arbitrary sway may discover benefits in a capital like Paris, which rules the nation; but those who can apprehend the dangers of uncontrolled power, whether political or commercial, cannot but admire the improvement in Great Britain, and the perfection here enjoyed in consequence of the division of these wide-spread benefits to the sovereignty of many States. Then, to counteract this disintegration, which, carried to an extreme, would give no power to cope with other great cities and nations of the earth, we

---

Mr. McChesney. Use of his *Merch. Mag.* Its value.

* It is proper to express acknowledgment to Mr. Robert McChesney, Chairman for several years of the Commercial Committee of the Board of Trade, for the privilege of using his complete set of that invaluable publication, the *Merchants' Magazine.* Mr. Hunt, the founder, gave me a set of some twenty volumes, and exchanged for the *Prairie Farmer* for years. But only a few volumes remain. If business men as well as merchants would cultivate a habit of studying standard works of this kind, they would find the benefit in the expansion of views and calculations, and a realization of the dignity of their calling, besides obtaining a vast amount of knowledge of the most practical kind, and indispensable to an eminent business character.

have our Federal bond of Union, which, instead of "independence," as Mr. Baxter imagines,* binds these States to each other by indissoluble obligations irrepealably extending equal rights to all these States, and to their citizens respectively, in their joint and several domains. State autonomy, not "Federal independence," has its influence, at once healthy and stimulating and powerful, to create many centres. The ease with which requisite charters are obtained for associated efforts, in many States authorized by general laws, affords full scope to enterprise and capital. So that while State interest promotes many operations calculated for individual or local advantage, yet in their commercial relations these citizens having almost the same rights they would have in a consolidated State, the trade of the Nation is left free, as in no other, to seek its natural centre or centres. Yet, besides pride in our States, which has more influence than we are aware of, the diversity of interest from large extent of area, and variety of configuration with lakes and rivers and mountains, has still greater power. Covering a continent, and with abounding advantages in all sections, we must in the beginning have various important trade centres. Still, nothing is more centripetal than trade; and we shall find in due time that we have the best possible system to leave trade free to its natural course among ourselves, creating only such restrictions on foreign commerce as wise national policy shall render expedient, which is the measure of justice in this regard. In evidence of this, we have in our own country, and especially here in the mighty West, abundant demonstrations of the centralizing power of railways.

Federal Union binds together.

Benefit of State divisions.

Charters easy to obtain.

Trade free.

Many centres.

Trade centripetal.

Railways in the West.

After exhibiting the different divisions of British railways, and their cost, Mr. Baxter considers—

Traffic and Benefit of Railways in the United Kingdom.—In order to appreciate the wonderful increase of traffic which has resulted from railways, it is necessary to know the traffic of the kingdom before their introduction. * * *

The effect of railways was very remarkable. It might reasonably be supposed that the new means of communication would have supplanted and destroyed the old. Singular to relate, no diminution has taken place either in the road or canal traffic. As fast as coaches were run off the main roads they were put on the side roads, or reappeared in the shape of omnibuses. At the present moment there is probably a larger mileage of road passenger traffic than in 1834. The railway traffic is new and additional traffic. But railways reduced the fares very materially. For instance, the journey from Doncaster to London by mail used to cost £5 inside and £3 outside (exclusive of food), for 156 miles, performed in twenty hours. The railway fares are now 27*s* 6*d*, first class, and 21*s* second class for the same distance, performed in four hours. The average fares now paid by first, second and third class passengers are $1\frac{1}{3}d$ per mile, against an average of 5*d* in the coaching days, being little more than one-fourth of the former amounts.

On canals the effect of railway competition was also to lower the rates to one-fourth of the former charges. In consequence the canal tonnage actually increased, and is now considerably larger than it was before the competition of railways. Hence the railway goods traffic, like its passenger traffic, is entirely a new traffic.

Benefit of railways in England.

Did not supplant other means.

Created its traffic.

Reduced fares.

Canal traffic increased.

Railway, new traffic.

* "*Federal* independence" is a misnomer, a palpable contradiction. *Federal* itself means covenant, being derived from *fœdus*. But this intelligent Englishman has doubtless given more attention to railways than politics, very much after our own fashion; and most of us having such insufficient conception of National Union based upon State Sovereignty, as to believe these terms themselves a contradiction, it is not singular that foreigners should misapprehend our system and its nature.

Federal not understood—not by ourselves.

Its saving. The saving in cost is also very great; goods are carried by rail at an average of $1\frac{1}{3}d$ per ton, or 40 per cent. of the old canal rates.

Rapid growth. Now observe the growth of this new railway traffic. The Parliamentary returns (except for 1865) show the receipts from passenger and goods traffic on railways in the following years: 1843, total receipts, £4,535,000; 1848, £9,933,000; average annual increase, £1,079,000. 1855, receipts, £21,507,000; annual increase, £1,653,000. 1860, receipts, £27,766,000; annual increase, £1,252,000. 1865, receipts, £35,890,000; annual increase, £1,619,000. Thus the average annual increase for the whole 22 years was £1,423,000; and the increase was largest in the latest years. * * *

Saving to country. Now let us examine the saving to the country. Had the railway traffic of 1865 been conveyed by canal and road at the pre-railway rates, it would have cost three times as much. Instead of £36,000,000 it would have cost £108,000,000. Hence there is a saving of £72,000,000 a year, or more than the whole taxation of the United Kingdom.

Still greater benefit— But the real benefit is far beyond even this vast saving. If the traffic had been already in existence, it would have been cheapened to this extent. But it was not previously in existence; it was a new traffic, created by railways, and impossible —created its own traffic. without railways. To create such a traffic, or to furnish the machinery by which alone it could exist, is a far higher merit than to cheapen an existing traffic, and has had far greater influence on the prosperity of the nation.

Following a statement of increase of exports and imports from 1853 to 1865, which is omitted, it is observed:—

Causes of increase. I am far from attributing the whole of this increase to railways. Free trade, steamboats, the improvements in machinery, and other causes contributed powerfully to accelerate its progress. But I wish to call attention to two facts.

Railways indispensable. 1. This increase could not have taken place without railways. It would have been physically impossible to convey the quantity of goods, still less to do so with the necessary rapidity. * *

Business increases with railways. 2. The increase of imports and exports was in strict proportion to the development of railways. The following table shows the miles of railway and navigation opened, and the total exports and imports. It must be remembered that there are about 4,000 miles of navigation and that the exports and imports had been for some time stationary before 1833—

Proportion of exports and imports to railway and navigation.

Proportion of Exports and Imports to Railways and Navigation.

Year.	Miles of railway and navigation.	Total exports and imports.	Exports and Imports, per mile.
1833	4,000	£ 85,500,000	£ 21,375
1840	5,200	119,000,000	22,884
1845	6,441	135,000,000	20,959
1850	10,733	171,800,000	16,206
1855	12,334	260,234,000	21,098
1860	14,433	375,052,000	25,985
1865	17,289	490,000,000	28,341

Even pace of trade with rise of railways. Here the increase in exports and imports keeps pace with railway development from 1833 to 1845, falls below it during the enormous multiplication of railways and the railway distress from 1845 to 1850, rises again to the former level in 1855, and outstrips it after that year, aided by the lowering of fares and the greater facilities for through booking and interchange of traffic. I cannot think that this correspondence within the two increases is accidental, especially as I shall show that it exists also in France.

This explained. But, it may be said, how do exports and imports depend on the development of the railway system? I answer because they depend on the goods traffic, and the goods traffic increases visibly with the increase of railway mileage and the per-

What is goods traffic. fecting of railway facilities. Goods traffic means raw material and food brought from ports, or mines, or farms, to the producing population, and manufactured articles carried back from the producers to the inland or foreign consumers. The exports and imports bear a variable but appreciable proportion to the inland traffic. Every mineral railway clearly increases them; every agricultural railway increases them less clearly but not less centainly. Hence I claim it as an axiom, that the commerce of a country increases in distinct proportion to the improvement of its railway system, and that railway development is one of the most powerful and evident causes of the increase of commerce. Commerce increases.

Now let us turn to the benefits which railways have conferred on the working classes. * * Increased facilities of transit led to increased trade; increased trade gave greater employment and improved wages; the diminution in the cost of transit and the repeal of fiscal duties cheapened provisions; and the immense flood of commerce which set in since 1850 has raised the incomes and the prosperity of the working classes to an unprecedented height. Railways were the first cause of this great change, and are entitled to share largely with free trade the glory of its subsequent increase and of the national benefit. But one portion of the result is entirely their own. Free trade benefited the manufacturing population, but had little to do with the agriculturists. Yet the distress in the rural districts was as great or greater than in the towns, and this under a system of the most rigid protection. How did the country population attain their present prosperity? Simply by the emigration to the towns or colonies of the redundant laborers. This emigration was scarcely possible till the construction of railways. Up to that time the farm laborer was unable to migrate; from that time he became a migratory animal. The increase of population in agricultural counties stopped, or was changed into a decrease, and the laborers ceased to be too numerous for the work. To this cause is principally owing the sufficiency of employment and wages throughout the agricultural portion of the kingdom. If I may venture on a comparison, England was, in 1830, like a wide-spreading plain flooded with stagnant waters, which were the cause of malaria and distress. Railways were a grand system of drainage, carrying away to the running streams, or to the ocean, the redundant moisture, and restoring the country to fertility and prosperity. Benefits to laborers. Especially farmers. Surplus labor relieved. Wages equalized. Railways like drainage.

Cost and Results of French Railways. * * * The Revolution of 1848 accounts for the small increase between 1845 and 1850, but it is plain that the great increase in French commerce was between 1850 and 1860, contemporaneously with the great development of railways. When travelling in France I have always heard railways assigned as the cause of their present commercial prosperity. French railways. Cause of prosperity.

The proportion which the exports and imports bore to the means of communication is shown in the following table:—

Proportion of Exports and Imports to Railways and Navigation. Proportion of trade to transportation in France—

Year.	Navigation (7700 miles and railways.	Exports and Imports.	Exports and Imports, per mile open.
1840	8,264	£ 82,520,000	£ 9,985
1845	8,547	97,080,000	11,358
1850	9,507	102,204,000	10,750
1855	11,015	173,076,000	15,712
1860	13,286	232,192,000	17,476
1865	15,830	293,144,000	18,518

Here there is a steady rise in the amount per mile, checked only by the revolution of 1848. But the principle that there is a distinct correspondence between the means of communication and the exports and imports is already shown. —clearly shown.

The effect of railways on the condition of the working classes has also been very beneficial. The extreme lowness of fares enables them to travel cheaply, and the opportunity is largely used. The number of third-class passengers in France is 75 per cent. of the total passengers, against only 58 per cent. in England. (M. Flachat, p. 60). The result of these facilities of motion has been an equalization of wages throughout the country, to the great benefit of the rural populations. M. Flachat says: Labor benefited. Equalized. *Dr. Flachat.*

"Railways found in France great inequality in the wages of laborers; but they are constantly remedying it. Wherever they were constructed in a district of low wages, employment was eagerly sought. The working classes rapidly learned to deserve high wages by the greater quantity of work done. Agriculture

Drawn from agriculture. had been unable to draw out the capabilities of its workmen, and was for the moment paralyzed for want of hands; but industry developed fresh resources. The total amount of work done was considerably increased all over the country. The difficulties of agriculture were removed by obtaining in return for higher wages a larger amount of work than before, and also because machines began to be used in cultivation. Everywhere it was evident that increased energy accompanied increased remuneration. This is the point in which the railways have most powerfully increased the wealth of France. The moral result of this improvement in the means of existence of the working class has been to diminish the distance which separates the man who works only for himself from the man who works for a master. In the education of the workman's children, in his clothing, in his domestic life, and even in his amusements, there is now an improvement which raises him nearer to his master."—pp. 78 and 79.

Increased energy. Elevation of labor.

Other benefits to France. I am sure we shall all rejoice at this evidence of the benefits conferred by railways upon the working classes of that great neighboring nation. I wish there was time to give you additional extracts, showing the immense services of railways to the industry of France, showing that France was kept back by the difficulty of communication, by the immense distances to be traversed, and the impossibility of conveying cheaply and rapidly the raw materials of manufactures. Railways have supplied this want, and have given a new impetus to production and new outlets for produce. * * *

France and England compared. Profits between France and England are compared, and the different financial management; also the effect of open competition as in England, or government control as in France.

Belgium and Holland. *Railways in Belgium and Holland.*—Belgium is one of the most striking instances of the benefits of railways. In 1830 she separated from Holland, a country which possessed a much larger commerce and superior means of communication with other nations by sea and by canals. * * *

Proportion of trade to transportation in Belgium.

Proportion of Exports and Imports to Railways and Navigation.

Year.	Canals (910 miles) and Railways open.	Exports and Imports.	Exp'ts and Imp'ts per mile open.
1839	1,055	£15,680,000	£14,862
1845	1,205	26,920,000	22,340
1853	1,590	47,760,000	30,037
1860	1,907	72,120,000	37,818
1864	2,220	97,280,000	42,919

Large increase. This enormous increase of Belgian commerce must be ascribed to her wise system of railway development, and it is not difficult to see how it arises. Before railways, Belgium was shut out from the continent of Europe by the expensive rates of land carriage and her want of water communication. She had no colonies and but little shipping. Railways gave her direct and rapid access to Germany, Austria and France, and made Ostend and Antwerp great continental ports. One of her chief manufactures is that of wool, of which she imports 21,000 tons, valued at £2,250,000, from Saxony, Prussia, etc., of which she returns a large proportion in a manufactured state. She is rapidly becoming the principal workshop of the continent, and every development of railways in Europe must increase her means of access to her trade.

Due to railways. Chief in mnfrs.

Holland surpassed. Her advantages. Now look at Holland, which in 1835 was much her superior. Holland was possessed of immense advantages in the perfection of her canals, which are the finest and most numerous in the world; in the large tonnage of her shipping; in her access by the Rhine to the heart of Germany; and in the command of the German trade, which was brought to her ships at Amsterdam and Rotterdam. The Dutch relied on these advantages and neglected railways. The consequence was that by 1850 they found themselves rapidly losing the German trade, which was being diverted to Ostend and Antwerp. The Dutch Rhenish railway was constructed to remedy this loss, and was partly opened in 1853, but *not fully till 1856. It succeeded in regaining part of the former connection.* But now observe the result. In 1839, the Dutch exports and imports were £28,500,000 or nearly double those of Belgium. In 1862 they were £59,000,000, when those of Belgium were £78,000,000. Thus, while Holland had doubled her commerce, Belgium had increased five-fold, and had completely passed her in the race.

She neglected railways. In 1839 her trade largest. In 1862 Belgium largest.

Holland depended upon her canals, as St. Louis has upon her rivers; while railways have wrought their legitimate result for Chicago, as for Belgium. Mr. Baxter here reaches— Holland like St. Louis.

Railways in the United States.—In any paper on foreign railways it is impossible to omit the United States, a country where they have attained such gigantic proportions. The increase of United States lines is as follows:— Railways in U. S.

Miles Constructed and Annual Increase from the Beginning. Miles from 1828 to 1868.

Year.	Miles.	Increase.	Year.	Miles.	Increase.	Year.	Miles.	Increase.
1828	3		1842	3,877	558	1856	19,251	1,853
1829	28	25	1843	4,174	297	1857	22.625	3,374
1830*	41	13	1844	4,311	137	1858	25,090	2,465
1831	54	13	1845*	4,522	211	1859	26,755	1,665
1832	131	77	1846	4,870	348	1860*	28,771	2,016
1833	576	445	1847	5,336	466	1861	30,593	2,822
1834	762	186	1848	5,682	346	1862	31,769	1,176
1835	918	156	1849	6,350	668	1863	32,471	702
1836	1,102	184	1850*	7,475	1,125	1864*	33,860	1,389
1837	1,421	319	1851	8,589	1,114	1865	34,442	582
1838	1,843	422	1852	11,027	2,438	1866	35,361	919
1839	1,920	77	1853	13,497	2,470	1867	36,896	1,535
1840*	2,197	277	1854	15,672	2,175	1868	38,822	1,926
1841	3,319	1,122	1855*	17,398	1,726			

* These are the years cited by Mr. Baxter, which were correct, and other years are taken from the *Railroad Journal*

The mileage here shown is something enormous; four times that of France, two and a half times that of England, and nearly as large as the total mileage of the United Kingdom and Europe, which is about 42,000 miles. Nearly equals Europe.

In so young a country inland traffic gives these lines the greater part of their employment, and there are no masses of expensive manufactured goods as in England or Belgium to swell the total value of foreign trade. Foreign commerce is still in its infancy, but an infancy of herculean proportions, as the following table shows: Traffic inland. Foreign to come.

Increase of Exports and Imports. Increase of exports and imports.

Year.	Total exports and imports.	Increase per cent.	Inc. per cent. per annum.
1830	£ 31,000,000		
		47.60	3.40
1844	45,759,000		
		50.00	8.33
1850	68,758,000		
		62.60	12.52
1855	111,791,000		
		42.00	8.40
1860	158,610,000		

The advance in the annual increase is very striking, being from 3½ per cent. per annum in the infancy of railways to 8 and 12 per cent. when their extension was proceeding rapidly. Before the introduction of railways America possessed a very extensive system of canals, which amounts to nearly 6,000 miles. At the present time both canals and railways are crowded with traffic. The following table shows the relation between the growth of trade and the increase of means of communication. Rapid increase of railways. 6,000 miles canals.

Proportion of Exports and Imports to Railways and Canals. Proportion of trade to transportation.

Year.	Canals (6,000 miles) and railways open.	Total Exports and Imports.	Exp'ts and Imp'ts per mile.
1830	6,040	£ 31,000,000	£5,130
1844	10,310	45,759,000	4,437
1850	13,475	68,758,000	5,102
1855	23,398	111,797,000	4,778
1860	34,770	158,810,000	4,567

Equal as in France and Belgium.

Thus, in the United States, as well as in England, France and Belgium, the exports and imports bear a distinct relation to the miles of communication open, but lower in amount than in the European countries, as was only likely from the thinner population.

15,000 miles now in progress.

Vast as is the mileage of American railways, it is by no means near its highest point. The lines in construction, but not yet completed, are stated to be more than 15,000 miles in length, a larger number than the whole mileage of the United Kingdom, completed and uncompleted. * * *

Pacific railways.

I must not omit to mention the great Pacific railways, one of which is now being constructed from the State of Missouri for a distance of 2,400 miles across Kansas, Nebraska, Utah, and Nevada, to San Francisco, in California. It receives from the general government subsidies of £3,300, £6,600, or £9,900 per mile, according to the difficulty of the ground, besides enormous grants of land on each side of the line. When this railway is completed, the journey from Hong Kong to England will be made in thirty-three days instead of the present time of six weeks, and it is anticipated that a large portion of our Chinese traffic will pass by this route.

Government aid.

33 days from Hong Kong to Europe.

Great future for railways in U. S.

No one can study the United States without being struck by the great railway future which lies before them, when their immense territories are more thickly peopled, and their mineral resources and manufactures have been developed. The distances to be traversed are so vast, and the traffic to be carried will be so enormous that the railways of the United States will far exceed in extent, and in the trade which will pass over them, anything that has hitherto been known in the history of the world.

Free trade and national debt.

"Railways and Free Trade," and "Railways and National Debt," are discussed, and we reach,—

Railway extension.

Further Railway Extension.—England is undoubtedly the country in the world best provided with railways. The statistical comparison stood thus at the end of 1865:

Railways compared with area and population.

Railways compared with Area and Population.

Miles open. Sq. miles to railway. Population to railway.

Country.	Railway miles open.	Square miles per Railway mile.	Population per Railway mile.
England and Wales	9,251	6¼	2,186
1. Belgium	1,350	8	3,625
2. United Kingdom	13,289	9	2,206
3. Switzerland	778	19	3,257
4. Prussia and Germany (except Austria)	8,589	20	3,525
5. Northern United States (except Kansas, Nebraska and Oregon)	24,883	25	801
6. France	8,134	26	4,607
7. Holland	372	29	9,066
8. Italy	2,389	41	9,084
9. Austria	3,735	63	9,375
10. Spain	2,721	67	5,991
11. Portugal	419	87	8,555
12. Southern United States	10,300	92	1,025
13. Canada	2,539	136	987
14. India	3,186	287	42,572
Total of the 14 Countries	82,495		

Our deficiency.

That is a very instructive table. We have yet to build four times our present miles to be as well supplied as England; and though in the eastern States the land is too much broken and mountainous to render it expedient, yet in the whole Mississippi Valley it will be done. We already exceed

France, Holland, Italy, Austria, etc. Then, too, observe how small our population per mile. This Great Interior is doubtless to be one of the most densely peopled regions of the globe, and if railroads increase half as fast as population, we shall be abundantly supplied. None has superior capacity of production of all life's essentials, or of many of its chief luxuries; and although our lines are already abundantly remunerative, yet receipts are small compared with what they will be when from 801 people to a mile, we rise to that of England of 2,186. That will be done rapidly, and then we shall go on to overtake Prussia and Belgium. Settlements to be dense. Receipts to augment.

Nor are preceding tables less significant. Observe how small are our exports and imports per mile of navigation and railway. Our navigation is only estimated at 6,000 miles, yet our exports and imports in 1860 were but £4,567, to £17,476 in France, £25,985 in England, and £37,818 in Belgium. Observe, also, how large and rapid the increase in those countries, keeping even pace with increase of railways, while we have even failed to keep them equal, the former being actually largest in 1830. This is to be accounted for in that as a new country, we naturally produce first the essentials of life; and if produced advantageously for our own country, we should have but small surplus in any article for which we had not superior advantages. Hence cotton has been our chief export; and it is most satisfactory evidence that we have pursued precisely the right course, consuming nearly all we produce, and producing nearly all we consume. But as we develope, especially here in the Great Interior, we shall produce of food, particularly in the condensed forms of pork, beef and mutton, to feed Europe cheaper than she can herself, just as soon as we can have adequate facilities for transport. Wealth is to be more diffused, and the masses will be equal consumers of luxuries from foreign lands with the aristocratic of other countries. Notwithstanding the small proportion of exports and imports, we are beyond all question among the strongest nations in commerce, and but for the war would probably have been on the lead. It is the enormous multiplication of railways that reduces our average of exports and imports; and the low rate of these only serves to exhibit the extent of traffic yet to be thrown upon our rail and water facilities. Foreign traffic yet small. Increase less than railways. Good reason. Cotton chief export. Food to increase. Strong in commerce. Rapid increase of railways renders traffic small in proportion.

Mr. Baxter follows the table with remarks upon England and Belgium, showing the large prospective increase over them, and remarks :— Holland and Belgium.

* * * Deducting the manufacturing districts, which are crowded with a railway net-work, the remainder of the country gives an average of about fifteen miles between each mile of railway. The average ought not to be more than eight or ten miles. Railways 15 miles apart. 10 enough.

The advantage of a railway to agriculture may be estimated by the following facts: A new line would, on an average, give fresh accomodation to three and a-half miles on each side, being a total of seven square miles, or 4,560 acres for each mile of railway. It would be a very moderate estimate to supppose that cartage would be saved on one ton of produce, manure, or other articles for each acre, and that the saving per ton would be five miles at 8*d* per mile. Hence the total annual saving would be £768 per mile of railway, which is 5 per cent. interest on £15,000. Thus it is almost impossible to construct a railway through a new district Benefits to agriculture. Saving—

—whole cost. of fair agricultural capabilities without saving to the land owner and farmer alone the whole cost of the line. Besides this, there is the benefit to the laborer of cheap coal and better access to the market. Benefits towns. There is also the benefit to the small towns of being put into railway communication with larger towns and wholesale producers. And there is the possibility of opening up sources of mineral wealth.

Dividends not essential. Somebody ought to make these agricultural lines, even though they may not pay a dividend to the shareholder. But who is that somebody to be? The great companies will not take the main burden, lest they should lower their own dividends. Who to build branches. The general public will not subscribe, for they know the uncertainty of the investment turning out profitable. And notwithstanding the able letters signed "H," in the *Times* some months ago, I cannot advocate the necessarily wasteful system of contractors' lines, or believe in the principle, "Never mind who is the loser, so that the public is benefited." Railway extension is not promoted in the long run by wasteful financing and ruinous projects. On the contrary, such lines injure railway extension, by making railways a bye-word and depreciating railway property, and they render it impossible to find supporters for sound and beneficial schemes.

Route-owners to build branches. The proper parties to pay for country lines are the proprietors and inhabitants of the districts through which they pass. They are benefited even if the line does not pay a dividend. They have every motive for economical construction and management, and can make a line pay where no one else can. But they will not Not directly— subscribe any large portion of the capital as individuals. Very few will make a poor investment of any magnitude for the public good, though all might be ready to take their part in a general rate. Almost every country but our own has recognized the fact, and legislated on this basis, by empowering the inhabitants of a district which would be benefited to tax themselves for the construction of a railway. —but by loans of credit. I have shown that in France either the department or the commune may vote a subvention out of their public funds, and that in the United States the municipalities vote subsidies of municipal bonds. In Spain the provinces and the municipalities Examples. have the power to take shares or debentures, or if they prefer it, to vote subventions or a guarantee of interest. In Italy the municipalities do the same thing. Why should not England follow their example, and authorize the inhabitants of parishes and boroughs to rate themselves for a railway which will improve their property, or empower them to raise loans on the security of the rates, to be paid off in a certain number of years by a sinking fund, as is done for sanitary Only way. improvements? I see no other way of raising the nucleus of funds for carrying out many rural lines which would be most beneficial to the country. * * *

Future of railways. I cannot conclude without saying a word on the future of railways. The progress of the last thirty-six years has been wonderful, since that period has witnessed 85,000 miles in 36 years. the construction of about 85,000 miles of railway. The next thirty-six years are likely to witness a still greater development, and the construction of more than More next 36 years. 85,000 miles. We may look forward to England possessing at no distant date, more than 20,000 miles, France an equal number, and the other nations of the continent increasing their mileage till it will bear the proportion of one railway mile to every ten square miles of area, instead of the very much less satisfactory proportions North America to have 100,000 miles stated in the comparative table. We may expect the period when the immense continent of North America will boast of 100,000 miles of line, clustered in the thickly populated eastern States, and spreading plentifully through the western to the base of the Rocky Mountains, and over to California and the Pacific. We may Russia. anticipate the time when Russia will bend her energies to consolidating her vast From Dover to China. empire by an equally vast railway network. We may predict the day when a continuous railroad will run from Dover to the Bosphorus, from the Bosphorus down the Euphrates, across Persia and Beloochistan to India, and from India to China. We may look for the age when China, with her 350,000,000 inhabitants, will turn her intelligence and industry to railroad communication.

Important results. But who shall estimate the consequences that will follow, the prodigious increase of commerce, the activity of national intercourse, the spread of civilization, and that advance of human intelligence foretold thousands of years ago by the prophet upon the lonely plains of Palestine, "when many shall run to and fro on the earth, and knowledge shall be increased."

Note.—Confirmation as to France, by M. Lavollee. NOTE.—Since reading this paper before the Society, my attention has been called to an article on French railways in the *Revue des deux Mondes* of January 1st, 1866, by M. Lavollee, which, written many months previously, confirms most strikingly my conclusions, especially those which relate to the effect of railways on French commerce and on the welfare of the working classes. It adds many eloquent reflections on railways in relation to civilization and progress, which are well worth perusal.

These facts and views afford a safe basis of judgment for the future of American railways. According thereto we must have 2½ times more than at present, to equal the proportion of mileage to population in England, and 4½ times to equal Belgium; for who doubts the demand of go-ahead Americans for as much railway as any other people can use? To make mileage equal to area in Belgium, we must have three-fold increase; to equal England, four-fold. Like begets like; and when we consider that only 35 years ago we had less than 600 miles for the 38,800 in actual use to-day, who can doubt that fifteen years will at least double the present mileage?

Such our future increase.

3 and 4-fold.

15 years to double present lines.

Shall we cease progress when we shall have attained to what England and Belgium have already attained unto? Mr. Baxter argues in an unquoted paragraph, that whereas English lines are now about 15 miles apart, they should not be more than 8 or 10. That would require a third to a half increase. Shall we be satisfied with less than Europe? M. Poussin, French Minister to our Government some 30 years ago, published a work in 1843 entitled "The United States; its Power and Progress," and remarks in the introduction:—

Shall we then stop?

The U. S., its power and progress.

M. Poussin.

But on the other side of the Atlantic, a nation is now rising, which though by the same race, and moved by the same ambition, is in every respect better adapted to become one of the greatest powers among the commercial nations of the world. Day by day it is advancing farther and farther into the lists, and already menaces with disastrous competition the former queen of the seas, its only rival. But yesterday the American nation was a people of consumers; to-day it reveals its power and its just pretensions to lavish on the other nations of the world its immense natural wealth, and the marvelous products of its industry. Why should it not covet the rich inheritance of Great Britain, of which it will one day be able to dispossess it?

To become a chief com. nation.

Rival to Gt. Britain.

Be able to dispossess her.

To consumate these ambitious views, it pursues a course entirely the opposite of that which has so well served the interests of England. The ascending movement of the one has been occasioned by the energy of its compact aristocracy. The supremacy of the ocean will be obtained by the other through the force of democratic principles. On the banner of the one is inscribed the motto, *Dieu et mon droit*; on that of the other will be inscribed the freedom of the seas, thus recognizing that grand and salutary principle, that *the flag of a vessel protects its merchandise.* This sacred principle will powerfully contribute to the reconstruction of the social edifice.

Pursues an opposite course.

Democracy rules.

Sailors rights.

In its defence, the American nation will rely not only on its navy, but on its ambition and its commercial interests. Its strength lies in the sovereignty of the people. To this, in fact, it owes its origin and its unexampled prosperity. Founded, principally, on the love of liberty, on patriotism, on the attachment of the citizen to the constitution of his choice, the Union presents the imposing spectacle of a compact nation provided with all the elements of strength and durability. Its citizens, happy under the empire of their institutions, would only lose by modifying them; and they will not risk the experiment—for they would thus compromise the future, of which their present prosperity is the most solid guarantee.

Sovereignty of people.

No change desired.

M. Poussin describes with great accuracy our lines of interior communication, rivers, lakes, canals and railways, judiciously considering them as a means of military defence. He says of—

Internal improvements.

Railroads.—The distinctive character of the American people is that of being eminently productive. In this respect, no country, perhaps, with the same population, has equaled them. But in no country has an equal degree of activity and

Railroads.

constant application been exhibited with the object of procuring means of exchange for the products of the soil, or additional facilities for their transportation.

American skill in their use. Development of our resources.

In the gigantic application, so to speak, of that important means of communication and transportation, the railroad, the Americans have especially manifested their characteristic intelligence and their unerring instinct. The employment of all the resources which nature has so generously distributed throughout their vast and magnificent territory, for the development of commerce and wealth, the principal sources of public happiness, would seem to have been the principal and almost exclusive objects of their lives.

Democratic liberalism and railroads

The American seems to consider the words democracy, liberalism, and railroads as synonymous terms, whether because they all equally express the constant object of human effort in the gradual amelioration of the social condition of man, or because of the happy influence of the diffusion of knowledge on all classes of society.

People decided about railroads, not States.

When the question concerning the construction of the railroad—an improvement which was so powerfully to second the active genins of the Americans—was agitated, public opinion was alone invoked. It was no business of the State to decide whether the innovation, such as it presented itself, should immediately be introduced into the country, with all the imperfections attached to a recent discovery, or whether postponement of action until some other country should commence the experiment would be the wiser course. I well remember this circumstance. The Americans did not hesitate a moment. They adopted the discovery at its inception, and immediately applied it to their necessities, with due relation to locality.

At once adopted.

Experience the test.

This mode of proceeding was rational, for it is difficult to judge properly of the merits of any invention, or of the improvements of which it is susceptible, apart from direct experience. This course the Americans have invariably pursued in all their enterprises. They have never believed they could import anything in a state of perfection. For the suggestions of improvements which experience alone can supply in the varied circumstances peculiar to each country, they have considered experiment the only safe dependence.

Only dependence.

Practical in all things.

These practical views are exhibited in everything the Americans undertake; a circumstance which, among others, must, in my opinion, place the United States at the head of all other nations in everything that relates to the industrial arts. At all events, they have applied steam more extensively, in every branch of industry, than any nation in the world.

Steam largely used.

Moderate cost of railroads.

Our practical good sense has not only been shown in the abundant use of the railway, but in building them according to our means. We could better serve the public and make more money by building and furnishing two miles of road imperfectly than one mile thoroughly. Improvements of road-bed, rail and machinery are more cheaply made after a road is in full operation. Especially is this the case in the West. A road in a new country sparsely settled, if quite inferior, is of incalculable value for its developing powers; and as they are felt, and the local traffic augments, the railway can be and is improved to meet demands.

Improvements easy after.

Most miles wanted.

Views 25 years old.

M. Poussin wrote his views, it must be remembered, in 1843, before the West had begun to understand the worth of railways, or the East to appreciate the adaptation of this region to their use, and the resulting profits. In 1842, of 4,863 miles, Kentucky had 28, Ohio 84, and Michigan 138; and no increase to 1844, except 68 miles in Michigan. In 1843 the editor of the *Railroad Journal*, Mr. Poor, exhibiting the difficulties encountered and changes in 11 years subsequent to its establishment, remarked:—

222 miles in N. W. 1842.

Mr. Poor, Railroad Journal, '43.

Difficulties in starting it.

The editor also thought it necessary to refer to several gentlemen of the city as guaranties for the continuance of the work. Before many numbers had been issued, information from all quarters poured in, and a very lively interest was felt in the undertaking. The demand for railroads throughout the country increased, and popular as well as scientific information was in request.

Let us now compare the present state of affairs with this humble commencement. There are now between four and five thousand miles of railroad in use in the United States, built by the expenditure of nearly one hundred millions of dollars. Eleven years ago there were but about one hundred miles in use. There are now probably more than five hundred locomotive engines in use, nearly all of them made in this country. Eleven years ago, the few engines in use were imported from England, and were of the oldest patterns. Since then fifty or more American engines have been sent abroad—some to Russia, some to Austria, and several to England. Had this fact been predicted, even in the most indirect manner, in the first number of the *Railroad Journal*, it would have sealed its doom.

Change in 11 years, to 1843.

100 miles in 1832, 4,500 in 1843.

Engines exported.

Eleven years ago, a dead level was, by many, deemed necessary on a railroad, and grades of thirty feet to the mile were hardly thought admissable. Now, engines are in daily use which surmount grades of sixty and eighty feet to the mile.

High grade ascended.

Eleven years ago, inclined planes with stationary power were considered the *ne plus ultra* of engineering science. Now, they are discarded as expensive, inconvenient, and incompatible with the free use of a railroad.

Inclined planes abandoned.

Eleven years ago, it was thought that railroads could not compete with canals in carrying heavy freight; and even much more recently statements to this effect have been put forth by authority. Now, we know that the most profitable of the eastern railroads derive one-half of its income from bulky freight, and that coal can be carried more cheaply upon a railroad than in canals.

Compete with canals.

Eleven years ago, the profitableness of railroads was not established; and, discouraged by the vast expenditure in several cases of experiment in an untried field, many predicted that they would be unprofitable. Now, it is already demonstrated, by declared dividends, that well constructed railroads, when divested of extraneous incumbrances, are the most profitable investments in our country. The New England railroads have paid, since their completion, 6 to 8 per cent.; several other roads, 6 and 10 per cent. The Hudson and Mohawk (of fifteen and a-half miles, costing about one million one hundred thousand dollars) paid, in 1840, 7 per cent. on that enormous outlay. The Utica and Schenectady, and Syracuse and Utica, pay 10 to 12 per cent. The stock of the Utica and Schenectady Railroad has never been down to par since operations were commenced in 1836, and has maintained its stand, without fluctuation, at a higher rate than any other species of stock during all our commercial revolutions.

Are profitable.

New England 6 to 8, others 6 to 10 per cent. profit.

Eleven years ago, there were but six miles of railroad in use in the vicinity of Boston. Now, Boston has direct connection with a web of railways one thousand two hundred and three miles in length; all of which, except about twenty-four miles, are actually in use—being a greater length of railroad than there was in the whole world eleven years ago.

6 miles at Boston—now 1,203.

It is difficult to realize that one generation should have witnessed the creation of such a power as the railway, so soon attaining its huge proportions. Had any man predicted the work, who would have given credit? Would not the universal inquiry, and conclusive against even possibility of accomplishment, have been—Whence shall the money come to do this? Yet done it is; and most here in the West, where the largest expenditure according to population has been made, though not of our own money by considerable. Mr. Ruggles told us, p. 317, of the consequent fabulous increase of property. It is with the West we have to do; and though the information quoted was necessary to understand that progess here is not exceptional, in order to be certain of continuance, we need to have information about the West itself in order to judge accurately concerning the future.

Railway progress wonderful.

Increase of property.

Knowledge of the West wanted.

Nor is this a departure from our plan, introducing an hypothetical basis. Unless new forces are invented to supplant the railway—and no section can employ more advantageously a superior means than the Great Interior—the investments must go on indefinitely. The chief lines have become gigantic corporations with almost unlimited credit, and all strong competitors in

Investments must go on.

Corporations strong.

Atlantic cities seek their own advantage. — Their net-work. — The West a safe reliance. — Trade with East increase. — Perseverance sure. — Western railways pay well.

extending trunks and multipyling branches. The seaboard cities, extending their railways throughout the West for their own advancement, have little realized that the effect must be ultimately to build up greater cities inland; but with jealous rivalry between themselves, they have had honorable and strong contention as to which should grasp most of this chief producing region. They have spread a complete net-work of railway over this entire Old Northwest, expecting to draw all the fish to the seaboard. From the beginning the trade of the West has been the coveted prize. This built the Erie canal and the many great works which have more than fulfilled sanguine anticipations relating to Atlantic cities, and will indefinitely in the future be their chief and safe reliance. But it is one thing to be satisfied with a moderate part; quite another to expect the chief. The trade of East and West, however extensive the home trade in our respective sections, will constantly increase, and very many new lines into the West will be needed, and with them they will build many more throughout the Great Interior. The course has been so far advanced upon, that from the building of western railways no seaboard city would withdraw if it could, or could if it would. The trifling amount of grain exported is with them an abundant object to continue railway construction; and as that shall diminish by direct shipments from lake ports to Europe, other business will doubtless take its place. At all events, western railways which have proper management pay so abundantly, that capital will seek out other good routes until lines shall not be more than 20 to 25 miles apart.

West will build its own centres. — *Merch. Mag.*

But while the West will always be the main reliance of the Atlantic cities, its benefits cannot be there chiefly bestowed. Its own chief centres will most profit from its advantages. The census of 1860 developed the effects of railways in the West, which it is evident that of 1870 will confirm. An unknown writer in the *Merchants' Magazine* for January, 1861, considered—

City population.

City Population.—The comparative growth of cities is always an interesting branch of statistical research, and the late returns of the census give many important facts in relation to the leading cities of the Union. The enumeration of the leading Atlantic cities show the following result:—

Growth of chief cities, 1810 to 1860.

	1810.	1820.	1830.	1840,	1850.	1860.
Boston	33,250	43,298	61,392	93,383	136,881	177,902
Providence	10,071	11,767	16,382	23,171	41,513	49,914
New York	96,373	123,706	202,589	312,710	515,547	821,113
Brooklyn	4,402	7,175	15,396	36,233	96,838	273,325
Newark	....	6,507	10,958	17,290	38,894	72,055
Philadelphia	111,210	137,097	188,961	258,037	408,762	568,034
Baltimore	35,387	62,738	80,625	102,313	169,054	218,612
Richmond	9,735	12,067	16,060	20,153	27,570	37,968
Washington	8,208	13,247	18,827	23,364	40,001	61,400
Charleston	24,711	24,780	30,289	29,261	42,985	40,195
New Orleans	17,242	27,176	46,310	102,193	116,375	170,766
Savannah	5,215	7,523	7,776	11,214	15,312	16,000
Total	355,800	478,075	695,560	1,029,322	1,649,732	2,518,484

These aggregates show that the twelve cities named had five per cent. of the whole population of the Union in 1810, and the proportion rose regularly to 6½ per cent. in 1850, to 8¼ per cent. in 1860. In nearly all these cities, however, the population since the era of railroads has flowed over into the surrounding country, thus spreading the dwellings of those who carry on the business for which the city is important. In the neighborhood of Boston there are thirteen towns that are commanded by railroads, and which contain the dwellings of Boston business men. [We omit the statement comparing towns and State.] Increase of 12 cities. Suburban population. Boston—

Thus Boston may be said to contain one-fourth of the population of the State. The thirteen cities of Massachusetts have a population of 441,987, or 35 per cent. of the whole population; in 1850 the same cities had a population of 324,845, or 33½ per cent of the whole population. It is to be borne in mind, however, that the towns around Boston are those which concentrated the population the most rapidly, and one-third of the whole State population lives within a radius of twelve miles of Boston, dependent upon its commerce and manufactures. —¼th of Mass. ⅓ of Mass. within 12 miles of Boston.

The population and valuation of the city of New York have probably received the most marked development. The increase of the population from 1850 to 1860 nearly equaled the sum of the entire population in 1840. The progress of the population has, however, been in the upper part of the island, following the course of the railroads, which, since 1852, have so powerfully aided in the expansion of the city in a northerly direction. New York.

The growth of New York, Brooklyn, Philadelphia, Newark and Baltimore is noticed, and— Other eastern cities.

The Chief Valley Cities. Valley cities.

Growth from 1810 to 1860.

	1810.	1820.	1830.	1840.	1850.	1860.
St. Louis	1,600	4,598	5,852	16,469	77,860	160,577
Louisville	1,357	4,012	10,341	21,210	43,194	70,226
Nashville	......	......	5,566	6,929	10,478	23,715
Cincinnati	2,540	9,642	24,831	46,338	115,436	158,851
Pittsburgh	4,768	7,248	12,568	21,115	46,601	48,804
Total	10,265	25,500	59,158	112,051	293,569	462,173

The five leading cities of the valley increased in the decade to 1850, during which the canals began to exert an influence on their trade, about 181,000 souls, of which the largest portion was in Cincinnati. In the last decade, railroad building, land speculation, and immigration, have all exerted an influence upon the tributary country, driving trade in upon each of these centres, and the increase has been 168,000 souls, of which the largest proportion is in St. Louis. But during the last ten years those cities have encountered a more active rivalry in the growth of the lake cities, which have successfully attracted a large portion of the business of the belt of country bounded by the lakes, the Ohio river, and the Mississippi river, by means of the railroads and the attraction of capital operating through those points. 5 cities increase in 10 years, 181,000. St. Louis largest. Rivalry of—

Chief Lake Cities. —lake cities.

Growth of 6 chief, 1840 to 1860.

	1840.	1850.	1860.
Buffalo	18,213	42,261	81,541
Lockport	6,500	12,323	9,962
Cleveland	6,071	17,034	43,550
Detroit	9,102	21,019	46,834
Chicago	4,479	28,269	109,420
Milwaukee	1,700	20,061	45,326
Total	46,065	140,967	335,633

22

Chi. and Buffalo.

The increase in those cities has been, it appears, to 1850, 95,000 persons, of which increase Chicago, at the other end of the lakes, had as large a share as Buffalo at this end. In the last ten years the aggregate increase has been 194,700 souls, of which 81,000 has inured to Chicago, while Buffalo has increased but 39,000, or less than half the increase of Chicago. This great apparent prosperity of the former city has grown out of the immense concentration, not only of railroads at that point, but of the expenditure for railroad construction on a radius of 100 miles, all of which has reflected upon Chicago as a focus. That region is now to a considerable extent settled, and every year must add to the immense quantities of produce that will seek Chicago as the primary point of shipment. This growth of lake cities is very remarkable, and more so if we compare it with the population of the prominent Internal cities of the Atlantic States, where manufacturing may be assumed as the chief element of growth. [We omit the table of the twelve interior cities.]

Railroads help Chi.

Produce to increase. Growth compared with eastern cities.

All the cities compared from 1840 to 1860.

The growth here presented has been but 62,672, or 36 per cent. only in the last ten years. The whole growth of all the cities in the last twenty years have been as follows:—

	1840.	1850.	1860.	Increase per cent.
Twelve Atlantic Cities	1,029,322	1,649 732	2,518,984	50
Five Valley	112,051	293,569	462,173	58
Six Lake	46,065	140,967	335,633	130
Twelve Interior	101,014	171,112	233,784	36
Total Growth	1,288,452	2,255,380	3,550,574	52

Lake cities largest increase. Causes.

Thus the lake cities have shown by far the largest proportional increase, and the increase of the valley cities, as well as those of the Atlantic and the interior, have been in a declining ratio. The large railroad expenditure, migration and speculative movement during the last ten years, have made the lake country the focus of migration, and St. Louis has largely benefited by the same state of affairs, since the affluents that feed its trade have been swollen by the settlement and improvement of the whole northwest region. That region is now well supplied with rails, that will require a large production of grain and other produce to pay the interest on the cost of their construction, and their competition for the freights will no doubt reduce the rates of transportation to a *minimum*, and therefore favor the business of cities at their termini. The value of the produce will be governed, as a matter of course, by the state of the markets of sale. In other words its value must fluctuate with the crops of Europe. The resources of that region are, however, equal to any demand, and it is, by the continued smoothing of the way to market, brought daily nearer to the European centres of demand.

St. Louis benefited.

N. W. supplied with railroads.

Smoothing her way to market.

Why not lake cities grow?

Mr. Scott's predictions—

What shall stop the relative progress of the lake cities, until even the chief Atlantic cities shall have been passed? With results like these to confirm Mr. Scott's predictions, obtained eight years ago, ought not the fair and prudent reader to consider further confirmation quite probable? With an addition in the Northwest of 4,430 miles in the last eight years, over two-fifths increase notwithstanding the retarding influences of civil war unexampled in magnitude, ought not fulfillment of the predictions to be more than probable?

—more than probable.

Adaptation of this region to railways.

It is a most important point in considering this topic, as first presented, that never was the railway brought to bear upon such a country. No other area exists so perfectly adapted to railways, in which the bed can be laid so cheaply, and so nearly level. Then, no other has equal capacity to support them. These influences conjoined are no doubt the prime cause of the unexampled increase, and must operate until the Old Northwest of 600,000 square miles shall be spread over with a closer net work of railway than any

Capacity to support them

100,000 square miles in one body elsewhere on the globe. To discuss this important point would be to write the book over again. Let the reader run through the marginal readings of the relating topics, and its application and force will be perceived. In no other region have equal results been witnessed from railroads; and as we shall see, their centralizing power has only begun. The country must be developed before it is centralized. Still, in this respect its effects in the West are already wonderful. To what other instrumentality are we indebted for the marvelous statistics of produce and trade increase at Chicago? Surely we have had abundant testimony in general of the *Power of the Railway to Develope and Centralize*, and of its application in particular to the Great West and its chief emporium. Yet still, one other point is important to the completeness of the argument—that there is—

These points discussed.

Large results

Yet only begun.

Testimony for present topic.

NO OTHER POINT OF EQUAL CONVERGENCE, OF EITHER RAIL OR WATER COMMUNICATION, OR OF BOTH, ON THE GLOBE.

Convergence here of rail and water unequaled.

The prime cause of Chicago's advancement is her possession of the farthest extremity of the lakes, the head of the grandest inland navigation of the world. The close confluence of lakes with the mighty rivers of the West, is another powerful cause; nor has any other internal port equal advantages in regard to water alone. This, together with the peculiar position of Lake Michigan, stretching with Lake Superior nearly 600 miles north and south, forcing the fertile region beyond into tribute, was no doubt the cause of railway convergence.

Head of lakes is 1st point.

Conjunction with rivers another.

But these unequaled water facilities are altogether subordinate to railways. They have become mere adjuncts to the latter, their value lying chiefly in moving the most bulky articles, as grain, lumber, coal, pig iron, iron ore, etc. Beyond the railways, as on the upper Missouri, they are still valuable for all commerce; but where the railway reaches, the steamboat is entirely subordinate. For internal commerce the sail or steam vessel renders chief service by competition with railways in carrying bulky articles of small value per ton, which, if cast upon the railroad, would greatly enhance prices of all transportation. Not, however, that water transportation is valueless. It is worth more than ever in itself, and will go on to increase indefinitely with the growth of the entire country. Yet nevertheless, we have a means of inter-communication still more valuable in the railway. And instead of the latter reducing in utility the former, it actually increases it. Mr. Edmunds, in the census report, said in introducing the Influence of Railroads upon Agriculture, quoted p. 315:—

Still, railways superior.

Water facilities valuable in conjunction with railways.

Increased by railways. *Mr. Edmunds.*

Although but slightly connected with the interests of agriculture, we may here state another fact, that since the introduction of railroads, the building and employment of steamboats on our interior rivers have also increased largely, so that, even where railroads have competed directly with them, the steamboat interest has continued to increase in value and importance. This has not been always, we

Increased demand for steamboats.

Doubled in West from 1850 to 1860.

admit, in direct proportion to the growth of the country, but enough to show that, even where competition was greatest, this interest has not been injuriously affected. More than double the number of steamers were built on the waters of the interior. west in 1861 than were in 1850.

Boating business changed

Aided by railways.

Upper Missouri.

A St. Louis argument. *Mo. Dem.*

But the railway has changed, and will change still more on the rivers, the character of boating business. As on the lakes, for passengers and light freights, boats cannot compete successfully; but the railway stimulates all departments to such an extent that it generates more than it takes away. But there are sections which railways will not traverse for some years, where they will be greatly serviceable to the water business itself. The upper Missouri is a case in point. From Sioux City about 1000 miles to the mouth, it is a difficult, dangerous stream. We saw, p. 119, the interest Montanans take in being relieved of that part of the trip, hitherto not avoidable. Numerous other similar expressions have been seen since that was stereotyped which have not been saved, nor are they wanted. A St. Louis argument, together with the spirit inspiring, is better. The *Missouri Democrat*, April 21st, had this article :—

St. Louis and Chicag .

Efforts must be fair.

N. Y. Ship. List not so.

St. Louis and Chicago.—We do not object to a brisk competition in business, nor to an honorable rivalry, either between individual merchants or competing cities The life of trade and the benefit of communities lie in healthy contests for business, as they develope resources and stimulate enterprise. But to be healthy they should be confined to legitimate efforts, and be stimulated only by truthful representations. Otherwise somebody is deceived, and deception in matters of trade is at best a swindle. Of the latter character is the following paragraph from the New York *Shipping and Commercial List :*

Competition of Chi. and St. L. for far West trade.

Chi. has advantage.

The competition between Chicago and St. Louis for the Far West is exceedingly sharp, and it is difficult to tell which will ultimately come out ahead. At present Chicago seems to have the inside track, as the "mountain trade," worth last year $8,000,000, promises to be diverted to the Lake City from St. Louis. By the competition of seventy miles of railroad from Sioux City to St. Johns (which seventy miles, though running southeastwardly, were subsidized by government as a branch Pacific railroad), Chicago has direct communication with Sioux City. The distance by rail from Chicago to Sioux City is 540 miles. The distance from St. Louis to Sioux City by way of the Missouri river is about a thousand miles, and the navigation of which is difficult and hazardous. As 540 miles of railroad is to a treacherous river, so is Chicago.to-St. Louis in the prospect of selling annually $8,000,000 worth of goods to Montana.

Same wrong in other papers.

Waited for a respectable one.

St. L. in no danger.

Mountain trade increasing.

St. L's water superiority.

N. Y. editor to inquire to learn truth.

We have met a similar statement several times before, floating about in exchanges, but originated in Chicago for the purpose of giving a false impression both of its own facilities for trade and its superior enterprise, as well as for a reflection upon St. Louis in regard to either. We have not felt it worth while to correct the statements until we find them indorsed by so respectable a paper as that from which the paragraph is quoted, and which ought, from its pretensions, to be both candid and truthful. In this instance it is neither. Whatever may be the wishes of Chicago as to the "mountain trade," St. Louis is in no danger of losing it. We can sell goods cheaper than Chicago, as we have direct water communication with the East and with foreign markets. Western traders understand this, and parties who have not had their eyes opened in season, have found that they have paid much higher for goods bought in eastern markets than they could have purchased for in St. Louis, besides paying an unnecessary freight. Then, as to the actual facts, we have been, ever since the early spring, selling largely to the "mountain trade," and the Missouri has been traversed by a fleet of steamers all the season with goods for the far West. In fact there has been an unusual activity in this trade, amounting to an increase rather than a falling off, as compared with previous years. St. Louis stands in no danger of losing this business until the advantages of water communication cease to be more commodious than land transit, to say nothing of the difference in freight. A little inquiry would have satisfied the New York paper of these facts and prevented it from becoming a party to dishonorable attempts to build up one large city at the expense of another, which is certainly entitled, in such matters at least, to have the truth told concerning her.

It is utterly impossible, from natural causes, that Chicago can ever become a dangerous competitor to St. Louis. Temporary advantages, from factitous circumstances, have been given to Chicago, but they are only temporary. Chicago must always get her goods by overland transit of nearly a thousand miles, which inevitably enhances the costs. Her lake and water communication is closed during a large portion of the year, and from November to May, she can get no freight except by rail. The "mountain trade" is all over by May, and all Chicago can sell to it is from last year's stocks, or from high cost land freights. The simple statements of that fact carries more weight than a world full of windy boasting. With St. Louis, on the contrary, the facts are infinitely different. We have direct water communication with the whole world, cheap and reliable. Some winters navigation of the river below us is never closed, and at the worst from only four to eight weeks, which is not an appreciable obstacle to direct foreign importation of our goods. Even this slight interruption will be soon remedied by the extension of the Iron Mountain road to New Madrid, or some point on the river below the ice line. Hence, at no distant day, St. Louis is as sure to become the great importing center for the entire western trade, on both sides of the Mississippi, as the world is sure to revolve on its axis, and in five years from this date Chicago must come to St. Louis to purchase the greatest portion of her goods, because she can buy cheaper here than in New York, and save some hundreds of miles of heavy freightage. These are the results that nature settles, and time will explode all fallacious pretensions opposed to the facts.

Naturally St. L. superior to Chi.

Her advantages.

Direct water communication.

Iron Mt. railroad. Great importing city.

Chi. to get goods there.

Upon another topic, however, the same article does us justice in relation to a subject upon which we have more than once recently written. We extract the following remarks:

Yet justice done.

Considerable quantities of corn from the West are coming forward via New Orleans—the time occupied in the transit from St. Lonis being from twenty-five to thirty days. Facilities for rapid handling and drying have been provided at St. Louis, and elevators and warehouses are in process of erection at New Orleans. When all the arrangements shall have been perfected, a new era in the transportation business will be inaugurated, and the vexatious delays connected with the grain movement will be to a great extent obviated. As ships cannot take on board full cargoes of grain at New Orleans, owing to the obstructions at the mouth of the Mississippi, it is not improbable that a large number of small, light-draft vessels will be called into requisition in this branch of the coasting trade.

Barge trade

A new era.

This illustrates the importance of the new movement, and shows that eastern communities are awake to the benefits to result from St. Louis becoming a great grain center. We are pleased to know that a lively impulse characterizes this new branch of enterprise, and its fruits are daily becoming more and more apparent. In every view our city is advancing in prosperity and in a sure growth of commercial importance. We do nothing spasmodically, and perhaps are too cautious. But our advance is healthy, steady and strong, and as one great enterprise after another culminates, we have every possible assurance of a glorious future, in spite of all invidious jealousies that seek to agrandize rivals be circulating incorrect and false statements.

The East interested in St. L.

Nothing spasmodic.

Glorious future.

The editor is excusable for substituting assertion for argument, for he has no basis for the latter. Quite a revolution in the coming five years is to be effected from the past five, it appears; yet nevertheless, our merchants will probably keep on for a year or two in unconscious security of the ruin so inevitable. Making so large calculations ourselves upon the benefits of the rivers, it is encouraging to us that St. Louis, who thoroughly knows her advantage, is still willing to trust them so entirely, and we are happy to give St. Louis the benefit of that statement without comment. We also cordially endorse the concluding paragraphs, hoping sincerely that their strongest hopes will be realized in the barge trade. As before said, if Chicago prospers, it must be on the prosperity of the farmers; and we need all the competition possible with the New Orleans route to keep down rates by the lakes and railways. Mr. J. S. C. Knowlton, of Massachusetts, in

Assertion not argument.

We, too, rely upon the rivers.

Wish success to barge trade.

Mr. J. S. C. Knowlton.

his letter to the Ship-Canal Convention, 1863, expressed Chicago sentiments perfectly:—

Great benefits of Mississippi—

—for man's advancement.

We hear much said, and we talk much ourselves, of the great natural outlet of the magnificent Valley of the West, the Mississippi river, and its 80 to 100 tributaries or bayous—all employed in promoting a most healthful communication between the interior points and the exterior lines of this great and growing empire, whose destiny, it is scarcely too much to hope or believe, is the development and rounding-out, in their full proportions, of the industry of freedom, and the intellectual and moral elevation and improvement of the race as individuals and in communities; so that it shall be an empire of MEN, and not alone of material interests.

Monopolies adverse to our genius.

East and West have centres—

—to be brought into harmonious action.

Chi. a centre.

Monopolies are adverse to the spirit of our institutions. None of us want to be limited to one dull routine, either of business or of enjoyment. Freedom of choice, the cheapest production, and the readiest sale, are the rules of industrial success; and equally true is the declaration that "*two markets are better than one.*" We of the East have our manufacturing and commercial centres; and you of the West have your agricultural and mercantile centres. The relations of these centres to each other are those of mutuality, and their action, one upon another, is that of reciprocity. It is, and must be a great question in political economy, how to bring these centres, as representatives of great communities around them, into the easiest and quickest action, without any jarring collisions of interest or of passion. The city of Chicago, sitting in queenly majesty, by the side of an internal sea, out of whose placid waters the sun seems to shoot its morning beams, is one of the most important of these great agricultural and commercial centres. Situated, as it is, at the most southern point of the great system of northern lakes and rivers, it must be, for one-half of the year, the common highway for the trade and travel between the populous East and the great region that lies beyond Lake Michigan, and around Superior; and will continue to be, when the Atlantic and Pacific shall be bound together with bands of iron, for commerce between Western Europe and the great Eastern Empires of China and Japan.

Long railways show Miss. no monopolist.

South a competitor—

—with the East.

Water wanted besides railways.

Water never wears out.

If the Mississippi river is so far the cheapest and best communication with the Ocean as to be regarded as a monopoly, why is it that we see upon every modern map of the United States, long lines of railway, stretching towards various points of the Upper Valley of the Mississippi, from the ports of New Orleans, and Mobile, Charleston and Savannah? What is the purpose of these railways, and what are they reaching after? There can be but one answer to the question. The South wants to drain the great Mississippi Basin of its vast wealth of agricultural and mineral products, and it feels the necessity of possessing itself of them in a shorter and more expeditious manner than by the slow and circuitous route of the Mississippi river, giant as it is among rivers, for the heavy burden it bears. The East also has its railways grappling the Mississippi Valley; but it feels that something more is wanted, as of *great national, commercial, and military importance to the country*" It has the advantage of thousands of miles in the route from the Mississippi to the Ocean and to Europe. That is not enough; it wants a *cheap* as well as an expeditious route. It wants a WATER track as well as an IRON track, and for this simple reason, that while the cost of the *iron* track, originally and continuously, is, of necessity, an immense expenditure, the *water* track, when once constructed, *never wears out.* The difference in the expense of operating the two routes is manifestly great.

Railways for travel. Water for heavy operations.

While railways between the East and the West will always be preferred for travel, and for light and quick freight, a water-communication intermediate between the Mississippi and the St. Lawrence direct, easy, and of sufficient capacity for large operations, both in peace and in war, seems to have been left, by Divine Providence, for the employment of the inventive genius, the constructive skill, the industrial power of a great people, whose progress is to be obtained by a combined force of physical, intellectual, and moral activities.

East wants the shortest water communication.

I have no means of judging of the feasibility of the plans of improvement which are in contemplation, nor of their cost, nor of the extent to which such improvement would be generally, or even locally useful. I only know the general fact, that we want, if we can have it, *an ample* WATER-COMMUNICATION, *over the shortest route possible, between the Mississippi and the sea-ports of the East.*

Means of union our object.

A slight survey of the great physical features of the United States is an assurance that "*the development, prosperity, and unity of our whole country,*" should be the ambition alike of East and West, North and South; since every consideration of national progress, strength, and unity urges the whole people as with an irresistible logic to find their highest prosperity and happiness in a common brotherhood of sentiments, of rights, of duties, and of obligations.

But the want of the East even more than of the West, is to open the route from the Georgian Bay through Lake Simcoe into Lake Ontario. Then New York can compete successfully by the shorter canal route from Oswego with the St. Lawrence, and New England will have its best accommodation from Ogdensburg or Montreal by rail, and by the Champlain canal by water. Hon. John A. Poor, of Maine, who has well studied this question as I happen to know, said in his letter to the Ship-Canal Convention:—

Lake Simcoe route wanted by all.

Hon. J. A. Poor.

Your call seems to limit the object of the Convention to the single purpose of an enlargement of the existing canals between the valley of the Mississippi and the Atlantic ocean—works of obvious value, if not all of them of immediate necessity—yet, it may fairly open the entire question of the internal commerce of the country, and the means of transit between the grain-producing regions of the interior of the continent—the great Northwest—and their place of market.

Ship-Canal convention—object to enlarge present canals.

Questions of this character are of interest to all, and must, for years, if not for generations to come, become the most engrossing topics of public concern; from the physical configuration of the North American continent, the limited capacity of its natural channels of trade, and the political difficulties in the way of all efforts at the opening of adequate avenues, by artificial means, to meet the wants of a rapidly increasing business.

These important questions.

Great as is now the internal trade of the country, it is a little only of what it will, in a few years, attain to. The production of food is not, at this time, equal to one-tenth of the capacity of the Northwestern States, without resort to the artificial stimulants that are common in the British Isles. Besides this one-half of all the grain raised in the United States is produced at points so remote from market, that its value would be consumed in the mere cost of transportation by the ordinary channels. With the aid of all existing canals and railroads, a bushel of wheat in the Northwest is only worth one-half its value in Liverpool, so enormous is the cost of present transportation. The question is, how shall this difficulty be overcome? And it is this question alone, that will engage the time and thoughts of the members of this Convention.

Internal trade yet small.

Grain consumed in transport.

Remedy of this the object.

It has seemed to me that the great difficulty lies in the way of outlets *from* Chicago, Milwaukee, and other lake ports, rather than in the lack of means to bring produce to the lake-shores. Cheaply-built and economically worked lines of sailers, with other means of transit, bring into these great granaries—the lake-ports—more produce than the outlets can economically take away.

Outlets from Chi. wanted.

What is wanted, are cheap and expeditious means of transit, from the Upper Lakes to the open sea. To secure this most effectually, we must make the St. Lawrence-waters AN OPEN MEDITERRANEAN SEA; so that, from the head of Lake Superior and from Chicago, ships of useful size for navigating the ocean can pass, free of duty, and with dispatch, to the Atlantic ports and Europe, and backward to the same places, fully laden. By this means, you could diminish by one-half the cost of transit for the benefit of the farmers of the Northwestern States, and indirectly, for the advantage of the entire population of the country.

Ample navigation from lakes to ocean.

Save half cost of freight.

This is a matter of easy accomplishment, if undertaken in the right spirit and temper. The *English-speaking people* of this continent are, for all commercial purposes, *one people*, holding a territory twice the size of the continent of Europe, capable of sustaining as dense a population as that which now occupies that favored portion of the globe. This territory is held in nearly equal shares by the people of the United States and of the British North American Provinces, lying mainly on opposite sides of this great Mediterranean Sea, formed by the waters of the Lakes and the St. Lawrence.

English-speaking people one.

The laws of commerce disregard political boundaries, and the people of the Northwest should have their choice of routes to the open sea. Ships should load at Chicago for any port into which an Atlantic sailor can enter, and by so many

Commerce disregards national boundaries.

Advance in one crop would pay whole cost of improvement from Chi. to the ocean.

routes as can be created, from the St. Lawrence, by the way of Lake Champlain, into the Hudson, by the Ottawa, and by Lake Ontario. The advance in the price of *a single crop of wheat* would pay for making all these routes, from Chicago to the Atlantic navigable for ocean-going sailing-ships and steamers. Montreal harbor could be made for the trade of New York, what Albany is now; and that, too, while the St. Lawrence basin, below the Victoria bridge, should be crowded, like the Thames in our day, from London to the sea, when this continent is as fully peopled as Europe.

Lake navigation cheap as ocean.

From Chicago to the Atlantic, for nearly the whole distance, navigation is as cheap as on the ocean. Short canals and lockage would not detain ships more than the average adverse winds of the Atlantic, so that the transit of goods, to and from Chicago and Liverpool, would be nearly as cheap as to and from New York. At one-tenth of the cost of transportation by railway, such a line of navigation would supply an outlet to the trade of the Northwest. To transport a ton of goods, by ordinary highways, costs on an average twenty dollars per one hundred miles. The railroads will perform this service for two dollars, the sailing-vessel for one-tenth of this, or twenty cents per ton. Open a ship-canal by the way of the St. Lawrence to Chicago, and the cost of freight will scarcely, if at all, exceed the cost of transit on the ocean, or the Lakes. * * * *

Not 1-10 of railway.

If not yet continental commerce—

If, however, the time has not arrived when we can treat the English-speaking people of the continent as properly subject to our commercial law—a result not very far distant from our day—when an ocean-tariff shall extend with uniform permission, for the collection of duties from Quebec to the Rio Grande, and upon the Pacific coast, with unrestricted power of internal trade; or, in other words, if the British North American Provinces are not ready to adopt with us *an American Zoll-Verin*, we must make use of our own independent advantages. We can, more cheaply than the Canadians have built theirs, construct a ship-canal around Niagara Falls, and from Oswego to the Hudson, that shall, for years to come, take away from the Lakes the surplus produce of the interior. We should further, with the same broad view, deepen the channel of the St. Clair, and extend this water-line, with a capacity equal to the passage of an ocean steamer, from Chicago to the navigable waters of the Mississippi, so that produce can pass by either route to the sea.

—let us do our best.

Niagara canal, Amer.

Improve St. Clair river.

We deal with great subjects.

The people of the great Republic of the North American continent have been unexpectedly called upon to deal with great enterprises, vast and undefinable in their extent; and while expending, without discontent or embarrassment, large sums in suppressing insurrection, and guarding against foreign invasion, they have found time to contemplate, as necessary practical measures, a railway from the Missouri to the Pacific, and a line of ocean-steamers from San Francisco to the shore of the densely populated continent of Asia. A further knowledge of the capacities of our country and of the capabilities of its people will ensure for them all full and complete success.

Prosecute war and build Pacific railway.

Do other works.

Chief grain and provision market will be reached.

A route so important to the eastern States and to Europe as that which opens to them free access for large vessels to the chief grain and provision market of the world, surely cannot long continue unimproved so as to afford requisite transportation. As Mr. Poor remarks, with ample knowledge and sound judgment, the necessities of both producers and consumers are best served by increasing facilities *from* lake ports to the East, rather than *to* them, from the West. Whatever the cost, a channel will be opened from lakes to ocean. For the Lake Simcoe route, $40,000,000 is estimated; and what would that be to the sea-board interest compared with the saving of over 300 miles around through Lake Erie, and avoiding Niagara? Either the British or American interest could well afford the cost for themselves individually. But to say nothing of Canada, neither New York nor Boston can use capital in any way equally as profitable to promote their separate interests, as would the opening of the route between Huron and

Facilities from lakes needed.

Lake Simcoe route.

N. Y. and Boston need it.

Ontario promote their joint interests. To New York it not only saves the detour around through Lake Erie, but nearly one-half of the canal transportation. To make this improvement between Huron and Ontario, the whole sea-board is equally interested; and that done, the competition between Quebec, Boston and New York would create all needed facilities. Nor need New York fear because she would lose half the tolls of the Erie canal. Increased traffic would more than equal the loss, to say nothing of the immense stimulus to trade in all departments.

Whole sea-board interested. N. Y. need not fear loss.

The advantages of the lake route will then be so increased, that it would now be difficult to estimate its value too highly. Yet, be it observed, we are not obliged to anticipate that to make good this caption; for as already remarked, no other city has equal advantages in water communication with what Chicago now has. Because of superior facilities already possessed, has the lake route drawn from the rivers. But no proper view of the future of Chicago can be taken, which ignores the certain passage from here to the ocean of vessels of 1,500 tons, and at least a quarter as large from Oswego to New York. It is not in the least hypothetical. Nor are our own canals to be overlooked. The *Chicago Times*, April 29th, remarked :—

Advantages of lakes improved. Yet superior as they are. Still, improvements to be regarded. Western canals. *Chi- Times*

The American "Head Centre."—The supposition of some people, since railways have become the great popular medium of travel and transportation, that canals are "played out," is a very great error.

Am. Head centre.

Notwithstanding the multiplication of railways in New York, parallel to the canals of that State, the business and receipts of the latter have steadily increased, until any considerable further increase would require an enlargement of their carrying capacity. Notwithstanding the bisection by numerous railways of the whole region that formerly had no convenient outlet to Chicago but the Illinois and Michigan canal, the business of that canal has steadily augmented, every new railway in its vicinity seeming to increase, rather than to diminish, the carrying trade which the canal has been called in requisition to do.

Canals still valuable. Traffic of Ill. & Mich. canal increas'd

A similar state of facts will probably be found wherever similar conditions of comparison exist. Railways, by affording the means of swift travel and quick exchanges of ideas—whether in mental or material forms,—supply to the body politic its nervous system, while water-courses may be aptly styled the muscular system of the same body. It is only where the nervous and the muscular systems exist together in full development that the highest state of human organism is found.

Railways the nerves— —canals the muscles of the body politic.

The great importance of canals, in connection with railways, is made more apparent at the present time by monopolizing tendencies which have made their appearance so generally in railway management. Between railways and canals there can be no such rivalry as will beget consolidation or combination upon rate-tariffs. As the safety-valve prevents steam from overcoming the resisting power of iron, so a canal, parallel to an important line of railway, will prevent the latter from overcoming, in its greed of high charges, the resisting power of the people.

Railways monopolize. Consolidation with canals impracticable.

The West is "the land of railways." The West also might be—and, some day or other, must become—the land of canals. The great ship canal from Chicago to the Mississippi river, already partially provided for, is certain to be a reality at a future day. So also is the more direct canal from Chicago to the Mississippi at Rock Island. Likewise, the projected canal from Rock river to Green Bay, which may be designated as the "stern-wheel canal."

West the land of both. Its canals.

The report of General Wilson on the survey of Rock river (constituting executive document No. 15, of the present Congress,) shows the practicability of that project, at a cost of $5,252,013 for an ordinary canal; or a cost of $14,783,370 for a canal suited to the navigation of small "stern-wheel" steamboats. For the navigation of any larger craft, the report sets forth the fact that the summit reservoir (Lake Horicon) cannot be made to supply enough water. As the natural

Canal from lake to Rock river.

Only 4ft. possible.

supply of water is apt to diminish, rather than increase, as the country grows older, the argument is in favor of a canal rather below the capacity which any present theoretical calculation may show to be practicable. For a canal with the usual four-feet channel, the supply of water would be unquestionably abundant for all times.

Chi. canal only one for large boats. Lake Mich. a sure head. Only 12 feet cut.

From all the surveys for ship canals to connect the navigation of the northern lakes with the navigation of the Mississippi and its tributaries, the very significant fact appears that the Chicago ship canal is the only one which can be made a ship canal in reality, as well as in name. The "summit reservoir" from which the Chicago canal will be supplied is Lake Michigan,—an "inland sea," on which the navies of the world might ride, and find "ample scope and verge enough." No lack of water here. The "summit level" which must be cut down to receive this supply is less than twenty miles long, and requires to be sunk less than a dozen feet to give a permanent depth of water on which the largest New Orleans steamboat may enter the port of Chicago.

Chi. the centre of interior navigation— —despite St. Louis' growling.

Chicago, the present commercial centre of the Continent, is surely destined to be the central point on a system of interior navigation that shall stretch from the Gulf of St. Lawrence to the Gulf of Mexico, and from the base of the Rocky Mountains to the Bay of New York. The great railway centre of the Continent is destined to be the grand centre of water navigation also, at once the heart and the brain—the head (and) centre,—where continental arteries and nerves conjoin. Nothing is more certain to be realized, notwithstanding that some of the present inhabitants of St. Louis may not live to growl over the reality.

St. L's self adulation because we seek further improvements.

"Growling" scarcely expresses the spite which some St. Louis papers exhibit. She seems to think we ought to rest satisfied with present attainments, and that it betokens admission of her superiority that we should deem it necessary to seek for any additional channels of communication. Were the measure of our ambition merely to supplant the Queen of the Rivers, we could be satisfied with what we have, or much less; but as the emporium of the Great Interior, we would lay plans and make efforts correspondingly.* Chicago characteristics are so totally different from those

---

We pursue our own course. *Mo. Dem.*

* We pursue the even tenor of our way, endeavoring to show what ought to be done, and rendering such aid as may be in our power. Evidently in response to that manly article, the *Missouri Democrat* of May 1st, contained the following characteristic travesty:—

Chi. wants a ditch— —is unhappy— —because St. Louis sends grain to N.Y. Smiles, too.

Wanted, a Ditch?—Something must be the matter. That great city, that Babylon of houses that fall down, located on a flat along the lake shore, which was to become the one and only great commercial city of *this* World, if not of another as well, and the iron arms of which were stretched out in all directions, reaching after trade to support its fast horses, faster men, falling houses and fallen women, has at this present moment a very evident touch of "the blues." Chicago is unhappy. Neither fast horses nor any other fast creature has power to charm away the melancholy which over-shadows with its dark wings the depressed spirit of the Chicago merchant. Because, laugh as much as he may, St. Louis is sending grain to New York and Liverpool. When Milwaukee stole the larger half of the trade, Chicago people said, "ah, well, the little town is only a suburb of this city; it has to come here for goods." But now Milwaukee itself is ir a panic, and passes resolutions by the bushel, while Chicago, with not less real apprehension but with more pluck, puts on a smile, sneers at big and muddy ditches, and talks in private very anxiously of ship-canals.

What can Chi. want of canals? She decries the rivers— —yet wants a ship-canal to reach them.

"Ship-canals!" What on earth can Chicago want of canals? Has she not that miraculous provision of nature in her behalf, the chain of lakes and rivers which make her a "port of entry?" Of course she has. And has she not told us a thousand times how utterly useless the Mississippi was and would be—how it freezes up in winter, dries up in summer, and runs the wrong way all the year round; how impossible it is for trade ever to run north and south; how "eternal laws" send all the grain for all future time straight to those big elevators which sometimes make mistakes in weighing or delivering; how absurd it was for a small town on the banks of that muddy ditch to think of becoming a commercial town, because Chicago could and would build railroads all around it, and the like? Nevertheless, here is Chicago talking about the expenditure of ever so many millions for a ship-canal to give that city an outlet into the Mississippi river!

Why? Current in St. L's favor.

Now can any one tell why these busy men of the modern Babylon are so anxious to get water connection with the Mississippi? Is it because somebody having proved that grain can be sent from St. Louis to Liverpool by river cheaper than from Chicago to New York, the busy men aforesaid begin to apprehend that one day they may be left out altogether, switched off on a side track at a way station. If the commerce of the Mississippi valley *will* go by the Mississippi river—in spite of all the "eternal laws of nature" quoted by philosophers and poets of the lake school—possibly it may be well to get access to the said stream, even if it is muddy!

of St. Louis, she cannot judge us fairly. As shown in the article, April 21st, p. 340, she is still entirely confident that nature having designed that she should have the mountain trade, it must come to her. On the other hand, while we are sure Hercules is moving our wheel of commerce, yet we realize the necessity of lifting ourselves to have the full strength of Hercules. One would suppose she would profit by her experience in the loss of the upper Mississippi trade, which was not in consequence of the war, as she now misrepresents, but as she herself showed in 1861 (pp. 111–113), the railways and canal had wrought their legitimate effect, drawing away her very life's blood. The same appliances to the Missouri will produce the same result; and the more effectually because of the dangerous navigation of the lower Missouri. The *St. Joseph* (Mo.) *Register*, of May 22d, giving a list of the boats *en route* for the mountains adds:—

She cannot judge fairly. Still relies on nature. We help our ourselves. As we drew Miss. trade— —so the Mo. trade. Navigation dangerous. *St. Jo. Register.*

As far as reported, but two of these mountain boats have as yet met with a disaster. The Carrie was snagged near Sioux City, and the Arabian sunk and lost near Atchison.

2 boats lost.

St. Louisians imagine that because they are sending not only as many, but more boats to the mountains, they are having the bulk of the trade. Doubtless the trade this year is more than doubled. Where has the increase gone to? Our merchants are well satisfied with their beginnings. The hold St. Louis has had is not at once to be shaken off; but that trade is to be done mainly by railroads, and by so much as Chicago excels in these facilities, will she excel in the mining traffic. St. Louis will doubtless have a good deal, if she prove more energetic in her railway building; but Chicago must have a good deal more.

St. L. has more mountain trade. Chi. satisfied with hers. To be done by rail.

We do not, however, expect railways to do all for us. Though the days of boating expensive goods up stream below Omaha and Sioux City are about ended, still the great rivers of the Interior are to be used more and more for down freighting by barges. To enable these to reach the lakes without transfer, we seek improvement of the Illinois and Michigan Canal and River, and also the cutting of the canal from La Salle to Rock Island. These works will surely be constructed on a scale commensurate with the joining of the grandest lake navigation, with the largest river navigation of the world.

Rivers also valuable. Down freight by barges. Canals wanted for these to reach lakes.

The different characteristics of the two cities seem to be well apprehended by parties who at all events ought to know St. Louis. The *Atchison* (Kansas) *Free Press*, says of—

Difference between St. L. and Chi. *Atchison Free Press.*

Chicago and St. Louis.—There are two great business centres in the West—Chicago and St. Louis. Each of them is extending its arms to draw to its bosom the trade which otherwise will fall to its rival. There was a time when St. Louis

Chi. and St. L. two great centres.

Beware, O Chica-geese! That river dries up in summer. It freezes up in winter, especially above this point. Your canal will be of no sort of use to you, for it will only send all your dealers to St. Louis to buy iron and goods of foreign manufacture, imported directly by river. It is a frightfully dangerous experiment. "But," mutters Chicago, "something must be done. Business is dull: not enough produce moving to employ the loanable money of the banks." Ah! Those houses of yours are built of remarkably slender splinters, O philosophers of the lake school.

Chica-geese beware! Especially of your houses.

St. L. had all. Cin. a hamlet. Fur trade. Merchants staid, substantial. No Yankees. So it is to-day.

was the centre of all the trade of the West;—that was when nearly everything depended upon the trade in furs, and the French were the only white inhabitants of the Mississippi Valley, and the region of the upper lakes. When Cincinnati was but a hamlet, gathered around Fort Washington, and but a few pioneers from Pennsylvania and Virginia had begun to penetrate the forests of southern Ohio and Indiana, the French had already an occupancy of all the tributaries of the Mississippi, and St. Louis was the focus of all their traffic. Merchandise found its way up that stream from New Orleans, and was at St. Louis exchanged for furs and peltries, which the *voyageurs* brought in from every valley of the West. Long after the West was transferred from the French to the Government of the United States, and emigration had poured its myriads from the eastern States into the Mississippi Valley, St. Louis continued to retain the character it had early formed. Its merchants were staid, substantial men. The current of their business flowed on as smoothly as the placid waters upon which all their commerce floated. The nervous, far-sighted, often reckless Yankee, was not there, or if he came he could not unloose the purse-strings of those whose wealth was necessary to extend speedily from that point, the arms of railroad system over the West. And so it is, in a great measure, to this day.

Chi. not begun. Active merchants buy grain by wagon load. Then railroads begin. Chi. cuts off St. L. to the east, the north, now west.

Chicago had not begun to spring up till long after St. Louis had become opulent in her quiet wealth and ease. But at length shrewd and active merchants set their stakes at Chicago. At first they bought grain by the wagon-load, and sent it all by schooners down the lakes. Then they commenced the construction of railroads. In all directions they caused them to push their way out over the prairies to bring in the productions of the ten thonsand farms, opened upon the exhaustless soil of all the States over which the ordinance of 1787 had spread its ægis of freedom. St. Louis merchants clung to the fogyism and the faith of their correspondents away down the Mississippi. Chicago merchants comprehended the most progressive ideas of modern commerce; and they sent out their iron rails, and erected their towering castles for the reception of all the grain of the Northwest. Chicago railroads cut St. Louis off on the east, away down to Cairo, long ago; cut across the State of Missouri to the Missouri river, long ago, and penetrated to the heart of Iowa, and cut across Wisconsin to Minnesota. Now they reach across Kansas by two lines—one by the way of Cameron, Kansas City, and the Eastern division, Pacific; the other by the Central branch Pacific, from Atchison. They cross Nebraska by the Pacific Trunk to the Rocky Mountains. They reach the Territory of Dacotah at Sioux City. And everywhere these iron arms are being rapidly lengthened out.

Nebraska trade secured. Provision trade.

Chicago merchants bought Nebraska grain two years ago, and paid more for it than would St. Louis merchants, though the latter could bring it to their own mills without change of bulk. And it is not only grain but the beef and the pork of the Northwest that the Chicago merchants monopolize by their superior enterprise. We published the other day the statistics of Chicago beef and pork-packing. St. Louis can make no such showing.

Exchange operations.

While Chicago has gathered up the produce of the West and marketed it in every eastern city and in Europe, she has kept her exchange accounts even. The grain merchant does not from his sales bring currency to buy more grain with. He gets a bill of exchange. This is transferred to the Chicago dry goods and grocery merchant.

Activity of Chicago merchants. Facilities of transport. Streams bridged.

To every point from whence comes grain to the Chicago market, Chicago dry goods and grocery merchants sent bills of goods. Every northwestern town is visited by the Chicago merchant, and orders solicited. Every newspaper in the Northwest teems with inducements offered by Chicago merchants to retail dealers. These inducements are real and they are accepted. The Chicago merchant has his arrangements for shipping complete. His transfers, if any, are made with the utmost facility. Every stream is bridged or being bridged. Not many months hence Chicago will reach the furthermost confines of every northwestern State without breaking bulk.

St. L. works, but slow. Wants Chi. enterprise.

Modern St. Louis men are working out a railroad system,—but at a slow pace. St. Louis merchants, at the spring rise in the river, manifest much spasmodic life; and then they sell considerable bills of goods. But the unceasing enterprise, the unfailing energy of the Chicago merchant is wanting among the merchants of St. Louis.

This gives over-credit on one important point. Chicago merchants have not at all built our railroads. Many of them could be named who are among our wealthiest men, who from the first opposed them as an injury to the City. They could appreciate the benefits of 1,000 to 1,500 "prairie schooners" making advent daily to the City, and with nervous energy, inspired by the loss of dollars—the only lode-stone to move their sensibilities—they would declare that "grass will grow in the streets when the railroads stop the teams." But most of our merchants and active business men have not been of that miserable set, or Chicago would not be here. Still, they have not built the railroads. They have had no money for them; and nothing but the strongest public spirit led to the initiation of the efforts which in only about 20 years from the very beginning, have made Chicago the greatest railroad centre of the world. In the "First annual report of the Galena & Chicago Union Railroad Company," dated 5th April, 1848, Mr. W. B. Ogden, the President, said:—

Over-credit to Chi. Many merchants opposed railroads. Most not of that sort. No money for railroads. *1st Rep. Gal. & Chi. R. R.* *Mr. Ogden.*

The Michigan Central Railroad Company, decided to terminate their road at New Buffalo in July last, and steps were taken preparing the way for an extension of their road to Chicago about the same time. Upon this, your Directors proceeded at once, to announce their intention of opening books of subscription to stock, for the extension of this continuous line of railroad from Chicago westward to Galena.

Mich. Cen. at New Buffalo. Galena to connect.

Books were accordingly opened at Chicago and Galena, and at the towns intermediate, on the 10th day of August last, and about $250,000 of stock were then subscribed.

$250,000 stock taken.

The first expectation of the Board was to obtain a general subscription from the citizens of Northern Illinois and Southern Wisconsin, residing along the line of the contemplated road, and in its vicinity, as indicative of their faith in the profitable character of the road when constructed, and of the general interest of the people in its construction; and, with the aid of this subscription, to open negotiations with, and solicit other subscriptions or loans from eastern capitalists, sufficient in amount to justify the commencement of the work.

Subscriptions in the country to show confidence—to obtain eastern capital.

The amount subscribed, however, on the opening of the books, was so liberal, and the feeling manifested along the line, so ardent, and so universal, that it was quite apparent the country and the people immediately interested in the construction of the road, were able to, and would increase their subscriptions to an amount sufficient, in connection with the credits on iron and engines then offered us, to build the road from Chicago to Elgin at once, and own it themselves.

Subscriptions suffice to build road-bed to Elgin.

Experienced parties at the East, largely interested in Railroad stock, and decidedly friendly to the success of the Galena and Chicago road, were consulted, and made acquainted with the particulars of our position at this juncture, and with the proposed plan for obtaining the additional means at the East, necessary to secure the completion of the road to Fox river.

Eastern capitalists consulted.

They were clearly and decidedly of the opinion, that the wisest and surest way to accomplish the speedy extension and completion of the entire route to Galena, was, for the inhabitants along the line of the road, to raise the means themselves, for its commencement and completion to the Fox river and Elgin, 41 miles, when there was every thing to assure us that the comparatively small cost of construction and extreme productiveness of the country tributary to the road, would secure such large returns as would enable us to command capital from any quarter or loans or increased subscriptions to stock for the extension of the road to Rock River, and to Galena, without delay.

Advise the people to complete 41 miles themselves. Would secure extension.

This course was adopted, the object explained and approved by subscribers, and further subscriptions solicited and obtained on this basis of operation, to an extent exceeding altogether, the sum of $350,000 (about $10,000 of stock subscriptions have since been added,) and the work was commenced in earnest.

$360,000 subscribed.

A Corps of Engineers was then (September last) immediately employed to survey and locate the line from Chicago to the Fox River, and prepare it for letting. The

Route surveyed.

time occupied in doing so, has somewhat exceeded what was at first supposed to be necessary, and the road, except the first seven miles, was not prepared for letting until the first of March last, when the grading and bridging of the first 31 miles (inclusive of the seven miles let last fall,) was put under contract, and on very favorable terms, as will appear by reference to the report of the Chief Engineer herewith submitted. [31 miles contracted.]

[Timber and ties for 41 miles.] By reference to that report, it will also be seen, that all the timber and ties necessary for the entire superstructure to Elgin, 41 miles, have been contracted for on favorable terms.

[A thorough road with T rail—] It has always been the desire and intention of the Directors, to commence the road in a thorough and substantial manner, and if possible, with our means, to finish it with an edge rail, which all experience seems to have approved, as being greatly preferable, and in the end more economical.

[—if possible.] A superstructure—cross ties—suited to such a rail has accordingly been adopted, and an edge rail will be procured if the means of the Company shall prove sufficient to obtain it. * * *

[Flat rail at first.] It is also proper to remark, that many considerations suggestive of the propriety of adopting a flat or plate rail, in the first instance, as far as Fox River, have presented themselves.

[Economy indispensable.] In a country where money is worth as much as it is here, and where the means of a company are as limited as ours are, and the necessity for the immediate construction of a railroad is so great, in consequence of the very bad character of our common roads, and of the great amount of produce to be transported over them; there are reasons favoring a commencement with a plate rail, which would not be entitled to consideration under better circumstances.

[T rail can be substituted for flat.] Should the future Board find themselves at any time hereafter, relieved from the necessity of adopting a flat rail, in consequence of the fall of iron, or of increased funds or credit suited to their circumstances, they will, no doubt, avail themselves of a rail of greater weight and more improved form.

[Extension will make it necessary.] Upon the extension of the road beyond Elgin, a greater necessity will exist for a heavier rail, from the increased business that will result from such extension; and the flat rail and the timber upon which it is placed between Chicago and Elgin, if used there, can then be taken up and relaid on a branch road to Beloit or to other points to which there will be occasion for branches.

[Our railways began thus moderately— —yet the future was anticipated.] With these moderate plans the first Chicago railroad was begun. Yet the report of the preliminary survey the previous year by Col. R. P. Morgan exhibits ample conception of the magnitude of the undertaking and ultimate benefits to the public and to shareholders. After speaking of eastern works and the pressure of travel and freight, the route was described, an estimate made of cost and receipts, and a comparison instituted between this and the Western Railroad of Massachusetts, concluding with the connexion at New Buffalo with the Michigan Central. Extracts would be interesting. Upon this connexion with the Michigan Central Mr. Ogden said in his report of 1848:— [*Mr. Ogden.*]

[Connexion with Mich. Cen.] It cannot have escaped the observation of all acquainted with the region of country to be affected by the construction of this important work, that if constructed now and extended east from Chicago, around the head of Lake Michigan till it meets the Michigan Central Railroad, as it soon will be, it secures to the country through which it passes, the *great Northwestern Railroad thoroughfare, for all time to come.* [The N. W. thoroughfare certain.]

[No possible competition.] No other continuous route of railroad will ever be made to that great and rapidly improving country lying west and northwest of Lake Michigan, to the north of the southern end of that lake, if this road is established there first. No line to the south of it, near enough to compete with it, will be at all likely to be built while the business of the country can be prosecuted upon the road in which we are now engaged. Indeed no other line to the south of it can compete with it, for the trade and travel of more than half a million of people now at the north and west of it, and tributary to it; and the only struggle we have to secure all the great considerations and ends we have in view, lies in the completion of the road to [41 miles to Elgin makes all sure.]

Elgin. Once finished to that point, it will promptly demonstrate its profitable character and usefulness and command the confidence of all, and the means necessary to ensure its immediate extension to its termination at Galena.

That italicized declaration of Mr. Ogden's he has emphatically repudiated. The location of another truer Northwestern, both in name and location, of which he has been chief patron, has not only been built, but has actually absorbed and wiped out of existence even the pioneer Galena. How much is due to public considerations, how much to personal retaliation for opposing his enlarged plans, and removing him from the Presidency, he knows, and I do not. But the change as yet seems to have been beneficial to the public, and especially to Chicago. Notwithstanding stockholders grumble for want of dividends, if necessary to have withheld them to make connection with the Pacific road from Omaha, what reasonable man can doubt the wisdom? In this land of great enterprises, developing with railroad speed, plans and means adapted to former measures of progress, are wholly misplaced, injurious to the public, unwise to stockholders. To forego dividends of 10 or 20 per cent, such as the old Galena paid, may be quite unpleasant, yet it may be very wise. The *Chicago Tribune*, February 18th, had a full account of railroads from which we quote largely. It thus spoke of the Galena—

Mr. Ogden repudiates his declaration. Built a true N. Western.

Change a public good.

Dividends well used.

Old measures will not answer.

Chi. Tribune.

Our First Railroad.—The organization of the first line of our present magnificent railway system dates back thirty-one years, to 1836, when the Galena & Chicago Union Railroad—the pioneer road of Illinois—was incorporated by the Legislature. At that time there were only about 1,000 miles of railroad in the United States. The time proved a disastrous one for public undertakings, as the financial crash came in the year following, making it impossible to go on with the work. It lay dormant for ten years, when, in 1847, the first rail of strap iron was laid on the present line to Freeport. In 1850 it had reached Elgin, forty-two miles from Chicago, and from there it was soon built to Freeport, where it connects with the Illinois Central Road for Dunlieth and Dubuque. About this time the Company purchased the Mississippi & Rock River Junction Railroad and completed it as the Dixon Air Line Road, to the Mississippi at Fulton, in 1855.

Old Galena railroad.

In 1836 1,000 miles in U. S.

1850 at Elgin, 42 miles.

Dixon Air Line, 1855.

In 1864 this parent road was purchased by its young and ambitious son, the Chicago & Northwestern, and absorbed in it, losing its old and honored name.

1864 absorbed by N. W.

Although the road was projected from a little trading town back upon the almost unsettled prairie, its coming caused villages and farm houses to rise along the way with marvelous rapidity, furnishing to it, almost from the very first year, a liberal and profitable business. In 1850 the dividends of the road were 10 per cent.; in 1851, 15 per cent.; in 1852, 15 per cent.; in 1853, 20 per cent.; 1854, 21 per cent.; in 1855, 17 per cent.; in 1856, 22 per cent.; and previous to its sale to the Northwestern Company, its stock was in demand at as high as 24 per cent. above par.

Its developing the country.

Large dividends.

Thus this parent road of Chicago, built as an experiment, and with much misgiving and doubt, proved to be very profitable, returning handsome dividends to the men who had the courage to inaugurate the bold system of railways which has made Chicago what she is, and whose receipts from this city alone reached, in 1867, the immense sum of $11,680,938.

Its great success.

The Chicago & Northwestern Railroad.—In 1848 a charter was procured by the officers of the Galena & Chicago Union Railroad Company for a branch of their road into Wisconsin, to be called the Beloit & Madison Railroad. Various changes and combinations took place, the Illinois & Wisconsin Railroad Company being incorporated 1851 and merged in 1855 with the Rock River Valley Railroad (formerly the Beloit & Madison,) into the Chicago, St. Paul & Fond du Lac. In 1857 this road was consolidated with the Wisconsin & Superior Railroad, which had received valuable land grants for a line to the great iron and copper regions of

Chi. & N. W.

Changes and combinations.

Re-organized 1859.

Lake Superior. In the revulsion of 1857 the Chicago, St. Paul & Fond du Lac Railroad was mostly ruined. It survived the storm, though badly shattered, and in 1859 was organized as the Chicago & Northwestern Railroad.

1864 bought the Galena.

In 1864 the Chicago & Northwestern achieved a great step in obtaining control of the Galena & Chicago Union Railroad, then one of the best paying roads in the country.

Dixon Air Line, or Fulton branch.

Bridge over Mississippi.

Connects with Pacific at Omaha.

The Fulton branch, which was included in this consolidation, is, with its extension across Iowa, perhaps the most important branch of the great line, on account of the vast westward region which it will open up. It runs due West 136 miles almost on an air line to the Mississippi, at Fulton, where it crosses on a splendid bridge, erected in a rapid current, in some places forty feet deep, at a cost of $400,000, and pushes on across the rich fields of Iowa towards the Missouri River at Omaha, which place it reached early in 1867, being 500 miles west of Chicago. Here it connects with the Great Union Pacific Railroad, which is already built 540 miles westward, over the plains towards the gold mines of the Rocky Mountains, and the rich valleys of the Pacific coast. When this great enterprise is completed, which will be probably by 1871, the whole immense territory from Lake Michigan to San Francisco will be bound by a continuous line of rail.

Chi. & Mil. absorbed.

Peninsula road.

Steamers connect from Green Bay.

In 1865 the Chicago & Milwaukee became a permanent part of the great Chicago & Northwestern system by virtue of a perpetual lease. In 1862 the Peninsula Railroad was chartered by the Legislature of Michigan, to run from Escanaba, or Green Bay, to the great iron region at Negaunee, sixty-two miles, and thirteen miles south of Marquette, and in 1864 the Chicago & Northwestern Company obtained control of this also. The remaining link to Marquette on Lake Superior is supplied by the Michigan & Bay de Noquet Railroad. This line, in connection with the fine steamers which run from Escanaba and Green Bay, one hundred miles, where the main line of the Chicago & Northwestern Railroad terminates, forms a delightful route for summer travel, and opens up the great lumber and mining regions of Wisconsin and Michigan.

Extension from Madison to St. Paul.

An enterprise of scarcely less importance than any of those already mentioned, is now on foot to extend the Madison Division of the great Northwestern system to Winona, and thence up the Mississippi to St. Paul, tapping the immense fur and other business of the Northwest. The distance from Madison to Winona is about 130 miles, and from thence to St. Paul about 90 more—making 220 to be built. Negotiations are now pending in regard to the construction of this important line, which, it is hoped, will be successful.

Officers.

The principal officers of the Chicago & Northwestern Railway are: President, Wm. B. Ogden. Vice President, Perry H. Smith. Secretary, James R. Young. Treasurer, Albert L. Pritchard. General Superintendent, George L. Dunlap.

Takes all points from N. to W.

A dangerous power.

Charter granted without experience.

Rival lines should not be consolidated.

Subject cannot be discussed.

Truly northwestern is that, for it runs to all points from due north to due west. No such corporation ought to have existence, for it is too dangerous a power to entrust to any one directory. Still it exists, and exists according to law, and until it unduly encroaches upon public rights and interests, it must and will be continued to the end of its charter. This charter was granted before any experience with railways, and my letters to the *Boston Courier* in 1847 (p. 21) urged as an inducement to invest in the Galena Company, that they could build a branch down Fox River, connecting with Alton and St. Louis. But experience teaches us the dangers of consolidating what should be separate if not rival lines to protect public interests. The risk of excessive competition to the injury of stockholders is very slight; at all events can never countervail for the danger of exorbitant rates where companies have no competition. But although it was my design to discuss this question here, and exhibit the propriety of consolidating longitudinal lines, not parallel, it is not essential to the present purpose and must be passed over.* Yet even this gigantic scheme, the consummation of which has given Mr. Ogden the cognomen of Railway King, has competition from other powerful corporations.

The Illinois Central, having the continuation of the line from Freeport to Dunleith, which is continuing across Iowa, is a strong competitor with the Northwestern. As business shall increase from the west, the Illinois Central will find it necessary to construct an independent and direct line to Chicago from Freeport. It is well for the public, and especially for Chicago, that two such powerful corporations should be rivals in the field beyond the Mississippi, as well as this side. Said the *Tribune*:—

Illinois Cent.

An independent line from Freeport.

Chi. Tribune.

The Illinois Central Railroad.—This road had its origin in the year 1850, when Stephen A. Douglas and General Shields obtained from Congress a grant of alternate sections of land on both sides of the proposed route, through the richest portions of the Garden State, giving it an immense and increasing revenue from their sale, without which encouragement the road would not have been undertaken. In 1852 the officers of the road applied for permission to enter the city along the lake shore, which was granted, and the Illinois Central, fifteen years ago, was added to our railroad system.

Origin of Ill. Cent.

Land grant.

Began 15 years ago.

This is our southern line penetrating the State from the west to its extreme limit at the point formed by the Ohio and Mississippi Rivers at Cairo, 363 miles from Chicago. After pursuing a southwesterly direction from this city the road unites at Centralia, 253 miles distant, with the North Division, which starts at Dunleith, 343 miles away, at the extreme northern limit of the State, and thence runs due south to its terminus. The total length of this immense line is 706 miles, and, with its vast grants of government land, which are gradually being sold and settled, it is one of the most wealthy and important corporations in the country. The value of this road in opening up and developing the agricultural and mineral wealth of the State can hardly be over-estimated. At Cairo connections are made with the trade of the great rivers and the Southern cotton and sugar fields, while the lower portion of this State, with their high temperature and varied productions of fruit and grain, pour in an unfailing supply of necessaries and luxuries to our northern market. The Illinois Central very materially facititated the speedy and safe transfer of fruit from this garden region by placing upon their road fast fruit-trains in the strawberry and peach seasons, bringing these delicious products fresh from the garden and orchard, so that they could be in the hands of the dealers, and perhaps on the tables of our citizens, in the early morning, twelve or fifteen hours after they left the vines or trees. The amount of fruit shipped during the last season was 14,000 bushels of berries and 389,000 baskets of peaches, which, with small lots of other fruits and vegetables, made nearly *nine millions* of pounds. Of this vast aggregate Chicago received 12,500 bushels of berries and 289,191 boxes of peaches, the larger part of which were consumed in this city.

Runs 363 miles to Cairo.

Line from Centralia to Dunleith 343 miles.

Developed the State.

River connections south.

Fruit traffic.

14,000 bushels berries. 389,000 baskets peaches.

The Central effected an important extension on Oct. 1, 1867, by leasing for twenty years, for a rent of thirty-five per cent of the gross earnings, the Dubuque & Sioux City Railroad, which is already completed due west from Dubuque 143 miles to Iowa Falls, with a branch fifty-three miles long running southwest from Farley to Cedar Rapids, on the Chicago & Northwestern Railroad. It also connects at Cedar

Dubuque and Sioux City extension.

* Yet I cannot forbear to observe, that beyond a doubt we shall find we have a sovereign remedy for oppressive monopolies, in the judicious exercise of State Sovereignty; as in the rightful annihilation by the Sovereignty of New York, of the manorial rights. And only let it be well understood that the remedy exists, and its application will seldom be necessary. It is true that a State may come under the domination of a corporation, as New Jersey is ruled by the Camden & Amboy monopoly. But as before observed, when we come to apprehend the doctrine of State Rights, and the strength of covenant obligations, guaranteeing equal rights and privileges to all the citizens of all these States; most assuredly we shall find means without resorting to Congress, which hasno right to interfere in the premises, to remedy the outrage. Would the two great States of New York and Pennsylvania submit to the discrimination against them which New Jersey authorizes, if they apprehended the principles of National Union based upon State Sovereignty? But it is equally unjust to all these States.

A relief from monopolies in State Sovereignty.

Camden & Amboy to be righted.

Falls, ninety-nine miles from Dubuque, with the Cedar Falls & Mineapolis Railroad, which is being built northward through Western Iowa and Minnesota. The Illinois Central thus gains a large and constantly increasing amount of travel and trade from these two fine States. The company is now perfecting facilities for shipping freight across the Mississippi, between Dubuque and Dunleith, without breaking bulk, and is building for this purpose barges capable of carrying five loaded cars each. The company has also contracted for a new first-class ferry-steamer, to be delivered at the opening of navigation next spring. It is their intention to have facilities for transferring, both ways, two hundred and twenty freight cars a day, if necessary.

Important region. Large ferry-boat.

The original grant of land to this company was for 2,595,000 acres. These lands have been in the market for twelve years, during which time 1,885,000 acres have been disposed of. In the early days the sales were made upon long time and at a low rate of interest, to induce settlers of small means to start and bring the lands into immediate cultivation and production. For the last three years the terms of payment have been either cash or upon short credit. No actual settler has ever been deprived of his home through harsh measures of the company, and up to January 1 last, full title papers have been passed for 907,365 acres. The number of deeds and contracts for farm lands issued to the same time has been 37,144, for an aggregate of over twenty millions of dollars. The business of the last year has been 203,834 acres, sold to 2,633 settlers, at an average of 10.67 per acre. One hundred and thirty-five thousand acres of these lands sold in 1867 lie on the Chicago Branch, in the great corn, cattle, hog and fruit producing districts directly tributary in business to the city of Chicago.

Land grant 2,595,000 acres. Credit sales. No forfeitures. Present sales.

The lands are sold in tracts of forty acres and upwards, at from $6 to $12 per acre, and are being taken up by a thrifty class of settlers who soon cover the wild prairie with waving cornfields and blossoming orchards. The road is thus developing the country, which will in turn support the road.

Price $6 to $12.

The Land Department in itself furnishes an immense business, as the foregoing figures show, though its operations make but little noise. It has a handsome stone building on Michigan avenue, built by the Illinois Central Railroad Company for its use, at a cost of $80,000, and employs some twenty-five persons in the Chicago offices. The Land Commissioner is John B. Calhoun, and the Salesman, C. P Holden.

Land Department heavy.

The chief officers of the Illinois Central are: President, John M. Douglas. General Superintendent, M. P. Hughitt. Secretary and Treasurer, M. K. Ackerman. General Passenger Agent, W. P. Johnson.

Officers.

Mich. Cent. Difficulties with Ia. and Ill. to reach Chi.

The Michigan Central was obliged to come in upon the Illinois Central line. It is difficult to account for the opposition which that important road had, both from Indiana and Illinois. Indiana refusing a charter, the New Albany & Salem charter for a railroad 35 miles long from the Ohio river was obtained, and an amendment procured from the Legislature, with the right of indefinite extension. The Michigan Central supplied funds to extend it 255 miles to Michigan City, thence to the Illinois line. To make the three miles connexion with the Illinois Central, a blind charter for a Union Railroad had been obtained from the Illinois Legislature. Jointly the Michigan and Illinois Centrals have constructed the breakwater, shielding the shore from abrasion by the lake, and at an immense expense have raised out of the water the extensive depot grounds, affording the very best facilities by lake and canal, and rail. This is one of the railroads which is in the hands chiefly of the original stockholders, and has paid regular dividends.

Union with Ills. Cent. in depots.

Chi. Tribune. Says the *Tribune*:—

Progress of Mich. Cent.

It was projected in 1842 and built in that year, from Detroit eastward to Ypsilanti, but did not reach Chicago until May 21st, 1852, previous to which time passengers between Chicago and Buffalo crossed the lake to St. Joseph, and travelled by stage until they reached its terminus. For more than twenty years this road has gone steadily on in prosperity, with hardly a change in its management. Its total length is 284 miles. Four through trains are run daily, besides a local between Detroit and Dexter, and the Cincinnati express, between Michigan City and Chicago. 20 years of success.

In December last a party of business men from this city, and from places along the line of the excursion, celebrated the opening of the Jackson, Lansing & Saginaw Railroad, which now constitutes an important branch of the Michigan Central, and brings a large amount of business to this city. It runs from Jackson, on the latter road, and 202 miles from Chicago, nearly north, through Lansing, the capital of Michigan, Owasso, on the Detroit & Milwaukee Railroad, and other growing towns, to Saginaw City and Bay City, near Saginaw Bay, tapping the great lumber and salt regions of the Saginaw Valley, which already contains many populous towns and cities, and looks to Chicago as its most advantageous market for the sale of products and the purchase of supplies. The new road is 100 miles long. Line to Saginaw. Route. Looks to Chi. for market.

The Michigan Central is, with many, the favorite route to the East, being always splendidly managed, and connecting, as it does at Detroit, with the Great Western Railroad, through a fine portion of Canada, and at Niagara, where the traveller has an opportunity to view the watery wonder of the world, with the New York Central railroad for the metropolis. Pullman's celebrated hotel and sleeping cars take the passenger from Chicago to Rochester without a single change, and it is intended soon to run them through to New York direct. Favorite route for travel.

The principal officers of the road are: President—James F. Joy. General Superintendent—H. E. Sargent. Assistant General Superintendent—W. K. Muir. The Passenger Agent at Chicago is H. C. Wentworth. Officers.

One of the strongest points of this argument in favor of the certain continuation of the railway system as now instituted, and its spread indefinitely into the Great Interior, is the direct interest which capitalists of eastern roads, mainly residents in New York and New England, have in the construction of extending lines with ramifying branches. An off-shoot of the Michigan Central, running into its depot, a large part of the stock held by the same parties, with the same capable President over both, is— An important point is the interest eastern capitalists have in Chi. roads.

The Chicago, Burlington & Quincy. Said the *Tribune*:— *Tribune.*

This road justly claims to be one of the best managed and most profitable roads in the West, and is one of the very few railroads in the West which is in the hands of the original stockholders, who, in this case, are receiving handsome dividends on their investments. Its friends are in the habit of saying that its initials, "C. B. & Q.," properly indicate its characteristics as the "Cheapest, Best and Quickest." The line runs southwest, through some of the finest and best developed agricultural regions of the State, to Burlington, 210 miles from Chicago, with a branch of 100 miles, from Galesburg to Quincy, a branch from Galesburg to Peoria, 54 miles, and a branch from Yates City to Rushville, 62 miles, making entire length 426 miles. Chi., Burlington & Quincy. "C.,B. & Q." Route.

The part of what is now the Chicago, Burlington & Quincy Railroad which was first operated was the Aurora Branch Railroad, which in the fall of 1852 was completed thirteen miles, from Aurora to the Junction, on the Galena & Chicago Union road. In the fall of 1853 it was completed southwest to Mendota, forty-five miles from Aurora. About 1856, the Chicago & Aurora road was consolidated with the Central Military Tract Railroad, from Mendota to Galesburg, and with the Peoria & Oquawka Railroad, the western part of which was between Galesburg and Burlington. About the same time a consolidation was effected with the Northern Cross Railroad, from Galesburg to Burlington, thus completing the Chicago, Burlington & Quincy Railroad. Until 1863, the trains of this road ran into the city over the Galena & Chicago Railroad track, from the Junction, thirty miles out, but in that year the Company completed its own track, entering the city along Sixteenth street. Beginning in 1852, 13 miles to Aurora. Consolidation with others. 1863, built track into city.

Iowa extension. Burlington & Mo. road. Hannibal & St. Joe. Atchison and Kansas City. 3 bridges.

The road is now virtually extended into Iowa by a contract made with the Burlington & Missouri Railroad, which is already built 156 miles west of Burlington, forming a very important connection, as it taps the richest portion of Iowa, and is rapidly extending toward the Missouri, at or near Omaha. The Hannibal & St. Joseph Railroad, which runs across the great State of Missouri, from opposite Quincy, is also a very important feeder, connecting with Atchison, Kansas, and thence with the Central Branch of the Union Pacific Railroad. Costly and extensive iron bridges at Burlington, Quincy and Kansas City, each about 2,000 feet long, are now being erected across the Mississippi, and their completion will greatly facilitate the business of the road.

Mo. Valley railroad. Connects with Pacific at Omaha.

The Council Bluffs & St. Joseph Railroad, which runs parallel to the Missouri, between these two cities, is being rapidly pushed from both ends, fifty-five miles being already in operation from Council Bluffs. The entire road will probably be completed during the coming summer, and will then prove a valuable feeder to the Chicago, Burlington & Quincy Railroad, through its immediate connection with the Hannibal & St. Joseph Railroad, and will undoubtedly attract a considerable share of business from the Union Pacific Road at Omaha.

Officers.

The officers of the road are as follows: President, James F. Joy. Secretary and Treasurer, Amos T. Hall. Superintendent, Robert Harris. Assistant Superintendents, A. N. Towne, H. Hitchcock and S. S. Greeley. General Freight Agent, E. R. Wadsworth. General Ticket Agent, Samuel Powell.

Old Aurora road. Advantage of diagonal line. Atchison road. Kansas Pacific. Lawrence and Galveston.

When it was determined fourteen years ago by Mr. Stephen F. Gale and a few others, that the Aurora road should be continued on to Quincy, it required no great foresight to perceive the advantages which a southwest road through such a region as the Military Tract, must have. Its diagonal course gives it great advantage over a direct line west, and it is already fed by the important lines, the Burlington & Missouri, which will connect with the Pacific at Omaha, and with the Hannibal & St. Joseph, which is also fed by the Atchison, a road already in use about 100 miles, and also with the Kansas Pacific. With the latter road, too, it has another connection, by the Cameron road and a bridge now building at Kansas City. And at Lawrence it connects with the Galveston road, now in use 30 miles, which is to be finished through to the State line this autumn.*

Chi. R. I. & Pacific. Prophecy fulfilled.

The Chicago, Rock Island & Pacific Railroad.—This is one of the roads urged upon Boston capitalists in 1847, (see p. 22,) the completion of which to Council Bluffs I predicted "within 20 years." Though wrong as to the road, yet the prophecy held good. The Rock Island is only a little behind, and will be there within a year, unless stock-jobbers prevent.

Mr. Farnum. Mr. Sheffield. Charter obtained. Road built.

In 1850 Mr. Henry Farnum came out at Mr. Ogden's invitation to look at the Galena road, with reference to engaging in its construction. Not arranging to his satisfaction, he considered the Rock Island route, and proposed to his friend, Mr. Joseph E. Sheffield of New Haven, Conn., to come out and examine it. The result was they obtained a charter and built the road. They had a very few subscriptions along the route, but most of the funds they raised themselves, Mr. Sheffield being a large capitalist and able to control funds for any enterprise he would undertake. Mr. Farnum

---

Osage Indian lands sold to U. S.

* The *Chicago Times* has advices from Kansas, May 30, that a treaty has just been concluded with the Osage Indians, who cede to the United States 8,000,000 acres of land through which the Galveston road is to pass. It is a very beneficial transaction to this road.

carefully superintended the construction. It has almost uniformly paid dividends. The *Tribune* observed :— *Chi. Tribune*

This road bears off in a southwesterly direction to Rock Island, on the Mississippi, at the mouth of Rock River, 82 miles from Chicago. It was commenced in April, 1852, and completed in February, 1854, being only one year and ten months. Here it crosses the river on a fine and costly bridge, and joins what was formerly the Mississippi & Missouri Railroad, with which the Chicago & Rock Island Road was consolidated August 20, 1865, the name being changed to the present one. The great consolidated line, therefore, will eventually reach from Chicago to the Mississippi, and thence directly across the broad and fertile State of Iowa to Council Bluffs, opposite Omaha, on the Missouri River. The road is already in operation to DesMoines, the Capital of Iowa, and is being rapidly pushed northwesterly to Council Bluffs. Within a few weeks the directors of the road have issued additional stock to the amount of $4,900,000, for the completion of this important part of the line, and a large portion of it has been sold at nearly par value, the road ranking among the most prosperous roads in the West. When the line is completed it will be the shortest route from Chicago to the Missouri, and of course receive a large addition to its business. It is already graded about fifty miles beyond DesMoines. The company has now 182 miles of main line in operation in Illinois, and a branch of forty-six miles from Bureau to Peoria, and by its consolidation with the Mississippi & Missouri, it now operates 450 miles of road.

Commenced 1852, finished 1854. 1 year 10 months.

Extension to Council Bluffs.

Shortest line.

Has now 450 miles.

The last annual report, dated April 1st, 1867, shows the following facts: The cost of the road, equipments, land and all other property was $15,313,822. This includes the cost of the two consolidated lines, the Chicago & Rock Island and the Mississippi & Missouri. To aid the latter a large amount of land was granted by the acts of Congress and the Legislature of Iowa, of which there has been certified by the Government of the United States to the company $481,000.

Cost $15,313,-822.

Land grant

There has been a large amount of rolling stock placed upon the line during the year, and a splendid depot in Chicago has been built in common with the Michigan Southern Railroad. The receipts of the road last year amounted to $3,574,033; the expenditures, $1,995,034; leaving as the net earnings $1,578,999. The company have 92 engines, 46 passenger coaches, 20 baggage and express cars, and 880 other cars. The amount of freight transported was 1,197,824,158 pounds.

Improvements.

Receipts and net earnings

During the year the company have built, about two miles south of the city limits, a large round house and very extensive car shops, which will probable employ nearly a thousand men, and quite a village has already begun to spring up there. Speculators have bought up tracts of land adjoining the works and divided them into lots, which they have sold, or still hold, at almost city prices, and when, as in due time no doubt will be the case, frequent "dummy" trains are run to this point, stopping at every street for passengers, a populous suburb will grow up along the line.

Work-shops at Chi.

Increased value of property.

The principal officers of the Chicago, Rock Island & Pacific Railroad Company, are as follows: President and General Superintendent, John F. Tracy. Treasurer, E. W. Dunham. Secretary, Francis H. Tows. Assistant General Superintendent, P. A. Hall.

Officers.

This mammoth corporation, however, is at present in the hands of stock-gamblers. It would seem that "a pool" has been made up to "bull" the Northwestern; and after obtaining a majority of that stock, in order to give it greater buoyancy, they endeavored to obtain control also of the Rock Island, in order to stop the road at Des Moines, giving the Northwestern the advantage of sole connection with the Pacific at Omaha. But Mr. Tracy, the able President of the Rock Island, very shrewdly took advantage of this new demand, and put 49,000 shares, $4.900,000 of stock, quietly upon the market, to obtain funds to build the road from Des Moines to Omaha. This being precisely what the Wall street sharks did not want, they have resorted to the New York courts to advance their schemes, and Mr. Tracy to the Iowa courts and Legislature to protect public interests and

Stock-gamblers at work.

Injuring R. I. to benefit N. W.

Mr. Tracy too sharp for them.

Courts used.

Iowa Legislature.

secure the completion of the road. The Legislature legalized the sale of stock, which was a fair and legitimate operation, and also required the immediate construction of the road through to Omaha.

N. Y. Sun.

The *New York Sun* of 29th May, had this sensible view:—

Objects of Wall street sharks.

The Approaching Annual Meeting of the Chicago, Rock Island & Pacific.—The approaching Rock Island meeting, called on the 3d prox., is assuming great importance. The promised success of the disaffected is supposed by some to have run the stock up to 98½ to-day; but others believe that the market was made active for the purpose of unloading the stock, not having confidence in a satisfactory result from the meeting. Disguise it as we may, it is known by all interested in Wall street, that the parties initiating this call were induced to make their purchases of Rock Island under the belief that they could prevent the extension of the road to Council Bluffs, which would afford a more direct communication with the Pacific road than that already built in connection with the Chicago & Northwestern road; but being defeated by the issue of 49,000 shares, they were foiled in their purpose, and now are attempting to gain an advantage for their investment in the Chicago & Northwestern pool. The Chicago & Northwestern railroad, with its large earnings, showing an increase of two and one-half millions over the previous year, and earning more net income than the New York Central, its managers can well afford to allow the Rock Island extension, without attempting to swallow a competing corporation, by a system of devices which, although admirable in Wall street, cannot be commended in other walks of life.

To prevent continuation of R. I. to Omaha.

N. W. can afford to let it be built.

Purchasers inimical to R. I.

If legitimate purchasers of Rock Island stock, why desire to prevent the building of the most important part of the line, through to Omaha, giving it the large share of that immense traffic to which it is entitled as the direct road? Is it not evident that ulterior, unnatural purposes controlled these new purchases? Nor was it the present directory of the Northwestern, or the shareholders which elected them, who are these buyers. An entire change in the Directory of the Northwestern is to be effected that these stock-gamblers may create a factitious demand for the Northwestern. It is doubtless for that purpose that the operation has been made, and not, as the *Sun* says, that having been foiled in regard to the Rock Island, they "now are attempting to gain an advantage in the Northwestern pool."

New interests in N. W.

Stock. gambling.

Mere surmise.

This, of course, is mere surmise, which events only can determine. * Another solution is made, in that the holders in Milwaukee roads are endeavoring to obtain the control of the Northwestern, to prevent the construction of the line from Madison to St. Paul, and other diversions adverse to Milwaukee. It is one of the evils of these railways, that the corporations can thus be used for private schemes, adverse to public interests. But these general interests will eventually rule, and the capital will be employed to construct all lines which are important to the traffic of the country; and if there be a natural converging point, as the existing system so plainly indicates, it will become so more and more as the present lines are extended and new ones created.

Public interests can be made subservient. Yet will rule ultimately.

Stockholders' meeting of N. W. Change of Directors.

* Since that was in type, the annual meeting of the Northwestern Company has been held 4th June. Incorrectness is acknowledged with pleasure, in saying there was to be an entire change in the Directors. Mr. Ogden with usual grace, withdraws from the Presidency; but Messrs. Smith, Dunlap, Turner and Ferry are elected Directors, and very likely may be continued in their offices. Should there be an opportunity to correct further anticipations of perversion of the road from its legitimate purposes, and from public interests, it will be cheerfully embraced. But it is foreign to the purposes of this effort to enter into the projects of stock-operators, farther than is necessary to exhibit their effects upon public interests.

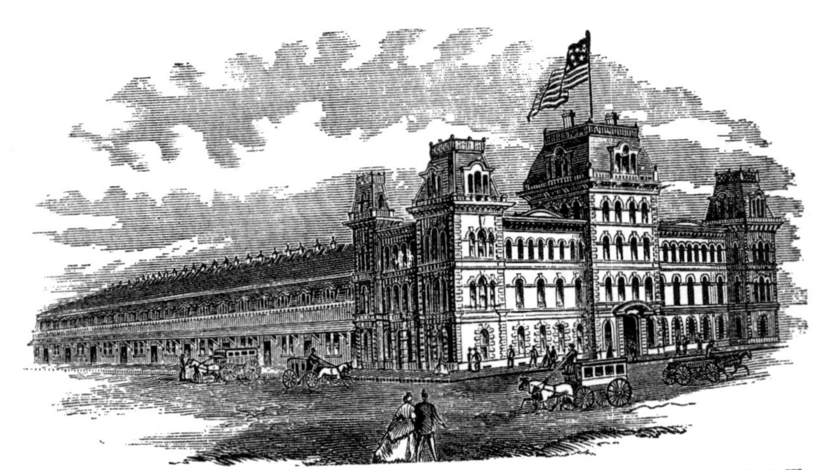

MICHIGAN SOUTHERN AND ROCK ISLAND DEPOT.

Mich. South. & North. Ind. Trains from Chi. 20 Feb. 1852. Chi. Tribune.

The Michigan Southern & Northern Indiana Railroad.—This important road, next to the Galena in running trains from Chicago, which was done 20th February, 1852, has had its ups and downs, its stock having been almost valueless, though for several years approaching par, notwithstanding dividends have been withheld to make necessary improvements in the road. Its elegant depot is thus described by the *Tribune* :—

Depot. Cost $250,000 Description. Fr't depot.

This company, in conjunction with the Chicago, Rock Island & Pacific Railroad Company, completed, in May last, on Van Buren street, between Griswold and Sherman streets, an immense and magnificent union passenger depot; the finest, it is said in the whole country, in point of size and accommodations. It is of stone, in the Italian style, and cost $250,000. The length is 594 feet, the width 160 feet. The front section, which contains the general offices of both companies, is 52 feet deep by 160 feet wide, and three stories high. On the front are three towers, the middle one eighty feet high, and the two at the corners each 74½ feet high. The Michigan Southern Road has also built during the year an immense brick freight depot, south of the passenger depot, on Griswold street, north of Polk, 51 feet wide and 603 feet long, containing standing room for twenty cars, and storage room for two thousand tons. The front portion is two stories high and contains the freight offices. The building cost $47,000.

Officers.

Its chief officers are, President, E. B. Phillips, Chicago; Treasurer, Le Grand Lockwood, New York; General Superintendent, Charles F. Hatch, Chicago; and Chief Engineer, Chas. Paine, Chicago; Com. Freight Agent, Chas. M. Gray, Chicago.

Chi. Rep.

The *Chicago Republican* of January 22d, 1867, gave an elaborate history of the road from which the following is taken :—

2 companies consolidated.

The Michigan Southern & Northern Indiana Railroad Company was formed April 25, 1855, by the consolidation of two previously existing companies, viz: the Michigan Southern Railroad Company and the Northern Indiana Railroad Company.

Mich. South. chartered 1846.

The Michigan Southern Railroad Company was chartered by the State of Michigan May 9, 1846, in pursuance of an act authorizing the sale to them of the Michigan Southern Railroad, and Tecumseh (now Jackson) branch, both owned and operated by the State of Michigan. The organiaztion was completed, and the conditions of the act complied with, in December, 1846, so that the Michigan Southern railroad entered into possession of said road and branch that year.

North. Ind. chartered 1835: Buffalo & Miss. Co

The Northern Indiana railroad, as it stood at the time of the consolidation with the Michigan Southern Railroad Company, in 1855, originated in a company first chartered in Indiana, in 1835, as the "Buffalo and Mississippi Railroad Company," which, with a company chartered in Ohio, March 3d, 1851, as the "Northern Indiana Railroad Company," and another organized in Illinois, under the general railroad law of that State, as the "Northern Indiana and Chicago Railroad Company," had become merged into one, known as the Northern Indiana Railroad Company.

Mich. South. begun 1838. Through to Chi. 1852.

The Michigan Southern Railroad, from Monroe westward, was commenced by the State of Michigan about 1838, but was only finished to Hillsdale at the time of the sale to the Michigan Southern Railroad Company, in 1846. It was extended by that company, in 1852, to the Indiana State line, near Middlebury, and connected there with the Northern Indiana railroad, which was completed to Chicago in June, 1852.

Mich. branches. Goshen branch.

The Tecumseh (or Jackson) branch was extended to Jackson, from 1853 to 1856; and a branch was built from Constantine, the terminus of the old Michigan Southern railroad, to Three Rivers, in Michigan, in 1853. The Goshen branch (formerly so called) forms part of the Goshen Air Line, from Toledo to Elkhart, where it connects with the old line from Monroe to Chicago.

Several roads consolidated.

The Erie and Kalamazoo railroad, from Toledo to Adrian, leased from the Erie and Kalamazoo Railroad Company, is run and used as part of the old or main line from Toledo to Chicago; and part of the Detroit, Monroe and Toledo railroad, mostly built by the Michigan Southern and Northern Indiana Railroad Company, and exclusively controlled and operated by them, is used as far as Monroe as part of the Michigan Southern railroad line from Detroit to Chicago—said Detroit, Monroe, and Toledo railroad being also used as a line from Detroit to Toledo, connecting there with roads to Cincinnati, Cleveland, and all points east, south, and southwest.

Through to Chi. 22 May, 1852. On the 22d of May, 1852, the entire line was opened, and a passenger train went through to Chicago. A large portion of the track was laid in the very severe winter of 1851–2, and consequently was in poor order, and had to be run over with care. The work of adjusting and ballasting the track, with the road in operation, involved a heavy expense.

Line built in 20 months. In the space of twenty months, embracing two winters (one particularly severe for such work) and one summer, the company constructed about one hundred and sixty miles of new road, and relaid, and nearly re-built, fifty miles of old road. The construction of a line of railroad of this length, in so short a time, was then looked upon as without precedent.

Early difficulties. Should this article meet the eye of any of the old stockholders, they will recollect the difficulty of procuring subscriptions to the stock. The Directors had strong confidence in the success of the undertaking, but the general feeling of Distrust of West capitalists was distrust of Western investments, and very few men were disposed to hazard any considerable amount in the undertaking. And, in addition to this, the financial crisis of 1851 came at a time most embarrassing to the affairs of the companies. During the whole progress of the work they encountered an active hostility, which was directed against their credit, assailing their securities, discrediting their finances, and, as far as possible, impairing the confidence of those Triumph over obstacles. engaged in the work. It is sufficient, at this time, to say that all obstacles were surmounted, active progress maintained, and the work brought into use with unprecedented rapidity.

Chi. & Alton. *The Chicago & Alton Railroad.*—This is another of the important lines anticipated in 1847, which fell into the hands of speculators, but is now a *Chi. Tribune.* completely equipped, well managed railroad. Says the *Tribune:*—

Length 275 miles. This road strikes the Mississippi at Alton, 275 miles from Chicago, where it connects with the Alton & St. Louis Railroad, which is operated and virtually owned by the same company, (the payments of $800,000 for its purchase being nearly To St. Louis 7 miles. completed) and follows the river to St. Louis, 282 miles from Chicago. Here connections are made with lines of steamers up and down the Mississippi and up the Connections there. Missouri to the wilds and gold fields of the northern Territories, and with the Missouri and Kansas Pacific Railroads and other lines through the great State of Consolidation of roads. Missouri. The road is formed by the consolidation of several distinct lines of which the first was the Joliet & Chicago, to which the right to enter the city on the Archer road was given January 5th, 1857. The earnings are reported below from the organization of the road in 1855.

Changes of Co. The Chicago & Alton Railroad proper was built under two charters—the first to the Alton & Sangamon Railroad, granted February 27, 1847, and the second to the Chicago & Mississippi Railroad, granted June 19, 1852. In 1855 the name of the road was changed to the Chicago, Alton & St. Louis Railroad; the company was again reorganized under the title of the St. Louis, Alton & Chicago Railroad in 1857, and again, for the third time, reorganized in October, 1862, as the Chicago & Alton Railroad

Alton to Springfield, 1853. The first portion of the present line that was constructed was the Alton & Sangamon Railroad, from Alton to Springfield, which was completed in 1853. The Chicago & Mississippi Railroad, from Springfield to Joliet, was next built, in 1854, Springfield to Joliet, 1854. and arrangements were made with the Chicago & Rock Island Railroad, from this city to Joliet, and with the Terre Haute, Alton & St. Louis, between the two last named places, completed the line from Chicago to St. Louis. In 1857 the Joliet & Joliet to Chi. 1857. Chicago Railroad was built under a separate charter, and the trains of the Alton Road run over it until January, 1864, when it was perpetually leased by the latter, and in the same year the Alton & St. Louis Railroad was purchased, completing the ownership of the present Chicago & Alton Railroad Company of the entire road from Chicago to St. Louis.

Its vicissitudes. The road has passed through many financial vicissitudes since its organization, which seemed for a time to have utterly wrecked it. In December, 1859, its heavy Forclosure 1862. mortgages were foreclosed, and it passed into the hands of a receiver. In September, 1862, the road was sold at Joliet, under a decree of the United States Court,

Messrs. Samuel J. Tilden and S. H. Meyer becoming the purchasers for the bondholders. The road was then reorganized, the first mortgage bondholders receiving new bonds, the second mortgage bondholders receiving preferred stock, and the third mortgage bondholders receiving common stock. A large amount was spent in repairing and equipping the road, and it is now in splendid running condition, and is a first-class road, running through some of the best farming country in the State, most of which is thoroughly improved, and connecting the two principal cities of the West, between which there is a large and increasing amount of travel and business. Present firm condition.

The principal event of the year, in connection with the Chicago & Alton Road, has been the opening of the Chicago, Jacksonville & St. Louis Railroad, which runs from Bloomington, on this road, through Jacksonville, 150 miles, to Monticello, eight miles above Alton, where it connects again with the main line. This new line was opened September 23d, by a very pleasant excursion from this city, and it has since proved a very important feeder, as it taps a wide belt of splendid agricultural land which has been settled and developed for many years, but until this had no railroad communication. Although lying much nearer to St. Louis than to Chicago, by far the largest part of its grain and cattle are sent to this market, from which merchandise of all kinds are sent in return, to the profit of both seller and buyer. The fact that Chicago can draw trade from within forty or fifty miles of St. Louis, paying better prices for products and selling goods at lower rates, shows its superior advantages as a market. Jacksonville branch. Taps a fine country. Takes trade from near St. Louis to Chi.

The principal officers now are: President and General Superintendent, T. B. Blackstone; Secretary and Treasurer, W. M. Larrabee; Chief Engineer, K. F Booth. Officers.

The Pittsburgh, Fort Wayne & Chicago Railroad, connects with the Alton & St. Louis road, and have their depots together. It is in contemplation that these roads and the Northwestern shall join in erecting a depot of more gigantic dimensions and greater splendor than anything before conceived, much less executed. But even these gigantic corporations are so entirely subject to the most selfish schemes of heavy and unprincipled capitalists, that until a work is accomplished, it is impossible to say who may be favorable and who inimical. The *Tribune* says:— Pitts., Ft. W. & Chi. Fine depot in prospect. Railroads uncertain. *Chi. Tribune.*

This line is one of the longest roads in the country, running from Chicago to Pittsburgh, 468, miles, where it makes direct connection with the Pennsylvania Central Railroad across the Alleghanies to Harrisburgh, Philadelphia, Baltimore and New York. Long line, 468 miles.

The road was incorporated in 1852 as the Fort Wayne & Chicago Railroad. The work progressed slowly, the company not being able to make a free sale of its securities. In 1856 it was consolidated with the Pittsburgh Division under its present name and completed November 10th of the same year. In 1861 it met the fate of many Western roads, and was sold by a decree of the United States Circuit Court; being reorganized and placed in the hands of Trustees in February, 1862. Since then it has been very prosperous, doing an immense through as well as local business. Incorporated 1852. Foreclosed and sold 1861. Line prosperous.

The company has in contemplation the erection, in connection with the Chicago & Northwestern and the Chicago & Alton Railroad Companies, a splendid passenger depot, in the West Division near the river, and somewhere between Lake and Adams streets. The plans, which are already made, describe a massive stone structure *thirteen hundred* feet long, and costing nearly *two millions* of dollars, forming by far the finest railroad depot in the world. It was thought when this work was planned that the Chicago, Burlington & Quincy, the Michigan Central, and one or two other roads, would unite in the project, forming one grand union depot, into which trains from all directions should centre, obviating the great inconvenience and expense of omnibus and baggage transfer. Although the combination will not be as general as was first thought of, it will at least include three prominent lines which, with their branches, cover all points of the compass, and will prove a great convenience to the traveling public, as our two principal union depots now do. It may be some time before this immense work is commenced, but the three companies interested in it all need better depot accommodations, and will probably not defer it long. Large depot to be constructed. $2,000,000. Several will unite. Must be built.

Officers. The officers of the road mainly reside in Pittsburgh. They are: Geo. W Cass, President; J. N. McCullough, General Superintendent; J. P. Farley, Auditor; . P. Henderson, Secretary. The passenger agent in this city is W. C. Clelland.

Earnings, 1857 to 1867. The earnings of this road have been as follows: 1857, $1,660,424; 1858, $1,567,232; 1859, $1,965,987; 1860, $2,335,353; 1861, $3,031,787; 1862, $3,745,310; 1863, $5,132,933; 1864, $7,120,465; 1865, $8,489,062; 1866, $7,467,217; and 1867, $7,242,125.*

Pa. Cent., its support and Phila. This important road is supported by the capital and efforts of the Pennsylvania Central of which it is the main feeder, and by the capital and business of Philadelphia, as the previous named roads are by the capital of Competition with N. Y. and N. E. New York and New England. They are competitors with the Pennsylvania interest, in drawing business to Chicago, in order that they may obtain their due share of traffic, the natural course of which, to the extent that it is destined for the East, would be south of this. And this road is a competitor with them for both freight and passage for the region northwest Large Revenues of here. Its enormous revenues bespeak at once its importance, and the superiority of Chicago as the gathering point.

Col. Chi. & Ind. Cent. Baltimore & Ohio a competitor. *The Columbus, Chicago & Indiana Central Railroad Company.*—A close competitor with the Pennsylvania Central is the Baltimore & Ohio, in connexion with the Ohio & Indiana Central Roads, which has had its connexion with Chicago by lines which have several times been changed, as the Chi. Tribune. *Tribune* describes:—

Chi. & Gt. East. *The Chicago & Great Eastern Railroad.*—This is the most westerly of the roads radiating to the southeast, and is the most recent of the trunk lines of Chicago. It was formerly known as the Chicago & Cincinnati Air Line Railroad, and entered the city over the Pittsburgh & Fort Wayne Railroad from Valparaiso, forty miles Present route, 224 miles. distant. It now has its own track the entire distance from Richmond, Indiana, to Chicago, 224 miles, running parallel with and just west of the city limits to Kinzie street, and thence using the track of the C. & N. W. R. R., to the depot on the corner of Kinzie and West Water streets. The company propose, eventually, to erect a Richmond connections. fine passenger depot in Carroll street. At Richmond the road connects with the Cincinnati, Eaton & Richmond Railroad for Cincinnati, to which place it is the shortest route from Chicago, and where it connects with main lines for the West and South.

Consolidated with Col. & Ind. Cent. At a meeting of the stockholders on January 15th, it was voted to consolidate the road with the Columbus & Indiana Central Railroad, which runs from Columbus, Ohio, to Indianapolis, Ind., *via* Richmond, the terminus of the Chicago & Great Eastern Road, and has a branch which is just completed, running from Union, Ohio, through Logansport to the State line between Indiana and Illinois.

New Co. The stockholders of the Columbus & Indianapolis Central also voted, unanimously, on the 17th for the consolidation, which is therefore assured, and the directors of both roads will meet in Columbus on the 12th of February to elect Directors for the new company, which will be known as the

Col., Chi. & Ind. Cent. *The Columbus, Chicago & Indiana Central Railroad Company*, the name of the Chicago & Great Eastern Railroad thus passing out of existence.

Last link finished. The last rail in the Union & Logansport Railroad which forms a part of the new line, was laid on the 16th of January, making the connecting line for another and the next to the shortest route between Chicago and New York. It is expected that

---

This omitted in former table. * The list of earnings of Chicago roads, p. 41, did not contain this important road, the reports not having been received. Then, forgetting that another road was to be added, the page was stereotyped without leaving space for the addition.

the road will be opened for passenger travel about the last of February. The new line will embrace 718 miles of track, as follows: Chicago and Great Eastern, 224 miles; Indiana Central, 88 miles; Peoria, Logansport & Burlington, 183 miles; Union & Logansport, 93 miles. The main shops of the new company will be located at Logansport. 718 miles.

The officers are: B. E. Smith, President; W. D. Judson, Assistant President; J. E. Young, Vice President; James Alexander, Treasurer; G. Moodie, Secretary; J. M. Lunt, General Superintendent; C. W. Smith General Freight Agent. Officers.

It is the intention of the company to put the whole property in perfect order at the earliest possible moment, and to largely increase the equipments. The new portion of the line is being thoroughly ballasted, and, as soon as completed will be open as a through line between Chicago and Pittsburgh, New York, Philadelphia, Baltimore and Washington. A through line to seaboard.

The Directors are now in the city for the purpose of taking initiatory steps toward putting the whole of their long line of road, as well as their rolling stock, in the best possible repair. It is their intention, also, as soon as it is practicable, to erect depot buildings in this city, of a character that shall be commensurate with the importance of the line, and with Chicago as one of its terminal points. Thorough condition. Depot at Chi.

This line is now opened through and sending freight and passengers in large amounts directly to Pittsburgh, and will be almost as good a feeder to the Pennsylvania Central, as the Pittsburgh & Ft. Wayne. Is in full operation.

Although this Central route would seem to belong legitimately to the Baltimore & Ohio, yet that corporation seems to have lost the enterprise for which it was formerly distinguished, and the Pennsylvania Central now eclipses all others in enterprise, and far-reaching and wide spreading plans. It happens, too, that from Chicago to Pittsburgh is only 29 miles further by this Columbus route than by Ft. Wayne. So that it is not singular that the energetic Pennsylvania corporation should have secured this line to its interests also. If Baltimore is to avail itself of its advantages and obtain its part of the trade of the Great Interior, which formerly was duly appreciated, she must see to it that some of the old spirit be revived in the Baltimore & Ohio Railroad. Pa. supersedes Balt. & Ohio. Only 29 miles further to Pitts. Balt. to be more energetic.

The Louisville, New Albany & Chicago Railroad, not having had the management which the Michigan Central has given to its own line, nor the business to support it, is in trouble, and the *New Albany Commercial* says:— Louis., New Albany & Chi. *New Albany Com.*

We learn that the plaintiffs, Horner et al., in the recent suit against the Louisville, New Albany & Chicago Railroad, have, in accordance with the decision rendered by Judge La Rue, nominated as Receiver of the road, William Foster, Esq., the present Superintendent of the Logansport & Peoria railroad. It is said that Mr. Foster's appointment will not be opposed by the defendants in the suit, and it is probable that he will be confirmed by Judge La Rue by common consent. Receiver appointed.

It is understood, we learn, that in the event of his appointment, Mr. Foster will tender the Superintendency of the road to A. B. Culver, Esq., and that he will accept it. We give these reports without vouching for their truth. We are inclined, however, to give them full credit. Both Mr. Foster and Mr. Culver formerly occupied the position of Superintendent of the road; both are gentlemen of large experience, mature judgment, liberal and energetic enterprise, and their appointment would insure the inauguration of such an era of prosperity to the road as it has never heretofore enjoyed. Mr. Culver to be Superintendent.

This completes the list of fifteen trunk lines, enumerated p. 36; the Northwestern having four of them besides the Galena, and the Burlington 15 trunk lines enumerated.

Earnings $49,816,419.

& Quincy two. Adding the earnings of the Pittsburgh & Ft. Wayne, $7,242,125.96 to the earnings of the others, p. 41, makes a total of those which have their centre here, $49,816,419.85. Surely it is moderate to

Other roads estimated $10,183,580.

estimate the earnings of other lines and branches which fairly belong to Chicago, though not reckoned in our reports, $10,183,580,15, making a grand total of $60,000,000.

18 years from $27,418 to $60,000,000.

Is it not more like magic than reality, that from $27,418 of earnings in 1849, the railways should in 1867 have increased over $49,700,000 ? in fact over $60,000,000 ? To exhibit the relative increase of the States and sections these tables are prepared :—

Mileage in different States from 1838 to 1868.

Railway Mileage in the several States from 1838 *to* 1868.*

States and Territories.	1838	1842	1846	1848	1850	1852	1854	1856	1858	1860	1865	1868
Maine	12	37	64	112	245	822	359	429	467	472	509	512
New Hampshire	....	....	19	263	465	567	643	656	656	656	659	667
Vermont	....	....	....	92	279	471	511	529	529	556	597	588
Massachusetts	126	435	626	893	1,035	1,047	1,144	1,272	1,272	1,272	1,324	1,400
Rhode Island	50	50	50	68	68	68	94	107	107	107	152	119
Connecticut	36	238	238	270	412	506	506	589	589	603	668	637
New York	325	590	873	1,019	1,403	2,249	2,567	2,641	2,675	2,701	2,956	3,244
New Jersey	108	186	186	239	205	317	375	485	516	559	867	911
Pennsylvania	562	893	893	981	822	1,113	1,404	1,799	2,081	2,442	3,967	4,252
Delaware	16	16	16	16	39	39	44	79	123	136	140	160
Maryland & D. C.	181	223	285	324	253	326	326	326	361	380	487	626
West Virginia	....	....	....	....	....	21	....	....	....	....	365	364
Virginia	125	223	223	306	515	954	1,218	1,341	1,594	1,771	1,379	1,494
North Carolina	....	87	87	155	248	311	534	638	789	889	977	1,000
South "	137	204	204	204	289	598	669	847	906	987	989	1,007
Georgia	57	323	576	602	643	909	983	1,165	1,297	1,404	1,421	1,547
Florida	....	....		23	21	21	....	56	198	401	402	639
Alabama	46	46	46	111	182	161	304	454	531	743	898	850
Mississippi	....	....	....	75	....	96	222	413	604	872	867	897
Tennessee	....	....	....	....	....	185	329	541	887	1,197	1,318	1,326
Arkansas	....	....	....	....	....	....	....	....	....	38	38	113
Louisiana	40	40	40	50	79	79	198	249	281	334	336	333
Texas	....	....	....	....	....	....	32	71	205	306	452	495
Kentucky	22	28	28	28	78	94	241	267	458	567	614	634
Ohio	....	84	84	274	575	1,385	2,001	2,522	2,651	2,900	3,393	3,397
Michigan	....	138	238	264	342	430	444	500	642	799	959	1,462
Indiana	....	....	30	86	228	755	1,317	1,806	1,994	2,125	2,196	2,386
Illinois	....	22	22	22	110	412	788	2,135	2,733	2,867	3,206	3,224
Wisconsin	....	....	....	....	20	70	97	276	647	922	1,045	1,036
Minnesota	....	....	....	....	....	....	....	....	....	....	281	419
Iowa	....	....	....	....	....	....	....	253	379	679	1,001	1,283
Missouri	....	....	....	....	....	....	37	144	547	817	925	984
Kansas	....	....	....	....	....	....	....	....	....	....	112	494
Nebraska Ter.	....	....	....	....	....	....	....	....	....	....	108	555
California	....	....	....	....	....	....	....	22	22	70	307	382
Nevada and Utah.	....	....	....	....	....	....	....	....	....	....	....	30
Oregon	....	....	....	....	....	....	....	....	....	3	20	19
Aggregate in U. S.	1,848	4,863	4,828	6,491	8,588	13,497	17,397	22,625	26,751	30,592	35,935	38,821

Sources of information.

Incorrectness.

* This table is made up from 1838 to 1848 and also for 1865, from Appleton's Encyclopedia; from 1850 to 1860, from U. S. Census; and for 1867 from the *Railroad Journal.* It will be observed there is a difference between these figures and those p. 329 from the *Railroad Journal.* Not only so, but my figures are carefully quoted from the U. S. Census volume, and it will be seen that the amounts in the annual columns, do not agree with the summary of sections. All pains possible have been taken to quote correctly, but I do not take responsibility usually to correct figures quoted. One exception, however, is in the column of the *Railroad Journal* above for 1867, which is footed both in that column and in its sectional summary, 38,821,81 miles. But if the mileage of the different States be correct, the amounts above are correct, except that not having space for the decimals, they are left off the columns but are added in the amounts. Corrections corresponding are made in tables following.

Progress of Railways in North Interior States, and in U. S., 1850–1868.

Miles and cost of railways in North Interior States, 1850, '60, '68.

North Interior States.	Mileage.*			Cost of construction, &c.*			Per mile.
	1850	1860	1868	1850	1860	1868	
Ohio	575,27	2,999,45	3,397,84	$10,684.400	$111,896,351	$149,540,950	44,008
Indiana	228,00	2,125,90	2,306,05	3,380,533	70,295,148	89,560,722	38.838
Michigan	342,00	799 30	1,462,82	8.945,749	31,012,399	45,043,870	42,374
Illinois	110,50	2,867,90	3,224,49	1,440,507	104,944,561	149,000,667	46,216
Wisconsin	20,00	922,61	1,036,50	612,382	38,555,606	40.966,182	39,523
Minnesota	....	....	419 50	....	....	11,250,000	26 817
Iowa	....	679,77	1,283,00	....	19,494,633	51,191,450	39.900
Missouri	....	817,45	984.75	....	42,342,812	55,754,105	56,603
Kansas	....	....	494,00	....	....	22,500,000	49.595
Nebraska	....	....	555,00	....	....	25,000,000	45,045
Interior States, North	1,275,77	11,212,38	15,163,95	$25,063,571	$413,541,510	$639,807,946	42,891

Miles and cost of railways in U. S, 1850, '60, '68.

Section.	Mileage.*			Cost of Construction.*			Per. mile.
	1850.	1860.	1868,	1850.	1860.	1868.	
6 New Eng. States	2,507,48	3,669 39	3,925.71	$ 97,254,201	$ 148,366,514	$ 166,435,366	$42,367
6 Mid. East. States	2,723,96	6,321.22	9,559.78	130,350,170	329,528,231	526,113,091	55,033
5 South. At. States	1,717,37	5,454.27	5,489.27	36,875,456	141,739,629	140,453,949	25,589
4 Gulf States	287,00	2,256.21	2,576.90	5.286,209	64.943,746	82,363,666	33,477
3 Int. States, South	78.21	1,806.35	2,074.25	1,830,541	49.761,199	75.696,791	33,477
10 Int. States, North	1,275,77	11,212.38	15,163.95	25,063,571	413,541,510	639.807,946	43,336
3 Pacific States	....	73.85	432.00	....	3,680,000	29,590,000	68,495
Total U. S.	8,589.79	30,793.67	39,421.81	$296,660.148	$1,151,560,829	$1,660,460,809	$42,797

* For 1850 and 1860, the figures are taken from U. S. Census; for 1868, from the *Railroad Journal*.

Instructive tables. Railway building retarded by war. More rapid hereafter.

These figures are very instructive notwithstanding they may be imperfect. No doubt the war has much retarded railway building in every section, yet no where more than in the West. Our railroad building has not been done by us, having very little capital therefor; and such operations on the part of non-residents, the war would greatly retard, except those needed for war purposes. Consequently the seven years of the present decade show an increase of expenditure in the North Interior of only $226,266,436, against an increase of $388,477,939 the previous decade; and previous to 1850 the total expenditure was only $25,063,571. Because of this retarding of construction, it must and will advance with greater rapidity in future.

Less cost of western roads. Cost in several States. Most building in the West. Branches in Ind. and Ill.

Another favorable feature pertaining to lines not further west than Missouri and Iowa, is their less cost of construction. The above figures of cost include incomplete mileage, though the divisor of miles is the completed mileage, and the *Railroad Journal* gives another total allowing for incompletions, and showing the cost per mile in New York, $54,646; in Pennsylvania, $50,029; in Indiana, $34,954; in Illinois, $41,595; Wisconsin, $37,551; Minnesota, $26,817; Iowa, $35,910; Nebraska, $45,045; Missouri, $53,773; and Kansas, $36,676. These are the States, especially the last six, wherein railway building is to be chiefly prosecuted for the next ten years; and within that time the supply will equal the rest of the North Interior. In Indiana and Illinois, the work is mainly to fill in branches to existing trunks; though a few trunk lines will be made as intimated p. 283.

Concentrate at Chi.

These branches, as with the Jacksonville branch of the Alton and St. Louis road, (see pp. 95 and 360,) will aid no less effectively than the trunks to concentrate business at Chicago.

New trunk lines.

In other States, however, trunk lines are to be supplied which will be done with more rapidity than has ever been witnessed; and branches will multiply along with them. Not only shall we have the same influences operating from the East in favor of railway extension, which have produced

Consoldating eastern roads aids them.

the existing marvelous system; but the consolidation of eastern roads into long lines will go on more and more, supplying unlimited capital and credit to extend and strengthen their relations. From this centre at the head of

Portland to Norfolk.

lake navigation, they are wide-spreading on the ocean from Portland to Baltimore, and soon to Norfolk; every one of the Atlantic cities, as heretofore shown, having more interest in multiplying facilities of intercourse with

Southern cities draw it directly east.

Chicago, than with any other business centre. Philadelphia, Baltimore and Norfolk, it is true, could best serve their purposes by preventing trade south and southwest from coming to the lakes. This they in vain have essayed to do, and find their best interest in yielding to the natural current.

Traffic seeks the lakes.

As has been abundantly substantiated, the grain and pork and cattle trade has a natural lake-ward tendency, which will operate with increasing power, so that less and less of it will be drawn eastwardly without coming to Chi-

Will find its centre.

cago. If this Great Interior has its natural centre, as seems to have been pretty well proved, its traffic will more and more there concentrate; for buyers will go to the chief market to purchase, and sellers will go where

Southern cities to seek it.

they can have most competition in buying. So that, as heretofore shown, even seaboard cities south of here are to derive far more benefit from traffic with

Rivalry of cities to reach Chi.

Chicago than from any other one point. And this one object to reach Chicago, is already creating rivalry between the Atlantic cities and their chief railways to the West, in absorbing the short lines, and constructing some links to make new, continuous lines hither. Nor has the West any more direct interest in the success of these efforts than have those cities

Competition our safety.

themselves. Herein lies the safety of the Great Interior and of its emporium. The lines of railway to one Atlantic city may possibly come under one directory, as attempted by that wonderful genius of great enterprises,

Cities must oppose consolidation.

Mr. Vanderbilt. But the rival cities are not to be consolidated. Nor can any one of them favor any such schemes as Mr. Vanderbilt's. The interest of each city is identical with that of the West, to create the greatest number of

All must seek the centre—

lines into the whole producing area. To the extent that the traffic of the Great Interior needs to seek a centre, with that centre they need to have the greatest possible facilities of intercourse; and for what can be taken

—yet trade to go by cheapest route.

direct from the producer to the consumer, on the seaboard or in foreign lands, not only the producer and the Atlantic city want it to be carried at

Prosperity of Chi. rests upon whole country.

the least possible cost, but Chicago also. The prosperity of Chicago, then, is closely identified with and is based upon that of the whole country. Need we a more solid ground-work?

The time is not long since Baltimore and its chief corporation, the Baltimore and Ohio Railroad; and Philadelphia and its chief corporation, the Pennsylvania Central, labored with all their might to counteract the centripetal forces of commerce in the West, to draw to themselves directly the rich traffic of the Great Interior; to control which created beyond any doubt the great commercial city of the Atlantic. It was a prize worthy of the mighty efforts which those cities and corporations have put forth, and which have been the chief promoters of the many east and west lines stretching across Ohio, Indiana and Illinois. But every degree of longitude west, the lake-ward draft increases in force, so that in Illinois the east and west lines feed more into Chicago than any other city.

Balt. and Phila. labored to draw trade directly east.

Prize worthy

Lake-ward tendency.

But the intelligent, sagacious, active business men of the eastern cities, are evidently coming to apprehend the important truth, that the Great Interior has and must have a centre of its own; and that Atlantic port which can furnish the best and cheapest facilities of intercourse with that centre, has a large advantage. As to Philadelphia and the Pennsylvania Central, no fact is more significant of their views than the consolidation of that important road with the Pittsburgh and Ft. Wayne. The whole subject is fairly presented, at once motives, means and results, by the *United States Railroad and Mining Register, for May 30th*, for which space must be taken to quote entire:—

Interior must have its centre.

East. rivalry to reach it.

Pa. Cent. & Pitts. & Ft. Wayne consolidated.

U. S. R. R. & Mining Reg.

The railroad situation in the United States is made reassuring to investers at the same time that it is made intelligible to the intertrading public. The insolvency, in one place, of a railroad corporation whose line failed to command traffic sufficient to yield profit equal to interest on cost of construction, and the duplication of a road at another place, at enormous cost, on a route parallel to an existing line capable of moving all the buisness offered, has had the wholesome effect of causing railroad managers, whose works are necessities to the public and sources of income to their owners, to turn their experience and judgment to practical account for the security of their constituents, and also for the vindication of the system of transportation by rail, which they administer, and in which is invested capital next in amount to the national debt.

Railway system to be understood.

Means of correction.

Great capital

Of the great roads in America, first and foremost, among the Atlantic trunk lines, is the Pennsylvania Railroad; and first and foremost among Western lines is the Pittsburgh, Ft. Wayne and Chicago Railway. The Pennsylvania Railroad, 354 9-10 miles long, covers the ground between Philadelphia and Pittsburgh, reaching from tidal docks to the Ohio River. The Pittsburgh, Ft. Wayne & Chicago Railway, 468 3-10 miles long, covers the ground between Pittsburgh and Chicago. *Together these two roads 823 2-10 miles long, make the shortest and best route between Chicago and the seaports*, for the combinations of the Pennsylvania Railroad Company include the Northern Central Railway of Baltimore and the Camden & Amboy Railroad to Jersey City.

Pa. road first in East—Pitts. & Ft. Wayne in West.

823 miles, shortest route to seaboard.

From Chicago *via* Pittsburgh, Harrisburgh, West Philadephia and Trenton to New York, the distance is 900 miles, whereas from Chicago *via* Toledo, Cleveland, Erie City and Dunkirk to New York the distance is 950 miles, or fifty miles more!

900 miles to N. Y.

From Chicago *via* Harrisburgh to Baltimore the distance is only four miles greater than will be the distance over the Connellsville route, when the latter shall have been completed—a small item in mileage, which is more than offset by the superior character and larger capacity of the Harrisburgh route.

To Baltimore only 4 miles more than Connellsville

At Pittsburgh, by a contract with the Pennsylvania Railroad Company, the Pittsburgh, Ft. Wayne & Chicago Railway Company puts itself in communication with Philadelphia, New York and Baltimore, over the Pennsylvania Railroad, the Camden & Amboy Railroad, and the Northern Central Railway—all works of the first class, in excellent condition, operated in unity and reciprocity, with efficiency, dilligence and success.

First-class roads to N. Y. and Balt

Benefit of combining this interest with Pitts. & Ft. Wayne. To the Pennsylvania Railroad Company, in which interest is included the Northern Central Railway to Baltimore, and also the Pittsburgh, Cincinnati and St. Louis Railroad, 192 miles long, from Pittsburgh to Columbus, the alliance with the Pittsburgh, Ft. Wayne & Chicago Railway assures peaceful and profitable communication with Chicago, St. Louis, Cincinnati, in fact with the whole Western country accessible from Pittsburgh, over diverging roads according to a scale and plan adjusted to geographical distribution and the avoidance of illegitimate competition. And considering that St. Louis is three degrees fifteen minutes due South of Chicago, whereas Washington is only one degree forty-nine minutes south of New York—the railroad distance from New York to Washington being 226 miles, whilst from Chicago to St. Louis it is 280 miles, 54 miles more—it follows that a direct route from Pittsburgh to St. Louis traverses a different base from a direct route from Pittsburgh to Chicago; and that, consequently, there is no valid reason for antagonism between two lines so divergent westward. Hence the case is one which is reconcilable, where the parties are animated by a common purpose to promote joint corporation objects and interests.

Avoids injurious competition.

St. L and Chi. on different base.

Chi. terminus of Union Pacific R. R. Chicago and San Francisco will be the practical termini of the Union Pacific Railroad; and at Chicago rather than at Omaha the seaports will compete for Union Pacific Railroad traffic. In combination with the Pennsylvania Railroad and its allies, the Pittsburgh, Ft. Wayne & Chicago Railway will be a power in Chicago, because from Chicago it is a long part of the best route to Philadelphia, New York and Baltimore.

Pitts., Ft. Wayne & Chi. a power.

St. L. terminus of Kan. Pacific. And as St. Louis, in like manner, will be the practical eastern terminus of the Kansas Pacific Railroad, the Pan Handle line will be part of the best route from the Eastern Division Pacific Railroad to the same three seaport cities.

Benefit of uniting Pa. Cent. and Pitts. & Ft. Wayne. Moreover, with the Pennsylvania Railroad and the Pittsburgh, Ft. Wayne & Chicago Railway *made a unit by compact*, the Pennsylvania Railroad Company can the sooner carry its plan for putting the Philadelphia & Erie Road in connection with the Western Pennsylvania Railroad, thereby to open and operate a cheap freight railway line from the Ohio to the Susquehanna and through to tidewater. With the Juniata route for passengers, fast freights, etc., and the West Branch for cheap and heavy freights, the two parties to the combination will both be in unrivalled condition to handle traffic and command travel between the East and the West—between New York, Philadelphia and Baltimore on one side, and Chicago, St. Louis and San Francisco on the other side.

Accommodate whole country.

N. Y. route. The negotiations, as reported, stipulate that the through business, for New York account, shall be carried *via* (West) Philadelphia, thereby including in the programme the whole mileage of the lines in interest; this route is only nine miles longer than the Allentown route—a consideration of no moment in a joint mileage of 909 miles—especially when considered in offset to the fact that the Allentown route evades the Camden & Amboy Railroad, 88 miles, and also 103 miles of the Pennsylvania Railroad. This stipulation will doubtless stimulate the work of reducing the curvature and adding more straight line to the old State road between Haverford and Downingtown—an improvement long contemplated and greatly needed.

Allentown bad because it evades Camden & Amboy!

Terms of union. The joint roads of the respective parties in the negotiation, it is said, are made a through route to the exclusive use of which, between certain points or areas, both are bound, whilst, too, both are pledged against granting material aid to rival lines or interests, within limitations set forth; and to insure equitable results to the contracting companies a commission or bureau is created, composed of representatives appointed by the respective parties, with a remedy for final adjudication in case of misunderstanding or dispute. The contract, in short, as may be supposed, is in effect an alliance, offensive and defensive, entered into to protect the investments of the Pennsylvania Railroad Company and the Pittsburgh, Ft. Wayne & Chicago Railway Company, made and to be made, and also to increase the business and income of the two roads considered as one for through transactions, within judicious boundaries.

Alliance offensive and defensive.

One party has Pitts.——the other Chi. The single consideration that one party is owner of the shortest and best road to *Pittsburgh*, and the other party owner of the shortest and best route to *Chicago*, makes the two roads jointly the shortest between Philadelphia and Chicago, and causes a common interest to prevade the entire mileage from end to end.

A unit of good feeling. Looked at as an unit, under a contract grounded in mutual appreciation and good feeling, and founded in a reciprocated desire and determination to do justice and lasting good service to the parties to it—what a magnificent iron way looms in the vista, in direct course 823 miles, hence to Chicago? Stand at Chicago and look seaward through Pittsburgh, to the three great cities on tidewater. Remember that,

Iron way 823 miles.

henceforward, the Pittsburgh, Ft. Wayne & Chicago Railway is in alliance reaching to three seaports, in a way which will allow its owners to expand its capacity between its termini, with faces turned "Westward," whither "the course of empire takes its way," leaving an ally in the rear, operating a trunk line from Pittsburgh to tidewater, with roots spreading to and into three cities, on three open and free ways to the sea. A view from Chi.

Stand at Philadelphia, remembering, meanwhile, that on your right hand is the New York and the Camden and Amboy Railroad; on your left hand Baltimore and the Northern Central Railway; contemplate Pittsburgh as the technical terminus of the Pennsylvania Railroad, at the head of Ohio river navigation and the starting point of two friendly roads reaching out West, and spreading wider and wider apart—St. Louis the final goal of one—Chicago the actual goal of the other; immagine the length and breadth of the Mississippi valley; see it as a checkered expanse of populous and potential States; conceive it as the seat of future empire, ruling the destinies of the continent; turn back through the short span of time which has developed the Pennsylvania Railroad; note the growth of that work; then turn forward to the anticipation of events of years to come; in their foreshadowed results see the Pennsylvania Railroad, then as now the great highway of the nation, its operations expanded, its totals multiplied, its domination as the paramount Atlantic trunk line a demonstration and confession. A Phil. view. At Pitts. 2 roads, St. L. and Chi. Points worth more consideration than they will have.

All honor to railroad officials of comprehensive minds who make peace for universal good to the transportation of interest; who make strength for mutual benefit by wisely joining hands and influence together. The general railroad interest of the country is commended more and more to the popular confidence by compacts akin to that which has welded into one line two great roads, with a single policy for through transactions, between the seaboard and interior cities of the State. Benefits of consolidation.

Consolidation of the Pittsburgh & Ft. Wayne with the Pennsylvania Central, is not the only evidence of appreciation of Chicago. Control of the late Great Eastern, Pennsylvania has also deemed important; though Chicago self-conceit is not sufficiently blinding to prevent our seeing that this point is less the aim in that enterprise, than is the direct connexion from Logansport through to Omaha. Still, we cannot but accord them the sincerity claimed for ourselves in the belief that "at Chicago rather than at Omaha the seaports will compete for Union Pacific Railroad traffic." But if "St. Louis, in like manner, will be the practical eastern terminus of the Kansas Pacific Railroad;" Omaha will as certainly be of the central route. It is at all events a sagacious move of that energetic corporation to secure the two strings to its bow; for Chicago will either be the practical terminus of all the three projected Pacific roads, or she will be of none. One would imagine that far more than our own produce, Asiatic trade, especially for the Great Interior which is to have unequaled distributing facilities, would seek a centre for distribution. Should it lack usual centripetal force, however, then the northern trade will doubtless concentrate at St. Paul, the central at Omaha, and the New Mexican at the Big Bend of the Missouri or at St. Louis. At all events, this energetic, ambitious corporation, next to absorbing the late Great Eastern, never did a wiser thing than to unite its interests indissolubly with a railway like the Ft. Wayne, the revenues of which have risen from $1,600,000 in 1857, to $8,400,000 in 1865, for the temporary diminution of which good reasons are given in the reports. The able President, Mr. Cass, remarks in his last report:— More evidence that Pa. appreciates Chi. Chi. not Omaha termination of Pacific road Well to have two strings to one's bow. Asiatic trade will concentrate. Effect of division. 2 wise acts of Pa. Central. *Mr. Cass' Report.*

The marked characteristic in railway policy the past year has been to the aggregation of capital and roads, and this policy is likely to continue through the current year. Within certain limits the policy is well enough both for the interest Tendency of railroads to consolidation.

Policy good sometimes. of shareholders to secure permanent income, and for the public to bring the leading avenues under such a unit of management that they can be worked with greater efficiency and economy, and thereby better serve the purposes of the public. The Objections. objectionable feature to this aggregation is the rapidity with which the controlling interest in these great corporations change ownership, without consulting the wishes or interest of minority holders, and sometimes without any considerations Avoided except once. of public policy. Your Board of Directors have avoided all such alliances and combinations, excepting in the case of the St. Louis, Alton and Terre Haute Road, heretofore noticed, and which cannot be regarded as of the character just described.

Chip of old block. A true "chip of the old block," overflowing with generous zeal to protect railroads on all sides from the rapacity and selfishness which these Disinterested. corporations are so apt to manifest, Mr. Cass had already explained the disinterestedness of the Pittsburgh & Ft. Wayne arrangement with the *Mr. Cass' Report.* St. L., A. & T. H. road in the same report :—

Reason for arranging with St.L.,A. and T. H. road. The object of your Board of Directors in entering into the arrangement for operating the St. Louis, Alton and Terre Haute Railroad was to harmonize all interests east of Indianapolis in the working of the single line of roads from Indianapolis to St. Louis, in such a way as to give to the several roads and lines east of Indianapolis their several fair and equitable proportions of the business east from St. Louis by this route, and at the same time remove all temptation from the parties in an effort, each for itself, to get an exclusive contract of the single Other roads selfish. Railway line west of Indianapolis. For nearly a year previous to the consummation of the arrangement each of the lines of road north and south of your road had been engaged in efforts to obtain exclusive control west of Indianapolis, the Would cut off Pitts., Ft. Wayne. effect of which, if accomplished, would have been to cut this Company off from all St. Louis business excepting by the way of Chicago. When, therefore, the plan She operates for common benefit. was suggested to your Board of Directors to join with all the other interests in an arrangement for working the line between Indianapolis and St. Louis for the common benefit on an equitable basis, it seemed so eminently to the interests of this Company, as well as to all, that they did not hesitate to commit this Company to the plan. Unfortunately before the final signing of the papers, and the formal taking possession of the property, the Pennsylvania Railroad Company withdrew from the arrangements for reasons which the other parties were not, and have not yet been, able to appreciate, and consequently they were unwilling to adopt them, and thus break the pledge entered into by them with the St. Louis, Alton and Terre Haute Railroad Company. It is hoped, as it is very desirable, that the Pennsylvania Railroad Company will yet join in the arrangement, and thus harmonize all interests, as was originally designed.

Pa. Cent. disinterestedness not appreciated. Probably the continued stupidity "of the lines of road north and south" preventing them still from appreciating the disinterestedness of the Pennsylvania Central, is doubtless the reason why that paternal road takes its worthy off-shoot, the P. & Ft. W., into consolidated union. At this rate, N. Y. reliev'd of anxiety. before New York is aware, she will find herself relieved of all anxiety about western railways, for the Pennsylvania Central and the Ft. Wayne Pa. Cent. and Ft. Wayne take care of all. will have taken them all into their *holy* keeping. Mr. Cass had frankly said in his report for 1866 :—

Railroad responsibility. To provide for the future wants of this very important line of road which you own, and to meet the just demands which will be made on you for transportation, by the people of the several States from which you obtained your corporate existence, is a question which has ever been pressing, and to-day as important as ever. A private individual can be limited— A private individual or firm, and corporations of certain kinds, may, and often do set bounds to their business and their desires for acquisition ; but a Railway corporation owning a line of road such as you own, cannot say "thus far it will go and No limit for railways. no further." Neither public policy, public duty or private rights and interests will permit you to stand still so long as the world around you moves. * *

Why not wait? In view of the results accomplished, and the large expenditures made, many shareholders may enquire: why not wait a period before embarking any more capital in the road? Our reply to this question is that unless the capabilities of the road keep pace with the trade and commerce of the country, and it is fully satisfied as to rates and manner of conducting it, the increasing business will seek other channels, and so deepen and widen them as even to draw off a portion of the present business of the road, and also bring unhealthy competition and non-remunerative prices for such as you will be able to retain. Road must keep pace.

Nor is New York without another equal competitor in Baltimore. That city used to appreciate the trade of the West, and made commensurate efforts to obtain her share. She seems hardly to have recovered yet from the effects of the war, and too many of her excellent citizens have fully believed that the country would never be what it has been, and that efforts to reinstate the old status of mutual confidence and prosperity between the sections was idle and visionary. As they witness the power of the country applied in recuperation, with equal potency as in destruction; they will once more put forth endeavors as of yore to obtain their part of the trade of the Great Interior, which of late has been neglected because of other engrossments. Straight avenues to its chief gateway will surely and speedily be secured. Baltimore another competitor with N. Y. Not efficient as formerly. Will renew efforts. Have routes to Chi.

In a volume of pamphlets I happen to have the account of the laying of the foundation stone of the Baltimore & Ohio Railroad by the last surviving signer of the Declaration of Independence, Charles Carroll of Carrollton. The ceremony was performed before 50,000 spectators 4th July, 1828, and Mr. John B. Morris said in his address on the part of the President and directors of the Company:— Laying foundation of Balt. & O. road, 1828. *Mr. Morris'* address.

Fellow Citizens: The occasion which has assembled us, is one of great and momentous interest. We have met to celebrate the laying of the first stone of the Baltimore and Ohio Railroad, and if there be anything which could render the day we have chosen more interesting in our eyes, than it already seems, it is that we now commence the construction of a work which is to raise our native city to that rank which the advantages of her situation and the enterprise of her citizens entitle her to hold. The result of our labors will be felt, not only by ourselves, but also by posterity, not only by Baltimore, but also by Maryland and by the United States. We are about opening the channel through which the commerce of the mighty country beyond the Alleghany must seek the ocean—we are about affording facilities of intercourse between the East and the West, which will bind the one more closely to the other, beyond the power of an increased population or sectional differences to disunite. We are in fact commencing a new era in our history; for there are none present who even doubt the great and beneficial influence which the intended road will have in promoting the agriculture, manufactures and inland commerce of our country. It is but a few years since the introduction of steam-boats effected powerful changes, and made those neighbors, who were before far distant from each other. Of a similar and equally important effect will be the Baltimore and Ohio Railroad. While the one will have stemmed the torrent of the Mississippi, the other will have surmounted and reduced the heights of the Alleghany; and those obstacles, before considered insuperable, will have ceased to be so, as the ingenuity and industry of man shall have been exerted to overcome them. * * * * Occasion interest. Work to advance Balt. Benefit Md. and U. S. Unite East and West. Benefits of steamboats. Railway equal.

This day fifty-two years since, two millions of people, the population of the provinces of Great Britain, proclaimed themselves independent States, and commenced the task of self government. Our native city was then an inconsiderable village, with few and difficult means of communication with the interior, and with a scanty and slowly increasing commerce. The inhabitants of these States now number ten millions! and Baltimore has increased in her full proportion of population. Wide avenues now radiate in every direction through the surrounding country—she has risen to the rank of the third city of the Union, and there are but few sections of the world where her commercial enterprise has not made her Changes of 52 years. In 1828 population 10,000,000.

Mr. Carroll. known. Fifty-two years since, he, who is this day to lay the first stone of the *great road*, was one among a band of fearless and noble spirits who resolved and declared that freedom which has been transmitted unimpaired to us.

N. Y. no sluggard. Nor will New York be a laggard in the contest to maintain her supremacy. What she lacks in railway facilities she more than makes good in water. Combines rail and water. Combination of the two being indispensable to great commercial attainments; and her wisdom not only being more apparent, day by day and year by year, in creating the closest possible connections with the lakes and with Chicago, but in drawing business from the South up to the lakes; what shall prevent her from pursuing the same wise policy which has undoubtedly been the prime cause of her prosperity? Past efforts at union with the West. With the immense outlay of means and effort hitherto judiciously bestowed to connect herself with and to develope the Great Interior; will it be easy or natural for her to stop endeavors now that the magnitude of the prize for which she has struggled begins to be developed. Realizing as they may and should do better than anybody else, the value of water communication, how much longer Must see importance of lake improvements. will the able statesmen of both State and city be blinded to the advantages they could have by cutting a canal around Niagara Falls, and by opening the Lake Simcoe route and making a large canal for steam tugs from Oswego to the Hudson? Will the fear of a little loss of tolls from Buffalo to Syra- Railway is absorbing. cuse much longer prevent this national work? The railway interest has grown upon them with such rapidity, and has yielded such abundant fruits, that the silently moving canal boat is not perceived among the rushing, clattering locomotives. They can see the dangers of railway consolidation, but *N. Y. Chamber of Commerce* memorial to Legislature. fail to consider the perfect antidote in improving water facilities. A committee of the New York Chamber of Commerce prepared an able report against railroad monopolies, and a memorial to the New York Legislature in which they said among other things:—

N. Y. has done nothing. While New York has made no progress in extending its railway connection with the West since the consolidation of the New York Central road in 1853, excepting only the extension of the Erie by the Atlantic & Great Western, to Cincinnati and St. Louis, the two great lines from Philadelphia and Baltimore have been actively engaged in perfecting a great system of roads designed to cover and control the whole trade of the West, and in this enterprise they have been backed by the whole Pa. Cent. has stolen march strength of the cities which they are expected to benefit. The Pennsylvania Central is extended to all portions of the West, by two lines run exclusively in their interest—the Pittsburgh, Ft. Wayne & Chicago, with a branch to Cleveland, and the Pan-Handle, both of which roads reach Chicago, and by roads which they have leased, consolidated with, or otherwise control, reach St. Louis, and are now being extended to the Mississippi at Keokuk; they are also known to control the southern branch of the Pacific Road, and their plans, when perfected, will complete a network of feeders covering the whole region between the Ohio and the lakes, which is finally designed to extend to the Pacific.

Balt. & O. not idle. The Baltimore & Ohio have not been idle, and within a few months have perfected connections with Chicago and St. Louis which will enable them to transport on their own terms from and to all the principal Western points. Both the Baltimore & Extension to Toledo. Ohio and the Pennsylvania Central are now agitating an extension to Toledo, which if carried out, will tap at that point the only railway on which New York now relies Railway competition with water. to maintain its trade with Chicago. For several years after the opening of the through lines to Chicago and the Mississippi, which were first formed by connecting many short and independent lines, it was deemed impossible to compete with the lakes, rivers and canals, particularly in the transportation of grain, flour and heavy freight, the great obstacle to such competition arising from difference of gauges and necessity of frequent transfer, which was expensive and injurious to the articles moved—the gauges of the Ohio roads differing from those east and west of them. This difficulty has now been completely removed by the use of what is called compromise cars, and cars are now run over the New York Central, Pennsylvania Central and Baltimore & Ohio road without change from the seaboard to the Mississippi, and when that river and the Missouri shall be bridged, will be run as far as the railway system extends.

Freight cars transferred.

The Erie Railway has but one connection of the broad gauge and in transporting to Chicago, and all parts excepting those reached by it, must necessarily break bulk over—a difficulty which can only be removed by an extension of their gauge to Chicago. The testimony of experienced railway managers is unanimous that in very long lines where through cars are used, where there is no immediate transfer and the only element of expense is that of mere haulage and wear of rail, through freights can be hauled at very low rates, hardly exceeding by the amount of insurance the cost of transportation by water, while the advantage to the owner in time saved is very great. The managers of the two Southern lines seem to have appreciated this fact much earlier than those of our New York lines, and have for some time quietly nursed the policy of securing all the business they could reach at a small profit, while those of the New York roads, relying on a continuance of the trade which they once exclusively enjoyed, have practically aided them by an attempt to establish arbitrary prices, so high, as in fact, to be prohibitory—an attempt in which they have been warmly seconded by the Pennsylvania Central. As an instance of this it may be stated that large quantities of grain have laid over at Toledo and Buffalo, its transportation being stopped by the excessive charges of the New York lines; while at the same time grain was continually being moved to the seaboard by the Southern lines from the interior of Indiana and Illinois at prices proportionately very much lower than would have been acceptable to Toledo and Buffalo forwarders. It is clear, therefore, that New York can no longer exclusively rely upon its river and canal advantages, but must in a great measure be dependent upon its rural connections for its share of Western trade, and that it will be benefited or prejudiced as those roads are liberally managed or the reverse. Indeed, it may almost be claimed that the property and progress of the city, and the material interests of the State, are under the control of two corporations, and if a consolidation of those be effected, will lie in the hands of a great moneyed monopoly.

Erie road no connection with Chi. Disadvantage. Pa. & Balt. alert. N. Y. too confident. Grain waiting at Toledo N. Y. cannot rely upon water. Injury of railway consolidation.

On the other hand, the facts also show that a full share of Western trade can be retained, or rather regained, and the railroads receive, under judicious management, an ample return. Having thus set forth the causes of injury to the people of this State and city, we now propose to lay before your honorable bodies a statement of its extent. In January, 1868, while prices from New York were governed by a combination of three of the trunk lines, the following were the comparative rates from New York and from Baltimore to the principal Western cities. The extent of the discrimination against New York trade is also shown.

Western trade regained by railways. Discrimination against N. Y.

Comparative rates from New York and from Baltimore to St. Louis:

Rates from N. Y. and Balt. to St. L.

	PER CENT.			
	1st Class.	2d Class.	3d Class.	5th Class.
New York	$2 62	$2 21	$1 81	$1 15
Baltimore	1 62	1 35	1 00	55
Difference	$1 00	86	81	59

Contracts have been made from Baltimore without regard to classification as follows:

Special rates

	Raisins.	Pepper.	Tea.	Rice and Flour.
New York	$2 21	$1 81	$ 62	$1 14
Baltimore	70	70	70	55
Difference	$1 51	$1 11	$1 92	59

Rates from N. Y. and Balt. to Cin.

Comparative Rates to Cincinnati:

	1st Class.	2d Class.	3d Class.	4th Class.
New York	$1 90	$1 60	$1 30	80
Baltimore	1 10	90	70	30
Difference	80	70	60	50

Rates from N. Y. and Balt. to Chi.

Comparative Rates to Chicago:

	1st Class.	2d Class.	3d Class.	4th Class.
New York	$2 02	$1 70	$1 38	86
Baltimore	1 40	1 15	75	38
Difference	62	55	63	17

Change requisite to N. Y.

If the commercial supremacy of New York is to be maintained, and the diversion of its trade to other cities averted, instant and adequate means must be taken to regain its lost advantages. So serious did this question seem to the convention which recently met to revise the constitution of the State that it reported as one of the proposed amendments to the same, in article 10, "On Corporations," the following: "The Legislature shall not authorize the consolidation of railroad corporations owning parallel or competing lines of road."*

Consolidating competing railroads failed.

N. Y. Legislature invoked to prevent consolidation, aid competition.

In consideration of the facts above set forth, your petitioners earnestly urge upon your honorable bodies to take such early and efficient measures as will prevent the control of the various lines which connect this city with the West from passing, by way of combination or consolidation of management, into the hands of a restrictive monopoly, and to grant every facility to existing roads to improve their condition, to extend their lines, and in every way to compete with the established systems above referred to, and your petitioners as in duty bonnd will ever pray.

Advantage of Balt and Philadelphia over N. Y.

To the extent that railways are relied upon for transportation, New York is not even on a par with Baltimore, and is altogether at a disadvantage with Philadelphia. The shortest, cheapest, best railway routes from Chicago to New York are through Pennsylvania, in close proximity to Philadelphia. Though lying on her oars for years, and having to labor under great disadvantage in railway transportation, this sluggishness is foreign to her nature, and New York will soon create new and better railways than any yet in use, through northern Pennsylvania. Though she can never remove the disadvantage of more mileage, yet her marketing facilities are a full equivalent. In these she must sustain herself, or she speedily falls in the rear; and to do this she must use more efficaciously the water routes in which she has decided advantages over every Atlantic city. The activity and energy of New York and New England have created avenues to conduct business from the entire West to the lakes, so that the amount is far beyond the capacities to bear it eastward. As Mr. Poor judiciously observed p. 343, "the great difficulty lies in the way of outlets from Chicago, Milwaukee and other lake ports, rather than in the lack of means to bring produce to the lake shore." The railway system is now thoroughly established throughout the Great Interior, and must grow of itself, and will

N. Y. will bestir herself.

Superior as a market.

N. Y. and N. Eng. need greater avenues to the lakes.

Railways will take care of themselves.

To regulate consolidation difficult.

* The Consolidation of parallel lines is everywhere to be discountenanced; but it is a very difficult question to govern by specific rules. Generally it is considered enough to control trunk lines, leaving branches to the several roads to manage at will. But many branches in the West soon become trunk lines. Which is the trunk of the Burlington & Quincy, the Hannibal & St. Joe, or the Burlington & Missouri?

constantly press its claims, and offer such superior investments for eastern capital, that its rapid expansion will require great activity to provide avenues for the traffic which unchecked would flow onward to the seaboard. For lack of proper facilities, and only for their lack, must much produce go to New Orleans, and even we at Chicago must and will further this relief as far as in our power.

Traffic to go to N. O.

Increased facilities are needed much less for transportation specially adapted to railroads, as light expensive articles, than for grain in bulk and for barreled provisions, which railways can least afford to carry, and the withdrawal of which in the main would be a great relief. Nor are they very urgently wanted for immediate use; but looking forward only a few years and the grain and provision exports will double and treble; and what seaboard city will afford means to handle them? Certainly more railways will then be needed for light freight themselves; but yet more must the increase of bulky and heavy produce be provided for, for which water channels are by far most advantageous. So that besides more railways, New York and New England need much more to have a ship-canal around Niagara, and an improvement of the Lake Simcoe route, and also of Lake Champlain. New York and Boston must and will coöperate in these national enterprises.

Transportation for bulky articles wanted. **Future necessities.** **Railways needed— —yet water more.** **Routes to Lake Ontario.**

Mr. Edward Crane of Boston, has given much attention to this important subject of "cheapening freights between the West and East," and last winter delivered an address before the legislature, merchants, etc., of which the *Advertiser*, Feb. 19th, presented a summary of 13 points. These are the first six and the 13th:—

***Mr. Crane's* address at Boston.** **13 points**

1 It is now well established that there is no means of transportation so cheap as by vessels on free navigable waters; whether the lakes or the ocean.

1. Free water cheapest.

2. The point of competition between the East and the West is not at Newburg, the terminus of the Boston, Hartford & Erie Railroad, nor at Albany or Troy, the western terminus of the Boston & Albany Railroad, nor at Schenectady, the terminus of the Fitchburg & Rutland line of railroad, but since the completion of the Welland Canal, the point of competition is at the eastern end of Lake Ontario.

2. Competition with N. Y. at east end of Lake Ontario.

3. The Ogdensburg line of railroad from Boston through Lowell, Nashua, Concord, etc., after fifteen years of trial, has failed in securing the results for which it was created, for the reason that its management is divided among seven distinct corporations without that unity of action which can alone make it a successful aid to our commerce; but after the opening of the Atlantic and Ontario line, they would be forced to unite, and would become a great aid to the commerce of New England.

3. Ogdensburg R. R. insufficient.

4. Under the laws of the State of New York, the Atlantic and Ontario Railroad, a new line, may be constructed without further legislation by that State; making the whole distance from Boston to Lake Ontario, by way of Fitchburg, Vermont and Massachusetts, Troy and Greenfield, and this new line, 360 miles, about the same distance as it is by the Erie Canal from Buffalo to Albany.

4. A new line, Atlantic & Ontario.

5. A double track railroad from Lake Ontario to Saratoga with the natural barriers to be overcome by this route, is capable of moving at the rate of six miles per hour, eight million tons of freight from West to East, which can be delivered to the Boston & Albany, the Rutland & Burlington, and Fitchburg, and (when completed) to the Hoosac Tunnel lines, as fast as they can move it with present increasing and local business, at a rate of cost per ton per mile, including interest and expenses of maintaining and operating the road, not exceedin the Erie canal charges for 1866 and 1867.

5. Capacity of road.

6. Reliable transportation essential.

6. An essential element for a prosperous commerce and the largest development of agricultural production is in the establishment of a line of communication, always reliable, with fixed rates for transportation, and perfect unity of action in its management.

13. Gov't to examine route. U. S. ship canal around Niagara.

13. In consideration of the foregoing facts, ought not the government of the State to forthwith appoint a commission to officially examine this route to Lake Ontario, make the necessary surveys, with full power in the premises, and report to the next legislature; and further, that this commission be directed to examine and report what legislation is necessary to enable our citizens to avail themselves of the use of the empty cars going West over our several lines of railroad? Should not the general government at once construct a free ship-canal on American soil, connecting the water of Lake Erie and Ontario, for the purpose of the full development of the agricultural, commercial and manufacturing interests of the country, as well as for the protection of the mercantile marine of the lakes in case of war.

Mass. should lead.

The government of Massachusetts should lead the commercial and manufacturing interests of New England, and the agricultural industries of the West, in memorializing Congress in favor of speedily constructing a ship-canal uniting Lakes Ontario and Erie, and requesting our Senators and Representatives to coöperate to this end.

N. Y. and Boston moving. Must have cheap food. Best relief by propellers of 1,500 tons to Ontario and Champlain. Balt. and Phila. will draw trade direct. *Pitts. Gaz.* and *North American.*

These views show that New York and Boston perceive the necessity of doing something, though they put too little stress upon the best means. Not only do the Atlantic States need to increase facilities for transportation in order to export advantageously, but to hold their own in the onward progress. The tendency as we have seen is for mouths to come to food, which can only be counteracted by cheap transportation, for the East can never compete in production. It is bulky food, too, that is to be carried; and though they must make the most of railways, and create new lines, yet far more efficacious, and a never-failing source of relief would it be to give a free course to propellers of 1,500 tons to reach lakes Ontario and Champlain from Lake Michigan. This is a means in which New York and Boston can have no competition with their southern rivals. And although Baltimore and Philadelphia acquiesce in the lake-ward tendency of trade, and must make Chicago their chief objective point, yet they will never cease their efforts to draw business straight to them, and keep all from the lakes which they can. The *Pittsburgh Gazette* quoted some time ago from the Philadelphia *North American* and remarked as follows:—

St. L. bridge important. Connects Balt. and Phila. with Pacific road. Is essential. Steel arches. Wide span.

"*Importance of the Railroad Bridge at St. Louis.*—The St. Louis bridge will be, in many respects, the greatest wonder, in the bridge line, of the present day, as well by reason of its length and height above the river as of the huge steel arches and the monstrous tunnel that are to form parts of it. This vast structure is intended to connect the long lines of railroad reaching Illinoistown, from Baltimore and Philadelphia, with the Pacific railroad of Missouri, and so make the connection with the Great Union Pacific railroad, now building across the wilderness to California. Without the completion of this bridge the working of the through line will be imperfect, as it is impossible to tranship across the river all the freight and passenger business of a highway such as this is destined to be. It is, therefore, essential to the plans of most of the great railroads that this bridge should be built at once; that it should be of a solid and substantial character, and able to bear any amount of strain that may be put upon it. It is for this reason that the arches are to be of steel ribs; but the span of these arches, between four hundred and five hundred feet each, will be immense." * * *

A necessity.

The *North American* justly characterizes the construction of a bridge over the Mississippi at St. Louis *a necessity.* The Union Pacific railway of the Kansas, which is destined to be the great national highway to the Pacific, is opening up a region of incalculable resources and value. By means of the bridge now building at Quincy, and another across the Missouri at Kansas City, Chicago will have at once an uninterrupted connection with that road, of uniform gauge, and thus the entire system of roads converging at Chicago will be united with that road. Trains may be run from New York, or Boston, or Portland, or Philadelphia, or Baltimore, or Pittsburgh, by way of Chicago, to the farthest extremity of that road. There would be no break in the line in any place. Thus, although the country is mainly indebted to the enterprise of the capitalists of St. Louis for the Union Pacific railway of the Kansas, that city, without a bridge, would be thrown off the unbroken line of its eastern connections. To it, therefore, that bridge is an imperative necessity.

Chi. connected with Pa. road. Cars through from Atlantic. Advantage taken of St. L.

But to Pennslyvania, and its two principal cities, it is almost equally a necessity; for St. Louis, rather than Chicago, is on our natural and most direct line of commercial intercourse. Give us a good bridge at St. Louis, and it will be a virtual extension of our own magnificent Pennsylvania Central entirely across the continent by the smoothest, the richest and the most salubrious route that exists. As beyond the Mississippi we believe the Kansas route will be the most popular and most successful, so on this side we are satisfied that the Pennsylvania route will be the same thing. But to all this a bridge at St. Louis is essential.

Equally important to Phila. and Balt. Kansas best route—so Pa. Bridge essential.

Ere long New York and New England will be again aroused to the necessity of increasing means of transportation, and will appreciate the advantages they possess by water. Their interests are still ours; and though we rejoice in close connection with Baltimore and Philadelphia, and that they begin to appreciate the importance of this centre, yet our reliance as hitherto is mainly upon the joint interest of New York and New England in drawing business to the lakes; and this depends very much upon means of transport from the lakes.

N. Y. and N. Eng. will arouse. Their interests ours.

Great, then, unequaled as are our present facilities by rail and water eastward, they are small compared with what they must yet be made. And what are our prospects westward?

Facilities east to increase. How west?

1. The conjoint interest of New York and New England with Chicago, as we saw, has been the basis of our calculations for future increase from the very beginning. Has it failed us? Have their reasonable expectations of profit to themselves from their endeavors, been disappointed? The lakes, it is true, have aided mightily, yet they would have been powerless but for the liberal expenditure of eastern capital. What has been done is a pledge for more doing of the same sort. Not only the same general object of securing the trade of the West operates, but the gains from the long avenues owned by them in the East and in the West will be largely augmented by addition of other lines; and far more influential is the immensity of trade obtained and to be obtained, which already surpasses the wildest expectations. We welcome the aid which we have from the Atlantic regions south, which will steadily augment as they find the traffic of the Great Interior seeks more and more its natural centre; but what they do for us is compelled by what the region north of them has done and will do. Our reliance, therefore, in the future as in the past, is upon the conjoint interest with Chicago of New York and New England? Can it fail us?

1. Joint interest of N. Y. and N. Eng. Their capital indispensable. Motives to enlargement. Welcome southern aid—rely upon northern.

2. Capitalists have invested over $75,000,000 per annum in railways for eighteen years, and never was there more surplus capital than now. The old States are quite well supplied already, except a few more lines into the

2. Railway investments to go on—

—must come west.

West; and where shall capital in that use more likely find investment than here in the Great Interior, so admirably adapted to railways, and where profits are at least equal to any other section?

3. Capital of West increased.

3. East of the Mississippi the benefits of railways are already very great in the enhanced value of real estate, and increase of agricultural profits. Nowhere is Mr. Baxter's correct judgment, (see p. 332) upon the interest of land owners in constructing branch railways, more applicable than here in the West.

Co. bonds to aid railroads.

County bonds will be the means employed, which the farmers themselves can take in large measure. Much information has been hereinbefore presented, to bear particularly upon this point. Nowhere else has the railway equally augmented capital; nor can any more profitable investment be found by the farmers, for their surplus, than these branch railways.

Ease of extension.

Present lines afford abundant facilities, by a small expenditure, to extend the benefits to every neighborhood. A large amount of favorable testimony could be supplied, but space will only be taken for two examples, and these

2 examples.

in regions hitherto wholly foreign to Chicago; one in southeastern Illinois,

Letter from Effingham Co. Ill.

and another in western Missouri. A letter was published in one of our papers, from Mason, Effingham county, Ills., May 4th, as follows:

Southeastern Ill. railroad.

The Southeastern Illinois Railway.—The points on the Southeastern Illinois Railway are now determined and made permanent. The last point (Mason) voted donations on the 27th and 28th of April last, amounting to $40,000. The several

County subscriptions.

counties, townships and towns along the line of the road have voted subscriptions and donations to the capital stock of the company, as follows: Gallatin County, $100,000 stock, and $100,000 donation, besides donating swamp lands to the amount of not less than $20,000; White County, $100,000 stock, and $100,000 donation; Wayne County, $100,000 stock and $100,000 donation, besides donating swamp lands worth now $20,000; Clay County, $100,000 stock, and $40,000 donation; Mason Township, Effingham County, $30,000 donation, and the town of Mason, Effingham County, $10,000—the total amount being: Stock, $400,000; donations, including swamp lands, $430,000. It is expected that the four towns of Shawneetown, Fairfield, Flora, and Louisville will donate $10,000 each, which will make an aggregate

$870,000.

of $870,000. The stock subscriptions amount to donations virtually.

Points of line.

The points determined upon are: Beginning at Mason, on the Chicago Branch of the Illinois Central Railroad; thence to Louisville, in Clay County; thence to Flora; thence to Fairfield, in Wayne County; thence to Carmi, in White County;

100 miles.

thence to Shawneetown, in Gallatin County. The road will be about one hundred miles in length, and will pass through some of the finest and best wheat, corn, grass, grazing, and fruit lands in the West.

Being surveyed.

Corps of engineers are now in the field, and the road will be located between the points named above within the next sixty days; and it is expected that a full force of men will be at work upon the road bed by the 1st of August next. The company start out with a good financial basis from which to operate, and it is intended to rush the work something after the style in which the Union Pacific road is now

Built in 18 months.

being built. The road will certainly be built and in full working order from this place to Shawneetown within eighteen months from this date.

Connects Ky. roads—

From opposite Shawneetown to Madisonville, Ky., a distance of about thirty-five miles, a road is now being built to connect with the Henderson & Nashville Railroad, and which is intended as a continuation of the Mason & Shawneetown Road, both roads being owned and controlled by the same company. The Kentucky road con-

—with all the South.

nects the Shawneetown road with the whole system of Southern roads, and gives us rail communication with the whole South and Southwest.

Leavenworth to Des Moines most important.

But of all prospective branches, none probably is of equal importance to Chicago with that from Leavenworth, Ka., to Des Moines, Iowa. Not only because the local traffic is very large; not merely because it affords an avenue for the immense business beyond; but because while supplying these, it creates healthy competition with the Quincy, Hannibal & St. Joe route for the business of the Atchison, the Kansas Pacific, and the Galveston, and the other roads which must converge at the Big Bend of the Missouri, do we esteem this the most important branch line contemplated. The following is inserted in our papers with strong commendation:—

Competition with Han. & St. Joe. route

Co's. circular

The Leavenworth and Des Moines Railway Company have determined to construct and complete their railroad, without delay, from Leavenworth to Des Moines—direct. The located line is through the wealthy counties of Platte, Clinton, De Kalb, Daviess, and Harrison, in Missouri; and Decatur, Clark, Warren, and Polk, of Iowa—a distance of 168 and 8-10 miles.

Leav. & Des Moines road to be built at once.

Route.

At Leavenworth, it connects with the Union Pacific railroad, eastern division, now completed over four hundred miles towards the west; and with the Leavenworth, Lawrence and Galveston railroad completed 35 miles south from Lawrence, and rapidly extending onward towards the gulf, under the direction of Chicago capital, energy and enterprise.

Connects with Union Pacific. With Lawrence and Galveston.

At Des Moines—its northern terminus—it will connect with the Chicago, Rock Island and Pacific railroad, to which it will give, and from which it will receive, the immense trade between Chicago, southern Kansas, and northern Missouri.

Connects with Rock Island.

The whole of the rich country traversed by this road has ever been tributary to St. Louis; but now, as the most satisfactory evidence of the wish of the people to bring their valuable trade to Chicago, it may be stated that they have voted bonds of Leavenworth, Clinton, DeKalb, Jo Daviess, and Harrison counties to the Leavenworth and Des Moines Railway Company to the amount of $800,000; while by private and individual subscriptions in land and money, the amount is now above $1,000,000, exclusive of the liberal aid certain to be obtained in the counties of Decatur, Warren, and Polk, in Iowa.

Sends St. L's. trade to Chicago.

$1,000,000 raised.

The work of construction was commenced last fall and has been actively prosecuted since that time, with the exception of two months during the winter; and within 30 days the force now in the field will complete the first division of 50 miles. Track-laying will then be immediately commenced.

Work begun.

Thus far the work has been carried on by individual subscriptions. None of the county bonds issued and delivered to the company have been offered for sale, but the time has come when a sale of these securities is absolutely necessary. The completion of the road must be delayed unless a market for them can be found. In their negotiation, and the consequent completion of this railroad, the representative men of Chicago are respectfully asked to give a hearty support. It is not expected nor desired that they will invest large sums of their active capital; but if each will subscribe for ten, five, or even one bond, they will so establish their currency in the market that a ready sale of the balance can be made elsewhere—where investments are eagerly sought at 7 per cent. per annum.

No county bonds sold.

Sale necessary.

Chi. to aid.

If only one hundred of the bonds be taken in Chicago, the directory of the company, now at the Tremont house, will undertake to vouch for the rest, and the completion of the road to Des Moines before the close of the present year. The assurances of material aid from other strong companies controlling the great lines with which this will be operated in harmony, leave no doubt that such a pledge would be fully redeemed.

100 bonds to be taken.

Railroads will aid.

Besides aiding in the construction of a railroad, so important to every interest of Chicago, the subscriber for these bonds gets as good and safe paper as was ever discounted. He gets the full worth of his money. The bonds have been regularly issued and delivered upon a vote of the people, and in accordance with the constitution and laws of the States. The interest has been fully paid for more than a year, and there remains no possible chance of insolvency or repudiation on the part of any county.

Bonds safe.

Interest paid.

But, if every bond were worthless, this loss would be more than compensated in one year by the additional trade that their road would bring to Chicago. In the single item of lumber, it has been carefully estimated that the completion of this road will increase that department of business in Chicago to double its present immense proportions. So of other branches of business.

If lo t, no matter.

Increase of business.

The cattle, hogs and grain that this road will bring to the superior market in Chicago, will almost equal the entire trade in that line left to St. Louis. Well acquainted with this fact, that city, by means of a branch road from the west

Take St. L.'s trade.

Her North Mo. road.

Trade destined for Chi.

branch of the North Missouri railroad at Brunswick, is now actively endeavoring to be the first to extend to this trade the means of communication, and to delay and defeat the construction of this road to Des Moines. With great faith and confidence in the ultimate destiny of Chicago, it is believed that ultimately, this trade, will in any event, be secured to this city; but the history of railroad communications justify the confident opinion that should St. Louis beat Chicago into this disputed territory, it will take many years to shake off her command of the trade, so rightfully the heritage of Chicago.

This an example.

Creates competition.

All not Chi. roads.

This is a fair sample of what will be done all through the West. No outline of a great plan could possibly be devised more perfectly adapted to filling in with laterals and a few more trunk lines. While this Des Moines line will create competition with the St. Joe. & Quincy route, it will have competition from the Omaha & Burlington line. So will it be all over the Great Interior. New lines are by no means to be altogether in the interest of Chicago, but some will run directly to St. Louis and to various other centres, building up important cities throughout this entire area.

Benefit of roads to farmers.

They want to do as well as their neighbors.

Chi. do her part.

Because all around them farms are made valuable by contiguity to a railway, will farmers midway combine to obtain the same advantages. To many farmers who used to haul produce 100 and 200 miles to Chicago, their 10 or 20 miles are more tedious than the trip of a week or two used to be. Then they were satisfied because their neighbors could do no better. And any one who knows the farmers of the West will say, that with the abundant trunk lines, very few farmers east of the Mississippi, or 500 miles west, will long be five miles from a railway station. Nor will Chicago fail to do her part of the bond-taking to encourage these enterprises upon which her business increase largely depends. Her bankers and merchants can take a lot and work them off to eastern capitalists who want a good investment, and take another lot.

4. More Chi. lines West.

East roads will aid them.

4. As the East must have several more trunk lines to Chicago, so we must have the six or seven from Chicago, enumerated, p. 283. A glance at the map will show their necessity. The new lines from the east will furnish requisite aid to every one of them to become equal competitors with the old lines; and Chicago is fast accumulating capital which will be liberally invested both in branches and new trunks.

5. Competition west of Miss.

Only 7 lines for 300 miles.

More needed

East and West roads preferred.

5. Beyond the Mississippi the seven Chicago roads already built are being extended with that energy which has distinguished the corporations this side; which are now more than ever in strong competition to obtain the lead and secure the largest tributary region. They diverge so rapidly, that from Quincy to St. Paul is over 300 miles air line, which our seven railways will not long accommodate. The same reasons which operated upon the East to construct these seven, will have greater power to construct intermediate lines; and more and more will the few cross lines which St. Louis will be driven to build, become feeders of them all. More railways, either north and south or east and west, must be built to accommodate the country; and because the railway system is already too thoroughly established in the natural currents of latitudinal trade for longitudinal lines to

have much power against them, will preference be given to these intermediate roads; and because the country must have them, will the connecting roads to Chicago, with their eastward continuing lines, be necessary and profitable, and therefore will be built.

That would only carry out the present system to its completion, the intrinsic excellence of which has not only been well tested to entire satisfaction, but which has attained a ponderosity that cannot be swayed, an inherent force that is irresistible, a rapidity of execution that defies competition. As before inquired, suppose a change be desired, whence shall come the power to work it? But the entire country yet traversed would have no change if it could; and the lines are approaching precisely right to traverse the entire region to the Rocky Mountains and beyond. Nor does any region nor any city of mark in such enterprises, desire any change. St. Louis is by far the most important personage who seeks to alter in any essential respect. But it is one thing to seek, quite another to do; and though we would say nothing detracting, may we not inquire whether she be a city of mark in railways? Nor is it detracting even to that great and wealthy city to intimate, that it is quite a task for any one city to endeavor to oppose and overthrow a system established by the combined wisdom and capital of the entire country. This wisdom is shown, as before observed, in that although each corporation has sought its own interests; yet so perfectly is the system arranged to accommodate the entire region, that no important change could be made in any line advantageously to the public. Only some new lines are wanted.

Complete present system. **What power can change it?** **No change desired—except by St. L.** **Quite a job for her.** **Perfection of present system.**

6. These east and west lines have an important advantage over those north and south, in Government aid rendered in Kansas and Nebraska. No further grants of bonds can there be expected; but alternate sections of land may undoubtedly be relied upon, which, as with the Illinois Central, will ultimately pay the cost of building. This policy is too thoroughly established, and its benefits too abundantly ascertained, both by the government as a land proprietor, and by the whole country in the development and settlement of the Great Interior, for that policy now to be abandoned. These grants would not be restricted to east and west lines; but west of Iowa and Missouri north and south lines are not now wanted, except for branches, as from Denver to Cheyenne, which will be built this year.

6. Gov't aid. **More land grants** **Policy fixed.** **Grants to east and west lines.**

A few niggardly members of Congress vote against these projects, for which the best reason, miserable as it is, is that they help the West too rapidly to power. Very poor representatives are they of the East, that noble section which has done so much to develope and improve the West, giving us not only nearly all the money requisite, but their very best sons and daughters. Better men will usually be sent to Congress, but should a constituency favor the selfish policy, there is strength enough already to carry every proper project; and what is lacking the West will surely supply after apportionment under the next census.

Some M. C.'s oppose. **Misrepresent East.** **West soon take care of itself.**

2 other Pacific roads. Northern one Chi. road. St. L. fears about Kansas road. *Chi. Board of Trade.*

Two other Pacific roads one from St. Paul, the other from Kansas City, are no doubt to be built with the same aid from the Government which has been given to that from Omaha. The northern one of course will be a Chicago road; and although St. Louis has not till recently supposed there was any doubt that the Kansas road would operate in her favor, she seems to have some fears already. We are willing at all events to take our chances. Whether we have chief benefits or not, it is beyond any doubt the most important of the three routes to the entire country, and we are doing what we can for its furtherance. The Board of Trade, upon motion of Mr. Murry Nelson, adopted these resolutions the 13th May:—

Resolution asking aid of Congress for Kansas Pacific. Co. needs aid. Road important to nation.

Whereas, The Kansas Pacific Railway has approached within a few miles of the point to which the aid granted by the Government under existing laws extends, and

Whereas, The work is one of national importance, and cannot be successfully prosecuted without the assistance of the Government, therefore be it

Resolved, That we regard the extension of this road through New Mexico, Arizona and California to the Pacific coast, as a measure of sound national policy, both to insure military economy and the development of a vast area of territory filled with mineral, pastoral and other wealth, situated six to seven degrees south of the Union Pacific Railroad, and is in no way tapped or developed thereby;

Solution of Indians. Reach Cent. Mexico. Important advantage.

That it will lead to a peaceful solution of the Indian question, and, while gradually but surely removing the necessity of maintaining expensive military forces in the region traversed, will permit the country to be settled up, and vastly increase the taxable wealth of the nation. That it will afford an avenue of approach to the rich mines and semi-tropical productions of Northern and Central Mexico, insuring the trade of these districts for our own Western and Northwestern States, and avoiding the possibility of future complications from foreign aggressions in that disturbed country, and that it will secure a line of communication across the continent, directly accessible by rail connection with all parts of the United States, and especially recommended by the abundance of timber and coal along the route, and by the mildness of its climate.

Only a loan needed. Gov't saving.

Therefore, since only a loan of the public credit is needed to insure these advantages, and the past history of the company shows that the annual saving to the Government in the transportation of troops and supplies alone largely exceeds the interest upon the aid required to build the road, we respectfully urge our Senators and Representatives in Congress to assist, by their votes and influence, in securing the aid required from Government to insure the immediate extension of the Kansas Pacific Railroad from its present terminus to the Pacific Ocean.

Chi. Republican. St. L. fears Kansas road.

The *Chicago Republican* in an able article, the 30th March, exhibited the importance of a movement in behalf of this road, showing the benefits already resulting from our Kansas roads, and the fears of St. Louis that the Pacific would prove to be another "Chicago road"; and on the 7th May, in another long article, said:—

2d Pacific road. Chi. and Ill. most interested.

Another road to the Pacific, by the way of Chicago, Quincy, Kansas City, Fort Wallace, Santa Fe, and thence on the thirty-fifth parallel to the Pacific shore and San Francisco, has been projected and is being pushed forward with characteristic Western energy. No city or section of the country is more interested in this new project than Chicago and the State of Illinois. This road to Fort Wallace, a distance of some nine hundred miles from this city, is already in operation. Over the new bridge across the Mississippi at Quincy, and the Missouri at Kansas City, to be completed in September, cars loaded with the cattle and productions of the country far to the west and south of Fort Wallace, without change or break of bulk, will come.

This road, the Legislature of Missouri, at its last session, and the people of St. Louis through it, refused to approve, or endorse, or give the least encouragement to, on the ground that it would be "a Chicago road," and would carry the productions of that vast country by St. Louis into Chicago. No better evidence of the truth that Chicago has a deep interest in this enterprise could be had. It, however, does not need this, for it is apparent that by this route Chicago reaches the Pacific coast and the commerce of the Indies over country unsurpassed in every mineral and agricultural resource. The immense prairies and the valleys crossed by this road have the advantage of perpetual summer, and for pasturage, cultivation of the fruits, and production of cereals, is, perhaps, not equaled by any other of our States and Territories.

Mo. Legislature refused to aid. Road important. Its advantages.

The question is, will Chicago countenance and favor this enterprise, which is to furnish it with the productions of this great country, and the commerce of the fifty millions of people who shall soon populate the vast and most attractive region.

Will Chi. aid it?

The *Chicago Times* of the 9th May, had a pithy article urging Congressional aid for this road, and on the 14th, the following:—

Chi. Times

The most prominent fact that has been developed by the opening of the Pacific Railway to the Rocky Mountains is, that two Railways to the Pacific are more needful than one. In the nature of things, a single road will be an oppressive, unbearable monopoly. The road from Omaha to the mountains is such a monopoly already. The cost of transportation on that road is little, if any, less than the former cost by ox-team express. Practically, all that private enterprise is able to save by its construction is time. That, to be sure, is something; but it is not all that the country has expected, and has the right to expect.

2 Pacific roads needed. One a monopoly, as Omaha.

Another important fact appears; that is, that the Cheyenne road, notwithstanding its enormous charges, finds plenty to do. It is not scarcity of freights that makes high charges necessary to an adequate remuneration; it is simply because the road, having no rival, may get whatever prices its managers choose to demand. There is no practical remedy for this state of things but in the building of a second road.

Has plenty work. Needs competition.

In the matter of local freights, the Kansas Pacific road (Chicago and Santa Fe line) may not be put in immediate competition with the more northern roads. Such competition will be created by the construction of lateral branch roads. Such branches will follow the construction of the main line as naturally as the tree puts forth its branches; and thus while two main trunks prevent an oppressive monopoly over the through traffic by either, their respective branches will carry the same beneficent effects to all important localities in the broad belt of territory that stretches between them.

Kansas Pacific not direct competition. Branches create competition.

By July the Kansas road will be finished to the eastern boundary of Colorado; and there, "in a wild prairie, a thousand miles from Denver or any other place, the government subsidy ends."

Kansas road to stop, where?

The government ought never to have granted a subsidy to a railway which was to be chopped off in the wilderness and have its western end tied up to the four hundred and eleventh mile-post. If the present proposition were to subsidize the road in that shape, it would be one of the projects concerning which it might be righteously said: "Not another bond."

Tie up at 411th mile post.

To do no more is to throw away that which is done. The proposition is to make that portion of the road already built of national value, by building the rest of it; to save the subsidy already granted and expended,—and which else might as well have been thrown away,—by extending to this Pacific road the same measure of government aid that was granted to the other.

Past aid thrown away.

General Sherman has shown that the saving to government by continuing this road to the Rio Grande will be $2,500,000 per annum on military transportation, and $70,000 per annum on mails. Not only will this saving cover the interest on the whole amount of Pacific railway subsidies, but, in less than a decade, it will reimburse the government for the outlay, with its lien on the road as a surety for reimbursement besides.

Saving to Gov't. Its safety besides.

That the completion of this road will beneficially affect the interests of Cincinnati, may be a good reason for its advocacy by Cincinnati gentlemen who "don't want to move to Chicago." A better reason is, that it will benefit the interests of

Cin's. reason. Chi's. reason better.

the whole country,—more especially of the whole west; and whatever will benefit the west, Chicago, as the present and future commercial metropolis of the West, naturally advocates. The history of Chicago is not a history of enterprises abandoned halfway to completion. The example of Chicago is one that the nation which would thrive must emulate.

Chi. example.

Character of the route.

Every few days some of our papers publish articles of the sort which have not been preserved. Having had a son engaged in the survey of this road about 12 months, I have some knowledge of the route; and although his letters are given more to description of the curious people in Mexico and Arizona, and the remarkable scenery, and other interesting objects, than to the railway, yet he writes that the route has been found favorable beyond expectation. The last letter is from near Albuqurque on his return, dated 24th May, and he says:—

Son in the survey.

Route favorable.

Lines practicable though some high grades.

All the distance through from Kansas, practicable lines have been obtained; although through some sections of country the work will require a large outlay of capital, and the grades will attain the highest rate allowed by law, which is 116 feet per mile. Yet most of the distance the work and grades are very light; for instance where they follow a valley or *cañeda.* Much of the country is capable of being farmed to advantage; and around the San Francisco mountains there are large forests of pine and cedar. The country will prove rich in minerals. There is plenty of gold and silver, and fine beds of coal have been found, and we saw one immense bed of white marble, covering five miles of ground. The latter when first exposed to the air is soft, but hardens in a short time, and will then receive a high polish. I have a specimen to take home.

Arable land.

Rich in minerals, coal, marble.

No opposition to grants.

No newspaper opposes the grant by Government, and most are its strenuous advocates; and the propriety of continuing what has been so well begun would seem to preclude any fear of failure. Sooner or later, at all events, the roads will in some way be built.

Roads will be built.

London and Paris as railroad centres.

To establish this topic futher, it was my purpose to have given a table of the railways centering at London and Paris; but it is unnecessary. Every railway of England and Wales as given by Mr. Baxter, p. 330, make a total of only 9,251 miles; and we have already shown (p. 37) that the trunk lines and branches of Chicago may fairly be reckoned at 9,465 miles, besides 1,546 miles paying some tribute. Since that table was prepared last February, several hundred miles have been added, and this season will add 1,500 or 2,000 miles. London is much less a centre than Paris; but all France has only 8,134 miles. What city in our country can be named in comparison with Chicago in railway facilities already existing? The *Chicago Tribune* gave this statement, Feb. 17th, of—

Eng. and Wales 9,251 miles.

Chi. 9,465 miles.

All France 8,134 miles.

Chi. Tribune.

Trains at Chi. daily.

Number of Trains Daily.—The following figures taken, from the time tables of the different roads for January, show the number of regular trains only arriving and departing daily over the different roading from Chicago, and that, too, at one of the dullest seasons of the year. In the summer and fall, when the fruit and grain crops are moving, an immense number of extra freight trains are added, amounting probably at some times to 150 or more additional trains. Then, also, many of the trains that leave our depots are double, though drawn by but one

More in summer and fall.

Double trains counted one.

engine, and shoot off on branches a little distance out to their separate destinations. It would be proper to count these separately, but this has not been done in the table.

Chi. trains daily.

Railroad	Passenger.	Freight.	Total.
Chicago & N. W.—Milwaukee Division	12	2	14
Wisconsin Division	6	8	14
Galena and Iowa Division	16	14	30
Chicago & Rock Island	6	8	14
Chicago & Alton	6	12	18
Chicago, Burlington & Quincy	8	14	22
Illinois Central	6	8	14
Chicago & Great Eastern	8	6	14
Chicago, P. & Ft. Wayne	6	8	14
Michigan Southern	8	8	16
Michigan Central	8	8	16
Totals	90	96	186

Passenger 90. Freight 96. Total, 186.

Adding the probable average number of extra trains the year round—freight, excursion, pay, etc.,—and it is fair to estimate the number of trains ariving at and leaving the depots of the twelve main lines of this city at 250 daily.

Extra trains. 250 daily.

The Galena and Iowa Divisions of the C. & N. W. Railway are separate lines, but the trains run a little way from the city on the same track, and they are therefore counted together.

2 divisions, 1 count.

Less than *every three minutes* of the twenty-four hours, a train arrives or departs. Nor do most of them come and go on short routes, but on long lines to Green Bay, La Crosse, St. Paul, Iowa Falls, Rocky Mountains, Des Moines, Chariton, Ft. Wallace, St. Louis, Cairo, Louisville, Cincinnati, Wheeling, Pittsburgh, Toledo, Detroit, and numerous intermediate routes.

A train every 3 minutes of 24 hours. Long routes.

As to water facilities, there is no comparison with any other city. Therefore, we need only to take existing facts to establish this caption; though it is very evident that water facilities must be greatly augmented, and that the mileage of railways in the Great Interior will be doubled within five years, of which Chicago will have even a greater proportion than what she now has, besides numerous additions eastward. With the abundant evidence we have had of the power of the railway to develope and centralize, and that it never traversed a region better adapted to its use; with a certainty of increase of facilities on all sides, and a rapidity of development never witnessed; with these powers brought to bear upon the best body of arable land upon the globe, and in the middle of the temperate zone; with the largest and richest area of mineral wealth, and of greatest diversity; with a railway system of over 11,000 miles already so located as that no essential change is possible, converging at one centre the traffic of this unequaled area of agricultural and mineral wealth, over a million five hundred thousand square miles in extent, it must also be remembered, that—

Water facilities unequaled. To be increased. Railways doubled. Some of Chi's. advantages present a certainty.

The Northwest and West are hereafter the Great Interior.

The N. W. and W. Great Interior.

Although chief actors in the mighty changes the New World is making, we ourselves have not perceived that we were converting the ancient Orient into our Occident. The wilderness which has seemed almost illimitable to

Change of Orient not perceived.

the west, has kept our points of compass as brought from the Old World. Although discoveries of gold and silver gave us the Pacific States, still the vast area intermediate ceased not to be to us the West. But now, and before the most gigantic of civil wars is closed, we begin and carry forward with railroad speed that enterprise which is acknowledged on all sides to be

Pacific railways.

the grandest, most important project of all time, the Pacific Railway; and ere one is finished, another line commenced as a branch, is to be pushed through as an independent trunk. Soon the iron horse travels on several roads from the Atlantic to the Pacific; and where to this young continental

Change our West.

Nation, has our West been placed? Where can we look for our West, except across the Pacific? Hence in the U. S. Census for 1850 we have (p. 365,) the proper classification of the Valley States into North and South Interior.

Great Interior.

These are all a unit in interest, as will be those adding to the westward of them, and will henceforth be known as the Great Interior.

To be a unit.

More and more will this section be found a unit as against the rest, however we may differ among ourselves; though there will be some important exceptions, as, for instance, in the removal of the National Capitol.

National capital should not be moved

Upon such a question it is to be hoped that State jealousy, if no other and better influence operate, may prevent the injustice of taking from the Old Thirteen the Capital, sacred with the name and hallowed associations of the Father of his Country.*

Sac. Union.

* Said the *Sacramento* (Cal.) *Union*, upon—

Aspiring West. St. L. wants national capital.

The Aspiring West.—The good people of St. Louis appear to be in earnest expectation that at some day, not distant, they may influence Congress to remove the capital of the nation to that city. They have resolved, through their Common Council, to that end, and operated on the State Legislature with good effect. They have already fixed upon the site of the new building, and are preparing to survey the needful "ten miles square," to include the beautiful location of Jefferson Barracks and the classic precincts of "Vide Poche."

Chi. claims.

Chicago has her pretensions as well as St. Louis, and she will hardly compromise them away. The Northwest is outgrowing the Southwest, and the Northwest will go for Chicago. They will be apt to find upon trial that the measure cannot carry yet. Sooner or later, however, the national capital must go to the West. That vast region, bound together by a common system of rivers and lakes. with a mild climate, rich soil, and incomparably enterprising population, made up from the contributions of New England, the Middle and Southern States, with a goodly mixture of Celt, Teuton, and Scandinavian elements, all

West seat of empire. Its characteristics.

fusing into one people, if it is not now, must in a few years become the seat of empire of this continent. The Great West is as sure to give her civilization and laws to America, as any event not yet decided. There is nothiug provincial in the West. When the young man from New England meets his brother Americans from the Southern aud Middle States, the first thing each party sets about is to take the measure of the other. Criticisms of speech and ideas are mutually exchanged in a friendly way, and it is not long till the three comprehend that each has something to learn, something to forget, and some provincial prejudices to abandon. It may seem a bold assertion, but we make it, nevertheless, that the best and purest English spoken is that which one hears from the man of Western or California education. The reason is clear enough to those who have resided for several years in that or this country. Our spoken language improves by criticism or deteriorates from lack of criticism. The provincial man is insensible to his errors till some one from the outside world takes him up and corrects them. This is what is constantly going on here and at the West, because the provinces all regularly contribute to our

Cal. and Ill. alike.

population. California is cosmopolitan. So is Illinois. Both are eminently national. In a population so mixed and constantly fusing by intermarriages, by attendance at the same schools and churches, and participation in the same industries, there can be no time or taste for the narrow, provincial philosophy which in the retired and excluding retreat of Abbeyville produced such bitter fruit from the brain of Calhoun. Everything in the west is on a grand scale—is national. Foreigners become Americanized

West national.

there quicker than anywhere else, because they see America in her grandest aspects, and are always cordially welcomed by the people who need population, but have land to spare for the taking. For the next quarter of a century the Eastern and Middle States must needs increase slowly, while the Great West will twice double her wealth and inhabitants. At the end of that time, if the West should work

Its power.

harmoniously, there is nothing she could demand but what she would receive—national capital, Niagara Ship Canal, ship canal from the Illinois to Lake Michigan, or anything else. She will then have at least

3 cities of a million in 25 years.

three cities of each more than a million inhabitants, and one, perhaps, as large as New York, toward which will always tend the wealth and fashion of the great heart of the nation. Something like this we remember to have seen prophesied about fifteen years ago. We were incredulous then; but times have changed, and the prophecy seems no longer extravagant. The West has only to wait and work together to get all it desires and to rule the destiny of America

Upon every question affecting commerce, manufactures, means of intercommunication, and other similar concerns bearing upon sectional progress, the Great Interior will be united. Having confluence of interest fully equal to that of New England; remarkable homogeneity of character; an absolute necessity that we should have more traffic with each other than all the world beside; possessed already of greater facilities for that traffic than any other region, and multiplying with unexampled speed; with the political power in our own hands, so completely after the next apportionment, that, unless all other sections combine against us, we can adopt any measures of progress which the Constitution will warrant; with the entire country most benefited as the Great Interior advances—what reason can be imagined why, without selfish purposes, but merely working out our destiny in the most natural manner, we should not carry onward the means already so effectually inaugurated, and which, from their beginning, have given marvelous growth to the chief centres? If nature and art conjoin to give that region a city so superior in advantages that we may reasonably expect it to become chief of the continent in commerce and manufactures, will it not be an object for its every part to advance its emporium?

Reasons of union. Means of prosperity. Work for our country. Work for ourselves. Have centres— —one chief.

As we saw, p. 116, of the Old Northwest, of the 378,000,000 acres, 273,000,000 are yet wild lands, and of the 105,000,000 in farms, so styled, only 52,000,000 are improved. These have not only built up Cincinnati, St. Louis, and Chicago, but twenty or thirty other large towns and cities. When the census of 1870 shall exhibit city and sectional growth, will not relative changes of 1860, and especially of lake cities, be even more remarkable, than those commented upon? (pp. 336–38.) Shall not immigration from Europe vastly exceed that hitherto, nearly the whole seeking this region? Shall we not have of Asiatic laborers five or ten to one from Europe? As millions upon millions of acres of rich arable land are brought under the plough; as hundreds of thousands square miles of rich mineral land are developed, and mining scientifically prosecuted with improved machinery, must not products of agriculture and of mines give an impetus to city growth never known before? Must not such a region have several of the largest cities on the continent? If there be one city central to all others and which each will have more traffic with than any other — one city, with which every town and village and neighborhood will trade more or less — must not the combined power of the Great Interior give its emporium such ascendancy, that with its central position in the Union, every city and section on the continent will have more occasion to resort to it than to any other city? Is it, then, unresaonable to affirm? that —

Little land yet tilled. Has built up cities. Rapid improvements. Stimulate city growth. Several large cities. Chief one will draw from others.

Other Cities are no Measure for Chicago.

Other cities no measure for Chi. This the conclusion.

This heading appears to be a natural and just conclusion unless the argument be fallacious. Therefore it is not to be proved as most other points have been. If not established already, further attempt would be

No boasting. It is excluded, and how?

fruitless. Nor is it presented in a spirit of vain-glorious boasting. However weak and imperfect the writer, he is not so bad, I trust, that a six month's study of such a subject should fail to awaken a sense of weighty responsibility, as it will in nearly every Citizen-reader; a spirit of dependence upon that Infinite Power which alone could bring about the unity of effort which from the first has been our most prominent characteristic; that energy in execution which is indispensable in the accomplishment of the unexampled results here witnessed.

Still, proud of our city. We should appreciate our position. This book to aid. Will cultivate pride.

Still, we have a pride in our City, or this book would never be distributed, would never have been written. And we have a right to be proud of the growth which is the wonder of the world, and which nearly every Citizen has helped to promote. We should not be the men to have accomplished this manly work, could we not better than any others appreciate the importance of the duties entrusted to us, and properly estimate the consequences to ourselves, to our State, to our Nation, to the world. It is to aid in making this estimate with exactness, that the book has its chief value; and so far as it shall have influence, it will surely cultivate pride in every soul of us—pride most ennobling, stimulating us to all needed efforts, that the destiny we know that faithfulness will ensure to us, fail not through our unfaithfulness.

Best studied views. *Mr. Scott*, '48.

Instead of quoting from other writers touching this important subject, it is better to consider yet more the thoughts of Mr. Scott, who doubtless had more thoroughly studied this important subject of city progress than any other man; and they are better than any present views could possibly be, the many years which have intervened having tested the soundness of his theory. In *Hunt's Merchants' Magazine*, October, 1848, he considered—

Our cities—Atlantic and Interior.

OUR CITIES—ATLANTIC AND INTERIOR.

All proud of our cities.

All people take pride in their cities. In them naturally concentrate the great minds and the great wealth of the nation. There the arts that adorn life are cultivated, and from them flow out the knowledge that gives its current of thought to the national mind.

Large cities hoped for. Yet not believed in. N. Y. not to equal London.

The United States, until recently, have had large cities in the hope rather than in the reality. It is but a few years since our largest city reached a population of one hundred thousand. Long before that period, sagacious men saw, in the rapid growth of the country, and the aptitude of our people for commerce, that such positions as those occupied by Philadelphia and New York, must rapidly grow up to be great cities. This, however, was by no means the common belief in this country; and our transatlantic brethren treated with undisguised ridicule the idea that these places could even rival in magnitude the leading cities of their own countries. New York is now sometimes called the London of America. Not that those calling her so, suppose she will ever come up to that mammoth in size and importance, but because she holds in the New World the relative rank which London holds on the old Continent.

N. Y. not appreciated. 150 years to have 5,000,000.

It is believed that few persons, at this time, have a sufficiently high appreciation of the future grandeur of New York; and yet fewer can be found who doubt that she will always continue to be the commercial capital of America. If this should be her destiny, the imagination could hardly set a limit to her future growth and grandeur It would be presumptuous to say that her population might not reach five millions, within the next century and a half. Of the few persons who have doubted her continual supremacy, most have given the benefit of the doubt to New

Orleans. This outport of the great central valley of North America was believed to command a destiny, when this valley should become well peopled, that might eclipse the island city of the Hudson. N. O. expected to grow.

Some twenty years ago the writer then living in a southeastern State, was convinced that the greatest city must, in the nature of things, at a not very distant day, grow up in the interior of the continent. Of this opinion he thinks he was the *inventor* and, for many years, the *sole proprietor*. It it had been the subject of a patent, no one would have been found to dispute his claim to the exclusive right to make and vend, (if that could be said to be vendible which no one would be prevailed on to take as a gift.) That such an opinion should appear absurd and ridiculous, may very well be credited by most people, who consider it not much less so now. The largest city of the interior was then Cincinnati, having scarcely 20,000 inhabitants; and the sum total of all the towns in the great valley scarcely exceeded 50,000. St. Louis at that time had but 5,000, and Buffalo about the same number. Here, then, was a basis very small for so large an anticipation. Who could believe that St. Louis, with 5,000 people could possibly, within the short period of 150 years, become greater than New York, with a population of near 200,000? But what seemed most ridiculous of all was, that the future rival of the great commercial emporium should be placed a thousand miles from the ocean, where neither a ship of war nor a Liverpool packet could ever be expected to arrive. In 1828 expected largest city to be inland. Opinion considered absurd. Cin. the largest. St. L. small How could she pass N. Y.?

Since 1828, some changes of magnitude have taken place; and the writer's exclusive right might now be questioned. There are now other men, considered sane men, who believe the great city of the nation is to be west of the mountains, and quite away from the salt sea. Governor Bebb, in a late address before the Young Men's Library Association of Cincinnati, expressed his decided belief that Cincinnati would, in the course of a century become "the greatest agricultural, manufacturing, and commercial emporium on the continent." There are other men, now, not much less distinguished for knowledge and forecast than Governor Bebb, who entertain the same belief. What has wrought this change of opinion? Time, whose business it is to unfold truth and expose error, has given proofs which can no longer be blinked. The interior towns have commenced a growth so gigantic that men must believe there is a power of corresponding magnitude urging them forward;—a power yet in its infancy, but unfolding its energies with astonishing rapidity. Changes since 1828. Gov. Bebb's confidence in Cincinnati. Others now believe. How the change? Rapid growth of interior towns.

Let us make some comparisons of the leading eastern and western cities. New York was commenced nearly 200 years before it increased to 100,000 people. Cincinnati according to Governor Bebb, has now, fifty years from its commencement, 100,000 inhabitants. Boston was 200 years in acquiring its first 50,000. New York since 1790, when it numbered 33,131, has had an average duplication every fifteen years. This would make her population in 1850, 530,096. This is very near what it will be including her suburb, Brooklyn. Eastern and western cities compared.

Cincinnati has on the average since 1800, when it had 750, doubled her numbers every seven years. Cincinnati doubled in 7 years.

New York.

1790	33,131	1820	132,524	1850	530,096
1805	66,262	1835	265,048		

N. Y. from 1790 to 1850.

Cincinnati.

1800	750	1821	6,000	1842	48,000
1807	1,500	1828	12,000	1849	96,000
1814	3,000	1835	24,000		

Cincinnati from 1800 to 1849.

It appears from this table, that, on the average of fifty years, Cincinnati, the leading interior town, has doubled her population every seven years; while New York, on the average of sixty years, has scarcely doubled hers in every period of fifteen years. If New York is compared with Cincinnati during the same fifty years, it will be seen that the period of her duplication averages over fifteen years, she had, in 1800, 60,489. Doubling this every fifteen years, she should have, in 1850, nearly 650,000. This number will exceed her actual population more than 100,000, whereas Cincinnati in 1850 will certainly exceed 96,000. Cincinnati doubled in 7 years. N. Y. in 15.

For 54 years N. Y. doubles in 18, Cincinnati in 10 years.

Let us now suppose that, for the next fifty four years after 1850, the ratio of increase of New York will be such as to make a duplication every eighteen years, and that of Cincinnati every ten years. New York will commence with about 500,000, which will increase by the year

N. Y. 1904 have 4,000,000.

1868 to.........1,000,000 1886 to.........2,000,000 1904 to.........4,000,000.

Cincinnati will commence in 1850 with at least 100,000, which will double every ten years; so that in

Cincinnati have 4,066,667.

1860 it will be...200,000	1880 it will be...800,000	1900 it will be...3,200,000
1870 " ...400,000	1890 " ..1,600,000	1904 " 4,066,667

The resulting figures look very large, and, to most readers, will appear extravagant.

For 100 years N. Y. double in 20, Cincinnati in 12.

Let us suppose the duplication of New York, for the next 100 years, to be effected on an average of twenty years, and that of Cincinnati of twelve years.

New York in

N. Y. have 1950, 16,000,000.

1850............ 500,000	1890............2,000,000	1930............. 8,000,000
1870............1,000,000	1910............4,000,000	1950...... ......16,000,000.

Cincinnati in

Cincinnati have 25,600,000.

1850............100,000	1886............ 800,000	1922............. 6,400,000
1862............200,000	1898............1,600,000	1934.............12,800,000
1874............400,000	1910............3,200,000	1946.............25,600,000

Surroundings included.

This looks like carrying the argument to absurdity, but if these two leading cities be allowed to represent all the cities in their sections respectively, the result of the calculation is not unreasonable. It is not beyond possibility, and is not even improbable.

Growth of interior cities equal to Cincinnati

The growth of the leading interior marts, since 1840, has been about equal to the average growth of Cincinnati for fifty years past. This growth for the last eight years, according to the best information to be obtained, has been more than 115 per cent., as the following table will show:

Interior cities in 1840 and 1848, 115 per cent.

	1840.	1848.		1840.	1848.
Cincinnati.................46,000		95,000	Detroit...............	9,000	17,000
St. Louis...................16,000		45,000	Milwaukee...	2,000	15,000
Louisville..................21,000		40,000	Chicago......	5,000	17,000
Buffalo.......................18,000		42,000	Oswego..............	5,000	11,000
Pittsburgh.................31,000		58,000	Rochester...	20,000	30,000
Cleveland................ 6,000		14,000			
Columbus................ 6,000		14,000	Total	191,000	412,000
Dayton.................... 6,000		14,000			

Exterior cities.

The growth of the exterior cities for the same period has been about 38 per cent., according to the following figures :—

Growth in 1840, 1848, 38 per cent.

	1840.	1848.		1840.	1848.
New York..............	312,000	425,000	Savannah.........	11,000	14,000
Philadelphia...........	228,000	350,000	Mobile......	12,000	12,000
Baltimore........	102,000	140,000	Brooklyn.........	36,000	72,000
New Orleans...........	102,000	102,000	Portland..........	15,000	24,000
Boston...................	93,000	130,000			
Charleston......... ...	29,000	31,000	Total	940,000	1,300,000

Authorities.

The census for 1840 is our authority for that year. For 1848 we have late enumerations of most of the cities. The others we estimate.

Inaccuracies.

There are doubtless a few inaccuracies in the details, but not enough to vary the result in any important degree.

Interior 3-fold faster than Atlantic cities.

In the aggregate our interior cities, depending for their growth on internal trade and home manufacture, increase three times as fast as the eastern cities, which carry on nearly all the foreign commerce of the country, and monopolize the home commerce of the Atlantic coast. This is a fact of significance. It proves that our fertile fields, after supplying food to everybody in foreign lands who will buy, and feeding the cities and towns of the Atlantic States, have sufficed to feed a rapidly growing town population at home. It proves, also, that the western people are not disposed to accept the destiny kindly offered them by their eastern brethren, of confining themselves to the handwork of agriculture—leaving to the old States the whole field of machine labor. Although the land on which the people of the great valley have but recently entered is new, the civil, social, and commercial condition of this people is advanced nearly to the highest point of the oldest communities. The contriving brain and skilful hand are here in their maturity. The raw materials necessary to the artizan and the manufacturer, in the production of whatever ministers to comfort and elegance, are here. The bulkiness of food and raw materials makes it the interest of the artizan and manufacturer to locate himself near the place of their production. It is this interest, constantly operating, which peoples our western towns and cities with emmigrants from the eastern States and Europe. When food and raw materials for manufacture are no longer cheaper in the great valley than in the States of the Atlantic and the nations of western Europe, then, and not till then, will it cease to be the interest of artizans and manufacturers to prefer a location in western towns and cities. This time will probably be about the period when the Mississippi shall flow towards its head.

West not confined to agriculture.

Advanced civilization.

Cost of transport an help.

Mnfrs. prefer West.

The chief points for the exchange of the varied productions in our western valley will, necessarily, give employment to a great population. Indeed the locations of our future great cities have been made with reference to their commercial capabilities. Commerce has laid the foundation on which manufactures have been, to a great extent instrumental in rearing the superstructure. Together, these departments of labor are destined to build up, in our fertile valley, the greatest cities of the world.

Points of western commerce to be great cities.

Joined with mnfrs.

The only point to which exception can be taken in the above is that the ratio of increase is continued the same through so long a period. Neither New York nor Cincinnati, nor any other city, can keep up its ratio. Why it cannot is difficult to determine. But. Mr. Scott is guarded and makes these cities inclusive of surroundings; and no doubt the predictions as to New York will thus be realized. They are far more so as yet, and even New York City alone has nearly 1,000,000 already. So, too, will Cincinnati have its 400,000 and more, by 1874. But will the causes which have thus far operated to keep up their ratio as well as actual increase, continue thus to operate in future? Mr. Scott wrote before it was possible to have anticipated the rapid multiplication of railways, or to have foreseen their effects. Who would have imagined that such diversion could have so soon been made adverse to Cincinnati? The chief mistake in the remarkable papers we have seen, pp. 300–313, was in taking too mnch time to effect changes that he foresaw would ultimately be realized, the results of which he attempted not to develope. With railroad power and speed they have come, and we only need to change his line of argument accordingly. The underlying principle, the power of the Great West to build up the chief cities of the land, has been thoroughly tested and is unquestionable; and the incidental point also is unanswerably established, the superiority of the lakes to the rivers.

Ratio of increase cannot be kept up.

Surroundings included.

Will ratio continue?

Rapidity of change not foreseen.

Power of West.

Lake superiority.

These points are the main reliance of this argument. While the traffic of the Great Interior is without doubt indefinitely to be the chief support of eastern cities, and will never fail them but steadily increase many fold; yet relatively it is to be confined more and more to ourselves. At first new settlers must obtain supplies of every description from older sections. They begin to make for themselves the simplest implements, bulky and

These main points.

West trade most with itself.

costing heavily for transport, and go on in quite regular succession according to the value of labor to build and cost of freight. Towns and cities grow as they can obtain materials advantageously together with labor, and be supplied with distributing facilities. Railways, as we have seen, more than any other means, supply facilities both to gather and to distribute. For this water transport is not essential, though more or less advantageous. With few railroads, and those centering at few points, their centres would be rapidly created into great cities. But here they are, in the very infancy of settlement of Indiana and Michigan and the States west, spread like a net-work all over them. Cincinnati had obtained the lead so effectually that they aided more and more in Ohio, Indiana and Kentucky to advance her above surrounding places; and though some of her trade may be drawn from her, yet doubtless she will continue to be the chief city of a radius of 250 miles around her.

Towns grow with mnfrs. and commerce. Railways best means. Spread over the West. Aid to Cincinnati.

Along Lake Erie there are too many railway centres for any one to attain great prominence. Mr. Scott still argues that Toledo is to lead; but its being at the head of Lake Erie is very different from being at the extremity of lake navigation, and appears not to be a sufficient advantage over what Cleveland has in her railways and large trade; and though climate favors lake towns, yet unless one of them is able to attain considerable ascendancy over the others, Cincinnati will always be chief of that region. Indeed, it seems that the effect of railways must be to centre the trade of their respective regions more and more at Cincinnati, St. Louis and Chicago. The only question as to St. Louis is, whether there shall not be at the Big Bend of the Missouri, a more important railway centre. She has enough intermediate, and south and southwest to make her a great city; and there is a doubt whether influences can be converged at one point which are now divided to Kansas City, Leavenworth and Lawrence. Should Kansas City obtain ascendancy, as she should, the chief city of that region will be there. But however large that city, the time will never come in which St. Louis will not be the centre of an area which will keep her in a state of rapid progress.

Lake Erie too many centres. Cincinnati probably largest. Cin., St. L. and Chi. chief of their regions. Kansas City may be large. St. L. sure.

Because the Great Interior has the power to create many large cities and will surely do it, is precisely the reason why there is no measure for Chicago in any thing which has preceded in the progress of the human race. In a region which is traversed by a perfect net-work of railroads converging at one centre; with an absolute certainty that the system can never be changed, but is so laid that its expansion and filling up must more and more converge traffic toward that centre; with that railway centre also the strongest point of conjunction of inland navigation, and certain to be opened in a few years to ocean commerce for vessels of 1,500 tons; is it not quite certain that so far as commerce influences, however numerous and large the cities of that region, the central one must have proportionate superiority?

Many large cities make Chi. sure. Reasons for commercial superiority.

If to commercial superiority be added unequaled advantages to gather every important material for manufacturing, with the cheapest food of the world, a climate unsurpassed, an abundance of purest water, and many other important advantages with no drawbacks; is it not certain that unless other places possess the same advantages, such a centre of manufactures and commerce must be first of its region? **Mnfg. advantages.** **Must be first**

If there be elsewhere another region—not a little tract of a few thousand square miles—that civilized man has ever occupied comparable to the Great Interior either in extent, in agricultural wealth, in mineral wealth, in facilities of inter-communication, there might be a chance to compare, though it would be reasonable to require at least two of the points. But there being none other equal to it in any one of these respects; is it reasonable to limit its prospective growth to any previous example? **Where another equal region?** **No measure for Chi.**

Besides, the whole region tributary is in the early stages of settlement; that forming period when the people have the fewest possible wants. The demand for expensive furniture, carriages, etc., is very slight, and that demand cannot be supplied by manufacturers in the region, but in the older States. What little manufacturing is done, being of the plainest kind, with little machinery, every county town, at least, has the usual variety. But as a country developes, a demand arises for better articles than can be had except in extensive establishments where machinery can be used to save labor. Where are they so likely to go for such articles as to the city they know is chief in those respects, and which they can go to or return from twice a day or oftener, and most of them on direct roads where they do not fear to miss connexions? Is not an enterprising manufacturer who wishes to change location, likely to seek a city where he has already at least 8,000 miles of railway upon which to send his wares daily or oftener without change of cars, and 3,000 miles more with one change, and with a certainty that five years will double these facilities? What else brought to us 2,848 manufacturing establishments, listed p. 204, when all Cook County had but 469 in 1860? The subject begins to be understood not only in the West but in the East. A correspondent of an eastern paper said:— **West in its developing state.** **Mnfg. now distributed.** **To have a centre.** **One easily reached.** **That the city a mnfr. would seek.** **What gave Chi. 2,848 shops?** ***Eastern paper.***

In a conversation with one of the Western delegates at the recent National Commercial Convention, your correspondent gained much interesting information concerning the lively interest felt by Western capitalists is regard to the future of manufacturers and their establishments in the Western States. It is natural for manufacturers to find their way to the market place of the country, at or near the commercial centres, instead of to the waterfalls, far away from the seaboard. Goods are, for the most part, made near cheap fuel and railroads, to obviate the expense of freights, commissions, agencies, etc., thus enabling the Eastern manufacturers to realize larger profits on the labor of every operative they employ. But Western men now urge that with the coal and water facilities offered by nature at the West, with the removal of the tax on manufactures, and cheap freight facilities and cheap labor, goods can be manufactured as cheaply as in the East, and that the time is not far distant when the large cities of the West will be in competition with those of the East; that the true places for manufacturing industry—those **Western expectations of mnfrs.** **Natural to seek a centre.** **Advantages of West.**

Trade centres best for mnfrs.

places which will be hereafter the true places for manufacturing industry—are the chief centres of trade; that it is not the possession of abundant water power, or coal near at hand which will determine the question, but that the question will be determined by the advantages held out by these great centres of supply for disposing of products when manufactured.

Report of Sec'y of Int. East and West compared.

The last report of the Secretary of the Interior develops the tendency of manufacturing industry. From a large number of places, East and West, selected to give a comparative view of the productive power of that industry in the place named, it was shown that the amount of earnings averaged by the operatives is less at points where steam power is not used and coal mines are not at hand. The average earnings of each operative in Lowell, Manchester, Paterson, Pittsburgh, Philadelphia and Reading are considerably less when compared with the average earnings for those places where there is no water power and an easy access to coal. It is also claimed that industry is more productive in money value at the West than in the East. The completion of the Pacific Railroad, it is prophesied, will tend to make the West the great seat of manufacturing industry, as it will be the centre of civilization. The question is one of political economy.

Effect of Pacific roads.

Views of western press. Disinterested judgment better. 11 years' test. *Mr. Scott, 1857.*

Numerous extracts from our own papers bearing upon this point must be omitted. That a live press like ours would be earnest and constant in calling attention to this important interest, is too much a matter of course to make it necessary to take further space for their testimony. Much better than any judgment of our own upon this essential point, we have another paper from Mr. Scott, which nine years more of observation enabled him to prepare, based upon the progress which a few years of railway power had developed. Eleven years more, notwithstanding the retarding influences of war, abundantly confirm the soundness of his reasoning, and the moderation of his conclusion, notwithstanding it has been and still is deemed improbable even by our own Citizens. In the February number of the *Merchants' Magazine* for 1857, Mr. Scott discussed this subject:—

West. movement of centre of population and industry.

WESTWARD MOVEMENT OF THE CENTER OF POPULATION, AND OF INDUSTRIAL POWER IN NORTH AMERICA.

An interesting subject.

In the rapidly developing greatness of North America, it is interesting to look to the future, and speculate on the most probable points of centralization of its commercial and social power. I leave out the political element, because, in the long run, it will not be very potential, and will wait upon industrial developments. I also omit Mexico, so poor and so disconnected in her relations to the great body of the continent.

U. S., Canadas. Movement of centres west. Come together— —on Lake Michigan. Then be permanent.

Including with our nation as forming an important part of its commercial community, the Canadas, and contiguous provinces, the centre of population, white and black, is a little west of Pittsburgh. The movement of this centre is north of west, about in the direction of Chicago. The centre of productive power cannot be ascertained with any degree of precision. We know it must be a considerable distance east, and north of the centre of population. That centre, too, is on its grand march westward. Both, in their regular progress, will reach Lake Michigan. The centre of industrial power will touch Lake Erie, and possibly, but not probably, the centre of population may move so far northward as to reach Lake Erie also. Their tendency will be to come together; but a considerable time will be required to bring them into near proximity. Will the movement of these centres be arrested before they reach Lake Michigan? I think no one expects it to stop eastward of that lake; few will claim that it will go far beyond it. Is it not, then, as certain as anything in the future can be, that the central power of the continent will move to, and become permanent on the border of the great lakes? Around

Toledo benefited.

these pure waters will gather the densest population, and on their borders, will grow up the best towns and cities. As the centers of population and wealth approach, and pass Cleveland, that city should swell to large size. Toledo will be still nearer the lines of their movement, and should be more favorably affected by them, as the aggregate power of the continent will, by that time, be greatly increased. As these lines move westward towards Chicago, the influence of their position will be divided between that city and Toledo, distributing benefits according to the degree of proximity.

Foreign commerce an element.

Chief essentials of centres.

If we had no foreign commerce, and all other circumstances were equal, the greatest cities would grow up along the line of the central industrial power, in its westward progress, each new city becoming greater than its predecessor, by the amount of power accumulated on the continent, for concentration from point to point of its progress. But as there are points, from one resting-place to another, possessing greatly superior advantages for commerce over all others, and near enough the centre line of industrial power to appropriate the commerce which it offers, to these points we must look for our future great cities. To become chief of these, there must be united in them the best facilities for transport, by water and by land. It is too plain, to need proof, that these positions are occupied by Cleveland, Toledo and Chicago.

Foreign commerce 1 to 20 of domestic.

But we have a foreign commerce beyond the continent of North America, by means of the Atlantic Ocean, bearing the proportion, we will allow, of one to twenty of the domestic commerce within the continent. This proportion will seem small to persons who have not directed particular attention to the subject. It is, nevertheless, within the truth. The proof of this is difficult, only because we cannot get the figures that represent the numberless exchanges of equivalents among each other, in such a community as ours.

Annual product, $4,000,000,000.

This reliable

If we suppose ten of the twenty-nine millions of our North American community to earn, on an average, $1,25 per day, 312 days in the year, it will make an aggregate of nearly four thousand millions of dollars. If we divide the yearly profits of industry equally between capital and labor, the proportion of labor would be but $1,25 per day, for five millions of the twenty-nine millions. The average earnings of the twenty-nine millions, men, women and children to produce two thousand millions yearly, would be twenty-two cents a day, for 312 working days. This is rather under than over the true amount; for it would furnish less than $70 each for yearly support, without allowing anything for accumulation.

$3,000,000,000 for exchange.

Superiority to foreign.

Of the four thousand millions of yearly production, we cannot suppose that more than one thousand million is consumed by the producers, without being made the subject of exchange. This will leave three thousand millions as the subjects of commerce, internal and external. Of this, all must be set down for internal commerce, inasmuch as most of that which enters the channel of external commerce, first passes through several hands, between the producer and exporter. Foreign commerce represents but one transaction: The export is sold, and the import is bought with the means the export furnishes. Not so with domestic commerce. Most of the products which are its subjects, are bought and sold many times, between the producer and ultimate consumer. Let us state a case:—

Course of domestic trade.

Importing one transaction.

Several domestic result.

I purchase a pair of boots from a boot dealer in Toledo. He has purchased them from a wholesale dealer in New York, who has bought them of the manufacturer in Newark. The manufacturer has bought the chief material of a leather dealer in New York, who has made the purchases which fill his large establishment from small dealers in hides. These have received their supplies from butchers. The butchers have bought of the drovers, and the drovers of the farmers. The boots purchased are of French manufacture, they have been the subject of one transaction represented in foreign trade, to wit: their purchase in Paris by the American importer; whereas, they are the subject of several transactions in our domestic trade. The importer sells them to the jobber in New York, the jobber sells them to the Toledo dealer who sells them to me.

Domestic 20 to 1 that of foreign traffic.

All commerce equal.

It can scarcely admit of a doubt, that the domestic commerce of North America bears a proportion as large as twenty to one of its foreign commerce. Has internal commerce a tendency to concentrate in few points, like foreign commerce? Is its tendency to concentration less than foreign commerce? No difference in this respect can be perceived. All commerce developes that law of its nature, to the extent of its means. Foreign commerce concentrates chiefly at those ports where it meets the greatest internal commerce. The domestic commerce being the great body,

N. Y. chief of foreign as of domestic. draws to it the smaller body of foreign commerce. New York, by her canals, her railroads, and her superior position for coast-wise navigation, has drawn to herself most of our foreign commerce, because she has become the most convenient point for the concentration of our domestic trade. It is absurd to suppose that she can always, or even for half a century, remain the *best* point for the concentration of domestic trade; and, as the foreign commerce will every year bear a less and less proportion to the domestic commerce, it can hardly be doubted, that before the end of one century from this time, the great centre of commerce of all kinds, for North America will be on a lake harbor. Supposing the centre of population (now west of Pittsburgh) shall average a yearly movement westward, for the next fifty years, of twenty miles; this would carry it one thousand miles northwest-ward from Pittsburgh, and some five hundred or more miles beyond the central point of the natural resources of the country. It would pass Cleveland in five years, and Toledo in eleven years, reaching Chicago, or some point south of it, in less than twenty five years. The geographical center of industrial power, is probably now in northeastern Pennsylvania, having but recently left the city of New York, where it partially, now for a time remains. This centre will move at a somewhat slower rate than the centre of population. Supposing its movement to be fifteen miles a year, it will reach Cleveland in twenty years, Toledo in twenty seven years, and Chicago in forty-five years. If ten years be the measure of the annual movement northwestward of the industrial central point of the continent, Cleveland would be reached in thirty years, Toledo in forty, and, Chicago in sixty-three years.

(Margin notes: Change certain. Supposed N. W. direction and rapidity. Where it strikes.)

Population moving more rapidly. It is well known, that the rate at which the centre of population in the United States is now moving westward, is over fifteen miles a year, and that it is moving with an accelerated speed. It is obvious that the centre of population, and the centre of industrial power, now widely separated by the nature of the country between New York and Cleveland, by the superiority in productive power of the old northern and middle States, over the new States of the Northwest; and still more, by the inferiority of industrial power of the plantation States, compared with the region lying north of them, will have a constant tendency to approximate, but can never become identical, so long as the inferior African race forms a large proportion of the population of the great southern section of our Union. The constant tendency of the centre of industrial power will be northward, as well as westward. This will be determined by the superiority of the natural resources of the Northwest, over the Southwestern section, by the use of a far greater proportion of machine labor, in substitution for muscular labor, in the northern regions, and also by the superior muscular and mental power, of the inhabitants of the colder climate. To these might be added the immense advantage of a vastly greater accumulated industrial power, in every branch of industry, and the tendency of the superabundant capital of the old world to flow into the free States, and the country north of them.

(Margin notes: Population and industrial power to come together. Tendency of latter north and west. Advantages of the region.)

British Provinces, Mexico and Cal. not affect result. In the view of the subject which has been taken here, it will be seen that the trade with the British Provinces north of us has been considered a portion of our domestic trade, and that Mexico and California have been left out of our calculation. These may be allowed to balance each other. But together or apart, they will not be of sufficient importance to our continental commerce, to vary materially the results of its future for the next fifty years, as developed in this paper.

U. S. and Canada in 50 years to have 120,-000,000. At their present rate of increase, the United States and the Canadas, fifty years from this time, will contain over one hundred and twenty millions of people. If we suppose it to be one hundred and five millions, and that these shall be distributed so that the Pacific States have ten millions, and the Atlantic border twenty-five millions, there will be left for the great interior plain seventy millions. These seventy millions will have twenty times as much commercial intercourse with each other as with all the world beside. It is obvious, then, that there must be built up in their midst the great city of the continent; and not only so, but that they will sustain several cities greater than those which can be sustained on the ocean border.

(Margin notes: Great Interior, 70,000,000. Must have the great city.)

Era of great cities. This is the era of great cities. London has nearly trebled in numbers and business since the commencement of the current century. The augmentation of her population in that time has been a million and a half. This increase is equal to the whole population of New York and Philadelphia; and yet it is probable that New York will be as populous as London in about fifty years. A liberal but not improbable estimate of the period of duplication of the number of these great cities would be, for London, thirty years, and for New York, fifteen years. At this rate,

(Margin note: Estimate of London and N. Y.)

London will have four millions and seven hundred thousand, and New York three millions four hundred thousand, at the end of thirty years. At the end of the third duplication of New York—that is, in forty-five years—she will have become more populous than London and number nearly seven millions. This is beyond belief, but it shows the probability of New York overtaking London in about fifty years.

N. Y. beat London in 50 years.

A similar comparison of New York and the leading interior city—Chicago—will show a like result in favor of Chicago. The census returns show the average period of duplication to be fifteen years for New York, and less than four years for Chicago. Suppose that of New York for the future should be sixteen years, and that of Chicago eight years, and that New York now has, with her suburbs, nine hundred thousand, and Chicago one hundred thousand people. In three duplications New York would contain six millions two hundred thousand, and Chicago, in six duplications, occupying the same length of time, would have six millions four hundred thousand. It is not asserted, as probable, that either city will be swelled to such an extraordinary size in forty-eight years, if ever, but it is more than probable that the leading interior city will be greater than New York fifty years from this time.

N. Y. and Chi.

N.Y. doubles in 16 years, Chi. in 8.

48 years Chi. largest.

A few words as to the estimation in which such anticipations are held. The general mind is faithless of what goes much beyond its own experience. It refuses to receive, or it receives with distrust, conclusions, however strongly sustained by facts and fair deductions, which go much beyond its ordinary range of thought. It is especially skeptical and intolerant towards the avowal of opinions, however well founded, which are sanguine of great future changes. It does not comprehend them, and therefore refuses to believe; but it sometimes goes further, and without examination, scornfully rejects. To seek for the truth, is the proper object of those who, from the past and present, undertake to say what will be in the future, and, when the truth is found, to express it with as little reference to what will be thought of it, as if putting forth the solution of a mathematical problem.

Doubt as to such predictions.

If it were asked, whose anticipations of what has been done to advance civilization, for the past fifty years, have come nearest the truth,—those of the sanguine and hopeful, or of the cautious and fearful, must it not be answered that, no one of the former class had been sanguine and hopeful enough to anticipate the full measure of human progress, since the opening of the present century? May it not be the most sanguine, and hopeful only, who, in anticipation, can attain a due estimation of the measure of future change and improvement, in the grand march of society and civilization westward over our continent?

Most sanguine nearest right.

What is fanciful, unreasonable in that sagacious paper? Notwithstanding the war has greatly retarded such enterprises as railways, has drawn very heavily upon the West in agricultural laborers, and every way has deranged the natural current of events; yet, have not the eleven years past given good evidence that those predictions are to be realized? Is not "this the era of great cities?" Was there ever such a power as the railway brought to bear upon cities? Has it ever existed in equal power to work upon any city as Chicago? Did it ever operate in any country where it had equal opportunity at once to develope and to centralize? Is not this gigantic railway system sustained and promoted by the lakes, the grandest inland navigation of the world? Is it not closely conjoined to and aided by the longest river navigation of the world? Is it not absolutely certain as the continuance of man and the globe in present condition, that in all these respects there can be no drawbacks, but steady, rapid progress? Has any city ever arisen upon which any such influences were ever brought to bear? Why then should it not be admitted that no other city can be a measure for Chicago? At all events, duplication has

These views thus far realized.

Reasons why Chi. has no precedent.

Why deny the fact?

Chi. has doubled in 8 years.

been made and more the last 8 years. The following is an abstract of a census just finished by the Board of Health for sanitary purposes, under the supervision of our capable head of the Board, J. H. Rauch, M.D.*

Census of Chi. April 1st, 1868.

Population 242,129. Buildings, 40,315.

Census of Buildings and of Population of Chicago, 1st April, 1868.

Ward.	Brick Buildings.	Stone or Iron Buildings.	Wooden Buildings.	Total Buildings.	Dwellings.	Stores.	Shops and Factories.	Public Buildings.	Americans.	Foreigners.	Colored.	Total Population.
1	1,122	310	505	1,937	196	1,128	224	146	3,688	7,022	789	11,499
2	215	10	1.301	1,526	822	336	59	8	4,166	8,187	1,186	13,539
3	299	87	2,127	2,513	1.905	232	73	29	8,052	7.689	879	16,620
4	312	25	2,355	2,692	2,635	118	109	28	11,007	5,372	120	16,499
5	44	2	2,106	2,152	2,011	50	50	31	1,588	11,837	9	13,434
6	25	1	2,096	2,122	1,240	198	144	5	1,519	10,879	9	12,407
7	25	....	3,402	3,427	3,359	222	25	18	10,702	10,948	7	21,657
8	52	....	2,312	2,364	2,133	72	107	10	6,983	7,009	11	14,003
9	388	....	3,859	4,247	3,136	145	77	17	11,097	6,812	141	18,050
10	209	....	2,259	2,468	1,779	299	90	39	8,812	4,751	81	13,644
11	70	....	2,084	2,154	1,627	381	184	23	2,142	10,946	29	13,117
12	37	1	2,948	2,986	2,584	93	80	16	2,408	12,317	14	14,739
13	44	....	1,807	1,851	1,617	80	3	00	1,498	9,590	30	11,113
14	218	....	2,493	2,711	2,257	92	61	9	6.197	7,968	8	14,168
15	127	6	2,888	3,021	2,927	81	24	24	10,044	10,367	18	20,429
16	293	....	1,751	2,044	1,819	411	81	14	9,066	6,909	36	16,011
	3,480	442	36,393	40,315	32,047	3,938	1,391	417	100,164	138,603	3.362	242,129

Population 1860 was 109,260.

Predictions 1848.

Not realized.

Census moderate.

The population in 1860 was 109,260, (see table p., 288) so that in this eight years, increase is 133,000, almost 11 per cent. on the average. My predictions in 1848 for 30 years were that we should increase 20 per cent. per annum for five years, and 18 per cent. for the next five. These were realized. But 16 for the next, and 14 for the next five have not been realized by considerable; and is not the war an abundant reason? I then calculated for 12 per cent. for five years, and then ten per cent. per annum indefinitely. The present census must be moderate, for it allows only six and a fraction to a building.

Views 1861.

These remarks in my circular of 1861 are here appropriate:—

Rapid growth of cities.

Railway power even in old countries.

Railways here in the beginning.

Looking back only twenty or thirty years, within which all [railroads] have been built in this country and mostly abroad, we are amazed at the growth of London, Paris, New York, Philadelphia, etc. The locomotive more than any other influence has been the operating cause, notwithstanding the regions tributary to them being old or comparatively so, various places had by efforts of many years, and the gradual accumulation of capital, become fixed as important business centres. The concentrating power of railroads, however, in even these old countries, has given to the focal points a sudden and remarkable growth.

But here, almost in the day-dawn of settlement of these heaven-favored States, has the best of means of intercommunication and of exchanging products, been spread all over them, and of necessity business will chiefly concentrate at central places. Also, the six thousand miles of railway in use, are so laid over one hundred and fifty thousand square miles contiguous to us, that *three-forths—forty-five hundred miles—have this one city for their centre;* and so admirably has the system been

* A vast amount of information has been collected in detail important to show the condition of the city. The area is computed, showing the square yards in the blocks and in streets and alleys; the grade, and condition of the surface; the drainage, length and size, and what houses connect with public drains and what do not; the kind of privies and their condition; the hygiene; and full descriptions of the buildings, material and use, and also the population. It being yet not wholly completed, some errors may be made in the above which will be corrected in the next edition.

planned to accomodate the country, that but few farms are over twenty miles from a railway leading directly hither, and more than half within ten miles. Had our best minds been employed in the begining to locate the roads with a view alone to concentrate at Chicago, the existing arrangement could hardly have been bettered, either for city or country, though each company has independently made its location, seeking its own interests solely. Perfection of system

Tnese lines, too, are constantly extending , and five to ten thousand square miles and over, will annually be brought into the same close proximity with us, till a hundred thousand to two hundred thousand more are added to our domain. This could now hardly be prevented. Expanding.

The knowledge of this railway system, and of the relations Chicago bears to it, is being widely extended and must be more fully appreciated. But even now, a New Englander who desires to remove his capital, materials and workmen into the midst of his western consumers, unless he preferred to do a small and restricted business, or had peculiar influences to control him, would of course seek Chicago. Before the day of railroads, he might have hesitated and erred in his decision, but not now. If he changed to another location in the old States, a choice must be made with care, but not in the West if he have energy and enterprise to meet competition,—without which he had better avoid Chicago. Advantages of Chi. knowledge. New England seeks Chi.

On the other hand, these farmers will soon be rich, erecting fine houses and barns, getting furniture and carriages and other things to correspond, and living not only in comfort but luxury. There will be a city within one to eighteen hours' ride of all of them, where they can go and be certain to find every article wanted, or of soon having it made, and that competition will insure fair prices, and that a choice can be made in different establishments. Is it not according to the ordinary course of trade, that the large city should be resorted to for all considerable purchases? Ability of country to trade. One city all can reach.

In this direct way do railroads bring together manufacturers and consumers to their mutual advantage. Can it be doubted that such must be their inevitable effect in the West, a field in which nearly all manufacturing establishments are yet to be located, and which has *par excellence*, one great centre? Railroads create a centre for Commerce and mnfrs.

Not only is the railway powerful to centralize, but nothing equals it to advance settlements and develope a new country. This region had attractions, that even before the advent of the locomotive, multiplied inhabitants as in no other, and when it cost more to get produce to Chicago, then as now the chief market, than to raise it. But the increase of profits to the farmer is immense since the time when five hundred to a thousand teams could be seen daily entering our city from their tedious journeys of thirty to a hundred miles and over. Wool would hardly compensate for such trips now-a-days, though wheat, corn, fruit, etc., were then the articles brought. Their power to develope. Increase farmer's profits.

Agriculture being the chief occupation in the West, its advantage is of first importance, and no other has had its direct profits so increased by railroads. It is a literal truth that even corn, which consumes more of its money-worth in transportation than almost any important article of farm produce, and is most valuable of all, western farmers can now supply cheaper to eastern farmers, transportation included, than they can possibiy raise it. For transporting live stock, too, and perishable articles, the railway is of much importance. It has doubled and trebled, and more, the profits of western agriculture. And the various lines connecting us with the old States, enable their citizens to come cheaply and easily to examine for themselves, and to remove their familes and effects. It cannot be questioned, that ten years will now advance the West in population and wealth and social progress, more than thirty would have done without this most influential of modern inventions. Can now send corn. Live stock. Can come and see.

Other Cities no Measure for Chicago.—Hence, in anticipating the future of Chicago, its progress is not to be limited to that of the most favored city, ancient or modern. None ever arose with which to compare it. Not only this new-found motive power of the railroad operates with unexampled force and effect, but no other ever had so vast, so rich a region, for its support. Besides, the whole country has made great progress, and its multiplied wealth and population, must with accelerating power and speed, advance this, its most growing section, and this, its most growing city. Other cities no measure for Chi.

The Destiny of Chicago—Predictions for Twenty-Five Years.—If hitherto you have not particularly investigated the subject, you have probably entertained the general belief that Chicago is to grow along with other western cities to a large size, having, perhaps, in twenty-five to fifty years, two to five hundred thousand people! But in the preceding views and those of Mr. Scott following | the article quoted, Its destiny.

p. 380 was referred to,] do you discover anything unfair or improbable, except that the result is so incredible? Does a single valid reason occur to you for rejecting the conclusions, that Chicago in half a century will be second only to New York, if so even to her, and among the largest cities in the world? If not, then let the views in favor, which are certainly fair and powerful, establish your belief that *probably* it is so to be.

If reasonable, admit the results.

Predictions 1861, that 20 to 25 years gives 1,000,000 to Chi.

Heretofore I have had considerable credit for good judgment as to the future of this city, my predictions having been found nearly correct. I mean these shall prove equally so. Calling the population 110,000, sixteen per cent. per annum compounded, would give in five years in round numbers, 230,000; fourteen per cent. for the next five years gives 380,000; twelve per cent. for the next five gives 650,000; and ten per cent. for the next five gives 1,000,000. *Probably* these figures will be reached within each five years or less, but to be surely within bounds, I allow a quarter more time to attain each amount, and say that *twenty-five years will give Chicago over a million inhabitants.*

Near 20 per cent. per annum from '48 to 1858.

From 1848 to '58, we gained almost 20 per cent., and compounded each year; and though other classes have come in, so large a part of the floating and laboring population have left, that the total has not since increased, if it be as large. But that strengthens the probabilities of future increase, for with a return of prosperity, these or other laborers come back in a crowd.

Another estimate for 1,000,000.

Take another estimate. Suppose we double in five years—as we surely will—gives 220,000; double again the next seven years, gives 440,000, and double the next ten years, gives 880,000; and three years are left of my twenty-five to reach the million. However improbable this may seem to others, it is very reasonable with my view of Chicago interests.

N. Y. compared.

The Progress of New York.—This prediction will not seem so very improbable, after glancing at the growth of New York. In 1810, it contained 96,373, and in 1830 had only reached 197,112. Brooklyn, Jersey City, Staten Island, Newark, and other places within ten or fifteen miles, are but appendages, and in a locality like Chicago, would not have a separate existence. In such a comparison they are properly to be reckoned as part of the metropolis, and in 1810 would not have made a much greater population for New York than Chicago now has. The late census gives New York city 814,277, and the surroundings have probably 700,000 more, making a total of about a million and a half.

1860, 814,277. Suburbs, 700,000.

Greater facilities would have increased her progress.

It will not be controverted, that could New York be put back to her 110,000, and be possessed of only the advantages and means of intercommunication she had acquired fifteen years ago, that her progress would be two or three fold what it has been—that on the average one year would accomplish for her what two or three have done since 1810. Why, then, if there be any soundness in the preceding views, should it be deemed extravagant to expect a growth for Chicago that would be moderate for New York?

All the Union aids N. Y.

It may be said, that New York has been built up by the whole Union—that even this West, upon which Chicago depends, has contributed largely to its prosperity, and must in future. That is so; but look at the immense territory directly tributary to Chicago, which is vastly greater than that of New York only fifteen years since. That city never had—has not even now—150,000 square miles of territory, and a population of three millions, so closely identified with her and dependent upon her, as Chicago has to-day; and this area is fast enlarging, and this three millions will more than double each ten years for several decades; and though New York has received tribute from the whole Union, it cannot be claimed that only fifteen years ago it was the equal of what Chicago now receives.

Chi. has a larger dependent area—stronger than that of N. Y. in 1845.

Greater power of the whole country.

Then consider the rich and numerous advantages of this region, so far excelling the old States—the means of intercommunication and concentration at Chicago, so much more powerful than were possessed by New York only ten years since—the general advancement of the whole country, and the augmented power to people and develope its newer and most desirable region—the large foreign immigration, which, though diminished of late, is far greater than ten or fifteen years ago, and every way more desirable, and chiefly seeks the West—and then consider the important point, that in the East, not only New York, but several cities not a hundred miles apart, have grown to a large size, and that here for a circuit of several hundred miles, there can be no considerable rival to this great centre of the West.

No rivalry.

25 years at Chi. equal to 50 at N. Y.

In view of all these influential considerations, is it unreasonable to believe that twenty-five years will advance Chicago equal to what the last fifty have advanced New York? Yet if only two-thirds that is realized, the above prediction is verified.

We saw (p. 321) in Prof. Tucker's able notes on the censuses from 1810 to 1840, the much greater increase of towns than of country. Up to 1840 the West had only 3 cities of over 10,000; Cincinnati, 46,000; Louisville, 21,000; St. Louis, 16,000. Since that period, railways having been spread like magic over the Old Northwest, instead of creating a few centres, their power has been applied far better to the creating of many centres. This, as has been so often observed, and by various writers, is because the first demands of settlers are for articles which they can make near home, and which cost largely for transportation. This diffusion of common manufactures affords of all things the surest basis of prosperity. Then each of these towns needs some articles which it cannot produce advantageously, and goes to the larger city; and these cities to the larger. These common manufactures are now widely diffused, and the time is fast coming when this Great Interior will have all the wants of the highest civilization. Are they much longer to go away off to Philadelphia and New York to get these articles? Besides the convenience of obtaining them at Chicago, pride in building up our own region, and rendering the Great Interior as important in manufactures as in agricultural productions, will more and more operate. Then the remarks upon the census of 1860, p. 338, exhibited the effects of railways in their first decade, showing the growth of 6 lake cities to be 130 per cent., of five river valley cities to be 58 per cent., of twelve Atlantic cities 50 per cent.; and will the census of 1870 show any retrograding on the part of the Old Northwest, or of its emporium?

Prof. Tucker's views, 1840.

Railway centres in West.

Mnfrs. diffused.

High civilization in the West.

Will they go to seaboard for traffic?

Growth of cities to 1860

Therefore, while we admit that former ratio of increase cannot be maintained and is not calculated upon, yet beyond any city that ever grew must it be kept up at Chicago. This city is in all respects exceptional. What has been witnessed elsewhere to compare with what is to be developed in this 600,000 square miles of richest arable land; and 900,000 miles yet beyond of richest mineral land which must make this City their emporium? Were it not for the constant and rapid addition of thousands upon thousands of miles, to go on year after year until the whole Great Interior shall be as effectually united to it as is the Old Northwest, ratio would further diminish. But as it is, I hold to my former predictions.

Though former ratio not maintained—

—present will be.

Besides, as before remarked, Coolie labor will be brought into the South as well as West, and the old system of cotton and sugar production will be revived. They are not going to the East altogether for their purchases as hitherto. They like the West; and give them an equal opportunity to obtain supplies at Chicago and they will give it preference to Atlantic cities. Facilities already are very good, and will be constantly increased; and for a cotton market we shall not only have the demand of western manufacturers to supply, but also, direct shipments to Europe.

Improvement of the South.

Will trade with the West.

If Chi. surpasses other cities— But while we thus present the claims of this City, and it would seem that no other cities are a measure for Chicago, yet an important point in the calculation is, that—

—room for them and us.

THERE IS ROOM FOR THEM AND US.

No pent up Utica contracts our powers,
The whole unbounded continent is ours.

We are continental. Unfortunately, and greatly to the misapprehension of our manifest destiny, and the contraction of our plans, that good old word of our fathers, CONTINENTAL, has been abandoned. We need to realize that this our Nation, stretching from the torrid to the frigid zone—the Atlantic ocean to connect us with Europe, the Pacific with Asia—is not to be measured by the progress of the contracted nations of the old world. With the Nation must its cities have corresponding superiority. And what is more, never did any land possess such a system of Government as this of ours for the development of its powers. Upon the Confederations of ancient Greece, whereby those petty States of that little country became the first powers in the world; we have improved by adding the Republicanism of Rome, that principle of Representation, which enables the most extended States and Nations to conduct their affairs with the same unity and equality which can be obtained in the smallest State.

Europe no measure for us.

Influence of our Gov'ts.

Our improvements.

We must regard both State Sovereignty and National Union. Hence it is that only between the coats of arms of my State as the basis, of my Nation as the defender, can the Past, Present and Future of my city be properly placed for consideration. This compound but not complex system of Government, is the prime cause, under Providence, of our unexampled progress. Under and by means of State Sovereignty, we have the strongest National Union that can be conceived. We have all the benefits of State Government to direct our local affairs, the most effective National Government in the world, as our civil war has demonstrated, to care for us against foreign dangers. This wonderful system of Government which we so little apprehend, is no doubt the main cause of our advance. With State Sovereignty as the basis of our every right, we have the ægis of *E Pluribus Unum* over us, not only to protect from abroad but to leave the currents of commerce and of manufactures free to flow in their channels, and to find their natural centres.

State Govt. for local— —National Govt. for foreign affairs.

Basis not apprehended. As we study into these great questions—as we surely shall—we shall find that the solid basis of our prosperity has not been apprehended, could not be appreciated. Very certain is it that the examination will have an influence inconceivable in drawing to us from the Nations of Europe. Then Asia, by means of the Pacific railroads will pour upon us millions of laborers, our chief deficiency. The effect of Pacific railways it is impossible to over-estimate, especially upon city growth. A glance at the map of the world, which backs* the railway map, exhibits the directness of the routes.

Foreign influx.

Mr. Blanchard's maps.

Traffic with Asia. * As before observed, I have no idea that we are going to bring by rail the traffic of Asia with Europe, or even for the Atlantic. It is enough for us that it must come that way for the Great Interior. Therefore it is regarded a good *backer* to add the map of the world which Mr. Blanchard, our enterprising map publisher, has kindly allowed me to use.

Mr. Blanchard's maps.

But it is more certain that the internal trade of the Great Interior itself, has been, is, and will continue to be the main means of progress of the whole country. If this shall build up great cities on the Atlantic, much more will it build them up in the Interior itself. Yet intennai trade the reliance.

Though I want to write a good deal more, yet the book is surely sufficiently expanded for a beginning; and I am happy to permit my efficient coadjutor, Mr. Scott, to conclude with appropriate thoughts which 22 years have well tested, as they have the other articles, written for the *Merchants' Magazine*, February 1846, upon— I want to write more. *Mr. Scott* concludes. Views 1846.

THE PROGRESS OF THE WEST CONSIDERED WITH REFERENCE TO GREAT COMMERCIAL CITIES IN THE UNITED STATES. Progress of West—Commercial cities.

The *Albany Argus* says, in the conclusion of an interesting article on the dependence of eastern towns on the West, for their growth— *Albany Argus.*

"New York, if she wills, can still hold her present command over the western trade; but this will require immediate efforts, such as will test the energies of her merchants. He is blind who does not see that, at the present time, she is menaced by a spirit of competition on the part of wealthy, enterprising, and powerful cities, such as never before occurred in her past history. But, with an effort, she holds the game in her own hands. The western trade is a prize worthy of those who would struggle for the colossal commercial power of America. A city sustained by that trade, can never languish; for the increase of production of the western States is almost boundless. Its city must be far greater than even Alexandria or Thebes. So long as New York remains at the head of the western trade, where our State pride and her own commanding position justly place her, she must irresistibly advance in wealth, influence and population, until she will be known not only as the great city of America but as the great city of the world." N. Y. can hold western trade. A worthy prize. With it N.Y. advances.

Most of the positions of the *Argus* are sound. New York undoubtedly has it in her power to hold more of the western trade than any other *eastern* city; but it should be remembered that the centre of trade in this country is likely to follow the centre of population, which has already, in its westward course, reached the top of the Alleghanies. We lay it down as susceptible of demonstration, that the great city of America will be in the midst of, and not far from, the centre of the great *population* of America. Every man of tolerable intelligence knows that the centre is shortly to be in the great western valley. Including Canada, the North American Valley, already has eleven of the twenty-one millions under the Anglo-Saxon dominion. This valley will have— N. Y. best chance of eastern cities. Great city to be in centre of population.

In 10 years	16,500,000	In 60 years	88,600,960	Progress of American Valley, 100 years.
" 20 "	23,100,000	" 70 "	124,040,134	
" 30 "	32,340,000	" 80 "	173,656,000	
" 40 "	45,276,000	" 90 "	231,540,333	
" 50 "	63,286,400	" 100 "	308,721,777	

To come to this result, we have allowed the increase for the first ten years to be 50 per cent., being nearly 24 per cent. less than the increase of the western states from 1830 to 1840. After that and down to eighty years, we have allowed 40 per cent. being 4 per cent. more than the increase of the white population of all the free States, old and new, from 1830 to 1840. From eighty years down, the rate allowed for each ten years is $33\frac{1}{3}$ per cent., being the present rate of increase of the whole country. The Atlantic border will increase nearly as follows Rate of increase.

From 10 millions in	10	years, at	15	per cent	11,500,000	Increase of Atlantic border 100 years.
" " "	20	"	"	"	13,225,000	
" " "	30	"	"	"	15,208,750	
" " "	40	"	"	"	17,490,062	
" " "	50	"	10	"	19,239,068	
" " "	60	"	"	"	21,162,964	
" " "	70	"	"	"	23,279,250	
" " "	80	"	"	"	25,607,175	
" " "	90	"	"	"	28,167,892	
" " "	100	"	"	"	30,984.681	

Rate of increase.

Fifteen per cent. increase, each decade, is allowed for the first forty years, and 10 per cent. afterwards. The increase of the Atlantic States, from 1830 to 1840, was 16.3 per cent.; but this included the western portion of New York, Pennsylvania, and Virginia, which are in our valley.

Argus allows 100 years for N. Y. to beat London.

So Cin. beats N. Y.

It is fair to presume that the *Argus* expected at least one hundred years to pass away before New York should become the greatest city in the world. London has now about five times as many people as New York, and New York something less than five times the number of Cincinnati. To suppose the latter will surpass New York, is not a more extravagant anticipation than that New York will go ahead of London.

N. Y. centre of domestic trade.

This 15 times greater than foreign.

Will 300,000,000 west go to N. Y. to trade?

The internal exchanges of this country constitute the greatest part of the commerce even of New York, at which so large a part of our foreign commerce is carried on. The values transported on the Erie canal, alone nearly come up to the values of all the exports of the United States. Our foreign commerce is increasing slowly; our home trade is expanding and augmenting rapidly. The latter, in all its branches, probably, now, is not less than fifteen times as great as the former. The home trade of the western valley, at the end of one hundred years, will be a trade of three hundred millions of people with each other, of the productions of their various climates, and more various industry; and also with the thirty millions of the Atlantic border. Will these three hundred millions go to New York to make their exchanges with each other? Is it even certain that half the product of the eastern slope, intended for western use, will not be brought to leading western marts for sale? or that western products intended for eastern consumption, will not be distributed from the western marts? Certainly, the three hundred millions will be backward children if they cannot make their exchanges with each other, without going eastward to the old homestead, a thousand miles out of the way.

Old ideas hard to eradicate.

Progress not realized.

Estimate reduced to 200,000,000.

Old ideas, whether hereditary, or the fruit of early education, are hard to eradicate or supplant. The salt sea, and commerce, and great cities, are naturally associated together in the minds of Western Europeans, and their descendants in America. As natnrally is the interior of a broad continent associated, in their minds, with gloomy forests, desert prairies, and slow movements in all the channels of business. The idea of easy and rapid and cheap movements of commercial equivalents, over the face of the continent, by means of river and lake steamers, and locomotives on railroads, with interlocking McAdam highways and canals, is slow to enter the minds of the present generation. That land commerce has become so facile, as to compare with ocean commerce, may be acknowledged in the abstract, but its results have but just commenced a lodgment in the public mind. If our estimate of the increase of the western valley should seem too large, let the reader reduce the aggregate for one hundred years hence, to two hundred millions; and then, lest the Atlantic border should seem stinted in her allowance, set that section down for forty millions;—still our deduction in favor of western cities, stands on a firm foundation.

Direct trade from lakes to Europe.

350 tons propellers.

Miss. route.

Change less than last 50 years.

We might make out a strong case for western cities, independent of the above considerations, by exhibiting the means providing for a direct foreign commerce, away from the eastern cities. Little more than one year from this time will elapse, before the completion of the locks and canals around the falls of the St. Lawrence; by means of which, the ocean commerce will be accessible from the ports of the great lakes, in vessels of 350 tons burthen. With iron vessels of the propeller kind, voyages to all the ports of the word may be made from the interior of our country; from Toledo, Chicago, and Fond du Lac. In the south by means of the Mississippi, a direct intercourse may be opened from Natchez, Memphis, and Evansville; and in high water from St. Louis, Louisville and Cincinnati with the West Indies, and the extensive coasts of the Gulf and Carribean sea, carried on in iron vessels, moved by steam and sail. Are these events as improbable as, fifty years ago, would have been deemed the changes that have taken place within that period? Are improvements to make slower progress the next fifty years than they have during the last fifty?

INDEX.

Use of the Facts. Chicago has by no means used up this mass of fact and testimony in applying them to her own case. The entire catalogue relates directly to every city in the Great Interior, and more or less so to every city on the continent. That the items may be available, and be used effectively to promote each city's interests, this index is annexed; Chicago's prosperity depending entirely upon that of all the cities of the Great Interior. It will be seen that the information is less flattering to St. Louis than we would desire; but that is less the fault of the facts and testimony, than a natural consequence of her having mistaken her proper rank. Still, the evidence is very strong that she is to be a great city. As hitherto the chief, of course she is most prominent.

The Generalization. Though care was taken to bring together the items in their appropriate sections, each heading being a premise in the argument which is established by the fact and testimony thereunder, yet different sections contain closely related information which the Index would bring together. Prepared for busy men who want the points presented at a glance, the generalization by the Index, and its presentation of the disinterested sources of fact and opinion, will enable them to appreciate the strength and worth of the details, and the certainty of the conclusions. Although the plan is poorly executed, it has had more than twice the labor spent in preparing the materials, and yet is the most unsatisfactory part of the work.

Abbreviations. Ap., appendix. C. and Ch., Chicago. Cin., Cincinnati. Gt. In., Great Interior. Mnfr., Manufacture. An *n* after page figures, a foot-note. R., railroads. St. L., St. Louis. N., S., E., W., the cardinal points.

Full face Type indicates that the words are referred to in their places in the Index. Antique type indicates sectional headings, under which the side-notes on the margin of the pages give the substance, repetition in the Index being unnecessary.

ADAMS, C. F. Jr., Boston and C., *N. Am. Rev.* 66 *n*.

ADVANTAGES, Local, and City Expansion, margin, 249–288. **Site** of C. favorable, 249. Ground, **grade** 250. **Docks,** 251. **Health, Climate, Water, Sewerage,** 252. **Building** *Materials*, 256. **Finances,** 259. **Population,** 260. **Churches,** 262. **Education,** 263. **Science and Art,** 267. Fine **Arts,** 277. **Newspapers,** 280. **Parks,** *Public*, 281. **Ventilation,** 281. **Horse** Railroads, 282. Steam **Railways,** 283. **Expansion,** *Room for Indefinite—its Benefits*, 285.

AGRICULTURE. **Grain. Provisions. Stock.** The basis of our prosperity, 399. Farmers' interest that of C, 3 *n*, 53, 62, 65, 179, 184, 341, 366. Advantages of N. W. for, 114. ☞ See whole volume. Figures in commerce large, 113, 131, 314, 319. Lands of N. W. in farms and out, table; small per cent. 193; 187, 319, 387. W'n farmers independent. 140. Products of lake basin, 131. *Edmunds*, U. S Census; farmer works in nature's order; his products, 193; benefits of land culture, 194; reciprocal benefits of Ag. and Mnfs., 195, 314, 399. Corn put into hogs and cattle saves transportation; stock raising improves farms, 209, *Scott*, internal trade: variety of products of Lake and river valleys, 301; exchanges n. and s.; something besides ag.; a. the basis; cheap food brings cheap labor, 302; ⅓ in a.; rapid tendency to towns, 308. *Edmunds*, U. S. Census; "Influence of Railroads upon A.;" positive benefits of r's to grain growers; means; carry ⅔, 315; give W. market; increase profits; N. Y. market not reduced; $1,000,000 profit more on N. Eng. flour; $3,000,000 gain to Ohio on hogs; railroads stimulate a. especially in N. W.; all built since 1850, 316; per cent. increase of produce in 5 N. W. States, 1850–60; land enhanced; I. C. R. R.; advance of farm value, 1850-60; half effect of r's; greater W. of Miss., 317; a. most benfited by r's; a chief interest in W.; feed Europe; mouths come to food, 318. *Ruggles*, Rep. to Berlin Cong., 318; great increase, especially of W. in population, farms, wealth; capacity to supply food, cereals, swine, cattle; figures difficult to realize, 319. *Baxter*, "Railway Extension and its results;" benefits laborers; especially farmers; benefits in France, 327; save in transportation total cost, 331; somebody to make ag. lines; dividends not essential, land-owners to build their branches by loans of credit; examples; only way; Am. to have 100,000 m's., 332....Fruit traffic I. C. R. R., 353. Benefits of r's to farmers; one wants as good as his neighbors, 380; a. promotes city growth, 387, 399.

ALBANY, N. Y., lumber trade half that of Ch., 170.

ALTON, *Telegraph*, Joliet cut-off, 70. A better natural site than St. L., 84.

ALLEN, Hon. THOMAS, purchases Cairo and Fulton r. 40, 98.

AREA, tributary and to be so. The Northwest is the Prize contested—its Extent and Resources, Margin, 111–131. 600,000 Square Miles of Arable Lands, and Water Courses, unequalled in Advantages, natural and acquired, must give unexampled Growth to their Emporium, m'gin, 131-140. 1,500,000 sq. m's; **pop.** 1860; part tributary 1861; do. 1868; what constitutes C. territory, 115. Reasons for the claims, 117. Rapidly expanding, 399. That closely depending larger than of N. Y., and doubling each 10 y., 400. Continental, xix, 402. **Mich.; Ia.; Ills.; Wis.; Min.; Iowa; Mo.; Kas.; Neb.; Dak.; Mon.; Wy.; Col.; N. Mex.; Arizona; Utah; Idaho.**

ARGUMENT, present. Aims; vii, xvi—xxvi: *Not to promote Speculation, but Confidence in the Real Estate,* xvi; *to show that the Great In. must build up many Great Cities,* xvii; *to show that the Great In., a complete Unit in Interest, must have its own Centre, which is found and established; to show that the chief City of the Great Int. must, probably, be Emporium of the Continent,* xix; *to show that Ch. has a Population equal to her Advantages,* xx; to gather facts and statistics of Gt. In. valuable for reference, vii; addition after each census; for foreign not home use, viii; traces marvellous city growth; object to lead not to drive men, ix.

BASIS, vii-xiv: *Fact not Hypothesis,* xii; *our political Institutions,* xi; *Co-operation of Nature and Art from abroad,* xii; *our Railway System is immovable,* xiv,; *the whole Capital of N. Y. and N. Eng. supports Ch.,* xv.

DUTIES, xxxiii—xliii: *to Ourselves and Families,* xxxii; *to the Church,* xxxv; *to our City,* xxxvi; *to our State,* xxxix; *to the Gt. In.,* xl; *to our Nation,* xli; *to our God,* xlii.

EFFECTS, xliv-xlvi: *upon the Bodies Politic,* xliv; *upon the Individual Citizen,* xlv.

OBJECTIONS, xxvii-xxxiii: *too much Puffing of Ch. already,* xxvii; *Invidious Comparisons render us odious,* xxix; *every Body already knows about Ch.,* xxx; *it tends to create a Spirit of Speculation,* xxxii; *too long a Story,* xxxiii.

USE. A *vade mecum* to editors and others; should be sent to them to use for our benefit, viii. For foreign, not home distribution; prepared to obtain capital for use here; what every citizen may use, ix. Men to be led, not driven to regard their interests; wide distribution, x. Exhibits the safety and profit of investments in the realty, xvii. Supply other cities with needed information, xviii, 405. Cultivate *esprit de corps* in the Gt. In., xviii.

MERITS. A gathering of facts for busy men, vii. A permanent record of past growth, not to be repeated; become more and more valuable, viii. Approved by Ch. press, viii, Ap. 19-22. City growth itself important; means and index of civilization; Ch. most marvelous example; her relation to the Gt. In., ix. Negative testimony of Cin. and St. Louis editors, leaving it severely alone, xviii. Endorsement by the Board of Trade, vii. Action by the Board, pages preceding the title. Endorsement general not special, N. B., xxvi. Indifference of citizens, ix. Ap. 1-72.

Study the Past to understand the Future and improve the Present, 1, 2. Former Opinions and Predictions were based upon a reasonable Hypothesis, 2-14. Real Estate, especially in a growing City, is the best Investment, 14-16. General pecuniary Revulsions may intervene, but can not change the Result, 16-21. Public Improvements anticipated 20 and 10 years ago as a Basis, 21-24. The Basis of our Prosperity is no longer hypothetical, 25, 28, 72, 104, 283, 335, 345. (For continuation, See Table of Contents, pp. v., vi.,) Views not overwrought; basis what is realized, 72. Affirmative as well as negative to Ch. superiority, 92. The negative the weak side; treated for men of observation and judgment, 102. Pac. and montanic trade not the basis, 104 Affirmative has nine points, 102-106. St. L. miscalculated; promises to be tested, 106; C. changes from promise to fact; has 9 sure points; a rival must have several of her points; system of improvements natural; ordinary influences considered; causes traced to effects, results to causes; St. L. to invent new forces; C. will use them; growth uncertain without a majority of the 9 points, 107; no city having any 3 of them growth uncertain. Great W. will build up cities, yet man must work; benefits of State and Nation considered, (**Politics**), 108, 109; were union broken C. would grow; with union no favors asked; this an example of general considerations; the W. a unit, proud of its queen; no city having 3 of the 9 points, C. has no rival; emporium of N. W. must be of the continent 110. Mining developments promising; no hypothetic basis; reality suffices, 243, 248. Advantages of art and nature actually secured, 249. Existing railway system in 1861 a solid basis, 290. Must argue from past to future, 318. St. L. having no basis employs assertion, 341. C.'s advantages present a certainty, 385.

ARMOUR DOLE and CO.'S Elevator, described by Mr. Baker, 157.

ART. **Agriculture. Canal. City. Commerce. Manufactures. Railways. Trade.** *Co-operation of* **Nature** *and of A. from abroad.* This a basis of argument, next to political institutions; converges facts like a lens; shows our sources of supplies, not in ourselves, but in God and country. Nature never makes a city; Cain built first (title page); is wholly artificial, xii. Yet nature aids a., as index shows. Still, index exhibits art's results; effects prove perfect co-operation between a. and nature, xiii. Conjunction of a. and nature at C. should be investigated, xxxi, xli, 70, 142, 249. No other equal Point of Convergence of either Rail or Water, or of both, on the Globe, margin, 339—385.

A. not nature makes a commercial centre, 85, 90, 92, 176. Triumph of a. in C. wheel of commerce, 106. Means of nature to be employed, 193. Public Improvements anticipated 20 and 10 Years ago as a Basis, margin, 22—25. The Basis of our Prosperity is no longer hypothetical, margin, 25—28. Art following Nature's Lead, C. has no Taxes for Railways, though she has several times more than any Rival, and nearly two-thirds of all W. of the Tol. and Cin. Railroad, and N. of the Ohio River, margin, 28—36, 105, 106. The focal Point of the Great West is fixed immovably by over 7,500 of its 11,000 miles of Railway, centering at Chicago, margin, 36-42. The Pacific Railways in Progress—their Effects, margin, 42—52. The Illinois and Michigan Canal to the Illinois River--its possible Continuation to Rock Island on the Mississippi margin, 42—52. Five rival Railways eastward, margin, 53—58. The difference between Ch. and other western Centres, margin, 66—73. The Rivals of the West, Cin., St. L. and Ch., margin, 73—111 The Commerce of Chi. compared with St. L., margin, 140, 191. Abundant Mnfg. Advantages of Ch, margin, 191—222. Power of the internal Trade to build up great Cities, margin, 300—313. Power of the Railway to develop and centralize, margin, 313—339. Other cities no Measure for Chicago, margin, 385—399. Room for them and us, margin, 399—404.

ST. LOUIS admits superiority of a.: admission general, 93; *Blow,* 29, 82; *Cobb,* 40; *Fagin,* 67; *Mo. Dem.,* 27, 34, 35, 69, 83, 96, 111—114, 119, 120; *Mo. Rep.,* 35, 49, 54, 89; Cor. *Spr.* (Mass.) *Rep.,* 85; *Waterhouse.* 174—178. St. L. must revolutionize a. or nature, 90, 102. One or the other blunders; are barges perfection of a.? 178.

ARTESIAN wells, **Water**, 169, 254, 255.

ARTS, Fine. **Science** and a. C. a centre; Mr. Healey's opinion; 21 painters; sculptors. *Ch. Jour.,* mural monuments; Mr. Volk, 278. Crosby's opera house, country patronage. *Ch. Cour.,* Root & Cady's music establishment an example, 279.

ASHMUN, Hon. GEORGE, of Mass., favored Ills. Cent. R. R. grant, 138 *n.*

ASIA to furnish us labor, 139, 197, 198, 218, 219. Commerce opens our path; A. to depend on us, 219. Commerce with A., 221. **Pacific.**

ATCHISON (Kas.) *Free Press.* Comparison of Ch. and St. L., 187, 347.

ATLANTIC. **Cities. East.** Rivalry of A. cities for W. trade, 30, 52, 54, 56, 103, 133, 336, 362, 366, 367, 376, 377, 403. To seek trade of W. at C., 56, 103, 362, 366. Trade of W. makes chief cities, xx, 336. *Scott:* 304. *Mo. Rep. Cor.:* St. L. wants straight road to Omaha; who to build; fighting for life; St. L. natural terminus on Miss. of Phila., Terre Haute line, and of Balt. and Cin.; at Ch. compete with N. Y. and Bost.; Pacific Co. and East connections able, 54; not to build gives Cal. and mountain trade to C.; central cities with St. L. against C.; to whip out C. from Mo., a new road from St. Joe; kills Han. and St. Joe C. road; look out for anti-St. L. grooves; E. equally concerned; is this understood, 55...... Home difficulties recognized: such narrow views to end, 55. *Rep. P. and Ft. Wayne R. R.:* Importance of Pac. trade through C., 55..... Acquiesce in things settled; take trade in natural channels; northern cities advantage in capital; competition strong; State Rights our defence. *N. Y. World.* "*East and West—The Port of New York.*" Cunard line taken from Bost.; N. Y. chief exporter. 56; Erie canal made N. Y.; N. Y. needs railroads W.; wants corn for freight; Balt. a strong rival to N. Y.; Boston increasing Wn. lines; advantages over N. Y., 57...... Competition must be met; Balt. has advantage, 57; table of rates; improvements in railways; in water, 58. The Lake Route to the East and Europe, margin, 58. Short roads E. to be consolidated into trunks; contest from Portland to Norfolk; s'n cities against n'n; traffic seeks the lakes; will find its centre; rivalry to reach C.; competition our safety; cities must oppose consolidation; to seek the centre; yet trade to go by cheapest route; prosperity of C. rests upon whole country, 366; Balt. and Phila. to draw trade directly E.; w'n prize worthy; lakeward tendency; interior must have its centre; rivalry to reach it, 367.
A. Monthly,—Mr. Parton upon Ch., 58 *n*, 66.

BAKER, WILLIAM, builds Elevators; describes Armour, Dole's and Co.'s, 157.

BALDWIN, S. C., of Mich., reports shipments of Lake Superior iron ore, 227, 239; cost of ore and freight, 241.

BALLANTYNE, JAMES F., list of Ch. manufactures 1855, 200.

BALTIMORE had advantage for C. trade, 53, 57. To have more roads, 54, 374. Joint interest with Phil. and St. L., 54, 366, 376. A rival to N. Y., 57, 367, 371, 374. Must revive old spirit, 363, 367, 371. B. and Phila. will draw trade direct, 376. Losing former energy; trade diverted, 363, 371. Rates of freight from N. Y. and B. to St. L., 373; to Cin., to Ch., 374.

BANKING facilities of St. L. superior, 189.

BARGE trade. **Trade** *of St. L., its difficulties.* On rivers benefits C., 53, 65, 161, 179, 185, 347. Advantages, 177. Origin, 184. Reliance of **St. Louis**, 176, 178, 180, 341. How benefit St. L.? 178, 181, 183, 184. C. desires its success, 184, 341. Canals wanted to facilitate bs., 347.

BASIS **Argument.** The B. of our Prosperity is no longer hypothetical, margin, 25-28, 26, 104, 106.

BATES, Judge, of Mo., N. Mo. road perverted to Ch., 96..

BAUGH & Sons, establishment utilizing offal, 214.

BEACH, H. H. grain dryer, 163.

BEAUBIEN, MARK, early settler, 208 *n*.

BEEF raising in Texas, 123 *n*. **Stock, Live. Provisions.**

BELGIUM & HOLLAND, railways in, 328. Growth of mnfrs., 328.

BESSEMER process of smelting iron. 225.

BIBLE. **Religion.** *Gen.*, iv, 16, 17; *Is.*, i, 24—26; *Mat.*, v. 13—16, Title-page. *Phil.*, ii, 12. xxii. 1 *Cor.*, x, 23, 24, xxiv. 1 *Tim.*, vii, 9, xxv. *Job*, xii, 2, xxxii, *Mal.*, iii, 7—11, xliv. *Eccl.*, i, 9—11, l. *Matt.*, xiii, 12; *Luke*, xviii, 8, 73. *Is.*, xl, 3—5, 108. *Ez.*, xxvii, 3—14, 114. *Micah*, vi, 8; *Eccl.*, ix, 10, 261. 1 *Tim.*, v, 8, 289 *n*. *Prov.*, xi, 25, 297. *Dan.*, xii, 4, 315, 332.

BLACKSTONE, SIR WM., his nonsense of the sovereignty of the legislature our bane, 196 *n*.

BLAKE, J. A. "*Mines and Manufactures of Mississippi Valley.*" 223, 224.

BLANCHARD, RUFUS, map of the world, 402.

BLANEY, Dr. J. V. Z., opinion of Lasalle fire clay, 268. Address at dedication of Medical College, 268.

BLOW, H. T., Inaugural as Mayor of St. L., 28, 82.

BOARD OF TRADE. Endorsement of the work by a liberal subscription, vii, xxvi. *Privilege and Duty of the B. of T. to maintain their plighted Faith in regard to this Work.* Ap., 1—72.
Annual reports: not appreciated, xxvii. Grain inspection, 161, 162. Increase of C. trade, 1860, 151. Grain shipments, 1838—'67, 153. Grain and Flour, routes and receipts 1866, '7, 154. Receipts and shipments 1866, '7, 155. Elevators and capacity, 158. Routes and receipts of hogs and cattle, 3 years, 166. Receipts and shipments of salt, 12 years, 172. Do. wool, 12 years, 172. River routes, early shipments, 183. Flour manufacture, 7 years, 215. Highwines manufacture, 11 years, 215.

BOND, HEMAN, built second brick building, 99.

BOOMER, L. B., building St. L. bridge, 94.

BOOT and SHOE mnfr. *C. Times:* extent of business; Mass. chief; Phila. next city out of N. E.; began in C. 1859; increase 206; C. work preferred. Chief mnfrers.; machinery used; superiority over hand labor; division of labor; female labor, 207. Increase of mnfr. in Ills., and Cook co., 208.

BOSTON. **Cities. East.** B. and Chicago joint interest, 22, 24, 29, 30, 31, 32. *Mo. Dem.*. 34, 50, 51, 105. *Courier*, letters to 1847, 21, 22, 29. *Mining Journal*, letters to, 1848, 31. B. aiding St. Louis, *Mo. Rep.*, 49. This doubtful, 50. To improve Lake Simcoe route, 62. 344. *Atlantic Monthly*, Mr. Parton upon C., 58. 66. *North American Review*, C. F. Adams, Jr., comparing B. and Ch.. 66. Cause of large trade report, 144. Railways bridged over, 285. 6 ms. railway 1832, 1,203 in 1843, 335. Needs Lake Simcoe route, 344. B. and N. Y. without competition for w'n trade by water, 376.

BRAINARD, Dr. D., founder of Rush Med. Col., 268.

BREADSTUFFS, export to Europe, 186. **Grain.**

BRICK, made by digging city canals, 251, 258.

BRIDGES for C. over Miss. and Mo. rivers, 40, 52, 90, 94, 348, 356. Over Miss. essential, 34, 90, 94, 176. Hurt St. L., 91, 94, 348. Mr. Boomer, of Ch., building at St. L., 94. At St. L., C. wants one, 94, 176. Necessary to St. L., yet poor as a main reliance; will bear more trade to C. than St. L.; C. wants half-a-dozen, 94. *Pitts. Gaz.* quotes *N. Amer.*, "Importance of Railroad Bridges at St. L.," 376. B. over railroad tracks in city, 285.

BRISTOL, R. C., first steam elevator, 157.

BRONSON, FREDERIC, sells 1½ block, 9,292; sells block 1, O. T. 291.

BRUNSWICK (Mo.), *Central City.* Trade tending to C. 34.

BUFFALO *Com. Adv.* Railway and water carriage, 59. *Board of Trade Rep.* upon N. W., 131.

BUILDINGS, First in Ch., 99 *n*. Oldest built by Mr. Peck, 100 *n*. Materials, brick, stone, and lumber; "Balloon," Mr. Snow invented: makes way for better 257. St. L.'s spite; "a C. house," 257 *n*. Joliet stone, its abundance and beauty, architects good, City being well-built; wide streets favor exhibition of architecture, 258. Mr. Palmer's marble block the finest commercial building in the world, 258, *n*. Some of the erections 1867, 259. Census of bs., 1868, of brick, stone and wood; of dwellings, stores, shops and public b's., 398. Bond built second brick b., 99 *n*.

BURLINGAME, Hon. ANSON S., Chinese Plenipotentiary, 219.

BUSINESS men of C. should buy real-estate, xv. 170. In b. affairs, principles important, 1.

CAIRO a better natural site than St. L., 84.

CANADA. Immigration from; their fears, 137. Canals to be improved, 132. *Poor*, St. Law. waters to be an open Mediter. Sea; English-speaking people one; commerce disregards National boundaries, 343; do our best to have continental commerce, 344......... Lake Simcoe route to be opened, 62, 343, 344, 345, 375.

CANALS. N. W. to have rapid increase in c's; Canadian to be improved, 132. Their traffic in Eng. increased by railways, 325. Railways compete with c's, 335. *Ch. Times:* Canals still valuable; muscles of body politic; no consolidation with railways; W. the land for both, 345; Ch. c. only one for large boats; Lake Mich. sure bead; Ch. centre of interior navigation, 346...... Rivers benefited by canals, giving barges access to lakes, 347. First Eng. 1760, 322.

ERIE made N. Y., 57. Enlargement necessary, 58, 60, 304. Made for the W., 304. From 1825 to 1838 only eastern outlet, 131. Takes about one-seventh western produce, 319. To be enlarged for ships from Oswego to Hudson, 344.

ILL. AND MICH. projected when Ills. became a State; a strong ligament of union, **xxxix**. *Circ. 1848.* That year to be opened; its value, 23. **Illinois and Michigan Canal to the Illinois River--its possible Continuation to Rock Island on the Miss.**, margin, 52, 53, 104. Deepened by city for sanitary purposes; corn and lumber trade, 53. *Rep. of Wilson and Gooding*, upon "adapting c. and Ills. River to military purposes:" Question settled; this route best; old natural connection; 7 ft. depth required; Ills. River a natural canal, 64 *n*.......Extension to Rock Isl., 53, 63, 64, 65, 104, 312, 345, 347. Deepening by city to cleanse Ch. River, 252 *n*. *Scott*, route compared with Maumee and Cin., 306.

Lake Simcoe, Huron to Ontario, to be opened, 62, 343, 344, 345, 375. Canadian c's to be improved, 132. Niagara, U. S. needed, 62, 375, 376. More cheaply built than Welland, 344. St. Lawrence waters to be an open Mediter. sea, 62, 343. Advance in one crop pay whole cost of improvement from Ch. to ocean, 344. Mass. should lead in the construction, 376. Sault St. Marie opened 1855, 240. Virginia, from Ohio River projected, 132. Welland Canal, *Mark Lane Exp.*, enlargement necessary, 66. Ottawa River route, 62, 344. Champlain Canal to St. Law., 343. Ohio Canals, 306. Green Bay to Rock River, 345. South Branch C. Co. an important improvement, 296.

CAPITAL. **Money.** **Real Estate, especially in a growing City, is the best Investment**, 14-16. Ch. lacks c., xiv, 27, 28, 35, 70, 190, 198, 200, 217, 349, 377, This work to draw to her c., xx. *The whole c. of N. Y. and N. Eng. supports Ch.*, xv, 22, 24, 29, 30, 31. 32, 35, 50, 51, 56, 71, 105. 120, 344, 349, 335, 374, 376, 377; *Mo. Dem.*, 26, 27, 34; *Mo Rep.*, 39; *Cobb*, St. L., 40; *Fagin*, St. L., 68; *Hammond*, St. L., 81. Ch. begins to have c., 99, 120, 378, 380. National securities supply c., 15. C. seeks and finds safety, 28, 29, Safety of the W., 28. N. Y. and N. Eng., have chief surplus, 29. Interested to maintain present railway system, 29, 38, 42, 56. C. for mnfrs. to be drawn from Europe, 198. C. will find profitable employment, 199, 244. Lack of c., felt specially in mnfrs., 200. *Rail. Jour.*: c. of W. in lands and improvements; railroad mnfg. at C. a good investment, 217. Investments in Ch. real estate, 296-299. *Ruggles:* Increase of property by railways and canals; chief in W., 318, 335.......... National securities supply c., 15. Immense draft of c. for railways, 335. *Baxter:* Land-owners to supply c. for branch railways, 332.

ST. LOUIS to get c., East, 27, 85, 90. Can get c. in Europe, 28. Has large c., 28, 83, 88, 189, 190, 200. She boasts of it, 153; *Cor. Mo. Dem.*, 83; *Prof. Waterhouse*, 189. This to her shame. *N. Y. Evening Post*, "*St. L. versus C.:*" St. L. rather worsted in the contest, 189; asserts superiority in banks; she exults, 190..........Ch. needs c.; to prove this our object; no city offers equal inducements, 190.

CARNOT'S Judgment of the permanence of our republic, 195.

CARROLL, CHARLES, laid corner stone of B. & O. R. R., 371.

CATTLE, Growth of trade at C., 164. **Stock, Live. Provisions.**

CAUSES, combination of in favor of Ch., 102. C's of Ch. growth traced to results, 107.

CEMETERIES, present inadequate; one wanted N. W., must have one large and permanent, 297, *n*.

CENSUS of **Buildings** and **Population** of C., 1868, 398.

CENTRE. **City.** AIMS: *To show that the Great Interior must build up many great Cities*, xvii, xxix, 59 *n*, 71, 108, 109, 110, 146, 217, 325, 387, 391. *To show that the Gt. Int, a complete Unit in Interest, must have its own Centre, which is found and established*, xviii, 92, 110, 130, 136, 138, 140, 218. 336, 367, 387. *To show that the chief City of the Gt. Int. must, probably, be Emporium of the Continent*, xix, 92, 110, 387, 392, 396.

The Difference between Ch. and other western C's, margin, 66, 73. No railway c. possible W. of C., 25, 49, 71, 120. Ch. was a c. for 150 to 200 ms. before railroads, 11, 72, 74. A c. draws trade from a distance, 110, 150. Trade seeks a c. for distribution, 56, 70, 87, 105, 110, 130, 155, 325.

Atch. (Kan.), Free Press "A Comparison;" W. has two c's., Ch. and St. L.; St. L. was c. of whole W.; on her dignity, 187; strong before Ch. started; relative changes in favor of Ch., 188. *Mr. Baxter*, "*Railway Extension and its Results:*" London a centre of other railway centres; national characteristics manifested in railway systems; "U. S. federal independence in many centres;" Manchester maufg., Liverpool commercial, London monetary and political centre 324......Commerce and mnfs. centralize, 324. Centralization like Paris dangerous; State sovereignty here counteracts; yet Federal union binds together; benefit of State divisions; yet trade centralizes, 325. Centres E. and W. to be in harmony, 342. All sections do and will seek it, 366, 387. *Scott*, "*Westward Movement of the Centre of Population and Industrial Power in N. Am.:*" C's moving W.; come together on L. Mich., 394; chief essentials; commerce important; domestic exceeds foreign 20 to 1, 395. N. Y. now chief; change certain; Gr. In. have 70,000,000, and chief city, 396. 1,905, Ch. beat N. Y., 397.

REGION OF WHICH CH. IS CENTRE.—**Great Interior. Northwest. West.** States by name. What is Ch. territory? Why not now Emporium of entire W? 115. **The Northwest is the Prize contested—its Extent and Resources**, margin, 111-131. **600,000 sq. m's of arable land and watercourses, unequaled in Advantages, natural and acquired, rapidly settling with the best of Men, must give unexampled growth to their Emporium**, margin, 131—140.

BY **Nature** Ch. is made chief c., 28, 74, 92, 150, 342. Ch. the c. of interior navigation, 346. **Lakes.** **The Lake Route to the East and Europe**, margin 58-65, 103. Ch. at the head of the grandest inland navigation on the globe, 101, 103, 339. Centre of Republic at head of lake navigation, 92, 101, 396. **Rivers.** Extent of navigation, 100-174. Not to be detracted, 64, 184. Yet lakes superior, 64, 75, 79, 88, 184, 304, 342. Convergence of lake and river valleys, Ch. the natural point of, 53, 58, 62, 70, 93, 104, 304, 393, 342.

BY **Art.** A, not nature, makes a commercial c., 85, 90, 176, 392. Geographical centrality of small account, 92, 130. **Canal.** **The Illinois and Mich. Canal to the Ills. River—its possible continuation to Rock Island on the Miss**, 52, 53, 104. **Railway.** Ch. system proves natural centrality, 28, 29, 40, 42, 65, 71, 120, 221, 346, 399. Chief r. centre of the world, xiii, 24, 384. Centralizing power of r's, 398, 399. **Art following Nature's Lead, C. has no Taxes for Railways, though she has several times more than any Rival, and nearly Two-Thirds of all west of the Toledo & Cincinnati Road, and north of the Ohio River**, margin, 28-36. **The Focal Point of the Great West is fixed immovably by over 7,500 of its 11,000 miles of Railway centring at Ch.**, margin, 36—42, 105. **The Pacific Railways in Progress—their Effects**, margin 42—52. **Five rival Railways eastward**, margin, 53—58. **Power of the Railway to develop and centralize**, margin, 313—339. **No other Point of equal Convergence of either Rail or Water, or of both, on the Globe**, margin, 339—385. **Agriculture. Commerce. Education. Fine Arts. Market. Manufactures. Mining. Science and Art. Trade.**

ST. LOUIS. *Prof. Waterhouse*, "*Missouri: St. L. the commercial C. of North America:*" Ordained by nature, 173; geog. c.; N. Mo. road; 10,000 ms. railway contemplated; chief terminal points. Lake Superior, Gulf, Pacific, etc.; N. W. trade may be diverted; S. W. sure; mining trade not monopolized; rebellion hurt St. L.; Sn. trade destroyed; St. L. paralyzed; purchase of Govt. supplies proves centrality; peace restores advantages, 175; difficulties of St. L.; C.

energetic; her railroads; trust in nature not safe; what St. L. must do, 176; barge trade begun; steamboats compared; cheapness to N. O.; thence to Europe; revolutionize river trade; Miss. to be improved; St. L. to work for it, 177; Europe to help fulfil prophecy; St. L. to keep pace with W.; growth immense; universal friendship 178.

CHANNING. W. E., D. D., the nobility of Commerce, 190.

CHARTER, Land Improvement Co., 13.

CHESBROUGH, E. S., Civ. Eng., planned lake tunnel, 213. Indebtedness to him for City improvements, 257. Proper liberality of citizens, 257, *n.*

CHESTER, Ills., coal fields, *Prof. Waterhouse*, 224.

CHICAGOAN. C. as a literary centre, 280.

CHISHOLM *vs.* Ga., its *obiter dicta* have misled us, 196, *n.*

CHURCH. **Religion.**

CINCINNATI. Distribution of copies of work to papers, viii, xviii. Not disparaged, xxix. Comparison of advantages with Ch. *Advt. 1847*, 15 y. for Ch. equal to 27 for Cin., 7. **Rivals of the West, Cincinnati St. L. and Ch.,** margin, 73-111. Superiority not claimed for Ch., 15 y. ago; cities at 3 corners of a triangle, sides 280 ms., 73......*Cir. 1848*, "*Ch. compared with Cin:*" Cin. no special river advantages; Ch. a centre of 200 miles; mnfg. advantages; 900,000 people in Ohio made Cin.; 800,000 in Ills. with more improvements, do more for Ch.; growth of whole country; 15 y. for Ch. equal to 20 for Cin. 74. *Cir. 1861:* 9 chief cities, relative changes in 10 y.; Ch. 18th, now 9th; in 1870 to be 4th or 3d; views of '48 tame; Cin. passed next; not till 1853 was it supposed possible to beat St. L; changes made; railroad advantages; lakes better than rivers, 75. *N. Y. Eve. Post*, Triangular fight; Cin. losing ground; refuses railroad connection; lines consolidating; avoid Cin......This imaginary excuse; other reasons. *Cor. Cin. Gaz.*, "*Business between Cin., Ch. and the Northwest:*" Business N. W. over, S. W. under-estimated, 76. Affinities of people adverse to Cin.; N. trade lost; try to keep 70 ms.; seek S. and S. W. business......Cin. modest; she formerly prized N. W. trade; prospects S. W., 77. Judge Wright's estimate of N W. trade, 77, *n.* *Mo. Rep.*, "South. Ills. Railroad." A Cin. meeting announced about Vin. & Cairo railroad; 8 attended; cut off St. L. and Ch.; same arguments apply to St. L.; railroad apathy..... Ch. takes care of S. E. Ills.; Cin. abandons triangular duel; St. L. reposes; her task difficult, 78. *N. Y. Mail* quoted by *Mo. Dem.*, comparing Cin., St. L. and Ch., 87, *n.* *C. Times*: Cin. distracted about heat and water; river down; coal up; trouble semi-annual, 88. To be chief in her region, 392. Rates of freight from N. Y. and Balt., 374. *Railroad Record*, aid of railroads by Congress, 127. Packing business natural to her, 209. Cin. admits her inferiority to Ch., 146, 173. *Cin. Enq.:* trade sales less; why so; press responsible; old Hunkers rule; Ch. not so; differences, 146. *Scott:* will C. equal N. Y., 301. mnfrs. and trade in C., 308. To be chief of rivers till 1890, 309.

CITY. **Advantages,** Local. **Atlantic. Centre. St. Louis,** and other cities by name. **Province, Government and Responsibility:** First Caucasian city, man's institution, significant name, *Gen.* iv, 16, 17; The best national government for a city, *Is.* i., 25—27; Responsibility according to strength, prominence and illumination, *Matt.* 5. 13—16. Title-page. Remarks thereon, xii, xiii. A work of art, not nature, xii, xiii.

BENEFITS OF THE CITY.—Real estate, especially in a growing C., the best **Investment,** margin, 14—16. **General Pecuniary Revulsions may intervene, but can not change the Result,** margin, 16—21. City an ulcer on the body politic; does not make itself; a vent for corruption; centres of civilization; associated effort needed; worth of a true city; modern tendency to towns, 320 Triple government not wanted, 287, *n.* Jealousy between c. and country. *Jacksonville* (Ills.) *Jour.*, "*Chicago at Home and Abroad:*" Illinoisan praises it abroad; why jealous at home; example worthy; activity; others plod; rich men of Jacksonville to use their capital; Ch. enterprise beats St. L., 109.

GROWTH OF CITIES.—Importance of this subject; this the most marvelous example, ix. St. L. or Ch. to be chief of W., xxix. No disparagement or injustice to any, xxx. *Duty to our City:* commensurate with advantages; foundations being laid, xxxvi; inroads by death; some run away; rich too neglectful; active business men do nearly all; to perform duty must well know C's future; mistakes expensive to children, xxxvii; a city of millions; work to be done; make known advantages in real estate; Gr. Interior will make its city chief of continent; Mr. Scott's predictions of Ch. 25 years ago confirmed, xxxviii. Information to be distrib'd at home and abroad, viii, xxxix. If one is to be chief others wish to know it, xliv. Growth of others doubtful, 26, 84, 108, 392. Rivalry of seaboard cs. for trade of W. xv., 30, 52, 54, 56, 103, 133, 336, 362, 366, 367, 376, 403. Increase of 9 chief, 1850–60, 75. State division creates many cities, 109. National Union permits trade to seek its centre, 110, 402. Commerce builds great cs., 141, 392. Wholesale trade of 20 chief, 1866-7, 142—145. *Edmunds:* cs. and towns mark our progress, 194. *Scott*, 1843, "*Internal Trade of the U. S.:*" interior cs. to have some foreign trade; large cs. inland, 303; lake trade makes Atlantic c. chief, 304; growth of lake cs., 1830–40, 305; tendency to cs.; effect of modern improvements, 307; estimates of relative growth of cs. and country for 50 y., from 1840, 308; lake to beat river valley, 309; Cleveland, Maumee and Ch. compared, 312......... Mr. Scott miscalculated rapidity of changes, 313. Railroads centralize; c. an ulcer; does not make itself; its benefits; modern tendency to towns, 320. *Tucker:* "*Cities and Towns:*" growth of cities marks progress; evils countervailed; progressive countries tend to; proportion of town-population in each section and in each Wn. State, 321; ⅛ in towns; railways stimulate their growth, 322, 401. *Scott*, 1843, "Effect of Improvements on Growth of towns:" Eng., first canal 1760, spinning jenny 1767, mule 1775, Watts' steam engine 1785; m'cad. roads, canals and railways since 1810; consequent increase in towns, 322; effect of railways; London to grow; growth in Eng. chiefly in towns; so in Mass., N. Y., Pa., O.; more rapid hereafter, 323. *Merch. Mag.:* growth of 12 Atl. and Gulf, 1810–60, 336; steady increase, p. c. over country increase; Boston ¼ of Mass.; N. Y. most remarkable; 5 Miss. val. c's, growth 1810–60; great increase; St. Louis largest; 6 lakes c's, growth, 1840–60, 337; greater increase of C. over Buff.; railroads help C.; produce to increase; growth remarkable compared with E'n c's.; comparison with lake and others, 1840–60; causes of lake superiority; St. L. benefited; N W. supplied with railroads; smoothing her way to market, 338.......... What shall stop growth of lake c's.? Mr. Scott's predictions confirmed, 338, 391. W. has already built up large c's; their growth to be stimulated; have several large ones; chief will be sought by all others, 387, 392. C. growth stimulated by modern improvements, 387, 398.—Why Ch. has no precedent, 397, 400.

AIMS:—*To show that the Gt. Int. must build up many great c's*, xvii, xxix, 59 *n*, 71, 108, 109, 110, 146, 217, 325, 386, 387, 391. *To show that the Gr. Int., a complete Unit in interest, must have its own Centre, which is found and established*, xviii, 92, 110, 130, 136, 138, 140, 218, 326, 366, 367, 387, 396. *To show that the chief City of the Gt. Int. must, probably, be Emporium of the Continent*, xix, 92, 110, 366, 387, 392, 396.

NINE POINTS, THE BASIS OF CHICAGO'S CERTAIN GROWTH. 1. **The Basis of our Prosperity is no longer hypothetical,** margin, 25-28. Ch. changes from promise to fact; she has these 9 points; a c. must have several of them to be a rival, 107; no city has 3; relative growth therefore problematical, 108. 2. **Art following Nature's lead, Chicago has no taxes for Railways, tho' she has several times more than any Rival, and nearly Two-thirds of all W. of the Tol. & Cin. Road, and N. of the Ohio River,** margin, 28-36. Art follows nature; joint interest of E'n **capital** with Ch., 105; spokes put in independently; wheel artistic; no Ch. work; common sense ruled; no power to change what all interests desire; can St. L. work a change; wheel sure to revolve,, 106. 3. The Focal Point of the Great West is fixed immovably [1868], by over 7,500 of its 11,000 miles of Railway centering at Ch., margin, 36-42. 15 trunks, 242 to 974 ms.; Ch. artificial hub of N. W.; felloes secure; adapted to stockholders' interest and to public; hibernaters not to change the wheel, 105. 4. The Pacific Railways in Progress—their Effects, margin, 42-52. Several to be built; Ch. sure of most of the trade; still hypothetical; therefore not the basis; nor mountain trade, 104. 5. The Illinois & Michigan **Canal,** margin, 52-53, Unites lakes and rivers; to be enlarged, 104. 6. Five rival Railways Eastward,, margin, 53-58.→No city sought by seaboard as is Ch., 103. 7. The **Lake** Route to the East and Europe, margin, 66-73. Head of lake navigation, lakes superior to rivers; chief grain and provision market sought by Europe; chief for imports and exports of the W., 103. 8. The difference between Ch. and other Western **Centres,** margin, 66-73. Combination of causes of **nature** and of **art.** 102. 9. The **Rivals** of the West, **Cincinnati, St. Louis,** and Chicago, margin, 111-131. The weakest beats the strongest, 102.

TEN POINTS TO CALCULATE THE MEASURE OF CHICAGO'S GROWTH. 1. The **Northwest** is the Prize contested—its Extent and Resources, margin, 111-131 St. L. a good witness; shows the value of N. W. trade, 111. 1,500,000 sq. ms. tributary and becoming so, 115. 2. 600,000 square miles [the Old Northwest,] of arable land and Water Courses, unequaled in Advantages, natural and acquired, rapidly settling with the best of Men, must give unexampled Growth to their Emporium, margin, 131-140. This already secured by r's; equal to 7 Englands, 131. 3. The **Commerce** of Chi. compared with **St. Louis,** margin, 140-191. Decline of St. L. relative, not actual, 142. 4. **Manufacturing** advantages of Ch., Rapid Progress, margin, 191-222. W. to mnfr. for itself; have its centre for this, 221. 5. Conjunction of **Coal, Iron,** and other **Minerals,** margin, 222-249. Chief minerals gathered at Ch.; insures mnfg. largely, 248 6. Local **Advantages** and City Expansion, margin, 249-300. With these unequaled advantages, does nature fail in site? 249. 7. Power of the Internal **Trade** to build up great Cities, margin, 300-313. *Scott's* discussion in *Hunt's Merch. Mag.*, 1843, of the "Internal Trade of the U. S.," 300. 8. Power of the **Railway** to Develope and Centralize, margin, 313-339. No other equal power; no such area to work upon, 313. 9. No other equal Point of Convergence, of either Rail or Water, or of both, on the Globe, margin, 339-385. Head of lakes is 1st point; conjunction with rivers another; still railways superior; water facilities valuable in conjunction with railways, 339. A train every 3 minutes, hundreds of miles; water facilities unequaled, to be increased; railways doubled; some of Ch.'s advantages present a certainty, 385. 10. The **Northwest** and **West** are hereafter the **Great Interior,** margin, 385-387. To be a unit, 386. Reasons of union; means of prosperity; work for our country; work for ourselves; have centres; one chief; little land yet tilled has built up c's; rapid improvements stimulate city growth; several large c's; chief will draw from others, 387.

TWO RESULTS OF THE **Argument.** 1. Other **Cities** are no Measure for Ch., margin, 387-402. This the natural and just conclusion, 387. No boasting; it is excluded, and how, 388; *Co-operation of nature and of art from abroad*, xii. *The whole capital of New York and New England supports Ch.*, xv *Obligations of City and Citizens in view of the unparalleled Benefits showered by God and Country*, xxiii. Still, proud of our c.; we should appreciate our position; this book to aid; will cultivate pride, 388 *Scott*, 1848, "*Our Cities, Atlantic and Interior*:" Pride in our c's; large ones hoped for; N. Y. not appreciated: exportations of N. O. 388; 1828 predicted inland c. largest; changes since; Cin. and N. Y. compared; past and future, 389; growth 13 interior c's, 1840-48; of 10 Atl. c's, 1840-48; int. 3-fold faster, 390; W. not confined to ag.; commerce and mnfrs. build great c's in W., 391. *Scott*, 1857, "*Westward movement of Centre of Pop., and of Industrial Power in N. Am.*": movement of centres W.; come together on L. Mich., 394; foreign commerce: domestic 20 to 1, 395; C. centre of commerce in 100 y.; Gt. Int. have chief city; era of great c's, 396; N. Y, equal Lon., and C. equal N. Y. in 50 y., 397......Ratio of increase not sustainable, 391; At C. more sustainable, 401. Census of Ch., 1st April, 1868. 398. Rapid growth of c's, 398. More rapid in future, 401. 2. "There is Room for them and us," margin, 402-404. We continental; Europe no measure for us; influence of our governments; our improvements, 402. *Scott*, 1846, "*The Progress of the West considered, with reference to great Commercial Cities in the U. S.*:" *Alb. Argus*, N. Y. can hold Wn trade; N. Y. best chance of en. c's; great city to be in centre of population; progress of Am. Val. 100 y., 300,000,000; Atl. border 31,000,000, 403. N. Y. now centre of dom. trade; this 15 times greater than foreign; will 300,000,000 go to N. Y. to trade; progress not realized; estimate reduced to 200,000,000; direct trade from lakes to Europe; 350 ton propellers; change less than last 50 y., 404.

CIVILIZATION promotes growth of cities, 321.

CLARKE, GEORGE C., Pres. Board of Ed., upon the progress of our schools, 267.

CLARKE, WILLIAM H., Civ. Eng., aid in lake tunnel, 253.

CLAY CO., MO., St. L. may lose its trade, 97. Its situation, 98.

CLEVELAND, trade of, 1867, 151. Trade with Lake Sup., 246.

CLIMATE. Heat unfavorable to N. O. exports of grain and provisions, 183, 306. Against river route, *U. S. Census Rep.*, 184. Of Ch. invigorating; cool summer nights brace for labor; a contrast with St. L., 252.

CLINTON, DE WITT, predicted importance of Ch. 101.

COAL. Conjunction of C, **Iron** and other **Minerals.** Margin 222-249. *Blake*, Mo. and Ills., 223; fields of the world, extent, 223; Belleville and La Salle seams, 223. *Waterhouse*, "Illinois Chester Coalfields," 225; contiguous to Missouri Iron Mountain; quality superior; Pittsburgh coal and other Pa.; Analysis of Chester coal by Dr. Litton, 225; coking is not necessary; benefit to St. L., 226...... Pa. and Ohio are sure, 241. Brazil probably next, 242. Wilmington coal good, 242. *Chi. and Alton R. R. Rep.* Coal traffic, 146,050 tons; 230 miles road over coal-field; only 55 miles from C., 242...... Competition with other railroads, canal and river in coal traffic, 242. Chester coal a reliance, trial at St. L., 243. *St. L. Board of Trade* resolutions, success in smelting Mo. iron with Chester coal, 243...... Greatest known field will yield good qualities; explorations just begun; yet no hypothetic basis; reality, suffices, 243. Lake Erie c. to cost $4 to $6, 244.

COBB, HENRY, in *Rep.*, Ch. a Delilah, manipulating the Samson, St. L., 40.

COBDEN, RICHARD, opinion of Ch., 66.

COGSWELL, Dr., selected Astor Library—would select one for C., 274, *n.*

COLORADO trade leaving St. L. for Ch., 117. *Mo. Dem.*; C. and N. Y. now have it; its extent; St. L. has very little; ox trains too slow; St. L. beats C., trade of W., beat her still more; fast frt. line wanted, 119. *Mo. Dem.*, "The Denver Pac. R. R. movement": quotes *Denver News'* account of action about road to Cheyenne which said: sorry to embarrass St. L. road; will welcome and aid them; but will have their own road, 120.

COMBINATION of commerce and mnfrs., ag. and min. wealth, etc., at Ch., 72, 249. A c. of causes gives superiority to a city, 70, 72, 73, 102. C. adverse to St. L., 84. St. L. eschews c., 159.

COMMERCE. **Market. Trade.** Immense growth, 59. Lake exceeds foreign, 62. Lake and ocean to be immense, 62, 103. Centripetal power, 70, 105,

110 130, 324, 366. Ch. wheel of c., triumph of art, 106. Hercules moves it, but man must help, 347. *N. Y. Eve. Post,* "The strong N. W.": feel pulse at Ch.; injury to E. helps Ch.; increase of c., 140. A city must have c., 140; builds great cities; division of labor requires c.; God ennobles it; *Ez. xxvii,* 3-14. Tyre renowned; influence of merchants; responsibility, 141. *Channing:* c. noble; makes peace; Christianizes, 190. Merchants to be generous; extend civilization; not to corrupt; teach Christ in acts: free trade for man's interest; we tend toward it......This at present doubtful; the reasons, 191. C. to be cared for; c. and mnfrs. both needed, 192. C. seldom makes a large city; but a commercial point draws other business, 199; as N. Y. draws mnfrs., 216. C. of Ch. compared with St. L., margin, 140-191. Power of the Internal trade to build up great cities, *Scott, in Hunt's Merch Mag.,* 1843, margin, 300-313. Danger of vassalage from mere c., 220. *Baxter:* Railways create their traffic, 325; proportion of ex. and imp. to r. ways and navigation. Gt. Br., 326; France, 327; Belgium, 328; U. S.; increase of U. S. imports and exports, 1830-60, 329. *Poussin:* U. S. to become chief com. nation; rival Gt. Br., 333......If not yet continental, must do our best, 344. *Atch.* (Kas.) *Free Press:* "Ch. and St. L."; two great centres; St. L. had all; Ch. not begun; cut-offs by C. of St. L.; Ch. activity, 348. Currents latitudinal, 380. *Scott:* Points of in W. to be great cities, 391. Advantages of C. 392. Foreign C. to domestic as 1 to 20, 395.

FACILITIES. What belong to Ch, 37. Advantages of **nature** and **art**, 142. **Canal. Lakes. Railways. Rivers. Water.**

REGION TRIBUTARY. **Area. Gt. Int. North-west. Valley. Lake. River.**

CHIEF BRANCHES. **Trade,** *wholesale.* **Grain. Live-Stock. Lumber. Mining. Provisions.**

COMMERCIAL EXPRESS, facilities for slaughtering and packing, 211.

COMMERCIAL REP. AND MARKET REVIEW upon pork packing, 211.

COMPARISONS. *Invidious* cs. *render us odious,* xxix.

COMPETITION. Ch. wants the largest c., 44, 222, 366.

CONGRESS to aid Pacific road, 46, 48; *Cin. Rail. Rec.,* 127. *San. Fran. Bulletin* opposes except as to land grants, 47. Justice never done the W., 138. A Mass. M. C. opposed Ills. Cent. R. R. grant, 138, *n.* C. to aid St. L. as well as Ch. roads, 80.

COOK CO., ILLS., U. S. census of mnfrs. 1860, 201.

COPPER. **Minerals.**

CORN **Grain.** Rec'd. by canal, 6 y., 53.

COTTON transported by rail, 57.

COURIER, CH., Reference to our City, excusable, xxxi. Root & Cady's music publications, 279.

CRANE, EDWARD, of Boston, cheapening freights, E. and W., 375.

CROSBY'S OPERA HOUSE, with cut, 279.

CUTT OFF, Ch. feared, St. L. hoped for, 69. The Joliet, 70. Of St. L., *Kas. Free Press,* 348. **Railroads:** *Cairo and Fulton; Cameron and Kas. City; Han. and St. Joe.*

DELILAH. C. a D., victimizing St. L., the Sampson, 39. Instead of D., she is in the grasp of a Procrustes, on a stretcher of iron rails, 82.

DEMOCRATIC PRESS, mnfs. of C. 1855, 200.

DENVER NEWS. Branch to Pacific railroad, 120.

DESERT, the American, a picture, 122 *n.*

DETROIT, C. compared with, 1834-5. Trade of 1867, 151. Had Lake Sup. trade, 246.

DIFFERENCE. The D. between Chicago and other Western Centres, margin, 66—73, 102.

DOCK fronts extensive; increasing; C. Dock and Canal Imp. Co.; officers; plan remedies harbor difficulties; description, 251. South Branch Canal Co. an important improvement, 96.

DOLE, GEORGE W., built 2d framed building, 99 Horse-power elevator, 157.

DORE, J. C., first superintendent of schools, 266.

DOUGLAS, STHEPHEN A., donation for University of Ch., 272. Patron of Mr. Volk, 278.

DUBUQUE *Herald.* Montana trade, 118.

DULL & GOWAN, contractors of lake tunnel, 253.

DYER, THOMAS, sells block 1, O. T., 7.

EAST, JOINT INTEREST OF C. WITH.—This main point affirmed, 20 y. ago, 27, 29, 32, 377. *The whole Capital of N. Y. and N. Eng. support C.,* xiv., 29, 35, 51, 56, 71, 105, 120, 336, 344, 349, 355, 374, 377. Gt. Int. the prize contested, 366, 367. Too much credit to C., not enough to N. Y. and N. Eng., 35. Rivalry of Phil. and Balt. with N. Y. and N. Eng. 53, 55. N. Y. and N. Eng. made C. the focal railway point, 56. Injury to E. helps C., 140. E. changed to W., to pursue our destiny, 197, 218.

Letters to Boston Courier, 1847: Bost., to build Galena r. and branches, one to Ia. State line, connecting Bost. and C. by Mich. Cent. within 3 years; Galena road with branch to Alton & St. L.; important to Boston, 21; lake shore road; B. to draw business N. to lakes; best do it soon; En. cities interested; B. especially; to Rock Island, and on to Council Bluffs within 20 ys.; Va. appreciated, but Mass. and W. united; B. and C. identified in interest: a strong basis of prosperity, 22. Why other Wn. cities can not get railroads; this a natural centre; examination confirms this, 29. *Let. to Bost. Cour.* (similar to that above), 30. *Let. to Bost. Min. Jour. and N. Y. Cour. and Enq.,* 1848: railroads a bond of union; iron arms encircling trade; W. the prize; N. Y. and Bost. to co-operate to draw business to the lakes; several railroads considered; Pacific possible; get one then to Council Bluffs; E. benefited as well as W., 31. N. Y. and N. Eng. to get trade thro' C.; railway predictions not visionary; results of 15 y.; what 15 y. to come; with aid of Cong. will reach Council Bluffs in 15 y. Predictions of 20 y. verified; joint interest the right string; effect of reiteration, 32. *Knowlton, of Mass.,* Letter to Ship Canal Convention: Miss. River vaunted; monopolies adverse to our genius; E. and W. have centres; to be brought into harmonious action; C. an important centre; long railways show Miss. no monopolist; S. and E. competitors; water wanted besides railways; it never wears out; railways for travel, water for heavy transportation; E. wants shortest communication; means of union our object, 342. *Poor, of Maine,* letter to same Con.; object embraces all means of communication with great N. W.; question important; internal trade, tho' great, small as to future; grain consumed in transport; to remedy this the object; outlets wanted from rather than to C.; make St. Law. waters a Mediter. sea; save half cost of freight; Eng. speaking people one; commerce disregards national boundaries, 343; advance in one crop pay whole cost; lake navigation cheap as ocean; not 1-10 of railway; if our commerce be not yet continental, let us do our best; Am. Niagara canal; improve St. Clair river; dealing with great subjects; prosecute war and build Pac. railway; capacities and capabilities ample, 344 .... N. Y. and N. Eng. need Lake Simcoe route, 345; without competition for W. trade by water, 376; will appreciate their superiority by water, 377.

ST. L. VIEWS.—"*A flank movement:*" Cameron road not aided by Ch., but by E.; road built; connects Pac. r. with Ch., 26; trade like water; work for St. L.; E'n capital protects C.; to be got for St. L., 27. *Mo. Dem. 1861:* St. L. trade decreasing; victim of illusion; Ch. trade increasing; N. Y. and Bost. in competition with St. L., thro' Ch.; Wall St. plans adverse, 34. *Cor. Mo. Rep.,* "*Ch. St. L., the Bridge:*" How does Ch. outstrip St. L.? has trade of N. W.; who helps Ch.; no advantages, no capital, all things supplied; different management in St. L. and Ch., 35. *Mr. Henry Cobb in Mo. Rep.:* the East, Philistines, victimizing the Sampson St. L., thro' Ch. the Delilah, 40. *Mo. Rep.:* E. capital aiding St. L, 49. *Cor. Mo. Rep.:* Central cities with St. L., against Ch. and N'n cities. 55. *Mr. Fagin's speech to St. L. Board of Trade:* E'n capital helps Ch, 68. *Cor. Springfield* (Mass.) *Rep.,* reliance on E. for capital. 85. *Cor. Mo. Rep.,* get capital E., 90.

EDMUNDS, J. W., Editor U. S. Census, 1860. 184, 193, 218, 315, 317.

EDUCATION. **Science. Art.** Donations of the U. S. for, 193. Energy of Methodists in, 271.

PUBLIC SCHOOLS. First public school house, 263. List and value of school houses, 1867; more to be done; dedication of Carpenter School, 264. *Ald. Holden's* remarks; schools, cost money; items expended, 1867–'8....Incomes; school fund; land rapidly enhancing; income from land rents; other receipts, 265; expenditures, 1867–'8; attention to schools; ridicule of Mr. Miltimore for first "barn" school house; superintendents, Dore, Wells and Pickard......*Mr. Wells' Rep.:* early workers to be honored......Public schools our bulwark, 266. *Mr. Geo. C. Clarke, Pres. Rep.:* change in, 40 y.; lead other cities; Mr. Wells' graded course; normal school; teachers' institute; list school houses; evening schools; teachers salaries, 267.

ELEVATORS. **Grain.** Steam at C. & St. L., 157–160.

EMIGRATION. **Immigration.**

EMPORIUM of a region has obligations to all sections, xli.; 600,000 sq. miles of arable land and water courses, unequaled in advantages natural and acquired, rapidly settling with the best of men, must give unexampled growth to their Emporium, margin 131–140. N. Y. e. of whole country; why C. is not yet e. of the whole west, 115.

ENGLAND. **Great Britain.** Opinion of C., *Mark Lane Exp.*, 1857*:* First called Eng. attention to C.; first vessel to Eng. in 1856; enlarging Welland Canal; rapid growth of C.; exports; railways; resources, commerce......*Mr. Parton* quotes *Mr. Cobden's* opinion of Niagara and C. Col. Hough's beef at World's Fair, 167.

ESCANABA, facilities to receive and ship iron ore, 237.

EUROPE. Direct trade with lakes, 62. Will reach chief grain and provision market of the world, 103, 344. Immigrants from, 1867, 137. Émmigrants to increase, 197. Direct shipments wanted, 184. Exports of breadstuffs to, 186. E. cannot have our governmental system, 197. Capital to be drawn from E. 198. Increased demand for meats, 211, 213. Labor from, 219. We can feed E. 318.

EVANS, JOHN, M. D., Educational efforts at Evanston; Gov. of Colorado. 270, *n.*

EVANSTON, N. W. University at, 270.

EXAGGERATION in this discussion would be a blunder, xxix.

EXPANSION, *Room for indefinite E., its Benefits.* **Suburbs.** 285.

EXPATRIATION, Britain wrong about—we fight for it if necessary, 197.

EXPERIENCE, disregarded, 1. This paper for those who regard, 2. Former opinions tested by E, 3, 12, 13, 294. Bible teaches by E. 3. *Poussin:* E. the only test; only safe dependence; upon this Americans rely, 334.

FACTS. Give value to volume viii. *F., not hypothesis the Basis;* xi.

FAGIN, Mr., Speech comparing St. L. with Chicago, 67.

FAMILY. *Duty to ourselves and f.*, xxxiv.

FARMERS. **Agriculture.** Their interest that of C., 3 *n*, 53, 32. 65, 179, 184, 341, 366.

FARNUM, HENRY, projects and builds R. I. railroad, 356.

FINANCES. **Capital. Money. Taxes.**

CITY. Cost of water works, income; cost of pipes, 5 y., 254. *Mayor Rice's Mess.*, 1868: total debt; water debt pays its way; real debt; improvements wanted; city prosperous; taxes faithfully applied, 259......Estimate for City expenses, 1868–'9, 260. Value of churches, 263. Value of public schools, lots and buildings, 264. Expenditure for schools, 1867; property of school fund; income, 265. Valuations, real and personal, and amount of taxes, 1837 to 1866, 288; do. for 1867, 289.

Ruggles, ten y. increase of property and population in U. S.; economy of railways in transportation, 318. *Baxter*, "Railway extension and its results:" proportion of exports and imports to railways and navigation, Gr. Bri., 326; France, 327; Holland and Belgium, 328; U. S., 329......Railway investments to increase, especially in W., 377. County bonds to aid railroads, 378.

FIRE CLAY, in La Salle Co., Ills., 248.

FLACHAT, M., benefit of railways upon land in France, 327.

FLOUR. **Grain.** Mnfr. at Ch. 7 years; St. L. 17 years, 215.

FOOD. *Scott*, population not 10 p. c. over f., 302. Mouths go to f., 302, 318.

FOSTER, J. W., Report of Ship Canal Convention, 188. Criticism of Prof. Waterhouse, 227, *n.* Report upon Lake Sup. iron, 228–234.

FRANCE, why its Republic failed, 195, *n.* Cost and results of railways, 327.

FRAUD in grain, guards against, 161.

FREEMAN, Rev. Mr., 1st Bap. clergyman, 262.

FUR trade started St. L., 85, 88, 187, 348.

FUTURE. Study the Past to understand the F., and improve the Present, 1-2. F. of C. not foreseen by some citizens, 3 *n.* Its certain growth, 26. Past and present, reasoning from to f., 140.

GALE, STEPHEN F., a projector of Aurora road to Quincy, 356.

GALENA lead mines, 223.

GARRETT, Mrs. AGUSTUS, founded Biblical (Meth. Epis.) Inst. at Evanston, 271.

GEOGRAPHICAL centre of small account, 92.

GIBBS & GRIFFIN'S elevators, 157.

GILLETTE, Mr., Sec. Pork Packers' Ass., report upon beef, 211.

GOD. **Religion.** *Duty to our God*, xlii.

GOODING, WILLIAM, report upon I & M. canal, 63, *n.*

GOODRICH, Hon. GRANT, obituary address of Mrs. Garrett, 271.

GOVERNMENT. **Politics.**

GRADE of C. favorable; our blunders; dug out streets; basements not valued; grade should be raised, at least out of the centre; benefits to drayage; give railways independent lines, 250, 284; avoid calamities; give high speed, 251, 284; Mr. Palmer wants higher, 251 *n.* Change of grade only protection to life and limb; benefits seen in Boston and here; all favor change; give C. unequal advantages; delay intolerable, 285. G. at Harlem and Lyons, 286

GRAIN. C. chief market of the world, 62, 103, 162, 166. Loss of g. trade at St. L., increase at C., 34, 67, 68, 83, 111, 114, 181. *Buf. Trade Rep.* First shipment from Lake Mich. 1836, from Ch. 1839; surplus 1862; product of lake basin 1840, '50, '60, 131. Product and per cent. increase in 5 N. W. States, 1850–60, 317, 319. Shipments g. and flour from Ch., 1838–67, 153. Receipts of g. and flour at St. L. from 1856–67; routes and receipts of g. and flour at C. 1866-7, 154; do at St. L., 1867; routes and shipments of g. and flour from C. 1866–7, 155. Receipts of leading articles at St. L. 12 y., 156. Trade began by wagon loads, then railroads, 348. Exports to Europe from various ports, 186.

STEAM ELEVATORS. Machinery necessary to handle such amounts; 1 in 1848, 17 in 1867; structure of frame; Armour, Dole & Co.'s described by *Mr. Baker:* advantages of C. site for es; speed of handling; building and machinery; 10 cars unloaded in 8 ms.; ship 180,000 bu. in 10 hours; 11 more large, 5 smaller ones, 157.......List of owners and capacity of C. es., 158. THE St. L. e. *Mr. Fagin:* 1 at St. L. to compete with C., up hats to C., 68. *Trade Rep.:* wheat statistics small compared with neighbors, lack of handling facilities; advantages of river route; N. O. e. built by St. L.; grain to be handled in bulk; some toting. *Prof. Waterhouse*, benefits of the, 159. Honest rather than keen to exhibit St. L.'s dependence on C. *Trade Rep.:* wheat receipts; increase due to elevator, 159.......St. L. wants more than one; its receipts; another at E. St. L., 160; St. L. should build one a year, 161.

INSPECTION. Guards against fraud; none yet in elevator business. *Mr. O. L. Parker, Chief Inspector:* 10 y. experience; system grain conveyed into store and out; differences arbitrated; No. of inspectors; cabinet of samples, 161. *Mr. Gurney:* inspection system cordially sustained; some mistakes.

GRAIN DRYING, Mr. Marsh's used by Mr. E. K. Hubbard, and Messrs. Munn & Scott; wheat curing; corn curing; losses by heating; spoilt for food; should be better prepared, 162; Messrs. Murry, Nelson & Co.'s dryer; Beach's pat.: 2,000 bu. per hour; any grain cured; mode of operation; grain not to be wasted; what is requisite will be done, 163.

MISS. RIVER ROUTE. **Barges.** *Col. Foster's Rep.:* N. O. route unfavorable to g. and provisions; exports from N. Y. and N. O., 183. *U. S. Census Rep.:* "G. Trade of Miss. River:" formerly rivers used; barges; change of trade to lakes, 184; Miss. almost abandoned for g.: 5 reasons; N. O. and C. receipts; N. O. and N. Y. exports, 185. *Mr. Scott:* N. O. route cheapest; climate injures flour; lake route safest. 306.

Railway Benefits to Grower. *Mr. Edmunds, U. S. Census:* Positive benefits; means; only railways adequate for transit, 316; to grain indispensable; give W. market; increase raiser's profit; N. Y. price not reduced; old country to be fed; $1,000,000 increased profit on N. Eng. flour, 316, etc.

Corn. Rec'd by canal, 1860, 52; 6 y. 53; N. Y. wants more, 57; raised in 5 N. W. States, 1840–60, 135; c. curing, advantages of, 162; great Wn. staple; put into hogs and cattle saves transportation, 209; John Taylor's "bread, meat and manure," 212. *Ruggles:* grain raising in W. just begun, 212; exceeds Gt. Brit. already; new world to feed the old; cheap transit wanted; hog—don't laugh at him; great corn carrier; corn incarnate, 213.

Wheat. (See *Grain* above.) *Mo. Dem.*, 1861, decrease at St. L.; increase at C., 34, 113; shipments from Min. 1867; product of 5 States, 1850-'60, 135. *St. L. Trade Rep.*, statistics small compared with neighbors, 158; increase 1866, 159.

Flour. (See *Grain* above.) St. L. excels C. in mnfr. of f.; yield 7 y.; product of each mill, 1865–7; St. L. mnfr. 17 y., 215.

Highwines, mnfr. 11 y., 215. Disadvantage in grain mnfr. in W., offal being worth more E., 215.

GT. BRITAIN. **England.** Export of breadstuffs to, 186; of cut meats, of provisions, 211. Progress in mnfrs. 194; excellent checks in its govt. 195 *n.*; wrong about expatriation, 197. Grain crop of W. already exceeds G. B., 213. Eng. supremacy on account of mnfrs.; cheap labor the means, 220. *Mr. Baxter:* railway distribution; centres, 324; traffic and benefit of railways, 325.

GREAT INTERIOR. The Territory Embraced. The **Northwest** and **West** are hereafter the Great Interior, margin, 385, 387. Old N. W., 591,000 sq. ms; present N. W., 1,082,000 sq. ms.; the W., 1,538,000 sq. ms.; population by States, 1860; part estimated tributary 1861, and 1868; what is Ch. territory? why Ch. is not yet emporium of the West, 115; area difficult to realise; small per cent. yet in farms; U. S. census returns, 1850, 1860, 116. Ancient Orient our Occident, 385. Our W. across the Pacific; change in U. S. census to N. and S. interior sections; to be a unit, 386. Causes of unity; power in our hands; other sections benefited with our growth; must have a chief city; small area tilled has built present cities; rapid progress; stimulate city growth; many large cities; one chief, 387.

Natural and Artificial Advantages and Capacity. **Agriculture. Commerce. Lakes. Manufactures. Minerals. Railways. Rivers.** Of the small part now tributary, not one acre in 5 has yet been ploughed, 116. Small estimate for mining trade, 117. Value of Rocky Mts. trade, 122. Extent of wealth unknown, 126. *Cin. R. R. Record,* "Govt. lands for rs.," 127. *Wilson's Rep.*, Com. U. S. Land Office, 128, 129. *Buf. Trade Rep., 1863:* Increase of population from 1800 to 1860; increase of cereals of lake basin, 131; rapidity of settlement; increase of int. improvements; extent; mineral wealth; rich arable land; division of labor to ag., mnfrs. and commerce; no country equal; St. Lawrence and Miss. lake arms; Va. canal; St. Law. strongest, 132......Rapid Progress, *Mess. Gov. of Mo.; Gov. of Kas.*, 133. *Merch. Mag.* upon Minn., 134. Corn and wheat of 5 States, 1850–'60, 135. General satisfaction of settlers, 136. Total **Immigration,** 1841–60, 137. *Waterhouse:* extent of river navigation, 174......Not 40 y. since first r.; N. W. already best accommodated, 314; effect here difficult to estimate; must be its own measure; we have our experience, 315. *Edmunds' U. S. Census,* "*Influence of Railways upon Agriculture:*" Positive benefits to grain-growers, 315; give W. a market; increase farmer's profits; N. Y. prices not reduced; W. prices grown to E.; rs. stimulate agr., especially in N. W.; all built since 1850; their effects, 316. *Ruggles Rep. to Berlin Cong.:* 10 y. increase, 1850-60; 11,212 ms. railway; saved $44 000,000 in transportation; comparative increase of sections, 318; population, farms, wealth; capacity to supply food; figures difficult to realise, 319.......Adaptation of this region to rs.; capacity to support them, 338; large results, yet only begun, 339.

The Gt. Int. must build up many great Cities. C. no monopolist; being chiefest, wants many chief, xvii.; each 200 or 300 ms. builds a large city, xviii. Other cities not disparaged; only the truth exhibited, xxx. Other and many great cities certain, 59 *n.* W. will build many great cities; must help themselves; national division into States, tends to great cities, 108. Room for all 3 cities; Cin. graceful; St. L. spiteful, 146. No city to monopolise mnfrs.; W. have many centres; yet one chief; save profits to themselves, 218. *Edmunds' U. S. Census:* increase of mnfrs. in W., 218. Railway building must go on, build many great cities inland; Atlantic cities made by W.; trade constantly increase; yet wn. cities most benefited, 336. *Merch. Mag.*, 1861, "*City Population:*" This an important branch of research; growth of 12 chief Atl. and Gulf cities, 1810–60, 336; 5 p. c. of pop. 1810, 6½ 1850, 8¼ 1860; suburbs still greater; ⅓ of Mass. within 12 ms. of Boston; growth of 5 chief river cities, 1810–60; St. L. chief; lake cities their rivals; growth of chief lake cities, 1840–60, 337; Ch. and Buffalo; Ch. railroad focus; produce to increase; growth compared from 1840–60, 12 Atl., 50 p. c. increase; 5 river, 58; 6 lake, 130; 12 int., 36 p. c.; lake cities largest increase; causes; St. L. benefited; N. W. supplied with rs.; smoothing her way to market, 338. *Scott,* 1848, "*Our Cities, Atlantic and Interior:*" Pride in our cities; large hoped for, not believed in; N. Y. not possible to equal London, 388; he predicted, 1828, largest city to be inland; opinion then absurd; others now believe; growth of N. Y. and Cin. compared from 1800, 389; estimates of the future upon the past; growth of other interior cities equal to Cin.; average over 115 p. c.; of seaboard cities only 58 p. c., 390; W. not confined to ag.; advanced civilization; cost of transportation a help; mnfrs. to prefer W.; commercial and manfg. points of W. to be great cities, 391...... Caution of these estimates; ratio of increase not sustainable; he could not calculate the power of railways; that the only change needed; power of W., and lake superiority over rivers, main points; W. trade most with itself 391; towns grow with mnfrs. and com.; Cin. to be a centre of 250 ms.; Cin., St. L. and Ch. chief of their regions; Kas. City may be another, 392.

The Gt. In., a complete Unit in Interest, must have its own Centre, which is found and established: This the chief point of the book; centralising trade by new currents; who change them, xix. Nature and art conjoin; Lake Michigan essential; natural connection of rivers and lakes, 70; art avails of them naturally; conjoint interest of capital; L. Michigan concentrates railways; no other rival site, 71; other cities rivals to reach the lakes, 72. Certain superiority to St. L. not claimed till 1853, 73, 75. The affirmative has nine points, 102-106. [See **City,** *nine Points the Basis of Chicago's certain Growth.* For the negative see **St. Louis.**] Ch. artificial hub of N. W.; felloes secure; each spoke put in independently; adapted to public and private interests; hard to change, 105. No Ch. work; common sense ruled; who can change it, 106. Causes traced to effects, effects to causes; St. L. to invent new forces; Ch. will use them; a prominent city should have a majority of the points, 107; no city has 3, 108. St. L. a chief and good witness; does she seek trade of N. W? 111. The Northwest is the Prize contested—its Extent and Resources, margin, 111–131. *Cir. 1861,* "*Rivalry of St. L. and Ch.*" 111. (**St. Louis,** *admissions against herself.*) N. W. a prize to be coveted; its own city should have it; trade obeys laws; 26 Engs., 7 Frances, neither has a centre so marked as that of N. W.; N. W. able to build up its Emporium, 130. 600,000 sq. ms. of arable Land and water Courses, unequaled in Advantages natural and acquired, rapidly settling with the best of Men, must give unexampled Growth to their Emporium, margin, 131-140.

N. W. to have political power, *Cir., 1861, Census Returns of Illinois, Iowa and Wis*: gained 10 M. C's., other new States 9, old States lost 24; same to continue; relative increase compared; Mr. Scott's prediction; its moderation; of this "great Interior plain" C. is centre, 138. *N. Y. Eve. Post*, "*The Strong Northwest*:" Prosperity general; out of debt; farmers independent; feel N. W. pulse at Ch.; injury to E. helps Ch.; increase of commerce; of mnfrs., 140. *Prof. Waterhouse*: Difficulties of St. L.; Ch. energetic; her railroads; trust in nature unsafe; what St. L. must do, 176. *Atch.* (Kas.) *Free Press*, "*A Comparison*:" St. L. had trade; fur trade; on its dignity, 187; strong before C. started; C. railroads, merchants, elevators; St. L. cut off on the S.; on W.; Nebraska trade turned; Ch. enterprise; St. L. spasmodic, 188. Balt. and Phil. endeavored to draw trade directly E.; lakeward tendency too strong; finds the Gr. In. has its centre, 367; many large cities make Ch. sure; reasons for commercial superiority, 392; mnfg. advantages superior; no other equal region; W. yet developing; mnfg. distributed; to have a centre; one easily reached; this the cause of our growth, 393. *East. Paper*: West to mnfr.; natural to seek a centre; advantages of W.; trade centres best for mnfrs.; Sec. of Int. shows relative increase E. and W., 394.

THE CHIEF CITY OF THE GT. IN., MUST, PROBABLY, BE EMPORIUM OF THE CONTINENT: Trade of Gt. In. the object of all cities; its domestic trade chief; to be more and more a primary market; centre of mnfrs.; centre of all the sections, xx. Ch. natural hub of the continent; lake not to be moved; Mahomet must go to the mountain; Ch. centre by art and nature, 92. Miss valley being heart of Union, does not make St. L. so; N. W., its chief part, lost to her; Miss. no head, benefits indefinite; Ch. at head of lakes; Clinton predicted its importance; centre of Republic at that head, 101. States to create large cities, yet trade left to natural channels, 109; were Union broken, C. would grow; with union no favors asked; the W. a unit, proud of its queen; no favors asked except to abide by principles of Union. To be emporium of N. W. is to be so of continent; trade centripetal, 110; Ch. continental, 111. *Scott*, "*Internal Trade of the U. S.*, 1843: Population hitherto on seaboard; imagined superiority of foreign commerce; internal not realized, 300; immense superiority of latter; narrow sea-coast made all hitherto; domestic profitable as foreign trade; will coast cities have advantages over inland, 301; agricultural exchanges N. and S.; mineral products; will they be on sea-coast; valley not confined to ag.; that the basis; food brings cheap labor, 302; inland cities have some foreign trade; large cities inland; railways, etc., yet new invention; a bold man to foretell their effect; no inland country like ours, 303. Close connection of lake and river valleys; facilities to ocean; lake trade makes Atl. city chief; emporium of rivers the city that has best avenue to lakes; takes trade of river valley, 304; growth of lake cities, 1830–40; increase of sectional trade; domestic increases most, 305; immense trade of lake and river valleys; routes compared; Ch. route to increase in importance; trade N. and S.; N. O. route cheapest; climate injures flour; lake route best, safest, 306; foreign imports for W. will be direct, not through N. Y.: superiority of lake over gulf route; saves 1,100 ms.; own their vessels. Tendency of population to cities; strengthened by modern inventions; man's constant progress, 307; growth of towns more than country; estimates of relative growth for 50 y.; hitherto less tendency to towns in U. S. than in old countries; reasons; change coming, 308; 26,000,000 in 1890 to be in towns, and where; Cin. chief of Miss. valley for 47 y.; a lake town beat Cin.; reasons; river avenues; relative growth of lake and river regions, 309-311; lake towns superior; which to lead; advantages of Maumee over Cleveland; Ch. market extensive, 311; only rival; their comparison; Ch. may equal Maumee in area; not in 47 y.; Ch. in future power unknown; canal to Rock Island; after 47 y. may be second, possibly first; conclusions not popular, facts incontrovertible, 312; let critics be moderate; not give hasty judgment, 312......25 years confirms these views; Mr. Scott's slight mistake; rapidity of changes in favor of Ch. not calculated, 313. Federal Union binds together; State autonomy creates many centres; yet trade is free and centripetal, 325. What shall stop the relative increase of lake over Atl. cities? 338. **No other Point of equal Convergence of Either Rail or Water Communication, or of both, on the Globe**, margin, 339-385. All Atlantic cities seek closest connection with Ch.; traffic seeks the lakes; will find its centre; S. will also seek it; competition of rs. our safety; Ch. wants free trade; her prosperity rests upon that of the whole country, 366. **Other Cities are no Measure for Ch.**, margin, 387-399. *Scott, 1857*, "*Westward Movement of the Centre of Population and of Industrial Power in N. Am.*: An interesting subject; come together on L. Mich.; there be permanent, 394; foreign commerce 1 to 20 of domestic; foreign one transaction; domestic manifold; all commerce equal, 395; N. Y. now chief; change certain; centres of pop. and industrial power moving N. W.; now separated, will come together; advantages of N. W. help; in 50 y. Gt. In. have 70,000,000; trade 20 fold more with itself than the rest of the world; must have the chief city; the era of great cities, 396; N. Y. beat Lon. in 50 y.; Ch. beat N. Y. in 48 y.; doubt as to such predictions; most sanguine nearest right, 397......These views thus far realized; reasons why Ch. has no precedent, 397. *Cir.*, 1861: Rapid growth of cities; effect of rs; here a net-work spread in outset, 398; perfection of system; expansion; ability of country; one city all can reach; rs. centralise commerce and mnfrs.; power to develope; other cities no measure for Ch.; its destiny, 399; progress of N. Y. compared; our facilities greater than were hers; Ch. has larger dependent area than N. Y. in 1845; greater power of the whole country; no rivalry; 25 y. at Ch., equal to 50 at N. Y., 400......**There is Room for Them and Us**, 402-404. Our nation continental; Europe no measure for us; influence of our governments; our improvements; regard both State sovereignty, national Union; influx from Europe and Asia, 402. *Scott*, in conclusion, "*The Progress of the West considered with reference to great Commercial Cities in the U. S.*," 1846: Quotes *Alb. Argus* that N. Y. can hold wn. trade, a worthy prize with which N. Y. advances; N. Y. best chance of en. cities; great city to be in centre of population; growth of lake and river valleys, and Atlantic border estimated for 100 y., 403; as in 100 y. N. Y. beats Lon., so Cin. beats N. Y.; domestic trade builds up N. Y.; will 300,000,000 W. go to N. Y. to trade; old idea hard to eradicate; progress not realized; direct trade from lake to Europe; Miss. route; change less than last 50 y., 404.

GROUND of C. favorable for a great city, 249, 250. **Grade.**

GROWTH. **Predictions. City** g. an important subject, ix. Ch. the most marvelous example, ix. Its g. not made by itself, xxi. Obligations to God and country, xxiii. No wonder when investigated, xxviii. Needs no exaggeration, xxix. Causes to be examined, xxix, xxxii.

GYPSUM in Illinois, 224.

GULF OF MEXICO, grain beats that route, 183.

HALE & AYRES, sale of nails, 244.

HALLAM, Rev. Mr., organized 1st. Epis. ch., 262.

HAMMOND, Gen. J. H., speech upon St. L. and Omaha railroad, 79.

HARBOR and river frontage. **Docks. Canals.** Extent; constant increase; difficulties; remedy, 251. Purifying river by deepening canal and feeding from L. Mich., 252.

HARLEM, Grade at, 286.

HEALTH of C. **Climate. Sewerage. Ventilation. Water,** 252.

HEALEY, G. P. A., Ch. a centre for fine arts. His skill, 277.

HELENA, (Montana) *Gazette, Ch. vs. St. L.*, 118.

HENNING, Major, V. Pres. Leav., Law. & Gal. R. R. 100.

HIBBARD & SPENCER, sale of nails, 244.

HIDES, receipts and shipments, 206.

HIGHWINES manufactured at C. 11 years, 215.

HJORTSBERG, Mr., C. E., statement relative to C. B & Q. railroad, 284.

HOGS, receipts and shipments at C. 10 years, 164.

Stock, *Live.* **Provisions.**
HOLLAND, neglect of railways, 328. Depends upon canals as St. L. upon rivers, 329.
HORSE-RAILROADS, wide streets favorable; have Phila. plan; improvements in; traffic 1867, 282.
HOUGH, Col., beef at world's fair, Lon. 167.
HOUGHTON (Mich.) *Gazette*, Lake Superior copper, 244.
HOUSTON, (Texas,) *Tel.* "St. Louis and Texas." St. L. and C. rivals, 100.
HUBBARD, Gurdon, S. passed thro. by boat from lakes to Ills. river, 93. Built 3d brick building, 99. First provision packer, 208.
HUBBARD, Elijah K., his foresight of C., 105.
HUBBARD, Elijah K., Jr., uses Marsh's grain-dryer, 162.
HUNT, Freeman, founder of *Merch. Mag.*: its excellence, 324, *n.*
HYPOTHESIS. **Argument.** *Basis, not H., but Fact*, xi. 107. My former Opinions and **Predictions** were based upon a reasonable H., margin, 2-14. A sound one important; not to be accidental; past a basis 2; Bible a record of past; old arguments reapplied; motives and experience important; some move hap-hazard, 3; evidence of past sound judgment, 4. Hypothesis changed to fact, 24. The Basis of our Prosperity is no longer hypothetical, margin 25–28. Guess-work not the basis of these calculations, 216, 335. Lake improvement not hypothetical, 345. Mineral dependence not hypothetical, 243.
ILLINOIS. Obligations of C. citizens to their State; admitted 1818; its extent; bond of Union, xxxix. Motto, "State Sovereignty, National Union," xxxix, 110. Has always favored C.; benefited by C.; to be empire State of Gt. Int.; C. should not seek for its capital, xx. Petitions to Cong. for land grant for Cent. R. R., 23. Grant no gratuity, 23 *n.* Benefits, 353. Amount, sales, prices, 354. Ch. cares for S. E. part, 78. Ch. centre of State, 92. Pride in Ch.: *Jacksonville Jour.*, "Ch. at Home and Abroad:" an Illinoisan praises her abroad; why jealous at home; example worthy; activity; thus C. grows; others plod; her enterprise; beats St. L., 109......Area, population, 115. Land in farms; not one-fifth under fence, 116. Ills. true to its motto, 110. Wheat and corn crop 1840-60, 135. Rank as grain-grower, 136. Changes of census, 1860, 128. Character of its settlers, 139 *n.* Trade of central I. turned to C., *C. & Alton R. R. Rep.*, 1867: Jacksonville branch completed; takes trade from St. L. to C., 95; *do.* 1868. increase 1867, due to freight on Jacksonville branch; not yet full freight, 187......Rapid-increase of mnfrs, 202; of boots and shoes, 208. Variety of minerals, 223. Coal, extent, chief seams Belleville and La Salle, 223. Lead mines, 223. Iron abundant, 224. Silex, salt, copper, gypsum, etc., 224. Chester Coal Fields, *Waterhouse*, 224. Sangamon Co. coal tried successfully, 243. Farm values, 1850, 1860, 317. National in Character, 386 *n.*
IMMIGRATION. Population. Influence of Govt. upon i., 136, 137, 139, 196, 402. National advantages chief influence, 136. Total of U. S., 1840–60, 137. At New York, 1848–67, 137. From Europe, 1867, 137, 219; from Canada, 137; from Europe to increase, 137, 197, 219, 387. General satisfaction of settlers, 136. Character of settlers, 138, 139, 303. Foreign to be improved, 139. From Asia, 139, 197, 219, 387, 402. Into the S. to be large, 123 *n*, 138, 139. Gt. Br. wrong about expatriation; if denied, we fight if necessary, 197. *Merch. Mag.*, "*Am. Manfrs. and Emigration:*" mnfrs essential to a nation, 219; commerce made a means of vassalage; dependencies not allowed to mnfr.; Eng. supremacy; a change coming; loss by emigration; cheap labor made Eng.; wages increasing; better living; laborers leaving; others better paid; cheap labor enables her to control; no sudden change, 220. Labor our difficulty; materials abundant; immigration our relief; price of labor not to be low; our advantage in transportation; commerce with Asia; Pac. railway, 221. *Scott*, mouths go to food, 302. 318.
IMPROVEMENTS, Public, anticipated 20 and 10 years ago, margin 21–24. Favor domestic as well as foreign trade, 303. Railways, etc., new, 303, 307, 315, 322. A man bold to predict effects, 303. Affect town-growth, 307.
IMPORTS, Foreign, Ch. chief for the West, 103. *Baxter*: I. and exports in proportion to railways and navigation, Gt. Br., 326; France, 327; Belgium and Holland, 328; U. S., 329.
INDIANA, Ch. centre of northern, 26. Area and pop. 114. Land in farms, 116. Wheat and corn crop, 1840–'60, 135. Good coal, 240. Farm values, 1850, 1860, 317.
INSPECTION of grain at Ch. 161. System sustained, 162.
IOWA, Ch. centre for, 25, 92. Area and pop., 115. In farm and out, 116. Changes of census 1860, 138. Trade turned to Ch., *Cin. Com.*, 33; *C. B. & Q. R. R. Rep.*, 48, 94; *Mo. Dem.* 1861, 112. Will take care of itself, 97 *n.* Variety of minerals, 224.
IRON. **Minerals.** Conjunction of Coal, I. and other Minerals, margin, 222–249. Mo. ores, 223. Abundance in Ills., 224. Bessemer process, 225, 231. Cost of iron at Pitts. from Mo. ore, 226. *St. L. Board of Trade* resolutions: smelting Mo. ore with Chester, Ills. coal, 243......*Ills. State Jour.*: iron made with Sangamon coal......These points promising to C.; no hypothetic basis, 243. Highest cost at C. from Lake Superior ore, $30 to $25; this the iron age, 244. Bog ores near C., 247.
LAKE SUPERIOR. Advantage of C. in its ore, 217, 244. This our chief dependence, 227. *Merch. Mag.*, 1857: superiority of ore, tested with others; one-third better; fibre tough, 227; 70 p. c. iron, 228. *Foster*: area of ores; mode of occurrence; varieties; localities, 228; mode of mining; peculiar uses and application; foreign analogous, Sweden nearest, 229; analysis; admixture with other ores at Buf. and Pitts., 230; benefits of mixing; steel mnfr.; Bessemer process; U. S. to make, 231; strength compared with others; points of distribution, N. Y., Pa., O., 232; prospective demand; product of principal States, ore and pig, 1850, '60, 233; competing ores; freight favors L. Sup., 234......These views trustworthy; advantage of Ch. in transportation and mixing ores, 235. *Lamborn*, "*advantages of L. Sup. Region for producing Charcoal Pig*:" large demand for this kind; supply east diminishing; Lake S. rich in minerals; supplied 1865 ⅛ U. S. iron; first made 1847, charcoal 1858; increase, 235. Total 8 years; mines inexhaustible; ease of mining; handling and shipping; cost of freight; process of mnfr.; cost; future encouraging; competition in freights and mining cos., 236. *Cor. Ch. Republican*: Shipping facilities at Escanaba; increase of shipments; energy N. W. railroad; good harbor; early navigation; trade valuable to C., 237. Shipments ore and pig; other products, 245. *Marquette Mining Jour.*: "The future supply of L. Sup. ore." 67 per cent. ores abundant, 237; supply increasing; machinery aids; mines improving downwards; new discoveries; more hæmatite; demand increases with supply. "Products of Marquette co," 1867, 238. Error that L. Sup. supplies one-fourth of the iron of the U. S., 238 *n.* Business full; increased capital; product of mines severally, 1867; of pig iron; of ore and pig 10 years, 239. First export, 1855. *Meeker*: Routes for ore; first cargo at Chicago, 1867; less freight to this port; Ia. coal to smelt; Ills. coal; mining trade of C. 240. *Ch. Jour.*: Mr. Meeker's Iron co., $250,000, 240; stockholders; Ch. best shipping port for ore; Wis. and Ills. ore; coal; C. great manufacturing point. *Baldwin*: Cost of Lake Sup. ore and freight.......Cost of pig with Brazil coal, $30; to be reduced, 241.
JACKSONVILLE, (Ills.) *Journal*: "Chicago at home and abroad." 108.
JOLIET building stone, 258.
JONES, WILLIAM, subscription for Ch. Univ., 272.
JOURNAL, EVENING. Ch. and the Upper Missouri, 117. U. S. export of breadstuffs to Gt. Britain, 186. Notice of Mr. Volk. 278.
JOY, Hon. JAMES F., C. B. & Q. road interested in Bur. & Mo., 48. Is Mr. J. in St. L's interest, 51. Purchase of Indian lands, 51. Aid in railway building at C., 298.
KANSAS. Trade turned to C., *Mo. Dem.*, "*A Flank Movement*:" Cameron and K. road not built by C.

but E.; no change of cars; connects Pac. with C., 27; trade not run up hill; work for St. L.......*Mo. Rep.*, "*K. City and Cam. R. R.*:" Another connection with the East; cheapen C. lumber; roads at K. City; rival St. L., 27......*K cor.Pitts. Gaz.*, "*The C. Yankee on his westward way*:" All business men from C.; also goods; C. entrenching to reach S. territory; present C. route; Cameron road to C., 51; bridge Mo. river; no breaking bulk, 52. *Col. Vliet*: superior region of L., L. and Gal. railroad, 121 *n.* Trade going to C., 51. Rapid progress of the State, *Gov's Mess.*, 133.

KANSAS CITY, an important site, 27, 71, 84, 121, 392.

KENNICOTT, ROBT., chief founder of Acad. of Sci.; his death; address of Mr. Geo. C. Walker, 276.

KINZIE, R. A., built first frame building in C., 99.

KNOWLTON, J. S. C., letter to Ship Canal Convention, 342.

LABOR. Division of in the W. to ag., mnfrs., and trade, 132. Division of requires commerce, 141, 192. All branches to be cared for, 191. W. wants l. for mnfg., 218, 221. To come from Europe, 137, 197, 218, 219. To come from Asia, 139, 197, 218, 219, 221. Knowledge of the principles of our government will bring l., 196-198. Will be equalized in demand, 199. Superiority of machinery over hand l. in boots and shoes; division of l.; 16 operations; female l., 207. *Merch. Mag.*: Cheap labor made Eng.; wages increasing; no sudden change, 220; labor our difficulty; immigration relieves; price of labor not to be low; advantage in transportation, 221. *Baxter*: Benefits of railways to l. in Gt. B.; surplus relieved; wages equalized; like drainage; benefits in France; 327. Cheap food brings cheap l., 302. Coolies to be supplied, in S. and W., 401.

LAKE FOREST University, 275. **Education.**

LAKES. **Valley. Water.** The Lake Route to the East and Europe, margin, 58–66, 103. Ch. at the head of the grandest inland navigation on the globe, 101, 103, 339. Interest of Bost., N. Y., and **East** to draw trade to l's., 22, 24, 29, 30. Interest of S. W. in a railroad to, 23, 100. Ch. natural point of conjunction with l's and rivers, 53, 58, 62, 70, 93, 104, 304 306, 339. Mr G. S. Hubbard passed loaded boats from lake to river before 1826, 93, *n.* To be opened for propellers of 1,000 to 1,500 tons, 62, 66, 376. L. navigation superior to rivers, 64, 75, 79, 103, 184, 185, 304, 307, 345, 391. Still to be improved, 345. Change of trade from rivers to ls, 183, 184, 304, 366, 367. Queen of l. queen of rivers, 93, 304. C. at head of l's, 101, 103, 339, 342. That the centre of the Republic, 101. *Mr. Scott* predicted, 1843, its importance when country tributary was settled, 306, 312. Importance of navigation and its improvement, *Knowlton*, 342; *Poor*, 343. Navigation cheap as ocean, 344, 375. Facilities from l's E. most needed, 344, 372. Interest of E. in improving l. facilities, 372, 374, 375. L's would have been powerless but for e'n capital, 377. Shipments and receipts of chief articles at C. by l. 6y., 66; arrivals and tonnage, 6ys; No. vessels and tonnage, 10y; No. class and owners of vessels entered at C. 1867, 61. Ls compel 500 ms, N. and S., to bend trade S. to C., 103. *Buf. Trade Rep.*, 1863. Lake basin, population 1800, 1860; grain, 1840–62; first grain from C. 1839; surplus 1862; what changes next 25 y., 131; area; rapidity of settlement; 1900, half in lake and river vallies; increase of internal improvements; water facilities; minerals; rich land; division of labor; no country equal; St. Law. and Miss. lake arms; St. Law. strongest, 132. River towns preceded those of lakes, 184......Lakes probably fed from Rocky mts., 256 *n.* *Scott*: ocean and inland navigation and value of trade compared, 301; stretch of ls. N. and S.; close connection with rivers; varied surface; minerals; outlets E.; l. trade makes Atl. city chief; shore lines; takes trade of river valley, 304; other eastern routes; business not to be over-estimated; immense growth of 13 l. cities, 1830-40; l. trade exceeds that of colonies; trade of ls. and rivers valuable; routes from the Atl. compared; N. O. cheapest; climate injures flour; l. valley beats river val., 309–311. Greater growth of lake over river cities, 337, 338.

CHAMPLAIN, ship canal to St. Law. and to Hudson, 343, 344, 375. HURON, canal to Lake Simcoe, and Lake Ontario, 62, 344, 345. MICHIGAN, makes C. by concentrating railways, 58, 71, 92. Boats from Green Bay to Escanaba, 246. ONTARIO, 300 ms. saved by canals to Lake Simcoe and Lake Huron, 62, 344, 345. Competition begins for trade of W. at end of Lake O., *Crane*, 375.

SUPERIOR, 227-241. **Iron. Copper.** Minerals to be distributed thro' C.; C. has $\frac{3}{4}$ the trade, 240. Value of trade, 237, 240, 245. *Anon.*: Trade; mining the dependence; purchase everything; Detroit first interested, and Cleveland; C. did nothing; Leopold & Austrian's line begun 1865; 7,000 tons of merchandise from C., 1867; 3 other propellers; Cleve. and Det. line declining; C. to furnish supplies, 246. Boats from Green Bay to Escanaba, 241. Sault St. Marie Canal, 240.

LAMBORN, Dr. R. H. "Advantages of Lake Superior region for producing charcoal pig," 235.

LAND IMPROVEMENT CO., Charter of, 13. Plan to organize, 14. 287, 299.

LAND. **Real Estate.** Grants to railroads, 23, 24, 25, 45, 46, 47, 127. Railroads enhance value of, 127, 317. Advance in farm values in 5 N. W. States, 1850–60, 317.

LA SALLE, Ills., Zinc works described, 247.

LATH, trade in, 170. **Lumber.**

LAW SCHOOL, **Science** *and Art, University of Ch.*

LAWRENCE, (Kas.) *Tribune*, difference between St. L. and Ch., 85.

LEAD. **Minerals.** Mnfr. at Ch., 247.

LEATHER, mnfr. at C. *Times*: ignorance of our progress in mechanic arts; mnfrs. rapidly increasing; already a success; 35 tanneries; substantial arrangements; advantages here, 205; product of chief tanneries; enlarging......Reasons for success; receipts and shipments of hides, 206.

LEOPOLD & AUSTRIAN, in Lake Sup. trade, 246.

LIBERTY, (Clay Co., Mo.,) *Tribune.* West Br. Mo. R. R., 97.

LIBRARY, Ch. should have a large one for the Gt. Int.; Astor, Dr. Cogswell, 27, *n.*

LILL & DIVERSEY, donation to Pres. Theo. Sem., 270.

LITERATURE, Ch. to be a centre. *Chicagoan*: No. of publications; slow growth; tendency to concentration, 281.

LIVE Stock. **Stock, Live.**

LONDON *Daily Telegraph* upon Pacific trade, 43. *Mark Lane Express*, 1857, upon C., 66. Its growth to continue, 323. A centre of other railway centres, 324. A less centre of railways than C, 384. Beaten by N. Y. in 50 y., 397.

LUMBER, C. chief market of the world, 166, 170. Home consumption, 171. Cheapened in Kansas by railroads to C., 27. Shipped by canal, 1860, 6 y., 52, 53. Trade 11 years, 170. Albany half of C., 170. St. L. market, *Mo. Dem.*: other cities larger in l. trade; upper Miss.; receipts 1867, 171......5 p. c. of C.; ungrateful to C., 171.

LYONS, grade at, 286.

McGUFFEY, W. H., L. L.D., opinion of Illinois settlers, 139, *n.*

McCHESNEY, ROBERT, use of Merchants Mag., 324, *n.*

McCORMICK, C. H., donation to Pres. Theol. Sem., 270.

MAGOFFIN, Dr., in charge of Cath. Theol. Sem., 275.

MANN, Gen'l O. L., Collector of C.; official statement of trade, 145.

MAN to work, **xxii.**, 91, 108. Inferior races to be cared for, 190. With Hercules to help, must help himself, 347.

MANUFACTURES. THEIR IMPORTANCE AND MEANS OF PROGRESS: Free trade at present doubtful; various interests to be cared for; duties vary; nature and obligations of States, 191; States to seek peace by being prepared for war; seek independence; commerce and mnfrs., both needed; States no philanthropists; gov't to care for all interests; ag. and mnfrs. more important than commerce; ag. diffuses, mnfrs. concentrate population, 192. *Mr. Edmunds, U. S. Census Report*: Nature gives means, man employs them; farmers' work and products; security of our constitution and laws; Eng. security her basis of prosperity; same element ours; free competition; benefits, 193; raw materials abound; labor gives them value; converts to use and ornament; benefits of land culture; cities and towns; manufactories; all linked by railways; Adam Smith considers mnfrs. chief means; British example, 194; U. S. progress in 50 y., 10-fold; in population, 4½; reciprocal benefits of agr. and mnfrs.; general advantages of our nation; Carnot's exception of the Am. Republic; its success, 195; changes 1800 to 1860, 196......**Politics** and physics wisely blended; effect on mnfrs., 196; labor to come from Asia, 197; capital from Europe, 198. *Merch. Mag.*, "*Am. mnfrs. and Immigration:*" ms. essential to a nation, 220; commerce made a means of vassalage; dependencies not allowed to M.; Eng. supremacy in mg.; a change coming; loss by emigration; cheap labor made Eng.; wages increasing; better living; laborers leaving; others better paid; cheap labor enables her to control; no sudden change, 220; labor our difficulty; materials abundant; immigration our relief; price of labor not to be low; our advantage in transportation; commerce with Asia; Pacific railway, 221. ......Steam power and machinery modern invention, 307. Not 40 years since first railroads, 314.

ADVANTAGES OF GT. INT. FOR MG. W. to be less dependent on E.; make one transportation of men and machinery, 74. W. to M. for itself, 199, 203, 218, 221, 302, 314, 393, 394. St. L. depends on mg.; means supplied by N. W., 113 Mnfrs. growing in the W., *N. Y. Eve. Post*, "The Strong N. W.:" prosperity general; out of debt; farmers independent; feel N. W. pulse at C.; injury to E. helps C.; increase of commerce; mnfrs.; grain, 140......Ills. in 1850 was 15th State in mnfrs.; 1860 was 8th; Mo. in 1850 was 10th; in 1860 was 11th, 202. *Rail. Jour.*, 1857, "Mufrs. of Machinery in the W.:" capital of the W. in lands and improvements; large railroad demands; C. a good point; many cities......Ms. have a foothold and will strenghen; greatest increase to be in W., 217. No city to monopolize; yet the W. to have a centre; save profit to themselves. *Edmunds' U. S. Census:* Increase of ms. in the W.; causes operating; immense mineral resources; benefits of home ms......Cost of labor chief obstacle; Asiatics to be our hewers of wood and drawers of water, 219. Begin examination of mineral resources with views favorale to St. L.; each locality to have ms., 222. *Scott:* Will exchange of mineral products be on seaboard; valley have something beside agr.; the seat of materials and food the place for mg.; food brings cheap labor, 302. N. W. best accommodated with rs.; in ag. products would glut the world; ms. to save from that; gathering and distributing facilities; duty to develope, 314. *East. paper:* Wn. expectations of mnfrs.; natural to seek a centre; advantages of W., 393; trade centres best for mnfrs.; Rep. of Sec. of Int., E. and W. compared; effect of Pac. roads, 394.

CHICAGO MG. CENTRE OF THE GT. INTERIOR. In **Provisions** chief of the world, 62, 103, 162, 166, 208, 214, 221. *Cir., 1848,* "Ch. compared with Cin.:" No advantage over Ch.; gathering materials; provisions; relative power of States; internal improvements; natural advantages; growth of whole country, 74. Mg. Advantages of Chicago—Rapid Progress, margin, 191-222. *Cir., 1861:* Ms. not commerce build great cities; N. Y. an example; same at C.; raw materials abound; unequaled gathering and distributing facilities; W. to mnfr. for itself; various advantages; m. some for E.; capital and labor will come; large railroad mg.; already great variety, 199. By census of 1860, C. was 16th city in mnfrs., 9th in pop., 202. Cook Co. then had 469 establishments, and 87 branches; in May, 1867, C. alone had 2,848 establishments, and 318 branches, 204. **Provisions** an index of other branches, 208, 216. Obstacles in starting ms.; present increase remarkable; N. Y. chief in ms., yet imports everything; no advantage over C. but age and capital; C excels N. Y. in distributing facilities, Phil. in gathering raw materials; rapid increase already, 216. Mg. here for railways immense, 199, 217, 233. West to m. for itself; to have its centre for this; advantages over N. Y. and Phila.; pre-eminent in others as in provisions; 600,000 sq. miles dependent; 1,000,000 sq. ms. also of mining region; railways a clincher; 15 daily routes of distribution, 221. No materials on the spot; nor has N. Y. nor Phil.; easily gathered; C. desires no monopoly; must be the great city of the continent; each locality to have mnfrs.; country to use its wealth to advance C., 222. Chief minerals gathered at C.; insures mg. largely; further mineral development, 248; their certainty; 1,000,000 sq. ms. of mining; what other equal point of convergence, 249. Gathering and distributing advantages; both commerce and ms.; agr. and mineral wealth; has nature failed in the site for the city, 249. Many large cities in Gt. In. make C. sure, 392; to commercial advantages, add mg.; where another equal region; no measure for C.; W. yet developing; mg. now distributed; to have a centre; one easily reached; that mnfrs. will seek, 393.

FACILITIES. GATHERING AND DISTRIBUTING. **Canal. Lakes. Railways. Rivers.** 74, 199, 221, 249, 314, 393. RAW MATERIALS ABOUND. **Coal. Iron. Lumber. Minerals.** 74, 218, 219, 221. Facilities to gather materials superior to Phila., to distribute surperior to N. Y., 216, 221, 222. No point equal to gather iron, coal, copper, lead and zinc; this not the only advantage; great variety of minerals; this not hypothetic, 248. Conjunction of Coal, Iron and other Minerals, margin, 222-249. CHEAP FOOD. Chief grain and provision market of the world, 62, 103, 162, 166, 208, 214, 221. LOCAL **Advantages,** margin, 249-300. **Capital. Climate. Labor.**

CHIEF BRANCHES. List of mnfrs., 1855, capital, hands, value; increase over 1854, 200. *U. S. Census* of Cook co., 1860: No. of establishments; cost of raw material; capital; No. hands; cost of labor; value of products, 201, 202. List of ms. and No. of establishments, May, 1867, 203, 204. **Boots** and **Shoes,** 206-208. **Flour,** 215. **Highwines,** 215. **Leather,** 205. **Provisions.** This branch an index of others in the future; C. chief packing city of the world, 208, 221. Facilities for slaughtering and packing, 211. Railroads require much at C., 199, 217. "Chicago Iron Co.," a blasting furnace, 240.

MARKET, C. chief of the world in **Grain,** 62, 103, 162, 166; in **Provisions,** 62, 103, 162, 208; in live **Stock,** 164, 166; in **Lumber,** 166, 170. Europe will provide means to reach such a m. 62, 204, 244. St. L. prefers a vibrating, C. a steady, 160.

MARSH, SYLVESTER, grain dryer, 162, 163.

MARTIN, Rev. Mr., the claims of Nevada, &c. 141 *n.*

MARQUETTE Co. Mich, its products, 1867, 238, 239. *Mining Journal.* Future supply of Lake Sup. iron ore, 237. Business of Marquette Co., 1867, 238.

MASSACHUSETTS and the West united, 22. Funny if in St. L. interest, 50. M. C. voted against Ill. Cent. R. R. grant, 138 *n.* M. and South Carolina conflicting teachings, 196. Growth of towns in, 323. Should lead in making Niagara U. S. canal, 375.

MATHIESON & HEGEHLER'S, La Salle Zinc Works, 247.

MAUMEE canal to Cin. compared with C. and Ill. and Mich. canal, 306. Superior to C. for 47 y., future unknown, 312.

MAYORS of C., list from 1837 to 1866, 288.

MEDICAL SCHOOLS. **Science** *and Art.* No. graduates next to Phila. and N. Y., 269.

MEEKER, A. B., upon Lake Superior Iron trade; his iron Co., 240.

MEEKER, JOSEPH, erected first school house, 264.

MERCHANTS, their power and responsibility, 141. Of C. refused to aid railroads; most not of that sort, 349.

MICHIGAN, trade with C., from Saginaw, 355. From Lake Superior, 246. Farm values, 1850, 1860, 317.

MILTIMORE, IRA, advised Dearborn school-house, 266.

MINERALS. Wealth as yet little known, 123, 126, 228. Railroads will develop, 44, 117, 121, 127, 130. Variety and abundance of the Union, 194; exchange of to be chiefly inland, 302. Mineral wealth promotes mnfrs. in the W., 223, 224; chief easily gathered at C., 248; 1,000,000 sq. ms. mining area tributary to C., 249. Conjunction of Coal, Iron and other Minerals, margin, 222, 249. Rocky Mts. *Cor. C. Rep.:* Sweetwater mines in Wyoming Ter.; gold discoveries; Cereso lode; long list of mines opened; estimates moderate; 150 leads; gold yield; new discoveries; field unknown; improves with development; 3 cities; various minerals; natural advantages; Pacific road in 15 ms.; coal, iron, silver,

124; resources unknown; trade going to C.; 50,000 people in a year; chance for busy men, not drones; act prudently; all depends on effort; all sorts of minerals, 125. *Cor. Va. City Enter.:* new discoveries in Sweetwater mines; rich placers; towns growing; good chance for prospectors, 126.

COAL, Ills., 223; 240, 241, 242, Chester, 224–226; 243; Ia., 240, 241, 242,; Mo., 223; Iowa, 224; Ohio, 225, 233, 241. COPPER, Ills., 223, 234; Mo., 223; Iowa, 224. Mich., Lake Sup., 244, 245. FIRE CLAY, Ills., 248; Mo., 223. IRON, Ills., 223, 224, 241, 243; Mo., 223, 225, 243; Iowa, 224. Mich., Lake Superior, 227–241; charcoal pig, 235, 245; Wis., 241. Advantages of C. in transportation; in mixing ores, 234. Product of principal States, 1850, '60, 233. Bog ores, 247. LEAD, Ills., 223; Mo., 223; Wis., 224; Iowa, 224. SILEX, Ills., 224, 248. ZINC, Ills., 247; Mo., 223; Wis., 247.

MINNESOTA, trade turned to C., *Mo. Dem.*. 1861, 112. *Merch. Mag.:* a territory, 1849, of 4,049; 1865, 250,000 population; newer States grow fastest; facilities greater; one day work of 30; progress in population and property, annually from 1858 to '64, 134. *Mo. Dem.,* "Wheat shipped, 1867," 135. *C. Rep.:* three-fourths comes to C., 135 *n.*

MISSOURI, of n. part C. is centre, 25, 34. Trade turned to C., *Mo. Dem*, 34, 35; *Cobb,* 40; *Hammond,* 80; Liberty, (Clay co.,) *Trib.,* 97; *Mo. Dem.,* 1861, 112. How to whip C. out of M., 55. Mnfrs. 1850 and 1860, 202. Variety of minerals, 223, 225, 243. *Gov's Mess., 1868:* progress since war; religion and education; great prosperity; debt reduced; population increased, 133. **River.**

MISSISSIPPI **River.**

MOBILE railroad to be helped, 23 *n.*

MONEY, increase of affects values, 11, 15. 16. Increase 1852 by gold not paper, 16. National indebtness to be currency; good in Europe, 15; debt to be paid by posterity, 16. N. Y. m. will not control to the prejudice of the W. against State sovereignty, 56. Capital to be drawn from Europe; confidence in our promises to pay; State-rights our safeguard; dispute about part of the bonds; return to specie payments; loss upon our securities; pay dearly for capital, 198; get rid of national banks, use greenbacks, pay specie, 199. **Capital.**

MONOPOLY, C. desires no m., xvii., 44, 222. Would promote barge trade to Gulf, 184. No city of W. monopolise mnfrs, 218. M. adverse to our genius, 342. Remedy for Camden and Amboy in State-rights, 353 *n.*

MONTANA trade coming to C., *Mon. paper:* Many streams; long trips from St. L., 118. *Hel. Gaz.,* C. *vs.* St. L.: Trade goes to best bidder; St. L. inert; C. active; Sioux City road; steamboats to connect; benefits to Montana; mountain trade large; C. seeks; St. L regrets; trade like water, 119. *C. Rep.:* Sioux City route best; cuts off St. L.; best for C.; increase of Mon. trade, 119.

MORGAN, R. P., first Gal. railroad report, 350.

MULLIGAN, General, graduate of St. Mary of the Lakes, 275.

MUNN & SCOTT, elevator and grain dryer, 162.

MUSIC, Culture of, *Chi. Cour.:* Root & Cady's publishing house, 279.

NAILS, sales of chief houses at C., 244.

NATION. **Politics.** Prosperity of C. thoroughly identified with that of the n., 366. Duty to our n., xli.

NATIONAL Union based upon State Sovereignty i, xii., 15 19, 56, 108, 110, 137, 195 *n.*, 198-333, 353 *n.*, 402. Nl. gatherings at C.; capitol should not be moved, 8 *n.*, 386, *Sac. (Cal.) Union,* "The Aspiring W.:" St. L. wants nl. capital; C. claims; W. seat of empire; Cal. and Ills. alike; W. national; its power; 3 cities of a million in 25 y., 386 *n.* Debt to be paid by posterity, 16. War difficulties considered, 1861, 17.

NATURE. **Agricultural** fertility. **Climate. Health. Lakes. Minerals. Rivers. Site.** Co-operation of n. and of art from abroad our basis, xiv. Conjunction of n. and art at C. should be examined, xxxi., xli., 70, 142, 249. Art following n's Lead C. has no Taxes for Railways, though she has several times more than any Rival, and nearly two-thirds of all W. of the Tol. & Cin. Railroad, and N. of the Ohio River, margin, 28–36, 105, 106. The Lake Route to the East and Europe, margin, 58 66. The Northwest is the Prize contested—its Extent and Resources, margin, 111, 131. 600,000 square miles of arable Land and water Courses, unequaled in Advantages natural and acquired, rapidly settling with the best of Men, must give unexampled Growth to their Emporium, margin, 131–140. Conjunction of Coal, Iron and other Minerals, margin, 222–249. Local Advantages and City Expansion, margin, 249–300. *Conjunction of n.'s benefits at C.:* Head of lake navigation, 58, 65, 70, 71; close proximity to valley of great rivers, 58, 70; largest and richest agricultural area of the globe, 114, etc.; minerals in greatest variety and abundance, 222, 249; pure water, 252, 255; good climate; health, 252; favorable site, 249. *Edmunds:* n. gives means, man employs them for his good, 193.

NO PROMINENCE GIVEN BY N. TO ST. L.: has no important natural location; if she had, why is not capital and energy effective? Cairo better site; also Alton, 84; fur trade started her; this not nature; also steamboats; are these nature? 85. Her claims to natural location examined, 86–88. Not n. but art makes a commercial centre, 90: she must revolutionize art and n., 90, 102. N. impairs her own advantages, 91. Miss. has no head or tail; an indefinite viaduct, 101. Why does n. fail at St. L.? 176. N. not to be proved false; yet art or n. blunders at St. L., 178. Has n. failed at C. as at St. L.? 249

NEBRASKA trade turned to C., *Cin. Com.,* 33. *Atch.,* (Kas.,) *Free Press,* 188.

NELSON, MURRY & Co.'s., Grain dryer, 163.

NEW ALBANY, (Ia.,) *Commercial:* Lou., N. Alb. & Salem road, receiver appointed; Mr. Culver to be superintendent, 363.

NEW ENGLAND, error that she is to mnfr. for W., 302. Profit on flour to N. E. increased $1,000,000 by railroads, 316. Their interest ours, 377. **East.**

NEWSPAPERS. Obligations of our city to the Press in general; should have a copy of this vol., viii. Press of the city: annual statistics valuable, xxvii. Character of our press; none more national; metropolitan. *Chicagoan,* "C. as a business centre:" proud of its business; to be literary metropolis; much done, 280; 75 publications; ability; literature slow growth; taste to grow rapidly; tendency to concentration; C. publishing centre of W., 281. *Cin. Enq.:* press wide awake, 146.

NEW ORLEANS, why trade report exceeds C., 144. Exports compared with N. Y., 183, 185, 186. Climate unfavorable to exports of grain and provisions, 183. Why produce goes there, and C. desires it, 375.

NEW YORK, growth of towns in, 323. *The whole capital of N. Y. and N. Eng. supports C.,* xv.

CITY. Joint interest with C., xv., 24, 29, 31, 32, 34, 51, 105, 377. *World:* "E. and W.—the port of N. Y.;" transfer of the Cunard Line; N. Y. chief exporter; business aggregates, 56; Erie canal made N. Y.; N. Y. and N. O. in tobacco; N. Y. needs railroads W.; wants corn; no freight for ships; Balt. a strong rival; cotton by rail; Boston increasing Wn. lines; advantages over N. Y., 57.......Not to depend on railways, 58, 377. Distance to C. and St. L., 80. Emporium of whole country, 115. Exports compared with N. O., 1860, 183, 185, 186. Advantages of C. over N. Y. in jobbing trade, 152. An example in manufacturing, 199. C. excels her in distributing facilities, 221. Draws mnfrs. tho' all materials are imported; relies on mnfrs., not commerce; no advantage over C. but age and capital; advantages of C. over N. Y. and Phil.; soon reach them, 216. Will N. Y. have advantage over Cin. for internal trade, 301. Competition with Phil., 370, 373; with Balt., 57, 371, 373, 374. No laggard; combines rail and water; past efforts for union with W.; must see importance of lake improvements; railway absorbing energies; water facilities a defence against railway monopolies, 372. Needs Lake Simcoe route. 344. Need not fear for canal tolls, 345. Superiority of N. Y. as a market, 374. Needs more avenues to lakes, 374. N. Y. and Bost. advantage over S. by water for wn. trade, 376. *Scott:* N. Y. beat Lou. and C. beat N.

Y. in 50 y., 398......*Cir.* 1861, comparison of N. Y. with C., 400. *Tribune*, Growth of C. compared with N. Y. and Brooklyn, xxxi. North Pacific railway, 45. *Cour. and Enq.*, letters to, 1848, 31. *Times*, Pacific road built 1870, 42. *Com. and Finan. Chron.* "New route to the Pacific," 43. *Ev. Post:* "The strong northwest," 140. *Railroad Journal:* "Manufactures of machinery in the West," 217. "Early difficulties of railways to 1843; progress, 11 y.," 334. *Hunt's Merch. Mag.:* "The C. beef trade," 1857, 211. "American monopolies and Emigration," 219. "Mines and manufactures in the Miss. Valley," J. A. Blake, 223. "The Ills. Chester Coal Fields," Prof. Waterhouse, 224. "Iron of Lake Superior," 227. "Zinc. mnfr. in Ill.," 247. A standard work of reference, 324 *n.* *Ship List:* C. draining Rocky Mts. trade, 340; barge trade a new era, 341. *Sun:* Gamblers in Rock Isl. stock, 358. *Memorial N. Y. Cham. of Com. to Legis.:* N. Y. done nothing in railways since 1853; Pa. Cent. has stolen march; Balt. & O. not idle; consolidation of short lines gives through trade, 372; Erie road should connect with C.; Phil. and Balt. alert; N. Y. too confident; cannot rely upon water; consolidation injurious; wn. trade regained by railways; comparative rates from N. Y. and Balt. to St. L., 373; to Cin.; to C.; change requisite to N. Y.; consolidation of parallel lines to be prohibited, 374.

NIAGARA Falls canal to be built, 62.

NON-RESIDENTS should buy C. property; they help the city, 297. Should share in benefits; railway men to have a share; do more than citizens, 298. Chartered co.'s desirable for them, 299.

NORFOLK to compete for trade of lakes, 54, 58. Railroad to C. to be built, 103, 366.

NORTHWEST. **Great Interior. West.** *Cor. Cin. Gaz.;* "Business between Cin.,C. and the N. W.": Trade of N. W. overestimated; products same as lat. of Cin, 76; line of trade n. of Cin.; large trade during war; N. trade lost; try to keep 70 ms.; seek S. & S. W. business, 77. Emporium of N. W. must be of the continent, 110. The N. W. is the Prize contested—Its Extent and Resources, margin, 131. The old N. W.: 600,000 sq. ms. of arable Land and water Courses, unequaled in Advantages natural and acquired, rapidly settling with the best of Men, must give unexampled Growth to their Emporium, margin, 131-140. Able to build up its emporium, 136. *C. Rep.*, "The N. W. and transportation:" Minn. to seek Atlantic not Pac.; barge system on trial; probable success; for C. interest with farmers; have railroads by and by; meanwhile use rivers, 179. The Northwest and West hereafter the Great Interior, margin, 385-387.

OBJECTIONS to the Work, xxvii. "*Too much Puffing of C. already:*" True; therefore make known the truth; truth considered bombast; other cities present claims; trade figures should be contrasted; newspapers inadequate to examine philosophy of growth, xxviii; examination indispensable; exaggeration a blunder. "*Invidious Comparisons render us odious:*" A just one not invidious; comparisons with St L. proper; show superiority of C.; St. L. and Cin. not disparaged, xxix; bubble of centrality pricked; this claim her only hook for complaint; Prof. Waterhouse's paper. "*Every body already knows about C:*" Not true; St. L. believed superior; West to have great cities; comparison of water and railroads necessary; C. considered smart; *N. Y. Trib.* upon her growth, xxxi; not abnormal; causes to be examined; effect results. "*It tends to create a spirit of Speculation:*" Truth no injury, xxxii. "*Too long a Story:*" No topic superfluous; every extract important; information valuable for reference, xxxiii.

OBLIGATIONS. *Aim to invite Consideration of the O's of City and Citizens, in view of the unparalleled benefits showered by God and Country:* we are here to make money; yet citizens of no mean city; our advantage in exhibiting the operations of art and nature; honor and self-interest conjoin, xxiii.

OCCIDENT, Ancient Orient changed to American Oc., 197, 218, 314.

OCEAN, Atlantic O., trade with lakes to be immense, 62. Direct between C. and Europe for 1500 tons, 62. First vessel to England, 66. O. and inland navigation compared, 301.

OFFAL, utilizing, 214.

OGDEN, W. B., railway king, 105. Plan of dock improvement, 251. Engagement for C. University, 272. Donation to Pres. Theol. Sem, 270. Aids to C. railroads, 298. Pres. and 1st report G. & C. U. R. R., 349. Predicts Galena to be only N. W. R. R., 350. That he repudiates, 351.

OHIO, area and population, 115. Proportion in farms, 116. Farm values, 1850, 1860, 317. Benefited on hogs, $3,000,000 by railroads 316. Facilities of trade and town growth, 323.

OMAHA *Register.* Large trade with C. Temporary bridge built over Mo., 96.

OPINIONS tested by experience, 3. Former O. and Predictions were based upon a reasonable Hypothesis, 2.

ORIENT, Trade of valuable, 43, 104. Being hypothetical not calculated upon, 104. C. to have trade with, 150. American occident, 197, 218, 314.

OSAGE Indians. value of their lands, 121 *n.* Treaty with for 8,000,000 as., 356 *n.*

OTTAWA river (Can.) to be improved for lake navigation, 62, 344.

PACIFIC. **Asia.** Trade, its magnitude, 42 44, 128, 221. European travel, 43. For the Great Interior sufficient for C., 43. *Lond. Daily Telegraph* upon, 43. *N. Y. Com. & Finan. Chron:* New route to Pac. 43. Several roads needed, 44, 47, 79, 104. C. wants no monopoly, 44, 47. C. centre of this trade, 44, 104, 342: 369. This trade being hypothetic, is not made a basis, 104. *Pitts. & Ft. W. Rep:* Get P. trade thro' C., 55, 369. Asiatic trade will concentrate, 369.

PAINTERS, chief artists of C., 278.

PALMER, POTTER, approves higher grade, 250. Marble building finest for commerce in the world, 258.

PANIC, 1857, causeless, 12, 16, 17.

PARIS, a less railway centre than C., 384.

PARKER, O. L., rules of grain inspection at C., 161.

PAST, Study the P. to understand the Future and improve the Present, margin, 1, 2. *Solomon*, "the thing that hath been," etc.; no new principle; experience disregarded; value of principles in business, 1; this book for regarders of experience; p. a basis, 2. Former Opinions and Predictions were based upon a reasonable Hypothesis. The Bible teaches mainly from the past, 3. P. proves certainty of C.'s growth, 21, 72. Reasoning from p. and present to future the basis of the argument, 140.

PECK, P. F. W., in Galveston road. Built 3d frame building. 1st Prs. Church there convened, 99 *n.*

PENNSYLVANIA, mnfrs., rails and locomotives of Pacific road, 52. Growth of towns in, 323.

PERKINS, C. E., Sup. Bur. & Mo. Road, Rep., 48.

PETROLEUM in Illinois, 224.

PHILADELPHIA has advantage of N. Y. and Bost., 54. P., Balt. and St. L. joint interest, 54, 376. Comparison of manufactures with C., 216. C. excels in gathering facilities, 221. Increase of domestic trade, 305. Competition with N. Y., 370, 373. *U. S. Rail. & Mining Reg.*, upon consolidation of Pitts., Ft. W. & C. with Pa. Cent., 367. *N. Amer:* "Importance of railroad bridge at St. L.," 376.

PICKARD, JOSIAH L., superintendent of schools, 266.

PIKE co., Mo.; railroad projected due west, 97.

PITTSBURGH *Gazette*, Kansas Cor., "Ch. Yankee on his westward way," 51. Quotes *N. Amer.*, "Importance of railroad bridge at St. L.," 376. *P. & Ft. Wayne R. R. Report.*, 1867. Pac. Trade thro. C., 55. *P. Commercial*, unanimity of C., 70. Trade of, 1867, 151. *Prof. Waterhouse's* estimated cost of iron, 226.

POLITICS. *Our Political Institutions the Basis of the Argument*, xii. *Duty to our State*, xxxix *Duty to our Nation*, xli. Coats of arms of U. S. and of Ills., i., 402. Man's various *stati* to be regarded, xxxiv., 191. P. properly introduced, 20 *n.*, 193. Politics and physics to consider mnfrs., 196. Safety of national indebtedness and currency, 15. Confidence in our institutions, 15, 137, 193, 195. *Cir.*, 1861, "Effects of Secession and War," 17. State sovereignty defends our rights, 56. Nature of Union not apprehended; secures national rights; benefits resulting from State experiments in govt.; State pride to operate; build great cities, 108. Creating large cities, yet trade must be left to natural channels; Cam. & Am. righted by State sovereignty, 109. Were Union broken C. would grow; with Union no favors asked; the West a unit; C. and Ills. true to State motto, 110. M. C.'s must do their duty to whole republic, 127. Influence of govt. in promoting commerce and mnfrs.; ignorance of principles; its cause; superiority of institutions not appreciated; foreigners will not display their inferiority 136; confidence in our institutions; strength of govt. demonstrated; State sovereignty to be apprehended, 137, 198. N. W. to have power; great responsibility; relative changes of M. C.'s from 1850–60; same to continue, 138; knowledge of our superior govt. will bring settlers, 139. Dr. Channing advocates free-trade; present doubtful; all interests to be cared for; duties vary; nature of State different from individual, 191; in every *status* laws to be regarded; States seek peace; independence best means; commerce not to be disregarded; future free-trade; commerce and mnfrs. both needed; States no philanthropists; govt. to care for all interests, 192. *U. S. Census Rep.:* Security of our Constitution and laws; Eng. security basis of prosperity; same elements ours, 193; maintaining Republics difficult; *Carnot's* exception of U. S., 105......Too little attention to p.; rights of conquest compel to study; final basis State Sovereignty. 193 *n.* Why failure of France as a Republic and our success? study requisite to appreciate our system; checks essential in Gt. Br.'s Monarchy; in our democracy; State sovereignty our basis; representation the basis of Republicanism; superiority of our checks and balances, 195 *n.* Politics and physics wisely blended; our contrary teachings prove egregious errors exist; discussion here impossible; effect of examination upon mnfrs., 196. Common sense has ruled; errors of the fathers; Chisholm *vs.* Ga.; Blackstone's nonsense, sovereignty of the legislature, our bane; error of 11th amendment to Const.; courts of claims to settle our disputes, 196 *n.* No difference in forms of Govt. an error; obligations to God for our system; strength of covenant to be apprehended; Europe cannot have our system; our teaching of the right of revolution; Europeans to come here; Gt. Br. wrong about expatriation; we fight if necessary, 197. Capital to be drawn from Europe; confidence in our promises to pay; State-rights our safeguard; State Sovereignty to be apprehended; dispute about part of the bonds, 198. Must understand rights and duties as States, as a Nation, 219 *n.* Our power as citizens; a city an ulcer; does not make itself; a vent for corruption; centres of civilization; associate effort needed: worth of a true city, 320. Checks upon power in Gt. Br., and U. S., 324. Fed. Un. binds together; benefits of State divisions; yet trade national, 325, 402. Federal not understood, 325 *n.* *Poussin:* Am. to become a chief com. nation; rival and dispossess Gt. Br.; pursues an opposite course; democracy rules; sailor's rights; sovereignty of people; no change desired, 333; democratic liberalism and railroads; people decided about railroads, not States. 334......A relief from monopolies in State Sovereignty, 353. *Sac* (Cal.) *Union:* St. Louis wants national capitol; claims of C., 386 *n.*......National capitol should not be mov. d. 386. State Sovereignty and National Union the basis of our growth; knowledge will draw immigrants, 402.

POOR, H. V., Ed. *Railroad Jour.*, changes, 11 y. to 1843, 334.

POOR, Hon. JOHN A., letter to Ship-Canal Conv.; importance of improving avenues from C. to the ocean, 343.

POPULATION. **Immigration.** *Aim to show that C. has a Population equal her advantages:* Character of a city important; difficult to change; "actions speak louder than words;" undue credit given C; site rather than citizens have made it, xxi. We believe in work; want different faith, xxii. Wealthy citizens do little for their city, xxxiii Some run away and stay away to shirk their duty, xxxvii. P. of the N. W. States, 1860, and proportion tributary to C., 1861–'68, 115. P. of U. S. in 1900 to be 100,000,000, 129, 132; half to be in lake and river valleys, 132. Progress of Min., 134; increase in Ills., Iowa and Wis., compared with Union; Mr. Scott's predictions, 138. Agriculture diffuses, manufactures concentrate, 192. P. of U. S. increased 4½ fold in 50 y., mnfrs. 10-fold, 195. Character of our p.; energy and enterprise; character made by active men; private men selfish; obligations increase with leisure, 260; exceptions; work done gives promise; C. an example; adornment beginning; old and new settlers to work, 262. Censuses from 1837 to 1866, 288. Not 10 p. c. over food, 302. Increase of P. in W., 1850–60, 319. Proportion in towns, 1840, in different sections and States, 321. P. 1810–60 of 12 Atl. and Gulf cities, 336; 5 river cities; 1840–60 of 6 lake cities, 337, 338. Superiority of W. in p., causes, 386, *n.* Census of C. 1868; p. c. increase, 398.

PORK. **Provisions. Stock.** Entire crop of country, 18 y, 165.

PORTER, Rev. JEREMIAH, organized 1st Pres. ch. 1832, 99, 262.

POST EVENING, C. Street Railway traffic, 1867, 282

POUSIN, M., upon U. S., its power and progress, 333

PRAIRIE FARMER, extent of area from which its friends came, 72, *n.* Traveling for, 139 *n.* Advises curing of corn, 162. Its beginning, 290.

PREDICTIONS. My former Opinions and P. were based upon a reasonable **Hypothesis,** margin, 2–14. Former, reasonable, 2, 24, 26, 27, 32, 65, 72 290, 292, 295, 296, 313. Present rest upon what has been done, 72. *Basis not Hypothesis but Fact,* xi. C. growth not foreseen by many citizens, 3 *n.*, 349. Ps. of C.'s growth, 1834: In 5 y. C. equal Detroit then, 5. 1847; 15 y. for C. equal to 27 for Cin., 7. 1848: ps. for 30 y.; realized for 10 y.; failed for next 10 y., 398. 1852: 7 y. give C. 100,000, 11. 1861: C. in 1870 to be 4th or 3d city in the U. S., 75. That 20 to 25 y. give C. 1,000,000, 400. 1868: that in 1880 7 figures will be required for enumeration, 67. *Scott,* 1843: when C. is to grow, 306. C. may equal Maumee; not for 47 y.; future power unknown; may be second or first after 47 y., 312. 1848: Relative growth of Atl. and interior cities, 388-391. 1857: N. Y. and C. compared for 48 y., 397. 1846: N. Y. to beat London in 100 y.; Cin. to beat N. Y., 403. His slight mistake, 313. His views confirmed, 138, 313, 338. 397.

PRESENT. Study the Past to apprehend the Future and improve the P., 1.

PRIDE of citizens in C. proper, xxxi, 388. *Scott:* All proud of their cities, 388. *Jacksonville* (Ill.) *Journal,* "C. at Home and Abroad:" Illinoisan praises it abroad; why jealous at home; her example worthy; activity; thus C. grows; others plod; C. enterprise beats St. L., 109.

PRINCIPLES. None new; to be known and used; needed in business, 1.

PRODUCE, Trade follows channels of, 83, 152, 181. This denied, 186. Increased facilities of transport wanted, 375.

PROCRUSTES, instead of a Delilah has St. L. in hand, 82

PROMISES to be tested, 106. C. changes from p. to fact, 107.

PROPELLERS superseding sail, 62.

PROSPERITY of C. thoroughly identified with Gt. Int. and the Nation, 366.

PROVISIONS. **Stock,** Live. C. chief market of the world, 62, 103, 162, 208, 214. This chief mnfr. of C.; indicates success in other branches more centralizing, 208. *Wing:* Growth of live-stock trade; this a branch; steady increase over other cities; dealers come here; basis solid, 208. *Edmunds:* Prices at N. Y. not reduced by railroads, but in W. growing to E., 316.

PORK AND BEEF PACKING: *Merch. Mag.,* quotes *C. Times,* "History of the business:" "G. S. Hubbard first packer; increase; C. chief packing city; advantages in transportation and food, 208; corn put into hogs and cattle; saves in freight, packing business at C. & Cin. natural; to increase; stock-raising improves farms, 209.

BEEF PACKING. Col. Hough's at Lon. World's Fair, 167. List of packers and statistics, 1867–8. *Merch. Mag.*, 1857, "C. Beef Trade:" rapid changes in the wilderness; high estimation; contracts for the allied army; amt. packed 1855, 211.

PORK PACKING, earliest recollections, 1832–'3, 208, *n*. List of packers and statistics for 1867–8, 210, 211. Cut meats instead of barrelled for Eng. and South, 211.

FACILITIES. Reflex influence of stock trade and packing; creates great facilities, 211; advantages of a large stock-market to a packer. *Com. Exp.*: description of largest packing house; slaughter 300 cattle, 2,000 hogs daily; machinery; floors for cooling, etc.; lard tanks and purifier; skillful workmen, 212.

UTILIZING OFFAL, Baugh & Sons establishment, 214.

FUTURE INCREASE. Illinois and adjoining States chief corn producers; must be concentrated to transport. *Ruggles:* Grain-raising in W. only just begun, 212; exceeds Gt. Brit.; benefits not home restricted; new world to feed the old: cheap transit wanted; hog—don't laugh at him; corn incarnate; new mode of curing; Eur. trade, 213; cut meats exported, 1859–60; fiscal effects; lard into oil; increased use......Facilities to be supplied to reach chief provision market of the world; live stock to be more and more manufactured here, 214.

AT ST. L. *Mo. Dem.*: St. L. exceeded by other cities; to swear less by her rivers......Consolation for present losses in future hopes. How can St. L. draw from C., what C. has drawn from Cin., 209.

PUFFING *of C., Too much already.* Therefore, is this work necessary; xxvii. Fair examination is not p., xxviii. Folly to desert truth for p., xxix.

QUARTER, Rt. Rev WILLIAM, 1st bishop of C., 275.

QUARTZ crystal in Illinois, 224.

RAILWAYS. CHICAGO AS A RAILWAY CENTRE—chief of the world, xiii, 384. Was so in 1858, 24. Art following Nature's Lead, C. has no Taxes for Railways, though she has several Times more than any Rival, and nearly Two-thirds of all west of the Tol. & Cin. R., and north of the Ohio River, margin, 28–36. Power of the Railway to Develope and centralize, margin, 313–339. No other equal Point of Convergence of either Rail or Water, or of both, on the Globe, margin, 339–385. Area tributary by r's., **Gt. Int. North-west. West.** Those are C. roads which send her more business than to any other city, 37. C. a natural centre, 24, 28, 29. 36, 41, 42, 65, 71, 92, 105, 106, 120, 221, 338, 346, 399. London and Paris inferior as centres; C. system greater than that of Eng. or France, 384. 250 daily trains; 1 each 3 ms.; long routes, 385.

EASTWARD LINES. Five Rival Railways Eastward, margin, 53–58, 103. (See below, Mich. Cent.; Mich South.; Pitts. & Ft. Wayne; Gt. East.; Balt & Ohio; Norfolk.) *N. Y. World*: N. Y. needs more rs., 57. Competitors with Miss. River, 342. Competition of En. lines, 362. New trunks by consolidating short lines; compete from Portland to Norfolk, 366. *Crane:* Ogdensburg road insufficient for Bost.; a new line to Lake O. wanted; capacity and cheap transportation, 375.

SOUTH AND S. WEST LINES. (See below, Louis., N. Alb. & C.; Evansville, Crawfordsville & Danville; Vincennes and Cairo; Ills. Central; C., Alton & St. L.; Jacksonville branch, do.; C., Bur. & Quincy; Han. & St. Joe; St. Joe & Leavenworth; Leavenworth, Law. & Gal.; Cameron & Kas. City; Kas. Pac., En. Div.; South W. Pacific; N. Mo.; Mo. Valley; Cairo & Fulton.) Ills. Cent., and Alton & St. L. predicted, 21, 23, 29–31. N. and S. lines E. of Miss. aid C., 37, 67, 95, 187, 361. So will lines W. of Miss. still more, 81, 95, 96. 150 ms. C. lines along Mo. River, 95. Prospective trunks, 283. Power of Ills. Cent. 98.

WEST AND NORTHWEST LINES. The Pacific Railways in Progress—their Effects, margin, 42–52, 104. (See below, Bur. & Mo.; Atchison & Pike's Peak; C. & Rock Island; Mississippi & Mo.; Galena & C.; C. & Northwestern; Ills. Cent.; Dubuque & Sioux City; Central Pacific; Pacific; Northern Pacific; Union Pacific; Kas. Pacific; Denver & Cheyenne; Sioux City & Omaha.) Galena and Rock Isl. to Council Bluffs predicted, 21-24, 30-32. W. chief field for rs., 71, 132, 338. Wn. rs. pay well, 72, 336. R's. E. of Miss. interested in extensions W., 48, 133. C. now able to aid the E. to extend the r. system; her 7 lines W. will continue to Rocky Mts., and beyond; their competition; other competition difficult, 120; equal divergence of C. lines from Mex. to British boundary, 121; parallel lines to be built each 50 or 100 ms., 122. C. lines will extend, 130. Progress in N. W., 132. Next 10 y. will double the increase of last 10 y., 133. Prospective trunks, 283.

ATCHISON AND PIKE'S PEAK. **C., B. & Quincy.** (Central Branch, Union Pacific route), Grant and length, 45; connects with Omaha road at Fort Kearney, 46, 49. *Cor. Mo. Rep.*: Connects with Han. & St. Joe, 49, 50, 356.

BALTIMORE & OHIO. Pa. Cent. diverts trade from, 363. Account of laying foundation stone, 1828, 371. Perfecting connections W., 372, 373.

BURLINGTON & MISSOURI ROAD. **Burlington and Q.** Has a land grant, 25; Mr. Perkins upon importance of C. B. & Q. road, 48; a feeder of C. B. & Q., 356.

CAIRO & FULTON, Mo. **Ills. Cent.** Bought up by Mr. Thomas Allen; more inimical to St L. than Han. & St. Joe road; cut-off prevented, 40. A villainous scheme nipped; Ills. Central in competition, 98.

CAIRO & VINCENNES. **Vincennes.**

CAMERON & KANSAS CITY. **C., B. and Quincy.** Built, 26, 51. *Mo. Dem.*, "A flank movement:" Not built by C. but by East; connects C. with Pacific road, 26; St. L. at disadvantage; must work; E'n capital aids C.; will change, 27, 99. *Mo. Rep.*, another road E.; cheapens C. lumber; roads centering at K. City; a rival to St. L., 27. *C. Times:* No aid from C., 33......Its value to C., 52. St. L. ignorant of it, 97; puts her in a dilemma, 98.

CAMDEN & AMBOY monopoly, remedy for, 109, 353, *n*.

CENTRAL PACIFIC (from Sacramento) Route, grant and length, 45, 122. Route favorable, progress, 79.

C. & N. WESTERN. **Galena.** Has a land grant, 25. Trunks, branches and lengths, 36. Earnings, 10 y., 41. *Rep. 1867:* Sioux City Road to Omaha; connects with N. W. at St. Johns; takes Upper Mo. trade; Omaha to St. Joe in rapid progress; 150 ms. C. lines, 95.......Facilities for receiving and shipping iron ore at Escanaba, 236, 237; energy, 237; boats to Escanaba, 246, 352. Mr. Ogden predicts Galena to be the N. W'n road, 350; this repudiated, 351. Chartered 1848; changes and combinations, 351; re-organized, 1859; 1864, buys Galena; Fulton branch to Omaha, connects with Pac.; C. and Mil. absorbed; Peninsular road; steamers connect at Green Bay; extension from Mad. to St. Paul; officers, 352. Truly N. W'n road; a dangerous power, 352. Endeavor of N. W. to control R. I. road, 357, 358. Change of directors, 358, *n*.

C., ALTON & ST. L. predicted, 21, 31. Earnings 10 y., 41. *Rep., 1867*: Jack. branch takes trade to C., 95. *Rep., 1868:* freight increase due to new Jack. road; not yet full trade; increase of passengers; local travel and freight, 187. Coal traffic, 242. *Trib.*: length; consolidations; changes of Co.; progress; vicissitudes, foreclosure; present firm condition; Jack. branch taps fine country; takes trade from near St. L. to C.; officers, 361.

C., BURLINGTON & QUINCY, trunks and branches and length, 36. Earnings 10 y., 41. *Hon. J. F. Joy's Report*, 1868: their interest in Bur. & Mo. road; earnings west of Miss.; settlement of country, 48. *Report*, 1867: Freight west of Miss; large local trade, 94. Depot grounds at C.; length of city track, 284. *Trib.*: Stock in original hands; well managed; route fine; 13 ms. to Aurora, 1852; consolidation with others; track into C. 1863, 355; Iowa extension, Bur. & Mo. road; Han. & St. Joe; Atchison and Kas. City: 3 bridges; Mo. Val. road connects with Pac. at Omaha; officers; 356......Mr. Gale a projector; S. W. and diagonal route desirable; connects with Pac. at Omaha; with Atchison & Pike's Peak; Kas. Pac.; Leav., Law. & Gal., 356.

C., ROCK ISL. & PAC., predicted, 22, 23, 31. Has land grant in Iowa, 25. Trunks, branches and length, 36. Earnings 10 y., 41. To connect Boston with Council Bluffs "within 20 y," predicted 1847; Messrs. Farnam & Sheffield examine, get charter and build road, 356. *Trib.:* commenced 1852, finished 1854; extension to Council Bluffs; shortest line; has now 450 ms.; land grant; receipts and net earnings; work-shops at C.; increased value of property; officers, 357. Endeavor to prevent extension to Omaha; a stock-gambling operation; Mr. Tracy defeats it, 357. *N. Y. Sun* upon the contest; objects and results, 358. Elegant depot, with cut, 359.

COLUMBUS, C. & IA. CENT. **Great Eastern** changed to; length of roads; officers; a through line to seaboard; thorough condition, 362. Pa. Cent. superseding Balt. & Ohio; only 29 ms. further than Ft. Wayne route to Pitts., 363.

DENVER & CHEYENNE, 117. (*Mo. Dem.,*) 120. **Un. Pac.**

DUBUQUE & SIOUX CITY. **Ills. Cent.** *Hel.* (Mon.) *Gaz.,* "C. *vs.* St. L.: Trade goes to best bidder; St. L. inert; C. active; Sioux City road leased to Ills. Cent.; steamboats to connect; benefits to Montana; her trade sought, 118; C. seeks; St. L. regrets; trade like water, 119. *Cor. C. Rep.:* Sioux City route best; cuts off St. L.; best for C.; increase of Mon. trade, 119.

EASTERN DIVISION, UNION PACIFIC. **Kansas Pac. C. B. & Quincy.**

EVANSVILLE & CRAWFORDSVILLE, via Danville. Built to Danville; there strikes Brazil coal beds; 22 ms. to Danville; 120 to C., 283.

GALENA & C. UNION, **C., & N. Western.** Predicted with branches, 21, 23, 31; large profits 29; trunk and branches and length, 36. *Mr. Ogden's* first rep.: Small beginnings; Mich. Cent. at New Buf.; Gal. to connect, $250,000 stock taken; En. capital to be obtained; W. to build first 41 ms., $360,000 subscribed; route surveyed, 349; 31 ms. contracted; thorough road with T. rail if possible; flat rail at first; economy indispensable; T. rail can be substituted for flat; extension will make it necessary; connection with Mich. Cent.; road to Elgin secures for all time the whole N. W., 350. *Trib.:* Chartered 1836; then 1,000 ms. in U. S.; 1850 reaches Elgin, 42 ms.; Dixon air line, 1855; 1864 absorbed by N. W.; developed the country; large dividends; great success; inaugurated our system, 351.

GREAT EASTERN. **Columbus, C. & Ia. Cent.** Length and branches; earnings 10 years, 36, 41.

HANNIBAL & ST. JOE. **C. B. & Quincy.** Inimical to St. L., 34, 40, 50, 55, 80, 81, 93, 97, 112; length and branches, 36; connects with Atch., & Pike's Peak, 50; present route from Kas. City to C., 51; seeks its own interest, 112; important feeder of C., B. & Q., 356. A road from St. Joe to Jef. City to dispose of H. & St. Joe, 55.

ILLINOIS CENT. Three petitions to Cong., 1848, for land grant, 22; S. W. interested in a road to the lakes; this the first; help Mobile road; no gratuity asked, 23. *Circ., 1848:* importance and certain construction. *Let. to Bost. Cour.* in favor of I. C., 31. ......Trunks, branches and their lengths, 36. St. L. dependent on, 39. Earnings 10 y., 41. Works for C., 81, 98. Lessee of Dub. & Sioux City; soon connect at St. Johns, 118, 353. Grant of lands by Cong. a good precedent, 127. Power S. and S. W., 98. Mass. M. C. voted against land grant; Hon. Geo. Ashmun favored, 138, *n.* Liberal to La Salle Zinc Co., 248. Effect of construction upon land value, 317. Wants its own line from Freeport, 353. *Trib:* Land grant 1850; length and route; developed State; river connections S.; fruit traffic; Dubuque & Sioux City extension, 353; extent of land grant; credit sales; no forfeitures; prices; land department heavy; officers, 354.

IRON MOUNTAIN, St. L. must push, 68, 83.

JACKSONVILLE BRANCH, **C., Alton & St. L.** road; takes trade to C., 95, 361. This is a fair example of other roads, 95.

KANSAS PACIFIC. (**Union Pacific, Eastern Division.**) **C. B. & Quincy.** Route, grant and length, 46. *Santa Fe Cor. San Francisco Bulletin:* Change of route thro' New Mexico; another line to San Francisco; coal, water, iron; no snow; Congress to aid, 47......*San Fran. Bulletin:* No contest with Omaha route; route feasible; country to build its own roads; only land grants from Cong., 47......Trade already large, 52. Route to New Mexico suits C., 50. Securing this easier than the Han. & St. Joe, 51. *Cor. Pitts. Gaz.:* trade already large, 52. Genl. Hammond: Route favorable; company energetic, 79. Best line to Pac. for Phil. and Balt., 377. *Resolutions of C. Board of Trade:* Ask Cong. to aid; solve Indian difficulty; reach Cent. Mexico; route advantageous; Govt. saving, 382. *C. Rep.:* C. and Ills. most interested in the road; Mo. Legis. refused aid; road important, 382. *C. Times:* two P. roads better than one; competition; benefit of branches; K. road tied up at 411th mile post; past aid lost; saving to govt.; Cin.'s reasons, and C.'s, 383. *A. W. Wright,* on the survey of route: lines practicable, tho' some high grades; arable land; minerals, 384.

KANSAS CITY & CAMERON. (**Cameron**), **C., B. & Quincy.**

LEAVENWORTH, LAWRENCE & GALVESTON. **C., B. & Quincy,** 36, 99. Col. Vliet's description of the route, 121 *n.* A C. road, 99, 121. 180 ms. built, from Gal., 100. Connects with C., B. & Q., 356.

LEAVENWORTH & DESMOINES, Co.'s circular upon construction of road, 379.

LOUISVILLE, NEW ALBANY & C. **Mich. Cent.,** and branches, 36. Little Rock, Ark., connected with, 98. Receiver appointed, 363.

MICHIGAN CENTRAL predicted, 21; length and branches, 36. Earnings 10 ys., 41; origin, difficulties and progress, 354. Desire of Galena road to connect with, 349, 350. Difficulties with Ia. and Ills. to reach C.; stock in original hands; regular dividends, 354. *Trib.:* built to Ypsilanti, 1842; to C. 1852, 354. 20 y. of success; line to Saginaw; looks to C. for market; favorite route for travel; officers, 355.

MICHIGAN SOUTHERN, & N. INDIANA, predicted, 23, 31. Length of branches, 36. Earnings 10 ys., 41. Second road into C., 20th Feb., 1852. Depot cost $250,000; description, with cut; officers, 359. *C. Rep.:* 2 Cos. consolidated; begun 1838; finished 1852; Mich. branches; Goshen do.; built in 20 mos.; early difficulties; distrust of W.; final triumph, 360.

MISSISSIPPI & MO. consolidated with **C., Rock Isl. & Pac.,** 357.

MISSOURI VALLEY to aid C., 95. Important feeder of **C. B. & Q.,** 356.

MOBILE & OHIO, **Ill. Cent.** land grant, to be aided, 23.

NEW Y. & ERIE wants broad guage to C., 373.

NORFOLK, Va., equi-distant with N. Y.; important port; to have r. to C., 54, 58, 103, 366.

NORTHERN PACIFIC, (St. Paul.) *N. Y. Trib.,* route has advantage, its importance, N. Y. and N. Eng. interested, 45.

NORTH MISSOURI to Omaha, 54, 79, 174. General Hammond's speech, 79; most important of all to St. L., 67, 68; connects with C. roads, 67; danger of perversion to C., 96 *n.* Cuts off C., 83. West Branch; *Liberty* (Clay co.) *Trib.,* 97.

OMAHA to **Sioux City.** To St. Joe in rapid construction, 95.

PACIFIC. **Northern Pac.** St. Paul. **Union Pac.,** Omaha, and **Central** Sacramento. **E. Div., Kansas City. South W. Pac.** *Let. to Bost. Cour.,* 1848: P. railway possible; get one then to Council Bluffs; insure continuation W.; route E. of Mo. river will pay well; Atlantic cities should aid to get it, 31. *Circ. 1858:* P. road will be built, 24. The Pacific Railways in Progress—their Effects, margin 42-52, 104. Several necessary; C. wants several, 44, 47, 104, 127. P. connections the object; Omaha Road in rapid progress; takes trade of Neb., Col., Mon. and Dac.; trade immense; Pac. end in rapid progress; finished by 1870, 79. *Merch. Mag.,* opens commerce with all Asia, 221. Roads begun will be finished, 384. One begun in the midst of war; another begun before that is finished, 386. Make W. seats of mnfrs., 394.

PENNSYLVANIA CENT. **Pitts. & Ft. W.** Stole a march on N. Y., 372.

PEORIA & BUREAU VALLEY, connects with **C., Rock Isl. and Pac.,** 357.

PIKE Co., Mo., projected due West, 97, 98. Remember this road; a new and proper one for C., 98.

PITTSBURGH & FT. WAYNE, length, 36. Mr. Cass' report, 1867, trade thro' C. from Pacific, 55. *Trib.:* incorporated, 1852; foreclosed and sold 1861; now prosperous; large depot proposed; officers, 361. Earnings, 11 y.; Pa. Cent. & Phil. its support; competition with N. Y. and N. Eng.; large revenues, 352. *U. S. Railroad and Min. Reg.:* r. system to be understood; means of correction; great capital; Pa. chief in E., P. & Ft. W. in W.; shortest to seaboard, 367; benefits of combination; C. & St. L. on different basis; C. terminus of Omaha Pac.; St. L. of Kas. Pac.; terms of union; one has Pitts.; the other C. 368; a C. view; a Phil. view; benefits of a consolidation, 369.......Seeks Pac. trade; 2 wise acts 369. *Mr. Cass' Rep.:* tendency to consolidation; policy good sometimes; objections; avoided except once; arrangement with St. L., A. & T. H. road; other roads selfish; P. & Ft. W. seeks common benefit; railroad responsibility; a person limited, not railways; must keep pace with trade, 370.

SIOUX CITY and the Pacific Route, grant and length, 45.

SIOUX CITY & OMAHA. **C. & Northwestern.** Is building; connect with N. W. at St. Johns'; take Up. Mo. trade, 95, 117, 118; steamboat line in connection, 117.

SOUTH WEST PACIFIC, its route, 50. St. L. must look after this road; another flank movement, 51.

UNION PACIFIC. (Omaha.) *N. Y. Times:* To be finished by 1870; already 525 ms., 42......Route, grant and length, 45, 79. Connect with St. L., 49, 79; effects of, 127. *Lon. Tel.:* importance of project. *N. Y. Com. Chron.:* its effect; develope the W., 43; increase mining and Pac. trade, 44; opens a fine country; trade immense.

CENTRAL PACIFIC (from Sacramento), route and length, 45, 128; C., not Omaha, the terminus, 368, 369.

VINCENNES TO CAIRO. A Cin. meeting to cut off St. L. and C.; 8 attended, 77.

BENEFITS AND EFFECTS OF RAILWAYS. Power of the R. to Develope and Centralize, margin, 313–319. Create their own traffic, 315, 325, 329. *Baxter:* Proportion of exports and imports to rs. and navigation in Gt. Br., 326; in France, 327; in Belg. and Hol., 328; in U. S. 329. *Edmunds:* Rs. increase the value of steamboats, 329......Rs. more important than **Rivers,** 33, 75, 83, 85, 89, 104, 112, 339, 347, 373. Valuable with **Water,** 63, 339, 340, 372. Water and rs, both indispensable, 59, 93, 319, 339, 342, 347, 375. *Buf. Com.:* Advantages compared, 59......Iron arms to draw trade, 31. The nerves of body-politic, 345. High freights derange trade, injure rs., 164. Power increased by consolidation, 47, 76, 335, 366, 369. Dangers, 352, 370, 373. Parallel lines should not be consolidated, 352, 374. Remedy in State-rights, 56, 353 *n.* Difficult to regulate consolidation, 374, *n.* Rivalry of cities opposes consolidation, 366. Water competition effective, 372. Public interests, tho' made subservient, will rule ultimately, 358. Increase of property by r's., 127, 318, 335. Economy in transportation, 315—317, 318, 320, 326, 399. Direct benefits to **Agriculture,** 314, 315—319, 327, 328, 331, 332, 399. Stimulate growth of **cities,** 307, 320, 322, 323, 398. Expansion of the city, **Suburbs,** 283—286. No means equal to develope, 313, 315, 399. To centralize, 320, 398. Settle a country, 48; farming lands enhanced, 317. R. stock pays well, 336. Balt. & O. R. unites E. and W., 371. Mining trade to be done by railroads, 347. Disadvantage of short lines in transferring freight, 373. Advantages to C. of constructing Des Moines and Leavenworth road, 279. R's. require much mnfg. at C., 199, 217, 223. Value in distributing mnfrs. at C., 221, 314.

RAILWAYS YET A NEW INVENTION. Not 40 y. since Quincy horse-road 3 ms., and Mauch Chunk, 9 ms., 314. The work of only one generation, 335. Mileage and annual increase in U. S. from 1828 to 1868, 329. *Scott:* Invention favors dom. trade; rs. yet new; 20 y. employed in constructing; bold man to foretell effects, 303; man's constant progress; effect of modern improvements upon towns, 307.......Our increase of mileage greater than imports and exports; good reason; therefore immense increase of traffic sure, 331; first roads cheaply built; after improvements easy; most mileage wanted at first, 334. Galena first C. road, chartered 1836, 350; first rep. 1848, extracts showing difficulties, 349, 350; first 42 ms. to Elgin, 1850, 351. Account of laying the foundation stone of Balt. & O., 1828, 371. *Rail. Jour.*, 1843: difficulties in starting, 334; changes of 11 y. from 1832; now export engines; ascend high grades; compete with canals; are profitable; pay 6 to 10 p. c.; 6 ms. at Boston, 1832, 1,208 in 1843, 336.

THE WEST CHIEF FIELD—RAPID PROGRESS. Table of C. roads, 36; other roads W. of Tol. and Cin. road; total in N. W., 37. Extension chiefly in W., 71. No such area for rs. to work upon; kept back for r. and telegraph, 313, 338, 339. *Ruggles*, Report to Berlin Congress: 10 y. increase of property in U. S., to 1860; cause railways and canals; large proportion in W.; saved 5 times cost in transportation; increase of property in several sections; W., $2,800,000,000, 318; area; increase of population, of farms; capacity 8-fold, 319......N. W. best accommodated, 314, 338. Progress in W. difficult to estimate; W. its own measure, 315, 335. Moderate cost of our roads; subsequent improvements easy; most mileage wanted; mileage, 1842, 334. Knowledge of W. wanted; no hypothetic basis; investments must go on; strong corporations will compete, 335. No inland country like ours, 303. Miss. Val. have r's equal to population as in Europe; receipts to augment; food to increase; immense increase of traffic, 331. We shall equal Eng.; then Belgium; 15 y. double present lines of U.S.; shall we then stop? 333. Rapidity of progress difficult to realize; whence the capital? done it is; investments must go on; corporations strong, 335. Adaptation of N. W. to r's; capacity to support them, 338; these points discussed; no equal results, yet only begun, 339. Old measures inapplicable to West, 351. Early difficulties; distrust of West, 360. Mich S'n. line built in 20 mos., 360. Mileage of the several States, 1838–'68, 364. Mileage and cost in Interior States, 365. Tables instructive; war retards construction; more rapid hereafter; less cost of W'n roads; most roads to be built in W., 365. System so established will grow of itself, 374, 377

PERFECTION AND IMMOBILITY OF THE CHICAGO SYSTEM. *Being natural and reasonable; it was foreseen: Let. to Bost. Cour., 1847*, Alton & C. road; 3 y. connects Boston and C. by Mich. Cent.; Galena road and branch to Alton & St. L.; important to B., 21; lake-shore route sure; Boston to draw business N. to lakes; best do it soon; E'n cities interested, especially B.; Rock Island road; 20 y. connect B. and Council Bluffs; Va. appreciated, but Mass. united to C. & W.; B. & C. identified in interest; a strong basis of prosperity for C., 22. Interest of N. Y. and Bost. identical with C.; rivalry with S'n cities; they must get business to the lakes; dog-in-the-manger policy will not do; road to Alton first wanted; best route for N. Y. & Bost.: C.'s interest that of those cities; does that injure N. Y. or Bost.; their direct interest in C., 30 *Circ. 1848:* R's prospective; 4 [5] certain; Mich. Cent., Galena, Buf. & Miss., and Ills. Cent., 23; national character; Bos. and N. Y. interested; 15 y. build them, 24. Predictions realized; prove the system to be natural, 24, 26, 27, 29, 71, 107, 377, 399.

Hypothesis changed to Fact: Public Improvements anticipated 20 and 10 years ago as a Basis, margin, 22—25. The Basis of our Prosperity is no longer hypothetical, 25—28. Chief roads secured, 25, 72, 107. Rival roads more difficult, 25, 96, 106, 120. *Cir. 1858*, "Railroads now built—focal Point now fixed:" Hypothesis changed to fact; annual earnings $18,000,000; other roads to be feeders; 6 W. of Miss.; Pac. road, 24. *Cin., 1861*, "4,500 ms. now tributary to C.:" list of trunks and branches; chief roads secured; others more difficult; land grants to 5; of Iowa and N. Mo. C. is centre; no railway centre W. of C. possible; States tributary; growth of other cities doubtful; former predictions reasonable; realised and more, 25. Basis not problematical; future of C. sure, 26. No tax for C. roads an item; reason more so; shows C. a natural centre; lacks capital; could not build her roads; St. L. rich, 28; yet C. roads never stopped; why other cities not sought by capitalists; this a natural centre, 29. Art follows nature; policy to continue, 36. Mileage of 15 trunks, and 45 roads centering in C. with 20 branches 36. Length of 15 continuous trunk lines, 38. Where the power to work a change? 38. Country well accommodated; same doing W. of Miss.; plan perfect to concentrate; each road sought its own interest, 40; yet best promotes public good; focal point surely found; earnings strong evidence; earnings 10 y.; future increase, 41. ☞ For conclusive evidence as to the power and effects of existing system thus far, look at **St. Louis**—*Results of Contest hitherto.*

Focal Point Immovable because **Capital** *rules:* **East,** *Joint Interest of C. with.* No tax for all our railroads an item; reasons more so; determines whether C. is a natural centre; C. lacks capital; St. L. rich, 28; C. roads never stopped in war; capital finds safety; profits on Galena, the first road: other cities supposed to have equal advantages; why not sought by capitalists? their sagacity shows what is best; surplus capital of nation in N. Y. and N. Eng., 29. N. Y. and N. Eng. identified in interest with C., *Cir., 1861: No tax for r. indebtedness:* C. roads built by foreign capitalists; other cities loaded with debt for their few; C. has more rs. than all her rivals, 32. 15 trunk lines, and 45 rs. centering in C. with 20 branches more or less tributary, (the length and terminus of each,) 36. The whole business not claimed; should cross roads be reckoned; those which give C. more benefit than ony other city; table of other rs. in N. W. giving C. some trade; all these excluded, and also over one-fifth of actual C. roads, 37; still leaves C. two-thirds of all in N. W.; 15 straight trunks of 5,960 ms.; where the power to work a change? capital interested to maintain present plans; 38. A master mind in the outset would have planned the system as it is, either to accommodate the country traversed, or to have centralized the business; each road has sought its own interests, 40; yet best promotes the public good; the true focal point must be found, 41. The interest of capitalists to carry out their investments; where the power to change? whole wealth of N. Y. and N. Eng. interested to prevent innovations; South best served by keeping things as they are, 42. Only 42 ms. 18y. ago; now 15 trunk lines and many branches, 342 to 974 ms.; C. artificial hub of N. W.; felloes secure; best for stockholders; for the public; C. a sure hub: wheel not to be changed; joint interest of e'n capital, 105; spokes put in independently; no C. work; common sense ruled; no power to work a change, 106. Greater facilities at C. by rail than water, 104, 339. C. feared cut-offs, 69; *St. L. Intelligencer*, 1853, quoted *Alton Tel.* upon the Joliet cut-off, 70. Perfection of present system to accommodate country traversed, to profit stockholders, to benefit the public, to build one great city, 40, 105, 339. Change of Wn. system impossible, 38, 42, 105, 106. No important r. centre W. of C. now possible, 25, 49. 71, 120. The Focal Point of the Great West is fixed immovably, by over 7,500 of its 11,000 ms. of Railway centering at C., margin, 36–42.

MEANS AND CERTAINTY OF EXPANSION. *Chicago has not built her Railways, but begins to help herself.* **Atlantic.** **Capital. East.** *Co-operation of Nature and of Art from abroad,* xii, xiii. *Our Railway System is immovable:* A new power must supplant the r.; system extends naturally; rivalry in future more difficult; if difficult E. of Miss., more so W.; had C. built her system, change might be easy; what has been done compels to more doing of the same sort; chief r. investments for 10 y. to be in C. lines, xiv; poverty of C. strongest reason in our favor; all capital invested calls for more; C. getting wealth to use for her advantage; this of small account—*The whole capital of N. Y. and N. Eng. supports C.:* E. seeks its own interest; hard work to get into C.; yet the E. has made her the focus of three-fourths the W'n system; C's weakness made strong by the E; they have all the surplus capital. xv.; C. ridiculed for her poverty; and dependence on E'n capital; we thank them; make the E. see more their direct interest with C.; they must back up the Queen of the Lakes although it make her larger than any ocean city, xvi. *C. Times* quotes a letter from Omaha to *Cin. Com.*, describing the turning of trade from St. L. to C. by the first r., boxes in the cellar marked "St. L.," on the sidewalk "Chicago," and comments thus: Cor. right as to effect of r., but wrong as to constructing power; C. did not build this r. nor any other; never has contributed to them; let others build for our profit; r's create the city, not the city r's; no aid for a Min. r.; nor for Cameron & Kas. City; she permits them to come in, 33......St. L. confirmation, *Mo. Dem. 1861:* Admits loss of trade right in her own State; gives figures; cause for alarm; victim of illusion; C. trade increasing; N. Y. and Bost. in competition with St. L. thro' C.; Wall st. plans adverse; treason right at home; Mo. dismembered by Han. & St. Joe r., 34...... Art follows nature; policy to continue; Solomon followed, 38. To develope the W. more important than Pac. trade; one Pac. r. insufficient; C. wants several; no monopoly; trade must come here if C. be the natural centre, 44. Competition of two Pac. roads; have several, 47. Routes East; to Balt. and Norfolk to be improved, 54. Take trade in natural channels; Atl. ports compete to reach C.; N. Y. and N. Eng. made C. the focal point; strong competition with Phil., Balt. and Norfolk, 56; must be met; advantage of Balt., 58. C. now begins to help her self, 99, 120. Encourage the E. to do more; continue her 7 W. lines into and over the Rocky Mts.; rival roads difficult, 120. Immense mining area to be supplied, 114-126. Facilities will be afforded, 126.

Aid by Federal Government: Cin. Railroad Rec., "Government lands for rs:" Should not be a party question; they create wealth; settle a country; effects of a Pac. road; aid taxation; sale of lands no object. Govt. should give something; several Pacific roads needed; Ills. Cent. an example; give to make money; for higher objects; immense area to be reached; must have 3 Pac. r's......These views judicious; must have 5 to 7 to Rocky Mts., 127. Land grants hitherto, 23, 24, 25, 45-47, 127. Resolutions of C. Board of Trade in favor of grant to Kas. Pac., 382. *C. Rep., C. Times* in their favor, 383. Consolidating short lines E makes strong corporations to push W.; have several more, 47, 366.

Baxter, "*Railway Extension and its Results:*" Distribution of Eng. r's; centres in Europe and U. S., 324; traffic and benefit of rs. in Gt. Br.; do not supplant other means; create their own traffic; proportion of exports and imports to railways and navigation in Gt. Br., 326; France, 327; Belgium, 328. In U. S.: miles built each year and annual increase from 1828–1868; nearly equals all Europe; traffic mainly domestic; foreign to come; increase p. c. of exports and imports from 1830–1860; proportion of exports and imports to railways and canals, 329; 15,000 ms. in progress; Pac. rs.; great future for U. S.; mileage of Europe and U. S. compared with area and population, 330; lines in Eng. and Belgium 15 ms. apart; 10 enough; benefits to agr., save whole cost, 331; benefits to towns; dividends not essential; route owners of land to build branches; not directly, but by loans of credit; only way; future of railways; 85,000 ms. in 36 years; more next 36. N. Amer. have 100,000 ms.; Europe a line from Dover to China; wonderful results, 332......Such our future increase; 15 y. to double present lines; shall we then stop? 333. Moderate cost of our first roads; subsequent improvements easy; most mileage wanted, 334.

The Controlling Cities demand Pursuance of their own Plans: Railway progress wonderful; whence the capital? largest expenditure in W.; knowledge of W. wanted; investments must go on; corporations strong, 335. Atlantic cities seek their own advantage; their net-work; the W. a safe reliance; trade increase; they must pursue the policy established; no Atlantic city would withdraw if it could, or could if it would; Wn. rs. pay well; W. build its own centres, 336. Less cost of Wn. roads; most building in W.; east of Mo. River main trunks built; chief work to make branches, 365; new trunk lines from the E. to be formed by consolidating short lines; competition to reach C. from Portland to Norfolk; the competition our safety, 367. *Memorial N. Y. Chamber of Commerce to N. Y. Legis.:* N. Y. has done nothing in rs. since 1853; Pa. Cent. has stolen march; B. & O. not idle; their extension to Toledo, 372; by transfer of cars between roads, the advantage by water is lost; Erie road no connection with C.; disadvantage; Pa. and Balt. alert; N. Y. too confident; cannot rely upon water; injury of railway consolidation; Wn. trade regained by rs., 373; must prevent consolidation; promote competition, 374...... *Crane's Address at Boston:* A new road to Lake Ontario, 375. ......N. Y. and N. Eng. will arouse; their interest ours; facilities E. to increase, 377.

6 Points in favor of expanding present Chicago System: 1st. Joint interest of N. Y. and N. Eng: still the basis; what has been done a pledge for more of the same sort; increased profits on their own roads by extension. 2d. Surplus capital, railway profits, must be invested; old States mostly supplied; must come W., 377. 3d. W. getting capital of its own to invest; county bonds to aid; interest of farmers to build branch roads and connect with whole r. system; examples, S. Eastern Ills. Railway, 378, Leavenworth & Desmoines, 379; branches strengthen competition by connecting between main trunks; all not C. roads; benefit of roads to farmers; want equal advantages with their neighbors; C. getting capital and will help. 4th. More C. lines to the W. and S. needed; Six probable ones; new lines from the E. will take hold of them. 5th. Competition W. of the Miss. between existing lines; divergence expands the 7 C. lines, Quincy and St. Paul being over 300 ms. apart; their competition to control the trade by extending branches; these 7 lines wholly inadequate; more rs. must be built; tendency to latitudinal lines irresistible, 380; new E. lines will build them; only completing present system, which gives entire satisfaction, and has ponderosity not to be swayed, inherent force irresistible, rapidity of execution that defies competition; whence the power to work a change? only St. L. desires change; quite a job for her, 381. 6th. Govt. aid rendered in Kas. and Neb.; bonds not expected but land grants; this policy well tried and established; some M. C.'s oppose; misrepresent E.; W. soon take care of itself, 381. Two other Pac. rs. sure; N'n of course a C. road; St. L. fears about Kas. Pac., and our confidence, 382. Mileage in Gt. Int. will be doubled in 5 years, 385.

RAUCH, J. H., Pres. Board of Health, census statistics, 1868, 398.

REAL ESTATE. **Suburbs.** *Aim not to promote Speculation, but Confidence in the Real Estate:* The running title, "Past, Present and Future of C. Investments," closely adhered to, xvi. The chief benefit of C. is to participate in the real e.; wish to invite consideration to the opportunity of investing in a city most certain to grow, xvii. **Objection.** "*The work tends to create a Spirit of Speculation:*" Is truth or falsehood speculative? Business men should own their homes and business lots, xxxii, 170, 289, 300. Most large owners do little for city; business men do most, xxxiii. The man a fool to build up a city and not have his part of the realty, xxxiv, 289. Its value large compared with personal, xiv, 288. Appraisals of r. and personal, 1837–66, 288; for 1867, 289. R. is the solid basis of our prosperity, xxxiv, 289. Its opportunities should draw citizens, xxxv, 289. Time good as ever to buy, 2, 4, 7, 8, 9, 10, 11, 12, 14, 296.

FIRST PURCHASES AND PREDICTIONS. Arrival at C. 1832, with my father; his opinion of C.; my early impressions; first purchases 1834, 290. *Letter to A. Wright*, 1834: lot 4 B. 17, O. T., bought for $3,500; reasons for purchase; C. to equal Detroit in 5 y.; 90½ as. bought for $3,500; option to take purchases, 5. Benefits to A. W.; sound reasons; railroads not foreseen; now a sure basis, 290. Other purchases, 1834; sales 1835–6, and present value, 6, 290. Purchase of B. 1, O. T., 1846, for $37,500; expectations realized, 291. Sold 1850 for $60,000, 293. *Circular*, 1847, "Safe and profitable investment:" part of B. 1 offered; profits assured; comparison with Cin.; 15 y. for C. equal to 27 for Cin., 7. *Cir.*, 1848, "Investments in C. property:" Speculation not proposed; a sure income; annual rent of lots; rent of stores; suburb lots, 8; money safe; also profits; growth of Ills.; personal examination urged; share of profits; my desire to avoid debt; invest for your children, 9. A block and a half bo't of Mr. Bronson; long credit; rents more than paid principal and interest; thoroughly calculated in advance, 292. *Circular*, 1849: proposal for funds to use in improvements; estimate of annual surplus of rents to 1864, 10. No body could see the result, 9, 10, 292, 293. This property still a desirable purchase, 292 *n.* Full endorsement of my estimates; yet not believed, 293. *Cir.*, 1852, real estate at auction: prices still low compared with other cities; railroads sure; no revulsion; why I sell, 20 p. c. guarantee, 11. Collapse of 1857, not occasioned by real estate, 12, 294 *n.* *Cir.*, 1858: money panic affords good chances to buy property; former advice should have been heeded. *Cir.*, 1860: prices depreciated by panic; desire to buy property, yet avoid debt, 12; invest on shares; my experience; capital and profit sure; charter for Land Improvement Co., 13.

ADVANTAGES OF C. Real Estate, especially in a growing City, is the best Investment, margin, 14-16. General Pecuniary Revulsions may Intervene, but cannot change the Result, margin, 16-21. The stock-yards, chief profit in the lands; that a C advantage, 169. Small cost of grading, 250. Sewerage paid by city, 252 *n.* Large owners have ample opportunity for enterprise, 252. To own C. lots a local advantage, 299. Wide streets and horse railroads, 282; steam railways to reach suburbs, 283; expansive power of railways, 284; room for indefinite expansion, its benefits, 285. Many a blacksmith and shoemaker made rich, 288; certain advance of city and suburban property, 288, 300. Opinions not visionary hitherto nor now; C. safer than ever; business localities changing; opportunities great, 296.

NON-RESIDENTS SHOULD BUY. They help C., 297; should have a share in real estate, especially railroad men; C. wants more roads; further stimulus to own C. lots; Hon. J. F. Joy's aid, 298. Difficulties of non-residents, 297. Companies desirable 298; improve suburbs; strength of associated capital; best for non-residents; advantages of a company; neglect of non-residents injudicious, 299.

LAND IMPROVEMENT CO., its charter, 13; advantages; time to use it; foreign capital wanted, 299. Features of the plan; dividend optional; management offset to capital; 20 p. c. per annum may be assured, 299 *n.*

REAPER business begun, 11, 294. Was my ruin, 12, 295; causes of failure, 295, *n.*

RELIGION. *Province, Government and Responsibility of the City*, Title Page. *Aim to invite Consideration of the* **Obligations** *of City and Citizens, in view of the unparalleled Benefits showered by God and Country*, xxiii. *To show Fellow-Citizens their right to prefer Expediency to Command, Privilege to Duty*, xxiv-xxvi: Get from under command by regard for expediency; regard our own dignity and honor, xxiv. Godliness profitable not only for eternity but time; subject closely related to making money; applied not to religion but business; self-interest and honor entirely concordant; be diligent in money-making, yet make it not the end; be not servants in subjection, but sons in honor, xxv; "Seek every man another's wealth;" C. to seek the wealth of other cities; best promote her own; desirable to convert duty into privilege, command into expediency, xxvi. *Duty to our* GOD: Study of our growth induces reverence; the work of conjoint wills; the province of the city in man's restoration, xlii; too much absorbed in getting the means; do not give our tythes; not even in death, xliii. The Bible teaches *a priori*, 3. Religion properly introduced, 20 *n.* Bible rule, he that hath shall have, 73. Man to work, 91, 108. Rev. Mr. Martin, of Nevada, on the claims of the mining region; tythes God's due and sufficient, 141, *n*, 263. God ennobles labor; Tyre's renown for commerce; responsibility of C. merchants, 141. Show thankfulness in giving; responsibility for, 142, 190. *Dr. Channing:* commerce ennobles; a peace-maker; Christianizing; merchants to be generous; extend civilization; do not corrupt; teach Christ in acts; free trade the interest of man; we tend towards it, 191......Obligations to God for our system of Govt., 197. Character of our population; energy and enterprise; character made by busy men; private men selfish; their shame and wrong; obligations to city increase with leisure; exceptions to their meanness; work done gives promise; C. to be an example; tythes supply means abundant; to be used for Divine objects; man's benefit, as Old Test. and Gospel teach; tythes not half given; old settlers to work and new, 261. Attention to religion from the beginning; no denominational jealousy; 262; duty of fellowship; benevolent societies organized, 263. A good resolution that should have been kept, 263 *n.*; diverse sects no injury; we must agree to differ 274; think less of sect; associated humanity less imperfect, 275. Gt. Int. kept back for r's.; Providence directs; man's duty and privilege; recognize the Giver; work for our fellow; a coworker with God, 314; r. and telegraph most efficient means; pecuniary profit least, 315. No boasting of C.'s growth; it is excluded; our dependence upon the Power controlling these diverse wills, 385.

CHURCHES. First Pres. met in Mr. Peck's loft, 99 *n.* First Meth., Pres., Bap., Cath., and Epis. clergymen and churches; unanimity; Baptists and Pres. in same church and Sunday school, 262. Present list of churches, 263. Meth. energy in education; 271. Catholics pioneers in education, 275.

THEOLOGICAL SEMINARIES. **Science** and art.

REPUBLICAN, THE C., A temporary bridge at Omaha, 96. Montana trade, 119. Mining in Wyoming Ter., 124. C. and the Territories, 129. Wholesale trade of C., 1866-7, 147, 149. The Northwest and Transportation, 179. Lake Superior Iron, 237, 245. Lake Superior Copper, 245. Buildings, 1867, 259.

REVULSIONS, temporary in effect, 11. **General Pecuniary R's. may intervene but cannot change the Result**, margin, 16–21. Only an event like removing Niagara's rocks, affects the destiny of C., 16. *Cir., 1861: Effects of Secession and War*, 17. Blessings resulting affect this question, 19; adversity to come; affects all property; yet real estate certain to rise; is most permanent, 20.

RICE, Mayor, JOHN B., a model message, 259; address at dedication of Rush Med. Col., 268.

RICHARDS, J. J., estimate of C. trade, 1860, 152.

RIVALRY of Nn. and Sn. Atlantic cities for Wn. trade, 30, 54. R. of Wn. cities to reach the lakes, 72. C. has no rival, 71, 72, 110. Other cities rivals, 71. When C. can have one, 72, 107. Combination gives superiority; rivals seemed to have; have not, 73. **The Rivals of the West, Cin., St. L. and C.**, margin, 73–111, 102. Nine points of which a prominent city should have a majority, 107; except C. no city in the W. has three, 108, 110. R. of St. L. and C., 1861, 111; began 1857, *Mo. Dem.*, 112.

RIVERS. **Trade. Water.** Extent of navigation, 100, 174. Conjunction with lakes at C., 58, 62, 70, 93, 104, 319, 338, 342, 347. Ills. and Mich. Canal shortest connection, 53. Lakes superior to rs., 64, 75, 79, 88, 184, 342. Queen of lakes queen of rivers, 93. Superiority of railroads to, 83, 85, 89, 112, 339, 347. Conjunction with railways, 63, 339, 340. Their navigation not to be detracted, 53, 63, 64, 184. St. L's. reliance, 88, 89, 111, 173, 182. Tillage ruins them, 88. Their decadence, 88, 89, 112, 184. Tonnage at St. L., 1866, 1867, 180. **Barge** trade, 65, 180, 184, 341. A benefit to C., 65, 184, 185, 341. St. Law. and Miss. lake arms; St. Law. strongest, 132. *Col. Foster's Rep.*, *Ship Canal Conv.:* Miss. formerly a necessary route; gulf difficulties; only local demand at S.; exports from N. Y. and N. O., 1860; N. O. equal to Mil. or Tol.; grain seeks other channels, 183......St. L. depends on direct shipments to Europe; C. wants it; our interest with the farmers; generosity costs C. nothing; climate against river route. *U. S. Census Rep.:* grain trade of Miss. and Ohio rivers unimportant; river towns before lake towns; Miss. natural outlet; settlements on rivers; barges used; change of trade from r. to lakes, 184; artificial channels E.; Miss. bridges; railroads taking grain to lakes; Miss. almost abandoned for grain; 5 reasons; N. O. receipts and C. compared; N. O. and N. Y. exports, 185. *C. Jour.:* N. O. and N. Y. exports 1867, 186. *Scott:* N. O. route cheapest; climate injures flour; lake route best and safest, 306. Superiority of N. route; saves 1,100 ms.; owns their vessels, 307. *Knowlton, to Ship Canal Conv.:* Great benefits of Miss.; man to improve them; "two markets better than one;" long railways show the Miss. is not monopolized; S. a competitor with E., 342.

ILLS. R. good for navigation, 52, 89; improved by deepening canal, 52.

MISSOURI R. dangerous, 89, 117, 347. Used in conjunction with railways, 117, 118, 199, 340, 347.

MISSISSIPPI R., St. L. affirms it is not a safe dependence, 85, 89, 93. Is an indefinite viaduct, without head or tail; benefits indefinite, 101. Competition by N. O. keeps down rates by lakes and rivers, 184, 341.

ROCK ISLAND. Extension of I. & M. Canal to, 104, 312.

ROCKY MTS. trade valuable, 122; centres at C., 117, 122, 125, 129, 340. 1,000,000 miles tributary to C., 22. Mining in Wyoming Ter., 124; claims of mining region on C., 141 *n.*

ROOT & CADY'S music establishment, 279.

RUGGLES, Hon. S. B., grain of the West, pork, etc., 212. Report upon U. S. to Berlin Congress, 318.

RUSH MEDICAL COLLEGE. **Science.** Its progress, 268. Faculty, 269.

SACRAMENTO, *Cal. Union*, "The aspiring W.:" St. L. wants national capital; the claims of C., 386.

ST. JOSEPH (Mo.), *Register:* Boats lost on Mo. River, 347.

ST. LAWRENCE route to be improved, 62.

ST. LOUIS AND C. SURE TO BE AMONG THE CHIEF CITIES OF THE GT. INT. AND CONTINENT; WHICH MUST BE CHIEFEST? "The three cities that have been generally considered"—**The Rivals of the West, Cincinnati, St. Louis and Chicago**, margin, 73–111. C. has no **rival,** 71, 72, 110. When can have one, 72, 107. St. L to be a great city, xxix, 76, 146, 173, 243, 392. She is spiteful, xxviii, 145, 257 *n.*, 340. Meanness of *Mo. Dem.* about a blunder in amounts of **trade** statistics, 142–145. *Cor. Mo. Rep.:* C's business based on borrowed money; when dull sells to insurance co's; efficient fire dep't, plenty water, yet $3,000,000 burnt in 3 hours; don't want fire put out; insurance co's buy, 146. *Mo. Dem.*, "*Wanted, a Ditch?*" Babylon of balloon houses has the blues; cause, St. L. sends grain to N. Y.; yet assumes a smile; talks anxiously of ship-canal; what necessity? she decries rivers; yet wants ship-canal to reach them; why is Babylon so anxious? current in St. L.'s favor; "Beware, O Chicag-eese!" houses of slender splinters, 347 *n.*......Should be philosophic like Cin., xviii, 146, 173. She cannot judge us fairly, 347. She is on a Procrustean stretcher, instead of dallying with a Delilah, 82. We rejoice in her prosperity, 226. St. L. excelled C. in mnfrs., 200. Amt., 1860, 202. Beef and pork packing less than other cities, 209. Large flour mnfr., 215. Growth from 1810 to 1890, 337. General belief in her superiority, xxx, 39, 114, 173, 175. Comparison of claims to greatness necessary, xxix, 114, 142. No exaggeration; no disparagement, xviii, xxix. Only bubble of centrality pricked, xxx, 87, 90, 101, 175, 188. Copies of the vol. sent St. L. editors, their negative endorsement, leaving it severely alone, xviii. Superiority to her not claimed till 1853, 74, 75. *Cir. 1861:* Made a comparison in 1848 between C. and Cin.; then too visionary to compare with St. L.; till 1853 supposed her size, large wealth, established business and river advantages would continue her superiority; railroads came; locomotives take the place of steamboats, and C. must have pre-eminence; lakes better than rivers; our rapid overtaking, 75; St. L. to be a great city; C. greater; reader to compare advantages, 76......Her decrease only relative, 142, 146, 173, 174. Her disadvantages no cause of prosperity to C., but its direct effect, 92. C. the mainspring of her troubles, 26, 33, 34, 35, 38, 39, 40, 51, 54, 67, 79, 82, 83, 85, 95, 96, 97, 111–114, 118, 119, 176, 187, 189. *Mo. Dem.*, "*St. L. and C:*" Competition the life of trade; efforts must be fair; *N. Y. Ship. List* not so; quotes it telling of the competition of the two cities for W. trade, and showing C's advantage; same wrong in other papers; waited for endorsement by a respectable paper; St. L. in no danger; mountain trade increasing; St. L.'s superiority by water; N. Y. editor inquire to learn the truth, 340. St. L. naturally superior to C.; overland transit of 1,000 ms. expensive to C.; from Nov. to May navigation closed; mountain trade over by May, and C. only old stock to sell; St. L. has direct water communication; sure to be great importer for W.; C. must come to St. L. for her goods; these results nature settles; time explodes fallacious pretensions. Paper does justice concerning barge trade; "a new era will be inaugurated;" this illustrates the importance of this movement in E'n judgment; "a lively impulse characterizes this new enterprise;" "nothing spasmodic;" "advance healthy, strong," "in spite of all invidious jealousies that seek to aggrandize rivals by circulating incorrect and false statements," 341......Joint interest of St. L. with Phil. and Balt., 54, 376. Natural location affirmed, 38, 39, 69, 83, 85, 112, 173, 340. This denied with reasons, 71, 84, 85, 112, 173, 340. Fur trade started her, 85, 88, 187. Then steamboats 34, 38, 67, 68, 88, 111, 112. Rivers her reliance, 68, 69, 85, 88, 89, 111, 173, 182, 329, 341, 347. They fail her, 85, 88, 89, 93, 112, 184. Tonnage not half that of C., 181. Other cities may beat her, 26, 71, 84. Kas. City may surpass her, 27, 121, 173. She prefers a vibrating, C. a steady market, 159, 160. False assumption injures her, *Hon. H. T. Blow*, 29; *Mo. Dem.*, 1861, 34; *Cor. Mo. Rep.*, 39. To assume to be a rival of C., must have at least 3 of C.'s nine points, 107, 110. St. L.'s superiority in wealth, 28, 39, 68, 75, 83, 85, 89, 176, 188, 189. She boasted of it, *N. Y. Eve. Post*, "St. L. *vs.* C.:" St. L. worsted in the contest; is satisfied with superiority in banks; she exults, 190......Her advantages from Chester coal and her iron mountain ore, 225. To be a great mnfg. city, 226. We begin to consider mnfg. in her interest, 222. Success in smelting Iron Mt. ore with Chester coal, 243. THE St. L. elevator, 158, 160. She ought to need more, 160. Extracts from her Trade Reports, 154, 155, 156, 158, 159, 160, 165, 172, 173, 174, 175, 176, 177, 178, 180, 181, 182. Her own admissions most effective, xxxiii, 67, 102. Is our chief witness, 111, 114.

EPITOME OF POINTS AND CONCLUSIONS RESULTING FROM THE INVESTIGATION. 1st. *St. L. sees her Difficulties:* 26, 27, 34, 35, 38, 39, 40, 46, 49, 54, 67, 69, 79, 80, 82, 83, 89, 96, 97, 111, 173–189.

2d. *Her Advantages are unavailing and lost:* 34, 35, 39, 40, 46, 68, 69, 71, 75, 83, 85, 89, 111, 113, 175, 176, 181, 188.

3d. *She must Revolutionize Art or Nature or both:* 86, 90, 101, 102, 107, 176, 178, 181, 182.

4th. *Though she relies on Rivers, she wants Railroads:* 27, 34, 35, 36, 40, 46, 49, 55, 62, 78, 79, 82, 83, 85, 89, 93, 111, 113, 174, 176, 182.

5th. *Railways injure her:* 26, 27, 34, 35, 46, 51, 55, 67, 79, 81, 83, 85, 93, 95, 96, 98, 112, 113, 176, 187, 188.

6th. *Her closely contiguous Territory trenched upon: Mo. Dem.*, "A flank movement" in W. Mo., 26; *Mo. Rep.*, do., 27; *Brunswick*, (Mo.) *Central City*, and *Mo. Dem.*, of N. Mo., 34; *Law.* (Kas.) *Trib.*, and *Mo. Dem.*, of Mo. and all N. W., 35; *Kas. Cor. Pitts. Gaz.*, of Kas., Denver and Santa Fe, 51; *Cor. Mo. Rep.*, of Mo., 55; *Genl. Hammond*, of N. Mo., Kas. & S. W., 79; *C. & Alton R. R. Rep.*, of Cent. Ills., 95; *Liberty* (Clay co., Mo.) *Trib.*, of W. Mo., 97; *C. & Alton R. R. Rep.*, of Central Ills., 187; *Atchison* (Kas.) *Free Press*, of the W., 187.

7th. *The War her Excuse for Losses:* 175, 182.

8th. *Admissions that the Contest began and Changes were in Progress before the War: Mo. Dem., 1861:* A large decrease of cereals; figures given; cause for alarm; victim of illusion; C. trade increasing; N. Y. and Bost. in competition with St. L. thro' C.; Wall st. plans adverse; Mo. dismembered by Han. & St. Joe R. *Cir. 1861*, "*Rivalry of St. L. & C.:*" To show that the N. W. was the prize contested, extracts were made from the *Mo. Dem.* 1861, "Commerce of St. L., Trade N. and S.:" theory well, facts better; has St. L. a commerce; if so, it flows down like the river; not to be forced up-stream; advantages of N. W.; outstrips the S.; uses its powers, 111; St. L. no hope but in securing that trade; what is the N. W.; rivalry for it began in 1857; action of St. L. and C. compared; must know the truth; Iowa trade gone to C.; reason for diversion; trade of whole W. lost; whence comes trade?......*Comments*, 1861: N. W. her reliance, rivers the means; railways anomalous; her natural highways more unsafe in future; she wants N. W. roads; Han. and St. Joe adverse; N. roads difficult; not equal to E. lines 112.......*Mo. Dem.*, 1861, "Commerce of St. L.—comparative receipts, N. & S.:" figures of chief articles, 1860; do not vary much from those of previous year; N. nearly six-fold; also the dependence for manufactures; "trade of the mighty N. W. to be sought."......*Comments*, 1861: C. receipts of same articles of N. W. for 1859 and '60; figures nearly 4-fold; no increase at St. L. though C. doubles; canal (common to both) brought C. nearly a quarter more corn than her total receipts, 113; general opinion that St. L. is to lead; study railroad map, 114.

9th. *Results of contest hitherto.* **Trade** *turned from St. L. to C.:* 35, 39, 55, 67, 69, 75, 80, 89, 95, 96, 111, 113, 117, 118, 119, 176, 181, 183, 184, 185, 361.

10th. *How can she change results?* **Commerce. Trade.** 36, 38, 41, 42, 50, 69, 82, 84, 88, 92, 95, 96, 106, 114, 120, 130, 174, 181, 186, 209.

ADMISSIONS AGAINST HERSELF. *Mo. Dem.*, "A flank Movement:" Cameron and Kas. City road not aided by C., but the E.; connects Pac. with C. 26; trade not run up hill: St. L. must work; C. protected by E.'n capital; a change coming. *Mo. Rep.*, "Kas. City & Cameron Railroad:" gives Kas. another connection E.; cheapen C. lumber; roads centering at K.; rival to St. L., 27. *Mo. Rep.*, "C.—St. L.—the Bridge:" how does C. outstrip St. L.? Has trade of N. W.; who helps C.? no advantages, no capital, all things supplied; different management in St. L. and C., 35. *Cor. Mo. Rep.*, "St. L. and her Flatterers:" natural position of St. L.; she could have held it; grew rich and powerful; new sites in competition; means they adopt; St. L. too good to do any thing; plains trade gone to C.; even Kas.; tickled with hair of flattery; sceptre departing; inconveniences of St. L., 39. *Chariton Cor. Rep.:* how does C. get money for railroads, St. L. not? 39. *Mr. Henry Cobb* in *Mo. Rep.:* St. L. a Sampson, C. a Delilah; E. supplies means of shaving; what St. L. has lost; even Pitts. trade comes *via* C.; bridges over Miss. and Mo. rivers; threatened loss of even southern trade, but for Mr. Allen; St. L. in fetters, 40. *Mo. Rep.*, "St. L. and her W.'n connections:" 4 Pac. roads; Boston aiding St. L. to compete with C.! routes described, 50; St. L.'s near future; C. Pac. hers; some gaps at home to fill, 50. *A St. Louisian from N. Y. to Mo. Rep.:* St. L. wants straight road to Omaha; who to build; Phil. and Balt. interested; Pac. co. able, perhaps loth; St. L. to urge; is nearest the E. end of Pac., 54; danger from C.; central cities with St. L. against C.; all want this Omaha road; St. L.'s vital point; a new road to St. Joe to whip C. out of Mo.; look out for anti-St. L. grooves; central route E. equally concerned; is this understood? 55. *Mr. Fagin's speech to St L. Board of Trade:* commerce languishes for want of railroads to N. W.; grain trade lost; N. Mo. road most important; connect with C. roads; W. of Miss. roads benefit St. L.; E. of Miss. injure her; C. strong in railway influence, 67; St. L. must go ahead or men leave; wait no longer for Miss. river; E.'n capital help C.; 2 railways to help St. L.; grain receipts only 3,000,000; 15 y. ago 8,000,000; one elevator to compete with C.; tip hats to C.; St. L. to do something. *Hon. Erastus Wells* endorses Mr. Fagin, 68. *Cor. Mo. Dem.*, "The needs of St. L.:" to know cause of depression; natural advantages; why not effective; C. and Cin. more energy; State liberal, but bad results; men beggars and leaving; what the cause and remedy? 69. *Gen. Hammond's speech before St. L. Board of Trade*, "Importance of St. L., Chillicothe and Omaha road:" Pac. connections the great object; strife with C. at Omaha; lakes equal to rivers; her railroads superior; trade now sure to C. from N. Mo., and on to Texas; will St. L. regain it? distances, 79; route and means; present roads "out and out C. routes;" distances to N. Y., 80; Ills. Cent. aids C.; no peace; St. L. must help; all help C.; what a future to St. L.; to realize, work, 81. *Hon. H. T Blow's inaugural address of the Board of Trade:* immense t. compels another organization; deliberate consideration imperative; wisest men to submit plans attractive to capitalists; a deliberate court of strong influences; while Merch. Exch. has dignified trade, etc., yet no co-operation as in C. and N. Y.; economy in C.; with 5 times her area, must use her principles; room for both cities; both to grow, 82. *Cor. Mo. Dem.*, "What St. L. has, what she has lost, and what she needs:" St. L. wants something; opinions various; this trial to ascertain truth; natural location for trade and mnfrs.; St. L. rich; men good; now what is lost; grain trade, merchandise, southern trade; C. taps all around; sells cheaper; then what St. L. needs; everything; mnfrs., and to push railroads; N. Mo. cuts off C.; Iron Mt. road wanted; railway combinations to be prevented; improve river; remove cotton tax, 83; combination of adverse circumstances, 84 *Cor. Springfield* (Mass.), *Rep.:* natural hub of continent; rivers old fogies; Miss. nearly ruins St. L.; railroads come; they cause progress; slow to build them; Chicago around Robin Hood's barn, 85. *Cor. Mo. Rep.*, "Railroads *vs.* Rivers:" St. L. chief of W. because of rivers; now a drawback; railroads neglected; St. L. old fogy: must build roads along Miss.; territory limited, 89; get new; get capital E. or merchants leave: bridges essential, 90. *Mo. Dem.* quotes *Omaha Reg.:* increase of C. trade, 96. *Judge Bates:* danger of perversion of N. and S. roads to C., 96 *n.*

HER CLAIMS—SHE STILL RELIES UPON NATURE AND RIVERS, BARGES COMING TO THE RESCUE. *Prof. Waterhouse in Merch. Mag., 1866,* "MISSOURI: ST. LOUIS THE COMMERCIAL CENTRE OF NORTH AMERICA. St. Louis is ordained by the decrees of physical nature to become the great inland metropolis of this continent. It cannot escape the magnificence of its destiny. Greatness is the necessity of its position. New York may be the head, but St. Louis will be the heart of America. The stream of traffic which must flow through this mart will enrich it with alluvial deposits of gold. Its central location and facilities of communication unmistakably indicate the leading part which this city will take in the exchange and distribution of the products of the Mississippi Valley," 173. Thus demonstrated:

St. L's bisections of thousands of miles; she is mistress of 16,500 ms. of river navigation......What else is necessary to prove her centrality? A magnificent prospective of railways......N. Mo. railroad; 10,000 ms. to be added W. of Miss.; chief terminal points, Superior City and N. O., *via* St. Paul, St L. and Memphis; St. L. and San Fran., *via* Kas. City and Salt Lake; Kas. City and Ft. Benton, *via* Omaha; Leav. and Gal., *via* Lawrence; St. L. and San Diego, *via* Springfield; N. W. roads may be partially diverted, S. W. sure......St. L. learns prudence, and with Cin. depends on trade S. and S. W.; Prof. W. recites the wonderful achievements hitherto, yet relative progress not being maintained, is thus accounted for, 174......Pac. road needed; mining trade not monopolized, yet goods originally purchased in St. L.; rebellion sent trade to Cin. and C; Sn. trade destroyed, Nn. injured; St. L. paralyzed; this important in comparing claims; yet govt. choosing St. L. for its depot of supplies proves centrality......Prevalent absurdity of centrality helps St. L.; currents changed before war; why no return with peace; relative figures, 1865-'6-'7; same area supplies both. ......Government choice proves commercial superiority; peace restores "use of natural facilities;" trade "navigates every stream," 175......Is that true? Prof. W. goes directly on to see......difficulties of St. L.; C. energetic; pushing rs.; trust in nature not safe; what St. L. must do; build a bridge to "bear the transit of continental commerce."......Why does nature so fail at St. L.? Barge trade the remedy, 176......"Our elevator gives rise to a new system of transportation;" The Miss. Val. Trans. Co.; "simply the motive power;" its operation and saving; relative delay and cost of steamboats; lessens fire risks; cheapness; "*grain from St. Paul will not be handled again until it reaches N. O.;*" thence to Europe; Minnesota surplus; "this new scheme bids fair to revolutionize the whole carrying trade of the wn. waters;" "shows what great results a spirit of progressive energy may accomplish;" Miss. to be improved; "for the accomplishment of an undertaking so vital to its municipal interests St. L. should exert its mightiest energies," 177; "if the emigrant merchants of America and Europe, ☞ who recognize in the geographical position of St. L the guarantee of mercantile supremacy will become citizens of this metropolis they will aid in bringing to a speedier fulfillment the prophecies of its greatness." St. L. to keep pace with the W.; growth immense; universal friendship......Why is *Missouri* put at the head of that argument? Nature not to be proved false; yet art or nature blunders at St. L.; does nature depend upon barges to fulfill her ordinations; how help St. L.; they dispense with even "toting" at St. L., carrying trade on to N. O. ☞ **Trade** will show that the Reports of the Board of Trade confirm this argument and conclusion.

ST. MARY of the Lakes, University of, 275.

ST. PALAIS, Father, Bishop of Vincennes, instituted first Catholic ch., 262.

SAILS being supplanted by propellers, 62.

SALT in southern Illinois, 224. Trade of C. 12 y.; St. L. do., 172.

SAMSON, St. L. a S., C. a Delilah, 40. No genuine S., hair (natural advantages) proved false; shorn of even this, supremacy vanishes, 173.

SAN FRANCISCO to N. Y., mail in 14 days, Dec. 4, 1868, 42. *Bulletin*, Kas. Pac. Railroad, 46; Sweetwater Mines, 126.

SCAMMON, J. YOUNG, built observatory of C. Univ., 272; his liberality, 272 *n.*

SCATES, Hon. W. B., Collector, port entries at C., 1867, 61.

SCIENCE AND ART. **Arts. Education. Newspapers.** Have attention; time indispensable; material interests not alone cared for, 267. MEDICAL COLLEGES—*The Rush.* Dr. Blaney's address at dedication of new edifice: opened 1843; Dr. Brainard; C. an important site; other schools beaten; new building 1867; wise location, 268. *Mayor Rice:* 20 y. ago 22 students; 1866, 300; paid its own way; cost $70,000......Total graduates 1,150; faculty; lectures and spring instructors. *Chicago Med. Col.*, well established; began 1856; graduates 222; faculty. C. next to N. Y. and Phil. in Med. graduates, 269. THEOLOGICAL SEMINARIES. *Congregational:* Endowment; alumni; directors, 269; faculty, 270. *Presbyterian, O. S.:* Land and endowment; graduates; trustees; faculty, 270. *Garrett Biblical Institute, Methodist:* Founded by Mrs. Augustus Garrett; her noble example. *Hon. Grant Goodrich's address* commemorative; man a coworker with God......Opened 1855; graduates; trustees; faculty, 271. *Baptist:* Connected with N. W. University; trustees; faculty; 272. *Catholic:* Begun by Bishop Quarter, in charge of Dr. Magoffin, 275. UNIVERSITIES. *Northwestern:* Meth. Epis., funds, officers, 270. *University of Chicago:* Baptist. Initiated by Judge Douglas, funds, officers, faculty, Law Department, 272. *Lake Forest Univ.:* N. S. Pres., property, delay. *St. Mary of the Lakes:* Catholic. Founded by Bishop Quarter; graduates, 37. LAW SCHOOL, Department of Univ. of Chicago, officers, graduates, 272. HISTORICAL SOCIETY, building, collection, officers, 276. ACADEMY OF SCIENCE, Major Kennicott chief founder, 276. *Mr. Walker's address;* Maj. K.'s death; his devotion to science; an example to be followed......Mr. Walker's example, 276 *n.* Dr. Stimpson, director; property; No. specimens; officers, 277. Episcopalians will have their seminary; no equal aggregation of seminaries. *Dr. Hague:* Paul an example; elements in education to be combined; C. a centre; Baptist headquarters. *Dr. Ide*, generals and ministers made not born; W. to educate its own men; have few seminaries; essentials other than money; a scholarly atmosphere; educate among men, 273...... East no index to W.; no centre there; here a focus; whole W. aid C. institutions; E. also different sects no injury; agree to differ, 274; think less of sect; associated humanity less imperfect; 4 universities begun, and schools of theology, medicine and law, historical society, 275, and academy of science, 276. These samples; attention to intellectual and religious culture; the E. aids; this the place. Fine Arts not neglected, 277. **Arts.**

SCOTT, J. W., of Ohio, his arguments in favor of Chicago 25 years old, xxxviii. "Internal Trade of the U. S.," 1843, I. 300, II. 304, III. 307. Effect of improvements on growth of towns, 1843, 322. "Our Cities, Atlantic and Interior," 1848, 388–391. "Westward Movement of the Centre of Population and Industrial Power in N. America," 1857, 394–397. "The Progress of the West considered with reference to great Commercial Cities in the U. S.," 1846, 403, 404. Noble spirit, 25 years sustain him; slight mistake; rapidity of changes not calculated, 313. His predictions moderate, 138, 338, 391, 397.

SCULPTORS, Messrs. Volk & Siebert, 278.

SECESSION, effect upon West, 17.

SEIBERT, Mr., sculptor, 278.

SETTLERS. **Immigration.**

SEWERAGE. System excellent; more needed; paid by city; the debt judicious, 252 *n.*, 259.

SHEFFIELD, JOS. E., donation to Pres. Theo. Sem., 270. Projected and built R. I. R. R, 356.

SHINGLES, trade in, 170. **Lumber.**

SHUFELDT, GEO. A., bored first artesian wells, 254.

SILEX in Alexander and Pulaski co.'s, Ills., 224. In LaSalle co., Ills., 248.

SILVER in Stevenson co., Ills., 224.

SIMCOE. Lake S. route from Georgian Bay to Lake Ontario, 62, 344.

SIOUX CITY, an important point for Upper Mo. trade, 95.

SITE. **Grade.** S. of C. favorable, 249; no swamp; solid foundation; rich soil, 250.

SMITH, ADAM, mnfrs. chief element of progress, 194.

SNOW, GEORGE W., inventor of "balloon" frames, 257.

SOLOMON upon the Past, 1.

SOUTH, trade changing to the West, 110, 139, 401. Immigration to be large, 123 *n.*, 401. S. to grow, 138, 139, 401. Benefit the North, 138, 139. Coolies instead of negroes, 139. S. & S. W. trade, Cin. to seek, 77; also St. Louis, 174.

SOUTH BRANCH Canal Co., an important improvement, 296.

SOUTH CAROLINA and Mass., conflicting teachings, 196.

SOUTHWEST trade contested with St. L., *Mo. Dem.*, 26; *Mo. Rep.*, 27, 34; *Law.* (Kas.) *Trib.*, 35; Mr. Cobb in *Mo. Rep.*, 40; *Cor. Pitts. Gaz.*, from Kas., 51; *Cor. Mo. Rep.*, 55; Gen. Hammond, 79; *Liberty* (Clay co. Mo.,) *Trib.*, 97, 98; *Houston* (Texas) *Tel.*, 100, 121, 186; Mr. Blackstone, Pres. C. A. & St. L.; road, 187, 195; *Atchison* (Kas.) *Free Press.*, 187; *C. Times*, 189.

SPRINGFIELD (Mass.) *Rep.*, *St. L. Cor.*, St. L. natural hub, 85.

SPRINGFIELD (Ills.) *Journal*, experiment with Sangamon coal and iron, 243.

STATE, *Duty to our*, xxxviii. Nature of the, 191. No philanthropist, 192. State Sovereignty, National Union the motto of Illinois, i, xii, xxxix. S. Sovereignty basis of Nat. Union, 15, 108, 193 *n.*, 195 *n*, 198; secures full competition, 56, 108; will correct Camden and Amboy, 109. S. pride to operate, 108, 109.

STEAM. Propellers fast superseding sails, 62.

STIMPSON, WILLIAM, M. D., Director of Academy of Science, 276.

STOCK, LIVE. C. largest market of the world, 166. Swine by the million, 164; yet no Porkopolis. Cattle by the hundred thousand. *C. Trib.*: rapid growth since 1860; causes; States tributary; receipts, 1855–'64; small area yet producing......Receipts and shipments of hogs at C., 10 y., 164. Stock raising improves farms, 209.

CATTLE. Receipts 11 y., shipments 15 y. at C.; routes and receipts at C., 3 seasons, 166. Receipts at St. L., 1856 to 1867, 156; 1867, 165. Increase of No. in W., 1850–60, 319.

HOGS. Receipts and shipments at C. 10 y., 164. Routes and receipts at St. L., 1866 and 1867, 165. Entire pork crop of U. S., 18 y., 165. Routes and receipts of hogs at C. 3 seasons, 166. *Ruggles*: Corn surplus in W.; new world to feed the old; cheap transit wanted; hog—don't laugh at him; great corn-carrier; corn incarnate, 213. Increase, 1850–60, 319.

STOCK-YARDS described: C. largest live stock market in the world; union of rival railways; early sales; increase; dealers congregate from other cities; basis solid; yards begun last June; 30 ms. sewers, 167; 345 acres; streets and alleys; 500 yards and pens; barns and cribs; 15 ms. railway track; ample depot arrangements, 168; load and unload entire train; 500 cars at once; artesian well, 440,000 gals. per day. Large trade affords large facilities; none equal; herds from Texas; add other improvements, 169. Another artesian well, 265.

STONE, Joliet building; its superiority, 258.

STORY, Too long a, xxxiii.

STREETS, Wide, give ventilation, 281; favor horse-railways, 282.

STURGES, WILLIAM, Pres. Leav., Law. & Gal. R. R., 99.

SUBURBS. Facilities to reach by wide streets and horse railroads, 282. Ordinary railways, 15 lines; 4 to 7 more within 5 y.; sharp competition to accommodate citizens; no city equal facilities, 283. *Expansive power of railways*: use large area; grounds of C. B. & Q. road; roads should buy ample grounds; afford facilities to reach suburbs; must run quick; have their independent grade; guard against casualties; these will multiply, 284; change of grade only protection; give C. unequaled advantages, 385. *Room for indefinite expansion, its benefits*: prairie grandeur, 285; no expense to prepare site; no choice of land; grade at Harlem and Lyons; benefits of expansion, health, low price of lots, beauty of landscape; plan desirable, 286; obstacles; obviated by chartered cos.; Land Imp. Co.; others to come; extend city limits to tax property benefited, 287. To be improved by chartered companies, 299. Tendency of city population to suburbs, 337.

SUGAR, Texas to supply deficiency in, 123 *n.*

SWEET WATER mines, *Cor. C. Rep.*, 124. *Cor. San. Bul.*, 126.

TAXES. **Art following Nature's Lead, C. has no T. for Railways, though she has several Times more than any Rival, and nearly Two-Thirds of all west of the Toledo & Cincinnati Road, and north of the Ohio River**, margin, 28–36, 105. Suburbs should pay city t., 287.

TAYLOR, JOHN, of Caroline, value of corn, 212.

TELEGRAPH, a most efficient means of progress, yet modern, 315.

TERRITORIES, The, and C., *C. Rep.*, 129.

TEXAS looks to connection with C. *Houst. Tel.*: growth of St. L. wonderful; metropolis of Miss. Val.; rivers 11,000 ms.; St. L. & C. rivals, 100; railroad connections with them important; Texas then to fill like the N.W., 101......Beef raising large; T. to supply deficiency in sugar, 123 *n.* Herds of cattle to be marketed at C., 169.

THEOLOGICAL SEMINARIES. **Science** and Art.

TIMES, THE C., Laudation of City, xxxviii. C. builds no railroads, 33. Cin. troubles about Ohio river, 88. St. L. to tap trade at C., 91. C. to be Phil., St. L., N. Y., 93. "What is a conduit?" 147. "The troubles of St. L.," 189. Leather mnfr. at C., 205. Boots and Shoes mnfr. at C., 206. "Beef and pork packing," 208. Description of stockyard artesian wells, 255. Importance of canals, 345.

TONNAGE. Arrivals at C. for 6 y.; engaged in C. trade, 10 y.; domestic and foreign vessels entered in port of C., 1867, 61. Of St. L., July 1, 1866; departures, 1867, 180. T. of C. over twice and a fourth that of St. L.; old figures wanted to exhibit relative changes, 181.

TOPOGRAPHICAL Bureau, Reports valuable, 61.

TRACY, J. F., Pres. R. I. Railroad, defeats stock-gamblers in preventing extension of R. I. road, 357.

TRADE. ST. L. OR C. TO BE TRADE **Centre** FOR THE GT. INT. **The Commerce of C. compared with St. L.**, margin, 140–191. C's greatness depends upon the greatness of other cities which support her, 59 *n* Tonnage of C., 61; St. L., 180. St. L. not half that of C., old figures would show relative changes, 181. Trade sales of C. over 50 p. c. greater than St. L., 144. How can St. L. regain her lost trade? 186. T. to be taken in natural channels, 27, 56, 91, 109, 366. C. was a centre of some 100 or 200 ms. before railroads, 72. T. seeks a centre for distribution, 56, 70, 87, 105, 110, 130, 155, 325, 336, 369. T. obeys laws, 130. T. follows produce, 83, 152, 181. This denied, 186. C. desires produce to run in channels saving most to farmers, whether coming to her or not, 3 *n.*, 53, 62 65, 179, 184, 341. 366. Competition of Atl. cities for trade of W., 30, 56, 57, 103, 133, 336, 344, 366, 367, 376, 377. Interest of Nn. cities to draw it N. to the lakes, 22, 24, 30, 31, 32, 34, 52, 54, 362, 376, 377. **Cincinnati** gives up contest for N. W. trade, 77. C. desires no monopoly, 44. Free trade not at present expedient, 191, 192. Transportation facilities to constantly increase, 58; rapid improvements, 59. Domestic trade $5,000,000,000, 128.

FOREIGN. EUROPE. The Lake Route to the East and **Europe,** margin, 58–65. Lake trade with Europe to be immense, 62. *Mark Lane Exp.*, 1857: First Eng. paper to call attention to C. as a grain depot; first vessel from C. to Eng., "Dean Richmond," 1856; Welland canal to be enlarged; trade requires it; rapid growth of C.; large exports; beef superior; railways increased; resources exhaustless; commerce marvelous, 66......Ocean t. to be immense; improvement of St. Law. interest of Gt. Br.; U. S. canal around Niagara; propellers superseding sails; grain not to go from C. to N. Y., for export, 62. Europe will reach chief grain and provision market of the world, 103, 344. St. L. depends upon direct shipments to Europe; C. desires her success, 184. Ports of exports of breadstuffs, and amounts to Gr. Br. and Continent, 186. Increasing demand for provisions, 211, 213. We can feed Wn. Eu. cheaper than any other country, 318. ASIA. The Pacific Railways in Progress—their Effects, margin, 42–52. T. of Orient valuable, 43, 44, 104, 128, 150, 221. *Lon. Daily Tel.*: importance of Pac. road; extravagant expectations; results to be immense, 43......With several roads it will centre at C. for Gt. Interior, 44, 47, 104, 342, 369. *Pitts. and F. W. Rep.*: get Pac. trade thro' C., 55. Trade of Orient being hypothetical is not the basis, 104. Commerce opens our path to power in A., 219.

DOMESTIC, INTERNAL T. CHIEF. **Great Interior.** The Northwest is the Prize Contested—its Extent and Resources, margin, 111–131. 600,000 sq. ms. of arable Land and Water Courses, unequaled in Advantages natural and acquired, rapidly settling with the best of Men, must give unexampled Growth to their Emporium, margin, 131–140. Power of the Internal Trade to build up great Cities, margin, 300–313. *Scott*, 1843: Population hitherto on seaboard; imagined superiority of foreign commerce; internal trade not realized, 300; domestic 9-fold advantage of foreign; coast trade 5-fold foreign; inland advantages superior to coast; narrow Atl. coast has made all its cities; domestic t. equally as profitable as foreign; advantage of Cin. over N. Y. in Sn. trade, 301; advantages of interior in agr., 302; interior cities have foreign trade; N. Y. and N. O. be outports; large cities inland, effect of railroads, etc., facilitating trade; no inland country like ours, 303; natural advantages of interior; admission general that trade of lakes makes chief Atl. city, 304; trade between different sections to grow; domestic increases more than foreign, 305; valley trade to be more important than with En. States or Europe; C. route; trade N. & S., 306; foreign products to be imported for W. by Nn. route, 307; future power of C. unknown; may be first or second city, 312.

CHIEF BRANCHES. WHOLESALE. Dispute with St. L. as to relative amounts. *C. Trib.*, 8th Jan.: Mr. Wells' error reporting C. 8th city; his statement of 9 cities; C. given for only 6 mos.; the correct figures 12 mos.; C. 4th city, 142. *Mo. Dem.*, Jan. 16th: Trade of large cities; St. L. exceeds C.; 20 cities given; St. L. exults; C. blows; Cin. beats her. *C. Trib.*, 16th Jan.: correction of Mr. Wells' report; changed as to C., 143; was 8th, is 5th; why New Orleans is larger; Boston trade; changes in other cities; traders included; trade of 20 cities, just and corrected statement. *Mo. Dem.*, 4th Feb., "A Chicago Story:" Mr. Wells' report denied; authority demanded; C. pretends to correct; mere blowing; no voucher; invention to hide C. nakedness, 144......St. L. to keep her temper; proper contempt for her charges. Collector's official statement of C. sales. St. L. below Cin. instead of C.; she wants philosophic endurance, 145. Sales of leading houses of C. 1866 and '67, 148. Do. of Cin. and St. L.; sales of 6 western cities, 1867, 151. C. trade, 1860; keeps pace with produce; advantages of C. over N. Y., 152. Receipts leading articles at St. L. 12 y. 156. **Grain.** C. chief market of the world, 62, 103, 162, 166. Shipments from C. different kinds, 26 y., 153. Receipts at St. L. 12 y., 154. Routes and receipts of flour and g. at C., 1866–'7, 154. Do. do. at St. L., 155. Routes and shipments from C., 1866–'7, 155. *Mo. Dem.*, 1861, receipts at St. L. about equal in 1859 and 1860...... C. doubled receipts, and over 3-fold her amts., 111. **Live-stock.** C. chief market of the world, 164, 166. Receipts and shipments of hogs at C. 10 y., 164. Routes and receipts of hogs at St L., 2 y. Entire pork crop of U. S. 18 y., 165. Receipts of cattle at C. 11 y., shipments, 15 y. Routes and receipts of hogs and cattle at C. 3 y., 166. **Lumber.** C. chief market of the world, 166, 176. Shipments by canal, 6 y., 53. Receipts 11 y., shipments 8 y., 170. **Mining.** C. must be certain of mining trade, 122. **Provisions.** C. chief market of the world, 103, 162, 208, 214. List of pork-packers and statistics, 1867–'8, 210, 211. Do. do. of beef, 211.

TRADE TURNED FROM ST. L. TO C. *Mo. Dem.*, of Kas., 26; *Mo. Rep.*, of Kas., and W. Mo., 27. *Cor. Cin. Com.*, of trade of Iowa and Nebraska; *Cor. Mo. Rep.*, of N. W., 35; *Cor. Mo. Rep.*, of Up. Miss. Val. and the plains, 38; *Mr. Cobb*, in *Mo. Rep.*, of Up. Miss. and Mo., Rocky Mts. and L'r Miss., 39; *Rep. C. B. & Q. Railroad*, of Iowa; *Cor. Mo. Rep.*, of the Omaha Pac., 55; *Mr. Fagin*, of Miss. Val., 67; *Cor. Mo. Dem.*, losing enterprising men, 69: *Pitts. Com.*, loss of trade, 70; *Circ. 1861*, of whole W., 75; *Gen. Hammond*, of Iowa, Neb. and Pac. road, 80; *Cor. Mo. Rep.*, of Miss. Val., 89; *N. W. R. R. Rep.*, of Mo. Valley, 95; *Omaha Reg.*, of Neb., 96; *Mo. Dem.*, 1861, of N.W., 111–113; *C. Jour.*, of Up. Mo., 117; *Helena* (Mon.) *Gaz.*, of Montana, 118; *Cor. Rep.*, of Montana; *Mo. Dem.*, of Colorado, 119; *Prof. Waterhouse*, of mining region, 176; *St. L. Trade Rep.*, of Up. Miss. Val., 181; *Col. Foster's Rep.*, of Miss., 183; *U. S. Census*, 1860, of Miss. and O. Rivers, 184, 185; *Atchison* (Kas.) *Free Press*, of entire W., 348; *Trib.*, 361.

ST. L. TRADE [illegible] 1866 and 1867: Grain receipts 12 y., 154 Routes and receipts of flour and grain, 1867, 155. Receipts of leading articles 12 y., 156. THE St. L. elevator, *Sec. Rep.*, 1866: some increase in wheat over 1865; figures small compared with neighbors; facilities to handle wanting; the "elevator has demonstrated the fact that grain can be handled in bulk advantageously;" facilitate shipments to E. and foreign ports; some "toting" yet, 158......*Prof. Waterhouse* gives cost and benefit of the elevator, and says "its receipts amounted to 600,000 bushels, 200,000 *of which were brought directly from C.*"......Prof. rather honest than keen to exhibit St. L.'s dependence on C.; italicising not mine, shows her sure reliance......*Sec. Rep.*: increase of 1866 nearly 1,000,000 over 1865; increase due to elevator; "prices have ruled as high and oftentimes higher than in other markets, and have been governed entirely by the demand and supply;" "has no combination of railroads or other interest to control her wheat market;"......St. L. eschews combination; C. desperate, 159; what the effect on her market of a week's C. supplies; C. likes a stable, St. L. a vibrating market......Elevator receipts, Oct., 1865, to Jan., 1868; an elevator building in East St. L., 160. Routes and receipts of hogs, 1866, 1867; entire pork crop of the country 18 y., 165. Receipts of salt 12 y., of wool 11 y., 172. Tonnage, 1866, 1867, 180. *Sec. Rep.*, 1866: Up. Miss. Val. wants to trade with St. L., but can't; railroads prevent, 181.

Sec. Rep., 1867 : Trade follows produce; trust too much to the natural advantages, and retarded by the late war; S. hitherto her market; must find another; must have facilities; then "the trade will flow to St. L. as naturally as the great river flows to the Gulf." *Rep. of Directors :* Circumstances had been adverse; causes considered; several conventions; good feeling; visitors call their attention to railroads, 182.

TRANSPORTATION. High rates derange trade, injure railroads, 164. C. depends not on mere carriage; a small commission makes her rich, 65. Positive benefits of railways to grain growers, *Mr. Edmunds*, 315; *Mr. Ruggles*, 318; *Mr. Baxter*, 324. Proportion of exports and imports to railways and navigation, in Gt. B., 326; France, 327; Belgium and Holland, 328. Reliable means essential, 376.

TRIBUNE, THE C. Arrivals and tonnage by lake for 6 y.; No. vessels and tonnage 10 y., 61. Wholesale trade of C., 1867, 142, 143, 147, 150. Business of the cities, important correction, 143. Growth of live-stock trade, 164. Railroad progress, numerous extracts. 351–363. No. railway trains, 384.

TRIBUNE, N. Y., Growth of C. compared with N. Y. and Brooklyn, xxxi.

TUCKER, Prof. GEORGE, upon the growth of cities, and towns, 320, 322.

TUNNEL, Lake, for water supply, description, 252.

UNANIMITY of C. *Pitts. Com.*, 70, 262.

UNITED STATES. **Politics.** Currency to be greenbacks, 15; good in Europe, 15, 198. Confidence in our institutions, 15, 193, 195. 198, 402. Nature of our Union not apprehended, xii, 15, 108, 136, 139, 196, 325 *n.* Dignity of citizenship, 20. Govt. to aid railroads, 45, 47, 48. *Cin. R. R. Rec.*, in favor of grants, 127, 128. *Wash. Chronicle*, a summary of a report by *Mr. Wilson, Comr. Govt. Land Office*, "The Future of our Country;" area; minerals; Pacific slope and railways; trade of East; ms. of railroad; aids by Congress; value of domestic trade; Asiatic trade with San Francisco and N. Y.; advantages of water, 128; we get this trade; ancient trade described; also our country; have 100 States by 1900; 100,000,000 people; value of the report, 129. Donations for educational objects, 193. Half the population in lake and river valleys in 1900, 132. Progress in 50 years, 194; general advantages, 195. Why our Government a success and France a failure, 195 *n.* Return to specie payments; loss upon our securities, 198. *Census :* Remarks upon "The Grain Trade of the Miss. River," 184; progress of mnfrs., 193. Statistics of Cook co., 160, 201. Competition of Gt. Br. for trade of W., 308. *Baxter :* Railroads in, 329. *Poussin :* "The U. S.; its Power and Progress," 1843: to become a chief com. nation; rival to Gt. Br.; able to dispossess her; pursues an opposite course; Dem. rules; sovereignty of people; railroads 333; skill in use; resources developed; dem. liberalism and railroads, at once adopted; experience the test; practical in all things; steam largely used, 334.... Were Union broken C. would grow; with it no favors asked, 110.

UNIVERSITIES, **Science** and Art.

VALLEY OF MISS. being heart of Union does not make St. L. so; the N. W., its chief part, lost to her; Miss. has no head; its benefits indefinite, 101.

Of Lakes, *Rep. Buff. Board of Trade*, 1863: pop. 1800, '40, '50, '60; cereals surplus 1840–62; Erie canal and Miss. R. only avenues, 1825; 1st grain from L. Mich, 1836, C. 1839; surplus 1862; what changes next 25 y., 132.

Lake and River V's. C. at the point of natural conjunction, 53, 58, 62, 70, 93, 104, 304, 307, 345, 391. This the site for the continental city on the hill that cannot be hid, xiii. *Buf. Trade Rep.:* Have half population of Union, 1900; internal improvements; area; mineral wealth; rich arable land; division of labor; outlets by St. Law. and Miss.; St. Law. strongest, 132. *Scott:* ocean and inland navigation compared; variety of products, 301; exchanges N. and S.; valley have something besides agriculture, 302; best of settlers, 303; lake valley will draw trade of rivers, 304; trade in valleys N. and S. to increase, 305; lake v. beats rivers, 309–311. Competition of river route regulates transportation by lakes and railways, 341. Vs. left by Providence to incite man to use his skill, 342.

VAN OSDEL, JOHN M., architect of Mr. Palmer's buildings, 258.

VENTILATION, Lake and river and wide streets for, 281.

VICE of C. needs counteracting influences, 262 *n.*

VINCENT, NELSON & Co.'s, grain dryer and elevator, 163.

VLIET, Col., chief eng. Leav. Law & Gal. R. R., 100. Letter about road, 121 *n.*, 123 *n.*

VOLK, L. W., sculptor, 278.

WALKER, Rev. Father, 1st. Meth. clergn., 262.

WALKER, Mr. GEORGE C., Pres. Acad. of Sci. Address upon decease of Maj. Robt. Kennicott, 276.

WAR. Effects of Secession and War Upon C. *Cir. 1861 :* West prosper with peace—or even war, 17; W. suffer least from war; large armies; W. not to be devastated except on the border, and perhaps St. L.; war on large scale, whether long or short; demand for agr. products; W. soonest recuperate; pay its part of cost easiest; S. not to be conquered; those views in March before the war; war begun; N. a unit; result sure unless foreign governments interfere; war long and fierce; errors S. & N.; S. can sustain war; border States to be injured; effect changes in a year or two that would have taken 5; calamity deplorable; W. & C. would have prospered with peace; most certain to prosper relatively in war, 19. War worth the cost, 20. War the cause of St. L.'s decline, this denied, 175.

WASHINGTON CHRONICLE, summary of Hon. Jos. S. Wilson's Land Office report, 128, 129.

WATER. **Lakes. Rivers.** No equal Point of Convergence of either Rail or Water Communication, or of both, on the Globe, margin, 339, 385. W. and railroads both needed, 59, 93, 319, 342, 372, 375. W. not to be supplanted, 59, 60, 128, 342, 375. W. valuable in conjunction with railways, 319, 340, 372. Free water cheapest, 375. *Buf. Com.:* W. and railroads compared. R.'s important; w. more so, cost compared, 59; vessels large; canal enlargement; w. carriage never superseded, 69......Boston must improve w. facilities, 62. Propellers superseding sails, 62. W. to counteract railroad monopolies, 62, 372. W. inferior to railroad facilities at C., 104. N. Y. cannot rely upon w., 372. Demand for steamboats increased by railroads, 339. *Knowlton*, to Ship-Canal Conv.: no monopolies; C. a centre; water wanted besides railways; never wears out; for heavy transportation; E. wants shortest water communication, 342. *Poor*, to Ship-Canal Conv.: Production of food in N. W. to increase; value consumed in transport; outlets from C. wanted; make St. Lawrence waters an open Mediterranean, 343; cheap as ocean; Am. Niagara canal; improve St. Clair river, 344.

City Supply. Lake Tunnel. City supplied with water from L. Mich.; tunnel 2 ms.; water 30 feet deep; Mr. E. S. Chesbrough, originator; Mr. W. H. Clarke, assistant; progress of the work, 253. Water-works: cost, income; pipes laid 5 y., 254. Water loan, amt.; pays its way, 259. Artesian Wells. Mr. Shufeldt's first, 711 ft. deep; 600,000 gals. *per diem*, 254; a 2d well 694 ft., 600,000 gals. *per diem*, analysis. Stock yard wells, 169; 1st, 1,032 ft., 65,000 gals., 255; 2d well, 1,190 ft. 600,000 gals. Value of these wells; promise others, perhaps throughout W., 256. C. River, purified by pumping into canal, 252. City now sinking the canal to feed it from the lake; State to pay cost, 252 *n.* N. Branch also to be purified. 282 *n.*

WATERHOUSE, Prof. S., paper about St.Louis, xi, xxv, 158, 173, 174, 175, 176, 177, 178. Endorsed in Trade Report, 178 *n.* Illinois Chester Coal Fields, 224. Criticised by Col. Foster, 225 *n.* Hard on Pitts., 226 *n.*

WELLS, Hon. ERASTUS, endorses Mr. Fagin's speech, 68.

WELLS, W. H., superintendent of schools, 263 *n.* Extract from Rep., 266. Grading schools, 267.

WEST. **Great Interior. Northwest.** The focal Point of the Great W. is fixed immovably by over 7,500 of its 11,000 ms. of Railways centering at C., margin, 36–42. The Rivals of the

West, Cin., St. L. and C., margin 73–111. The W. and N. W. hereafter the Great Interior, margin, 385–387. W. a unit in interest, 110. Old measures here inapplicable, 351. W. its own measure, 273, 315, 335, 393. W. able to build up many great cities, xvii, xxix, xxx, 9 *n.*, 71, 108, 109, 110, 146, 217, 222, 325, 387, 391. W. has a natural centre, xviii, 92, 110, 130, 136, 138, 140, 218, 222, 336, 367, 387. Trade of W. the prize, 30, 31, 54, 56, 377. Chief field for railway extension, 71, 313, 338, 365, 376. Wn. railroads pay well, 72, 336, 351. Pacific roads will develope W., 43. This the first object, 44. Effect of railroads in settling W., 48. Settlers superior, 138, 303. Dr. McGuffey's opinion, 139 *n.* Atl. cities to seek trade of W. at C., 56. C. chief mart for foreign imports for W., 103. Capital safe in W., 28. Justice never done to the W. in Cong., 138. Trade of S. changing to W.; their natural affiliation, 110. *Ruggles:* grain-raising first begun, 212. To mnfr. for itself, 199, 219, 221. *Edmunds:* increase of mnfrs. in the W.; immense mineral resources; lack of labor chief drawback, 218......W. changed to E. to pursue our destiny, 197, 218. W. to rule, our responsibility, 43, 138, 281, 387. *Dr. Ide:* W. to educate its own men; should have few seminaries, 273. ......W. aid C. institutions, 274. Effects of secession and **War** upon W., 17, 18, 140. W. and Mass a united interest, 22. Change of ancient Orient to our Occident not perceived, 385. Our W. across Pacific; lake and river valley States henceforth the Gt. Int.; will be a unit, 386; reasons of union; means of prosperity; have many centres; one chief; small part yet tilled has built several cities; city growth to be stimulated; chief will draw from others, 387. *Sacramento* (Cal.) *Union*, "The aspiring West:" St. L. wants national capitol; claims of C.; W. seat of empire; characteristics, Cal. and Ills. alike; W. national; its power; 3 cities of a million in 25 y., 386.

WHEAT. **Grain.**

WHEEL of commerce, St. L. no hub, 88. C. a hub, ii, 92, 105, 130. Centripetal in effects, 105.

WILSON, Genl. J. H. Report upon Ills. and Mich. Canal, 63.

WILSON, Hon. J. S., Future of our Country, 128.

WISCONSIN, changes of U. S. Census, 1860, 138. Farm values, 1850, 1860, 317.

WOOL, receipts and shipments at C. 12 y., 172. At St. L. 11 y., 172.

WOOLNER & GARRICKS, lumber circular, 170.

WRIGHT, AUGUSTINE W., a surveyor on Kas. Pac. railroad, extract from letter, 384.

WRIGHT JOHN, arrived at C, Oct.. 1832; removed his family to C., 1834, 289. His judgment of C. 4 *n.* His death, 1840, 289.

WRIGHT, Hon. JOHN C., of Ohio, expected to draw trade to Cin. thro' C. 77 *n.*

WRIGHT, JOHN S., came to C. 29th Oct., 1832, 289. First purchases of **Real Estate**, 4–7, 289–291. Letters to *Boston Courier* about railroads, 1847, 21, 29. To *Boston Mining Jour.*, and *N. Y. Cour. & Enquirer*, 1848, 31.

WYOMING TER., Sweetwater mines described, 123–126.

ZINC. *Merch. Mag.* La Salle (Ills.) works, progress and success—ore from Galena mines, 247.

NO APPENDIX.

In preparing this volume *currente calamo*, it was expected to add an appendix, some points needing more investigation than it was possible to give under the pressure of preparing copy to keep ahead of the printer. But in this long and unexpected delay in issuing a complete edition, material has so accumulated that to attempt an appendix would too long postpone publication. Besides, the plan having been to issue an additional volume after the census of 1870, the time is so near that it is better to incorporate in the body of that, the information which in an appendix would have less consideration, though of much importance. So that although this index is not as full under some important topics as was expected, it is hoped it will suffice to induce the reader to look for its successor. It will be a gathering of information about the whole Great Interior; and the comparison of the relative changes in the last decennial period which the census will disclose, will be of profound interest to all sections, and especially to all cities of this continental republic. We need to reason about and to know our destiny, in order to realize our obligations.

In the preface, pp., viii. and x., reference is made to the argument with the Board of Trade which was to have been added, but which is left out for the reasons given in the acknowledgment to the Board preceding the title-page.

www.ingramcontent.com/pod-product-compliance
Lightning Source LLC
LaVergne TN
LVHW020915110826
845150LV00004B/677

* 9 7 8 1 4 2 5 5 5 5 2 1 4 *